HMRC Investigations Handbook 2018/19

HMRC Investigations Handbook 2018/19

General Editor
Mark McLaughlin
Mark McLaughlin Associates Limited

Authors

Helen Adams
BDO LLP

Gary Ashford
Harbottle and Lewis LLP

Phil Berwick
Berwick Tax Limited

Russell Cockburn
Taxation consultant, lecturer and author

Hartley Foster
Fieldfisher LLP

Andrew Gotch
TaxAction Consulting Limited

Talia Greenbaum
BDO LLP

Kendra Hann
Deloitte LLP

Julian Hickey
Temple Tax Chambers

Andrew Hinsley
RSM

Jennifer Jones
BDO LLP

Alastair Kendrick
MHA MacIntyre Hudson LLP

Mark McLaughlin
Mark McLaughlin Associates Limited

Simon Oakes
Simon Oakes Consultancy Services

Dawn Register
BDO LLP

Ian Roberts
The TACS Partnership

Bloomsbury Professional
LONDON · DUBLIN · EDINBURGH · NEW YORK · NEW DELHI · SYDNEY

BLOOMSBURY PROFESSIONAL
Bloomsbury Publishing Plc
41–43 Boltro Road, Haywards Heath, RH16 1BJ, UK

BLOOMSBURY and the Diana logo are trademarks of Bloomsbury Publishing Plc

First published in Great Britain 2018

Copyright © Bloomsbury Professional Ltd 2018

All rights reserved. No part of this publication may be reproduced or transmitted in any form or by any means, electronic or mechanical, including photocopying, recording, or any information storage or retrieval system, without prior permission in writing from the publishers.

While every care has been taken to ensure the accuracy of this work, no responsibility for loss or damage occasioned to any person acting or refraining from action as a result of any statement in it can be accepted by the authors, editors or publishers.

All UK Government legislation and other public sector information used in the work is Crown Copyright ©. All House of Lords and House of Commons information used in the work is Parliamentary Copyright ©. This information is reused under the terms of the Open Government Licence v3.0 (http://www.nationalarchives.gov.uk/doc/open-government-licence/version/3) except where otherwise stated.

All Eur-lex material used in the work is © European Union, http://eur-lex.europa.eu/, 1998–2018.

British Library Cataloguing-in-Publication Data

A catalogue record for this book is available from the British Library.

ISBN: 978 1 52650 624 5

Typeset by Compuscript Ltd, Shannon
Printed and bound by CPI Group (UK) Ltd, Croydon, CR0 4YY

To find out more about our authors and books visit www.bloomsburyprofessional.com. Here you will find extracts, author information, details of forthcoming events and the option to sign up for our newsletters

Preface

Welcome to *HMRC Investigations Handbook 2018/19*.

When writing this Preface, I noted that the Preface for the previous edition of this book was written in November 2016. That is a long time ago in tax terms generally, and even more so when considering developments in tax administration, compliance and enforcement as it applies to HMRC enquiries and investigations.

For example, since the previous edition of *HMRC Investigations Handbook* there have been three Finance Acts (and draft legislation was also published for what will eventually become Finance Act 2019). Those Finance Acts included (among other things) legislation on the requirement to correct certain offshore tax non-compliance, partial closure notices in relation to HMRC enquiries, errors in tax returns etc. related to tax avoidance arrangements, and a new penalty on enablers of defeated tax avoidance. In addition, new tax cases are published regularly, which inform how tax legislation should be applied as it affects the work of professionals and specialists engaged in HMRC investigation and enquiry work. Practitioners must also be aware of relevant changes in HMRC policy and practice. Hopefully, readers will find that *HMRC Investigations Handbook 2018/19* makes it easier to stay up-to-date with important developments.

HMRC's activity in its investigation and enquiry work is extensive, and it shows no sign of abating. In fact, there is likely to be significant activity specifically in terms of HMRC investigations into offshore non-compliance following expiry of the 'requirement to correct' deadline of 30 September 2018.

As in previous editions, *HMRC Investigations Handbook 2018/19* covers practical aspects of dealing with HMRC enquiries from beginning to end. The book also covers HMRC investigations into suspected tax fraud, which have always been very serious matters normally best left to specialists. Nevertheless, non-specialists need to be alert and aware of the processes involved, in case a client is subject to an HMRC investigation.

HMRC Investigations Handbook has continued to evolve in response to changes in legislation, case law and HMRC practice, and also to make the publication as practical and relevant to practitioners as possible. The 2018/19 edition features two new chapters, on discovery and penalty mitigation

Preface

respectively. I hope that readers will find these new chapters informative and useful.

The authors of *HMRC Investigations Handbook 2018/19* include some of the more well-known and respected experts in their fields. They bring a wealth of practical experience, which they have endeavoured to share with readers of this publication. The term 'handbook' in the title reflects that its purpose is, as indicated above, to provide practitioners with practical guidance to help them in their exposure to issues covered in this publication; it is structured so that (for example) each stage of an HMRC enquiry is separately covered, from selection to settlement. I hope readers will agree that the authors have achieved the purpose of this publication in a clear and concise manner.

On behalf of all the authors, I would like to thank everyone at Bloomsbury Professional who has been involved in the production of *HMRC Investigations Handbook 2018/19*, in particular Dave Wright for his considerable efforts and support during its publication.

Last but not least, many thanks to you, the reader, for picking up and reading this publication. I hope that you find it a useful source of reference. Constructive comments and suggestions for future editions of *HMRC Investigations Handbook* are always welcome.

The law in this book is stated as at 31 August 2018.

Whilst every care has been taken to ensure that the contents of this work are complete and accurate, no responsibility for loss occasioned by any person acting or refraining from action as a result of any statement in it can be accepted by the authors or the publishers.

Mark McLaughlin
General Editor

Manchester, 24 September 2018

Contents

Preface	*v*
Table of Statutes	*xxxi*
Table of Statutory Instruments	*xliii*
Table of Cases	*xlix*
Abbreviations	*lxv*

Section 1: Investigations and enquiries

Chapter 1 HMRC enquiries: outline and recent developments   1

Signposts	1
Introduction	2
Disclosure	5
Handling an enquiry	7
The start of an enquiry	9
Meetings	15
Books and records	22
Information powers	24
Information and documents	24
Business premises inspections etc	27
Other ways to obtain information	28
Completion of enquiry	29
Partial closure notices	33
Discovery	34
Key points	37

Chapter 2 Serious civil tax investigations into fraud and avoidance: Code of Practice 9 (Contractual Disclosure Facility) and Code of Practice 8   39

Signposts	39
Fraud Investigation Service	40
The role of Special Investigations (Fraud and Avoidance)	41
Types of SI investigation	42
Code of Practice 9 (Contractual Disclosure Facility procedures)	42
Cases other than suspected serious fraud (COP8)	42

Contents

Serious tax fraud (evasion)	42
Definition of fraud	44
The Fraud Act 2006	46
Code of Practice 9 (cases of suspected fraud)	46
Civil investigations of fraud procedures	48
The nine questions of COP9	50
Contractual Disclosure Facility	51
Changes to the Contractual Disclosure Facility from June 2014	54
Outline disclosure	54
Voluntary disclosure	54
Formal questions	55
Meetings under CDF	55
Closing the investigation	58
Settlement	58
Code of Practice 8: cases where civil investigation of fraud procedures are not used	58
Handling SI investigations (practice management and professional indemnity insurance)	59
Specialists within SI	60
Key points	64

Chapter 3 Tax fraud: criminal investigations and litigation – direct tax **65**

Signposts	65
Overview	66
Tax fraud: offences in overview	69
New criminal offences	70
Offence for failure to prevent facilitation of tax evasion	70
Offences for failure to give notice of being chargeable to tax, of failing to deliver a return, of making an inaccurate return	74
Government policy	76
Tax prosecution: offenders' perspective	78
Civil investigation of suspected tax fraud	79
Prosecution policy	81
Factors suggesting the likelihood of criminal investigation	81
HMRC organisation for criminal investigation	84
Overview of a criminal investigation and prosecution	85
HMRC's criminal investigation powers and safeguards	87
PACE 1984	88
Training and support	90
Intrusive surveillance	91
Safeguards	91
Search warrants and production orders	92
Evidential material: items subject to legal privilege and special procedure material	94

Order for the delivery of documents under TMA 1970, s 20BA	98
Complying with a s 20BA production order	99
PACE 1984, Sch 1 production order	100
SOCPA 2005 production order	102
Dealing with a dawn raid	103
Legal privilege	105
Interviews	106
The anatomy of a criminal trial	107
Use of information by HMRC	118
Money laundering	121
Introduction	121
The money laundering legislation	122
Guidance for financial intermediaries and professional advisers	147
The role of the fiscal authorities	152
The risk to financial intermediaries and professionals	156
Conclusion	159
Key points	160

Chapter 4 Contentious tax planning enquiries   162

Introduction	162
Background	162
Tax planning arrangements	163
HMRC's strategy for dealing with tax avoidance	165
Introduction	165
The moral dimension	165
Operational initiatives	165
Legislative initiatives	166
International Tax Planning	184
Personal tax	184
Liability for penalty for failure to correct	184
Companies	186
The role of specialist directorates	190
Background	190
Counter Avoidance	190
The evolution and importance of avoidance case law	191
Introduction	191
Domestic planning: a potted history	192
Trading and loss generation schemes	207
Employee benefit trust (EBT) arrangements	209
Unallowable purpose	211
International planning	218
The avoidance versus evasion distinction	222
HMRC's approach to working complex tax enquiries	223
Case identification	223
Case profiling	224

Contents

HMRC approach to fact finding: general	224
Approach to fact finding: domestic planning	226
Case sampling	234
Approach to fact finding: international planning	235
Recommended responses to HMRC's approach: overview	239
Introduction: impact of operational and legislative changes	239
Recommended responses: overview	240
Managing the enquiry	245
Introduction	245
The importance of maintaining a compelling narrative throughout the enquiry	245
Framing contentions	246
Evidencing facts/purpose	247
Engaging with HMRC	249
Formal challenges to information requests	254
Resolving an impasse	259
Resolving disputes	262
Introduction: litigation and settlement strategy	262
The Increased threat of discovery	264
Increased threat of penalties	272
HMRC's approach where fraud is suspected	273

Chapter 5 Offshore tax investigations, disclosure campaigns and tax cooperation agreements — 274

Signposts	274
Background	277
Residence and domicile matters	277
Individuals	278
Trustee residence	279
Company residence	279
Anti-avoidance legislation	279
Other notable international tax investigation cases	280
Exchange of information	280
Organisation for Economic Cooperation and Development	280
European Union Savings Directive	281
Foreign Account Tax Compliance Act/Intergovernmental Agreement	282
Common Reporting Standard for automatic exchange of tax information	283
HMRC offshore disclosure campaigns	283
Offshore coordination unit	284
Liechtenstein Disclosure Facility	284
Five-year Taxpayer Assistance Compliance Program	285
Relevant persons	286

Definition of 'beneficial interest'	286
Eligible persons	288
The LDF as a tax disclosure facility of worldwide issues	288
Tax liabilities	289
Composite rate option	290
Single rate charge	290
Late payment interest	290
Penalties	291
Criminal prosecution	291
The Liechtenstein Disclosure Facility developments	291
New tax disclosure facility	292
UK/Swiss tax cooperation agreement	293
Swiss paying agent	293
Relevant assets	293
Relevant person	294
Regularising the past	294
The one-off payment	294
Non UK domiciliaries and the past	295
Clearance	295
The post-1 January 2013 withholding tax	296
Non-domiciliary certification	296
Inheritance tax changes by protocol	297
Crown Dependency disclosure facilities	297
Offshore penalties	298
An offshore matter could relate to income, an asset or activities offshore	298
Finance Act 2016	299
Further developments in relation to offshore tax investigations	299
Criminal Finances Act 2017	302
Failure to prevent facilitation of UK tax evasion offences	302
Failure to prevent facilitation of foreign tax evasion offences	303
The Foreign Offence	304
Associated Person	304
Defence of Reasonable Procedures	304
HMRC Guidance	305
Worldwide Disclosure Facility (WDF)	305
Who can use the facility?	305
Registering for the facility	306
The terms of the facility	306
Pre-disclosure agreement	307
Legal interpretation	307
Assets	307

Contents

Requirement to Correct Offence (RTC) (Finance Act (2) 2017)	308
Correcting the offence and disclosure	309
Assessments	310
Penalties	311
Reduction in penalties	311
Appeals	312
Reasonable Excuse	312
Key points	315

Section 2: The progress of an enquiry

Chapter 6 Practical aspects of an enquiry — 316

Signposts	316
Introduction	318
Preliminary issues: Costs	319
Recognise the signs	320
Practice management	321
The people involved	322
The taxpayer	322
The HMRC officer	322
The professional adviser	325
Practical issues	325
Be prepared	325
During the enquiry	327
The formalities	327
Information notices	330
Controversial points	331
Private records	331
Unannounced visits	332
Meetings	333
The venue	334
The agenda	335
Meeting notes	336
Appointment diaries	337
Other professionals	338
Resolving disputes	338
Appeals to the tribunal	340
Re-opening other years ('presumption of continuity')	340
Closure notice applications	342
Settlement	344
Final points	348
Complaints procedures	349
Key points	350

Contents

Chapter 7 Selection for enquiry   **352**

Signposts	352
Where are we now? – Selection in context	352
The enquiry regime and its problems	352
The compliance checking regime	353
The risk analysis environment	355
HMRC's wealthy and mid-sized business compliance teams ('WMBC') – demonstrating the power of computerised risk analysis	357
Disclosure of selection parameters	359
Toolkits: how to use them properly	359
The importance of identifying 'changes'	360
Behavioural risk	360
Record keeping	361
Selection at a local level	362
The selection process	364
Accounts and return review	365
Accounts review	365
Estimates and percentage abatements	366
Turnover	366
Gross profit	367
Deductions from income	368
Net profit	370
Balance sheet	371
Return review	374
Practice management	375
The future	375
Key points	377

Chapter 8 Conduct of enquires   **378**

Signposts	378
Introduction	380
Gathering information	381
Enquiry triggers	383
Cases where no return is submitted	385
Criminal tax investigations	387
Encouraging voluntary disclosures	388
Multi-tax enquiries	393
Collaborative working	396
Countering tax avoidance	398
Maintaining progress despite delays	406
Estimating in the absence of full information	408
Expanding enquiries into other tax years: discovery and time limits	410

Contents

Key forms that HMRC may request	413
Deadlock: what is the way forward?	416
Penalties	419
Settling the case	424
Tax Debt Collection	427
Carrots and sticks: publishing taxpayer's details and the Managing Serious Defaulters programme	429
Sanctions on tax advisers	431
Key points	433

Chapter 9 Meetings with HMRC — 434

Signposts	434
Introduction	434
Purpose of the meeting	436
Is a meeting the best way forward?	438
Preparing for the meeting	439
The adviser's knowledge of the client	440
Identify any problem areas	440
Pre-meeting issues	441
What the HMRC officer wants	443
Checklist for preparing for a meeting	444
The meeting itself	445
Format of the meeting	445
Who will be present?	446
Where and when should the meeting be held?	447
Conduct of the meeting	448
How should the meeting conclude?	449
Notes of meetings	450
Ten key areas	450
Employer compliance checks	451
Pre-planning checklist	456
During the visit itself	457
Checklist for areas the compliance officers are likely to review	458
Conclusions	459
Key points	459

Chapter 10 Conduct of a full enquiry — 461

Signposts	461
Why is control important?	462
The purpose of this chapter	462
Who and what are to be controlled?	462
Case studies	463
Controlling the client	464
The client must have confidence	465

Take a realistic look at the client	466
The adviser should be fair but firm with the taxpayer	468
Honesty is paramount	468
Get disclosure in early	469
Keep client to a timetable	469
Sort out fees	470
Explain what is happening	470
Conclusions of the initial discussions with the taxpayer	471
Dealing with HMRC	471
How does an adviser get control of HMRC?	472
Ten commandments to ensure control	472
1 Plan	472
2 Control paper	473
3 Don't cause delay	474
4 Know what you have to do	474
5 Be realistic	475
6 Is formal action being taken?	476
7 Know where you are going	476
8 Use reminders and powers	476
9 Pay the tax	477
10 Behave yourself	477
The eleventh commandment	478
The twelfth commandment	478
Think about meetings	479
Is it cost effective?	479
Can the client cope?	480
Organising the venue	480
Preparation is vital	481
Control the meeting	482
Get your disclosure in first	482
Watch your body language	483
Keep control of the client	483
Taking notes	484
Action points	484
After the meeting	484
Control of paper	484
Setting up an investigation file	485
Correspondence file	485
Working files	486
Dealing with information requests	487
Third party notices	488
Dealing with HMRC inspections	489
Bringing matters to a conclusion	491
Planning for penalties	493
Conclusion	496
Key points	496

Contents

Chapter 11 Settlement negotiations — 498

Signposts	498
Introduction	501
Start the negotiating groundwork early	502
Are interest and penalties due?	503
Calculation of interest	503
Penalty negotiation	503
Payments on account	505
VAT disclosure	506
Professional costs	506
Why negotiate?	507
Reduce the length of the investigation period	507
Finality for the client	508
Financial (professional fees)	508
Financial (tax, etc savings for the client)	508
Finality for the practitioner	508
What is negotiable?	509
Consideration of grey areas	509
Litigation and settlement strategy	510
The art of negotiation	511
Negotiate	511
Pitch at the right level	511
How strong is the client's case?	512
Consider the outcome	512
The officer is not the enemy	512
Agree on minor issues	513
No two cases are the same	513
Avoid premature concessions	513
Previous experience	513
Claims, allowances and reliefs	514
Remittances by non-domiciled individuals	514
Reasonable care and reasonable excuse	514
Advantages for the officer	515
Time	516
Workload	516
When agreement cannot be reached	516
The settlement package	517
Funding the settlement and time to pay	518
The letter of offer	520
Making sub-standard offers	521
Settlement meetings	521
Relationship with the officer	522
Relationship with the client	522
Key points	524

Chapter 12 Alternative Dispute Resolution — 525

Signposts	525
Introduction	526
HMRC's ADR procedure	526
Background	526
What is ADR?	527
Learning from the ADR feedback to date	529
How does ADR fit into the litigation and settlement strategy?	531
Suitable cases	535
How to ask for ADR	536
Guiding principles and Mediation Agreement	537
The 'without prejudice' rule	537
Full disclosure	538
Flexibility	538
Confidentiality	538
Key decision makers	539
Costs	539
The mediation day	540
Opening phase	540
Exploration phase	540
Bargaining phase	541
Concluding phase	541
Mediation techniques	543
Relationship building	543
Managing the mediation process	543
Facilitating a workable solution	543
Conclusion	544
Still a role for the Tax Tribunal?	544
Success and the future	544
Appendix: template mediation agreement	546

Section 3: Practical issues

Chapter 13 Discovery — 549

Signposts	549
Introduction	551
When is discovery irrelevant?	552
Discovery enquiries	553
Discovery overview	554
When does a discovery occur?	556
Assessment time limits	559
Assessment time limits – deceased taxpayers	560
Assessment time limits – offshore non-compliance	561

Contents

When is a discovery assessment made?	562
Discoveries can become stale	563
Discovery in the absence of a tax return	564
Discovery where a tax return was submitted?	566
Generally prevailing practice exemption	567
The careless or deliberate behaviour requirement	569
The situation must be 'brought about'	569
Who is 'a person acting on his behalf'?	570
What does 'deliberate' mean?	572
What does carelessness mean?	574
Reliance on advice	576
Discovery without culpable behaviour	577
Conditions	578
The 'hypothetical' officer	578
When does the officer cease to be entitled?	580
Available information	580
The level of awareness	582
HMRC's statements of practice	584
Presumption of continuity	584
Estimating liabilities in the absence of evidence	586
What format should a discovery assessment take?	586
Challenging discovery assessments	588
Burden of proof	591
When is tax payable following a discovery assessment?	594
Consequential claims	594
Key points	598
Chapter 14 Voluntary disclosures	**600**
Signposts	600
Introduction	602
Early considerations	603
Triggers for making a voluntary disclosure	605
Sleepless nights	605
HMRC contact	605
The world is changing	606
'Had a good run'/Risk of getting caught	606
'Snowball' effect	606
Advantages of making a voluntary disclosure	606
Professional fees	606
Civil resolution	607
Penalty reduction	607
The 'naming and shaming' provisions	608
The old penalty regime	608

Contents

HMRC's view	609
Failure to file on time	612
VAT wrongdoing	612
Options for making the disclosure	613
The investigating officer (or usual HMRC office)	613
Voluntary disclosure opportunities	613
The Contractual Disclosure Facility	614
Making the disclosure	616
HMRC's response to the disclosure	618
Key points	619

Chapter 15 Private records: are they 'private'?   **621**

Signposts	621
Introduction	621
The power to obtain information and documents	622
HMRC's conduct of enquiries	623
Non-business information and documents	623
Business models	625
Private finances	626
Progressing the enquiry	628
Tax cases	629
First-tier Tribunal	629
Special Commissioners and the courts	630
Key points	632

Chapter 16 HMRC's information powers   **633**

Signposts	633
Introduction	634
The rationale for change	636
Finance Act 2007	637
Finance Acts 2008 and 2009	639
Finance Act 2008, Sch 36	640
Summary	640
Scope of HMRC's information and inspection powers	640
The power to obtain information and documents	641
HMRC's powers in relation to data-holders (FA 2011, Sch 23)	657
Categories of data and data-holders	658
Money service businesses	662
Data-holder notices	663
Power to inspect taxpayer's business premises (Sch 36, para 10)	664
What can be inspected?	664
Timing of inspections	666

Contents

Inspection of premises used in connection with taxable supplies (Sch 36, para 11)	667
Power to inspect premises of involved third parties (Sch 36, para 10A)	667
Power to inspect premises for valuation (Sch 36, para 12A)	668
Restrictions on the use of the powers by HMRC	668
Possession or power	669
Possession	669
Power	670
Territorial limits of Schedule 36	673
Legal professional privilege	674
Litigation privilege	678
Resolving privilege disputes	679
Schedule 36, para 19(1)(a)	681
Auditors and tax advisers' documents (FA 2008, Sch 36, para 24)	681
Penalties	683
The criminal investigatory powers of HMRC	685
PACE powers	685
Key points in respect of the PACE search powers	689
Section 20BA offences	694
Tax accountants and agents	694
Key points	696

Chapter 17 Preparing reports for HMRC   697

Signposts	697
Introduction	700
The case for preparing a report	701
Professional fees	701
Additional liabilities	702
Control	702
Tactics	703
The ground rules: planning the report and agreeing the parameters with HMRC	704
Preparing and completing the report	706
Common methodologies used in preparing the report	707
Analyses of banking accounts	707
Review of lodgements	708
Analyses of withdrawals from banking accounts	708
Scheduling income for comparison with submitted tax returns	709
Directors' loan or current accounts	709
Cash flow tests	710
Analyses of credit card expenditure	711
Review of P11Ds and potential benefits in kind	712
Schedules of assets and liabilities and/or capital statements	712

Contents

Working papers	712
Disclosure reports in COP9 cases	713
Voluntary disclosures	714
Disclosure facility submissions	715
Formal certificates	715
Key points	716

Chapter 18 Penalties for error and failure to notify — 718

Introduction	718
History	718
Objectives of this chapter	719
HMRC guidance	719
The relevant penalties legislation	719
Finance Act 2007, Sch 24	719
Finance Act 2008	720
Finance Act 2009	720
The statute	720
The types of 'inaccuracy'	721
Documents subject to the penalty regime	721
Documents relevant for income tax	722
Documents relevant for corporation tax	722
Documents relevant for VAT	722
Documents relevant for all taxes	723
Assessments	723
Penalty periods	723
The 'relevant person'	723
The previous penalties regime	724
Penalties for incorrect returns/inaccuracies	725
Introduction	725
The scale of penalties	725
Assessing the taxpayer's 'culpability'	726
Where are there no penalties?	727
Penalties for careless errors	733
Penalties for 'deliberate errors'	735
Penalties for deliberate errors with 'concealment'	736
Failure to notify penalties	738
Other penalties	739
Failure to notify an under-assessment	739
Errors by third parties	739
Computer records	739
HMRC information powers	739
Senior accounting officers	740
Notices for details of debtors	741
Failures to make returns	741
Amount of these penalties	741

xxi

Contents

Failure to pay taxes	742
Breach of minimum wage rules	742
The common causes of penalties	742
Late returns	743
Inaccuracies in documents	743
Failure to notify chargeability	744
Compliance with information notices	745
Are company officers liable for penalties?	746
Penalties and tax avoidance schemes	747
Recent developments	750
2015 Consultation on Penalties	750
Making Tax Digital – penalty proposals	751
Finance Act 2016 changes	753
Other changes introduced in 2017	754
Partial Closure Notices	754
Presumption of 'carelessness'	754
Penalties for enablers of tax avoidance	755
More VAT penalties for breaches of VAT record-keeping rules	756
Penalties for offshore matters	756
Offshore disclosure facility cases	756
General approach to offshore evasion penalties	756
Other consequences of 'deliberate' penalties	758
Managing serious defaulters	758
Naming and shaming	759
Administrative matters: deadlines for imposing penalties	761
Assessments	761
Time limits	762
Appeals	762
Multiple penalties	762
Transition	762
Some miscellaneous penalty matters	763
Group relief	763
Losses	763
Multiple penalties	764
The double jeopardy rule	765
Key points	765

Chapter 19 Penalty mitigation   767

Reductions for disclosure	767
Mitigation of penalties for failure to make returns	768
Mitigating penalties by making good quality 'disclosure'	769
Mitigation by 'special reduction' or 'special relief'	773
Calculating penalties and potential lost revenue	774

Contents

Suspended penalties	777
Case decisions on suspension	778
Examples	780
Mitigation for 'reasonable excuse'	782
Key points	785
Checklist	785
Appendix: list of statutes	786

Chapter 20 Tax appeals — 788

Signposts	788
Introduction	790
The tax appeals system	790
Use of litigation as a tactic	791
Litigation and Settlement Strategy	792
Introduction of the tribunal system	794
The origin for change	794
The Leggatt Inquiry	795
The Tribunals, Courts and Enforcement Act 2007	796
Summary of the tax tribunal system	797
The overriding objective	798
Alternative Dispute Resolution	800
Pre-appeal procedures	802
Introduction	802
Starting an appeal: direct taxes	802
Self-assessment closure procedure	803
Closure notice applications	803
The purpose of a closure notice	804
Referral of questions during enquiry	810
Partial Closure Notices	810
Starting an appeal: indirect taxes	811
The review procedure	812
Introduction	812
Indirect taxes	813
Direct taxes	813
Appealing to the tax tribunal after the review process	816
Application for postponement of tax	817
Withdrawal of an appeal	829
The First-tier Tribunal	830
Introduction	830
The categories	831
Statement of case/exchange of documents	835
Case management powers	835
Strike out	837
BPP Holdings	839

Contents

Jurisdiction of the First-tier Tribunal in respect of public law matters	842
Hearings	843
The position before the predecessor tribunals	844
Approach of the High Court	845
Approach of the First-tier Tribunal	846
Decisions	847
Review of decisions	849
Costs	850
The Upper Tribunal	856
The function of the Upper Tribunal	856
Direct referrals to the Upper Tribunal	857
Appeals from the First-tier Tribunal	857
Judicial review	859
Case management powers	861
Hearings	862
Decisions	863
Costs in the Upper Tribunal	863
Appeals from the Upper Tribunal	863
The tax courts	864
The High Court	864
Court of Justice of the European Union	866
Key points	869

Chapter 21 Tackling 'tax avoidance' — 870

Signposts	870
Introduction	871
Primary targets for APNs	873
Target list	873
Taxes covered	874
Accelerated payment notices	875
Qualifying conditions	875
Process and timeline	877
The notice	878
Calculating the tax due	878
Payment	879
Resolving the underlying tax dispute	880
Follower notices	881
Purpose of an FN	881
Qualifying conditions	881
Process and timeline	882
The notice	882
Amended returns	883
Outstanding appeals	883

Contents

Penalties for failure to comply with a follower notice	883
Payment and resolving the dispute	884
Promoters of tax avoidance schemes	884
Conduct notices	885
Monitoring notices	885
Enablers of Tax Avoidance	886
Offshore enablers	886
PCRT & HMRC Spotlights	888
The General Anti-Abuse Rule (GAAR)	889
Contesting an APN or FN	891
Differences for partnerships	892
Practical issues for partnerships	893
Serial Tax Avoidance Regime	893
Disguised Remuneration	895
Penalties on tax avoidance arrangements	896
Tax geared penalties for errors in tax returns	896
Failures to deal with APNs or FNs on time	897
GAAR Penalty	897
Serial Tax Avoiders Regime (STAR)	898
The taxpayer's options	898
Where are we now?	898
Judicial review	899
Early stage options	899
Key points	903
Appendix: an example of an accelerated payment notice	904

Chapter 22 Tax debt collection   912

Signposts	912
Introduction	913
Managed payment plans – pre-empting cashflow issues	914
The early collection stages	915
Identifying the debt and debtor	915
Transfer of debt to other parties	915
Tax collection via coding notices	917
Reminders	917
Accelerated payment notices for Scheme users	918
Time to pay agreements	918
Direct recovery of debts from taxpayer's bank accounts	920
Information and hold notices	921
Objecting to and appealing against hold notices	924
Deduction notices	924
Penalties	925
Court action	926

Contents

Notice of enforcement – taking control of goods	926
Who is the bailiff?	928
Liquidation and bankruptcy	928
HMRC procedure for dealing with tax debts for companies in insolvency	929
Requirement to give security for tax	930
HMRC enforcement of non-UK tax debts	932
European Union Mutual Assistance for Recovery of Debts (MARD)	932
Mutual Assistance to non-EU countries for tax debts	933
HMRC mutual assistance teams	934
Key points	935

Chapter 23 Complaints about HMRC — 937

Signposts	937
Introduction	938
What does HMRC's complaints process cover?	940
Mistakes	940
Unreasonable delays	941
Unreasonable/misinformed decisions	941
Disproportionate/unfair/inconsistent decisions	942
HMRC not following its published guidance	943
Misleading advice	944
Unacceptable HMRC staff behaviour	945
Any mishandling by HMRC of the complaint	945
What HMRC's complaints process does not cover	945
Handling issues associated with how HMRC interprets tax legislation and court decisions	946
Interest charges arising from unreasonable delays by HMRC	946
Unnecessary or vexatious complaints	948
Complaints concerning serious and/or potentially criminal misbehaviour by HMRC staff	948
Other factors that need to be taken in to account when deciding to complain	949
Impact on the client	949
Management of expectations	949
When to complain: ongoing investigations and the seeking of other outcomes	950
Other implications of complaining	951
Interaction with legal routes to securing redress	952
Interaction with tribunal hearings	952
Interaction with Judicial Review	952
HMRC's complaints process	953
Time limits for complaining	953
What if there is more than one area of HMRC involved?	954

Contents

Tier 1	954
Tier 2	954
Tier 3: the Adjudicator	954
The Parliamentary Ombudsman	955
Redress available if the complaint is upheld	956
Compensation for financial losses	956
The writing off of tax, interest or a tax credit repayment	957

Section 4: VAT, NIC, employment income

Chapter 24 VAT aspects — 958

Signposts	958
Overall concept	959
Assurance visits	961
General questions	962
Review of VAT returns submitted	963
Credibility queries	966
Business records checks	967
Intrastat visits	968
Mutual assistance through exchange of information	969
Preparing for visits	970
Search and entry	974
Surveillance operations	975
Role of the professional adviser	976
Business review	976
Assessments and disputes	976
Assessments	976
Appeals	977
Appeal time limits	977
Alternative dispute resolution	978
The Revenue and Customs adjudicator	979
Judicial review	979
Key points	980

Chapter 25 National Insurance aspects — 981

Signposts	981
Introduction	982
Inspectorate powers	985
National Insurance funding	986
Triggers for investigations	988
Triggers for visit	988
Which employers are chosen for investigation?	989
RTI submissions	990

Contents

End-of-year returns (pre-RTI)	992
Category X notations	995
Complaints from employees	999
Regional initiatives	999
National programme	1000
Routine visits	1000
Failing to reply to correspondence	1001
Large employers	1001
Employers with an international exposure	1002
Unlucky	1003
HMRC visits	1003
Purpose of visit	1003
Timing of visit	1004
Notification of visit	1004
Length of visit	1005
Place of visit	1005
Preparation for the visit	1005
Commencement of the visit	1006
Records to be made available	1006
Record keeping	1010
Errors and omissions	1011
Inspection report	1013
Future visits	1015
Offences and penalties	1015
Background	1015
False information, delays and obstruction	1015
Contravention of regulations	1016
Offences relating to contributions	1016
Offences by bodies corporate	1017
Employer failing to pay Class 1 and Class 1A contributions	1017
Class 1, Class 1A and PAYE penalties	1020
Interest	1027
Overdue contributions	1027
Repaid contributions	1028
Repayment and remission of interest	1029
Interest on Class 4 and Class 2 contributions	1029
Appeals	1029
Decisions of officers of HMRC	1031
The subject matter of a decision	1031
Giving notice of the decision	1034
Appeals against officer's decisions	1036
Manner of making an appeal	1036
Place of hearing of appeal	1037
Late appeals	1037
Determination by tax tribunal	1037
Settling appeals by agreement	1037

Dissatisfaction with tribunal's determination	1038
Decisions under the Pension Schemes Act 1993 and in respect of the award of credits, etc	1039
Class 4 appeals	1039
Conclusions	1040
Key points	1042

Chapter 26 Employment tax issues   1043

Signposts	1043
Introduction	1044
PAYE compliance issues	1046
Subjecting earnings to PAYE/NICs	1049
Calculation of the correct amounts of PAYE/NICs	1060
Including all employees and directors on the payroll	1063
Self-employment v employment: basic principles	1063
Self-employment v employment: the audit approach	1066
Casual workers	1069
Agency workers	1070
One-man companies	1072
Students	1075
Cleaners	1076
Directors	1076
Schedule E benefits and reimbursed expenses	1076
Dispensations	1076
Working rule agreements	1078
Scope of benefits	1079
Value of benefits	1081
Areas likely to be investigated	1082
Liability for tax arising	1103

Index   *1107*

Table of Statutes

Access to Justice Act 1999 .... 20.254
  s 54(4) 20.257
  55(1) 20.255
Accessories and Abettors Act 1861
  s 8 .... 3.7
Capital Allowances Act 2001
  s 45 .... 20.61, 20.62, 20.63, 20.69, 20.70
  (4) 20.61, 20.62, 20.63,
                 20.65, 20.67, 20.68, 20.70
  Sch 2
    para 51(1)(a) 26.146
Children Act 1989
  Pt IV (ss 31–42) 16.166
Commissioners for Revenue and
  Customs Act 2005 .... 3.159; 11.2;
                 16.5, 16.6, 16.9; 22.1
  s 5 .... 6.109; 23.38
    6(2) 3.159
    7(3) 3.159
    17 .... 3.159
      (1), (2), (3) 3.159
    18 .... 3.159
      (2)–(7) 3.159
      (2), (3) 3.159
    20 .... 3.159
      (9) 3.159
    21 .... 3.159
      (2A) 3.5
      (3) 3.159
    22 .... 3.159
    35 .... 16.6
Companies Act 2006 .... 3.179
  Pt 42 (ss 1209–1264) 3.170
  s 1210 .... 3.170
Constitutional Reform Act 2005
  Sch 2
    Pt 1 (paras 4–9) 20.239
Corporation Tax Act 2009
  s 14 .... 4.90; 5.17
    276 .... 16.92
    441 .... 4.78
    1313 .... 16.92
Corporation Tax Act 2010
  s 455 .... 17.42
    750 .... 21.6
    1033 .... 16.92

Criminal Finances Act 2017 .... 3.8; 5.122,
                5.123, 5.124; 8.30, 8.169
  s 45 .... 3.8; 5.122
    (4), (5) 3.8
    46 .... 3.8; 5.122
    (6) 3.8
Criminal Justice Act 1982
  s 37(2) 25.113
Criminal Justice Act 1988 .... 3.31
Criminal Justice Act 1993 .... 3.166
Criminal Justice Act 2003
  s 281(5) 3.9
Criminal Justice and Police
  Act 2001 .... 3.84, 3.131; 16.200
  s 50 .... 16.201, 16.203
    52 .... 16.203
  Sch 1
    Pt 1 (paras 1–74) 16.201
Criminal Justice and Public Order
  Act 1994
  s 34 .... 3.43, 3.136
Criminal Justice (International
  Co-operation) Act 1990
  s 4 .... 3.186
Criminal Law (Consolidation)
  (Scotland) Act 1995 .... 3.53
Criminal Procedure and Investigations
  Act 1996 .... 3.60, 3.142
  ss 5, 6 .... 3.145
  s 6A 3.144
    11 .... 3.145
Criminal Procedure (Attendance of
  Witnesses) Act 1965 .... 3.146
Criminal Procedure (Legal
  Assistance, Detention and
  Appeals) (Scotland) Act 2010 .... 3.54
Criminal Procedure (Scotland) Act
  1995 .... 3.53
Customs and Excise Management
  Act 1979
  s 139 .... 22.60
Debtors (Scotland) Act 1987
  Sch 5 .... 25.123
Employment Act 2002
  ss 11, 12 .... 25.111
  Sch 1 .... 25.111

Table of Statutes

European Union Notification of Withdrawal Act 2017	20.279
Finance Act 1989	25.126
s 178	25.161
Finance Act 1994	
Sch 7	
para 24	22.80
Finance Act 1995	
s 106(9)(b), (c)	26.176
Finance Act 1996	
s 54	20.83
Sch 5	
para 31	22.80
Sch 9	
para 13	4.78, 4.83
Sch 13	
paras 2, 3	4.61
Finance Act 1998	18.165; 26.43, 26.180
s 58	26.42
127	16.36
Sch 18	1.125
para 2	8.17; 18.91
3	1.26; 18.18
paras 4–16	1.26
para 17	1.26; 18.199
(2), (3)	20.129
18	1.26; 18.199
paras 19, 20	1.26
para 21	1.26; 6.15
(1), (5)	1.71
paras 22, 23	1.26
para 24	1.1, 1.2, 1.26, 1.36, 1.89; 6.4, 6.34; 13.1, 13.179; 21.6
(2)	6.43
paras 25, 26	1.26
para 27	1.26, 1.81; 16.144
paras 28, 29	1.26
para 30	1.26; 8.146
31	1.26
(3)	21.9
paras 31A–31D	20.78
para 31A	1.123; 8.127
32	1.26; 6.34; 20.51, 20.81
(1)	1.106
33	1.26, 1.109, 1.113; 6.95, 6.99; 8.99; 20.54, 20.81
(3)	6.96
34	1.26
(1)	1.108
(3)	1.111; 21.6
(4)	1.108
35	1.26
36	8.22; 13.55
paras 41–46	13.14, 13.15
Finance Act 1998 – *contd*	
Sch 18 – *contd*	
paras 41–45	4.185
para 41	1.133; 6.34, 6.43; 8.24; 13.110, 13.146
paras 42–45	1.133
42–46	8.107
para 43	13.71, 13.84, 13.98, 13.99, 13.160
44	13.105, 13.107, 13.114, 13.115, 13.121, 13.160
(1)	13.109
(2)	13.107, 13.116
(d)(i)	13.118
45	13.66, 13.163
46	1.130; 13.29
(1), (2), (2A)	8.109
(2B)(a), (b)	13.32
47	13.142, 13.146
48	20.49; 21.6
52	13.19
paras 61–63	13.173
61–64	8.113
para 62(1)(a)	13.173
(2), (3)	13.174
64	13.175
65	13.176
74(2)	13.179
76	13.20
Finance Act 1999	26.161
Finance Act 2000	4.97
s 144	3.17, 3.190
149(1)	16.223
Sch 6	
para 139(1)	22.80
Sch 10	
para 5(1)	26.159
Finance Act 2001	20.78
s 26(1)	22.80
Finance Act 2003	
s 42	3.170
Sch 10	
para 12	21.6
28	13.20
31	13.33
35	20.49; 21.6
Finance Act 2004	4.12; 16.3
ss 306–319	4.13
s 307(1A)	4.17
ss 308–310	4.15
309, 310, 313	13.28
s 313C	4.17, 4.20
316C	4.21; 8.71
Finance Act 2006	
s 173	16.91; 22.90
175	22.90

Table of Statutes

Finance Act 2007	3.48, 3.49, 3.53, 3.57, 3.58, 3.97; 4.18; 6.115; 11.9, 11.55; 16.2, 16.10, 16.11, 16.12, 16.14, 16.15, 16.226, 16.235; 18.8, 18.17, 18.25, 18.31, 18.33, 18.43, 18.204; 19.9
ss 82–86	3.73
s 87	3.73; 19.72
97	5.72, 5.113; 18.31
Sch 24	4.36; 5.72, 5.113, 5.116, 5.120; 6.34, 6.104, 6.106, 6.110, 6.113; 7.73; 8.88, 8.132, 8.133; 14.2; 16.15, 16.16, 16.22, 16.189; 18.7, 18.10, 18.11, 18.31; 19.40, 19.72; 21.35; 25.104, 25.127, 25.141, 25.150, 25.151, 25.152
para 1	11.9, 11.55; 18.14
1A	8.139
paras 3A, 3B	6.112; 8.93
para 4AA	21.24
5(1)	19.29
9	13.58
(1)	6.110; 19.13
(2)(a), (b)	14.2
11	6.112
13(3)	8.137
14	6.112
Finance Act 2008	1.129; 5.14; 15.2; 16.2, 16.3, 16.19, 16.235; 18.8, 18.9, 18.25, 18.210; 24.61
s 113	5.42; 19.72
114	16.34; 18.95; 19.72
115	19.72
118	5.64; 19.72
ss 119, 122	19.72
s 123	5.113; 18.87; 19.72
Sch 36	1.13, 1.40, 1.41, 1.44, 1.46, 1.81, 1.83, 1.96, 1.140; 4.23, 4.108, 4.168; 6.17, 6.34, 6.45, 6.46, 6.49, 6.50, 6.53, 6.81, 6.88; 7.10, 7.21, 7.27; 8.57, 8.73, 8.96, 8.97, 8.111, 8.138; 10.117; 13.13; 15.2, 15.12, 15.24, 15.33; 16.3, 16.4, 16.19, 16.20, 16.21, 16.24, 16.25, 16.28, 16.39, 16.40, 16.46, 16.48, 16.59, 16.63, 16.65, 16.80, 16.84, 16.102, 16.116, 16.126, 16.149, 16.151, 16.161, 16.172, 16.188, 16.190; 18.105; 19.72; 21.24; 24.59; 25.14, 25.79, 25.85
Pt 1 (paras 1–9)	1.84, 1.86; 21.21
para 1	1.47, 1.84; 3.134; 6.54, 6.103; 15.5; 16.36, 16.42, 16.43
2	1.47, 1.85, 1.105; 8.12; 16.50

Finance Act 2008 – *contd*	
Sch 36 – *contd*	
Pt 1 (paras 1–9) – *contd*	
para 3	1.85
(2A)	16.46
(3)	16.56
(b)	16.54
4	10.118
5	2.95; 5.39, 5.42; 8.12; 16.66, 16.77, 16.78, 16.79, 16.85, 16.86, 16.142, 16.185
5A	8.12; 16.83, 16.84, 16.86
(2), (3), (4)	16.85
6(2)	16.32
(3)	16.57
(4)	16.47, 16.57
7	16.31, 16.49
(2)	1.85; 16.31, 16.35
8	1.85
Pt 2 (paras 10–14)	1.56, 1.61, 1.98, 1.100; 7.3; 16.103
para 10	6.55, 6.66; 16.104, 16.107
(1)	1.98
(4)	16.108
10A	16.89, 16.120
11	16.117, 16.119
12	6.56; 16.113
(2)(b)	16.115
12A	16.123
12B	16.125
13	1.99; 6.56; 16.125
(1)	16.111
Pt 4 (paras 18–28)	1.100; 15.24
para 18	16.32, 16.128
19	16.171
(1)	4.117
(a)	16.180, 16.181
(2)	15.24
(3)	6.53; 15.26, 15.27
21	7.4, 7.5; 8.111; 13.13; 16.43; 20.74
(1)–(3)	1.87
(4)	1.88, 1.89, 1.111; 6.103
(6)	1.90, 1.132
(7)	1.91
paras 23–26	4.116; 16.164
para 23	1.93; 4.107, 4.115; 16.152
24	1.93; 16.171, 16.182
25	1.93; 4.115; 16.171, 16.184
26	1.93; 4.115
(1), (2)	16.185, 16.186
(3)	16.186

Table of Statutes

Finance Act 2008 – *contd*
  Sch 36 – *contd*
    Pt 4 (paras 18–28) – *contd*
      para 27 .... 1.93
      28 .... 1.100; 16.110, 16.152
    Pt 5 (paras 29–33) 1.94
      para 29 .... 1.48; 6.50
        (2) 1.94
        (3) 1.94; 6.58; 16.58
      30 .... 16.82
        (1) 16.60
        (3) 1.94; 16.58
      32 .... 16.59
        (5) 16.59
    Pt 6 (paras 34–38) 1.95
      para 34A 16.87, 16.88
    Pt 7 (paras 39–52) 1.95
      para 39 .... 6.58, 6.59; 16.112,
                     16.176, 16.190, 16.191
        (2) 18.96
      40 .... 6.58; 16.112,
                     16.190, 16.191
        (2) 16.191
      40A 16.192
      44 .... 16.190
      45 ...... 6.58; 16.112, 16.176, 16.191
      47 .... 16.191
        (b) 16.191
      50 .... 16.190; 20.221
    Pt 8 (paras 53–55) 1.95
    Pt 9 (paras 56–64) 1.95
      para 58 .... 16.48
      59 .... 16.194
      61A 16.87, 16.121
      62 .... 1.94; 16.108
        (1) 16.61
        (2) 16.62
        (3) 16.64
      64 .... 1.85; 16.29
        (2), (2A) 1.92
    Pt 10 (paras 65–92) 1.95
      para 84 .... 25.14
Sch 37 .... 19.72; 25.85
Sch 38 .... 19.72
Sch 39 .... 5.64; 19.72
Sch 40 .... 19.72
Sch 41 .... 4.36; 5.72, 5.113, 5.120;
          8.25, 8.131, 8.133; 18.94; 19.72
    para 1 .... 18.90
    2 .... 18.89
    12 .... 13.58; 19.2
    13 .... 19.2
    16(4) 8.137
    22 .... 18.134
Sch 50
    para 36 .... 20.219

Finance Act 2009 .... 16.3, 16.87,
           16.118, 16.120, 16.123;
           18.10; 18.97, 18.210;
           19.72; 20.265
s 93 .... 18.100
Sch 46 .... 19.72
s 94 .... 3.19; 5.120; 6.112, 6.120;
           8.159; 13.58; 14.18;
           18.162; 19.72
ss 95, 96 .... 16.21; 19.72
s 97 .... 18.105; 19.72
ss 98, 99, 100 .... 19.72
101–103 .... 6.34
101–105 .... 6.108; 19.72
106–109 .... 19.72
s 106 .... 18.106; 19.72
107 .... 18.110; 19.72
108 .... 19.72
Sch 47 .... 16.21; 19.72
    para 4 .... 16.47, 16.57
    5 .... 16.108
    6 .... 16.118
    15 .... 16.192
Sch 48 .... 16.21, 16.23, 16.41; 19.72
    para 3 .... 16.120
    5 .... 16.123
    6 .... 16.125
    14 .... 16.121
Sch 49 .... 18.105; 19.72; 22.7
Sch 50 .... 19.72
Sch 51 .... 19.72
Sch 52 .... 19.72
Sch 53 .... 6.108; 19.72
Sch 54 .... 19.72
Sch 55 .... 8.23, 8.131, 18.106;
           19.72; 25.127, 25.139
    para 17(3) 8.141
Sch 56 .... 8.131; 18.110; 19.72
    para 9A 8.141
Sch 57 .... 19.72
    para 6 .... 18.196
Finance Act 2010 .... 4.18; 5.120;
           16.3, 16.16
s 35 .... 5.113
Sch 6 .... 16.92
Sch 10 .... 5.113; 11.10; 19.72
Finance (No 2) Act 2010
    Sch 10 .... 19.72
    Sch 11 .... 19.72
Finance (No 3) Act 2010 .... 16.3
Finance Act 2011 .... 16.3, 16.92
s 87 .... 22.83
Sch 23 .... 16.41, 16.89, 16.90, 16.91
    para 13A 16.93
    13D 16.97
Sch 25 .... 22.83

Table of Statutes

Finance Act 2012	16.3, 16.41
s 218	5.83
223	16.234
224	16.83
Sch 36	5.83
Sch 37	16.243
Sch 38	8.170, 8.171; 16.234
para 8	16.234
9(2)	16.234
Finance Act 2013	16.3, 16.93
s 204	4.37
Pt 5 (ss 206–215)	4.25; 8.72
s 207(2)	4.26, 4.27
218	5.7
230	25.139
Sch 29	4.25
Sch 33	
para 8	21.6
21	13.20
25	13.33
35	21.6
Sch 43C	8.72
para 8	8.141
Sch 45	5.7
Sch 50	19.72
paras 3, 4	25.139
Finance Act 2014	4.19; 8.78, 8.79; 16.3; 20.117; 21.2, 21.5, 21.7; 25.124
s 17	22.11
Pt 4 (ss 199–233)	4.11, 4.29; 20.115, 20.116; 21.19
Pt 4 Ch 2 (ss 204–218)	4.130, 4.271
s 204	4.29; 20.119
(3)	20.119
205(3)	20.119
(b)	20.119
(4)	20.119
207	20.119
214	20.119
ss 219–229	21.6; 22.21
s 219	20.117
(4)(b)	4.22
ss 220, 221	21.9
s 222	20.117
ss 230, 231	21.30
Pt 5 (ss 234–283)	4.23; 8.170; 21.20
s 253	13.28
Sch 31	21.29
Sch 32	21.29
Sch 33	21.6
Sch 34	4.15, 4.23; 8.170
Sch 35	4.15, 4.23; 8.170
Sch 36	4.15, 4.23; 8.170

Finance Act 2015	4.19, 4.38; 16.3; 18.90; 21.9
s 118	21.19
Sch 18	21.5, 21.19
Sch 20	5.115
Sch 21	5.116; 8.35, 8.131, 8.133, 8.136
Finance (No 2) Act 2015	22.1, 22.36
s 51	8.157; 22.32
Sch 8	8.157; 22.32
para 2	1.136; 22.34
3	22.36
(3)	22.36
4(4)	22.38
(6)	22.37
5(1), (2)	22.43
6(2)	22.37
7	22.39
(2), (5)	22.40
8	22.41
(10)	22.41
(c)	22.41
(11)	22.41
9	22.42
10	22.44
(3), (6)–(8)	22.44
11	22.45
12	22.46
(9)	22.46
13	22.47
(2)(c)	22.47
(10)	22.48
(11)	22.47
14	22.49
(1)(g)	22.51
(4), (5), (6)	22.50
15(3)	22.52
16	22.53
18	22.48
paras 19–21	22.33
Finance Act 2016	3.9, 3.10; 4.19, 4.23, 4.28; 5.117, 5.120; 16.3, 6.120; 8.35; 18.160, 18.161, 18.162, 18.163, 18.164
s 94	6.119
159	4.32; 8.82; 21.32
160	4.23
161	4.33
162	3.10; 5.119
163	3.10; 5.120
164	3.10
165	3.10; 5.121
166	5.118
Sch 18	4.32; 8.82; 21.32
para 55	21.32
64(2)	8.86

Table of Statutes

Finance Act 2016 – *contd*
Sch 20...................... 8.170, 8.174; 21.24
  para 1(2)(b) 8.174
    (3), (4), (5)...................... 8.174
Sch 21............... 3.10; 8.133, 8.136, 8.160
Sch 22.. 8.136
Finance Act 2017 .... 20.80, 20.81
s 24 .... 4.23
Sch 16 .... 4.24
Finance (No 2) Act 2017.......... 1.123, 1.125;
4.15, 4.18; 6.85, 6.103,
6.112; 16.3; 21.34
s 63 .... 8.127; 18.165
64 .... 8.93; 18.166; 21.35
65 .... 18.167
68 .... 18.168
69 .... 16.97
Sch 11 .... 21.33
Sch 15 .... 8.127, 8.137; 18.165
Sch 16 .... 8.170, 8.173; 18.167; 21.23
Sch 18 .... 4.36; 5.135; 8.35, 8.44; 21.33
  para 7 .... 8.110
    23(5) 4.36
    26 .... 8.110; 13.31
    30 .... 8.44
Finance Act 2018
Sch 1 .... 21.33
Forgery Act 1861 .... 4.97
Fraud Act 2006..................... 2.19, 2.20; 3.2;
4.97; 18.209
s 1 .... 3.6
Freedom of Information Act
2000............. 6.2; 7.15, 7.16, 7.17; 9.89
Human Rights Act 1998..................... 6.57
Sch 1
  art 8 .... 15.14
Income and Corporation Taxes
Act 1988 .... 4.62, 4.63; 5.7
s 18 Sch D 26.79, 26.81
19 Sch E 26.3, 26.79, 26.101,
26.135, 26.146, 26.165
66 .... 5.17
148 .... 26.42
ss 167, 168 .... 26.120
s 202B(6).. 26.58
203A(1)(c) 26.58
Pt XIII Ch II (ss 539–554) 4.63
s 574 .... 4.72
577 .... 26.150
  (1)(a), (b) 26.151
  (3) 26.149, 26.151
  (5) 26.150
ss 703–709 .... 4.42
s 703 .... 4.50, 4.110
706 .... 4.81, 4.110; 20.2, 20.3,
20.31, 20.258

Income and Corporation Taxes
Act 1988 – *contd*
s 727A 4.58
730A 4.59
737A 4.59
ss 739, 741 .... 4.148
s 747 .... 5.20
Sch 6
  paras 6, 9 .... 26.135
Sch 11A.............................. 26.166, 26.169
Sch 28AA 5.20
Income Tax Act 2007
s 132 .... 4.72
475 .... 5.15
Pt 13 (ss 682–809ZR) 5.18
ss 682–713 .... 4.42
s 705 .... 21.6
ss 731, 732 .... 5.18
829–835 .... 5.7
Income Tax (Earnings and Pensions)
Act 2003................................... 25.124
s 6 .... 26.4
7 .... 26.4, 26.112, 26.140
  (5) 26.159
10 .... 26.56
  (2) 26.4
44 .... 26.88
  (4)–(6) 22.10
46A 22.10
62(2) 26.4
66(4) 26.118
71 .... 26.121, 26.158
ss 97, 98 .... 26.129
s 99 .... 26.129
  (1) 26.129
ss 100–113 .... 26.129
125, 126, 132 .... 26.135
s 167(1) 26.135
174(1) 26.159
175 .... 17.42
180 .... 26.159
  (5) 26.159
188(2) 26.159
203(2) 26.124
  (3) 26.132
204 .... 26.124
216(3) 26.135
223(7) 26.182
225 .... 26.38
237(2) 26.135
240 .... 26.162
264 .... 26.170
288(4) 26.168
315 .... 26.129
316(1) 26.161
320 .... 26.132

Income Tax (Earnings and Pensions) Act 2003 – contd

s 321	26.173
328	26.162, 26.172
(1)	26.147, 26.150, 26.154, 26.159, 26.161
336	26.108, 26.111
337	26.177, 26.179
356(1)	26.146
357	26.147
386	20.243
394	26.40
403	26.34, 26.37, 26.39, 26.42, 26.45
413	26.46
Pt 7 (ss 417–554)	4.66
Pt 7 Ch 2 (ss 422–434)	4.64, 4.65, 4.67
Pt 7 Chs 3A–3D (ss 446A–446Z)	4.67
s 423	4.64, 4.66, 4.67
(1), (2)–(4)	4.67
429	4.64
Pt 7A (ss 554A–554Z21)	21.33
Pt 11 (ss 682–712)	21.6
s 684	25.124; 26.68
ss 688A–688B	25.136
s 688A(2)	22.8
721(5)	26.122, 26.145

Income Tax Management Act 1964

s 5(6)	20.261
29(6)	20.261

Income Tax (Trading and Other Income) Act 2005

Pt 2 Ch 2 (ss 5–23)	25.164
s 58	4.74
Pt 5 (ss 574–689A)	5.19
s 696	16.92
Pt 8 (ss 829–845)	5.12
s 874	16.92

Inheritance Tax Act 1984

ss 216, 217	21.6
s 218	16.151
222	21.6
(3)	20.266
240	8.109; 13.9
256	21.6

Insolvency Act 1986	3.179; 16.65
s 388	3.170

Interpretation Act 1978

s 7	6.41; 13.166

Jobseekers Act 1995

s 27	25.173

Juries Act 1974

s 17	3.148

Land and Buildings Transaction Tax (Scotland) Act 2013

s 1	3.170

Landlord and Tenant Act 1985

s 11	26.129

Legal Aid, Sentencing and Punishment of Offenders Act 2012

s 85	25.113

Legal Services Act 2007	8.74, 8.150
Limitation Act 1980	25.52, 25.93
ss 9, 24, 37	22.20

Local Audit and Accountability Act 2014

s 4(1)	3.170

National Insurance Contributions Act 2011

s 8(6)	25.174

National Insurance Contributions Act 2015

	4.37; 21.6; 25.3, 25.125, 25.163
s 4	21.19
Sch 2	21.19, 25.124
Sch 6	
para 4	21.6

Oil Taxation Act 1975	16.92

Pension Schemes Act 1993

s 170(1)	25.210

Perjury Act 1911	4.97

Petroleum Act 1998

Pt 1 (ss 1–9)	16.92

Police Act 1996

s 2	3.170

Police Act 1997	3.62
s 2(2)	3.159

Police and Criminal Evidence Act 1984

	1.34; 2.28; 3.42, 3.43, 3.48, 3.49, 3.50, 3.51, 3.52, 3.53, 3.55, 3.59, 3.62, 3.70, 3.71, 3.73, 3.94, 3.116, 3.117, 3.120, 3.123, 3.124, 3.131, 3.135; 8.28; 16.2, 16.4, 16.9, 16.10, 16.12, 16.13, 16.193, 16.194, 16.201, 16.209, 16.210
s 8	3.48, 3.50, 3.69, 3.76, 3.80, 3.83, 3.84, 3.119, 3.124; 16.13, 16.201, 16.205, 16.209, 16.225
(1)	3.75
(b)–(d)	3.77
(2)	3.69
(3)	3.77
9	3.69, 3.93, 3.112
10	3.79, 3.129
(2)	3.79
11(1)	3.81
12	15.25; 16.234
14	16.210
(2)	3.82

Table of Statutes

Police and Criminal Evidence
Act 1984 – contd
- ss 14A, 14B 16.213
- s 15 .... 3.76
- 17 .... 3.50
- 18 .... 3.50, 3.85
- ss 19, 20 .... 3.50
- s 21(1)–(8) 3.86
- 22 .... 3.69
- (2) 3.50
- 23 .... 3.70
- 24(2) 3.50
- 37 .... 3.44
- ss 46, 58 .... 3.43
- s 67 .... 16.214
- (11) 16.214
- 78 .... 3.42
- Sch 1 .... 3.76, 3.80, 3.84,
  3.93, 3.112, 3.114, 3.121,
  3.125; 16.13, 16.213, 16.226
- para 4 .... 3.48, 3.89, 3.91, 3.92, 3.97
- paras 7–11 .... 16.212
- para 12 .... 3.48, 3.69, 3.83, 3.88,
  3.124; 16.211
- 13 .... 3.69

Prescription and Limitation
(Scotland) Act 1984 .... 25.52

Proceeds of Crime Act 2002 .... 3.27, 3.31,
3.164, 3.166, 3.171, 3.178, 3.187,
3.207, 3.211, 3.212, 3.213, 3.228,
3.235; 5.62; 14.15; 16.3
- s 6 .... 3.151
- 76(4) 14.15
- Pt 5 (ss 240–316) 3.159; 8.31
- Pt 7 (ss 327–340) 3.173, 3.171
- s 327 .... 3.172, 3.176, 3.184
- 328 ..... 3.173, 3.176, 3.184, 3.229, 3.231
- 329 .... 3.173, 3.174, 3.176, 3.184
- ss 330–331 .... 3.194
- s 330 .... 3.179
- (10), (14) 3.179
- 337 .... 3.191
- 340 .... 3.175
- (2)(b) 3.182, 3.184, 3.185
- (11) 3.178
- Pt 8 (ss 341–416) 3.159

Regulation of Investigatory Powers
Act 2000 .... 3.62

Serious Crime Act 2007
- s 45 .... 3.7

Serious Organised Crime and Police
Act 2005 .... 3.117, 3.120; 8.28;
16.4, 16.219
- ss 60, 61 .... 16.221
- s 62 .... 3.118; 16.221
- (3) 16.217

Serious Organised Crime and Police
Act 2005 – contd
- ss 63–65 .... 16.221
- s 66 .... 3.48, 3.121; 16.221
- (2) 16.221
- ss 67–70 .... 16.215
- Sch 1
- Pt 2 (paras 8–14) 16.215

Social Security Act 1998 .... 25.113, 25.122
- s 12 .... 25.210
- 60 .... 25.110
- 61 .... 25.113
- 63 .... 25.123
- 64 .... 25.133, 25.194

Social Security Administration
Act 1992
- s 113 .... 25.110
- ss 113A, 113B 25.111
- s 114 .... 25.113
- 115 .... 25.115
- (1), (2) 25.114
- 121A 25.122
- 121B 25.123
- 121C 25.133
- 121D 25.194

Social Security Contributions and
Benefits Act 1992
- s 15(1), (2), (5) 25.212
- 16 .... 25.156
- 17(1), (3)–(6) 25.215
- 18 .... 25.215
- Pt V (ss 94–111) 25.173
- s 110ZA 25.13, 25.14
- 121C 25.173
- Sch 1
- para 3(1) 22.13
- paras 3A, 3B 25.112
- para 6(3) 25.161
- 7 .... 25.126, 25.141
- (2) 25.143
- (3), (4), (5) 25.126
- (6), (8) 25.132
- Sch 2
- para 6 .... 25.164
- Sch 8 .... 25.212

Social Security Contributions
(Transfer of Functions etc)
Act 1999 .... 25.171
- s 8 .... 25.103, 25.172, 25.179,
  25.197, 25.216
- (1) 25.173
- (c) 25.185
- (2) 25.175
- (3) 25.177
- 9(1), (2), (3) 25.179

Table of Statutes

Social Security Contributions (Transfer of Functions etc) Act 1999 – *contd*
- s 10 .... 25.179
- 11(1), (2), (4) 25.194
- 12(1), (2) 25.196
- (3) 25.198
- ss 13, 14 .... 25.199
- s 16(1), (6) 25.210

Taxation (International and Other Provisions) Act 2010
- s 81(2) 13.65
- Pt 6A (ss 259A–259NF) 4.39
- Pt 9A (ss 371AA–371VJ) 5.20

Taxation of Chargeable Gains Act 1992 .... 5.19
- s 12 .... 5.12
- 13 .... 5.19
- 16(2A) 13.179
- ss 68, 86 .... 4.60
- 144A, 149AA 4.72
- s 276 .... 16.92
- Sch 5 .... 4.60

Taxes Management Act 1970 .... 1.125; 6.34; 11.2; 13.179; 16.161; 18.165; 20.60; 25.140
- s 1(1) 11.2
- 7 .... 3.9; 8.21, 8.24; 18.91, 18.199
- 8 .... 1.26; 3.9; 8.21; 13.55, 13.61; 18.17; 25.124
- 8A 13.55, 13.61; 18.17
- 9 .... 1.26
- 9A 1.1, 1.89; 6.4, 6.41, 6.43; 6.88; 9.42; 13.1; 21.6
- (1) 1.2, 1.36
- 9C 8.146
- ss 10–12 .... 1.26
- s 12ZM 13.1
- 12AA 18.17
- 12AB 18.17
- 12AC 1.2, 1.89; 6.4, 6.34; 13.1; 21.6
- (1) 1.2, 1.36
- (6) 1.2; 21.6
- 12B 1.75, 1.77; 6.15; 7.27; 20.74
- (1) 1.71
- (3) 1.71
- ss 13–18 .... 1.26
- s 19 .... 1.26; 15.35
- 19A 1.81; 6.47, 6.49, 6.88; 16.22, 16.49, 16.126
- 20 .... 1.26, 1.81, 1.96; 3.159; 4.168; 15.35; 16.22, 16.49, 16.53, 16.126, 16.131, 16.134, 16.146, 16.147, 16.148, 16.187, 16.189; 25.13

Taxes Management Act 1970 – *contd*
- s 20(2) 3.159
- (3) 3.159; 16.70
- (7) 16.69
- (8A) 2.95; 5.39; 16.67, 16.69, 16.70, 16.72, 16.75, 16.76, 16.79, 16.82, 16.142
- (8B) 16.70, 16.85
- 20B 4.116; 16.164; 25.13
- (6) 16.53
- 20BA 3.17, 3.48, 3.87, 3.96, 3.97, 3.98, 3.103, 3.108, 3.125; 16.4, 16.212, 16.213, 16.223, 16.224, 16.225, 16.226, 16.228, 16.230, 16.233
- (1)(a), (b) 3.98
- (2) 16.227
- (b) 3.105
- 20BB 25.13
- 20C 3.48, 3.74, 3.80, 3.87, 3.119; 16.12, 16.13, 16.202, 16.225, 16.230
- (1AA) 16.225
- (3)(b) 16.202
- (4) 16.206, 16.218, 16.230
- 20CC 16.232
- 20D(1) 16.224
- ss 21–28 .... 1.26
- s 28ZA 1.123; 8.127; 20.80
- ss 28ZB–28ZE 20.78
- s 28A 1.26, 1.107; 6.34, 6.95; 10.52; 20.48, 20.51, 20.73, 20.81; 21.6
- (1) 1.106
- (2) 1.107
- (3) 1.106
- (4) 1.107, 1.110; 8.99; 20.54
- (5) 1.109; 11.82
- (6) 1.109; 6.96
- 28B 1.26; 6.34, 6.95; 20.48, 20.56, 20.66, 20.81; 21.6
- (1A) 20.81
- (5) 20.54, 20.81
- (7) 6.96
- 28C 1.26; 8.22; 13.55
- (3), (5) 8.23
- ss 28D–28G 1.26
- s 28G 13.55
- ss 28H–28J 8.21
- s 29 .... 1.133; 4.185, 4.188; 6.34, 6.43; 8.24, 8.107; 13.15, 13.19, 13.30, 13.118, 13.123, 13.144
- (1) 4.188, 4.196, 4.197; 13.14, 13.25, 13.50, 13.56, 13.57, 13.59, 13.71, 13.110, 13.155
- (a)–(c) 13.22

Table of Statutes

Taxes Management Act 1970 – *contd*
s 29(2) 13.25, 13.57, 13.60,
13.66, 13.67, 13.70,
13.71, 13.161, 13.163
   (3) 11.67; 13.25, 13.57, 13.61
   (4) 13.61, 13.64, 13.65, 13.69,
13.71, 13.74, 13.80, 13.84,
13.87, 13.98, 13.99, 13.160
   (5) 1.17; 4.188, 4.191,
4.196, 4.197; 6.75; 13.59, 13.61,
13.64, 13.65, 13.69, 13.98,
13.105, 13.107, 13.108, 13.109,
13.114, 13.115, 13.118, 13.121,
13.160, 13.180
   (6) 1.18; 4.188; 6.75; 13.107,
13.111, 13.116, 13.128
      (a)–(c) 13.117
      (d) 13.117
         (i) 13.117, 13.118
         (ii) 13.120
   (7A) 13.65
   (8) 13.148
29A 13.20, 13.30
30 .... 13.19
30A 8.21; 13.43
   (2) 13.25
   (3) 13.142, 13.146
   (4) 13.149
30AA 13.143
30B 1.133; 4.185; 13.20
   (1) 20.48
   (7) 1.1
31 .... 1.11; 21.6
   (1) 20.48
     (b) 20.57, 20.66, 20.74
     (d) 13.148
31A(1) 13.148
31AA 8.21
33 .... 20.261
ss 34–36 .... 1.130; 13.36
s 34 .... 2.97; 5.64, 5.66; 8.109; 13.28
   (1) 13.50
   (1A) 13.30
35 .... 13.34, 13.40
36 .... 1.13; 2.97; 5.64, 5.65,
5.66; 6.34; 8.109
   (1) 13.28
   (1A) 6.119; 13.28
     (b) 14.3
     (d) 8.70
   (1B) 13.32
   (3) 8.113; 13.176
40 .... 8.109; 13.40
   (1), (2) 13.36
42 .... 13.179
   (1) 13.179

Taxes Management Act 1970 – *contd*
s 43 .... 13.179
   (2) 13.170, 13.175, 13.176
43A 8.113; 13.171, 13.174
   (3), (4) 13.174
43B 13.171
   (3) 13.175
Pt V (ss 44–59) 25.212
s 46(2) 20.120
49 .... 8.130; 25.201
ss 49A–49I 20.100
s 49A 6.87; 20.100
49B(2) 20.96
49C 8.130
   (2) 20.96
   (4) 20.98
49D(2) 20.50
49E 8.130; 20.102
   (4) 8.130
49F(2) 13.149
49G(3) 20.106
   (5)(a), (b) 20.100
s 49H 20.100
s 50 .... 8.130; 13.149; 20.66, 20.71,
20.72, 20.75
   (6) 13.153, 13.154
   (7) 11.67; 13.153, 13.154
54 .... 8.130, 8.148; 11.4;
13.149, 13.179; 20.120,
20.121; 21.42
   (4) 8.130
55 .... 8.130; 13.168; 20.112,
20.136; 22.67
   (3) 8.158; 13.148, 13.157
   (3A) 20.112
   (5) 20.114
56 .... 8.77; 22.67
56A 20.228
59A 11.18
   (2) 22.3
   (4B) 13.167
59B 22.3
   (6) 13.166
59C 11.18; 20.129
   (4) 11.18
59D 22.3
59G 22.3
   (2)(b) 22.4
   (4) 22.5
59H 22.4
60(1) 22.18
   (2) 22.19
61 .... 22.57
65 .... 22.54
   (3) 25.124
ss 66, 68, 69 .... 22.55

Table of Statutes

Taxes Management Act 1970 – *contd*
s 86 .... 6.34, 6.108; 11.8; 25.164
ss 87–92 .... 6.34
Pt X (ss 93–107)............................ 25.156
s 93 .... 18.199
  (2), (4).................................... 20.129
95 .... 6.104; 11.55;
                             18.199; 21.35
97 .... 11.59
98 .... 16.22, 16.189
98A 25.126, 25.128, 25.138
  (4) 25.143
106A 3.6, 3.18; 8.29
ss 106B–106H............................ 3.9; 8.29
s 106F(4) 3.9
113(1B).. 13.44
114 .... 1.38; 6.43; 13.146
  (1), (2).................................... 13.145
118(2) 11.56; 13.177
  (7) 13.84, 13.87
Sch 1A
  para 5.................................. 1.89; 21.6
  9.. 21.6
Sch 1AA 3.98; 16.223
  para 3.. 16.228
    (1) 3.101
    4 .... 16.229, 16.233
      (1)(b) 3.103
      (2), (3) 3.104
    5 .... 3.129; 16.230
    8 .... 16.232
Sch 1AB.. 20.265
Terrorism Act 2000
  Pt III (ss 14–31) 3.170
Theft Act 1968 .... 3.2
  s 17 .... 3.6, 3.184; 16.215
Theft Act 1978 .... 3.2
Tribunals, Courts and Enforcement
  Act 2007 .... 20.3, 20.25, 20.150,
                       20.177, 20.236
  Pt 1 (ss 1–49) 20.25
  s 9.. 25.209

Tribunals, Courts and Enforcement
  Act 2007 – *contd*
  s 11 .... 16.59
    (1) 20.227
    (4)(b) 20.229
  12 .... 20.227
    (4)(a) 20.235
  13 .... 16.59
  14(3)(a) 20.235
  18 .... 20.237, 20.238,
                              20.239
  19(3) 20.237
  29(4) 20.204
  Pt 2 (ss 50–61) 20.25
  Pt 3 (ss 62–90) 22.56
  Sch 2... 20.26
  Sch 3... 20.26
Value Added Tax Act 1994........ 16.61, 16.67
  s 82(2) 16.12
  83 .... 20.83, 20.86
    (1)(c) 20.174
    (2) 16.12
  ss 83C, 83E 20.91
  s 83F(4) 20.102
    (8), (9) 20.109
  84(3), (3B) 20.111
  85 .... 20.122
  Sch 11 .... 16.14; 24.61
    para 4(2)(a).............................. 22.80
    6 .... 16.63; 24.61
    10(2) 16.118
    (3) 16.12, 16.13
    11 .... 16.122, 16.212,
                          16.213; 24.61
SWITZERLAND
Banking Act 1934 .... 5.86
Stock Exchange Act 1995 .... 5.86
UNITED STATES
Foreign Account Tax Compliance
  Act... 5.31
Hiring Incentives to Restore
  Employment Act 2010 .... 5.31

xli

Table of Statutory Instruments

Annual Tax on Enveloped Dwellings Avoidance Schemes (Prescribed Descriptions of Arrangements) Regulations 2013, SI 2013/2571 .... 4.13
Appeals (Excluded Decisions) Order 2009, SI 2009/275 .... 20.226
Appeals from the Upper Tribunal to the Court of Appeal Order 2008, SI 2008/2834
  art 2 .... 20.254
Civil Procedure Rules 1998, SI 1998/3132 .... 16.131; 20.39, 20.168, 20.172
  r 1 .... 20.34
  1.1 .... 20.153
  3.9 .... 20.38, 20.171
  5.4C 20.192
Criminal Finances Act 2017 (Commencement No 1) Regulations 2017, SI 2017/739 .... 8.169
Criminal Finances Act 2017 (Commencement No 4) Regulations 2018, SI 2018/78 .... 8.30
Criminal Procedure and Investigations Act 1996 (Defence Disclosure Time Limits) Regulations 2011, SI 2011/209 .... 3.145
Criminal Procedure (Legal Assistance, Detention and Appeals) (Scotland) Act 2010 (Consequential Provisions) Order 2011, SI 2011/1739 .... 3.54
Criminal Procedure Rules 2015, SI 2015/1490
  r 22.4 .... 3.145
Data-gathering Powers (Relevant Data) Regulations 2012, SI 2012/847 .... 16.90
Data-gathering Powers (Relevant Data) (Amendment) Regulations 2013, SI 2013/1811 .... 16.95
Data-gathering Powers (Relevant Data) (Amendment) Regulations 2016, SI 2016/979 .... 16.95

Enforcement by Deduction from Accounts (Imposition of Charges by Deposit-takers) Regulations 2016, SI 2016/44.... 22.33
Facilitation of Tax Evasion Offences (Guidance About Prevention) Regulations 2017, SI 2017/876.... 5.127
Finance Act 2007, Schedule 24 (Commencement and Transitional Provisions) Order 2008, SI 2008/568 .... 16.15
Finance Act 2008, Schedule 36 (Appointed Day and Savings) Order 2009, SI 2009/404 .... 16.20, 16.22
Finance Act 2008, Schedule 39 (Appointed Day, Transitional Provision and Savings) Order 2009, SI 2009/403
  art 3 .... 13.28
Finance Act 2016, Section 162(1) and Schedule 20 (Appointed Day) Regulations 2016, SI 2016/1249 .... 21.24
Finance Act 2016, Section 166 (Appointed Day) Regulations 2017, SI 2017/970 .... 3.9; 8.29
Finance Act 2016, Schedule 21 (Appointed Days) Regulations 2017, SI 2017/259 .... 8.160
General Commissioners (Jurisdiction and Procedure) Regulations 1994, SI 1994/1812
  reg 13 .... 20.184
Income Tax (Employments) Regulations 1993, SI 1993/744
  reg 49 .... 25.157
Income Tax (Pay As You Earn) Regulations 2003, SI 2003/2682 ..... 25.124, 25.136; 26.10
  reg 80 .... 25.103, 25.173
  97 .... 9.77
  Pt 4A (regs 97M–97X) 22.80
  reg 97V(5) 22.78
  regs 97ZA–97ZF 22.11

xliii

Table of Statutory Instruments

Information Notice: Resolution of Disputes as to Privileged Communications Regulations 2009, SI 2009/1916	4.107; 16.172
Inheritance Tax Avoidance Schemes (Prescribed Descriptions of Arrangements) Regulations 2011, SI 2011/170	4.13
Insolvency (Northern Ireland) Order 1989, SI 1989/2405 (NI 19)	
art 3	3.170
International Mutual Administrative Assistance in Tax Matters Order 2007, SI 2007/2126	22.89
International Tax Compliance Regulations 2015, SI 2015/878	
reg 12H	3.170
MARD Regulations 2011, SI 2011/2931	22.83
Money Laundering, Terrorist Financing and Transfer of Funds (Information on the Payer) Regulations 2017, SI 2017/692	3.170; 16.97
Pts 1–6 (regs 1–60)	3.170
reg 5	16.97
(1)	3.170
6	16.97
7	3.170
regs 8–15	3.170
reg 8(1), (2)	3.170
regs 11, 12	3.170
reg 15	3.170
Pt 2 (regs 16–25)	3.170
reg 17(9)	3.170
18(1), (4)	3.170
19(1), (2), (4), (6)	3.170
regs 21–24	3.170
21, 24	3.170
Pt 3 (regs 26–38)	3.170
reg 26	3.170
regs 27–32	3.170
27–38	3.170
reg 27	3.170
(1)	3.170
28	3.170
(1)	3.170
29	3.170
31(1), (3)	3.170, 3.198
31(4)	3.170
regs 33–36	3.170
33–37	3.170
reg 33(1)	3.170
regs 34, 35	3.170
37–38	3.170

Money Laundering, Terrorist Financing and Transfer of Funds (Information on the Payer) Regulations 2017, SI 2017/692 – *contd*	
Pt 4 (regs 39–41)	3.170
regs 39–40	3.170
Pt 5 (regs 42–45)	3.170
reg 40	3.170; 16.97
(3)	3.170
(b)(i)	3.170
41(1), (5), 6), (7), (14)	3.170
42	3.170
(1)	3.170
(a)(vi)	3.170
(4)	3.170
43	3.170
(1)	3.170
44	3.170
(1)	3.170
(2)(b)	3.170
(4)	3.170
(5)	3.170
(b)	3.170
(10)	3.170
45	3.170
(2)(b)–(d)	3.170
(5)(f), (g)	3.170
(14)	3.170
Pt 6 (regs 46–60)	3.170
reg 47	3.170
Pt 7 (regs 61–64)	3.170
Pts 8–11	3.170
Pt 8 (regs 65–74)	3.170
regs 65–68	3.170
69–70	3.170
71–73	3.170
Pt 9 (regs 75–92)	3.170
reg 75	3.170
regs 76–85	3.170
86–92	3.170
86, 87, 88	3.170
89–92	3.170
Pt 10 (regs 93–100)	3.170
reg 93	3.170
regs 94–100	3.170
Sch 1	3.170
Sch 6	3.170
Money Laundering Regulations 2007, SI 2007/2157	3.164, 3.169, 3.176, 3.199
reg 14	3.188
Money Laundering and Transfer of Funds (Information on the Payer) Regulations 2017, SI 2017/692	3.169

National Insurance (Contributions) Regulations 1969, SI 1969/1696.................................. 25.176
National Insurance Contributions (Application of Part 7 of the Finance Act 2004) Regulations 2012, SI 2012/1868................... 4.13
Orders for the Delivery of Documents (Procedure) Regulations 2000, SI 2000/2875............................ 3.99
   reg 4(2)....................................... 3.100
      5(1)–(3)................................ 3.106
      6(1)–(3)................................ 3.111
      7... 16.231
        (1)–(7)................................. 3.131
Penalties Relating to Offshore Matters and Offshore Transfers (Additional Information) Regulations 2017, SI 2017/345.. 8.136
Police and Criminal Evidence Act 1984 (Application to Revenue and Customs) Order 2007, SI 2007/3175............. 3.42, 3.50, 3.97; 16.12; 16.193, 16.195, 16.232
   art 4... 16.193
      7............................... 3.96; 16.213
     18.. 3.52
   Sch 2
     Pt 2... 3.55
Police and Criminal Evidence Act 1984 (Application to Revenue and Customs) Order 2015, SI 2015/1783
   art 4... 16.193
     6............................... 16.213, 16.226
Police and Criminal Evidence (Northern Ireland) Order 1989, SI 1989/1341............................ 3.49
Recovery of Foreign Taxes Regulations 2007, SI 2007/3507... 22.90
Recovery of Foreign Taxes (Amendment) Regulations 2010, SI 2010/794...................... 22.90
Recovery of Social Security Contributions Due in Other Member States Regulations 2010, SI 2010/926..................... 22.87
Rules of the Supreme Court 1965, SI 1965/1776
   Ord 24.. 16.138
     r 2.. 16.137
Social Security (Adjudication) Regulations 1986, SI 1986/2218
   reg 16(1)....................................... 25.217

Social Security (Categorisation of Earners) Regulations 1978, SI 1978/1689............................. 25.89
Social Security (Contributions) Regulations 2001, SI 2001/1004
   reg 3(2B)...................................... 25.178
      21.. 25.178
      21A.. 25.128
        (8)... 25.127
   regs 21D, 21EA............................. 25.128
   reg 21F(12)................................... 25.127
      26.. 9.77
      31.. 25.178
      50(2)....................................... 25.178
      52(1)(a), (b)............................ 25.178
        (8)... 25.178
      54(3)....................................... 25.178
      55(3)....................................... 25.178
      60.. 25.178
      61(2)....................................... 25.178
      65(2), (3), (4)......................... 25.178
      67(1)....................................... 25.124
      67A.. 25.145
      67B............................ 25.150, 25.151
      71.. 25.160
      76.. 25.160
      77.. 25.162
   regs 78, 79................................... 25.163
   reg 81(1), (2), (3), (4).................. 25.149
      86(1)(a)................................... 22.13
   regs 90F–90H................................ 25.144
   reg 110(3)..................................... 25.178
   Sch 4......................... 9.77; 22.80; 25.128
     para 6(2), (3)............................ 25.112
        14(1), (3)............................ 25.116
        15(1)................................... 25.117
          (4)..................................... 25.121
        17....................................... 25.158
          (1)(a)................................. 25.161
          (3)..................................... 25.161
        18....................................... 25.162
     paras 19, 20.............................. 25.163
     para 26.. 25.85
Social Security Contributions (Decisions and Appeals) Regulations 1999, SI 1999/1027.. 25.171
   reg 3(1).. 25.180
      (2)... 25.181
      4.. 25.185
        (1)... 25.182
        (2), (3).................................. 25.189
      5(1), (2), (4)........................... 25.190
      6(1), (2).................................. 25.191
      9.. 25.201
      10.. 25.203

Table of Statutory Instruments

Social Security Contributions (Decisions and Appeals) Regulations 1999, SI 1999/1027 – *contd*
reg 11(1), (2), (3) 25.204
    (4) 25.205
    (5) 25.206
    (6) 25.207
Social Security (Crediting and Treatment of Contributions, and National Insurance Numbers) Regulations 2001, SI 2001/769
regs 5, 6 .... 25.178
Special Commissioners (Jurisdiction and Procedure) Regulations 1994, SI 1994/1811
reg 15 .... 20.184
    (2)(i), (ii) 20.187
21 .... 20.206
Stamp Duty Land Tax (Avoidance Schemes) (Specified Proposals or Arrangements) Regulations 2012, SI 2012/2396 .... 4.13
Stamp Duty Land Tax Avoidance Schemes (Prescribed Descriptions of Arrangements) Regulations 2005, SI 2005/1868 .... 4.13
Statistics of Trade (Customs and Excise) Regulations 1992, SI 1992/2790 .... 24.60
Taking Control of Goods Regulations 2013, SI 2013/1894 .... 22.57
Tax Avoidance Schemes (Information) Regulations 2012, SI 2012/1836 .... 4.13
Tax Avoidance Schemes (Penalty) Regulations 2007, SI 2007/3104 .... 4.13
Tax Avoidance Schemes (Prescribed Descriptions of Arrangements) Regulations 2006, SI 2006/1543 .... 4.16
reg 10 .... 4.16
Tax Avoidance Schemes (Prescribed Descriptions of Arrangements) (Amendment) Regulations 2016, SI 2016/99 .... 4.16
Tax Avoidance Schemes (Promoters and Prescribed Circumstances) Regulations 2015, SI 2015/130 .... 4.13
Transfer of Funds (Information on the Payer) Regulations 2007, SI 2007/3298 .... 3.169

Transfer of Tribunal Functions and Revenue and Customs Appeals Order 2009, SI 2009/56
arts 3, 4 .... 20.3
Sch 3
    para 7(3), (7) 20.213
Tribunal Procedure (Amendment) Rules 2009, SI 2009/274
r 14 .... 20.231
Tribunal Procedure (First-tier Tribunal) (Tax Chamber) Rules 2009, SI 2009/273 .... 20.4, 20.161, 20.168, 20.193
r 2 .... 20.36
3 .... 20.39
5 .... 20.150
    (3) 20.209
    (a) 20.200
8 .... 20.38, 20.166
    (2)(a) 20.77
    (7) 20.165
    (9) 20.166
10 .... 20.203
    (1) 20.209
    (b) 20.206, 20.207
11 .... 20.178
15(2) 20.154
16(1)(b) 3.134
17 .... 20.123, 20.126
    (1), (2) 20.126
18 .... 4.119; 8.77
23 .... 20.208, 20.211, 20.212
    (4) 20.142
    (c) 20.145
24(3), (4) 20.138
25(1)(b) 20.149
    (3) 20.130
26(3)(c) 20.132
27 .... 20.149
28 .... 20.147, 20.222
32 .... 20.180
33 .... 20.179
35 .... 20.193
    (6) 20.194
37 .... 20.196
38 .... 20.197
    (3) 20.198
39(2) 20.199
40 .... 20.201
41 .... 25.209
    (1)(b) 20.201

Table of Statutory Instruments

Tribunal Procedure (Upper Tribunal) Rules 2008, SI 2008/2698	
	20.4, 20.168
r 2	20.36
(2)	20.36
(4)	20.38
3	20.39
5	20.244
7	20.245
11	20.246
21(3)(b)	20.230
22(2)(b)	20.232
(3)–(5)	20.229
rr 24, 25	20.233

Tribunal Procedure (Upper Tribunal) Rules 2008, SI 2008/2698 – *contd*	
r 34	20.246
40	20.248
(2)	20.248
42	20.250
43	20.251
44(1)	20.252
Value Added Tax Regulations 1995, SI 1995/2518	16.61
reg 31	16.63
Value Added Tax Tribunals Rules 1986, SI 1986/590	
r 24	20.188

xlvii

Table of Cases

A

A v R & C Comrs [2012] UKFTT 541 (TC), [2012] SFTD 1257, [2013] STI 65.. 20.181, 20.182, 20.191
AB (a firm) v R & C Comrs [2007] STC (SCD) 99, [2007] STI 157.................... 13.101
Accountant v Inspector of Taxes [2000] STC (SCD) 522, [2000] STI 1518..................... 15.35
A Divorcee v R & C Comrs [2010] UKFTT 612 (TC), [2011] STI 1344 .... 8.130
Addison v London Philharmonic Orchestra [1981] ICR 261 .... 26.76
Addo v R & C Comrs [2018] UKFTT 93 (TC) 13.156
Aeroassistance Logistics Ltd v R & C Comrs [2013] UKFTT 214 (TC).......................... 6.92
AH Field (Holdings) Ltd v R & C Comrs [2012] UKFTT 104 (TC), 81 TC 1, [2012] STI 1461... 4.78, 4.111, 4.147
Al-Fayed v A-G for Scotland [2004] STC 1703, 2004 SC 745, 2004 SLT 798 .... 20.121
Alexander Duncan v C & E Comrs [2016] UKFTT 709 (TC) 8.126
Alfred Crompton Amusement Machines Ltd v C & E Comrs (No 2) [1974] AC 405, [1973] 3 WLR 268, [1972] 1 WLR 833.. 16.168
Allan v R & C Comrs [2016] UKFTT 504 (TC) 6.94
Alvi v R & C Comrs [2016] UKFTT 201 (TC)... 15.33
Anderson v Bank of British Columbia (1876) 2 Ch D 644 .... 16.153
Anderson v R & C Comrs [2009] UKFTT 258 (TC), [2009] STI 2938............................ 13.95
Anderson v R & C Comrs [2016] UKFTT 335 (TC), [2017] SFTD 100, [2016] STI 2319... 13.103
Anderson v R & C Comrs [2016] UKFTT 565 (TC)... 4.196
Anderson v R & C Comrs [2018] UKUT 159 (TCC), [2018] 4 WLR 90, [2018] STC 1210, [2018] BTC 516... 13.25
Anstock v R & C Comrs [2017] UKFTT 307 (TC).. 16.191
Aria Technology Ltd v R & C Comrs [2018] UKUT 111 (TCC), [2018] BTC 511, [2018] STI 822.. 20.192
Ashraf v R & C Comrs [2018] UKFTT 97 (TC), [2018] SFTD 901, [2018] STI 951... 8.105; 13.162
Astall v R & C Comrs [2009] EWCA Civ 1010, [2010] STC 137, 80 TC 22.............. 4.58, 4.61
ATEC Associates Ltd v R & C Comrs (unreported, 4 December 2009).............................. 20.229
Atherton v R & C Comrs [2016] UKFTT 831 (TC)... 13.64, 13.82, 13.98
Atkins' Executors v R & C Comrs [2011] UKFTT 468 (TC), [2011] WTLR 1675 .... 20.207
Atlantic Electronics v R & C Comrs [2012] UKUT 45 (TCC), [2012] STC 931, [2012] BVC 1577... 20.209, 20.215, 20.217
Auxilium Project Management Ltd v R & C Comrs [2016] UKFTT 249 (TC), [2016] STI 1442.. 13.90, 13.97; 18.58
Ayrshire Pullman Motor Services & DM Ritchie v IRC (1929) 14 TC 754......................... 4.48
Aziz v R & C Comrs [2018] UKFTT 153 (TC).. 13.164

B

B v B (Matrimonial Proceedings: Discovery) [1978] Fam 181, [1978] 3 WLR 624, [1979] 1 All ER 801... 4.165, 4.167; 16.132
B v R & C Comrs [2014] UKFTT 256 (TC), [2014] STI 1982... 20.195
B & K Lavery Property Trading Partnership v R & C Comrs [2015] UKFTT 470 (TC); [2016] STI 315... 20.77

Table of Cases

Babergh District Council [2011] UKFTT 341 (TC), [2011] SFTD 709, [2011] STI 1915.. 20.214, 20.217
Baines-Stiller v R & C Comrs [2016] UKFTT 481 (TC)... 19.23
Ball UK Holdings Ltd v R & C Comrs [2017] UKFTT 457 (TC), [2018] 1 BCLC. 229, [2017] STI 1775.. 8.62
Barclays Mercantile Business Finance Ltd v Mawson (Inspector of Taxes) [2004] UKHL 1, [2005] 1 AC 684, [2005] STC 1... 4.54, 4.57, 4.75
Barkham v R & C Comrs [2012] UKFTT 519 (TC)................................... 6.93; 13.139, 13.164
Barnes v R & C Comrs [2014] EWCA Civ 31, [2014] BTC 5.. 4.58
Barraclough v Brown [1897] AC 615... 20.261
Bastionspark LLP v R & C Comrs [2016] UKUT 425 (TCC), [2016] STC 2549, [2016] BTC 519... 20.203
BAT Industries Plc v R & C Comrs [2017] UKFTT 558 (TC)................................... 20.279
Bayfine UK Products v R & C Comrs [2009] STC (SCD) 43, 11 ITL Rep 440, [2008] STI 2735... 20.72
Bayliss v R & C Comrs [2016] UKFTT 500 (TC)... 8.91
Beagles v R & C Comrs [2017] UKFTT 462 (TC)... 13.52
Beckwith v R & C Comrs [2012] UKFTT 181 (TC), [2012] STI 1842................. 1.48; 6.53; 15.33; 16.39, 16.63
Behague v R & C Comrs [2013] UKFTT 596 (TC), [2014] WTLR 187, [2013] STI 3577.. 16.178
Behague v R & C Comrs [2013] UKFTT 647 (TC)... 16.38, 16.179
Bekoe v R & C Comrs [2017] UKFTT 772 (TC).. 6.90
Bennett v IRC [1995] STC 54, [1995] STI 13.. 20.267
Berry v R & C Comrs [2011] UKUT 81 (TCC), [2011] STC 1057, [2011] BTC 1623...... 4.69
Bessie Taube Discretionary Settlement Trust (Trustees of) v R & C Comrs [2010] UKFTT 473 (TC), [2011] SFTD 153, [2011] WTLR 1, [2011] STI 268......... 13.79
Betts v R & C Comrs [2013] UKFTT 430 (TC).. 1.131; 7.5, 7.7; 13.13; 15.34
Biffin Ltd v R & C Comrs [2016] EWHC 2926 (Admin), [2016] BTC 48............... 8.158; 22.64
Birkett (t/a Orchards Residential Home) v R & C Comrs [2017] UKUT 89 (TCC), [2017] BTC 511... 16.191
BJH Building & Plumbing v R & C Comrs [2010] UKFTT 60 (TC)............................... 6.97
Bloomfield v R & C Comrs [2013] UKFTT 593 (TC).. 1.118; 6.98
Blum v R & C Comrs [2018] UKFTT 152 (TC).. 13.98, 13.117, 13.119
Blyth v Birmingham Waterworks Co [1856] 20 JP 247.. 8.91
BNP Paribas SA (London Branch) v R & C Comrs [2017] UKFTT 487 (TC); [2017] STI 1933... 20.77
Bogle v R & C Comrs [2014] UKFTT 201 (TC).. 20.207
Boughey v R & C Comrs [2012] UKFTT 398 (TC)... 19.49
Bowman v Fels [2005] EWCA Civ 226, [2005] 1 WLR 3083, [2005] 4 All ER 609, [2005] 2 Cr App R 19, [2005] 2 CMLR 23, [2005] 2 FLR 247, [2005] WTLR 481, [2005] Fam Law 546, (2005) 102(18) LSG 24, (2005) 155 NLJ 413, (2005) 149 SJLB 357, [2005] NPC 36... 3.173
BPP Holdings Ltd v R & C Comrs [2016] EWCA Civ 121, [2016] 1 WLR 1915, [2016] 3 All ER 245, [2016] STC 841, [2017] RVR 132, [2016] BVC 9, [2016] STI 516; [2017] UKSC 55, [2017] 1 WLR 2945, [2017] 4 All ER 756, [2017] STC 1655, [2018] RVR 8, [2017] BVC 36, [2017] STI 1742.. 8.130; 20.168
Brady (Inspector of Taxes) v Hart (t/a Jaclyn Model Agency) [1985] STC 498, 58 TC 518... 26.89
Brown v R & C Comrs [2012] UKFTT 425 (TC)... 13.119
Bubb v R & C Comrs [2016] UKFTT 216 (TC).. 13.76
Bullock (Inspector of Taxes) v Unit Construction Co *see* Unit Construction Co Ltd v Bullock (Inspector of Taxes)
Burgess, Brimheath Developments Ltd v R & C Comrs [2015] UKUT 578 (TCC), [2016] STC 579, [2015] BTC 533, [2015] STI 3368.................................. 13.158, 13.160

1

Table of Cases

Burns & Neil v R & C Comrs [2009] STC (SCD) 165, [2009] STI 262............................ 4.148
Buxton v Public Trustee (1962) 41 TC 235 .... 20.263
Buyco Ltd & Sellco Ltd v R & C Comrs [2006] VTD 19752... 20.111
BW Hills Southbank Limited v R & C Comrs [2016] UKFTT 423 (TC)........................ 22.26

C

C & E Comrs v ApS Samex (Hanil Synthetic Fiber Industrial Co Ltd) [1983]
   1 All ER 1042, [1983] Com LR 72, [1983] 3 CMLR 194.. 20.275
C & E Comrs v National Westminster Bank plc *see* National Westminster Bank plc v C
   & E Comrs (Unjust Enrichment)
C & E Comrs v Young [1993] STC 394.. 20.164
Cannon v R & C Comrs [2017] UKFTT 859 (TC), [2018] SFTD 667 .... 8.141
Cansick (Murphy's Executor) v Hochstrasser (Inspector of Taxes) (1961) 40 TC 151,
   (1961) 40 ATC 46, [1961] TR 23... 13.25
Cape Brandy Syndicate v IRC [1921] 2 KB 403, 12 TC 358.. 4.48
Capital Air Services Ltd v R & C Comrs [2010] UKFTT 160 (TC), [2010]
   SFTD 671, [2010] STI 2546; [2010] UKUT 373 (TCC), [2010] STC 2726,
   [2011] 1 Costs LO 21... 20.143, 20.147
Cardazzone (t/a Mediterranean Ices) v R & C Comrs [2014] UKFTT 357 (TC)................ 6.90,
   6.92; 13.134
Cenlon Finance Co Ltd v Ellwood (Inspector of Taxes) [1962] AC 782,
   [1962] 2 WLR 871, [1962] 1 All ER 854, 40 TC 176 .... 4.187; 13.21, 13.23
Chadwick (as trustee in bankruptcy of Mrs Gloria Oduneye-Braniffe) v National
   Crime Agency [2017] UKFTT 656 (TC), [2017] BPIR 1429, [2017] STI 2103........ 13.146
Chan v R & C Comrs *see* B v R & C Comrs
Changtel Solutions UK Ltd (formerly Enta Technologies Ltd) v R & C Comrs [2015]
   EWCA Civ 29, [2015] 1 WLR 3911, [2015] STC 931.. 22.65
Changtel Solutions UK Ltd (formerly Enta Technologies Ltd) v R & C Comrs [2016]
   UKFTT 399 (TC)... 13.91
Chapman v R & C Comrs [2011] UKFTT 756 (TC)....................................... 6.90, 6.94
Chohan v R & C Comrs [2017] UKFTT 779 (TC)... 16.191
Charlton v R & C Comrs *see* R & C Comrs v Charlton
Clark (Inspector of Taxes) v Oceanic Contractors Ltd [1983] 2 AC 130, [1983] 2 WLR
   94, [1983] STC 35... 16.151
Clark v R & C Comrs [2017] UKFTT 392 (TC) 13.25, 13.154, 13.155
Clunes v R & C Comrs [2017] UKFTT 204 (TC); [2017] STI 1070............................... 20.192
Clynes v R & C Comrs [2016] UKFTT 369 (TC), [2016] STI 1678 .... 13.92
Cobb v R & C Comrs [2012] UKFTT 40 (TC) 19.50
Coffee Republic plc v R & C Comrs (VAT Decision 20150) [2007] STI 2245............ 4.84, 4.86
Collector of Stamp Revenue v Arrowtown Assets Ltd (2003) 6 ITLR 454 .... 4.55
Commane v R & C Comrs [2006] STC (SCD) 81, [2006] STI 459 .... 16.39
Connaught Contracts v R & C Comrs [2010] UKFTT 545 (TC), [2011] STI 140............. 18.62
Consortium International Ltd (VTD 824)... 20.188
Cooke v R & C Comrs [2017] UKFTT 844 (TC), [2018] SFTD 633, [2018] STI 454...... 13.98
Coombes v R & C Comrs [2007] EWHC 3160 (Ch), [2008] STC 2984,
   [2008] BTC 884 .... 4.60
Cooper v Cadwalader (1904) 7 F 146, (1904) 12 SLT 449, 5 TC 101 .... 5.8
Corbally-Stourton v R & C Comrs [2008] STC (SCD) 907................ 1.23; 4.189, 4.190, 4.191,
   4.195; 13.44, 13.46, 13.47, 13.49
Craven (Inspector of Taxes) v White [1989] AC 398, [1988] 3 WLR 423,
   [1988] STC 476.. 4.52

D

D'Arcy v R & C Comrs *see* R & C Comrs v D'Arcy
D'Souza v R & C Comrs [2012] UKFTT 210 (TC).. 14.53
D-Media Communications v R & C Comrs [2016] UKFTT 430 (TC) 22.78

Table of Cases

D Midgley & Sons Ltd v R & C Comrs [2011] UKFTT 187 (TC) 15.33
Daniel v R & C Comrs [2014] UKFTT 173 (TC) 13.69
Davies v R & C Comrs [2011] UKFTT 303 (TC) 19.64
DB Group Services (UK) Ltd v R & C Comrs *see* UBS AG v R & C Comrs
De Beers Consolidated Mines Ltd v Howe (Surveyor of Taxes) [1906] AC 455,
 5 TC 198 .... 4.91; 5.17
Degorce v R & C Comrs [2013] UKFTT 178 (TC), [2013] SFTD 806,
 [2013] STI 2050 .... 20.160
Demibourne Ltd v R & C Comrs [2005] STC (SCD) 667 .... 26.79, 26.81
Derry v Peek (1889) 14 App Cas 337, (1889) 5 TLR 625 .... 2.16; 8.91
Deutsche Morgan Grenfell Group plc v IRC [2006] UKHL 49, [2007] 1 AC 558,
 [2006] 3 WLR 781 .... 20.263
Dickinson (t/a John Dickinson Equipment Finance) v Rushmer (t/a FJ Associates)
 (Costs) [2002] 1 Costs LR 128, (2002) 152 NLJ 58 .... 16.178
Direct Cosmetics v C & E Comrs (No 2) [1984] 1 CMLR 99 .... 20.274
Dock & Let Ltd v R & C Comrs [2014] UKFTT 943 (TC), [2015] STI 160 .... 6.42
Dormeuil Trade Mark [1983] RPC 131 .... 16.161
Dosanjh v R & C Comrs [2014] UKFTT 973 (TC) 1.76
Dreams plc v R & C Comrs [2012] UKFTT 614 (TC), [2013] SFTD 111,
 [2013] STI 224 .... 20.145, 20.147
Drummond v R & C Comrs [2008] EWHC 1758 (Ch), [2008] STC 2707,
 [2008] BTC 473 .... 4.192, 4.193
DSG Retail Ltd v R & C Comrs [2009] UKFTT 31 (TC), [2009] STC (SCD) 397,
 11 ITL Rep 869 .... 4.89
DTE Financial Services Ltd v Wilson (Inspector of Taxes) [1999] STC 1061,
 [1999] BTC 415, (1999) 96 (44) LSG 41 .... 26.29
Duchy Maternity Ltd v Hodgson (Inspector of Taxes) [1985] STC 764, 59 TC 85,
 (1985) 135 NLJ 3175 .... 11.67
Duffy v R & C Comrs [2007] STC (SCD) 377, [2007] STI 1176 .... 6.77; 9.75
Duke of Westminster v IRC [1936] AC 1, 19 TC 490 .... 4.48
Duncan v R & C Comrs [2016] UKFTT 709 (TC) 8.143, 8.144

E

Easinghall Ltd v R & C Comrs [2016] UKUT 105 (TCC) 20.120
Eastman v R & C Comrs [2016] UKFTT 527 (TC) 19.52
Eclipse Film Partners No 35 LLP v R & C Comrs [2009] STC (SCD) 293,
 [2009] STI 627 .... 20.56
Eclipse Film Partners No 35 LLP v R & C Comrs [2014] EWCA Civ 184,
 [2014] CP Rep 26, [2014] BTC 10; [2016] UKSC 24, [2016] 1 WLR 1839,
 [2016] 3 All ER 719, [2016] STC 1385, [2017] RVR 105, [2016] BTC 20,
 [2016] STI 1531 .... 4.73; 20.209
Edwards (Inspector of Taxes) v Bairstow [1956] AC 14, [1955] 3 WLR 410,
 [1955] 3 All ER 48 .... 20.228
Elbrook Cash & Carry Ltd v R & C Comrs [2016] UKFTT 191(TC), [2016] STI 1415;
 [2017] UKUT 181 (TCC), [2017] BVC 514 .... 20.111
EMI Group Electronics Ltd v Coldicott (Inspector of Taxes) [2000] 1 WLR 540,
 [1999] STC 803, [1999] IRLR 630 .... 26.37
Ensign Tankers (Leasing) Ltd v Stokes (Inspector of Taxes) [1992] 1 AC 655,
 [1992] 2 WLR 469, [1992] STC 226 .... 4.75
Estate 4 Ltd v R & C Comrs [2011] UKFTT 269 (TC) 6.99
Everest Ltd v R & C Comrs [2010] UKFTT 621 (TC), [2011] SFTD 217,
 [2011] STI 349 .... 20.214

F

Fane v R & C Comrs [2011] UKFTT 210 (TC) 8.143; 19.27
Ferguson v Noble (1919) 7 TC 176, [1919] SC 534 .... 26.20

Table of Cases

Fidex Ltd v R & C Comrs [2014] UKUT 454 (TCC), [2015] STC 702, [2014] BTC 530; [2016] EWCA Civ 385; [2016] 4 All ER 1063, [2016] STC 1920, [2016] BTC 16 .... 1.117; 4.87; 20.77
FJ Chalke Ltd v R & C Comrs [2009] EWHC 952 (Ch), [2009] STC 2027, [2009] 3 CMLR 14.. 20.224
Flanagan v R & C Comrs [2014] UKFTT 175 (TC), 82 TC 392, [2014] SFTD 881 .... 4.74
Forde & McHugh Ltd v R & C Comrs [2014] UKSC 14, [2014] 1 WLR 810, [2014] 2 All ER 356.. 25.48
Furniss (Inspector of Taxes) v Dawson [1984] AC 474, [1984] 2 WLR 226, [1984] STC 153.. 3.75, 4.51

G

Gaines-Cooper v R & C Comrs [2007] STC (SCD) 23, 9 ITL Rep 274, [2007] WTLR 101.. 5.11
Gardiner v R & C Comrs [2015] UKFTT 115 (TC).. 8.141
Gedir v R & C Comrs [2016] UKFTT 188 (TC).. 8.91
George v Ward [1995] STC (SCD) 230.. 26.44
Gilbert (Inspector of Taxes) v Hemsley [1981] STC 703, [1981] IRLR 501, 55 TC 419.. 26.132
Glyn v HMRC [2013] UKFTT 645 (TC), [2014] STI 630.. 4.126
Godman v Crofton [1914] 3 KB 803, [1913] 110 LT 387.. 25.110
Gold Nuts Ltd and others v R & C Comrs [2017] UKFTT 354 (TC), [2017] STI 1326.. 16.33
Goldsmith v R & C Comrs [2018] UKFTT 5 (TC), [2018] STI 590.. 8.27; 16.191
Gordon v R & C Comrs [2018] UKFTT 307 (TC).. 13.54, 13.161
Grace v R & C Comrs [2011] UKFTT 36 (TC), [2011] SFTD 669, [2011] STI 1581 ...... 5.11
Grant v Downs [1976] 135 CLR 674.. 16.167
Grogan v R & C Comrs (unreported, 20 November 2010).. 20.253
Group One (Arshad Mehmood) [2016] UKFTT 198 (TC).. 19.27
Guest House Proprietor v Kendall (Inspector of Taxes) [2005] STC (SCD) 280, [2005] STI 160.. 6.89; 15.35
Guide Dogs for the Blind Association v R & C Comrs [2012] UKFTT 687 (TC), [2012] STI 3302.. 6.93
Gunn v R & C Comrs [2011] UKUT 59 (TCC), [2011] STC 1119, [2011] BTC 1608, [2011] STI 530.. 13.144
Guyer v Walton (Inspector of Taxes) [2001] STC (SCD) 75, [2001] STI 732 .... 15.35

H

Hall (Inspector of Taxes) v Lorimer [1994] 1 WLR 209, [1994] 1 All ER 250, [1994] STC 23.. 26.76, 26.87
Hall v R & C Comrs [2016] UKFTT 412 (TC).. 19.51
Hankinson v R & C Comrs [2011] EWCA Civ 1566, [2012] 1 WLR 2322, [2012] STC 485, 81 TC 424, [2012] BTC 1, [2012] STI 29 .... 13.159
Hanover Co Services Ltd v R & C Comrs [2010] UKFTT 256 (TC), [2010] SFTD 1047, [2010] STI 2575.. 20.175
Hanson v R & C Comrs [2012] UKFTT 314 (TC), [2012] WTLR 1769 .... 4.199; 8.91, 8.141; 13.102; 18.56
Harding v R & C Comrs [2013] UKUT 575 (TCC), [2014] STC 891, [2013] BTC 2088, [2013] STI 3773.. 13.96
Hargreaves v R & C Comrs [2016] EWCA Civ 174, [2016] 1 WLR 2981, [2017] 1 All ER 129, [2016] STC 1652, [2016] BTC 13, [2016] STI 1154 .... 13.156, 13.161
Hartland v Diggines (Inspector of Taxes) [1926] AC 289, (1926) 24 Ll L Rep 94, 10 TC 247.. 26.112
Hawkeye Communications Ltd v R & C Comrs [2010] UKFTT 636 (TC), [2011] SFTD 250, [2011] STI 1447.. 20.214
Haythornthwaite (T) & Sons Ltd v Kelly (Inspector of Taxes) (1927) 11 TC 657.............. 4.171

liii

Table of Cases

Health Response UK Ltd v R & C Comrs [2010] UKFTT 123 (TC), [2010] STI 2303 .... 20.176
Henke v R & C Comrs [2006] STC (SCD) 561, [2006] STI 1888 .... 13.57
Henn v DPP; R v Henn (Maurice Donald); R v Darby (John Frederick) [1981] AC 850, (1980) 71 Cr App R 44, [1980] 2 CMLR 229 .... 20.271
Herefordshire Property Co Ltd v R & C Comrs [2015] UKFTT 79 (TC) 8.90
Hicks v R & C Comrs [2018] UKFTT 22 (TC) 1.130; 13.51, 13.80, 13.104
HL Bolton (Engineering) Co Ltd v TJ Graham & Sons Ltd [1957] 1 QB 159, [1956] 3 WLR 804, [1956] 3 All ER 624 .... 22.15
Hochstrasser (Inspector of Taxes) v Mayes [1960] AC 376, [1960] 2 LR 63, (1959) 38 TC 673 .... 26.121, 26.159
Holly v HM Inspector of Taxes [200] STC (SCD) 50, [2000] STI 161 .... 6.88
Homeowners Friendly Society Ltd v Barrett (Inspector of Taxes) [1995] STC (SCD) 90 .... 20.206
Honig v Sarsfield (Inspector of Taxes) [1986] STC 246, 59 TC 337, (1986) 83 LSG 1399 .... 13.45
Horton v Young (Inspector of Taxes) [1972] Ch 157, [1971] 3 WLR 348, 47 TC 60 .... 26.180
Howell v Trippier (Inspector of Taxes) [2004] STC (SCD) 132, [2004] WTLR 437, [2004] STI 314; [2004] EWCA Civ 885, [2004] STC 1245, 76 TC 415 .... 20.186, 20.187
Humbles v Brooks (1962) 40 TC 500, 41 ATC 309. [1962] TR 297 .... 26.144
Humphreys v R & C Comrs [2010] UKFTT 204 (TC) 15.35
Hutchings v R & C Comrs [2015] UKFTT 9 (TC), [2015] WTLR 1359, [2015] STI 1260 .... 8.139

I

IRC v Alexander von Glehn & Co Ltd [1920] 2 KB 553, (1920) 2 Ll L Rep 556, 12 TC 232 .... 26.135
IRC v Botnar [1998] STC 38, [1997] BTC 613 .... 5.21
IRC v Brebner [1967] 2 AC 18, [1967] 2 WLR 1001, [1967] 1 All ER 779 .... 4.86
IRC v Brown (1926) 11 TC 292 .... 5.8
IRC v Nuttall [1990] 1 WLR 631, [1990] STC 194 .... 11.4
IRC v Scottish Provident Institution [2004] UKHL 52, [2004] 1 WLR 3172, [2005] STC 15 .... 4.54, 4.56, 4.57, 4.61
IRC v Willoughby [1997] 1 WLR 1071, [1997] 4 All ER 65, [1997] STC 995 .... 4.3
IRC v Zorab (1926) 11 TC 289 .... 5.8
India v Taylor [1955] AC 491, [1955] 2 WLR 303, [1955] 1 All ER 292 .... 3.183
Inzani v R & C Comrs [2006] STC (SCD) 279, [2006] STI 1354 .... 25.135

J

J & W Brown v R & C Comrs [2016] UKFTT 343 (TC), [2016] STI 1610 .... 18.68
Jackson v R & C Comrs [2018] UKFTT 64 (TC) 8.141
Jacobs Construction (Holdings) Ltd v R & C Comrs [2016] UKFTT 555 (TC) 13.68
Jade Palace Ltd v R & C Comrs [2006] STC (SCD) 419, [2006] STI 1623 .... 1.112; 20.55
John Wilkins (Motor Engineers) Ltd v R & C Comrs [2009] UKUT 175 (TCC), [2009] STC 2485, [2009] STI 2714 .... 20.147, 20.224
Jonas v Bamford (Inspector of Taxes) [1973] STC 519, 51 TC 1, [1973] TR 225 .... 6.90, 6.91; 8.108; 13.132
Jordan v R & C Comrs [2015] STC 2314 .... 16.59
JSM Construction Ltd v R & C Comrs [2015] UKFTT 474 (TC), [2015] STI 2904 .... 20.146
Jumbogate Ltd v R & C Comrs [2015] UKFTT 64 (TC) 20.197

K

Kemp (Peter & Linda) v C & E Comrs (VTD 19479) 20.111
Kempton v Special Comrs of Income Tax [1992] STC 823, 66 TC 249, [1992] STI 891 .... 15.35
Kennerley v R & C Comrs [2007] STC (SCD) 188, [2007] STI 265 .... 13.25
Khagram v R & C Comrs [2012] UKFTT 494 .... 7.28

Table of Cases

Khan v R & C Comrs [2014] UKFTT 18 (TC) 1.120; 6.98
Khan Properties Ltd v R & C Comrs (TC 6225) 19.65
Khazenifar v R & C Comrs [2013] UKFTT 752 (TC) 1.119; 6.98
Kilbride v R & C Comrs [2008] STC (SCD) 517, [2008] STI 224..................... 1.114
Kopecky v Slovakia (2005) 41 EHRR 43 .... 20.118
Kyte v R & C Comrs [2018] EWHC 1146 (Ch), [2018] BTC 20, [2018] STI 1048 .... 1.136

L

L (A Minor) (Police Investigation: Privilege), Re [1997] AC 16, [1996] 2 WLR 395,
  [1996] 2 All ER 78.. 16.166
Laerstate BV v R & C Comrs [2009] UKFTT 209 (TC), [2009] SFTD 551,
  [2009] STI 2669 .... 4.95, 4.142
Langham (Inspector of Taxes) v Veltema [2004] EWCA Civ 193, [2004] STC 544,
  76 TC 259 .... 1.23; 4.188, 4.191, 4.194;
    13.111, 13.123
Lee v R & C Comrs [2009] STC (SCD) 1, [2008] STI 2675 .... 1.115
Lee v R & C Comrs [2012] UKFTT 312 (TC) 15.33
Lee Ting Sang v Chung Chi-Keung [1990] 2 AC 374, [1990] 2 WLR 1173,
  [1990] ICR 409 .... 26.84
Leeds City Council v R & C Comrs [2014] UKUT 350 (TCC), [2015] STC 168,
  [2014] BVC 531... 20.169
Levene v IRC [1928] AC 217, [1928] All ER Rep 746, 13 TC 486 .... 5.8
Lithgow v R & C Comrs [2012] UKFTT 620 (TC), [2013] STI 267................. 18.65
Litman v R & C Comrs [2014] UKFTT 89 (TC), [2015] WTLR 857.......... 4.199; 8.89; 18.146
Livewire Telecom Ltd v R & C Comrs [2008] BVC 2208, [2008] V & DR 131,
  [2008] STI 1161... 20.85
Livingstone v R & C Comrs [2010] UKFTT 56 (TC)... 25.135
Long v R & C Comrs [2014] UKFTT 199 (TC).. 1.48; 6.81; 16.30
Lonrho Ltd v Shell Petroleum Co Ltd [1980] QB 358, [1980] 2 WLR 367, (1980)
  124 SJ 205, CA; [1980] 1 WLR 627, (1980) 124 SJ 412, HL............ 4.167, 4.169; 16.137,
    16.138, 16.142, 16.143, 16.144, 16.147
Lucas v Cattell (1972) 48 TC 353, [1972] TR 83 .... 26.174
Lyth v R & C Comrs [2017] UKFTT 549 (TC).. 13.150

M

McCloskey v R & C Comrs [2018] UKFTT 352 (TC).. 13.91
MacDonald v R & C Comrs [2016] UKFTT 496 (TC) 19.23
MacNiven (Inspector of Taxes) v Westmoreland Investments Ltd [2001] UKHL 6,
  [2003] 1 AC 311, [2001] STC 237.. 4.53; 20.120
Mairs (Inspector of Taxes) v Haughey [1994] 1 AC 303, [1993] 3 WLR 393,
  [1993] STC 569.. 26.121
Mariner v R & C Comrs [2013] UKFTT 657 (TC), [2014] SFTD 504,
  [2014] WTLR 293 .... 13.80; 18.66
Market Investigations Ltd v Minister of Social Security [1969] 2 QB 173,
  [1969] 2 WLR 1, [1968] 3 All ER 732 .... 26.72, 26.76
Marks & Spencer plc v Halsey (Inspector of Taxes) [2003] Eu LR 46,
  [2003] STC (SCD) 70, 5 ITL Rep 536 .... 20.275
Marks & Spencer v Halsey (Inspector of Taxes) (Case C-446/03) [2006] Ch 184,
  [2006] 2 WLR 250, [2006] STC 237, ECJ; [2006] EWHC 811 (Ch), [2006] STC
  1235, [2006] 3 CMLR 8, [2006] BTC 346, 8 ITL Rep 1012, [2006] STI 1352;
  [2007] EWCA Civ 117, [2008] STC 526, [2007] 2 CMLR 21, [2007] Eu LR 577,
  [2007] BTC 204, 9 ITL Rep 739, [2007] STI 410, (2007) 151 SJLB 300 .... 20.279
Marsh (Elizabeth) v R & C Comrs [2017] UKFTT 320 (TC)................................. 13.25, 13.150
Martin v R & C Comrs [2017] UKFTT 488 (TC) 1.110
Marwood Homes Ltd v IRC [1997] STC (SCD) 37, [1998] STC (SCD) 53,
  [1999] STC (SCD) 44 .... 4.81, 4.109, 4.110

lv

Table of Cases

Mathew v R & C Comrs [2015] UKFTT 139 (TC) 6.51; 16.37
Mayes v R & C Comrs [2011] EWCA Civ 407, [2011] STC 1269, 81 TC 247 .... 4.58, 4.62, 4.64
Meditor Capital Management Ltd v Feigan (Inspector of Taxes) [2004] STC (SCD) 273, [2004] STI 1280 .... 4.169; 16.143, 16.144, 16.145, 16.147
Mehdvi v R & C Comrs [2013] UKFTT 173 (TC) 6.93
Miesegaes v R & C Comrs [2016] UKFTT 375 (TC), [2016] SFTD 719, [2016] STI 2444 .... 13.48, 13.119
Mistral Promotions & Marketing (UK) Ltd v R & C Comrs [2015] UKFTT 112 (TC) 22.77
Mitchell v News Group Newspapers Ltd [2013] EWCA Civ 1537, [2014] 1 WLR 795, [2014] 2 All ER 430 .... 20.168, 20.169, 20.170, 20.171
MJP Media Services Ltd v R & C Comrs [2012] EWCA Civ 1558, [2013] STC 2218, [2012] BTC 477 .... 20.228
Mobile Export 365 Ltd v R & C Comrs [2007] EWHC 1737 (Ch), [2007] STC 1794, [2008] BVC 125 .... 20.153
Monarch Assurance Co Ltd v Special Comrs [1986] STC 311, 59 TC 594 .... 15.35; 16.181
Moore v R & C Comrs [2011] UKUT 239 (TCC).. 8.91; 13.68, 13.95
Morren v Swinton & Pendlebury Borough Council [1965] 1 WLR 576, [1965] 2 All ER 349, 63 LGR 288 .... 26.76
Morris v R & C Comrs [2017] UKFTT 749 (TC) 19.66
Morris v Roberts (Inspector of Taxes) [2005] EWHC 1040 (Ch), [2006] STC 135, [2005] PNLR 41 .... 20.205
Mother v HM Inspector of Taxes [1999] STC (SCD) 279 .... 15.35
Munford v R & C Comrs [2017] UKFTT 19 (TC) 1.130
Murat v HM Inspector of Taxes see Accountant v Inspector of Taxes
Murphy v Gowers (Inspector of Taxes) [2005] STC (SCD) 44, [2004] STI 2267 .... 15.35
Murray Group Holdings Ltd v R & C Comrs [2015] CSIH 77, [2016] STC 468, 2016 SC 201, 2015 SLT 765, 2016 SCLR 485, [2015] BTC 36 .... 4.76

N

N Ltd v Inspector of Taxes [1996] STC (SCD) 346 .... 4.149
National Exhibition Centre Ltd v R & C Comrs [2013] UKFTT 289 (TC), [2014] SFTD 107, [2013] STI 2003; [2015] UKUT 23 (TCC), [2015] STC 1185, [2015] BVC 506 .... 20.217, 20.218, 20.220
National Westminster Bank plc v C & E Comrs (Unjust Enrichment) [2003] EWHC 1822 (Ch), [2003] STC 1072, [2003] BTC 5578 .... 20.173
Needs v R & C Comrs [2011] UKFTT 434 (TC) 19.59
Nelson (t/a Sandvale Licensed Grocers) v R & C Comrs [2012] UKFTT 551 (TC) 7.53
Newell (t/a Tanya's Takeaway) v R & C Comrs [2013] UKFTT 742 (TC) 1.76; 6.90; 9.46
New Victoria Hospital v Ryan [1993] ICR 201, [1993] IRLR 202 .... 16.161
News Datacom Ltd v Atkinson (Inspector of Taxes) [2006] STC (SCD) 732, [2006] STI 2346 .... 4.92
Nichols v R & C Comrs [2016] UKFTT 155 (TC) 1.118
Nicoll v Austin (1935) 19 TC 531 .... 26.112
Nijjar Dairies Ltd v R & C Comrs [2013] UKFTT 434 (TC), [2013] STI 3372 ..... 13.45, 13.146
NMB Holdings v Secretary of State (2000) 73 TC 85 .... 26.29
Norman v R & C Comrs [2015] UKFTT 303 (TC), [2015] SFTD 868 .... 13.119

O

O'Kelly v Trusthouse Forte plc [1984] QB 90, [1983] 3 WLR 605, [1983] 3 All ER 456 .... 26.83, 26.87
O'Rorke v R & C Comrs [2011] UKFTT 839 (TC), [2012] SFTD 553, [2012] STI 354; [2013] UKUT 499 (TCC), [2014] STC 279, [2013] BTC 2096, [2014] STI 253 .... 22.12; 25.136

Table of Cases

Onillon v R & C Comrs [2018] UKFTT 33 (TC), [2018] SFTD 728, [2018] STI 826.. 20.119
Osborne (dec'd) v Dickinson (Inspector of Taxes) [2004] STC (SCD) 104, [2004] STI 150... 13.57, 13.62
Owen v Burden [1972] 1 All ER 356, 47 TC 476, (1971) 50 ATC 172............................ 26.144
Oxfam v R & C Comrs [2009] EWHC 3078 (Ch), [2010] STC 686, [2010] BVC 108.. 20.173, 20.174, 20.175, 20.177

P

PA Holdings Ltd v R & C Comrs [2011] EWCA Civ 1414, [2012] STC 582, 82 TC 1.. 20.197
Parikh v Back (Inspector of Taxes) [1985] STC 232... 20.114
Parikh v Sleeman (Inspector of Taxes) [1990] STC 233, 63 TC 75, [1990] BTC 142...... 26.144
Parkin v Cattell (1971) 48 TC 462, [1971] TR 177... 4.186
Parkwell v Wilson; Parkwell Investments Ltd, Re [2014] EWHC 3381 (Ch), [2015] Bus LR 40, [2014] BCC 721.. 8.157; 22.64
Patel v R & C Comrs [2014] UKFTT 167 (TC), [2014] WTLR 1183.......... 1.48; 4.169; 16.150
Pattullo v R & C Comrs [2016] UKUT 270 (TCC).. 1.23; 13.50, 13.51, 13.113, 13.122
Pendergate Ltd (t/a Ridge Crest Cleaning Services) v R & C Comrs [2016] UKFTT 166 (TC).. 18.85
Pepper (Inspector of Taxes) v Hart [1993] AC 593, [1992] 3 WLR 1032, [1993] 1 All ER 42.. 26.125, 26.126, 26.129, 26.141, 26.174
PML Accounting Ltd v R & C Comrs [2015] UKFTT 440 (TC); [2017] EWHC 733 (Admin), [2017] STC 1091, [2017] BTC 10, [2017] STI 1101...................... 1.105; 16.191
Pook (Inspector of Taxes) v Owen [1969] 1 Ch 535, [1968] 2 WLR 591, 45 TC 571....... 26.180
Porter v R & C Comrs [2016] UKFTT 401 (TC).. 19.27
Practice Direction (Sup Ct: References to the Court of Justice of the European Communities) [1999] 1 WLR 260, [1999] 1 Cr App R 452, [1999] 2 CMLR 799... 20.276
Price v R & C Comrs [2011] UKFTT 624 (TC)... 6.97
Price v R & C Comrs [2013] UKFTT 297 (TC), [2013] STI 2510.................................. 4.72
Price Waterhouse v BCCI Holdings (Luxembourg) SA [1992] BCLC 583..................... 16.164
Prince v R & C Comrs [2012] UKFTT 157 (TC), [2012] SFTD 786, [2012] STI 1666.... 20.163
Providence Health Consultants Ltd v R & C Comrs [2013] UKFTT 601 (TC)................ 13.82
Prudential plc v R & C Comrs [2008] STC (SCD) 239, [2007] STI 2412; [2008] EWHC 1839 (Ch), [2008] STC 2820, [2008] BTC 739, [2008] STI 1919; [2009] EWCA Civ 622, [2009] STC 2459, 79 TC 691... 4.58, 4.109
Pumahaven Ltd v Williams (Inspector of Taxes) [2001] STC (SCD) 206, [2001] STI 1502... 20.113

R

R v Allen [2001] UKHL 45, [2002] 1 AC 509, [2001] 3 WLR 843................................. 2.24
R v Charlton [1996] STC 1418, 67 TC 500....................................... 3.36, 3.218; 4.98; 5.21
R v Da Silva [2006] EWCA Crim 1654, [2007] 1 WLR 303, [2006] 4 All ER 900.......... 3.189
R v Dimsey [2001] UKHL 46, [2002] 1 AC 509, [2001] STC 1520................................. 5.21
R v Ghosh [1982] QB 1053, [1982] 3 WLR 110, [1982] 2 All ER 689............................ 3.1
R v Gill [2003] EWCA Crim 2256, [2004] 1 WLR 469, [2003] 4 All ER 681.... 2.26, 2.27, 2.28
R v H [2004] UKHL 3, [2004] 2 AC 134, [2004] 2 WLR 335, [2004] 1 All ER 1269, [2004] 2 Cr App R 10, [2004] HRLR 20, 16 BHRC 332, (2004) 101(8) LSG 29, (2004) 148 SJLB 183.. 3.142
R v Hepworth (George Alfred); R v Fearnley (Norman) [1955] 2 QB 600, [1955] 3 WLR 331, 39 Cr App R 152.. 3.140
R v Hudson (Alan Harry) [1956] 2 QB 252, [1956] 2 WLR 914, (1956) 40 Cr App R 55... 3.7

lvii

Table of Cases

R v IK [2007] EWCA Crim 491, [2007] 2 Cr App R 15, [2007] Crim LR 882 .... 3.156
R v IRC, ex p Banque International a Luxembourg SA [2000] STC 708, 72 TC 597, [2000] BTC 228 .... 15.35
R v IRC, ex p Chisolm [1981] 2 All ER 602, [1981] STC 253, 54 TC 722 .... 22.14
R v IRC, ex p Cook & Keys [1987] STC 434, 60 TC 405, [1987] BTC 339 .... 22.14
R v IRC, ex p Davis Frankel & Mead [2000] STC 595, 73 TC 185, [2000] BTC 203 ...... 15.35
R v IRC, ex p McVeigh [1996] STC 91, 68 TC 121 .... 22.14
R v IRC, ex p Mead [1993] 1 All ER 772, [1992] STC 482, [1992] COD 361 .... 3.36
R v IRC, ex p Sims [1987] STC 211, 60 TC 398 .... 22.14
R v IRC, ex p Ulster Bank Ltd [1997] STC 832, 69 TC 211, [1997] BTC 314 .... 5.39; 15.35
R v IRC & Connolly, ex p Mohammed [1999] STC 129, (1998) 73 TC 128, [1999] BTC 20 .... 15.35
R v IRC & Middlesex Guildhall Crown Court, ex p Tamosius & Partners [2000] 1 WLR 453, [1999] STC 1077, [1999] BTC 404 .... 16.206
R v International Stock Exchange of the United Kingdom & the Republic of Ireland Ltd, ex p Else (1982) Ltd [1993] QB 534, [1993] 2 WLR 70, [1993] 1 All ER 420 .... 20.274
R v Kensington Income Tax Comrs, ex p Aramayo [1913] 3 KB 870, 6 TC 279 .... 4.186
R v Mavji (Ramniklal Nathoo) [1987] 1 WLR 1388, [1987] 2 All ER 758, 84 Cr App R 34 .... 3.7
R v NW; SW, RC and CC [2008] EWCA Crim 2, [2009] 1 WLR 965, [2008] 3 All ER 533 .... 3.157
R v O'Kane & Clarke, ex p Northern Bank Ltd [1996] STC 1249, 69 TC 187 .... 15.35
R v Special Comrs of Income Tax, ex p Morgan Grenfell & Co Ltd *see* R (on the application of Morgan Grenfell & Co Ltd) v Special Comrs of Income Tax
R v Steed [2011] EWCA Crim 75, [2011] Lloyd's Rep FC 238 .... 14.15
R v Werner (Laurence Ian) [1998] STC 550, [1998] BTC 202, (1998) 95 (16) LSG 24 .... 2.24; 3.26
R (on the application of Broomfield) v R & C Comrs [2017] EWHC 2926 (Admin), [2017] BTC 38 .... 20.119
R (on the application of de Silva) v R & C Comrs [2017] UKSC 74, [2017] 1 WLR 4384, [2018] 1 All ER 280, [2017] STC 2483, [2017] BTC 37, [2017] STI 2269 .... 13.8
R (on the application of Derrin Brother Properties Ltd) v R & C Comrs [2014] EWHC 1152 (Admin), [2014] STC 2238, [2014] BTC 21 .... 16.37
R (on the application of DFS Furniture Co plc) v C & E Comrs (No 1) [2002] EWCA Civ 1708, [2003] STC 1, [2003] BTC 5003 .... 20.122
R (on the application of F, J & K) v Blackfriars Crown Court & Comr of Police of the Metropolis) [2014] EWHC 1541 (Admin) 3.95
R (on the application of Graham) v R & C Comrs [2016] EWHC 1197 (Admin), [2017] STC 1, [2016] BTC 23, [2016] STI 1653 .... 20.117
R (on the application of H) v IRC [2002] EWHC 2164 (Admin), [2002] STC 1354, 75 TC 277 .... 16.202
R (on the application of Haworth) v R & C Comrs [2018] EWHC 1271 (Admin), [2018] STC 1326, [2018] BTC 22, [2018] STI 1045 .... 14.77
R (on the application of Jimenez) v First Tier Tribunal (Tax Chamber) [2017] EWHC 2585 (Admin), [2018] 1 WLR 2017, [2018] STC 132, [2017] BTC 35, [2017] ACD 136, [2017] STI 2204 .... 8.97; 16.151
R (on the application of Morgan Grenfell & Co Ltd) v Special Comrs of Income Tax [2002] UKHL 21, [2003] 1 AC 563, [2002] 2 WLR 1299, [2002] 3 All ER 1, [2002] STC 786, [2002] HRLR 42, 74 TC 511, [2002] BTC 223, 4 ITL Rep 809, [2002] STI 806, (2002) 99(25) LSG 35, (2002) 146 SJLB 126, [2002] NPC 70 .... 4.112, 4.115; 16.155
R (on the Application of NCM 2000 Ltd) v R & C Comrs [2015] EWHC 1342 (Admin), [2015] BVC 28 .... 23.63
R (on the application of Pattullo) v R & C Comrs [2009] CSOH 137, [2010] STC 107 .... 4.195

lviii

Table of Cases

R (on the application of Prudential plc) v Special Comr of Income Tax [2009] EWHC 2494 (Admin), [2010] 3 WLR 1042, [2010] 1 All ER 1113; [2010] EWCA Civ 1094, [2011] QB 669, [2011] 2 WLR 50; [2013] UKSC 1, [2013] 2 AC 185, [2013] 2 WLR 325 .... 3.104; 4.112, 4.114, 4.115, 4.148; 16.159, 16.160

R (on the application of Rawlinson & Hunter Trustees) v Central Crown Court & Serious Fraud Office [2012] EWHC 2254 (Admin), [2013] 1 WLR 1634, [2013] Lloyd's Rep FC 132 .... 3.95

R (on the application of Rowe) v R & C Comrs [2015] EWHC 2293 (Admin), [2015] BTC 27; [2017] EWCA Civ 2105; [2018] 1 WLR 3039, [2018] STC 462, [2018] BTC 4 .... 20.117, 20.118; 21.9

R (on the application of S, F & L) v Chief Constable of British Transport Police [2013] EWHC 2189 (Admin), [2014] 1 WLR 1647, [2014] 1 All ER 268 .... 3.93

R (on the application of ToTel Ltd) v First-tier Tribunal (Tax Chamber) [2011] EWHC 652 (Admin) (ToTel 1) 20.111

R (on the application of Vital Nut Co Ltd) v R & C Comrs [2016] EWHC 1797 (Admin), [2016] 4 WLR 144 .... 20.117, 20.118

R (on the application of Werner) v IRC [2002] EWCA Civ 979, [2002] STC 1213, [2002] BTC 319 .... 15.35

R & C Comrs v Ariel [2016] EWHC 1674 (Ch), [2017] 1 WLR 319, [2016] BPIR 1144, [2016] BTC 27 .... 16.65

R & C Comrs v Atlantic Electronics *see* Atlantic Electronics Ltd v R & C Comrs

R & C Comrs v Banerjee [2009] EWHC 1229 (Ch), [2009] 3 All ER 930, [2009] STC 1930.. 8.130; 20.189, 20.192

R & C Comrs v Bank of Ireland Britain Holdings Ltd [2008] EWCA Civ 58, [2008] STC 398, [2008] BTC 126 .... 4.58, 4.59

R & C Comrs v BPP Holdings Ltd; BPP University College of Professional Studies v R & C Comrs [2014] UKUT 496 (TC), [2015] STC 415, [2014] BVC 544 .... 20.169

R & C Comrs v Charlton [2012] UKUT 770 (TCC), [2013] STC 866, [2013] BTC 1634 .... 1.23; 4.189, 4.191, 4.192, 4.193, 4.195, 4.196; 13.2, 13.22, 13.49, 13.59, 13.112, 13.118, 13.124, 13.126

R & C Comrs v CM Utilities Ltd [2017] UKUT 305 (TCC), [2017] BTC 527 .... 8.130

R & C Comrs v Cotter [2013] UKSC 69, [2013] 1 WLR 3514, [2014] 1 All ER 1, [2013] STC 2480, [2013] BTC 837, [2013] STI 3450 .... 13.8

R & C Comrs v D'Arcy [2006] STC (SCD) 543, [2006] STI 1856; [2007] EWHC 163 (Ch), [2008] STC 1329, [2007] BTC 257.............................. 4.58; 20.56, 20.58, 20.72

R & C Comrs v DCC Holdings (UK) Ltd [2010] UKSC 58, [2011] 1 WLR 44, [2011] 1 All ER 537.. 4.58

R & C Comrs v Dhanak [2014] UKUT 68 (TCC), [2014] STC 1525, [2014] BTC 506 .... 20.243

R & C Comrs v Household Estate Agents Ltd [2007] EWHC 1684 (Ch), [2008] STC 2045, 78 TC 705, [2008] BTC 502, [2007] STI 1815 .... 13.68, 13.127, 13.160, 13.163

R & C Comrs v Lansdowne Partners LP [2011] EWCA Civ 1578, [2012] STC 544, 81 TC 318.. 1.23 ; 4.190, 4.195; 13.25, 13.111, 13.120

R & C Comrs v Mabbutt [2016] UKFTT 306 (TC); [2017] UKUT 289 (TCC), [2017] STC 1873, [2017] BTC 528, [2017] STI 1868 .... 1.38; 6.43; 11.5

R & C Comrs v McCarthy & Stone (Developments) Ltd [2014] UKUT 196 (TCC), [2014] STC 973, [2014] BVC 504.. 20.169, 20.230

R & C Comrs v Mercury Tax Group Ltd [2009] STC (SCD) 307, [2009] STI 628 .... 4.198

R & C Comrs v Morrison [2013] UKUT 497 (TCC), [2014] STC 574, [2013] BTC 2065 .... 20.247

Table of Cases

R & C Comrs v Munir [2015] EWHC 1366 (Ch), [2015] BCC 425 .... 22.66
R & C Comrs v Noor [2011] UKFTT 349 (TC), [2011] STI 1950; *revs'd*
 [2013] UKUT 71 (TCC), [2013] STC 998, [2013] BVC 1571 .... 20.175, 20.177; 23.60
R & C Comrs v Parissis [2011] UKFTT 218 (TC), [2011] SFTD 757,
 13 ITELR 934 .... 4.168, 4.169, 4.170, 4.171; 16.136,
 16.143, 16.146, 16.148
R & C Comrs v Raftopoulou [2018] EWCA Civ 818, [2018] STC 988,
 [2018] BTC 17, [2018] STI 943 .... 13.177
R & C Comrs v Rochdale Drinks Distributors Ltd [2011] EWCA Civ 1116,
 [2012] STC 186, [2013] BCC 419 .... 22.64, 22.65
R & C Comrs v Root2tax Ltd [2017] UKFTT 696 (TC) 8.70
R & C Comrs v Tager [2015] UKUT 40 (TCC), [2015] STC 1687, [2015] BTC 509;
 [2018] EWCA Civ 1727 .... 6.59; 16.191
R & C Comrs v TGH (Commercial) Ltd [2017] UKUT 116 (TCC), [2017] BVC 511 ..... 8.130
R & C Comrs v Tooth [2018] UKUT 38 (TCC), [2018] STC 824,
 [2018] BTC 505, [2018] STI 1052 .... 6.119; 13.24, 13.53, 13.84, 13.89
R & C Comrs v Vodafone 2 [2005] EWHC 3040 (Ch), [2006] STC 483,
 [2006] BTC 406 .... 20.56
R & C Comrs' Application (Section 20 Notice: Financial Institution), Re (SpC 517)
 [2006] STC (SCD) 71, [2006] WTLR 277, [2006] STI 241 .... 5.39; 16.73
R & C Comrs' Application (Section 20 Notice: Financial Institution), Re (SpC 536)
 [2006] STC (SCD) 360, [2006] STI 1497 .... 16.73, 16.76
R & C Comrs' Application (Section 20 Notice: Financial Institution No 1), Re (SpC 580)
 [2007] STC (SCD) 202, [2007] WTLR 777, [2007] STI 351 .... 5.39; 16.73
R & C Comrs' Application (Section 20 Notice: Financial Institution No 2), Re (SpC 581)
 [2007] STC (SCD) 208, [2007] STI 295 .... 16.73
R & C Comrs' Application (Section 20 Notice: Financial Institution No 3), Re (SpC 582)
 [2007] STC (SCD) 216, [2007] STI 297 .... 16.73
R & C Comrs' Application (Section 20 Notice: Financial Institution No 4), Re (SpC 583)
 [2007] STC (SCD) 222, [2007] STI 352 .... 16.73
R & C Comrs' Application (Section 20 Notice: Financial Institution Nos 6 & 7),
 Re (TC 10) [2009] UKFTT 69 (TC), [2009] STC (SCD) 493, [2009] STI 1803 .... 16.76
R & C Comrs' Application (Approval to Serve 308 Notices on Financial
 Institutions), Re (TC 174) [2009] UKFTT 224 (TC), [2009] SFTD 780,
 [2009] STI 2717 .... 16.77, 16.78
Rafferty v R & C Comrs [2005] STC (SCD) 484 .... 13.67
Rankin v R & C Comrs [2016] UKFTT 541 (TC) 6.103
RD Utilities Ltd v R & C Comrs [2014] UKFTT 303 (TC) 16.33
Ready Mixed Concrete (South East) Ltd v Minister of Pensions & National Insurance
 [1968] 2 QB 497, [1968] 2 WLR 775, [1968] 1 All ER 433 .... 26.76
Red Discretionary Trustees v Inspector of Taxes *see* Howell v Trippier (Inspector
 of Taxes)
Red Star v R & C Comrs [2011] UKFTT 812 (TC) 6.90
Reddleman Properties Ltd v R & C Comrs [2011] UKFTT 395 (TC) 20.195
Reed (Inspector of Taxes) v Seymour (1927) 11 TC 625 .... 26.112
Reed Employment plc v R & C Comrs [2010] UKFTT 596 (TC), [2011] STC 695,
 [2011] BTC 1517 .... 20.242; 25.24, 25.26
RFC 2012 Plc (in liquidation) (formerly Rangers Football Club Plc) v Advocate
 General for Scotland [2017] UKSC 45, [2017] 1 WLR 2767, [2017] 4 All ER
 654, [2017] STC 1556, 2018 SC (UKSC) 15, 2017 SLT 799, 2017 SCLR 517,
 [2017] BTC 22, [2017] WTLR 1093, [2017] STI 1610 .... 21.33
Rheinmuhlen-Dusseldorf v Einfuhr-und Vorratsstelle fur Getreide und Futtermittel
 (Case 166/373) [1974] ECR 33, [1974] 1 CMLR 523 .... 20.274
Rich v R & C Comrs [2011] UKFTT 533 (TC) 18.64
Richter v R & C Comrs [2017] UKFTT 339 (TC) 19.68

Table of Cases

Rincham Ltd v R & C Comrs [2010] UKFTT 502 (TC), [2010] STI 3177 .... 16.82
Ritchie v R & C Comrs [2017] UKFTT 449 (TC).. 13.25
Roberts v R & C Comrs [2012] UKFTT 308 (TC)... 25.136
Roberts and Martin v R & C Commrs [2011] UKFTT 268 (TC)............................. 25.136
Roche v R & C Comrs [2012] UKFTT 333 (TC), [2012] STI 2364 .... 19.27
Rowe v R & C Comrs [2015] EWHC 2293 Admin, [2015] BTC 27 .... 4.30
Royal Institute of Navigation v R & C Comrs [2012] UKFTT 472 (TC) 20.134
Rumbelow v R & C Comrs [2013] UKFTT 637 (TC)... 4.127
Rusling v R & C Comrs [2014] UKFTT 692 (TC).. 13.98

S

Sanderson v R & C Comrs [2013] UKUT 623 (TCC), [2014] STC 915, [2014] BTC 502; [2016] EWCA Civ 19, [2016] 4 WLR 67, [2016] 3 All ER 203, [2016] STC 638, [2016] BTC 3, [2016] STI 237 .... 4.189, 4.196; 13.25, 13.103, 13.111, 13.124, 13.128
Saunders v R & C Comrs [2017] UKFTT 765 (TC), [2018] SFTD 487, [2018] STI 95.. 19.67
SCA Packaging Ltd v R & C Comrs [2007] EWHC 270 (Ch), [2007] STC 1640, [2007] BTC 308 .... 26.35
School Estates Consultancy Ltd v R & C Comrs [2018] UKFTT 4 (TC) 22.77
Schotten & Hansen (UK) Ltd v R & C Comrs [2017] UKFTT 191 (TC), [2017] STI 1044.. 18.69
Secretary of State for Trade and Industry v Baker [1988] Ch 356, [1998] 2 WLR 667, [1998] 1 All ER 673, [1998] BCC 888, [1998] 1 BCLC 16............................ 16.170
Self-Assessed v HM Inspector of Taxes [1999] STC (SCD) 253............................ 6.47
Seymour Limousines Ltd v R & C Comrs [2009] STI 845 .... 20.111
Shakoor v R & C Comrs [2012] UKFTT 532 (TC), [2012] SFTD 1391, [2012] STI 3334.. 18.59
Shepherd v R & C Comrs [2005] STC (SCD) 644 .... 5.11
Shimlas Ltd v R & C Comrs [2016] UKFTT 670 (TC)... 16.61
Singh v R & C Comrs [2014] UKFTT 299 (TC)... 15.34
Siwek v IRC [2002] STC (SCD) 247, [2002] STI 899.. 15.35
Skoye v Bailey [1971] 1 WWR 144 .... 16.135
Slade v Tucker (1880) 14 Ch D 824 .... 16.161
Smith v R & C Comrs [2011] UKUT 270 (TCC), [2011] STC 1724, [2011] BTC 1742, [2011] STI 2172 .... 13.99
Smith v R & C Comrs [2012] UKFTT 428 (TC)... 25.136
Smith v R & C Comrs [2015] UKFTT 200 (TC)... 6.53; 15.27
Snell v R & C Comrs [2008] STC (SCD) 1094, [2008] STI 1926.......................... 4.147
Sokoya v HMRC [2008] EWHC 2132 (Ch), [2008] STC 3332, [2008] BTC 635............. 15.35
Space 2 Build Ltd v R & C Comrs [2010] UKFTT 66 (TC), [2010] STI 2260 .... 20.176
Sparrow Ltd v Inspector of Taxes *see* Pumahaven Ltd v Williams (Inspector of Taxes)
Spring Capital Ltd v R & C Comrs [2015] UKFTT 8 (TC); [2016] UKFTT 671 (TC).. 6.103; 8.157; 15.34
St Anne's Distributors Ltd v R & C Comrs [2010] UKUT 458 (TC), [2011] STC 708, [2011] BVC 1539.. 20.126
Stanford International Bank Ltd (in receivership), Re [2010] EWCA Civ 137, [2011] Ch 33, [2010] 3 WLR 941 .... 3.94
Steady v R & C Comrs [2016] UKFTT 473 (TC) 19.52
Steiner v R & C Comrs [2017] UKFTT 157 (TC)... 18.69
Surestone Ltd v R & C Comrs [2009] UKFTT 352 (TC), [2010] STI 682, [2010] STI 1649.. 20.214, 20.217
Swedish Central Rail Co Ltd v Thompson [1925] AC 495 .... 4.92
Syed v R & C Comrs [2011] UKFTT 315 (TC) 6.91; 13.133

Table of Cases

T

Tager v R & C Comrs [2015] UKUT 663 (TCC), [2015] BTC 538 .... 6.59
Tanfern Ltd v Cameron-MacDonald [2000] 1 WLR 1311, [2000] 2 All ER 801, [2001] CP Rep 8 .... 20.255
Taylor v Bratherton (Inspector of Taxes) [2005] STC (SCD) 230, [2005] STI 107 .... 6.89; 15.35; 16.39
Taylor (dec'd) v R & C Comrs [2013] UKFTT 483 (TC), [2014] WTLR 357 .... 20.163
TelNG Ltd v R & C Comrs [2015] UKFTT 327 (TC), [2015] STI 2416 .... 16.35
Thomas Mawdsley & Son v R & C Comrs (TC/2010/05147) 20.207
Thorpe v R & C Comrs [2010] EWCA Civ 339, [2010] STC 964, [2010] BTC 425 .... 20.175
Three Rivers District Council v Governor & Co of the Bank of England [2004] UKHL 48, [2005] 1 AC 610, [2004] 3 WLR 1274 .... 16.170
Tinkler v R & C Comrs [2018] UKUT 73 (TCC), [2018] BTC 506 .... 1.38; 6.41
Tod (Inspector of Taxes) v South Essex Motors (Basildon) Ltd [1988] STC 392, 60 TC 598 .... 20.120
ToTel Ltd v R & C Comrs [2014] UKUT 485 (TCC) (ToTel 2) 20.111
Tower MCashback LLP 1 v R & C Comrs [2011] UKSC 19, [2011] 2 AC 457, [2011] 2 WLR 1131 .... 1.116, 1.117; 4.58, 4.75; 20.56, 20.58, 20.59, 20.72, 20.77
Towers Watson Ltd v R & C Comrs [2017] UKFTT 846 (TC) 20.77
Tricell (UK) Ltd v C & E Comrs [2003] V & DR 333, [2003] STI 1516 .... 20.111

U

UBS AG v R & C Comrs [2014] EWCA Civ 452, [2014] STC 2278, [2014] BTC 20 .... 4.62, 4.64, 4.67
Unit Construction Co Ltd v Bullock (Inspector of Taxes) [1960] AC 351, [1959] 3 WLR 1022, 38 TC 712 .... 4.91; 5.17
Untelrab Ltd v McGregor (Inspector of Taxes) [1996] STC (SCD) 1 .... 4.93

V

Van Boeckel v C & E Comrs [1981] 2 All ER 505, [1981] STC 290, [1980] TR 477 .... 13.25
Vandervell's Trusts (No 1), Re [1971] AC 912, [1970] 3 WLR 452, [1970] 3 All ER 16 .... 20.261
Versteegh Ltd v R & C Comrs [2013] UKFTT 642 (TC), [2014] SFTD 547, [2014] STI 475 .... 4.83, 4.109, 4.111

W

Walapu v R & C Comrs [2016] EWHC 658 (Admin), [2016] 4 All ER 955, [2016] STC 1682, [2016] BTC 14, [2016] STI 1336 .... 20.117
Waugh v British Rlys Board [1980] AC 521, [1979] 3 WLR 150, [1979] 2 All ER 1169 .... 16.167
Westbeach Apparel UK Ltd v R & C Comrs [2011] UKFTT 561 (TC) 19.60
Westek Ltd v R & C Comrs [2008] STC (SCD) 169, [2007] STI 2145 .... 25.184
Whight (Paul) v R & C Comrs [2011] UKFTT 60 (TC) 15.33
While v R & C Comrs [2012] UKFTT 58 (TC) 6.75; 13.120, 13.164
White v R & C Comrs [2012] UKFTT 364 (TC), [2012] STI 2502 .... 19.27
Whitefields Golf Club Ltd v R &C Comrs [2014] UKFTT 458 (TC), [2014] STI 2051 .... 16.36, 16.58
Whittle v R & C Comrs [2014] UKFTT 254 (TC) 8.106
Wickens v Champion Employment [1984] ICR 365, (1984) 134 NLJ 544 .... 26.76
Wilden Pump Engineering Co v Fusfeld [1985] FSR 159 .... 4.115; 16.161
Williams v Ingram (1900) 16 TLR 451 .... 16.135, 16.167
Williams & Glyn's Bank v C & E Comrs [1974] VATTR 262 .... 20.86
Wing Hung Lai v Bale [1999] STC (SCD) 238 .... 6.88
Wong Yau Lam v R & C Comrs [2012] UKFTT 118 (TC) 15.33

Table of Cases

Wood v Holden (Inspector of Taxes) [2005] EWHC 547 (Ch), [2005] STC 789, [2005] BTC 253; [2006] EWCA Civ 26, [2006] 1 WLR 1393, [2006] STC 443.. 4.93, 4.94
Wood v R & C Comrs [2015] UKFTT 282 (TC), [2015] SFTD 806 .... 13.151
Woolmington v DPP [1935] AC 462, (1936) 25 Cr App R 72 .... 3.140
Woolwich Equitable Building Society v IRC [1993] AC 70, [1992] 3 WLR 366, [1992] STC 657.. 20.263
WT Ramsay Ltd v IRC [1982] AC 300, [1981] 2 WLR 449, 54 TC 101 .... 4.49, 4.51, 4.53, 4.54, 4.55, 4.57, 4.61, 4.63, 4.64, 4.68, 4.69, 4.70, 4.106

Abbreviations

AAG	Anti-Avoidance Group
ADR	Alternative Dispute Resolution
AMAP	approved mileage allowance payments
APB	Auditing Practices Board
APN	accelerated payment notices
BEIS	Department of Business, Energy and Industrial Strategy
BEPS	Base Erosion Profit Shifting
BPT	Basic PAYE Tools package
BRC	business records check
CA	Contributions Agency
CAD	Counter-Avoidance Directorate
CAR	Charity Assets and Residence
CC	customer coordinator
CCAB	Consultative Committee of Accountancy Bodies
CDF	Contractual Disclosure Facility
CEDR	Centre for Effective Dispute Resolution
CEP	Criminal and Enforcement Policy
CF	criminal finance
CFC	controlled foreign companies
CGT	capital gains tax
CH	Compliance Handbook
CHG	Complaints Handling Guidance
CIF	Civil Investigations of Fraud
CIOT	Chartered Institute of Taxation
CIS	construction industry scheme
CJA 1993	Criminal Justice Act 1993
CJPA 2001	Criminal Justice and Police Act 2001
COG	Compliance Operational Guidance manual
COP8	Code of Practice 8
COP9	Code of Practice 9
COR	Confirmation of Relevance
CPS	Crown Prosecution Service
CRCA 2005	Commissioners for Revenue and Customs Act 2005
CRG	Complaints Remedy Guidance
CRM	client/customer relationship manager
CRO	composite rate option
CRS	common reporting standard
CTA 2009	Corporation Tax Act 2009
DMB	HMRC's Debt Management and Banking department

lxv

Abbreviations

DDS	Digital Disclosure Service
DOTAS	disclosure of tax avoidance schemes
DPP	Director of Public Prosecutions
DPT	Diverted profits tax
DRD	direct recovery of debts
DTC	Double Taxation Convention
DWP	Department for Work and Pensions
EAS	employer alignment submission
EBT	employee benefit trust
EBTSO	EBT settlement offer
ECAT	Enforcement and Compliance Assurance Team
ECJ	European Court of Justice
EH	Enquiry Handbook
EM	Enquiry manual
EPS	Employer Payment Summaries
ESC	Extra-Statutory concession
ESL	EC Sales List
ESM	Employment Status manual
EUSD	European Union Savings Directive
EYU	earlier year update
FA	Finance Act
FATCA	Foreign Account Tax Compliance Act
FCIM	Fraud Civil Investigation manual
FEU	Foreign Entertainers Unit
FI	financial institution
FIS	Fraud Investigation Service
FN	follower notice
FPS	Full Payment Submission
FTT	First-tier Tribunal
FYA	first-year allowance
GAAP	generally accepted accounting practice
GAAR	general anti-abuse rule
GNS	generic notification system
GPR	gross profit rate
HNWU	High Net Worth Unit
HRCP	High Risk Corporate Programme
IGA	Intergovernmental Agreement
IRU	Interest Review Unit
ITTOIA 2005	Income Tax (Trading and Other Income) Act 2005
JP	justice of the peace
KAI	Knowledge, Analysis and Intelligence
KYC	Know Your Client
LB	Large Business
LAP	legal advice privilege
LCD	Lord Chancellor's Department

Abbreviations

LDF	Liechtenstein Disclosure Facility
LEL	lower earnings limit
LPP	legal professional privilege
LPU	Large Payers Unit
LSS	Litigation and Settlement Strategy
LVO	local VAT office
MARD	European Union Mutual Assistance for Recovery of Debts
MCR	Managing Complex Risk
MLR 2007	Money Laundering Regulations 2007, SI 2007/2157
MOU	Memorandum of Understanding
MPP	managed payment plan
MSC	managed service company
MSD	managing serious defaulters
MTD	Making Tax Digital Project
MTIC	missing trader intra-community
NCA	National Crime Agency
NCIS	National Criminal Intelligence Service
NDO	New Disclosure Opportunity
NFE	non-financial entity
NIC	National Insurance contributions
NICA 2015	National Insurance Contributions Act 2015
NIC&EO	National Insurance Contributions and Employer Office
NIM	National Insurance manual
NINO	National Insurance number
NMW	national minimum wage
NPS	National Insurance and PAYE System
NVR	National Insurance number verification request
NVS	non-voting shares
OCU	Offshore Coordination Unit
ODF	offshore disclosure facility
OECD	Organisation for Economic Co-operation and Development
PACE 1984	Police and Criminal Evidence Act 1984
PAYE	pay as you earn
PFN	partnership follower notice
PILONs	payments in lieu of notice
PLR	potential lost revenue
POCA 2002	Proceeds of Crime Act 2002
POTAS	promoters of tax avoidance schemes
PPN	partnership payment notice
PRN	promoter reference number
RCPO	Revenue and Customs Prosecutions Office
RIS	Risk and Intelligence Service
RTC	Requirement to correct legislation
RTI	Real Time Information
SA	self-assessment

lxvii

Abbreviations

SAP	statutory adoption pay
SAO	senior accounting officer
SAR	Suspicious Activity Report
SCI	Special Civil Investigations Office
SCO	Special Compliance Office
SCON	scheme contracting out number
SCP	single compliance process
SDLT	stamp duty land tax
SI	Special Investigations
SLA	service level agreement
SME	small and medium-sized enterprise
SMP	statutory maternity pay
SO	Senior Officer
SOAL	statement of assets and liabilities
SOCA	Serious Organised Crime Agency
SOCPA 2005	Serious Organised Crime and Police Act 2005
SPP	statutory paternity pay
SRN	scheme reference number
SRT	statutory residence test
SSCBA 1992	Social Security Contributions and Benefits Act 1992
SSCTFA 1999	Social Security Contributions (Transfer of Functions, etc) Act 1999
SShPP	statutory shared parental pay
SSP	statutory sick pay
TCEA 2007	Tribunals, Courts and Enforcement Act 2007
TCGA 1992	Taxation of Chargeable Gains Act 1992
TCRM	Tax Compliance Risk Management manual
TIEA	Tax Information Exchange Agreement
TMA 1970	Taxes Management Act 1970
TTP	time to pay
UC	Universal Credit
UEL	upper earnings limit
UN	United Nations
UT	Upper Tribunal
VAT	value added tax
VATA 1994	Value Added Tax Act 1994
VIES	VAT Information Exchange System
WDF	Worldwide Disclosure Facility
WRA	working rule agreement

Chapter 1

HMRC enquiries: outline and recent developments

Mark McLaughlin CTA (Fellow) ATT (Fellow) TEP
Mark McLaughlin Associates Ltd, Chartered Tax Advisers; Consultant, The TACS Partnership LLP

SIGNPOSTS

- **Introduction** – An HMRC enquiry may be random, but the vast majority of enquiries are opened because HMRC suspects that there is something wrong with the return. A 'nudge' letter from HMRC is not an enquiry, but can be followed by one. (See **1.1–1.13**.)

- **Disclosure** – The risk of an HMRC enquiry (or discovery) outside the enquiry window can be reduced by anticipating possible questions about the return and providing explanations in the form of appropriate tax return disclosures. (See **1.14–1.23**.)

- **Handling an enquiry** – The statutory provisions governing the enquiry process must be distinguished from any non-statutory procedures applied by HMRC. It is important to recognise and distinguish standard tax return enquiries from enquiries into tax avoidance or tax fraud. (See **1.24–1.35**.)

- **The start of an enquiry** – HMRC must start an enquiry by giving notice to the taxpayer within the statutory time limit for doing so. In some cases, HMRC may use its information powers during the course of the enquiry to compel the provision of information, etc. Consideration should be given to whether the information requested falls within those powers. (See **1.36–1.50**.)

- **Meetings** – HMRC generally attaches importance to meetings with taxpayers in the course of enquiries, although there is no statutory power to compel a meeting. If it is decided that a meeting is appropriate, HMRC should be asked in advance to produce a detailed agenda. Meetings should normally be held at the accountant's office or HMRC's office. It is generally unwise to sign HMRC's notes of meetings. (See **1.51–1.70**.)

1.1 *HMRC enquiries: outline and recent developments*

> - **Books and records** – A person must keep all such records as may be requisite for the purpose of enabling him to make and deliver a correct and complete return, and retain them for statutory time periods. Penalties may be imposed for failure to keep appropriate records. (See **1.71–1.80**.)
>
> - **Information powers** – HMRC's information powers (in *FA 2008, Sch 36*) apply to information, documents and inspections of business premises, subject to certain restrictions and exclusions. A person's statutory right of appeal does not apply in some instances, such as where information or any document forms part of the taxpayer's statutory records. Penalties can be imposed for compliance failures. (See **1.81–1.105**.)
>
> - **Completion of enquiry** – An enquiry is completed when HMRC issues a closure notice to the taxpayer. At any time during the course of an enquiry the taxpayer can apply to the tribunal for a direction requiring HMRC to issue a closure notice within a specified period. (See **1.106–1.125**.)
>
> - **Discovery** – The discovery powers enable HMRC to assess tax in relation to 'closed' years in certain circumstances, within statutory time limits. Disputes over the requirements for a valid discovery by HMRC have resulted in a number of cases. (See **1.126–1.139**.)
>
> - **Key points** – For a list of key points from this chapter, see **1.139**.

INTRODUCTION

1.1 This chapter concerns HMRC enquiries into the self-assessment returns of individuals or trustees (under *TMA 1970, s 9A*) and companies (under *FA 1998, Sch 18, para 24*).

1.2 Partnerships are subject to separate but broadly similar enquiry provisions as individuals (*TMA 1970, s 12AC*) and much of the commentary in this chapter therefore applies equally to HMRC enquiries into partnership tax returns. It should be noted that an HMRC enquiry notice given under *s 12AC(1)* is deemed to include the giving of an enquiry notice to each partner under *TMA 1970, s 9A(1)* (for individuals or trustees) or *FA 1998, Sch 18, para 24* (for companies) as the case may be (*TMA 1970, s 12AC(6)*).

1.3 Subsequent chapters of this book separately deal with HMRC investigations under Code of Practice 8 'Specialist investigations for fraud and bespoke avoidance' and Code of Practice 9 'HM Revenue & Customs investigations where we suspect tax fraud' (**CHAPTER 2**), criminal investigations (**CHAPTER 3**) and tax avoidance investigations (**CHAPTER 4**). HMRC's conduct of enquiries is considered further in **CHAPTER 8**.

HMRC enquiries: outline and recent developments 1.9

1.4 An enquiry power is an essential element of a self-assessment system. Enquiries have two objectives. The first, and most obvious one, is to seek to detect fraud, errors and areas in which the applicable legal principles may be open to different interpretations so that HMRC may wish to challenge that adopted by the taxpayer.

1.5 The second, less obvious, one is to test the system. If different taxpayers make the same error this may be due to poor design of the returns and guidance notes, or may suggest that an HMRC interpretation of the legislation needs to be reconsidered.

1.6 Direct tax enquiries are often categorised into 'full', 'aspect' and 'random' enquiries. These are not statutory divisions, but convenient descriptions.

1.7 A full enquiry is one in which HMRC enquires into every aspect of the return – and in many cases seeks to enquire into matters outside the return (albeit that it is questionable whether in most cases it has power to do so) to obtain an overall view of the taxpayer's financial affairs against which it can test what is shown in the return.

1.8 An aspect enquiry is one that relates to only one, or selected, entries in the return. It is important to realise that an aspect enquiry can develop into a full enquiry, particularly if it is not handled well.

> **Example 1.1 – Escalated enquiry**
>
> HMRC raised a number of questions in relation to estimates used in arriving at the figures entered in the self-employment pages of the taxpayer's return. Conscious of costs, that estimates are to some extent a matter of opinion, and that the figures involved were all fairly trivial, the accountant made little effort to justify his figures but accepted without much protest the figures suggested by HMRC.
>
> The HMRC officer, not surprisingly, finding that every figure he had challenged was conceded, concluded that the rest of the figures shown in the return might well be unreliable and the enquiry, which had started in relation to fairly trivial issues, turned into a full enquiry.

1.9 The vast majority of enquiries begin because HMRC suspects that there is something wrong with the return. In other words, there is either something on the face of the return that gives cause for concern, or HMRC has information from other sources (eg 'Connect' – see **1.11**) that conflict with what is shown on the return (eg an apparent omission of income or gains).

1.10 *HMRC enquiries: outline and recent developments*

1.10 A small number of returns are selected randomly for enquiry by the HMRC computer before the start of the tax year. These random enquiries are designed to test the tax system. They are not selected on the basis of risk (they are selected in advance of the return being submitted) and there could well be cases where the HMRC risk assessment would not identify that anything might be wrong with the return. Random enquiries are full enquiries – although the officer working the case may be able to verify some of the entries on the return from internal sources, so would not necessarily raise questions on every aspect.

HMRC officers are instructed to proceed with random enquiries in exactly the same way as risk-based full enquiries (see HMRC's Enquiry manual at EM0093).

1.11 Where an enquiry is opened into a return, some accountants seem to assume that the enquiry is a random enquiry because they have absolute faith in both their client's honesty and their own ability to avoid errors. This is a dangerous position to take. It has been estimated that around one in a thousand enquiries is a random enquiry.

If there is no obvious reason why HMRC has opened an enquiry it is accordingly likely that it has been opened 'for cause' and that the factor or factors that caused the enquiry are simply not apparent to the accountant.

For example, HMRC has sophisticated analytical tools at its disposal including 'Connect', a computer system that cross-references business and individual tax records with other databases to assist in identifying fraudulent or undisclosed activity. The data intelligence available to HMRC is formidable, and should not be underestimated (see **8.6–8.16**).

1.12 HMRC may seek to apply the process of 'nudge' letters in some cases. This process is used by HMRC to prompt taxpayers to check an entry, or the lack of an entry, on a self-assessment return in a particular area (eg untaxed income); no formal enquiry notice is issued.

1.13 It should be recognised that the process does not constitute a formal enquiry, and may arguably be outside HMRC's information powers under *FA 2008, Sch 36*. It remains possible, of course, for HMRC to change direction whether or not a response is made, by issuing a formal enquiry notice within the statutory time limits (possibly followed by a formal information notice) or by commencing an investigation, claiming to have made a 'discovery'.

If any information is given to HMRC in response to a nudge letter, great care should be taken to ensure that the information is complete and correct, as incomplete and/or incorrect information could lead to a criminal investigation.

For detailed commentary on the selection process in enquiries, see **CHAPTER 7**. See also **CHAPTER 16** regarding HMRC's information powers.

DISCLOSURE

1.14 Whilst it is not possible to avoid the risk of HMRC opening an enquiry into a tax return, the risk of an aspect enquiry at least can be reduced by anticipating which items in a return are likely to raise questions and forestalling such questions by providing the answer with the return. HMRC does not then need to open an enquiry in order to elicit that information.

1.15 It needs to be appreciated that even if, when challenged, a convincing explanation can easily be given in relation to an item that looks odd, HMRC has only 'one bite of the cherry' in relation to enquiries. Once it closes an enquiry it cannot raise enquiries on any other issues in relation to the return (unless it can make a discovery).

Accordingly, if something in a return looks odd and HMRC has to open an enquiry to elicit why it does so, it is likely to review the remainder of the return much more thoroughly than it otherwise would have done, as once it closes the enquiry it will reduce its ability to raise any other issues relating to that year.

1.16 Thus, heading off an enquiry by forestalling questions about the oddity is also likely to head off the review of the return that would have been prompted by an enquiry into that item.

> **Focus**
>
> The strategy of not volunteering information, but leaving it to HMRC to inspect the return, is dangerous. Returns are selected for enquiry on the basis of an HMRC assessment of the risk that the return may not be wholly correct. Anything that can be done to reduce HMRC's perception of such risk therefore ought to be done.
>
> Explaining in advance items that are likely to call for an explanation might well eliminate the perception of risk in relation to such items, thus reducing the overall risk that HMRC places on the return.

1.17 Volunteering information can also have a second benefit of making it more difficult for HMRC to make a discovery in relation to the return at a later date. Unless it can establish careless or deliberate conduct HMRC cannot make a discovery assessment unless, at the time when the 'enquiry window' closed, it could not have been reasonably expected, on the basis of the information made available to it before that time, to be aware of errors or omissions that it subsequently discovers (*TMA 1970, s 29(5)*).

1.18 Information which is contained in the tax return, or in any accounts, statements or documents accompanying the return (or in the return for either of the two previous years) is deemed to have been made available for this

1.19 *HMRC enquiries: outline and recent developments*

purpose, even if the officer who reviewed the return at that time chose not to look at it. It therefore makes sense to volunteer relevant accounts, dividend schedules, capital gains tax computations and other information created or used in arriving at the figures to be included in the return in order to enhance protection from discovery (*TMA 1970, s 29(6)*). The same considerations apply in relation to partnership statements (*TMA 1970, s 30B(7)*).

1.19 HMRC sometimes seeks to discourage the submission of such information, but it has no power to prohibit a taxpayer from providing it. In the early days of self-assessment, HMRC sometimes returned such information. If it does so, it is sensible to send it back again and point out that it has no statutory power to refuse to accept it, and that *s 29(6)* clearly envisages a taxpayer being entitled to submit accompanying documents. Indeed the legislation requires no more than that the document accompanies the return. What HMRC then does with it cannot thwart the statutory protection given to the taxpayer; that is already in place before HMRC sends it back, although it is probably easier to convince the appeal tribunal of this if it can be shown that efforts were made to seek to persuade HMRC to accept the information and to clearly explain its relevance.

1.20 HMRC considers that 'reasonably be expected' requires a taxpayer to point out that information sent to it is relevant to the return, but it is hard to imagine a tribunal holding that an HMRC officer could not have expected something sent with the return to be relevant to it. Of course, an officer might well not be expected to read through a long document only part of which is clearly relevant, so if the taxpayer wants protection for something else in it he may well be prudent to point it out.

1.21 For example, if shares in a private company are sold and the sale agreement is sent with the return, it should be obvious that the name of the vendor, the date, and the existence or otherwise of warranties and indemnities that might give rise to contingent liabilities are relevant to the return.

1.22 However, if HMRC later discovers that the gain was declared in the wrong year because the contract was a conditional one, the tribunal could uphold HMRC's right to make a discovery assessment on the basis that the taxpayer could be expected to have pointed out the relevant clause.

1.23 A number of cases have considered what constitutes a valid discovery by HMRC, including *Veltema v Langham (Inspector of Taxes)* [2004] EWCA Civ 193; *Corbally-Stourton v Revenue and Customs Comrs* [2008] STC (SCD) 907; *Revenue and Customs Comrs v Charlton* [2012] UKUT 866; *Revenue and Customs Comrs v Lansdowne Partners Ltd Partnership* [2011] EWCA Civ 1578; and *Pattullo v Revenue and Customs Comrs* [2016] UKUT 270 (TCC).

Discovery is considered further at **1.126** *et seq* and in **CHAPTER 13**.

HANDLING AN ENQUIRY

1.24 The enquiry process is laid down in the statute. However, HMRC has overlaid the statutory rules with its own, non-statutory, procedures. It is important to distinguish the two. A taxpayer is required to comply with a statutory request; if he wishes to comply with a non-statutory request or procedure he is free to do so, but is equally free not to do so.

1.25 That is not to say that he ought not to, but rather to make the point that a taxpayer should volunteer something in the full knowledge that he is volunteering and having made a positive decision to do so, rather than volunteering it under the mistaken impression that he is required to provide it.

1.26 It is unwise to seek to deal with an enquiry without first familiarising oneself with the statutory rules. For income tax purposes, these can mainly be found in *TMA 1970, Pts II–IV* and for corporation tax in *FA 1998, Sch 18, Pts II–IV*. These provisions do not relate solely to enquiries. They also cover the rules on tax returns. It is important to be aware of these, as the requirements for what is to be included in a return set the parameters for what HMRC might need in order to check that return.

There are no similar statutory rules for VAT enquiries. These are dealt with elsewhere in this work (see **CHAPTER 24**), and are not considered further here.

1.27 It is also important to know who you are dealing with. HMRC's Fraud Investigation Service (FIS) was formed in autumn 2015, following the merger of its specialist investigations (SI) and criminal investigations teams.

1.28 Whilst the enquiry legislation applies to all tax enquiries, the FIS adopts a different approach to inspectors in local area offices and needs to be approached in a different manner.

1.29 Historically, SI (and its predecessors the Special Civil Investigations Office (SCI) and Special Compliance Office (SCO) which merged the old Special Offices and Enquiry Branch) generally dealt with two distinct areas, tax avoidance and serious civil tax fraud. Whilst dealing with both, it seemed to concentrate on the former, and would take on new fraud cases only if it believed that the tax underpaid was at least £500,000. However, it is understood that this threshold no longer exists.

1.30 Smaller cases of suspected serious fraud, which used to be dealt with by SCI, were being dealt with by local Civil Investigations of Fraud (CIF) offices. These were headed by former SCI investigators. Their staff were trained by SCI, and their cases would be handled in the same way as SCI cases. Whilst it was easy to recognise if a case was being handled by SCI, it became more difficult to identify where a CIF office was involved as this was

1.31 *HMRC enquiries: outline and recent developments*

not always apparent from the letterhead. CIF offices did not only deal with serious suspected fraud though.

1.31 Where FIS (previously SI or a CIF office) is dealing with such a case it will say that it is dealing with the case under Code of Practice 9 (COP9). This is a procedure that replaced the old 'Hansard' procedure. The contractual disclosure facility (CDF) currently applies to COP9 procedures. Where the CDF is offered and COP9 is issued, HMRC will not normally prosecute the taxpayer for the fraud where this is fully disclosed; it is looking for a cash settlement. However, it may prosecute if, for example, false documents are given to it, or false statements made to it, in the course of the investigation.

1.32 CIF offices usually worked cases in the range of £100,000 to £500,000. However, once a case was opened it usually remained with the office responsible for taking it on.

1.33 Smaller cases of serious suspected fraud (which was previously measured where the tax at risk was initially thought to be under around £100,000), are dealt with in the area office network. Area offices are not empowered to offer the CDF and issue COP9. Only FIS can do so. This is not necessarily a good thing, as these procedures can afford protection against prosecution.

1.34 In practice, a network enquiry is unlikely to result in prosecution, if only because unless the case is identified as warranting prosecution at a very early stage, network enquiries are likely to seriously prejudice the taxpayer's rights under the *Police and Criminal Evidence Act 1984 (PACE 1984)* (as network officers are not trained in *PACE 1984*), which would make a prosecution very difficult.

1.35 The following HMRC publications may be helpful in handling an enquiry:

- *HMRC's Enquiry manual* – This is available via the GOV.UK website (www.gov.uk/hmrc-internal-manuals/enquiry-manual) and is HMRC's internal staff guidance. It not only gives an invaluable insight into how HMRC expects an enquiry to be conducted, but also highlights areas where there may be doubt about the legal position and points out the limitations on HMRC's powers.

- *HMRC's Compliance Handbook manual* – this deals with penalties and compliance powers (www.gov.uk/hmrc-internal-manuals/compliance-handbook).

- *Codes of Practice* – COP9 (tinyurl.com/HMRC-COP9) is used in cases of serious suspected tax fraud and COP8 (tinyurl.com/HMRC-COP8) for other cases. See also HMRC's Specialist Investigations

HMRC enquiries: outline and recent developments **1.38**

Operational Guidance manual (www.gov.uk/hmrc-internal-manuals/specialist-investigations-operational-guidance).

- *HMRC's Fraud Civil Investigation manual* – this guidance deals with COP9 and the CDF (www.gov.uk/hmrc-internal-manuals/fraud-civil-investigation).

- *Compliance checks factsheets* – HMRC has published a series of factsheets containing general information about compliance checks (tinyurl.com/HMRC-Comp-Checks-Factsheets). The subjects in other factsheets include HMRC's information and inspection powers, penalties, tax avoidance schemes, tax defaulters and alternative dispute resolution.

For detailed commentary on COP8 and COP9 investigations and the CDF, see **CHAPTER 2**.

THE START OF AN ENQUIRY

1.36 HMRC must start an enquiry by giving notice to the taxpayer of its intention to do so (*TMA 1970, ss 9A(1), 12AC(1); FA 1998, Sch 18, para 24*). The notice must normally be given by the first anniversary of the date on which the return was filed. However, HMRC's enquiry window may be extended if the return was filed late, or was amended.

1.37 There is no right of appeal against such a notice. If there is something wrong with it, such as being given out of time, it is not a valid notice. The best option is to discuss matters with the HMRC officer responsible or his manager.

1.38 Should this fail, the only practical way to establish whether or not it is valid is in the course of an appeal later in the enquiry process, such as an appeal against an information notice, or an appeal against an HMRC amendment to the return, because if the original enquiry notice is not valid it will invalidate the entire enquiry process. A judicial review is unlikely to be a viable option. However, an error in an enquiry notice will not necessarily result in the enquiry being invalid.

For example, in *Mabbutt v Revenue and Customs* [2017] UKUT 289 (TCC), the First-tier Tribunal ([2016] UKFTT 306 (TC)) held that an enquiry notice which incorrectly referred to a tax return for the year ended 6 April 2009 was not a valid notice of enquiry into the appellant's tax return for the year ended 5 April 2009 (following an appeal against HMRC's later closure notice), and that the notice was not 'saved' by *TMA 1970, s 114* ('Want of form or errors

1.39 *HMRC enquiries: outline and recent developments*

not to invalidate assessments, etc'). HMRC was out of time to issue a new, correct tax return enquiry notice, or to raise a discovery assessment outside the normal tax return enquiry window. However, the Upper Tribunal allowed HMRC's subsequent appeal, concluding (among other things) that the mistaken reference to the 'year ended 6 April 2009' did not, in the circumstances, render the enquiry notice invalid.

In addition, in *Tinkler v Revenue and Customs* [2018] UKUT 73 (TCC), a preliminary issue in an appeal against a closure notice amending the taxpayer's tax return for 2003/04 was whether HMRC had properly opened an enquiry. The Upper Tribunal noted that HMRC had given notification of the intention to open an enquiry into the taxpayer's return by sending a copy of the enquiry notice to the taxpayer's agent, and held in the circumstances that this was sufficient notice to the taxpayer.

1.39 The formal enquiry notice is normally accompanied by a letter asking for the information that the HMRC officer requires for the purpose of the enquiry. Officers are encouraged to ask upfront for everything they are likely to require, although they can, and often do, of course, ask for further information at any time during the course of the enquiry.

The letter will normally give a time limit within which the officer expects the information to be supplied. This is normally a minimum of 30 days.

> **Focus**
>
> This opening letter is not part of the statutory enquiry process. Accordingly, the time limit is not a statutory one: it is a figure plucked out of the air by the officer. No penalty or other statutory sanctions arise if this time limit is not met.

1.40 The officer's only recourse is either to chase for a reply or to issue a formal notice under *FA 2008, Sch 36* for the information.

It is obviously courteous to tell the officer as early as possible if his target date cannot be met, and often this will elicit further time if reasons are properly advanced. However, there is no need to panic if the time limit is overlooked or, although the taxpayer or his agent aims to comply with it, he does not manage to do so.

1.41 Similarly, the HMRC officer is not entitled to compel the provision of information in response to the opening letter. He will need to use the information powers contained in *FA 2008, Sch 36*. Accordingly, in reality in his opening letter the officer is requesting the taxpayer to volunteer information, and indeed this will normally be the appropriate response.

1.42 That is not to say that the taxpayer should not volunteer to do so but instead insist on the use of the formal information powers. It is pointless to waste time on a statutory procedure when it is clear that at the end of that procedure the information is statutorily required to be provided. It will also clearly irritate the officer, which may well influence his approach to doubtful issues that arise during the enquiry, and any penalty position.

1.43 However, it is sensible to consider each item of information requested by the officer in the context of the information powers. If it is clear that the item can be reasonably required under those provisions, then it should be provided. If it is not clear, the taxpayer or his agent ought to consider whether he believes it to be in his best interest to provide it.

1.44 For example, a trial balance prepared by the taxpayer's agent is unlikely to be within *Sch 36*, as in most cases it is likely to belong to the agent and therefore will not be within the taxpayer's power to provide it. Nevertheless, it is difficult to conceive of a reason not to volunteer it. Without it the officer will be forced to ask far more questions than he otherwise would have done and may make incorrect assumptions that needlessly prolong the enquiry and thus increase its cost.

1.45 Where it is decided to volunteer information, it is sensible to make the point to HMRC that the taxpayer or agent does not believe that it falls within *Sch 36*, but that the taxpayer has agreed nevertheless to provide it. This indicates co-operation and helpfulness.

1.46 If the taxpayer or agent does not believe that the information requested falls within *Sch 36* and he chooses not to volunteer it, there is nothing to prevent his declining to provide it. It is sensible to do so politely, such as telling the officer that its relevance to the tax return is not readily apparent and asking why he believes it to be relevant.

1.47 Each enquiry obviously depends on its individual facts. It is accordingly not possible to list what may or may not fall within *FA 2008, Sch 36, para 1*. Information that belongs to third parties, such as the taxpayer's spouse or children, or to his agent, clearly does not fall within these provisions (but might fall within *FA 2008, Sch 36, para 2*).

1.48 Consideration should generally be given to challenging requests for certain types of information, such as the following:

- *An analysis of drawings or of a proprietor's capital account or a director's loan account*

    There are things that do not impact on the quantification of profit. They relate to how the profit is spent and how funds to finance the business are raised. Normally, neither of these things has any relevance to the enquiry into the tax return, which is a return of income.

1.48 *HMRC enquiries: outline and recent developments*

HMRC often argues that if drawings are minimal that may be an indication that income has been diverted from the business. However, that is far too wide a generalisation. The proprietor's or director's spouse may be generating the income to meet living expenses; parents may be helping to support an adult child whose business acumen is such that he cannot generate adequate income; a person may be living off borrowings such as a bank overdraft or may be realising past savings or using an inheritance to supplement his living expenses. It is hard to see a justification for HMRC to pry into a taxpayer's private life on the off chance that he may be diverting income from his business. Many taxpayers strongly resent such an intrusion and it does not seem right to ask them to submit to it merely to seek to prove the negative that income has not been diverted.

Where a business does not handle cash at all but receives all of its income by cheque, diversion is clearly improbable, as banks do not allow a cheque made out to one person to be banked in the account of another, but that fact does not seem to deter HMRC requests for analyses of drawings or loan accounts. Furthermore, even if such information is volunteered, this may not necessarily satisfy HMRC, and it may go on to raise further questions on the information provided because the officer is searching for the possibility, no matter how remote, of some other theoretical source of undisclosed income.

- *Personal bank statements of a sole trader or partnership where he keeps his personal finances separate from those of his business, or personal bank statements of a director of a company*

Again, these have nothing to do with the tax return under enquiry and have probably been requested on the off chance that something in them may suggest diverted takings. In this connection it needs to be appreciated that if such bank statements are volunteered the officer will often take the stance that, as it is for the taxpayer to disprove an assessment, he intends to assess every single receipt in the personal bank account as diverted business income and leave it to the taxpayer to prove that it is not. Very few people can identify – and evidence – the source of small payments into their bank accounts two years earlier. In most cases, these are things like refunds from utilities or from mail order or online retailers for goods that are no longer available, receipts from friends for their share of a restaurant bill, premium bond or online gambling winnings, insurance claims, and cheques as birthday or wedding presents and similar day-to-day personal receipts.

It is, of course, highly improbable that if a person were to divert money from his business he would divert (say) £8.46 or some other tiny sum, so the likelihood of such an item in a person's personal bank account representing diverted income is inherently improbable. However, such an improbability does not seem to deter some HMRC officers from making the allegation which, in appropriate cases, should be firmly resisted.

Sometimes an HMRC officer will put forward a non-business reason for needing to see personal bank statements. In such cases, it is worth considering whether there is an alternative means to do what the officer says that he is trying to do.

Example 1.2 – Private bank statements and dividends

In the course of an enquiry into an individual's tax return, the enquiring HMRC officer stated that he needed to see the taxpayer's personal bank statements, to check the receipt of dividends from quoted companies, and to check the amount of bank interest earned.

However, the taxpayer's agent submitted to the HMRC officer the dividend counterfoils that his client had retained. It was pointed out that they provided far better evidence of the dividends than the bank statements, particularly as the receipt of a dividend warrant is a receipt of income even if the warrant is not banked or is banked in a later year.

In the case of interest, most banks give a figure of interest for the year as a note on the first bank statement after 5 April, or provide a certificate of interest paid. Thus that one document or statement, rather than all of the statements for the tax year, will evidence that figure. A letter from the bank might be an alternative source of evidence.

The provision of such alternative evidence does not prevent HMRC from claiming that in the particular circumstances of the case the personal bank statements come within *FA 2008, Sch 36*, but it is likely to make it difficult for HMRC to convince an appeal tribunal that the information is 'reasonably required' for that purpose when it already holds better evidence of the item that it has said that it wishes to check.

It goes without saying that entirely separate accounts should be maintained for business and personal transactions, and that great care should be taken to ensure that such transactions remain separate. Failure to do so may leave the taxpayer open to an HMRC information notice requiring private bank statements to be produced, on the basis that they constitute statutory records. There is no right of appeal against an information notice requiring the production of a document that forms part of the taxpayer's statutory records (*FA 2008, Sch 36, para 29*); for example, see *Beckwith v Revenue and Customs Comrs* [2012] UKFTT 181 (TC).

- *Appointment diaries*

Most people do not keep their business and personal life separate. Appointment diaries therefore invariably contain personal data for which the taxpayer is entitled to privacy.

1.48 *HMRC enquiries: outline and recent developments*

Furthermore, the author's diary is not necessarily an accurate historical record. It is merely a reminder of future engagements. If a client does not turn up for an appointment it does not get crossed out of the diary. If a client phones for an urgent appointment in a couple of hours' time, it will probably not get put in the diary. Some of the appointments are of meetings that the author will attend if he has time, but not if he is too busy at the time, and those that are missed may well not be crossed out. The diary is therefore a wholly inappropriate tool as a basis for HMRC to assume that every item in it should have generated a fee and, if it does not, to assume that income has been diverted. Electronic diaries may sometimes delete past entries on a monthly basis.

Clearly, whether a diary is kept manually or electronically can have no bearing on the accuracy of a business's accounts. If accounts can be assumed to be reliable if the diary is electronic and does not retain past data, they ought to be assumed to be equally reliable if the diary is kept in a different manner.

In *Long v Revenue and Customs Comrs* [2014] UKFTT 199 (TC), the First-tier Tribunal held that a doctor's appointment diaries did not need to be produced to HMRC. The diaries contained clinical and personal details, but no financial information whatsoever, and the information included in them did not enable a calculation of income to be made from the patients identified in them. It was therefore impossible for the tribunal to hold that the business appointment diaries were 'reasonably required' in order to check the taxpayer's position.

- *An accountant's working papers*

  These may be the property of the accountant and if so not in the possession or power of the client to obtain. However, see **16.187** as to the possibility of information notices requiring accountants to provide information or produce documents such as working papers.

- *A statement of a director's or proprietor's personal assets and liabilities*

  Such a statement has no bearing on the tax return of a company or on the profits of an unincorporated business. Even where the individual has non-business income it is hard to see how a statement of assets can say anything about his income.

- *Joint bank account*

  This is altogether much more difficult. Whereas the joint account holder is entitled to privacy and it may be unclear whether or not the bank statements of such an account are in the possession or power of the taxpayer, it is quite likely to be the case.

- *Income of spouses or children*

    These are not normally in the possession or power of the taxpayer. They may be if the child is a minor and the taxpayer is the child's guardian, but the position is unclear.

- *Assets not producing taxable income or gains*

    Investments such as premium bonds or National Savings certificates which do not produce taxable income or capital gains will not feature in tax returns.

- *Assets held by the taxpayer as a trustee*

    It is not clear whether these are in a taxpayer's possession or power in relation to his personal affairs. In the case of information or documents held by third party trustees, HMRC may argue that a settlor has the power to influence and require the trustees to comply with lawful and reasonable requests, such that the information or documents are considered to be in the settlor's possession or power (*H A Patel & K Patel (a partnership) v Revenue and Customs Comrs* [2014] UKFTT 167 (TC)).

- *Overseas assets and income of a non-UK domiciled taxpayer where there have been no remittances of the income generated by such assets*

    It is hard to see how these can have any relevance to his UK tax return.

1.49 It does, however, need to be borne in mind that whether or not something is relevant depends on the circumstances. Although the above items are rarely relevant when an officer opens an enquiry, if during the course of the enquiry it were to become apparent that the business accounts are unreliable and the only satisfactory way to arrive at the taxable profits is to reconstruct what probably happened from some other source, then it clearly becomes relevant to look at whether one of the above sources provides an appropriate means to do this. However, this becomes the case only when the accounts are unreliable – what HMRC used to call 'breaking the accounts'.

1.50 A handful of small errors or a few small unexplained items do not necessarily suggest that the accounts are unreliable as a basis for measuring the profits for the year.

MEETINGS

1.51 HMRC instructs its staff (at EM1821) that in 'more complex cases' they will need to consider whether holding a meeting with the taxpayer or their

1.52 *HMRC enquiries: outline and recent developments*

book-keeper/accountant will be the most effective way of establishing all the relevant facts. HMRC also states:

> 'Meetings with the taxpayer are a vital part of any enquiry work. Correspondence or meetings with the accountant are not normally an adequate substitute. The best way to get the facts about a business and the proprietor's or director's private affairs is face to face' (EM1822).

However, Parliament does not appear to have regarded meetings as vital when it introduced self-assessment. Had it done so, the government would surely have given HMRC power to require a taxpayer to attend meetings and answer questions, which it did not do.

1.52 Furthermore, some agents refuse to countenance meetings, either at all or except where there is a good reason for a meeting, and such agents seem to settle enquiries as much as anyone else without recourse to the tribunal. Accordingly, 'vital' seems a wholly inappropriate adjective for HMRC to use.

1.53 HMRC's guidance states that meetings enable its staff to do the following (EM1822):

- 'obtain facts from the taxpayer about their business, how they run it and the records that they keep

- obtain the facts in non-business enquiries

- explain the purpose of your enquiry. Taxpayers may not always be fully aware of the extent of HMRC enquiries

- establish whether the taxpayer wishes to disclose omissions

- agree what action is required and by whom to move the enquiry towards conclusion

- ensure that, where omissions have been found, the taxpayer is aware what offence has been committed, the likelihood of penalties and of the benefits of co-operating in bringing about an appropriate settlement at the earliest possible date. But you should make it clear that it is entirely a matter for them to decide whether and to what extent they co-operate. At this stage you should also give them the HRA message at EM1375 and advise them that public funding or legal aid for penalty appeals may be available. You should also issue the relevant penalty factsheets, including CC/FS15 "Compliance checks – Self Assessment and old penalty rules", see EM1605

- quantify and agree omissions/inaccuracies and establish the underlying behaviours that led to them

- settle the enquiry.'

1.54 Curiously, HMRC also tells its staff (at EM1861) that if they encounter resistance to a meeting from an agent they might reduce or overcome this by:

- '– explaining that meetings can actually reduce the costs and length of an enquiry, because so much more can be covered at a meeting than in protracted correspondence.

- – saying why you want to meet the taxpayer. You should make it clear that: you are entitled to enquire into the taxpayer's return; the information you need can only be given by the taxpayer in person; and in the absence of co-operation, you will not give up.

- – asking if the agent has passed on your views about the desirability of a meeting to the taxpayer.

- – confirming to the agent that he or she will be provided with a copy of your notes following the meeting. The agent and taxpayer will be able to correct any misunderstanding of what was said and will be able to revise any explanations or information given at the time if, on reflection, these are felt to be inaccurate. If this happens, you will have to consider whether what was said at the meeting was correct. Was it the sort of detail a trader would need to know at all times in order to run the business? Is there any documentary or third party evidence to back up some, or all, of what was said at the meeting or the revised explanation or information now offered?

- – stating there may come a point at which further progress by correspondence seems difficult or impossible without a meeting. When this point arrives, you will have to close your enquiry with amendments or assessments as appropriate. The taxpayer can appeal against the amendments or assessments and ask for a review or notify their appeal to the tribunal. At a tribunal hearing the taxpayer may need to give evidence to support the returns and accounts submitted and can then be questioned as part of your cross examination.'

It seems curious that the reasons that HMRC staff are told to give agents for wanting a meeting seem to bear little relationship to their actual purpose in wanting it.

1.55 HMRC also tells its staff that 'wherever possible' meetings should be held at business premises, or at the accountant's office (EM1830). This is on the basis that it will normally be easier to examine the business records there.

Again, it is odd that when self-assessment was introduced, HMRC did not seek to convince Parliament that it should be given power to hold meetings at business premises and this remains the case.

1.56 *HMRC enquiries: outline and recent developments*

1.56 HMRC has the power to inspect business premises (*FA 2008, Sch 36, Pt 2*). Nevertheless, this does not compel 'a meeting', although one might expect the situation to develop particularly when the taxpayer is not represented. HMRC's Enquiry manual (at EM1861) confirms: 'ultimately you do not have a power to compel a taxpayer or accountant to attend a meeting'.

1.57 In fact, the tax legislation contains no references at all to meetings. These are purely voluntary. It follows that the terms on which they are held are equally voluntary. Sadly, most accountants can relate many horror stories of what has happened at meetings. Anecdotes include the inspector who, when the client started to give an explanation, jumped in and said 'Don't try to explain; just answer yes or no to my questions'; the inspector who asked the client how often his wife changed her underwear; and a number of inspectors who sought to put words into the client's mouth or harangued a client because the inspector seemed to think it incredible that a client could not remember details of a small transaction two or three years earlier.

Clearly, an agent's reaction to a request for a meeting is likely to be coloured by his past experiences.

1.58 The author's approach from personal experience is to welcome meetings between himself and HMRC, but to agree to meetings with the client present only where there is a good reason for doing so, and where a detailed agenda has been agreed in advance.

1.59 HMRC's Enquiry manual tells its staff (at EM1821):

> 'A meeting with the business's book-keeper or accountant may also be valuable in understanding how the records were built up and link together and how the accounts have been prepared. In some cases a meeting with the book-keeper or accountant may enable you to resolve issues without troubling the taxpayer.'

Such meetings seem sensible. Unfortunately, the author's experience is that they are rarely offered and where the agent himself suggests such a meeting that suggestion is invariably rebuffed. In many cases, such a meeting could actually achieve virtually all of the purposes set out above for which HMRC believe meetings vital.

1.60

Focus

What about taking clients to meetings with HMRC? The circumstances in which (in the author's view) such meetings might be considered include those listed below.

HMRC enquiries: outline and recent developments **1.60**

- HMRC has issued in advance a detailed agenda of what it wishes to cover at the meeting. It is unrealistic to expect a list of questions, as these ought, to a large extent, to be dependent on the answers to earlier questions. On the other hand, 'I wish to discuss how the business operates and the taxpayer's lifestyle' (or 'the gross profit percentage and living expenses') is not a detailed agenda. Indeed it is so vague that it probably does not justify a meeting at all.

   A detailed agenda is important because it indicates that the officer has identified what issues require help that only the taxpayer can give, and enables the accountant to satisfy himself that that is indeed the case and that some of the issues cannot be better resolved in advance of the meeting.

- All of the accounting issues and other issues that can be dealt with by the accountant have been resolved. HMRC tells its staff, 'The number of meetings, the subject matter, and who attends will depend on the circumstances but you should bear in mind that meetings can be expensive and inconvenient for taxpayers.' (EM1821).

   Sadly, officers rarely seem to take much notice of this. The reality is that many clients have no knowledge of how the detailed figures in their accounts have been put together. Nor, indeed, is there any rational reason why they should. It is not information that they need to manage the business. It is information that has been generated partly by their book-keeper and partly by their accountant and it is therefore understandable that they seek to rely on the expertise of such people.

   It is unreasonable for an officer to expect a taxpayer to put aside running his business and attend a three-hour meeting, much of which is taken up by accounting issues that are outside the taxpayer's own knowledge and competence and which his accountant can deal with without the taxpayer's intervention.

- The taxpayer is the most appropriate person to deal with the remaining issues. Many HMRC officers seem to take the view that, as the taxpayer has ultimate responsibility for his tax affairs, they need to interview him because he ought to know precisely how the business operates. Such officers often become extremely suspicious when the client is unable to provide detailed explanations for things that his book-keeper or another staff member could well have been able to answer readily.

   If the taxpayer or company director is not the most appropriate person to provide the information that the officer says that he is seeking from the meeting, consider offering a meeting with the appropriate staff member instead. If such an offer is rebuffed, the reasons the officer has given for wanting a meeting are probably not his real reasons. It is clearly inappropriate to subject a client to a meeting where the agent has any

1.61 *HMRC enquiries: outline and recent developments*

suspicion that the reasons the officer has given for wanting a meeting are either spurious or incomplete.

- If the agenda includes detailed questions on entries in the records that the accountant has been given an opportunity to deal with but has been unable to answer fully because the books and records were sent to HMRC at the start of the enquiry but have not been returned prior to the meeting. It is unreasonable to expect anyone to answer questions on individual transactions that occurred two or three years earlier without his having been able to review the records to refresh his memory in advance of the meeting.

- The issues that the HMRC officer wishes to discuss need to be of sufficient importance in the context of the accounts to justify taking the taxpayer or director away from his business. A meeting for the sake of having one is never justifiable.

1.61

Focus

If it has been decided that a meeting is appropriate, where should it be held?

The answer is normally at either the accountant's office or an HMRC office, generally depending on which is more convenient. HMRC increasingly deals with a taxpayer's affairs a long distance away. In such a case, a meeting at the accountant's office is usually sensible, although the officer can usually arrange to hold a meeting at a local HMRC office, if this is desired.

In the author's experience, on balance meetings should probably be held at the professional adviser's office (eg because these will often be comfortably familiar surroundings for the taxpayer), if possible and practical.

What about the HMRC desire to meet at the client's premises absent a notice under *FA 2008, Sch 36, Pt 2*? If the records are voluminous, or it is clear that a number of staff members are likely to be called on to deal with specific issues, this may be sensible.

1.62 However, in most cases a taxpayer does not want someone arriving at his office and announcing to the receptionist that he is from HMRC. Even less do clients want to risk people wandering round the building, perhaps looking for the toilets, and telling other staff that they are from HMRC. The business staff are likely to wonder why the tax authorities are visiting the business and could well draw incorrect conclusions from the presence of such people, which can be damaging to the operation of the business. There is also the risk an officer might add to his list of questions things that he notices while at the

HMRC enquiries: outline and recent developments 1.67

business premises but which actually have no bearing on the enquiry (other, of course, than to needlessly prolong the meeting).

1.63 However, in practice these tactics are probably less common than before HMRC's information powers were introduced, as those powers are likely to be exercised first and the request for a meeting will follow.

1.64 HMRC usually makes detailed notes of meetings. It is prepared to provide a taxpayer or his agent with a copy of such notes, but does not always volunteer to do so. If it does not send a copy of its notes after the meeting, it is sensible to request a copy.

Where HMRC sends notes, it tends to sign them and ask the taxpayer and his agent to read them, sign them if they agree with them and send back a signed copy. It is unwise to sign such notes. Many firms of accountants decline to do so as a matter of policy and explain to HMRC that it is their policy never to ask clients to sign such notes.

Some HMRC officers get upset when notes are not signed. However, there are two good reasons not to do so.

1.65 First, the notes tend to be slanted towards what the officer wanted to know. That is probably not deliberate. Meeting notes do not purport to be a transcript of what was said. They are a summary. Any summariser is likely to include in his summary the things that he regards as important and to omit things that he considers trivial. When people take notes of a meeting they do the same thing; their notes tend to cover only the points they consider significant. The result is that the notes often downplay or omit entirely things that may have been said, the relevance of which may not assume any importance until a later date. If the taxpayer has signed the notes as a complete and correct record of the meeting it becomes difficult, if not impossible, subsequently to convince a tribunal that he said something at the meeting that is not covered in the notes.

1.66 The language adopted can itself slant the emphasis of what was said. The obvious example is that taxpayers seem often not to 'say' anything at HMRC meetings; they 'allege' things. To many people 'allege' carries a connotation that what was said is not readily believable.

1.67 Second, the reason that HMRC wants the notes signed is that in the event of a later dispute it can point to the signature as evidence that what the taxpayer is then claiming that he said at the meeting was not said. There is no advantage to the taxpayer in signing HMRC's notes. Accordingly, why risk them being regarded at a later date as evidence of precisely what was said at the meeting?

1.68 *HMRC enquiries: outline and recent developments*

1.68 The HMRC notes should, of course, be read and any significant errors or omissions pointed out to the officer. This is important because HMRC may seek to rely on the notes, if the enquiry becomes contentious (*Duffy v Revenue and Customs Comrs* [2007] SpC 596; see **6.77**).

Where the notes do not properly explain a point which the taxpayer was seeking to make, it is sensible to re-explain that point. If the notes correctly reflect what was said but it has subsequently been found that the taxpayer's recollection was at fault, the information given at the meeting should of course be corrected. It is sensible to send HMRC any documentary evidence that shows that the corrected position reflects the facts.

1.69 Often, if a taxpayer or his agent challenges what was said in an officer's notes the officer will seek to argue over what was said. Try not to get drawn into such a debate over the notes. At the end of the day, enquiries are resolved on the basis of the facts. If the tribunal is presented with a set of notes and a contemporary letter challenging aspects of those notes, they are likely to recognise that the issue is disputed and not regard the notes as evidence of what was said but look for alternative evidence to resolve the matter.

1.70 If the purpose of a meeting is to ascertain the facts, it is also curious that the HMRC officer should seem more concerned about what was and was not said than what the facts actually are.

Meetings with HMRC are an important and sometimes difficult matter. A separate chapter is therefore devoted to the subject (see **CHAPTER 9**).

BOOKS AND RECORDS

1.71 A person must keep all such records as may be requisite for the purpose of enabling him to make and deliver a correct and complete return (*TMA 1970, s 12B(1); FA 1998, Sch 18, para 21(1)*). In the case of a person carrying on a business, such records must include records of the following (*TMA 1970, s 12B(3); FA 1998, Sch 18, para 21(5)*):

- all amounts received and expended in the course of the trade, profession or business and the matters in respect of which the receipts and expenditure take place; and
- in the case of a trade involving dealing in goods, all sales and purchases of goods made in the course of the trade.

The impending introduction of 'making tax digital' is likely to add to existing compliance obligations in many cases.

1.72 The records must be retained until the fifth anniversary of 31 January following the end of the tax year (the first anniversary for non-business records) or, if later, the completion of any HMRC enquiry. In the case of a company, the records must be kept for six years after the end of the accounting period (or the close of any HMRC enquiry, if later).

1.73 It is a question of fact what records 'may be requisite' for the purpose of delivering a correct and complete return. Unless and until it is demonstrated that the return is not correct and complete, there is a strong inference that the records that were in fact kept satisfy the statutory obligation as they have enabled the statutory objective to be achieved.

Focus

Comments in the course of an enquiry that the HMRC officer considers the business records to be inadequate should be approached in the context of this statutory requirement. The records a taxpayer needs to keep are those that he considers appropriate, not those which the officer considers appropriate.

1.74 The HMRC officer has no real knowledge of either the needs of the business or the abilities of its staff. Records that a person finds easy to keep are likely to be more accurate than more complex records that he finds difficult to complete. It is possible that HMRC officers may expect records to be kept that are inappropriate to the circumstances of the particular business.

1.75 For example, if cheques received are entered into a cash book and copied from there to a paying-in book, and the bankings agree with the cash book, it is hard to see any justification for keeping the paying-in book, as that is not the prime record but is something prepared simply for the bank. Even if the paying-in book is completed first, it is difficult to see why it should form part of the records under *s 12B* once it is ascertained that the bankings agree with the cash book (although in that case it may be a supporting document).

Similarly, cheque book stubs are unlikely to come within *s 12B* if they are not the prime document.

1.76 HMRC will generally expect owners of cash-based businesses to retain till rolls, and may consider that failure to do so breaches statutory record-keeping requirements. However, in *Newell t/a Tanya's Takeaway v Revenue and Customs Comrs* [2013] UKFTT 742 (TC), the taxpayers invariably transferred the information from their till rolls to a Simplex book each day. The First-tier Tribunal considered that the taxpayers had generally met their statutory obligations by doing so (by contrast, see *Dosanjh v Revenue and Customs Comrs* [2014] UKFTT 973 (TC)).

1.77 *HMRC enquiries: outline and recent developments*

1.77 HMRC officers sometimes contend that the use of estimates breaches the requirement of *s 12B*. If the starting point for taxable profits is accounts prepared in accordance with generally accepted accounting practice (GAAP), and if GAAP permits estimates, that contention cannot be right provided that the estimate can be justified under GAAP. Accounts that satisfy GAAP also satisfy the test of being correct and complete (subject to any adjustments required by law).

Of course, if HMRC amends a taxpayer's return it is then up to him to justify any estimate used, but that is a different obligation from the record-keeping requirement.

1.78 For PAYE purposes, employers are required to keep specified records. For VAT, income tax, capital gains tax and corporation tax the requirement is for taxable persons to keep adequate business and accounting records. Adequate does not mean excessive or prescriptive – it means keeping records to be sure that the right profit, loss, tax declaration or claim is made.

1.79 There are penalties for failure to keep appropriate records. One of the key elements in the current framework is the ability to inspect records before a return is submitted if such inspection is reasonably required to check a tax position. The basic requirements in relation to record keeping have not changed, but rules have been aligned on how things are kept. HMRC's powers include: a generic requirement in primary legislation, the power to make regulations by secondary legislation, where necessary, to specify additional records, and published non-statutory HMRC guidance as to what is likely to meet the generic requirement, tailored to business, non-business and particular cases such as capital gains.

1.80 Where there has been a failure to comply with statutory record-keeping requirements for self-assessment tax return purposes, HMRC indicates in its Enquiry manual (at EM4650) that penalties will only be sought in the more 'serious cases' (eg where records have been destroyed deliberately to obstruct an enquiry, or where there has been a history of record-keeping failures).

Business record checks and examinations are discussed in **CHAPTER 16**.

INFORMATION POWERS

Information and documents

1.81 Historically, HMRC's original self-assessment information powers were principally under *TMA 1970, ss 19A, 20* and *FA 1998, Sch 18, para 27*. Those powers were repealed with effect from 1 April 2009. In their place new information powers were introduced (*FA 2008, Sch 36*).

Those powers were initially applicable to enquiries and investigations in relation to income tax, capital gains tax, corporation tax, PAYE and VAT, but their scope was extended (eg to inheritance tax and stamp duty land tax) from 1 April 2010.

1.82 Whilst HMRC's present powers are probably more straightforward than those under the previous regime, they are wider in their application.

1.83 A separate chapter of this book is dedicated to HMRC's information and inspection powers (see **CHAPTER 16**). The scope of *FA 2008, Sch 36* is therefore not considered in detail in this chapter, which deals solely with self-assessment enquiries.

1.84 The powers to obtain information and documents are contained within *FA 2008 Sch 36, Pt 1*. *Paragraph 1* provides that an HMRC officer may by notice in writing require a person ('the taxpayer') to provide information, or to produce a document, if the information is *reasonably required* by the officer for the purpose of *checking the taxpayer's tax position* ('a taxpayer notice').

1.85 *Paragraph 2* applies similarly to third-party notices, which may only be issued with the agreement of the taxpayer or the approval of the First-tier Tribunal, and are subject to certain conditions (see *para 3*). *Paragraph 7(2)* specifies the place at which documents may be produced. Clearly this could be specified as the business premises. *Paragraph 8* relates to the production of copied and original documents. Note that 'checking' is defined as including the carrying out of an investigation or enquiry of any kind (*para 58*). 'Tax position' is defined in *para 64*.

1.86 Part 1 of *FA 2008, Sch 36* is subject to various restrictions in *Pt 4*. *Paragraph 18* retains the important stipulation that a person can only be required to produce a document if it is in his possession or power.

1.87 *Paragraphs 21(1)* and *(2)* provide that where a person has made a return a taxpayer notice may not be given. Alas, this is too good to be true, as *para 21(3)* states that *sub-paras (1)* and *(2)* do not apply where, or to the extent that, any of the conditions in A to D is met.

1.88 Condition A is that a notice of enquiry has been given in respect of:

- the return; or
- a claim or election (or an amendment of a claim or election) made by the person in relation to the chargeable period in respect of the tax (or one of the taxes) to which the return relates ('relevant tax'), and the enquiry has not been completed so far as relating to the matters to which the taxpayer notice relates (*para 21(4)*).

1.89 *HMRC enquiries: outline and recent developments*

1.89 In *sub-para (4)*, 'notice of enquiry' means a notice under:

- *TMA 1970, s 9A* or *s 12AC*, or *Sch 1A, para 5*; or
- *FA 1998, Sch 18, para 24*.

1.90 Condition B is that an officer of Revenue and Customs has reason to suspect that, as regards the person:

- an amount that ought to have been assessed to relevant tax for the chargeable period may not have been assessed;
- an assessment to relevant tax for the chargeable period may be or have become insufficient; or
- relief from relevant tax given for the chargeable period may be or have become excessive *(para 21(6))*.

1.91 Condition C is that the notice is given for the purpose of obtaining any information or document that is also required for the purpose of checking the person's position as regards any tax other than income tax, capital gains tax or corporation tax *(para 21(7))*.

1.92 Condition D is that the notice is given for the purpose of obtaining any information or document that is required (or also required) for the purpose of checking the person's position as regards any deductions or repayments of tax, or withholdings of income referred to in *para 64(2)* or *(2A)* (PAYE, etc) *(para 21(8))*.

1.93 There is a time limit in relation to the giving of an information notice for the purpose of checking the tax position of a deceased person of four years after the person's death *(para 22)*. *Paragraphs 23–27* deal with certain limitations of information notices in relation to privileged communications, auditors and tax advisers.

1.94 *FA 2008, Sch 36, Pt 5* deals with appeals against information notices. Note that there is no right of appeal against a taxpayer notice to provide any information or document that forms part of the taxpayer's statutory records *(para 29(2))*. There are similar provisions for third-party notices *(para 30)*.

In addition, there is no right of appeal against an information notice that has been approved by the First-tier Tribunal *(paras 29(3), 30(3))*.

'Statutory records' are defined in *para 62*.

1.95 *FA 2008, Sch 36, Pt 6* relates to special cases including groups. *FA 2008, Sch 36, Pt 7* deals with penalties for non-compliance, *FA 2008, Sch 36, Pt 8* deals with offences, *FA 2008, Sch 36, Pt 9* deals with miscellaneous provisions and interpretation, and *FA 2008, Sch 36, Pt 10* deals with consequential provisions.

1.96 The Sch 36 information powers combine, reinforce and widen those previously available to HMRC. Whereas HMRC's previous powers (in *TMA 1970, s 20*) were used sparingly, it appears that Sch 36 powers are being used far more widely across the various taxes.

1.97 The meaning of such terms as 'reasonably required' and 'possession or power' which continue to be undefined in statute will remain as interpreted by case law.

Business premises inspections etc

1.98 HMRC's powers to inspect business premises (and other property) are a significant weapon in relation to self-assessment enquiries and 'compliance checks'. *FA 2008, Sch 36, Pt 2* broadly allows an authorised officer of HMRC to enter business premises and inspect the premises, business assets and business documents that are on the premises. There is a requirement that the inspection is 'reasonably required' for the purpose of checking that person's tax position (*FA 2008, Sch 36, para 10(1)*).

1.99 If an information notice has been issued, the documents required in the notice can be inspected at the same time. The powers do not extend to any part of the premises which is used solely as a dwelling. Inspections will normally be carried out at a time agreed with the taxpayer or at any reasonable time with a minimum of seven days' notice, which may be given in writing or otherwise. There is also provision for an unannounced visit if a prearranged visit is considered to be inappropriate.

There is no right of appeal against an inspection notice but the taxpayer can refuse entry and prevent the inspection being completed. The taxpayer can be penalised for such an obstruction, but only if the inspection has been approved by the First-tier Tribunal under *FA 2008, Sch 36, para 13* (see *FA 2008, Sch 36, para 39(1)(b)*). The inspection powers are in no way a substitute for a *PACE 1984* search warrant either as conferring the right of entry or conduct whilst on the premises.

1.100 *FA 2008, Sch 36, Pt 2* is subject to the restrictions in *FA 2008, Sch 36, Pt 4*. Significantly, *para 28* provides that:

> 'An officer of Revenue and Customs may not inspect a business document under Part 2 of this Schedule if or to the extent that, by virtue of this Part of this Schedule, an information notice given at the time of the inspection to the occupier of the premises could not require the occupier to produce the document.'

1.101 *HMRC enquiries: outline and recent developments*

1.101 HMRC internal instructions relating to business inspections may be found in HMRC's Compliance Handbook at CH25000–CH25700.

1.102 Historically, it was perhaps rare for professional advisers even to learn of a PAYE or VAT inspection visit, or at least not until howls of anguish were to be heard from distraught clients when they received a tax bill at its conclusion.

The rules of the game are now different, and professionals should therefore encourage clients to let them know when they receive a request for a visit from HMRC.

Focus

Best practice suggests that it would normally be prudent for advisers to attend these events, at least in part so that they might ensure that the proper procedures are followed.

In the rarer case where an unannounced visit is made, the alarm bells should ring and HMRC should be refused entry until such time as proper professional advice has been taken. This process need not be rushed.

1.103 In the even rarer case where a notice is issued with the approval of the First-tier Tribunal should entry be refused so that the taxpayer can take professional advice, so potentially incurring a penalty?

A commercial view should be considered, albeit that this could well result in entry being refused so that advice may be taken. This may result not only in a penalty – there is no commentary in HMRC guidance as to whether this would constitute a 'reasonable excuse' (within *FA 2008, Sch 36, para 45(1)*) – but in the most serious cases where HMRC is contemplating criminal proceedings could lead to HMRC applying for a *PACE 1984* search warrant where entry is not negotiable and reasonable force can be used to enter.

Other ways to obtain information

1.104 HMRC have sometimes asked for a mandate from the taxpayer authorising his bank or another third party to provide direct to HMRC such information as it may request. This is not a statutory procedure. It is wholly voluntary. A taxpayer should think carefully before agreeing to provide such a mandate. It is normally better for the taxpayer to volunteer to obtain information from the bank himself. If HMRC obtains information direct from the bank the taxpayer may well not know what information it has been given, which places him at a potential disadvantage.

HMRC enquiries: outline and recent developments **1.110**

1.105 Furthermore, in practice banks make available information to HMRC under the authority of a mandate which they would not make available to the taxpayer himself. The obvious example is the bank's own file notes of telephone conversations with the taxpayer.

Note, however, that HMRC may decide to use its third-party notice powers under *FA 2008, Sch 36, para 2* to obtain information it reasonably requires for the purpose of checking the taxpayer's tax position directly from the bank or other third party.

COMPLETION OF ENQUIRY

1.106 An enquiry is completed when the officer issues a closure notice to the taxpayer (*TMA 1970, s 28A(1), (3); FA 1998, Sch 18, para 32(1)*). The closure notice takes effect when it is issued. An income tax closure notice must inform the taxpayer that the officer has completed his enquiries and state his conclusions. It must also state that in his opinion no amendment to the return is required, or must make the amendments to the return that are required to give effect to his conclusions (*TMA 1970, s 28A(1), (3)*). This clearly implies that the conclusions must incorporate the amount of any adjustment that the officer concludes is required, as otherwise he would not be able to amend the return.

1.107 The provisions dealing with the completion of a partnership tax return enquiry (*TMA 1970, s 28B*) are similar to those in *s 28A* above. In addition, where a partnership return is amended (under *s 28B(2)*), HMRC will also amend the partners' tax returns so as to give effect to the amendments of the partnership tax return (*s 28B(4)*).

1.108 A corporation tax closure notice must either state that no amendment is required to the return under enquiry, or alternatively make any amendments to give effect to HMRC's conclusions in the closure notice (*FA 1998, Sch 18, para 34(1)*). An appeal against an amendment may be made in writing within 30 days after the amendment was notified to the company (*FA 1998, Sch 18, para 34(4)*).

1.109 At any time during the course of an enquiry the taxpayer can apply to the tribunal for a direction requiring HMRC to issue a closure notice within a specified period. Such an application is heard and determined in the same way as an appeal. The tribunal must give the direction applied for unless it is satisfied that there are reasonable grounds for not issuing a closure notice within a specified period (*TMA 1970, ss 28A(4)–(6), 28B(5); FA 1998, Sch 18, para 33*).

1.110 This places the onus on the HMRC officer to convince the tribunal that it ought not to direct a closure. The purpose of this provision is to prevent

1.111 *HMRC enquiries: outline and recent developments*

HMRC leaving an enquiry open indefinitely and thus defeating the taxpayer's right to finality in his tax affairs within a reasonable time.

A taxpayer might make such an application where he considers that HMRC delays are unreasonable (eg in *Martin v Revenue and Customs* [2017] UKFTT 488 (TC), the First-tier Tribunal ordered HMRC to close an enquiry into a tax return when no progress had been made in the enquiry for nearly three years until HMRC requested information and documents), or where the taxpayer feels that HMRC is raising new questions in relation to areas that have already been fully dealt with.

Focus

Such an application should not be made lightly. If successful, it does not force the HMRC officer to abandon his enquiry; it forces him to reach a conclusion on the basis of the information that is available to him by the specified date.

If there is incomplete information, the HMRC officer is likely to conclude that a greater adjustment to the self-assessment ought to be made than he would have concluded had he been able to obtain the missing information. Accordingly, a successful application is likely to force the taxpayer to appeal against the officer's amendment and on the appeal to disprove a larger assessment than he would have faced had he let the officer continue with his investigation. As usual, timing is everything.

1.111 There is, of course, a right of appeal against the amendment to the self-assessment as a result of the closure notice or against HMRC's amendment of the assessment (*TMA 1970, s 31; FA 1998, Sch 18, para 34(3)*). Notice of such an appeal must be made in writing within 30 days in the normal way.

However, the issue of the closure notice brings to an end the self-assessment process and, in particular, may reduce the officer's ability to seek information under *FA 2008, Sch 36, Pt 1* (see *FA 2008, Sch 36, para 21(4)*). Thus if HMRC suspects that the taxpayer may be contemplating an application to the tribunal for the issue of a closure notice, there is a danger that this may prompt an information notice to be issued as a pre-emptive measure.

A closure notice does not, of course, prevent the taxpayer volunteering further information or the officer asking for further information informally.

1.112 Case law dealing with closure notices include the selection below.

In *Jade Palace Ltd v Revenue and Customs Comrs* [2006] SpC 540, it was held that the legislation did not require the officer to be satisfied – he might never

HMRC enquiries: outline and recent developments 1.116

be, so that would undermine the purpose of the provision – but merely to form a conclusion. It also held that the Commissioner does not have to require the closure by the date requested by the taxpayer, but can reach his own decision as to the appropriate date.

1.113 In *Revenue and Customs Comrs v Vodafone (No 2)* [2006] EWCA Civ 1132, which was concerned with the validity of the UK's controlled foreign companies rules, the company asked for a closure notice so that the case could be brought before the ECJ. The Commissioners decided that the substantive issue was one that ought to be referred and ordered the closure. HMRC appealed on the basis that the Commissioners had no power to decide the substantive point so ought not to have ordered the closure. The Court of Appeal held that *FA 1998, Sch 18, para 33* gives the Commissioners power to do anything they consider reasonably necessary to decide whether or not to require a closure and that included deciding incidental points of law.

1.114 In *Kilbride v Revenue and Customs Comrs* [2008] SpC 660, HMRC opened enquiries into two directors and their company, suspecting that the directors had not accounted for all their income, as they had both declared considerably less income than was in their bank accounts. The taxpayers applied for closure notices arguing that HMRC had produced no evidence of any tax loss. The Special Commissioner dismissed the application. He held that there were reasonable grounds for not issuing closure notices with immediate effect, including the failure of the taxpayers to disclose the identity of directors of a related overseas company even though they were not under a legal obligation to do so.

1.115 In *Lee v Revenue and Customs Comrs* [2009] STC (SCD) 1, the Special Commissioner decided that as there were unresolved questions about whether the taxpayer had made timely disclosure of savings income, it was not appropriate to direct closure at this stage of the enquiry.

1.116 In *Tower MCashback LLP v Revenue and Customs Comrs* [2011] UKSC 19, the Supreme Court considered a procedural question concerning the scope of appeals against closure notices: could an appeal be heard on grounds other than those set out in the closure notice? HMRC had issued a closure notice that stated that the LLPs were not entitled to the first-year allowances that had been claimed because the qualifying expenditure fell within one of the statutory exceptions. However, HMRC subsequently pursued other lines of attack. The court held that there is no express requirement that the HMRC officer must set out or state the reasons which have led him to his conclusions. There was no basis for implying any obligation to give reasons in the closure notice. What matters at that stage is the conclusion that the officer has reached upon completion of his investigation of the matters in dispute, not the process of reasoning by which he has reached those conclusions.

1.117 *HMRC enquiries: outline and recent developments*

Furthermore, Lord Walker commented:

> 'In issuing a closure notice an officer is performing an important public function in which fairness to the taxpayer must be matched by a proper regard for the public interest in the recovery of the full amount of tax payable. In a case in which it is clear that only a single, specific point is in issue, that point should be identified in the closure notice. But if, as in the present case, the facts are complicated and have not been fully investigated, and if their analysis is controversial, the public interest may require the notice to be expressed in more general terms.'

1.117 The Supreme Court's decision in *Tower MCashback* was subsequently applied in *Fidex Ltd v Revenue and Customs Comrs* [2014] UKUT 454 (TCC), in which it was held that the conclusion in a closure notice following an enquiry into a company's tax return did not prevent HMRC from arguing for an adjustment to the company's return on different grounds. However, it is worth noting that the Upper Tribunal commented: 'The [HMRC] officer has a duty to make the closure notice as helpful to the taxpayer as is possible or appropriate in the circumstances.'

1.118 Even if the tribunal directs HMRC to issue a closure notice within a specified period, in practice that period will depend on the particular circumstances of the case. For example, in *Bloomfield v Revenue and Customs Comrs* [2013] UKFTT 593 (TC), HMRC's enquiry had lasted for over three years. The tribunal directed on the facts of the case that HMRC should issue a closure notice in respect of its enquiry within 30 days.

In *Nichols & Anor v Revenue & Customs* [2016] UKFTT 155 (TC), the First-tier Tribunal considered what would be a 'reasonable period' for closure notices to be issued. Having regard to all the circumstances, the tribunal directed that HMRC must issue closure notices in respect of each application by three months from the date of the hearing.

1.119 In *Khazenifar v Revenue and Customs Comrs* [2013] UKFTT 752 (TC), the tribunal decided that HMRC had reasonable grounds for not issuing a closure notice straightaway, but directed that it must do so within six months of the tribunal's decision.

1.120 In *Khan v Revenue and Customs Comrs* [2014] UKFTT 18 (TC), the tribunal considered that the taxpayer still needed to provide HMRC with genuinely significant information. It held that nine months was an adequate period for the enquiry to be concluded properly.

1.121 HMRC guidance states that if a taxpayer applies to the tribunal for a closure notice (or is considering applying for one), the HMRC officer should consider whether to offer alternative dispute resolution (ADR) to the taxpayer (EM1976).

1.122 ADR is broadly a voluntary procedure for resolving tax disputes in compliance checks if appropriate, whereby a trained mediator from HMRC who was not previously involved in the case mediates between the taxpayer and the HMRC officer dealing with the case with a view to reaching an agreement between them. The attraction of ADR is that it may help to resolve any disputes between the taxpayer and HMRC in the enquiry without a tribunal hearing. If the dispute cannot be resolved, the taxpayer could still go to the tribunal. ADR is therefore potentially helpful, and should be considered in appropriate cases.

Further information on ADR is available on the GOV.UK website (www.gov.uk/tax-disputes-alternative-dispute-resolution-adr).

ADR is covered in depth in **Chapter 12**.

PARTIAL CLOSURE NOTICES

1.123 Prior to legislation on partial closure notices (introduced in *F(No 2)A 2017*), HMRC could only issue a closure notice once it had reached a conclusion in respect of all areas of dispute within the enquiry.

However, there are provisions which allow HMRC and the taxpayer to jointly agree to refer an issue (or multiple issues) to the tribunal whilst the enquiry is in progress (*TMA 1970, s 28ZA* for individuals and partnerships, and *FA 1998, Sch 18, para 31A* for companies). Those provisions were suitably amended but remain a potential option following the introduction of the partial closure notice facility.

1.124 The partial closure notice provisions followed a period of consultation. HMRC published a consultation document 'Tax Enquiries: Closure Rules' in December 2014 on the proposed introduction of a new power to enable HMRC to achieve early resolution and closure of one or more aspects of a tax enquiry whilst leaving other aspects open. This consultation indicated that the above joint applications to the tribunal were insufficient for HMRC, particularly in 'complex cases where there is significant tax under consideration or which involve issues which are novel or have wider impacts'.

1.125 The consultation document indicated that the option of mutual referral to the tribunal by the taxpayer and HMRC would be retained. However, if the taxpayer did not wish to proceed on that basis, HMRC would have the option to consider a 'sole referral' to the tribunal.

HMRC subsequently published a summary of responses to the consultation document in September 2015. There was widespread opposition to the measure as originally announced, on the grounds that it favoured HMRC and did not

1.126 *HMRC enquiries: outline and recent developments*

offer taxpayers the same option to apply to the tribunal for particular disputed aspect(s) to be heard.

Subsequently, the legislation introduced in *F(No 2)A 2017* amended *TMA 1970* and *FA 1998, Sch 18* and introduced the power to allow HMRC (and taxpayers, upon a successful application to the tribunal) to resolve particular matters during a tax return enquiry in advance of a full closure notice, through the issue of a partial closure notice. Those provisions generally apply from 16 November 2017 in relation to tax return enquiries opened on or after that date, or to existing enquiries in progress immediately before that date.

For further commentary on closure notices generally, see, **6.95–6.103** and **CHAPTER 20**.

DISCOVERY

1.126 Self-assessment is designed to give finality to the taxpayer. The general principle is that once an enquiry has been closed, or the enquiry window has passed without HMRC having opened an enquiry, it can no longer challenge the return.

1.127 The discovery power provides an exception to this general principle. It broadly enables HMRC to assess tax in relation to closed years if it discovers that tax has been under-assessed and the under-assessment is attributable either to:

- careless or deliberate conduct of the taxpayer or a person acting on his behalf; or
- something of which the officer could not have been reasonably expected to be aware at the time the enquiry window closed on the basis of the information made available to him before that time.

1.128 The lack of clarity in the requirements for a valid discovery by HMRC has resulted in a number of cases, including those noted at **1.23**.

1.129 Prior to *FA 2008*, a discovery assessment could be made at any time up to the fifth anniversary of 31 January following the tax year to which it relates (or up to six years after the end of the accounting period in relation to a company).

In the case of fraud or negligence, a discovery assessment can be made up to 20 years after 31 January following the tax year to which it relates or, in the case of a company up to 21 years after the end of the accounting period.

HMRC enquiries: outline and recent developments **1.133**

1.130 Under the present discovery regime, the basic rules for income tax, capital gains tax and corporation tax are as follows (*TMA 1970, ss 34–36; FA 1998, Sch 18, para 46*):

- four years – normal time limit;
- six years – careless error; and
- 20 years – deliberate error.

These time limits apply from the end of the accounting period or tax year. The general time limits for taxpayer claims are also aligned at four years.

HMRC sometimes contend that a tax return error was careless or deliberate where the normal four-year time limit for a discovery assessment has passed, even though it may be highly arguable that the taxpayer's behaviour did not fall into those categories. However, the burden of proving (for example) a deliberate loss of tax rests initially with HMRC (EM3348), and in some cases this burden may not be satisfied (eg see *Hicks v Revenue and Customs* [2018] UKFTT 22 (TC); *Munford v Revenue and Customs* [2017] UKFTT 19 (TC)).

1.131 As discovery is not part of self-assessment, the self-assessment enquiry procedures do not apply. Under the information powers regime, HMRC can issue a notice to compel the production of documents or information (*FA 2008, Sch 36, para 21(6)*). However, for these purposes see **1.90** as to the requirement for HMRC to 'suspect' (for example) a loss of tax; this represents a potentially difficult hurdle, which HMRC must successfully overcome (eg see *Kevin Betts v Revenue and Customs* [2013] UKFTT 430, and **7.5**).

1.132 The discovery provisions (in *TMA 1970, ss 29, 30B; FA 1998, Sch 18, paras 41–45*), and the often difficult matter of what constitutes a valid discovery, are important issues, and a separate chapter is therefore devoted to the subject of discovery (see **CHAPTER 13**).

The reason for mentioning discovery in the context of enquiries is that HMRC takes the view that in the absence of evidence to the contrary 'a presumption of continuity' can be made where an enquiry suggests that there is an understatement of income in the enquiry year and the reasons for that understatement suggest under-declarations in earlier years (EM3309).

1.133 In practice, HMRC invariably seeks to adjust up to the previous six years in addition to the enquiry year where it believes that a presumption of continuity can reasonably be made. In general, it does not seek to investigate the omissions for such earlier years, but quantifies the supposed omissions by assuming that the figure quantified for the enquiry year is representative of the level of under-declaration in earlier years, and adjusting it on some rough and ready basis to allow for inflation.

1.134 *HMRC enquiries: outline and recent developments*

> **Focus**
>
> There are two points that need to be borne in mind:
>
> - Before agreeing to an adjustment in an enquiry for the sake of an easy life when the taxpayer does not believe any adjustment to be legally due, it needs to be appreciated that the adjustment may result in a tax bill seven times the size of that which was anticipated when agreeing it.
>
> - If the taxpayer does not believe that adjusting the current year's amendment to reflect the effect of inflation is likely to give a reasonable approximation of any underpayment for earlier years, he ought to seek to establish the size of any appropriate adjustment on a more accurate basis using whatever information he has available in relation to the years in question, and seek to persuade the officer to agree his calculation.

It should be noted that the taxpayer has had some success before the First-tier Tribunal in appealing against assessments based on the presumption of continuity (see **6.91** and **13.125**).

1.134 Where, in the course of a self-assessment enquiry, HMRC makes a discovery in relation to earlier years it normally seeks 'a contract settlement' rather than raise formal discovery and penalty assessments. A contract settlement is a contract between HMRC and the taxpayer under which the taxpayer offers to pay HMRC an agreed sum in respect of tax, interest and penalties in consideration of HMRC agreeing not to institute proceedings against him. The contract settlement will normally cover the enquiry year as well as the discovery years.

A contract settlement between the taxpayer and HMRC will generally take the form of a signed letter of offer and acceptance (which is sometimes referred to as a 'simple contract'). However, in certain cases HMRC conclude contract settlements using signed and witnessed deeds. Where possible, HMRC will use a simple contract rather than a deed, but it reserves the right to use a deed in appropriate cases (eg where HMRC has doubts about whether the consideration in a letter of offer would be adequate to form a binding contract, or where a taxpayer insists on reaching a settlement using a deed (see EM6001a)).

1.135 Where a contract settlement has been entered into, the amount due is not tax; it is a civil debt. However, note that a contract settlement liability is a 'relevant sum' for the purposes of the provisions for HMRC enforcement by deduction from accounts (ie the 'direct recovery of debt' legislation; see *F(No 2)A 2015, Sch 8, para 2(b)*).

1.136 Where a contract settlement is entered into, HMRC does not in practice issue a closure notice. The main reason appears to be administrative convenience (eg a contract settlement obviates the necessity for formalities such as amendments, assessments etc.). In theory, this leaves the enquiry window open indefinitely.

A contract settlement is a binding legal agreement. The elements of a binding contract were considered in *Kyte v Revenue and Customs* [2018] EWHC 1146 (Ch), in the context of a purported agreement for the settlement of a taxpayer's liabilities arising from participation in a tax avoidance scheme. The requirement for offer and acceptance between the parties to constitute a valid contract means that if the taxpayer or agent insists on a formal closure notice being issued, this should be done. Where a formal notice is under appeal, it is still possible to settle through a contract settlement once the dispute is resolved (EM6001),

1.137 HMRC tells its staff, 'Once a contract offer has been accepted, it has the same effect as the issue of a closure notice. The year(s) included in the contract become final and you will not be able to make any further enquiries into those years ... unless you consider that the conditions for making a discovery assessment are satisfied'. Whilst the legal basis for this statement may be dubious, the taxpayer can probably safely rely on it.

1.138 Clients should be asked whether they have the benefit (albeit sometimes limited) of a professional fee protection policy in relation to HMRC enquiries. Unless they have taken out such a policy themselves, or are covered by a group scheme, they might not realise that they may have cover from other insurance products such as commercial or house insurance. The relevant policy documents should therefore be reviewed, where appropriate.

KEY POINTS

1.139

1   HMRC enquiries are the 'bread and butter' of HMRC's compliance function.

2   A timely enquiry notice within the statutory 'window' represents the legal starting point.

3   Enquiries can be either 'aspect' or 'full'; reasons for the enquiry should be provided by HMRC.

4   Where the enquiry window is missed, HMRC can re-open earlier years if it can claim to have made a 'discovery' of new facts.

1.139 *HMRC enquiries: outline and recent developments*

5   In practice it is often not too difficult to demonstrate a valid discovery; however, the matter requires careful consideration.

6   HMRC can use its formal powers (under *FA 2008, Sch 36*) to require the production of information.

7   Requests for meetings need careful consideration.

8   Where a meeting is to be held, a comprehensive agenda should be obtained from HMRC.

9   Culpability and assessment time limits should be considered.

Chapter 2

Serious civil tax investigations into fraud and avoidance: Code of Practice 9 (Contractual Disclosure Facility) and Code of Practice 8

Gary Ashford CTA (Fellow), ATT, TEP
Partner, Harbottle and Lewis LLP

SIGNPOSTS

- **The role of Special Investigations (Fraud and Avoidance)** – Special Investigations (Fraud and Avoidance) handles the more complex tax investigations, and cases of suspected serious fraud. At the time of writing, SI and the Criminal Investigation Directorate have recently been brought back together to form the Fraud Investigation Service. (See **2.1–2.7**.)

- **Types of serious fraud investigations** – HMRC has a published criminal investigation policy. HMRC maintains a policy of selective prosecution, selecting the more heinous and public interest cases of suspected serious fraud for criminal investigation. Where it chooses not to proceed using its criminal powers, HMRC will use its civil powers, and in cases of suspected serious fraud, it can proceed under Code of Practice 9. Where cases are complex but do not hold sufficient evidence of suspected serious fraud, HMRC may proceed within Special Investigations (Fraud and Avoidance) by way of Code of Practice 8. (See **2.8–2.9**.)

- **Serious tax fraud** – Serious tax fraud is tax matters which are of a fraudulent nature. Fraud usually involves some sort of mistruth or deception and there is a great deal of case law and much reference material on the matter. (See **2.10–2.20**.)

- **Code of Practice 9** – Code of Practice 9 is the main Code of Practice used by Special Investigations (Fraud and Avoidance) to investigate

2.1 *Serious civil tax investigations into fraud and avoidance*

> cases of suspected tax fraud where it has chosen not to proceed by way of a criminal investigation. It is very important to appreciate that under the current COP9 (the Contractual Disclosure Facility) if the client does not cooperate and meet the terms of the CDF, HMRC has the power to cancel the contract, and potentially proceed by way of a criminal investigation. (See **2.21–2.81**.)
>
> - **Code of Practice 8** – HMRC Special Investigations (Fraud and Avoidance) investigates cases where it does not have evidence of suspected fraud under Code of Practice 8. It is important to recognise that, if during a Code of Practice 8 investigation, HMRC identifies the presence of fraud, it could withdraw Code of Practice 8 and potentially progress under Code of Practice 9 or commence a criminal investigation with a view to prosecution. (See **2.82–2.84**.)
> - **Managing professional risk** – Tax investigations or disclosures involving serious tax fraud contain specific risks for clients. HMRC could choose to undertake a criminal investigation with a view to prosecution. Alternatively, as well as more significant tax-geared penalties, HMRC could use its powers to publish the details of the client. It is essential that these risks are taken into account before taking on such work. (See **2.85–2.97**.)
> - **Key points** – For a list of key points from this chapter, see **2.98**.

> **Focus**
>
> This chapter aims to provide practical guidance and experience when it comes to handling HMRC serious fraud investigations. It is very important to fully appreciate that this work is highly contentious and contains many risks for clients.

FRAUD INVESTIGATION SERVICE

2.1 The Fraud Investigation Service (FIS) was created in Autumn 2015. This office brings together all HMRC's serious fraud investigation teams (Criminal Investigation Directorate and Special Investigations (Fraud and Avoidance) Office), and in part returns HMRC's serious fraud investigation functions back into one unit with more than 4,000 staff.

At the time of writing, the changes which will result from the creation of FIS are still being developed and so we will concentrate on the structures prior to the creation of FIS.

The role of Special Investigations (Fraud and Avoidance)

2.2 The Special Investigations (Fraud and Avoidance) Office (SI) is the office within HMRC with responsibility for larger and more serious civil investigation cases, including cases of suspected fraud and complex avoidance.

2.3 Cases of suspected serious fraud are investigated under Code of Practice 9 (COP9) (currently the Contractual Disclosure Facility (CDF)). Cases of complex avoidance matters, where fraud is not suspected, are investigated under Code of Practice 8 (COP8). Large scale avoidance cases may sometimes be taken over by SI from other HMRC offices under the original Codes of Practice issued.

2.4 SI also conducts sensitive projects, looking at groups like high-profile entertainers or sportsmen; sectors where significant amounts of PAYE and NIC or other taxes are at risk; for example in relation to city traders, the pharmaceutical industry, umbrella companies, etc.

2.5 SI was previously known as the Special Compliance Office (SCO) and was before that in two parts: Enquiry Branch and Special Office. The old SCO was the home of the (HMRC) Board's Investigation Office and Criminal Investigation teams and also previously had responsibility for teams such as the Foreign Entertainers Unit (FEU). FEU, however, moved to the Centre for Non-Residents, which then became part of Charity Assets and Residence (CAR).

2.6 On 1 April 2005, the criminal investigation functions of the former Inland Revenue and the former Customs and Excise were placed within a new independent prosecuting authority, the Revenue and Customs Prosecution Office (RCPO). This led the way for the criminal investigation teams to be removed to a new HMRC department, the Criminal Investigation Directorate. Whilst the Criminal Investigation Directorate, as a separate function, remains within HMRC, any prosecution is carried out by Crown Prosecution Service (CPS).

2.7 There are SI offices strategically located throughout the UK: in London, Bristol, Manchester, Solihull, Edinburgh, Nottingham and Leeds. Various subsidiary SI offices have been created to handle the large increase in workload on tax-avoidance scheme arrangements.

2.8 *Serious civil tax investigations into fraud and avoidance*

TYPES OF SI INVESTIGATION

Code of Practice 9 (Contractual Disclosure Facility procedures)

2.8 Where SI investigates cases of suspected tax fraud by way of civil procedures, it does this under COP9 (Contractual Disclosure Facility). CDF investigations can arise in the following circumstances:

- from an investigation being conducted in the local area office where the local investigator identifies significant evasion, or activities which suggest that serious fraud may have taken place;
- from an investigation opened directly by SI or as a result of its own intelligence and research work;
- alternatively, where a taxpayer or his adviser identifies an issue or issues where evasion has taken place, he might wish to approach the relevant SI team direct to seek the protection of CDF procedures.

Cases other than suspected serious fraud (COP8)

2.9 SI also investigates non-evasion cases as follows:

- where significant tax is at risk, perhaps as a result of the use of offshore structures or trusts;
- where SI conducts projects, for example to identify high-profile individuals, entertainers and sportsmen whose tax affairs may be complex or not up to date, or who have failed to register for tax altogether (an example of this is the well-publicised football and rugby project of the late 1980s and 1990s);
- where SI has been tasked to support local offices or, for example, the Anti Avoidance Group (AAG) by raising investigations into marketed avoidance schemes.

SERIOUS TAX FRAUD (EVASION)

2.10 When considering cases of suspected serious tax fraud, it is important to understand HMRC's approach to criminal investigation. Where HMRC considers whether a case is suitable for CDF procedures, it will first look at the suspected offences committed and whether they are sufficiently heinous (or in the public interest) to warrant a criminal investigation.

Serious civil tax investigations into fraud and avoidance **2.12**

2.11 HMRC's published criminal prosecution policy states the following:

'HMRC's aim is to secure the highest level of compliance with the law and regulations governing direct and indirect taxes and other regimes for which they are responsible. Criminal investigation, with a view to prosecution by the Crown Prosecution Service in England and Wales (CPS), or the Crown Office and Procurator Fiscal Service in Scotland (COPFS), or the Public Prosecution Service Northern Ireland (PPSNI) – is an important part of HMRC's overall enforcement strategy.

It is HMRC's policy to deal with fraud by use of the cost-effective Civil Fraud Investigation procedures under Code of Practice 9, wherever appropriate. Criminal Investigation will be reserved for cases where HMRC needs to send a strong deterrent message or where the conduct involved is such that only a criminal sanction is appropriate.

However, HMRC reserves complete discretion to conduct a criminal investigation in any case and to carry out these investigations across a range of offences and in all the areas for which the Commissioners of HMRC have responsibility.'

2.12 Examples of the kind of circumstances in which HMRC will generally consider commencing a criminal, rather than civil, investigation are:

- cases of organised criminal gangs attacking the tax system, or systematic frauds where losses represent a serious threat to the tax base, including conspiracy;
- where an individual holds a position of trust or responsibility;
- where materially false statements are made or materially false documents are provided in the course of a civil investigation;
- where, pursuing an avoidance scheme, reliance is placed on a false or altered document or such reliance or material facts are misrepresented to enhance the credibility of a scheme;
- where deliberate concealment, deception, conspiracy or corruption is suspected;
- cases involving the use of false or forged documents;
- cases involving importation or exportation breaching prohibitions and restrictions;
- cases involving money laundering with particular focus on advisers, accountants, solicitors and others acting in a 'professional' capacity who provide the means to put tainted money out of the reach of law enforcement;

2.13 *Serious civil tax investigations into fraud and avoidance*

- where the perpetrator has committed previous offences or there is a repeated course of unlawful conduct or previous civil action;
- cases involving theft, or the misuse or unlawful destruction, of HMRC documents;
- where there is evidence of assault on, threats to, or the impersonation of HMRC officials;
- where there is a link to suspected wider criminality, whether domestic or international, involving offences not under the administration of HMRC.

2.13 When considering whether a case should be investigated using the civil fraud investigation procedures under COP9 or is to be the subject of a criminal investigation, one important factor will be whether the taxpayer has made a complete and unprompted disclosure of the offences committed.

2.14 However, there are certain fiscal offences where HMRC will not usually adopt the civil fraud investigation procedures under COP9. Examples of these are:

- VAT missing trader intra-community (MTIC) fraud;
- VAT 'bogus' registration repayment fraud;
- organised tax credit fraud.

Definition of fraud

2.15 As well as understanding the HMRC Board's policy on criminal prosecution, when considering cases of suspected serious fraud some understanding of what constitutes fraud is also clearly helpful. There is an abundance of common law (both tax and non-tax related) on this subject.

2.16 HMRC's Enquiry manual (at EM5106) publishes the following extract from *Halsbury's Laws of England* (LexisNexis), in relation to 'Misrepresentation and Fraud':

> **'Section 757 What Constitutes Fraud?**
>
> Not only is a misrepresentation fraudulent if it was known or believed by the representor to be false when made, but mere non-belief in the truth is also indicative of fraud. Thus, whenever a person makes a false statement which he does not actually and honestly believe to be true, for purposes of civil liability, that statement is as fraudulent as if he had stated that which he did not know to be true, or knew or believed to be false.* Proof of absence of actual and honest belief is all that is necessary to satisfy the requirements of the law, whether the representation has been made recklessly or deliberately;

Serious civil tax investigations into fraud and avoidance **2.16**

indifference or recklessness on the part of the representor as to the truth or falsity of the representation affords merely an instance of absence of such a belief.

A representor will not, however, be fraudulent if he believed the statement to be true in the sense in which he understood it, provided that was a meaning which might reasonably be attached to it, even though the court later holds that the statement objectively bears another meaning, which the representor did not believe.

[* See *Derry v Peek* 14 App Cas 337, p 374, per Lord Herschell: fraud is proved when it is shown that a false representation has been made (1) knowingly, or (2) without belief in its truth, or (3) recklessly, careless whether it be true or false; the third case being but an instance of the second.]

Section 759 Irrelevancy of Representor's Motive

It follows from the meaning of fraudulent misrepresentation that, given absence of actual and honest belief by the representor in the truth of the misrepresentation, his motive in making the misrepresentation is wholly irrelevant. It may be that he intended to injure the representee without benefiting himself, or to benefit himself without injuring the representee; it may be that he did not intend to do either, but solely to benefit a third person, or even the representee himself, or otherwise to do right. Lastly, he may have acted with no intelligible or rational notice whatsoever and told a lie from mere caprice, mischievousness or stupidity. In all these cases, provided that there was an absence of actual and honest belief in the truth of his assertion, the misrepresentation is accounted fraudulent and no proof of any wicked or other intention (other than an intention to induce) on the part of the representor is required by the law; or if it is necessary to establish an intention to deceive or injure, that intention is immediately and irrebuttably presumed in law from the mere act of making the misrepresentation without such belief.

Section 760 Representation Subsequently Discovered by Representor to be False

Where a representation is a continuing one and where, between the time when it was made and the time when the representee altered his position on the faith of it, either (1) the representor discovers that his original statement which, when he made it, he honestly believed to be true, was false, or (2) supervening events render, to the knowledge of the representor, his statement no longer true, a duty to disclose the changed situation to the representee may arise. In such cases the mere fact that the statement may have been innocently made, though false, or true when made, will not, it seems, prevent the representee from establishing fraud where he can show that the representor dishonestly failed to discharge the duty of disclosing the change in the situation.'

2.17 *Serious civil tax investigations into fraud and avoidance*

The above demonstrates that, particularly in terms of civil liability, the term 'fraud' is widely drawn. For example, it extends to the deliberate submission of understated accounts and incorrect tax returns.

2.17 HMRC has also recently included within its latest COP9 booklet (June 2014) a definition of tax fraud. It states that for the purposes of COP9 '"fraud" means the dishonest behaviour that led to or was intended to lead to the loss of tax'. The document states that the clarification covers all matters for which HMRC has administrative responsibility and could commence a criminal investigation. It also states that 'a person commits an offence if they are knowingly concerned in the fraudulent evasion of tax or duty by themselves or another person'.

2.18 Examples set out in the document include:

- concealing or withholding relevant facts;
- failing to disclose a liability to tax or duty;
- misrepresenting your tax affairs.

The statement also confirms that the person might not have actually gained from the deliberate conduct.

The Fraud Act 2006

2.19 Further guidance on fraud can also be drawn from the *Fraud Act 2006*. The *Fraud Act 2006* defines fraud in three categories:

- fraud by false representation;
- fraud by failing to disclose information;
- fraud by abuse of position.

2.20 The Act states in all three categories that there must be an act of dishonesty. In relation to the Fraud Act itself, the person committing the offence must have an intention to make a gain or loss, temporary or permanent, and defines loss or gain as extending only to money or other property (real or personal) but including things in action or other intangible property.

Code of Practice 9 (cases of suspected fraud)

History

2.21 COP9 has been around for a long time. We have seen parliamentary statements made by the Chancellor of the Exchequer in relation to tax fraud

Serious civil tax investigations into fraud and avoidance **2.27**

since 1923. Many people would associate a COP9 investigation with the term 'Hansard' investigation, which reflects the fact that at various points in time HMRC's policy towards the civil investigation of serious tax fraud has been set out to Parliament.

2.22 Early versions of COP9 stated that where a person made a full disclosure of all tax irregularities as part of the formal Hansard process, the Board of the ex-Inland Revenue would take this into account when considering whether to accept a money settlement or institute criminal proceedings.

2.23 Whilst this provided no actual commitment that criminal proceedings would not result from what amounted to disclosure of fraud, in practice, the then Inland Revenue would generally not commence criminal investigations in such cases despite having legal authority to do so. (The approach of the ex-Customs and Excise was more clear-cut, in that once a case had been categorised as civil, only in very defined circumstances could a criminal investigation occur.)

2.24 The position came to a head in *R v W* [1998] STC 550. In this case the Crown did institute criminal proceedings, despite the custom and practice of HMRC for many years of not doing so where full disclosure was made. In the case of *R v Allen* [2001] UKHL 45, the court judgments referred to the inducement contained within the wording of the COP9 effectively saying that a criminal investigation might not be undertaken where a full disclosure was made.

2.25 In order to clarify the position, a new statement was made by the Chancellor of Exchequer in November 2002 which resulted in the issuing of a revised version of COP9. This statement explicitly confirmed for the first time (for direct tax purposes) that no criminal investigation would result where a full disclosure was made.

2.26 Further changes took place following the case of *R v Gill* [2003] EWCA Crim 2256. In this case, the courts criticised the ex-Inland Revenue for not having formally cautioned the defendants before offering them an inducement to make a disclosure (however, the courts did not free the defendants from their prison sentence, notwithstanding the criticism of the ex-Revenue procedures, as they found that the defendants had deceived despite the absence of the caution).

2.27 As a result of *R v Gill* all COP9 procedures were suspended for a period of time in Autumn 2003. New COP9 procedures were formulated to take account of the issues raised in *R v Gill*. It is worth recognising that, in terms of investigating the extent of any irregularities and preparing disclosure reports, there was little difference in all of these variations of the COP9 procedures. The differences largely affected the procedures adopted in the formal opening of a case by SI, and, although the potential impact was significant, in practical

2.28 *Serious civil tax investigations into fraud and avoidance*

terms the position only changed for those who did not make a full and complete disclosure when offered the protection of COP9.

2.28 Under the changes made as a result of *R v Gill*, new procedures were adopted, such that at the opening of any meeting under the new procedures, the person under investigation was reminded of his rights under *PACE 1984*, Code C. A formal tape recording would be taken of the meeting. The person would be advised that the investigation under COP9 was not a criminal investigation, but that if at a later date HMRC did undertake a criminal investigation as it believed a full and complete disclosure had not been made, the tape-recorded interview could be used in evidence. As a result of this, it became common for taxpayers and their advisers to attend the opening meetings with a criminal lawyer who could advise as to whether any self-incriminatory discussions could take place following the reading of the caution under *PACE 1984* and the COP9 questions. Consequently, some opening meetings were very short, and were limited merely to the formal questions (see **2.61**) with no other discussion of the issues in the case.

2.29 Following the merger of the Inland Revenue and HM Customs and Excise in April 2005, further changes were required to the COP9 procedures, given the different approaches that each department had to civil investigation of fraud.

2.30 The Customs and Excise approach (730 procedures) made very clear that once the decision had been made to go down either the civil or criminal route there was no ambiguity about the protection, or otherwise, available to the taxpayer when making a disclosure of irregularities.

There was also the cumbersome approach of applying both COP9 and the 730 procedures to the same case where both direct and indirect taxes arose from the same irregularity.

Civil investigations of fraud procedures

2.31 On 1 September 2005, a new COP9 was published, introducing the new Civil Investigation of Fraud (CIF) procedures to cover all taxes. The CIF procedures replaced all previous former Inland Revenue or former Customs and Excise procedures for conducting investigations into serious fraud on a civil basis.

2.32 The most significant feature in the new CIF procedures from 1 September 2005 was an upfront commitment by HMRC that it would not conduct a criminal investigation in relation to the initial tax offence. The need to remind the person of his rights under PACE and for taped recorded meetings were dispensed with.

Serious civil tax investigations into fraud and avoidance **2.37**

2.33 A criminal investigation might still be commenced where the person under investigation misled or deceived HMRC or provided false documents as part of the COP9 investigation and this was made clear at the start of the investigation.

2.34 As with previous COP9 procedures, the person under investigation would receive formal notification in writing from HMRC that his affairs were to be investigated in line with the CIF procedures under COP9. A copy of the COP9 booklet would be enclosed with that letter. The leaflet suggested that the person under investigation should consider seeking specialist advice (this remains good advice for any investigations conducted under COP9).

2.35 The person under investigation under the CIF procedures would be invited to attend a meeting with specialist investigators from a CIF team or from SI. The purpose of the meeting was for the HMRC investigator to set out in very prescribed terms the Board of HMRC's approach to suspected serious fraud. Investigators were trained not to deviate from the Board's published statement.

2.36 The HMRC investigator would repeat the published statement in relation to HMRC's approach to the civil investigation of fraud:

'The Commissioners reserve complete discretion to pursue a criminal investigation with a view to prosecution where they consider it necessary and appropriate.

Where a criminal investigation is not considered necessary or appropriate, the Commissioners may decide to investigate using the CIF procedure.

Where the Commissioners decide to investigate using the CIF procedure they will not seek a prosecution for the tax fraud which is the subject of that investigation.

The taxpayer will be given an opportunity to make a full and complete disclosure of all irregularities in their tax affairs.

However, where materially false statements are made or materially false documents are provided with intent to deceive in the course of a civil investigation, the Commissioners may conduct a criminal investigation with a view to a prosecution of that conduct.

If the Commissioners decide to investigate using the CIF procedures the taxpayer will be given a copy of this statement by an authorised officer.'

Having set out the formal policy, the investigator would provide a printed copy of that policy to the person under investigation.

2.37 The meeting would then progress, to the point where the investigator would ask a series of questions in relation to the person's affairs which were designed to elicit 'yes' or 'no' replies.

2.38 *Serious civil tax investigations into fraud and avoidance*

2.38 For investigations commenced before 1 September 2005 there were essentially five questions, which extended to all direct taxes and were without time limit (although HMRC was effectively time barred from action beyond its 20-year assessing time limit, clients could still be invited to pay out-of-date liabilities through voluntary restitution).

From 1 September 2005, the CIF procedures included indirect taxes and there was also a series of four questions covering indirect taxes (see **2.42** for the nine questions).

2.39 Depending on whether the CIF investigation resulted from a voluntary disclosure or from HMRC's own investigation work, the meeting would then move to discussions of the irregularities, so that the CIF or SI investigator was able to understand more of the background to any disclosure.

2.40 At the centre of any COP9 investigation is the aim to secure a disclosure of historical tax irregularities. If the person was denying that he had perpetrated a fraud, then while the investigation could continue on a civil investigation basis, that investigation would be undertaken by HMRC.

The nine questions of COP9

2.41 There were five direct tax and four indirect tax questions.

The five direct tax questions were:

1   Have any transactions been omitted from or incorrectly recorded in the books of any business with which you are or have been concerned whether as a director, partner or sole proprietor to the best of your knowledge or belief?

2   Are the accounts sent to the HMRC for each and every business with which you are or have been concerned whether as a director, partner or sole proprietor, correct and complete to the best of your knowledge and belief?

3   Are all the tax returns of each and every business with which you are or have been concerned whether as a director, partner or sole proprietor correct and complete to the best of your knowledge and belief?

4   Are all your personal tax returns correct and complete to the best of your knowledge and belief?

5   Will you allow an examination of all business books, and private statements and any other business and private records in order that HMRC may be satisfied that your answers to the first four questions are correct?

2.42 The four indirect tax questions were:

1 Have any transactions been omitted from, or incorrectly recorded, in the books and records of [name of legal entity] for which you are [responsible status]?

2 Are the books and records you are required to keep by HMRC for [name of legal entity] for which you are [responsible status], correct and complete to the best of your knowledge and belief?

3 Are all the VAT returns of the [name of legal entity] for which you are [responsible status] correct and complete to the best of your knowledge and belief?

4 Were you aware that any of the VAT returns were incorrect or incomplete at the time they were submitted?

In cases where the main offence is failure to notify chargeability, HMRC may also include an extra direct tax question.

Contractual Disclosure Facility

2.43 HMRC introduced new COP9 procedures from 31 January 2012. This introduced the CDF. With the introduction of the CDF came a new COP9.

Many felt that the CIF procedures (see **2.31** *et seq*) had lost some of their deterrent effect, in part because of the assurances given under CIF that once a CIF investigation had commenced there would not be a criminal investigation for the original offence and where a full and complete disclosure was made. This approach, whilst still effective for those who were prepared to cooperate with HMRC, was less so for those who did not wish to cooperate, because they believed (and this was to some extent the reality) that the threat of a criminal investigation was largely gone.

2.44 With the introduction of the CDF a greater threat of criminal investigation exists, not just where a full and complete disclosure is not forthcoming, but also where the person denies fraud, does not cooperate from the start of the investigation, or withdraws cooperation later.

2.45 The CDF amounts to a contract between the person under investigation and HMRC. HMRC has stated that the CDF is suitable only for people who are prepared to confess to tax fraud. While strictly in line with the fundamental objectives of previous COP9 investigations, this statement is more clear. HMRC states that the CDF is not for people who want to disclose errors, mistakes or avoidance schemes where there is no fraud.

2.46 *Serious civil tax investigations into fraud and avoidance*

2.46 This approach may have the impact of reducing the number of people volunteering to be investigated under COP9 in order to secure the inherent protections in relation to civil investigation treatment.

The HMRC Investigation of Fraud Statement

2.47 A revised Statement on the HMRC investigation of fraud is provided in a new COP9 booklet which was issued on 31 January 2012.

> 'The Commissioners of HMRC reserve complete discretion to pursue a criminal investigation with a view to prosecution where they consider it necessary and appropriate.
>
> In cases where a criminal investigation is not commenced, the Commissioners may decide to investigate using the Code of Practice 9 investigation of fraud procedure.
>
> Under the investigation of fraud procedure, the recipient of Code of Practice 9 is given the opportunity to make a complete and accurate disclosure of all irregularities in their tax affairs.
>
> Where the recipient fails to make a full disclosure of the tax frauds they have committed, the Commissioners reserve the right to commence a criminal investigation with a view to prosecution.
>
> In the course of the Code of Practice 9 investigation, if the recipient makes materially false or misleading statements, or provides materially false documents the Commissioners reserve the right to commence a criminal investigation into that conduct as a separate criminal offence.'

2.48 CDF effectively presents the person under investigation with three options:

- owning up to fraud (the disclosure route);
- denying that there has been a fraud (the denial route);
- not replying to HMRC (the non-cooperation route).

Denial of irregularities with cooperation is possible but there is a chance that by adopting such an approach HMRC will treat this as a denial in line with the above.

The disclosure route

2.49 If the person satisfies himself that the CDF is appropriate (he has committed fraud and is prepared to make a confession of this), he is required to sign an acceptance letter and complete the outline disclosure form.

Under the CDF contract, HMRC confirms that it will agree not to criminally investigate and prosecute the person in relation to the fraud that has been disclosed.

In return for this commitment, HMRC is seeking that the person disclose the tax that has been evaded (see **2.57** *et seq*).

2.50 There is a time limit of 60 days in which to do this. Given the relatively tight deadline, disclosure within the 60-day timeline may amount to an initial disclosure, to be followed up with a full and complete disclosure perhaps by way of a disclosure report.

The initial disclosure needs to be of sufficient detail so as not to be treated as a denial or non-cooperation under the terms of the CDF.

2.51 The person must also sign a statement to say that he:

- has provided accurate and complete details of the tax fraud;
- will pay all taxes, duties, interest and penalties due.

The person must also confirm that he has ceased any continuing fraudulent behaviour.

The denial route (cooperation offered)

2.52 (See **2.54** *et seq*, as this route was discontinued on 1 June 2014.) Where the person denies that he has committed a fraud, but offers to cooperate, he can sign and return a CDF denial letter, again within the 60-day time limit.

However, HMRC has stated that it will review matters, and this could result in matters being progressed as a criminal investigation.

The non-cooperation route

2.53 If the person does not respond to HMRC within the 60-day time limit, HMRC has stated it will treat this as a denial under the terms of the CDF.

HMRC has stated that, as with denial cases, it will then proceed to undertake its own investigation, either as a criminal investigation or civil one.

2.54   *Serious civil tax investigations into fraud and avoidance*

Changes to the Contractual Disclosure Facility from June 2014

2.54   From June 2014 certain fundamental changes were introduced to the CDF, in that the opportunity to cooperate with HMRC but not to make an outright admission of fraud was withdrawn (the denial with cooperation).

2.55   From the introduction of the CDF in January 2012, HMRC announced that where a person elected for the route of denial with cooperation, HMRC reserved the right to commence a criminal tax investigation.

2.56   Despite that inherent risk, some clients and advisers still took this approach, viewing it as less of a risk than formally acknowledging that they had committed fraud. They took this approach on many cases where, in particular, they were concerned about the implications for their membership of a professional body or regulated industry.

Outline disclosure

2.57   The deadline and the content of an outline disclosure under the CDF is extremely important.

HMRC expects the following to be included:

- what the person has done (there is an expectation that this will include a confession that he has committed fraud);
- how the fraud was committed;
- the involvement of other people and entities;
- how they benefited from the conduct.

2.58   HMRC has advised that where it believes (based on the information that it is holding) that an incomplete disclosure has been made it reserves the right to commence a criminal investigation.

It is recommended that sufficient time is spent at the earliest point in the 60 days in order to ensure that any disclosure made is as comprehensive as possible.

Voluntary disclosure

2.59   The CDF does allow for those who have committed tax fraud to approach HMRC voluntarily and ask HMRC to offer them the CDF contract.

Serious civil tax investigations into fraud and avoidance **2.64**

However, it is important to appreciate that HMRC is under no obligation and has given no assurance that it will offer the CDF contract. There is therefore a risk of criminal investigation.

The person contemplating making a voluntary disclosure and seeking the CDF might therefore want to fully explore his options.

2.60 When making voluntary disclosures under CDF, it is also worthwhile considering whether HMRC has any other disclosure facilities available at the time. for example, where untaxed assets were of an offshore nature and held at 1 September 2009, the client may have wished to explore the benefits of the Liechtenstein Disclosure Facility (LDF), which is referred to in **CHAPTER 5**. In that case, providing the person held a Liechtenstein asset at the point of approaching HMRC, he would potentially be able to gain the assurances given by HMRC in relation to that disclosure facility that HMRC would not commence any criminal investigation.

Formal questions

2.61 Under the CDF the formal questions which were very much part of COP9 have been dispensed with.

Meetings under CDF

2.62 Meetings under CDF are different to previous COP9 meetings because the formal questions have been dispensed with. Meetings will instead concentrate on the disclosure as set out in the outline disclosure, and will then progress to look at general matters such as discussing the business (if appropriate) and the personal financial affairs of the person under investigation.

2.63 Meetings are still an opportunity for SI investigators to set out the importance of continued cooperation and the format of any disclosure report, including the expected accompanying documents such as: adoption of report certificate, statement of assets and liabilities, certificates of bank and credit card accounts operated and the certificate of disclosure.

Preparation for COP9 meetings

2.64 Prior to any meeting under COP9 it is good practice to assist the taxpayer in preparing for the meeting.

2.65 *Serious civil tax investigations into fraud and avoidance*

Such meetings can be very stressful for clients, and without any preparation they might inadvertently answer some or all of the questions incorrectly or provide misleading information to the investigator.

In some cases there is scope to hold the meeting without the attendance of the client, particularly where the client's health is an issue.

2.65 It is also good practice for the adviser to try to understand more about the client's affairs and identify any potential tax liabilities which might have arisen and which may have been overlooked by the client in compiling the disclosure.

This should include a full review of all areas where a liability might have resulted, including from technical points, as well as any liabilities that have arisen from any potential fraudulent activities.

2.66 The purpose of this is to assist the taxpayer in making an early disclosure of any such items, thus securing the maximum mitigation for penalties, but more importantly to demonstrate full cooperation and to ensure that there is no reason for HMRC to suspect that false or misleading statements will be made, which might risk the withdrawal of COP9 and its replacement with a criminal investigation.

2.67 A denial of any wrongdoing will result in the investigator conducting his own investigation. At this point HMRC could escalate matters to a criminal investigation. Alternatively, it might still proceed under COP9.

2.68 If HMRC subsequently demonstrates that there are additional liabilities which were not disclosed, there is a risk of the withdrawal of COP9 if it can demonstrate that it was misled or was provided with false documents. Also, mitigation for tax-geared penalties will be greatly reduced even if the case remains on a civil basis with COP9.

2.69 The HMRC investigator will use the meeting to seek to understand the following about the taxpayer's business:

- detailed explanations around any disclosure being made;
- the client's response to any specific allegations being put before him;
- the nature and structure of the client's business (if appropriate);
- the business records maintained and controls applied;
- the accounting areas or practices where income/purchases may have been understated/overstated, etc;
- any other areas where there might be a risk of a tax liability.

Serious civil tax investigations into fraud and avoidance **2.76**

2.70 The HMRC investigator will use the meeting to understand fully the personal tax affairs of the client, including:

- personal history and background, including family relationships, etc;
- details of sources of personal income and expenditure;
- details of personal assets and liabilities;
- any links to perceived tax-sheltering vehicles such as offshore trusts.

2.71 After the fact-finding part of the meeting, the investigator will ask whether the client formally wishes to instruct his adviser to prepare a disclosure report. If the client confirms that he does wish this to happen, the investigator will make it very clear that HMRC will expect the disclosure report within six months of the date of the opening COP9 meeting.

2.72 A client does not have to commission a disclosure report. However, on more complex matters it is suggested that a disclosure report is the preferred approach. This is because it will generally ensure that a fully considered and complete disclosure is made.

2.73 Following the formal meeting there will generally be a separate meeting with the adviser who has been commissioned to prepare the disclosure report, in order for both parties to agree on what should be covered and what work should be undertaken.

2.74 This is an opportunity for the adviser to set out to SI or the CIF team any practical difficulties that he may anticipate. This might include discussions on whether the six-month deadline for the report should be extended because of special circumstances, ie the case involves exceptional circumstances or is particularly large or complex.

2.75 Throughout the period of preparing the disclosure report it is expected that there will be update meetings or telephone calls with the SI or CIF team investigator and again this is also an opportunity to set out any difficulties that the adviser is experiencing.

2.76 HMRC will generally expect the final disclosure report to include the following completed certificates:

- a certificate of bank and credit card accounts operated;
- a statement of personal assets and liabilities;
- a certificate of full disclosure.

The disclosure report will be required to be adopted by the taxpayer as his own full and complete disclosure.

2.77 *Serious civil tax investigations into fraud and avoidance*

2.77 The importance for absolute accuracy in these certificates cannot be overstated. Very often, where a COP9 disclosure report is rejected and a criminal investigation commenced, HMRC will refer to incorrect certificates.

Closing the investigation

2.78 Once the disclosure report has been submitted to HMRC, the investigator might accept the report straightaway, seek to test the contents, or reject the report. In the last of these circumstances he could pass the report to his colleagues at the Criminal Investigation Directorate to commence a criminal investigation.

Settlement

2.79 Where HMRC accepts, either straight away or in due course, that a full and complete disclosure has been made, it will progress matters towards a negotiated financial settlement, including tax, interest and penalties.

2.80 All the general administrative legislation, guidelines and practice relating to civil settlements will apply when calculating any settlement. The general approach of settling civil tax investigations by way of a letter of offer also is exactly the same for settlement of a COP9 investigation.

2.81 Where a deliberate penalty is charged HMRC may also seek to apply its Managing Deliberate Defaulters or Publishing Details of Deliberate Defaulters procedures. Again, the general administrative legislation, guidelines and practice relating to such matters will apply.

CODE OF PRACTICE 8: CASES WHERE CIVIL INVESTIGATION OF FRAUD PROCEDURES ARE NOT USED

2.82 As well as cases of suspected serious fraud, SI also carries out other types of investigation. COP8 has historically been the code used by SI to investigate complex tax-planning structures, and high-profile taxpayers with complex tax affairs, particularly involving offshore aspects, where HMRC believes there is a significant risk of substantial unpaid liabilities, but where it does not at that point hold evidence to warrant the use of the civil investigation of fraud procedures under COP9.

2.83 It is important to recognise that COP8 does not bring with it any of the protections or commitments of COP9 (ie HMRC's commitment to not making a criminal investigation where CDF is taken on disclosure and cooperation is met). If SI identifies fraud during any COP8 investigation, it cannot be assumed that a civil settlement will result, and the enquiry could instead be handed over to the Criminal Investigation Directorate to commence a criminal investigation. A COP8 investigation can also be withdrawn and replaced by COP9 during the investigation where it suspects fraud is in point.

2.84 With HMRC's recent drive against marketed avoidance schemes, COP8 has been used to conduct investigations in this field.

COP8 investigations should be treated seriously and with care. It is strongly advised that these cases should be handled by a specialist tax adviser.

HANDLING SI INVESTIGATIONS (PRACTICE MANAGEMENT AND PROFESSIONAL INDEMNITY INSURANCE)

2.85 SI investigations involve highly specialised work and should only be handled in consultation with or by tax advisers with the appropriate specialist skills.

Most professional indemnity insurers will state that they will not cover this work unless it is handled by specialists.

2.86 It is very important to recognise that all inspectors operating within SI teams have been selected for their specific flair and interest in investigation work. These investigators are also recognised as possessing excellent negotiating skills.

2.87 New staff joining SI will shadow colleagues and work closely with experienced investigators and team leaders to ensure that they meet the standards required. One should therefore never view inspectors who have recently joined SI as less experienced. There is a huge support network there to protect them.

2.88 SI investigators will not be easily deflected where they believe there is a need for an explanation. SI is recognised as expert in the use of civil information powers in terms of information notices within the UK and overseas.

2.89 It is also important to recognise that any case which is taken on by SI will have been reviewed and identified as one where there is a clear risk of a significant loss of tax either as a result of fraud or otherwise.

2.90 Any case registered by SI must be viewed within the tax profession as one that has passed all the appropriate internal registration tests and where the

2.91 *Serious civil tax investigations into fraud and avoidance*

investigator believes that there are substantial further liabilities. In cases under COP9, this includes strong evidence pointing towards fraud.

2.91 It is good practice to ensure the person under investigation is aware of this. As soon as an enquiry notice under either COP8 or COP9 is received, it is always worthwhile spending time with the person to explore whether there is any reason he can think of why he is the subject of an SI investigation.

2.92 SI teams, like any other government agency, can occasionally get things wrong. However, the process of CDF does not provide scope to hold a discussion about why SI has registered the case for COP9. The person would have to make what amounts to an effective denial.

Specialists within SI

2.93 SI is staffed not only by direct and indirect tax investigators. In each office, there is also a team of qualified accountants whose role is to assist the investigators in understanding accountancy issues.

2.94 SI is also the home of a number of the liaison points for HMRC with other UK government agencies or overseas fiscal authorities. For example, SI is the HMRC home for all UK exchange of information requests with other foreign fiscal authorities with whom the UK has reciprocal arrangements via agreements such as the OECD tax convention, double taxation treaties, etc.

2.95 SI Liverpool was the home of the teams that were responsible for the *TMA 1970, s 20(8A)* success against financial institutions which supported the 2007 Offshore Disclosure Facility. They were also responsible for the *FA 2008, Sch 36, para 5* notices against financial institutions in support of the 2009 New Disclosure Opportunity. From October 2011 HMRC set up a new Offshore Coordination Unit (OCU). OCU will hold responsibility for coordinating HMRC's activities on offshore matters. It is not formally part of SI but will work very closely with it.

SI is also home to HMRC's liaison with the National Crime Agency (NCA) (previously the Serious Organised Crime Agency (SOCA)), specifically in terms of money laundering.

2.96 Where the NCA receives a suspicious activity report (SAR) and tax offences are the main offence, the relevant SAR will be passed to SI for consideration of a tax investigation. Where SI decides it will not mount its own investigation, the SAR may then be handed over to the local tax office.

Whilst the criminal work of HMRC is no longer housed within SI, SI is the civil liaison point for the Criminal Investigation Directorate.

Serious civil tax investigations into fraud and avoidance **2.97**

2.97 It is good practice to treat SI staff professionally and courteously at all times, whilst remaining firm and positive when representing a client. As experienced investigators, SI staff will not be put off track by an overly aggressive approach; SI inspectors are well trained, well supported and more than capable of holding their own in difficult and uncomfortable situations. Conversely, professionalism and experience will generally result in mutual respect and will be more likely to lead to a successful resolution of the COP9 investigation.

Further guidance on interacting with HMRC is contained within the Professional Conduct in Relation to Taxation issued by the main tax professional bodies in the UK.

Case study 2.1 – Disclosure and outcome

Mrs X asks to visit your office.

When she arrives she provides you with a copy of a letter she has received from HMRC stating that she is under investigation under COP9. The letter encloses a copy of the relevant code of practice.

Mrs X states that the letter refers to her having committed fraud. She does not feel this has been the case.

The first step is to spend some time with Mrs X to understand whether fraud may have actually been committed even though her views are that this has not been the case.

COP9 covers the tax affairs of the person under investigation effectively without time limit (with the taxation of any omission being limited to relevant assessing time limits under *TMA 1970, s 34* or *36*).

Mrs X states that she did do some writing work over a period of five years around four or five years ago. She was earning quite good money but didn't have time to register with the tax authorities and given the time that had lapsed forgot all about it.

This is the sort of thing that, should HMRC have become aware of it, could easily result in a COP9 investigation. (COP9 is generally reserved for more significant cases of tax fraud, so you would expect the potential omissions to be sizeable. Otherwise HMRC may conduct the investigation under a lesser code of practice, at least initially.)

Complete the outline disclosure within 60 days

Having identified what amounts to tax fraud, the next stage with the client wishing to take advantage of the protection afforded by COP9 is to complete the outline disclosure and return it to HMRC within 60 days. The time limit

2.97 *Serious civil tax investigations into fraud and avoidance*

is extremely important. If the deadline is missed HMRC will potentially treat the person as denying that there has been any fraud, running the risk that HMRC will conduct a criminal investigation.

It is also best, where there has been fraud, and where the client is happy to make a confession to that effect, to make this clear within the outline disclosure.

Having returned the outline disclosure within the time limit, there will be a short wait while HMRC reviews the outline disclosure to decide whether it is satisfied with the disclosure made, in part against the information HMRC already holds and the basis of why it opened the COP9 investigation in the first place.

You next meet Mrs X the following week and she confirms she was resident in the UK for the years in question and was also UK domiciled during that time. She provides the following information which you set down on the outline disclosure:

> 'I Mrs X would like to disclose to HMRC that over the period 2005 to 2010 I earned the following amounts from writing assignments I undertook as a journalist for the *Geneva Post*:
>
> These sums were not disclosed to HMRC and no Income Tax, National Insurance or VAT was paid.
>
> I would like to correct my tax position with HMRC and will be making a payment on account of the potential liabilities as soon as practicable.
>
> I would also like to disclose a bank account that I have in Geneva with Geneva Bank AG where the funds are retained.
>
> I would like to disclose interest which arose on that account as follows:
>
> | | |
> |---|---|
> | 2005 | £4,000 |
> | 2006 | £15,000 |
> | 2007 | £15,000 |
> | 2008 | £35,000 |
> | 2009 | £22,000' |

Acceptance by HMRC of the outline disclosure

Once HMRC has decided to accept the outline disclosure, it will write a letter to that effect.

The next stage may involve HMRC wanting to hold a meeting with the client. This would certainly have been the case under the CIF procedures, as HMRC would have wished to read the 'formal questions' to the client. With the replacement of CIF by CDF and the demise of the 'formal questions', the need for a meeting may be less important but there might still be very good reasons to hold a meeting.

If a payment on account has already been provided with the outline disclosure it should be considered at all times and more importantly that the potential meeting will be an essential part of demonstrating good cooperation.

Disclosure report

If there was nothing further to disclose it may have been possible to set out the tax liabilities within the outline disclosure or shortly thereafter. However, if there is a risk that that approach may not ensure a full and complete disclosure (perhaps because the client is not 100% sure of the background facts, etc) then it may be prudent to prepare a disclosure report.

If that approach is agreed, then a meeting between the adviser and HMRC to agree on the scope of the report is recommended.

Generally the contents of the report will include the following:

- background;
- further details of the original or subsequent disclosure;
- details of work done and documentation reviewed;
- executive summary of liabilities;
- certificates –
    - statement of personal assets and liabilities,
    - certificate of bank accounts operated,
    - certificate of credit card accounts operated,
    - certificate adopting the report by the client as his full and complete disclosure.

Conclusion

Once the disclosure report has been submitted to HMRC, ideally it will accept the disclosure and progress to settling the investigation.

There will be a period of correspondence, while HMRC and the advisers agree on the liability; tax, interest and any penalty.

Discussions may also have to take place to establish whether the client should be considered for the Naming of Deliberate Defaulters or Managing Deliberate Defaulters regimes.

Once agreement has been reached, HMRC may wish to meet with Mrs X to finalise matters, perhaps including the signing of a letter of offer and a certificate of full disclosure.

2.98 *Serious civil tax investigations into fraud and avoidance*

KEY POINTS

2.98 The following key points are intended as a guide for the practitioner dealing with an HMRC serious fraud investigation:

1. Satisfy yourself that you are competent to handle this work and that you have adequate professional indemnity insurance. The work can be highly contentious and the risks to clients are significant and numerous.

2. Try to understand, if possible, by communicating with HMRC, its concerns.

3. Discuss with the client any past fraudulent activities, or tax exposures, and areas where a disclosure might be considered.

4. Objectively assess the strengths and weaknesses of the client's position.

5. Provide your advice on the best way to proceed, if necessary consulting with a fraud specialist or legal adviser with experience of criminal matters.

Chapter 3

Tax fraud: criminal investigations and litigation – direct tax

Julian Hickey, Barrister
Temple Tax Chambers

SIGNPOSTS

- **Introduction** – Investigations involving tax evasion are often started in consequence of matters identified during a civil investigation. The range of tax offences for evasion is broad, and the policy of the government is to increase prosecutions. Following enactment of *Finance Act 2016* and *Criminal Finances Act 2017* review policies and procedures to ensure that no issues arise following enactment of new criminal offences relating to corporate failure to prevent tax evasion (See **3.1–3.38**.)

- **Criminal investigation and prosecution** – A criminal investigation must be conducted by HMRC in accordance with the statutory scheme prescribed under the *Police and Criminal Evidence Act 1984*, which provides for specific safeguards in favour of suspects. (See **3.39–3.68**.)

- **Search warrants and productions orders** – The *Police and Criminal Evidence Act 1984* requires HMRC to obtain a warrant for the search of premises, and under the Act specific materials are protected from seizure (e.g. items subject to legal privilege). If the grounds for issue of a warrant are not established, then the validity of the order can be challenged. (See **3.69–3.121**.)

- **Dealing with a dawn raid and interviews** – if a client is the object of a dawn raid then the adviser must ensure that the search warrant is valid, and that the search is conducted in accordance with the requirements of the *Police and Criminal Evidence Act 1984*. Often a dawn raid is accompanied by a suspect being arrested and interviewed under caution at a police station. The adviser must ensure that his client is legally represented and that the interview is conducted in compliance with the duties imposed on HMRC. (See **3.122–3.138**.)

3.1 *Tax fraud: criminal investigations and litigation – direct tax*

- **Anatomy of a criminal trial** – If a suspect is charged with a criminal offence it will be necessary for the defendant to be represented at all stages by a legal team throughout the judicial process. The Crown will be subject to disclosure obligations in relation to evidence, and the defence team will have to serve a defence statement. (See **3.139–3.158**.)
- **Use of information** – The sharing of information within different parts of HMRC is permitted and controlled by *Commissioners for Revenue and Customs Act 2005*, HMRC cannot disclose information which is held by them in connection with a function of the Revenue and Customs, but the obligation of confidentiality is subject to exceptions which include public interest disclosure or disclosure to a prosecuting authority. (See **3.159**.)
- **Money laundering** – It is well established that tax evasion is caught by the 'all crimes' provisions of the *Proceeds of Crime Act 2002*. The benefit derived from tax evasion is almost invariably subject to restraint and confiscation proceedings following a criminal conviction. Criminal money laundering charges normally form part of an indictment together with the charges relating to the substantive offence based upon tax evasion. Third parties who dishonestly assist first parties in the process of tax evasion are exposed to criminal sanctions for money laundering in addition to substantive offences. (See **3.160–3.234**.) The new *Money Laundering, Terrorist Financing and Transfer of Funds Regulations 2017* take effect from 26 June 2017 and these impose obligations on relevant persons and there is now an obligation on HMRC to maintain a register relating to certain trusts and the beneficiaries (see **3.170**).
- **Key points** – For a list of key points from this chapter, see **3.235**.

OVERVIEW

3.1 Tax evasion (also known as tax fraud) is a criminal offence under UK law. The distinction between tax avoidance, which is lawful, and tax evasion, which is not, is therefore of critical importance both to taxpayers and their advisers. The key ingredient in any criminal offence, unless it is a strict liability offence relating to tax, is 'dishonesty'. The issue of what constitutes dishonesty has been considered by the Court of Appeal in the leading case of *R v Ghosh* [1982] 3 WLR 110. In that case the court held that, in considering whether a person has been dishonest, the jury must ask itself two questions:

- Would the defendant be regarded as dishonest by the standards of reasonable and honest people? If not, the defendant should be acquitted.

- If the above is answered in the affirmative, the jury must then ask itself whether the defendant realised that his conduct would be regarded as dishonest by the ordinary standards of reasonable and honest people? The defendant should be convicted if he had this realisation. If not, he should be acquitted.

Unlike a civil appeal, the Crown bears the legal burden of proof, which means that the Crown must prove that the accused person has committed the offence, and the standard of proof is beyond reasonable doubt. The governing principle of English criminal law is that the onus lies upon the prosecution in a criminal trial to prove all the elements of the offence with which the accused is charged.

3.2 Tax offences apply to the range of taxes, such as income tax, corporation tax and VAT, and also failing to make proper returns for the purpose of evading National Insurance contributions, while making false claims for state benefits or for the payment of government subsidies can constitute the offence of obtaining property by deception. All these offences can be prosecuted and punished under common or statute law such as the *Theft Acts 1968* and *1978*, and the *Fraud Act 2006*.

3.3 Tax offences carry potentially lengthy custodial terms and/or unlimited fines. In addition, the courts can order the confiscation of the benefit obtained from the crime. The measure used to calculate the quantum of benefit is usually punitive.

3.4 The Chief Secretary to the Treasury has stated 'Tax evasion is a crime like any other. If people help a burglar, they are accomplices and criminals too. Now it will be the same for those that help tax evaders' (19 March 2015). In the context of tax evasion, the number of prosecutions for tax evasion/tax fraud against individuals has increased markedly, and the figures do not reflect situations where a criminal investigation has been started and then subsequently a prosecution has not be brought by the CPS:

Year	Total number of persons prosecuted for tax evasion as result of HMRC criminal investigations
2010/11	372
2011/12	501
2012/13	739
2013/14	880

(HM Treasury response to a written Parliamentary question to Chancellor of the Exchequer, February 2015.)

The year 2016 provides an illustrative flavour of HMRC prosecutions relating to tax fraud. This saw 679 individuals being convicted for their part in tax

3.5 *Tax fraud: criminal investigations and litigation – direct tax*

crimes, with sentences for 2016 totalling more than 730 years. HMRC published their ten most significant cases for that year, which included the following prosecutions:

- a group of film producers, accountants, financial advisers and investment bankers jailed for a total of 36 years for their part in a £2.2 million film tax scheme fraud;

- three men jailed for a total of 27 years for a film fraud disguised as a tax avoidance scheme, which was intended to defraud taxpayers of £100 million;

- three men – including an accountant and a construction firm boss jailed for a total of 19 years, after stealing £6.9 million in a payroll fraud to fund lavish lifestyles;

- a criminal gang from the South East jailed for a total of 19 years, after getting caught red-handed with bundles of 'dirty' cash, as part of £15 million made from selling alcohol illegally;

- two charity con-men, who faked charitable donations to fraudulently claim more than £5 million in Gift Aid repayments, were jailed for a combined total of 19 years;

- a gang of five men from the north of England, who used free public Wi-Fi to try to hide their £10 million cigarette smuggling ring, were jailed for a total of 16 and a half years;

- a criminal gang, including a father and son, caught running a fuel fraud, evading more than £900,000 in duty and taxes by running an illegal filling station in the West Midlands, jailed for a combined total of more than nine and half years;

- a London couple who masterminded a nationwide counterfeit tobacco production racket capable of robbing the taxpayer of £1 million a week, were jailed for a total of eight years;

- a cheating accountant who advised the media industry, was jailed for five years for a £6 million tax fraud;

- four fraudsters from Forfar, Stoke-on-Trent and Spain, ordered to repay more than £111 million in criminal profits. The men, who were part of an 18-strong criminal gang involved in a mobile phone VAT fraud, were sentenced between 2012 and 2014 to a total of 135 years in prison.

3.5 The majority of criminal investigations are initiated following the commencement of HMRC enquiries into the tax affairs of an individual and/or company, which have identified factual circumstances indicating that a criminal investigation should be undertaken. For these purposes a 'criminal investigation' means any process:

(i) for considering whether an offence has been committed;

(ii) for discovering by whom an offence has been committed; or

(iii) as a result of which an offence is alleged to have been committed.

(see the *Commissioners for Revenue and Customs Act 2005, s 21(2A)*).

TAX FRAUD: OFFENCES IN OVERVIEW

3.6 There is no single criminal offence of committing tax evasion, i.e. tax fraud. A prosecution may be brought in either the magistrates' court or Crown Court but this depends on the nature of the offence. The most serious offences will be heard in the Crown Court. A prosecution for tax fraud in respect of direct taxes may be made under a variety of different offences, which are summarised below:

- Conspiracy to defraud (common law offence).

  Triable on indictment only.

- *Fraud Act 2006, (s 1)*.

  Triable either way.

  Maximum: ten years' custody.

- False accounting: *Theft Act 1968, (s 17)*.

- Fraudulent evasion of income tax: *TMA 1970, (s 106A)*.

  Triable either way.

  Maximum: seven years' custody.

- Cheating the public revenue (common law).

  Triable on indictment only.

  Maximum: life imprisonment.

(Fraud, Bribery and Money Laundering Offences, Sentencing Council (effective 1 October 2014))

- Offences relating to offshore income, assets and activities (see **3.8** and following below).

  Maximum: on summary conviction up to 51 weeks imprisonment.

3.7 The principal offence for evading tax is cheating the public revenue, which is making a false statement tending to prejudice the Queen and the Public Revenue with the intent to defraud the Queen (see *R v Hudson* [1956] 2 QB 252, cited with approval in *R v Mavji* [1987] 1 WLR 1388, 1391). The offence includes the offence of causing to be delivered to an inspector of taxes

3.8 *Tax fraud: criminal investigations and litigation – direct tax*

accounts relating to the profits of a business that falsely and fraudulently state the profits to be less than they actually are. Any individual who aids, abets, counsels or procures the cheating the public revenue offence is also guilty of the actual offence (*Accessories and Abettors Act 1861, s 8*). It is also an offence to attempt the above offences, conspire to commit them, or to perform an act capable of encouraging or assisting the commission of one of these offences, intending to encourage or assist in the offence, or believing that the offence will be committed and that the act will encourage or assist its commission (*Serious Crime Act 2007, s 45*).

NEW CRIMINAL OFFENCES

Offence for failure to prevent facilitation of tax evasion

3.8   On 16 July 2015 the Government published a consultation on holding corporations criminally responsible *for failing to prevent* their agents from facilitating tax evasion. Prosecutions are normally brought against an individual and not a corporate entity, but this new offence changes the position so that a corporation can be the subject of a criminal sanction, by way of imposition of a fine. The legislation was introduced by the *Criminal Finances Act 2017* (CFA), which came into force with effect from 30 September 2017. The legislation makes the following activities an offence:

1. Failure to prevent facilitation of UK tax evasion offences (*CFA, s 45*), which provides that the offence is committed where:

    '(1) A relevant body (B) is guilty of an offence if a person associated with B commits a UK tax evasion facilitation offence when acting in the capacity of a person associated with B.'

    In this regard, a UK tax evasion facilitation offence means (*CFA, s 45(5)*):

    '(5) In this Part "UK tax evasion facilitation offence" means an offence under the law of any part of the United Kingdom consisting of—

    (a) being knowingly concerned in, or in taking steps with a view to, the fraudulent evasion of a tax by another person,

    (b) aiding, abetting, counselling or procuring the commission of a UK tax evasion offence, or

    (c) being involved art and part in the commission of an offence consisting of being knowingly concerned in, or in taking steps with a view to, the fraudulent evasion of a tax.'

Tax fraud: criminal investigations and litigation – direct tax 3.8

The definition of UK tax evasion offence in the context of UK tax evasion facilitation offence means (*CFA, s 45(4)*):

'(4) In this Part "UK tax evasion offence" means—

(a) an offence of cheating the public revenue, or

(b) an offence under the law of any part of the United Kingdom consisting of being knowingly concerned in, or in taking steps with a view to, the fraudulent evasion of a tax.'

2. Failure to prevent facilitation of foreign tax evasion offences (*CFA, s 46*), which provides that the offence is committed where:

'(1) A relevant body (B) is guilty of an offence if at any time—

(a) a person commits a foreign tax evasion facilitation offence when acting in the capacity of a person associated with B, and

(b) any of the conditions in subsection (2) is satisfied.

(2) The conditions are—

(a) that B is a body incorporated, or a partnership formed, under the law of any part of the United Kingdom;

(b) that B carries on business or part of a business in the United Kingdom;

(c) that any conduct constituting part of the foreign tax evasion facilitation offence takes place in the United Kingdom.'

For this purpose, the term 'foreign tax evasion facilitation offence' is defined as meaning (*CFA, s 46(6)*)

'… conduct which—

(a) amounts to an offence under the law of a foreign country,

(b) relates to the commission by another person of a foreign tax evasion offence under that law, and

(c) would, if the foreign tax evasion offence were a UK tax evasion offence, amount to a UK tax evasion facilitation offence (see section 45(5) and (6)).'

The scope of the new offences is explained in the Government's guidance (published 1 September 2017), which is available at: https://assets.publishing.service.gov.uk/government/uploads/system/uploads/attachment_data/file/672231/Tackling-tax-evasion-corporate-offences.pdf.

The Guidance provides the following overview of the offences (at para 1.3), stating that there are three stages that apply to both the domestic and foreign

3.8 *Tax fraud: criminal investigations and litigation – direct tax*

tax evasion facilitation offences (although it should be noted that there are additional requirements for the foreign offence set out above (including the 'dual criminality' requirement)):

> 'Stage one: criminal tax evasion by a taxpayer (either a legal or natural person) under the existing law' (for example an offence of cheating the public revenue, or fraudulently evading the liability to pay VAT);

> 'Stage two: the criminal facilitation of the tax evasion by an "associated person" of the relevant body acting in that capacity' (this is criminal facilitation of the offence by a person acting on behalf of the corporation, whether by taking steps with a view to: being knowingly concerned in; or aiding, abetting, counselling, or procuring the tax evasion by the taxpayer);

> 'Stage three: the relevant body failed to prevent its representative from committing the criminal facilitation act' (this is the corporation's failure to take reasonable steps to prevent those who acted on its behalf from committing the criminal act outlined at stage two.

Accordingly, as is apparent from the above for a corporation to be liable it is necessary for there to be criminal tax evasion by a person, and for that evasion to have been facilitated by a person acting on behalf of the company. The material defence for the corporation will be that it took reasonable steps to prevent the criminal facilitation. The legislation provides for the following defence for the corporate in respect of the UK tax evasion facilitation offence (*CFA, s 45*):

> '(2) It is a defence for B to prove that, when the UK tax evasion facilitation offence was committed—
>
> (a) B had in place such prevention procedures as it was reasonable in all the circumstances to expect B to have in place, or
>
> (b) it was not reasonable in all the circumstances to expect B to have any prevention procedures in place.
>
> (3) In subsection (2) "prevention procedures" means procedures designed to prevent persons acting in the capacity of a person associated with B from committing UK tax evasion facilitation offences.'

A similar defence applies for the purposes of the foreign tax facilitation offence (see *CFA, s 46*).

HMRC's document *Tackling tax evasion: Government guidance for the corporate offences of failure to prevent the criminal facilitation of tax evasion* (published 1 September 2017) contains guidance on the new offence, and the following aspects are particularly noteworthy in the context of the defence relating to taking reasonable steps to prevent criminal facilitation. In this regard, the document provides guidance on the type of approach that a corporation

Tax fraud: criminal investigations and litigation – direct tax **3.8**

should consider adopting in order to ensure it has appropriate procedures in place. The specific nature of any procedures adopted must be reasonable in all the circumstances, and this will be specific to each organisation. On this point the guidance states that the prevention procedures which should be adopted by a person must be informed by reference to six specific principles: (see Chapter 2 of the guidance):

'The Government considers that prevention procedures put in place by relevant bodies to prevent tax evasion from being committed on their behalf should be informed by the following six principles.

- Risk assessment.
- Proportionality of risk-based prevention procedures.
- Top level commitment.
- Due diligence.
- Communication (including training).
- Monitoring and review.'

The guidance sets out the following principles for each organisation to consider in order to determine whether it has reasonable procedures in place to prevent criminal facilitation:

- **'Principle 1 – Risk assessment**

    The relevant body assesses the nature and extent of its exposure to the risk of those who act in the capacity of a person associated with it criminally facilitating tax evasion offences. The risk assessment is documented and kept under review.'

- **'Principle 2 – Proportionality of risk-based prevention procedures**

    Reasonable procedures for a relevant body to adopt to prevent persons acting in the capacity of a person associated with it from criminally facilitating tax evasion will be proportionate to the risk the relevant body faces of persons associated with it committing tax evasion facilitation offences. This will depend on the nature, scale and complexity of the relevant body's activities. We recognise that the reasonableness of prevention procedures should take account of the level of control and supervision the organisation is able to exercise over a particular person acting on its behalf, and the proximity of the person to the relevant body. The new offences do not require relevant bodies to undertake excessively burdensome procedures in order to eradicate all risk, but they do demand more than mere lip-service to preventing the criminal facilitation of tax evasion.'

- **'Principles 3 – Top level commitment**

    The top-level management of a relevant body should be committed to preventing persons acting in the capacity of a person associated with

3.9 *Tax fraud: criminal investigations and litigation – direct tax*

it from engaging in criminal facilitation of tax evasion. They should foster a culture within the relevant body in which activity intended to facilitate tax evasion is never acceptable.'

- **'Principle 4 – Due diligence**

The organisation applies due diligence procedures, taking an appropriate and risk-based approach, in respect of persons who perform or will perform services on behalf of the organisation, in order to mitigate identified risks.'

- **'Principle 5 – Communication (including training)**

The organisation seeks to ensure that its prevention policies and procedures are communicated, embedded and understood throughout the organisation, through internal and external communication, including training. This is proportionate to the risk to which the organisation assesses that it is exposed.'

- **'Principle 6 – Monitoring and review**

The organisation monitors and reviews its preventative procedures and makes improvements where necessary.'

Offences for failure to give notice of being chargeable to tax, of failing to deliver a return, of making an inaccurate return

3.9 Strict liability offences apply for failing to declare taxable offshore income and gains over a threshold amount to be defined in regulations on a per tax year basis (imposed by *TMA 1970, ss 106B–106H*). The penalties for conviction are an unlimited fine in England and Wales and/or a custodial sentence of up to six months for offences committed before the *Criminal Justice Act 2003, s 281(5)* comes into force (once it is brought into force the custodial sentence increases to 51 weeks thereafter). A fine not exceeding level 5 on the standard scale can be imposed in Scotland or Northern Ireland and/or a custodial sentence of no more than 6 months.

These offences were introduced by *Finance Act 2016* in consequence of government consultation *Tackling Offshore Tax Evasion: A New Criminal Offence for Offshore Evaders* (published on 16 July 2015). The purpose of the new criminal offence is to make prosecution of offshore evaders easier. The offences apply for the purposes of income tax and capital gains tax. The provisions came into force on 6 April 2017 and subsequent tax years. The offence does not apply retrospectively.

The reference to strict liability means that the state of mind of the defendant is irrelevant to guilt. In this regard, it is intended that the offence applies only to income tax and capital gains tax, to all offshore income and gains, only if a minimum threshold amount is met, and that there should be an option for a prison sentence of up to six months. The offences are committed in three possible ways (in each case where this leads to an understatement or underpayment of tax relating to relevant offshore income, assets or activities), namely:

(i) Failing to notify HMRC of chargeability to tax as required by *TMA, s 7 (TMA 1970, s 106B)*. There is a defence to the offence if the person accused proves they had a reasonable excuse for failing to notify as required;

(ii) Failing to file a return when required by a notice under *TMA, s 8* and an accurate return would have shown income or capital gains tax chargeable by reference to offshore income, assets or activities, and that amount of tax exceeds the threshold amount *(TMA 1970, s 106C)*. There is a defence to the offence if the person proves they had a reasonable excuse for failing to deliver the tax return; and

(iii) Filing an inaccurate return *(TMA 1970, s 106D)*. There is a defence to the offence if the person proves they took reasonable care to ensure that the return was correct.

The new offences apply to 'offshore income, assets or activities', which is defined as meaning *(TMA 1970, s 106F(4))*:

(a) income arising from a source in a territory outside the UK;

(b) assets situated or held in a territory outside the UK; or

(c) activities carried on wholly or mainly in a territory outside the UK.

In addition to the defences provided by *FA 2016 (TMA 1970 ss 106B–106D)*, *FA 2016* confers on the Treasury a power to issue regulations specifying further circumstances when a person will not be guilty of the new offences. By virtue of the new s 106H, the regulations may make different provisions for different cases and make other consequential and transitional provisions.

The financial threshold for the offences to be in issue must not be less than £25,000 (see *SI 2017/970*). Regulations may also set out how to calculate whether the threshold has been exceeded for the purposes of the offences.

3.10 *FA 2016* also contains, in addition to the new criminal offences, further measures designed to deter tax evasion. These measures are:

- civil penalties for offshore tax evaders *(FA 2016, s 163, Sch 21)*: increased civil penalties for deliberate offshore tax evasion, including the introduction of a new penalty linked to the value of the asset on which tax was evaded and increased public naming of tax evaders *(FA 2016, ss 164, 165)*;

3.11 *Tax fraud: criminal investigations and litigation – direct tax*

- civil penalties for those who enable offshore evasion (*FA 2016, s 162*) new civil penalties for those who enable offshore tax evasion, including public naming of those who have enabled the evasion.

The new civil penalty linked to the value of the asset on which tax was evaded (*FA 2016, s 165*) applies for the purposes of income tax, capital gains tax and inheritance tax. The penalty will only apply if a penalty for an inaccuracy in a document, failure to notify or failure to submit a return has been levied in respect of an offshore matter or transfer, and the behaviour that led to the penalty was deliberate, or deliberate and concealed, and the tax or liability underpaid or understated is over a threshold amount.

GOVERNMENT POLICY

3.11 The expressed aim of the government is to secure the highest level of compliance with the law and regulations governing direct and indirect taxes and other regimes for which it is responsible. Criminal investigation, with a view to prosecution by the Specialist Fraud Division of the Crown Prosecution Service in England and Wales – or the Crown Office and Procurator Fiscal Service in Scotland, or the Public Prosecution Service for Northern Ireland – is an important part of HMRC's overall enforcement strategy.

3.12 Traditionally, limited manpower resources, and the time required to bring criminal investigations to fruition, mean that HMRC's policy is to deal with fraud by use of the cost effective Code of Practice 9 procedure (investigations where HMRC suspects tax fraud), wherever appropriate. Criminal investigation has therefore been reserved for cases where HMRC needs to send a strong deterrent message or where the conduct involved is such that only a criminal sanction is appropriate. However, in recent years, the government has allocated more resources to identify and deal with tax evasion cases being brought before the criminal courts. Government figures indicate an additional 200 criminal investigators were recruited to increase the number of people prosecuted for tax evasion from 165 in 2010 to 2011, to 565 in 2012 to 2013, and to 1,165 in 2014 to 2015 (Policy paper, '2010 to 2015 Government Policy: Tax Evasion and Avoidance', 8 May 2015). There can be little doubt that the trend towards increasing use of criminal prosecutions will continue.

3.13 The tax gap – the difference between the amount HMRC should collect if everyone did what was required of them by law and the amount actually collected – was estimated by HMRC in its most recent annual report to have been £33 billion, which is 5.7% of tax liabilities in 2016/17 (*Measuring Tax Gaps*, 2018 edition). For 2016/17, tax evasion accounted for £5.3 billion, the hidden economy £3.2 billion and criminal attacks against the revenue gathering system accounted for £5.4 billion of the gap.

Tax fraud: criminal investigations and litigation – direct tax 3.16

3.14 There is no question that HMRC faces significant problems in closing the gap which unquestionably exists and it was given more than £150 million of additional investment in the December 2013 Autumn Statement to spend over the next three years to tackle avoidance and evasion. This is in addition to £917 million of efficiency savings which the Chancellor agreed should be re-invested over the four-year period from 2012/13 into tackling evasion, avoidance and criminal attacks on the revenue gathering system. The positive outcomes of HMRC's compliance activities in 2012/13 include cash collected or protected amounting to £20.7 billion and £8.8 billion in the first half of 2013/14 – the best ever performance at that point in the fiscal year. 'Revenue protected' in this context means illicit goods seized, erroneous payments prevented, future non-compliance deterred and avoidance loopholes plugged. In the July 2015 Budget the Chancellor announced:

> 'We're boosting HMRC's capacity with three quarters of a billion pounds of investment to go after tax fraud, offshore trusts and the businesses of the hidden economy, tripling the number of wealthy evaders they pursue for prosecution – raising £7.2 billion in extra tax.'

Since 2007, HMRC has collected over £1 billion from disclosures under various campaigns and initiatives, some of which targeted assets hidden offshore.

3.15 In addition, in January 2013, an agreement with Switzerland, aimed at untaxed funds held in banks there, came into effect and led to an upfront payment of £342 million to the Exchequer. HMRC forecasts that £4.4 billion will be recovered over the next three years in respect of past liabilities, either directly from individuals or through the levy by the Swiss banks. The Liechtenstein Disclosure Facility, which ended in 2016, has (to March 2016) yielded over £1.2 billion. On 31 December 2015 all offshore facilities closed. Up to that date, HMRC gave incentives to encourage people to come forward and clear up their tax affairs. A new Worldwide Disclosure Facility (WDF) opened on 5 September 2016. However, after 30 September 2018 new sanctions will come into effect in respect of offshore non-compliance. Anyone who wishes to disclose a UK tax liability that relates wholly or in part to an offshore issue is eligible to use the WDF under the terms, namely: (a) to make a full disclosure of all previously undisclosed UK tax liabilities within 90 days of notifying an intention to disclose, (b) calculate interest and penalties due based on the existing legislation. Use of the WDF may not result in a reduction of penalties, where the person has failed to make use of prior disclosure facilities.

3.16 The target for prosecutions for 2013/14 was 765 and for 2014/15 it was 1,165. There are no current statistics but the targets are likely to be substantially similar. The total amount of additional receipts and revenue loss prevented as a result of these criminal investigations in 2012/13 was in excess of £1 billion. HMRC provides no breakdown of these figures but information

3.17 *Tax fraud: criminal investigations and litigation – direct tax*

published elsewhere indicates that there were ten criminal investigations in the wake of the New Disclosure Opportunity (relating to offshore bank accounts) and six following the disclosure campaign aimed at medical professionals.

3.17 With a view to speeding up the criminal investigation process, the government gave the Revenue the power to require the production of documents under the authority of an order from a circuit judge (in England and Wales) (*TMA 1970, s 20BA*). Furthermore, following the report by Lord Grabiner QC entitled *The Informal Economy* published in March 2000, the government introduced the statutory offence of evading income tax. This is contained in *FA 2000, s 144* which came into force on 1 January 2001. The offence may be tried either summarily in the magistrates' court or on indictment in the Crown Court (and in the appropriate courts in Scotland and Northern Ireland).

3.18 The power (now in *TMA 1970, s 106A*) was originally intended to facilitate joint prosecutions of those who defraud the Benefits Agency and the Revenue at the same time, for example where wages are paid to employees 'cash in hand' to avoid income tax deductions, and then suppressed in claims to income-related benefits.

3.19 In addition, HMRC has authority to publicly name tax defaulters where there is more than £25,000 of tax at risk and to put known tax evaders under close scrutiny for five years (*FA 2009, s 94*).

TAX PROSECUTION: OFFENDERS' PERSPECTIVE

3.20 In September 2015 HMRC published a report, which was produced by the NatCen Social Research, entitled 'HMRC Report 396: Qualitative Research with People Convicted of Tax Evasion' ('the Report'). The Report's primary conclusions based on interviews with participants identified the following motivating factors for those committing tax evasion (see para 5.1):

- personal financial gain;
- to support their business and help keep it afloat at a time of financial difficulty;
- altruism; and
- unknowingly committing tax evasion by following the advice of others (accountants or co-defendants).

3.21 The Report also identified the following perceptions from offenders:

'While not a reason for tax evasion as such, views of tax and tax compliance appeared to facilitate some participants' offending. A key perception was that the tax system in the UK is inherently unfair, with large companies

Tax fraud: criminal investigations and litigation – direct tax **3.25**

and wealthy celebrities allowed to avoid tax with no repercussions. ... Tax evasion being seen as common place in some participants' industries either facilitated offending or allowed participants to rationalise their offending after the event.' (para 5.1)

3.22 It is interesting to note that some participants in the research claimed to be unaware of their offending and those who described evading tax to support their business said they would not reoffend. However, the reason for stating that they would not reoffend was not because the prosecution acted as a specific deterrent, 'but because they would not have reoffended anyway as, in their words, they were not a "criminal"'. (see para. 5.4 of the Report). The research tended to 'suggest that the experience of prosecution was less effective as a deterrent for some participants who had evaded tax for personal financial gain'. However, the principal effect of a prosecution was on the immediate family of the offender, and the Report commented that HMRC should emphasise this as a potential deterrent. The Report comments:

> 'one of the most striking impacts of the prosecution was on participants' relationships with family and friends, and on the health and wellbeing of their loved ones. Given this and to encourage deterrence, it might be worthwhile for HMRC to highlight these impacts in future communication.' (para. 5.4)

CIVIL INVESTIGATION OF SUSPECTED TAX FRAUD

3.23 HMRC's civil investigation unit is Specialist Investigations (SI), which investigates tax avoidance and cases of suspected tax fraud involving both direct and indirect taxes. Cases of suspected tax fraud are investigated under Code of Practice 9 (COP9) (June 2014) using the Contractual Disclosure Facility (CDF) procedure initiated on 31 January 2012. COP9 is also used by SI in investigating perceived avoidance schemes which it suspects have transgressed the boundary into fraud.

3.24 Whereas the COP9 regime as previously revised in September 2005 had appeared to reduce the threat of criminal investigation, the new CDF process goes some way to redress the balance by emphasising the significant possibility of criminal action where the taxpayer fails to make a full disclosure of the tax frauds he has committed or where he makes materially false or misleading statements or provides materially false documents in the course of an investigation.

3.25 Under the CDF procedure the taxpayer has 60 days from being offered to enter into a contract, in accordance with which he will agree to:
- give HMRC details of tax deliberately evaded, within 60 calendar days from receipt of the CDF letter;

3.26 *Tax fraud: criminal investigations and litigation – direct tax*

- sign a statement to say accurate and complete details of the tax fraud have been provided;
- pay all taxes, interest and penalties due; and
- stop any fraud immediately.

In return HMRC will agree not to criminally investigate the fraud disclosed in the CDF contract.

HMRC emphasises that a formal written denial of tax fraud or a complete failure to co-operate in the process may lead to a criminal investigation.

3.26 It should be noted that, although taxpayers have historically taken comfort from the fact that HMRC cannot accept a monetary settlement and institute criminal proceedings, the case of *R v W* [1998] STC 550 (CA) established that a pecuniary settlement negotiated by the Revenue in relation to tax liability did not preclude the Crown Prosecution Service (CPS) from instituting proceedings for false accounting. The reasoning of the court in that case was that one part of the Crown does not bind another. In this case the charge of false accounting was severed from an indictment alleging conspiracy to defraud and was ordered to be tried first. The authors understand that the alleged false accounting arose solely in relation to a scheme designed to facilitate tax evasion and was not part of separate alleged criminal conduct by the defendants which was the subject of the conspiracy counts.

3.27 The decision has potentially serious ramifications. Say, for reasons of public interest, the CPS chose to institute proceedings against a taxpayer who had already reached a monetary settlement with the Revenue. If the CPS was able to gain access to statements and documents produced in connection with the tax investigation, it might for example have little difficulty in bringing a successful prosecution for non-tax-related predicate offences or money laundering. In theory, this could lead to cases where, as a result of a monetary settlement reached with HMRC in respect of tax evasion, sufficient admissible evidence is generated to enable, for example, a money laundering charge to be brought by the CPS (or any other prosecuting authority such as the Serious Fraud Office), where the predicate crime upon which the money laundering charge is based was related to tax evasion. Thus, a tax evader may find that having paid a sizeable amount of tax, interest and penalties to HMRC, he is charged with false accounting under the *Theft Act 1968, s 17* and a money laundering offence under *POCA 2002*. A money laundering charge would mean that the taxpayer is faced with the possibility of 14 years' imprisonment and/or an unlimited fine (interestingly, the charge of false accounting carries a maximum sentence of only seven years).

PROSECUTION POLICY

3.28 As discussed above not all criminal activity will result in a prosecution because HMRC will seek to resolve the position by use of COP8. However, HMRC are clear as to the circumstances in which they will prosecute. The Board of Inland Revenue's approach to prosecution was clearly stated in a paper entitled 'Prosecution Policy' published in September 1980 in which it was said:

> 'In the main ... the Department deals with the tax evader not by prosecution but by money penalties graded according to the gravity of the offence ... criminal prosecution for tax offences is undertaken only in a small minority of ... the more serious cases of fraud.'

3.29 Underlying this policy of selectivity is a philosophy of deterrence. This was expressed in the same paper thus:

> 'to prosecute in some examples of all classes of tax fraud. This policy is essential because it is the possibility of prosecution which prevents the spread of tax fraud to unacceptable limits.'

This ethos is still reflected in HMRC's approach to criminal investigations.

3.30 The Board of Inland Revenue's report for the year to 31 March 1999 reaffirmed the intention to continue the policy of selective prosecution. To date, challenges to this approach under the *Human Rights Act 1998* have been largely unsuccessful.

3.31 It is important to note that the offences which constitute tax evasion may also constitute money laundering offences. Increasingly, HMRC is using the powers contained in the *Criminal Justice Act 1988* to confiscate assets which are deemed to be the proceeds of criminal conduct. In addition, *POCA 2002* introduced radical new powers to deprive criminals of their assets.

3.32 While HMRC is responsible for investigating suspected criminality in relation to tax, the decision as to whether or not to prosecute in England and Wales has since 1 January 2010 been made by the Crown Prosecution Service. In Northern Ireland this function is fulfilled by the Public Prosecution Service for Northern Ireland and in Scotland by the Crown Office and the Procurator Fiscal Service.

FACTORS SUGGESTING THE LIKELIHOOD OF CRIMINAL INVESTIGATION

3.33 Beginning with their evidence in 1983 to the Committee on enforcement powers of the Revenue Departments (the Keith Committee),

3.34 *Tax fraud: criminal investigations and litigation – direct tax*

HMRC has set out the indices of serious fraud regarded as heinous, the presence of any one of which in a case would make the possibility of prosecution more likely. These have been altered and modified over the years as the threats to the tax-gathering system have changed.

3.34 For example, in recent years significant losses were sustained as a result of large scale frauds on the tax system perpetrated by organised criminal gangs. To put this into perspective HMRC estimates that for 2016/17 tax evasion accounted for £5.3 billion.

With these criminal attacks in mind HMRC has created specialist cybercrime teams to protect the exchequer from cyber fraud perpetrated by organised criminals.

3.35 HMRC reserves the right to conduct a criminal investigation in *any* case and to carry out these investigations across a range of offences and in all the areas for which it has responsibility. When considering whether a case should be investigated under the CDF procedure or should be the subject of a criminal investigation, one important factor to be considered will be whether the taxpayer has made a complete and unprompted disclosure of the offences committed.

Professional advisers should have this in mind at all times. Apart from prosecution considerations, an unprompted, voluntary disclosure will attract significant mitigation of any civil penalties.

3.36 Clearly, HMRC simply does not have the resources to investigate with a view to prosecution more than a minority of tax fraudsters, and the following are examples of the sorts of circumstances which might lead HMRC to consider using the most potent weapon at its disposal (based on HMRC's Criminal Investigation Policy, published on 6 November 2011):

- cases of organised criminal gangs attacking the tax system or systematic frauds where losses represent a serious threat to the tax base, including conspiracy;

- where an individual holds a position of trust or responsibility. Where the suspected offender is a professional tax adviser (eg an accountant or a solicitor) HMRC takes a particularly stringent view. A dishonest accountant is particularly reprehensible in HMRC's eyes, being a source of 'infection' who is likely to have assisted a number of clients in the commission of serious fraud. However, the Board will not necessarily prosecute all the adviser's clients who may have been involved in fraudulent activities along with their adviser. This principle was tested in an application for judicial review *R v IRC, ex p Mead* [1992] STC 482. In its judgment, the High Court upheld the Board's right to be selective in prosecuting persons alleged to have committed serious fraud.

Tax fraud: criminal investigations and litigation – direct tax **3.36**

From 1 April 2013, HMRC has had the power to investigate dishonest conduct by tax agents, charge civil penalties ranging from £5,000 to £50,000 and to publish the details of tax agents who have acted dishonestly. As part of that process HMRC will ask for access to working papers.

Another case which highlights the dangers of prosecution for professional advisers is *R v Charlton* [1996] STC 1418. One of the defendants convicted on two counts of cheating the Revenue, for which he served a term in prison, was a barrister who had advised a corporate client on tax avoidance arrangements involving operations in a low-tax jurisdiction. In the case of *R v Chipping*, a UK solicitor and a Jersey-resident accountant were convicted of conspiracy to cheat the public revenue and received custodial sentences;

- where materially false statements are made or materially false documents are provided in the course of a civil investigation. It is this determination which underpins the COP9 procedure introduced in January 2012. In 1987, the case of *R v Piggott* (widely reported in the press) culminated in a former British champion jockey receiving a three-year term of imprisonment after pleading guilty to serious tax fraud charges. One of the aggravating features of the case had been that the defendant had undergone two previous tax investigations, at the conclusion of which he had signed false statements of assets;

- where, pursuing an avoidance scheme, reliance is placed on a false or altered document or such reliance or material facts are misrepresented to enhance the credibility of a scheme. This underlines the fact that although an avoidance scheme would normally be pursued under Code of Practice 8 (cases where serious fraud is not suspected), HMRC will not be inhibited from changing tack and initiating a prosecution in appropriate circumstances.

In a speech made in January 2013 the then Director of Public Prosecutions, Keir Starmer QC, identified a new category of criminal offender: 'those who devise and operate sophisticated schemes to abuse direct tax regimes: dishonest tax avoidance schemes'. In January 2014, HMRC established the Counter-Avoidance Directorate to lead a more focused attack on avoidance;

- where deliberate concealment, deception, conspiracy or corruption is suspected. The siphoning off of profits into an offshore bank account in a false name would be one such example;

- cases involving the use of false or forged documents. Modern technology has brought this particular fraud within easy reach of anyone with access to a computer and printer. The use of false invoices or the keeping of a second set of books is likely to lead HMRC to at least consider applying the ultimate sanction;

3.37 *Tax fraud: criminal investigations and litigation – direct tax*

- cases involving importation or exportation breaching prohibitions and restrictions;
- cases involving money laundering with particular focus on advisers, accountants, solicitors and others acting in a professional capacity that provide the means to put tainted money out of reach of law enforcement;
- where the perpetrator has committed previous offences, or there is a repeated course of unlawful conduct or previous civil action;
- cases involving theft, or the misuse or unlawful destruction of HMRC documents;
- where there is evidence of assault on, or threats to, or the impersonation of HMRC officials;
- where there is a link to suspected wider criminality, whether domestic or international, involving offences not under the administration of HMRC.

HMRC's published policy views are available at: www.gov.uk/government/publications/criminal-investigation/hmrc-criminal-investigation-policy.

3.37 HMRC has made absolutely clear its unbending attitude to certain offences which it will almost always seek to prosecute rather than offer the COP9 approach. These are:

- VAT missing trader intra-community (MTIC) fraud – generally involving the importation and onward sale of small high-value components such as mobile phones and computer chips;
- VAT bogus registration repayment fraud;
- organised tax credit fraud.

3.38 On the other hand HMRC makes it clear that in considering whether a case should be investigated under the COP9 procedure or be the subject of a criminal investigation, an important factor taken into account will be whether the taxpayer has made a complete and unprompted disclosure of the offences committed.

HMRC ORGANISATION FOR CRIMINAL INVESTIGATION

3.39 HMRC Criminal Division has three directorates in which staff are authorised to use criminal investigation powers:

- Criminal Investigation including Internal Governance is responsible for all of the department's criminal investigations. Internal Governance is responsible for undertaking investigations into potentially serious

Tax fraud: criminal investigations and litigation – direct tax **3.42**

disciplinary and criminal allegations involving HMRC staff. Following the creation of HMRC, responsibility for dealing with drug trafficking and associated criminal finance and organised immigration crime, was transferred, along with a large number of Customs and Excise investigators, to the Serious Organised Crime Agency.

- Specialist Investigations – Road Fuel Testing is responsible for the detection and disruption of the illicit supply, distribution, sale, storage and misuse of fuel for road vehicles.

- Risk and Intelligence Service – Criminal Intelligence Group is responsible for profiling and intelligence work. It uses criminal investigation powers to develop cases and highlight areas of potential criminal activity.

3.40 Within HMRC, Criminal and Enforcement Policy (CEP) has oversight of the criminal legislation and powers that are at HMRC's disposal. The application of these powers is subject to review and assurance by an Enforcement and Compliance Assurance Team (ECAT).

3.41 In addition, each of the directorates using criminal powers maintains professional standards functions that oversee management assurance of these powers. Together CEP, ECAT and directorate standards functions work to ensure compliance with the many safeguards that are built into the legislation and associated Codes of Practice.

OVERVIEW OF A CRIMINAL INVESTIGATION AND PROSECUTION

3.42 A criminal investigation will typically arise out of a pre-existing HMRC civil tax enquiry, since factual circumstances examined during an enquiry are likely to identify to a potential criminal offence. A typical investigation will involve the responsible officers undertaking a review and evaluation of the documents and other information that has already been obtained, including working with specialists (such as accountants and lawyers) to understand the particular issues involved. In the early stages of a tax related fraud investigation it is likely that there will be a suspect who is thought to have committed an offence (ie the individual under civil investigation). The criminal investigating officers will have to determine whether it is necessary to undertake a search of premises for the purpose of gathering information to help their investigation, interview witnesses and whether there is sufficient material to justify interviewing the suspect under caution. As discussed below, the *Police and Criminal Evidence Act 1984* (*PACE 1984*) and its accompanying codes of practice establish the powers of investigating officers to combat crimes whilst protecting the rights of the public. These powers,

3.43 *Tax fraud: criminal investigations and litigation – direct tax*

with modifications, are extended to HMRC by *PACE 1984* (Application to Revenue and Customs) Order 2007, SI 2007/3175 ('the PACE Regulations'). This means that specific obligations are imposed on an investigating officer in order to search premises and question a suspect. For example, where premises are searched, some forms of material are protected (such as that covered by legal professional privilege). Where there is a failure to meet the requirements of *PACE 1984* it may result in the contents of a suspect's statement being ruled inadmissible at trial (see *s 78*).

3.43 Where a suspect is to be interviewed, Guidance 10A of the Codes of Practice to PACE 1984 requires there to be some reasonable, objective grounds, based on known facts or information, which are relevant to the likelihood that the offence has been committed and the person to be questioned committed it. The interview must occur at a police station, and must comply with Codes C and E of *PACE 1984*. The interview will be recorded (normally on two tapes, one of which is sealed at the end of the interview in the presence of the suspect). At the start of the interview the suspect will be cautioned. The suspect has the right to remain silent and he cannot be compelled to answer questions. However, if the suspect exercises his right to silence but then subsequently raises facts as part of his defence which could have been mentioned during the interview, the court may draw an 'adverse inference' from the silence (under the *Criminal Justice and Public Order Act 1994, s 34*). Where an individual is held at a police station, he cannot be kept in police detention for more than 24 hours without being charged (authorisation for continued detention is tightly controlled under *s 46*). A person arrested and held in custody in a police station or other premises is entitled to consult a solicitor privately at any time (*PACE 1984, s 58*).

3.44 The decision pattern following an arrest is whether the suspect should be charged. The options available to the custody officer are (*PACE 1984, s 37*):

(a)   release without charge;

(b)   release without charge but on bail whilst further enquiries are made;

(c)   release the suspect without charge but on bail for the purpose of enabling the CPS to make a decision on charges; or

(d)   charge the suspect.

3.45 For tax fraud it will be the CPS who decides whether or not to charge the suspect. Once a suspect has been charged no further interviews can be carried out with the suspect by the investigating officers (subject to certain limitations).

3.46 Once charged the defendant's first court appearance will be before the magistrates' court. If the defendant has been charged with an indictable offence (eg conspiracy to defraud or cheat the public revenue) then the magistrates will immediately send the case to the Crown Court for trial. If the defendant is charged with an either way offence then either the defendant may enter:

(a) a guilty plea with the result that the magistrates must determine whether they or the Crown Court should pass sentence due to the seriousness of the offence;

(b) a not guilty plea with the result that the magistrates must determine whether the defendant is tried before them or in the Crown Court.

3.47 The allocation of the court will depend on a variety of factors, including the seriousness of the offence and whether if convicted the court will have appropriate sentencing powers. An overview of the criminal trial process is provided in at **3.139**.

HMRC'S CRIMINAL INVESTIGATION POWERS AND SAFEGUARDS

3.48 The creation of the new department in 2005 brought into sharp focus the disparity between the respective powers of the former Inland Revenue and Customs and Excise criminal investigators. The latter had historically always had significantly greater powers than their counterparts and it is understandable that this situation could not be allowed to continue. Following an extensive consultation process, *FA 2007* enacted a number of amendments to *PACE 1984* aligning the powers of criminal investigators across the department. These mainly affected the powers of HMRC investigators to:

- apply for production orders requiring information to be produced. Revenue investigators had previously relied solely on *TMA 1970, s 20BA*, which remains on the statute book. However, HMRC is now required to use *PACE 1984, Sch 1, para 4* if it requires the production of 'special procedure material' (see **3.82** and **3.89** *et seq*);

- apply for search warrants. *TMA 1970, s 20C* has been repealed and all HMRC investigators will now normally rely on *PACE 1984, s 8 or Sch 1, para 12* or, in certain circumstances, the Serious Organised *Crime and Police Act 2005 (SOCPA 2005), s 66*;

- make arrests. Revenue investigators had previously relied on the presence of police officers to carry out this function on their behalf;

- search suspects and premises following arrest.

3.49 In Northern Ireland these powers derive from the Police and Criminal Evidence (Northern Ireland) Order 1989, SI 1989/1341 which has also been amended. *PACE 1984* does not apply in Scotland, but similar powers have been introduced for HMRC investigators there (see **3.53–3.54**). *FA 2007* amended

3.50 *Tax fraud: criminal investigations and litigation – direct tax*

PACE 1984 and the PACE (Northern Ireland) Order so that they can be used for all HMRC criminal investigations, but there are a small number of former Inland Revenue functions for which *PACE 1984* powers are not available. The advantage of using *PACE 1984* is that it provides a set of powers that are designed for use by law enforcement agencies. It means that tax crime is tackled in the same way as any other crime.

PACE 1984

3.50 *PACE 1984* and its accompanying Codes of Practice establish the powers of the police to combat crimes whilst protecting the rights of the public. These powers, with modifications, are extended to HMRC by the PACE Regulations. Broadly, the powers available in respect of relevant investigations conducted by officers of Revenue and Customs are:

- to enter and search premises provided this is authorised by a warrant granted by a magistrate (*s 8*), and to seize items such as computers (*s 20*);
- to enter and search any premises for the purpose of arresting a person for an indictable offence (*s 17*);
- to enter and search any premises occupied or controlled by a person who is under arrest for an indictable offence (*s 18*);
- if already on the premises lawfully, to seize anything that the officer has reasonable grounds for believing –
    - was obtained in consequence of the commission of an offence; or
    - is evidence in relation to an offence that the officer is investigating; and is necessary to seize it to prevent it being lost (*s 19*);
- to seize anything that is on the premises if the officer has reasonable grounds for believing –
    - that it has been obtained in consequence of the commission of an offence, and
    - that it is necessary to seize it in order to prevent it being concealed, lost, damaged, altered or destroyed, provided that the officer is lawfully on the premises (*s 19*),

    and to retain anything which has been seized under this power 'for so long as is necessary in all the circumstances' (*s 22(2)*);
- to arrest without a warrant if the officer has reasonable grounds for suspecting that an offence has been committed, in which case he may arrest without a warrant anyone whom he has reasonable grounds to suspect of being guilty of it (*s 24(2)*);

- to search an arrested person in any case where the person to be searched has been arrested at a place other than a police station, if the constable has reasonable grounds for believing that the arrested person may present a danger to himself or others (*s 32*).

3.51 Various safeguards are included in *PACE 1984* such as in respect of the requirements for obtaining a warrant, and the method of execution of the warrant (see discussion below at **3.66** *et seq*). There are also limits on the type of material that can be obtained in the execution of a warrant, for example items subject to legal privilege.

3.52 Not all of the powers in *PACE 1984* are made available to HMRC. For example, HMRC does not have the power to take fingerprints, charge or bail suspects. This has to be done by the police. Some of the powers in *PACE 1984* are modified for HMRC. For example, a search warrant may allow HMRC to search persons found on premises without the need for an arrest. This allows HMRC to search a bookkeeper, who is not considered a suspect, but who may have evidence in a briefcase or laptop when a company's premises are searched (see the PACE Regulations, art 18).

3.53 *PACE 1984* does not apply in Scotland. *FA 2007* introduced a special set of powers that apply in Scotland within the *Criminal Law (Consolidation) (Scotland) Act 1995* and the *Criminal Procedure (Scotland) Act 1995*. These powers address the same areas as *PACE 1984*.

3.54 Following the Cider Review to assess the rights and safeguards available to persons arrested by the police, with particular reference to evidence obtained during police interviews where the suspect had no access to a lawyer, the *Criminal Procedure (Legal Assistance Detention and Appeals) (Scotland) Act 2010* was introduced, which is only applicable to the police. However, HMRC has introduced the Criminal Procedure (Legal Assistance, Detention and Appeals) (Scotland) Act 2010 (Consequential Provisions) Order 2011, SI 2011/1739, to extend these rights and safeguards to suspects arrested for tax offences.

3.55 The criminal investigation powers can only be used by officers who are authorised to use them (ie by HMRC officers who have been appropriately trained and are engaged on operational duties in the various Directorates mentioned above). *PACE 1984* stipulates that certain powers can be exercised only by police officers of a particular rank. These ranks are converted to HMRC grades of an equivalent authority (see the PACE Regulations, Sch 2, Pt 2):

- Sergeant (Officer).
- Inspector (Higher Officer).

3.56 *Tax fraud: criminal investigations and litigation – direct tax*

- Chief Inspector (Higher Officer).
- Superintendent (Senior Officer).

3.56   HMRC has set internal authorisation levels requiring an authorised officer to obtain the approval of a higher graded officer before using certain powers. The authority levels within HMRC are no lower than those set in the police force. Indeed, in most cases HMRC has set the main authority level at a minimum of Senior Officer grade. By contrast, most authorities within the police force are held at the equivalent of a Higher Officer in HMRC.

3.57   Usually it is obvious fairly early in an investigation where a crime has been committed and that the investigation may require evidence to be gathered in different parts of the UK. This means that it is necessary to take account of the differences between the legal systems in England and Wales, Scotland and Northern Ireland. In particular there are significant differences between the legal systems in Scotland and those in other parts of the UK. Cross-border powers contained in *FA 2007* enable HMRC's criminal investigation powers to be exercised in all parts of the UK. Thus, a search warrant issued by a court in Scotland can be exercised in England, if it is endorsed by an English court, and vice versa.

3.58   However, cross-border powers contained in *FA 2007* only apply to UK borders and not to EU or international borders. It may be possible to prosecute an offence in more than one part of the UK and the prosecuting authorities have generated guidance on how to determine in which UK country the offence is to be prosecuted. This is available through the CPS website at www.cps.gov.uk.

TRAINING AND SUPPORT

3.59   Officers serving in the Criminal Investigation Directorate are trained before they can be authorised to use any of the criminal investigation powers and that training must be kept up to date. The training covers the *PACE 1984* Codes of Practice and the Scottish powers, changes to relevant legislation and HMRC policy and procedures.

3.60   The broad range of subjects covered includes:

- entry, search and seizure powers;
- powers of arrest. Approximately 1,570 officers in Criminal Investigations and 118 in the Road Fuel Testing Unit have powers of arrest which can only be exercised for HMRC offences, and are not general powers of arrest. As with all of HMRC's criminal investigation powers, arrests are made only by authorised officers who have been appropriately trained;
- cautioning and interviews;

- the law of evidence;
- personal safety and the use of handcuffs; and
- responsibility for disclosure under the *Criminal Procedure and Investigations Act 1996*.

3.61 Comprehensive operating procedures are provided in internal guidance. Investigators can also ask for the advice of HMRC criminal lawyers. An HMRC lawyer will be assigned to work on the larger investigations and investigators and HMRC lawyers will also consult the prosecuting authorities at an early stage on major prosecutions.

INTRUSIVE SURVEILLANCE

3.62 HMRC is empowered to apply for authority to use surveillance powers in the *Regulation of Investigatory Powers Act 2000* and the *Police Act 1997*. These are principally:

- the interception of post and telecommunications;
- intrusive surveillance;
- property interference.

These powers are very effective in the fight against serious and organised crime. Because they are so intrusive their use is subject to strict safeguards.

3.63 They can be used only when investigating serious crime. The interception of communications has to be approved personally by the Home Secretary. The use of this power is overseen by the independent Interception of Communications Commissioner.

3.64 The most intrusive surveillance requires prior approval of a surveillance commissioner. All other cases of intrusive surveillance have to be reviewed by a surveillance commissioner, who can revoke the authorisation. The use of intrusive surveillance is overseen by the Surveillance Commissioners.

3.65 The use of these powers has to be approved at the highest levels in Criminal Investigation. Only certain members of the senior management team can approve applications for the use of any of these powers.

SAFEGUARDS

3.66 There are numerous statutory and non-statutory safeguards on HMRC's use of its criminal investigation powers.

3.67 *Tax fraud: criminal investigations and litigation – direct tax*

HMRC's criminal investigation powers are used only in its criminal work and are not used in civil investigations or other HMRC activities. HMRC is not responsible for prosecuting the crimes it investigates. The decision whether or not to prosecute is taken by the relevant independent prosecuting authority.

Like all other aspects of HMRC's work, criminal investigation is subject to review by HMRC's Internal Audit directorate.

3.67 External oversight is provided by HM Inspectors of Constabulary, the Scottish and Northern Ireland inspectors and the National Audit Office. Complaints can be made to the Independent Police Complaints Commission, the Ombudsman and the Adjudicator.

3.68 Many of the powers require external independent approval before they can be used. The person granting approval has to be satisfied that the relevant conditions are met. Production orders and search warrants have to be issued by a magistrate or a judge. The use of intrusive surveillance powers is subject to external approval at the highest level, as described at **3.62** *et seq*.

SEARCH WARRANTS AND PRODUCTION ORDERS

3.69 The clearest possible signal of the Revenue's intention to investigate with a view to prosecution is a 'dawn raid' (so called because the search operation generally begins early in the morning) carried out under *PACE 1984*, s 8, or s 9 and *Sch 1, para 12*, when HMRC invokes its powers to enter premises, by force if necessary, to search the premises and 'seize and retain anything for which a search has been authorised' (*s 8(2), Sch 1, para 13* and *s 22*), notwithstanding the fact that the thing found is not evidence of an offence which relates to a matter in relation to which HMRC has functions. A failure to comply with a warrant or order will be treated as contempt of court. Where a dawn raid is carried out it is absolutely critical to obtain immediate legal advice and to arrange for a suitably qualified lawyer to be in attendance at the premises so that he can monitor the search and most importantly review the terms of the warrant/production order. At a practical level it is also important to give an explanation to any employees at the business premises in the event that their assistance is needed to identify relevant materials, and also crucially for the legal representative to observe the search for the purpose of ensuring that there is no contamination of evidence being collected by the investigating officers.

3.70 The warrant will identify the premises covered by the order. Under *PACE 1984* the term 'premises' includes any place and in particular:

- any vehicle, vessel, aircraft or hovercraft;

Tax fraud: criminal investigations and litigation – direct tax **3.76**

- any offshore installation;
- any renewable energy installation;
- any tent or moveable structure (*s 23*).

3.71 Where an HMRC officer is conducting a search under the authority of a *PACE 1984* warrant, he may also carry out a same-sex search of any person found on the premises where he has reasonable cause to believe that person to be in possession of material likely to be of substantial value (by itself or together with other material) to the investigation of the offence.

3.72 In the past it was almost certain that not only would the suspect taxpayer's home be raided, but also his business premises and quite probably the offices of his professional advisers – both accountants and lawyers. This was so even if neither set of advisers was suspected of wrongdoing, since the Revenue wished to obtain documentary evidence at as early a stage as possible. This approach has changed significantly now that HMRC has a production order power available to it.

3.73 It is arguable that in some respects the amendments to *PACE 1984* introduced by *FA 2007, ss 82–87* and as applied by the PACE Regulations have made life more difficult for those HMRC criminal investigators accustomed to dealing with direct tax investigations.

3.74 To obtain a search warrant under the now defunct *TMA 1970, s 20C*, HMRC had to persuade a circuit judge in England and Wales (a sheriff in Scotland or a county court judge in Northern Ireland) that there was 'reasonable ground for *suspecting* that an offence involving serious fraud in connection with ... tax is being, has been or is about to be committed'.

3.75 Now HMRC has to surmount a higher hurdle by convincing a justice of the peace (JP) that 'there are reasonable grounds for *believing* that an indictable offence has been committed' (*s 8(1)*).

3.76 The reality, however, is that whereas an application for a search warrant under *TMA 1970, s 20C* had to be approved by the Board of Inland Revenue, which duty was taken very seriously by the Board, an application under *PACE 1984, s 8* or *Sch 1* will be approved at a much lower level. The application for a *s 8* warrant is made *ex parte* and must be supported by information in writing. Various safeguards, mainly relating to the identification of the premises to be searched, are set out in *s 15*.

Note: actions preparatory to committing a tax offence are now no longer grounds applying for a warrant to raid premises.

3.77 *Tax fraud: criminal investigations and litigation – direct tax*

Evidential material: items subject to legal privilege and special procedure material

3.77 Evidential material which is likely to be relevant, and of substantial value, to the investigation can be seized (*PACE 1984, s 8(1)(b)(c)*). However, there is a protection for items subject to legal privilege, excluded material and special procedure material (*s 8(1)(d)*). The search warrant application must also specify that there are no reasonable grounds for believing that the material on the premises to be searched consists of or includes items subject to legal privilege, excluded material or special procedure material. The JP also has to be satisfied that either it is not practicable to communicate with any person entitled to grant access to the evidence, or that entry to the premises will not be granted without a warrant, or that the purpose of the search is likely to be seriously prejudiced unless HMRC can gain instant access (*s 8(3)*).

3.78 Computerised information must be provided in a form in which it can be taken away and in which it is visible and legible, or from which it can readily be produced in a visible and legible form.

3.79 The term 'items subject to legal privilege' means (*PACE 1984, s 10*):

'(a) communications between a professional legal adviser and his client or any person representing his client made in connection with the giving of legal advice to the client;

(b) communications between a professional legal adviser and his client or any person representing his client or between such an adviser or his client or any such representative and any other person made in connection with or in contemplation of legal proceedings and for the purposes of such proceedings; and

(c) items enclosed with or referred to in such communications and made –

   (i) in connection with the giving of legal advice; or

   (ii) in connection with or in contemplation of legal proceedings and for the purposes of such proceedings,

when they are in the possession of a person who is entitled to possession of them.'

Something held with the intention of furthering a criminal purpose is not subject to privilege (*PACE, 1984, s 10(2)*).

3.80 The legal privilege protection applicable to both *PACE 1984, s 8* and *Sch 1* search warrants is contained in s 10 and is worded in the same way as it was in *TMA 1970, s 20C*.

3.81 'Excluded material' is defined in *s 11(1)* as personal records which a person has acquired or created in the course of trade, business, profession or other occupation or for the purpose of any paid or unpaid office and which he holds in confidence. Also included are human tissue and the like. Material of such a description would clearly include a patient's records held by a GP or psychiatrist. Excluded material also includes a journalist's notes or information obtained from a confidential source and held in confidence, or records other than documents.

3.82 'Special procedure material' is defined in *s 14(2)* as meaning material, other than material subject to legal privilege, acquired or created in the course of any trade, business, profession or other occupation and held subject to an express or implied undertaking that it is to be held in confidence or under a legal obligation of secrecy or restriction on disclosure. This would include business records held, for example, by an accountant on a client's behalf and an accountant's working papers. Also included is journalistic material other than the type of journalistic material, which is classed as 'excluded material'.

3.83 Where a search is likely to uncover special procedure material which may be required as evidence, HMRC will have to obtain a warrant signed by a circuit judge under *PACE 1984, Sch 1, para 12*.

As with *s 8*, material subject to legal privilege cannot be seized under a *PACE 1984, Sch 1, para 12* warrant.

3.84 Under the *Criminal Justice and Police Act 2001*, officers faced with large volumes of material during a search under a *s 8* warrant, may take it from the premises to be sifted and examined elsewhere. Legally privileged, excluded or special procedure material seized under a *s 8* warrant and which cannot be retained, must be returned as soon as practicable. Similarly, legally privileged and excluded material seized under a *Sch 1* warrant must also be returned.

3.85 An officer of HMRC may, without a warrant, enter and search any premises occupied or controlled by a person who is under arrest for any relevant indictable offence if he has reasonable grounds for suspecting that there is on the premises evidence, other than items subject to legal privilege, that relates:

- to that offence; or
- to some other indictable offence which is connected with or similar to that offence (*s 18*).

3.86 Following a *PACE 1984* raid, HMRC must supply a record of what was seized within a reasonable time of being so requested (*s 21(1), (2)*). And unless any investigation or criminal proceedings would be prejudiced, HMRC is also required to allow access under supervision to, and provide copies of, documents seized (*s 21(3)–(8)*).

3.87 *Tax fraud: criminal investigations and litigation – direct tax*

3.87 The introduction in 2000 of a production order power in the form of *TMA 1970, s 20BA* was intended, at least in part, to obviate the need to execute a *s 20C* raid on a professional firm, such as a lawyer or an accountant, or on a bank that was not viewed as being implicated in criminal activity, but where speedy access to information held by it was required. At the same time as *s 20BA* was enacted, *s 20C* was amended to say that the Board should not authorise an application for a search warrant unless it believed a request for a production order would seriously prejudice the investigation. HMRC is now bound by a similar provision in *PACE 1984*.

3.88 If, for instance, access to an accountant's working papers is required, and an application for a production order might seriously prejudice the investigation, HMRC may apply to a circuit judge under *PACE 1984, Sch 1 para 12*, for a search warrant. The application must make it clear why HMRC believes a production order may seriously prejudice the investigation.

3.89 Where HMRC requires access to 'special procedure material' such as an accountant's working papers or a solicitor's conveyancing files and it does not wish to invoke its search powers, it can seek leave of a circuit judge to serve a production order under *PACE 1984, Sch 1, para 4*.

3.90 The target of such an order is entitled to be present at the hearing before the judge. The material must be produced to HMRC within seven days from the date of the order or such longer period as is specified in the order and, if it is stored in any electronic form, must be produced in a form in which it is visible and legible.

3.91 A para 4 production order may be served on a person—whether an individual, company or any one of the partners in a partnership—either by delivering it to, or by leaving it at, the proper address or by sending it by registered post or recorded delivery. The proper address for a company is the registered or principal office; for a partnership it is the principal office of the firm; and in any other case it is the last known address of the person concerned.

3.92 Any person in receipt of a notice of an application for a para 4 production order must not conceal, destroy, alter or dispose of the material without the leave of a judge or written permission of HMRC until either the application is dismissed or an order made following the application has been complied with. Failure to comply with an order will be treated as contempt of the Crown Court.

3.93 The target of a search warrant may seek to challenge its validity by way of judicial review, which may result in the quashing of the warrant. The courts have emphasised that for a search warrant to be issued it is necessary to properly meet the onerous requirements imposed under the legislation.

Tax fraud: criminal investigations and litigation – direct tax **3.94**

This was emphasised by the High Court in *R (S, F and L) v Chief Constable of British Transport Police* [2013] EWHC 2189 (Admin). This case involved S who was a practising solicitor and a partner in the claimant solicitors' firm 'F'. The claimant 'L' was another firm of solicitors. All three claimants sought to quash search warrants issued in respect of their home (in the case of S) or professional premises (in the cases of F and L). The search warrants had been issued under the powers provided by *PACE 1984, s 9 et seq* and *Sch 1* (in respect of the search for and seize of 'excluded material' and 'special procedure material'). The court quashed the search warrants in the particular circumstances. The court commented that the safeguards imposed by *PACE 1984* in respect of the conditions for granting a warrant means that 'there has to be a very rigorous procedure both in preparing an information for the application for a search warrant and also when a judge is considering it'. The court emphasised:

> 'First, as a matter of practice all hearings for a search warrant, whether for a warrant under section 8 of PACE or of the "special procedure" type, must be recorded so that there can be no dispute about what was or was not said to and by the judge. Secondly, the circuit judge making the decision leading to the issue of the search warrant must give reasons for either granting or refusing the warrant.' (para 46 of the judgment)

3.94 In relation to the information provided by the investigating officer applying for the warrant, the court emphasised that it is clear from the statutory provisions of *PACE 1984* that it must deal with the following (para 45):

1 It must set out each of the statutory requirements which has to be satisfied in the particular case before the warrant in question can be granted.

2 It must show, for each of the relevant statutory requirements, how that requirement is satisfied by setting out all the relevant facts relied on including all facts and matters which are said to show that a particular 'reasonable belief' is justified. It is not enough to assert that a particular requirement is satisfied without explaining how it is said to be so.

3 It must state whether, despite there being 'reasonable grounds' for the constable believing that the material sought consists of or contains 'special procedure material' or 'excluded material', there might be a claim for legal privilege in respect of any communication sought and, if so, how and why that would arise together with precise details of the arrangements which are to be taken to ensure that there will be an independent supervising lawyer present at the time of the search.

4 It must make full and frank disclosure. This means, in the words of Hughes LJ in *Re Stanford International Limited* [2010] EWCA Civ 137 at para 191 that:

> 'in effect a prosecution seeking an ex parte order must put on his defence hat and ask himself what, if he was representing the defendant

3.95 *Tax fraud: criminal investigations and litigation – direct tax*

or a third party with the relevant interest, he would be saying to the judge, and, having answered that question, that is precisely what he must tell.'

This is a heavy burden but a vital safeguard. Full details must be given. It is a useful reminder to the person laying the information to state expressly which information is given pursuant to the duty of full and frank disclosure.

5   If further information is supplied to the circuit judge during the hearing of the application, whether as a result of judicial questioning or otherwise, the information should be supplemented by a witness statement or a further information setting out such further information.

3.95 Other recent examples of challenges to the issue of search warrants are: *R (F, J and K) v Blackfriars Crown Court and Commissioner of Police of the Metropolis* [2014] EWHC 1541 (Admin) and *R (Rawlinson and Hunter) v Central Crown Court and Serious Fraud Office* [2013] 1 WLR 1634. As part of a judicial review challenge it may also be possible to seek damages and payment of costs on an indemnity basis (eg where there was material non-disclosure by the investigating officer on application for the warrant).

3.96 Where HMRC require production of documents which are not special procedure material, it must continue to use *TMA 1970, s 20BA* (PACE Regulations, art 7). Such documents will be those which, although acquired or created in the course of business, are not held under a duty of confidentiality. Copy sales invoices may be examples of such documents.

ORDER FOR THE DELIVERY OF DOCUMENTS UNDER TMA 1970, s 20BA

3.97 Following the changes introduced by *FA 2007*, HMRC may only use its powers under *TMA 1970, s 20BA* if the officer thinks that an application under *PACE 1984, Sch 1, para 4* would not succeed because the material required does not consist of, or include, special procedure material (*PACE 1984, s 14B* as inserted by the PACE Regulations).

3.98 *Section 20BA* and *Sch 1AA* give HMRC authority to order the production of documents 'which may be required as evidence for the purpose of any proceedings in respect of an offence ... involving serious fraud in connection with, or in relation to, tax' (*TMA 1970, s 20BA(1)(a), (b)*).

3.99 The Orders for the Delivery of Documents (Procedure) Regulations 2000, SI 2000/2875, contain procedural rules governing the application for a production order and the resolution of disputes as to legal privilege.

3.100 An order to produce documents has to be made by 'the appropriate judicial authority' (a circuit judge in England and Wales). The person against whom the order is sought must be given not less than five working days' notice before the hearing of the application (SI 2000/2875, reg 4(2)).

3.101 Exceptionally, the right of the target of an order to appear and be heard at the hearing of the application can be waived if the appropriate judicial authority is satisfied that this would seriously prejudice the investigation of the offence (*TMA 1970, Sch1AA, para 3(1)*).

3.102 It is generally unlikely that a production order would be served on a professional firm in relation to a client of that firm without there being a simultaneous search operation on the client. However, there are additional safeguards to protect the security of HMRC's investigation in the form of an anti-'tipping-off' provision on similar lines to that contained in the money laundering legislation.

Complying with a s 20BA production order

3.103 A person who has been given notice of the Revenue's intention to apply for an order must not, on pain of proceedings for contempt of court 'disclose to any other person information or any other matter likely to prejudice the investigation of the offence to which the application relates' (*Sch 1AA, para 4(1)(b)*).

3.104 On the other hand, where the intended recipient of a notice is a 'professional legal adviser' there is no let or hindrance on him 'disclosing any information or other matter' to a client or his representative in connection with the giving of legal advice to the client or to any other person in contemplation of, or in connection with, legal proceedings and for the purpose of those proceedings (*Sch 1AA, para 4(2), (3)*).

There is no such protection for an accountant – see *R (on an application of Prudential plc) v Special Commissioner of Income Tax* [2013] UKSC 1.

3.105 The legislation envisages that the person who has the documents required by HMRC in his power or possession will be given ten working days to comply with the order or 'such shorter or longer period as may be specified' (*s 20BA(2)(b)*).

3.106 The time limits for giving notice of the intention to apply for an order and for the recipient to comply, run from the day of receipt at the 'proper address' (usually the last known place of residence, or business, or employment or a company's registered office) or, where that day is not a working day, from the next working day. There is also provision for such notices to be delivered

3.107 *Tax fraud: criminal investigations and litigation – direct tax*

'by facsimile ... or other similar means' (but only by agreement of the intended recipient (COP22)), in which case the notice is deemed to have been given when 'the text is received in legible form' (SI 2000/2875, regs 5(1), (2), (3)).

3.107 The order must specify or describe the documents that are the subject of the application, which will limit the scope for the over-zealous investigator to embark on an over-speculative enquiry. The order must also describe the suspected offence – 'serious fraud in connection with, or in relation to, tax' will no doubt suffice – and must also name the person suspected of having committed the suspected offence.

3.108 It is an offence, punishable by up to two years' imprisonment and a fine, to falsify, conceal, destroy or otherwise dispose of (or permit the same to happen) any document required by a *s 20BA* order.

3.109 The statutory instrument, possibly anticipating the almost inevitable challenges, goes into fairly minute detail in setting down the procedures for complying with an order.

3.110 For example, the order is complied with if the documents (originals, not photocopies) are delivered to the officer of the Board specified in the order, either by delivering them to him directly, or by leaving them marked for his attention at the address specified in the order. Should compliance within the time specified cause a problem, the target should not hesitate to agree an extension with HMRC. But, of course, do not wait until the time limit is about to expire or, even worse, has already expired, before asking for an extension.

3.111 Where documents are sent by post, they will be treated, in the absence of evidence to the contrary, as having been produced on the second working day after first class posting and on the fourth working day if posted second class (SI 2000/2875, reg 6(1), (2), (3)). One can imagine that a production order, particularly on a sole practitioner where the documents may already be in storage, could impose an almost intolerable strain on the business. Again, there must be a very real possibility of a challenge being mounted under human rights legislation.

PACE 1984, Sch 1 production order

3.112 There are a number of conditions which must be satisfied before a *PACE 1984, s 9, Sch 1* production order or search warrant can be applied for. These include:

- the application must be supported by a signed written authority from a Higher Officer of HMRC;
- HMRC must also have reasonable grounds for believing that –
  – an indictable offence has been committed;

- there is material which consists of or includes special procedure material, and does not also include excluded material, on premises specified in the application or on premises controlled by a person specified in the application;
- the material is likely to be of substantial value (on its own or together with other material) to the investigation; and
- the material is likely to be relevant evidence.

In addition, other methods of obtaining the material must have been tried without success, or have not been tried because it appeared that they were bound to fail.

3.113 It must also be in the public interest that the material should be produced or that access should be given to it, having regard both to the benefit which is likely to accrue to the investigation if the material is obtained and the circumstances under which the person in possession of the material holds it.

3.114 There are, in addition, further conditions which have to be satisfied before a *Sch 1* search warrant can be issued.

Rather than specifying all the premises which it wishes to search, HMRC may seek an 'all premises warrant', but the judge must not issue such a warrant unless he is satisfied:

- that there are reasonable grounds for believing that it is necessary to search premises occupied or controlled by the person in question which are not specified in the application, as well as those which are, in order to find the material in question; and
- that it is not reasonably practicable to specify all the premises which that person occupies or controls which might need to be searched.

3.115 The judge must also be satisfied that:

- it is not practicable to communicate with any person entitled to grant entry to the premises;
- it is practicable to communicate with a person entitled to grant entry to the premises but not with any person entitled to grant access to the material;
- the material includes excluded material in the form of medical records held subject to a statutory obligation of secrecy which would be breached by disclosure other than as a result of a search under warrant;

3.116   *Tax fraud: criminal investigations and litigation – direct tax*

- service of an application for a production order might seriously prejudice the investigation.

3.116   Code of Practice B of *PACE 1984* gives extensive guidance to those using or intending to invoke the PACE search and production order powers. The Code should also be consulted by those whose clients are subject to a raid or are, or are themselves, in receipt of a production order.

SOCPA 2005 production order

3.117   As was said earlier, most HMRC raids are likely to be conducted under *PACE 1984*. However, the *Serious Organised Crime and Police Act 2005* (*SOCPA 2005*) created a number of powers of investigation, including the power to force witnesses to answer questions or to provide documents or information. These powers are to be exercised by, among others, the Director of Public Prosecutions (DPP), who may delegate these powers to a Revenue and Customs prosecutor who is any one of a number of senior officials and lawyers in HMRC.

3.118   Where someone has been served with a disclosure notice to produce documents under *SOCPA 2005, s 62* and has not complied, or it is not practicable to give a disclosure notice, or the giving of a disclosure notice might seriously prejudice the investigation, a JP may issue a warrant to enter premises and seize documents (including computer disks) (*SOCPA 2005, s 66*).

3.119   Such a warrant may be applied for where the prosecutors 'suspect' (as for the repealed *TMA 1970, s 20C*, rather than 'believe' as for *PACE 1984, s 8*) that, for instance, the common law offence of cheating the public revenue has been committed. A very low threshold of loss of revenue of not less than £5,000 is stipulated; not quite the 'substantial financial gain' according to which 'serious fraud' was defined in *s 20C*.

3.120   However, it is understood that the DPP will in fact exercise its powers under *SOCPA 2005* only in cases involving serious fraud, ie where the fraud has in fact resulted in substantial loss to the public revenue. The areas envisaged are tax credit and MTIC fraud. In other cases where HMRC has an existing power, *PACE 1984* will almost certainly be applied.

3.121   As with other search powers, there is a protection for privileged material, but apparently none for excluded or special procedure material. Accordingly, a search warrant obtained under *SOCPA 2005, s 66*, on application to a JP might cover, say, an accountant's working papers. To gain access to these by a search under *PACE 1984, Sch 1* would require an application to a circuit judge.

DEALING WITH A DAWN RAID

3.122 The adviser's role on learning that his client is the object of a dawn raid is clear. First, he must immediately arrange for a legal professional with detailed knowledge of the search provisions to stand by his client both at his home and at the business premises. The instructed lawyer will then contact the HMRC officer in charge of the searches and commence a dialogue. If it is likely that legally privileged materials are to be found on any premises then HMRC should be requested to delay the search to allow time for a solicitor to be present from the start.

Without doubt the client, his family and, possibly to a lesser extent his staff, will be in a state of some fear and trepidation when faced with a determined search crew of HMRC investigators.

3.123 Arrests will frequently be carried out at a very early stage of the raid process. If that happens, arrangements must be put in hand immediately for clients to be represented by a suitably qualified solicitor, since HMRC will be looking to conduct interviews under caution as soon as practicable. Certain officers of HMRC have been authorised to carry out arrests and to search and detain the persons arrested. Offices of HMRC may be designated as being suitable to be used for the purpose of detaining arrested persons. However, officers are not empowered to charge a person with an offence, to release a person on bail, or to detain or fingerprint a person after he has been charged with an offence (this is strictly controlled by *PACE 1984*).

The Commissioners of HMRC are required to keep records relating to detentions and charges and to include the information in their annual reports.

3.124 Needless to say, nothing should or can be done physically to impede the search. However, that does not mean that the warrant itself must not be scrutinised in minute detail to ensure that the search is being conducted strictly in accordance with the terms on which it has been issued. Section 16 stipulates several requirements in relation to the execution of *PACE 1984* search warrants:

- A warrant is valid for three months from the date of issue.
- A warrant may be executed by any officer of HMRC.
- Entry and search must be at a reasonable hour, unless the purpose of the search might be frustrated on entry at a reasonable hour. Criticism of the early morning raid was considered by the Keith Committee. One expert, in evidence to the Committee, maintained that the hours between 4am and 7am were the only hours when the hardened criminal could be guaranteed to be found at home. Thus the Revenue continues with its practice of commencing such raids in the early hours of the morning – usually 7am.

3.125 *Tax fraud: criminal investigations and litigation – direct tax*

- The warrant may authorise persons to accompany the investigator. Such persons have the same power as the officer they are accompanying but they may exercise these powers only in the company, and under the supervision, of an officer. The presence during a raid of unauthorised persons has been successfully challenged in judicial review proceedings.

- If the warrant is an all-premises warrant, premises which are not specified may not be entered or searched unless a senior officer has given written authority; nor may premises be entered or searched for a second or subsequent time under a warrant which authorises multiple entries unless a senior officer has given written authority.

- The officer must identify himself to the occupier of the premises if he is present at the time the warrant is executed, and if not, to any other who is present, and provide him with a copy of the warrant.

- If no person is present a copy of the warrant must be left in a prominent place.

- A search may only be carried out to the extent required for the purpose for which the warrant was issued.

- HMRC may download information from computers or it may remove them if necessary. This highlights the need for regular backing up of data.

- The officer must endorse the warrant, stating whether the articles sought were found and whether any articles were seized other than articles which were sought. HMRC must not remove documents which are subject to legal professional privilege. Disputed documents should be separately bagged and sealed for adjudication at a later date.

- On completion of the search, a *s 8* warrant has to be returned to the designated officer for the local justice area and a *Sch 1, para 12* warrant to the appropriate officer of the court.

- A returned warrant must be kept for 12 months from its return, during which time it must be available for inspection by the occupier of the premises entered and searched.

3.125 The award of costs of any application under *Sch 1* and of anything done in pursuance of an order are entirely at the discretion of the judge granting the order. By contrast there is no provision for the award of costs of complying with a *s 20BA* order.

3.126 Although the officers of HMRC must not be obstructed in any way, they should be accompanied at all times whilst on the premises and not left unattended. A detailed note of the progress of the search should be taken. The IT systems will be examined by HMRC and this should be done in the presence of the taxpayer's solicitor. Staff should be instructed not to answer any questions put to them by the officers of HMRC.

3.127 Advisers should consider whether clients should draw up a Raid Protection Plan under which, amongst other precautions, staff – particularly reception staff and those who normally arrive at work early – are made fully aware of the contact details of senior staff who should be alerted immediately in the event of *any* unannounced visit.

LEGAL PRIVILEGE

3.128 Potentially one of the most difficult areas of the legislation relates to items which may be considered to be protected from disclosure by legal privilege and it is worth repeating the appropriate paragraph in its entirety.

3.129 *TMA 1970, Sch 1AA, para 5* states:

'(1) Section 20BA does not apply to items subject to legal privilege.

(2) For this purpose "items subject to legal privilege" means:

(a) communications between a professional legal adviser and his client or any person representing his client made in connection with the giving of legal advice to his client;

(b) communications between a professional legal adviser and his client or any person representing his client or between such an adviser or his client or any such representative and any other person made in connection with or in contemplation of legal proceedings and for the purposes of such proceedings; and

(c) items enclosed with or referred to in such communications and made:

   (i) in connection with the giving of legal advice; or

   (ii) in connection with or in contemplation of legal proceedings and for the purposes of such proceedings, when they are in possession of a person who is entitled to possession of them.

(3) Items held with the intention of furthering a criminal purpose are not subject to legal privilege.'

The definition of legal privilege in *PACE 1984, s 10* is identical.

3.130 Readers will immediately note that, as far as production orders are concerned, the first arbiter as to whether or not a document is subject to legal privilege is the recipient of the notice himself.

3.131 *Tax fraud: criminal investigations and litigation – direct tax*

3.131 SI 2000/2875, reg 7(1)–(7) contains detailed provisions aimed at resolving disputes as to legal privilege which are far from being weighted in HMRC's favour (in contrast to the legislation in the *Criminal Justice and Police Act 2001* which will allow investigators – including HMRC – to remove, in the course of a raid and in certain circumstances, privileged material from the premises for sifting). It is likely that these regulations will also apply to disputes over legal privilege arising out of orders under *PACE 1984*.

3.132 Where a dispute arises in a production order case, the person in receipt of the order can apply to the appropriate judicial authority to resolve the dispute. The disputed documents must be lodged with the court at the same time. Naturally, HMRC will have the right to be present and be heard at the hearing of the application and costs may be awarded against HMRC, except where the court holds that no document, or no part of a document, is subject to legal privilege.

3.133 There is an alternative and less formal means of resolving disputes as to privilege suggested in COP22. This envisages an independent counsel (or exceptionally an HMRC solicitor) considering the disputed documents in the light of the information previously seen by the judge who granted the order, to enable him to give a considered view on the claim to privilege and thus to enable HMRC to decide whether to challenge that claim.

INTERVIEWS

3.134 Not every prosecution, of course, is preceded by the drama of a dawn raid.

Frequently, HMRC will feel that it already has sufficient evidence indicating the commission of serious fraud. The source of this material could be a spin-off from another investigation, information and possibly documents provided by an informer and by potential witnesses, or quite possibly documents supplied by the taxpayer during the course of an investigation whether voluntarily or in response to a notice under *FA 2008, Sch 36(1)* or in obedience to an order issued under the Tribunal Procedure (First-tier Tribunal) (Tax Chamber) Rules 2009, SI 2009/273, r 16(1)(b), or by a third party such as a bank under *FA 2008, Sch 36(2)*.

3.135 In such circumstances as these HMRC's evidential jigsaw may be all but complete. All that is required to complete the final piece and guarantee the required standard of proof to convince a jury beyond reasonable doubt may be the evidence obtainable under caution from the suspect's own mouth. The letter from HMRC inviting the taxpayer to an interview will make it clear that the taxpayer is to be cautioned and indeed will suggest that he may wish to be legally represented. Until 9 April 1995, the caution which investigators were required to administer in accordance with para 10 of the Code of Practice for the detention, treatment and questioning of persons issued under *PACE 1984* read as follows:

> 'You are not obliged to say anything but anything you do say may be taken down in writing and given in evidence.'

3.136 Since that date, as a result of a change brought in by the *Criminal Justice and Public Order Act 1994, s 34*, the caution now reads:

> 'You do not have to say anything. But it may harm your defence if you do not mention when questioned something which you later rely on in court. Anything you do say may be given in evidence.'

At the same time, if the person cautioned is not under arrest, he must be told that this is the case, that he is not obliged to remain with the investigator and that he may obtain legal advice (if he is not already legally represented).

3.137 This shift in the balance towards the investigating authorities requires careful consideration by the taxpayer and his advisers, who must by this time include a specialist criminal solicitor and quite possibly a barrister.

Whereas under the old caution, the taxpayer was well advised to exercise his right to remain silent, the same cannot be said of the new regime.

3.138 However, before submitting to interview, HMRC, which has probably already had many months prior to the meeting to examine documents and speak to witnesses and generally to formulate the case, should be asked to provide details of the questions which it would like to be answered and copies of the documents which it wishes to put to the taxpayer for comment during the course of the interview under caution.

THE ANATOMY OF A CRIMINAL TRIAL

3.139 A criminal investigation by HMRC can last for many months and indeed can run into years before the matter is put to the CPS for consideration of whether charges should be laid against the taxpayer. In such cases charges will generally be:

- the common law charge of cheating HMRC;
- offences under the Theft Acts;
- forgery, perjury or conspiracy; or
- fraudulent evasion of income tax.

3.140 *Tax fraud: criminal investigations and litigation – direct tax*

3.140 An outline of these offences is provided in the introduction to this chapter. A conviction can only be obtained if the Crown can prove beyond a reasonable doubt that the defendant committed the offence (see *Woolmington v DPP* [1935] AC 462). In *Hepworth & Fearnley* (1955) 39 Cr App R 152 at 154, Lord Goddward put the nature of the standard of proof as follows:

> 'one would be on safe ground if one said in a criminal case to a jury: "You must be satisfied beyond reasonable doubt" and one could also say: "You must be completely satisfied" or better still: "You must feel sure of the prisoner's guilt." But I desire to repeat what I said in the case of Kritz (33 Cr.App.R. 169, at p. 177; [1950] 1 K.B. 82, at p. 89): "It is not the particular formula of words that matters; it is the effect of the summing-up. If the jury are charged whether in one set of words or in another and are made to understand that they have to be satisfied and must not return a verdict against a defendant unless they feel sure, and that the onus is all the time on the prosecution and not on the defence," that is enough. I should be very sorry if it were thought that cases should depend on the use of a particular formula or particular word or words. **The point is that the jury should be directed first, that the onus is always on the prosecution; secondly, that before they convict they must feel sure of the prisoner's guilt. If that is done, that is enough.**'

(Emphasis added)

The Judicial Studies Board *Crown Court Compendium* (May 2016) provides for the following specimen direction to be given by the judge to the jury on the nature of the legal test:

> 'The prosecution must prove that D is guilty. D does not have to prove anything to you. He does not have to prove that he is innocent. The prosecution will only succeed in proving that D is guilty if you have been made sure of his guilt. If, after considering all of the evidence, you are sure that D is guilty, your verdict must be "Guilty". If you are not sure that he is guilty, or sure that he is innocent, your verdict must be "Not Guilty".'

It is therefore clear that the jury must decide that they are 'sure of' a person's guilt in respect of a specific criminal offence before a conviction is made.

3.141 Accordingly, unlike a civil tax appeal where the burden of proof is almost universally on the taxpayer and that burden must be discharged to the civil standard (more likely than not), a criminal case imposes the burden on the Crown, which must be proved beyond a reasonable doubt. The standard that must be met is, therefore, a high one.

3.142 Where the suspect has been charged, if it is demonstrated that the taxpayer has a case to answer, he will be committed for trial in the Crown Court in due course. HMRC will serve bundles on the defendant incorporating

Tax fraud: criminal investigations and litigation – direct tax 3.142

documentary evidence upon which the prosecution intend to rely, including statements from witnesses. These can run to many thousands of pages and can be, and indeed frequently are, added to right up to the commencement of the trial in the Crown Court. A rigorous regime applies to the disclosure of documents to the defendant which are relied upon by the Crown for the purposes of its prosecution. Moreover, the Crown is required to give access to unused documents obtained during the course of the investigation. The House of Lords stated in *R v H and C* [2004] UKHL 3; [2004] 2 AC 134; [2004] 2 Cr App R 10:

> 'Fairness ordinarily requires that any material held by the prosecution which weakens its case or strengthens that of the defendant, if not relied on as part of its formal case against the defendant, should be disclosed to the defence. Bitter experience has shown that miscarriages of justice may occur where such material is withheld from disclosure. The golden rule is that full disclosure of such material should be made.' ([2004] 2 AC 134, at 147)

Under the *Criminal Procedure and Investigations Act 1996*, the Crown must provide the defence with copies of, or access to, any material which might reasonably be considered capable of undermining the case for the prosecution against the accused, or of assisting the case for the accused, and which has not previously been disclosed. In this regard, the following guidance has been published by the Attorney General (*Attorney General's Guidelines on Disclosure, see: https://www.gov.uk/government/publications/attorney-generals-guidelines-on-disclosure-2013*):

'4. Disclosure refers to providing the defence with copies of, or access to, any prosecution material which might reasonably be considered capable of undermining the case for the prosecution against the accused, or of assisting the case for the accused, and which has not previously been disclosed (section 3 CPIA).

5. Prosecutors will only be expected to anticipate what material might undermine their case or strengthen the defence in the light of information available at the time of the disclosure decision, and they may take into account information revealed during questioning.

6. In deciding whether material satisfies the disclosure test, consideration should be given amongst other things to:

    a. the use that might be made of it in cross-examination;

    b. its capacity to support submissions that could lead to:

        (i) the exclusion of evidence;

        (ii) a stay of proceedings, where the material is required to allow a proper application to be made;

3.142 *Tax fraud: criminal investigations and litigation – direct tax*

    (iii) a court or tribunal finding that any public authority had acted incompatibly with the accused's rights under the ECHR;

  c. its capacity to suggest an explanation or partial explanation of the accused's actions;

  d. the capacity of the material to have a bearing on scientific or medical evidence in the case.

7. It should also be borne in mind that while items of material viewed in isolation may not be reasonably considered to be capable of undermining the prosecution case or assisting the accused, several items together can have that effect.

8. Material relating to the accused's mental or physical health, intellectual capacity, or to any ill treatment which the accused may have suffered when in the investigator's custody is likely to fall within the test for disclosure set out in paragraph 4 above.

9. Disclosure must not be an open-ended trawl of unused material. A critical element to fair and proper disclosure is that the defence play their role to ensure that the prosecution are directed to material which might reasonably be considered capable of undermining the prosecution case or assisting the case for the accused. This process is key to ensuring prosecutors make informed determinations about disclosure of unused material. The defence statement is important in identifying the issues in the case and why it is suggested that the material meets the test for disclosure.

...

Annex: Attorney General's Guidelines on Disclosure: Supplementary Guidelines on Digitally Stored Material (2011)

...

A38. In complying with its duty of disclosure, the prosecution should follow the procedure as outlined below.

A39. Where digital material is examined, the extent and manner of inspecting, viewing or listening will depend on the nature of the material and its form.

A40. It is important for investigators and prosecutors to remember that the duty under the CPIA Code of Practice is to "pursue all reasonable lines of enquiry including those that point away from the suspect". Lines of enquiry, of whatever kind, should be pursued only if they are reasonable in the context of the individual case. It is not the duty of the prosecution to comb through all the material in its possession – e.g. every word or byte of computer material – on the

Tax fraud: criminal investigations and litigation – direct tax **3.144**

look out for anything which might conceivably or speculatively assist the defence. The duty of the prosecution is to disclose material which might reasonably be considered capable of undermining its case or assisting the case for the accused which they become aware of, or to which their attention is drawn.

A41. In some cases the sift may be conducted by an investigator/ disclosure officer manually assessing the content of the computer or other digital material from its directory and determining which files are relevant and should be retained for evidence or unused material.

A42. In other cases such an approach may not be feasible. Where there is an enormous volume of material it is perfectly proper for the investigator/disclosure officer to search it by sample, key words, or other appropriate search tools or analytical techniques to locate relevant passages, phrases and identifiers.

A43. In cases involving very large quantities of data, the person in charge of the investigation will develop a strategy setting out how the material should be analysed or searched to identify categories of data. Where search tools are used to examine digital material it will usually be appropriate to provide the accused and his or her legal representative with a copy of reasonable search terms used, or to be used, and invite them to suggest any further reasonable search terms. If search terms are suggested which the investigator or prosecutor believes will not be productive – for example because of the use of common words that are likely to identify a mass of irrelevant material, the investigator or prosecutor is entitled to open a dialogue with the defence representative with a view to agreeing sensible refinements. The purpose of this dialogue is to ensure that reasonable and proportionate searches can be carried out.'

3.143 Accordingly, it is necessary from a very early stage for lawyers to be instructed so as to properly prepare for the trial, and have the time to review materials that are disclosed by the Crown. At a practical level, managing these bundles is of crucial importance, and the option of scanning them on to a computer should be considered since this process can greatly facilitate the constant referral to those documents, which is usually necessary, and the transfer of documents between the defence team.

3.144 It is also necessary for the defence team to serve a defence statement, which must be provided within 14 days (in a magistrates' court case) or 28 days (in a Crown Court case) after the initial prosecution disclosure (or notice from the prosecutor that there is no material to disclose). If more time is required then an application must be made to the court, giving reasons for

3.145 *Tax fraud: criminal investigations and litigation – direct tax*

the application. The contents of the defence statement are governed by the *Criminal Procedure and Investigations Act 1996, s 6A*, so that it must:

(a) set out the nature of the defence, including any particular defences;

(b) indicate the matters of fact on which the defence takes issue with the prosecutor, and in respect of each explain why;

(c) set out particulars of the matters of fact on which the defence intend to rely for the purposes of defence;

(d) indicate any point of law that the defence wishes to take, including any point about the admissibility of evidence or about abuse of process, and any authority relied on; and

(e) if the defence statement includes an alibi (ie an assertion that the defendant was in a place, at a time, inconsistent with the defendant having committed the offence), give particulars, including:

   (i) the name, address and date of birth of any witness who the defence believe can give evidence in support of that alibi,

   (ii) if the defence does not know all of those details, any information that might help identify or find that witness.

3.145 The consequence of failing to serve a defence statement are provided by the *Criminal Procedure and Investigations Act 1996, s 11*. This provides that if a defendant:

(a) does not disclose what the Act requires;

(b) does not give a defence statement before the time limit expires;

(c) at trial, relies on a defence, or facts, that the defendant has not disclosed; or

(d) at trial, calls an alibi witness whom the defendant has not identified in advance,

the court, the prosecutor or another defendant may comment on that, and the court may draw such inferences as it thinks proper in deciding whether the defendant is guilty. For further details on the nature of the defence statement see generally the Criminal Procedure and Investigations Act 1996, ss 5 and 6; the Criminal Procedure and Investigations Act 1996 (Defence Disclosure Time Limits) Regulations 2011, SI 2011/209; and the Criminal Procedure Rules, r 22.4.

3.146 It will be necessary for the defence team to identify any potential witnesses who will be able to support the defendant at trial for the purposes of assisting in his defence. This task can only properly be undertaken by a lawyer, who will need to meet with any prospective witness and take a witness

Tax fraud: criminal investigations and litigation – direct tax **3.148**

statement of his proof of evidence (which will be signed by the witness). Such witness statements that will be relied upon by the defence team will be disclosed to the prosecution in accordance with a trial timetable that will have been imposed by the court. If necessary, the defence team may also have to consider whether it is necessary to compel a prospective witness to attend court by the issue of a court summons under the *Criminal Procedure (Attendance of Witnesses) Act 1965*. It is also possible for the court to compel an individual to produce documents for the purposes of the trial.

3.147 Any opportunity to attack HMRC's case must not be overlooked and the services of a forensic accountant will frequently be invaluable. It is important also to bear in mind at all times that it is not enough, to secure a conviction, for HMRC to demonstrate that tax that could have been paid has not been tendered to the Exchequer. What must be proven is *dishonesty*. The tax code is extremely complicated and in the pressures of commercial life many taxpayers get themselves into difficulties; this does not necessarily mean that they have acted dishonestly according to the test in *R v Ghosh* above.

All this requires close co-operation between accountants and lawyers, and the concept of the team surrounding and supporting the taxpayer cannot be overemphasised.

3.148 In a criminal trial the judge has the right to determine issues of law (ie to rule on the nature of the legal offence and the requirements that must be met as a matter of law for the defendant to be found guilty by the jury). The jury will solely determine whether the defendant is guilty of the offence. The overall order of events for a criminal trial in the Crown Court will be as follows:

- swearing in of the jury (comprising 12 individuals);
- opening speech from the prosecution counsel (outlining the nature of the case against the defendant);
- prosecution witnesses called to give evidence (then cross-examined by the defence);
- opening speech from the defence counsel (outlining the nature of the defence);
- defence witnesses called to give evidence (then cross-examined by the prosecution);
- prosecution closing speech;
- defence closing speech;
- summing up by the judge on the issues of fact and law;

3.149 *Tax fraud: criminal investigations and litigation – direct tax*

- the jury then considers its verdict in private;
- verdict: this must be unanimous, but a majority verdict of 11:1 or 10:2 will be accepted in certain circumstances. A majority verdict will not be accepted unless it appears to the court that the jury has had such period of time for deliberation as the court thinks reasonable having regard to the nature and complexity of the case; and the Crown Court shall in any event not accept such a verdict unless it appears to the court that the jury has had at least two hours for deliberation (*Juries Act 1974, s 17*);
- no verdict: if the jury cannot reach a verdict then the judge has power to discharge the jury. The CPS is then likely to seek a re-trial with a new jury;
- guilty verdict: the judge will proceed to sentence the defendant usually after an adjournment so that pre-sentence reports can be obtained prior to sentencing. Defence and prosecution counsel will be able to make submissions on the length of the sentence;
- not guilty verdict: the defendant will be discharged and is free to leave court.

3.149 If the accused is convicted it will then be necessary for the judge to determine the appropriate sentence by reference to hearing submissions on mitigation by the Defence and consideration of the relevant sentencing guidelines. The Sentencing Council has published its guidance for tax fraud in *Fraud, Bribery and Money Laundering Offences* (1 October 2014). Broadly, the court will have regard to the following matters:

1. The court will determine the offence category with reference to sentencing guidelines. In order to determine the category, the court should assess culpability and harm. The level of culpability is determined by weighing up all the factors of the case to determine the offender's role and the extent to which the offending was planned and the sophistication with which it was carried out.

2. Once the court has determined the category at step one, the court will then use the appropriate starting point as referenced in the guidance to reach a sentence within the category range. The starting point applies to all offenders irrespective of plea or previous convictions. Where the value is larger or smaller than the amount on which the starting point is based, should lead to upward or downward adjustment as appropriate.

3. The guidance contains a non-exhaustive list of additional factual elements providing the context of the offence and factors relating to the offender. The court should identify whether any combination of these or other relevant factors should result in any further upward or downward adjustment from the starting point. It should also be noted that

Tax fraud: criminal investigations and litigation – direct tax **3.149**

consecutive sentences for multiple offences may be appropriate where large sums are involved. In this regard:

a. Factors increasing the seriousness of an offence are:

Statutory aggravating factors: Previous convictions, having regard to a) the nature of the offence to which the conviction relates and its relevance to the current offence; and b) the time that has elapsed since the conviction Offence committed whilst on bail

Other aggravating factors:

- Involves multiple frauds,
- Number of false declarations Attempts to conceal/dispose of evidence,
- Failure to comply with current court orders,
- Offence committed on licence,
- Offences taken into consideration,
- Failure to respond to warnings about behaviour,
- Blame wrongly placed on others,
- Damage to third party (for example as a result of identity theft),
- Dealing with goods with an additional health risk,
- Disposing of goods to under age purchasers.

b. Factors reducing seriousness or reflecting personal mitigation

- No previous convictions or no relevant/recent convictions,
- Remorse Good character and/or exemplary conduct,
- Little or no prospect of success,
- Serious medical condition requiring urgent, intensive or long-term treatment,
- Age and/or lack of maturity where it affects the responsibility of the offender,
- Lapse of time since apprehension where this does not arise from the conduct of the offender,
- Mental disorder or learning disability,
- Sole or primary carer for dependent relatives,

3.150 *Tax fraud: criminal investigations and litigation – direct tax*

- Offender co-operated with investigation, made early admissions and/or voluntarily reported offending,
- Determination and/or demonstration of steps having been taken to address addiction or offending behaviour,
- Activity originally legitimate.

3.150 The conclusion of the trial, whatever the outcome, is not the end of the matter. First, HMRC will seek to recover any tax lost as a result of the fraud (even if the taxpayer has been acquitted of any criminal offence). Inevitably on conviction the prosecution will seek to obtain a confiscation order in respect of the proceeds of crime.

3.151 Under *POCA 2002, s 6* the Crown court is, in certain circumstances, required to make a confiscation order. The court will make an order if two conditions are satisfied:

- the defendant has been convicted of an offence in proceedings before the Crown Court, or has been committed to the Crown Court; and
- either the prosecutor is seeking a confiscation order or the court is of the view that it is appropriate to proceed under *s 6*.

3.152 If both conditions above are satisfied, a confiscation order may then be made if the defendant is found to have a 'criminal lifestyle' and if so to have benefited from his 'general criminal conduct' (or, if he does not have a criminal lifestyle, he has nonetheless benefitted from his 'particular criminal conduct').

Any question arising in connection with whether the defendant has a criminal lifestyle or has benefited from his criminal conduct must be decided on the balance of probabilities.

3.153 Broadly, a person has a 'criminal lifestyle' if he is either convicted of one of a number of prescribed offences, including money laundering, or the offence constitutes conduct forming part of a course of criminal activity or was committed over a period of at least six months.

Broadly, 'general criminal conduct' is all the defendant's criminal conduct, whenever it occurred.

3.154 In deciding whether a defendant with a criminal lifestyle has benefited from his general criminal conduct, the court may make certain assumptions (these may be challenged by the defence) as follows:

- Any property transferred to the defendant within the period of six years ending on the day on which proceedings were started was obtained by him as a result of his general criminal conduct.

Tax fraud: criminal investigations and litigation – direct tax **3.158**

- Any property held by him at any time after the date of conviction was obtained by him as a result of his general criminal conduct.
- Any expenditure incurred by him within a period of six years ending with the date on which the proceedings were started against him was met from property obtained by him as a result of his general criminal conduct.
- Any property obtained or assumed to have been obtained by the defendant is free of any other interest in the property.

3.155 The recoverable amount is broadly equal to the defendant's benefit from the conduct concerned. The amount may be reduced if the defendant can show that the realizable value of his assets are less than the recoverable amount.

3.156 In the case of *R v IK* [2007] EWCA Crim 491 the Court of Appeal held that profits from a legitimate trade upon which tax had been evaded could, in part, represent the proceeds of crime. In this case the criminal property was represented by the tax evaded. Dyson LJ said that cheating the public revenue had to have already taken place for the funds to represent the proceeds of crime (ie the date for payment of tax due must have passed).

3.157 In the case of *R v NW, SW, RC and CC* [2008] EWCA Crim 2 the Court of Appeal confirmed that the Crown could not simply point to unexplained wealth and assert that there was no legitimate explanation and therefore it must be from the proceeds of crime. The Crown had to identify the criminal conduct or at least the category of criminal conduct alleged to have generated the money.

3.158 The approach of HMRC regarding penalties is usually:

(a) to refrain from taking steps to recover civil money penalties on the basis of fraud in respect of an offence which has been before the criminal courts;

(b) to seek appropriate civil money penalties in respect of any offence which has not been brought before the courts; and

(c) to reserve the right to seek, where there are grounds to do so, a civil penalty in respect of negligence by a taxpayer who has been acquitted of criminal intent in respect of a prosecution for fraud.

Another tool in HMRC's asset recovery armoury is the Criminal Taxes Unit, which uses the tax system to disrupt serious criminality often in collaboration with other law enforcement agencies.

3.159   *Tax fraud: criminal investigations and litigation – direct tax*

USE OF INFORMATION BY HMRC

3.159   *Use in connection with any HMRC function:* The sharing of information within different parts of HMRC is permitted and controlled by the *Commissioners for Revenue and Customs Act 2005* (*CRCA 2005*). The starting point is that any information acquired by HMRC in connection with a function may be used by them in connection with any other function (*CRCA 2005, s 17(1)*). However, this is subject to any restriction or prohibition on the use of information which is contained in *CRCA 2005* or any other enactment or an international or other agreement to which the United Kingdom or Her Majesty's Government is party (*CRCA 2005, s 17(2)*). For the purpose of *CRCA 2005, s 17(1)* the reference to a 'function' of HMRC means a function of any of the persons listed in *CRCA 2005, s 17(3)*, including:

(a)   the Commissioners;

(b)   an officer of Revenue and Customs;

(c)   a person acting on behalf of the Commissioners or an officer of Revenue and Customs;

(d)   a committee established by the Commissioners;

(e)   a member of a committee established by the Commissioners;

(f)   the Commissioners of Inland Revenue (or any committee or staff of theirs or anyone acting on their behalf);

(g)   the Commissioners of Customs and Excise (or any committee or staff of theirs or anyone acting on their behalf).

HMRC's guidance expresses the transfer of information to another part of HMRC in the context of there being a 'business need' (and also recognising the restrictions of legal privilege). HMRC state (IDG20000) in respect of *CRCA 2005, s 17(1)*:

> 'This means that, with a few exceptions ... any information held by one part of the department may be passed to any other part of the department provided there is a business need. Business need means that there is a valid reason, directly connected to HMRC's functions, for information to be passed from one person to another. There will not be a business need where information is passed from one person to another because that information may be personally interesting.
>
> Information that is properly obtained under a Section 20 Taxes Management Act (TMA) notice is also covered by Section 17 CRCA and may be passed to another part of the department where there is a valid business need. The business need may be in respect of the same taxpayer or in relation to the tax affairs of others. You may only disclose the minimum information required to enable another business area to carry out its functions.

Tax fraud: criminal investigations and litigation – direct tax 3.159

Information obtained under a S20(2) TMA notice cannot be used elsewhere if a claim to Legal Professional Privilege could be sustained e.g. information obtained from a lawyer under a S 20(2) TMA notice cannot be used in relation to a client's tax affairs where the information could not be obtained under a S20(3) TMA notice.'

Obligation of confidentiality: CRCA 2005, s 18 imposes on HMRC an obligation of confidentiality, which provides that '... officials may not disclose information which is held by the Revenue and Customs in connection with a function of the Revenue and Customs'.

Permitted disclosures: The obligation of confidentiality is subject to exceptions (*CRCA 2005, s 18(2)*), which include the following:

(a) a disclosure which:

    (i) is made for the purposes of a function of the Revenue and Customs; and

    (ii) does not contravene any restriction imposed by the Commissioners,

(b) which is made in accordance with *CRCA 2005, s 20* (public interest disclosure) or *CRCA 2005, s 22* (disclosure to a prosecuting authority),

(c) which is made for the purposes of civil proceedings (whether or not within the United Kingdom) relating to a matter in respect of which the Revenue and Customs have functions,

(d) which is made for the purposes of a criminal investigation or criminal proceedings (whether or not within the United Kingdom) relating to a matter in respect of which the Revenue and Customs have functions,

(e) which is made in pursuance of an order of a court,

(f) which is made with the consent of each person to whom the information relates.

Further, the restriction on confidentiality is subject to any other enactment permitting disclosure (*CRCA 2005, s 18(3)*).

Public interest disclosure: As referred to above, under *CRCA 2005, s 20*, HMRC are permitted to make a disclosure if:

(a) it is made on the instructions of the Commissioners (which may be general or specific),

(b) it is of a kind to which (i) any of *CRCA 2005, ss 18(2)–(7)* apply; or (ii) specified in regulations made by the Treasury, and

(c) the Commissioners are satisfied that it is in the public interest.

3.159 *Tax fraud: criminal investigations and litigation – direct tax*

The categories referred to in *CRCA 2005, ss 18(2)–(7)* cover the following matters:

- *s 18(2)* A disclosure made:
    - (a) to a person exercising public functions (whether or not within the United Kingdom),
    - (b) for the purposes of the prevention or detection of crime, and
    - (c) in order to comply with an obligation of the United Kingdom, or Her Majesty's Government, under an international or other agreement relating to the movement of persons, goods or services.
- *s 18(3)* A disclosure if:
    - (a) it is made to a body which has responsibility for the regulation of a profession,
    - (b) it relates to misconduct on the part of a member of the profession, and
    - (c) the misconduct relates to a function of the Revenue and Customs.
- *s 18(4)* A disclosure if:
    - (a) it is made to a constable, and
    - (b) either:
        - (i) the constable is exercising functions which relate to the movement of persons or goods into or out of the United Kingdom, or
        - (ii) the disclosure is made for the purposes of the prevention or detection of crime.
- *s 18(5)* A disclosure if it is made:
    - (a) to the National Criminal Intelligence Service, and
    - (b) for a purpose connected with its functions under section 2(2) of the Police Act 1997 (c 50) (criminal intelligence).
- *s 18(6))* A disclosure if it is made:
    - (a) to a person exercising public functions in relation to public safety or public health, and
    - (b) for the purposes of those functions.
- *s 18(7)* A disclosure if it:
    - (a) is made to the Secretary of State for the purpose of enabling information to be entered in a computerised database, and

(b) relates to:
- (i) a person suspected of an offence,
- (ii) a person arrested for an offence,
- (iii) the results of an investigation, or
- (iv) anything seized.

Information disclosed in reliance on public interest disclosure may not be further disclosed without the consent of the Commissioners (which may be general or specific) (*CRCA 2005, s 20(9)*).

Disclosure to prosecuting authority: As discussed above, HMRC are permitted to disclose information in accordance with *CRCA 2005, s 21* to a prosecuting authority and for the purpose of enabling the authority:

- (i) to consider whether to institute criminal proceedings in respect of a matter considered in the course of an investigation conducted by or on behalf of Her Majesty's Revenue and Customs,
- (ii) to give advice in connection with a criminal investigation or criminal proceedings, or
- (iii) in the case of the Director of Public Prosecutions, to exercise his functions under, or in relation to, Part 5 or 8 of the *Proceeds of Crime Act 2002*.

For this purpose, 'prosecuting authority' means:

- (a) the Director of Public Prosecutions,
- (b) in Scotland, the Lord Advocate or a procurator fiscal, and
- (c) in Northern Ireland, the Director of Public Prosecutions for Northern Ireland.

Where information is disclosed to a prosecuting authority it may not be further disclosed (*CRCA 2005, s 21(3)* except: (*a*) for a purpose connected with the exercise of the prosecuting authority's functions, or (*b*) with the consent of the Commissioners (which may be general or specific).

MONEY LAUNDERING

Introduction

3.160 The purpose of this part is to provide an appreciation of the relationship between tax evasion and money laundering. Historically it was a widely held view that the money laundering legislation exists solely to deal with those

3.161 *Tax fraud: criminal investigations and litigation – direct tax*

involved in drug trafficking, terrorism or other 'serious crimes'. There was a prolonged and sometimes fierce debate as to whether money laundering extended to tax evasion and if so the appropriate measure, but it is now clear that tax evasion is covered.

3.161 The structure of this part is as follows:

- the money laundering legislation: details its applicability to the proceeds of domestic and foreign tax evasion;
- guidance for financial intermediaries and professional advisers: considers some of the existing guidance available;
- the role of the fiscal authorities: considers how the money laundering legislation is being and may be used by the fiscal authorities in enhancing tax compliance and in prosecutions for tax-related money laundering offences;
- the risk to intermediaries and professionals: considers some of the risks posed to intermediaries by the tax evasion/money laundering issue;
- conclusion.

The money laundering legislation

European Union Directives

3.162 The First Directive of the Council of the European Community dated 10 June 1991 on the prevention of the use of the financial system for the purpose of money laundering provides the foundation for the domestic money laundering legislation of the member states.

3.163 Nowhere in the Directive is the issue of tax evasion specifically exempted from the list of prohibited activities. Nowhere in the First Directive are the activities of those professionals who usually give advice on fiscal matters excluded from the list of persons subject thereto. On the contrary, the Second and Third Directives focused attention specifically on the professions.

3.164 UK domestic legislation on money laundering is based on the European Directives and, again, nowhere is the issue of tax evasion specifically exempted from those activities which are prohibited. The latest (2005 and Third Directive) entered into force in the UK on 15 December 2007 with the implementation of the Money Laundering Regulations 2007, SI 2007/2157 (MLR 2007). In the EU the Fourth Anti-Money Laundering Directive (Directive No 2015/849/EU) and an EU Regulation on reporting obligations

Tax fraud: criminal investigations and litigation – direct tax **3.167**

connected to money transfers (Regulation No 2015/847/EU) were passed on 20 May 2015. The Fourth Directive must be transposed by the member states into national legislation by 26 June 2017 (with the Regulation taking effect from the same date). This part does not consider the history of substantive anti-money laundering legislation and addresses only the regime imposed by *POCA 2002* (as amended) and MLR 2007.

3.165 As with the First and subsequent Directives, criminal activity means 'any kind of criminal involvement in the commission of a serious crime'. Certain serious offences are specified. Beyond this, member states may designate any other offence as a criminal activity for the purposes of the Directives (ie the Directives set a minimum standard).

3.166 In the UK, legislation such as the *Criminal Justice Act 1993* (*CJA 1993*) has long since been extended to cover the proceeds of all crime (including tax offences) and *POCA 2002* closes many legal loopholes which may have existed previously.

3.167 The Fourth Money Laundering Directive will considerably widen the scope of domestic regulations. The proposals will have greater effect in some continental European states and will help to level the playing field across the EU. Article 1 of the Fourth Directive provides that member states shall ensure money laundering and terrorist financing are prohibited. Specifically, Art 1(3) provides that for the purposes of the Directive, the following forms of conduct, when committed intentionally, will be regarded as money laundering (Art 1(3)):

(a) the conversion or transfer of property, knowing that such property is derived from criminal activity or from an act of participation in such activity, for the purpose of concealing or disguising the illicit origin of the property or of assisting any person who is involved in the commission of such an activity to evade the legal consequences of that person's action;

(b) the concealment or disguise of the true nature, source, location, disposition, movement, rights with respect to, or ownership of, property, knowing that such property is derived from criminal activity or from an act of participation in such an activity;

(c) the acquisition, possession or use of property, knowing, at the time of receipt, that such property was derived from criminal activity or from an act of participation in such an activity;

(d) participation in, association to commit, attempts to commit and aiding, abetting, facilitating and counselling the commission of any of the actions referred to in points (a), (b) and (c).

3.168 *Tax fraud: criminal investigations and litigation – direct tax*

3.168 The purpose of the Fourth Directive is to:

- facilitate the work of Financial Intelligence Units from different member states to identify and follow suspicious transfers of money and facilitate the exchange of information;

- establish a coherent policy towards non-EU countries that have deficient anti-money laundering and counter-terrorist financing regimes;

- ensure full traceability of funds transfers within, to and from the European Union.

3.169 The Directive requires registers to be kept detailing the identities of beneficial owners behind companies and trusts. The measures should improve transparency and enable tax authorities to establish who is behind legal ownership in such structures. The Government carried out a consultation exercise on how to implement the Directive into national law. As part of the consultation, the Government implemented the Money Laundering and Transfer of Funds (Information on the Payer) Regulations 2017 in order to transpose both the directive and the Fund Transfer Regulations. These regulations came into force on 26 June 2017. The previous Money Laundering Regulations 2007 and Transfer of Funds Regulations 2007 were revoked with appropriate transitional provision being made to the new Regulation.

The Money Laundering, Terrorist Financing and Transfer of Funds (Information on the Payer) Regulations 2017

3.170 The new regulations implement in part the Fourth Money Laundering Directive (2015/849/EU) on the prevention of the use of the financial system for the purpose of money laundering or terrorist financing, and the Funds Transfer Regulation (2015/847/EU). These regulations came into force on 26 June 2017. In overview the regulations cover the following matters:

1. *Part 2* (money laundering and terrorist financing) identifies the 'relevant persons' to whom the money laundering provisions apply (regs 8–15). Regulations 16–25 impose requirements for risk assessments to be carried out by the Treasury and the Home Office, the supervisory authorities and relevant persons to identify and assess the risks of money laundering and terrorist financing. They also require relevant persons to have policies, controls and procedures to mitigate and manage effectively the risks of money laundering and terrorist financing identified through the risk assessments. Regulation 26 prohibits any person from being the beneficial owner, officer or manager of certain firms or a sole practitioner unless that person has been approved by the appropriate supervisory authority. For instance, the ICAEW must approve all beneficial owners, officers and managers ('BOOMs') in supervised firms. Any person who continues to be a BOOM after 26 June 2018 without approval (i.e. any person with relevant unspent convictions) will be committing a criminal

offence punishable by imprisonment of up to three years and/or a financial penalty.

2. *Part 3* (customer due diligence) makes provision for customer due diligence measures. Regulations 27–32 identify what customer due diligence measures must be undertaken by relevant persons, and when those measures must be undertaken. Regulations 33–36 identify when enhanced customer due diligence measures must be applied by the relevant person in addition to the general customer due diligence measures required by regs 27–32. Regulations 37–39 identify when simplified customer due diligence measures may be applied by the relevant person (reg 37) and what customer due diligence measures are required in relation to electronic money (reg 39). Simplified customer due diligence measures are customer due diligence measures that may be adjusted by the relevant person provided there is sufficient monitoring in place to detect any unusual or suspicious transactions.

3. *Part 4* (reliance and record keeping) sets out the circumstances in which a relevant person may rely on another person to apply customer due diligence measures (reg 39). It also makes provision as to which records relevant persons are required to keep, and when they are to be deleted (reg 40) and clarifies the requirements as to data protection (reg 41).

4. *Part 5* (beneficial ownership information) applies to UK bodies corporate and to trustees. It requires trustees to inform the relevant person of their status, and corporate bodies and trustees to provide specified information to a relevant person in certain circumstances and to provide information to law enforcement authorities (regs 43 and 44). The trustee is under additional requirements to provide certain information to the Commissioners for Her Majesty's Revenue and Customs in certain circumstances. The Commissioners are under a requirement to hold the information that has been received from the trustee in a register (reg 45).

5. *Part 6* (money laundering and terrorist financing: supervision and registration) makes provision in relation to supervisory authorities and the registration of certain relevant persons. Regulations 46–52 provide for duties on supervisory authorities in relation to their own sector (regs 46, 47 and 48). The self-regulatory organisations listed in Sch 1 are subject to additional duties (reg 49). All supervisory authorities are subject to a duty to cooperate with other supervisory authorities, the Treasury, law enforcement authorities and overseas authorities (reg 50), and a duty to collect information (reg 51). Provision is made for the circumstances in which a supervisory authority may disclose information it holds for supervisory purposes (reg 52). Regulations 53–60 require the Financial Conduct Authority ('FCA') and the Commissioners to maintain registers of certain relevant persons and impose corresponding requirements on relevant persons to apply for registration.

3.170 *Tax fraud: criminal investigations and litigation – direct tax*

6. *Part 7* (transfer of funds (information on the payer) regulations) sets out the transfer of funds supervisory authorities for a payment service provider and the duties of the authorities (regs 61–64). There are only two transfer of funds supervisory authorities for service providers: the FCA and the Commissioners.

7. *Part 8* (information and investigation) gives supervisory authorities (including transfer of funds supervisory authorities) information gathering powers (regs 65–68), gives the FCA and the Commissioners further investigatory powers (regs 69–70) and makes provision for the way in which the powers in Part 8 may be exercised (regs 71–73).

8. *Part 9* (enforcement) identifies 'relevant requirements' for the purpose of these regulations (reg 75 and Sch 6) and gives the FCA and the Commissioners powers to impose civil penalties on any person who has contravened a relevant requirement (regs 76–85). Regulations 86 to 92 provide for criminal offences where a person has contravened a relevant requirement (reg 86); prejudiced an investigation (reg 87) or provided false or misleading information to any person in purported compliance with a requirement imposed by or under these Regulations (reg 88) and make provision in relation to criminal proceedings (regs 89–92).

8. *Part 10* (appeals) provides for an appeal from a decision by the FCA under these regulations (reg 93), and for reviews and appeals in relation to decisions of the Commissioners (regs 94–100).

For the foregoing purposes, under reg 7 and Sch 1 the following professional bodies are designated as supervisory authorities for relevant persons who are members of it, or regulated or supervised by it:

1. Association of Accounting Technicians
2. Association of Chartered Certified Accountants
3. Association of International Accountants
4. Association of Taxation Technicians
5. Chartered Institute of Legal Executives
6. Chartered Institute of Management Accountants
7. Chartered Institute of Taxation
8. Council for Licensed Conveyancers
9. Faculty of Advocates
10. Faculty Office of the Archbishop of Canterbury

Tax fraud: criminal investigations and litigation – direct tax **3.170**

11. General Council of the Bar
12. General Council of the Bar of Northern Ireland
13. Insolvency Practitioners Association
14. Institute of Certified Bookkeepers
15. Institute of Chartered Accountants in England and Wales
16. Institute of Chartered Accountants in Ireland
17. Institute of Chartered Accountants of Scotland
18. Institute of Financial Accountants
19. International Association of Bookkeepers
20. Law Society
21. Law Society of Northern Ireland
22. Law Society of Scotland

The Commissioners are the supervisory authority for auditors, external accountants and tax advisers who are not supervised by one of the professional bodies listed in Sch 1.

Relevant persons

As outlined above, Parts 1–6 and 8–11 apply to persons ('relevant persons') acting in the course of business carried on by them in the United Kingdom, who are listed below and are not within the exclusions provided for in reg 15 (e.g. a registered co-operative society, industrial and provident society (reg 8(1)). The persons who are relevant persons are:

(a) credit institutions;
(b) financial institutions;
(c) auditors, insolvency practitioners, external accountants and tax advisers;
(d) independent legal professionals;
(e) trust or company service providers;
(f) estate agents;
(g) high value dealers;
(h) casinos.

3.170 *Tax fraud: criminal investigations and litigation – direct tax*

The Regulations define the foregoing which includes, in so far as relevant to this book, the following:

Under reg 11:

(a) 'auditor' means any firm or individual who is:

    (i) a statutory auditor within the meaning of Part 42 of the *Companies Act 2006* (statutory auditors), when carrying out statutory audit work, or

    (ii) a local auditor within the meaning of section 4(1) of the *Local Audit and Accountability Act 2014* (general requirements for audit), when carrying out an audit required by that Act.

(b) 'insolvency practitioner' means any firm or individual who acts as an insolvency practitioner within the meaning of *Insolvency Act 1986, s 388* or article 3 of the Insolvency (Northern Ireland) Order 1989 (meaning of 'act as insolvency practitioner').

(c) 'external accountant' means a firm or sole practitioner who by way of business provides accountancy services to other persons, when providing such services.

(d) 'tax adviser' means a firm or sole practitioner who by way of business provides advice about the tax affairs of other persons, when providing such services.

Under reg 12:

'independent legal professional' means a firm or sole practitioner who by way of business provides legal or notarial services to other persons, when participating in financial or real property transactions concerning:

(a) the buying and selling of real property or business entities;

(b) the managing of client money, securities or other assets;

(c) the opening or management of bank, savings or securities accounts;

(d) the organisation of contributions necessary for the creation, operation or management of companies; or

(e) the creation, operation or management of trusts, companies, foundations or similar structures,

and, for this purpose, a person participates in a transaction by assisting in the planning or execution of the transaction or otherwise acting for or on behalf of a client in the transaction.

'trust or company service provider' means a firm or sole practitioner who by way of business provides any of the following services to other persons, when that firm or practitioner is providing such services:

(a) forming companies or other legal persons;

(b) acting, or arranging for another person to act:

    (i) as a director or secretary of a company;

    (ii) as a partner of a partnership; or

    (iii) in a similar capacity in relation to other legal persons;

(c) providing a registered office, business address, correspondence or administrative address or other related services for a company, partnership or any other legal person or legal arrangement;

(d) acting, or arranging for another person to act, as:

    (i) a trustee of an express trust or similar legal arrangement; or

    (ii) a nominee shareholder for a person other than a company whose securities are listed on a regulated market.

By reg 4(1) 'business relationship' means a business, professional or commercial relationship between a relevant person and a customer, which:

(a) arises out of the business of the relevant person, and

(b) is expected by the relevant person, at the time when contact is established, to have an element of duration.

Obligations imposed on Relevant persons

In overview, the following obligations are imposed on relevant persons:

1   *Risk assessment by relevant persons.* Under reg 18(1) a relevant person must take appropriate steps to identify and assess the risks of money laundering and terrorist financing to which its business is subject. In carrying out the risk assessment a relevant person must take into account:

    a. information made available to them by the supervisory authority, and

    b. risk factors including factors relating to:

        (i) its customers;

        (ii) the countries or geographic areas in which it operates;

        (iii) its products or services;

        (iv) its transactions; and

        (v) its delivery channels.

3.170 *Tax fraud: criminal investigations and litigation – direct tax*

A relevant person must keep an up-to-date record in writing of all the steps it has taken in compliance with the foregoing (reg 18(4)), unless its supervisory authority notifies it in writing that such a record is not required.

2 *Policies, controls and procedures.* By reg 19(1) a relevant person must:

   a. Establish policies, controls and procedures, and maintain policies, controls and procedures to mitigate and manage effectively the risks of money laundering and terrorist financing identified in any risk assessment undertaken by the relevant person under reg 18(1);

   b. regularly review and update the policies, controls and procedures established;

   c. maintain a record in writing of:

      (i) the policies, controls and procedures established;

      (ii) any changes to those policies, controls and procedures made as a result of any review and update; and

      (iii) the steps taken to communicate those policies, controls and procedures, or any changes to them, within the relevant person's business.

By reg 19(2) the policies, controls and procedures adopted by a relevant person must be (a) proportionate with regard to the size and nature of the relevant person's business, and (b) approved by its senior management. Further, the policies, controls and procedures must include (reg 19(4)):

(a) risk management practices;

(b) internal controls (see regs 21–24);

(c) customer due diligence (see regs 27–38);

(d) reliance and record keeping (see regs 39–40);

(e) the monitoring and management of compliance with, and the internal communication of, such policies, controls and procedures. The policies, controls and procedures must include policies, controls and procedures (reg 19(4)), inter alia:

   a. which provide for the identification and scrutiny of:

      (i) any case where (aa) a transaction is complex and unusually large, or there is an unusual pattern of transactions, and (bb) the transaction or transactions have no apparent economic or legal purpose; and

      (ii) any other activity or situation which the relevant person regards as particularly likely by its nature to be related to money laundering or terrorist financing;

Tax fraud: criminal investigations and litigation – direct tax **3.170**

- b. which specify the taking of additional measures, where appropriate, to prevent the use for money laundering or terrorist financing of products and transactions which might favour anonymity; and
- c. under which anyone in the relevant person's organisation who knows or suspects (or has reasonable grounds for knowing or suspecting) that a person is engaged in money laundering or terrorist financing as a result of information received in the course of the business or otherwise through carrying on that business is required to comply with:
    - (i) the *Terrorism Act 2000, Part 3*; or
    - (ii) the *Proceeds of Crime Act 2002, Part 7*.

Under reg 19(6) a relevant person must, where relevant, communicate the policies, controls and procedures which it establishes and maintains in accordance with this regulation to its branches and subsidiary undertakings which are located outside the United Kingdom.

By reg 21 where appropriate with regard to the size and nature of its business, a relevant person must:

(a) appoint one individual who is a member of the board of directors (or if there is no board, of its equivalent management body) or of its senior management as the officer responsible for the relevant person's compliance with the regulations;

(b) carry out screening of relevant employees appointed by the relevant person, both before the appointment is made and during the course of the appointment;

(c) establish an independent audit function with the responsibility:
   - (i) to examine and evaluate the adequacy and effectiveness of the policies, controls and procedures adopted by the relevant person to comply with the requirements of the Regulations;
   - (ii) to make recommendations in relation to those policies, controls and procedures; and
   - (iii) to monitor the relevant person's compliance with those recommendations.

By reg 24 a relevant person must:

(a) take appropriate measures to ensure that its relevant employees are:
   - (i) made aware of the law relating to money laundering and terrorist financing, and to the requirements of data protection, which are relevant to the implementation of the regulations; and

3.170 *Tax fraud: criminal investigations and litigation – direct tax*

        (ii)   regularly given training in how to recognise and deal with transactions and other activities or situations which may be related to money laundering or terrorist financing; and

   (b)   maintain a record in writing of the measures taken in respect of training, and in particular, of the training given to its relevant employees.

3   *Customer due diligence.* By reg 27(1) a relevant person must apply customer due diligence measures if the person:

   (a)   establishes a business relationship;

   (b)   carries out an occasional transaction that amounts to a transfer of funds within the meaning of Article 3.9 of the funds transfer regulation exceeding 1,000 euros;

   (c)   suspects money laundering or terrorist financing; or

   (d)   doubts the veracity or adequacy of documents or information previously obtained for the purposes of identification or verification.

Under reg 28(1) when a relevant person is required by reg 27 to apply customer due diligence measures the relevant person must:

   (a)   identify the customer unless the identity of that customer is known to, and has been verified by, the relevant person;

   (b)   verify the customer's identity unless the customer's identity has already been verified by the relevant person; and

   (c)   assess and, where appropriate, obtain information on, the purpose and intended nature of the business relationship or occasional transaction.

Where the customer is a body corporate, the relevant person must obtain and verify:

   (i)   the name of the body corporate;

   (ii)   its company number or other registration number;

   (iii)   the address of its registered office, and if different, its principal place of business;

Where the customer is beneficially owned by another person, the relevant person must:

   (a)   identify the beneficial owner;

   (b)   take reasonable measures to verify the identity of the beneficial owner so that the relevant person is satisfied that it knows who the beneficial owner is; and

Tax fraud: criminal investigations and litigation – direct tax **3.170**

(c) if the beneficial owner is a legal person, trust, company, foundation or similar legal arrangement take reasonable measures to understand the ownership and control structure of that legal person, trust, company, foundation or similar legal arrangement. However, this obligation does not apply where the customer is a company which is listed on a regulated market.

The relevant person must conduct ongoing monitoring of a business relationship (reg 27(8)):

(a) at other appropriate times to existing customers on a risk based approach;

(b) when the relevant person becomes aware that the circumstances of an existing customer relevant to its risk assessment for that customer have changed.

For the purposes of determining when it is appropriate to take customer due diligence measures in relation to existing customers, a relevant person must take into account, among other things:

(a) any indication that the identity of the customer, or of the customer's beneficial owner, has changed;

(b) any transactions which are not reasonably consistent with the relevant person's knowledge of the customer;

(c) any change in the purpose or intended nature of the relevant person's relationship with the customer;

(d) any other matter which might affect the relevant person's assessment of the money laundering or terrorist financing risk in relation to the customer.

Under reg 39(1) a relevant person may rely on a person who falls within reg 39(3) ('the third party') to apply any of the customer due diligence measures required by regs 28(2)–(6), (10) but, notwithstanding the relevant person's reliance on the other person, the relevant person remains liable for any failure to apply such measures. The persons within reg 39(3) are:

(a) another relevant person who is subject to the Regulations under reg 8 (e.g. Solicitor, Accountant, Chartered Tax Adviser);

(b) a person who carries on business in another EEA state who is:

(i) subject to requirements in national legislation implementing the fourth money laundering directive; and

(ii) supervised for compliance with the requirements laid down in the fourth money laundering directive in accordance with section 2 of Chapter VI of that directive; or

3.170 *Tax fraud: criminal investigations and litigation – direct tax*

- (c) a person who carries on business in a third country who is:
  - (i) subject to requirements in relation to customer due diligence and record keeping which are equivalent to those laid down in the fourth money laundering directive; and
  - (ii) supervised for compliance with those requirements in a manner equivalent to section 2 of Chapter VI of the fourth money laundering directive;
- (d) organisations whose members consist of persons within sub-paragraph (a), (b) or (c).

Where a relevant person is entitled to rely on a third party to apply customer due diligence measures (under reg 39(1) (see above), the following requirements must be met (reg 39(2)):

- (a) the relevant person must immediately obtain from the third party all the information needed to satisfy the requirements of regulation 28(2)–(6), (10) (see above);
- (b) the relevant person must enter into written arrangements with the third party which:
  - (i) enable the relevant person to obtain from the third party immediately on request copies of any identification and verification data and any other relevant documentation on the identity of the customer or its beneficial owner;
  - (ii) require the third party to retain copies of the data and documents referred to in paragraph (i) for the period referred to in reg 40.

However, by reg 39(4) a relevant person may not rely on a third party established in a country which has been identified by the European Commission as a high-risk third country under the fourth money laundering directive.

By reg 31(1) there is a requirement to cease transactions where, in relation to any customer, a relevant person is unable to apply customer due diligence measures as required by reg 28, that person:

- (a) must not carry out any transaction through a bank account with the customer or on behalf of the customer;
- (b) must not establish a business relationship or carry out a transaction with the customer otherwise than through a bank account;
- (c) must terminate any existing business relationship with the customer; and

Tax fraud: criminal investigations and litigation – direct tax **3.170**

(d) must consider whether the relevant person is required to make a disclosure (or to make further disclosure) by:

   (i) the *Terrorism Act 2000, Part 3*; or

   (ii) the *Proceeds of Crime Act 2002, Part 7*.

However, under reg 31(3) the obligation under reg 31(1) does not apply where an independent legal professional or other professional adviser is in the course of ascertaining the legal position for a client or performing the task of defending or representing that client in, or concerning, legal proceedings, including giving advice on the institution or avoidance of proceedings. Under reg 31(4) the term 'other professional adviser' means an auditor, external accountant or tax adviser who is a member of a professional body which is established for any such persons and which makes provision for:

(a) testing the competence of those seeking admission to membership of such a body as a condition for such admission; and

(b) imposing and maintaining professional and ethical standards for its members, as well as well as imposing sanctions for non-compliance with those standards.

By reg 33(1) a relevant person must apply enhanced customer due diligence measures and enhanced ongoing monitoring, in addition to the customer due diligence measures required under reg 28 and, if applicable, reg 29, to manage and mitigate the risks arising:

(a) in any case identified as one where there is a high risk of money laundering or terrorist financing:

   (i) by the relevant person under reg 18(1); or

   (ii) in information made available to the relevant person under regs 17(9) and 47;

(b) in any business relationship or transaction with a person established in a high-risk third country;

(c) in relation to correspondent relationships with a credit institution or a financial institution (in accordance with reg 34);

(d) if a relevant person has determined that a customer or potential customer is a politically exposed person ('PEP'), or a family member or known close associate of a PEP (in accordance with reg 35);

(e) in any case where the relevant person discovers that a customer has provided false or stolen identification documentation or information and the relevant person proposes to continue to deal with that customer;

3.170 *Tax fraud: criminal investigations and litigation – direct tax*

- (f) in any case where:
  - (i) a transaction is complex and unusually large, or there is an unusual pattern of transactions; and
  - (ii) the transaction or transactions have no apparent economic or legal purpose; and
- (g) in any other case which by its nature can present a higher risk of money laundering or terrorist financing.

The regulations impose record-keeping requirements under reg 40. Broadly, a relevant person must keep the records specified below for at least the period specified in reg 40(3).

The records are:

- (a) a copy of any documents and information obtained by the relevant person to satisfy the customer due diligence requirements in regs 28, 29 and 33–37;
- (b) sufficient supporting records (consisting of the original documents or copies) in respect of a transaction (whether or not the transaction is an occasional transaction) which is the subject of customer due diligence measures or ongoing monitoring to enable the transaction to be reconstructed.

By reg 40(3) the period is five years beginning on the date on which the relevant person knows, or has reasonable grounds to believe:

- (a) that the transaction is complete, for records relating to an occasional transaction; or
- (b) that the business relationship has come to an end for records relating to:
  - (i) any transaction which occurs as part of a business relationship; or
  - (ii) customer due diligence measures taken in connection with that relationship.

A relevant person is not required to keep the records referred to in para (3)(b)(i) for more than 10 years.

4 *Beneficial ownership information.* Under regs 43 and 44 certain obligations are imposed on UK bodies corporate and relevant trusts relating to the provision of information on beneficial ownership. In this regard, reg 42 provides that:

- (a) a 'UK body corporate' is a body corporate which is incorporated under the law of the United Kingdom or any part of the United Kingdom, and includes an eligible Scottish partnership;

Tax fraud: criminal investigations and litigation – direct tax **3.170**

    (b)   a 'relevant trust' is:

          (i)   a UK trust which is an express trust; or

          (ii)   a non-UK trust which is an express trust; and

                (aa)   receives income from a source in the United Kingdom; or

                (bb)   has assets in the United Kingdom, on which it is liable to pay one or more of the taxes referred to in reg 45(14);

    (c)   a trust is a 'UK trust' if:

          (i)   all the trustees are resident in the United Kingdom; or

          (ii)   sub-paragraph (d) applies;

    (d)   this sub-paragraph applies if:

          (i)   at least one trustee is resident in the United Kingdom, and

          (ii)   the settlor was resident and domiciled in the United Kingdom at the time when:

                (aa)   the trust was set up; or

                (bb)   the settlor added funds to the trust;

    (e)   a trust is a 'non-UK trust' if it is not a UK trust;

    (f)   a 'collective investment scheme' has the meaning given in the International Tax Compliance Regulations 2015, reg 12H.

A trustee or settlor is resident in the United Kingdom:

    (a)   in the case of a body corporate, if it is a UK body corporate;

    (b)   in the case of an individual, if the individual is resident in the United Kingdom for the purposes of one or more of the taxes referred to in reg 45(14).

5   *Corporate bodies: obligations:* By reg 43(1) when a UK body corporate which is not listed on a regulated market enters into a relevant transaction with a relevant person, or forms a business relationship with a relevant person, the body corporate must on request from the relevant person provide the relevant person with:

    (a)   information identifying:

          (i)   its name, registered number, registered office and principal place of business;

          (ii)   its board of directors, or if there is no board, the members of the equivalent management body;

          (iii)   the senior persons responsible for its operations;

3.170 *Tax fraud: criminal investigations and litigation – direct tax*

        (iv)   the law to which it is subject;

        (v)   its legal owners;

        (vi)   its beneficial owners; and

   (b)   its articles of association or other governing documents.

For the purposes of reg 43 references to the legal owners and beneficial owners of a UK body corporate include a reference to the legal owners and beneficial owners of any body corporate or trust which is directly or indirectly a legal owner or beneficial owner of that body corporate. Reg 43(1) (a)(vi) (beneficial owners information) does not apply if no person qualifies as a beneficial owner (within the meaning of reg 5(1)) of the UK body corporate; or any body corporate which is directly or indirectly the owner of that UK body corporate.

By reg. 5(1) the term 'beneficial owner', in relation to a body corporate which is not a company whose securities are listed on a regulated market, means:

(a)   any individual who exercises ultimate control over the management of the body corporate;

(b)   any individual who ultimately owns or controls (in each case whether directly or indirectly), including through bearer share holdings or by other means, more than 25% of the shares or voting rights in the body corporate; or

(c)   an individual who controls the body corporate.

By reg 43(4) if, during the course of a business relationship, there is any change in the identity of the individuals or information falling within reg 43(1), the UK body corporate must notify the relevant person of the change and the date on which it occurred within fourteen days from the date on which the body corporate becomes aware of the change.

6   *Trustee obligations.* By reg 44(1) the trustees of a relevant trust must maintain accurate and up-to-date records in writing of all the beneficial owners of the trust, and of any potential beneficiaries, containing the information required by regs 45(2)(b)–(d) and (5)(f), (g). When a trustee of a relevant trust, acting as trustee, enters into a relevant transaction with a relevant person, or forms a business relationship with a relevant person, the trustee must:

   (a)   inform the relevant person that it is acting as trustee; and

   (b)   on request from the relevant person, provide the relevant person with information identifying all the beneficial owners of the trust (which, in the case of a class of beneficiaries, may be done by describing the class of persons who are beneficiaries or potential beneficiaries under the trust). If, during the course of a business

Tax fraud: criminal investigations and litigation – direct tax **3.170**

relationship, there is any change in the information provided previously, the trustees must notify the relevant person of the change and the date on which it occurred within fourteen days from the date on which any one of the trustees became aware of the change.

By reg 44(4) a 'relevant transaction' means a transaction in relation to which the relevant person is required to apply customer due diligence measures under reg 27.

By reg 44(5) the trustees of a relevant trust must on request provide information to any law enforcement authority:

(a) about the beneficial owners of the trust; and

(b) about any other individual referred to as a potential beneficiary in a document from the settlor relating to the trust such as a letter of wishes.

If the trustees of a relevant trust are relevant persons who are being paid to act as trustees of that trust, they must:

(a) retain the records referred to in para 44(1) for a period of five years after the date on which the final distribution is made under the trust; and

(b) make arrangements for those records to be deleted at the end of that period, unless:

   (i) the trustees are required to retain them by or under any enactment or for the purpose of court proceedings;

   (ii) any person to whom information in a record relates consents to the retention of that information; or

   (iii) the trustees have reasonable grounds for believing that records containing the personal data need to be retained for the purpose of legal proceedings.

By reg 44(10) any of the following authorities is a law enforcement authority:

(a) the Commissioners;

(b) the FCA;

(c) the NCA;

(d) police forces maintained under the *Police Act 1996, s 2*;

(e) the Police of the Metropolis;

(f) the Police for the City of London;

(g) the Police Service of Scotland;

3.170 *Tax fraud: criminal investigations and litigation – direct tax*

- (h) the Police Service of Northern Ireland;
- (i) the Serious Fraud Office.

7 *Register of beneficial ownership*: By reg 45(1) the Commissioners must maintain a register ('the register') of:

- (a) beneficial owners of taxable relevant trusts; and
- (b) potential beneficiaries (referred to in reg 44(5)(b)) of taxable relevant trusts.

The trustees of a taxable relevant trust must within the time specified provide the Commissioners with:

- (a) the information specified below in relation to the trust; and
- (b) the information specified in below in relation to each of the individuals referred to in regs 44(2)(b) and (5)(b) (but if sub-paragraph (d) applies, this information does not need to be provided in relation to the beneficiaries of the trust).

By reg 45(14) a taxable relevant trust is a relevant trust in any year in which its trustees are liable to pay any of the following taxes in the United Kingdom in relation to assets or income of the trust:

- (a) income tax;
- (b) capital gains tax;
- (c) inheritance tax;
- (d) stamp duty land tax (within the meaning of the *Finance Act 2003, s 42*);
- (e) land and buildings transaction tax (within the meaning of the *Land and Buildings Transaction Tax (Scotland) Act 2013, s 1*);
- (f) stamp duty reserve tax.

The information required to be provided to the Commissioners must be provided on or before:

- (a) 31st January 2018; or
- (b) 31st January after the tax year in which the trustees were first liable to pay any of the taxes referred to in para (14) ('UK taxes').

By reg 45(5) the information to be provided to the Commissioners is:

- (a) the full name of the trust;
- (b) the date on which the trust was set up;
- (c) a statement of accounts for the trust, describing the trust assets and identifying the value of each category of the trust assets at the date

Tax fraud: criminal investigations and litigation – direct tax 3.170

on which the information is first provided to the Commissioners (including the address of any property held by the trust);

(d) the country where the trust is considered to be resident for tax purposes;

(e) the place where the trust is administered;

(f) a contact address for the trustees;

(g) the full name of any advisers who are being paid to provide legal, financial or tax advice to the trustees in relation to the trust.

By reg 45(6) the information as to the beneficiaries which is to be provided to the Commissioners is

(a) the individual's full name;

(b) the individual's national insurance number or unique taxpayer reference, if any;

(c) if the individual does not have a national insurance number or unique taxpayer reference, the individual's usual residential address;

(d) if the address provided under sub-paragraph (c) is not in the United Kingdom:

   (i) the individual's passport number or identification card number, with the country of issue and the expiry date of the passport or identification card; or

   (ii) if the individual does not have a passport or identification card, the number, country of issue and expiry date of any equivalent form of identification;

(e) the individual's date of birth;

(f) the nature of the individual's role in relation to the trust.

As to information to be provided in respect of a company by reg 45(7) the information is:

(a) the legal entity's corporate or firm name;

(b) the legal entity's unique taxpayer reference, if any;

(c) the registered or principal office of the legal entity;

(d) the legal form of the legal entity and the law by which it is governed;

(e) if applicable, the name of the register of companies in which the legal entity is entered (including details of the EEA state or third country in which it is registered), and its registration number in that register; and

(f) the nature of the entity's role in relation to the trust.

3.171 *Tax fraud: criminal investigations and litigation – direct tax*

POCA 2002

3.171 Part 7 of *POCA 2002* consolidates, replaces and expands the previous anti-money laundering legislation. There are three specific offences of money laundering.

Section 327 – concealing

3.172 A person commits an offence if he conceals, disguises, converts, transfers or removes criminal property from England and Wales or from Scotland or from Northern Ireland.

Section 328 – arrangements

3.173 A person commits an offence if he enters into or becomes concerned in an arrangement which he knows or suspects facilitates (by whatever means) the acquisition, retention, use or control of criminal property by or on behalf of another person. The anti-money laundering (AML) guidance (March 2018) produced by the legal sector AML supervisors, including the Law Society, has received the approval of HM Treasury. It is available at: http://www.lawsociety.org.uk/policy-campaigns/articles/anti-money-laundering-guidance/. For those involved in litigation the guidance states (at p 89):

> '**What is an arrangement?**
>
> Arrangement is not defined in Part 7 of POCA. The arrangement must exist and have practical effects relating to the acquisition, retention, use or control of property.
>
> An agreement to make an arrangement will not always be an arrangement. The test is whether the arrangement does in fact, in the present and not the future, have the effect of facilitating the acquisition, retention, use or control of criminal property by or on behalf of another person.
>
> **What is not an arrangement?**
>
> *Bowman v Fels* [2005] EWCA Civ 226 held that section 328 does not cover or affect the ordinary conduct of litigation by legal professionals, including any step taken in litigation from the issue of proceedings and the securing of injunctive relief or a freezing order up to its final disposal by judgment.
>
> Our view, supported by Counsel's opinion, is that dividing assets in accordance with the judgment, including the handling of the assets which are criminal property, is not an arrangement. Further, settlements, negotiations, out of court settlements, alternative dispute resolution and tribunal representation are not arrangements.

However, the property will generally still remain criminal property and you may need to consider referring your client for specialist advice regarding possible offences they may commit once they come into possession of the property after completion of the settlement.

The recovery of property by a victim of an acquisitive offence will not be committing an offence under either section 328 or section 329 of the Act.'

Section 329 – acquisition, use and possession

3.174 A person commits an offence if he acquires, uses or has possession of criminal property.

Section 340 – interpretation

3.175 Criminal conduct is conduct which constitutes an offence in any part of the UK or would constitute an offence in any part of the UK if it occurred there. Property is criminal property if it constitutes a person's benefit from criminal conduct, or it represents such a benefit (in whole or part and whether directly or indirectly), and the alleged offender knows or suspects that it constitutes or represents such a benefit.

3.176 Money laundering is an act which:

(a) constitutes an offence under *ss 327, 328* or *329*;

(b) constitutes an attempt, conspiracy or inducement to commit an offence specified in (a) above;

(c) constitutes aiding, abetting, counselling or procuring the commission of an offence specified in (a) above; or

(d) would constitute an offence specified in (a), (b) or (c) above if done in the UK.

3.177 The Serious Organised Crime Agency (SOCA) (now the National Crime Agency (NCA)) defines money laundering as follows (SOCA website, 4 August 2009):

'Money laundering is any action taken to conceal, arrange, use or possess the proceeds of any criminal conduct. Criminals try to launder "dirty money" in an attempt to make it look "clean" in order to be able to use the proceeds without detection and to put them beyond the reach of law enforcement *and taxation agencies*.' (emphasis added)

3.178 It should be noted that this primary legislation is drafted in extremely wide terms sufficient to embrace the conduct of the person involved in the

3.179 *Tax fraud: criminal investigations and litigation – direct tax*

criminal conduct himself; *POCA 2002* is not directed solely at intermediaries. Similarly, the primary legislation fails to provide any *de minimis* limit in relation to criminal property and applies to all criminal conduct no matter how petty.

3.179 In relation to the regulated sector as defined by MLR 2017, *POCA 2002, s 330* creates a criminal offence for any person within the scope of MLR 2017 if they do not report their knowledge, suspicion or information which gives reasonable grounds for knowing or suspecting that another person is laundering the proceeds of any criminal conduct, where the information comes to them in the course of a business in the regulated sector. *POCA, s 330(10)* contains a privileged circumstances reporting exemption. Members of relevant professional bodies (referred to as 'relevant professional advisers') who know about or suspect money laundering or terrorist financing (MLTF) offences (or have reasonable grounds for either) are not required to submit a SAR if the information came to them in privileged circumstances (ie during the provision of legal advice and acting in respect of litigation). As recognised in the AML guidance (CCAB, March 2018):

> '… in these circumstances, and as long as the information was not provided with the intention of advancing a crime, then the information must not be reported.'

The privileged reporting exemption only covers SARs and should not be confused with legal professional privilege, which also extends to other documentation and advice. In *POCA, s 330(14)*, 'relevant professional adviser' is defined as an accountant, auditor or tax adviser:

(i) who is a member of a relevant professional body; and

(ii) that body makes provision for: testing professional competence as a condition of admission; and imposing and maintaining professional and ethical standards for members along with sanctions for failures to comply.

The AML guidance (CCAB, March 2018) provides the following examples of work which may fall within privileged circumstances (see 6.2.25);

- Advice on tax law to assist a client in understanding their tax position;
- Advice on the legal aspects of a take-over bid;
- Advice on duties of directors under the *Companies Act*;
- Advice to directors on legal issues relating to the *Insolvency Act 1986*;
- Advice on employment law;
- Assisting a client by taking witness statements from him or from third parties in respect of litigation;

- Representing a client, as permitted, at a tax tribunal; and
- When instructed as an expert witness by a solicitor on behalf of a client in respect of litigation.

However, audit work, book-keeping, preparation of accounts or tax compliance assignments are unlikely to take place in privileged circumstances (see 6.2.26).

3.180 The legislation embraces all criminal conduct (including summary offences) which constitutes an offence in the UK or elsewhere if the offence would be recognised in the UK. In relation to criminal conduct there is no exception in relation to tax evasion, which is capable of being charged in a multitude of ways under common or statute law.

3.181 Similarly, the long and learned debate concerning the identity of funds representing the proceeds of crime under previous legislation (ie whether the proceeds represented the profits or gains not declared for tax purposes or a lesser amount, namely the tax due thereon) is now put to rest completely by the new statutory definition of criminal property referred to above. Any earlier doubt concerning the point at which funds became the proceeds of crime (ie before or after a tax return or other false account or document was submitted to the Revenue) are potentially overcome by the new definition of money laundering referred to in *POCA 2002, s 340(11)* and, in particular, paras (b) and (c) thereof. It remains necessary for the Crown to demonstrate that an act of alleged money laundering involved both criminal conduct and the proceeds of crime.

Foreign tax evasion

3.182 *POCA 2002, s 340(2)(b)* extends the money laundering legislation to funds derived from criminal conduct in foreign jurisdictions to the extent that such conduct would constitute an offence in any part of the UK had it occurred there.

Historically, some have questioned whether the money laundering legislation applies to the proceeds of foreign tax evasion that pass through the UK.

3.183 There is case law to support the general principle that UK courts will not enforce foreign revenue law (*Government of India v Taylor* [1955] AC 491). It was therefore suggested that to bring the proceeds of foreign tax evasion within the ambit of the money laundering legislation would violate this principle. In many cases, evading foreign tax will involve conduct which breaches the general criminal law as well as specific revenue law.

3.184 *Tax fraud: criminal investigations and litigation – direct tax*

Obvious examples are false accounting, conspiracy to defraud and obtaining a pecuniary advantage by deception.

3.184 The offence of widest application is likely to be false accounting under the *Theft Act 1968, s 17*. If an offence of false accounting is committed in a foreign jurisdiction (albeit as part of a wider scheme to defraud the foreign fiscal authority) *POCA 2002, s 340(2)(b)* treats this as having occurred in the UK. Hence it would seem difficult to argue that *ss 327, 328* or *329* do not apply.

3.185 It is important to note that the test laid down by *s 340(2)(b)* is whether the criminal conduct would constitute an offence if it had taken place in any part of the UK. There is no need to enquire into the workings of foreign tax systems to determine whether a client's actions may amount to a criminal offence in the foreign jurisdiction. The only question which needs to be addressed when considering the applicability of *s 340(2)(b)* is 'If the conduct had taken place in the UK, would it constitute a criminal offence?'

3.186 The *Criminal Justice (International Cooperation) Act 1990, s 4*, which originally related to drug trafficking offences, gives the Serious Fraud Office the power to investigate UK aspects of foreign tax offences and to assist foreign fiscal/prosecuting authorities in this regard. These powers have been used with substantial effect.

What constitutes knowledge or suspicion?

3.187 Under *POCA 2002*, it is an offence for those in the regulated sector to fail to report where, inter alia, they have reasonable grounds to suspect someone has committed a money laundering offence.

3.188 What would constitute the requisite degree of 'knowledge or suspicion' for these purposes given the new objective test imposed on the regulated sector? For example, is anecdotal evidence that the vast majority of a country's inhabitants routinely evade tax sufficient to sustain the argument that the individual should have 'known or suspected' that the foreign national seeking help with a transaction or advice was guilty of an offence? If the individual is aware of such anecdotal evidence, does this equate with 'knowledge or suspicion' based on the objective standard now imposed on the regulated sector. Certainly not; however, this may indicate a need for enhanced due diligence following MLR 2007, reg 14.

3.189 In *R v Da Silva* [2006] EWCA Crim 1654, the Court of Appeal held that 'suspicion' meant that 'there is a possibility, which is more than fanciful, that the relevant facts exist. A vague feeling of unease would not suffice'.

Guidance for financial intermediaries and professional advisers

Institute of Chartered Accountants in England and Wales

3.190 ICAEW Guidance entitled 'Anti-Money Laundering Guidance for the Accountancy Sector' (TECH 04/08) provides in section 9 as follows:

'9.1.1 Where a tax practitioner knows or suspects, or has reasonable grounds for knowing or suspecting, that a client or other party is engaged in tax evasion in the UK or overseas, this will clearly amount to one or more of a number of possible criminal offences, such as theft, obtaining pecuniary advantage by fraud, false accounting, cheating HMRC, the offence of fraudulent evasion of income tax under s 144 Finance Act 2000 or a range of specific indirect tax offences .... Unless the privilege reporting exemption applies ... a tax practitioner should report the matter to SOCA (or to his firm's MLRO where he is not a sole practitioner) immediately.

9.1.2 If the suspected evasion is of taxes outside the UK, in circumstances which would be a criminal offence if the conduct occurred in the UK, this should also be reported immediately unless it is known to be lawful under the criminal law applying in that country and that conduct, if carried out in the UK, would attract a maximum sentence in the UK of less than twelve months, except as prescribed by order.'

3.191 *POCA 2002, s 337* on protected disclosures exempts a person who receives information in the course of his trade, profession, business or employment from any legal or other obligations (ie professional) that would otherwise prevent him from making disclosures to the authorities. There are, however, three conditions:

1. that the information came to the attention of the discloser in the course of his trade, profession, business or employment;
2. that the information:
    (a) causes the discloser to know or suspect, or
    (b) gives him reasonable grounds for knowing or suspecting that another person is engaged in money laundering; and
3. the disclosure was made as soon as is practicable after the information comes to the discloser.

3.192 The disclosure must be made in good faith and as soon as practicable. It is possible that ill-considered disclosures would not be protected from suit. The potential for civil litigation must not be overlooked; for example, there may be exposure to claims predicated upon constructive trusteeship – knowing receipt or knowing assistance.

3.193   *Tax fraud: criminal investigations and litigation – direct tax*

3.193   However, a detailed consideration of the risk of civil liability is beyond the scope of this chapter. Professional advisers who are considering a report to SOCA (now the NCA) and are concerned about the risk of litigation should seek specialist advice.

The Consultative Committee of Accountancy Bodies

3.194   The Consultative Committee of Accountancy Bodies (CCAB) issued Anti-Money Laundering Guidance for the accountancy sector, which has been approved by HM Treasury (see para 1.3.1 of the guidance). Because this guidance has been approved by HM Treasury, the UK courts must take account of its contents when deciding whether a business subject to it has committed an offence under the 2017 Regulations, or *POCA, ss 330–331*. Guidance on tax matters is included in Appendix A of the Guidance. The guidance (May 2018) is available at: https://www.icaew.com/en/membership/regulations-standards-and-guidance/practice-management/anti-money-laundering-guidance OR https://www.ccab.org.uk/documents/FinalAMLGuidance2018.pdf

The guidance has been approved and adopted by the following supervisory bodies:

- Institute of Chartered Accountants in England and Wales – www.icaew.com
- Association of Accounting Technicians – www.aat.org.uk
- Association of Taxation Technicians – www.att.org.uk
- Association of International Accountants – www.aiaworldwide.com
- Institute of Certified Bookkeepers – www.bookkeepers.org.uk
- Chartered Institute of Management Accountants – www.cimaglobal.com
- Institute of Financial Accountants – www.ifa.org.uk
- International Association of Bookkeepers – www.iab.org.uk
- Association of Chartered Certified Accountants – www.accaglobal.com/uk/en.html
- Chartered Institute of Taxation – www.tax.org.uk
- Insolvency Practitioners Association – www.insolvency-practitioners.org.uk
- Insolvency Service – www.gov.uk/government/organisations/insolvency-service

Tax fraud: criminal investigations and litigation – direct tax **3.198**

- HM Revenue & Customs – www.gov.uk/government/organisations/hm-revenue-customs
- Institute of Chartered Accountants in Scotland – www.icas.com
- Chartered Accountants Ireland - https://www.charteredaccountants.ie/

Chartered Institute of Taxation

3.195 The Chartered Institute of Taxation (CIOT) has issued 'Supplementary Anti-Money Laundering Guidance for the Tax Practitioner' as Appendix A to the CCAB main guidance. The Guidance is available at: https://www.icaew.com/en/restrictedmedia?mediaItemId=8cc5c3e6-ca7c-4ecf-9778-c5b754534d7f or here: https://www.ccab.org.uk/documents/FinalAMLGuidance2018.pdf

The guidance note dated May 2018 (as referred to above) has been approved by HM Treasury.

Auditing Practices Board

3.196 The Auditing Practices Board (APB) issued Practice Note 12 (Revised) 'Money Laundering – Interim Guidance for Auditors on UK Legislation' on September 2010. The purpose of the Practice Note is to provide auditors with information on the money laundering legislation and guidance on its relationship with their responsibilities as auditors. Any subsequent update will be available at: https://www.frc.org.uk/auditors/audit-assurance/standards-and-guidance/practice-notes.

3.197 The practice note offers some extremely useful guidance on money laundering legislation (but prior to the 2017 changes), but is now silent on the subject of tax offences.

The Law Society

3.198 The anti-money laundering (AML) guidance (March 2018) produced by the legal sector AML supervisors, including the Law Society, has received the approval of HM Treasury. It is available at: http://www.lawsociety.org.uk/policy-campaigns/articles/anti-money-laundering-guidance/. For those involved in litigation the guidance states (at p 17):

'Activities not covered by the Regulations

HM Treasury has confirmed that the following would not generally be viewed as participation in a financial transaction:
- payment on account of costs to a legal professional or payment of a legal professional's bill

3.199 *Tax fraud: criminal investigations and litigation – direct tax*

- provision of legal advice
- ***participation in litigation or a form of alternative dispute resolution***
- will-writing, although you should consider whether any accompanying taxation advice is covered
- work funded by the Legal Services Commission

If you are uncertain whether the Regulations apply to your work, you should seek legal advice on the individual circumstances of your practice or simply take the broadest possible approach to compliance with the Regulations.'

(Emphasis added)

Further, the guidance states in respect of litigation (at p 49):

'Ascertaining legal position

Regulation 31(3) provides that the prohibition in 31(1) does not apply where:

An independent legal professional or other professional adviser is in the course of ascertaining the legal position for their client or performing the task of defending or representing that client in, or concerning, legal proceedings, including giving advice on the institution or avoidance of proceedings.

The requirement to cease acting and consider making a report to the NCA when you cannot complete CDD does not apply when you are providing legal advice or preparing for or engaging in litigation or alternative dispute resolution.

This exception does not apply to transactional work, so take a cautious approach to the distinction between advice and litigation work, and transactional work.'

HM Revenue & Customs

3.199 Following their appointment as a supervisory authority under MLR 2007 and now MLR 2017, HMRC issued guidance for those parts of the regulated sector in respect of which it was responsible. The guidance was contained in HMRC Notice MLR8 which was revised in August 2008 and withdrawn in July 2010.

3.200 Paragraph 1.1 stated: 'All auditors, insolvency practitioners, external accountants and tax advisers, including those that are supervised by HMRC, should follow the guidance published by the Consultative Committee of Accountancy Bodies (CCAB)': see above. No specific guidance on tax matters was provided; however, HMRC has adopted the CCAB guidance referred to above (see https://www.gov.uk/government/publications/anti-money-laundering-guidance-for-the-accountancy-sector). HMRC refers to the CCAB Guidance in relation to the accountancy sector.

3.201 HMRC has published the following guidance:

(a) Guidance to assist in identifying whether a trust or company service provider needs to register for supervision with HMRC under the Money Laundering Regulations: see https://www.gov.uk/guidance/money-laundering-regulations-trust-or-company-service-provider-registration.

(b) Trust or company service provider guidance for money laundering supervision. This guidance was finalised on 7 March 2018 and has been approved by HM Treasury. See https://www.gov.uk/government/publications/anti-money-laundering-guidance-for-trust-or-company-service-providers.

(c) Guidance to assist in identifying whether an estate agency business needs to register with HMRC under the Money Laundering Regulations: https://www.gov.uk/guidance/registration-guide-for-estate-agency-businesses.

(d) Money service business guidance for money laundering supervision. This guidance was finalised on 7 March 2018 and has been approved by HM Treasury. See https://www.gov.uk/government/publications/anti-money-laundering-guidance-for-money-service-businesses.

Knowledge or suspicion of an offence

3.202 As with other offences, there is no requirement under the money laundering legislation for a UK financial institution, or a professional adviser, to investigate the affairs of its customers or clients to ascertain whether an offence has been committed. Financial institutions may not be in a position to judge whether a customer has paid tax due in the UK or in any other country. The money laundering legislation does not require a report to the NCA where there is a suspicion that a customer may be considering evading tax in the future. There has to be knowledge or suspicion that the conduct which has generated the proceeds of tax evasion has already occurred or is continuing.

3.203 If knowledge or a suspicion does arise that the relevant conduct has taken place, then a report should be made to the NCA unless the client enjoys the benefit of legal professional privilege or the more limited benefits of the regulations relating to accountants. In these cases specialist advice should be

3.204 *Tax fraud: criminal investigations and litigation – direct tax*

obtained where necessary as these exceptions are limited in their application and certainly will not apply at all where conduct is capable of furthering a crime (known as the crime exception).

Procedures for processing the reports

3.204 It is possible that a special form will be prescribed for reporting suspicions of tax evasion. For the time being the NCA requests that one of the two general forms in issue be used. The reporting procedure is outlined at www.nationalcrimeagency.gov.uk/publications/517-submitting-a-suspicious-activity-report-sar-within-the-regulated-sector/file.

Guidance on the completion of a SAR can be found at http://www.nationalcrimeagency.gov.uk/publications/suspicious-activity-reports-sars.

3.205 The NCA will consider the disclosures received and will pass all or some of the intelligence contained in the suspicious transaction report to the enforcement agency with the power to investigate further. Disclosures which appear to provide evidence of a tax-related crime will be passed to HMRC. Each case will be judged on its merits and not necessarily on the amount of tax at risk.

3.206 Where the intelligence relates to offences committed overseas, the NCA will have the power to disclose the intelligence to Financial Intelligence Units overseas, subject to ensuring suitable safeguards. HMRC may also pass information to an overseas tax authority under various provisions, for example the double taxation agreements or the EU Mutual Assistance Directive.

The role of the fiscal authorities

3.207 Historically, whereas HM Customs and Excise charged money laundering offences in addition to predicate tax offences, the Revenue did not.

The quality of the intelligence flowing to the Revenue from 1998, and the results that quickly followed therefrom, led to a change of attitude, which broadly coincided with *POCA 2002* entering into force. The Revenue Publication 'Working Together' Issue 13 commented on *POCA 2002* both generally and specifically where there was an impact from the tax perspective. The following extracts are of interest:

> '*Requirement for Professional Advisers to Report Knowledge or Suspicion of Tax Evasion*
>
> All SAR forms must be submitted direct to NCIS. This is the case whether the report concerns the proceeds of tax evasion or any other form of criminal

Tax fraud: criminal investigations and litigation – direct tax **3.208**

activity. NCIS is the government body to receive these reports as only they have the information to check whether there are links to wider criminality.

The Inland Revenue is not a receiving body for these reports. Where a voluntary disclosure about unpaid liabilities due to tax evasion is intended to be made to the Revenue the professional adviser is still required to make a SAR to NCIS at the earliest opportunity.

Reports that Concern Tax Evasion

Reports that relate to tax evasion will be referred within the NCA to an Inland Revenue team who will analyse and evaluate them. Where the only criminality identified from this analysis is tax evasion, the reports will be forwarded by NCIS to the Inland Revenue or HM Customs & Excise as appropriate. For offences of evading direct taxes or NICs the Inland Revenue will be the investigating body and, in England and Wales, the prosecuting body for these offences. In Scotland the Procurator Fiscal and in Northern Ireland the Director of Public Prosecutions are the prosecuting bodies. Reports forwarded by NCIS to the Revenue will be received by Special Compliance Office (SCO) (now Specialist Investigations).

Effect on Inland Revenue Enquiries and Hansard (now Code of Practice 9)

Any Inland Revenue enquiries that result from or are informed by disclosures forwarded by NCIS will be carried out in the same manner as any other Inland Revenue enquiry.

In particular reporting a case to NCIS ahead of notifying the Revenue will have no bearing on how the Revenue may treat a case, if the taxpayer is actively seeking to set their affairs straight. This also applies to cases dealt with under the Inland Revenue approach to civil settlements known as "Hansard".

Confidentiality of information received by the Inland Revenue will of course remain of uppermost importance. In cases other than criminal investigations by SCO, procedures are in place such that investigators receive only the factual information from a SAR with no knowledge of who made the original disclosure.

Tipping Off

Approaching the Inland Revenue to make a disclosure on behalf of a client about unpaid tax liabilities after the SAR has been sent to the NCA does not constitute tipping off.'

3.208 In 2017 the NCA published the Suspicious Activity Reports (SARs) Annual Report 2017. The following is an extract:

'**HMRC increasing the use of SARs**

HMRC's criminal finance strategy is based around identification and intervention against key risk areas using the full range of the department's

3.209 *Tax fraud: criminal investigations and litigation – direct tax*

capabilities. This includes civil or criminal investigation, asset disruption, denial and recovery techniques, policy and legislative amendment and, in relation to MLRs risks, the full range of anti-money laundering supervisory interventions, including criminal sanction. Intelligence and organisational learning is extracted from these activities and used to inform the overall risk and threat picture, which in turn influences future operational activity.

A key component of risk identification is the SARs regime. SARs, and the intelligence derived from them, play a fundamental part in HMRC's drive to maximise intervention opportunities afforded by the criminal finance intelligence strategy and the full range of asset disruption, denial and recovery techniques available to HMRC. The 2016–17 financial year witnessed a change in HMRC's operational response to DAML SARs, with a number of interventions secured using non-POCA capability such as civil freezing orders or civil insolvency interventions. These represent a new way of working which HMRC wishes to build upon during 2017–18 when a number of new provisions are made available within the Criminal Finances Act.

HMRC has continued to work with the NCA using a data matching tool that enables the cross referencing of HMRC and third party data with SARs data. This has matched risk profiles to SARs data and continues to generate cases for both criminal and civil investigation. Yield from civil enquires between April 2016 and March 2017 amounted to £48.7m. Further exploitation of this capability has also enhanced civil investigations profiled for HMRC's risk-led taskforces by generating intelligence to support a yield of £22.1m between July 2016 and March 2017.

Progress to expand the capability continues and has enabled the exchange of new information, including interest markers and enhanced data to improve risk assessment from the Elmer database. HMRC's embedded staff in the UKFIU continue to work with the NCA to identify and develop sensitive SAR intelligence. This aims to identify undeclared and unreported assets and income hidden overseas and to recover unpaid taxes, along with any penalties due.'

The full report may be found at http://www.nationalcrimeagency.gov.uk/publications/suspicious-activity-reports-sars

HMRC's strategy

3.209 These fresh sources of intelligence have served as significant new sources of investigation cases and will undoubtedly enhance existing investigations. The flow of intelligence will also inform HMRC's risk-assessment processes, which are used as a basis for case selection. HMRC has stated in unequivocal terms that its first consideration in receiving intelligence will be to identify targets for criminal proceedings.

3.210 In its statement of Criminal Investigation Policy, HMRC notes that it will consider a criminal investigation 'In cases involving money laundering with particular focus on advisers, accountants, solicitors and others acting in a professional capacity who provide the means to put tainted money out of reach of law enforcement'.

3.211 HMRC has responsibility for investigating money laundering cases where tax evasion is the predicate crime and will operate a selective prosecution policy. To this end a specialist unit has been established (the Criminal Taxes Unit). Officers within the unit will use powers under *POCA 2002* and will work closely with other law-enforcement agencies exchanging information under the legal gateways available. The prosecution of tax-related money laundering offences is now the responsibility of the Revenue and Customs Prosecutions Office.

3.212 In 2004 SOCA (now the NCA) stated: 'the Inland Revenue indicates that around a fifth of disclosures received from SOCA identify a new target and a quarter lead to new enquiries'.

In November 2004, the Revenue published a press release concerning the Proceeds of Crime Act and money laundering. This document also contained a statement of the Revenue's anti money-laundering strategy. In 2007 this was followed by the publication of the HMRC Criminal Finances Strategic Framework. The statements expand on the principles outlined above and are significant documents worthy of being read in full.

3.213 Of the second document, paras 71–73 are of particular note:

> 'HMRC operates a discerning approach to prosecution in respect of all offences within its remit. Where evidence of money laundering is uncovered during the course of the criminal investigation of a predicate offence, HMRC will ask the prosecutor to consider the addition of money laundering charges to the indictment in order to further dent an individual or gang's capacity to fund or commit future illegitimate activity. Equally, stand-alone money laundering prosecutions are valid where there is sufficient evidence to support charges under the Proceeds of Crime Act. There is no monetary threshold for prosecution.
>
> Where the suspicion of money laundering mounts during a civil investigation, and there is evidence of other serious illegal activities which are not assigned matters, HMRC will consider disclosing this information to other agencies under statutory gateway provisions, either in the CRC Act or other legislation.

3.214 *Tax fraud: criminal investigations and litigation – direct tax*

HMRC will normally investigate money laundering cases criminally where the money flows (benefit) are derived from fraud against HMRC regimes. HMRC will also investigate cases that will identify and investigate those persons benefiting from fraud by providing the means to launder the proceeds of crime, with particular focus on advisers, accountants, solicitors and others acting in a "professional" capacity who provide the means to put tainted money out of reach of law enforcement. The focus will be on cases where investigation and referral to RCPO will do most to promote compliance with the law and where HMRC can make a contribution to the over-arching HMG anti-money laundering strategy. HMRC will utilise all of the investigative powers in the Proceeds of Crime Act 2002 in the course of investigating money laundering. It will devote effort to counter the use of trusts, offshore mechanisms, internet banking and other devices in the cleansing of criminal monies and will refer appropriate cases to RCPO who will consider prosecution.'

The risk to financial intermediaries and professionals

3.214 Historically, UK professionals involved in giving tax advice should always have considered the subtle difference between (legal) tax avoidance and (illegal) tax evasion. Recently, the concept has widened to include a further category, tax mitigation, which relates to very simple statutory relief which is available to reduce tax liabilities (personal allowances, etc).

3.215 However, tax avoidance can involve an artificial series of apparently commercial transactions which may have little or no substance, and which are designed merely to avoid taxation. Conversely, tax evasion is where someone deliberately sets out to defraud the fiscal authorities. This can represent an act of commission, or one of omission. An offence may be committed where information is deliberately withheld or misrepresented to the fiscal authorities (ie there is an inadequate disclosure of material facts that prevents a properly informed decision from being taken). As always, the key indicia of tax evasion is dishonesty.

3.216 The dividing line between avoidance and evasion has become thinner and more dangerous to cross. Professional advisers have historically taken the view that tax avoidance is capable of being recognised by the civil courts (or even in some circumstances, condoned by HMRC) and is therefore legitimate, safe from the dangers of criminal litigation. This view is no longer necessarily accurate. The political view of tax avoidance and the need for instigating criminal proceedings to combat the more egregious practices, has reached an unprecedented level. Of particular note is that HMRC has alleged fraudulent conduct in the use of certain marketed avoidance schemes.

3.217 When avoidance schemes are put before the criminal courts the focus of the prosecution is likely to be on the bona fides of the scheme and whether the transactions involved have any commercial substance or purpose. Should such transactions not pass the test of commerciality (reality), a criminal court, which will have little or no concept of the civil law distinction between avoidance and evasion, is unlikely to be sympathetic to the accused. Former Labour Chancellor, Denis Healey, is reported to have commented that 'the distinction between tax avoidance and tax evasion is the thickness of a prison cell wall'.

3.218 This lack of distinction became apparent in a case in the criminal courts, *R v Charlton* [1996] STC 1418, which challenged an offshore invoicing scheme which had always been regarded (by some) as tax avoidance rather than evasion. The jury disagreed and some of the professional advisers were duly convicted and imprisoned.

3.219 How then does the layman distinguish between lawful tax mitigation or tax avoidance and unlawful tax evasion which may involve the proceeds of crime? Generally speaking, the more aggressive a 'tax planning' arrangement, particularly where it is accompanied by a reluctance to make a full and transparent disclosure of documents or facts to the fiscal authorities, either in filing a tax return, or on subsequent enquiry, the greater the risk of a criminal offence.

3.220 Consideration should be given to the activities with which professional advisers are often associated, namely:

- establishing and administering offshore corporate structures and trusts;
- handling cash for clients and/or the provision of client account facilities; and
- the provision of investment advice.

Such activities are capable of being involved in laundering the proceeds of crime (including tax crime) and therefore potentially expose the professional adviser concerned to prosecution under the money laundering legislation.

3.221 In the UK the fiscal authorities have always regarded suspect tax practitioners as desirable targets for criminal proceedings because they occupy a position of trust in relation to the fiscal authorities (and also because they tend to produce high-profile criminal prosecutions).

3.222 However, one problem for the fiscal authorities has always been proving (to criminal standards) that there has been a conspiracy between a taxpayer and his professional adviser. Informed application of the money laundering legislation to tax evasion may make it easier to bring criminal charges against financial intermediaries and professional advisers.

3.223 *Tax fraud: criminal investigations and litigation – direct tax*

Developments in law and practice

3.223 There is little doubt that the European Directives on money laundering and the UK domestic legislation has imposed a huge burden on the financial community, both in terms of management time and the direct cost of compliance.

3.224 Ostensibly, these burdens and costs were introduced in order to make it impossible for those involved in organised crime to launder their profits and acquire a cloak of respectability. However, some cynics will assert that the underlying purpose of the money laundering legislation is to flush out the 'untaxed' rather than the criminal economy with a view to reducing losses to the Exchequer relating to tax evasion.

3.225 In the UK there is little evidence that the introduction of the legislation has had any material effect on organised crime. The fact is that since the 1930s organised crime has developed highly sophisticated money laundering techniques and, while the new legislation may make things more difficult, it also creates a greater degree of awareness of risk, which will tend to drive the activities further underground.

3.226 It is also a fact that since the anti-money laundering legislation was introduced in the UK, there have been very few successful prosecutions (the exceptions have been mainly for drugs-related transactions), although this is by no means the only measure of success.

3.227 Having said this, it is right to say that the situation may be changing following the current HMRC strategy. Today it is by no means unusual to see charges of money laundering accompanying those of substantive tax offences. Certainly, the authorities intend to target the professional services sector, from which there have been comparatively few disclosures of suspicious transactions. Slowly but surely it appears that life is becoming more difficult for the sophisticated tax evader, particularly where he has been established in business for some time. For example, former secretive tax havens such as Liechtenstein and Switzerland have tightened their banking rules and entered into international agreements that have hampered money laundering activities.

3.228 For the legislation to become an effective deterrent there must be successful and high-profile prosecutions. The legal framework and public interest policy is now in place to enable this. Certainly in this climate it would be foolhardy for a financial intermediary or professional adviser to claim a statutory defence based on the assertion that tax evasion does not constitute 'criminal conduct' for the purposes of money laundering legislation.

Life for the alleged tax evader who enjoys a criminal lifestyle will be made more difficult by other provisions of *POCA 2002* (ie the civil recovery process or revenue functions of the NCA).

3.229 It is now clear that HMRC will make use of the money laundering legislation. HMRC will be tempted to utilise the money laundering legislation in the most serious cases where financial institutions and/or professional advisers have assisted in or have otherwise facilitated tax evasion.

Example 3.1 – False accounting and money laundering

An individual is criminally investigated by HMRC and found to have dishonestly evaded tax on profits of £500,000. The evaded income was deposited in various undisclosed bank accounts, both UK and overseas, and investments. No dishonest assistance in the process was provided by third parties. The quantum of tax evaded was £200,000.

The person is charged with false accounting in relation to his false business accounts and money laundering in relation to the investment of the bank deposits and investments.

He pleads guilty to the charges and is sentenced to three years imprisonment for the false accounting offences and a concurrent two years for the money laundering offences. HMRC take confiscation proceedings and the judge makes an order for confiscation of £200,000 with a further two years of imprisonment if unpaid.

Example 3.2 – Professional third party involvement

The facts are similar to those in Example 4.1 above, however the investment is made with dishonest assistance from a professional third party who, together with the first party, is charged with conspiracy to cheat the public revenue, and the money laundering offence of assisting the first party (*POCA 2002, s 328*).

Both parties are convicted with the first party receiving a greater sentence of four years on the substantive offences (reflecting the conspiracy with another) and a concurrent three years on the money laundering offences. The third party receives a sentence of three years' imprisonment on the conspiracy offences and a concurrent three years for assisting in money laundering. HMRC takes confiscation proceedings against the first party and the judge makes an order for confiscation of £200,000 with a further two years of imprisonment if unpaid.

CONCLUSION

3.230 It is beyond doubt that tax evasion, or offences related to it, are predicate crimes for money laundering purposes. Financial intermediaries and

3.231 *Tax fraud: criminal investigations and litigation – direct tax*

professional advisers must acquaint themselves with the relevant legislation and establish procedures to deal with situations where they suspect their clients are involved in tax evasion (and hence, potentially, money laundering).

It is also vital that professional advisers ensure that their action or inaction, once they know or suspect money laundering is taking place, does not risk implicating them in any criminality.

3.231 Professional advisers should note that the money laundering legislation does not prevent them from acting on behalf of a client seeking to make a full disclosure of irregularities to one or more of the fiscal authorities. However, advisers acting for such clients should ensure that they do not give any 'transactional advice' which may implicate them in an 'arrangement' for the purposes of *POCA 2002, s 328*.

3.232 In this context, consider a professional adviser representing a client seeking to make a disclosure to HMRC whilst at the same time offering the client some hypothetical advice on how to 'ring fence' certain assets from the fiscal authorities. In the author's opinion, this is unlawful.

3.233 A former version of ICAEW's 'Professional Conduct in Relation to Taxation' points out at para 2.32:

> 'The money-laundering legislation does not prevent a member from advising clients on negotiations with the tax authorities in respect of evaded tax liabilities, *on a bona fide basis of full disclosure* in accordance with the guidelines.' (emphasis added)

3.234 As the dividing line between tax avoidance and tax evasion becomes increasingly important, the money laundering legislation adds a 'double jeopardy' dimension for those who either cross the line or assist another to do so. In the current economic and political climate professional advisers involved in devising and/or implementing aggressive tax avoidance schemes would be well advised to ensure that they genuinely deserve the 'avoidance' label, although this label is far less comforting than it once was. Perhaps the test for any scheme should be whether a credible explanation could be provided to a Crown Court judge and a jury of 12 lay people. If in doubt, it may be prudent to seek counsel from a member of the criminal bar.

KEY POINTS

3.235

1   It is now well established that tax evasion is caught by the 'all crimes' provisions of *POCA 2002*.

Tax fraud: criminal investigations and litigation – direct tax **3.235**

2 Allegations of money laundering related to substantive tax offences (usually charged in indirect tax cases as cheating the public revenue or false accounting) will assist UK investigators in cases with an international dimension.

3 The measure of benefit gained from unlawful tax evasion is the quantum of tax evaded.

4 The benefit derived from tax evasion is almost invariably subject to restraint and confiscation proceedings following a criminal conviction.

5 Criminal money laundering charges normally form part of an indictment together with the charges relating to the substantive offence based upon tax evasion.

6 Third parties who dishonestly assist first parties in the process of tax evasion are exposed to criminal sanctions for money laundering in addition to substantive offences.

Chapter 4

Contentious tax planning enquiries

Andrew Hinsley
RSM

INTRODUCTION

4.1 For the purpose of this chapter, 'contentious tax planning enquiries' is the term given to enquiries which are more likely to result in a significant dispute with HMRC.

Background

4.2 Contentious tax planning enquiries typically have the following features, which mean disputes are more likely to arise as a result:

- large amounts of tax are at stake;
- the facts are complex and/or difficult to establish and/or agree;
- the tax analysis is complex, and/or has little precedent and/or is difficult to apply to the specific facts, or avoidance (see below) is suspected.

Transactions which are likely to result in contentious tax planning enquiries will typically fall within one of the following categories:

- company acquisitions/disposals/reorganisations;
- asset acquisitions/disposals;
- financing and treasury activities;
- significant business projects (for example, business combinations, capex programmes);
- cross-border transactions.

Although this chapter focuses on in-depth enquiries into tax planning arrangements, many of the features and issues found in tax planning disputes will be applicable to all complex technical enquiries. The key differences between transactions are the applicable statute, the case law environment, the attitude of the courts and HMRC, and the specific departments dealing with the particular transactions.

Tax planning arrangements

4.3 Tax planning is a broad and emotive subject and one man's legitimate tax planning could be another's unacceptable tax avoidance. The terms tax planning and tax 'avoidance' are used interchangeably throughout this chapter and the latter should be taken to mean any form of legal planning, whether acceptable or unacceptable from the perspective of HMRC.

The term tax avoidance is not specifically defined in statute and the judiciary has tended to shy away from attempts at a universally applicable definition. Lord Nolan in *IRC v Willoughby* [1997] STC 995 defined tax avoidance as 'a course of action designed to conflict with the evident intention of Parliament'. The essence of this definition was adopted by the joint HM Treasury/HMRC briefing '*Tackling Tax Avoidance*' March 2011. HMRC describes tax avoidance as bending the rules of the tax system to gain a tax advantage that Parliament never intended. Although this seems to be a sensible working definition, divining the intention of Parliament has proved problematic over the years and it still does.

Lord Templeman sought to differentiate between 'acceptable' and 'unacceptable' avoidance but this proposition has since been rejected, although arguably it persists but without formal judicial approval.

Globalisation and the revolution in information technology mean that tax planning is not restricted to UK-based activity and transactions. Businesses can potentially take advantage of low tax rates in particular jurisdictions in order to arrange their affairs in a manner that reduces their overall tax burden.

4.4 This chapter looks at tax avoidance arrangements under two headings:

- **Domestic tax planning**: transactions undertaken by UK entities or individuals which are structured in a particular way so as to achieve a tax advantage;
- **International tax planning**: (or 'substance based' planning as it is often known) involves moving people (and related decision-taking), activities, risks, contractual arrangements and assets to low tax jurisdictions in order to achieve tax savings.

In 2007 HMRC's Anti-Avoidance Group (now Counter Avoidance: see below) published guidance (available on its website (which can be accessed by the

4.5 *Contentious tax planning enquiries*

search facility on the HMRC site)) to enable taxpayers to better understand how it addresses the risks it perceives as arising from tax planning. The guidance originally took the form of 'signposts' or features of transactions that HMRC is likely to challenge.

HMRC has taken this concept a stage further by highlighting in its 'Spotlights' section of its 'Avoidance' web pages (https://www.gov.uk/government/collections/tax-avoidance-schemes-currently-in-the-spotlight) the types of arrangement it believes are ineffective. Taxpayers entering into transactions with the same hallmarks should expect their planning to be litigated.

4.5 Although this chapter aims to provide practical guidance and experience, when it comes to handling tax planning enquiries, one of the most important considerations is how the courts are likely to react to a particular arrangement. This is because there is a much greater likelihood that the enquiry will lead to litigation.

A detailed review and analysis of tax avoidance, related statute and case law, is beyond the scope and purpose of this chapter (although a number of key cases will be considered). The aim is to provide an insight into the current tax avoidance environment in terms of the attitude of the tribunals and courts and the implications of this environment for practitioners.

4.6 It is also important to understand the bigger picture in terms of HMRC's strategic and operational approach to dealing with tax planning arrangements, since the practitioner will not be dealing with just the typical HMRC officer. HMRC will usually have a number of specialist technical and operational departments with comprehensive expertise in the particular area, either supporting the local officer or actually working the case.

This chapter therefore attempts to cover a mixture of strategic, technical and practical dimensions in relation to domestic and international planning under the following headings:

- HMRC's strategy for dealing with tax avoidance;
- the role of specialist Directorates;
- the evolution and importance of tax avoidance case law;
- HMRC's approach to working complex tax enquiries;
- managing the enquiry;
- resolving disputes; and
- discovery and the increased threat of penalties.

HMRC'S STRATEGY FOR DEALING WITH TAX AVOIDANCE

Introduction

4.7 HMRC's approach to tackling tax avoidance schemes is to:

- prevent tax avoidance where possible, by designing tax law effectively and underpinning this with clearly-stated policy objectives: so called 'up-stream' solutions;
- detect it early where it arises, through the Disclosure of Tax Avoidance Schemes (DOTAS) rules;
- counteract it effectively through investigation and legal challenge or legislative change, including, exceptionally, retrospective change.

At a strategic level HMRC's approach has involved:

- a fight to win 'hearts and minds' over the notion that tax avoidance is morally unacceptable;
- a raft of anti-avoidance legislation;
- operational changes to improve the effectiveness and consistency of HMRC's working of tax avoidance cases.

The moral dimension

4.8 Tax and in particular tax planning has been the subject of intense media interest and public debate in recent years which shows no sign of abating. HMRC and the government have embarked upon a battle to win hearts and minds by seeking to make tax avoidance a moral issue and positioning themselves on what they see as the moral high ground, requiring taxpayers to pay their 'fair share'. Other stakeholders such as the media, pressure groups and Public Accounts Committee are all taking a keen interest in the tax affairs of high-profile businesses and personalities. Taxpayers therefore need to be aware of the potential reputational risk arising from scrutiny of their affairs when entering into tax planning arrangements.

The intense scrutiny of tax planning arrangements has also led to much greater scrutiny and stronger governance over the settlement of significant tax disputes, which now have to pass through various levels of approval before being agreed or rejected.

Operational initiatives

4.9 In order to implement the strategic objective of clamping down on tax avoidance, HMRC continues to refine its operational efforts, both to focus

4.10 *Contentious tax planning enquiries*

resource on where it perceives the greatest risk to be and to improve the overall effectiveness of the resource so targeted.

Originally this effort was focused on the corporate sector but is now mirrored in relation to individual taxpayers with the High Net Worth Unit dealing with the wealthiest taxpayers (those with net assets of over £20 million). In 2011–12 HMRC set up a series of teams to improve its coverage of wealthy taxpayers (whose assets are between £2 million and £40 million and who (should) pay tax at the highest rate). These 'affluent teams', unlike the High Net Worth Unit, intervene in specific tax risks as they arise but do not undertake responsibility for all aspects of the taxpayer's affairs whether contentious or not.

4.10 Key changes being noted in practice include:
- a more rigorous approach to information gathering, with ever wider requests for information and much tighter timeframes for compliance;
- greater coordination, team working and centralisation, involving advice from specialist resources (including external sources, such as earlier consultation with counsel);
- increased resource, revised working methods and better supporting technology;
- a greater willingness to litigate;
- settlement programmes such as the High Risk Corporate Programme (HRCP), Managing Complex Risk (MCR), and various settlement initiatives;
- an increased threat of penalties where planning fails, especially as a result of poor implementation;
- enhanced governance around the settlement of disputes; and
- avoidance is worked on a project basis to achieve greater consistency of outcome for all users of particular 'schemes'.

Legislative initiatives

4.11 The legislative approach has involved:
- the disclosure regime first introduced in 2004 with subsequent tightening of the rules aimed at identifying avoidance arrangements at an earlier stage and counteracting the perceived abuse;
- the introduction of numerous targeted anti-avoidance provisions within new legislation;
- the introduction of principles-based anti-avoidance legislation (for example, the group mismatch rules);

Contentious tax planning enquiries **4.12**

- a general anti abuse rule (GAAR) from July 2013;
- the introduction of 'Follower Notices and Accelerated Payments' under *FA 2014, Part 4*, which require the upfront payment of tax in advance of resolution by HMRC or the courts in respect of a notifiable tax scheme under the Disclosure of Tax Avoidance Schemes (DOTAS) provisions (see below) or where a case has been decided in relation to an arrangement whose main purpose is to secure a tax advantage and HMRC believes the ruling involves a principle which is applicable to another taxpayer, or is subject to the GAAR. The provisions also provide for tax geared penalties for failing to make the upfront payment; the measures apply from 17 July 2014;
- the Promoters of Tax Avoidance Scheme (POTAS) legislation targeting persistent promoters of tax avoidance schemes who are uncooperative, and/or whose schemes are regularly defeated;
- penalties for taxpayers using schemes counteracted by the GAAR;
- a requirement for large business to publish their Tax Strategy;
- proposed sanctions for serial avoiders and promoters;
- significantly enhanced exchange of information with overseas territories including low tax jurisdictions; and
- various G20 driven/OECD led initiatives aimed at countering perceived tax avoidance by multinational companies – so called Base Erosion Profit Shifting (BEPS).

Disclosure of Tax Avoidance Scheme rules (DOTAS)

Background

4.12 The *Finance Act 2004* introduced a set of disclosure requirements that are imposed on promoters and users of certain tax schemes and arrangements. They were designed to enable HMRC to identify at a much earlier stage tax-avoidance schemes it was likely to find unacceptable, with a view to introducing swifter and more targeted legislation in response. They have gone through various amendments to widen and strengthen their effect and have been very effective in enabling HMRC to close down tax avoidance arrangements much quicker than in the past. The original scope of the rules has been extended to cover a much wider range of transactions and apply to a much broader range of transactions.

Where practitioners consider the rules may be in point, a more detailed review of the provisions will be required, and in areas of doubt further advice should be sought. A high level overview, including recent developments, is set out below.

4.13 *Contentious tax planning enquiries*

4.13 The primary legislation, set out at *FA 2004, ss 306–319*, provides the basic framework and definitions for the regime. The majority of the detail is found in secondary legislation. Key secondary provisions which have been subject to various amendments over the years are:

- The Tax Avoidance Schemes (Promoters and Prescribed Circumstances) Regulations
- The Tax Avoidance Schemes (Information) Regulations
- The SDLT Avoidance Schemes (Prescribed Descriptions of Arrangements) Regulations
- The SDLT (Avoidance Schemes) (Specified Proposals or Arrangements) Regulations
- The ATED Avoidance Schemes (Prescribed Descriptions of Arrangements) Regulations
- The IHT Avoidance Schemes (Prescribed Descriptions of Arrangements) Regulations
- The NICs (Application of Part 7 of the *Finance Act 2004*) Regulations
- The Tax Avoidance Schemes (Penalty) Regulations

Arrangements impacted

4.14 The basic structure of the legislation is based on the concept of a 'notifiable arrangement'. A notifiable arrangement is an arrangement:

- that falls within any one of the descriptions ('hallmarks') provided by the Treasury (in secondary legislation);
- that enables a person to obtain a tax advantage; and
- where the tax advantage is the main benefit of the arrangement.

A 'notifiable proposal' is a proposal for notifiable arrangements. For example, where a promoter tells a client about a notifiable arrangement that is a notifiable proposal.

Promoter

4.15 A person is a promoter in relation to a notifiable proposal if, in the course of carrying on a business which involves the provision to others of services related to taxation or certain other services, he:

- has any responsibility for designing any notifiable proposal or arrangements except in excluded circumstances;

Contentious tax planning enquiries **4.16**

- makes a notifiable proposal available to another person (for example, by marketing or promoting arrangements designed by another person); or
- has any responsibility for the organisation or management of the notifiable arrangement but only if they are connected with the design of the arrangement.

Further provisions have been introduced in relation to 'high risk' tax scheme promoters in the *Finance Act 2014, Schs 34–36*, including certain penalty measures.

Under *FA 2004, ss 308–310*, disclosure must be made to HMRC by the promoter within 5 days of the scheme being made available.

The scheme user may need to make a disclosure where:

- the promoter is based outside the UK;
- the promoter is a lawyer and legal privilege applies; or
- there is no promoter.

Where a person designs and implements their own hallmarked scheme, the person must disclose the scheme within 30 days of it being implemented.

A person who is only involved in the design of a scheme, and does not make the scheme available for implementation by others or organise or manage it, is not a promoter if any one of the following three tests is passed:

- the benign test;
- the non-advisor test;
- the ignorance test.

This is not to say that the person who is only involved in the design of the scheme is not subject to any penalty regime (see comments at **4.24** below concerning the penalty regime for Enablers of defeated tax avoidance schemes introduced under *F(No 2)A, 2017*).

Hallmarks

4.16 When there is a promoter of the arrangement, the scheme is hallmarked if any one of the following hallmarks applies:

- hallmark 1(a): Confidentiality from other promoters;
- hallmark 1(b): Confidentiality from HMRC;

4.16 *Contentious tax planning enquiries*

- hallmark 3: Premium fee;
- hallmark 4: off market terms no longer applicable;
- hallmark 5: Standardised tax products;
- hallmark 6: Loss schemes;
- hallmark 7: Leasing arrangements;
- hallmark 8: Employment income;
- hallmark 9: Financial products.

When the arrangement is designed 'in-house', it is a hallmarked scheme when any one of the hallmarks 2, 3, 7 and 8 apply.

Hallmark 9 – Financial products was introduced by SI 2016/99 which amended SI 2006/1543 with effect from 23 February 2016. The Hallmark will be satisfied if the arrangements include at least one specified financial product, and it would be reasonable to expect an informed observer (having studied the arrangements and having regard to all relevant circumstances) to conclude that the main benefit, or one of the main benefits, of including a specified financial product in the arrangements is to give rise to a tax advantage and it would be reasonable to expect such an observer to conclude that:

- a specified financial product included in the arrangements contains at least one term which is unlikely to have been entered into by the persons concerned were it not for the tax advantage; or
- the arrangements involve one or more contrived or abnormal steps without which the tax advantage could not be obtained.

At its most basic level the definition of a financial product includes a loan or a share which will feature in many commercial transactions. For this reason many advisers have expressed concerns that the DOTAS provisions have been unduly widened. This is particularly so as the courts approach to construing certain anti-avoidance provisions such as 'unallowable purpose' has highlighted the degree of subjectivity in applying the concept of a 'main or one of the main' tests. The same can be said of a benefit test even when the test is to be applied by an objective observer.

Some comfort may be gleaned from HMRC's comments on the purpose of the new hallmark which was to 'catch schemes using financial products where there is a direct link between the financial product and the gaining of the tax advantage i.e. where the inclusion of the financial product is not merely incidental to the tax advantage'.

Contentious tax planning enquiries **4.18**

The 'standardised products' hallmark (Regulation 10, SI 2006/1543) is rewritten by SI 2016/99, from 23 February 2016. This was done to counteract arguments that it does not apply where there are minor changes for individual clients but the arrangements remain subject to standardised or substantially standardised documentation. This is achieved by requiring 'the informed observer' to consider all aspects of the test, rather than only the 'purpose of the arrangements'. It also removes grandfathering of standardised products that were made available before introduction of this hallmark (1 August 2006).

Introducers

4.17 *FA 2010* included a new category of person for information power purposes, an 'introducer,' to describe persons who advertise notifiable schemes on behalf of a promoter but whose role does not extend to that of a promoter. 'Introducer' is defined in *FA 2004, s 307(1A)* as a person who 'makes a marketing contact' in relation to a notifiable scheme.

The disclosure rules do not impose any automatic reporting obligations on an introducer. However an introducer can be required to provide HMRC with information in response to an information notice under *FA 2004, s 313C* (see 'information from introducers' below).

Penalties

4.18 Failure to comply with the above requirements attracts a maximum penalty of £5,000 together with a further maximum penalty of £600 each day for continued failure to disclose after the imposition of the initial penalty. Where there has been one previous failure to disclose in the previous 36 months the maximum penalty is £7,500 and £10,000 where there has been more than one failure in the previous 36 months. *FA 2010* introduced the potential for a penalty of up to £1 million where the penalty under the existing provisions would be inappropriately low.

FA 2007, Sch 24 ('Penalties for Errors') was amended by *F(No 2)A 2017* to include provisions for penalties for errors in taxpayers' documents which are given to HMRC and are related to avoidance arrangements.

In addition to the financial penalties there is reputational risk attached to failure to comply with these disclosure requirements, as penalty proceedings will be heard before the Tax Tribunal (some types before the Upper Tribunal).

No penalty should be charged where the promoter or user has a reasonable excuse and the failure to comply is remedied within a reasonable time after the excuse ceased.

4.19 *Contentious tax planning enquiries*

Information powers

4.19 HMRC's various DOTAS information powers (introduced in *FA 2007, FA 2010, FA 2013, FA 2014*, and *FA 2015*) enable them to:

- require an introducer (a person who introduces clients to a promoter) to identify the person who provided them with information relating to the scheme or to identify persons with whom they have made a marketing contact in relation to a scheme;
- enquire into reasons why a promoter has not disclosed a scheme;
- enforce disclosure in appropriate cases;
- call for more information where a disclosure is incomplete or where HMRC considers that further information about the scheme is needed; and
- request further information from the promoter about clients using schemes.

Information from introducers

4.20 *Finance Act 2004, s 313C*, with effect from 26 March 2015 applies where HMRC suspects a person of acting as an introducer for a notifiable scheme which has not been disclosed. It may require them to provide the name and address of:

- any person who has provided them with information about that scheme; and
- each person with whom they have made a marketing contact in relation to the proposal.

Publication of schemes and/or promoters

4.21 *Finance Act 2004, s 316C*, with effect from 26 March 2015 provided HMRC with new powers to publish information, in any manner HMRC believes appropriate, about:

- notified schemes that have been allocated a scheme reference number on or after 26 March 2015; and
- the promoters of those schemes (ie 'naming and shaming' provisions).

Changing role of DOTAS – practical issues

4.22 A key point to note about recent changes impacting arrangements subject to DOTAS is that they are no longer simply an 'early warning system'

Contentious tax planning enquiries **4.23**

for HMRC as originally envisaged, but are now a trigger for a number of significant issues affecting taxpayers and their advisers for example:

- Accelerated payment notices – clients may be issued with an accelerated payment notice under *Finance Act 2014, s 219(4)(b)* from 17 July 2014, for arrangements that assert a tax advantage that are DOTAS arrangements.

- Entry into the serial avoidance regime. A DOTAS arrangement that has been counteracted will constitute a 'relevant defeat' for the purposes of the serial tax avoidance regime. Taxpayers subject to a warning notice are subject to additional compliance obligations, including a requirement to submit an annual information notice. Also the possibility, if they incur a further 'relevant defeat' within a five year warning period, that they may be subject to public naming, restrictions from claiming tax reliefs during a three-year period and additional penalties.

- Entry into the Promoters of Tax Avoidance Schemes (POTAS) rules. The counteraction of a DOTAS arrangement will constitute a 'relevant defeat' for purposes of the new threshold condition in the POTAS rules. Such a relevant defeat is a trigger for HMRC to consider whether a tax adviser should be issued with a conduct notice under the POTAS rules. The consequences of a firm receiving a POTAS conduct notice are significant and, if its conditions are not complied with, the firm may be subject to a monitoring notice, requiring it to publicise and advise its clients that it is a monitored promoter.

The Promoters of Tax Avoidance Schemes (POTAS)

4.23 The POTAS legislation at *FA 2014, Pt 5, Schs 34–36* was originally introduced to target and change the behaviour of what HMRC described as 'a small number of promoters who operate in a culture of non-disclosure, non-co-operation and secrecy'. The legislation applies a graduated series of sanctions for those promoters who trigger a threshold condition. Up until FA 2016 these threshold conditions would only apply to a small number of promoters, however, the introduction of a new threshold condition – the concept of a relevant defeat, potentially significantly widens the scope (see below).

The provision can only be applied where an authorised HMRC officer believes the triggering of the regime is 'significant, in view of the purposes of the rules and where, having regard to the extent the promoter's activities are likely to have on the collection of tax, it is appropriate to issue a conduct notice'.

The provision applies to any 'person' (including companies and LLPs) that has promoted or introduced tax avoidance arrangements that meets a 'threshold condition'.

4.23 *Contentious tax planning enquiries*

Once a 'threshold condition' is met, HMRC can, within three years, issue a 'conduct notice', requiring the promoter to comply with specified conditions for two years, including providing 'adequate' information to clients and intermediaries and meeting disclosure obligations.

If the promoter fails to comply with a current 'conduct notice', HMRC can apply to the tribunal to issue a 'monitoring notice'. This brings a number of specific requirements, including allowing HMRC to:

- publish details of the promoter;
- require the promoter to notify their clients that they are a monitored promoter and provide their clients and intermediaries with their allocated promoter reference number (clients that expect to obtain a tax advantage from arrangements promoted by a monitored promoter must notify HMRC of that fact together with the promoter reference number); and
- apply severe penalties for failure to meet the monitoring notice conditions (eg up to £1 million for a failure to publicise that the promoter is a monitored promoter on the internet if required to do so).

The 'threshold conditions' are:

(1) Publication of the promoter's name by HMRC as a deliberate tax defaulter.

(2) Publication of the promoter's name because of a breach of the banking code of practice.

(3) The promoter receiving a notice under the Tax Agents: Dishonest Conduct legislation.

(4) Failure to disclose arrangements under the DOTAS rules.

(5) Being charged with a criminal offence relating to fraud, failure to comply with money laundering regulations or tax evasion etc, unless acquitted.

(6) Promotion of arrangements on which two or members of the GAAR panel have given an opinion that the arrangements are not reasonable.

(7) Being subject to disciplinary action by a professional body.

(8) Being subject to disciplinary action by a regulatory authority.

(9) Failure to comply with an information notice under *FA 2008, Sch 36*.

(10) Imposing confidentiality terms on a client preventing disclosure to HMRC or requiring clients to contribute to a 'fighting fund'.

(11) Continuing to promote arrangements for which a follower notice has been issued following an adverse judicial decision.

(12) Promoter whose schemes are regularly.

Contentious tax planning enquiries **4.24**

Conditions 1, 2, 3, 5 and 6 are automatically regarded as 'significant'.

The concept of a 'relevant defeat' was introduced by *FA 2016, s 160* and includes 'schemes defeated' under the GAAR or a TAAR, or following the issue of a follower notice. A relevant defeat is very widely defined and includes not just instances of a court finding against a taxpayer, but any circumstance where the taxpayer concedes (including by agreement) that the arrangement does not achieve the desired tax effect. This would, therefore, include circumstances where a taxpayer decides to concede irrespective of the technical position (eg because of commercial criteria such as the cost of litigation as reputational risk). A conduct notice may be given where there are three relevant defeats in a period of eight years.

Whilst the legislation was originally targeted to a minority of promoters, there is a concern that the very wide definition of arrangement to which the provision applies could catch bespoke tax planning, as opposed to highly artificial and or generic schemes. There is for example, no requirement for an arrangement to be disclosable under the DOTAS provisions for the legislation to bite – though with the recent additional Financial Products DOTAS Hallmark it is likely to be disclosable. The legislation is effectively retrospective and applies to schemes put in place many years ago, thus EBT planning where a taxpayer concedes under the settlement opportunity, could, at least in theory, be caught. Other areas of concern are the changes to the transactions in securities legislation where there is a concern that bona fide commercial arrangements could be caught by the new transactions in securities rules. It would be hoped that in such circumstances HMRC would exercise its discretion sensibly given the apparent lack of statutory protection.

FA 2017, s 24 has widened the concept of 'control' in respect of body corporates (companies and LLPs) to prevent promoters avoiding the rules by setting up a promoter entity that has not itself met a threshold condition. Under these provisions, HMRC can issue a promoter with a conduct notice where, within the previous three years, a threshold condition has been met by someone with a defined type of connection, via a company or partnership, to the promoter. This 'connection' is defined by reference to control or significant influence.

Enablers of defeated tax avoidance schemes

4.24 *F(No 2)A 2017, Sch 16* introduced a penalty for any person who enables the use of abusive tax arrangements, which are later defeated. The legislation only applies to a person if they enable abusive tax arrangements that are entered into on or after 16 November 2017. HMRC now has more power to tackle all aspects of the marketed avoidance supply chains, complementing the suite of anti-avoidance measures already in place.

4.25   *Contentious tax planning enquiries*

An enabler is defined within the legislation as a person who is:

(*a*)   a designer of the arrangements;

(*b*)   a manager of the arrangements;

(*c*)   a person who has marketed the arrangements;

(*d*)   an enabling participant in the arrangements; or

(*e*)   a financial enabler in relation to the arrangements.

Arrangements are 'tax arrangements' if, having regard to all the circumstances, it would be reasonable to conclude that the obtaining of a tax advantage was the main purpose, or one of the main purposes, of the arrangements. Tax arrangements are 'abusive' if they are arrangements the entering into or carrying out of which cannot reasonably be regarded as a reasonable course of action in relation to the relevant tax provisions, having regard to all the circumstances.

The penalty for each enabler is equal to the amount of consideration either received or receivable by them for enabling those arrangements.

It should be noted that the GAAR Advisory Panel provides an important safeguard for the purpose of the legislation: no penalty can be charged unless HMRC has obtained an opinion from the GAAR Advisory Panel in relation to the tax arrangements.

Whilst drafted widely to potentially impact all tax agents, intermediaries and others who benefit financially from designing, marketing or facilitating the use of abusive tax arrangements that are defeated, HMRC has confirmed the legislation is not targeted at those who provide clients with services in respect of genuine commercial arrangements.

General anti-abuse rule

4.25   The specific anti-avoidance provisions are too numerous to mention here given the scope of this chapter. However, it is important to note that the general anti-abuse rule (GAAR) introduced at *FA 2013, ss 206–215, Sch 29*, will have a significant impact on certain types of tax avoidance arrangements.

The original intention was for a targeted GAAR aimed at the most abusive schemes. However, as drafted, the legislation could apply to a much wider set of transactions than envisaged at the time of the consultation.

The rule applies to income tax, corporation tax, capital gains tax, petroleum revenue tax, inheritance tax, stamp duty land tax, and annual tax on enveloped dwellings. The GAAR can also apply to arrangements where UK tax advantages have been obtained from the rights or benefits under any Double Tax Agreement.

4.26 The GAAR is intended to be a freestanding provision which comes into operation when the application of all other tax rules (including targeted anti-avoidance rules) applied purposively may not defeat the planning. HMRC envisages that the application of the rule will run in parallel or be argued in the alternative.

The purpose of the GAAR is to counteract tax advantages arising from tax arrangements that are abusive. The rule aims to capture 'abusive' arrangements which have the securing of a tax advantage as the main or one of the main purposes of entering into the arrangement. However, it is not enough that the arrangement seeks to secure a tax advantage; it must do so in a way that is considered to be abusive. Thus there is a relatively high threshold for showing schemes are abusive. *FA 2013, s 207(2)* reads as follows:

> '(2) Tax arrangements are "abusive" if they are arrangements the entering into or carrying out of which cannot reasonably be regarded as a reasonable course of action in relation to the relevant tax provisions, having regard to all the circumstances including:
>
> (a) whether the substantive results of the arrangements are consistent with any principles on which those provisions are based (whether express or implied) and the policy objectives of those provisions,
>
> (b) whether the means of achieving those results involves one or more contrived or abnormal steps, and
>
> (c) whether the arrangements are intended to exploit any shortcomings in those provisions.'

This provision is intended as a safeguard to protect arrangements that can reasonably be regarded as a reasonable response to choices of conduct which are made available by the relevant tax legislation. An example given in the consultation document is the choice between debt and equity.

4.27 HMRC also considers that the requirement to have regard to all relevant circumstances is important to counter the proposition that any course of action intended to improve the taxpayer's economic position must be reasonable. This is because the test is not solely about whether it is a reasonable approach to pay less tax (along Duke of Westminster lines). Rather, the test considers whether it can be regarded as a reasonable course of action to pay less tax in the way the taxpayer is seeking to pay less tax.

HMRC's approved GAAR guidance (Part C) gives examples of what is considered to be abusive and non-abusive (ie what conforms to established practice).

4.28 *Contentious tax planning enquiries*

The legislation at *s 207(2)* is providing guidance on what 'all the circumstances' might include:

- are results consistent with policy?
- do the means of achieving the result have contrived or abnormal steps?
- are they intended to exploit loopholes?

4.28 The burden of proof rests with HMRC to demonstrate that all the elements of the GAAR are satisfied. The procedure for HMRC to apply the GAAR is as follows:

- **Stage one:** The designated officer writes to the taxpayer giving reasons for believing that the GAAR applies to arrangements and the proposed counteraction. The officer invites a written response from the taxpayer as to why the GAAR may not apply.
- **Stage two:** The taxpayer either responds in writing or does not respond.
- **Stage three:** The designated officer refers the matter to the advisory panel if the taxpayer does not respond in writing. Otherwise, the designated officer considers the response. The officer refers the matter to the advisory panel if he or she still believes that the GAAR applies.
- **Stage four:** Three members of the advisory panel give their opinion(s) to the designated officer and to the taxpayer.
- **Stage five:** The designated officer decides whether the relevant tax advantage should be counteracted after considering the opinion(s) and notifies the taxpayer of the decision. If the relevant tax advantages are to be counteracted, the adjustments required are also set out in the decision and the taxpayer has the normal rights of appeal against the adjustments.

There is provision for HMRC and the taxpayer to provide further comments to the panel on each other's views.

If the GAAR is invoked in litigation, HMRC must show the court or tribunal that the tax arrangements are abusive and that the adjustments made to counteract the tax advantages arising from the arrangements are just and reasonable.

Finance Act 2016 introduced a new penalty for all cases successfully counteracted under the GAAR. A penalty of 60% of the counteracted tax will be charged in respect of an arrangements entered into after 15 September 2016 (the date of Royal Assent).

Accelerated tax payment rules

4.29 The Government introduced legislation ('Follower Notices and Accelerated Payments' under *FA 2014, Pt 4*) to allow HMRC to demand upfront payment of disputed tax before tax enquiries and disputes have been resolved where tax avoidance is in point. The provisions are retrospective in that any tax previously postponed pending resolution of an appeal ceases to be once a notice is issued.

The original intention behind the legislation was to enable HMRC to secure tax they believed was due in circumstances where a large number of taxpayers had participated in a highly generic scheme that had been defeated in the courts but large numbers still refused to concede. However, the scope of the legislation was subsequently widened to require upfront payment in relation to notifiable arrangements under DOTAS or those to which the GAAR applies.

The circumstances (conditions A–C in the legislation) in which an accelerated payment notice may be issued are:

- a 'Follower Notice' has been issued in circumstances where HMRC believes that there is a final judicial ruling in another case which would deny the tax treatment adopted (*FA 2014, s 204*);
- the tax treatment adopted is notifiable under the Disclosure of Tax Avoidance Schemes (DOTAS) rules;
- the tax treatment adopted is subject to HMRC counteraction under the General Anti-Abuse Rule (GAAR).

In addition, there must be an enquiry in progress or an open appeal (condition A) and the return, claim or appeal is made of the basis that a particular tax advantage ('the asserted tax advantage') results from particular arrangements (condition B).

Follower notices

4.30 HMRC may issue a 'Follower Notice' if conditions A–D are satisfied. Conditions A and B are essentially those described at para **4.29** above. Condition C is that if HMRC is of the opinion that there is a final judicial decision which is relevant to the (chosen) arrangement.

A judicial ruling is only relevant to the chosen arrangement if:

- it relates to tax arrangements (these are arrangements which having regard to all the circumstances, it would be reasonable to conclude that the obtaining of a tax advantage was the main, or one of the main purposes, of the arrangement);
- the principles laid down, or reasoning given in the ruling would, if applied to the chosen arrangements, deny the asserted advantage (or part of); and
- it is a final ruling.

4.30 *Contentious tax planning enquiries*

Thus, the judicial ruling need not emerge from the same arrangement providing the principles of or reasons for the judicial ruling would, if applied to the chosen arrangements deny their asserted tax advantage. This measure is intentionally wide and HMRC has given some guidance to narrow its scope. The measure has retrospective effect (for two years from Royal Assent) as they include judicial decisions delivered before the legislation comes into effect and matters currently under enquiry/appeal.

Condition D is simply that a previous Follower Notice has not been given to the same person (and not withdrawn) by reference to the same tax advantage, tax arrangement, judicial ruling and period.

The Follower Notice would inform the recipients that in HMRC's opinion they should either settle their dispute (where a closure notice has been issued) or amend their return (if an enquiry is ongoing) in line with HMRC's view. This is known as corrective action and the SA rules have been altered to allow SA returns to be amended after the normal time permitted for this purpose.

There is no right of appeal to the Tribunal against the issue of a Follower Notice but representations can be made to HMRC objecting to the notice on the grounds that conditions A, B or D are not met; the judicial ruling in the notice is not relevant to the chosen arrangements; or the notice was not given within the relevant period. However, if the notice is not overturned there is no opportunity to appeal that decision, leaving a judicial review application the only avenue.

It is not yet clear whether HMRC intends to issue an Accelerated Payment Notice at the same time as a Follower Notice, or whether it will wait to see whether the taxpayer takes corrective action that would have the same effect of bringing the tax into charge (though HMRC would not be able to issue a closure notice in respect of that corrective action where other issues are still open).

If the users do not take corrective action to counteract the denied tax advantage within 90 days of the notice being given (or if representations are made 30 days from HMRC's determination following the representations, if later), they risk being liable to a penalty. The penalty is up to 50% of the denied advantage (though this may be mitigated for cooperation in certain circumstances). An appeal may be made against a penalty for failing to take corrective action in response to a Follower Notice on the grounds that condition A, B or D was not met; the judicial ruling in the notice is not relevant to the chosen arrangements; the notice was not given within the relevant period; or that it was reasonable in all the circumstances for corrective action not to have been taken.

Contentious tax planning enquiries **4.31**

There have been a number of legal challenges to APNs via judicial review. For the most part these have been singularly unsuccessful. The first case *Rowe and others v HMRC* [2015] EWHC 2293 Admin involved a partner payment notice (PPN) involved a challenge to the notice on typical judicial review grounds namely:

- it breached natural justice in failing to afford the opportunity to make representations;
- it breached the legitimate expectation that arose from the previous postponement disputed by HMRC of the tax;
- irrationality/unreasonableness;
- unlawful breach of article 1 (right to enjoyment of property) and article 6 (right to a fair trial).

There was also a specific technical ground on the basis that the tax advantage did not arise from an item in the partnership return itself (a requirement for a PPN) but from a separate claim by the individual partner to carry back the loss relief. The appeal was dismissed on all grounds.

Subsequent cases sought to distinguish themselves from *Rowe* on their facts with emphasis being placed on whether the arrangement in question giving rise to the tax advantage was disclosable under the DOTAS rules but these arguments were also rejected.

However, HMRC decided to withdraw hundreds of APNs as a result of judicial review proceedings which included a challenge on the basis that Condition C was not met in respect of an employee benefit trust implemented in 2003 and notified to HMRC in 2004 under the DOTAS provisions. This was because although the arrangement was notified, it was not in fact notifiable under the DOTAS provisions, having been first made available prior to those provisions coming into force. It is, therefore, necessary to check whether the respective conditions have been satisfied, in particular, Condition C.

DOTAS and GAAR

4.31 As mentioned above, the accelerated payment measures apply to DOTAS and GAAR counteraction arrangements. This is irrespective of whether or not there has been prior consideration of any similar tax treatment or arrangements by the courts or tribunals. The measures apply to both legacy and future arrangements.

The measures apply to taxpayers who have open enquiries or open appeals involving arrangements notifiable under DOTAS, or in respect of which HMRC has decided to proceed to counteraction under the GAAR.

4.32 *Contentious tax planning enquiries*

In practice, this means that a taxpayer who engaged in tax planning which was notifiable under DOTAS and who would not have expected to pay any additional tax until this was determined following the enquiry and appeals process, will be required to pay the disputed tax upfront once an accelerated payment notice has been issued.

As with the Follower Notice, representations can be made to HMRC on the basis that the relevant conditions are not met or by objecting to the amount specified in the notice. However, if following those representations, the notice and amount are confirmed, the only basis of redress is an application for judicial review.

There is a tax geared penalty of 5% for failing to pay the tax within the 90-day payment period (which increases by a further 5% if this remains unpaid 5 months after this date and a further 5% if unpaid 11 months after the 90 days).

HMRC has estimated that as a result of these new measures it will issue accelerated payment notices to around 33,000 individual and 10,000 corporate taxpayers (the majority of which are expected to relate to DOTAS). This may in turn also impact a number of third parties (such as trustees) who may have indemnities in place and any tax liabilities that are sought in advance could, therefore, be the responsibility of the trustee.

HMRC has published a list of DOTAS reference numbers to which the provisions may be applied.

Serial Tax Avoiders

4.32 *Finance Act 2016, s 159 and Sch 18* introduced a new regime of warnings and escalating sanctions for those who persistently engage in tax avoidance schemes that are defeated by HMRC. Following the first defeat of a tax avoidance scheme, HMRC will place the taxpayer on warning that the use of any avoidance scheme in the following five years which HMRC defeats, will result in a penalty based on percentage of the tax arising as a result of the defeat. The warning must be given within 90 days of the defeat.

If the taxpayer uses any further schemes while under warning which HMRC defeats, the rate of penalty increases from 20% for the first defeat up to a maximum of 60% of the counteracted tax advantage if warning has been given for two or more relevant defeats.

If HMRC defeat three tax avoidance schemes while the taxpayer is on warning, the taxpayer's details can be published.

Contentious tax planning enquiries **4.34**

Requirement to publish tax strategy

4.33 As part of HMRC's desire to foster greater transparency in respect of the approach of large businesses to tax including planning, legislation was introduced at *FA 2016, s 161* requiring these businesses to publish their tax strategy on the internet

The tax strategy must set out the organisation's:

- approach to risk management and governance arrangements in relation to UK taxation;
- attitude towards tax planning (so far as affecting UK taxation);
- level of risk in relation to UK taxation that it is prepared to accept; and
- approach towards its dealings with HMRC.

The following businesses are within the scope of the rules:

- standalone companies incorporated in the UK, partnerships and LLPs with annual turnover of more than £200 million and/or a balance sheet total of more than £2 billion on the last day of their previous financial year.
- UK incorporated companies who are members of a group (including groups headed by a non-UK company) and whose UK aggregate group turnover and/or balance sheet total meets the qualifying test above.
- Multi-national enterprise (MNE) groups per the OECD definition with a global annual consolidated turnover of more than €750 million which are subject to country-by-reporting requirements in the UK (or would be if their head of group were tax resident in the UK). This test brings within scope some comparatively small UK subsidiaries of large MNEs.

These businesses now have to set out publically how they approach tax planning and therefore are likely to come under even greater media and pressure group scrutiny to ensure what they say accords with what they do in practice. The typically over-simplistic analysis of tax matters that takes place in the media means business will have to pay particularly close attention to how they word there publically available tax strategy document.

Further sanctions for promoters, enablers and users of tax avoidance schemes

4.34 Not content with the above sanctions, HMRC has issued a consultation on further proposed measures aimed at those who promote, enable and use tax avoidance schemes. The aim is to widen the net from promoters to all those in

4.35 *Contentious tax planning enquiries*

the supply chain who enable or facilitate tax avoidance. The proposal borrows much of its terminology from the existing DOTAS and POTAS legislation, as well as the enablers of offshore tax evasion legislation. In essence the proposal adopts the concept of a relevant defeat (see the POTAS legislation above) of an arrangement and suggests applying a tax geared penalty on the promoter, enabler and taxpayer (or a penalty based on the financial benefit derived by the promoter and enabler).

The same concerns apply as to the extension the POTAS arrangements given the very wide definition of arrangement, the approach to a relevant defeat and the retrospective effect of the proposals which could include planning under taken many years before the proposed legislation.

INTERNATIONAL TAX PLANNING

Personal tax

4.35 HMRC announced a new Worldwide Disclosure Facility (WDF) available from 5 September 2016 in advance of new sanctions under the requirement to correct legislation (RTC) announced in the Autumn statement and the receipt of offshore bank details under automatic exchange of information provisions from over 100 countries that have signed up to the Common Reporting Standard.

These developments mark a step change in HMRC's approach to offshore tax compliance from encouraging taxpayers to make voluntary disclosures in return for favourable settlement terms to far tougher sanctions for those who do not regularise their tax affairs.

Liability for penalty for failure to correct

4.36 *F(No 2)A 2017, Sch 18* introduced a specific penalty regime for taxpayers who failed to correct offshore tax non-compliance before 30 September 2018.

The penalty payable under this regime is 200% of the offshore potential lost revenue ('PLR') attributable to the uncorrected offshore tax non-compliance (or so much of it as is uncorrected at 30 September 2018). PLR is determined as it is under *FA 2007, Sch 24* ('Penalties for errors') where the non-compliance is a failure to deliver a return or other document or the documents are delivered but contain an inaccuracy. If the non-compliance is a failure to notify chargeability, the PLR is determined as it is under the provisions of *FA 2008, Sch 41*.

The legislation provides for a reduction in the penalty if the person who is liable to the penalty discloses any matter that is relevant to the non-compliance

Contentious tax planning enquiries **4.36**

or its correct to HMRC. HMRC must reduce the penalty to one that reflects the quality of the disclosure, but it may not be reduced to below 100% of the offshore PLR. No penalty will apply if a taxpayer has a reasonable excuse for their failure.

Where a penalty is payable, it must be paid before the end of the period of 30 days beginning with the day on which notification of the penalty is issued.

> **Focus**
>
> *F(No 2)A 2017* impacts offshore planning arrangements that for whatever reason do not work, as well as deliberate tax evasion.

HMRC hopes the measure will drive taxpayers with offshore interests to review their affairs to either:

- assure themselves that their offshore interests have been treated correctly for tax purposes, or
- to identify the incorrect tax treatment and put it right by notifying HMRC to ensure the appropriate tax, interest and penalties can be charged.

The RTC is essentially a window in which to correct inaccuracies in a taxpayer's return relating to offshore matters before much tougher sanctions are apply.

Under these new measures HMRC is simply targeting tax loss from offshore arrangements. The terminology is deliberately more neutral in their view of taxpayer behaviour by simply focusing on a UK tax loss rather than evasion. HMRC recognise that people with overseas assets are often those with the most complex tax affairs and this can include tax structures which were compliant when they were set up but are not now.

RTC represents a final chance to put right anything that may be amiss and act as a driver for taxpayers with international affairs to review their tax position. The taxes that are currently in scope for the offshore penalties are within the scope of the RTC namely:

- Income Tax (IT);
- Capital Gains Tax (CGT);
- Inheritance Tax (IHT; in scope of offshore penalties from April 2016).

The 'correction' is expected to cover any outstanding UK tax liabilities that are within the time limits for assessment under the existing rules for tax assessment.

4.37 *Contentious tax planning enquiries*

In effect the RTC will create an additional offence on top of their original non-compliance by not correcting that situation by the end of the relevant window.

Anyone who does not correct errors and is identified by HMRC will have to rely on the reasonable excuse defence. The taxpayer cannot, however, rely on the typical defence of placing reliance on taking appropriate professional advice if the advice was given by an 'interested person' (as defined in para 23(5)) or did not take account of the taxpayer's specific circumstances.

Companies

Background

4.37 In response to political pressure from governments facing budget deficits and media scrutiny of whether global corporations are paying their 'fair share' of tax, G20 finance ministers sponsored the OECD to undertake an exercise for the preparation of action points to address the issue of Base Erosion Profit Shifting (BEPS). This involved strengthening and reshaping the existing international tax landscape to prevent the exploitation of low tax jurisdictions' beneficial tax regimes and tax mismatches between different countries' rules.

The OECD published its final 'action points' from the BEPS review in October 2015 and some recommendations have already been incorporated into domestic provisions by many countries (including the UK – most notably the UK 'anti-hybrid' provisions) or the principles are being adopted in practice in tax audits and examinations.

Diverted profits tax

4.38 *FA 2015* introduced the Diverted Profits Tax (DPT) (commonly referred to as the 'Google Tax'). A unilateral action taken by the UK government before the release of the final BEPS report in response to increased pressure by the public to counter aggressive tax planning

DPT seeks to prevent multinational enterprises from taking artificial steps to avoid creating a UK permanent establishment or eroding the UK tax base through the use of payments (royalties, technical, management, and services fees etc) to parties outside the UK. The tax is commonly referred to as the 'Google Tax'.

It is a separate tax to corporation tax and is chargeable at 25% (plus interest) (current rate of UK corporation tax being 19% with 17% enacted from 1 April 2020).

The provisions contained within *FA 2015* are extremely complex and detailed consideration is outside the scope of this chapter. However, broadly the provisions target two scenarios:

- non-UK resident companies who are regarding as artificially avoiding having a permanent establishment in the UK

- UK resident companies that are considered to use transactions with insufficient economic substance which result in a tax mismatch outcome through the creation of intra-group expenditure or the diversion of income.

BEPS action plan

4.39 The OECD's BEPS project considered actions under the following headings:

Concept	Action	Risk Area
Coherence: Country tax laws should be coherent and not leave any opportunity for income to be inappropriately untaxed or double taxed	2 Hybrid mismatch arrangements 3 CFC rules 4 Interest deductions 5 Harmful tax practices	Inappropriate use of international and domestic legislation to exploit preferential tax regimes and/or obtain unintended tax benefits
Substance: Profits should be attributed to the locations where people performing the value creating activity are located	6 Preventing treaty base 7 Avoidance of Permanent Establishment status 8 Transfer pricing aspects of intangibles 9 Transfer pricing aspects of high risk transactions	Activities and operating models which reflect a mismatch between where profits are taxed and where the people who generate those profits are based.
Transparency: Tax authorities should obtain information about global operations and share with each other to be able to carry out better risk assessments and audits.	11 Methodologies and data analysis 12 Disclosure rules 13 Documentation and country by country reporting 14 Dispute resolution	Mismatches in the reporting of profits and the location of people and other value drivers in the supply chain.

4.39 *Contentious tax planning enquiries*

In addition to the above actions, the OECD also looked at addressing the challenges of the digital economy (Action 1) and concluded that it cannot be subject to a special regime and further work will be undertaken in consultation with key stakeholders.

Action 15 considers the practicality of a multi-lateral instrument ('MLI') to enable the necessary modification to bilateral treaties to be undertaken to implement the treaty related aspects of the various actions. The MLI is effective from 1 January 2019, and has been ratified by the UK government. It should be noted that the MLI must be considered together with a bilateral treaty where both jurisdictions to the treaty have agreed to the modification; where a jurisdiction has reserved on a modification, the modification recommended under the MLI is not in point (unless the government which has not reserved to the modification incorporates the recommendation within its domestic legislation).

As well as modifying the application of bilateral tax treaties, the MLI also implements agreed minimum standards to counter treaty abuse as well as improving dispute resolution mechanisms.

The key UK impact of the BEPS recommendations are as follows:

- Action 2: Hybrid mismatch arrangements have been targeted by legislation at *TIOPA 2010, Pt 6A* 'Hybrid and Other Mismatches'. The regime applies to payments (of money or money's worth) made and transactions entered into on or after 1 January 2017, where it is reasonable to suppose that an arrangement will rise to:

   Relief/deduction for a payer with no taxable inclusion (a 'deduction/non-inclusion outcome'); or

   Relief/deduction in multiple jurisdictions in respect of the same item of expenditure ('double deductions').

A commercial arrangement is not outside the scope of the UK anti-hybrid legislation; in contrast to the UK anti-arbitrage legislation, now repealed, which did not apply if it could be argued that the arrangement was commercial or the tax benefit was not a UK benefit.

- Action 4: Legislation restricting interest deductions based on a fixed group ratio ('Corporate Interest Restriction' legislation).

- Action 5: Countering harmful tax practices more effectively having regard to substance and transparency. The substance requirement is addressed by the 'nexus approach' which requires that research and development (R&D) activity must be carried out by the taxpayer in the relevant jurisdiction. The transparency aspect involves exchange of information on certain rulings. A monitoring programme will ensure countries comply with the requirements.

Contentious tax planning enquiries **4.40**

- Action 6: Amendments to the OECD model treaty and related commentary addressing inappropriate granting of treaty benefits and other potential treaty abuse (so called 'treaty shopping'). In this respect the final report notes that countries have committed to a 'minimum standard involving a principle purpose test; a Limitation of Benefits (LOB) rule and combination of the two or a LOB rule supplemented by specific rules aimed at conduit financing arrangements'.

- Action 7: Prevention of artificial Avoidance of Permanent Establishment through changes to the PE definition in Article 5 of the OECD Model convention. This is aimed at Commissionaire and other similar arrangements and the use of preparatory or auxiliary activity exemptions. Changes to Article 5(4) include an anti-fragmentation rule to prevent the fragmentation of a cohesive operating business into a number of smaller operations in order to argue that each one individually is only conducting preparatory or auxiliary activities.

- Actions 8–10: Aligning transfer pricing outcomes with value creation. Work under this heading covered three key areas: transactions involving intangibles (8); contractual allocation of risks (9); high risk areas (10). The guidance aims to ensure operational profits are allocated to the economic activities that generate them. Specific areas covered are:

New guidance on comparability factors

4.40 *Intangibles:* Key aspects of the guidance are (1) the reaffirmation that legal ownership of itself does not confer any right to return from the assets exploitation. Rather the return accrues to the entities performing the key value creating functions of developing, enhancing, maintaining and exploiting the intangible, (2) that funding only, without the management of risk associated with that funding, does not entitle the lender to any more than a risk free capital return and (3) guidance on hard-to-value intangibles

Cost contribution arrangements: the existing guidance is replaced with the report seeking to ensure that the guidance on cost contribution arrangements is consistent with the rest of the guidance on the approach to risk and intangibles

- Action 13: A standardised approach to transfer pricing documentation involving a 'master file' that includes high level information on the groups global operations, including the key value drivers and a 'local file' that includes more detailed information regarding material related party transactions and how they have been priced in accordance with the arm's length principle. In addition a country by country template that requires large MNE's (worldwide group turnover €750 million) to report various information to assist tax authorities carry out a risk assessment.

4.41 *Contentious tax planning enquiries*

THE ROLE OF SPECIALIST DIRECTORATES

Background

4.41 There are a number of different HMRC specialists who may be consulted with regard to tax avoidance arrangements, but with the creation of the Counter Avoidance Directorate HMRC combines in working or coordinating cases the former roles of the old Anti Avoidance Group (AAG) and avoidance work of Specialist Investigations (SI).

Counter Avoidance

4.42 Counter Avoidance (CA) took over the role and functions of the Anti Avoidance Group (AAG) in 2013 and the operational staff of SI who worked on avoidance schemes. Its role is set out on HMRC's website and broadly involves:

- providing advice and support to Ministers, HM Treasury and HMRC colleagues on anti-avoidance policy issues;
- developing, delivering and maintaining an anti-avoidance strategy;
- leading the investigation by operational colleagues of those avoidance cases judged to be the most serious;
- risk assessing disclosed avoidance schemes and co-ordinating responses;
- providing the statutory clearance procedures;
- applying the provisions in *Income Tax Act 2007, ss 682–713* (formerly *ICTA 1988, ss 703–709*) to counteract tax avoidance by transactions in securities.

4.43 CA comprises several hundred people and aims to fully cover avoidance activity from policy, identification, intervention to resolution. It is arranged into three sections:

- intelligence, clearance and counteraction;
- policy; and
- delivery or operational response (investigation, litigation and resolution providing an end-to-end service).

The intelligence group is responsible for the review and dissemination of disclosures. Clearance and counteraction handles applications for clearance in mergers and acquisitions, applying the long-standing Transactions in Securities, purchase of own shares, etc, rules.

Contentious tax planning enquiries **4.45**

The policy group is responsible for monitoring the impact of avoidance arrangements, including the disclosure regime and liaising with the Treasury and technical divisions to coordinate responses where necessary.

The investigations arm is the operational department working the cases, including cases to be litigated. This is organised on themed and project lines, though investigation for example in Large Business cases may be conducted by the LB tax specialist or Customer Relationship Manager.

4.44 Whilst CA, in conjunction with the Solicitor's Office, has overall responsibility for arrangements which will be litigated, the actual allocation of cases identified through the disclosure regime is determined for day-to-day working by a committee representing a number of departments such as the Large Business office (LB), the High Net Worth Unit (HNWU) and Specialist Investigations (SI). The LB and HNWU teams have responsibility for the taxpayer's affairs and, therefore, it can be seen that it makes sense for these departments to work these cases with support from CA whilst CA concentrates on mass market avoidance.

Following the model used by Anti Avoidance Group, in CA schemes are worked by project teams who are running a stable of similar arrangements (eg film partnerships, intellectual property, forex, loan relationships, leasing, etc). In practice, the exact dynamics of the various departmental interactions will often come down to personalities and individual effectiveness.

For significant cross-border avoidance arrangements, the head office department 'Business International' retains full control of the case management.

THE EVOLUTION AND IMPORTANCE OF AVOIDANCE CASE LAW

Introduction

4.45 Ultimately the courts will decide the success or otherwise of a particular arrangement if agreement cannot be reached with HMRC. This aspect has become increasingly important in recent years as HMRC is more likely to litigate tax avoidance arrangements.

As stated at the outset, a detailed analysis of avoidance case law is beyond the scope of this chapter. However, given that it is the courts that are the ultimate arbiters of whether a particular arrangement is effective, it is essential that practitioners take a realistic (as opposed to 'rose-tinted') view of how the courts may react to a particular arrangement and whether it has the characteristics of an arrangement that is likely to be litigated by HMRC.

4.46 *Contentious tax planning enquiries*

4.46 The long lead time between the decision to enter into the planning arrangement and any litigation can result in views evolving considerably from when the planning was conceived and implemented to when its fate is ultimately decided in the courts (assuming a negotiated settlement cannot be reached).

The evolution of the courts' approach and thinking over time is currently demonstrated by the debate over the extent to which the courts will adopt a literal or purposive construction in their interpretation of the statutes. The potted history below shows that whilst some clear principles have emerged over recent years, significant uncertainty remains as to how they will be applied in specific circumstances. Consequently, practitioners face a difficult task in predicting outcomes and determining a clear and consistent rationale for decision making.

Domestic planning: a potted history

4.47 To know where we stand today it is helpful to understand the history of how judicial thinking has evolved over time.

Planning based on a literal interpretation of statute

4.48 In answering issues of artificiality (and to some extent morality) when seeking to defend a client's right to plan their tax affairs so as to reduce their liability, tax advisers often rely on the classic dicta of Lord Tomlin in *Duke of Westminster v IRC* (1936) 19 TC 490:

> 'Every man is entitled if he can to order his affairs so that the tax attaching under the appropriate Acts is less than it otherwise would be. If he succeeds in ordering them so as to secure this result, then, however unappreciative the Commissioners of Inland Revenue or his fellow taxpayers may be of his ingenuity, he cannot be compelled to pay an increased tax'.

In a similar vein, the comments of Lord Clyde in *Ayrshire Pullman Motor Services and DM Ritchie v IRC* (1929) 14 TC 754 imply that the courts at the time perceived tax avoidance as something of a game between the taxpayer and the authorities. He commented:

> 'No man in this country is under the smallest obligation, moral or other, so to arrange his legal relations to his business or to his property so as to enable the Inland Revenue to put the largest possible shovel into his stores. The Inland Revenue is not slow—and quite rightly—to take every advantage which is open to it under the taxing statutes for the purpose of depleting the taxpayer's pocket. And the taxpayer is, in like manner, entitled to be astute to prevent, so far as he honestly can, the depletion of his mean by the Revenue'.

Contentious tax planning enquiries **4.49**

The strict legalistic approach to statutory interpretation favoured in early decisions is perhaps best summed up by Rowlatt J in *Cape Brandy Syndicate v IRC* 1921 12 TC 358:

'In a taxing Act one has to look merely at what is clearly said. There is no room for any intendment. There is no equity about a tax. There is no presumption as to tax. Nothing is to be read in, nothing is to be implied. One can only look fairly at the language used'.

The *Ramsay* principle: a watershed in judicial thinking

4.49 The explosion of highly artificial tax-avoidance arrangements during the 1970s ultimately led to the House of Lords case of *WT Ramsay Ltd v Inland Revenue Commissioners* 1981 54 TC 101. The case marked a watershed in judicial thinking in relation to avoidance arrangements. The taxpayer sought to avoid capital gains tax by the creation of a loss via a series of pre-ordained, self-cancelling transactions which had no commercial purpose other than the avoidance of tax. It was accepted by the courts that all the transactions were genuine and not a sham.

Lord Justice Templeman in the Court of Appeal, while finding for the Crown on the narrow technical point of whether a loan was a debt on a security, in his opening comments reflected how, in the writer's experience, many if not most HMRC officers view many of the tax avoidance arrangements they come across. It is so apt in this respect, and in the sense that a number of the observations remain pertinent today, that the relevant passage has been included in full below:

'The facts set out in the case stated by the Special Commissioners demonstrate yet another circular game in which the taxpayer and a few hired performers act out a play; nothing happens save that the Houdini taxpayer appears to escape from the manacles of tax. The game is recognisable by four rules. First, the play is devised and scripted prior to performance. Secondly, real money and real documents are circulated and exchanged. Thirdly, the money is returned by the end of the performance. Fourthly, the financial position of the actors is the same at the end as it was at the beginning save that the taxpayer in the course of the performance pays the hired actors for their services. The object of the performance is to create the illusion that something has happened, that Hamlet has been killed and that Bottom did don an asses head, so that tax advantages can be claimed as if something had happened. The audience are informed that the actors reserve the right to walk out in the middle of the performance but in fact they are the creatures of the consultant who has sold and the taxpayer who has bought the play: the actors are never in a position to make a profit and there is no chance that they will go on strike. The critics are mistakenly

4.50 *Contentious tax planning enquiries*

informed that the play is based on a classic masterpiece called 'The Duke of Westminster' but in that piece the old retainer entered the theatre with his salary and left with a genuine entitlement to his salary and to an additional annuity'.

4.50 The case was heard in the House of Lords where Lord Wilberforce set out four principles:

- a subject is only to be taxed on clear words, not upon 'intendment' or upon the 'equity' of an Act. Any taxing Act of Parliament is to be construed in accordance with this principle. What are 'clear words' is to be ascertained upon normal principles: these do not confine the courts to literal interpretation. They may, indeed should, be considered in the context and scheme of the relevant Act as a whole;

- a subject is entitled to arrange his affairs so as to reduce his liability to tax;

- it is for the Commissioners (now the Tax Tribunal) to find whether a document or transaction is a sham;

- if a document or transaction is genuine the court cannot go behind it to some supposed underlying substance.

Lord Wilberforce considered that his decision fully respected the first three principles but did, however, make an important clarification of the fourth principle. In this respect he said that:

'This is a cardinal principle but it must not be overstated or overextended ... for the Commissioners ... It is wrong and an unnecessary self limitation, to regard themselves as precluded by their own finding that documents or transactions are not "shams" from considering what the relevant transaction is. They are not, under the Westminster doctrine or any other authority, bound to consider individually each separate step in a composite transaction intended to be carried out as a whole'.

Lord Wilberforce also went on to consider the argument that because the capital gains tax code did not contain a wide-ranging anti-avoidance measure such as that which became *ICTA 1988, s 703* and because Parliament had never passed a general anti-avoidance rule, if loopholes remained in the capital gains tax system, these should be plugged by Parliament and not the courts. In response he stated:

'While the techniques of tax avoidance are technically improved, the courts are not obliged to stand still. The capital gains tax was created to operate in the real world not that of make belief ... it is a tax on gains, it is not a tax on arithmetical differences. To say that a loss which appears to arise at one stage in an individual process, and which is intended to be and is cancelled out by a later stage, so that at the end of what was bought as, and planned as, a single continuous operation is not such a loss as the legislation is dealing with, is in my opinion well ... within the judicial function'.

In this sense Lord Wilberforce was adopting a purposive interpretation of the legislation.

4.51 In the immediate aftermath of *Ramsay* it remained unclear whether its groundbreaking doctrine could be applied to schemes which were not 'circular' in their nature. Clarity, or so it seemed, arrived on this point in the case of *Furniss (Inspector of Taxes) v Dawson* [1984] STC 153.

In *Furniss v Dawson* the *Ramsay* principle was applied to establish the true parties to a transaction and its true nature. A sale which was a practical certainty was arranged between the taxpayer (Mr Dawson) and a particular purchaser, Wood Bastow Holdings Ltd, was held to be the true transaction and the inserted intermediary step of a sale solely for tax reasons to a wholly-owned creature company (Greenjacket Ltd) was to be ignored. Brightman J stated:

'First there must be a preordained series of transactions; or, if one likes, one single composite transaction. Secondly, there must be steps inserted which have no commercial purpose apart from the avoidance of tax. If those two ingredients exist, the inserted steps are to be disregarded for fiscal purposes'.

4.52 By way of contrast, in *Craven (Inspector of Taxes) v White* [1985] STC 476, which involved the same basic scheme as that which failed in *Furniss*, it was held that it was not sufficient that the inserted steps had a sole tax avoidance purpose for them to be ignored. The fundamental difference in the cases was that in *Craven v White* the inserted sale of shares to an intermediate company took place at a time when there was no preordained onward sale to an ultimate purchaser.

In *Craven v White*, Lord Keith said:

'In my opinion both the transactions in the series can properly be regarded as preordained if, but only if, at the time when the first of them is entered into the taxpayer is in a position for all practical purposes to secure that the second also is entered into'.

As a consequence of these cases the debate for many years often centred upon whether transactions with inserted steps were preordained or not.

Current status of *Ramsay* as a principle of purposive construction

4.53 Since 2001 a number of cases have been heard which again demonstrate the difficulty of achieving clarity as to where the goalposts lie in relation to tax planning and how difficult it can be to predict how the courts will react.

4.54 *Contentious tax planning enquiries*

Lord Hoffmann, in the case of *MacNiven (Inspector of Taxes) v Westmoreland Investments Ltd* [2001] STC 237, attempted to bring clarity to over 20 years of tax-avoidance case law. He confirmed that *Ramsay* is a principle of statutory construction which does not provide a general 'substance over form' doctrine but

> '… was a recognition that the statutory language was intended to refer to commercial concepts, so that in the case of a concept such as a "disposal" the court was required to take a view of the facts which transcended the juristic individuality of the various parts of a pre-planned series of transactions'.

Lord Hoffmann then went on to impose limitations to which commercial concepts could be applied to statutory language. He considered these limits were set by the purpose of the relevant statutory provision and the particular statutory language. Lord Hoffmann considered that there were many terms in the tax legislation which could not be construed in this way because they referred to purely legal concepts which have no broader commercial meaning. In these cases he considered that the *Ramsay* principle would have no application.

4.54 However, his attempt to distinguish between commercial and legal concepts was subsequently found to be unsustainable as a general proposition (see *Barclays Mercantile Business Finance Ltd v Mawson (Inspector of Taxes)* [2005] STC 1 (*BMBF*)).

In *BMBF* (and *IRC v Scottish Provident Institution (SPI)* [2005] STC 15, released on the same day) the House of Lords took the unusual step of giving a combined judgment which was clearly intended to bring some clarity to the confusion which had arisen from Lord Hoffmann's introduction of the commercial/legal division of statutory language.

In *BMBF*, the House confirmed that it was necessary to consider carefully the particular statutory provision and identify its requirements before deciding whether circular payments or elements inserted for tax avoidance should be disregarded or treated as irrelevant for the purposes of the statute. However, this did not justify the assumption that the answer to this analysis could be determined by classifying all concepts as either 'commercial' or 'legal' in the first instance. The House of Lords summarised [para 32] the *Ramsay* principles as follows:

> 'The essence of the new approach was to give the statutory provision a purposive construction in order to determine the nature of the transaction to which it was intended to apply and then decide whether the actual transaction (which might involve considering the overall effect of a number of elements designed to operate together) answered to the statutory description. Of course this does not mean that the courts have to put their reasoning into

Contentious tax planning enquiries **4.56**

the straight jacket of first construing the statute in the abstract and then looking at the facts. It might be more convenient to analyse the facts and then ask whether they satisfy the relevant requirements of the statute'.

4.55 Their Lordships dismissed as a general proposition that any elements inserted into transactions without any commercial purpose were to be treated as having no significance. Instead a purposive approach involved two steps: 'First to decide, on a purposive construction, exactly what transaction will answer to the statutory description and secondly, to decide whether the transaction in question does so.' Their Lordships went on to quote from Ribeiro PJ in the Hong Kong appeal *Collector of Stamp Revenue v Arrowtown Assets Ltd* (2003) 6 ITLR 454:

'The ultimate question is whether the relevant statutory provisions, construed purposively, were intended to apply to the transaction, viewed realistically.'

As a succinct summary of the *Ramsay* approach Ribeiro's words have not been bettered.

In applying this principle to BMBF's capital allowances claim, their Lordships appeared to have been swayed by the purpose of the capital allowances legislation in providing a tax deduction equivalent to accounting depreciation where the plant is used for the purpose of the trade. HMRC's claims that the funding arrangements were artificial and circular were dismissed as irrelevant or 'happenstances' which had no bearing on the creation of an entitlement to capital allowances. Moreover, the legislation was concerned with the acts of the lessor and said nothing about the lessee's position, in terms of how he should fund the rental payments.

4.56 By way of contrast, the loss claimed by Scottish Provident in *IRC v Scottish Provident Institution (SPI)* [2005] STC 15 did not answer the statutory description. In this case, the arrangement had no other purpose than seeking to take advantage of the legislative transition from the old pre-derivative contracts regime to the new regime.

The scheme involved Scottish Provident granting an option to buy gilts to the bank who devised the scheme at an 'off market' price in return for a large premium. This premium was not taxable under the old regime. Once the derivative contracts regime came into force, the option was exercised requiring Scottish Provident to sell the gilts at a loss, which was allowable for tax purposes under the new regime. Commercially the transactions cancelled each other out but in tax terms gave rise to an allowable loss and a non-taxable gain.

The Special Commissioners found as a fact that:

'There was a genuine commercial possibility and a real practical likelihood that the two options would be dealt with separately. Likewise, there was

4.57 *Contentious tax planning enquiries*

genuine commercial possibility and a real practical likelihood that the [Scottish Provident] option would not be exercised'.

The House of Lords recognised that it could not disturb this finding of fact but considered that a question of law was involved. The House of Lords concluded that the Commissioners had erred in law in concluding that a contingency which had been deliberately inserted in the documents to give a possibility that the transaction might not have happened prevented it from being construed as a composite transaction when that contingency did not in reality arise.

The House of Lords considered that the question to be answered was whether the option gave an entitlement to gilts which would then enable it to be a qualifying contract as defined in the legislation. Despite the argument that the legislation in question was highly prescriptive, the House of Lords ruled that the statutory language was to be given a 'wide practical meaning' and required the court to have regard to the whole series of transactions which were intended to have 'a commercial unity'.

4.57 In both of the above cases the application of the facts to the legislation was crucial in reaching the respective decisions. In *BMBF* the taxpayer's evidence as to what constituted its 'ordinary trade of finance leasing' was important; in *SPI* the fact that a commercially irrelevant contingency was inserted to ensure there was no prospect of arguing that the transaction was pre-ordained weighed heavily against the taxpayer.

However, it would appear that the courts regard the issue of what constitutes a composite transaction to be a question of law as opposed to fact. The courts continue to deny the existence of judicially created law. HMRC, however, appears to consider the decision in *SPI* as a strengthening of the *Ramsay* principle. This may well be the case with regard to schemes which have been entered into purely for tax-avoidance reasons with no commercial purpose. Irrespective of whether this is a principle of a statutory construction or judicially created law there remains a considerable degree of uncertainty as to what type of arrangement will, in the words of their Lordships in *SPI*, 'sail through the gap'.

4.58 There have been a significant number of cases since these two landmark House of Lords judgments, with decisions both for and against the taxpayer. HMRC has undoubtedly been encouraged by recent successes such as *Astall v Revenue and Customs Comrs* [2009] EWCA Civ 1010; *Prudential plc v HMRC* [2009] STC 2459; *Revenue and Customs Comrs v DCC Holdings (UK) Ltd* [2011] STC 326 and *Tower Mcashback v Revenue and Customs Comrs* [2011] STC 1143. But there have been equally significant wins for the taxpayer in cases such as *Revenue and Customs Comrs v D'Arcy* [2008] STC 1329; *Mayes v Revenue and Customs Comrs* [2011] STC 1269 and *Revenue and Customs Comrs v Bank of Ireland Britain Holdings Ltd* [2008] STC 398.

Contentious tax planning enquiries **4.60**

These latter three cases provide further recent evidence that the courts are prepared, in certain circumstances, to find for the taxpayer, notwithstanding that the transaction in question was designed with the exploitation of a perceived loophole in the legislation in mind. In *Revenue and Customs Comrs v D'Arcy* the taxpayer sought to take advantage of a mismatch between the tax legislation relating to the accrued income scheme and the manufactured interest payment regime in order to create a tax deduction with no corresponding charge. HMRC sought to argue that a purposive interpretation of the accrued income provisions should impose a charge on the taxpayer. However, the court found in favour of the taxpayer. Henderson J commented:

> 'The Revenue's real complaint, as it seems to me, is that the accrued income scheme does not throw up a charge to counterbalance the deduction admittedly available to Mrs D'Arcy for her manufactured interest payment. But the accrued income scheme and the provisions relating to manufactured interest were enacted at different times and with different statutory purposes. They do not form part of a single unified code, and their separation is indeed emphasised by section 727A. In short, this is in my view one of those cases, which will inevitably occur from time to time in a tax system as complicated as ours, where a well-advised taxpayer has been able to take advantage of an unintended gap left by the interaction between two different sets of statutory provisions'.

However, a more recent attempt to exploit a claimed mismatch between the accrued income scheme and the manufactured interest rules failed in *Barnes v CRC* [2014] EWCA Civ 31.

4.59 In *Revenue and Customs Comrs v Bank of Ireland Britain Holdings Ltd* [2008] STC 398, the taxpayer had entered into an arrangement (involving a tripartite repo) which exploited a mismatch between two sets of repo provisions (*ICTA 1988*, ss 730A and 737A). The legislation in question had not envisaged a tripartite repo involving a non-resident interim holder. HMRC argued that the taxpayer's interpretation gave a bizarre result and suggested that:

> 'If the court is presented with two alternative constructions, the construction which gives a result in line with the policy of the Act should be preferred to a construction which gives a result so bizarre it could not possibly have been intended'.

The Court of Appeal, however, rejected such an approach. Lawrence Collins LJ acknowledged that the scheme had been devised to take advantage of a mismatch between two sets of provisions but considered there was no legitimate process of interpretation that would solve HMRC's problem.

4.60 In a similar vein, in *Coombes v Revenue and Customs Comrs* [2008] STC 2984, HMRC sought to tax the taxpayer as if he was the settlor by virtue

4.61 *Contentious tax planning enquiries*

of him having provided the funds to purchase the settled property. As a settlor, the taxpayer would have been subject to tax under *TCGA 1992, s 86*. HMRC contended that the arrangement adopted by the taxpayer effectively emasculated the anti-avoidance effect of *TCGA 1992, s 86*. However, Sir Donald Rattee, whilst acknowledging this point, commented:

> 'That may be, but that fact does not, of course, enable me to do violence to the actual provisions of sections 68 and 86 of, and Sch 5 to, the 1992 Act'.

4.61 From HMRC's perspective, the Court of Appeal case of *Astall v Revenue and Customs Comrs* [2009] EWCA Civ 1010 appears to have further developed the concept of a 'commercially irrelevant contingency' which was introduced in *SPI*.

The taxpayers had, in separate transactions, sought to create an income tax loss by using a discounted security; both admitted that the transactions took place solely for tax avoidance purposes. The terms of the security were structured in such a way as to provide a 15% chance that the transaction would give rise to a gain on redemption. However, this contingency was considered to be commercially irrelevant to the security (given that it related to the dollar/sterling exchange rate when the security was in sterling) and as such, was viewed as an insertion to *Ramsay*-proof the transaction.

The Special Commissioner held that the conditions inserted to introduce uncertainty could be ignored under the *Ramsay* principle because they lacked reality. The Special Commissioner concluded:

> 'A purposive construction of the definition of relevant discounted security must have regard to real possibilities of redemption, not ones written into the document creating the security that the parties know, and any reasonable person having the knowledge available to the parties knows, will never occur'.

Both the High Court and Court of Appeal concurred with the Special Commissioner's view. In the Court of Appeal Arden LJ rejected counsel's argument for the taxpayer that regard should only be had to the terms of the security, not extraneous facts such as the likelihood of redemption. She considered the *FA 1996, Sch 13, paras 2* and *3* had to receive a purposive construction. That purpose was that there should be a real possibility of a deep gain if losses incurred on a relevant discount security were to be offsettable for income tax purposes.

Interestingly, while in Arden LJ's view the process probably started with determining the purpose of the statutory provision, she considered that it may be necessary to refine that purpose as and when the facts are more closely defined. She felt that this may have been what Lord Hoffmann had in mind

Contentious tax planning enquiries **4.62**

when he spoke in Privy Council judgment in *Carreras* of the need to find facts 'in the process of construction'. This is yet another reminder to advisers of the importance of the facts when considering how the courts are likely to view a particular avoidance transaction.

4.62 Although HMRC has, in recent years, been relatively successful in cases heard before the Special Commissioners and subsequently the First-Tier Tribunal, the two recent cases of *Mayes v Revenue and Customs Comrs* [2011] STC 1269 and *UBS AG* and *DB Group Services (UK) Ltd v Revenue and Customs Comrs* [2014] EWCA Civ 452 indicate the limits to which it is possible to take the concept of purposive construction in the context of a 'realistic view of the facts'.

The *Mayes* case involved a tax avoidance scheme using single premium 'non-qualifying' life assurance policies which had been designed to trigger a chargeable event (without incurring an actual charge to tax) as a result of their part-surrender, followed by a full surrender by the individual investor (Mayes) who could then claim the relief.

The scheme involved the following steps:

(1) on 2 April 2002 a Jersey resident individual purchased from an insurer, by means of single premiums of £5,000, two bonds comprising several policies on his life;

(2) on 6 March 2003 the Jersey individual assigned the bonds to a Luxembourg company ('JSI') for value;

(3) on 7 March 2003 JSI paid £375,000 to the insurer in respect of each policy in the first bond and £50,000 in respect of each policy in the second bond;

(4) on 31 March 2003 JSI withdrew from the bonds all the sums paid on 7 March;

(5) on 6 November 2003 JSI assigned the bonds to a limited liability partnership ('LLP') for value;

(6) on 18 December 2003 the LLP assigned the bonds to the taxpayer for value;

(7) the taxpayer surrendered both bonds to the insurer, receiving in return the remaining proceeds from the bonds.

The taxpayer claimed income tax relief arising from the surrender for the tax year 2003–04. HMRC contended that steps (3) and (4), which were needed to create the corresponding deficiency relief, did not, on a purposive construction, fall within the relevant provisions of *ICTA 1988* under which the relief was claimed.

4.63 *Contentious tax planning enquiries*

4.63 The Special Commissioner accepted HMRC's contention that steps (3) and (4) being pre-ordained, composite, self-cancelling transactions, devoid of commercial content, should be disregarded pursuant to the *Ramsay* principle. As such, the transaction viewed realistically should ignore the effect of these transactions as the creation of a 'corresponding deficiency' by such means would not be a rational application of the relevant Chapter. The Special Commissioner considered that this conclusion accepted and reflected a coherence of drafting of, and the purpose behind, the provisions in the Chapter.

The Special Commissioner's decision was overturned by the High Court and this decision was upheld by the Court of Appeal. Proudman J in the High Court agreed with the Special Commissioner's formulation of the statutory question to be answered in the words of Ribeiro PJ but considered that as the legislation does not seek to tax real or commercial gains it made no sense to say that the legislation must be construed to seek to apply to transactions by reference to their commercial substance. The judge considered that:

> 'Chapter II, Part XIII of the Taxes Acts adopted a formulaic and prescriptive approach. No overriding principle can be extracted from the legislation, or from the authorities, that some types of transaction should be ignored in the application of the chapter'.

Lord Justice Mummery in the Court of Appeal agreed with Proudman J that the Special Commissioner had erred in law in disregarding the payment of a premium at step (3) and the partial surrender at step (4) simply because they were self-cancelling steps inserted for tax advantage purposes. Mummery LJ considered:

> 'It was right to look at the overall effect of the composite step 3 and step 4 in the 7 step transaction in terms of ICTA to determine whether it answered to the legislative description of the transaction or fitted the requirement of the legislation for corresponding deficiency relief. So viewed, step 3 and step 4 answer the description of premium and partial surrender. On the true construction of the ICTA provisions, which do not readily lend themselves to a purposive commercial construction, step 3 was in its legal nature a premium to secure benefits under the bonds and step 4 was in its nature a withdrawal of funds in the form of a partial surrender within the meaning of those provisions. They were genuine legal events with real legal effects. The court cannot, as a matter of construction, deprive those events of their fiscal effects under ICTA because they were self-cancelling events that were commercially unreal and were inserted for a tax avoidance purpose …'

In the same case, Toulson LJ expressed a view that it was with some reluctance that he concurred with Mummery LJ, because the result instinctively seemed wrong as it bore no relation to commercial reality and produced a windfall for

Contentious tax planning enquiries **4.65**

the taxpayer which Parliament could not have foreseen or intended. Despite this conflict with Parliament's intention, he nevertheless concluded that the scheme worked.

4.64 Whilst the above cases show how difficult it can be to assess where the line is drawn in terms of the impact of purposive construction, the joined cases of *UBS AG* and *DB Group Services (UK) Ltd v Revenue and Customs Comrs* [2014] EWCA 452 reinforce the importance of purposive construction even in closely articulated legislation. In finding in favour of the taxpayer, the Court of Appeal drew upon the findings in *Mayes* to conclude that an arrangement described by the Upper Tribunal as a 'carefully planned tax avoidance scheme which was designed to enable the [banks] to provide substantial bonuses to employees in a way that would escape liability to both income tax and national insurance contributions' was effective in that aim.

The key issues identified by the Upper Tribunal were: (1) did the employees become entitled to be paid their bonuses in money before the sums allocated to them were applied in acquiring scheme shares? If yes, the bonuses were subject to tax; (2) if no, did any charge to tax arise under *ITEPA 2003*? This raised the questions of whether the scheme shares were 'restricted securities' within *s 423* and, if so, whether the employees were entitled to the tax exemption provided by *s 429*; (3) applying the *Ramsay* principle on a realistic appraisal of the facts, did the schemes fall outside Chapter 2 altogether?

4.65 HMRC considered the scheme to be a 'cash in, cash out' scheme whereby UBS would decide upon the intended bonus, which it would pay into the scheme and which the employee could take out a few weeks later. The Court of Appeal, however, considered that was a mis-description of the scheme.

The crux of HMRC's argument was that the arrangements were simply a tax avoidance scheme and it was not the intention of the legislature to extend the benefit of the provisions of Chapter 2 to artificial arrangements, such as the scheme, that have no commercial purpose.

HMRC considered the focus on the redemption of the shares for cash showed that the securities were not intended to function as securities in the normal sense. They were not granted as interests in companies with an independent business, the arrangement was simply a vehicle for passing to the employees the cash identified for them at the outset. The scheme had no commercial purpose, only a tax avoidance purpose and as its sole purpose was to reward the employees in cash, the shares were not, therefore, 'restricted securities' at all, they did not perform the function envisaged for 'restricted securities' and therefore, the scheme fell outside Chapter 2.

4.66 *Contentious tax planning enquiries*

4.66 UBS admitted that the forfeiture restriction imposed upon the shares issued to employees had no commercial purpose. It was, therefore, a commercially irrelevant provision inserted solely for the purpose of achieving the intended tax avoidance.

However on an analysis of *ITEPA 2003, Part 7* it was clear that there was nothing to suggest that the only securities contemplated by the provision are those given to an employee by way of an incentive. The definition was considered to extend to securities in companies unrelated to the employer and is, deliberately, spread very wide. Counsel for UBS accepted that it is legitimate to ask whether what the employee got was securities or money, but that it was not legitimate to ask whether he got what he did for tax avoidance reasons.

Counsel for UBS contended that the 'certain circumstances' that are a condition of *s 423* meant what they said and there was no basis for including only 'certain circumstances' other than those included for tax avoidance purposes. UBS accepted there must be a real, genuine possibility of the stated circumstances occurring: if they were never going to happen in the real world, a purposive interpretation of *s 423* would exclude them from its contemplation. In this case the FTT found there was a genuine possibility of a forfeiture happening on the facts of the scheme. The 'certain circumstances' were therefore real ones, even though their inclusion in the scheme was tax motivated.

4.67 The court considered that in cases in which, even though what was nominally awarded were shares, an objective interpretation of the true nature of the arrangements would justify the conclusion that in fact the employee was being paid money: for example, if the shares were required to be redeemed immediately for a pre-ordained cash sum, then on a realistic view of these facts the shares would not answer to the statutory description.

On the facts of the *UBS* case, the Court of Appeal considered there was no question of the scheme being one for the payment of money, and considered HMRC's efforts to suggest that it was as misconceived. The FTT found that the NVS were real shares, some of which were held by employees for more than two years, and real dividends were paid on them.

Moreover, although the employees had the right to redeem their shares for cash over a period of two years, the redemption money was not pre-ordained, but its amount varied with the fortunes of the UBS shares held by ESIP, which could have risen or fallen. The shares were therefore real shares which functioned as such.

The Supreme Court reversed the Court of Appeal's decision finding unanimously in HMRC's favour. Before setting out the basis for its conclusion

Contentious tax planning enquiries **4.67**

the Court set out in some detail the relevant background and context for the provisions in question. This background and context was key to the Supreme Court's reasoning based on a purposive construction. The Court acknowledged that there was weight to the argument that Part 2 and Chapter 2 in particular, are extensive and highly detailed; contain no explanation of the purpose of Chapter 2 upon which a purposive interpretation might be based; and do not indicate that restricted conditions attached to securities purely for tax avoidance purposes fall outside the scope of Chapter 2. It was also argued that parliament dealt with certain kinds of tax avoidance in Chapters 3A to 3D but made no provision in respect of schemes with which the appeals were concerned meant that it was impossible attribute to Parliament an unexpressed intention to exclude the taxpayers' schemes from the ambit of Chapter 2.

However, the Court considered the context of Chapter 2 provides some indication of what Parliament intended. The Court considered the purposes of part 7 were identified in broad terms in *Grays Timber Products* as being:

'(1) to promote employee share ownership, particularly by encouraging share incentive schemes;

(2) since such schemes require benefits to be contingent on future performance, creating a problem if tax is charged on the acquisition of the shares in accordance with *Abbott v Philbin*, to wait and see in such cases until the contingency has fallen away; and

(3) to counteract consequent opportunities for tax avoidance.'

The Court considered therefore that the reference in *s 423(1)* to 'any contract, agreement, arrangement or condition which makes provision to which any of subsections (2) to (4) applies' is to be construed as being limited to a provision having a business or commercial purpose, and not to commercially irrelevant conditions whose only purpose is the obtaining of the exemption.

The Court considered that the forfeiture condition – whether the FTSE 100 rose by a specified amount during a three-week period – was completely arbitrary. It had no business or commercial rationale beyond tax avoidance and therefore, was not relevant to the application of *s 423*. Applying *s 423* to the facts, viewed from a commercially realistic perspective, it followed that the condition to which the UBS shares were subject should be disregarded, with the consequence that the shares are not 'restricted securities' within the meaning of that section.

The Court considered that conclusion was also supported by the fact that the economic effect of the restrictive condition was in any event nullified by the hedging arrangements, except to an insignificant and pre-determined extent. So considered, the benefit to the employee was not truly dependent on the

4.68 *Contentious tax planning enquiries*

contingency set out in the condition. The Court considered this position was supported by the Supreme Court's decision in Scottish Provident.

Summary

4.68 These cases emphasise the difficulty in determining where the line is in terms of success and failure with regard to tax avoidance. They also serve to highlight the importance that HMRC will attach to establishing every last piece of information relating to the transactions in question, in order to give the most realistic view of the transaction, taken as a whole.

To sum up where we currently stand, the following key points appear to have emerged from recent decisions:

- the *Ramsay* principle is confirmed as a purposive approach to statutory construction involving a consideration of what the legislator intended that its requirements would be;

- the legal/commercial dichotomy formulated by Lord Hoffmann in *MacNiven* is not an unreasonable generalisation but does not provide a substitute for what the statute actually means;

- the effect of a single composite transaction should be considered as it was intended to operate without regard to the existence of commercially irrelevant contingencies;

- there is no universal rule that transactions or elements of a transaction which have no commercial purpose should be disregarded in construing the transaction as a whole.

In the context of what is a trade it is important to look at what was done and whether 'viewed realistically' it objectively amounts to a trade, not why it was done, which will not be determinative (though it may having a bearing where the other badges of trade do not point to an obvious answer).

4.69 A trading transaction cannot be re-characterised as non-trading simply because of the presence of a tax avoidance motive:

- Lewison J in *Berry v HMRC* [2011] UKUT FTC/29/2010 gave a helpful and up-to-date summary of the *Ramsay* principles with their judicial derivation at para 31.

Put simply, arrangements which involve a 'real' loss/profit and 'real' risk are likely to be successful, notwithstanding the fact that tax savings played a part in how the transaction was structured, whereas those involving artificial losses and only the appearance of risk are more likely to fail.

Contentious tax planning enquiries **4.73**

> **4.70** In addition, attempts to *'Ramsay* proof' a transaction by artificially creating an element of uncertainty are likely to undermine the chance of success before the courts. As would be expected, transactions with 'real' or 'genuine' legal and commercial consequences remain likely to be successful, irrespective of whether they contain a degree of circularity or tax-motivated elements within them.
>
> Planning around prescriptive closely articulated legislation or legislation which creates statutory 'fictions' (by 'deeming' provisions) will tend to succeed. Where the legislation applies a broader approach, most artificial tax planning is more likely to fail on a purposive interpretation by the courts.

Trading and loss generation schemes

4.71 There has been a raft of recent cases in the last few years where taxpayers have sought to claim significant losses and the issue has been whether the expenditure has been incurred and/or whether a trade has been conducted.

The courts have been unconvinced as to the commerciality of the arrangements, with the result that they have found that there was no trade with the result that to date, HMRC has been very successful in defeating the wide range of attempts to secure relief.

4.72 For example in *Price Myers & Lucas v HMRC* [2013] UKFTT 297 (TC) the three 'investors' claimed to carry on a plumbing trade (Stony Heating Ltd) but due to share identification rules they claimed for a modest outlay to generate large capital losses having subscribed for 'trading' company shares which under *ICTA 1988, s 574* (now *ITA 2007, s 132*) could be set against their income. As with other schemes, circular financing was part of the arrangement; preference share transactions occurred with offshore parties.

Though the company carried on a trade (the profit came from participation in the tax scheme) and was a qualifying company, the claims were reduced to minimal sums based on the Tribunal's reading of *TCGA 1992, ss 144A* and *149AA*.

Other promoted arrangements also failed for various reasons, with the trading question again being tested.

4.73 In *Eclipse Film Partners No 35 LLP v Revenue and Customs Comrs* [2014] EWCA Civ 184 the taxpayers needed to establish that a trade was carried on so that the partners could claim large sums 'paid' in the first period on borrowing to finance their 'investment' in film rights. The matter tested at the Tribunal was whether the partnership had traded. The First Tier and Upper

4.74 *Contentious tax planning enquiries*

Tier Tribunals found that Eclipse had not carried on a trade with a view to profit on the facts but carried on a non-trade business.

Eclipse 35 failed to persuade the tribunal that they had undertaken the risks, purchases and sales associated with that of trade in film rights or in films. What they acquired involved no prospect of loss or profit for the partnership. The scheme or 'business model' ignored the key ingredient that any person in business knows too well that they could make a profit or loss. This was because the speculative nature of the arrangement meant the prospect of a return was, over a period of 30 years, too unlikely to constitute a trade, especially having regard to the pre-negotiated, pre-ordained elements of the scheme, which together with the non-recourse loans gave an air of artificiality to the schemes.

4.74 *Working Wheels* [2014] UKFTT TC 00573, 980, 1070 was the loose name for some high-income individuals (Flanagan, Moyles and Sennett) who claimed to carry on second-hand car dealing trades via agents in the car trade. The cars bought and sold were of low value and the profits and losses minimal. However the participants claimed tax relief on large 'manufactured overseas dividend payments' under the repo rules as incidental costs of loan finance on which they hoped to obtain relief against their income. The repo element came in the assignment and re-assignment of securities and an extremely large fee was claimed. Indeed the fee was some 80,000 times the loan, on which basis it was found not to be 'representative' of the finance.

There was, however, no trade conducted by the individuals – they did not supply or trade in cars at all; they took no interest in the details of purchases or sales – the FTT said that each 'were instead engaged in an arrangement designed only to give the illusion of trading'. With no trade there was no sum which would meet the condition for relief of *ITTOIA 2005, s 58*.

The *Working Wheels* decision indicated that minimal levels of trade are not difficult to achieve but tax schemes sold to high income individuals are not trades unless the risk and daily involvement of the participants are genuine.

4.75 The Supreme Court in *Tower Mcashback LLP v Revenue and Customs Comrs* [2011] UKSC 19 held that arrangements whereby software expenditure quantified on the basis of future profits of speculative amounts against a background of limited recourse borrowing lacked commerciality, finding that the expenditure was not on software as claimed.

At first sight, the case has similarities to *BMBF v Mawson* (see para **4.54**) because of the circularity of the financing arrangements in both cases. However, in *BMBF*, despite the circularity, the cashflows had a genuineness to them which meant that the court was able to say that, viewed realistically, expenditure had been spent on an asset qualifying for capital allowances. Conversely, in *Tower*

Contentious tax planning enquiries **4.76**

Mcashback the amount paid for the software was considerably in excess of what the software was worth. In such circumstances it is relatively easy for the court to find that what was paid for was not the asset itself but something else. It was not the circularity that defeated the scheme, it was the fact that what was paid for did not, viewed realistically, answer the statutory description.

Tower Mcashback also seemingly confirms *Ensign Tankers (Leasing) Ltd v Stokes (Inspector of Taxes)* [1992] STC 226 as good law, though for different reasons. In *Ensign Tankers* the House of Lords held that whilst a tax avoidance purpose did not preclude the film production activity from being a trade no expenditure was incurred on interest because of the non-recourse nature of the arrangement. In *Tower Mcashback*, the Supreme Court accepted expenditure had been incurred but not on software. Perhaps if *Ensign Tankers* was heard today with the benefit of recent judgments, there would similarly be an acceptance of an expense but not on something that answered the statutory description to qualify for relief.

Where the common features of a marketed avoidance scheme are present, HMRC does not distinguish between the classification of the alleged trading activity, holding the view that they all follow the same blueprint of the planner.

Employee benefit trust (EBT) arrangements

4.76 HMRC has for a number of years been contending that payments into an EBT are taxable at the latest when the payments are allocated into a sub-trust for the benefit of a named beneficiary (usually the employee or family member). A large number of pre-disguised remuneration employee benefit trust arrangements remain under dispute despite the option to have settled via the Employee Benefit Trust Settlement Opportunity (EBTSO). This is because the EBTSO did not typically offer much of an incentive for arrangements where funds were placed in the trust and almost immediately loaned out to employees. In these circumstances taxpayers often preferred to take their chances and await the outcome of litigation (many gaining comfort from the decisions in *Murray Group Holdings Ltd and others v Revenue Customs and Commissioners* at both the FTT and UTT, which found that payments to employees via intermediary trust arrangements were not remuneration subject to PAYE). The Court of Session [2015] CSIH 77 overturned those decisions ruling in HMRC's favour that the payments were subject to PAYE. Although the decision is fact specific, HMRC will no doubt consider it will strengthen their hand in pursuing its PAYE argument on payments to EBTs.

However, perhaps even more significant will be the effect of the draft legislation published after the Autumn Statement in 2017 which would involve taxing loans from EBTs as if they were remuneration unless they are repaid by

4.77 *Contentious tax planning enquiries*

April 2019. This means that even if HMRC is ultimately unsuccessful litigating its PAYE arguments, it is likely to achieve its desired treatment by this alternative route.

In *Murray Group Holdings*, MGML set up an employees' remuneration trust ('the principal trust'), involving more than 100 sub-trusts that were established in the name of individual employees of companies in the group for the benefit of their families. Moneys were transferred into the principal trust with a direction to the trustees that a sub-trust should be established and funded for the benefit of the family of the company's employees. In addition, the trustees of the sub-trust made a loan facility available to the employee. The loan was repayable out of the employee's estate. The employee would be appointed protector of the sub-trust, with extended powers in respect of the trust, but without title to the trust assets and without the ability to confer any absolute beneficial right on the employee himself. After it was decided that a sub-trust should be created in the name of the particular employee, that employee would complete a letter of wishes, naming the family members that he wished to benefit on his death, and almost invariably a loan application requesting that moneys be advanced on loan to him by the trustees of the sub-trust. These were submitted to the trustee of the relevant sub-trust. The employing company would then pay a contribution to the principal trust which would then, at its discretion, set up a sub-trust in the name of the selected employee.

4.77 A sub-trust in the name of the employee was invariably set up. In almost all cases, loans for the full amount advanced from the employer to the trustees of the principal trust were granted by the trustees of the sub-trust to the relevant employee, for a term of ten years subject to extension and on a discounted basis. The employees' general expectation was that the terms of the loans would be renewed. In relation to employees other than footballers, they had no contractual right to a bonus. However, the practice was to pay annual bonuses on a discretionary basis (based on the employee's performance and profitability of the company) through the principal trust into a sub-trust. In the case of footballers, their terms of engagement were recorded in a contract of employment and a side letter. The side letter provided ordinarily for the constitution of a sub-trust in the name of the footballer, benefiting his family with the footballer as protector.

The Court of Session considered that the fundamental principle was that income derived from an employee's services as an employee was an emolument or earnings. It made no difference that the employee had requested or agreed that the payment was to be redirected to a third party (in this case a trust). Importantly, it was irrelevant that the trustees who received the payment exercised a genuine discretion as to what happened to the funds because the funds were ultimately derived as consideration for the employee's services. In relation to the employees, while the bonuses were discretionary, and there was no contractual entitlement to them, they were derived from and based on the work done by the particular employee. An obligation was created by the employer's decision to pay a bonus in recognition of the work performed by the relevant employee. It was not necessary that there should be any prior obligation provided that the payment itself could be shown to be remuneration for the employee's services. The mere making of a payment was sufficient to give rise to an emolument or earnings. On that basis, the sums received by the trustees of the principal trust and in due course by the trustees of the sub-trusts amounted to a mere redirection of income already earned.

While the bonuses to employees other than footballers were discretionary, and there was no contractual entitlement to them, the Court of Session considered it was very obvious that they were derived from and based on the work done by the particular employee.

In the case of the footballers, the same principle applied, perhaps even more so as the obligations in the side letter were part of the employee's employment package and as such were emoluments or earnings derived from their employment.

Despite debate about the significance and whether a new redirection principle has been established it is clear that the Court considered it was simply applying an existing principle to the facts viewed realistically. The case is due to be heard in the Supreme Court and the outcome is eagerly awaited.

Unallowable purpose

A H Field (Holdings) Ltd v Revenue and Customs Comrs

4.78 Despite the introduction in *FA 1996, Sch 9, para 13* (now *CTA 2009, s 441*) of an anti-avoidance 'unallowable purpose' rule relating to loan relationships entered into for the purpose of securing a tax advantage, there was no litigation on the application of the rule until 2012. The First-tier Tribunal case of *AH Field (Holdings) Ltd v Revenue and Customs Comrs* [2012] UKFTT 104 (TC), although fact specific, is helpful in illustrating the process adopted by the Tribunal to the consideration of purpose. The appellant was a UK resident investment company, holding residential property. All the shares of the appellant were ultimately owned by a Jersey resident company. The shares in the parent company were settled in trust primarily for the benefit of the owner's family.

Barclays Bank agreed to make a borrowing facility available for £2 million to the appellant for three days, for a fee of £2,500, in order to pay a dividend.

On 15 December 2003 the appellant borrowed £2 million from Barclays Bank. The appellant paid a dividend of £1,999,500 to Overseas on 17 December 2003.

4.79 *Contentious tax planning enquiries*

This was declared as a dividend and paid by Overseas to Holdings Jersey. On 19 December 2003 the appellant issued a zero coupon bond ('ZCN') to Holdings Jersey for £1,999,500, redeemable on 17 December 2004 for £2,150,000, effective interest rate 7.57%. The loan was for a period of one year minus two days. On 19 December 2003 the appellant repaid the loan from Barclays. On 10 December 2004, the appellant borrowed £2m from Barclays in order to repay the loan from Holdings Jersey. The ZCN was redeemed on the same day for £2,147,106, ie £147,606 more than the issue price. The structure was repeated in subsequent years.

4.79 The argument for the appellant was straightforward, the company was an asset rich but cash poor property company, under pressure to pay out cash in the form of dividends to shareholders. In response to this commercial pressure, the appellant took a decision to fund a dividend payment by way of a shareholder loan.

Evidence was provided to demonstrate that the company was 'prosperous but highly illiquid' and that the ZCN had a commercial purpose in responding to the shareholders' requirements for cash. The Tribunal were directed to a number of company documents evidencing the pressure which the appellant was under to pay out dividends to the shareholders, in particular a KPMG memo which stated that the shareholders and beneficiaries had some specific requirements for cash in 2003–04 including in order to finance property purchases for their offspring.

It was also contended that the business purposes of the ZCN were to introduce debt rather than equity financing for the appellant in order to conserve the appellant's working capital; to provide an assured return on equity ('ROE'); and to achieve this in a tax efficient manner.

4.80 Counsel for the appellant contended that HMRC was inferring, from the fact that a deduction for loan relationship debits had been claimed, that the obtaining of these debits must therefore be a purpose of the transaction, whereas counsel argued that the saving of tax was not the directors' reason for entering into the loan, rather this was a natural *consequence* of entering into the loan.

Counsel for HMRC contended that the main purpose of the loan structure being put in place was the anticipated tax saving for the group derived from the reduction of the group's liability to UK corporation tax.

Counsel for HMRC submitted that the structure set in place was largely self-cancelling, a view with which the Tribunal concurred, finding that all the bank was doing in reality was lending money for three days for a fee. In addition, the ultimate payment to the shareholders under the ZCN was an equivalent amount to the historic dividends which had been paid and therefore the beneficiaries did not receive a greater amount of cash than that which they had received in earlier years.

4.81 The onus is on the taxpayer to demonstrate that the 'unallowable purpose' test does not apply and in considering whether that burden was satisfied the Tribunal took a similar approach to that adopted by the *s 706* tribunal in *Marwood Homes* (see para **4.110**) in determining the purpose of the appellant company. Whilst acknowledging that the directors are the 'directing mind and will' of the company, the Tribunal considered that in carrying out their duties the directors are obliged to take into account the view of their shareholders and the advice given by external advisers. So while only the directors can act on behalf of the company and embody its purposes, 'embedded' within their purposes are the 'purposes' of all the stakeholders in the company. The directors' purpose cannot therefore be entirely divorced from them.

The Tribunal also felt it was legitimate to consider the consequences of the taxpayer's actions in order to determine his purpose. The Tribunal also considered that just because a tax result is a 'natural concomitant' of a transaction it does not necessarily mean that it cannot be a main purpose for entering into that transaction.

4.82 Although the case included some comments that HMRC will no doubt find helpful, ultimately it was decided in HMRC's favour because the taxpayer's facts were weak and the Tribunal was not persuaded by evidence of commercial benefits when weighed against the clear tax benefits of the arrangement.

Counsel for the appellant argued that a commercial purpose would always cancel out any fiscal purpose. The Tribunal disagreed with this assertion and considered the matter depended on the weight given to the commercial purpose. Whilst at first sight this appears a helpful formulation for HMRC, its impact is limited given that it stems from a tax planning arrangement that was unlikely to succeed given the lack of clear evidence as to the commercial benefits. It is not considered to be an authority for concluding that an arrangement which incorporates very significant tax benefits will fail the commercial purpose test; each case needs to be considered on its own merits, whether the 'unallowable purpose' rule applies is a question of fact.

The Tribunal considered that in order to decide whether para 13 applies it is not enough to point to the commercial purpose of the taxpayer; it is necessary to weigh up all the relevant factors which, on the basis of the evidence, the taxpayer took into account in coming to the decision to take a particular course of action, having regard both to the commercial and tax considerations.

4.83 *Contentious tax planning enquiries*

Versteegh Ltd v Revenue and Customs Comrs

4.83 The case of *Versteegh Ltd v Revenue and Customs Comrs* [2013] UKFTT 642 (TC) is of particular interest because of the unusual approach adopted by the parties to determining one particular point at issue. The case concerned a tax avoidance scheme designed to achieve a loan relationship debit in the borrowing company in a group without a corresponding tax charge elsewhere in the group. This involved structuring the loan to provide a return in the form of preference shares issued by the borrower, not to the lender but to another group company (the share recipient).

The parties agreed to put a narrow question to the Tribunal which required no further findings of fact by the Tribunal. The question was put in the following way:

'(1) Whether it necessarily follows that the borrower has a tax avoidance purpose which is a main purpose within the meaning of para 13, Sch 9 FA 1996 where, as in this case,

(a) the only reason for the borrowing's design structure or its terms was to obtain a tax advantage for the lender and/or the share recipient (in that the entirety of any payments made by the borrower would escape tax altogether in the hands of the lender and the share recipient),

(b) the lender, the share recipient and the borrower all knew at the time of entering into the borrowing that the borrowing was designed and structured so that the lender and/or the share recipient would obtain the tax advantage,

and irrespective of the further fact that the borrower had a commercial need for the borrowing, and irrespective also of any additional facts, whatever they may be, including for example that the borrower was not able to obtain the funds from any other source, and the lender was not willing to provide funding on any other terms, and the borrower would not obtain any financial or other benefit from the accrual of the tax advantage to the lender or the share recipient (the borrower having no shareholding or other interest in the lender or the share recipient), and there was a cash flow advantage to the borrower in issuing shares instead of paying interest in cash.

(2) If the answer to (1) is yes, whether the facts in paragraph (1)(a) and (b) entail that the entirety of the borrower's debit is disallowed, irrespective of any additional facts, whatever they may be'.

The judge noted that the way the issue had been put to the Tribunal was a little unusual, because they had not been provided with all the facts, nor heard evidence referable to the unallowable purpose issue. Instead, the Tribunal was asked to determine whether HMRC's argument must succeed on the basis of certain agreed facts only.

Contentious tax planning enquiries **4.85**

4.84 HMRC contended that the three facts, from which the Tribunal must arrive at the inevitable conclusion that para 13 operates to deny the borrower the loan relationship debit, were:

(a) the only reason for the borrowing's design, structure and terms was to obtain a tax advantage for the lender and/or share recipient;

(b) the lender, the share recipient and the borrower all knew at the time of entering into the borrowing that the borrowing was designed and structured so that the lender and/or the share recipient would obtain the tax advantage;

(c) the borrower had a commercial need for the borrowing.

HMRC's argument proceeded on the basis that in being a party to a loan relationship, which the borrower knew would have the inevitable consequence of securing a tax advantage (for the lender and/or for the share recipient), the borrower must have had an intention to secure a tax advantage, and such an intention could not be distinguished from the borrower's subjective purpose. That purpose was an important, and thus a main, purpose.

In support of the argument that the inevitable consequence of the tax advantage would necessarily translate into a purpose of the Borrower to secure that tax advantage, and thus be a tax avoidance purpose, counsel for HMRC referred to the decision of the VAT Duties Tribunal in *Coffee Republic plc v Revenue and Customs Commissioners* (VAT Decision 2150). That was a case concerning whether certain food had been heated for the purpose of enabling it to be consumed at a temperature above ambient air temperature; if so, then its supply when hot would be a standard rated supply for VAT (and not zero-rated). The purpose therefore needed to be ascertained. The appellant argued that its purpose in heating the products was not to enable them to be consumed hot, but to supply them in a crisp or toasted state, to melt cheese and to make the products more visually appealing.

4.85 In reaching its conclusions, the tribunal noted that there was a distinction between an inevitable result of the successful completion of a purpose and something which is necessary for or part of a stated purpose. The tribunal offered the following analogy:

> 'If with intent a person kills a fly by squashing it, it cannot be said that because his avowed purpose was 'to kill the fly', it was not also to squash it. His purposes may stop short at the killing: his purpose of killing the fly by squashing does not mean that he had a purpose of leaving a mess on the window, but it must encompass the intended means of achieving the killing'.

It was on this basis that the tribunal drew a distinction between the intention to provide a product that was crisp and the intention to enable the cheese to

4.86 *Contentious tax planning enquiries*

be consumed in a melted state. In the former case the intention encompassed a purpose of heating the product, but not that of enabling it to be consumed hot, even though that was a consequence.

4.86 The Tribunal considered *Coffee Republic* pointed in the opposite direction to that maintained by HMRC. The case suggested that, if the purpose of a borrower was to achieve tax avoidance by entering into a loan relationship, it could be said that the borrower had a purpose of entering into the loan relationship, because that was the means by which the tax avoidance purpose would be achieved. The tax avoidance purpose in this instance equated to the killing of the fly, and the loan relationship is the squashing if it. However, the tribunal considered that the converse did not hold.

> 'The fact that a tax advantage is an inevitable consequence of the entry into the loan relationship does not mean that it is a purpose of the borrower, even if he knows that will be a consequence; the tax advantage is merely the mess on the window'.

The tribunal considered the approach adopted in *Brebner* was the correct when considering whether something is a main object, or a main purpose, of a transaction or of a party to a transaction.

> 'As Lord Upjohn also said in *Brebner* (at p 718), that is a matter of the intention of the parties. The mere fact that tax informs the choice of transaction does not itself give rise to a necessary inference that the obtaining of a tax advantage was a main object or purpose. Such an inference may, of course, be drawn, but that will depend, as it did in *Brebner*, on the findings of fact made on consideration of all the relevant evidence'.

4.87 The Tribunal considered that the significance of the tax advantage to the taxpayer must be considered as a matter of subjective intention, which necessarily involves a careful analysis of all the reasons the taxpayer had for entering into the transaction.

The tribunal considered that the correct approach to the application of para 13 was to identify, in the first place, a purpose of the taxpayer, and secondly to determine whether that purpose is a main purpose. In the same way that the mere presence of a commercial purpose cannot rule out the existence of tax avoidance as being a main purpose, the mere existence of a tax advantage, known to the taxpayer does not on its own render the obtaining of that advantage a main purpose. The tribunal considered that all the authorities point to the question being one of degree and significance to the taxpayer, and that the question is one of fact for the tribunal, having regard to all the circumstances, which requires a full factual enquiry.

The tribunal did, however, find that it did not necessarily follow, from the fact that the only reason for the design, structure and terms of the borrowing was to obtain such a tax advantage, and that the parties, including the borrower, knew that was the case, meant that the borrower has a tax avoidance purpose which is a main purpose within the meaning of para 13.

In the case of *Fidex v HMRC* [2016] EWCA 385, the Court of Appeal rejected the taxpayers argument that if, in an accounting period the company had one or more allowable main purposes for being party to a loan relationship and one unallowable purpose, it was not just and reasonable to attribute the whole of the debit in question to the unallowable purpose. The Court accepted that Fidex may have continued to be a party to the loan relationship in question irrespective of the unallowable purpose, however that was not the issue. The key question was whether the relevant debit was attributable to the unallowable purpose for which the bonds were held. The court considered that without the bad purpose the debit would not have arisen so this was an easy conclusion for them to reach.

Summary

4.88

- Whether a main purpose is an unallowable purpose is a question of fact.
- It can only be answered by a careful analysis of all the subjective reasons the taxpayer had for entering the transaction.
- The above analysis involves weighing up all the relevant factors, which on the basis of the evidence, the taxpayer took into account in coming to a decision.
- The courts' suggested approach is to first identify a purpose of the taxpayer and secondly determine whether that purpose is a main purpose.
- A commercial motive will not automatically 'trump' a fiscal motive or rule out a tax avoidance main purpose and vice versa.
- If the tax advantage is the 'icing on the cake' as opposed to the cake itself, the tax advantage should not be a main purpose for entering the transaction.
- It is legitimate to have regard to other stakeholders who may influence the directors' subjective intentions.
- It is legitimate to ask whether the transaction would have been undertaken if the tax impact had been neutral (the 'but for' test).

4.89 *Contentious tax planning enquiries*

- Where there can be said to be commercial and tax avoidance purposes it will be a question of fact and degree as to whether the avoidance purpose is also a main purpose.

- *CIR v Brebner* has been confirmed as good law such that where the taxpayer is faced with a choice between two options one which involves paying less tax than the other, this will not necessarily mean that tax avoidance is a main purpose of the arrangement if there is a commercial purpose for the transactions.

International planning

Central management and control

4.89 As mentioned at para **4.4** above, international planning involves moving people, activities, risks and assets to low tax jurisdictions in order to achieve tax savings. Here the analysis is particularly focused on the facts. In this area of planning relatively few cases reach the courts.

Remarkably, there has only been one case in the UK dealing with a substantive transfer pricing dispute, *DSG Retail Ltd v Revenue and Customs Commissioners* [2009] STC (SCD) 397 and even in that case the Tribunal decided the case on a point of principle and referred the matter back to the parties to reach agreement on the specific pricing having regard to that principle.

Much of the case law dealing with international tax planning revolves around the issue of whether a company which is incorporated outside the UK is resident in the UK as a result of its central management and control being located here.

Given the extensive anti-avoidance provisions, case law is concerned with non-close companies or close companies controlled by non-domiciled individuals where the anti-avoidance provisions do not apply.

4.90 Under UK domestic law, a company is UK resident if:

- it is incorporated in the UK (*CTA 2009, s 14*); or

- if its 'central management and control' is exercised in the UK (see below).

As such, a non-UK incorporated company can only be resident in the UK under domestic law if it is centrally managed and controlled from the UK.

Central management and control: general principles

4.91 The principal authority on the 'central management and control' test for UK residence is *De Beers Consolidated Mines Ltd v Howe (Surveyor of Taxes)* [1906] 5 TC 198, in which Lord Loreburn stated:

> '... the principle that a company resides for purposes of income tax where its real business is carried on. ... I regard that as the true rule, and the real business is carried on where the central control and management actually abides'.

This principle has been widely followed and applied by the courts. It has, however, been modified in certain specific circumstances where central management and control cannot be shown to be in one country alone because acts of controlling power and authority are exercised to some substantial degree in another country (*Bullock (Inspector of Taxes) v Unit Construction Co* [1959] 38 TC 712). The courts have not fully developed the process to be adopted in the situation envisaged in *Bullock*.

4.92 Nevertheless, it is an established principle that a company may be resident in more than one territory as a consequence of control and management being exercised in more than one location (see *Swedish Central Rail Co v Thompson* [1925] AC 495). This is an argument HMRC occasionally raises where there is a significant presence in the UK, and was a contention initially pursued in the case of *News Datacom* [2006] STC (SCD) 732, but without much conviction before the Special Commissions.

In that case the presence of the CFO in the UK (amongst other factors) led HMRC to believe that what was regarded by the taxpayer as a peripatetic company was in fact UK resident. On a proper examination the Commissioners concluded the company was resident outside the UK and moreover, having reached this conclusion, it was not necessary to answer where it was in fact resident (as counsel for HMRC had requested).

4.93 In Statement of Practice 1/90 ('SP 1/90') HMRC states that '[t]he case law concept of central management and control is, in broad terms, directed at the highest level of control of the business of a company'. HMRC also notes that central management and control should '... be distinguished from the place where the main operations of a business are to be found, though those two places may often coincide.'

In *Untelrab Ltd v McGregor (Inspector of Taxes)* [1996] STC (SCD) 1, the Special Commissioners summarised the key principles in relation to company residence. Whilst *Untelrab* was a decision of the Special Commissioners and is therefore not binding on a higher court, in *Wood v Holden (Inspector of Taxes)*,

4.94 *Contentious tax planning enquiries*

Park J specifically stated that he agreed with counsel for the appellant that the *Untelrab* decision '... sets out correct and helpful statements of principle [regarding the common law of corporate residence] ...'

4.94 In *Wood v Holden (Inspector of Taxes)* [2005] STC 789, on the facts of the case, the Special Commissioners found as fact that '[t]he only acts of management and control ... were the making of the board resolutions and the signing or execution of documents in accordance with those resolutions'. In the High Court, Park J (as endorsed by the Court of Appeal) emphasised that, if these were the only acts of central management and control, whilst there may not have been much involved in them

> '... the test of a company's residence is still the central control and management test; it is not the law that the test is superseded by some different test if the business of a company is such that not a great deal is required for central control and management of its business to be carried out'.

However, Park J also stressed the importance of directors exercising their discretion and considering matters independently before approving or taking a decision:

> 'If directors of an overseas company sign documents mindlessly, without even thinking what the documents are, I accept that it would be difficult to say that the national jurisdiction in which the directors do that is the jurisdiction of residence of the company. But if they apply their minds to whether or not to sign the documents, the authorities ... indicate that it is a very different matter'.

In the Court of Appeal [2006] STC 443, Chadwick LJ stated the following at [27]:

> '... In seeking to determine where "central management and control" of a company incorporated outside the United Kingdom lies, it is essential to recognise the distinction between cases where management and control of the company is exercised through its own constitutional organs (the board of directors or the general meeting) and cases where the functions of those constitutional organs are "usurped"—in the sense that management and control is exercised independently of, or without regard to, those constitutional organs. And, in cases which fall within the former class, it is essential to recognise the distinction (in concept, at least) between the role of an "outsider" in proposing, advising and influencing the decisions which the constitutional organs take in fulfilling their functions and the role of an outsider who dictates the decisions which are to be taken. In that context an "outsider" is a person who is not, himself, a participant in the formal process (a board meeting or a general meeting) through which the relevant constitutional organ fulfils its function'.

Contentious tax planning enquiries **4.96**

4.95 In the case of *Laerstate BV v Revenue and Customs Comrs* [2009] UKFTT 209 (TC), the First-tier Tribunal applied these principles to find that the activities of the sole director based outside the UK were limited to signing documents when told to do so and that the business was managed in the UK by its controlling shareholder. In arriving at this conclusion the Tribunal analysed what would be required of a director for him to be regarded as managing and controlling the company following the principles set out above.

The Tribunal noted the distinction between the mere physical acts of signing resolutions or documents which do not suffice for actual management and the situation where the directors apply their minds to whether they sign, quoting Park J in *Wood v Holden (Inspector of Taxes)*.

The Tribunal recognised that there is nothing to prevent a majority shareholder, whether a parent company or an individual majority shareholder, indicating how the directors of the company should act. Providing the directors consider the wishes and act on them it is still their decision.

The Tribunal distinguished this situation from where there is no decision by the directors because nobody could have made a decision based on less than the absolute minimum of information necessary to make such a decision (constituting central management and control). Where there is at least such an absolute minimum of information there is a decision by the directors, although an ill-informed one.

Summary

4.96

- The residence of a company is where the directors meet and transact their business and exercise the powers conferred upon them.

- If the directors meet in two places then the company's residence is where its real business is carried on; and the business is carried on where the central management and control actually abides. This is a pure question of fact to be determined by a scrutiny of the course of business.

- The actual place of management, and not the place where the company ought to be managed, fixes the place of residence of a company.

- It is an exceptional case for a parent company to usurp control from its subsidiaries.

- A parent company usually operates through the Boards of its subsidiaries.

4.97 *Contentious tax planning enquiries*

> - Although a Board of Directors might do what it was told to do, it does not follow that the control and management lies with another, so long as the Board exercise their discretion when coming to decisions and would refuse to carry out an improper or unwise transaction.
>
> - When deciding the issue of residence, one should stand back from the detail and make up one's mind from the picture which the whole of the evidence presents.
>
> - If directors of an overseas company sign documents mindlessly, without even thinking what the documents are, that will not establish residence in the location where signed.
>
> It is, therefore, essential that evidence is retained showing the proper consideration by the directors and that adequate information was available to them to reach an informed decision.

The avoidance versus evasion distinction

4.97 It goes without saying that it is critical to keep on the 'right side of the line' between tax avoidance and evasion, the former being legal and the latter illegal. However, in recent years there have been attempts by HMRC and lobby groups to blur the distinction between tax evasion and fraud. There is, however, a very clear distinction.

A tax fraud will normally involve some pretence or deception; some form of dishonesty is necessary for tax avoidance to cross the line and constitute the criminal evasion. Offences range from the common law offence of 'cheat' (of the public revenue), to fraudulent evasion of tax (*Finance Act 2000, Fraud Act 2006, Forgery Act, Perjury Act* offences and so on). On the back of these offences, money laundering offences will commonly follow.

The effectiveness of avoidance schemes depends on the steps taken in them being real as distinct from a pretence or a sham. A sham is pretence, something which pretends to be something it is not. A forged document is a sham. Actions deliberately purported to be conducted by one person, but in fact conducted by someone else, possibly in a different location, are sham transactions. There will be occasions where genuine mistakes are made in documents or misunderstandings over the precise demarcation of responsibilities or difficult interpretations, but deliberate attempts to mislead or conceal the true facts are dishonest actions with the perpetrators being liable to criminal proceedings. The possibility that a transaction could have happened as envisaged in the planning, but in fact did not, would not diminish the seriousness of the offence.

Contentious tax planning enquiries **4.99**

4.98 The case of *R v Charlton* [1996] STC 1418 demonstrates the potential difficulties involved. The crux of the fraud involved interposing a Jersey company between the overseas supplier of tyres and a UK-based purchaser. Originally tyres were purchased directly from the original supplier, but following the incorporation of the Jersey company, they were subsequently bought from that source at an inflated price. It was contended on behalf of the defendant that the Jersey company was properly incorporated and contracted with the overseas supplier for the purchase of the tyres, the scheme although unsuccessful (technically speaking) was not fraudulent. The accounts properly reflected the transactions which had occurred. The Revenue successfully contended that the arrangement comprised a dishonest avoidance scheme.

The case was important as it lifted the corporate veil. The defence sought to argue that because the Jersey company was properly incorporated, transactions with that company did not cease to be real or bona fide simply because they were uncommercial. However, what seemed decisive in securing the defendants' conviction was the combination of the lack of commerciality of the transactions combined with the intention to keep the arrangements hidden from the attention of the tax authorities, whilst the financial benefits accrued to the directors.

HMRC'S APPROACH TO WORKING COMPLEX TAX ENQUIRIES

Case identification

4.99 HMRC will typically identify the types of transactions referred to at para **4.2** through a review of the tax return and in the case of larger companies via the annual risk assessment.

The key ways by which HMRC identifies tax avoidance cases are as follows:

- disclosure: schemes or arrangements which have been disclosed under the disclosure rules;
- profiling: the process of identifying avoidance in cases not disclosed from characteristics identified in particular schemes;
- reviewing information from various databases, exchange of information with overseas countries, media articles and even informers.

Avoidance identified through the last of the above points will typically be 'international' or 'substance' based planning and will often be worked by SI, often initially with the local office fronting for them by asking some initial

4.100 *Contentious tax planning enquiries*

questions, in order to build up a case for registering within SI under COP8 (cases other than suspected serious fraud).

4.100 The disclosure regime and improved risk assessment mean it should now be the exception that a tax avoidance arrangement escapes the attention of HMRC.

On the corporate side HMRC is using software to analyse results and identify indicators of avoidance arrangements (for example through the impact on various ratios).

On the personal tax side it is possible for HMRC analysts to conduct searches of specific boxes on tax returns or white space entries to ensure that they have captured all examples of particular avoidance arrangements and exercise central oversight to ensure they are dealt with appropriately. This reduces the discretion of network offices to ignore cases due to resource pressures or to enter into a settlement which Head Office considers is inappropriate.

Even where an avoidance arrangement has not been identified and challenged in the relevant enquiry period, it is not uncommon for HMRC to identify the arrangement in a subsequent year (possibly as a result of a change to, or unwinding of the planning). In these circumstances HMRC will usually seek to raise a discovery assessment or use its information powers to establish the facts to put it in a position to make a discovery assessment (see para **4.184**). In the absence of an enquiry or very full disclosure it is, therefore, very difficult for taxpayers to achieve certainty until the statutory time limit has expired (which, absent careless or deliberate behaviour, is four years).

Case profiling

4.101 Profiling is a structured process undertaken by a dedicated profiling unit. The team's work involves taking an undisclosed scheme, establishing key footprints considered to be linked to the avoidance arrangement and devising a program to identify other cases from those characteristics (eg British Virgin Islands companies, partnership structures, guarantee companies, etc).

Once identified, these cases can then be subjected to more detailed scrutiny.

HMRC approach to fact finding: general

4.102 The approach to fact finding taken by officers in relation to complex technical enquiries, particularly those into tax avoidance arrangements, is usually more rigorous than that encountered in standard enquiries. However, in the writer's experience, it is still not uncommon for the uninitiated practitioner

Contentious tax planning enquiries **4.104**

to be surprised by the extent of fact finding in what they may perceive to be a technical enquiry.

As a rule of thumb, HMRC regards any technical enquiry as 80% fact finding and 20% technical analysis, which is typically borne out in practice.

So what are the facts and how does HMRC seek to establish them? Facts are established when they are proven; the means of proof is evidence. Evidence is essentially anything which tends to persuade someone that a particular factual position exists. The most common forms of evidence are oral and documentary.

The focus of any HMRC enquiry into tax planning transactions has typically been to initially obtain all the evidence that might conceivably have some relevance in relation to the enquiry before entering into any form of technical debate on the basis that this would be premature without the facts. Striking a balance between unfocussed and seemingly endless requests for information on the one hand, and ensuring both parties have sufficient understanding of the relevant facts on the other, is key to the successful management of complex disputes.

4.103 In recent years HMRC has been prone to using wide ranging requests for information as a substitute for a sensible discussion about the respective technical differences. Although widely drawn requests for information are likely to continue in certain types of avoidance arrangements, the fact that HMRC is embracing collaborative working as a matter of strategic policy should help taxpayers and their advisers reach a decision point in a more cost effective manner where tax avoidance is not in issue.

The difficulty can be in persuading HMRC that because there is a tax advantage, tax avoidance is not the purpose. The key is to be able to show why commercially the transaction makes sense and, that the tax advantage is a consequence or outcome of structuring the transaction in a particular way, not the purpose of the transaction itself.

4.104 Guidance accompanying the revised Litigation and Settlement Strategy (LSS) (see para **4.154**) promotes a more targeted approach to information gathering than the previous widely drawn requests. The guidance advocates an approach that seeks to balance three factors:

(i) the need for HMRC to have a good understanding of the facts before it reaches firm conclusions on what it believes to be the right tax;

(ii) the need for requests for information to be well targeted, confined to the relevant facts, and framed with a view to making the fact-finding process as cost effective as possible for both HMRC and the customer; and

4.105 *Contentious tax planning enquiries*

(iii) the need to ensure that tax avoidance is not accepted as successful unless HMRC is satisfied that the relevant tax planning has indeed been implemented as described.

Whilst this encouraging, it should be remembered that the guidance is drafted to cover all disputes and also acknowledges that widely drawn requests will be appropriate in certain circumstances. These circumstances are likely to include tax avoidance arrangements, particularly in light of the comments of the First-tier Tribunal in *Versteegh* regarding the importance of the facts in determining purpose.

The evidence sought is invariably in two forms, documents and particulars (ie information).

Approach to fact finding: domestic planning

4.105 In relation to domestic planning, a standard information request in relation to a transaction will typically cover the following:

- all legal documents and board minutes;
- all communications including emails, notes of meeting, etc between the company and any other person concerning or referring directly or indirectly to the transaction (including with all advisers);
- opinions tax/accounting including 'details of substance of meetings, etc, where no notes taken';
- all instructions to banks, engagement letters;
- all calculations, all bank statements, all bookkeeping entries;
- chronology of events and explanation of commercial rationale;
- reasons for the amendments of documents;
- requests to see privileged information (albeit on a voluntary basis).

The aim of such a request is twofold: first, to try to establish the purpose behind the transaction, and possibly from HMRC's perspective, to find a 'smoking gun' email which undermines the commerciality of the transaction; second, to ascertain whether the transaction steps have been implemented as intended to give effect to the planned outcome and technical analysis.

4.106 The more recent letters from HMRC put as much emphasis on explanations (under the heading 'information') as they do on documents, particularly around the consideration of commercial versus tax-related factors in undertaking a particular transaction.

Examples of requests include:

- an explanation setting out why the arrangements connected to the disclosed scheme were undertaken;
- an explanation setting out why the arrangements connected to the disclosed scheme can be considered commercial and would have been entered into by third parties;
- what commercial benefits arose from borrowing in this way;
- an explanation of the commercial reasons the arrangements were structured in the way they were;
- an explanation of the extent to which tax was a factor in the arrangement.

Even in cases where there is no purpose test, or *Ramsay* challenge (see below) and the outcome is dependent on the interpretation of specific sections within the statute, there may still be factual information relating to the implementation of the transaction which HMRC will consider relevant. This is because it is not uncommon for an avoidance arrangement to work technically but be ineffective as a result of an implementation failure because certain steps have not taken place as envisaged. HMRC will wish to check for any such failures in the course of an enquiry. Indeed, HMRC will often seek documentation from third parties in order to build as complete a picture as possible of the transaction.

The time frame for responding to information requests is also typically becoming much shorter, especially where HMRC considers the transaction to be an avoidance arrangement. In relation to tax avoidance arrangements HMRC has come to expect that all necessary information would have been collated in anticipation of an enquiry and can, therefore, be reluctant to significantly extend deadlines.

4.107 Documents which are subject to Legal Professional Privilege are protected from disclosure to HMRC (*FA 2008, Sch 36, para 23*). However, HMRC is also paying much closer attention to the basis for claims to privilege over certain documents.

HMRC will now typically make a request for the taxpayer to provide a statement of the following in relation to privileged documents:

- date of document;
- details of sender/receiver;
- purpose of the document;
- reason why legal professional privilege (LPP) applies.

4.108 *Contentious tax planning enquiries*

This information is said to be required so that HMRC can consider a challenge and referral to the Tribunal under the Information Notice: Resolution of Disputes as to Privileged Communications Regulations 2009, SI 2009/1916 (under which, from August 2009, the First-tier Tribunal can examine withheld material and direct disclosure if it decides that an item is not protected by LPP and is relevant).

Requests for tax advice

4.108 One of the most difficult and sensitive areas of tax planning investigations is requests by HMRC to see the tax advice provided by the adviser in relation to a particular transaction.

Over recent years HMRC has been particularly persistent in requesting tax advice including the surrounding background information, such as an evaluation of the suitability of the arrangement to the client. This issue has been the subject of much debate in the courts, both in relation to whether the advice is relevant to the liability (or in relation to the current information powers provision (in *FA 2008, Sch 36*), reasonably required to check the taxpayer's 'tax position').

In relation to tax planning, access to tax advice is a sensitive area and is typically a source of contention between HMRC and taxpayers as regards its relevance to the determination of a tax liability. HMRC's view is that tax advice will be potentially relevant to the taxpayer's liability where tax avoidance is involved because it may shed light on the taxpayer's motive for entering into the transaction or the degree to which transactions are inevitable or a series of transactions is a composite. See para **4.160** regarding challenging HMRC's requests to see tax advice.

Legal basis for HMRC requesting tax advice

4.109 So what support is there for HMRC's stance of seeking access to confidential tax advice in avoidance enquiries? HMRC considers that Special Commissioners cases such as *Marwood Homes* [1997] STC [SCD] 37, [1998] STC [SCD] 53 and [1999] STC [SCD] 44 and the Special Commissioner's 2007 ruling in SpC 647 in the *Prudential* litigation (which was confirmed by the High Court), as well as the comments of the First-tier Tribunal in *Versteegh* (see para **4.83**) are supportive of its stance with regard to access to tax advice.

Whilst only Special Commissioners' decisions, it is easy to see why HMRC regards them as authority justifying its approach. It is, after all, the first level Tribunal that is the arbiter of fact and, therefore, arguably well placed to opine on whether HMRC's information requests can be justified from an evidential perspective. *Prudential* progressed all the way to the Supreme Court but in the High Court Charles J observed that the advice sought was not pure legal advice (on the meaning of the law) but whether transactions were pre ordained.

4.110 *Marwood Homes* concerned the issue of whether transactions in securities giving rise to a tax advantage were carried out for bona fide commercial reasons. It was first heard by Special Commissioners comprising the *s 703* tribunal who found in favour of the taxpayer. The former Inland Revenue subsequently gave notice to the Special Commissioners requiring the appeal to be reheard by a tribunal constituted under *s 706*, which found in favour of the Inland Revenue.

Prior to the second hearing an order for discovery of documents was issued. The tribunal noted that, to a large extent, the difference in the conclusion they reached was attributable to the substantial amount of additional written material relevant to the issue they were provided with. This material had not been disclosed to the Inland Revenue and had not been produced as evidence before the Special Commissioners at the *s 703* hearing.

In relation to the order for discovery, the Commissioners commented that:

> 'where [as here] the question of liability depends on the intentions of those responsible for implementing the transactions, the advice they acted on is crucial at every stages [sic] of the proceedings'.

In this respect the Commissioners appear to have been particularly influenced by the comments in communications and notes of meeting between the tax advisers and the taxpayer. These included references by the tax advisers to excluding the words 'some significant taxation savings' in a letter from the taxpayer company to its solicitors and references to 'beefing up' the commercial justification for the transactions in the necessary clearance applications to the Inland Revenue. They also appear to have been swayed to a considerable extent by the prevalence of the tax issues in the communications with the advisers.

The company's advisers maintained that the transaction was carried out for bone fide commercial reasons and the tax advantages were incidental to the commercial drivers.

4.111 Whilst the comments that the Commissioners noted were unhelpful to the taxpayers' cause, in the writer's view, the more significant point was that part of the steps undertaken to reorganise Marwood's two divisions could not (to the Commissioners' satisfaction) be rationally explained unless the requirement to obtain a tax advantage was taken into account.

4.112 *Contentious tax planning enquiries*

This was the ultimate nail in the taxpayer's case. In simple terms, there was nothing to 'beef up' commercially; had there been, the comments should have taken less significance. It is easy to overlook this aspect of the case and come away with the view that any comment in a document referring to a tax advantage is fatal. This is simply not the case; what is important is the context within which the comment and the tax advantage itself arise.

Nevertheless, the case is a useful indication of how the Tribunal (Commissioners) are likely to approach the issue of access to documentation where the purpose for entering into a transaction is potentially relevant to the determination of the tax treatment. The Commissioners considered that, as a general principle, intention should be determined by looking at the transactions as a whole in their proper commercial context; the relevant intention being that which led to the implementation. A company's object in this respect was to be determined from the intentions of those who govern its policy. The Commissioners considered this might involve looking at intentions of the directors, shareholders or, where appropriate, the company's professional advisers.

This position was also adopted in the First-tier Tribunal case of *A H Field* (see para **4.78**), with further endorsement by the First-tier Tribunal in *Versteegh* (see para **4.83**).

4.112 The issue of the relevance of certain emails was also considered by Charles J in the High Court in *R (on the application of Prudential plc) v Special Commissioner of Income Tax* [2009] EWHC 2494 (Admin). Before the Special Commissioners (case SpC647), it was contended on behalf of HMRC that the request was to enable HMRC to understand the relevant transactions, to see why they were entered into and, in its words, to see whether the statutory provisions, construed purposively, applied to the transactions as they actually were, viewed realistically.

On behalf of the taxpayer in relation to the relevance issue the point was made to the Special Commissioner that *R v A Special Comr, ex p Morgan Grenfell & Co Ltd* 74 TC 511 supported the company's claim. In particular, the view of Lord Hoffmann expressed at para 38 whereby he disagreed with the Revenue's argument that it was important for them to have access to legal advice in cases where the liability turns on the purpose for which a transaction was entered into, rather, 'the court must infer purpose from the facts'.

The Crown argued that *Morgan Grenfell* was solely about legal professional privilege and the case did not consider an extension to it. The Special Commissioner concurred with the Crown's view and considered that the taxpayer had misread the passage from *Morgan Grenfell*.

4.113 Before the High Court, counsel for Prudential argued that in seeking disclosure of skilled advice on tax law given by accountants, HMRC was unlawfully departing from its earlier stance and practice. This was essentially the practice contained in 'Tax Bulletin 46' and 'Tax Bulletin 62' albeit that these had subsequently been withdrawn. The judge rejected the argument that there had been a departure, and pointed out that in many cases HMRC accepts that pure legal advice will be irrelevant.

Both the Special Commissioner and High Court judge referred to certain emails which had been included in documents submitted to HMRC. The content of the emails included the following:

> 'As the preference is not to mention the declaration and payment of the dividend by PCAHL the "outline proposal" element of the note is brief and just details the intention to issue the warrants to SNC ... Just as a presentational point, we mention that the reasons for the issue of the warrants is to facilitate the winding up of PCAHL but we do not explain how the issue helps to achieve that ... perhaps a point to gloss over ...
>
> Please do NOT include reference to the dividend in the approvals note as that would give it an inevitability.
>
> As you know Robin has let us have a copy of the proposed steps to effect the payment of the charge by PGL. Myself and David have had discussions to try and "put a little flesh in the bones" and as a result have numerous questions for PwC, eg duration and terms of the warrant, are the Australian directors aware of the proposals, nature of the investment in the partnership—capital or debt—, does the partnership need a general partner, how does PCAHL reconcile the issue of the warrants which will include a provision that no dividends will be paid during the term of the warrant with the fact that it will propose to pay a dividend to PGL on the same day, etc ...'

The Special Commissioner considered the officer was 'entirely reasonable in his opinion that the documents sought contain or may contain information that shows the whole facts which are relevant to the tax liability of the subsidiary'. Similarly, in the High Court, the judge considered that the above extracts indicated that the content of the final transactional documents may not include all the facts. In the context of these particular emails it is perhaps not difficult to see why the Special Commissioner and High Court reached the conclusion they did in this instance.

4.114 In the High Court in *Prudential* Charles J (para 81) stressed that what HMRC sought was not pure legal advice on the meaning and effect of the relevant taxing provisions but information concerning the nature of the transactions and, in particular, what was and what was not pre-ordained.

For that reason, the *Prudential* case should not be regarded as a general precedent that all tax advice is disclosable. It is implicit in the judgement that pure tax advice on the meaning and effect of the statute will not be relevant.

4.115 *Contentious tax planning enquiries*

This view is further reflected in HMRC's own guidance CH22300 which states that:

'... the advice that a person has received from their tax adviser is not usually something that is reasonably required to check the tax position. We can normally come to our own conclusions based on the relevant facts.'

Each situation will need to be considered on its own facts.

Protection for tax advisers' papers

4.115 The issue of an officer's right to access from the taxpayer advice covered by legal professional privilege was covered in the case of *R (on the application of Morgan Grenfell & Co Ltd) v Comrs of Income Tax* [2002] STC 786.

Lord Hoffmann dismissed the Inland Revenue's contention that it was important for them to have access to the taxpayer's legal advice which was subject to legal professional privilege in those cases in which liability may turn upon the purpose with which he entered into a transaction.

He observed that there were many situations in both civil and criminal law in which liability depends upon the state of mind with which something was done. Apart from the exceptional case in which it appeared that the client had obtained the advice in furtherance of a crime, this was not sufficient reason for overriding legal professional privilege. Hoffmann considered 'the court must infer the purpose from the facts'. Consequently, tax advice which is covered by legal professional privilege is protected from disclosure. That is the common law.

FA 2008, Sch 36, para 23 codified that decision by providing a statutory protection for documents held by the client which are covered by legal professional privilege.

Paras 25 and *26* provide a similar but limited protection for accountants' tax advice but only in respect of advice held by the adviser, not advice held by the taxpayer and not where it would explain a tax return entry or accounts submitted to HMRC.

The Prudential was unsuccessful in its argument that common law legal professional privilege applied to tax advice from accountants. The High Court and Court of Appeal in *Prudential* considered themselves bound by the Court of Appeal decision in respect of patent agents in *Wilden Pump Engineering Co v Fusfeld* [1985] FSR 159. Patent lawyers provided legal advice but this did not justify extending the concept of LPP to any professional person who happened to provide legal advice in the course of their business.

4.116 Prudential's appeal was dismissed in the Supreme Court in January 2013 by a 5:2 majority. Lord Neuberger (with whom Lords Hope, Walker, Mance, and Reed agreed) delivered the lead judgment which rejected extending the common law scope of legal advice privilege (LAP) to include legal advice (on tax matters) given by accountants, notwithstanding a considerable degree of sympathy with the logic of such an extension.

Whilst the majority of the Lords considered there was no logical basis for the distinction in the modern world, such a change would have flown in the face of over 130 years of jurisprudence which had provided a very clear understanding of the concept of LAP and its limits. The three reasons for rejecting such an extension were:

- the consequences of allowing the appeal would be hard to assess and would be likely to lead to what is currently a clear and well understood principle becoming unclear and uncertain;

- such an extension raised questions of policy which should be left to Parliament;

- Parliament had enacted legislation relating to legal advice privilege (*TMA 1970, s 20B* and *FA 2008, Sch 36, paras 23–26*) on the basis that legal advice privilege applies only to advice given by lawyers, which implied that it would be inappropriate for the court to extend the law in the way proposed by Prudential.

4.117 As a result of this decision it is now clear that advice given by accountants is not protected by LPP in the hands of the client.

As stated above, there remains protection for tax advice papers in the hands of tax advisers but there is no protection for other third parties, such as banks, where they are merely a counterparty to a transaction. If a third party obtains it own legal advice (to assure itself of its own position) LPP will apply in the normal way.

Advice from accountant in litigation has a form of protection by virtue of *FA 2008, Sch 36, para 19(1)* if it refers to the conduct of a pending appeal. This is because accountants have the right of audience before tribunals to present their clients' appeals. Nevertheless, advice on litigation will not be required to check the tax position and therefore will not, in any event, be relevant.

Generally in addition to the question of whether the advice is protected by privilege, whether advice needs to be disclosed will also depend on whether it is potentially relevant to the taxpayer's liability (see para **4.108**).

4.118 *Contentious tax planning enquiries*

Case sampling

4.118 One development in certain tax-avoidance arrangements is that of case batching (representative sample enquiries). This involves the Anti-Avoidance Group (now Counter Avoidance) contacting advisers (or vice versa) with a view to securing their agreement to a sample-based approach to raising enquiries.

The approach is reserved for highly generic schemes with near identical (or relatively straightforward) fact patterns. In such cases, whilst all taxpayers who have availed themselves of a particular generic arrangement will have an enquiry notice issued, only a sample will be looked at in detail.

The proposal is voluntary and individual taxpayers are free to opt out of the arrangement, the idea being that the sample will be representative of the arrangements as a whole and will save both time and cost for both sides. The advantage for those that agree to the arrangement is the ability to share the adviser's costs amongst all those taking part. Anyone not agreeing to enter the sample arrangement will have their arrangements looked at in detail in the usual way.

Examples of arrangements where such an approach has been adopted include personal tax planning involving relevant discounted securities and gilt strips, certain intellectual property planning and certain arrangements involving share or other asset-based payments to employees.

4.119 The approach can be made more formal through an application to the Tax Tribunal (under the Tribunal Procedure (First tier Tribunal) (Tax Chamber) Rules 2009, SI 2009/273, r 18, as amended) to bind a group of cases to follow a lead case subject to any subsequent appeal to distinguish the related cases.

Whilst this approach has the practical advantage of convenience and a potential reduction in costs, there are dangers in making assumptions as to the uniformity of fact patterns. Decisions of the courts can differ in cases which appear on the face of it to have very similar facts. Tiny nuances can play an important part in why certain decisions are reached. In monitoring cases centrally HMRC is not only looking to apply consistency but also to identify what it regards as a representative case, in order that this may be litigated. Practitioners need to be aware that there is potential for a case with an excellent fact pattern to be undermined by HMRC successfully litigating a case with a weaker fact pattern. Whilst in theory it should be possible to distinguish a case based on the facts, in practice, the taxpayer is facing an uphill struggle to overturn an existing decision even with different facts. It is, therefore, important for practitioners to network in order to be aware of similar arrangements that may be heading for litigation, as the best policy may be for interested parties to seek to drive a more favourable case before the Tribunal judges.

Approach to fact finding: international planning

4.120 Planning involving overseas operations or entities typically falls into two camps: capital gains tax planning involving the holding of assets outside the UK tax net (generally for non-domiciliaries or companies which do not fall foul of the close company anti-avoidance rules); or substance basis planning involving the location of profit generating activities outside the UK in a low tax territory.

However, because of the comprehensive anti-avoidance provisions applicable to smaller companies and UK resident and domiciled individuals, this type of planning is only likely to work for larger companies (or those owned by non-domiciliaries) with certain activities where the connection with the UK from a practical management perspective can be severed.

Here, HMRC's focus is less on the purpose of the transaction and more on who did what, where and when.

Company residence

4.121 In reviewing residence, HMRC's approach (see INTM120120) is to first ascertain where and by whom a company ought to be managed and controlled according to its legal and constitutional framework. In the majority of cases the responsibility for the management of a company is charged to a Board of Directors.

Once this has been established, HMRC's approach is then to establish the following:

- Do those to whom management is legally entrusted in fact exercise central management and control?
- If so, where do they carry out their duties (which is not necessarily where they meet)?
- If those entitled to act do not exercise central management and control, where and by whom is it exercised?

Determining where central management and control is exercised is wholly a question of fact and HMRC acknowledges that 'the place of directors' meetings is significant only insofar as those meetings constitute the medium through which the central management and control is exercised' (SP1/90).

In reviewing residence, HMRC's internal instructions also emphasise the importance of 'build[ing] up a complete picture of just how the business is run, over a period of time'. They also state that meetings with those involved in the

4.122 *Contentious tax planning enquiries*

management and examination of records and correspondence are essential to a thorough examination.

4.122 In relation to capital gains tax planning via an offshore company, the information requested is likely to be along the lines of:

- details of all key decisions taken by the directors of the offshore holding company;
- copies of all resolutions and board meeting minutes;
- copies of all agendas, correspondence, emails, memos, and notes relating to these meetings.

In addition, where an enquiry is being conducted by a specialist office such as SI, there is a distinct possibility that the investigator will seek information from a third party (for example, a vendor, purchaser or tenant in the case of UK situs property).

HMRC may seek to use such information to help establish that a management decision in relation to the property has already been taken in the UK and is merely being rubber stamped overseas.

4.123 In relation to planning involving the movement of trading activities outside the UK the information requests can be particularly voluminous and in the more significant cases can run to tens of pages. Whilst the specific details of such requests are too fact specific and voluminous to include here, HMRC typically wants to know who did what, where, how, with what qualifications and how much they were paid for doing it.

The purpose of such requests is to establish whether the company is managed and controlled in the UK and/or in the case of a trade whether there is a tax presence in the UK in the form of a permanent establishment of a non-resident company. If it cannot be established that there is a permanent establishment, HMRC may still seek to argue that a trade is being conducted in the UK which may, nevertheless, be subject to income tax. Alternatively, activities are being conducted in the UK for which a transfer pricing adjustment should be made.

4.124 Examples of the categories of information requested are set out below:

- a detailed functional analysis of the entire business (distinguishing the business function and staff in each location) and identifying the key decision-making/value-adding functions;
- details of all recharges with regard to any functions provided by the UK and recharged;

Contentious tax planning enquiries **4.126**

- the pay structure, detailing the criteria used to determine any performance pay;
- a business structure chart identifying the reporting lines;
- details of all employees earning over a certain amount and where based;
- copies of employment contracts;
- copies of intercompany contracts, management/service level agreements;
- financial data showing re-charges posted;
- expenses claims;
- work diaries/calendars/appointment diaries (paper or electronic);
- hotel and travel invoices for all directors;
- details of any agreements under which expenses incurred by one company are recharged to another;
- all emails between certain individuals.

4.125 In relation to dual contract arrangements, the focus is similarly on who did what and where with requests to see:

- travel arrangements;
- travel and accommodation receipts;
- diaries/electronic calendars;
- emails;
- itemised telephone bills/logs.

Approach to determining residence for individuals

4.126 Two recent personal tax residence decisions by the Tribunal show the importance of evidence in determining disputed residence. Detailed factual enquiries underlaid each case in order to determine whether the individuals in question had sufficiently loosened their ties with the UK and made a distinct break to become non-resident.

In *Glyn v HM Revenue & Customs* [2013] UKFTT 645 (TC), it was found that the individual had sufficiently loosened his ties with the UK. In this case Mr Glynn left the UK on 5 April 2005 to live in Monaco, claiming that he became non-resident from that date. The court considered a number of different factors and found that overall it could be shown that Mr Glynn's lifestyle was sufficiently different once he moved to Monaco to demonstrate a clean break from the UK. Although he made a number of visits back to the

4.127 *Contentious tax planning enquiries*

UK and he retained property in the UK, this was not enough to demonstrate that he was maintaining a similar lifestyle. His business ties were effectively severed as he retired, withdrawing from the day-to-day running of the company he owned with his brother and having no significant role in the company.

The Tribunal found that his social life also altered sufficiently with a significant reduction on the number of social events he attended. His family ties also loosened sufficiently; prior to his departure he had been the main carer for his mother. HMRC placed a lot of importance on the traditional Jewish Friday night dinners which had been a regular occurrence prior to Mr Glynn's departure to Monaco, arguing that Mr Glynn specifically returned to the UK for these dinners on 15 occasions. The Tribunal found that as the dinner was an ingrained feature of Jewish family life there would be no requirement to abandon that on the basis that he had become non-resident, especially when the dinner might only have involved the family being together for two or three hours.

Overall the Tribunal found that the continuance of some family ties was of less significance when considered along with the almost complete severance of the business ties, a significant loosening of the social ties and the fact that Mr Glynn had left for Monaco with the intention of starting a new way of life. Whilst he made regular trips to the UK these were largely short stopovers and did not constitute making the UK property his habitual home.

The Tribunal also found that the fact that he retained a UK property with a housekeeper permanently living in the property was not an influencing factor. Mr Glynn had stated that his move outside of the UK was for an indefinite period but not a permanent one; it was a stated intention that he wanted to return to the UK in the future, it made economic sense for him to retain the property that he already had. Overall the Tribunal found that the case presented to them clearly showed that he had made a distinct break from the UK.

4.127 In contrast, in *Rumbelow v CRC* [2013] UK FTT 637 (TC) a husband and wife failed to provide enough documentary evidence to convince the court of their non-residence. In this case the couple decided to leave the UK for tax reasons in April 2001. Their intention was originally to move to Portugal but on advice from their accountants it was decided that, due to a potential tax liability in Portugal, it would be more tax efficient to live in Belgium. The couple saw Belgium as very much a stop gap whilst they were preparing to move to Portugal and never considered that they were settled there.

The couple could not produce sufficient documentary evidence regarding the days spent in the UK or the purpose of their visits to the UK. They had taken advice on how to become non-resident but could not provide any record of this advice. This, the Tribunal found, showed that they took the process of becoming non-resident casually.

The majority of time spent outside of the UK in the 2001/02 tax year was spent on holiday in a number of different locations. They did not enjoy spending time in Belgium and the time they spent there was only as a way of avoiding being in the UK. Whilst their time spent in the UK was often dictated by necessity in winding down their business interest it also served the dual purpose of allowing them to continue their family and social ties. The Tribunal found that despite the couple's stated intention of leaving the UK, Belgium did not become their settled and habitual abode and the nature of their stay in Belgium did not constitute a substantial loosening of social and family ties which remained in the UK.

4.128 With the introduction of the statutory residence test from 6 April 2013, an individual's residence should become easier to determine, with set tests which will automatically determine whether an individual is UK resident or not.

As with company residence, the two cases outlined above demonstrate the importance of the facts and the need to be able to demonstrate these through record keeping and having absolute clarity over what needs to be achieved for a successful outcome. Mr Glynn could clearly evidence when he had been in the UK, the dates and times of the flights, what he did whilst he was in the UK, and his reasons for visiting the UK. Mr Glynn was able to demonstrate a clear break in his lifestyle from the UK to Monaco. The Rumbelows in contrast could not provide the same clarity to demonstrate that they had made a clean break from the UK.

RECOMMENDED RESPONSES TO HMRC'S APPROACH: OVERVIEW

Introduction: impact of operational and legislative changes

4.129 The operational and legislative changes HMRC has made in recent years have tended to improve the standard and overall consistency of its working of complex enquiries, particularly tax avoidance investigations. The use of specialists and central oversight to maintain consistency of decision making, together with earlier and more frequent referral to leading counsel has also had a significant impact on the standard of case working.

The disclosure rules and improved risk assessment methods mean that HMRC is more likely to identify tax avoidance arrangements. Advisers should therefore proceed on the basis that the planning will be identified and challenged. If the

4.130 *Contentious tax planning enquiries*

scheme has been disclosed this is almost certain. Once identified HMRC will almost certainly mount an in-depth investigation, and the outcome could well result in litigation.

4.130 The GAAR will enable HMRC to tackle what it perceives are the most abusive schemes without needing to rely on existing case law principles, though these will still be used as alternatives.

The accelerated tax payment rules in the *Finance Act 2014, Pt 4, Ch 2* remove the potential cashflow advantage from any planning involving a notifiable (DOTAS) arrangement.

HMRC has put in place rigorous governance processes around the settlement of disputes in the face of intense media and political scrutiny and in light of allegations by pressure groups of 'sweet heart' deals having taken place with large companies. Advisers need to be aware of these arrangements in order to understand the decision-making process and to ensure that premature conclusions are not drawn. It is now more common for a caseworker's recommendation to be challenged by one of the review committees in place.

Full details of the different elements of the governance model as they apply to specific circumstances can be found in HMRC's document 'Code of governance for resolving tax disputes' which can be found at www.hmrc.gov.uk/adr/resolve-dispute.pdf.

Recommended responses: overview

4.131 Advisers also need to respond by ensuring that they do not underestimate the technical and fact finding rigour that will be deployed in challenging tax planning arrangements. In addition, the extent to which a purposive approach to statutory interpretation will be adopted by the courts adds an additional level of uncertainty.

The following responses are recommended:

- prepare for the worst by 'road testing' planning ideas and responses to questions/challenges;
- adopt a realistic view of the facts and ensure that they can be properly evidenced;
- be rigorous in execution;
- adopt a structured approach to framing contentions (and be clear as to the extent to which a purposive construction is likely to apply to the transaction in question);
- proactively manage the direction of the enquiry.

The first three recommendations are covered below; the fourth and fifth are dealt with at paras **4.143** and **4.152** ff.

Prepare for the worst

4.132 At the risk of stating the obvious, preparation is key to achieving a successful outcome. Forewarned is forearmed. Being prepared sounds easy but it is not uncommon for taxpayers and their advisers to be taken by surprise at some stage during an enquiry. The best preparation involves rigorous self challenge at every stage of the planning cycle, from inception and implementation of the idea to defending a HMRC challenge.

Counsel, when blessing an idea, will usually give an indication of the potential risks and possible challenges. However, this tends to focus on the theoretical as opposed to the likely practical questions or challenges from HMRC.

It is important to know exactly what to expect from the enquiry in terms of information requests, the types of technical challenge and how they can be answered. Advisers should ask themselves upfront what they would say if HMRC asks for certain information, asks a difficult question, or raises a sometimes obvious challenge.

This enables any potential weaknesses in the planning to be addressed before it is potentially too late or identifies transactions which should not be undertaken because the risk of a successful challenge is too high.

It is also essential to bear in mind and plan for the possibility that the planning undertaken may proceed to litigation no matter how well the particular points are articulated and argued with HMRC. The cost of the litigation process (including any potential reputational implications) should always be factored in to the cost/benefit and risk/reward analysis of whether to undertake the planning in question.

Adopt a realistic view of the facts and ensure they can be properly evidenced

4.133 The courts will take a realistic view of the facts which involves taking an unblinkered and robust approach to the examination of evidence (both oral and documentary). HMRC, the Tribunal and the courts cannot be 'hoodwinked' into accepting a version of events that is not able to withstand detailed scrutiny (typically involving rigorous cross-examination of witnesses).

It is important not to take false comfort from a failure to adopt the same level of rigour to the examination of a client's facts that will be applied by HMRC or

4.134 *Contentious tax planning enquiries*

the courts. If the documentary evidence or oral testimony does not stand up to detailed scrutiny, this will be readily exposed at a tribunal.

4.134 The following need to be considered in detail at the outset:

- the strength of the fact pattern, particularly the commercial rationale (if this has a significant bearing on the analysis);
- how the facts and legislation need to be presented to demonstrate that the transaction answers the relevant statutory provision;
- what evidence will be adduced to prove the facts to the satisfaction of HMRC or the Tribunal.

4.135 As noted above, in many instances, the presence of a tax avoidance motive will not necessarily be fatal to the taxpayer's case and attempts to deny the obvious will be counter-productive. It is far better to accept the obvious and deal with why the presence of a tax benefit should not have bearing on the analysis.

Where a tax benefit is incidental or secondary to a commercial purpose and this commercial objective is important to demonstrate because of a purpose test having appropriate evidence to demonstrate the commercial purpose is essential.

The same is true of a straightforward dispute into whether expenditure qualifies as a trading or management expense, where being able to persuade HMRC or the court as to the purpose of the expenditure is critical. In this respect the director's evidence and credibility is likely to be key.

Rigour in execution and documentation processes

4.136 If the planning is poorly implemented, the factual position can undermine the technical analysis to such an extent that no matter how well presented by the advocate, the argument is ultimately doomed to failure.

Domestic planning

4.137 It is not uncommon for planners to focus on the idea itself and not give its implementation the attention it requires. It is important to plan well ahead and ensure that the implementation step plan leaves no stone unturned. Effective execution requires a comprehensive implementation plan to cover every aspect of the planning from start to finish; nothing should be assumed or taken for granted.

Strong processes and controls are necessary to ensure all required actions are performed timeously, documented appropriately and are readily available in a well-organised and 'audit ready' format in anticipation of HMRC requests.

4.138 Adopting the following recommended actions should help ensure successful implementation:

- the implementation programme should foresee any potential pitfalls (ie what would undermine the technical conclusion reached) and ensure that any weaknesses are addressed;

- ensure all transaction steps are appropriately documented in a step plan;

- the step plan should assign the person responsible for each step with a date for completion and that person must evidence the fact that the required action has been completed. Ownership for implementation of each step in the planning is critical to ensuring success;

- commercial criteria should be clearly documented and supported by facts which can be evidenced to prove the assertions made;

- the step plan should include sign-off for correctly reflecting transactions in the accounting records and financial statements; this should include reference to the person responsible for the tax planning.

4.139 While HMRC may attempt to portray a step plan in an unhelpful light as evidence of pre-ordination, it is important to distinguish between pre-planned and pre-ordination. Advisers should not feel defensive about having taken the sensible approach of setting out the required actions to implement a commercially driven transaction which may have been structured to achieve the best tax outcome.

This is entirely different from a wholly artificial pre-ordained series of transactions undertaken solely or mainly to achieve a tax benefit. HMRC can be prone to tarring the two with the same brush and being able to distinguish is often critical to a successful outcome.

The documentation should be maintained on the basis that it may be adduced as evidence in court. As a rule of thumb taxpayers and their advisers should not write anything they would not be happy being read out in court.

Statements of fact should be carefully researched before being documented; advisers should not rely on verbal confirmation alone. Where necessary, independent documentary evidence should corroborate the facts.

4.140 Care must be taken to ensure that nothing is ever done which could be construed as misrepresentation of any factual information. Deliberate misrepresentation is dishonest conduct which potentially carries a criminal

4.141 *Contentious tax planning enquiries*

sanction. This includes the creation or destruction of documents with the intention to mislead the authorities.

Where the taxpayer's witness evidence is likely to be critical, this should be fully explained to the taxpayer at the outset. The taxpayer, company director, or other key employees should be made aware of the possibility of the need for them to give evidence, which may be subject to rigorous cross-examination in proceedings.

In anticipation of a HMRC challenge, documents should be categorised into those that are relevant, those that are covered by legal professional privilege (if applicable), and those which are not relevant. In maintaining the demarcation between relevant and irrelevant documents it is important to try, as far as is practical, to separate factual information from opinions.

Where documents contain a mixture of fact and opinion it may be impossible to prevent disclosure of the opinion unless the parts of the document containing the opinion are redacted. Redaction is best avoided if possible as it is often viewed very unfavourably by HMRC, even though it is a legally recognised and reasonable way of dealing with different types of material within the same document.

International planning

4.141 In the case of international (or substance-based) planning which relies upon specific actions or activities having been undertaken by specific individuals in particular locations, it is not uncommon for those activities to be carried out as envisaged at the outset of the planning, but for lapses to occur as time progresses.

It is essential that the operations of the business are fully appreciated and the key operations and related decisions that could impact the relevant tax analysis (such as the place of central management and control or whether a permanent establishment has been created) are fully understood. Once these activities have been established and mapped out, controls need to be established with clear action owners post implementation to ensure activities are properly monitored on an ongoing basis. This should ensure activities and decisions are implemented as planned and no lapses occur.

It is also important for advisers to be clear as to where the responsibility lies for maintaining this type of business structuring, as sometimes there may be an assumption on the client's part that the adviser is somehow responsible.

4.142 The case of *Laerstate BV v Revenue and Customs Comrs* [2009] UKFTT 209 (TC) demonstrates what can happen when the individuals take shortcuts and do not follow the necessary courses of actions which are essential for the success of the planning. The opportunity to achieve a tax-free gain was wasted as a result of poor implementation which could have been avoided by taking greater care.

It also demonstrates that merely relying on what at first sight appears to be a convincing set of resolutions and minutes will not suffice where there is conflicting evidence which casts doubt on their reliability as to what was done, by whom and where.

In addition, the case demonstrates the importance of being able to establish the important facts through a compelling trail of documentary evidence.

MANAGING THE ENQUIRY

Introduction

4.143 As noted above, HMRC has said that an enquiry typically comprises 80% fact finding and 20% technical argument. If execution of the planning is carried out as described above, responding to standard HMRC information requests should be straightforward, as the information will already have been categorised at the time, or shortly after the transaction and will be readily available.

Taxpayers and their advisers can fall into the trap of viewing the enquiry as a one-sided affair with HMRC in the driving seat. However, a lack of pro-activity and a failure to focus on the key points will unnecessarily prolong the enquiry by missing opportunities to close down an irrelevant line of enquiry.

Managing a complex enquiry is not about slavishly responding to HMRC's information requests and challenges to HMRC's timetable. It is about presenting the most persuasive narrative possible, backed by the best evidence in the most cost-effective manner.

The importance of maintaining a compelling narrative throughout the enquiry

4.144 Taxpayers should not focus only on what HMRC requests. HMRC is typically focused on establishing facts that support its contentions and will often have a pre-conceived notion of the facts in an avoidance case. Answering a set of unstructured questions does not usually present information effectively or persuasively. Slavishly following HMRC's requests can, therefore, often lead to a failure to identify helpful facts for the taxpayer.

4.145 *Contentious tax planning enquiries*

The adviser should consider what would be helpful to provide, irrespective of whether or how HMRC has requested it. The question advisers should ask themselves is not just whether they have answered all HMRC's questions, but whether they have put to HMRC all the relevant facts in a manner that is as persuasive as possible. This may involve departing from HMRC's question numbering in order to present information that flows consistently with the narrative and technical analysis which supports the desired conclusion. This may even involve changing the way the question is framed where it is designed in a leading way to elicit a response in a less than helpful light.

It can, therefore, be helpful to provide a narrative setting out the facts (including, if relevant, positioning the tax advantage in the context of a wider commercial transaction). This approach can be done in writing or via a presentation in a meeting. A failure to take the initiative over how the facts and technical analysis are presented can lead to HMRC forming an early unhelpful view of the transaction based on selective analysis of the facts, stemming from a less than objective perspective. Such a view can be more difficult to overcome once HMRC's view has become entrenched.

Framing contentions

4.145 The starting point of the tribunals and courts will be to adopt a purposive approach to construing the relevant provision. However, the extent to which a particular provision lends itself to a purposive construction will vary depending on the specific provision in question. The courts will also, in undertaking their analysis, view the facts realistically.

The following analytical approach is therefore recommended:

- establish the purpose of the statutory provision (including whether the provision readily lends itself to a commercial, purposive construction);
- determine the meaning of the statutory provision;
- determine the nature of the transaction to which it is intended to apply in a manner which reflects the provision's purpose;
- establish the true legal effect of the transaction(s) carried out taking account of how the facts will look to the courts 'viewed realistically' (including the impact of a composite series of transactions);
- determine whether the transaction 'viewed realistically' answers to the statutory provision (as construed purposively).

4.146 The dividing line between success and failure can be very small and difficult to determine, as the highlighted case law demonstrates. Recent cases have shown that whether steps were entered into for tax avoidance purpose

Contentious tax planning enquiries **4.147**

(absent a specific purposes test) is not necessarily a decisive consideration in how a particular provision should be construed.

In the *Mayes* case, the skilful articulation of the above elements by counsel for the taxpayer in the Court of Appeal of how the chargeable events provisions applied appeared decisive in persuading the judge that they operated mechanically according to a series of statutory formulae. This operation was capable of generating apparently legitimate avoidance possibilities or hardship. These possibilities illustrated the formulaic and prescriptive nature of the legislation, ie show how the regime worked. Once the provisions had been explained to work in this way, it is easy to see how both the High Court and Court of Appeal reached the conclusion they did.

This careful articulation goes for responses during the course of an enquiry. It is a mistake to rush a reply simply in order to meet an arbitrary deadline. It can be difficult to recover from an ill-conceived response (especially at a key juncture) and such responses can be very costly in terms of time, money or the ultimate outcome.

Evidencing facts/purpose

4.147 HMRC typically focuses on tax advice in order to seek to demonstrate that an arrangement is wholly tax motivated. This over-emphasis on tax advice can, however, lead to a less than objective assessment of the commercial drivers behind a transaction and to HMRC confusing the form of a transaction with its purpose.

A transaction can have a commercial driver but be structured in a tax-efficient way. Thus, whilst the form of the transaction may be tax motivated, it does not necessarily follow that the underlying purpose is tax driven. Advisers should not be overly defensive in relation to the tax benefits of a particular arrangement. Any planning which saves significant amounts of tax will contain references to this benefit; it would be surprising if it were otherwise. What is important is that these tax benefits are not allowed to be taken out of context, especially in a way that appears to undermine a genuine commercial purpose for the transaction as a whole.

In considering the influence of advisers, HMRC's attitude appears to be that a person intends the natural consequences of his actions; so where a taxpayer incurs significant tax advisers' fees and a tax advantage is secured as a result of the advice, then from HMRC's perspective, it seems to follow that the main purpose is tax avoidance. Whilst this is clearly a gross over-simplification, it should also be borne in mind that there will generally be an onus on the taxpayer to displace this prima facie assumption, and particularly so where the legislation contains a commercial purpose test.

4.148 *Contentious tax planning enquiries*

In *Vincent Alan Snell v Revenue and Customs Comrs* SpC 532 the Tribunal held that if the adviser's purpose is to avoid tax and the client understands that then the arrangement will have that (tax avoidance) purpose. This view similarly influenced the First-tier Tribunal in *A H Field* (see the reference to tax advice at paras **4.78** and **4.111**). Tax advisers need to have this at the forefront of their mind when implementing tax-planning arrangements. It is therefore critical for advisers to understand and gain comfort as to the commercial purpose in order to provide the advice in the relevant business context.

The approach of the courts to evidence

4.148 Recent tax cases have amply demonstrated that the courts take an 'unblinkered' approach when it comes to interpreting the facts. In some instances, this 'unblinkered' approach has gone as far as the fact-finding Tribunal undertaking a degree of speculation to draw a secondary inference to determine the facts.

For example, *Burns and Neil v Revenue & Customs Comrs* [2009] SPC 728 involved a Special Commissioner's decision on the bona fide defences under *ICTA 1988, s 741* against a liability under *s 739*. Two daughters of a family resident and domiciled in Jersey transferred their interest in settled property (investment property in the UK) to two Jersey companies, one owned by each. The transfers satisfied the conditions for a liability on the transferors and the only issue was whether the bona fide commercial transaction defences applied. Witness evidence from the girls' mother was that she and her husband did not want their daughters to have the responsibility of managing the investments at the age of 18. This, together with the aim of protecting the girls from the aspirations and bad influence of unwelcome boyfriends, was given to be the reason for the transfer of the properties into companies of which the girls' parents would be directors. However, this was undermined by evidence from cross-examination which showed that the girls' parents were not involved in managing the companies; this had always been done by the girls' grandfather who had established the family's wealth.

Consequently, the Special Commissioner did not accept that separation of ownership was the reason for the transfer. Nor did the Commissioner accept the 'gold digger' explanation as this protection could have been undone by any boyfriend prevailing on the daughters to sack the directors as a route to the companies' assets.

Even where the oral evidence provided has not been contested or remains unshaken in cross-examination it is not unknown for the Tribunal to form its own view on that evidence. For example in *R (on the application of Prudential plc) v Special Commissioner of Income Tax* [2010] STC 16 the company's witness said that had Prudential 'been ready to implement a swap, in the form in which we in fact entered into it, and there had been an announcement that altered the tax treatment in relation to the premium, I would still have gone ahead with the swap in this form'. Nevertheless, the Special Commissioner commented 'in parenthesis, we wonder, however, if this would really have been the case' again showing a scepticism regarding commercial motives where a significant tax advantage arises.

4.149 It is easy for advisers to become emotional over HMRC being unwilling to accept their client's stated commercial purpose, but what matters is either persuasive evidence or a case that is not dependent on the absence of a tax avoidance purpose. Seeking to build a case solely on the basis of the taxpayer's testimony in the face of significant evidence to the contrary is likely to be doomed to failure.

The Special Commissioners' case *N Ltd v Inspector of Taxes* [1996] STC (SCD) 346 demonstrates the dangers of such reliance. In that case, counsel for the taxpayer submitted that in relation to the evaluation of oral and documentary evidence, the Special Commissioners should conclude that the company was trading as the alternative conclusion was inescapably that the directors had embarked on what amounted to conspiracy to defraud by misrepresenting the extent to which the transaction was fiscally motivated. The Special Commissioners rejected this proposition stating:

'We wholly reject this artificial dichotomy. It is by no means unknown, or indeed uncommon, for taxpayers to focus their attention on the appearance rather than the substance the trappings rather than the underlying reality, in effecting transactions designed to achieve a saving of tax.'

The Tribunal will simply evaluate the evidence and determine which party to the proceedings has the most compelling and persuasive evidence.

Engaging with HMRC

Introduction

4.150 There are typically three key stages of engagement with HMRC:

- at the outset of the enquiry to understand HMRC's basis of challenge, explore what is required to address the issue, a timetable for key milestones, and the proposed approach to interaction (correspondence, presentations, meetings etc);
- exchanges and crystallisation of views; and
- determining how the matter is to be resolved.

4.151 In the past it was not uncommon for enquiries to drift if neither side was particularly focused on reaching a resolution either by agreement or litigation.

4.152 *Contentious tax planning enquiries*

Also a common complaint of taxpayers and their advisers was a general reluctance by HMRC to see the enquiry process as a two-way conversation. In particular, it has not always been a straightforward matter to persuade HMRC to provide its detailed technical argument in advance of proceedings before the tribunal, at least in a form substantially reflecting what would be argued if the matter went to litigation.

It is not uncommon for disputes to have been running for many years where neither party has been able to clearly articulate their position. This is clearly unacceptable for the client, who is unnecessarily incurring significant additional costs.

Constructive engagement: collaborative working

4.152 At the risk of stating the obvious, a clear understanding of each party's position is essential for meaningful progress to be made in the enquiry and for the parties to reach an informed conclusion. In addressing HMRC's contentions, a question can often be as, if not more, disarming than an assertion. Assertion, questioning and challenge are just as much a matter for the taxpayer as it is for HMRC. HMRC is keener to ask questions than to answer them; nevertheless, taxpayers are entitled to a clear articulation of the case against them, both in terms of factual and technical differences.

The previous somewhat one-sided approach described above was the subject of an internal review by HMRC which concluded that HMRC should be more transparent in articulating its position. This is further supported by experience to date from HMRC's alternative dispute resolution (ADR) programme that many disputes reach an impasse because neither side has properly understood the questions to be answered. HMRC's guidance on resolving disputes now recommends:

- discussing, sharing and testing of technical arguments to assess relative strengths and weaknesses in analyses (but see LSS guidance at para 13 about sharing copies of legal advice);
- establishing a decision tree: see below.

Techniques and features of collaborative working

Decision trees

4.153 A decision tree approach can be a helpful technique to help focus both sides on what needs to be addressed to resolve the dispute, or at least agree on what the key differences are and why. The idea of a decision tree is that it provides a logical sequence which successively narrows down differences and in so doing builds collaboration as both sides work together to address the same questions.

As noted above, HMRC's approach often lacks focus. In these circumstances, a decision tree can also be used effectively by one party as a means of taking the initiative by setting out the points that party wishes to focus on. In this sense the taxpayer can seize the initiative, by focusing on what it believes is relevant and approaching the decision tree in a way that leads to the inevitable conclusion the taxpayer is arguing for. HMRC can then either agree or, if not, it will quickly focus the officer's mind on where the differences are and provide the medium through which these differences can be expressed such that despite them, they can be addressed collaboratively.

It may not always be appropriate to share the decision tree with HMRC where it identifies avenues and questions HMRC may not themselves have considered. Nevertheless, working through the process is helpful to flush out the big picture and how HMRC's approach may develop.

Documenting facts and legal arguments agreed and those in dispute

4.154 The writer has often found it helpful in the course of an enquiry to take the proactive approach of setting out the agreed facts, the facts not agreed, HMRC's arguments and the taxpayer's arguments side by side, in order to focus on key differences and to highlight any unsubstantiated assertions by HMRC. This approach is now included in the LSS guidance examples at para 9, and shows how HMRC and the taxpayer can work collaboratively where a dispute is proceeding towards litigation.

This document can also be used to hone specific questions in order to obtain clarification as to HMRC's technical position.

The LSS states, at para 13, that 'HMRC will always seek to ensure that respective arguments are fully shared', though this does not extend to copies of counsel's opinions. Taxpayers and their advisers should not, therefore, be in a position of not understanding the detailed case they have to answer in the event agreement cannot be reached. HMRC should begin the process of sharing and testing the strengths of its arguments as soon as the risk being addressed has been articulated and sufficient information has been provided to enable the key facts to be established.

Challenging a failure to engage

4.155 As noted above, the reasons for differences of view can remain unresolved, and whilst arguments are exchanged their impact has been like

4.156 *Contentious tax planning enquiries*

'ships that pass in the night'. There can be a reluctance on both sides to challenge the reasons for differences but rather continue to assert respective positions.

Straightforward open questions with further direct questioning as required is often the best way to address this; for example:

- 'Do you agree with the facts as set out?' 'If not, why?'
- 'Based on these facts [which are not in dispute] why do you not agree with the conclusion we have reached on the tax analysis?'
- 'Precisely what aspects of the information provided to date leads you to reach that view and why?'
- 'Exactly what is it about the taxpayer's explanation of XYZ that you don't accept?'
- 'What further evidence would persuade you of this fact?'
- 'Given that there is no further evidence available do you agree that we will have to come to a conclusion on the information available?'

Meetings are often the best forum in which to raise these questions and to probe HMRC for a clear articulation of its position.

Use of meetings

4.156 Meetings can often be the most productive means of progressing an enquiry, as they provide the opportunity to explore, clarify and resolve differences on the day. On the other hand a meeting for a meetings sake will usually be unproductive and an unnecessary expense for the taxpayer.

In order to be effective it is important to have a clear objective of what the meeting is designed to achieve, a clear agenda and to have completed any preparatory work required to meet the objectives. Meetings can be useful to help clarify facts, and to explore and debate technical positions in an open and frank manner, whilst avoiding the polarisation of views which can ensue from correspondence. Once HMRC has committed itself in writing to a particular course of action it can be more difficult for the officer to retract from that position. A more informal exploration of views can sometimes prevent entrenched positions developing.

4.157 It is important that taxpayers and their advisers avoid preconceived ideas about whether to hold meetings but decide on the advantages based on the specific facts and circumstances. Reasons for meetings can include:

- at the outset of the enquiry: to determine the risk being addressed, agree what information is needed to address that risk and the key legislation that is in point;

Contentious tax planning enquiries **4.159**

- to provide/clarify facts: HMRC will often wish to meet the directors on the grounds that they wish to ascertain or clarify facts. However, advisers should also be wary of putting their client in a situation that could end up as a form of uncontrolled cross examination with adverse consequences later on;
- to crystallise/'fine tune' arguments with a view to reaching a decision point;
- to negotiate a settlement; this is usually easier face to face than in correspondence as positions can be explored through a fluid discussion. It is also possible to reserve a position or 'walk away' completely if agreement cannot to be reached.

4.158 Taxpayers should always be thoroughly prepared for any meeting with HMRC, particularly if factual information is being provided. This should involve a full exploration of the factual position with the client in advance of meeting HMRC, particularly in areas of dispute, so none of HMRC's questions come as a surprise.

In some instances it may be advisable to provide information from the directors in written form, as opposed to in a meeting, to ensure its accuracy can be checked before submission. It can be difficult to retract statements made in meetings which, being based on memory, are not always accurate or articulated as persuasively as they might be in writing. However, it is important that this it not presented as witness evidence but rather a summary of the key facts. Any evidence that could be used in litigation proceedings always needs great care. It is therefore important to ensure that written information is provided as an explanation or confirmation of key facts, as opposed to formal witness evidence, unless it has been taken with that purpose in mind (and this would typically require counsel's involvement in significant cases).

Summary

4.159 Constructive engagement should prevent HMRC from treating fact gathering as an end in itself, and from refusing to provide any articulation of its technical position; either an interim view in order to better distil the facts that need to be adduced and identify potential early differences of opinion, or a final view prior to a decision point being reached. HMRC's desire for a collaborative approach should involve a dialogue aimed at resolving a potential difference of view, not a one-sided 'fishing trip' or exercise aimed solely at demonstrating a preconceived view.

4.160 *Contentious tax planning enquiries*

> This is recognised in HMRC's commentary accompanying the LSS. However, it is not uncommon to find a disconnect between the guidance and the actions of officers on the ground. It is, therefore, almost inevitable that advisers will sometimes have to refer an officer to the guidance where it is felt the principles are not being adhered to.

Formal challenges to information requests

Introduction

4.160 If the case has been worked on the collaborative lines described above, then the need to mount a formal challenge to a HMRC request for information should be rare. It should also be borne in mind that HMRC's powers are extremely widely drawn and successfully challenging a notice is therefore difficult given the relatively low threshold HMRC has to satisfy to demand information. For this reason it is often more effective to agree through discussion at the outset what is likely to be needed and why.

This approach is also recommended in HMRC's guidance accompanying the LSS which makes it clear that HMRC should be clear about the risk it is addressing (ie the technical concern) and how the information is relevant to address that risk.

4.161 An information request can broadly be challenged on the following grounds:

- that the information is not reasonably required for the purpose of the Officer's enquiry (ie to enable the officer to check the taxpayer's tax position), ie it is not relevant to the tax in question;
- the information is subject to legal professional privilege;
- the information is not within the taxpayer's possession or power.

Information not reasonably required

4.162 The bar for HMRC to be able to successfully demand information is relatively low. In interpreting what is reasonably required, it is important to note that this is considered from the perspective of the HMRC officer and not the taxpayer's or adviser's perspective. HMRC will not always be able to know for certain that the information requested will definitely be relevant to a person's tax liability until it is obtained. The relevant test is whether it would be reasonable for any officer to hold that it might be relevant, not that it must be relevant.

Contentious tax planning enquiries **4.164**

In other words, the tribunal is only likely to reject a request on the grounds of relevance if it can be shown that the information requested could not, on any reasonable assessment, be relevant to the person's tax liability in the particular circumstances.

However, the 'reasonably required' test also involves considerations of proportionality. HMRC recognises that 'reasonably required' means getting the balance right between:

- the burden put on someone to provide the information; and
- how important the information is in deciding on the correct tax position.

4.163 As noted at para **4.108**, requests for tax advice are usually a source of contention. In challenging a request to see tax advice the dividing line is usually in respect of what constitutes pure opinion on the operation of the law, as distinct from what may be regarded as proactive advice that is likely to have influenced the taxpayer's behaviour.

The tribunal will almost certainly regard this latter type of advice as relevant where a purpose or motive test is in point. Even in scenarios where there is no purpose test it is possible that a tribunal would find such advice relevant in order to form a 'realistic view' of the facts. Where the advice relates solely to the analysis of how the law operates (ie pure opinion) it is considered that this should not be relevant to the liability.

In some instances the distinction can be particularly difficult to draw, as can be seen from the *Prudential* 'privilege' judicial review (see para **4.113**), particularly where advice is provided in emails. As noted at para **4.115**, it is permissible to redact (ie blank out) the irrelevant parts of the document. However, although HMRC acknowledges that redaction is possible, in practice it is viewed unfavourably and if possible is best avoided by ensuring at the outset that documents do not contain a mixture of relevant and irrelevant information.

In the writer's experience, a more successful outcome is achieved by negotiating with HMRC to reduce the scope of a request rather than blanket resistance, with a line being clearly drawn as to what is pure tax advice on the law rather than what should be done in a given situation.

Documents subject to legal professional privilege

4.164 As noted at para **4.115**, documents which are subject to legal professional privilege are protected from disclosure. However, this only applies to advice from lawyers, not accountants following the decision of the Supreme Court in the *Prudential* case.

4.165 *Contentious tax planning enquiries*

Documents not within power or possession

4.165 This issue most commonly arises in relation to documents held by overseas entities which it is asserted are not under the control of a UK entity or individual.

Possession, as defined in case law:

- includes documents in the mere custody of the person and '... the right to the possession of a document' (*B v B* [1979] 1 All ER 801). Thus physical control over the document will satisfy the test;

- includes company documents in the physical possession of an officer or employee of a company, if held as servant or agent of the company, or by such an individual in their capacity as an officer or an employee of the company (*B v B*).

4.166 If a document which has been requested does not exist or has been lost, it cannot, of course, be provided. In these circumstances, HMRC should be advised of this fact and the notice should, as a consequence, be set aside by the officer.

If HMRC does not accept the validity of the taxpayer's claim to no longer have possession of the documents in question or the power to get them, ultimately it will be for the tribunal to determine as a fact whether this is so, either on hearing an appeal against the notice or the determination of a penalty.

4.167 Case law gives the following definitions of power:

- an enforceable right to inspect a document or to obtain possession or control of it from another person (*B v B*);

- a presently enforceable legal right to obtain from whoever actually holds the document inspection of it without the need to obtain the consent of anyone else (*Lonrho Ltd v Shell Petroleum Co Ltd* [1980] 1 WLR 627).

4.168 If a document is considered not to be within the power of the recipient of the request to provide, it may be necessary to seek specialist advice to determine the position.

In the case of *Revenue and Customs v Parissis* [2011] UKFTT 218 (TC), the First-tier Tribunal considered the meaning of 'power and possession' in the context of *TMA 1970, s 20* information notices on a number of individuals in relation to certain trust arrangements. The decision has direct application to HMRC's current information powers in *FA 2008, Sch 36*, which adopts the same terminology.

It was argued on behalf of the taxpayer that 'power' had the meaning decided in the leading non-tax case of *Lonrho Ltd v Shell Petroleum Co Ltd* in relation to the words 'possession', 'custody' or 'power'.

4.169 The Tribunal in *Panos Parissis*, taking the lead from the Special Commissioners' case of *Meditor Capital Management Ltd v Feighan (Inspector of Taxes)* [2004] STC (SCD) 273, considered that 'power' splits into two concepts: legal power and power in the practical sense (de facto power).

The Tribunal first considered 'power' in the context of the legal sense (per *Lonrho*) and concluded that whilst power in the legal sense may have a wider meaning than in *Lonrho* (on the facts of this particular case) it did not extend to include taking legal action that was likely to fail.

As to de facto power, the Tribunal held that documents are within a person's power if they can obtain them, by influence or otherwise, and without great expense, from another, even where that person has the legal right to refuse to produce them; in other words, a simple request to the other person for the information.

The Tribunal considered that HMRC had raised a prima facie case that the documents were within the power of the taxpayer and it was for the taxpayer to show that they had asked the trustee for the documents and been refused. Because that taxpayer had not done this, the Tribunal imposed a penalty for non-compliance with the notice. Again in *HA & K Patel Partnership v Revenue and Customs Comrs* [2014] UKFTT 167 (TC) the Tribunal was not impressed with the taxpayers who had set up an offshore structure and not pressed offshore parties for the requested documents.

4.170 Where HMRC is seeking information from the first party who may not possess or indeed have the power over the information in question, it is essential that care is taken in the approach to provision or non-provision depending on the circumstances.

In many cases the taxpayer will be keen to cooperate and try to ensure that third-parties such as overseas directors of companies which may be connected to UK companies or individuals (or similarly trustees) provide whatever is demanded. Indeed the apparent extension of the meaning of power per *Revenue and Customs v Parissis* to include practical power may mean that a tribunal might consider it is necessary to ask the person in possession of the information to provide it before asserting it is not within the first party's power.

However, taxpayers need to ensure that voluntary provision of information does not undermine the independence of the overseas entity's decision making process and thereby potentially its residence status. If information is sought

4.171 *Contentious tax planning enquiries*

from overseas directors or trustees it should be made clear that this is a request (assuming no enforceable right exists over the information) and that they are considering the matter in terms of what is in the best interests of the company/beneficiaries.

4.171 Also, the *Parissis* case should not necessarily be regarded as a green light for HMRC to demand that the taxpayer makes unreasonable requests of other parties that might have information that could be relevant to an HMRC enquiry. In the *Parissis* case it is likely that the Tribunal was influenced by HMRC's assertion that the UK individuals were the controlling influence behind the trusts at the centre of its enquiries in reaching their view.

The Tribunal also concluded on the facts that it was reasonable to suppose that the trustee would act in accordance with the wishes of the beneficiary and settlor of the trust. These influential factors will not always be present and the burden of any request HMRC makes should be proportional in the circumstances of the case and the risks being addressed.

Nevertheless, the *Panos Parissis* case is a further indication that the Tribunal is minded towards the fullest possible disclosure of the facts. The Tribunal imposed a penalty on the individuals for non-compliance with the information notice effectively for not asking the trustees to provide the information, whilst accepting that the taxpayer could not have legally compelled them to do so. The Tribunal also imposed a penalty despite the practical test being a significant extension of the *Lonrho* test.

The Tribunal also sounded a cautionary note of the adverse implications for the taxpayer of failing to disclose information. The Tribunal noted HMRC has wide powers to make a discovery assessment and then referred to the case of *Haythornthwaite (T) & Sons Ltd v Kelly (Inspector of Taxes)* (1927) 11 TC 657, where the taxpayer's refusal to produce requested documents which it could not lawfully be compelled to produce left the taxpayer without the evidence to challenge the assessment.

Summary

4.172 HMRC has very wide powers to demand information and generally the courts will favour provision.

Whilst the taxpayer and the adviser may consider the information is unnecessary, the statutory test is essentially whether it could potentially be reasonably held to be relevant, not that it is relevant.

> It is important to avoid a blinkered 'one size fits all' approach to information provision. In response to any request for information, it is essential to have regard to the bigger picture and where disclosure or push-back will lead. In some instances it may be tactically advisable to go beyond what can be compelled but in others it will not. To enable the right decision to be made, it is necessary to have regard to where each alternative action could lead in the context of the overall strategy and end plan.

Resolving an impasse

Introduction

4.173 There are essentially three routes to resolving an enquiry that has reached an impasse:

- escalation;
- ADR;
- formal closure and litigation.

Escalation

4.174 Before considering a formal approach for ADR or closure and litigation, the simple option of escalation should always be considered first. Whilst escalation should not be undertaken lightly or routinely, it can be a cost-effective way to overcome unprofessional and/or unreasonable behaviour by an individual officer. Any escalation should always be on the basis of an objective view of the actions and approach of the officer and not on the personal views of the taxpayer or adviser.

Senior HMRC officials will dismiss any approach that amounts to a general moan; it will be necessary to point to clear procedural or judgement errors which HMRC as a department would be unwilling to stand behind.

ADR

4.175 If the case has been worked collaboratively then there should, in theory, be no need for escalation or ADR. However, in practice, the personalities and/or experience of those working the case on both sides can mean a fresh pair of eyes and approach can bring renewed impetus to bring about a resolution or at least a better understanding of the reasons why agreement cannot be reached. In appropriate cases ADR can, therefore, be an effective means to break through apparent impasses in an enquiry.

4.176 *Contentious tax planning enquiries*

Having said this, in general HMRC will not wish to use ADR in tax avoidance cases, as typically HMRC will reach an established view having consulted with the relevant specialists and any basis of settlement will have been sanctioned by the relevant specialist.

HMRC also recognises that ADR should only be considered in cases where the process is likely to add value. Therefore, in general, ADR is unlikely to be appropriate unless the benefits of using it in the particular case can be clearly articulated (including how it might help the parties resolve a dispute). If the benefits cannot be clearly identified, articulated and agreed between the parties then ADR is unlikely to be suitable.

HMRC'S guidance sets out the type of circumstances where ADR is likely to be appropriate and where it is probably inappropriate.

4.176 ADR may be appropriate where any or all of the following points apply:

- the parties are seeking to work collaboratively, but
- it is proving difficult to pin down the essential point(s) of disagreement,
- HMRC and the customer appear to be at cross purposes, or
- there is uncertainty about the other party's position, underlying rationale or process for resolving disputes;
- the point at issue appears to be 'all or nothing' but there is a possibility that structured discussions might uncover (an) alternative approach(es) which would enable HMRC to resolve the dispute in accordance with the terms of the LSS;
- a narrowing or clarification of the facts or issues in the dispute is necessary. This may be particularly useful in fact-heavy disputes such as transfer pricing;
- complex or unique facts mean that a potentially costly and time-consuming judicial determination would be of little or limited precedent value.

4.177 Cases which HMRC considers are unlikely to be suitable for ADR include those where:

- it would be more efficient to have an issue judicially clarified so that the precedent gained can be applied to other cases;
- resolution can only be achieved by departure from an established 'HMRC view' on a technical issue, and no exceptional facts or circumstances exist to justify a departure from the law or practice;

Contentious tax planning enquiries **4.179**

- there is reason to suspect lack of integrity on the part of the customer, whether or not criminal proceedings are envisaged;
- there is doubt over the veracity or strength of evidence provided and HMRC wish to test it by cross-examination in a public tribunal.

Proceeding formally

4.178 If HMRC is unable to agree the position or, despite the requirements of the LSS guidance to clearly set out its own contrary position, proceeding formally may be a more cost-effective route to resolution than maintaining futile dialogue or exchanges of correspondence.

The first stage in that process would be to request a closure notice in order to crystallise the issue of whether HMRC's delay or further requests for information are unreasonable. If they are HMRC will be required to provide its conclusion, as the onus is on HMRC to demonstrate why a closure should not be given.

If HMRC does not accept the return and its reasons are disputed and/or they are unclear, the next step would be to appeal or ask for an independent review. Taxpayers have the legal right to have appealable tax decisions or assessments reviewed by another HMRC officer before appealing to the Tribunal.

However, the impact of this legislation is likely to be less important for cases involving tax avoidance because these cases are already subject to internal review by subject-matter specialists and in many instances HMRC's Solicitors Office. As such, it is unlikely that another officer would reach a different conclusion.

4.179 If by this stage HMRC has still not properly articulated its position, the officer's mind should be focused by the need to provide the taxpayer with a statement of case setting out the facts, law and contentions within 60 days of a standard Tribunal Direction. It will typically take around two months for the Tribunal to get around to this. In the meantime the taxpayer does not have to do any additional work or incur any additional costs and can simply await a properly articulated case.

Such an approach can trigger HMRC to review its position properly and concede the point. At the very least, the taxpayer will properly understand the case it has to answer and whether HMRC intends to pursue the matter to litigation. One of the difficulties taxpayers have is that they may wish to seek the view of counsel before deciding whether to pursue the dispute to litigation.

However, it is important to have the fullest possible articulation of HMRC's case before incurring the significant expense of a conference with counsel.

4.180 *Contentious tax planning enquiries*

HMRC should be prepared to articulate its case at least to the standard of a Statement of Case well before a closure notice is issued but this cannot always be taken as read. It is important to press for the fullest articulation before incurring costs prematurely.

RESOLVING DISPUTES

Introduction: litigation and settlement strategy

4.180 In 2007 HMRC sought to change its previous approach in relation to negotiated settlements (which it considered tacitly encouraged avoidance due to a lack of a downside) by introducing a new policy known as the Litigation and Settlement Strategy (LSS). This was re-issued on 12 July 2011 in order to refresh the strategy in the light of specific developments (eg changes to the Tribunal structure) and experience since its introduction. It also incorporates HMRC's latest thinking on resolving disputes cost effectively through collaborative working and attempts to clarify some of the misinterpretations of HMRC's key messages in the original document.

The key aims of the LSS when introduced were as follows:

- to resolve disputes consistently with HMRC's objectives of maximising revenues, reducing costs and improving customer experience;
- to resolve disputes consistently with HMRC's considered view of the law;
- to deal with each dispute on its own merits – ie 'Do not enter into package deals';
- to settle all or nothing issues on all or nothing terms;
- where HMRC has a strong case, to seek full value from any settlement, or take the matter to litigation;
- not to seek low value settlements where HMRC is not prepared to litigate; rather the case should be dropped.

4.181 The LSS has had a particularly significant impact over the conduct of disputes involving tax avoidance arrangements, as many HMRC officers took it to mean that such disputes could only be settled by litigation if the taxpayer refused to fully accept HMRC's position.

The revised LSS is shorter than the original but is supplemented by guidance for HMRC staff on how to implement the principles of the LSS in their day-to-day working of enquiries.

The revised LSS reinforces the previous messages that HMRC will not compromise its view of the law in order to reach a settlement. It also remains

Contentious tax planning enquiries **4.182**

committed to proceeding with litigation in cases where it believes it is likely to succeed and that litigation would be both effective and efficient. This caveat is a subtle but very important refinement of the previous LSS document, which many within HMRC and externally interpreted as requiring HMRC to litigate in all cases where it believed it had a greater than 50% chance of success.

HMRC has now clarified that the strength of opinion is only one factor to take into account. HMRC will not base its approach solely on its initial view on the strength of its argument but should be willing to test this view against the taxpayer's position before arriving at a conclusion. If both sides' estimate of success adds up to more than 100% then it is clear that one of the parties is over estimating its chance of success. HMRC acknowledges the need to explore this further before reaching a definitive view. This may provide scope for a negotiated settlement if the issue is not of an 'all or nothing' nature. In this respect the guidance also urges inspectors to explore whether the issue is truly of an 'all or nothing' nature, or whether there are a range of possible answers.

4.182 The LSS guidance (www.hmrc.gov.uk/practioners/lss-guidance-final.pdf) specifically recognises that the provisions in para 1 of the LSS allow HMRC to reach an out of court settlement on a basis which it believes gives the best overall return for the Exchequer, without going through the expense and uncertainty of taking the case to court.

The starting point for HMRC's view of what gives the best outcome to a tax dispute is what HMRC believes to be the likely outcome of litigation, though HMRC recognises that what is a 'likely outcome' (of litigation) is open to disagreement.

Broadly, where HMRC has reached a considered and definitive view of what is the right tax treatment of a particular transaction, and after having considered the full range of possible arguments, it will not settle out of court for any other tax treatment.

However the guidance goes on to state that:

> 'Where, having considered the facts and the range of arguments, HMRC is satisfied that there are alternative approaches which are each *reasonably likely* alternative outcomes to court proceedings, it may choose to settle out of court for one of the alternatives (though not necessarily for the lowest of the possible range of alternatives).
>
> HMRC will not however settle out of court for a result which it does not believe to be one of a range of likely alternative outcomes. Also, HMRC will not agree less tax, interest or penalties than it believes is within the range of outcomes in the interest of achieving a quick settlement, even if this would provide a good return on time spent on the case'.

4.183 *Contentious tax planning enquiries*

4.183 Thus the key to finding a resolution that does not involve litigation is either to persuade HMRC that it has a low prospect of success in litigation, or find a range of possible answers and articulate why at least one of the answers is a reasonable outcome; to be reasonable it does not necessarily have to be evenly weighted. To be an outcome which is LSS compliant, HMRC considers that it should be capable of being an answer that the Tribunal could theoretically have come to. In practice, what may be regarded as acceptable is often simply down to whether it is a technically tenable solution to reach a practical answer. The greater the desire on HMRC's part to reach a settlement, the greater the flexibility in terms of what would be regarded as a tenable outcome.

Some relatively recent and informative examples of how resolution may be reached (despite HMRC's stated policy position that it will not compromise its view of the law) are HMRC's settlement initiatives (see below). These demonstrate that where both sides are willing to compromise, a resolution can be reached even in cases where the issue seems to be black and white or where, at first sight, HMRC's offer appears singularly uninviting.

THE INCREASED THREAT OF DISCOVERY

4.184 The shortening of the 'normal' assessing time limit from six to four years has led to a significant increase in attempts by HMRC to raise discovery assessments. Even before this change, HMRC has been very keen to pursue discovery assessments in tax avoidance cases. There have been a number of recent cases where HMRC has established that a particular arrangement has been undertaken after the enquiry window has closed and where the planning is considered or shown to be ineffective, and has therefore, raised a discovery assessment. Advisers therefore need to understand that even where a year has closed and adequate disclosure was made at the time this may not be the end of the matter.

A detailed review of the disclosure provisions is beyond the scope of this chapter, rather this section aims to consider the implications of recent decisions.

4.185 Broadly stated, under the discovery provisions (contained in *TMA 1970, ss 29, 30B; s 30B; FA 1998, Sch 18 paras 41–45*), if HMRC discovers an assessment to tax should have been made, is insufficient, or relief is excessive, an officer may make an assessment in the amount which in his opinion ought to be charged. The power is only exercisable in the specified circumstances:

- the under-assessment ('insufficiency') is attributable to fraudulent or negligent conduct of the taxpayer or a person acting on his behalf; or
- HMRC could not have been reasonably expected, on the basis of the information made available to it, to be aware of the 'insufficiency'.

4.186 The meaning of 'discover' is well established and means:

- simply comes to the conclusion 'from the examination he makes, and, if he likes, from any information he receives' (*R v Kensington Income Tax Comrs, ex p Aramayo* 6 TC 279);

- 'finds out ... not only when he finds out new facts not known to predecessor but also when predecessor drew the wrong inference or where predecessor got the law wrong' (per Lord Denning in *Parkin v Cattell* 48 TC 462);

- it does not require any new facts to come to light.

4.187 In *Cenlon Finance Co Ltd v Ellwood* [1962] AC 782 Viscount Simonds said:

> 'I can see no reason for saying that a discovery of undercharge can only arise where a new fact has been discovered. The words are apt to include any case in which for any reason it newly appears that the taxpayer has been undercharged and the context supports rather than detracts from this interpretation.'

However, while the meaning of discover is very wide, this is cut down by the requirement that a 'notional officer' considering the return would not be able to reasonably infer that it was incorrect. If that notional officer could infer this then HMRC is prevented from making a discovery irrespective of how widely the term has been interpreted by the courts.

Thus in practice it is likely that new information will have come to light (either in relation to the taxpayer's facts or a decision in the courts that has a bearing on the taxpayer's affairs). Otherwise, the (reasonably competent) 'notional officer' should at the time the return was submitted have been able to infer that it was insufficient.

4.188 There has been a spate of discovery cases since the significant Court of Appeal case of *Veltema v Langham* [2004] STC 544 concerning what the officer could have inferred as to the existence of an insufficiency based on the information available to him at the time. In *Veltema* the Court of Appeal determined the test was not what the officer should have done to establish the insufficiency but what he could have reasonably been aware of from the information specified in *s 29* (in most instances the tax return).

Auld LJ concluded:

> '... it is plain from the wording of the statutory test in s 29(5) that it is concerned not with what an Inspector could reasonably have been expected to do but with what he could have been reasonably expected to be aware of.

4.189 *Contentious tax planning enquiries*

> It speaks of an Inspector's objective awareness, from the information made available to him by the taxpayer, of "the situation" mentioned in s 29(1), namely an actual insufficiency in the assessment.'

Some advisers took this reference to actual insufficiency to mean that the officer had to be absolutely certain that there was an insufficiency and a taxpayer was only protected from a discovery where this was the case if he had made it clear in the return that it contained an insufficiency. However, this was a misreading of Auld LJ's judgment, which has been clarified in later cases.

Auld LJ recognised in his judgment that a discovery could be made where the officer had less than actual knowledge of an insufficiency.

> 'It also allows as s 29(6) expressly does, for constructive awareness of insufficiency, that is, for something less than an awareness of an insufficiency, in the form of an inference of insufficiency'.

4.189 The cases of *Corbally-Stourton v Revenue and Customs Comrs* [2008] STC (SCD) 907, *Charlton v Revenue and Customs Comrs* [2012] UKUT 770 (TCC) and *Sanderson v Revenue and Customs Comrs* [2014] STC 915 illustrate the issues in relation to tax avoidance arrangements. All these cases concerned tax avoidance arrangements which were not challenged within the enquiry window but were identified at a later stage as a result of enquiries into other taxpayers who had undertaken the same or very similar planning.

In *Corbally-Stourton* and *Sanderson* the Special Commissioners/First-tier Tribunal found for HMRC, whereas in *Charlton* they found for the taxpayer despite very similar facts.

4.190 The decision in *Sanderson* broadly followed the rationale in *Corbally-Stourton* (whilst gaining additional comfort from the Court of Appeal case of *Revenue and Customs Comrs v Lansdowne Partners Ltd Partnership* [2012] STC 544, which was not concerned with tax avoidance).

In relation to the disclosure in that case the Special Commissioner said, at [66]:

> 'It seems to me that an inspector equipped with a reasonable knowledge of tax law could reasonably be expected to conclude from the Appellant's disclosure that something was going on, and that Mrs Corbally-Stourton had participated in a tax scheme. It would be reasonable to expect him to wish to question the workings of the scheme and the genesis and existence of the remarkable £1 billion loss. But he would also be aware that some tax schemes work and deliver the benefits claimed. There is nothing ... in the disclosure to suggest that this scheme did not work.

Contentious tax planning enquiries **4.191**

In my judgment an inspector could not reasonably be expected to conclude from the clear hints that there was a scheme that it was unlikely that it would work.'

4.191 In the case of *Charlton* the First-tier Tribunal considered it was a somewhat absurd test that led to a finding that the notional officer, faced with what was obviously a tax avoidance scheme, was required to be aware of the insufficiency from his own knowledge alone in order for HMRC to be precluded from making a discovery.

The Tribunal considered that the ban in *Veltema* on raising further enquiries did not extend to the notional officer dealing with a return which included a disclosed scheme taking the sensible step of seeking advice from a specialist colleague. The Tribunal judge stated:

'And if it is glaringly obvious either that the relevant officer should consider the law, and possibly refer to published material or, where an SRN number is disclosed, simply send an e-mail or make a phone call to colleagues and ask for guidance, this is precisely how we should treat the notional officer as proceeding.

This approach does not fall into the error of attributing to the "notional average officer" the views and knowledge of specialists as such. It only has this effect in those cases where any officer would inevitably seek guidance, and indeed know precisely where to seek that guidance. It simply deems the notional average officer to approach matters realistically, as HMRC would inevitably expect him to operate, and it avoids the absurdity of consigning the officer to his dark room, without legislation, books or other information, and with no opportunity to seek guidance from colleagues'.

The Tribunal also considered that even if this view was incorrect in relation to the operation of *s 29(5)*, HMRC was still precluded from making a discovery based on what was effectively a reversal of the *Corbally-Stourton* rationale:

'... but if we were wrong in the application of the sub-section 29(5) test that we have summarised above, we are still not entirely sure why the notional officer should be assumed, in his dark room, without guidance, law, Manuals or other published information, simply to dither, and then fail to assess because "some tax avoidance schemes fail and others do not". It seems, even on this seemingly ridiculous hypothesis, that the notional officer might more sensibly take the view that he should make an assessment, charging the gross gains and disallowing the losses, under the alternative expression, that "some assessments are sustained on appeal, and others are not". Equipped with the knowledge that many schemes, which taxpayers' counsel and advisers consider to be effective, actually fail, there might well be justification for making an assessment'.

4.192 *Contentious tax planning enquiries*

4.192 The *Charlton* case was heard by the Upper Tribunal in October 2012. The judge found in favour of the taxpayer of the basis that the officer should have been aware of the nature of the scheme and should have been sufficiently aware of the High Court judgment in *Drummond v Revenue and Customs Comrs* [2008] STC 2707 in favour of HMRC which defeated a very similar scheme.

However, the Upper Tribunal considered that the First-tier Tribunal had made an error of law in making the assumption that the notional officer would consult a more specialist colleague (see Upper Tribunal judgment paras 12, 46 and 53). The Upper Tribunal did, however, agree with the First-tier Tribunal that it was reasonable for the officer to be aware of the existence and relevance of form AAG1 from the DOTAS reference number (SRN). The extent to which this would have been relevant to the awareness of an actual insufficiency is debatable absent the decision in the *Drummond* case, which should have made the insufficiency clear.

4.193 What appears to have distinguished *Charlton* from the other two cases is the fact that the scheme was disclosed in that case, whereas the other cases predated the disclosure rules. In addition, in *Charlton*, by the time the three appellants had submitted their self-assessment tax returns, HMRC had challenged a broadly similar scheme in *Jason Drummond v HMRC* where it was decided in the courts that the scheme failed. Thus, despite the scheme having been disclosed under the DOTAS rules and a decision showing it did not work, HMRC failed to pick up on the insufficiency, raise an enquiry and amend the return in accordance with the decision in *Drummond*. In these circumstances it is not difficult to see why the Tribunal found as it did.

Absent the above fact pattern it seems more likely that HMRC will be able to make a discovery (where the year remains in date) unless it is reasonably clear at the time that the scheme does not work.

4.194 Central to whether HMRC can make a discovery is the degree of certainty the officer must have regarding an 'objective awareness' of the 'insufficiency' before being in a position to raise a discovery. As stated above, there have been many instances of HMRC raising 'protective discovery assessments', particularly around the time the normal assessing time limits changed from six to four years.

Practitioners need to be mindful that the term 'protective discovery assessment' is somewhat misleading. The reality is that HMRC either has grounds to make the assessment or it does not, it cannot raise an assessment simply to protect its position because a year is about to go out of date. This is clear from both case law and HMRC's own Statement of Practice (SP1/06) which was issued following the *Veltema* decision and which specified that 'mere suspicion' will not be sufficient for HMRC to make a discovery assessment.

Contentious tax planning enquiries **4.196**

4.195 Recent cases have considered what is meant by an objective awareness of an insufficiency (ie the level of certainty required that profits have been under-assessed). In the case of *Corbally-Stourton*, the Special Commissioner thought the test was that on the balance of probability there was an insufficiency. In the case of *Charlton*, the Tribunal thought this was broadly the correct test but thought the threshold was lower than the balance of probabilities.

However, the Court of Appeal in *Lansdowne Partners* expressed doubt as to the validity of this test. Moses stated that

'Awareness is a matter of perception and of understanding, not of conclusion. I wish, therefore, to express doubt as to the approach of the Special Commissioner in *Corbally-Stourton v Revenue and Customs Comrs* [2008] STC SCD 907 and of the Outer House in *R (on the application of Pattullo) v Revenue and Customs Comrs* [2009] STC 107, namely that to be aware of a situation is the same as concluding that it is more probable than not. The statutory context of the condition is the grant of a power to raise an assessment'.

Whilst this may be the correct statutory interpretation of the provision it is hardly a practical test and its subjectivity leaves considerable room for doubt and uncertainty. Perhaps the best rule of thumb test for practitioners to apply is that expressed by the Tribunal in *Charlton v HMRC* that the officer:

'... merely needs to consider, in a bona fide manner, that as he now views matters, he has "reason to believe" that there has been as under-assessment, and that an assessment is now justified and that there is a reasonable likelihood that, were the taxpayer to appeal, the new assessment would be sustained'.

4.196 The Court of Appeal in Sanderson upheld the decision of the FTT and UTT that the notional inspector could not have been aware of the insufficiency from the return. Counsel for the taxpayer had sought to rely on what he considered to be the circularity between *ss 29(1)* and *(5)*, contending that the UTT had overstated the level of knowledge required to be imputed to the notional officer under *s 29(5)* in order to justify a discovery assessment. Counsel argued that the threshold for discovery was a relatively low one and merely required the officer to be able to justify his belief that further tax was due. Counsel argued that unless the threshold was set relatively low HMRC would struggle to raise a discovery assessment in most cases. As such, the notional officer would, at the relevant time, have had sufficient awareness to meet that low threshold. However, the Court of Appeal considered that *s 29(1)* and *(5)* did not import the same test. A discovery assessment under *s 29(1)* was made by a real officer who was required to come to conclusion about a possible insufficiency based on all the available facts at the time the discovery

4.196 *Contentious tax planning enquiries*

assessment was made. The purpose of *s 29(5)* was to test the adequacy of the taxpayer's disclosures, not to prescribe the circumstances which would justify the real officer exercising the *s 29(1)* power.

Anderson v Revenue & Customs [2016] UKFTT 565 directly considered the issue of what level of knowledge is required to make a discovery assessment. It is noteworthy that the judge commented at para 22 that this basis of appeal had been taken in recognition that recent decisions (including Sanderson) gave the taxpayer a slim chance of success by arguing the condition at *s 29(5)* had not been met. The judge there reaffirmed the principle that there has to be a reasonable belief that there is an insufficiency quoting from *Charlton* that *'All that is required is that it has newly appeared to an officer, acting honestly and reasonably, that there is an insufficiency in the assessment'* [para 37].

The judge considered this meant: *'They [HMRC] just need to be sure of enough facts to enable them to determine a reasonable conclusion by the application of logic.'*

The judge also quoted with approval from Corbally-Stourton:

'It seems to me clear that both these judges and the legislation do not require the inspector to be certain beyond all doubt that there is an insufficiency; what is required is that he comes to the conclusion on the information available to him and the law as he understands it, that it is more likely than not that there is an insufficiency. I shall call this a conclusion that it is probable that there is an insufficiency. It is clear however that mere suspicion, something short of a conclusion that it is probable that there is an insufficiency, is not enough'. [paras 42–43].

The Appellant argued that the discovery assessment was based on a suspicion not a belief. The FTT considered: 'A suspicion becomes a belief when it is based on logical conclusions derived from what is known.'

On the facts the FTT considered HMRC did have sufficient information to come to a reasonable belief.

Notwithstanding the comments by the Court of Appeal in *Sanderson* regarding *s 29(1)* and *s 29(5)* the decision in *Anderson* reaffirms the rule of thumb threshold considered by the FTT in *Charlton* which, whilst lower than practitioners would have perhaps thought or liked, reflects current judicial thinking. If HMRC raises a discovery assessment and it appears this threshold has not been reached, then in the writer's experience the best course of action is to challenge the validity of the assessment without any further debate. In the context of a tax scheme in particular, taxpayers cannot, however, rely

Contentious tax planning enquiries 4.197

on the *ss 29(1), (5)* circularity argument that if HMRC has made a discovery on the basis of comparatively little information, then the corollary is that it must have had sufficient information at the relevant time.

At this stage, for an officer to be in a position to raise a valid discovery assessment, the officer should have a mindset that the assessment has a reasonable prospect of being sustained on appeal (without further information). The officer should not, therefore, be fishing for substantial further information once this state of mind has been reached and a discovery assessment made.

If the officer does not have this level of conviction, it is still open to him to seek additional information to potentially put him in that position, notwithstanding that there is no open enquiry. This is because HMRC's information powers entitle the officer to require the provision of information reasonably required for the purpose of checking the taxpayer's tax position even when the year is closed, providing he has reason to suspect profits have been under-assessed. This is clearly a much lower threshold than that required to make a discovery assessment.

However, once the officer has raised the discovery assessment he is no longer able to use HMRC's information powers to obtain further information. Any additional information could only be obtained by the Tribunal making a specific direction under its own powers on request by HMRC or of its own volition.

Summary

4.197

- 'Discover' is widely drawn and means 'finds out', 'comes to the conclusion' and does not require new facts.

- The current test is that it has newly appeared to an officer, acting honestly and reasonably, that there is an insufficiency in the assessment. This involves HMRC being sufficiently sure of enough facts to enable them to determine a reasonable conclusion by the application of logic.

- This wide scope is cut down by the fact that the officer must not have been able to infer from a relevant return (or enquiry into a relevant return) that the self-assessment was insufficient.

- The test is what the officer could infer from the relevant return **not** what the officer should have done (eg open an enquiry at the time).

- If the insufficiency was the result of careless or deliberate behaviour (including on the part of an agent) it does not matter what whether or

4.198 *Contentious tax planning enquiries*

> not the officer could have inferred there was an insufficiency from the relevant return.
>
> - The officer is a hypothetical (average) officer.
>
> - Sections *29(1)* and *(5)* do not import the same test, the former is concerned with a real officer's conclusion about a possible insufficiency based on all the available facts at the time the discovery assessment was made whereas the purpose of *s 29(5)* is to test the adequacy of the taxpayer's disclosures.

INCREASED THREAT OF PENALTIES

4.198 HMRC has made it clear that it will seek penalties where it believes the failure of an avoidance arrangement is the result of neglect (or from 1 April 2008, failing to take reasonable care).

Where a taxpayer has sought professional advice in relation to a particular arrangement, it should not generally be open to HMRC to charge a penalty should the advice ultimately prove to be wrong, either as a result of litigation or accepting HMRC's position, providing the position adopted was tenable. In relation to whether a scheme was disclosable the Special Commissioner in *Revenue and Customs Comrs v Mercury Tax Group Ltd* [2009] SWTI 628 held that as Mercury took counsel's advice on the question of disclosure, he would not penalise the taxpayer if that advice turned out to be wrong. They had done all they could in seeking such advice.

4.199 However, the First-tier Tribunal cases of *Hanson v Revenue and Customs Comrs* [2012] UKFTT 314 (TC) and *Bernard Peter Litman & Ann Newall v Revenue and Customs Comrs* [2014] UKFTT 089 (TC) show that the taxpayer cannot simply leave everything to his or her agent. In the latter case, the tribunal found that it was not reasonable for the taxpayer who had entered into a marketed tax avoidance scheme to have done no basic due diligence in respect of the payment flows or to ascertain whether a loan had in fact been made and to have acted on so little in the way of advice from the schemes promoter. As a result, the tribunal concluded the taxpayers were liable to a penalty.

Also, where HMRC is able to establish that the advice sought by the taxpayer was from a firm whose capability was clearly not commensurate with the technical complexity of the issue under consideration, it is likely HMRC would seek to charge a penalty for failing to take reasonable care.

Similarly, where the planning is ineffective because of an implementation failure (for example, funds did not move as envisaged) HMRC will contend that the taxpayer has failed to take reasonable care.

HMRC'S APPROACH WHERE FRAUD IS SUSPECTED

4.200 Where it is suspected that the taxpayer has acted fraudulently in implementing a planning arrangement the avoidance investigator will refer the matter elsewhere within HMRC. It may be decided that another office should pursue the matter, or indeed whether a criminal investigation should be instigated.

Examples of issues that would trigger such a referral are back-dating of documents or other forms of deliberate misrepresentation.

Chapter 5

Offshore tax investigations, disclosure campaigns and tax cooperation agreements

Gary Ashford CTA (Fellow), ATT, TEP
Partner (Non lawyer), Harbottle and Lewis LLP

> SIGNPOSTS
>
> - **Background** – For many years HMRC has challenged offshore tax matters, particularly involving low taxation offshore financial centres. This approach has developed as OECD member countries have taken similar approaches. HMRC introduced a Tax Evasion Strategy and is working with developed countries towards exchanging information with each other, with the aim of reducing international tax evasion. (See **5.1–5.4**.)
>
> - **Residence and domicile matters** – International tax matters are complex. There are different rules for individuals, companies and trusts. Prior to the introduction of the Statutory Residence Test for individuals in 2013, most precedent and guidance was by way of case law. The non-domicile rules for individuals are also very complex and provide good opportunities but also significant risks to clients. (See **5.5–5.17**.)
>
> - **Anti avoidance legislation** – Over the years, HMRC has tried to limit the opportunities of overseas tax planning, particularly, involving non-resident trusts. It is very important to keep up to date with the constantly changing legislation around international tax matters. (See **5.18–5.22**.)
>
> - **Exchange of information** – There has been a steady move towards greater transparency in the world of international tax matters. The European Union introduced the EU Savings Directive in 2005, the US introduced FACTA in 2010, and we are seeing the introduction of the OECD Common Reporting Standard, with first exchanges of

information in 2017. This trend will continue, as will the support given to each other by the fiscal authorities in the developed countries. It is a very important time to engage with clients so that they fully understand the risks and opportunities presented. (See **5.23–5.38**.)

- **HMRC disclosure campaigns** – Following OECD principles, HMRC introduced its first offshore disclosure facility in 2007. This was highly successful with over 45,000 disclosures. It was followed up in 2009 with a new disclosure facility, which resulted in at least another 5,000 disclosures. Such facilities have essentially been launched in most of the developed countries over the last ten years. The facilities provide a 'light touch', low-cost opportunity for those holding untaxed offshore assets to regularise those assets. (See **5.39–5.44**.)

- **Liechtenstein Disclosure Facility** – In August 2009, HMRC and the government of Liechtenstein reached an agreement whereby financial institutions would review their client files to identify UK resident persons holding accounts there and HMRC would provide an offshore disclosure facility enabling those UK persons to regularise those assets in return for favourable tax treatment. The LDF was not just limited to those holding Liechtenstein assets, so in effect it amounts to an HMRC worldwide disclosure facility for UK residents. The LDF was brought to an end on 31 December 2015. (See **5.45–5.80**.)

- **UK/Swiss tax cooperation agreement** – The UK and Swiss governments signed an agreement in 2011 introducing a tax cooperation agreement which came into force on 1 January 2013. The agreement contained three main parts: to regularise the past, on withholding tax for the future, and on exchange of information. Many UK residents holding untaxed assets in Switzerland made disclosures to HMRC, mainly by way of the LDF, however some chose the 'one off payment' method whereby the bank calculated a lump sum based on an agreed formula, to be taken to amount to the regularisation of the account. The agreement also allowed non-doms to opt out. (See **5.83–5.106**.)

- **Crown dependency disclosure facilities** – In the 2013 Budget, HMRC introduced tax disclosure facilities for the three Crown Dependencies, the Isle of Man, Jersey and Guernsey. Many aspects of these disclosure facilities were similar to the LDF, but crucially did not contain the assurance on criminal investigation. In the 2015 Budget, HMRC announced that these facilities would be closed on 31 December 2015. (See **5.107–5.112**.)

5.1 *Offshore tax investigations*

- **Offshore penalties** – FA 2011 introduced the offshore penalty regime. This brought in changes to the penalty regimes of *FA 2007, Sch 24* and *FA 2008, Sch 41* to increase penalties where the offence related to an offshore matter linked to category-specific jurisdictions. The offshore penalty regime effectively increases the level of penalty linked to the specific jurisdiction's approach to transparency and exchange of information. A new category of offshore penalty was introduced in *FA 2016*. (See **5.113–5.116**.)

- **Finance Act 2016** – This introduced a number of new developments, including a new criminal offence relating to offshore income, assets and activities, Penalties for enablers of offshore tax evasion or non-compliance, Penalties in connection with offshore matters and offshore transfers and asset-based penalties for offshore inaccuracies and failures. (See **5.117–5.121**.)

- **Criminal Finances Act 2017** – The *Criminal Finance Act 2017* introduces the new corporate criminal offences of Failure to Prevent the Facilitation of UK Tax Evasion and Overseas Tax Evasion. These are strict liability criminal offences. (See **5.122–5.127**.)

- **Worldwide Disclosure Facility** – On 5 September 2016 HMRC launched a new tax disclosure facility. There is now only one disclosure facility to disclose and regularise non tax compliant offshore assets. (See **5.128–5.134**.)

- **Requirement to Correct Offence (RTC)** – The Autumn Statement 2016 brought forward HMRC's proposals of a formal requirement in law to correct offshore tax non compliance. This requirement was brought in to run in parallel with the date for Common Reporting Standard (30 September 2018). Where offshore tax non compliance is not rectified significant penalties will flow. (See **5.135–5.143**.)

- **Key points** – For a list of key points from this chapter, see **5.144**.

Focus

This chapter aims to provide some historical context to the HMRC Offshore Evasion Strategy, and technical content over relevant issues, particularly into offshore disclosure campaigns and international exchange of information.

BACKGROUND

5.1 In recent times we have seen a significant increase in HMRC compliance activity in relation to overseas tax evasion and avoidance. In the 2013 Budget, HMRC published its offshore evasion strategy with the document 'No Safe Havens'. This was updated on 14 April 2014.

5.2 The HMRC objectives in relation to offshore tax evasion were set out as follows:

- there are no jurisdictions where UK taxpayers feel safe to hide their income and assets from HMRC;

- would-be offshore evaders realise that the balance of risk is against them;

- offshore evaders voluntarily pay the tax due and remain compliant;

- those who do not come forward are detected and face vigorously enforced sanctions;

- there will be no place for facilitators of offshore evasion.

5.3 However, despite the recent wave of media interest in this area, HMRC has long focused on non-compliance on offshore tax evasion and avoidance as part of its overall compliance strategy. The recent increase in activity is partly as a result of the globalisation of financial markets and mobility of taxpayers.

With the increased reliance and opportunities presented by globalised information technology by persons ever more internationally mobile, the risk to HMRC has increased.

5.4 The threats to the tax base mentioned above are not limited to the UK. The proliferation of international banking and trade has been such that all the large developed nations are having to face new and increasing challenges to taxation contribution. The Organisation for Economic Cooperation and Development (OECD) and the United Nations (UN) are at the forefront of tackling the challenges coming from this new global tax base.

RESIDENCE AND DOMICILE MATTERS

5.5 A key point for UK taxation is whether a person (individual or legal) is resident in the UK. If they are non-resident then they may well not be taxable at all, or taxable only on perhaps UK-source income.

5.6 This presents a significant opportunity for those who are internationally mobile or who conduct cross-border transactions to structure their affairs in such a way to limit the exposure to UK taxation. Many perfectly legal and

5.7 *Offshore tax investigations*

innocent commercial transactions can easily become the subject of an HMRC investigation.

Individuals

5.7 HMRC introduced a Statutory Residence Test (SRT) from 6 April 2013 (*FA 2013, s 218, Sch 45*). However, prior to the SRT, whether or not an individual was regarded as being UK resident for tax purposes largely relied on common law principles. There was limited legislation at *ITA 2007, ss 829–835* (and before that in *ICTA 1988*), but that essentially related to temporary visitors and leavers.

5.8 There are many tax cases setting out the principles of residence in the UK. A number of tax cases in the early twentieth century set the tone on residence (*Levene v IRC* [1928] AC 217; *IRC v Zorab* (1926) 11 TC 289; *Cooper v Cadwalader* (1904) 5 TC 101 and *IRC v Brown* (1926) 11 TC 292).

5.9 For individuals there were additional aspects such as not ordinarily residence status, which limited UK tax on foreign income only. From 6 April 2013, the concept of not ordinarily resident was replaced by Overseas Workday Relief (OWR).

5.10 As shown in the many tax cases and guidance provided over the years (IR20 and HMRC6), the above issues take account of both presence (number of days) but also pattern of life and wider facts when looking at these matters.

5.11 There have also been many notable recent cases on residence (*Shepherd v Revenue and Customs Comrs* [2005] STC (SCD) 644, *Gaines Cooper v Revenue and Customs Comrs* [2007] STC (SCD) 23 and *Grace v Revenue and Customs Comrs* [2011] UKFTT 36 (TC)).

Domicile

5.12 In the UK, the domicile of individuals can also have a significant impact on their tax position. Domicile is a legal issue; however, for tax purposes in the UK, there is scope to treat those who are not UK domiciled in different ways in relation to offshore income and capital gains (*ITTOIA 2005, Pt 8* and *TCGA 1992, s 12*).

5.13 Where a person is resident but not UK domiciled he can elect to pay tax on an arising worldwide basis or be taxed on a remittance basis for his offshore income and gains. Where he does this, providing the offshore income and gains are not remitted to the UK, no tax will be due on that unremitted income and gains.

5.14 Significant changes were introduced to the remittance basis regime by *FA 2008*. Those who qualified for the remittance basis, where offshore income exceeds £2,000 and they have lived in the UK for seven out of nine tax years, will have to pay the Remittance Basis Charge (RBC) of £30,000. From April 2013 where the person has lived in the UK for 12 out of 14 tax years the remittance basis charge increases to £50,000. April 2013 also introduced a further increase where a person has been resident in the UK for 17 out of 20 years. In that case, the RBC is £90,000 (this rate was effectively scrapped from 6 April 2017).

Trustee residence

5.15 There are different residence rules for the residence of trustees.

Changes were made from April 2007 (*ITA 2007, s 475*). The residence position of trustees relates to the residence of the trustees but also, on occasion, the residence of the settlor.

5.16 Where all the trustees are resident in the UK, the trust body will be treated as UK resident. Equally where all the trustees are resident outside the UK then the trust will also be treated as not resident for UK tax purposes. However, where there is a mixture of resident and non-resident trustees, the trust will be resident in the UK unless the settlor was not resident in the UK, not ordinarily resident in the UK, or not domiciled in the UK.

Company residence

5.17 Companies incorporated in the UK and those that are managed and controlled in the UK will be treated as resident for UK tax purposes (*CTA 2009, s 14*).

Where representatives of overseas companies are operating in the UK there may also be tax issues arising as a result of those representatives having created permanent establishment issues in the UK.

Significant cases in relation to company residence include *De Beers Consolidated Mines Ltd v Howe* [1906] AC 455 and *Bullock v Unit Construction Co Ltd* [1959] 38 TC 712.

ANTI-AVOIDANCE LEGISLATION

5.18 Over the years we have seen much anti-avoidance legislation introduced with the aim of taxing offshore income or assets which may

5.19 *Offshore tax investigations*

have escaped the net of HMRC. In relation to individuals, some of this is contained within *ITA 2007, Pt 13*, particularly the 'transfer of assets abroad' rules. *ITA 2007, s 721* taxes individuals (transferors) holding the relevant transactions. *ITA 2007, s 732* taxes individuals (non-transferors) where they receive a benefit as a result of relevant transactions.

5.19 Settlements legislation (within *ITTOIA 2005, Pt 5*) can, amongst many things, be used to tax settlors of offshore trusts. There are some similar rules for capital gains tax in the *TCGA 1992*. *TCGA 1992, s 13* can also allocate gains of non-resident companies to UK resident shareholders in certain circumstances.

5.20 Many other changes have been made over the years to the rules for offshore trusts, both in the UK and offshore. For companies, there is anti-avoidance in areas such as for controlled foreign companies (*ICTA 1988, s 747*; now *TIOPA 2010, Pt 9A*) and transfer pricing (*ICTA 1988, Sch 28AA* and now *TIOPA 2010, Pt 4*).

Other notable international tax investigation cases

5.21 There have been many cases which are of use when looking at HMRC's approach to offshore tax investigations. Notable cases include *R v Dimsey* [2001] UKHL 46, *R v Charlton* [1996] STC 1418 and *IRC v Botnar* [1998] STC 38.

5.22 The issues of residence, ordinary residence and domicile for both individuals and companies is complex and the aim of this chapter is merely to mention them as relevant issues when looking at overseas tax investigations.

EXCHANGE OF INFORMATION

Organisation for Economic Cooperation and Development

5.23 The OECD has for some time identified the risk to the development of member countries from international tax evasion and avoidance (what has been termed harmful tax practices of offshore financial centres).

5.24 At the centre of the OECD's response to counter this threat has been the issue of increased exchange of information between the various jurisdictions. Article 26 of the OECD Model Tax Convention sets the standards for double taxation agreements in relation to the issue of exchange of information.

There have been a number of enhancements to Article 26 in recent times.

Offshore tax investigations **5.29**

5.25 There has also been a significant increase in the use of Tax Information Exchange Agreements (TIEAs). TIEAs are bi-lateral information exchange agreements between individual states. This is to some extent as a result of various actions taken by the OECD to place pressure on states to become more transparent by way of a form of naming and shaming of uncooperative states in lists published by the OECD.

Most exchange of information provisions require fiscal authorities to make formal requests for information, in most cases requiring them to demonstrate a particular risk.

In 2014 the OECD introduced the concept of the Common Reporting Standard for international exchange of information.

European Union Savings Directive

5.26 Automatic exchange of information is the preferred approach of the EU in relation to exchanging information towards countering offshore tax evasion relating to savings. This approach circumvents the need to identify risks and make formal requests for information. The European Commission introduced the EU Savings Directive (2003/48/EC) (EUSD) from 1 July 2005.

5.27 The EUSD requires financial institutions in EU member states to collect and exchange data on those citizens receiving interest in that state where, according to the financial institutions' client acceptance procedures, the person is resident in another member state. On receipt of the data the other state can ensure that the information where appropriate has been properly declared to the fiscal authorities in the other state.

5.28 Austria, Belgium and Luxemburg initially applied a withholding tax instead. Belgium initiated automatic exchange from 1 January 2010. Austria and Luxemburg continue to operate withholding tax. Whilst outside the EU, the Isle of Man and Guernsey both agreed to automatic exchange from 1 January 2011. Jersey will apply automatic exchange of information in line with the EUSD from 1 January 2015.

5.29 The EUSD has provided significant data to respective fiscal authorities including HMRC. However, because it was limited to interest on savings and individuals, member states believe it is too limited. The EUSD has been significantly changed as a result of a long running review by the European Commission, with the introduction of Council Directive 2014/107/EU. The new Directive goes beyond interest and includes the following five non-financial categories of income and capital, with effect from 1 January 2015, ie for income from employment, director's fees,

5.30 *Offshore tax investigations*

life insurance products not covered by other Directives, pensions, and ownership of and income from immovable property.

5.30 From its amendment on 9 December 2014, the Directive also brings a list of financial information within the scope of the automatic exchange of information with effect from 1 January 2017. This information consists of interest, dividends and similar types of income, gross proceeds from the sale of financial assets and other income, and account balances.

Foreign Account Tax Compliance Act/Intergovernmental Agreement

5.31 The US introduced the Foreign Account Tax Compliance Act (FATCA) as part of the Hiring Incentives to Restore Employment Act 2010.

FATCA requires financial institutions outside the US to collect and exchange personal details where relevant persons (US citizens) hold accounts with those financial institutions overseas. Financial institutions outside the US are required to register for FATCA so that they will not be treated as non-participating foreign financial institutions.

5.32 The result of being treated as non-participating is that the financial institution will suffer withholding tax on all US dealings. However, the agreement's focus is triggered where a financial institution holds reportable accounts, ie accounts where the financial institution's procedures have identified the account as being held by a US specified person (potentially beneficial owner).

5.33 The EU held discussions with the US government to find practical ways to help EU financial institutions comply with FACTA and in many cases to seek that the US also collects and exchanges data on its own EU resident citizens.

5.34 The US and EU countries signed individual Intergovernmental Agreements (IGAs). These agreements require financial institutions still to collect data on US citizens but instead of handing this over to the US authorities, it is handed to the relevant fiscal authority in each country (in the UK, HMRC).

5.35 The various FATCA/IGA agreements introduce significant due diligence obligations on the various financial institutions to identify relevant persons. As well as individual accounts, accounts held in overseas companies must also be reviewed. Also, financial institutions includes trust companies and family offices.

Following the initial FATCA IGA agreements, many countries, particularly OECD member countries, started to look at introducing wider automatic exchange of information IGAs.

5.36 In Autumn 2013 the UK signed IGAs with the Crown Dependencies and Offshore Territories. These agreements followed FATCA principles of requiring financial institutions in the relevant overseas jurisdiction to capture and exchange information relating to relevant persons (UK or the reciprocal jurisdiction) resident in the other jurisdiction, to capture and exchange the relevant information.

The earliest period for which information was captured was calendar year 2014 and the first exchanges of information took place on 30 September 2016.

Common Reporting Standard for automatic exchange of tax information

5.37 As a further development of the FATCA/IGA principles, the OECD in 2013 introduced a new standard for automatic exchange of information for tax purposes. This is better known as the common reporting standard (CRS).

5.38 In 2014 all OECD member countries signed up to the new principles. Another 65 countries also agreed to apply the principles, 40 of which exchanged early, from 2017. Other countries started to exchange information from 2018.

HMRC OFFSHORE DISCLOSURE CAMPAIGNS

5.39 HMRC successfully applied its information powers (*TMA 1970, s 20(8A)* and *FA 2008, Sch 36, para 5*) to secure details of UK residents holding offshore assets over the years. This was demonstrated in the cases of *R v IRC, ex p Ulster Bank Ltd* (1997) 69 TC 211, *Revenue and Customs Comrs v Financial Institution* [2006] STC (SCD) 71 and *Financial Institution 1–4 v Revenue and Customs Comrs* (SpC 580–583).

5.40 At various points in time the OECD highlighted the opportunity for member countries to broaden the tax net by pragmatic means such as voluntary tax disclosure facilities. There have been various such campaigns in many developed countries. The UK offered its first disclosure facility in 2007 with the introduction of the offshore disclosure facility (ODF).

HMRC's offer, for a limited period, was that those holding untaxed offshore assets could make a disclosure to it, pay the tax (going back 20 years), late payment interest and a 10% penalty.

5.41 *Offshore tax investigations*

5.41 This campaign was extremely successful and HMRC announced that it had secured over £400 million in additional tax revenue that arguably might not otherwise have been collected. HMRC secured a further £100 million from follow-up work.

5.42 Because of the success of the ODF, and because HMRC still held significant amounts of personal data pointing towards others who might still have a disclosure to make, HMRC announced another similar tax disclosure campaign in 2009, the 'New Disclosure Opportunity' (NDO). Using the same unnamed third party information powers (updated by *FA 2008, s 113, Sch 36, para 5*) HMRC was successful in securing further formal notices against a great number of other financial institutions in the UK (around 308 notices were apparently issued).

The NDO was successful in securing a further £85 million of tax with a further £40 million from follow-up work.

5.43 HMRC's data store on those potentially holding offshore accounts continues to be replenished, particularly by way of information received from the EUSD, and in due course from the information available from the various intergovernmental agreements, mentioned earlier.

We have also seen significant client data thefts by offshore private bankers, with the information being handed over to fiscal authorities around the globe.

OFFSHORE COORDINATION UNIT

5.44 In October 2011, HMRC announced that as a result of the success achieved in its offshore tax investigations, it was bringing all this work together into one office in Birmingham, in the Offshore Coordination Unit (OCU).

This unit has taken on responsibility for all offshore investigation work, including the UK/Swiss tax cooperation agreements and liaising on the Liechtenstein Disclosure Facility with Specialist Investigations (Fraud and Avoidance).

LIECHTENSTEIN DISCLOSURE FACILITY

5.45 On 11 August 2009, HMRC (on behalf of the UK government) and the government of the Principality of Liechtenstein signed two tax cooperation agreements: a Tax information Exchange Agreement (TIEA) and a Memorandum of Understanding (MOU).

5.46 Both the MOU and the Joint Declaration issued at the time confirmed that a five-year taxpayer compliance assistance program was to be introduced and operated in Liechtenstein, together with a five-year tax disclosure facility to be introduced in the UK (the Liechtenstein Disclosure Facility (LDF)).

5.47 The MOU set out the objective for the agreement: by the end of the five-year period there should no persons holding assets in Liechtenstein that are not tax compliant. Any persons identified as part of the Taxpayer Assistance and Compliance Program will be required to demonstrate to the financial intermediary that there is no UK tax liability, or that they are tax compliant, within the five-year period, otherwise the financial intermediary will be required to cease to provide services or, in exceptional circumstances where this is not possible because of specific legal reason, will face sanctions.

5.48 The MOU defined the various criteria for the agreement, such as who is covered by the agreement (relevant persons), the assets covered (relevant assets) and the financial intermediaries involved.

The MOU also set out the terms of the UK tax disclosure facility (the LDF), including who can participate and the terms of the facility.

Five-year Taxpayer Assistance Compliance Program

5.49 The MOU stated that legislation was to be introduced by the government of Liechtenstein to carry into effect procedures in Liechtenstein for the identification of persons who had a beneficial interest and who were relevant persons. The purpose of the legislation was to support the Taxpayer Assistance and Compliance Program.

The legislation was passed in September 2010 (the Administrative Assistance in Tax Matters in the UK (UK TIEA) Act).

5.50 As part of the agreement and supporting legislation, financial intermediaries in Liechtenstein are under a duty:

(i) to identify relevant persons in respect of whom or which they are providing relevant services;

(ii) to contact those relevant persons who have a contractual relationship with the financial intermediary in relation to the respective relevant property;

(iii) to cease providing relevant services in respect of relevant persons who do not follow various certification procedures by the final compliance date.

The duties above are ongoing.

5.51 *Offshore tax investigations*

Relevant persons

5.51 For the purposes of the Taxpayer Compliance Assistance Program and the LDF, 'relevant persons' are defined as:

(a) in the case of natural persons, those who have a beneficial interest in relevant property and:

    (i) who, on 1 August 2009 the financial intermediary knows had a residential address in the UK which the financial intermediary is or was accustomed to treat as his principal address,

    (ii) who, on 1 August 2009 or at any time thereafter, the financial intermediary knows has been resident for tax purposes in the UK, or

    (iii) for whom, on 1 August 2009 or at any time thereafter, a UK address has been given in a form identifying those persons as the 'beneficial owners' provided to the financial intermediary under Liechtenstein anti-money laundering legislation;

(b) in the case of legal persons, persons who have a beneficial interest in relevant property and:

    (a) have their place of incorporation in the UK, or

    (b) which, on 1 August 2009 or at any time thereafter, the financial intermediary knows have been a resident of the UK for UK tax purposes.

Definition of 'beneficial interest'

5.52 A relevant person has a beneficial interest in relevant property where:

1   In the case of foundations, trusts or other fiduciary entities –

    (a) he is the person or one of the persons who established or funded it;

    (b) he is the person or one of the persons whom the financial intermediary regards as its principal beneficiary or principal beneficiaries;

    (c) he is a person entitled to 25% or more of its income or capital;

    (d) he is a person who has received a distribution or distributions, in a given UK tax year, in total amounting to £5,000 or more from such an entity since 1 August 2009; or

    (e) he is a person whom the financial intermediary knows has been provided with the benefit, in a given UK tax year, of an asset or any number of assets of a value equivalent to £25,000 or more from such an entity since 1 August 2009.

2   Where relevant services are provided in respect of bank and financial (portfolio) accounts (that are relevant property) –

   (a)   those persons in whose name the account is held if they are natural persons and are the beneficial owners of the account or are UK companies; or

   (b)   the account is held in the name of a natural person who is not the beneficial owner, any person identified as the 'beneficial owner' in forms provided to the financial intermediary by that legal person pursuant to Liechtenstein anti-money laundering legislation.

3   Where relevant services are provided to corporations (other than collective investment vehicles), those natural persons who, at any time since 1 August 2009 –

   (a)   have held or controlled a share or voting rights amounting to 5% or more in such entity; or

   (b)   have received 5% or more of the profits of such entity.

5.53   Relevant *property* means:

(i)   a bank or financial (portfolio) account in Liechtenstein; or

(ii) a company (including a corporation and an institution structured as a corporation as well as a company without a legal personality), partnership, foundation, establishment, trust, trust enterprise, or other fiduciary entity, estate, or insurance policy that is issued, formed, founded, settled, incorporated, administered, or managed in Liechtenstein.

5.54   Relevant *service* means any one or more of the following services provided by a financial intermediary in Liechtenstein with respect to relevant property:

(i)   serving as a board member or officer;

(ii)   providing a registered office;

(iii) holding powers of appointment of beneficiaries, trustees or property whether personal or fiduciary;

(iv)   providing custodianship of all forms of property whether on the terms of a trust or contract; or

(v)   providing banking services as defined under the applicable laws of Liechtenstein.

5.55   As indicated at **5.45**, HMRC launched the LDF on 11 August 2009. The formal commencement date was 1 September 2009. Originally

5.56 *Offshore tax investigations*

the agreement was set to end on 5 April 2015; this was then extended to 5 April 2016, however, in the Budget of 2015, HMRC brought forward the end of the LDF to 31 December 2015.

Eligible persons

5.56 Paragraph E of the MOU (Preamble) sets out the eligibility categories for the LDF. It states that the LDF is open to all persons with new or existing fiduciary, company or other holding structures or financial accounts in Liechtenstein during the five-year period subject to the following:

- '(a) any person already under investigation by HMRC as of the date of signing of this MOU cannot participate in the disclosure facility;
- (b) any person who was previously under investigation by HMRC and who knowingly did not disclose his interest in any relevant property will be able to participate in the disclosure facility but will not be able to benefit from the limited penalty provided for in the disclosure facility;
- (c) any person previously contacted by HMRC under the terms of the Offshore Disclosure Facility or the New Disclosure Opportunity will be able to participate in the disclosure facility but will not be able to benefit from the limited penalty provided for in the disclosure facility. The relevant penalty will not, however, be higher than the penalty provided for under the New Disclosure Opportunity; and
- (d) a person who participates in the disclosure facility and has a bank account, including a financial (portfolio) account, outside the UK or Liechtenstein which is in his name and was opened through a UK branch or agency of that bank, will not, in relation to that account, be eligible for the shorter limitation period, the fixed penalty and the composite rate option provided under the disclosure facility'

THE LDF AS A TAX DISCLOSURE FACILITY OF WORLDWIDE ISSUES

5.57 Paragraph E of the Preamble, above, particularly sub-para (d) (together with Sch 7, para 1(a) to the MOU) effectively state that the LDF is not just available to those holding historical assets in Liechtenstein.

5.58 Schedule 7, para 1(a) to the MOU states that the LDF is available:

(a) from 1 September 2009 for those relevant persons with an existing asset or interest in an asset in Liechtenstein at that date; and

Offshore tax investigations **5.65**

(b) from 1 December 2009 for relevant persons with an asset or an interest in an asset in Liechtenstein acquired between 2 September 2009 and the final compliance date (5 April 2016).

This effectively allows persons holding untaxed assets *anywhere in the world* wishing to avail themselves of the LDF, to acquire a new asset in Liechtenstein and register for the LDF.

5.59 The fact that a person did not hold an offshore asset as at 1 September 2009, or that the offshore asset was acquired via a UK branch or agency, does not prevent someone making use of the LDF. He can still register, but the full beneficial terms of the LDF will not be available.

5.60 Paragraphs (a)–(c) above set out other restrictions for those who can or cannot make use of the LDF or whose participation is restricted. Paragraph (a) states that a person who is already 'under investigation' at the point of signing the MOU cannot participate.

5.61 The MOU confirms that changes to LDF guidance may be provided in agreed frequently asked questions. Within those FAQs, it has been clarified that 'under investigation' relates to criminal investigations and tax investigations under Code of Practice 9 (COP9).

5.62 Anyone with an investigation which has already been closed, criminal or otherwise, may potentially still register and be eligible to participate but will potentially face greater penalties. The key to eligibility is that the investigation is not open at the point of registering.

HMRC has made it clear that where the disclosure is linked to criminal proceeds as set out in the *Proceeds of Crime Act 2002* (excluding tax matters), the protection of the LDF is not available.

5.63 Sub-paragraph (c) of para E of the Preamble relates to persons identified and written to at the time of the New Disclosure Opportunity. It states that these persons will pay a higher penalty (the FAQs have stated that this will be 20% up to 2009, after which the normal time limits apply).

Tax liabilities

5.64 Tax liabilities in the UK are calculated by reference to the statutory time limits set out at *TMA 1970, ss 34* and *36*. These time limits changed from 6 April 2009 as a result of *FA 2008, s 118, Sch 39*.

5.65 Where someone has deliberately not paid tax, under *TMA 1970, s 36*, HMRC has the power to assess back 20 years. Under the LDF, HMRC

5.66 *Offshore tax investigations*

will restrict any assessments relating to unpaid tax resulting from deliberate behaviour to periods after 6 April 1999.

5.66 In line with *ss 34* and *36*, where reasonable care has been taken, HMRC will limit its assessments to four years. Where carelessness has occurred, HMRC will limit its assessments to six years.

Composite rate option

5.67 Tax under the LDF can be calculated in two ways: the actual basis or under the composite rate option (CRO). The actual basis is the normal basis of taxation, taking into account reliefs, deductions, rate bands and exemptions.

5.68 The CRO requires the tax to be calculated at a straight 40% rate. The CRO is irrevocable. Where the CRO is selected, no reliefs, deductions, rate bands or exemptions are available to be set against the additional income assessed under the LDF. It does, however, ensure that liabilities are not effectively charged twice such as *CTA 2010, s 455* on cases of diverted takings, for example where there are additional company profits as a result of diverted takings and a resulting overdrawn loan account. The potential double liability will be met by making a payment using the CRO basis.

5.69 The CRO also extends to predecessor taxes so where so elected, historical IHT may be effectively cleared. An example of this might be where funds have passed down over a number of family generations and IHT has not been paid when due. The CRO is only available for years to 5 April 2009.

Single rate charge

5.70 HMRC introduced a single rate charge for 2010/11, at a rate of 50%. It is similar to the CRO, but is only available where there were historical assets in Liechtenstein at 1 September 2009.

Late payment interest

5.71 The LDF requires that late payment interest is paid as well as the historical tax. Where the actual basis is used for calculation, the strict basis of late payment interest is to be applied (including to additional payments on account).

Where the CRO is used for calculation, a single date for interest of 1 July following the end of the relevant tax year can be used.

Penalties

5.72 The LDF requires, where appropriate, the payment of penalties, as well as the historical tax and late payment interest.

HMRC has confirmed that where the full beneficial terms apply the penalty will be 10% up to 2009. Thereafter the *FA 2007, s 97, Sch 24* penalty regimes (and other relevant penalty rules such as *FA 2008, Sch 41* for failure to notify) apply. HMRC has indicated that it would expect a penalty of no less than 20% to be in point, where a penalty applies, for 2010 onwards.

HMRC acknowledges that in some cases innocent error might be possible, and so in such cases it will accept that no penalty applies.

Criminal prosecution

5.73 The LDF includes a commitment that HMRC will not conduct a criminal investigation where an eligible person registers and is accepted into the LDF.

THE LIECHTENSTEIN DISCLOSURE FACILITY DEVELOPMENTS

5.74 HMRC issued new guidance in relation to the LDF on 14 August 2014. A new Fourth Joint Declaration was also released at the same time.

The changes limit some of the favourable terms of the LDF. This means that the changes brought about limit the benefits of the LDF but do not exclude the new categories altogether.

5.75 The categories can be summarised as follows:

- those where no new disclosure is being made;
- cases where the issue being disclosed is already under investigation and that investigation began more than three months before the application for the LDF;
- cases where there is no substantial connection between the liabilities being disclosed and the offshore asset held as at 1 September 2009.

5.76 The changes effectively withdraw the following favourable terms for the categories above:

- the reduced 10% penalty for the period up to 5 April 2009;

5.77 *Offshore tax investigations*

- the reduced assessing period back to 1 April 1999;
- the opportunity to use the Composite Rate Option up to 5 April 2009 and the Single Charge Rate from 6 April 2010.

5.77 A significant change is the introduction of a form of 'materiality' test. HMRC has referred to the fact that in order to participate in the LDF, the person requires a Confirmation of Relevance (COR) as of 2011 provided by the financial intermediary, and the COR is issued subject to the financial intermediary's own materiality tests. HMRC will now only provide the full beneficial terms where the matter being disclosed is substantially material to the offshore asset held at 1 September 2009.

Changes in relation to avoidance matters are notable and show that HMRC is determined to hold a strong line in its ongoing battle in this area.

5.78 HMRC has stated that where a disclosure of tax avoidance schemes (DOTAS) number has or should have been issued (perhaps because the promoter did not disclose) it will not allow the full favourable terms. It has stated that where no DOTAS number was required then full favourable terms can still remain.

5.79 The issue of ongoing tax enquiries entering the LDF is also interesting. Before these changes came into effect, it had been possible to 'move' an ongoing local enquiry into the LDF to make a disclosure or simply to take advantage of the reduced assessing time limits or penalties. With these changes, however, this opportunity has been severely restricted, but may still be possible. The key is for the adviser to make a decision within those first three months. It is also necessary to keep a close eye on the new materiality test to make sure you don't fall foul of that additional hurdle.

5.80 As part of the Fourth Joint Declaration, it was announced that it will commence to give charitable tax relief where the charity is properly registered in Liechtenstein.

NEW TAX DISCLOSURE FACILITY

5.81 At the time of writing, HMRC is in the process of developing a new tax disclosure facility to replace the LDF.

Few details have been issued, but the understanding is that there will be one facility to cover the period 2016/17 (the exact dates have not been released), which will run up to around the introduction of the Common Reporting Standard.

5.82 HMRC has suggested that there will be no assurance in relation to criminal prosecution, penalties could be around a minimum of 30% and the time period for the disclosure facility could revert to a full 20-year period.

UK/SWISS TAX COOPERATION AGREEMENT

5.83 On 6 October 2011, the UK and Swiss governments signed a tax cooperation agreement. It was amended on 20 March 2012 by Protocol. The UK legislation supporting the agreement is at *FA 2012, s 218, Sch 36*.

The agreement came into force on 1 January 2013.

5.84 There are three main objectives of the agreement:

- regularisation of the past;
- withholding tax going forward;
- enhanced exchange of information.

5.85 The agreement is designed to be effectively implemented by financial intermediaries (mainly, but not limited to, the banks) in Switzerland.

For the agreement to apply there needs to be a relevant person holding relevant assets with a Swiss paying agent in Switzerland.

Swiss paying agent

5.86 The definitions chapter of the agreement states that 'Swiss paying agent' means banks under the Swiss Banking Act of 8 November 1934, securities dealers under the Swiss Stock Exchange Act of 24 March 1995 and natural and legal persons resident or established in Switzerland.

Relevant assets

5.87 The definitions chapter of the agreement states that 'relevant assets' means all forms of bankable assets booked or deposited with a Swiss paying agent including, cash and precious metals accounts, all forms of stocks, shares and securities, options, debts and forward contracts and other structured products traded by the banks (such as certificates and convertibles). Insurance contracts that are 'insurance wrappers' are relevant assets.

The following are not be regarded as relevant assets: contents of safe deposit boxes, real property, chattels.

5.88 *Offshore tax investigations*

Relevant person

5.88 The definitions chapter of the agreement states that 'relevant person' means any individual resident in the United Kingdom (at 31 December 2010) who is the account holder or deposit holder and beneficial owner of assets; or who (in accordance with the conclusions of a Swiss paying agent drawn in line with the prevailing Swiss due diligence obligations) is the beneficial owner of assets held by a domiciliary company.

5.89 A domiciliary company is defined to include legal entities, companies, institutions, foundations, trusts, fiduciary companies and other establishments not exercising a trading or manufacturing activity.

Regularising the past

5.90 In terms of addressing historical tax issues, the agreement provides several options:

(i) close the account (in which case there is no clearance);

(ii) a one-off payment on 31 May 2013 on an anonymous basis; or

(iii) authorise the Swiss paying agent to provide personal details of the account holder to the Swiss tax authorities, for onward transmission to the UK tax authorities.

The one-off payment

5.91 Relevant persons holding an account at 31 May 2013 (if they do not choose the option to exchange information) can elect for the Swiss paying agent to take an amount from the balance of the account at 31 May 2013 and this amount may be taken to clear past tax liabilities relating to the account.

5.92 The one-off payment is calculated by using the formula (see below) and results in an amount of between 21% (the minimum) and 41% (the maximum) of the capital balance on the account at 31 May 2013 (the maximum is 34% where the account is under £1 million).

The percentage formula effectively takes into account the relative balances (if the account is open at that time) at 31 December 2002, 2010 and 2012. This is called the 'capital method'.

The formula

5.93 The one-off payment is made by the Swiss paying agent and does not require the identity of the account holder to be made known to the tax authorities.

Non UK domiciliaries and the past

5.94 Non UK domiciliaries with a certificate from their tax adviser demonstrating that where appropriate they have claimed the remittance basis for 2001/11 or 2011/12 can opt out of the options to regularise the past.

They can also provide details of remittances made to the Swiss paying agent, who will then tax the amount at 34%. This is called the 'self-assessment method'.

Clearance

5.95 The historical one-off payment provides clearance over the funds on which the one-off payment has been paid. This is done by way of the Swiss paying agent providing a tax certificate to the client 30 days before the one-off payment is made. The relevant person has 30 days to challenge or approve the figure of the one-off payment.

5.96 As the payment relates to funds in the account at a specific date (31 December 2010 or 31 December 2012), funds that have been taken out of the account (and have not been replaced) will not be cleared. There is some scope to place new funds into the account before 31 December 2012, however there are many areas where clearance cannot be fully or partly achieved under the agreement.

5.97 For example, funds placed into the account to increase the balance at 31 December 2012 (to counter funds taken out previously), if they are made from the UK will be treated as a payment on account (if at some later stage they find themselves under enquiry with HMRC).

5.98 Where an individual was under investigation at 31 May 2013 or where the individual was investigated and the investigation was concluded before that date, and in the case of a criminal investigation was convicted or had a civil investigation concluded after 31 December 2002 and who did not disclose the Swiss account, this will again be treated as a payment on account.

5.99 The general approach of the one-off payment is that where HMRC opens a tax investigation, the person can provide it with a copy of the

5.100 *Offshore tax investigations*

one-off payment certificate as a method of demonstrating that the funds are tax compliant (subject to whether all funds are actually cleared).

5.100 Where a person falls into the categories set out above, the one-off payment cannot clear previous liabilities in the same way and instead can only be used as a certificate of tax paid, which can be used as a payment on account of the ongoing investigation.

This position is also the case for individuals who have been written to by HMRC as part of one of its tax campaigns.

The post-1 January 2013 withholding tax

5.101 Relevant persons receiving income, gains, etc on relevant assets from 1 January 2013 have two choices over payments made after the agreement comes into force.

They can either suffer withholding tax or authorise the Swiss paying agent to provide their personal details to the Swiss tax authorities for onward transmission to the UK tax authorities.

5.102 Tax is withheld at various rates depending on the source of the income: interest, dividends, capital gains, etc. The effective rates run in line with UK personal income tax rates but are slightly lower to take account of the fact that the payment is made earlier. The rates are: interest (48%), dividends (40%), capital gains (27%), other income 48%.

5.103 The way the withholding tax will work in practice is to complement any tax already being withheld under the European Savings Agreement with Switzerland (EUSA). Therefore where a person is also suffering the 35% withholding tax, an additional amount of 13% will be deducted as part of the UK/Swiss agreement.

5.104 If the relevant person does not wish to suffer withholding tax he must agree to exchange of information. Unlike the position in the past, whereby non UK domiciliaries were able to opt out from the one-off payment, this is not possible for future payments.

However, non-UK domiciled individuals can seek to ensure that withholding tax is limited to amounts remitted to the UK. This is administered by the bank.

Non-domiciliary certification

5.105 If a relevant person wishes to elect for the non-domiciliary options, either for the historical one-off payment or future payments, then it is necessary for him to provide a certificate to the Swiss paying agent.

The certificate must be provided by a qualified tax professional. The agreement sets out the list of professional bodies that are allowed to provide such certificates.

The tax professional must then confirm that the relevant person claimed non-domiciliary status in his tax returns for 2010/11 or 2011/12 and, where appropriate, claimed the remittance basis.

Inheritance tax changes by protocol

5.106 The one-off payment is taken to clear historical liabilities in relation to the capital on which it is made. This includes historical inheritance tax.

However, where the relevant person dies after the one-off payment is made, unless the personal representatives authorise the exchange of information approach at that time, then the account will suffer another payment of 40% of the capital balance at the time.

The UK/Swiss agreement came to an end on 31 December 2016.

This is essentially because it was no longer necessary given the intention of both UK and Switzerland to automatically exchange information under the Common Reporting Standard (CRS).

CROWN DEPENDENCY DISCLOSURE FACILITIES

5.107 In the Budget 2013, HMRC announced voluntary disclosure facilities with the Crown Dependencies of the Isle of Man, Jersey and Guernsey. Like other disclosure facilities (ODF, NDO and LDF) these disclosure facilities provide the opportunity for UK taxpayers holding untaxed assets in these jurisdictions to make a disclosure of past tax liabilities in return for a reduced financial settlement.

5.108 Originally the facilities were set to end on 30 September 2016, however, in the Budget of 2015, HMRC brought forward the end of the Crown Dependency to 31 December 2015.

5.109 The terms of the agreements are such that HMRC will limit any tax liabilities back to 6 April 1999, charge late payment interest only back that far, and also charge penalties of 10% up to 2009. The terms are similar to those of the LDF (see **5.21**), and so penalties increase slightly after 2009; 20% in the main, but could be 30% or 40%, subject to the Offshore Penalty regime (see **5.60**).

5.110 *Offshore tax investigations*

5.110 There are some significant differences between the Crown Dependency disclosure facilities and the LDF. The greatest difference is that only the LDF provides assurance that there will not be a criminal investigation, or prosecution, where there is a tax offence.

5.111 The Crown Dependency disclosure facilities require that disclosures are made within six months and that on registering with HMRC to make a disclosure the tax is paid on account within 30 days.

5.112 Where there are no historic assets in a Crown Dependency, unless new assets were secured before 31 December 2013, the facility is not open to those with untaxed assets in other jurisdictions.

Anyone under any kind of civil tax investigation cannot make a disclosure under these disclosure facilities.

OFFSHORE PENALTIES

5.113 *FA 2010, s 35* and *Sch 10* introduced amendments to the legislation for both incorrect and failure to notify penalties at *FA 2007, s 97, Sch 24* and *FA 2008, s 123, Sch 41* respectively.

Offshore penalties relate to income tax and capital gains matters only.

5.114 From 6 April 2011, where a penalty relates to an offshore matter, the penalty will be increased, by either 150% or 200% if the territory to which the offshore matter relates falls within a prescribed category within a list published by HMRC. The list takes into account tax cooperation agreements in place with the other territory.

AN OFFSHORE MATTER COULD RELATE TO INCOME, AN ASSET OR ACTIVITIES OFFSHORE

5.115 *FA 2015, Sch 20* introduced a new category of offshore penalty, a Category 0 penalty. Category 0 is equivalent in value (eg maximum 100%) to the old Category 1 penalty. Category 1 introduces a new range with a maximum to 125%.

5.116 *FA 2015, Sch 21* introduced a new additional offshore tax penalty. This penalty is known as an 'offshore move' penalty. The penalty is in point where:

- the person is liable to a penalty for an inaccuracy under *FA 2007, Sch 24* – this is the underlying penalty;

- the tax at stake in relation to the underlying penalty is income tax, capital gains tax or inheritance tax;
- there is a relevant offshore asset move connected with the inaccuracy that led to the underlying penalty. The relevant offshore asset move occurred after 26 March 2015;
- the relevant offshore asset move occurred after the relevant time;
- the main purpose or one of the main purposes of moving the asset to another territory was to prevent or delay discovery by HMRC of the inaccuracy that led to the underlying penalty.

The offshore asset move penalty is 50% of the amount of the underlying penalty and is in addition to that underlying penalty.

FINANCE ACT 2016

Further developments in relation to offshore tax investigations

5.117 The Government introduced yet further legislation within *Finance Act 2016* in the area of offshore tax, demonstrating their continued determination to ensure full tax compliance in this area, or some would say which might risk some from undertaking cross-border business altogether.

The changes within *Finance Act 2016* of particular interest are:

- Offences relating to offshore income, assets and activities;
- Penalties for enablers of offshore tax evasion or non-compliance;
- Penalties in connection with offshore matters and offshore transfers;
- Asset-based penalties for offshore inaccuracies and failures.

Offences relating to offshore income, assets and activities (*FA 2016, s 166*)

5.118 This offence is criminal in nature rather than civil, and is in point where a person fails to submit a tax return, fails to notify liability, or submits an incorrect return in relation to income tax or capital gains tax. The offence relates to offshore income, assets or activities.

The main significance of this offence is the lack of a link between the offence and the underlying behaviour (eg careless or deliberate), which in criminal standard terms generally require deliberate intent. With this new offence, there

5.119 *Offshore tax investigations*

is no requirement of HMRC to demonstrate that same link to behaviour, and so the worry is that taxpayers could potentially fall foul of this offence (which it is important to stress is a criminal one) by the mere fact they are non-compliant and offshore matters are involved.

There are some safeguards in that the person charged with the offence can argue 'reasonable excuse'. Also, HMRC has introduced a £25,000 threshold.

HMRC have suggested that they will limit this new offence to tax matters relating to offshore jurisdictions who have not signed up to automatic exchange of information under the Common Reporting Standard (CRS).

Penalties for enablers of offshore tax evasion or non-compliance (*FA 2016, s 162*)

5.119 This offence also brings in some very significant developments, this time for those who advise clients in relation to offshore tax matters.

Whilst this is a civil penalty, it focuses on what is essentially deliberate behaviour. An offence is committed when two conditions are met in relation to the adviser's relationship with the client, and the client commits a relevant offshore tax offence, or non-compliance.

The first condition is that the adviser knew that their actions could assist the client in committing tax evasion or offshore tax evasion.

The second condition is that the client has been convicted of a tax offence, or in the case of offshore tax evasion or non-compliance, the client is liable to a relevant penalty.

As a relevant penalty includes any offshore civil penalty relating to offshore tax matters, there could be circumstances where an adviser is caught under this legislation for actions they have taken that resulted in their client becoming liable to a civil penalty, including carelessness.

The offence effectively extends to tax advisers, legal advisers, trustees, private bankers, and any intermediary based in or outside the UK who holds clients with offshore UK tax matters. However, for those advisers located offshore, it may be difficult for HMRC to charge an enabling penalty, given that it is a civil offence.

The offshore enabling legislation has been developed to ensure that it also catches the 'turn a blind eye' scenario, as well as more significant deliberate offshore tax evasion assistance.

If found liable to a penalty under this legislation, the adviser could be liable to a penalty of the greater of £3,000 or 100% of the tax lost. Reductions are possible to these penalties for unprompted disclosures. In the case of an unprompted disclosure the penalty can be reduced to the greater of £1,000 or 10% of the tax lost, or in cases of prompted disclosures to the greater of £3,000 or 30% of the tax lost.

Penalties in connection with offshore matters and offshore transfers (*FA 2016, s 163*)

5.120 The civil penalty regime for offshore penalties is also further increased. Offshore civil penalties were introduced by *Finance Act 2010*, and essentially increase the civil penalties for errors regime (in *FA 2007, Sch 24*) and failure to notify regime (under *FA 2008, Sch 41*), where income tax and capital gains tax are in point and the offences relate to jurisdictions which HMRC have determined as falling into higher penalty categories. The categories are 0, 1, 2 and 3, ultimately arising from HMRC's view of that jurisdiction's commitment to exchange of information and transparency.

Whereas the general maximum penalty for inaccuracies and failure to notify is up to 100% of the 'potential lost revenue', the maximum penalty for (say) a category 3 jurisdiction penalty is 200%. The same principles apply for offshore penalties in relation to minimum penalties for prompted and unprompted disclosures. *Finance Act 2016* essentially increases those minimum penalties by 10% where the underlying behaviour is deliberate.

HMRC has also stated that it is introducing new requirements where reductions to penalties are sought, requiring details of structures used, how funds were transferred offshore and importantly requiring the identification of any enabler who facilitated the evasion.

Amendments have also been made to the 'publishing deliberate defaulter' legislation (*FA 2009, s 94*). This will enable HMRC to publish the details of those who control offshore companies and partnerships, where the person who is subject to the offshore deliberate penalty is the body itself.

Asset-based penalties (*FA 2016, s 165*)

5.121 HMRC has introduced a new asset-based civil penalty for cases involving civil offshore penalties and the potential lost revenue exceeds a threshold of £25,000.

The penalty is in point where the offshore penalties relate to deliberate behaviour and the tax involved is capital gains tax, inheritance tax and asset-based income tax.

5.122 *Offshore tax investigations*

The standard amount of the penalty will be limited to the lower of 10% of the value of the asset or ten times the potential lost revenue.

The legislation states that HMRC must reduce any penalty charged where the person makes a disclosure of the inaccuracy or failure relating to the standard offshore tax penalty, provides HMRC with a reasonable valuation of the asset, or provides HMRC with information or access to records that HMRC requires for the purposes of valuing the asset.

The reduction must reflect the quality of the disclosure, valuation and information provided (and for these purposes 'quality' includes timing, nature and extent). Further regulations are required setting out the maximum amount of the penalty reduction.

CRIMINAL FINANCES ACT 2017

5.122 The *Criminal Finances Act 2017* (CFA) introduced the Corporate Criminal Offences of Failure to prevent facilitation of UK tax evasion offences (*CFA, s 45*) and Failure to prevent facilitation of foreign tax evasion offences (*CFA, s 46*).

CFA attained Royal Assent on 27 April 2017.

The two offences are serious, in that they both carry sanctions of up to an unlimited fine against any legal body found guilty.

The offences can be applied to any 'relevant body', which essentially means any legal body (including companies and partnerships) wherever they are located or formed. Importantly, relevant bodies are responsible for actions of persons associated with them, as explained further below.

There is effectively a precondition for both forms of the offences requiring a person to have committed a criminal tax offence.

Failure to prevent facilitation of UK tax evasion offences

5.123 In terms of the UK offence, CFA states that a relevant body is guilty of an offence if a person commits a UK tax evasion facilitation offence when acting in the capacity of a person associated with the body.

A UK tax evasion facilitation offence is an offence under the law of:

(a) being knowingly concerned in, or in taking steps with a view to, the fraudulent evasion of a tax by another person;

(b) aiding, abetting, counselling or procuring the commission of a UK tax evasion offence; or

(c) being involved art and part in the commission of an offence consisting of being knowingly concerned in, or in taking steps with a view to, the fraudulent evasion of a tax.

UK tax evasion offence for the purposes of the offence means:

(a) an offence of cheating the public revenue; or

(b) an offence under the law of any part of the United Kingdom consisting of being knowingly concerned in, or in taking steps with a view to, the fraudulent evasion of a tax.

Failure to prevent facilitation of foreign tax evasion offences

5.124 In terms of the Foreign offence, CFA states that a relevant body is guilty of an offence if a person commits a foreign tax evasion facilitation offence when acting in the capacity of a person associated with the body, and:

(a) that body is incorporated, or a partnership formed, under the law of any part of the United Kingdom; or

(b) carries on business or part of a business in the United Kingdom; or

(c) any conduct constituting part of the foreign tax evasion facilitation offence takes place in the United Kingdom.

Foreign tax evasion facilitation offence is defined as conduct which:

(a) amounts to an offence under the law of a foreign country;

(b) relates to the commission by another person of a foreign tax evasion offence under that law; and

(c) would, if the foreign tax evasion offence were a UK tax evasion offence, amount to a UK tax evasion facilitation offence (see 5.122 above).

Foreign tax evasion offence means conduct which:

(a) amounts to an offence under the law of a foreign country;

(b relates to a breach of a duty relating to a tax imposed under the law of that country; and

(c) would be regarded by the courts of any part of the United Kingdom as amounting to being knowingly concerned in, or in taking steps with a view to, the fraudulent evasion of that tax.

5.125 *Offshore tax investigations*

THE FOREIGN OFFENCE

Associated Person

5.125 The definition wording of an Associated Person is quite broad.

The legislation states that a person is associated with a relevant body if it is:

(a) an employee, acting in that capacity;

(b) an agent of the body (other than an employee) who is acting in the capacity of an agent; or

(c) any other person who performs services for or on behalf of the body who is acting in the capacity of a person performing such services.

It is important to look at all relevant circumstances and not merely by the strict nature of the relationship between the person and the body. The contractual status or say, job title, of a person performing services for or on behalf of the relevant body does not necessarily matter; employees, agents and sub-contractors can be associated persons.

Defence of Reasonable Procedures

5.126 For both the UK and Foreign offence, the legislation states that it is a defence for the body to prove that, when the UK tax evasion facilitation offence was committed:

(a) it had in place such prevention procedures as it was reasonable in all the circumstances to expect B to have in place; or

(b) it was not reasonable in all the circumstances to expect B to have any prevention procedures in place.

The practical application of the offences involves looking at three stages:

- Stage one: there has been criminal tax evasion by a taxpayer (either an individual or a legal entity) under existing law.

- Stage two: there has been criminal facilitation of that tax evasion by an 'associated person' of the relevant body.

- Stage three: there has been criminal facilitation of the tax evasion by an "associated person" of the relevant body.

Without all three stages, the offences will not be triggered.

HMRC GUIDANCE

5.127 HMRC issued guidance on the new offences, including guidance on reasonable procedures, on 1 September 2017, and this became law on 30 September 2017, by virtue of the Facilitation of Tax Evasion Offences (Guidance About Prevention) Regulations 2017, SI 876. The HMRC guidance sets out that any Reasonable Procedures should incorporate consideration of the following areas:

– Proportionality of risk based prevention procedures.
– Top level commitment.
– Due diligence.
– Communication (including training).
– Monitoring and review.

A reasonable approach to developing reasonable procedures would be to undertake some sort of tax risk assessment of the body. There is clearly a cross over between for example Anti Money Laundering procedures, but one would suggest that that a tax risk review might cover areas, beyond specific AML threats.

Given the reference to Top Level Commitment, it would seem appropriate to develop any procedures in consultation with the senior management team of the relevant body.

Once the procedures have been developed, they should have 'life' and so one would expect those procedures to be reviewed regularly, and updated as necessary.

WORLDWIDE DISCLOSURE FACILITY (WDF)

5.128 On 5 September 2016, HMRC launched a new offshore disclosure facility, the Worldwide Disclosure Facility (WDF).

Who can use the facility?

5.129 The facility is open to anyone who wants to disclose a UK tax liability that relates wholly or partly to an offshore issue. For the terms of the facility this includes unpaid or omitted tax relating to:

- income arising from a source in a territory outside the UK;
- assets situated or held in a territory outside the UK;
- activities carried on wholly or mainly in a territory outside the UK.

5.130 *Offshore tax investigations*

The facility extends to funds connected to unpaid or omitted UK tax that have been transferred to a territory outside the UK or are owned in a territory outside the UK.

HMRC has stated that if a person has previously made a settlement following an in-depth enquiry or disclosure, they will consider the new disclosure for further investigation and if it covers the same period, higher penalties could be charged.

The facility carries no immunity from prosecution and so, depending on what is being disclosed HMRC could commence criminal investigation with a view to prosecution. This is also potentially the case where a second disclosure is being made, as set out above.

Registering for the facility

5.130 HMRC guidance links to HMRC's Digital Disclosure Service (DDS) (www.gov.uk/government/publications/hm-revenue-and-customs-disclosure-service) to register. It also states that the following is required:

- name;
- address;
- national insurance number;
- unique tax reference;
- date of birth;
- the name, reference and contact details of any agent acting for you.

Once registration has taken place, the person has 90 days to submit their disclosure.

The terms of the facility

5.131 The terms are that the person:

- must be eligible;
- must make a full disclosure of all previously undisclosed UK tax liabilities;
- must calculate interest and penalties based on the existing legislation.

Any disclosure requires self assessing of behaviours, assessing periods and penalties.

HMRC, however, makes it quite clear that if an incomplete disclosure is made, they may:

- apply a higher penalty than we would if you'd provided the information voluntarily;
- open a civil or criminal investigation;
- publish the person's details on the HMRC website.

They also stress the point that an incomplete disclosure could result in them commencing a criminal investigation.

Pre-disclosure agreement

5.132 One of the interesting aspects of the new Worldwide Disclosure Facility is the opportunity to seek clarification of complex issues before submitting the disclosure.

The pre-clearance route is only open to those who have already registered to make a disclosure of offshore liabilities through the Digital Disclosure Service.

Where the person has registered and pre-clearance is sought, the person will be allowed 90 days from the time that the application for clarification is finalised, rather than the from the date of registration.

Legal interpretation

5.133 One point of particular note for the Worldwide Disclosure Facility is that where any part of the liabilities within the disclosure have been reduced because of consideration and interpretation of the law, HMRC requires that as part of the disclosure, the person sets this out. This includes the following:

- residence;
- domicile;
- remittance basis;
- trust issues;
- inheritance tax issues.

Assets

5.134 HMRC also requires the person making a disclosure to set out the maximum value of assets they held overseas at any point in the five years prior

5.135 *Offshore tax investigations*

to the disclosure date. The value must be converted to sterling and the person is required to disclose the main location of these assets, and if there are multiple jurisdictions involved, the main three locations.

REQUIREMENT TO CORRECT OFFENCE (RTC) (FINANCE (NO. 2) ACT 2017)

5.135 *Finance (No. 2) Act 2017, Sch 18* sets out the legislation for the Requirement to Correct (RTC) Offence.

The new offence came into force from 6 April 2017 and requires those persons with offshore non compliance in relation to income tax, capital gains tax and inheritance tax to make good that non compliance before 30 September 2018.

The RTC is timed to coincide with automatic exchange of information through the Common Reporting Standard (CRS).

Any person who has not rectified past 'relevant offshore tax non-compliance' by 30 September 2018, covering periods up to and including 5 April 2017 will face significant penalties.

The person will have relevant offshore tax non-compliance if the following three conditions are met.

Condition A is that the original offshore tax non-compliance has not been fully corrected before the end of the 2016/17 tax year.

Condition B is that:
(a) the original offshore tax non-compliance involved a potential loss of revenue when it was committed; and
(b) if the original offshore tax non-compliance has been corrected in part by the end of the 2016/17 tax year, the uncorrected part involves a potential loss of revenue.

Condition C is that on 6 April 2017 it would have been lawful for HMRC to assess the person concerned to any tax the liability to which would have been disclosed to or discovered by HMRC:
(a) where the original offshore tax non-compliance has not been corrected before the end of the 2016/17 tax year, had that offshore tax non-compliance not occurred; or
(b) where the original offshore tax non-compliance has been corrected in part by that time, had the uncorrected part not occurred.

'Tax non-compliance' means any of the following in relation to income tax, capital gains tax or inheritance tax:

(a) a failure to notify chargeability;

(b) a failure to deliver a return or other document within the filing date; or

(c) delivering to HMRC a return or other document which contains an inaccuracy which amounts to, or leads to:

   (i) an understatement of a liability to tax;

   (ii) a false or inflated statement of a loss; or

   (iii) a false or inflated claim to repayment of tax.

Correcting the offence and disclosure

5.136 Historic offshore non-compliance can be rectified in a number of ways.

Where it involves failing to file a return or failing to notify chargeability, it can be corrected by simply filing or notifying. Also, where an incorrect document has been submitted, filing a corrected document corrects the offshore non-compliance.

Where there is an ongoing enquiry the person can bring the matter to the attention of the HMRC officer.

HMRC launched a new Worldwide Disclosure Facility (WDF) on 5 September 2016 (See **5.128** above). The WDF amounts to one route to disclose and regularise any historical offshore non-compliance.

The Worldwide Disclosure Facility provides no protection from prosecution, so where historical tax fraud is at issue, it may be better to consider making a disclosure under Code of Practice 9 (Contractual Disclosure Facility).

The penalty for not correcting the offshore non-compliance by 30 September 2018 is 200% of the potential lost revenue attributable to the uncorrected offshore non-compliance.

There is scope to appeal against the penalty, and the usual reasonable excuse defence is available.

It is possible to reduce the penalty by making a disclosure to HMRC. However, the penalty after reduction cannot be lower than 100% of the PLR.

5.137 *Offshore tax investigations*

In terms of correcting the offshore non-compliance, there are various ways to do this, depending on whether the offence relates to failure to notify, non-filing of a tax return or the previous submission of an incorrect document.

In the case of rectifying the offence by notifying chargeability, HMRC require the person to notify, or if they have received a return by making and delivering the tax return. They are also required to provide HMRC with the relevant information:

(a) using the digital disclosure service or any other service provided by HMRC as a means of correcting tax noncompliance;

(b) communicating it to an officer of Revenue and Customs in the course of an enquiry into the person's tax affairs; or

(c) using a method agreed with an officer of Revenue and Customs.

5.137 In terms of a failure to submit a return, correction is made by:

(a) making or delivering the requisite return or document;

(b) using the digital disclosure service or any other service provided by HMRC as a means of correcting tax non-compliance;

(c) communicating it to an officer of Revenue and Customs in the course of an enquiry into the person's tax affairs; or

(d) using a method agreed with an officer of Revenue and Customs.

5.138 In terms of an incorrect return, correction is made by:

(a) in the case of an inaccurate tax document, amending the document or delivering a new document;

(b) using the digital disclosure service or any other service provided by HMRC as a means of correcting tax non-compliance;

(c) communicating it to an officer of Revenue and Customs in the course of an enquiry into the person's tax affairs, or

(d) using a method agreed with an officer of Revenue and Customs.

Assessments

5.139 As the RTC relates to any year that it is lawful for HMRC to assess, an RTC correction effectively requires a correction of any past years within the normal assessing time limits, depending on relevant behaviour:

- Reasonable care.
- Careless.
- Deliberate.

The normal time limits apply: four years, six years or 20 years, however, the RTC extends the time to apply those time limits, such that HMRC has up until 4 April 2021 to assess any matters that were in time at 5 April 2017.

Penalties

5.140 The main penalty for failing to correct (FTC) offshore non-compliance is a 200% penalty of the potential lost revenue attributable to the uncorrected offshore noncompliance

There is a double jeopardy clause in the legislation that states where a penalty has already been charged on a matter, then there will not also be an FTC penalty.

However, where an FTC penalty can be charged, in parallel with the wider approach to offshore penalties, additional penalty measures can be considered, including:

- An asset-based penalty of up to 10% of the asset value, where the person was aware they had offshore non-compliance to correct and the amount was over £25,000.
- A further 50% penalty if assets have been moved to avoid exchange of information.
- Publishing the name of the person.

Reduction in penalties

5.141 The legislation allows for HMRC to reduce the penalty for any uncorrected relevant offshore tax non-compliance if the person who is liable to the penalty discloses the matter to HMRC.

A person discloses the matter to HMRC by:

(a) telling HMRC about it,

(b) giving HMRC reasonable help in relation to the matter (for example by quantifying an inaccuracy in a document),

(c) informing HMRC of any person who acted as an enabler of the relevant offshore tax non-compliance or the failure to correct it, and

(d) allowing HMRC access to records:

    (i) for any reasonable purpose connected with resolving the matter (for example for the purpose of ensuring that an inaccuracy in a document is fully corrected), and

5.142 *Offshore tax investigations*

(ii) for the purpose of ensuring that HMRC can identify all persons who may have acted as an enabler of the relevant offshore tax non-compliance or the failure to correct it.

Where a person is liable to a penalty and discloses the matter HMRC must reduce the penalty to one that reflects the quality of the disclosure, but the penalty may not be reduced below 100% of the offshore PLR.

The reduction will be calculated using the same principles for wider penalties, taking into account: Telling, Helping and Access.

Appeals

5.142 The legislation provides for appeals to be made in relation to either the decision to charge a penalty, or the amount of the penalty.

Reasonable Excuse

5.143 There is also scope to argue reasonable excuse.

However, as with other aspects of penalty legislation the legislation states that an insufficiency of funds is not a reasonable excuse.

The legislation also sets out that where the person who has failed to correct has relied on any other person to do anything, that cannot be a reasonable excuse unless they took reasonable care to avoid the failure and where they had a reasonable excuse but the excuse has ceased, the failure is remedied without unreasonable delay after the excuse ceased.

In line with the other proposed legislation for avoidance, reliance on advice is to be taken automatically not to be a reasonable excuse if it is disqualified. Advice is disqualified if

(a) the advice was given by an interested person,

(b) the advice was given as a result of arrangements made between an interested person and the person who gave the advice,

(c) the person who gave the advice did not have appropriate expertise for giving the advice,

(d) the advice failed to take account of the person's individual circumstances, or

(e) the advice was addressed to, or was given to, a person other than the person.

Offshore tax investigations **5.143**

An interested person, in relation to any relevant offshore tax non-compliance means:

(a) a person (other than P) who participated in relevant avoidance arrangements or any transaction forming part of them, or

(b) a person who for any consideration (whether or not in money) facilitated P's entering into relevant avoidance arrangements.

'Avoidance arrangements' means arrangements as respects which, in all the circumstances, it would be reasonable to conclude that their main purpose, or one of their main purposes, is the obtaining of a tax advantage.

A 'tax advantage' includes relief or increased relief, repayment, avoidance or deferral of tax.

Case study 5.1 – Undeclared Swiss bank account

UK resident/domicile holding Swiss bank account since 1992. Not declared to HMRC. Higher rate taxpayer.

Details of income

Opening balance £350,000

Interest

1992	£17,000
1993	£17,100
1994	£17,500
1995	£18,000
1996	£18,100
1997	£18,500
1998	£18,500
1999	£19,000
2000	£19,000
2001	£19,000
2002	£19,200
2003	£19,500
2004	£19,750
2005	£20,000
2006	£20,200

5.143 *Offshore tax investigations*

2007	£20,500
2008	£10,000
2009	£10,000
2010	£10,000
2011	£12,000
Balance 31/12/02	£550,000
Balance 31/12/10	£750,000
Balance 31/12/12	£780,000

General disclosure to HMRC

20-year disclosure (back to 1996)

Tax

Interest	£326,075
Tax (40%)	£130,430
Interest say	£83,000
Penalty (35%)	£45,000
Total	£258,430

LDF disclosure

Disclosure back to 1999

Tax

Interest	£199,150
Tax (40%)	£79,660
Interest say	£31,000
Penalty (10% to 2009)	
(20% 2010 onwards)	
Total	£110,660

UK/Swiss

Cb (balance at end 31/12/02)	£550,000
Cr (higher of balance 31/12/10 or 31/12/12)	£780,000
N (number of years before 31/12/10)	8

C9 (Cr times 103%)	£803,400
C10 (Cr times 106%)	£826,800
Average C9 and C10	£815,100

Apply formula

34%(2/3(Cr−n/8*Cb)+1/3(n/10*Cr+2/10*average C9/C10))
34%(2/3 (780,000−550000)+1/3(8/10*780,000+2/10*815,100))
34%(2/3 (230,000)+1/3(624,000+163,020))
34%(2/3(230,000)+1/3(460,980))
34%(153333+153,660)
34%(306,993)
Equals £104,377 (amounts to 13%, therefore minimum is 21%)
21% of £780,000 is £163,800

Comparison

20-year disclosure	£258,430
LDF disclosure	£110,660
UK/Swiss one-off payment for offshore investigations	£163,800

KEY POINTS

5.144 The following key points are intended as an aide to understanding the challenges practitioners need to consider, and assist clients in evaluating relevant tax exposures and whether some form of offshore disclosure might be required:

1. Establish the client's tax position, particularly in relation to overseas assets, including residence and domicile.

2. Establish whether the client has any tax exposure resulting from overseas assets.

3. Establish whether the client has received any correspondence from HMRC, recently or historically in relation to offshore assets.

4. Consider the risks from any exposure, particularly, in relation to criminal or civil offences.

5. Consider whether a disclosure should be made to HMRC to set out any exposure and minimise penalties, criminal or civil.

Chapter 6

Practical aspects of an enquiry

Mark McLaughlin CTA (Fellow) ATT (Fellow) TEP
Mark McLaughlin Associates Ltd, Chartered Tax Advisers; Consultant, The TACS Partnership

> **SIGNPOSTS**
>
> - **Scope** – The self-assessment enquiry process is part of statute law. HMRC enquiries can be 'full' or 'aspect'. Guidance on HMRC practice in enquiries is set out in the Enquiry manual. (See **6.1–6.5**.)
>
> - **Preliminary issues** – Enquiry work can often be time consuming for practitioners; fees can quickly escalate. The question of fees should be raised with clients at an early stage (see **6.6–6.9**). Practitioners should undertake their own critical analysis of client tax returns before they are submitted, and ensure that full explanations are given for any entries (eg low business drawings) which could trigger an HMRC enquiry (see **6.10–6.13**). Clients should be educated regarding record keeping, and practitioners should ensure wherever possible that clients keep and maintain adequate records from the outset. (see **6.14–6.18**).
>
> - **The people involved** – Enquiries can be highly stressful for some taxpayers; the practitioner's job is to support and represent his client through the enquiry to the best of his ability. HMRC officers are trained in enquiries and meeting procedures, so the practitioner must be fully prepared. Consideration should be given to whether it would be in the client's best interest for the enquiry or investigation to be handled in-house, or whether an external specialist should be engaged instead. (See **6.19–6.32**.)
>
> - **Practicalities** – Practitioners should have requisite knowledge and understanding of the tax legislation as it applies to enquiry work, and an awareness of HMRC practice from guidance such as the Enquiry manual and Compliance Handbook manual (see **6.33–6.37**). Most practices offer fee protection insurance to their clients, to wholly or partly cover the additional professional fees incurred in an enquiry (see **6.38–6.40**). The formalities of the enquiry should

be carefully checked and monitored (eg whether the enquiry notice has been given to the taxpayer within the statutory time limit). (see **6.41–6.51**).

- **Controversial points** – Areas of potential difficulty during an enquiry include HMRC requests for a taxpayer's private records (ie whether such requests are justified), and unannounced visits by HMRC officers to taxpayers' business premises. (see **6.52–6.60**).

- **Meetings** – HMRC officers often request meetings with taxpayers during an enquiry. The taxpayer is not obliged to accept such requests (note: criminal investigations are a different matter). The practitioner must decide whether a meeting is in the best interest of his client. If so, consideration should be given to the most appropriate venue. It is also important to obtain a detailed agenda from HMRC in advance of the meeting. Practitioners should take their own notes at meetings, if possible. If HMRC produces meeting notes, they should be reviewed carefully for any errors or omissions, but in general should not be formally approved or signed. (See **6.61–6.79**.)

- **Other issues** – Requests by HMRC for client business appointment diaries should be approached with caution, particularly where a diary also contains sensitive personal information (see **6.80–6.81**). Practitioners should be prepared to seek expert professional help in appropriate cases, such as where the enquiry has the potential to escalate into something more serious. (see **6.82–6.83**).

- **Resolving disputes** – If a dispute arises with HMRC during the enquiry, consideration should be given to whether the 'alternative dispute resolution' procedure might provide an effective solution. (see **6.84–6.87**).

- **Appeals to the tribunal** – Practitioners should not be afraid of taking a case to the tribunal where it is considered that the HMRC officer has exceeded his powers. There have been numerous cases dealing with issues such as the validity of enquiry notices and applications for the tribunal to direct HMRC to issue closure notices. Taxpayers have also achieved some success before the tribunal in challenging HMRC assessments of additional business profits. (See **6.88–6.103**.)

- **Settlement** – If penalties for inaccuracies are in point, it may be necessary to negotiate the level of such penalties with HMRC (although no penalty is in point if an error has arisen despite 'reasonable care' having been taken). Consideration should also be given to whether there are any 'special circumstances' giving rise to a possible reduction in penalties, and whether the circumstances are appropriate for penalties to be suspended in cases involving careless inaccuracy. (See **6.104–6.118**.)

6.1 *Practical aspects of an enquiry*

- **Final points** – For errors involving deliberate inaccuracy, HMRC's powers to 'name and shame' offenders should be noted where relevant, The taxpayer may also be subject to HMRC's 'managing serious defaulters' programme. (See **6.119–6.120**.)
- **Complaints procedures** – For clients and practitioners with genuine grievances about the way in which HMRC has handled the enquiry, there are possible alternative ways to lodge complaints. (see **6.121–6.127**).
- **Key points** – Ten suggestions for the enquiry practitioner are included at **6.128**.

INTRODUCTION

6.1 HMRC enquiries and investigations are not an exact science. HMRC has described self-assessment as a 'process now/check later' regime. HMRC practice in connection with tax enquiries and investigations has been built up and refined over many years.

6.2 HMRC's current practices when dealing with enquiries (insofar as not restricted under the *Freedom of Information Act 2000*) is contained in the Enquiry manual, which is readily accessible via the GOV.UK website (www.gov.uk/hmrc-internal-manuals/enquiry-manual).

HMRC's Compliance Handbook manual also provides useful guidance on matters including penalties for inaccuracies and record keeping (www.gov.uk/hmrc-internal-manuals/compliance-handbook).

6.3 Historically, HMRC always seems to be looking at ways of increasing its efficiency in activities including enquiry work. For example, its 'single compliance process' (SCP) was built around a single framework for dealing with the majority of small and medium-sized business compliance checks. The SCP was designed to concentrate solely on the risks identified in an enquiry, using four different levels of intensity proportionate to those risks. HMRC's operation of the SCP involves a five-stage process (ie planning, contact, process, resolve and close). HMRC's stated aim for the SCP was:

> 'improving the quality and consistency of our enquiry work by adopting a more collaborative approach with business and their agents, increasing the efficiency and effectiveness of our workforce, reducing unnecessary delays and focussing solely on the aspects that we need to.'

Following a trial of the SCP which ended on 31 March 2013, HMRC has now adopted the process as standard practice.

6.4 The self-assessment enquiry is part of statute law. *TMA 1970, ss 9A and 12AC* make provision for an enquiry into the tax return of an individual (eg a sole trader) or a partnership business. Company tax return enquiries are dealt with under *FA 1998, Sch 18, para 24*. This chapter is mainly concerned with individuals and partnerships, although many of the issues raised will similarly apply in relation to company tax return enquiries.

6.5 Self-assessment enquiries can be 'full' or 'aspect'. HMRC can investigate the affairs of a business or individual without reason. This is commonly known as the 'random' enquiry. Only a small number of such enquiries take place each year, but no professional practice can be sure that its clients will not be investigated under this criteria. HMRC staff are instructed to adopt a 'neutral' approach and not to distinguish random enquiries from other enquiries (EM1503), which perhaps removes some of the stigma that might otherwise attach to an individual (and his agent) who is subject to an HMRC enquiry.

> **Focus**
>
> Every firm of accountants, tax advisers and tax consultants therefore has to confront the idea that one or more of its clients will be subject to an enquiry in any given tax year. The purpose of this chapter is to highlight some of the practical points that professional advisers should consider both before and during an enquiry.

For guidance on the conduct of enquiries, see **CHAPTER 8**.

PRELIMINARY ISSUES: COSTS

6.6 Readers may be surprised that the subject of costs comes at the beginning of this chapter, but enquiry work is a costly business, and fees can escalate quickly due to the amount of time, effort and manpower put into the job. This presents a potentially significant problem, particularly where the client is of modest means.

6.7 Sadly, in some instances a commercial decision has to be made not to oppose HMRC's submissions regarding additional tax due, solely on the ground that additional work in representing the client would not be cost-effective.

In some instances, the practitioner should consider completing *pro bono* work for the client on principle where there is clear inequity simply to make a stand against HMRC, whose resources by comparison may seem relatively boundless. This will not only benefit the client, but taxpayers and the professions as a

6.8 *Practical aspects of an enquiry*

whole. It is not healthy for HMRC always to have its own way, and its officers will generally respect those practitioners who legitimately stand up to them.

6.8 Sometimes the taxpayer, and perhaps most or all of the clients in the practice, will have the benefit of fee protection insurance in connection with investigations. This may be helpful, and is considered further below (see **6.38–6.40**).

6.9 Whatever the position, the fee question must be discussed with the client at the outset of the enquiry or investigation, and not at the end. Some practices ask for a payment on account before any work at all is commenced. Others rely on monthly billing of fees. It must be recognised, however, that this is a crucial aspect of enquiry work, as untimely representation without discussion could result in a large unpaid fee.

RECOGNISE THE SIGNS

6.10 Most tax returns and accounts are not subject to enquiry. Those tax returns and accounts which are enquired into are examined by HMRC to see if there are any obvious flaws that could invite adjustments. The practitioner must be aware of these flaws.

6.11 Large, 'one-off' transactions, such as a business or share disposal by an individual where entrepreneurs' relief has been claimed, may attract HMRC's attention (eg in terms of checking that the relief conditions are satisfied).

6.12 In the case of business owners, varying, and low, profit ratios are an obvious target for HMRC. So are low business drawings in cases where the taxpayer's only living expenses come from that source. Unexplained increases in the capital account will also invite HMRC's attention.

6.13 It should be remembered that professional advisers have a duty under the money laundering legislation to consider reporting unexplained capital accretions, on pain of committing a criminal act if they do not do so.

For further information regarding selection criteria for an enquiry, see **CHAPTER 7**.

Focus

'Disclosure' must be the keyword of the tax practitioner. Aside from preventing an unnecessary enquiry, tax return disclosures must be sufficient to prevent HMRC invoking the 'discovery' legislation outside the normal enquiry window.

> Practitioners must therefore undertake their own critical analysis of tax returns and accounts before they are submitted. Will the material stand up to examination by a compliance officer? Judicious use of the 'white space' in the return is advised, as well as explanation in supporting documentation. However, it should be remembered that other documents may become separated from the return when it is processed by HMRC.

PRACTICE MANAGEMENT

6.14 It is important for the practitioner to maintain a good standard of office systems. This extends to 'clean' working papers and accessible files and correspondence. Copies of emails should be printed out and filed with client documents. Best practice would also involve maintaining separate files (preferably of a different colour to the client's correspondence, tax and other files) for enquiry work.

6.15 Most importantly, clients should be educated regarding record-keeping, both to assist the practice and comply with the provisions of *TMA 1970, s 12B* ('Records to be kept for purposes of returns'). For companies, the duty to keep and preserve records is contained in *FA 1998, Sch 18, para 21* ('Duty to keep and preserve records').

6.16 Every practice has its share of recalcitrant clients, but they are an increasing liability in these days of investigation and compliance, and may even invite the attention of HMRC to the practice. In some instances, it may be necessary for the practitioner to be strong and decline to act further for such taxpayers. The rules and practice guidelines of the practitioner's professional body should be closely followed.

6.17 Until relatively recently, HMRC could initiate business records checks (BRCs), which were targeted in-year compliance checks to test the adequacy of statutory business records. BRCs were designed to bring about record-keeping improvements in smaller businesses. Failure to keep adequate records could result in HMRC seeking to impose penalties for continued non-compliance. However, HMRC announced towards the end of 2015 that BRCs were being phased out, with no new ones being undertaken.

Nevertheless, HMRC can use its information powers to give written notice requiring a person to provide information or produce documents, and/or to inspect business premises etc., if reasonably required to check their tax position (*FA 2008, Sch 36*). Those powers effectively provide for in-year inspections in appropriate circumstances.

6.18 *Practical aspects of an enquiry*

Practitioners should ensure wherever possible that clients keep and maintain adequate records from the outset. For commentary on the examination of records and review of systems by HMRC, see **CHAPTER 16**.

6.18 Practitioners will also need to check whether their firm's existing client engagement letter covers HMRC enquiries, and if necessary issue a separate engagement letter to the client for the enquiry work.

The major tax and accounting bodies offer guidance for their members on engagement letters. For example, the Chartered Institute of Taxation's guidance on engagement letters can be accessed via its website (www.tax.org.uk/professional-standards/engagement-letters), featuring templates including an Appendix in respect of HMRC civil tax investigations and enquiries.

THE PEOPLE INVOLVED

The taxpayer

6.19 The taxpayer, who is also your client, may well be angry and aggrieved at being subject to an enquiry, and also stressed and fearful. It is your job to support him through the enquiry. You may not be trained in psychology, but enquiry work demands far more than number crunching.

6.20 The starting point is that the taxpayer must be persuaded to tell you the complete truth, even if he has not yet done so to HMRC. This should be made clear to him at your opening meeting, and any failure in this respect should result in you ceasing to act immediately.

6.21 You will then have a relationship which may last for months or even years, until the matter is concluded. It is your job to support a 'layman' taxpayer all the way to settlement, and to represent him to the very best of your ability. Enquiries and investigations are extremely stressful for taxpayers, and it is not unknown for a prolonged enquiry to affect the health of the client and/or his spouse. Practitioners need to be aware of such happenings, and if necessary to consider them in negotiations with HMRC.

The HMRC officer

6.22 The HMRC officer will be highly trained and will view a successful enquiry as a positive step in his career progress. HMRC officers are trained in enquiries and meeting procedures, and often in appeals to the tribunal. You face a formidable opponent, supported by the might of a large bureaucratic organisation. It is important to try and find out as much as possible about

Practical aspects of an enquiry **6.25**

your opponent. Is he fully trained? What were the previous posts held within HMRC? Has there been any connection in the past with the Fraud Investigation Service (FIS) (or its predecessors, special investigations (SI) or criminal investigations)? You are probably going to spend time negotiating with this person, so also spend some time in assessing the opposition.

6.23 There are variations in grades and experience. For example, officers who have started life at HMRC as collectors in what is now debt management and banking, or who previously worked on PAYE compliance checks, may have less of a technical background than others. Conversely, every area office has a compliance manager, who should be respected, if not feared. He may perhaps have an FIS (or SI) background, or have previously been the officer in charge of another area.

6.24 If you and your client agree to a meeting with the HMRC officer (see **6.61**), it is important to ascertain who will be present from HMRC. If someone will attend other than the enquiring officer, who is he? The area compliance manager perhaps, or even someone from FIS? Forewarned is forearmed.

Example 6.1 – Who are they?

HMRC officers often attend meetings with clients and agents in pairs (or more). A list of attendees should be requested in advance of meetings with HMRC. There may be an innocent explanation for multiple attendees (eg to enable one of them to ask questions, and the other to take notes). However, the specific reason why an HMRC officer is attending in addition to the case worker should be ascertained.

The author has attended a meeting in which the additional HMRC officer seemed unusually reluctant to reveal his identity or purpose, until insistence that he does so revealed that the officer was highly experienced in a particular technical area of the enquiry. Taxpayers have a right to know who is asking them questions, so agents should be persistent in the best interests of their client.

HMRC has previously stated that (what was then) SI inspectors would be assigned to local compliance offices, and would attend meetings with taxpayers in conjunction with the investigating officer. This may be considered a somewhat sinister development in an enquiry case, and makes it doubly important that the practitioner is prepared and equipped for the task.

6.25 Most HMRC officers deal with enquiry work in a professional and reasonable manner. A very small minority do not. It is possible to encounter

6.26 *Practical aspects of an enquiry*

an aggressive and confrontational individual who does not keep to HMRC guidelines. This makes it all the more important for the practitioner to 'know his stuff' and be able to deal with such a situation.

> **Focus**
>
> It is necessary to be aware of the taxpayer's charter (www.gov.uk/government/publications/your-charter/your-charter), and to ensure that it is properly applied.

6.26 'Your charter' was last amended in January 2016. The amended version broadly comprises seven taxpayer rights. It also contains seven obligations (ie what HMRC expects from taxpayers), namely: 'be honest and respect our staff; work with us to get things right; find out what you need to do and keep us informed; keep accurate records and protect your information; know what your representative does on your behalf; respond in good time; take reasonable care to avoid mistakes'.

The seven taxpayer rights (ie what the taxpayer can expect from HMRC) are reproduced below:

'Respect you and treat you as honest

Provide a helpful, efficient and effective service

Be professional and act with integrity

Protect your information and respect your privacy

Accept that someone else can represent you

Deal with complaints quickly and fairly

Tackle those who bend or break the rules'

6.27 In the context of a tax return enquiry, the taxpayer rights that practitioners should monitor in particular are the first and third above in respect of the HMRC officer's conduct during the enquiry, and the second in terms of HMRC's approach to the enquiry in general (eg in terms of helping to keep the practitioner's professional fees to the client as low as possible).

6.28 Do not be afraid to make a complaint if the HMRC officer has acted inappropriately during an enquiry. Guidance on making complaints ('Complaints about HMRC') is published on the GOV.UK website (www.gov.uk/complain-about-hmrc).

A separate chapter of this book is devoted to complaints about HMRC (see **CHAPTER 23**).

The professional adviser

6.29 The role of the professional adviser is to represent the client to the very best of his ability. Each practitioner has to face the issue of whether he really wants to do enquiry work. Is the time and effort involved to the best advantage of the practice? Will the time spent on enquiries and investigations be detrimental to the other types of work undertaken and the profitability of the practice? Will it be in the client's best interest for the enquiry or investigation to be handled in-house, instead of engaging an external specialist? These are issues that have to be faced.

6.30 Larger firms tend to have their own tax enquiry and investigation departments, so that these issues do not arise. There are also many specialist investigation consultants and firms in practice, so that you can always consider asking one of them to deal with enquiries or investigations for your firm. A good number of HMRC officers have now moved to the private sector and are engaged in such work. This may be an advantage, for example, in a Code of Practice 9 investigation case where a phone call to a former FIS (or SI) colleague may help.

6.31 On the other hand, some former HMRC employees retain something of an HMRC mindset, which may be less than helpful in enquiry work. It is essential that the adviser is firmly on the side of the client, in the same way that a lawyer is in a criminal prosecution.

6.32 What is quite evident is that enquiry and investigation work is not a pleasant occupation. There is a need to be assertive without being rude. Each practitioner has to decide whether he is cut out for it or not. If not, it is better to delegate it to someone else.

PRACTICAL ISSUES

Be prepared

Research and training

6.33 Assuming that the practitioner is committed to undertaking enquiry work, he must be prepared. There is no substitute for experience, but there is plenty of written and other material to assist those determined to learn.

6.34 The starting point for individuals, trustees and partnerships is *TMA 1970*, which contains the basic legislation about HMRC enquiries, production of documents, interest and penalties. For companies, the relevant legislation is contained in *FA 1998, Sch 18*. An extensive array of HMRC powers has also evolved in subsequent legislation.

6.35 *Practical aspects of an enquiry*

The current provisions which the practitioner should study include (but are not restricted to) the following:

- *TMA 1970, ss 9A, 12AC* (notices of enquiry for individuals, trustees and partnerships);
- *FA 1998, Sch 18, para 24* (notices of enquiry for companies);
- *TMA 1970, ss 28A, 28B* (completion of enquiry for individuals, trustees and partnerships);
- *FA 1998, Sch 18, para 32* (completion of enquiry for companies);
- *TMA 1970, s 29* (assessment where loss of tax discovered – individuals and trustees);
- *FA 1998, Sch 18, para 41* (assessment where loss of tax discovered or determination of amount discovered to be incorrect – companies);
- *TMA 1970, s 36* (loss of tax brought about carelessly or deliberately, etc – income tax and capital gains tax);
- *FA 1998, Sch 18, para 46* (general time limit for assessments – companies);
- *FA 2009, ss 101–103; TMA 1970, ss 86–92* (interest on overdue tax);
- *FA 2007, Sch 24* (penalties for errors); and
- *FA 2008, Sch 36* (information and inspection powers).

6.35 The next port of call is the HMRC manuals. The importance placed on investigation and enquiry work by HMRC is illustrated by the comprehensive contents of the Enquiry manual.

There is also a Specialist Investigations Operational Guidance manual, which is aimed at HMRC staff working in specialist investigations, and a Fraud Civil Investigation manual for investigations under Code of Practice 9 and the contractual disclosure facility.

In addition, practitioners may find HMRC's Compliance Handbook manual helpful when dealing with issues such as penalties and HMRC information notices.

6.36 HMRC has also published a series of factsheets on subjects including compliance checks, HMRC's information and inspection powers, and penalties (tinyurl.com/HMRC-CRF).

It must be appreciated that the contents of HMRC manuals and factsheets are not the law, but represent the position of HMRC on any particular issue, and this proviso should always be borne in mind.

Practical aspects of an enquiry **6.40**

6.37 There is also a large array of resources in the private sector. Most professional publishers have books on enquiries and investigations, and the subject is a popular focus in magazines and journals. Conferences, courses, seminars and lectures on enquiries and investigations are always available, some arranged by the professional institutions, others by conference providers, and some by publishers. There is no excuse for not taking advantage of these resources.

Fee protection insurance

6.38 Some practices will take advantage of professional expenses insurance (often referred to as fee protection insurance). This is an insurance product in the context of tax, which relates to the additional professional fees incurred in an investigation.

6.39 Various schemes are offered by the insurance providers, such as those covering the firm's clients as a whole, but it is possible for an individual taxpayer to insure, though perhaps for a higher premium. This type of insurance is not a panacea, and one should not expect limitless cover for a modest premium. The insurance provider is in business to make money, and will work on the basis of an expected average fee per investigation. Practitioners should not, therefore, be surprised if the insurer places an upper limit on fees covered by the insurance, or seeks to limit the amount of work undertaken or prevent additional work which it deems not to be cost effective. Some insurers will even insist on taking over the enquiry work through in-house specialists.

6.40 Factors that the practitioner will need to consider are the cover offered, premiums and claims procedure of the company involved. The policy document and its small print are very important, as are the detailed conditions and exclusions. It is wise to 'shop around' and perhaps arrange a face-to-face meeting with the insurer before committing the practice and its clients to any one company.

DURING THE ENQUIRY

The formalities

> **Focus**
>
> Once the HMRC officer has initiated the enquiry, the practitioner needs to be aware of the formalities, and ensure that they have been adhered to.
>
> For example, has the enquiry notice been framed correctly? Has the enquiry notice been given to the taxpayer within the statutory time limit?

6.41 *Practical aspects of an enquiry*

6.41 It is important to check that the enquiry notice has been received by the taxpayer within the statutory time limit. It is not sufficient for HMRC merely to post an enquiry notice before the time limit; it must be received within that deadline. Unless it can be proved to the contrary, a notice sent by post is deemed to be received when it would arrive 'in the ordinary course of post' (*Interpretation Act 1978, s 7*). HMRC guidance states (EM1506):

> 'Your notice must be **received** before the time limit. The Courts assume that second class post takes 4 working days to be delivered and first class post takes 2 working days. Working days do not include Saturdays, Sundays or Bank Holidays.'

HMRC often issues enquiry notices close to the statutory deadline for doing so. The default position is that HMRC has a 12-month 'window' in which to open a tax return enquiry, although the time limit may be extended in certain circumstances (eg if the return is filed late).

Communication between taxpayer and agent (if there is one), and the extent of authority given by taxpayers to agents, can be particularly important in this context. For example, in *Tinkler v Revenue & Customs* [2018] UKUT 73 (TCC), an HMRC enquiry notice (under *TMA 1970, s 9A*) was held to be validly given to the taxpayer, even though he did not receive it, because a copy of the enquiry notice, which was sent to his agents, was sufficient notice to the taxpayer.

6.42 In the case of a singleton company, the statutory period is generally 'up to twelve months from the day on which the return was delivered' (*FA 1998, Sch 18, para 24(2)*). In *Dock & Let Ltd v Revenue & Customs* [2014] UKFTT 943 (TC), a tax return enquiry notice given by HMRC on the anniversary of the day on which the company's return was filed was held to be within the statutory period of 12 months from the day on which the return was delivered, and was therefore valid. This was broadly on the basis that 'from' was akin to 'after'.

For examples of cases in which taxpayers have successfully appealed against the issue of enquiry notices, see **6.88** *et seq*.

Example 6.2 – 'Discovery enquiries'

The author has encountered instances of HMRC attempting to open enquiries into the tax returns of individuals and partnerships outside the normal enquiry window using the discovery provisions in *TMA 1970, s 29*, but without having made a valid 'discovery' (for companies, the discovery provisions are in *FA 1998, Sch 18, para 41*).

Practical aspects of an enquiry **6.45**

> There is no statutory basis for HMRC to open a speculative 'discovery enquiry' of this nature in the hope of making an actual discovery during the course of the enquiry, and any attempts to do so should therefore be firmly resisted.
>
> For detailed commentary on discovery, see **CHAPTER 13**.

6.43 Aside from the statutory time limit, the enquiry notice should be checked carefully for other procedural or clerical errors. However, such errors will not necessarily invalidate the enquiry notice.

For example, in *Revenue and Customs v Mabbutt* [2017] UKUT 289 (TCC), HMRC issued by letter a notice of its intention to enquire (under *TMA 1970, s 9A*) into the appellant's tax return 'for the year ending *6 April 2009*' (emphasis added). The taxpayer appealed against HMRC's conclusions in the subsequent closure notice, and contended that an enquiry was not opened because no valid notice of enquiry was given.

The First-tier Tribunal concluded that HMRC's enquiry notice did not constitute a valid notice of enquiry into the taxpayer's return for the tax year ended 5 April 2009. Furthermore, *TMA 1970, s 114* (which broadly provides that assessments etc are not invalidated by errors in certain circumstances) did not apply to save the disputed notice. Without a valid enquiry notice, there was no enquiry. HMRC's purported closure notice therefore had no standing, and the taxpayer's appeal was therefore allowed.

However, the Upper Tribunal allowed HMRC's subsequent appeal. It held (among other things) that a reasonable taxpayer would have concluded that HMRC intended to open an enquiry, and that the reference to the year ended 6 April 2009 was simply a minor clerical slip.

6.44 Is it clear whether the enquiry is an aspect or full one? Is there any clue as to whether this is a random enquiry, or does HMRC have grounds for investigating? This will normally become apparent. Following submissions through the 'Working Together' initiative, HMRC officers will normally disclose any concerns they have regarding tax returns and accounts at an early stage.

6.45 It should be remembered that while the practitioner and taxpayer will wish to co-operate in an enquiry, a time limit in the opening letter (eg 30 days) for the production of books and documents need not be adhered to if this creates difficulties, and a longer period should be requested within reason, if necessary. This is not a reference to a formal information notice under *FA 2008, Sch 36*, which is a quite different matter.

6.46 *Practical aspects of an enquiry*

Remember that your continuing obligation is to represent the client to the best of your abilities, while at the same time not deliberately provoking the HMRC officer. This is a fine line to tread.

Information notices

6.46 It is also important to monitor the receipt of any formal information notice under *FA 2008, Sch 36*, while bearing in mind that HMRC can issue as many of these as it considers necessary during an enquiry. HMRC must allow a person issued with an information notice a reasonable time to produce the information or documents.

6.47 In the context of the legislation which preceded the current HMRC information powers regime (*TMA 1970, s 19A*), the case *Self-Assessed v HM Inspector of Taxes* [1999] STC (SCD) 253 indicated that HMRC must allow at least 30 days for the production of documents and information.

6.48 HMRC guidance states (CH23420): 'As a general rule of thumb, it might be reasonable to expect that most information or documents could be provided or produced within 30 days from the date of the notice but may need to be longer around a business's seasonal peaks'. In practice, HMRC officers will often allow rather more than this period.

6.49 One should also remember that a valid appeal against an *FA 2008, Sch 36* notice 'stops the clock running'. Historically, some practitioners appealed routinely against notices under the predecessor legislation (in *TMA 1970, s 19A*), but never actually had to appear before the Commissioners. If such an appeal was taken, the grounds would be whether or not HMRC's request was reasonable in the circumstances.

6.50 However, in the context of *FA 2008, Sch 36* notices it is important to recognise that there is no right of appeal against a taxpayer notice to provide information or produce documents that forms part of the taxpayer's statutory records. The same applies to notices which have been approved by the tribunal (*FA 2008, Sch 36, para 29*).

6.51 Whether information or documents form part of a taxpayer's statutory records may not be altogether clear or straightforward to ascertain. This has resulted in the issue being considered by the tribunal in some cases (eg see *Mathew v Revenue and CustomsComrs (Rev 1)* [2015] UKFTT 139 (TC)).

For more detailed commentary on HMRC's information and inspection powers, see **CHAPTER 16**.

CONTROVERSIAL POINTS

Private records

6.52 A controversial area that has occupied the time of the professional bodies in their continuing dialogue with HMRC is private records. This aspect is covered in the Enquiry manual (eg in the context of private bank accounts at EM3560), but what has tended to happen in practice is that when a sole trader business undergoes a self-assessment enquiry a request has sometimes been made routinely for private bank statements in the opening letter.

6.53 However, in *Beckwith v Revenue and Customs Comrs* [2012] UKFTT 181 (TC) personal bank statements were held, on the particular facts of that case, to be part of the taxpayer's statutory records, and no appeal could therefore be made against an information notice under *FA 2008, Sch 36* in respect of them.

Even if personal statements do not constitute statutory records, it is not necessarily the end of the matter. For example, in *Smith v Revenue & Customs* [2015] UKFTT 200 (TC), the taxpayer did not operate separate business bank accounts; his bank accounts and credit cards were all private accounts. HMRC accepted that his statements were not statutory records, but maintained that they were reasonably required for the purposes of checking the taxpayer's tax position. The First-tier Tribunal agreed, but held that the information notice should be varied (in accordance with *FA 2008, Sch 36, para 19(3)*), such that the taxpayer was required to provide the bank and credit card statements, but omitting any 'personal information'.

6.54 Even if no business transactions have gone through the private accounts, HMRC officers may attempt to justify requests for such records by stating that drawings have been transferred from the business account to the private bank account. This supposition has been resisted strongly by many professional advisers. It should be remembered that details of drawings are not part of the accounts required for self-assessment purposes.

Focus

However, as mentioned, private bank statements may constitute a business record. Each practitioner will therefore have to decide based on the particular facts and circumstances, perhaps with the help of an investigation specialist, whether or not the private bank statements are part of the statutory records of the taxpayer in question, and if not, whether they are 'reasonably required' by HMRC for the purposes of checking that taxpayer's tax position (within *FA 2008, Sch 36, para 1*).

For more detailed commentary on private records, see **CHAPTER 14**.

6.55 *Practical aspects of an enquiry*

Unannounced visits

6.55 HMRC's information and inspection powers (see **CHAPTER 16**) allow an HMRC officer to (among other things) enter a person's business premises and inspect it, together with business assets and business documents that are on the premises. However, it must be emphasised that the inspection must be 'reasonably required' for the purpose of checking that person's tax position (*FA 2008, Sch 36, para 10*). Inspections will normally be arranged in advance at a convenient date and time (CH25480), or otherwise subject to at least seven days' notice being given.

6.56 Unannounced inspections are possible at any reasonable time, by or with the approval of an authorised HMRC officer, or with the approval of the tribunal (*FA 2008, Sch 36, paras 12, 13*). Written notice of the inspection must be given to the occupier of the premises, or to anyone who appears to be in charge of the premises if the occupier is not present. If no-one appears to be in charge, the notice must be left in a prominent place on the premises.

6.57 There is nothing controversial about unannounced inspections in the sense that there is statutory authority for HMRC to conduct them. However, the question of whether such inspections are 'reasonably required' in every case is rather less clear.

HMRC guidance states: 'Where an authorised officer has to give agreement ... they will be responsible for ... ensuring the use of information, data gathering and inspection powers is reasonable, proportionate and [Human Rights Act] compliant' (CH261000). Judgement calls such as whether a particular action is 'reasonable and proportionate to the risks identified' will often be subject to disagreement, thus making unannounced visits by HMRC a potentially emotive subject.

6.58 HMRC has no right to force entry to business premises. In addition, the taxpayer can refuse HMRC entry into the business premises. There is no penalty for such a refusal if the inspection was approved only by an authorised HMRC officer.

However, if the inspection was approved by the tribunal, a fixed penalty of £300 can be charged for deliberate obstruction, with further penalties of £60 for each day on which the obstruction continues (*FA 2008, Sch 36, paras 39, 40*). Such penalties are subject to a possible exception if there is a reasonable excuse for the obstruction (*para 45*).

There is no right of appeal against the issue of an inspection notice or a tribunal decision to approve one (*FA 2008, Sch 36, para 29(3)*), but there is a right of appeal against the decision to charge a penalty.

6.59 In cases of continued delay (ie after a £300 penalty has been imposed (under *para 39*)), HMRC may apply to the Upper Tribunal for the imposition of an additional, tax-related penalty in certain circumstances (see *para 50*). An application for a tax-related penalty will only be considered by HMRC in the most serious cases where the tax at risk because of the failure or obstruction is substantial (CH26720).

In *Revenue and Customs Comrs v Tager* [2015] UKUT 40 (TCC), the Upper Tribunal imposed penalties of 100% of the tax considered to be at risk, as a result of an individual failing to comply with HMRC information notices. However, the amount of the penalty (almost £1.25 million) was subsequently found to be incorrect (*Tager v Revenue and Customs Comrs* [2015] UKUT 663 (TCC)), and the Court of Appeal reduced the penalties for failing to comply with income tax notices and an IHT notice to £20,000 and £200,000 respectively (*Tager & Anor v Revenue and Customs* [2018] EWCA Civ 1727).

6.60 As always, it is important for taxpayers (and their advisers) to know their rights. HMRC factsheets CC/FS4 'Unannounced visits for inspections' (tinyurl.com/HMRC-CCFS4) and CC/FS5 'Unannounced visits for inspections approved by the tribunal' (tinyurl.com/HMRC-CCFS5) outline those rights.

MEETINGS

6.61 Meetings with the taxpayer present are generally favoured by HMRC in an enquiry or investigation. This is not surprising, as HMRC officers are trained in interview techniques. The practitioner has to decide whether such a meeting is in the best interests of his client, while at the same time not prejudicing the co-operation factor in any settlement involving penalties.

6.62 HMRC's approach to meetings in an enquiry is set out in its Enquiry manual (at EM1820 and following). HMRC states:

> 'Meetings with the taxpayer are a vital part of any enquiry work. Correspondence or meetings with the accountant are not normally an adequate substitute. The best way to get the facts about a business and the proprietor's or director's private affairs is face to face' (EM1822)

6.63 However, if the client does not wish to attend a meeting for any reason, HMRC should be duly informed. It should also be emphasised to HMRC that full cooperation will be given in correspondence. It would then be more difficult for HMRC to contend that the client's failure to attend a meeting constitutes a lack of cooperation. This may be an important point if it becomes necessary to negotiate an appropriate level of penalty for inaccuracies in the return (see **6.104**).

6.64 *Practical aspects of an enquiry*

6.64 An initial meeting between the HMRC officer and the professional adviser is generally a good move. Accounts questions can be dealt with without the client being present. HMRC acknowledges that a meeting with the taxpayer's bookkeeper or accountant may enable issues to be resolved in some cases without troubling the taxpayer (see EM1821).

If the practitioner decides that a meeting with the HMRC officer and the client would be beneficial, he then needs to prepare his client for this occasion. This is not to suggest that the taxpayer should be coached in any way, but, for example, it is important to make the client aware that if he is unsure of the answer to a question put by HMRC, he should say so instead of guessing. This will allow the adviser and client to research the answer properly and subsequently provide HMRC with a complete and correct response.

In addition, a meeting with HMRC is an occasion when psychological factors come very much into play. Can the client cope? An initial briefing with the client may help to answer this question.

6.65 As indicated at **6.24**, it should be ascertained who will represent HMRC at the meeting. If there will be two or more HMRC officers present, who are they? If the local compliance manager or a 'coach' from FIS will be there, this needs to be ascertained politely before the meeting, and the necessary action taken in the form of the presence of a solicitor or investigation specialist to support the practitioner and client.

The venue

6.66 The venue for any meeting then has to be agreed. HMRC has previously stated that normally the meeting should take place at the client's business premises. In the author's view, this suggestion should normally be resisted.

However, as mentioned at **6.55**, HMRC's powers extend to inspecting business premises, if the inspection is reasonably required to check the taxpayer's tax position (*FA 2008, Sch 36, para 10*).

6.67 The HMRC officer generally has no right to insist on the business premises being the venue for a meeting, and he should generally be dissuaded from doing so. This is not to suggest that the taxpayer will have anything to hide, but merely that such a visit could produce further irrelevant queries, etc.

6.68 The ideal venue is normally the offices of the professional adviser. Indeed, HMRC's current guidance states (at EM1830): 'Wherever possible, meetings should be held at business premises or accountant's office because it will normally be easier to examine the business records there.' The client will

Practical aspects of an enquiry **6.71**

feel relatively at home at the professional adviser's office and can obviously be supported by his adviser.

The initiative goes very much back in the HMRC officer's favour if the meeting is held at his office, but that is generally still a better venue than the client's business premises or home.

The agenda

6.69 Preparation for the meeting is very important. The professional adviser does not want to be seen thumbing through his papers repeatedly in order to answer the HMRC officer's questions on the day. Neither the adviser nor the client wants to be in the position of being faced by some completely unexpected questions.

6.70 The professions previously pressed for agreement of an agenda prior to the meeting for some time, and there was limited success in this campaign (eg see *Tax Bulletin* Special Edition 2a, 'A better approach to enquiry work under self-assessment (faster working)').

Focus

HMRC officers will often agree to provide a broad agenda. However, it is important to try and obtain a much more detailed agenda prior to the meeting, if possible.

6.71 The scenario where the HMRC officer has a long sheet of questions already prepared will be all too familiar to many practitioners.

Every effort needs to be made to ensure that the taxpayer and his adviser are not at a disadvantage. If an ostensibly detailed agenda is obtained and HMRC subsequently raises a subject not in the agenda, it should not seem unreasonable for the adviser and client to refuse to discuss the matter, without the opportunity to give it proper consideration. HMRC guidance confirms (at EM1827) that an agenda covering the main areas for discussion at a meeting with the taxpayer should always be provided, and states:

> 'It would ... be unusual for a completely new major agenda item to be introduced at the meeting unless something unexpected is revealed during the course of the meeting.'

If the meeting does take an unexpected turn, consideration should be given to adjourning (or, in exceptional circumstances, terminating) the meeting to discuss the matter with the client.

6.72 *Practical aspects of an enquiry*

6.72 In addition to requesting an agenda, the adviser should ask HMRC for some indication of how long the meeting is expected to last, and ensure that the HMRC officer adheres to that timescale as far as possible. This should help to ensure that the meeting runs efficiently, and is not unduly protracted. An indication of the timescale will also help to prepare the client in terms of the likely length of the meeting.

Meeting notes

6.73 Agreement of the notes of the meeting is another controversial area. Ideally, voice recording of the meeting would avoid arguments about what was discussed in the meeting. HMRC guidance states that if a taxpayer or agent wishes to make an audio recording of the meeting, the enquiring officer will normally allow this (see EM1835), although in practice they may be unhappy to do so.

Traditionally, the HMRC officer has provided notes of the meeting to the professional adviser some time after the event, and then asks for these to be signed by the taxpayer. However, it would be sensible for the adviser to take his own detailed notes, in the event that the HMRC officer's notes are not issued for any reason.

6.74 In the author's view, the HMRC officer's notes should not be signed, and should not be commented on without a thorough review. At the very least, the practitioner's notes should be compared with those prepared by the HMRC officer. Ideally, the practitioner should ask a colleague or assistant to attend the meeting and concentrate on writing detailed notes. The practitioner's notes can then be used as a basis for pointing out errors in the recollection of the HMRC officer. This illustrates clearly the time and effort that has to be put into this work. However, taking meeting notes seriously can benefit the taxpayer, or at least help prevent subsequent problems arising.

6.75 For example, in *While v Revenue and Customs Comrs* [2012] UKFTT 58 (TC), HMRC's meeting notes in the course of an enquiry were held to be within *TMA 1970, s 29(6)* as being information made available to HMRC, such that a subsequent discovery assessment could not be made under *s 29(5)*.

6.76 Furthermore, the client may have realised that some of his 'off the cuff' answers at the meeting were wrong, and corrections can be pointed out at the same time. The correction of wrong answers is important, because such answers given in meetings and recorded in the notes can amount to careless conduct, allowing HMRC an opportunity to make discovery assessments.

6.77 HMRC has cited the case of *Duffy v Revenue and Customs Comrs* [2007] SpC 596 as a cautionary tale to encourage taxpayers and advisers to check meeting notes carefully. In that case, HMRC opened an enquiry into the taxpayer's 2002/03 tax return. A meeting took place between an HMRC inspector and the taxpayer in March 2005. The HMRC inspector's meeting notes noted the taxpayer's responses to questions raised, including 'Mr Duffy said he had no investments or interests in property in Spain' and also 'Mr Duffy confirmed that he had held no other accounts and would be prepared to sign a statement to that effect'. In fact, the taxpayer did own a property in Spain, and also had a bank account there, although he did not possess either at the date of the interview. The inspector subsequently issued a closure notice amending the taxpayer's tax return for 2002/03, and also made discovery assessments for the tax years 1999/2000, 2000/01, 2001/02 and 2003/04. The taxpayer appealed.

Among the issues in the appeal was whether the inspector made a discovery that would justify the discovery assessments, and whether there was negligent conduct on the taxpayer's part.

6.78 In confirming the closure notice and discovery assessments, the Special Commissioners held (*inter alia*) that the taxpayer's answers to the HMRC inspector's questions amounted to negligent conduct, and commented:

> 'In relation to his answers relating to the Spanish property and bank account the appellant said in evidence that he thought the inspector was asking questions about Spanish property or non-UK bank accounts as at the date of the interview, which he answered correctly that there were none. We do not accept he thought this.'

6.79 The Commissioners added: 'If the appellant had really thought that the question related to the present he would surely have amended the statement to refer to the present rather than the past.'

For detailed commentary on meetings with HMRC and related issues, see **CHAPTER 9**.

APPOINTMENT DIARIES

6.80 HMRC officers are sometimes also keen on requesting appointment diaries during an enquiry or investigation. This is a typical tactic in a tax return enquiry in respect of, say, a hairdresser or alternative health therapist.

It is questionable whether such diaries are part of the books and records of the business, particularly if used for non-business purposes as well. More importantly, it could be pointed out to the HMRC officer that such diaries will contain details of meetings and appointments that never, in fact, ultimately took place, and also assignments that did not lead to any new business.

6.81 *Practical aspects of an enquiry*

6.81 Appointment diaries of those in the medical professional also raise the issue of patient confidentiality. In *Long v Revenue and Customs Comrs* [2014] UKFTT 199 (TC), the First-tier Tribunal expressed the view that an information notice under *FA 2008, Sch 36* could prevail over the duty of patient confidentiality in certain circumstances.

However, the tribunal also found (among other things) that the taxpayer's diaries contained no financial information whatsoever. The taxpayer's appeal was therefore allowed; she did not have to produce her business appointment diaries to HMRC.

OTHER PROFESSIONALS

6.82 During the course of an enquiry or investigation the practitioner needs to be aware of his limitations. This is particularly relevant if any kind of criminal behaviour by the taxpayer comes to light. In the extreme instance of criminal investigation involving a 'dawn raid' by HMRC, it goes without saying that a solicitor versed in criminal procedure should be engaged immediately.

The same applies if money laundering issues come to light.

6.83 Where HMRC issues either Code of Practice 8 or 9 to the taxpayer, it is also time for non-specialists to call for expert assistance in the form of a consultant experienced in such cases. There is nothing to be gained from a 'lone ranger' attitude in enquiry and investigation work. Indeed, it could make the inexperienced practitioner vulnerable to a claim for professional negligence.

RESOLVING DISPUTES

6.84 Disagreements often arise between taxpayers (or their advisers) and HMRC during enquiries, for example on a technical point about the tax treatment of a particular transaction. This can have a serious effect on the progress of the enquiry where the position of both parties becomes entrenched. If agreement cannot be reached, the approach to resolving such an impasse has traditionally been for HMRC to issue a closure notice based on its technical arguments, and for a subsequent appeal to be listed for hearing before the tax tribunal.

6.85 However, following legislation introduced in *F(No 2)A 2017*, HMRC can issue a partial closure notice in relation to particular matters during an ongoing tax return enquiry. Alternatively, the taxpayer can apply to the tribunal for the issue of a partial closure notice (see **1.123**).

> **Focus**
>
> HMRC's 'alternative dispute resolution' (ADR) procedure for large businesses, small and medium-sized enterprises (SMEs) and individual taxpayers offers an alternative way of resolving tax disputes in compliance checks in appropriate cases. The ADR for SMEs and individuals was originally a two-year pilot, but HMRC moved ADR into 'business as usual' from 2013/14.

6.86 ADR is potentially available where a tax issue is in dispute. It is possible to appeal or request a statutory review as well as asking for ADR, although ADR can be requested before HMRC has made a decision. The ADR process broadly involves an independent person from HMRC (a 'facilitator') who has not previously been involved in the dispute mediating between the taxpayer and the HMRC officer dealing with the case to try to broker an agreement between them. Entering into the ADR process does not affect the taxpayer's review and appeal rights.

Guidance on how ADR can be requested is available on the GOV.UK website (www.gov.uk/tax-disputes-alternative-dispute-resolution-adr).

6.87 As an alternative to the ADR process, or following it, if an appeal has been sent to HMRC the taxpayer may have the matter reviewed, whether by accepting HMRC's offer of a statutory review, or by requesting one (*TMA 1970, s 49A*). If an HMRC decision is to be reviewed, it will generally be good practice to make written (and possibly verbal) representations to the review officer, explaining why HMRC's previous decision should be overturned. HMRC guidance on the review process is included in HMRC's Appeals, Reviews and Tribunals manual at ARTG2000 *et seq*.

For more commentary on ADR see **CHAPTER 12**. For more commentary on statutory reviews see **CHAPTER 20**.

A tribunal hearing should normally be avoided if possible. Aside from the additional time and further fees potentially involved in preparing for and attending the hearing, the outcome of tribunal hearings is generally unpredictable. By entering into dialogue before the hearing, it may be possible to persuade HMRC's litigating officer that the taxpayer's case is sufficiently compelling that it should not proceed to a tribunal hearing. Whilst it might seem unlikely that the HMRC officer will agree and close the enquiry, this strategy has been known to produce a favourable outcome.

6.88 *Practical aspects of an enquiry*

APPEALS TO THE TRIBUNAL

6.88 A number of cases before the First-tier Tribunal (and the Commissioners before it) have considered appeals relating to HMRC enquiries. For instance, in *Wing Hung Lai v Bale* [1999] STC (SCD) 238 the validity of a *s* 9A notice was challenged successfully. A similar successful appeal took place in *Holly v HM Inspector of Taxes* [2000] STC (SCD) 50. There have also been appeals against information notices under *FA 2008, Sch 36* (and notices requiring the production of documents under the previous legislation in *TMA 1970, s 19A*).

6.89 Practitioners should not be afraid of taking a case to the tribunal where it is considered that the HMRC officer has exceeded his powers.

For example, in *Taylor v Bratherton* [2005] STC (SCD) 230, the Commissioner, in allowing the appeal partly, stated some of the inspector's requests were 'intrusive'. Similarly, in *Guest House Proprietor v Kendall* [2005] STC (SCD) 280, where most of the disputed issues were resolved before the appeal hearing, it was clear that the appeal had been worthwhile.

6.90 Taxpayers have achieved some success before the tribunal in challenging HMRC assessments of additional business profits, including *Chapman v Revenue and Customs Comrs* [2011] UKFTT 756 (TC), *The Red Star v Revenue and Customs Comrs* [2011] UKFTT 812 (TC), *Newell t/a Tanya's Takeaway v Revenue and Customs Comrs* [2013] UKFTT 742 (TC), *Cardazzone t/a Mediterranean Ices v Revenue and Customs Comrs* [2014] UKFTT 357 (TC) and *Bekoe v Revenue and Customs* [2017] UKFTT 772 (TC).

RE-OPENING OTHER YEARS ('PRESUMPTION OF CONTINUITY')

> **Focus**
>
> For cash-based businesses in particular, if additional business profits are assessed for the tax year of enquiry on the basis that disclosed profits were understated, HMRC may also seek to assess other years as well. This HMRC treatment is often referred to as 'spreading', and is based on a 'presumption of continuity' (see EM3309), following the case *Jonas v Bamford* ChD 1973, 51 TC 1. In that case, Walton J described the principle as follows:
>
> > 'Once the Inspector comes to the conclusion that, on the facts which he has discovered, [the appellant] has additional income beyond that which he has so far declared to the Inspector, then the usual presumption of continuity will apply. The situation will be presumed to go on until there is some change in the situation, the onus of proof of which is clearly upon the taxpayer.'

Practical aspects of an enquiry **6.94**

6.91 HMRC has applied the presumption of continuity to a number of other cases. However, the tribunal has not always accepted its application, and has on occasion expressed reservations about HMRC's use of it.

For example, in *Syed v Revenue and Customs Comrs* [2011] UKFTT 315 (TC), the tribunal observed:

'In our view this quotation [from Walton J in *Jonas v Bamford*] expresses no legal principle. It seems to us that it would be quite wrong as a matter of law to say that because X happened in Year A, it must be assumed that it happened in the prior year. An officer is not bound by law and in the absence of some change to make or to be treated as making a discovery in relation to last year merely because he makes one for this year. This tribunal is not bound to conclude that what happened this year will happen next year. It seems to us that Walton J is instead expressing a common sense view of what the evidence will show. In practice it will generally be reasonable and sensible to conclude that if there was a pattern of behaviour this year then the same behaviour will have been followed last year. Sometimes however that will not be a proper inference: there will be occasions when the behaviour related to a one off situation, perhaps a particular disposal, or particular expenses; in those circumstances continuity is unlikely to be present.'

6.92 If errors in tax returns and accounts are 'one-off' in nature and therefore unlikely to have been repeated in other years, a presumption of continuity will not be appropriate, and it may be possible to successfully challenge attempts by HMRC to spread adjustments for earlier or later years in an appeal to the tribunal (eg *Aeroassistance Logistics Ltd v Revenue and Customs Comrs* [2013] UKFTT 214 (TC) and *Cardazzone t/a Mediterranean Ices v Revenue and Customs Comrs* [2014] UKFTT 357 (TC)).

6.93 Furthermore, the tribunal in *Guide Dogs for the Blind Association v Revenue and Customs Comrs* [2012] UKFTT 687 (TC) pointed out that the presumption of continuity is only a presumption, which may be rebutted. Thus even if an error might have been repeated in other years, such that a presumption of continuity is potentially in point, taxpayers should not necessarily be deterred from appealing against HMRC assessments made on that basis, particularly if HMRC's methodology for calculating the additional profits is unfair, unreasonable, or unrealistic (eg *Barkham v Revenue and Customs Comrs* [2012] UKFTT 519 (TC) and *Mehdvi v Revenue and Customs Comrs* [2013] UKFTT 173 (TC)).

6.94 It should be noted that the presumption of continuity as expressed by Walton J in *Jonas v Bamford* provides for the possible assessment of additional profits for *later* years of assessment (eg for the tax year following the year of enquiry), as opposed to earlier ones. However, HMRC might seek to use the presumption of continuity as a basis for assessing earlier years as well.

6.95 *Practical aspects of an enquiry*

This approach has been rejected by the First-tier Tribunal. For example, in *Chapman v Revenue and Customs Comrs* (see **6.90**), the tribunal noted:

> 'The presumption goes on until there is some change. The presumption as expressed in that case looks to the future and not the past. It is difficult to see how one can apply such a presumption based on the Enquiry Year to the earlier years.'

However, in *Allan v Revenue and Customs Comrs* [2016] UKFTT 504 (TC), the tribunal stated: 'Once the threshold requirement is satisfied for there to be a "discovery" of loss of tax, the presumption of continuity applies in the raising of assessments for earlier years'. The taxpayer in that case was not represented. On the face of it, *Allan* extends the scope of the presumption of continuity to earlier years, although the decision does not set a binding legal precedent.

For more information on the presumption of continuity and other matters relevant to discovery see **CHAPTER 13**.

CLOSURE NOTICE APPLICATIONS

6.95 The practitioner should consider the possibility that a visit to the tribunal may be necessary during an enquiry. This may be particularly relevant where a case has continued to meander on when HMRC has failed to 'break the records' or find any other evidence of defaults. In such a case, an application under *TMA 1970, ss 28A* (for individuals and trustees), *28B* (for partnerships) or *FA 1998, Sch 18, para 33* (for companies) should be considered, with the intention of actually appearing before the tribunal to seek closure of the enquiry.

6.96 If such an application is successfully made, the tribunal is required to direct HMRC to issue the closure notice within a specified period, unless there are reasonable grounds for not doing so (*TMA 1970, ss 28A(6), 28B(7); FA 1998, Sch 18, para 33(3)*). Thus the onus is effectively on HMRC to show why the enquiry should be allowed to continue.

6.97 The patience of a taxpayer or his adviser will often be tested by HMRC's persistence in an enquiry. It may be tempting to apply to the tribunal for a closure notice, perhaps somewhat prematurely. However, this temptation should be resisted. Applications for closure notices have been dismissed in a number of First-tier Tribunal cases (eg in *BJH Building & Plumbing v Revenue and Customs Comrs* [2010] UKFTT 60 (TC) and *Price v Revenue and Customs Comrs* [2011] UKFTT 624 (TC)).

On the other hand, any attempt by HMRC to conduct a 'fishing expedition' is likely to extend the duration of the enquiry and should be resisted if possible (but see **6.103** below).

Practical aspects of an enquiry **6.102**

6.98 The period specified by the tribunal for HMRC to issue a closure notice following an application by the taxpayer may vary, as no time limit is mentioned in the legislation. In practice, such a period typically varies from 30 days (eg *Bloomfield v Revenue and Customs Comrs* [2013] UKFTT 593 (TC)) to several months (eg the First-tier Tribunal specified a period of six months in *Khazenifar v Revenue and Customs Comrs* [2013] UKFTT 752 (TC)). In *Khan v Revenue and Customs Comrs* [2014] UKFTT 18 (TC), HMRC opened an enquiry into the taxpayer's 2009/10 tax return. There were certain unusual features in this case (eg HMRC apparently mislaid the taxpayer's records, and the tribunal criticised HMRC for its 'poor administration' of the case). However, the tribunal was also critical of the taxpayer, indicating that his responses to HMRC's requests for information had 'frequently not been adequate or timely'. The tribunal held that the enquiry should be concluded within nine months.

6.99 Similar considerations regarding closure notices apply in the context of enquiries into company tax returns. In *Estate 4 Ltd v Revenue and Customs Comrs* [2011] UKFTT 269 (TC), the tribunal directed HMRC to issue a closure notice within 30 days, following an application for a closure notice (under *FA 1998, Sch 18, para 33*).

6.100 It is important for the taxpayer and also the professions themselves for professional advisers to take a stand in some instances where a principle is at stake or there is clear inequity. It is here that the costs issue raises its head again. The practitioner may have to consider some *pro bono* work.

6.101 The other issue in this connection is whether the adviser has experience of taking a case to the tribunal. Here again, there is nothing like experience, but Bloomsbury Professional have published helpful guidance on the subject (*Hamilton on Tax Appeals*, by Penny Hamilton).

If the practitioner is uncomfortable about appearing in a quasi-legal situation on behalf of his client then he should consider delegating this task, perhaps to a lawyer or an investigation specialist.

6.102 Even if the tribunal directs HMRC to issue a closure notice, the taxpayer's problems are unlikely to end there. The closure notice will set out HMRC's conclusions at the point where the enquiry is ended. If HMRC has no information or grounds for amending the taxpayer's return, the closure notice will state that there are no amendments to the original self-assessment. However, if the return is amended, HMRC's conclusion in the closure notice could be based on incomplete information, in which case any amendment to the taxpayer's return may be inaccurate. Additional tax (and possibly penalties) could therefore be wrongly charged, which may result in an appeal and potentially another hearing before the tribunal.

6.103 *Practical aspects of an enquiry*

6.103 Furthermore, HMRC's information powers include the power to inspect business records and premises during the course of an enquiry (*FA 2008, Sch 36, para 21(4)*). HMRC could seek to use these powers in cases where the taxpayer is considering an application to the tribunal for a direction that HMRC should issue a closure notice.

For example, HMRC may adopt this approach if the taxpayer is considering an application for a closure notice on the basis that HMRC is conducting a 'fishing expedition' (see **6.97**), ie broadly that HMRC is seeking to extend the scope of its enquiry without having any reason to suspect that anything was wrong. However, in *Spring Capital Ltd v Revenue and Customs* [2015] UKFTT 8 (TC), the tribunal commented (in the context of an information notice and alleged fishing expedition):

> 'There is nothing in [FA 2008, Sch 36, para 1] that requires HMRC to suspect that the return is incorrect before issuing an information notice. HMRC are entitled to check taxpayer's (sic) tax position and they are entitled to any documents or information reasonably required for the purpose of doing so. In other words, HMRC are entitled to undertake "fishing expeditions" when checking returns: they do not need suspicion in order to check a tax return.'

This conclusion was subsequently followed in *Rankin v Revenue and Customs* [2016] UKFTT 541 (TC).

As to the facility for the taxpayer to apply to the tribunal for a partial closure notice (following legislation introduced in *F(No 2)A 2017*), see **6.85**.

For further guidance on closure notices, tax appeals, tax tribunals and HMRC reviews, see **CHAPTER 20**.

SETTLEMENT

6.104 As the enquiry draws to a close the final negotiation with the HMRC officer will often concern the level of penalty. The current penalty regime (*FA 2007, Sch 24*) applies to inaccuracies in returns, etc with a filing date on or after 1 April 2009, where the return relates to a tax period beginning on or after 1 April 2008, such as personal tax returns for 2008/09 and later years. For previous years, incorrect returns and accounts may be subject to a penalty under *TMA 1970, s 95* for individuals.

6.105 The law and method of calculating and mitigating penalties under the current and previous regimes is completely different. Advisers may still need to be aware of both sets of rules and methodologies, eg if an enquiry results in adjustments for earlier years, or in the event of a 'discovery' by HMRC where deliberate behaviour is involved.

Practical aspects of an enquiry **6.111**

6.106 The current regime (*FA 2007, Sch 24*) provides that HMRC should issue an assessment where a person becomes liable to a penalty. However, in direct tax cases it is still possible to undertake a contract settlement with HMRC involving tax, interest and penalties as under the previous regime (CH83020).

6.107 With regard to interest, HMRC considers that if a contract is made, the amount payable by the taxpayer is due under the contract, so that if any tax specified in the contract is paid late, the interest provisions written into the contract apply, rather than the statutory interest provisions (CH140280).

6.108 The regime for interest charges in *FA 2009* (*ss 101–105, Sch 53*) applies for income tax self-assessment purposes from 31 October 2011 (ie to personal tax returns for 2010/11 and later years). The provisions are intended to create a 'harmonised' regime across all taxes and duties, replacing various interest provisions in stages, including *TMA 1970, s 86*.

6.109 HMRC regards the interest charge merely as commercial restitution and there is no right of appeal against it. HMRC may also point out that there is no specific power to mitigate interest charges. However, there is potential scope for HMRC to consider requests to review interest charges in appropriate circumstances under its general 'collection and management' responsibility in the Commissioners for Revenue and *Customs Act 2005* (*CRCA 2005*), *s 5*.

In addition, in a contract settlement interest may be reduced if there has been 'unreasonable' HMRC delay within the terms of its 'Complaints and putting things right' policy (www.gov.uk/complain-about-hmrc; see EM4040).

6.110 This then leaves the question of the penalty. In theory it could start at 100% of the tax found to be due (or higher in some cases, such as for tax return errors involving 'offshore matters'), but this is extremely rare. Under the *FA 2007, Sch 24* penalty regime for errors, the level of penalty broadly depends on the degree of culpability (ie 'careless', 'deliberate but not concealed' or 'deliberate and concealed'), whether the taxpayer's disclosure or the error, etc is 'prompted' or 'unprompted', and on the quality of the disclosure (ie broadly telling HMRC, helping HMRC, and giving HMRC access to records so that the accuracy of the disclosure can be checked: *FA 2007, Sch 24, para 9(1)*).

There is generally room to negotiate the level of penalty within these statutory boundaries, and the adviser should be prepared to do so.

6.111 HMRC has produced a series of factsheets concerning compliance checks. Factsheet CC/FS7a 'Compliance Checks – Penalties for Errors in Returns or Documents' provides an overview of the current penalty regime (http://tinyurl.com/CC-Penalties).

6.112 *Practical aspects of an enquiry*

More detailed information on penalties for inaccuracies is contained in HMRC's Compliance Handbook manual at CH80000 *et seq*, including a section dealing with penalty reductions for disclosure (CH82400–CH82470). Whilst HMRC's manuals are not legally binding, they can be helpful in terms of indicating HMRC's approach to dealing with issues such as penalties.

6.112 It is important to note that HMRC cannot impose penalties for errors where the taxpayer has taken reasonable care. What constitutes 'reasonable care' is often a moot point, which will generally depend on the specific circumstances of the case. However, HMRC cites specific examples of reasonable care in the Compliance Handbook manual at CH81131.

It should be noted that (following legislation introduced in *F(No 2)A 2017*) where a person receives 'disqualified' advice in relation to certain tax avoidance arrangements, they cannot rely on that advice to demonstrate that reasonable care has been taken to avoid an inaccuracy arising from their use of the arrangements, subject to certain limited exceptions (*FA 2007, Sch 24, paras 3A–3B*). This measure therefore makes it more difficult to demonstrate that reasonable care has been taken in some cases.

Focus

From a tactical perspective, the professional adviser may wish to consider the client's penalty position at an early stage in the enquiry. It is arguably easier to raise the issue of reasonable care at that point than in response to HMRC's later conclusion that the client's behaviour has been careless.

The current penalty regime has certain advantages over its predecessor (see below). For example:

- HMRC has the power to reduce a penalty under 'special circumstances' (*FA 2007, Sch 24, para 11*);
- there is also a provision to enable HMRC to suspend penalties for careless inaccuracies in appropriate cases (*FA 2007, Sch 24, para 14*).

The adviser should consider whether these provisions may be relevant.

There is anecdotal evidence of HMRC increasingly contending that inaccuracies in returns were attributable to the taxpayers' deliberate behaviour, whereas their behaviour was arguably only careless (at worst). Such a contention should be strongly resisted in appropriate cases. Aside from generally higher penalties (with no possibility of suspension), there are various other possible adverse consequences of deliberate behaviour compared with careless behaviour, including the potential for HMRC to raise discovery assessments for additional earlier years (see **6.119**), as well as the possibility of the taxpayer being placed in HMRC's 'managing serious defaulters' regime (see HMRC Factsheet CC/FS14) and the publication of the taxpayer's details (*FA 2009, s 94*). See **6.120**.

A separate chapter of this book is devoted to the current penalty regime for errors, etc (see **Chapter 18**).

6.113 For penalties arising from enquiries for tax years prior to the introduction of the *FA 2007, Sch 24* penalty regime, long-standing mitigation factors developed over many years by HMRC were set out in HMRC Code of Practice 11 and HMRC Leaflet IR160. However, this guidance was withdrawn, and replaced by HMRC Factsheet CC/FS15 'Self Assessment and Old Penalty Rules' (tinyurl.com/HMRC-CC-FS15).

6.114 More detailed guidance on penalties for incorrect returns, accounts, etc under the 'old' regime is available in HMRC's Enquiry manual (see EM4800 and following). There is also guidance on the mitigation (or 'abatement') of penalties in the context of contract settlements relating to direct tax (see EM6051–EM6089).

As mentioned, an understanding of how penalties are mitigated under this regime may be necessary in enquiries affecting earlier years. This aspect is therefore discussed briefly below.

6.115 The mitigation of penalties under the pre-*FA 2007* regime is divided into three elements. HMRC will award a mitigation factor of up to 20% for prompt and correct disclosure. In exceptional cases where the disclosure is entirely voluntary and without challenge by HMRC, this can rise to 30%. This is most unlikely in a self-assessment enquiry, where HMRC has initiated the matter.

6.116 A further mitigation of up to 40% is given for co-operation during the investigation or enquiry. Finally, a further 40% is available for the seriousness of the case. Readers will note that the possible mitigation percentages add up to 110, but of course it is not possible to obtain that percentage of mitigation.

6.117 What is clear is that this is an area where all the negotiating skills of the practitioner come into play, and where a successful outcome can benefit the client substantially. Suppose that the tax agreed to be due is £10,000. The HMRC officer is looking for a penalty mitigation of 75%, making the total penalty £2,500. The adviser is pressing for 90% mitigation in all the circumstances. Finally mitigation is agreed at 85%, making the penalty £1,500. £1,000 will have been saved by this negotiating, which should be swiftly communicated to the client before the fee is rendered.

6.118 *Practical aspects of an enquiry*

6.118 Settlement of the case should be in mind from the inception of the enquiry. This is difficult in principle because HMRC has a legal mandate for an enquiry, although anecdotally one practitioner used to ask the HMRC officer for a settlement figure at the very first meeting. His view was that it was better to settle early in order to save substantial professional fees. It would have been necessary for the adviser to have completed his own homework before that meeting, otherwise such an approach could be quite dangerous.

Settlement negotiations are discussed in greater detail in **Chapter 11**. See also **Chapters 18 and 19** regarding penalties.

FINAL POINTS

6.119 Once the enquiry has been completed and formally closed, there are loose ends to clear up. For example:

- any books and papers should be returned to the taxpayer by the HMRC officer;
- the practitioner should tidy up his files and submit an agreed fee to the client; and
- if fee protection insurance is in place, a claim will need to be finalised and submitted to the insurer.

An enquiry is a strain on the relationship between the parties, and the adviser should do his best to retain a good future relationship with his client.

Focus

For enquiries or investigations where errors were found to involve deliberate inaccuracy, there are further considerations to bear in mind aside from potentially significant higher levels of penalty.

For example, if a loss of income tax or capital gains tax was brought about by the taxpayer's careless behaviour, HMRC can assess the lost tax up to six years after the end of the tax year to which it relates (instead of the ordinary time limit of four years). However, if the loss of tax was brought about deliberately, the time limit is increased to 20 years (*TMA 1970, s 36(1A)*).

HMRC may seek to contend that a loss of tax has been brought about deliberately, where the time limit for a discovery assessment to be raised on the basis of carelessness has expired. Such a contention should be resisted if appropriate (eg see *Revenue and Customs v Tooth* [2018] UKUT 38 (TCC)).

6.120 In addition, the following points should be noted:

- HMRC may publish a person's details to identify that person as a deliberate tax defaulter, ie broadly where a tax penalty is incurred and the potential lost revenue in respect of that penalty exceeds £25,000 (*FA 2009, s 94*). The penalty must be what HMRC refers to as a 'qualifying relevant penalty', ie one for which the person has not earned the maximum reduction for the quality of disclosure (CH190704), but note that changes to *s 94* introduced in *Finance Act 2016* make it more difficult for a person to avoid being named where a penalty is charged for an 'offshore matter' or 'offshore transfer', with effect from 1 April 2017. The defaulter's details are at risk of publication when that penalty becomes final, unless representations are successfully made as to why such details should not be published. HMRC will issue Factsheet CC/FS13 'Compliance Checks: publishing details of deliberate defaulters' (tinyurl.com/HMRC-CC-FS13) and invite the taxpayer's representations against publication.

- A person who has been charged a penalty for a deliberate inaccuracy (or has been identified during a civil investigation of fraud as presenting a continuing high risk to HMRC) may be subject to HMRC's 'managing serious defaulters' (MSD) regime. Within this regime, the defaulter is subject to 'enhanced monitoring' by HMRC for a period of up to five years. Defaulters may be subject to criminal proceedings if the deliberate or dishonest activity continues. Further information about the MSD regime is contained in HMRC's Compliance Handbook manual (at CH480000 and following) and Factsheet CC/FS14 'Managing Serious Defaulters' (tinyurl.com/HMRC-CC-FS14).

For more information on these matters, see **8.159–8.166**.

A practitioner whose client has made a non-deliberate tax return error should therefore strongly resist any accusation by HMRC that the client's behaviour was 'deliberate'.

COMPLAINTS PROCEDURES

6.121 In some cases, both the client and practitioner will feel that they have a genuine grievance about the way in which the HMRC officer has handled the case. Technical tax issues have to be aired before the tribunal and courts, and the reference in this instance is to the administration of the case and the manner and attitude of the investigating officer. There is also the additional ingredient of human rights legislation to consider.

6.122 The GOV.UK website includes guidance on how to make a complaint (www.gov.uk/complain-about-hmrc).

6.123   *Practical aspects of an enquiry*

6.123   In practice, complaints are often made in the first instance to the complaints manager of the HMRC office or area which dealt with the enquiry. If this fails, the next port of call is the head of that HMRC office or area.

It is only after this point that the matter should be referred to one of two parties for further consideration.

6.124   The Adjudicator (www.adjudicatorsoffice.gov.uk/) may hear complaints regarding HMRC maladministration and has the power to recommend restitution in the form of apologies and modest financial payments, including reimbursement of professional fees. Those fees should have been rendered before the complaints process begins.

6.125   The other alternative is the Parliamentary and Health Service Ombudsman. In this instance access is via the taxpayer's Member of Parliament. For further information, visit https://ombudsman.org.uk/.

It is debatable as to which procedure is better. Both are likely to take some time. However, a case referred to the Ombudsman cannot then be referred back to the Adjudicator, although the reverse procedure is possible.

6.126   Be prepared to fight your client's corner whenever appropriate. There is anecdotal evidence of a case that was settled at local area office level. In that case, the enquiry was closed immediately by a senior officer and all professional costs refunded. In addition, the adviser was making a claim for a consolatory payment, as the health of a family member had been affected by the unacceptable behaviour of an HMRC officer.

6.127   HMRC's Complaints Handling Guidance manual sets out HMRC's general policy on and approach to complaints. In addition, the Complaints and Remedy Guidance manual covers HMRC's approach to considering whether they have made a mistake or given poor service, and if so, what the appropriate remedy might be. It sets out (at CRG6000 and following) the circumstances in which consolatory payments may be made, and includes guidance on the amounts that can be offered (see CRG6075).

For more detailed commentary on complaints about HMRC, see **Chapter 23**.

KEY POINTS

6.128   Finally, here are ten suggestions for practitioners dealing with HMRC tax return enquiries:

1   Reduce the client's risk of enquiry in the first place, such as by:
- ensuring compliance with statutory tax obligations;

Practical aspects of an enquiry **6.128**

- conducting analytical reviews of tax returns and accounts; and
- considering the level and nature of disclosures of additional information to HMRC (eg in the 'white space' on the return).

2   Be aware of your client's (and your) rights.

3   Act assertively, but politely – be prepared to challenge HMRC if appropriate, and to complain, if necessary.

4   Always act in the best interests of the client. This includes encouraging him to keep good records.

5   Check that the enquiry is being conducted in accordance with the law, within statutory time limits, etc.

6   Be aware of the powers of HMRC, and the limitations on those powers.

7   Know your own limitations; seek assistance if necessary.

8   Provide information 'reasonably required' by HMRC. Do not volunteer information naively and freely.

9   If penalties are charged, ask HMRC to reduce or suspend them in appropriate circumstances.

10 Always keep costs in mind; consider fee protection insurance.

Chapter 7

Selection for enquiry

Andrew Gotch BA MA CTA (Fellow)
TaxAction Consulting Ltd

SIGNPOSTS

- **The legal background** – The compliance checking regime in *FA 2008, Sch 36* needs to be fully understood. Read the legislation and keep an eye on how the tribunals and the courts are interpreting it. (See **7.3–7.7**.)

- **HMRC risk analysis** – It is becoming increasingly sophisticated and is at the initial stage almost entirely computerised. The new Connect software allows HMRC to keep an increasingly complex picture of taxpayers to enable potential risk to be identified. HMRC's Affluent Unit is a good example of what can be done to pursue losses of tax. (See **7.8–7.16**.)

- **Selection parameters** – HMRC does not disclose them but their nature can be inferred from published material and from practical experience. Advisers should learn to adapt their own reviewing processes to address the questions that HMRC will be asking. (See **7.17–7.40**.)

- **Accounts and return review** can be time consuming but it is never a waste of time. It is only by undertaking imaginative review that adequate disclosures can be made in the white space to pre-empt or mitigate the risk of an intervention by HMRC. (See **7.41–7.88**.)

- **Key points** – For a list of key points from this chapter, see **7.98**.

WHERE ARE WE NOW? – SELECTION IN CONTEXT

The enquiry regime and its problems

7.1 The introduction of self assessment in 1996 stood the whole approach to selection for investigation on its head. Taxpayers still had responsibility

Selection for enquiry **7.3**

for submitting correct and complete returns, but HMRC (as the then Inland Revenue later became) was given a broad power to enquire into those returns without a prior legal requirement of being dissatisfied with what the taxpayer had returned before doing so.

7.2 Despite the breadth of that power, the passage of time revealed that it was still insufficient to give HMRC the unfettered powers to review taxpayers' affairs that it wanted. In particular, the enquiry legislation was proving inadequate in two ways:

- First, as HMRC's risk analysis became increasingly sophisticated, an enquiry window of just one year meant that more cases were being identified than could be taken up for enquiry within in a 12-month period. The problem was exacerbated by the rate of attrition on HMRC staffing numbers, which meant that fewer HMRC officers were available to undertake enquiry work.

- Second, the introduction of the enquiry legislation meant that, in law, HMRC was no longer able to ask a question of a taxpayer without opening an enquiry. That gave rise to a problem unforeseen in 1996, in that if HMRC could not ask a question, it could not find anything out; and if it could not find anything out, it could not make a discovery. Thus HMRC was being fettered in its ability to use the discovery legislation, one of the most powerful tools in its investigative armoury.

The compliance checking regime

Focus

Make sure you understand what compliance checking means – it is radically different to enquiry and a much more powerful compliance tool for HMRC.

7.3 Both problems were swept aside by the compliance checking legislation contained in *FA 2008, Sch 36, Pt 2*. HMRC was granted unappealable powers of access to premises, assets and records where it was felt necessary to do so to check a taxpayer's 'tax position', a defined term covering a taxpayer's position in relation to any financial transaction with HMRC whether in the past, the present or the future. It is impossible to conceive of a more widely drawn power: it provides, in effect, for statutorily authorised fishing expeditions into any aspect of a person's tax affairs, including not just direct and indirect taxes, but also PAYE and CIS, double tax relief claims, interest and penalties. A 'compliance check' is now HMRC jargon for any intervention into a taxpayer's affairs. Checking does not mean that there is something wrong; it could, in theory, simply mean that HMRC is just checking that a return is right. However, given HMRC's stretched resources and intense

7.4 Selection for enquiry

focus on yield, an assumption that a taxpayer selected for a check falls within a higher risk population is a very sensible one.

7.4 The apparent safeguard contained in the limit to checking matters only in relation to years for which returns have not been submitted is qualified by the exception to the limitation contained in *Sch 36, para 21*, which allows exactly the same suite of powers to be engaged for an earlier year for which a return has been submitted if an HMRC officer has reason to suspect that income has not been assessed, a self assessment is inadequate or a relief become excessive.

> **Focus**
>
> Protect your client from unjustified compliance check risk for earlier years where HMRC is suspicious – but has no reason to suspect anything is wrong.

7.5 Perhaps unsurprisingly, 'reason to suspect' is a less onerous test than 'reason to believe', and the exception was plainly designed to allow HMRC unfettered access to records for earlier years if officers' suspicions are aroused by anything found in the course of checking records for a current year. Advisers familiar with tax compliance will know that HMRC's suspicions have a tendency to be aroused all too easily, often inappropriately and on the flimsiest of pretexts. However, the recent case of *Kevin Betts v Revenue and Customs Comrs* [2013] UKFTT 430 shows that mere suspicion is not enough: there have to be reasons for suspicion that have real substance and a 'gut feeling' on the part of HMRC will not be enough to justify a notice. Practitioners are therefore advised to scrutinise the basis for any request under *Sch 36, para 21* that is based on reason to suspect before acceding to the request and to appeal suitable cases accordingly.

> **Focus**
>
> Be present at on-site meetings and record reviews.

7.6 Real-time record review in a compliance check makes sense in the context of transaction-based tax functions like indirect taxes and employer obligations to account for tax and NIC under the PAYE system. However, it will normally be impossible, on a review of records for a current period at any given time, to identify what the direct tax consequences of those records, and therefore the 'tax position', will be: an accounting period will have to end, and accounts and computations be prepared, before that judgement can be made. It follows that there is a good case to be made that in a direct tax context the principal purpose of undertaking a compliance check will be to assess the vulnerability of earlier and later years' returns to an enquiry.

Selection for enquiry **7.9**

7.7 In that context, practitioners should bear in mind the decision in *Betts* and, if records are being reviewed on-site at a taxpayer's premises, should be present in order to scrutinise, evaluate, and if necessary rebut, any claims from HMRC officers that reasons for suspicion have been established. HMRC officers will be wholly unfamiliar with the particular profile of a taxpayer's records and explaining apparent anomalies in real time can curtail and sometimes prevent the potential for an enquiry being realised.

It is noteworthy as well as concerning that HMRC's first priority in its published strategic objectives is to 'maximise revenues due', so HMRC are now very motivated to seek as much extra tax from taxpayers as possible. Those familiar with HMRC compliance work know that yield is now the principal focus of HMRC case-workers and that we are firmly in the world of the maximum sustainable (and sometimes unsustainable) claim. In such a dismal world, it is more important than ever to do what one can to prevent taxpayers attracting HMRC's attention in any way in the first place. How can that be done?

The risk analysis environment

Focus

HMRC's electronic selection capacity is highly sophisticated and improving all the time. The only sensible assumption is that HMRC will find out about anything that clients are trying to hide! The introduction of the Common Reporting Standard brings a much-increased risk of overseas liabilities being brought to HMRC's attention and the threat of substantial penalties means that all advisers should take this seriously.

7.8 Until relatively recently, pre-enquiry reviews were carried out by painstakingly amassing information about taxpayers, with individual officers collating information from sources they could find and then evaluating the potential risk. Those days are gone: the selection exercise is now considerably automated and far more sophisticated. At the level of basic compliance, there is focus on new employers, who might be expected to be more likely to get things wrong; and employment intermediaries, which is likely to increase as and when the private and public sector treatment is aligned, as seems certain. Similarly, ATED limits are falling and many with properties owned by corporates may not have identified a new liability. Advisers with such clients should take particular care.

7.9 HMRC has a dedicated part of its organisation, the Risk and Intelligence Service (RIS), dedicated to collecting, analysing, interpreting and disseminating information to facilitate selection for enquiry. At a high level, HMRC is hungry for information (notoriously going as far as purchasing stolen

7.10 *Selection for enquiry*

information from informants in one highly publicised case) and is always happy to promote and support legislation that increases its information-gathering powers – even when, as with the new Foreign Account Tax Compliance Act (FATCA) legislation, it is promoted by an overseas government. The international angle is also important, and the Offshore Coordination Unit within HMRC exchanges huge quantities of information for that collected by overseas governments for submission to HMRC under the UK's burgeoning collection of Tax Information Exchange Agreements. All such information that HMRC receives is correlated and compared with return information. No taxpayer can safely believe that money or assets can be hidden from HMRC scrutiny.

The introduction of the Common Reporting Standard (CRS) introduces a fresh element of risk. A very wide range of overseas jurisdictions will be reporting a wide range of financial information to other fiscs. Advisers were required by regulation to warn customers of the increased access to offshore information and mandatory disclosure is required. So confident is HMRC in the efficacy of the CRS in supplying them with wide-ranging and accurate information that it has introduced the Worldwide Disclosure Facility (WDF) to give an opportunity for offshore disclosures before the first tranche of CRS information comes in in September 2018 – with severe penalties for those who are subsequently identified as having failed to disclose. 'Nudge' letters are already being issued by HMRC to taxpayers whom it feels might need to use the WDF, so the mechanisms for pursuing non-compliance are already in place.

7.10   To increase the accuracy of case selection, in 2009 (just in time to exploit *FA 2008, Sch 36*, the cynic might say!), HMRC brought online a new and sophisticated intelligent software tool, known as Connect, designed to seek out and correlate information from a vast range of sources and to build a picture of the taxpayer, facilitating evaluation for risk. Currently, Connect contains over 22 billion lines of data (the equivalent of a pile of A4 paper 158 miles high – 28 times the height of Mount Everest!) and 596 million compliance documents like tax returns – and has generated over £3 billion of additional revenues since it was introduced.

The information within Connect does not just come from predictable sources like returns of interest from banks and financial institutions at home and abroad, royalties from publishers and transaction details from auction houses: it also correlates information from non-tax sources like Companies House, the Land Registry and other government departments and law enforcement agencies locally and nationally, with the intention of producing a detailed picture of a taxpayer's circumstances and behaviour – not just income, but interests in property, involvement with companies and LLPs and more, including – for those alleging residence overseas – flight data from airlines.

7.11   HMRC now routinely analyses data from credit card providers to identify traders who may be mis-declaring receipts – or who do not use credit

Selection for enquiry **7.13**

cards and therefore may be transacting principally in cash, which in HMRC's view increases potential for diversion of income. Data can also be matched with business that have ceased trading to identify potential post-cessation income. The data can provide geographical norms for businesses in the split between card and cash transactions – for example, in some business sectors, those in London will have a much higher proportion of card transactions than those in the North, which allows for more accurate risk profiles to identify cases that fall outside the expected parameters.

It can be inferred from the recent interest in online trading through sites like eBay that HMRC is also mining the internet effectively and correlating that information with data on Connect. That is also reflected in proposals for legislation targeting 'digital wallet' businesses (eg PayPal) and Money Service Businesses (those which transfer money overseas without using the normal banking system), which will expose another tranche of economic activity to HMRC scrutiny.

7.12 Connect has revolutionised HMRC's approach to compliance checks: currently nearly 90% of cases taken up for investigation are generated from leads provided by Connect and the percentage rises every year. More than 13,000,000 requests for information are made annually by HMRC staff – all of which will be compliance-related. In practice, the advent of Connect means that it is now naïve to expect that any intervention from HMRC has been selected randomly, particularly within the relatively small databases of business taxpayers and the wealthy. The only sensible response is that every case selected must be assumed to have originated from an adverse risk report, with that assumption informing the response of the adviser – and the client. That is not to say that the information within Connect may not be clean – mistaken assumptions will still be made; but the chances of an enquiry being entirely without foundation is generally low.

HMRC's wealthy and mid-sized business compliance teams ('WMBC') – demonstrating the power of computerised risk analysis

Focus

All taxpayers paying tax at the additional rate will have their returns reviewed critically by HMRC – make sure you anticipate that risk with detailed review and full white space disclosure.

7.13 The power and potential of HMRC's information-gathering resources was shown in an article in *Taxation*, 21 March 2013, by Roger Atkinson, an Assistant Director of HMRC's 'Affluent Unit', where he described what the

7.14 *Selection for enquiry*

then newly-formed Unit would be looking for. In its current guise of Wealthy and Mid-sized Business Compliance, HMRC focuses on individuals with assets of more than £1 million and annual income of more than £150,000. That is a low threshold and means that any additional rate taxpayer needs to take extra care: latest figures show that HMRC has harvested £2 billion of extra revenues from the 500,000 wealthiest individuals in the UK.

The range and scope of HMRC's interest is instructive. High-level risk indicators include:

- use of avoidance schemes – HMRC's view, reasonably enough, is that more tax is at risk if the taxpayer has a proclivity to take uncommercial routes to escape liability;

- late filing – HMRC's view, born of long experience, is that apparently minor procedural failure can indicate a poor attitude to tax obligations leading to larger problems;

- Swiss bank accounts – the result of HMRC's acquisition of stolen bank details;

- multiple property ownership in the UK and overseas – suggestive of substantial resources and possible under-declared rental income: HMRC has a data-mining 'robot' that trawls the Internet looking for properties to let or for sale that appear to have a UK connection.

7.14 There are two principal models for selection of affluent cases that mesh with those risk indicators. The first models for predictive risk on the basis of information from tax returns and third party sources and combines the score with that for any spouse to produce an overall risk score. The second looks more closely at low effective rates of tax, on the basis that if total income is taxed at less than marginal rates of income tax there is a possibility of arrangements to reduce liability, including avoidance schemes. Low income and increased capital gains may indicate attempts to tax income as capital. This is combined with modelling of income trends: any wide variation in income from year to year will attract closer review.

The focus is not just on direct income taxes: HMRC recognises the scale of risk in inheritance tax and capital gains tax too; and recent changes to the rules penalising moving assets overseas and the impending changes to the domicile rules indicate the scale of the problems that HMRC perceive.

7.15 Once an affluent taxpayer has been identified as a tax risk, more focused research is undertaken by HMRC officers to inform the decision about whether an intervention is required – we do not yet appear to have reached the point where selection is entirely by computer, although it may well be that that day will come. It is at this stage that an evaluation will be made of 'white space' information, so it is therefore of prime importance that detailed disclosures should accompany any return that seems to contain any potentially anomalous characteristics – it could be the difference between a quiet life for another year and a costly and potentially avoidable intervention. The processes developed to address affluent taxpayers reflect, in many ways, the methods used for selecting any case for a compliance check. Return information is subjected to constant scrutiny; enquiry cases are analysed to extract relevant information; project work is undertaken into business and taxpayer sectors to identify risk, bearing fruit in the succession of disclosure opportunities aimed at specific groups of taxpayers; behaviour is analysed to identify potential rule breakers. So far as these activities relate to the SME sector, detailed information relating to HMRC's risk assessment strategy is, most unhelpfully, heavily censored using *Freedom of Information Act 2000* powers.

7.16 In a large business context, HMRC's approach is more sophisticated and more public. HMRC's Tax Compliance Risk Management Process is published and is one of the few compliance-related publications that have not been heavily censored using *Freedom of Information Act 2000* powers. However, a good deal of useful information can be gleaned from it about HMRC's approach to areas such as behavioural risk; after all, when it comes to human behaviour the difference between small and large businesses is often one of quantum rather than quality.

Disclosure of selection parameters

7.17 However, the general approach of HMRC is to keep its risk analysis cards close to its chest. That sits poorly with the obligation imposed by the Carter Report some years ago for HMRC to disclose its selection criteria. While some Carter requirements have been embraced with alacrity by HMRC, such as iXBRL reporting for company accounts, HMRC has been extremely reluctant to disclose the selection criteria that it uses.

7.18 Quite why is unclear. Any conscientious adviser would use that information to identify risk in his clients' returns that could form the basis of voluntary disclosure or enable constructive explanations that would save expensive investigative resource all round. However, it seems that for the time being taxpayers are faced with a traditional 'cat and mouse' approach to selection.

Toolkits: how to use them properly

> **Focus**
>
> Toolkits tell you what HMRC is looking for, so don't get it wrong in those areas.

7.19 *Selection for enquiry*

7.19 Whilst it has never been openly stated, it is likely that the publication of tax toolkits represents HMRC's lip service to the Carter disclosure requirement, disguised as an educational tool. The lists in each toolkit of matters that taxpayers tend to get wrong are drawn from HMRC's own analysis of return error, and so are indications in themselves of where in particular HMRC will be looking when returns are submitted. Thus, in effect, the toolkits are a clear checklist of areas that advisers and taxpayers should ensure they get right when submitting returns and preparing tax computations. A failure to do so is likely to be self-selecting for further compliance intervention.

The importance of identifying 'changes'

7.20 Anomalies in returns generate interest and advisers should consider the overall composition of the return from year to year. HMRC is known to target 'changes', and to enquire into returns where these beg questions. An example would be a taxpayer whose return has shown rental income for several years. Then a return is submitted and the rental income is no longer there. That difference of form as against previous years will generate a risk report to be pursued, because HMRC needs to know why the apparent anomaly has occurred. For example:

- Has the rental income simply been left off the return, deliberately or otherwise?
- Has the rental property been sold, and if so has the capital gain been returned?

7.21 The powers in *FA 2008, Sch 36* now make it easier for HMRC to ask what is going on, but that means that the taxpayer has already attracted attention as a compliance risk, which is undesirable. Advisers should therefore ensure that full explanations of any such anomalies are included in the white space on the return, so that HMRC's suspicions can be allayed and the risk of contact with HMRC minimised or obviated.

Behavioural risk

> **Focus**
>
> Getting basic procedural compliance right reduces risk profile – getting it wrong increases it.

7.22 In recent years, HMRC has invested a considerable amount of time and money in developing its predictive risk analysis capabilities. Although it can never be an exact science, HMRC's approach to model behaviour is to identify groups of taxpayers who are more likely than other groups to be 'rule-breakers'.

7.23 Some types of behaviour will be self-selecting. For example, taxpayers who consistently enter disclosure of tax avoidance schemes (DOTAS) reference numbers on their returns cannot be surprised if they are seen as having a higher level of tax risk than taxpayers who never do so.

7.24 On the other hand, there are other more everyday examples of behaviour that will affect risk profile adversely, for example late returns, returns with inaccuracies, late claims and elections, late payment, reluctance to engage with, or dilatoriness in dealing with, HMRC. In the modern world there is no *de minimis* for behaviour, and taxpayers and their advisers should always consider how their general attitude to tax compliance and to HMRC could be interpreted.

It is also important to identify potential new sources of exposure. An example is the new quarterly reporting requirement for employment intermediaries. Compliance across the target sector is variable and those who have failed to file returns when HMRC might expect them to do so by the nature of their business (eg the construction industry) are likely to receive HMRC attention – status cases are lucrative for HMRC. Similarly, it is often forgotten that those who no longer feel they need to make returns have to notify HMRC, and those who do so are again very likely to be reviewed. Advisers need to monitor compliance carefully to keep this risk low.

7.25 For large businesses, there are lengthy lists of criteria that affect risk rating set out in the Tax Compliance Risk Management manual (TCRM) at TCRM3320–TCRM3370. Some are focused on large business criteria, but many apply across the board and are relevant, *mutatis mutandis*, to small businesses as well and should be considered by all advisers of SMEs.

7.26 The extent to which that is true is shown by the tenor of the initial telephone questionnaire for business record checks. The initial questions seek to find out how familiar taxpayers are with the tax compliance obligations generally, and how comfortable they feel with form filling and similar procedural matters. That reflects a similar interest in TCRM in how large businesses deal with their obligations.

Record keeping

7.27 Business records were not a risk selection factor prior to the inception of the Business Record Checks project. Fortunately that project was withdrawn early in 2016 since it had proved a total failure, but that does not mean that HMRC has given up on its quest to eradicate incomplete records and pursue and penalise those who have them.

7.28 *Selection for enquiry*

The Making Tax Digital (MTD) project – postponed, but guaranteed to become a reality – contains a substantial requirement to notify business income and expenditure on a quarterly basis, and may well include a requirement to transmit copies of records to HMRC. HMRC has maintained a worrying silence about what it will do with this information, but it is undoubtedly something that will echo in HMRC's risk profiling. Taxpayers who make no or incomplete returns will see their risk profiles rise, and an erratic pattern of returns or a final accounts figure that differs materially from what quarterly returns have led HMRC to expect will suggest that underlying records and/or internal controls are chaotic. That will be easy for HMRC to review using their compliance checking powers under *FA 2008, Sch 36* and a significant upsurge in such checks can be expected once MTD becomes a reality. Advisers would be wise to advise their clients of this new risk – and of the related potential risk of penalties under *TMA 1970, s 12B*.

7.28 The consequences of inadequate record keeping were exemplified in the case of *Khagram v HMRC* [2012] UKFTT 494 TC 02171. Despite the fact that the taxpayer had engaged an accountant, records were wholly inadequate and did not support accounts entries to a material extent. Purchase invoices were only present in part, private expenditure was included in purchases, cash records were scanty and there was an incorrect allocation of goods between zero- and standard-rated purchases. Assessments to VAT and income tax were made totalling some £27,000 and before the tribunal the taxpayer was unable to discharge the burden of proving that the assessments should be discharged, as a direct result of her inadequate records.

Selection at a local level

7.29 Cases that RIS identifies as a compliance risk are sent through to compliance centres for review for possible intervention. Even though the RIS report will contain reasons for selection, it is still ultimately for HMRC officers locally to decide whether to take up the case for further compliance activity. Except in cases where there has been a clear statutory offence, selection for investigation has always been a matter of analysing the potential risk of tax being lost in a particular case.

7.30 Although the pilot of the single compliance process (SCP) did not result in a wholly new approach to compliance activity and the SCP project is no more, several core principles that were seen as successful in practice are being adopted across the board within HMRC so far as the selection process is concerned. The core idea is that HMRC should not indulge in speculative enquiries or fishing expeditions, on the grounds that it is not cost-effective to do so, and should disclose why the intervention is happening. So any case that is selected will (or should) have been chosen because of identified risks giving

Selection for enquiry **7.34**

rise to a loss of tax, not just because it doesn't generally 'smell right' to the compliance officer. If those risks are not disclosed then ask HMRC what they are. That is not to say that further risks will not be pursued if identified; but it does mean that a case selected for a compliance check or an enquiry can be expected to have characteristics that give justifiable or certain cause to believe there is a loss of tax.

7.31 Advisers should also bear in mind that HMRC is interested in compliance risk in all areas of tax. Selection is now a holistic undertaking and will consider not just direct tax issues, but also SDLT, VAT and PAYE/NIC risk, as well as tax credits, national minimum wage, child benefit charge, excess pension charges and any other matter for which HMRC has responsibility. Thus the adviser's role becomes correspondingly more difficult because risk has to be assessed in the broadest possible context; everything has to be right when the guiding principle of HMRC's compliance initiatives is alignment and cross-tax working across all its business streams.

7.32 After nearly 20 years of self-assessment, HMRC has abundant material in its possession in a computerised form to use in comparative analysis, both horizontally, as regards particular taxpayers from year to year, and vertically as between groups of taxpayers with common denominators, for example those who carry on the same or very similar trades. That form of 'bench-marking' is a productive source of potential enquiry cases, since anomalies are easy to identify. The advent of iXBRL reporting for companies, and the enormous and increasing amount of data it provides, will mean that comparative analysis becomes increasingly sophisticated as time passes.

7.33 Of course, this is a one-sided process, because HMRC officers have only the information before them and do not have the benefit of explanation at or before the time that the case is selected for further compliance intervention work. However, practitioners would be well advised to give HMRC officers the maximum opportunity to exercise their judgement and discretion before progressing a case by providing detailed supplementary information about any unusual, complicated or anomalous entry in a return in the white space to anticipate questions that might be raised in the HMRC officer's mind. Some suggestions for what commentary is required for accounts and return entries are made below.

7.34 Prudent advisers will be doing so anyway, of course, to protect their clients from the risk of discovery; but anticipating questions that might arise in a review is an equally important function of the white space. HMRC officers customarily have very little practical external information to go on when making judgements about selection, and white space entries can help to provide that essential background context to the return and tip the balance away from interventions that have no real justification.

7.35 *Selection for enquiry*

THE SELECTION PROCESS

7.35 The risk analysis of a taxpayer will take into account a very broad range of information. No one matter will necessarily tip the balance towards selection; it could be a combination of any number of factors building up a profile that suggests that tax could be at risk. What is not known, and what is unlikely ever to be known precisely, is exactly what the parameters for selection will be, or how often those parameters will be changed.

7.36 For example, it is commonly acknowledged that deviation from a particular rate of gross profit remains one of the biggest selectors for compliance intervention. But the degree of variation required to operate the trigger will not be known; it could be 3% from the norm one year, 7% the next year, or different for different businesses.

7.37 Additionally a normative rate of gross profit for a particular trade might be obtained by a national analysis of accounts for that trade, in which case the percentage trigger point will be one figure, or by an analysis on a regional or local basis, which will give different figures to act as potential triggers.

7.38 In one sense, then, taxpayers are in the dark about where HMRC will concentrate its interest. However, a suitable programme of prophylaxis can be devised by inferring where the likely focus of interest will be.

Consider clearance applications. If a statutory clearance application is made the following returns will always be checked to ensure that the transaction has taken place in the manner described. However, non-statutory applications for clearance will receive similar scrutiny and so full white space description should be used to minimise risk of selection.

7.39 There is little guidance now available in HMRC's published guidance to identify risk. However, in the now-withdrawn Enquiry Handbook (EH) there was a list of several kinds of issue that mandatorily selected a return for enquiry review. Thus any return that contains one of those features should receive extra attention to identify potential risk and explain anomalies in other areas. In particular the white space needs to be filled in expansively to provide context for the areas in question, particularly in the case of capital gains and losses. CGT is seen as a technically difficult tax that is not well understood and if (say) a claim for private residence relief, or entrepreneurs' or rollover relief is returned, the tax at stake can be substantial and checking the claim is the more attractive to HMRC for that. So justifying the claim in the white space can be a cost-effective step in reducing the risk of compliance intervention.

Selection for enquiry **7.44**

7.40 The particular areas that were mentioned in the EH are:

- provisional figures;
- capital gains/losses;
- Lloyds cases;
- tax-geared penalties for failure to notify or late return;
- post transaction rulings;
- change of accounting date more than once in any five years for an unincorporated business.

ACCOUNTS AND RETURN REVIEW

> **Focus**
>
> Imaginative review of the accounts and the return should be the norm. Put yourself in HMRC's shoes and ask what questions are begged. HMRC looks at accounts and returns as a text with a story to tell about the taxpayer – what story do they tell about your client?

7.41 From a practitioner's perspective, it is essential in today's hostile risk-aware tax environment to conduct pre-submission reviews in order to identify potentially anomalous features in accounts and returns that could give rise to compliance risk.

7.42 In the normal way, the pre-submission review should enable advisers to home in on anomalous or high-risk factors in accounts and returns so that action can be taken either to remedy any potential omissions or failures, or to confirm that the anomalies stem from bona fide commercial or personal circumstances so that they can be adequately described in white space entries.

7.43 It may not be possible to avert compliance action entirely, but the opportunity to mitigate should not be missed. Even if such a preliminary review discovers unrectifiable omissions or failures, then at least it will have provided the taxpayer with the opportunity to maximise his penalty reduction by means of a full unprompted disclosure followed by informed co-operation by the practitioner.

Accounts review

7.44 In non-commencement cases, compare the accounts to be submitted with those of previous years. Ideally a spreadsheet should be compiled and

7.45 *Selection for enquiry*

updated on an annual basis so that the fluctuation in accounting entries and ratios can be properly observed.

7.45 Any obvious differences in scale from the figures in the previous year's accounts should be queried with the taxpayer. In the same way, if there are material new deductions in the accounts, consider what they may mean. Has there been a change in the nature of the business, or has the business stayed the same but the manner of carrying it on changed?

7.46 If there has been a change it is essential that it is notified. HMRC classifies taxpayers in terms of the trade carried on, and analysis of a set of accounts will necessarily be inaccurate and anomalous if it is thought that the taxpayer has an entirely different kind of business.

7.47 Advisers will find it instructive to include within a spreadsheet functions to evaluate changes in ratios within the accounts. This type of review is particularly suited to computer analysis and the sheer breadth of the sample available to HMRC means that such ratios will become an increasingly important and accurate measure of the fiscal health of a business when pre-selecting for enquiry.

Estimates and percentage abatements

7.48 As a general precaution, advisers should ensure that the basis of any amounts disallowed by reference to a percentage, for instance, say, 20% motor expenses, is sustainable by reference to adequate records. Similar considerations apply to estimates of expenditure; make sure that these are calculated on a sustainable basis that reflects reality. Such an estimate will not render the return incorrect. Round sums and conventional unchanging estimates (£520, £2,080) are always conspicuous in a set of accounts and, once again, indicate that the records of the business are less than complete and/or that the professional work done by the accountant and the subsequent review by the business owner is less thorough than it should be. Now that compliance checking is here, nothing is easier for HMRC officers to check and, if the basis of the estimate is unsustainable, attack – and the recoveries could go back over many years.

Turnover

7.49 HMRC is interested in income trends. Consider the reason for any substantial increase or decrease in sales, examine critically the explanations put forward by the client and formulate an appropriate white space narrative. If the nature of the trade has changed, even if only by a little, make sure that the fact is included in the taxpayer's return.

Gross profit

7.50 The rate of gross profit should be reviewed both objectively and subjectively. First, is the achieved rate low for the type of trade carried on? Secondly, has the achieved rate varied within the business under review?

Low or variable gross profit rates have traditionally been a very common route into an investigation and with increasing validity of broadly based sampling, will remain so.

7.51 If there has been any more than minimal variation, commercial explanations should be sought. Is the trade one in which the trader can influence the margin at which he sells goods to any significant extent? To return to a familiar theme, does the change in gross profit rates (GPR) reflect a change in the nature of the trade? If so, say so to avoid an incorrect analysis being made.

> **Example 7.1**
>
> Your client is a retail butcher. Halfway through one year, he decides to start some wholesaling as well. That change will mean a GPR that diverges sharply from that of previous years. That will generate a risk report within HMRC. If you do not explain what has happened and how the change in the nature of the trade affects GPR, you will be guaranteeing your client an enquiry into that return.

It may be that the business whose accounts you are examining is not one for which GPR is a good indicator.

7.52 A flexible and imaginative approach is required in order to address the range of permutations which computer selection may apply to accounts analysis. For instance, in a distribution or carriage trade, ratios of vehicle or fuel costs to sales should be reviewed; and in construction industry trades, the ratio of sub-contractor costs to turnover can be instructive.

7.53 Weakness in support for a low GPR can leave clients vulnerable to excessive assessments. The case of *Nelson T/A Sandvale Grocers* [2012] UKFTT 551 (TC) is in point. Gross profit rates were very low and fluctuating from year to year, and HMRC's assessments following enquiry nearly tripled the taxpayer's GPR in arriving at revised figures for profits. The taxpayer's flimsy explanations were uniformly rejected by the tribunal and assessments confirmed bringing some £47,000 into charge.

7.54 *Selection for enquiry*

Deductions from income

7.54 The range of possible deductions is large, but those to which particular attention should be paid include the following.

Employee costs

7.55 HMRC assumes that in the majority of cases business owners will not be prepared to pay themselves less than their employees without very good reasons. If a client seems vulnerable to this sort of comparison, explore, and if necessary explain, the reasons behind the apparent anomaly.

7.56 Evaluate the amount of wages being paid in terms of turnover. Is productivity per employee so low that it seems uneconomical? HMRC's view could well be that sales are understated, or that the deduction for wages may include something other than employee costs. Narrative explanation is essential.

Premises costs

7.57 If this charge varies substantially from that in previous years, consider what that means in terms of the business. Does the variation mean that premises or working practices have changed in some way? If so, is this reflected in turnover? If not, why not? Advisers should include a justification for any significant increase or decrease on the return.

Repairs

7.58 This has always been a fertile ground for HMRC review and remains so. Consider whether there is any element of capital expenditure included in the debit. Is there an increase in fixed assets that might imply that the sums claimed as repairs are in fact part of a scheme of capital reconstruction or improvement? If so, ensure that the correct amount is added back for tax purposes. If not, state on the return that a proper evaluation of the amount deducted has been made and give an analysis if necessary to support that statement.

Motor expenses

7.59 Advisers should consider first whether there should be an abatement for private use in an unincorporated trade. As a general rule HMRC will expect to see such an abatement and if one is not made, a note should be put on the return to explain the position.

7.60 Similarly, HMRC will be able to make comparisons with similar businesses locally, regionally or nationally to give a benchmark for what is a broadly acceptable level of expenditure and private use. Examine critically any particularly high figure for motor expenses to ensure that it is fully justified and does not include, for example, expenditure on cars for family members.

Travel and subsistence

7.61 Consider any significant deduction within the context of the business. Is this the kind of business in which one would expect to see much travel and subsistence expenditure incurred? If advisers feel that the sum deducted is unusually high, an explanation should be provided on the return to demonstrate that there is no private or non-business element included.

Advertising, promotion and entertainment

7.62 These categories of expenditure are traditionally lucrative sources of adjustment and any substantial debit should be reviewed to ensure that it does not contain capital expenditure such as fees for corporate identity and other long-term design fees; and, more importantly, that all entertaining expenditure has been identified and added back. Entertaining expenditure is another matter that is vulnerable to real-time review in the course of a compliance check, with potential for lucrative recoveries in earlier years.

7.63 Businessmen customarily take a very narrow view of what is disallowable entertaining expenditure. HMRC analysis will be able to find out what an average level of entertaining expenditure is for a particular type of business. If little or none is shown in a particular set of accounts for that trade, then the natural inference is that the expenditure will have been made but is concealed under a different heading.

Legal and professional costs

7.64 Review any significant sum included under this heading. Review the balance sheet for signs of changes, such as additions to buildings, acquisitions of intangibles or share reorganisations of share capital that may have given rise to legal and professional costs. As with repairs and renewals, state on the return that a proper evaluation of the amount deducted has been made and give an analysis if necessary to support that statement.

7.65 *Selection for enquiry*

Bad debts

7.65 If the accounts show an excessive number of bad debts written off during a year, advisers should satisfy themselves that the debts are fully deductible for tax purposes. While in the past HMRC officers working alone may have been less inclined to undertake a potentially time-consuming review, HMRC's new team-working approach will mean that such reviews are easily undertaken within a compliance check context. Furthermore, comparative analysis will identify those businesses within unusual levels of bad debt.

Interest and other finance charges

7.66 Two elements within these categories should be considered by advisers:

(a) an addition for bank interest paid in respect of an overdrawn loan account should be considered in appropriate cases;

(b) credit card commission payments can be used to estimate the percentage of sales in the business that are not by credit card and which therefore may be cash sales, and the information HMRC is getting from credit card providers makes this an increasingly easy analysis to undertake. Businesses with substantial cash sales are inherently more likely to be subject to investigation than non-cash businesses and advisers may be able to perform a rough calculation to see whether the cash sales figure predicted by reference to stock sold is likely to be reflected in the recorded figure for turnover.

Other expenses

7.67 Consider the size of debits for miscellaneous and sundry items. Bear in mind that there is considerable statutory emphasis on record keeping under self-assessment and that items comprised within these debits are often under-supported by records. Consider re-analysing a disproportionately large debit under other more specific headings in the return. It is known that HMRC look specifically for accounts showing large amounts of expenditure under opaque general headings. If that approach is adopted, then detailed white space analysis and justification will be required.

Net profit

7.68 HMRC officers know that net profit is the most important indicator of how a business is doing in the eyes of many businessmen. The implication is that a consistently low level of net profit would be unlikely to be tolerated. A failure to address low profitability or a decline in profitability may be interpreted by HMRC to mean that profits are being understated.

Balance sheet

7.69 Advisers should not ignore the balance sheet (if there is one) in a pre-submission review of accounts. A great deal of information relevant to potential enquiry is contained there. Moreover, it is the kind of information that is easily subjected to computer analysis.

7.70 In general terms, advisers should consider – as HMRC will consider – what the balance sheet says about the return that the business is giving on capital employed. If this is low compared with other businesses carrying on that trade, and if the proprietors or shareholders (taking their drawings, remuneration and benefits into account) seem to be satisfied with a relatively low return, consider the reasons why return on capital is so low. Apparent continuing complacency about a low return on capital will increase the risk profile of a taxpayer since it suggests that profits may be being diverted from the business.

Fixed assets

7.71 Advisers should examine the fixed asset base of the company. If there has been an increase in these, the following points should be considered:

- If the acquisition was not funded by loans, where did the money come from? Are diverted profits being re-introduced into the business?
- If the business premises have been enlarged, does this mean that the trade has changed or that its size has been increased? If so notify the fact. Is the increased capacity reflected in turnover? If not, some justification should be included in the white space.
- If plant and machinery (including cars) have increased, is that investment reflected in increased turnover or profitability? Again, if not, include some justification in the white space.

Stock and work-in-progress

7.72 Reviews into stock valuations have traditionally been approached with caution by HMRC, largely because of the prodigious amount of work that a properly detailed review entailed. With a team-working approach to compliance checks HMRC has the resources to carry out detailed enquiries into stock valuations of even large concerns in a manner that is economical in terms of time and money.

7.73 *Selection for enquiry*

7.73 It follows that advisers should consider the accounts figures for stock and work-in-progress carefully. If the sums are round sums, particularly if they persist from year to year, then consider the basis upon which the figures were calculated. Calculate what the figures at the year-end actually represent in terms of a percentage of purchases. If the figure is not in accordance with what would be expected in the trade as a whole, the stock valuation may be wrong or, possibly, purchases have been understated to conceal diverted takings. However, if the trade is seasonal, allow for the impact of that on stock figures. The enactment in *FA 2007, Sch 24* of penalties specifically for teaming and lading offences signals renewed interest in pursuing adjustments of this kind.

7.74 If there is no figure for work-in-progress, consider the trade in question and evaluate whether work-in-progress would normally be expected in that trade. HMRC will know what is expected in the trade nationally and will be attracted to any case that is outwith the norm.

Debtors/prepayments/other current assets

7.75 Evaluate the interaction of debtors and sales. If the ratio of one to the other seems unusual in the context of the usual terms of credit in that line of business in general, or if it changes from year to year, find out why. Ostensibly illiquid businesses, or businesses that do not seem to mind when money comes in, will attract attention.

7.76 There may be a sound explanation; for example the trade may be, or have become, seasonal, such that the accounting date might influence the expected ratio. On the other hand there may be a cash aspect to the business that circumvents the need for rigorous credit control but that is also not being included in the accounts.

Cash

7.77 HMRC is always interested in the cash side of a business, and its approach to BRC shows that it sees small cash businesses as a particular compliance risk. Despite this, many balance sheets show no cash at all, or, if cash is shown, it is often a fairly small round sum. The natural inference is that cash records and cash control are poor or non-existent.

7.78 Advisers should consider whether it is likely that, on a particular accounting date, cash will actually have been a small round sum. If, for instance, the accounting date falls on a weekend, it may well be that cash takings were not banked on that day but were actually on hand. Similarly, if the trade is one where the proprietor is likely to need cash in order to make purchases of stock, it is unlikely that only a small amount of cash will be on hand.

In all cases a narrative relating to the cash aspect of a business is a sensible white space entry.

Loans and overdrawn bank accounts

7.79 Advisers should consider the level of security that would be required for any loans and overdrafts. Are there any assets suitable for use as security for any loans in the balance sheet? If there are not, and substantial loans are present, the natural inference is that the proprietors or directors have provided security themselves. If the business has shown low profitability for some years, consider how the proprietors or directors could have managed to acquire such a substantial capital base in the context of their declared drawings or remuneration. Suitable explanations of security for increased financing should be made in the white space.

Other liabilities: directors' current accounts

7.80 These have always been subject to scrutiny when they are overdrawn. However, advisers should also examine the source of any increase in a credit balance or decrease in a debit balance on such an account. The question that will be asked is where the money came from to account for the increase, if there is no obvious source within the accounts such as a bonus or a dividend. Consider whether the director's known liquid capital position can support any unexplained introduction of funds.

In this context advisers should bear in mind that HMRC will be able to correlate all of a director's income and capital details when analysing a current account critically.

Capital accounts

7.81 HMRC officers are always interested in details of capital introduced and drawings. If capital introduced is shown in the drawings account, advisers should make sure that the source of it can be identified. The HMRC view is, broadly, that capital introduced represents recycled profits of the business that have been diverted previously unless there is an identifiable source for the sum introduced.

7.82 Low drawings have always been a trigger for compliance action and are likely to remain so. Advisers should review not only the adequacy of drawings for a particular year, but also the pattern of drawings from year to year. HMRC's assumption is that it is very hard indeed to reduce one's standard of living to any significant extent, and that this applies especially to

7.83 *Selection for enquiry*

the business community whose lives are directed to the generation of their own income.

Return review

7.83 RIS analysis of a taxpayer's affairs will include not only the accounts of the business or company concerned, but also a review of the personal tax returns of the individuals who run that business.

7.84 In broad terms, tax returns provide an opportunity to assess the growth in personal wealth of an individual. Should this growth be out of step with the declared results for the taxpayer's business or with his remuneration, then compliance action becomes more likely.

Investment income

7.85 Does the pattern of investment income received suggest that the individual has been able to deposit significant sums at interest? If so, is it likely that those sums could have been saved out of known income, given a reasonable estimate of necessary outgoings?

7.86 Exponentially increasing investment income that is not matched by increased earned income or a capital disposal will contribute to an adverse risk profile. The inference will be that the taxpayer either has an undeclared income stream or has made an undisclosed capital disposal, either of which may mean that tax is at risk. Similarly, the appearance of dividend income on a return may also beg a question about the source of the funds needed to purchase the underlying shares.

Any sums received from non-taxable sources (inheritances, winnings) should be disclosed clearly in the white space.

Capital gains

7.87 Where a capital gain is shown on the return, the question to ask is whether the individual could reasonably have afforded the asset in the year when it was acquired.

With the effluxion of time, RIS analysis can draw on a very substantial picture of a taxpayer's financial position, and comparisons of that type will be easy to make. Advisers need to ensure that they keep sufficiently detailed records to make a similar comparison.

> **Example 7.2**
> Through Internet mining and other public information sources, HMRC identified that an affluent taxpayer had acquired several properties overseas worth more than £1 million, paying deposits of £100,000. Declared income from the tax return was only some £6,000 per year. The inevitable enquiry revealed substantial undeclared letting income and capital gains.

7.88 Where capital gains are at issue, substantial reliefs may also feature on the return. It is known that capital gains, losses and reliefs are subjected to review so particular care must be taken. These are always subject to complex conditions and advisers should always ensure that the relief claimed is actually available. Penalties may well follow on a negligent claim and the amount of tax – and therefore the tax-geared penalty – can be large.

PRACTICE MANAGEMENT

7.89 It is notorious – and true – that a bad professional relationship with HMRC has an adverse effect on the way in which HMRC deals with the tax affairs of a firm's clients. A review of a case always involves a consideration of the standing and reputation of the firm acting for a taxpayer, and as HMRC's spotlight focuses increasingly on agent behaviour, the impact of poor practice will increase.

It follows that advisers should consider reviewing their firms' working practices with a view to ensuring that relations with HMRC run as smoothly and professionally as possible.

7.90 A reputation as a dilatory, inept or unprofessional firm is easily acquired and hard to lose. HMRC will soon recognise those firms that are inclined to submit accounts and returns late, incomplete, or poorly presented; who habitually make technical mistakes; who are slow to reply to correspondence; or that are known for an habitually abrasive, 'anti-Revenue' approach.

THE FUTURE

7.91 There is no doubt that HMRC has embarked on a new phase of proactive engagement with compliance risk. The higher profile activities it undertakes, such as campaigns and taskforces, show just how extensive and thorough its risk analysis is, because each of those initiatives is underpinned by knowledge of expected yield, specifically so that the success of the campaigns can be measured. The signs are that HMRC's belief in the accuracy of its RIS information is justified.

7.92 *Selection for enquiry*

7.92 In such an environment, a checklist like the one above is useful but advisers cannot afford to stop there. Risk in the modern tax environment is a far more nebulous concept, involving not only items in accounts and returns but also behaviour and attitude, as inferred from a wide variety of information sources.

7.93 With discounted penalties available for unprompted disclosures, the role of advisers in the compliance matrix has changed radically and permanently and it is now incumbent upon all to advise clients of the range of potential risk and of what can be done should there be something amiss that requires disclosure.

7.94 Advisers should make it their business to become as well acquainted as possible with a client's business affairs, going well beyond mere accounts preparation, so that an informed view can be taken about what the accounts and returns say. For example, the practitioner who fails to visit the business premises regularly may not realise that some back-door cash sales are being made, or that a flat above the business premises is being rented out, or occupied by a relative of a director rent free. Now that HMRC has unfettered access to business premises, assets and records, compliance checks present real risks and advisers must adopt a suitably forensic approach in response.

7.95 Similarly, advisers should try to gain an impression of the lifestyles of their clients. Substantial property interests, expensive tastes and hobbies are all easy to identify for an HMRC officer conducting a pre-enquiry review or a compliance check. If these areas seem inconsistent with the taxpayer's known income and capital resources, this will be reflected in HMRC's risk profile of the client and advisers would be wise to address the matter with the client before HMRC does so. Know Your Client (KYC) is more than a social exercise!

7.96 Advisers are uniquely placed to gather a very broad range of information about the financial and personal affairs of their clients, and that background knowledge is a vital element in being able to evaluate the real meaning of apparently anomalous matters in accounts and returns and to give the essential factual detail and background context to HMRC in the form of white space narrative disclosure.

7.97 None of the foregoing is meant to suggest that advisers should forbear from fighting on behalf of their clients' best interests as strongly as possible should a compliance check commence. Indeed, more than ever before, managing client interaction with HMRC to keep risk profiles permanently low is a skill that any reputable adviser needs to develop and retain. But where selection is based on risk analysis, every effort should be made to ensure that clients'—and advisers'—heads are as far below the parapet as possible.

KEY POINTS

7.98 It's all about perceived risk, so think laterally:

1   Explain changes in the return and accounts profile.
2   Maintain good records.
3   Watch tax-related behaviour. Try to:
    (a)   comply on time;
    (b)   pay on time;
    (c)   steer clear of avoidance schemes.
4   Keep tabs on:
    (a)   how a client's business changes;
    (b)   how your clients invest the money they make;
    (c)   how clients present to the outside world and the press.
5   Review accounts and returns for:
    (a)   inconsistencies;
    (b)   anomalies.

Chapter 8

Conduct of enquiries

Helen Adams BSc (Hons) FCA CTA TEP CEDR Accredited Mediator
Tax Principal, BDO LLP

SIGNPOSTS

- **Gathering information** – it has never been easier for HMRC to search for and obtain data, from specific third party information to bulk data from other tax jurisdictions: it is all processed by Connect to identify enquiry targets (see **8.6–8.16**).

- **Enquiry triggers** – HMRC will open an enquiry when it believes a taxpayer has obtained more income or gains than he declared and there are a variety of circumstances where it knows there is a high risk of under or non-disclosure (see **8.17–8.19**).

- **Cases where no return is submitted** – HMRC may issue simple assessments, determinations or discovery assessments to assess tax where no return is submitted. Penalties may be charged for failures to notify (see **8.20–8.27**).

- **Criminal tax investigations** – HMRC may commence a criminal investigation with a view to prosecution for a number of offences including cheating the public revenue and fraudulent evasion of income tax as well as the new strict liability offences. Investigations may begin as criminal investigations or be converted to a criminal investigation from another type of case. HMRC may ask the High Court issue Unexplained Wealth Orders too (see **8.28–8.31**).

- **Encouraging voluntary disclosures** – Specific campaigns and voluntary disclosure facilities have proved an effective way for HMRC to increase the tax take from its risk-profiling work. These include the Worldwide Disclosure Facility which precedes and somewhat facilitates HMRC's proposed Requirement to Correct (see **8.32–8.47**).

- **Multi-tax enquiries** – Previously referred to as the Single Compliance Process, HMRC now operates multi-tax enquiries for many tax investigations – particularly for business taxpayers (see **8.48–8.62**);

Conduct of enquiries **8.1**

- **Collaborative working** – HMRC adopted a formal strategy of collaborative working to streamline and shorten the enquiry process to cut costs for all parties compared to traditional correspondence-based enquiries (see **8.63–8.68**).

- **Countering tax avoidance** – HMRC's Counter-Avoidance Directorate investigates a sample of users of particular tax avoidance arrangements (TAAs) to test the technical validity of the TAA and its implementation; accelerated payment notices may be issued to hasten the tax payment; the outcome of the test case can lead to HMRC issuing follower notices to other users of the TAA. HMRC may consider imposing penalties after some TAA failures and other consequences may follow due to the Serial Tax Avoidance and General Anti-Abuse Rule (GAAR) regimes (see **8.69–8.94**).

- **Maintaining progress despite delays** – Although a taxpayer who objects to HMRC delays in handling an enquiry can apply for a closure notice, HMRC has considerably more powers to take action that will help progress the enquiry (see **8.95–8.99**).

- **Estimating in the absence of full information** – Estimating exercises are, by their nature, little more than guess work but there are many ways to research and calculate figures that are accepted as credible by HMRC (see **8.100–8.106**).

- **Expanding enquiries into other years** – HMRC will invoke the presumption of continuity when it identifies an error in a tax return that may affect other years. HMRC will then make discovery assessments within the statutory time limits which vary according to the taxpayer's behaviour (see **8.107–8.113**).

- **Key forms that HMRC may request** – Where something has been omitted from a return, HMRC will usually want the taxpayer to sign one or more certificates before an enquiry is closed (see **8.114–8.125**).

- **Deadlock: what is the way forward?** – If progress on an enquiry becomes deadlocked, HMRC has more options than the taxpayer to push the case forward but both parties have the opportunity to use alternative dispute resolution (see **8.126–8.130**).

- **Penalties** – While HMRC bears the burden of proof to demonstrate the taxpayer's behaviour, as the nature of the taxpayer's behaviour affects the level of tax penalty charged, HMRC will often start by arguing that the taxpayer's behaviour was 'deliberate' – forcing the taxpayers' adviser to contest the point (see **8.131–8.144**).

- **Settling the case** – HMRC can issue closure notices, assessments and/or determinations to close an enquiry where time is of the essence or in other cases opt for a contract settlement (see **8.145–8.156**).

8.1 Conduct of enquiries

- **Tax debt collection** – HMRC has extensive debt collection powers including collecting debts direct from taxpayers' bank accounts and using bailiffs. Payment by instalments may be agreed via contract settlements or via time to pay arrangements (see **8.157–8.158**).

- **Carrots and sticks** – HMRC's enforcement powers include the option to publish taxpayer's details or enter the taxpayer into the Managing Serious Defaulters programme (see **8.159–8.166**).

- **Sanctions on tax advisers** – HMRC may penalise and publish the details of some tax agents. It is important for advisers to understand the triggers so they can identify what to do/not do and avoid conflicts of interest (see **8.167–8.175**).

- **Key points** – For a list of points in conclusion see **8.176**.

INTRODUCTION

8.1 HMRC, as a government organisation, has significant powers at its disposal to counter tax evasion, avoidance and simple errors. Its officers have the luxury of not having to complete time cards or justify fees to clients although the National Audit Office and parliamentary committees may review HMRC's activities to see if it is delivering value for money. While their officers work within boundaries set by HMRC, they do not have to compare the amount of tax at stake to the amount of time spent on an enquiry.

8.2 Having said all that, their goal is clear: to identify the taxpayers whose returns are not correct, investigate and collect the tax due. This does include checking whether taxpayers are getting things right, but increasingly this focus is falling away in favour of resourcing based on the perceived risk of a loss of tax.

8.3 The considerable powers at HMRC's officers' disposal, largely as a consequence of the changes in UK legislation from 2007 to date and developments in technology and international co-operation on tax over the same period, mean that the cards could be perceived as being stacked in HMRC's favour. HMRC also wins the majority of cases considered by the Tribunals and Courts.

8.4 The key for an adviser who is seeking to guide an anxious client through an in-depth enquiry is to understand where HMRC is coming from and what it may do next, and to use that knowledge to help bring the enquiry to an end as swiftly as possible.

8.5 This chapter provides an insight into HMRC's tactics from gathering data and deciding who to investigate, through the various stages of an enquiry to closing it. Knowing what HMRC may do at any stage can help tax advisers assist their clients in navigating through and emerging from an enquiry more speedily. The text also highlights some points at each of these stages that advisers may want to consider in order to progress the enquiry.

GATHERING INFORMATION

8.6 In today's Internet-dominated world it has never been easier for HMRC to search for and obtain data. It is common knowledge that HMRC has access to financial information such as interest credited to bank accounts, company information held at Companies House and, of course, the information in tax returns submitted to it, as well as information gleaned during tax enquiries.

8.7 However, HMRC can also obtain and access other information such as:

Source	Information
Land Registry and Zoopla	Purchase and sale price of properties, completion dates, names of owners and charges secured against the property as well as changes in property values over a period of time
Company websites	Products or services sold, where they are based, etc
Ebay, Amazon, Gumtree, etc	Information about people who sell goods online via these websites such as the number of transactions
Newspapers, magazines, Facebook	Articles on business, individual wealth and lifestyle as well as information in advertisements
Google Streetview	Type of house, neighbourhood, car on the drive
Google, Bing, Yahoo, etc	Search engines can locate information from anywhere in the world
gov.uk website	Tax evasion reports via Tax Evasion information report form or calls to the HMRC tax evasion hotline

8.8 In January 2018, HMRC updated some of its Compliance Check factsheets to warn taxpayers that:

'HMRC may observe, monitor, record and retain internet data which is available to anyone. This is known as "open source" material and includes news reports, internet sites, Companies House and Land registry records, blogs and social networking sites where no privacy settings have been applied.'

8.9 *Conduct of enquiries*

Such information will be factored into HMRC's decision-making about whether to investigate a taxpayer and, if so, the questions to ask.

8.9 HMRC can access records held at Companies House, including details of the companies for which an individual is/was a director. This information may also enable HMRC to identify companies and/or LLPs who are yet to submit tax returns.

Companies House now keeps data on persons who exert significant influence and/or control over the companies/LLPs registered there. This may help HMRC to more easily identify companies/LLPs that are part of larger structures or owned via trusts.

8.10 In 2017, HMRC required certain trusts to join the UK trusts register and disclose details such as a statement of accounts and details of each 'beneficial owner' for each trust. Such information may help HMRC identify trusts, settlors and/or beneficiaries who are yet to fully declare UK tax. This register arose from the EU's Fourth Money Laundering Directive so many other jurisdictions are also creating these registers.

8.11 In March 2018, the Government announced that it will legislate to introduce a public register showing who owns and controls overseas companies and other legal entities that own UK property or participate in UK government procurement. Failure to register or update information on the register will be a criminal offence after the register is in operation, which is expected in 2021, and other sanctions may also apply. This is part of cross-government efforts to crack down on tax evasion, money laundering and financial crime following press and public pressure. HMRC is likely to use the information on the register whilst conducting tax investigations and enquiries.

8.12 HMRC can also approach third parties using its powers under *FA 2008, Sch 36, paras 2, 5* and *5A*, such as UK branches of offshore banks, to ask for data regarding accounts held by anyone with a UK address or information on fees paid to medical consultants by private health insurance companies.

The same power can be used to obtain details of rental income paid by estate agents to landlords, for example.

8.13 From an offshore perspective, HMRC receives significant amounts of data provided under double taxation agreements and international tax information exchange agreements (including the Common Reporting Standard) and from other sources, eg offshore banks. HMRC may also receive information and documentation from overseas authorities under criminal investigation procedures.

Conduct of enquiries **8.17**

8.14 Once HMRC receives bulk and other data, it is fed into its sophisticated data analysis system (called Connect), which analyses and cross-references large volumes of data from third parties, HMRC's records and the internet to identify discrepancies, trends and connections. HMRC may then use this information when deciding whether to investigate or enquire into a taxpayer's affairs.

8.15 For example, HMRC compares information about property income or bank interest to entries on tax returns and identifies under-declarations of income. The output identifies high risk cases for investigation. HMRC can then make more focused information requests to the taxpayer, his bankers (including credit and debit purchase data from the UK's merchant acquirers), customers, suppliers, and other relevant bodies as necessary using its various information powers.

8.16 Developments in computerised data analysis techniques including artificial intelligence are beginning to further enhance HMRC's ability to identify discrepancies and cases for further investigation. Such analysis may involve the use of algorithms to consider and extrapolate information from government and third party databases including credit card transactions and internet usage to identify cases where outgoings exceed declared income.

Tips for the start of enquiries

- If HMRC opens a full enquiry or investigation into a taxpayer's affairs, consider doing a thorough internet search to see what is evident on the internet; it may help to show what triggered HMRC's concerns.

- Also, ask enough open questions of the client regarding their background, lifestyle, sources of income, capital and outgoings early in the investigation to help you identify issues, potential misunderstandings (perhaps caused by assumptions, preconceptions or extrapolation), or the answers to set HMRC's mind at rest.

ENQUIRY TRIGGERS

8.17 Enquiries take different forms. They may be self-assessment enquiries, eg focusing on an aspect of a taxpayer's return or a 'full' enquiry into all or almost all aspects of a taxpayer's affairs (see **CHAPTER 10**). Other enquiries will include investigations under the Contractual Disclosure Facility, also known as Code of Practice 9 (COP9) (see **CHAPTER 2**), in cases of suspected tax fraud and investigations under Code of Practice 8 (COP8)

8.18 *Conduct of enquiries*

(see **Chapter 2**) into other matters, eg avoidance. In extreme cases HMRC will investigate with a view to criminal prosecution (see **Chapter 3**). Which type of enquiry largely depends upon the extent, type and reason for the issues that HMRC perceives require resolution.

8.18 In the broadest sense, HMRC will open an enquiry when it believes a taxpayer has obtained more income, gains or profits than they declared.

Enquiry trigger	Reason why it is a trigger
Previous enquiries generating additional tax due especially where record keeping was inadequate	HMRC will want to check if the returns and accounts are accurate now
High earned income but no investment income	Unless the taxpayer has an expensive lifestyle, HMRC may want to check if he has undeclared investment income
Fluctuating income and/or expenses	Big changes in income or expenses in accounts may cause HMRC to ask why, in case the accounts are wrong
Different profit margins compared to average for that business type	This may indicate that not all the business transactions are reflected in the accounts
Accounts just not making sense, eg a new investor coming in but not charging interest at the market rate and/or allowing other finance to be removed (eg family/shareholder finance)	Uncommercial transactions may indicate funds being provided by or sent to an account that is undeclared
Perceived high risk areas, ie types of businesses which are perceived as failing to pay the right amount of tax	Examples may be businesses that have cash takings such as restaurants and taxi drivers as it is easy not to declare all the takings
Means issues, ie how does the taxpayer afford that asset, loan, lifestyle or support dependants given the income declared?	If the taxpayer has high outgoings then HMRC considers his income should be similarly high and will investigate if not
International issues, eg residence and domicile	This is a hot topic and HMRC will check if the person really is non-UK resident and/or non-UK domiciled

Conduct of enquiries **8.20**

Enquiry trigger	Reason why it is a trigger
DOTAS/DASVOIT numbers	HMRC will want to check its implementation and whether the tax avoidance arrangement works technically
Being in the 'Managing Serious Defaulters' regime	The taxpayer has paid a penalty for a deliberate error, so HMRC will be monitoring him more closely (including through enquiries) whilst he is in the regime

8.19 The suspicions may be generated from the Connect analysis. HMRC may then seek additional documents and information from third parties and/or undertake a business economics review before or during the enquiry, depending on its concerns, whether it is considering prosecuting the taxpayer and the level of co-operation it experiences during the enquiry.

Further information is available in **CHAPTER 7**.

Focus

- Help your client keep high quality financial records.
- If your client's tax return has unusual entries on it (or is missing entries that HMRC might expect) then consider making an explanatory note in the Additional Information box on the return in order to explain the reason and pre-empt an enquiry.
- If your client struggles to give you the information for his return (eg because of Alzheimer's disease or other medical conditions) then get formal permissions in place so you can get information direct from his banks, etc and consider adapting your work to do things like reviewing their bank statements so that transfers to new accounts or investments are identified at the tax return preparation stage.
- If you identify that something has gone wrong, assist the taxpayer to make a voluntary disclosure obtaining specialist advice where necessary, especially where there is any indication that the issues arise from deliberate or intentional actions or omissions.

CASES WHERE NO RETURN IS SUBMITTED

8.20 In cases where returns have not been submitted, HMRC may adapt its approach. The three most likely scenarios are:

- simple assessment;

8.21 *Conduct of enquiries*

- non-submission of a return despite being notified of the need to submit one; and
- failing to notify HMRC of the need to submit a return and failing to submit one.

8.21 Simple assessment was introduced by *TMA 1970, s 28H–J* with effect from 2016/17. It allows HMRC to assess income tax or CGT liabilities using information already it holds without the need for individuals or trustees to complete self-assessment tax returns.

If a person is sent a simple assessment then they no longer have an obligation to notify HMRC that they should be assessed to tax under *TMA 1970, s 7* for that tax year unless they are chargeable to income tax or capital gains tax for the year of assessment on any income or gain that is not included in the assessment. HMRC will not send a simple assessment if it has sent a notice to file a tax return (eg under *TMA 1970, s 8*) but HMRC may withdraw a notice to file a tax return and issue a simple assessment instead.

The standard procedure for issuing assessments (*TMA 1970, s 30A*) applies as does the standard assessment time limit. Each element of the simple assessment should be carefully checked. If the taxpayer disagrees with it, they must write to HMRC within 60 days to challenge incorrect information in a simple assessment (see *TMA 1970, s 31AA*). HMRC will then consider their comments, decide whether it needs more information and reply to the taxpayer. If the taxpayer disagrees with HMRC's response then taxpayers have 30 days to formally appeal against HMRC's decision.

8.22 If returns are requested but not submitted then HMRC can use its powers to issue determinations (eg *TMA 1970, s 28C, FA 1998, Sch 18, para 36*) to quantify and assess the estimated amount which it considers would be included on any return were it to be submitted. It therefore draws on information in its possession when estimating the liability.

8.23 The determination may only be displaced by submission of returns within the later of three years from the filing date and 12 months from the date of the determination (see *TMA 1970, s 28C(3)* and *(5)*). Once the tax debt is on the system as a consequence of the determination, the Collector of Taxes will proceed with its usual debt collection tactics (see **CHAPTER 22**). In addition, late payment interest will be charged as will penalties for late submission under *FA 2009, Sch 55* (see **19.24**).

8.24 Taxpayers are obligated to notify HMRC when they need to submit a return (*TMA 1970, s 7; FA 1998, Sch 18, para 2*). If a taxpayer fails to notify HMRC then it may take some time for HMRC to realise that there is a problem. When HMRC notices, eg through analysing information in Connect, it will either issue a number of years' tax returns for completion

Conduct of enquiries **8.29**

or open an investigation, eg under COP9. It can also use its information powers (see **Chapter 16**) to obtain the information necessary before issuing discovery assessments (*TMA 1970, s 29 and FA 1998, Sch 18, para 41*) or determinations to bring what it considers to be an appropriate amount of tax into charge.

8.25 Penalties can also be charged which, if issued under *FA 2008, Sch 41*, are tax geared and increase depending on the reason why the taxpayer failed to notify HMRC. Conversely, there may be no penalties if the taxpayer has a reasonable excuse for the failure and remedies it without undue delay after becoming aware of the issue (see **19.57–19.68**).

8.26 In such situations, advisers should seriously consider advising their client to make a voluntary disclosure to HMRC to bring his affairs up to date before HMRC identifies the issue; not least because it may reduce the risk of an investigation with a view to prosecution and enable further mitigation of any penalties (see **Chapter 14**).

8.27 Finally, *Goldsmith v Revenue & Customs Comrs* [2018] UKFTT 5 (TC) confirmed that HMRC cannot issue a tax return just to enforce the debt when it already knows the person's liability.

CRIMINAL TAX INVESTIGATIONS

8.28 HMRC's Fraud Investigations Service conducts tax investigations using criminal as well as civil law powers. **Chapter 3** describes direct tax criminal investigations with a view to prosecution. Criminal investigations are conducted using criminal law information powers eg the *Police & Criminal Evidence Act 1984* and the *Serious Organised Crime & Police Act 2005*.

In cases where HMRC believes that deliberate errors or omissions occurred then HMRC will consider whether to conduct a criminal investigation or to offer COP9 (Contractual Disclosure Facility) instead. HMRC may also convert an enquiry or investigation conducted under civil powers into a criminal investigation after becoming aware of something which suggests a criminal offence was committed.

8.29 Criminal law tax evasion offences include cheating the public revenue, fraud and false accounting. All of these offences require the jury to be satisfied beyond reasonable doubt that the person was dishonest and realised his conduct was dishonest.

The offence of fraudulent evasion of income tax (*TMA 1970, s 106A*) was joined by new strict liability offences (*TMA 1970, s 106B–H*). By their very nature of being 'strict liability' HMRC does not need to demonstrate that the

8.30 *Conduct of enquiries*

taxpayer intended to get their tax wrong by failing to notify, submitting an incorrect return etc i.e. a careless error will be sufficient. These new offences apply to income tax or capital gains tax chargeable wholly or partly by reference to offshore income, assets or activities for 2016/17 and subsequent years (*SI 2017/970*).

8.30 On 31 January 2018 the government introduced a new power via the *Criminal Finances Act 2017* and *SI 2018/78*: Unexplained Wealth Orders (UWOs). UWOs require a person to provide documents and explain the nature and extent of their interest in property (land, building, vehicles etc) exceeding £50,000, how it was acquired (including how its purchase was funded) and provide details of any settlement holding the property.

HMRC and other authorities such as the National Crime Agency can ask the High Court to issue a UWO where there are 'reasonable grounds to suspect' an inconsistency or disproportionality between a person's legitimate income and the extent of their assets. HMRC or the other authorities may ask the High Court to issue an interim freezing order when the UWO is issued.

8.31 If a satisfactory explanation is not given in response to the UWO then, in the absence of a reasonable excuse for that failure, the property will be confiscated (forfeited) under *the Proceeds of Crime Act 2002, Part 5*. If a false or misleading statement is made then this may be an offence resulting in a fine or prison sentence.

Focus

Advisers without suitable expertise must refer their client to an experienced solicitor specialising in criminal tax investigations if:

- HMRC opens a criminal investigation or invites a client to a meeting referencing one legislation relating to a criminal offence.

- A client admits that they previously incorrectly signed a Certificate of Full Disclosure (**8.114**, **8.115** and **8.122**) then they are at risk of prosecution.

ENCOURAGING VOLUNTARY DISCLOSURES

8.32 HMRC frequently launches campaigns and disclosure facilities to encourage particular taxpayers to make voluntary disclosures of errors.

8.33 Current campaigns include:

- the 'let property campaign' to encourage disclosure of rental income from properties in the UK and overseas;

Conduct of enquiries **8.36**

- the 'credit card sales campaign' aimed at individuals and businesses who accept credit or debit card payments who need to tell HMRC that they have not declared all their income.

8.34 Further details about current campaigns can be found by typing 'HMRC campaigns' into the search box on the GOV.UK website. However, some campaigns are conducted informally and so do not appear on the official list. An example is a campaign by HMRC's Offshore Co-ordination Unit that wrote to individuals who were identified as having an account with a specific Jersey bank who had not included any interest from their accounts on their UK tax returns. The letters asked each individual to complete forms confirming whether their UK returns were correct or whether they were going to make a disclosure of undisclosed income to HMRC. It is likely that the recipients for these letters were identified by HMRC's Connect system comparing bank account data against tax return data.

8.35 In addition to campaigns, on 5 September 2016, HMRC opened the Worldwide Disclosure Facility (WDF). The disclosure facility offers no 'deals' so taxpayers must disclose and pay the full tax, late payment interest and penalties due whilst making a disclosure (albeit time to pay arrangements may be requested). Penalties are calculated using existing statutory rules including uplifts for offshore matters and offshore asset moves penalties (*FA 2015, Sch 21*). HMRC perceives that no 'carrots' are needed to encourage taxpayers to use the WDF because:

- HMRC is now receiving information from overseas jurisdictions via automatic annual information exchanges such as those under the Common Reporting Standard;

- HMRC is confident that it will be able to analyse the data and efficiently identify taxpayers who have failed to fully disclose UK tax liability on offshore income and gains;

- HMRC introduced strict liability criminal offences (so that it no longer has to prove the taxpayer intended to get their tax wrong) for offshore matters via *FA 2016*, whilst maintaining the existing criminal offenses such as cheating the public revenue (**CHAPTER 3**); and

- Offshore penalties have been increased via several recent Finance Acts including through the introduction of the Offshore Asset Moves Penalty (**CHAPTER 5**) such that the maximum effective penalty rate in some situations will be 300% of the undisclosed tax plus an asset-based penalty. These sanctions are enhanced by the Failure to Correct sanctions (*F(No2)A 2017, Sch 18*) (**CHAPTER 5**).

8.36 Taxpayers may use the WDF to disclose UK tax which wholly or partly relates to offshore issues i.e. income arising, assets situated/held or activities carried out wholly or mainly in an offshore jurisdiction as well as

8.37 *Conduct of enquiries*

'anything having effect as if it were income, assets or activities of the kind described above'. Whilst there is no prosecution protection for taxpayers using the WDF, HMRC is unlikely to prosecute taxpayers who make full, accurate disclosures.

8.37 HMRC expects taxpayers or their agents to register online to make a disclosure. Taxpayers will then have 90 days within which to submit their full disclosure after their disclosure reference number is issued, although this period may be extended to 180 days for complex disclosures. In addition to disclosing tax, taxpayers will also have to detail the maximum value of offshore assets held at any time in the previous five years. For many with offshore issues this will be a tight deadline unless they hold all relevant information prior to registering. It should also be noted that IHT for periods more than 20 years ago, VAT and tax credits cannot be disclosed via the WDF. Tax, interest and penalties must be paid when the disclosure is submitted, unless time to pay is agreed. Guidance on using the WDF is available via: www.gov.uk/guidance/worldwide-disclosure-facility-make-a-disclosure.

8.38 An integral part of the WDF disclosure is a section in which the taxpayer must explain if they reduced the amount of tax due 'because of consideration and interpretation of the law'. This may be obvious steps such as non-UK domicile, non-UK residence for some or all of the period covered by the disclosure, use of the remittance basis or more complex areas such as Transfer of Assets legislation. Decisions as to the reason why the error or failure occurred which then affect assessment time limits and penalties through behavioural classifications can also be covered here. It is likely that HMRC will use the information gleaned for risk assessment purposes and to decide which disclosures to investigate post submission.

8.39 HMRC is aware that complex technical issues sometimes accompany offshore matters. For the first time for a disclosure facility, HMRC is offering a non-statutory clearance process. The clearance application must be made within 90 days of registration for the WDF. The final disclosure must be submitted within 90 days of the 'application for clarification [being] finalised'. Details of the clearance process are available via www.gov.uk/guidance/non-statutory-clearance-service-guidance (Annex E). HMRC expects the clearance application to give details of the issues for which clarification is needed, the taxpayer's view of the tax consequences arising and an explanation 'why you believe the tax treatment and application of the legislation is open to different possible interpretations'.

8.40 HMRC will not provide 'advice' via the clearance process if it 'doesn't think that there are genuine points of uncertainty – they will explain why they think this and direct you to the relevant online guidance'. According to its guidance, HMRC considers that most decisions it makes via its clearance process are not appealable.

Conduct of enquiries **8.44**

8.41 HMRC acknowledges disclosures within 15 days and aims to tell taxpayers within a further 90 days what HMRC's next steps will be eg accept the disclosure or enquire into it. In limited cases, such as those in which HMRC perceives the disclosure to materially incorrect, HMRC will launch an investigation (eg under Codes of Practice 8 or 9 or with a view to a criminal prosecution).

8.42 Disclosures using the WDF and via the campaigns listed at **8.33** above are to be made using HMRC's Digital Disclosure Service (DDS). This is an on-line portal. Once the form is drafted it may be printed so that the client can check it before it is signed and submitted. Given the limited space for entries on some parts of the form, agents are likely to need to prepare and submit a disclosure report describing the disclosure in full and the reasons why the errors or omissions occurred before submitting it by post at the same time as submitting the online disclosure forms. A tip is to make it clear in the online form's boxes that a disclosure is being submitted by post too, in order to help HMRC identify and match up the written and online submissions.

8.43 For those taxpayers who need to make a disclosure of a tax liability that is not encompassed by current campaigns or the WDF, HMRC offers a general voluntary disclosure opportunity via the DDS. Details can be found via: www.gov.uk/government/publications/hmrc-your-guide-to-making-a-disclosure . In addition, voluntary disclosures can be made via Customer Compliance Managers and by using the Contractual Disclosure Facility (also known as Code of Practice 9) where at least one deliberate errors or failures occurred. COP9, unlike the WDF, provides protection from prosecution in exchange for a full disclosure (see **CHAPTER 2**). Further details on making voluntary disclosures in general are available via **CHAPTER 14**.

8.44 *Finance (No 2) Act 2017, Sch 18* introduced a new Requirement to Correct (RTC) (see **CHAPTER 5**). The RTC required all taxpayers whose UK tax positions were not correctly disclosed previously to correct their UK tax position on or before 30 September 2018 with respect to income tax, capital gains tax and inheritance tax. Those who failed to correct their positions under the RTC will face higher penalties as well as having their details published, unless they have a 'reasonable excuse' for the failure to disclose. The legislation sets out what constitutes a reasonable excuse for these purposes, which is restricted compared to other instances of 'reasonable excuse'. The Failure to Correct (FTC) penalties (see **CHAPTER 5**) will effectively be a new regime that retrospectively supersedes all existing regimes for the offshore matter which was not declared by 30 September 2018. FTC sanctions also include HMRC publishing the details of people who failed to correct by the deadline despite being aware that they should correct their UK tax affairs (*F(No 2)A 2017, Sch 18, para 30*). Standard assessment time limits are modified (see **8.109–8.110** below).

8.45 *Conduct of enquiries*

8.45 HMRC expected all taxpayers with offshore interests to review their UK tax affairs to ensure their tax position (including any technical views eg their domicile status) were correct. Those taxpayers with open self assessment enquiries or other tax investigations for prior years were not excluded from the RTC.

8.46 Such disclosure facilities and campaigns are relatively cheap to run for HMRC and bring in revenue. HMRC then uses its information powers to gather data from third parties to enable it to identify people who did not come forward during the campaign who appear to have not disclosed all their income and gains. Decisions will then be taken as to whether to prosecute them or to open investigations instead.

8.47 In addition to formal campaigns and disclosure facilities, HMRC also undertakes publicity such as billboard advertisements, newspaper advertisements and comments in the press. The publicity often relates to successes in cases such as prosecutions for tax evasion or court decisions in HMRC's favour on significant tax avoidance cases. One reason for the publicity is to encourage taxpayers to resolve their tax affairs proactively (eg through voluntary disclosures) and to deter others from evasion and avoidance.

Focus

- If your client made an error on their tax returns in the past, encourage them to make a voluntary disclosure as soon as possible, as making a voluntary disclosure usually leads to reduced penalties and avoids the risk of a criminal investigation.

- Consider notifying HMRC immediately that you become aware that the client needs to make a disclosure, prior to the tax etc being quantified and the disclosure made. The reason for this is to protect the 'unprompted disclosure' penalty discount which will be lost should HMRC open an enquiry or investigation before it is aware that the taxpayer is making a disclosure. The WDF and Contractual Disclosure Facilities contain processes for this upfront notification, although consideration should also be given to the other deadlines within their process too.

- Careful consideration will need to be given to identify the most appropriate method for making a disclosure to HMRC depending on the taxpayer's circumstances, issues and amounts involved.

- If this is not your area of specialisation then do seek advice from a person experienced in such matters.

MULTI-TAX ENQUIRIES

8.48 In the past, HMRC visits to check the VAT or PAYE records of a business were regular affairs. If something amiss was identified, then it would be referred to the taxpayer's business/corporation tax district for follow up.

8.49 For many businesses, HMRC adapted its procedures so that it undertakes multi-tax enquiries (sometimes also referred to as cross-tax enquiries). This first appeared as trials for a single compliance process (SCP) approach for SME enquiries in approximately 2007. Trials were completed by 2012/13 and the SCP became 'business as usual' for HMRC, ie the elements of what was the SCP are absorbed within HMRC's workflow generally, eg within parts of its Litigation and Settlement Strategy (see the Collaborative Working section at **8.63–8.68** below), enquiry process and use of its powers. Consequently, additional information on multi-tax enquiries can also be found in the chapter on HMRC's information and inspection powers (**Chapter 16**).

8.50 A multi- or cross-tax enquiry is one in which HMRC focuses on more than one tax simultaneously. For example, business/corporation tax inspectors will be involved in an enquiry alongside specialists in VAT and/or PAYE and other taxes. This streamlining also enables HMRC to deal with the tax consequences of an error across a number of taxes simultaneously.

8.51 This can be seen in the Large Business Services' and WMBC's adoption of customer compliance managers (CCMs), formerly called customer relationship managers. Part of the CCM's role is to ensure that officers across the taxes work together to undertake enquiries and resolve issues within normal HMRC processes and powers.

8.52 In addition, HMRC targets resources at particular trades or professions in specific geographical areas through its taskforces. HMRC periodically announces new taskforces on its website. These taskforces will use all HMRC's standard powers and processes to ascertain whether the businesses targeted owe tax. They may focus on one tax but often they will focus on more than one. They will often visit the businesses involved (see **Chapter 16**).

8.53 One such taskforce is the Offshore Property Developers Task Force (OPDTF) launched in 2016. It is checking whether offshore companies that developed or are developing land and buildings in the UK are paying the correct amount of UK tax. The OPDTF is considering all taxes in its investigations, which are conducted by multi-disciplinary teams including HMRC's transfer pricing and large business specialists. For corporation tax, it considers issues such as whether the offshore company is actually UK resident or whether it has a permanent establishment generating profits which should be taxed in the UK. If companies failed to submit the necessary returns or

8.54 *Conduct of enquiries*

made incorrect returns then HMRC will seek the tax for all available periods taking into account assessment time limits together with late payment interest and penalties.

8.54 Occasionally, taskforces are cross agency involving the National Crime Agency, Financial Conduct Authority and/or Serious Fraud Office in addition to HMRC. An example of this is the Panama Papers Taskforce formed in April 2016 to investigate the data made available as a result of the International Consortium of Journalists investigation and the associated data leak. HMRC's part in such a taskforce is to establish whether any additional tax or duties are payable. This may be achieved using its civil or criminal powers.

8.55 The following table summarises departments within HMRC that use multi-tax enquiries:

HMRC office	Source of information	Other points
Local Compliance	Anywhere including Connect	Usually smaller cases, generally under self-assessment
Large Business Service	Anywhere including Connect	Large cases but not involving fraud or avoidance arrangements
Offshore Co-ordination Unit	Overseas tax authorities and financial institutions but also other information held by HMRC	The unit is part of HMRC's Fraud Investigation Service department
Fraud Investigation Service (formerly Specialist Investigations)	Anywhere including Connect	Deals with cases under COP8 and COP9
Taskforces/ campaigns hub	Anywhere including Connect	Targeted at different types of business for short periods to tackle perceived high risks of non-compliance

8.56 HMRC has finite resources and now tries to identify and focus on taxpayers which it perceives to be at a higher risk of issues. Usually HMRC begins an enquiry, particularly one covering multiple taxes, because it has specific information that indicates a problem with that taxpayer's tax position. For businesses, the enquiry begins with an opening letter detailing the areas of concern.

8.57 Increasingly that letter requests a meeting at the business premises with the business's owner/director combined with a review of business records from both direct and indirect tax perspectives. This is further detailed in **CHAPTER 16**, which also includes guidance on how to handle such inspections. Both the visit and the request for documents to be available that day are usually conducted under the auspices of *FA 2008, Sch 36*, unless the visit is a raid.

8.58 HMRC officers change departments during their careers. If HMRC opens what appears to be a 'full' self-assessment enquiry (ie one that looks into many aspects of a taxpayer's affairs) then it might be the case that the Local Compliance district has an officer in it who used to be part of HMRC's Fraud Investigation Service (formerly Specialist Investigations) department.

8.59 Officers in the Fraud Investigations Service receive extra investigative skills training and training in interviewing techniques. Those skills are useful in other districts to help them assess information provided during enquiries, identify questions to ask, and ask probing questions of taxpayers during meetings.

8.60 For meetings, it is advisable to carefully consider who the best person is to attend. It may be that the taxpayer's adviser is best placed to have the meeting but it could also be the case that it would be preferable to have the business owner or a director present. The latter would particularly be the case if HMRC wants to ask questions to help it understand the business and the role of key people within it. While there is no obligation to attend meetings with HMRC, it can sometimes be an efficient way of helping HMRC understand points, resolving misunderstandings and demonstrating a willingness to resolve the enquiry. This can help reduce tax-geared penalties if any errors are identified.

8.61 Further information regarding meetings is available in **CHAPTER 9** but, in terms of HMRC tactics, the HMRC team will consist of at least two people regardless of the size of the business. One of them will be the caseworker who will prepare a script of anticipated questions to cover a number of eventualities in advance of the meeting. HMRC will take notes of all the replies and produce notes of the meeting.

Tips for handling meetings

- Ask for an agenda detailing the topics for discussion.
- Ensure that the adviser is there too and that a good note is taken.
- If you know that there are issues, then tell HMRC at the start of the meeting/visit (ie what is wrong, why it is wrong, which years it affects and your proposed way to resolve it).
- Remind the client to answer the question that is asked and to say so if he does not know the answer.

8.62 *Conduct of enquiries*

> - Remind the client not to lie and not to guess: if he doesn't know then he should say so. The point can be followed up after the meeting.
>
> - Don't be lulled into a false sense of security by the pleasant nature of the HMRC officer: he is there to do a job.
>
> - Stay calm: if you need a break then take one.
>
> - If HMRC sends minutes after the meeting then you should check them and write to HMRC setting out any discrepancies between its version and your/the client's recollection of the discussion. If this is not done then HMRC's meeting notes may be taken as the final ones if the matter ends up in the tribunal at a later stage.

8.62 A common HMRC tactic is to ask questions about the director's personal tax affairs during an enquiry into a company. If HMRC has concerns about the director's personal affairs then that should be handled via an enquiry into the director, not via the company. Generally, personal records such as bank statements will not be relevant to a company's enquiry unless the personal bank account has been used for business transactions.

HMRC's usual approach is to understand the business's (or an individual's) affairs and gather information on the various points about which it is concerned before considering the tax technical aspects.

> **Focus**
>
> If you feel that HMRC is approaching matters on the wrong basis it may be that either it has some information that you do not, or it may be lacking information. If you believe it is the latter, then volunteer it and help HMRC understand the business or the particular issue. This should help HMRC identify what the key issues of concern are and shorten the enquiry. If there are errors then this approach should help minimise any penalties.
>
> Do not forget that HMRC may challenge the tax position by contesting the accounting treatment adopted for specific items in a company's audited accounts (see *Ball UK Holdings Limited v HMRC* [2017] UKFTT 457 (TC), for example). Specialist advice and/or an expert witness may be needed.

COLLABORATIVE WORKING

8.63 Collaborative working is a concept introduced by HMRC's Litigation and Settlement Strategy (LSS). It involves HMRC inspectors and tax advisers/taxpayers working together to resolve enquiries. Collaborative working involves:

- a discussion early in the enquiry as to what it is that concerns HMRC;
- a mutually agreed timetable for stages such as establishing facts, providing documentation, discussing queries and the way forward;
- providing regular progress updates;
- clarifying understanding of facts;
- agreeing key questions which need to be answered in order to resolve the dispute;
- agreeing the format in which information is to be provided;
- discussing technical arguments and interpretation and possible alternative interpretations; and
- working with the taxpayer/his adviser to agree the amount of tax, interest and penalties due.

Focus

- If HMRC asks for information or explanations and you are unsure why it is asking the question (ie what it is getting at) then call the caseworker, explain that if he can help you understand his concerns then you will be better able to identify the best way to answer them (eg with relevant explanations, etc). To the extent he can, albeit without revealing his sources, it is likely that he will explain his concerns.

- Read the LSS and associated guidance, particularly the collaborative working part.

8.64 However, one part of the collaborative working approach is not utilised in COP9 investigations; HMRC will not reveal its concerns as one central tenet of this type of investigation is that it is for the taxpayer to make a full disclosure and satisfy HMRC that there are no other unresolved issues.

8.65 While correspondence will be a key part of the process, meetings will also feature heavily. More progress can generally be made in a two-hour meeting (for which both sides are well prepared) than in three months of correspondence.

8.66 Most HMRC officers will also appreciate it if information is collated, analysed and presented to them rather than being given a bundle of documents, eg bank statements or complex contractual documentation, with no explanations.

8.67 *Conduct of enquiries*

Focus

Advisers can therefore help by:

- undertaking an analysis of transactions over a pre-agreed amount or for a pre-agreed sample period, providing explanations as to the source or destination of funds;

- combining and presenting results in a long letter or report to explain to HMRC the background, an overview of the work undertaken, the facts on the particular points under enquiry and explanations of complex transactions/documents together with any technical interpretations and the result in terms of any additional tax to pay (as demonstrated by computations and other documents submitted as appendices);

- anticipating the questions that HMRC may ask when reading the letter/report and answering them within the letter/report; and

- asking for an agenda of the key points for discussion for a meeting to discuss the way forward after HMRC has considered the contents of the report/letter.

8.67 This is a key part of collaborative working and should help demonstrate the 'telling', 'helping' and 'giving access' parts of the penalty reduction negotiation and, consequently, reduce the amount of any tax-geared penalties for errors.

8.68 This may appear resource intensive and costly in terms of fees for the client. However, the overall aim is to streamline the enquiry process and shorten it so the cost should be the same or less than the traditional correspondence-based approach when taken over the course of the entire enquiry.

COUNTERING TAX AVOIDANCE

8.69 HMRC's Counter-Avoidance Directorate (CAD) carries out most enquiries into Tax Avoidance Arrangements (TAAs). It identifies TAAs using the information provided to HMRC under the disclosure of tax avoidance schemes (DOTAS and DASVOIT) regimes and identifies other entries on tax returns that may relate to TAAs despite the omission of DOTAS numbers from the return. This enables CAD to identify new TAAs and group together similar TAAs being promoted by different firms.

8.70 HMRC challenges TAAs that it believes are disclosable under DOTAS. This is important as HMRC is able to take other steps to tackle

Conduct of enquiries **8.73**

TAAs which are disclosable eg Accelerated Payment Notices (see **8.78** below). Additionally, HMRC can use the extended time limits under *TMA 1970, s 36(1A)(d)* so that it has 20 years from the end of a tax year to issue discovery assessments where the loss of tax was attributable to TAAs which should be notified under DOTAS but which were not notified. For example, HMRC won *Root2Tax Limited v HMRC* [2017] UKFTT 696 (TC), in which the First-tier Tax Tribunal agreed with HMRC that the TAA was notifiable under DOTAS.

8.71 HMRC publishes details of tax avoidance arrangements (TAAs) that it believes do not work on the 'Tax Avoidance Schemes currently in the Spotlight' part of the GOV.UK website. The aim of this is to deter taxpayers from entering into the TAA in the first place or claiming relief on their return. Additionally, *FA 2004, s 316C* enables HMRC to publish details of the promoter and any TAA that is notified under DOTAS. This publishing can occur irrespective of whether the TAA achieves its intended aims or is ultimately defeated.

8.72 Another factor that HMRC hopes will deter taxpayers' use of TAAs is the introduction of the General Anti-Abuse Rule (GAAR) in *FA 2013, Part 5*. The aim of the GAAR is to deter new tax planning arrangements that are also likely to contravene the Professional Conduct in Relation to Taxation standards. The GAAR categorises arrangements as abusive 'if they are arrangements the entering into or carrying out of which cannot reasonably be regarded as a reasonable course of action in relation to the relevant tax provisions, having regard to all the circumstances …'. Further information on the GAAR can be found in **CHAPTER 18**.

An independent panel, the GAAR Advisory Panel, meets periodically. Its task is to review TAAs referred to it by HMRC and decide whether they fail the GAAR criteria. The Panel's rulings are published on the government website. HMRC can issue GAAR counter-action notices to taxpayers who used TAAs which are abusive. GAAR penalties of up to 60% of the tax advantage in the final counteraction notice for arrangements entered into on or after 15 September 2016 may also be charged (*FA 2013, Sch 43C*). These notices also enable HMRC to impose other sanctions such as APNs (see **8.78–8.81**) and the Serial Tax Avoidance regime (see **8.82–8.87**).

8.73 Each type of TAA is grouped together and all participants in the TAA are treated in the same way. Often CAD will select a small sample of taxpayers whose participation in the TAA will be subjected to scrutiny. It will initially informally request information before using its formal information powers (eg *FA 2008, Sch 36*) in order to obtain a full set of documents from the taxpayer or the promoter for all stages of the TAA from promotion to conclusion. This will be scrutinised, technical advice sought to determine if it works from a tax technical perspective, and a decision taken as to

8.74 *Conduct of enquiries*

whether it fails either from a technical or an implementation perspective, or both. Often investigations into TAAs take several years from the use of the TAA and its inclusion in a tax return through the opening of the enquiry (often as a self-assessment enquiry with a COP8 investigation into the TAA) to its conclusion, any appeals and tribunal/appeal court hearings. In a minority of cases, HMRC's Fraud Investigation Service investigate a TAA's participants using Code of Practice 9 or with a view to a criminal prosecution if it considers that tax fraud has been committed. Further information on tax avoidance investigations can be found in **Chapter 4**.

8.74 If HMRC believes that the TAA fails then the taxpayer will be invited to concede his position. If he concedes then HMRC will proceed to bring the tax into charge by way of enquiry closure notices or contract settlements (see **8.145–8.156**). More recently HMRC has issued settlement deeds in place of letters of offer on some TAAs (particularly those involving partnerships where the partnership's position remains open). The 'deeds' differ from a contract settlement in that they often do not cover penalties and also include clauses which clients may be reluctant to sign, such as confirming that they effectively will not undertake tax avoidance in future. Careful handling of such deeds and related negotiations is needed, particularly when what one person may deem 'tax avoidance' may differ from another's view. The drafting, preparation and execution of deeds is a 'reserved activity' under the *Legal Services Act 2007* so it can only be carried out by an authorised or an exempt person. Before undertaking any work on settlement deeds, advisers should ensure they understand the legal implications and whether legal advice is needed. Guidance is available for CIOT members on the CIOT's website.

8.75 Throughout this process, which may take several years, HMRC may occasionally use other tactics to encourage taxpayers to withdraw from the TAA. Such tactics include issuing what might be termed 'nudge' letters encouraging taxpayers to voluntarily withdraw because HMRC is, for example, winning most TAA cases taken to court, has won all cases taken against the particular promoter's TAAs to date or because HMRC wishes to remind taxpayers that the tax purportedly 'saved' by the TAA was funds which could be used elsewhere eg to fund the NHS. HMRC may also issue extensive information requests to all TAA participants at a similar time.

8.76 If taxpayers decline to withdraw from the TAA during the enquiry then HMRC will issue discovery assessments (see **Chapter 13**) or enquiry closure notices to bring the tax into charge. If the TAA was to generate a refund then it is standard practice for HMRC to withhold the refund whilst it ascertains whether the planning works.

8.77 If the taxpayer appeals against the assessment then the case proceeds to a hearing before the First-tier Tribunal. Often a small number of participants

Conduct of enquiries **8.83**

in the TAA are selected as the lead case(s) under the Tribunal Procedure (First-tier Tribunal) (Tax Chamber) Rules 2009, SI 2009/273, r 18. The tribunal's decision (and those of higher courts, if there are appeals) then binds the other participants in the TAA. If the TAA fails in the First-tier Tribunal then HMRC can require the tax to be paid even if there is an appeal to the Upper Tribunal, under *TMA 1970, s 56*. If the taxpayer ultimately succeeds then the tax will be repaid.

8.78 Legislation in *FA 2014* enables HMRC to issue 'accelerated payment notices' (APNs) to taxpayers who are participants in a TAA which was notifiable to HMRC under the DOTAS regime or fails under the GAAR, and whose tax affairs are under enquiry or the subject of an ongoing appeal on or after 17 July 2014. The aim of this legislation was to bring existing TAA enquiries to a close sooner, collect the tax, deter taxpayers from TAAs and to remove the cash flow advantage of undertaking a TAA.

Further information on APNs can be found in **Chapter 21**.

8.79 *FA 2014* also empowered HMRC to issue 'follower notices' (FNs) to participants in TAAs where a final decision was reached by the courts as to whether a TAA fails. These notices will instruct a TAA participant to amend their return in accordance with the court's decision, although there should be scope to ask HMRC to reconsider its decision.

8.80 The FN will require the taxpayer to amend their return to remove the entries relating to the TAA so that the liability becomes the amount that it would have been if the arrangement had not been utilised. In practice, if an APN has not already been issued by the time the FN is issued, an APN will be issued with the FN. Further information on FNs can be found in **Chapter 21**.

8.81 APNs and FNs may be challenged by making representations to HMRC as described in **Chapter 21**. There is no formal right of appeal to the First-tier Tribunal. However, it may be possible to seek judicial review of HMRC's decision to issue the notice(s). To date, most judicial review decisions are in favour of HMRC. Tax counsel should be engaged quickly in order that permission for judicial review may be sought before deadlines expire.

8.82 HMRC gained additional powers via the Serial Tax Avoidance (STA) legislation in *FA 2016 (Sch 18 and s 159)*. HMRC's aims in introducing this legislation were to deter taxpayers from entering into TAAs in future and to encourage those already in TAAs who were still to finalise their tax positions to consider withdrawing before 6 April 2017.

8.83 If a taxpayer participates in one or more TAAs which are 'defeated' after 5 April 2017 then the taxpayer will be affected by the STA regime. Within 90 days of the defeat HMRC will issue a warning notice to the taxpayer.

8.84 *Conduct of enquiries*

A 'defeat' for these purposes broadly occurs when a follower notice is complied with/becomes final or when DOTAS able (or the VAT equivalent) arrangements are counteracted eg via a final GAAR counteraction notice, an assessment or contract settlement.

8.84 A five year 'warning period' starts from the day after the warning notice is issued. The taxpayer must submit information notices to HMRC annually during the warning period. These annual information notices (AIN) give HMRC details of TAAs the taxpayer used during the year. Late submission of an AIN, submission of an incorrect AIN or a subsequent 'relevant defeat' will extend the warning period so that it finishes five years after this failure. Special rules will apply for corporate groups, associated persons and partnerships.

8.85 If a taxpayer 'uses' more TAAs during a warning period which HMRC subsequently defeats then the STA legislation enables:

- The imposition of STA penalties of 20–60% of the tax;
- The restriction of tax reliefs, after three or more defeats meeting certain legislative conditions; and
- Publishing of taxpayers' details, after three or more defeats.

8.86 The regime is somewhat retrospective and may affect taxpayers who participated in TAAs many years before 2016. According to *FA 16, Sch 18, para 64(2)*, if a taxpayer participated in a TAA prior to Royal Assent then they could only escape the STA regime if, before 6 April 2017, they:

- reached an agreement with HMRC to exit the TAA; or
- notified HMRC of their firm intention to make a full disclosure and then made the disclosure by a deadline set by HMRC; or
- fully disclosed to HMRC the matters to which the 'relevant counteraction' relates.

8.87 Taxpayers who didn't take one of these steps before 6 April 2017 will be issued with a warning notice if the TAA is defeated after 5 April 2017.

Further information on the Serial Tax Avoidance regime may be found in **CHAPTER 18**.

Focus

Advisers may therefore help by:

- reviewing a client's tax position back to the start of DOTAS to determine which TAAs may be affected by the STA regime;

> - making the client aware of the STA regime and helping the client consider their options (e.g. whether to remain in the TAA or whether to take steps to avoid the STA regime);
> - referring clients to specialist advisers where appropriate, including solicitors where non-tax legal issues arise;
> - helping clients implement the desired course of action; and
> - explaining STA and the steps HMRC takes to tackle tax avoidance to any clients considering using TAAs in future.

8.88 HMRC will also seek penalties for incorrect tax returns from taxpayers who participate in TAAs which fail. Penalties may be due if the taxpayer carelessly or deliberately failed to implement the TAA correctly (*FA 2007, Sch 24 and its predecessor in TMA 1970*). If the implementation was correct, penalties are unlikely to be due if the TAA fails on a technicality as long as detailed advice was taken from a suitably experienced adviser.

8.89 HMRC's success in the case of *Litman v HMRC* [2014] UKFTT 89 (TC) means that it will consider whether penalties may be due in every case where a TAA fails. In *Litman*, whilst the tribunal accepted that the taxpayers could rely on their advisers regarding the legal and tax technical aspects and the order in which the TAA's steps had to occur, the taxpayers were held to be negligent for failing to ensure that all the TAA's steps happened before they included the claims for relief on the tax return. HMRC will, therefore, expect taxpayers who are sophisticated enough to enter into such TAAs to carry out basic due diligence to ensure that everything happens as it is meant to.

8.90 However, HMRC's success was somewhat tempered by the taxpayer's win in *Herefordshire Property Company Ltd v HMRC* [2015] UKFTT 79 (TC) which focused on another participator in the identical TAA to that considered in *Litman*. The company's director was able to draw a parallel between the manner in which he conducts business on a day-to-day basis and the assumptions and verbal assurances on which he relied to assert that he had believed that all TAA's steps occurred as planned and to demonstrate that he had taken sufficient care such that a penalty was inappropriate.

8.91 The taxpayer won *Bayliss v HMRC* [2016] UKFTT 500 (TC 05251), which involved a Contracts for Differences arrangement. HMRC considered that the inclusion of the TAA on the taxpayer's return was fraud for several reasons including that the taxpayer knowingly misrepresented the key sequence of steps and claimed a tax loss despite not making a monetary loss of

8.92 *Conduct of enquiries*

the same amount. However, the Tribunal decided that the taxpayer was neither fraudulent nor negligent as HMRC failed to discharge the burden of proof in either area. The decision reminded readers that:

- HMRC must show that the taxpayer personally, not an adviser, was fraudulent or negligent for the purposes of penalties

- In determining whether penalties may be charged it is the taxpayer's conduct up to the filing of the return that is key AND there must be a 'causal nexus' between the alleged fraudulent/negligent conduct and the incorrect tax position stated in the return. Conduct after the return's submission is only relevant in so far as it provides evidence of whether that earlier conduct was fraudulent/negligent and in determining the level of the penalty.

- The test in *Derry v Peek* [1886–90] All ER Rep 1 (House of Lords) re: fraud is applicable ie in order to prove fraud HMRC must prove that the taxpayer did not have an honest belief that the return was correct when submitted.

- For negligence HMRC needed to demonstrate that B failed the test in *Blyth v Birmingham Waterworks Co* [1856] 20 JP 247 and *Colin Moore v HMRC* [2011] UKUT 239 (TCC) ie B must have fallen short of doing 'what a reasonable taxpayer, exercising reasonable diligence in the completion and submission of the return, would have done'. The judge also referred to the *Gedir v HMRC* [2016] UKFTT 188 (TC) and *J R Hanson v HMRC* [2012] UKFTT 314 cases re: reliance on an agent ie the taxpayer needs to consult an adviser who he reasonably believes to be competent, provides the adviser with the relevant information, checks the adviser's work to the extent possible and implements any advice.

Ultimately, the Tribunal considered that the taxpayer had 'an honest belief that his tax return was correct' not least due to the reassurances from the TAA provider. He relied upon his adviser who had acted for him for many years and on the TAA providers who his adviser recommended. In addition, uncommercial terms within the TAA did not constitute negligence and neither did the failure to get independent financial advice as it 'would not have informed [B] about how to fill in his tax return'.

8.92 Penalties in cases of TAAs may, therefore, be somewhat difficult for those who arguably delegated too much to their advisers and did not make basic checks to ensure that the TAA was implemented as they understood it would be. For the period ending before 6 April 2017 it is essential to check if the TAA was implemented properly and, if not, where the fault lies in order to establish the penalty position.

Conduct of enquiries **8.94**

8.93 The position changes for tax years commencing on or after 6 April 2017 by virtue of *F(No 2)A 2017, s 64* which inserted two paragraphs (*3A* and *3B*) into *FA 2007, Sch 24* (penalties for errors). Whilst the new provisions do not alter how any penalty for error is calculated when a TAA is defeated, the aim of the new legislation is to deem the defeat of the TAA to be due to careless behaviour rather than an innocent error, unless:

- it was due to deliberate behaviour; or
- the taxpayer demonstrates they took reasonable care without reference to any evidence which the legislation disqualifies.

8.94 It is clearly vital to identify if any of your clients participated in notifiable TAAs. Clients who have participated should be warned about APNs, FNs, penalties and the Serial Tax Avoidance regime so that they may make an informed decision whether to take action. Additionally, it is important to consider whether the work you undertake may fall within the enablers of tax avoidance scheme rules (see **8.173** below).

Focus

- Advisers should ensure that the client checks that all the TAA's steps are implemented correctly before relief is claimed on a tax return and that evidence is retained to demonstrate this.
- Copies of all documents regarding a TAA should be kept including the promotional material, counsel's opinion (and the instructions) and any related advice (so as to evidence that the client did not intend to submit an incorrect return such that deliberate penalties may be due).
- Clients should be made aware that:
  - HMRC may issue information notices (to obtain the TAA documentation) and enquire into their returns.
  - HMRC may challenge whether the TAA was notifiable under DOTAS/DASVOIT and, if so, what the consequences are.
  - If an APN is issued, then the cash flow advantage of participating in a TAA will be minimal as they will be required to make a payment on account of the tax.
  - They may be required to revise their return if another taxpayer's case is lost and HMRC issues a follower notice.
- Clients should be given proactive advice to enable them to consider:
  - whether to remain in or exit from the TAA;

8.95 *Conduct of enquiries*

> - how to fund the expected tax payment following an APN being issued – they may need to obtain bank finance or negotiate a time-to-pay arrangement and discussions with HMRC can be started before or after an APN is issued;
> - whether to pay the tax, make representations or seek further specialist legal advice when an APN is issued; and
> - what to do when an FN, GAAR counteraction notice or STAR warning notice is issued so that action can be taken within the statutory deadlines.

MAINTAINING PROGRESS DESPITE DELAYS

8.95 Occasionally, taxpayers are slow to respond to HMRC's requests for information. It may be the case that this is because the information and documentation is time consuming to collate, the taxpayer may be ill or he may just be trying to ignore HMRC's request, hoping it will go away. However, HMRC will not give up.

> **Focus**
>
> If there is a reason to expect slow progress, such as illness, delays by third parties or the sheer volume of documents to collate (eg in a company's busy season when there is little time for such activities), then best practice is to contact the HMRC officer soon after receiving the information request, explain the issue and negotiate a realistic revised deadline.

8.96 If HMRC considers that the taxpayer is not providing the information or documentation that HMRC believes it needs within a reasonable timescale, then HMRC will consider issuing a formal notice under *FA 2008, Sch 36* (see **CHAPTER 16**). This gives the taxpayer a limited time within which to respond before penalties are imposed. Such notices may sometimes be appealed. The additional disadvantage is that the issue of this notice means that the taxpayer will receive a higher tax geared penalty for any careless or deliberate errors as the penalty reductions will be lower (as set out in **CHAPTER 18**). However, HMRC should not use its *FA 2008, Sch 36* information powers to seek information from parties overseas (*Jimenez, R (on the application of) v The First Tier Tribunal (Tax Chamber) & Ors* [2017] EWHC 2585 (Admin)).

8.97 Should the HMRC officer consider that the taxpayer is still not providing what is required, the officer may consider issuing third party

Conduct of enquiries **8.97**

information notices under *FA 2008, Sch 36, para 2*, with or without the taxpayer's permission. In this way, HMRC obtains information direct from a taxpayer's customers, suppliers, banks, etc.

In extreme cases, HMRC may use its powers to inspect premises and obtain information in *FA 2008, Sch 36* (or its criminal investigation powers – see **8.28–8.31**) unexpectedly. Such visits are often termed 'dawn raids'. Depending on the powers used for the raid, HMRC may be able to seize business records, computers and mobile phones as well as questioning individuals.

Tips for handling dawn raids

- Do not panic: keep calm.

- Ask the officials to wait in a separate meeting room if possible, ensuring that the room does not contain confidential information.

- Call specialist legal advisers immediately.

- Politely ask the officials to wait until your legal advisers arrive before they begin any search or interviews. Re-assure them that co-operation is intended. They will usually wait a reasonable period of time.

- Do not interfere or obstruct the officials. Do not destroy or hide documents – it could be a criminal offence. Equally, do not casually provide or volunteer information.

- Request a copy of the information notice or warrant so that its terms and scope can be checked. Provide a copy of it to your legal advisers.

- Alert and assemble your internal response team in accordance with your existing procedures to deal with these situations. Arrange for them, or other team members, to shadow the officials taking notes of anything they say, ask or look at subject to any advice provided by your legal advisers.

- Try to establish whether similar visits are taking places at other locations eg other offices or the homes of key personnel where business documents or equipment may be stored.

- Ensure that a list of documents seized/copied/reviewed by the officials is retained. If possible, retain copies thereof including copies of any digital data downloaded by the officials.

- Alert your legal advisers to any potentially privileged information/ documents so that they can ensure (if possible) that protocols (eg *SI 2009/1916*) are followed and no such documents are copies/ seized. Disputed documents should be placed in a sealed envelope for later consideration by an independent third party.

8.98 *Conduct of enquiries*

8.98 If there is a lack of co-operation later in the enquiry and/or the parties cannot agree on the amount of tax due then HMRC may bring matters to a head by issuing enquiry closure notices, discovery assessments or determinations to bring what it considers to be the correct amount of tax into charge. The taxpayer then has to appeal in order to stop HMRC's figures becoming final.

8.99 In contrast, if the taxpayer considers HMRC is taking too long to respond towards the end of the enquiry, when the taxpayer has provided all available relevant information, then the taxpayer or his agent may apply for an enquiry closure notice (*TMA 1970, s 28A (4)* or *FA 1998, Sch 18, para 33*). If the First-tier Tribunal agrees with the taxpayer, then it will direct HMRC to close the enquiry within a specified length of time. For further information on closure notices, see **6.95–6.103** and **20.53–20.77**.

Focus

- If your client is frustrated by a lack of progress then consideration may be given to requesting a meeting with the HMRC caseworker and his superior to discuss the issues and ways forward to settle the case.

- If there is still no progress then consider mediation (alternative dispute resolution (ADR)) – see **8.126–8.130** below regarding overcoming deadlock – as well as whether to request a closure notice.

- Arguably the closure notice should be a last resort and works best where all available, relevant information and documentation has been provided to HMRC well in advance of the hearing. If information or documentation is outstanding, then it is much less likely that the First-tier Tribunal's decision will be in the taxpayer's favour.

ESTIMATING IN THE ABSENCE OF FULL INFORMATION

8.100 Sometimes taxpayers do not have all the information needed in order to quantify the additional tax due. This may be through no fault of their own; for example, the records may have been damaged by fire or a third party (like a bank) may not retain records after a certain number of years. In other cases, taxpayers may have deliberately failed to keep records or have destroyed those that they previously held. In all such cases, estimates and assumptions need to be made to bridge the gap unless the missing records can be obtained from third parties.

8.101 In other cases, for example, HMRC may be concerned that the taxpayer has not retained records of all sales. HMRC will use information at its disposal to calculate what the profits should be. This could mean observing a restaurant's lunchtime service, observing average spend, noting how many mints are on the plate with the bill, seeing from the records how many boxes of mints are purchased per month, counting how many mints are in a box and then calculating how many customers the restaurant has had over the period and multiplying it by the average spend. For businesses selling goods via internet marketplaces, HMRC may use data on sales available via the internet site.

8.102 Such estimating exercises are, by their nature, little more than guess work. The calculations may be challenged by finding the answers to questions such as: Do any of the staff eat the mints? Was the service they observed 'typical'? Do they always offer mints or do they know that some regular customers really like them and so give them extra?

8.103 As mentioned above, HMRC has access to large quantities of data. It can, therefore, calculate the gross profit percentage it expects different types of businesses to achieve. It will use test purchases and statistical information to fill in the gaps or test the records. If the taxpayer's business is not 'typical' then HMRC will need to understand the way in which it is different and the impact that has on its profitability. HMRC will use other statistics regarding spending by typical households such as those produced by the Office for National Statistics.

8.104 If HMRC believes that an owner-managed business's profits are too low then it may also enquire into the owner's tax affairs to see if his lifestyle and spending patterns match the business's profits and his declared income. HMRC tends to use the phrase 'breaking the records' to describe this type of analysis work. HMRC will be testing whether the business records are credible and complete or whether profits are under-declared and, if so, by how much.

8.105 Estimates and assumptions may be needed in other situations such as bank accounts showing deposits for which the source cannot easily be identified or payments to acquire assets or for expensive holidays for which the source of funds is unclear given the level of the taxpayer's assets and income. HMRC may make assumptions eg that the deposits are undisclosed takings or untaxed investment income. As *Mohammed Ashraf v HMRC* [2018] UKFTT 97 (TC) indicates, if it is not possible to identify the source of funds on the balance of probabilities then the Tribunal may cancel the discovery assessment.

8.106 Such estimates may then be used in enquiry closure notices or discovery assessments. If the taxpayer needs to appeal the assessment then detailed evidence is likely to be needed to persuade the Tribunal what the taxable profits should be in order to displace HMRC's assessment (see **13.141** *et seq*).

8.107 *Conduct of enquiries*

Tips for challenging assumptions and estimates

- Consider how else information may be found. For a person whose UK day count is in question, if he uses one travel company or airline for all flights, can that company provide a printout of the flights taken over a period? Did his employer retain records of his business travel? Alternatively, do the client's mobile telephone or credit card bills show where he was (as long as no-one else uses the card)? Does his passport contain legible border stamps or visas?

- Information provided by third parties is more credible than information summarised by the taxpayer or his agent. In some cases, no evidence exists so the client's best recollection is the only thing available. If HMRC cannot find evidence to disprove its credibility then it may be the key to resolving the case (see *Glen Whittle v Commissioners of Revenue & Customs* [2014] UKFTT 254 (TC) for an example of this).

- HMRC will listen to reasoned estimates and assumptions, particularly if the basis and reasoning for those estimates/assumptions is explained so it can test the underlying rationale. Put these forward proactively, rather than letting HMRC take the advantage by calculating its own.

- Talk with your client to establish why things may vary in such a way as to explain away any difference HMRC perceives exists. Perhaps expenditure has been lower because a family member has let the taxpayer stay at his holiday home or he had a gift from a relative? Was the industry having a bad year because of the weather, currency movements, etc and how did this impact the business? Then explain these things to HMRC with a calculation or extrapolation to demonstrate their effects.

- If the gaps in records are because third parties do not provide information, then ask the third party to confirm in writing that it is unable to provide it and then show the letter to HMRC so the officer can see that everything possible has been done.

EXPANDING ENQUIRIES INTO OTHER TAX YEARS: DISCOVERY AND TIME LIMITS

8.107 In simplistic terms, HMRC can issue a discovery assessment under *TMA 1970, s 29* or *FA 1998, Sch 18, paras 42–46* where:

- the loss of tax is attributable to deliberate or careless behaviour by or on behalf of the taxpayer; or

- HMRC could not have been expected, on the basis of the information available to it at the relevant time, to be aware of the potential loss of tax;
- *unless* the return was prepared in accordance with the generally accepted prevailing practice at the time.

More detailed information about the criteria for discovery assessments and how to challenge them is set out in **CHAPTER 13**.

8.108 If HMRC identifies an error in a tax return during an enquiry which may affect other years' tax returns then it will assert the presumption of continuity (from *Jonas v Bamford* (1973) 51 TC 1) thus suggesting that all those other returns are similarly incorrect. How many years' returns this might affect largely depends upon the reason for the error (ie is it an innocent, a careless or a deliberate error).

8.109 The standard time limits within which a discovery assessment may be issued for income tax, capital gains tax and corporation tax are:

- innocent error and failures to notify with a reasonable excuse: four years from the end of the tax year (*TMA 1970, s 34* and *FA 1998, Sch 18, para 46(1)*);
- careless error: six years from the end of the tax year (*TMA 1970, s 36* and *FA 1998, Sch 18, para 46(2)*);
- deliberate error: 20 years from the end of the tax year (*TMA 1970, s 36* and *FA 1998, Sch 18, para 46(2A)*); and
- failure to notify liability without a reasonable excuse: 20 years from the end of the tax year (*TMA 1970, s 36* and *FA 1998, Sch 18, para 46(2A)*).

However, it should be noted that these time limits vary for other taxes (such as for IHT at *IHTA 1984, s 240*) and for lifetime tax liabilities of deceased individuals (*TMA 1970, s 40*).

8.110 The assessment time limits for income tax, capital gains tax and inheritance tax in connection with offshore income, gains and profits are extended by the Requirement to Correct legislation. HMRC wanted more time to analyse data and investigate taxpayers following the start of automatic information exchange under the Common Reporting Standard. Consequently, any time limits which would expire during the period from 6 April 2017 to 4 April 2021 are extended so that they do not expire until 5 April 2021 (*F(No 2)A 2017, Sch 18, para 26*).

At the time of writing HMRC is consulting on further extending assessment time limits for income tax, capital gains tax, inheritance tax and corporation

8.111 *Conduct of enquiries*

tax. The expectation is that the time limits for reasonable excuse, innocent and careless errors will be extended to 12 years from the end of the tax year. This is expected to affect offshore matters and offshore transfers as defined in *F(No 2)A 2017, Sch 18, para 7*. If enacted, this change may apply to periods that are in date for assessment on or after April 2019.

8.111 HMRC will consider using its information powers in *FA 2008, Sch 36* (as detailed in **CHAPTER 16**) to obtain information and documentation to quantify any additional tax due for years for which there are no open self-assessment enquiries. This is possible in some circumstances even if a previous enquiry has been closed or where no enquiry was opened within the statutory time limit due to *FA 2008, Sch 36, para 21*.

8.112 Once HMRC quantifies the amount of tax it considers has been under-declared (or excessive loss or other claims made) then it will consider issuing a discovery assessment. It is worth noting that discovery is the power to issue an assessment, not open an enquiry, but when the assessing power is coupled with the information powers discussed above, the effect is somewhat similar to what happens under an enquiry.

8.113 The power to make discovery assessments is one of the most important powers that HMRC possesses. Officers will, therefore, consider their ability to use it in order to collect tax which may be due. This power is available to HMRC even where taxpayers have failed to submit tax returns or are making a voluntary disclosure. It is also used by HMRC as a way to bring other tax years into charge whilst an enquiry is ongoing into a more recent tax year.

Focus

- Apart from ensuring that careless and deliberate errors are not made by the taxpayer or anyone acting on his behalf, the other key way to prevent discoveries being made is to ensure that an adequate disclosure is included on tax returns. For example, include text explaining the point in detail and making it clear that HMRC may not agree with the technical position adopted so, consequently, may consider there to be an insufficiency in the tax assessed.

- If a discovery assessment is made and the taxpayer wants to make a consequential claim to reduce the tax charged, this is possible in some circumstances – such as those set out in *TMA 1970, ss 36(3), 43A* and *FA 1998, Sch 18, paras 61–64*.

KEY FORMS THAT HMRC MAY REQUEST

8.114 In cases where something has been omitted from a return, particularly where there is a full enquiry or COP9 (Contractual Disclosure Facility) investigation or voluntary disclosure, HMRC often wants one, two or all of the following forms to be completed and submitted either with a disclosure report or before the end of the enquiry:

- certificate of bank accounts operated;
- certificate of credit cards;
- statement of assets and liabilities; and
- certificate of full disclosure.

8.115 All these forms carry the warning that the signatory may face prosecution if the information on the form is incorrect. Consequently, great care needs to be taken to ensure that the forms are completed accurately, to the best of the knowledge and belief of the person signing the forms.

8.116 If a person signs the form and it later transpires that something material was not disclosed HMRC takes the matter extremely seriously: a criminal investigation may start. So, if a taxpayer realises he made a mistake, it is essential to approach HMRC voluntarily to make a disclosure, eg via the CDF.

8.117 The certificates of bank accounts operated and credit cards held detail the bank, building society and loan accounts and the credit cards that a person has in his name or had access to during a specific period.

Whilst HMRC has significant data on what accounts each person holds, it may not be complete, so this form is a key part of the reassurance that the caseworker will want from the taxpayer towards the end of the case.

8.118 The statement of assets and liabilities (SOAL) is effectively a personal balance sheet at a specific date. Often the date to be used is the last day of the final tax year covered by the disclosure or enquiry. Occasionally, HMRC will also want one completed on a date at the start of the period under investigation, so it can compare it with the one for the end of the investigation period, to reconcile the taxpayer's income, gains, net gifts and outgoings.

8.119 This may highlight discrepancies in the information disclosed, eg if the increase in net assets and expenses over the period is greater than the income and gains disclosed this may indicate that there is undisclosed income. More commonly, if a second SOAL is needed it will be required to substantiate that the taxpayer has insufficient funds to settle his liability.

8.120 *Conduct of enquiries*

8.120 The SOAL must list all assets and liabilities regardless of where in the world they are located. The only exception to this is that only UK situs assets and liabilities need to be listed if the taxpayer is accepted to be non-UK domiciled and taxable on the remittance basis. The assets and liabilities need to be listed at their value on the date for which the form is prepared. For some assets this is easy (eg bank account balances). While there is no requirement to get assets valued, HMRC will want to understand the basis of the figure given for each asset, such as insured value, cost on a particular date, a balance or valuation on a particular date (eg for shares or investments). Appropriate notes must be put on the form and any accompanying schedules.

8.121 HMRC will want information about the taxpayer's minor children's assets and liabilities in the final column of the form because some taxpayers have disguised undeclared income, etc by depositing funds or acquiring assets in their children's names. It is not necessary to include the taxpayer's spouse's assets and liabilities so, if an asset is held jointly, this needs to be noted on the form and the figure should reflect the taxpayer's interest in the asset.

8.122 The certificate of full disclosure is used at the end of an investigation/enquiry or on the submission of a disclosure to HMRC. There are different versions of the certificate and HMRC will issue the one it considers is appropriate. The simplest requires the taxpayer to certify that he has made a full disclosure of his sources of income and amounts arising plus all facts relevant to their tax liabilities for a specific period. The most complex (eg often used for COP9 investigations) requires the taxpayer to certify that he has also disclosed all his assets, investments, bank accounts and gifts.

As the name suggests, HMRC uses the form to get the taxpayer's confirmation that he has made a full disclosure.

8.123 Occasionally, particularly with a disclosure facility case, some or all of these forms may have been submitted earlier in the process. In such cases, HMRC will rarely ask for revised versions unless the taxpayer has insufficient funds to pay the tax, interest and penalties.

8.124 In limited circumstances, it may be appropriate to refuse to complete these forms. An example of this is a taxpayer who has medically diagnosed memory issues, eg memory loss due to an accident which resulted in brain damage. In such a case, HMRC may require a letter from the taxpayer's GP or consultant setting out the medical problem and how it affects the taxpayer's memory. If a taxpayer has no reliable medium/long-term memory then there really is no point in completing the forms as they could easily be incorrect.

8.125 HMRC also writes to some taxpayers identified from analysis of offshore data whom HMRC is concerned perhaps may not have made a full disclosure of all income and gains taxable in the UK. Some of these letters enclose a 'Certificate of Tax Position'. The certificate asks the taxpayer to tick a box to either confirm that they are going to make a WDF disclosure or confirm that they have already made a full disclosure of their 'worldwide income, assets and gains that are taxable in the UK'. The form does not have a de-minimis or limit the time period for which the confirmation is sought ie it appears to apply for all tax years and for all amounts. The form carries a prosecution warning (see **8.115**). When considering the next steps advisers should bear in mind that:

- There is no legal obligation to complete the form.

- A conversation with their client is essential to establish whether there are any issues to be disclosed.

- There are other ways to make a disclosure – the WDF is not always the most appropriate method.

- As the form is unlimited (ie is not restricted to, for example, the last 4 or 6 years and has no de minimis amount), many advisers may be uncomfortable asking their clients to sign it just in case a small error was made many years ago. In cases where there appears to be no reason for the client to make a disclosure then an alternative way forward may be to write to HMRC confirming that the client, to the best of their knowledge and belief, is not aware of anything that needs to be disclosed for a specific period. If the client has offshore assets/income which is not assessable here for some reason then adding an explanation about this may assist HMRC to decide whether to investigate further.

- Not replying may cause HMRC to open an enquiry or investigation to check the client's UK tax position.

Focus

- Ensure that the wording on each form is amended to reflect the circumstances of the case, ie it only covers the period of the enquiry or report and it does not require the listing of other parties' (including a spouse's) accounts unless the taxpayer can operate them.

- Check the information on the form to other information provided to HMRC, eg via tax returns and disclosure reports, to ensure that it is complete.

8.126 Conduct of enquiries

> - If some information is unobtainable (eg the details of a company's bank accounts for which a taxpayer was previously a director) then discuss this with the HMRC officer and agree revised wording.
>
> - Ensure that the client reads the warning on the forms regarding prosecution and understands the importance of the forms being correct and consequences of errors before he signs the forms.

DEADLOCK: WHAT IS THE WAY FORWARD?

8.126 If progress on an enquiry grinds to a halt, then the HMRC officer may ask himself:

- Are there any other documents or explanations that could reasonably be provided?
- Should an information notice be issued?
- What else am I concerned about?
- When did I last meet the taxpayer or his agent? Is it time for a meeting to discuss the possible ways forward?
- Would it be worth asking a colleague who has not been involved in the case to date to take a look in case he can suggest something?
- Is it time to issue assessments/determinations?

8.127 Of course, it may be the case that deadlock has been reached and neither side accepts each other's position. In such circumstances, the options that HMRC may consider are:

Way forward	Benefits and down-sides of this option
Issue enquiry closure notice	Brings the additional tax that HMRC considers is due into charge. Taxpayer can request an internal review or a hearing before the First-tier Tax Tribunal.
Issue discovery assessments or determinations	Brings additional tax into charge for periods where there is no open enquiry, subject to the statutory time limits. The taxpayer can request an internal review or a hearing before the First-tier Tribunal.
Offer Alternative Dispute Resolution (ADR), a form of mediation	This option offers both sides the chance to reach a facilitated agreement before assessments or closure notices are issued (and after).

Conduct of enquiries   8.130

Way forward	Benefits and down-sides of this option
Jointly refer questions to the Tribunal during an enquiry (*TMA 1970, s 28ZA and FA 1998, Sch 18, para 31A*)	Unlikely that both parties will be willing to do together. (This is one reason why partial closure notices were introduced by *F(No 2)A 2017, s 63 and Sch 15*).

Once the tax is in charge, HMRC can issue penalty determinations too.

8.128 The adviser or the HMRC Inspector may consider that ADR (see **Chapter 12**) is an appropriate option. The facilitated mediation process which is a key part of ADR may well unlock a case where progress has ground to a halt. A one-day mediation can be an extremely effective, efficient way to resolve an enquiry, particularly where progress has slowed following a couple of years of enquiry correspondence.

8.129 An adviser or taxpayer also has the option of applying to the First-tier Tribunal for an enquiry closure notice. The tribunal will consider the position based on both parties' evidence and will either direct that the enquiry should remain open (particularly where HMRC's concerns remain unanswered) or be closed within a specified period of time. This may be useful where all available information has been provided, but should be a last resort.

8.130 A taxpayer may appeal against HMRC's decision within 30 days of the date on the assessment or closure notice and request postponement of the tax due. At the same time as appealing, the options are to request an internal review by an independent officer within HMRC or to proceed to a hearing before the First-tier Tribunal.

It may also be possible to request ADR soon after opting for a Tribunal hearing so as to facilitate the exploration of issues and solutions with a view to either resolving the matter before both sides' Tribunal preparation is complete or narrowing the issues to be considered by the Tribunal.

Some tips for appeals

- When appealing, consider whether you wish to postpone collection of the tax. If so, request a postponement within the appeal letter following the criteria in *TMA 1970, s 55* as well as explaining the grounds for the appeal and whether an internal review or appeal to the First-tier Tribunal is preferred.
- Set out the grounds for the appeal clearly and comprehensively.
- Keep proof of postage of the appeal. If submitting by email too, keep delivery/read receipts.

8.130 *Conduct of enquiries*

- If a deadline for appealing HMRC's decision is missed, you can ask for HMRC to exercise its discretion to permit a late appeal. The criteria are set out in *TMA 1970, s 49* so you can use this list to explain why you consider the late appeal should be permitted. If HMRC refuses, permission may be sought from the Tribunal. Both HMRC and the Tribunal will consider whether, given the circumstances causing the late appeal, they will permit the appeal to be made.

- If HMRC offers an internal review when issuing a closure notice or assessment, then taxpayers must either accept that offer or reject it and request a tribunal hearing (*TMA 1970, s 49C*) in order to avoid HMRC's figures being confirmed as final. HMRC's Annual Report for 2016/17 confirmed that 52% of internal reviews result in HMRC's original decision being varied or cancelled.

- Don't forget to warn the client that:

  - If several matters were under enquiry and HMRC's decision on one of them is the reason why the client wishes to appeal the closure notice (for example) then the review officer may reconsider HMRC's conclusions on all the issues and may alter them (*TMA 1970, s 49E*).

  - It may be worth spending time making representations to the review officer (*TMA 1970, s 49E(4)*) who will consider them before making a conclusion. This can be particularly helpful in cases where the enquiry or investigation is prolonged as making representations enables the salient points to be collated and presented to HMRC in a cohesive way with relevant case law.

  - *TMA 1970, s 50* means that the Tribunal may increase or decrease the tax assessed if it decides that the taxpayer is under or over-charged, respectively, otherwise the assessment will be unchanged;

  - If they withdraw their appeal then the figures originally assessed are finalised even if the case has been heard by the First-tier Tribunal or other court (*TMA 1970, s 54(4)* and *HMRC v TGH (Commercial) Limited* [2017] UKUT 116 (TCC)). HMRC may also seek costs if it believes the taxpayer acted unreasonably.

  - In the unlikely event that HMRC refuses to let the appeal be withdrawn then the assessment could still increase (see for example *HMRC v C M Utilities Limited* [2017] UKUT 305 (TCC)).

- Once an appeal is made to the First-tier Tribunal, the client enters a process controlled by the Tribunal and Courts Service. Whilst it may be possible to maintain dialogue with HMRC with a view to reaching agreement (*TMA 1970, s 54*) there is no guarantee of success, court directions must be complied with and the Court will set the deadlines. Failing to meet the deadlines may result in being barred from the proceedings (*BPP Holdings Limited v HMRC* [2017] UKSC 55). Serious consideration should be given to engaging tax counsel at the earliest opportunity.

- It is difficult to obtain permission for decisions to be anonymised (*HMRC v Banerjee* [2009] EWHC 1229 (Ch)) or for hearings to be in private but not impossible depending on the circumstances (*A Divorcee v HMRC* [2010] UKFTT 612 (TC)).

Further information on internal review and appeals to the First-tier Tribunal can be found in **Chapter 20**.

PENALTIES

8.131 Whilst punishment is probably the first thing that comes to mind when considering why HMRC imposes penalties, aspects of the various penalty regimes are also designed to:

- improve taxpayer's ability to deal with their tax affairs (eg conditions for suspension of careless error penalties); and

- deter taxpayers from taking certain future actions, such as undertaking future tax avoidance arrangements, keeping funds in less transparent jurisdictions (the uplifts for offshore matters relating to category 2 or 3 jurisdictions) or moving funds to jurisdictions which are not adopting the common reporting standard so it may be harder for HMRC to find out about the money (eg Offshore Asset Moves Penalties – *FA 2015, Sch 21*).

8.132 The principal tax-geared penalties considered in this part of this chapter are penalties for errors (*FA 2007, Sch 24*). Others exist, including penalties for failures to notify (*FA 2008, Sch 41*), late submission (*FA 2009, Sch 55*), late payment (*FA 2009, Sch 56*), GAAR (**Chapter 18**), failing to comply with Follower Notices (see **Chapter 21**), late payment of APNs (see **Chapter 21**), and Serial Tax Avoidance (see **8.82–8.87** above).

8.133 *Conduct of enquiries*

8.133 For voluntary disclosures and investigation involving offshore matters or offshore transfers special care is needed due to the interaction of Failure to Correct (*F(No 2)A 2017, Sch 18, para 23*) penalties and sanctions – depending on whether the taxpayer had a reasonable excuse (within the meaning of for failing to correct by 30 September 2018 – and other penalty regimes depending on the years for which tax is assessed. This is made more complex to the alterations to *FA 2007, Sch 24* and *FA 2008, Sch 41* that are effective from different dates. Additionally, HMRC may seek to impose offshore asset moves penalties (*FA 2015, Sch 21*) and/or asset-based penalties (*FA 2016, Sch 21*).

8.134 Penalties for errors and failures to notify may be mitigated. Further reductions are possible if special circumstances exist which are not taken into account elsewhere in the penalty calculation and mitigation process.

Penalty reductions generally take into account the timing, nature and extent of the taxpayer's disclosure (telling HMRC about the issue and why it occurred), helping HMRC to quantify the tax and giving HMRC access to records.

8.135 In 2017 HMRC altered its Compliance Handbook manual (CH82444 and CH82465) to state:

> 'Where a person has taken a significant period to correct their non-compliance in relation to either an onshore or offshore matter, or they would previously have been able to make a disclosure through one of HMRC's offshore disclosure facilities, they can no longer expect HMRC to give them the full reduction for the quality of disclosure. A "significant period" is normally considered to be over 3 years but may be less where the overall disclosure covers a longer period.'

> 'You do this by restricting the maximum reduction by 10 percentage points to reflect the time that they have taken to begin telling us about the inaccuracy, before going on to work out any further reductions for the quality of telling, helping and giving.'

For example, for cases affected by this change of practice a minimum prompted careless error penalty becomes 25% (rather than 15%) where the maximum penalty is 30%. This change of practice by HMRC may make it less likely for taxpayers to receive the maximum reductions for the quality of their disclosure and thus increase the likelihood that taxpayers who made deliberate errors will have their details published (see **8.159–8.162** below). As the Tribunals and Courts base their decisions on legislation and case law, it is unclear how the Tribunals will view the above alteration in HMRC's practice.

8.136 For deliberate errors and failures relating to offshore matters and offshore transfers for tax years commencing on or after 6 April 2016 (or IHT transfers of value on or after 1 April 2017), taxpayers are expected to provide HMR with details of any person who enabled their deliberate conduct including a description of the enabler's actions (*SI 2017/345*). The minimum penalties for these types of error was also increased by 10 percentage points (*FA 2016, Sch 21*) and an asset-based penalty imposed (*FA 2016, Sch 22*) in addition to the offshore asset moves penalty (*FA 2015, Sch 21*).

8.137 Although strictly HMRC has 12 months after a tax liability is finalised to impose penalties for errors and failures to notify (*FA 2007, Sch 24, para 13(3)* and *FA 2008, Sch 41, para 16(4)*), HMRC will usually consider whether penalties are due towards the end of an enquiry or investigation. It will first ascertain whether it is a case of the taxpayer failing to notify his chargeability or of making errors in tax returns. Since the introduction of partial closure notices (PCNs) via *F(No 2)A 2017, Sch 15*, HMRC is able to issue penalties for tax finalised via PCNs whilst the rest of the enquiry continues.

8.138 HMRC will ask for information and for an explanation of why the error occurred in order to ascertain whether it was the taxpayer's error or that of a third party, including the taxpayer's agent, and whether the taxpayer took reasonable care. HMRC can use its powers under *FA 2008, Sch 36* to obtain such information.

8.139 *FA 2007, Sch 24, para 1A* enables HMRC to charge tax-geared penalties where a person deliberately provides or omits to provide information which results in an incorrect return being submitted. The only case on *para 1A* penalties to date is *Hutchings v HMRC* [2015] UKFTT 9 (TC) which may be a useful read should such a penalty be proposed by HMRC. Mr Hutchings was penalised for deliberately omitting to give his father's executors information on a lifetime gift which resulted in an incorrect IHT return being filed. The decision also clarified that 'deliberately' means 'intentionally'. More information on penalties can be found in **CHAPTERS 18 AND 19**.

8.140 HMRC's tactical approach is often to assert that taxpayers made careless or deliberate errors. It is then for the taxpayer, or his agent, to demonstrate whether:

- the error is an innocent error (so that no penalty applies);
- the error is that of a third party;
- the quality of disclosure is such that maximum reduction is appropriate;
- there are any 'special circumstances' that should be taken into account to reduce the penalty further; and
- there are any conditions that might be set, which would help the taxpayer avoid making careless errors of any type in future, such that a penalty for a careless error may be suspended.

8.141 *Conduct of enquiries*

8.141 However, it is worth also remembering that, strictly and certainly if the case is considered by the tribunals/courts, the burden of proof to demonstrate the taxpayer's behaviour is on HMRC but the burden of proof is on the taxpayer to demonstrate that he took reasonable care and that it was his agent's error (*J R Hanson v Revenue and Customs Comrs* [2012] UKFTT 314). The burden of proof is on the balance of probabilities (eg *Gardiner v Revenue and Customs Comrs* [2015] UKFTT 0115 (TC)).

It is also important to remember that "although there is only one civil standard of proof, it is a general requirement of a fair trial that the more serious the allegation relied upon by one party, such as an allegation of dishonesty or the making of a deliberate misrepresentation to the respondents, the fact-finding tribunal must be the more assiduous to ensure that the evidence relied upon by the person making that allegation is sufficiently credible, relevant and cogent to warrant such an adverse finding (*Cannon v HMRC* [2017] UKFTT 859 (TC)).

Some pointers for dealing with penalty challenges

When replying to HMRC's queries in this area, it is important for an adviser to:

- Spend time discussing the matter with the client and reviewing paperwork to establish why the failure or error occurred.

- Consider the knowledge and abilities of the client (including any mental or physical health issues) and how these impacted on the issue.

- Consider whether there are other extenuating circumstances which could be a basis for the penalty to be reduced under the 'special circumstances' provisions.

- Be careful not to muddle up 'reasonable excuse' and 'reasonable care' and associated case law.

- Look for parallels with decided cases to demonstrate why an error/failure is not deliberate or not careless on the part of the taxpayer. Discovery and penalty cases can both provide helpful examples.

There are numerous different penalty regimes in existence. It is not unusual that more than one type of penalty may be chargeable by reference to the same tax liability. Legislation provides the rules on the maximum levels of cumulative penalties that may be charged in each situation (e.g. those at *FA 2013, Sch 43C, para 8* and *FA 2009, Sch 56, para 9A*). Advisers may need to work through these rules carefully and systematically for each type of penalty applicable to the client's situation in order to establish the correct penalty level and agree it with HMRC.

Conduct of enquiries **8.144**

> Care should also be taken where several penalties of the same type are chargeable e.g. late submission of tax return penalties. There are rules limiting the maximum penalties *(FA 2009, Sch 55, para 17(3))* which may help limit the penalties (see *Alan Jackson v HMRC* [2018] UKFTT 64 (TC) for example).

8.142 If HMRC imposes penalties for deliberate failures then other consequences may follow; the taxpayer may be placed in HMRC's Managing Serious Defaulters Programme or have their details published (see **8.159–8.166** below).

8.143 As HMRC's Compliance Handbook (at CH83155) states, HMRC will always insist that one of the conditions of suspension of a penalty for a careless error is that the taxpayer must submit returns for all relevant taxes by the due dates (or words to that effect). Whilst this, in effect, duplicates penalties for late filing, HMRC is unwilling to agree to a suspension without it. However, it should be noted that in paragraph 16 of the First Tier Tribunal's decision in *Alexander Duncan v Revenue and Customs Comrs* [2016] UKFTT 709 (TC) the judge said 'compliance with filing obligations and payment of tax liabilities are both requirements of the law and cannot form suitable conditions for suspension of a penalty; it is clear from the context of the statute that something more than compliance with the law is required as a condition, as stated by Judge Brennan in *Fane* [2011] UKFTT 210 (paras 60–61)'. HMRC is, open to short suspension periods (of months rather than the two-year maximum) as long as the period is realistically long enough to enable compliance with the conditions.

8.144 HMRC places the responsibility for demonstrating compliance with the suspension conditions on the taxpayer. In some cases, letters of offer will require the taxpayer to demonstrate his compliance on or before the day the suspension period ends. In other cases, HMRC will approach the taxpayer soon after the end of the suspension period to obtain confirmation that the conditions are met. Failure to meet all the suspension conditions in full will result in the suspended penalty becoming payable.

> **Focus**
>
> - Discuss possible suspension conditions with your client. They need not only to meet the criteria for helping the client avoid future careless errors but also to be specific, measurable and achievable.
>
> - Ensure your client is aware that if he wants the penalty suspended then HMRC may insist on the condition that his returns must be submitted

8.145 *Conduct of enquiries*

> on time (until its guidance is updated to reflect the *Alexander Duncan* decision (see **8.143** above).
>
> - Identify the minimum suspension period in which the conditions can realistically be met.
>
> - Ensure that evidence is kept so that HMRC can be shown the client met the conditions (eg note of a meeting to review a tax return, supporting documents/schedules and computations before submission).
>
> - Make a diary note so that HMRC is told that the conditions have been met by the appropriate date (based on the wording in the letter of offer or penalty suspension notice).
>
> - Don't forget that meaningful and relevant payments on account of the tax due (when it is quantified for a particular error) can show co-operation which helps reduce penalties under the old (pre-*FA 2007*) rules and also limits late payment interest charges.

SETTLING THE CASE

8.145 HMRC will typically settle an enquiry or investigation where additional tax is due in one of two ways:

- issue partial/final closure notices, discovery assessments and/or determinations; or

- reach a contract settlement.

8.146 The former will often be used either when only one year's tax is affected by the adjustments (ie for simplicity) or when HMRC wishes to assert its position, three examples of which are:

- issuing a discovery assessment just before a year goes out of time for HMRC to assess the tax it considers is due;

- issuing a jeopardy assessment to prevent a loss of tax (*TMA 1970, s 9C* and *FA 1998, Sch 18, para 30*); or

- where a taxpayer is not co-operating with HMRC and/or HMRC wishes to bring the matter to a head eg issuing a partial closure notice (see **20.81**) to bring the tax into charge which HMRC believes is due if it considers that a tax avoidance arrangement is defeated.

The closure notices, assessments and determinations can all be appealed (see **CHAPTER 20**).

8.147 In contrast, a contract settlement involves the taxpayer making a formal offer to HMRC of an amount to settle the tax, late payment interest and penalties due during a specific period of time as a consequence of the enquiries. Forward interest will be charged if the liability is to be paid by instalments. HMRC will then formally consider the offer and will issue an acceptance letter if it agrees to close the enquiry or investigation.

It is often administratively more convenient for HMRC to adopt this approach where multiple years' tax liabilities (and/or more than one type of tax) are affected by the proposed settlement. However, it should be noted that the offer must comply with the LSS on every issue ie 'global' settlements covering multiple issues or 'splitting the difference' are discouraged.

8.148 Contract settlements are often used at the end of COP8 or COP9 (Contractual Disclosure Facility) investigations and for voluntary disclosures, such as those using the Worldwide Disclosure Facility. Together, the exchange of offer and acceptance letters closes the case via a *TMA 1970, s 54* agreement.

8.149 If HMRC has not already received it, the officer is likely to ask the taxpayer to complete and submit a certificate of full disclosure at the same time as the letter of offer (see **8.114**).

HMRC has a number of 'standard' versions of the letter of offer and the case worker will provide the one that is considered to be appropriate.

8.150 If a taxpayer wishes to withdraw from some types of tax avoidance arrangement (particularly those involving partnerships where the partnership's position remains open) then HMRC may insist upon using a settlement deed rather than letters of offer and acceptance. The drafting, preparation and execution of deeds is a 'reserved activity' under the *Legal Services Act 2007* so it can only be carried out by an authorised or an exempt person. Advisers must ensure they understand the legal implications and whether a lawyer should be consulted before undertaking any work on settlement deeds. Guidance is available for CIOT members on the CIOT's website.

Focus

Offer letters and settlement deeds are legally binding documents, so it is important that the taxpayer and his adviser read the proposed wording carefully to ensure that they understand it and it is appropriate/achievable for the taxpayer's circumstances. If anything gives cause for concern, ask HMRC to explain clauses or consider amendments to the letter (subject to the need to consult a lawyer re: settlement deeds).

8.151 *Conduct of enquiries*

> This is especially important because a liability, once confirmed by the contract settlement, cannot be appealed. The client must therefore be in agreement with the rationale and basis for the liability of tax, interest and penalties therein before signing it.

8.151 Contract settlements conclude a taxpayer's tax affairs up to a particular date. HMRC cannot enter into forward agreements to agree how it will treat an issue or agree a liability for any tax years which are yet to end when the settlement is reached.

8.152 In limited circumstances, HMRC may consider a 'sub-standard' offer from the taxpayer. This is one that is for less than the tax, interest and penalties due because the taxpayer has insufficient net assets to pay the full amount. HMRC will only do so if it receives an up-to-date statement of assets and liabilities form, usually with documentation to back up the entries on it, plus three months' statements for all bank accounts and any other relevant information about the taxpayer's circumstances. It is likely to request that a form detailing monthly income and outgoings is completed.

8.153 If HMRC rejects the sub-standard offer and issues assessments/determinations to bring the tax, interest and penalties into charge, then the taxpayer may ultimately be made bankrupt, so consideration should be given to obtaining suitable advice on this aspect at the appropriate time. Whilst HMRC ranks alongside all other unsecured creditors in a bankruptcy or liquidation, until that happens, HMRC will want reassurance that it is being prioritised rather than left at the end of the queue.

8.154 If the taxpayer has sufficient net assets to pay the full liability, then HMRC is extremely unlikely to accept a sub-standard offer even if the taxpayer does not have enough liquid funds to pay the tax. HMRC will expect the taxpayer to make serious efforts to reduce his outgoings, consider an instalment payment plan to settle the liability over a number of months and attempt to raise finance in other ways (eg obtaining or increasing a mortgage or selling assets).

> **Focus**
>
> It is better to ensure that the offer to HMRC is realistic and achievable for the taxpayer to pay than risk the taxpayer finding that he has over-committed and cannot pay what is owed on the due dates. If the latter happens then the matter will be passed to HMRC's Debt Management teams who have less leeway to agree payment terms than the original case team and the whole agreement could be repudiated, ie cancelled (depending upon the terms of the letter of offer).

8.155 It is important to remember that HMRC may not accept an offer, even after a negotiation process. The caseworker will prepare a report to his line manager setting out views on the issues, the amount of tax at stake, the impact of HMRC's litigation and settlements strategy and code of governance as well as the offer from the taxpayer.

8.156 Depending on the amounts involved, HMRC's governance process may mean that the offer must be considered by a specific panel, board or the Tax Disputes Resolution Board. Details on the governance process to be followed (depending on the type of issues and tax at stake) are documented in HMRC's *Code of Governance for Resolving Tax Disputes* which is available on the GOV.UK website. These boards and panels aim to ensure consistency of decision making across the various HMRC departments and take account of its Litigation and Settlement Strategy.

It is only when a formal acceptance letter is issued in response to a letter of offer that the taxpayer and his agent know that the matter is finalised.

TAX DEBT COLLECTION

8.157 HMRC wants taxpayer to pay what they owe without delay. HMRC's tactics for encouraging prompt payment in conjunction with enquiries and investigations include:

- writing letters to 'nudge' taxpayer's into paying liabilities relating to tax avoidance appeals. These may state that public services need the money;
- issuing Accelerated Payment Notices (see **CHAPTER 21**);
- challenging requests for postponement of direct tax collection whilst an appeal is ongoing (see *Spring Capital Ltd v HMRC* [2016] UKFTT 671 (TC) for example). For indirect tax, hardship applications may be made;
- telephone calls from HMRC's Debt Management team chasing payment;
- seeking to transfer debts to other parties such as directors;
- asking other countries to enforce collection of UK tax debts under international mutual assistance arrangements if taxpayers are overseas;
- applying to a Court under civil debt proceedings;
- calling in the bailiffs to take control of goods;

8.158 *Conduct of enquiries*

- using powers to collect debts directly from taxpayer's bank accounts (*F(No 2)A 2015, s 51* and *Sch 8*);

- pursuing insolvency or liquidation, even where the dispute about whether the tax is actually due is yet to be resolved (see for example *Parkwell v Wilson* [2014] EWHC 3381 (Ch); and

- reinstating companies to the register at Companies House.

Further information is available in **CHAPTER 22**.

8.158 Where HMRC identifies persistent non-payment of debts in current or previous businesses, HMRC may also seek advance payments as security for tax debts.

Consequently, it is advisable to take proactive action when client cannot pay a tax debt on time.

Focus

HMRC officers appear to have somewhat more leeway to agree instalment payment plans via contract settlements. Consequently, where clients do not have sufficient available funds to pay their liabilities in full at the end of an enquiry or investigation, it is probably better to raise this with the case officer with a view to arranging a payment plan as part of a contract settlement. They are likely to offer more favourable terms, depending on the client's circumstances, than would be available from HMRC's debt management teams under Time to Pay Arrangements after closure notices or assessments are finalised.

When appealing HMRC's decisions relating to direct taxes, revisit the criteria for postponement (*TMA 1970, s 55(3)*) and ensure that requests provide the information required by the legislation whilst managing the client's expectations on the potential outcome. If requests are refused, consider asking the First-tier Tribunal for permission to postpone the debt's payment pending the outcome of the appeal against the tax liability. Bear in mind that counsel's assistance may be beneficial and that an application to the High Court for interim relief may also be needed (see for example *Biffin Ltd & Others v Revenue and Customs Comrs* [2016] EWHC 2926 (Admin)).

CARROTS AND STICKS: PUBLISHING TAXPAYER'S DETAILS AND THE MANAGING SERIOUS DEFAULTERS PROGRAMME

8.159 HMRC wants to deter people from evading tax and duties. For periods after 1 April 2010, if HMRC charges a taxpayer a penalty for a 'deliberate' error, then it may publish information about the taxpayer if:

- as a consequence of a HMRC investigation, one or more penalties are found to have been incurred by a taxpayer;

- the tax at stake exceeds £25,000 in total across all periods to be settled (after 1 April 2010); or

- maximum reduction was not given for the quality of the taxpayer's disclosure when the penalties were calculated.

The legislation is set out in *FA 2009, s 94* and HMRC's guidance is available in its Compliance Handbook at CH190000 and CH500000. Care needs to be taken if, following a voluntary disclosure, HMRC considers it needs additional information in order to quantify the tax or penalties at stake. If this occurs, the penalties may be deemed to arise 'as a consequence of an investigation' such that the taxpayer's details may be published (CH190686–CH190692).

8.160 For offshore matters and offshore transfers for tax years commencing on or after 6 April 2016 for income tax and CGT (or for IHT transfers of value on or after 1 April 2017) the rules are tightened by *FA 2016, Sch 21* and SI 2017/259. Effectively this means that disclosures of deliberate errors and omissions will result in publishing if the disclosure is prompted. Voluntary disclosures will escape publishing if maximum penalty reductions are received, although this is made harder to achieve by the change in requirements (see **8.135–8.136** above).

8.161 The information published will include the name and address of the taxpayer, the nature of his business, the periods involved, the amount of tax and the amount of the penalty. HMRC publishes this information quarterly on the GOV.UK website and it remains on there for one year before it is deleted.

8.162 If a taxpayer is charged a penalty for a deliberate error or deliberately failing to notify his liability, and does not meet one of the conditions listed above, HMRC will consider whether the taxpayer's details should be published as a punishment and as a deterrent to other taxpayers (ie the 'stick'). It is not possible to appeal against HMRC's decision to publish a taxpayer's details, but representations may be submitted to HMRC.

8.163 *Conduct of enquiries*

> **Focus**
>
> If your client's details may be published, consider whether he might meet the limited requirements for non-publication and also warn him up front so that this does not come as a nasty shock at the end of the enquiry.
>
> Whilst working with clients on resolving enquiries and making voluntary disclosures it's important to ensure that full facts are disclosed including the reasons why any errors or omissions occurred. This is because the taxpayer's details will be published if any issues were 'deliberate' unless the minimum penalties are charged.

8.163 If the taxpayer is charged a penalty for a deliberate error or deliberately failing to notify his liability to tax, the HMRC officer will also arrange for the taxpayer to be placed in the Managing Serious Defaulters (MSD) regime. HMRC's aim is to monitor the taxpayer closely to ensure that he is now complying with his tax obligations.

8.164 Such taxpayers are notified by letter with an accompanying fact sheet. They may receive further correspondence detailing additional information and documentation to be submitted on or with their tax returns. They may also be informed that they cannot use some of the 'short' versions of the tax return pages.

8.165 HMRC will review everything submitted by or on behalf of taxpayers while they are in the MSD regime. It may use its information powers to obtain documents and information from taxpayers or third parties to enable it to check whether the returns are complete and correct. HMRC will also open self-assessment enquiries and undertake business records checks using its enquiry and inspection powers. If it finds errors, then it will bring the tax into charge and charge penalties.

8.166 The taxpayer will be in the MSD regime for at least two years and perhaps as many as five, ie long enough for HMRC to satisfy itself that the taxpayer is now compliant. So the 'carrot' for the taxpayer is if he submits complete and correct tax returns and pays his tax on time then he will be in the regime for a shorter period of time than someone who does not do so.

> **Focus**
>
> - If your client is placed in the MSD regime, ensure that you see all letters sent to him about it. In addition, check if new clients are in the programme and look at their letters.

> - The letters will tell you what additional information and documentation must be included on or submitted with the taxpayer's returns. Depending on what information is requested and because he is likely to face an enquiry after the return's submission, you may need to adapt your working practices (eg check his bank statements, check source documents rather than making estimates or assumptions) accordingly. This may change your fee quote too.
>
> - Consider undertaking a record-keeping review to ascertain whether such clients are keeping good quality records and identify what improvements could be made. It is also worth reading the FAQs on HMRC's website.

SANCTIONS ON TAX ADVISERS

8.167 Finally, it is important to remember that HMRC can sanction advisers. Professional bodies may also investigate the conduct of members, taking into account the Professional Conduct in relation to Taxation (PCRT) standards.

8.168 In the most serious cases, HMRC can use criminal powers to investigate whether an adviser was aided a client in committing any of the criminal offences listed in **8.29** above or committed one of those offences themselves.

8.169 The *Criminal Finances Act 2017* introduced the two offences of failing to prevent the facilitation of tax evasion with effect from 30 September 2017 (*SI 2017/739*). This applies to all businesses regardless of industry sector or size. A successful conviction may result in an unlimited fine, significant adverse publicity, reputational and regulatory impacts. The primary defence is to have reasonable prevention procedures in place. Further information on this can be found in **CHAPTER 3**.

8.170 HMRC may investigate, with a view to sanctioning advisers under:

- Dishonest tax agents (*FA 2012, Sch 38*)

- Promoters of tax avoidance Schemes (*FA 2014, Part 5 & Sch 34–36*)

- Sanctions against enablers of defeated tax avoidance (*F(No 2)A 2017, Sch 16*)

- Sanctions against enablers of offshore tax evasion and non-compliance (*FA 2016, Sch 20*)

8.171 HMRC is more likely to conduct a criminal investigation against a dishonest tax agent. However, the alternative since 1 April 2013 is for HMRC

8.172 *Conduct of enquiries*

to use *FA 2012, Sch 38* to investigate and, if necessary, issue a conduct notice to tax agents who do something dishonest with a view to bringing about a loss of tax. These powers also give HMRC access to working papers and enable them to penalise the dishonest agent and publish their details. Further information may be found in HMRC's Compliance Handbook manual at CH180000 and at **16.234**.

8.172 The promoters of tax avoidance schemes (POTAS) rules require monitored promoters to disclose details of their products and clients to HMRC and tell clients, potential clients and intermediaries that they are a monitored promoter. This is achieved by a system of conduct, stop and monitoring notices issued if specific criteria are breached backed up by information powers and significant penalties. Further information may be found in **CHAPTER 16**.

8.173 *F(No 2)A 2017, Sch 16* introduced additional sanctions against enablers of defeated tax avoidance entered into on or after 16 November 2017. These regulations are triggered if an abusive tax avoidance arrangement is defeated. Defeat for these purposes includes a person voluntarily reaching a contract settlement with HMRC, finalised assessment/closure notice, finalised counteraction via a Follower Notice or GAAR counter-action notice as well as a final court decision. The regulations are broadly drafted and there are no specific legislative exemptions for auditors, tax return preparers or advisers assisting clients to withdraw from tax avoidance arrangements. The sanctions involve penalties and publishing of the enabler's details. Further information may be found in **CHAPTER 18**.

8.174 If any tax agent or adviser, on or after 1 April 2017, enables offshore tax evasion or non-compliance by another person then HMRC may investigate, issue penalties and publish the agent's details *(FA 2016, Sch 20)*. Enabling occurs when a person encourages, assists or otherwise facilities another person's conduct *(FA 2016, Sch 20, para 1(2)(b))*.

The key test is whether the agent knew when carrying out their actions that they enabled or were likely to enable the other person to carry out tax evasion or non-compliance *FA 2016, Sch 20, para 1(5))*. The legislation lists various criminal offences plus civil penalties for errors and failures *(FA 2016, Sch 20, paras 1(3) & 1(4))* which, when final, effectively confirm that a person carried out offshore tax evasion or non-compliance. Further information may be found in HMRC's Compliance Handbook manual at CH124000 and **CHAPTER 18**.

8.175 If an adviser may be considered an enabler then serious consideration should be given to getting specialist legal advice and ceasing acting for the client in view of any conflicts of interest, especially given the PCRT's standards.

KEY POINTS

8.176

1. HMRC's powers are comprehensive and have been strengthened significantly over the last ten years or so. HMRC's officers are all trained in the new powers and penalty regimes. HMRC is also willing to take cases to the courts (in accordance with the LSS) in order to collect tax where necessary.

2. Although all of this may make advisers and taxpayers feel that the cards are stacked against them, a working knowledge of HMRC's processes and practices should help advisers anticipate HMRC's next move and guide their clients through enquiries.

3. The key is to remember that HMRC is challenging the taxpayer but it is not the enemy. It wants to close the enquiry too and it is easier (and better) for both sides to work together to close it than for an entrenched battle to commence. This does not mean that there should be capitulation on points like penalties (eg behaviour) but a pragmatic solution may be the best way forward (especially on points where the fees exceed the tax, interest and penalties).

4. Enquiries worry most taxpayers, so resolving them swiftly, with minimal penalties, usually takes a weight off their minds. During the enquiry, taxpayers need to help their adviser by providing documents and explanations, leave them to do the work, and then focus on their business/life rather than having sleepless nights.

5. Likewise, taxpayers may fear the consequences of admitting to HMRC that they made a mistake. However, HMRC's significant data analysis capabilities coupled by the sheer volume of data it receives from organisations and government bodies inside and outside the UK means that the chances of being found out are increasing. Where taxpayers make mistakes or fail to do things (eg fail to disclose a source of income), making a voluntary disclosure to HMRC before it investigates them is an important step. The variety of routes for voluntary disclosures means that specialist advice is needed to determine what is best for the client's specific circumstances. An accurate, complete disclosure should result in reduced penalties and peace of mind for the client.

Chapter 9

Meetings with HMRC

Ian Roberts BA
Partner, The TACS Partnership

Acknowledgement: This chapter includes commentary originally produced by Chris Chadburn BSc.

SIGNPOSTS

- **Establish why the meeting is taking place** – There must be clarity on the reasons why a meeting is taking place (see **9.7–9.22**).

- **Preparation for the meeting is crucial** – This will include not only mastering the facts and arguments to be put but also understanding what HMRC wants from the meeting (see **9.23–9.48**).

- **Control and manage the meeting** – The meeting will be crucial in establishing both the facts of the case and HMRC's view of the taxpayer's approach to his tax affairs. The meeting should present the best case possible for the taxpayer. (See **9.49–9.71**.)

- **Follow up the outcomes of the meeting** – The hard work of the meeting should not be diluted by any failure to ensure that the agreements and decisions arrived at in the meeting are followed up (see **9.72–9.75**).

- **Meetings with HMRC can be traumatic** – Preparing for the meeting will involve not only mastering the brief but also psychologically preparing the taxpayer for the challenges of the meeting. Technical expertise is necessary but not sufficient. (See **9.111–9.114**.)

- **Key points** – For a list of key points from this chapter, see **9.115**.

INTRODUCTION

9.1 Meetings with HMRC are a fact of life. This chapter looks at meetings that may take place between advisers, their clients and HMRC officers relating to day-to-day direct tax business return enquiries, interventions and compliance checks by the HMRC Local Compliance business units.

Meetings with HMRC **9.5**

For guidance on meetings with HMRC (and a mediator) in the context of alternative dispute resolution see **Chapter 12**.

9.2 Ensuring that any meeting is conducted properly can be crucial to getting the optimum result for the taxpayer. Many of the points made in this chapter are of general application. In particular **9.77** *et seq* covers meetings in the employer inspection context

9.3 HMRC's publicly stated approach to tackling non-compliance includes a commitment to work closely with the taxpayer in an open and collaborative way. In July 2015 the report of the Tax assurance Commissioner said

> 'HMRC should – wherever possible – handle disputes non-confrontationally and by working collaboratively with the taxpayer, no matter what the size or complexity of the risk or point at issue, to resolve them effectively and efficiently for taxpayers and HMRC.'

9.4 This echoes the words published in 2013 in HMRC's 'Resolving Tax Disputes', which was its commentary on the Litigation and Settlement Strategy that has guided its approach to enquiry work since 2007. In this it says:

> 'Collaborative working practices are already commonplace between HMRC and many of its customers, across the different customer groups.'

It should be noted that this stated approach is only relevant to disputes to be resolved through civil procedures: it does not apply to criminal prosecution cases.

9.5 HMRC acknowledges the importance of ensuring that fact finding should be undertaken proportionately. In 'Resolving Tax Disputes' it says:

> 'A common challenge in disputes is for HMRC to determine the most efficient and effective way of establishing the relevant facts and identifying the relevant information required to reach a decision on what is the right tax. Even after having identified a potential tax risk, HMRC may not know which facts are going to turn out to be relevant in resolving that risk. Where the risk is a generic one (for example, whether a customer's accounting records or systems are not sufficiently robust), opening questions may need to be widely drawn. But where the risk relates to the tax treatment of a particular transaction, a widely drawn request for information can lead to a significant amount of non-relevant information being provided. This can be time-consuming and costly, not only for the customer (in searching for/providing the information/documentation) but also for HMRC (in having to review everything provided, much of which might have limited or no relevance to helping to resolve the dispute).'

9.6 *Meetings with HMRC*

9.6 It goes on to consider the 'best approach' to address these issues:

'The best approach for doing this will vary from case to case, but could include:

- initial meeting to discuss the potential tax risk/issue
- presentation by the customer (eg summary of transaction, timeline, background, etc)
- meeting with particular individuals (eg owner of the business, those involved in implementing a transaction, etc)
- on site meeting (eg where the risk concerns a particular business asset, such as a piece of plant and machinery)'

The adviser might wish to consider if the request for a meeting with HMRC has been planned within this framework. If there is any doubt it may be appropriate to ask HMRC to explain how they have concluded that a meeting is required by reference to the above guidelines.

PURPOSE OF THE MEETING

9.7 Detailed guidance notes on meetings relating to enquiries are in HMRC's Enquiry manual (EM1820 *et seq*). Meetings are described as a vital part of full enquiries, and appropriate for any substantial aspect enquiry. In such cases explanations of fact and behaviour will invariably be needed from the taxpayer and it is suggested that these are best obtained directly at an early stage rather than by correspondence (EM1821).

9.8 HMRC's guidance to its compliance officers is that that they should know exactly why they are holding any meeting, what they want to achieve from that meeting and what information they want to obtain. Meetings are stated to be the best way to:

- explain the purpose of the enquiry;
- obtain facts about how the business is run and the records kept;
- establish whether the taxpayer wishes to make a disclosure;
- explain the position on interest and penalties where omissions are established;
- agree the action needed to move the enquiry forward;
- quantify the omissions;
- settle the enquiry.

Meetings with HMRC **9.12**

This list is from EM1822. It does not include some areas almost always included covered in enquiry meetings, such as facts about the taxpayer's private finances.

9.9 Although some full enquiries are randomly selected, the vast majority arise because HMRC considers that tax is at risk. When tackling non-compliance, officers are under constant pressure to deliver results in terms of yield and turnaround. So before any meeting it should be assumed that HMRC have given detailed consideration to the risk of something being wrong with the return and the likely scale of the problem and the potential yield if the investigation establishes a problem.

9.10 The typical opening enquiry letter from HMRC will involve a request for books and records together with some additional information. This will normally relate solely to the business rather than the personal finances of the proprietors. There is no compulsion on the officer to say why the enquiry has been started, but if no such explanation is forthcoming it may be appropriate to remind HMRC of its commitment to transparency. In larger cases there may be a request for a 'pre-meeting meeting' before any records are examined, typically be with the firm's accountant and the adviser. This can be helpful to agree on how the records can be most effectively examined by HMRC.

9.11 In examining the records the officer is seeking to establish whether there is evidence to support the initial doubts on the accuracy of the return. Unless the record review shows there to be no problem (or sometimes where the results are inconclusive), the officer will usually proceed by requesting a meeting with the client.

9.12 HMRC's guidance to its officers envisages that there may be a reluctance by the taxpayer to attend a meeting, and gives advice on how to overcome any such objections. EM1861 confirms that the officer should say why a meeting with the taxpayer is desirable. EM1827 says that 'an agenda covering the main areas for discussion should always be provided. This should enable the agent to carry out any necessary preparation or research in advance'. In practice at the outset there is usually little by way of explanation of the need for a meeting beyond the assertion that experience shows this is the most cost-effective way of dealing with HMRC's concerns. Comment on what the officer wants to talk about is often restricted to generalities or the need to know more about the business or the client's personal finances.

However, a detailed agenda can be requested if it is not offered, to assist the adviser in preparing the client for the meeting (see **9.35**).

9.13 *Meetings with HMRC*

Is a meeting the best way forward?

9.13 EM1861 concludes by saying that HMRC 'do not have a power to compel a taxpayer or accountant to attend a meeting'. Advisers will need to discuss the meeting request with their client, but invariably every effort should be made to establish with HMRC why a meeting is considered necessary and the aspects to be covered in the proposed meeting. If the officer considers the quality of the records to be, at best, indifferent, this alone may be a reason for him to say he needs to look at the business and private finances in more detail to validate the figures returned. Officers may well talk in generalities at this point and keep specific concerns to themselves until after the taxpayer has provided explanations without prior notice of the detailed questions.

9.14 If an adviser is not convinced that a meeting at this stage is the best way forward it may be suggested that many of the questions can be dealt with perfectly adequately by correspondence. At this early stage of an enquiry HMRC may take up this offer if they are still in fact gathering mode.

9.15 In practice, providing additional written details at this stage can take the enquiry forward and this approach does have the benefit of giving answers after deliberation and research which can help establish where HMRC's interest really lies and whether a meeting is actually appropriate.

9.16 HMRC's approach to enquiry work is outlined in a series of compliance checks factsheets which can be found at www.gov.uk/government/collections/hm-revenue-and-customs-leaflets-factsheets-and-booklets#compliance-checks-factsheets. It should be noted that attendance at meetings is seen by HMRC as one way to demonstrate that a taxpayer is helping HMRC with its enquiries, which is a factor that will be taken into consideration when the level of any penalty is being assessed at the end of an enquiry. See in particular factsheet CC/FS7a, where willingness to attend a meeting is said to be a factor in deciding on mitigation of penalties. That said, there is no suggestion that attendance at a meeting is compulsory.

9.17 The Compliance Handbook (CH) includes guidance on the penalty regime. CH82400 *et seq* covers penalty reductions dependent on the quality of disclosure and 'attending meetings where that is the best way to quantify the inaccuracy and test the disclosure can be seen as a positive step by HMRC'.

9.18 As HMRC evidently considers attendance at meetings to be a sign of taxpayer cooperation, if a meeting is declined for any reason it should also be made clear to HMRC that full cooperation will be given via correspondence.

9.19 Having said that, given that any taxpayer has a right not to attend a meeting it is difficult to see how the penalty reductions would be affected if everything was done that could reasonably have needed to be done without attendance at a meeting. It seems difficult to argue that proactively establishing the extent of any tax loss must involve a meeting with HMRC after the records review. To help in any future negotiation on penalties it should be made clear to the officer why a meeting at that particular time was not the 'best way' forward. See more detail on penalties in **CHAPTERS 18 AND 19**.

9.20 HMRC may, in a small minority of cases, take the line that if the taxpayer continues to refuse to attend a meeting then he will have to be questioned before the tax tribunal. But it will be rare for a case to follow that path. After the initial records examination the officer will invariably still be looking for a lot of information to determine whether suspicions are well founded and the likely extent of the problem. Advisers and taxpayers may be more than happy to provide information, but not at a meeting.

9.21 There may come a time where the officer says that progress of an enquiry will be made using formal means if there is to be no meeting. Experience shows that this approach will only usually arise several months after the start of the enquiry. By then the merits (or lack of them) of the HMRC case it should be clear and any meeting is likely to be on relatively narrow ground if information has been provided during the review process.

9.22 It is, of course, generally accepted that a co-operative and constructive approach to HMRC enquiries is adopted, but it must also be recognised that the objectives of the officer and those of the adviser and the client may not always coincide.

> **Focus**
>
> A meeting is a major step and there should be clarity on why the meeting is taking place and the desired outcomes.

PREPARING FOR THE MEETING

9.23 HMRC officers will prepare extensively for any meeting with a taxpayer and his adviser. HMRC does not have the direct cost constraints of the taxpayer in preparing for meetings and therefore will be able to devote significant time to such preparation. To ensure that the taxpayer's and adviser's preparation is cost effective there should be clarity before agreeing to any meeting on where preparation time should be focused. The following notes are really a counsel of perfection, but as a minimum:

- the taxpayer needs to be aware of:
    - the background to the enquiry and the meeting,

9.24 *Meetings with HMRC*

- the advantages of being cooperative and making early and complete disclosures;
- there needs to be consideration of the general areas to be covered at the meeting and the likely areas of particular interest to HMRC;
- the taxpayer needs to be briefed on:
  - what is likely to happen at the meeting,
  - how direct and open questions should be approached,
  - potentially difficult areas and how to deal with these,
  - the adviser's role.

The adviser's knowledge of the client

9.24 The adviser should generally review the case and identify both the strengths and weaknesses. Particular attention should be paid to those areas to which the officer's attention might usefully be directed if a speedy and beneficial resolution for the client is to be reached. There should be a focus on:

- the quality of the client's records;
- issues arising during the preparation of the accounts and/or tax returns and how these were dealt with;
- previous tax issues;
- the position on any previous enquiries;
- general knowledge of the adviser (and adviser's staff) of the business and private finances.

Identify any problem areas

9.25 If omissions or understatements are identified prior to a meeting with HMRC it is critical that these are considered in some detail and disclosed to HMRC at an early stage. This will signify a constructive and cooperative approach and will assist in optimising the penalty position. If disclosures are not made at an early stage of a meeting but are revealed in a piecemeal fashion, this will have a damaging effect not only on the penalty loading but also on the client's (and possibly the adviser's) credibility.

9.26 On making a disclosure it may be agreed that an early meeting with the client is dispensed with and the adviser agrees to provide details in writing. This might involve a meeting with the officer to agree the scope of such an approach and a provisional timescale.

9.27 If the review process identifies no particular issues it will be useful at some stage to detail the research which has been done and the conclusions reached. Care needs to be taken on the timing of this and usually it will be appropriate to do this once an adviser has established that HMRC have 'fired all the bullets' (or that there are none to fire....).

9.28 There may be advantages to an adviser starting the process by saying he has looked at the papers and discussed the position in some detail with the taxpayer and that on that basis the return is considered correct. If, however, the officer has strong evidence to the contrary then this risks both taxpayer and adviser looking less than competent (and possibly dishonest!).

Pre-meeting issues

9.29 At the time of receiving the opening letter the taxpayer should have been briefed on the background to HMRC enquiries and the likely course that will be taken. In particular the adviser should outline:

- the obligations to keep proper records;
- the absolute right to enquire into tax returns;
- the power to call for relevant documents and particulars;
- the rights of appeal and review.

9.30 The advantages of admitting problems at an early stage should have been spelled out. There will have been a subsequent dialogue on the upsides and downsides of having a meeting at this stage and the client should be reminded of all this.

9.31 The adviser may be thoroughly familiar with HMRC meetings but most taxpayers are not. The taxpayer will experience a fair degree of stress when face to face with an HMRC officer. To minimise this the taxpayer should be briefed as far as possible on what to expect on the day. Much of the meeting, certainly the opening explanations, issue of HMRC leaflets, etc. will follow a fairly predictable course.

9.32 An adviser who deals with HMRC in a mature and professional manner will help settle the client. Whilst representing the taxpayer is key, the role of the professional adviser is perhaps best described as a facilitator. The taxpayer will be expected to answer any appropriate questions and should understand this ahead of the meeting.

9.33 As a general rule taxpayers should be encouraged to keep answers to questions factual and concise and to avoid overly lengthy replies. In particular, they should be aware that if they do not know the answer to a specific question

9.34 *Meetings with HMRC*

then they should not guess and should only provide estimates when they are comfortable doing so. Any false impressions given at the initial meeting may be difficult to correct at a later stage. This is another excellent reason for establishing the key issues to be discussed at any meeting to avoid any surprises.

9.34 The taxpayer should be made aware that HMRC's usual objective in the early stages of the meeting is to put the taxpayer at ease and get him talking. The taxpayer should be encouraged to:

- remain calm and avoid aggravating the officer;
- participate actively and constructively;
- answer specific questions directly;
- answer more general questions with circumspection.

The adviser should be prepared to suggest a 'review and report back' approach which should be acceptable to HMRC.

9.35 The taxpayer cannot be expected to remember details from many years ago. Ideally the request for a detailed agenda will have resulted in identifying such questions before the meeting and appropriate answers given. Areas of weakness should be considered in detail. It is not possible to be prescriptive on what these will be but **9.8** above sets out the areas of interest for the officer and an open discussion ahead of the meeting between the taxpayer and his adviser may suggest some likely issues.

9.36 If the officer is looking at private finances in any detail at all then questions will invariably arise in relation to non-taxable sources. See EM2051:

> 'Taxpayers may claim that deficiencies ... or money introduced were funded from ... non-taxable receipts. You should at an early stage in an enquiry try to pre-empt such claims by asking the taxpayer about matters such as cash accumulation, loans and gifts received and so on. If the claim is first made at a meeting you should question the taxpayer closely about it, before he or she has had time to invent plausible circumstances to surround a false story.'

9.37 Further general guidance on such matters is given at EM2053 and more specific details are given at EM2056–EM2097. Common explanations of the source of funds are:

- cash hoards;
- betting wins;
- legacies and sales of personal effects;
- illegal or immoral activities.

9.38 Clearly an adviser should ask the taxpayer about such issues before the meeting, although it may be difficult to raise a specific query on illegal or immoral income. If there are matters of substance in the relevant period then these should be discussed in considerable detail. A good adviser will test whether, applying an appropriate degree of professional detachment, he is satisfied with the explanations given.

9.39 In any event the taxpayer needs to understand that HMRC will require evidence to substantiate any claims and the adviser needs to establish how best this can be obtained.

See **9.25** above regarding early disclosure of any irregularities.

9.40 One reason for the officer preferring to see the taxpayer is that it may help in forming a view on his overall credibility. The adviser should do all that is possible to ensure that the taxpayer comes across as honest, open, knowledgeable, and helpful. The aim will be to come out of the meeting feeling that the taxpayer would make a very credible witness if appeals were taken to the tax tribunal.

There is no substitute for sound preparation, but note that over-coaching can easily give the wrong impression.

WHAT THE HMRC OFFICER WANTS

9.41 The officer will have a combination of the following objectives which should be considered in the light of the reasons given for the meeting and the agenda:

- to obtain detailed information about the taxpayer's personal and financial background, the nature of the business being carried on and the economics on which it operates;
- to obtain detailed information about the business records with a view to testing their reliability;
- to obtain detailed and specific information about the individual's personal finances to establish whether these stack up with the returns and accounts;
- to check facts and explanations against third-party information held.

9.42 The officer has to be able to cast significant doubt on the accuracy of the return in order to justify continuing with the enquiry. *TMA 1970, s 9A* obliges the inspector to establish whether the return 'is incorrect or incomplete'.

9.43 *Meetings with HMRC*

9.43 It is important to HMRC officers to find problems with the records. They can then justify, for example, preparing a recalculation of the taxpayer's sales figure based on a business economics exercise which suggests that the figure in the accounts may have been understated. The preparation of a business economics exercise which casts doubt on the accuracy of the sales figure is not enough to justify displacing the accounts figures if there is no reason to dispute the accuracy of the records from which those accounts were prepared.

9.44 The officer may be able to show that evidence about the taxpayer's lifestyle (and the day-to-day expenditure of he and his family) suggests a significant difference between the cash available from the business and other sources for the client, and the sums apparently spent. Similarly, the funding of private assets may be unclear from the known borrowings and other established funds.

9.45 If the officer can show that any of these 'doubtful' features are present, there may well be a strong case for establishing omissions. Invariably, though, HMRC will be in a much stronger position if it can be shown that there is evidence of material inaccuracies in the records supporting the return.

9.46 Taxpayers and advisers should not be afraid to stand their ground in the face of challenges by HMRC as to the integrity of the taxpayers' business records and explanations, particularly if such challenges have little or no foundation. Whilst it may sometimes be necessary for taxpayers to defend their position before the tribunal (eg see *Newell (t/a Tanya's Takeaway) v Revenue and Customs Comrs* [2013] UKFTT 742 (TC)), it will clearly be preferable to circumvent such challenges by HMRC well before they get to that stage, if possible.

Focus

Taxpayers and their advisers should go into any meeting with HMRC as fully briefed and prepared as possible. HMRC will be fully prepared and failure to match or exceed its 'knowledge of the brief' will greatly increase the risk of failure.

CHECKLIST FOR PREPARING FOR A MEETING

9.47 The adviser should:
- review the case history;
- review all knowledge of the taxpayer and business;
- prepare and review schedules from the accounts and tax returns;

Meetings with HMRC **9.49**

- discuss the case with accounts and tax staff;
- identify areas of weakness;
- discuss briefly areas of interest with the compliance officer (consider a pre-meeting meeting);
- clear up any accountancy queries and brush up on relevant technical knowledge;
- agree with HMRC that accounts queries are to be handled before the meeting;
- agree an agenda for the meeting;
- agree who is to be present and a suitable place, date and time;
- agree what information should be brought to the meeting.

9.48 The adviser should cover the following points with the taxpayer:

- explain the reason for the meeting;
- outline the history of the case to date;
- explain what HMRC already knows;
- explain the officer's likely objectives;
- summarise the expected control and format of the meeting;
- advise on approach and demeanour;
- identify areas of weakness and strengths;
- identify and go through key questions and answers;
- provide briefing notes.

THE MEETING ITSELF

Format of the meeting

9.49 Most full HMRC enquiry meetings will follow a fairly predictable format, at least in outline and will cover some combination of the following:

- reasons for the interview, an outline of the relevant legislative provisions, the rights of HMRC to make enquiries into a return and the rights of the taxpayer to ask for an internal review and for the tax tribunal to determine when an enquiry should be terminated;
- background to the business, business history, particular expertise, types of products, types of goods sold, business performance over the years, problems encountered in running the business, wastage, expertise and

9.50 *Meetings with HMRC*

experience of the proprietor, specific nature of the trade, prices, pricing policies, stock-holding policies, cash-control policies, economics of the business, general trends;

- business records: who keeps them, where, how often, what they are, what they cover, nature of 'prime' records; details of any 'non-financial' records kept; points from the officer's initial review demonstrating a clear problem and profit adjustment;

- business economics in detail: how the business is organised;

- level and frequency of drawings from the business, personal and private expenditure, personal assets and liabilities, funding of major assets, etc, other sources of income, cash windfalls and legacies, etc;

- technical adjustments: own use and own goods, private car adjustments, private telephone, etc, other private benefits/expenses;

- any omissions or additions disclosed during the meeting, proposals for further investigation;

- agreements for subsequent action: information to be provided, records to be reviewed, investigations to be undertaken by the accountant, etc, scope of future enquiries and an agreed timetable for action.

Who will be present?

9.50 If possible it is helpful to ascertain before the meeting who is to attend on behalf of HMRC. There will usually be at least two officers, one essentially conducting the meeting and the other taking notes.

9.51 It is important to establish whether there will be anyone there outside the norm, eg a very senior officer or a qualified accountant. Why are they attending and does this affect your approach to the meeting?

9.52 The adviser should always consider who should attend on the taxpayer's behalf and ensure HMRC is aware of the position. If the meeting is likely to be protracted, complex and generally difficult, then assistance from the adviser's office may be necessary to take notes and provide general support.

9.53 It may be appropriate from time to time to get a specialist's technical input at the opening meeting if the agenda warrants it. If the taxpayer's personal finances are to be discussed it may be appropriate to consider if a spouse or partner might attend the meeting, although a clear line should be drawn with HMRC about whose tax affairs are being reviewed.

9.54 If a meeting is likely to cover detailed reviews of business records or particular areas of commercial expertise, it may be advisable to have an appropriate member of the taxpayer's staff available to join the meeting. Questions to be directed to the employee may have to be dealt with at a separate meeting or at the beginning of the discussion after which the employee can leave. He should be given clear guidelines and support in preparation for the meeting and his terms of reference and areas of expertise and knowledge about the business and the proprietor's affairs must be made clear to the officer.

9.55 Where the business is conducted by a husband and wife, civil partners or cohabiting couples in a business partnership or as directors in a limited company, it is important to verify before the meeting the exact degree of involvement of both parties in the business. Should any query about the level of involvement of one of the couple in the business be raised by the officer, it can then be addressed properly. Where omissions are to be disclosed it will be of considerable importance to ascertain the extent of the involvement and knowledge of both parties in the relevant events. HMRC's instructions tell the officer to offer separate interviews to both initially (EM1852 *et seq*). It may be necessary to insist on separate meetings where it is clear that one party has had no involvement in or no knowledge of what has gone on. In such cases, it may be necessary for one or both of the couple to seek independent advice.

9.56 For businesses run by partners or directors of a limited company the officer will indicate who it is believed should attend the meeting or meetings. There will usually be a clear line drawn between meetings where personal finances and business matters are to be discussed. At the former, only the relevant partner or director will be present with the adviser and at the latter either all partners and directors or those with specific responsibilities, eg the finance partner/director. Clearly the larger the organisation the more likely it is that not all partners/directors will attend the business side of the meeting.

9.57 The officer's views on which taxpayers should attend should be fully considered. Having a number of partners/directors tied up for several hours in a meeting with HMRC, together with essential preparatory time, may be a very significant commitment. The officer should be prepared fully to justify the assertion that the suggested attendees are necessary to progress the enquiry.

Where and when should the meeting be held?

9.58 HMRC's view is that 'Wherever possible, meetings should be held at business premises or accountant's office because it will normally be easier to examine the business records there'. (EM1830).

9.59 Given that there is no obligation to have a meeting with HMRC, the adviser and the taxpayer need to take a view on the advantages and disadvantages of holding a meeting at the business premises, in the tax office

9.60 *Meetings with HMRC*

or at the adviser's office. It will rarely be suggested that the meeting take place at the taxpayer's home and unless there are issues such as age and infirmity any such suggestion should normally be rejected.

9.60 The logistics and potential disruption to the business as well as lack of privacy from employees will be principal factors to consider, but deciding where the taxpayer is likely to feel most comfortable should usually be the key point. This is unlikely to be at the tax office. The adviser's office might sensibly be regarded as the venue of choice, where the taxpayer and adviser will be most at ease.

9.61 Although it will be sensible to have a degree of flexibility, the time and day best suiting the taxpayer should be 'the norm'.

9.62 Wherever and whenever the meeting is held, it should be arranged that the room and set up provide for a reasonable degree of comfort and minimal opportunity for disruption. It will usually be sensible to establish approximately how long the meeting is expected to last and manage expectations if necessary.

9.63 As a separate matter, it should be noted that under the compliance checks regime, HMRC has the power to enter a person's business premises and inspect business documents. Further information is given at **9.79** *et seq*.

Conduct of the meeting

9.64 EM1850 gives general points to compliance officers on meetings, and gives some insight into expected conduct. Whilst the guidelines are welcome it would be interesting to see how often the guidelines are fully applied in practice. For example, the guidelines say 'You are not there to trick the taxpayer' but often questions to the taxpayer early in the meeting asked 'innocently' will be returned to later in the meeting if the discussion has suggested differing facts.

9.65 All enquiries and all meetings are different, and however well the adviser and the taxpayer have prepared, unexpected and potentially difficult issues may be raised. The adviser should be alert to this and recognise potential stress points quickly.

9.66 Brief adjournments can be called for to reassure the taxpayer, to provide professional guidance and to review the progress of the meeting to establish whether or not the taxpayer wishes to proceed. There may be occasions on which the adviser deems it necessary to bring the meeting to a close either because new and unwelcome information has come to light, or because HMRC adopts specific procedures about which the adviser is unsure or unprepared.

Meetings with HMRC **9.71**

9.67 A good example of the latter situation would be where it appears from comments during the meeting that HMRC may regard this as a case of serious fraud. See www.hmrc.gov.uk/prosecutions/crim-inv-policy.htm and **CHAPTER 3** for details of HMRC policy on prosecutions. HMRC prosecutes few cases for false accounts/returns but the case may be taken over by an HMRC Fraud Investigation team if the yield is likely to be £75,000 or more.

9.68 Prolonged pauses or silence during a meeting are sometimes used by HMRC's officers and can appear oppressive and quite stressful for the taxpayer. Unnecessary or irrelevant statements simply to keep the meeting moving should be avoided, and the adviser should normally fill such silences if the client is uneasy.

9.69 The adviser should be prepared to participate actively or intervene in the meeting even if at times this is clearly not to the satisfaction of the officer. But be aware of HMRC's view at EM1850 that 'The agent may try to answer all or some of the questions on behalf of their client. Explain that the purpose of the meeting is to obtain facts which only the taxpayer knows'.

9.70 Officers should not tape or video record a meeting. If the taxpayer or adviser wants to tape record the meeting this should normally be allowed if it is agreed that an unedited copy of the tape be provided or a full typed transcript. Requests for video recordings will normally be refused on the basis that there is no obvious business advantage over an audio recording. See EM1835.

How should the meeting conclude?

9.71 The officer is told to ensure the taxpayer knows exactly where he stands at the end of the meeting. If there is likely to be additional liability then the taxpayer needs to be informed and reminded of the benefits of co-operation and what needs to be done next. The officer will most likely raise the possibility of a penalty being charged at this stage and is then obliged to issue factsheet CC/FS9 (the human rights factsheet). Factsheets CC/FS7a (concerning penalties) may also be issued. If further information is needed then the officer should make it clear what is needed; a realistic timescale should be agreed. The position should be summarised by letter shortly after the meeting. See EM1855.

Focus

The meeting should be conducted in a professionally polite manner, despite the sometimes raw issues being discussed. The coolest head often comes out on top,

---

9.72   *Meetings with HMRC*

Notes of meetings

9.72   The HMRC officer or his assistant will prepare a detailed (but not verbatim) note of the meeting usually shortly after it has been held. A copy should be sent to the adviser either:

- asking for the client to signify agreement to its accuracy by signing a copy and returning it; or

- asking for comments or any amendments that are considered necessary.

9.73   There will usually be no advantage to the taxpayer in signing the notes and there is no statutory obligation to do so. If, however, there are points of dispute or a particular spin on what was said then these should be pointed out reasonably quickly.

9.74   Similarly, if what was said is properly recorded but the taxpayer or the adviser on reflection wants to give better particulars then this may be an appropriate time to do so. Clearly if points on the notes are not raised until many months after the notes were sent out then their evidential value is likely to be substantially weakened.

9.75   HMRC may sometimes draw the attention of the taxpayer and his adviser to the case of *Duffy v Revenue and Customs Comrs* [2007] STC (SCD) 377 to underline the importance of checking meeting notes carefully and ensuring that they are complete and correct (see **6.77**).

Ten key areas

9.76

1   **Be prepared** – Lack of preparation and attention to detail will result in an inability to answer questions properly. Taxpayers may be faced with questions for which they are not ready, leaving them feeling exposed and vulnerable. This in turn may jeopardise the client/agent relationship.

2   **Be ready to negotiate** – Most enquiries are settled without recourse to formal appeal proceedings and the adviser should be aware throughout any meeting that he may have to reach a compromise settlement at some stage. Identifying strengths and weaknesses and continually reinforcing the best arguments with references to points and facts in the taxpayer's favour is a key area of negotiating.

3   **What are the key areas?** – A list of priorities and certain key points to make helps the adviser redirect the route a meeting is taking in some cases. The adviser must be prepared to insist that the discussion is moved on if it is felt that the meeting is bogged down.

4 **Be constructive but firm** – An ability to see the other side's viewpoint, to accept HMRC's statutory authority and to take a constructive approach towards resolving areas of doubt and difficulty is generally to be recommended. It is likely to prove more cost-effective in the long run. Advisers must, however, be prepared to exercise their judgement on where co-operation ends and obsequious collaboration begins. The taxpayer is entitled to representation and to feel that he has been afforded the correct level of support.

5 **Know the taxpayer's rights** – Many enquiries will at some stage cover or at least touch on areas where the inspector's right to information or to take certain action is not clear cut. Advisers must not be afraid to dispute these areas if needed.

6 **Research technical points** – A thorough awareness of the legislative provisions governing HMRC enquiries and the rights and obligations under the statute is needed. Cases may involve specific areas of the Taxes Acts and careful research should always be undertaken if such technical issues are to be the subject of discussion during any meeting.

7 **Be prepared to appeal** – The adviser who lets the HMRC officer know that he would not take a case to tribunal is sacrificing a solid negotiating tactic and, more fundamentally, is depriving the taxpayer of one of his basic rights under the enquiry process.

8 **End the meeting if necessary** – The adviser should always be prepared to call a halt during a meeting to be satisfied that the taxpayer fully understands the statutory position and what the various options are, even if this is just done to give breathing space (or indeed a comfort break!).

9 **Be polite and courteous** – The adviser should adopt a politely questioning and challenging approach to the officer's statements where appropriate.

10 **Review later** – Where detailed calculations are presented during an interview it will rarely be possible to test them properly. An interview is inevitably a pressurised situation and even simple points or errors can easily be overlooked. Generally no comment should be made on detailed calculations presented under these circumstances and they should be reviewed later. Similarly, any request for a taxpayer to sign any document at the meeting should be resisted; the document should be taken away for later review.

Employer compliance checks

9.77 All references to employers include contractors. A broad summary of the approach taken in employer compliance checks is given in HMRC's Compliance Operational Guidance manual (COG). The key statute governing

9.78 *Meetings with HMRC*

these issues is set out in the HMRC Compliance Handbook, and includes the requirement that PAYE records must be retained for at least three years after the end of the tax year to which they relate (Income Tax (Pay As You Earn) Regulations 2003, SI 2003/2682, reg 97 and Social Security (Contributions) Regulations 2001, SI 2001/1004, reg 26, Sch 4).

9.78 In general the points made in relation to the opening meetings in SA enquiries will apply to inspection visits for employers. The essential objectives of these inspections are to ensure that employers:

- pay what is due;
- keep accurate records;
- submit accurate returns;
- submit returns within the statutory time limits.

The framework for inspections generally is provided in the HMRC Compliance Handbook.

9.79 If an inspection is reasonably required to check the tax position of any person, an HMRC officer has the power to enter a person's business premises and inspect:

- the premises (see CH25180);
- the business assets on those premises (see CH25260);
- the business documents on those premises (see CH25280).

9.80 The employer may agree a time and date for an inspection but otherwise HMRC must give at least seven calendar days' notice unless the inspection is carried out by or with the agreement of a senior HMRC officer. Such unannounced visits will only take place where it has not been possible to make an appointment or there are identified concerns, such as a reason to believe tax is being deliberately evaded. See CH25520.

9.81 Entry into the premises may be refused and the officer may not force entry (CH25120). In these circumstances HMRC is likely to get approval for the inspection from the First-tier Tribunal. This allows HMRC to impose penalties for deliberately obstructing an officer in the course of an approved inspection. The initial penalty is £300 and up to £60 a day for continuing failure.

For detailed commentary on HMRC's information powers, see **CHAPTER 16**.

9.82 As in other areas of tackling non-compliance, it is clear that the selection of employers for inspection is based on risk assessment and that yield is the name of the game. An employer inspection may be undertaken if a full

Meetings with HMRC **9.88**

enquiry into a business and its principals is being considered. Full enquiries into larger businesses will often have a review of PAYE and benefits as part of the overall compliance check. In short these are not routine matters.

9.83 Detailed guidance on employer compliance checks can be found in Compliance Operational Guidance at COG900000. See also the compliance check factsheets at www.gov.uk/government/collections/hm-revenue-and-customs-leaflets-factsheets-and-booklets#compliance-checks-factsheets-general-information.

9.84 If there is to be a pre-arranged visit, clearly it makes sense to establish in advance exactly which records are needed and for which period. COG905015 says that an explanation of the types of records required should be given when making the appointment. Before inspecting the records the officer will want to talk about the business, the workforce and the systems.

9.85 HMRC should notify the adviser of the commencement of the compliance check (COG905020). It is common for advisers not to attend such visits and this may be appropriate. However, given the risk-based decision to undertake the check, the benefits and costs of the adviser attending the visit should be carefully discussed.

9.86 At the very least, clients need to know:

- how the review is likely to unfold;
- their risk areas;
- how to handle the visit.

9.87 COG905045 sets out details of the 'intervention plan' which provides a framework for the check and is produced before the visit. It is used to record:

- specific risks to be addressed;
- key steps planned to address those risks;
- results of the work/tests undertaken;
- outcomes, conclusions and yield.

9.88 COG905075 sets out details of HMRC's risk-based systems audit which gives a good idea of the questions likely to be asked and the approach to testing the systems allegedly operating in practice. COG905085 says that it is important that the 'talk through' of the systems is conducted:

- with the owner, partner, director or company secretary as they will have knowledge of the business; and, if applicable;
- the person with the knowledge of the systems in operation.

9.89 *Meetings with HMRC*

9.89 Where there is a request for copies of the intervention plan, etc the HMRC officer is told to consider whether 'any other information should [also] be released' although it is expected that the usual answer will be that a note of the meeting will be provided and other details are withheld under an exemption in the *Freedom of Information Act 2000*.

9.90 Where the employer or agent refuses to attend a meeting or cancels two pre-arranged meetings the HMRC officer is instructed to explain why a meeting is preferred, how it will assist the compliance check and encourage him to reconsider. A further letter may be issued, reminding the employer of his obligations. If there is still a refusal to co-operate then the officer and senior manager should consider forcing action in terms of:

- a formal notice of the visit with possible approval by the tribunal;
- an unannounced visit;
- a formal information notice;
- formal determinations or decisions of tax and National Insurance.

9.91 The HMRC factsheet CC/FS3 says that '[the taxpayer does] not have to be present at the visit' although it is helpful if he is available particularly at the beginning and at the end. The officer may ask to speak to the people who keep the records. COG905030 says that when making an appointment '[the officer] should ask that the proprietor or director and the person responsible for maintaining the records is present'.

9.92 Clearly, the officer has a right to inspect relevant records and it is sensible and practical to have someone senior at the meeting who can help the officer understand the systems and how they work in practice.

9.93 HMRC officers may not always highlight particular areas of interest before the meeting and in these circumstances it can be difficult to establish who should be around to answer detailed questions. For example, in terms of expenses policy that may be a director with responsibilities for human resources or for the arrangements with sub-contractors a director responsible for production. Whatever the situation, there should be a conscious decision as to who will be at or available for the meeting and they should all be fully briefed.

9.94 If there is any doubt it will usually be sensible to keep the meeting at a relatively low level to allow the officer to flag up areas of interest but to allow the employer not to go into any great detail on these without proper consideration. Because it is relatively unusual in smaller cases for advisers to be present during the visit, their presence may put the officer on notice that the employer has particular concerns.

9.95 The officer, either at the visit or in terms of follow up, may be very keen to meet a particular director or principal of the business. HMRC may overlook the fact that its rights relate purely to inspecting records. It has no rights to meet a particular client and every request needs to be considered on its merits. In short, it should meet the client when it suits the client (and the adviser), not when it suits HMRC. When referring to 'meetings' COG905165 seems to be referring to the visit rather than to the presence of any particular person at any part of the visit. There is no indication of forcing action to be taken (including a penalty for obstruction) unless there is a problem with the officer gaining access to the premises and records.

9.96 The visit will usually begin with general fact finding in terms of the nature of the business; number of directors and employees; responsibilities of key people; the payroll system used and who does what in relation to wages, PAYE returns, etc. This is basic information and may be more cost effectively covered by way of a detailed note provided by the employer and adviser before or at the meeting. With the notes in front of them the compliance officer can then focus on any particular points of detail or areas of concern.

9.97 HMRC may ask for sight of records kept electronically. CH23360 says that electronic documents and records can include the actual computer or server, including an internal hard drive system and an external storage device holding backed up information or scans of previously printed documents. If it is not possible to produce a copy electronically, then HMRC is instructed to accept a printed copy instead.

9.98 Status issues will often be a significant risk area and will be covered in detail. Note that compliance officers may approach workers or ex-workers to validate the client's version of the facts relating to the engagement. It is possible that such approaches may have been made before the compliance visit.

9.99 On the conclusion of the visit the compliance officer should ensure that all questions have been answered and relevant facts obtained. HMRC is empowered to copy, take extracts from or remove for a reasonable period documents relating to the inspection. If removing documents, the officer is advised to provide a written receipt.

9.100 At the end of a compliance check, if nothing is wrong then the employer will get a letter of confirmation. Otherwise the results of the check will be set out in a letter and the employer will be encouraged to co-operate in establishing the correct amount of tax and NIC payable.

9.101 Agents should note that HMRC may collect the amount owing from the date when the mistakes first started, although frequently HMRC will only

9.102 *Meetings with HMRC*

go back up to six years, provided it can establish that mistakes are due to at least careless inaccuracies. CC/FS7a sets out the position on penalties applicable. The factsheet makes no direct reference to attendance at the visit in relation to the penalty reduction.

9.102 COG906170 says the officer should consider further meetings as necessary to:

- see additional records;
- ask further questions;
- challenge explanations;
- avoid lengthy correspondence;
- maintain the initiative and continuity.

9.103 In practice the areas highlighted by the review will need to be looked at in detail to establish whether tax is likely to have been lost and arrive at a reasonable quantum. Sometimes the conclusions of the officer are sound and often they are not. The earlier the adviser provides input, the easier and less costly the visit is likely to be.

PRE-PLANNING CHECKLIST

9.104

- What records does HMRC want to see?
- What state are those records in?
- Is all relevant information easily accessible?
- Extract all irrelevant items.
- Is the suggested date too early? Consider postponement?
- Where is the meeting to be held?
- Arrange suitable accommodation.
- Who is to attend the meeting?
- Appoint someone to accompany the visitors?
- Find out exactly who is coming.
- Get a list of what/who they will want to see.
- Ask if there is a specific reason for the visit.

- Check up on statutory powers.
- Ascertain statutory obligations and rights.
- Identify any areas of risk or vulnerability.
- Quantify any problems, potential errors or omissions.
- Prepare statements for early disclosure if relevant.
- Prepare explanations in mitigation if necessary.
- Identify likely exposure to interest and penalties and quantify.

DURING THE VISIT ITSELF

9.105 General:

- be concise and factual;
- do not guess: if you're unsure, adopt a 'report back' approach;
- ensure that the officers have adequate accommodation;
- give access only to:
    - the relevant records;
    - parts of the premises;
    - relevant (and fully briefed) staff.

9.106 Review of records:

- agree a timetable;
- delegate secretarial assistance/copying facilities if needed;
- list all records seen and examined;
- resist removal of records and offer copies.

9.107 Conclusion of visit:

- establish when the results of the review will be explained: agree a timescale;
- agree a timescale within which the officers will report their conclusions;
- agree a schedule of any matters outstanding;
- identify the specific areas for further research;
- establish who is to do what, and when;
- ask for a copy of HMRC's meeting note.

9.108 *Meetings with HMRC*

CHECKLIST FOR AREAS THE COMPLIANCE OFFICERS ARE LIKELY TO REVIEW

9.108 Formal returns:
- P11Ds;
- VAT returns and the VAT account;
- wages books and records;
- cash records, nominal ledgers, private ledgers;
- subcontractor records.

9.109 General records:
- clock cards, timesheets, worksheets, job cards;
- sickness records, absence records;
- holiday pay records;
- cash books, bank books, expense invoices, etc.

9.110 The danger areas:
- directors' benefits and expenses payments;
- accommodation and related benefits;
- casual labour records, overtime records;
- bonuses paid and weekend working records;
- the subcontractors' scheme;
- students and part-time workers;
- status of subcontractors and consultants;
- travel and subsistence payments;
- overnight allowances and clothing allowances;
- Class 1A insurance records and mileage records;
- telephone logs;
- tips and gratuities systems;
- tronc systems in operation;
- seasonal workers;
- payments to wives;
- cars provided for family members, entertaining and gifts, staff canteens and vending machines.

> **Focus**
> Employer visits pose specific challenges to the taxpayer and adviser and the 'rules of the game' must be understood.

CONCLUSIONS

9.111 A meeting with HMRC is a potentially difficult experience for a client. The adviser's role is to participate actively and constructively during these meetings, to represent the client, to ensure that his rights are observed and upheld and to provide professional and positive guidance before and throughout the course of a meeting on the legal, technical and practical aspects of any case.

9.112 The adviser needs to be familiar with:

- relevant legislation;
- HMRC's statutory rights and duties;
- the client's rights and obligations;
- codes of practice on investigations and relevant parts of HMRC manuals.

9.113 This chapter is not an exhaustive review of all the aspects of HMRC meetings. It aims to provide some guidelines on how such meetings are best conducted. There can be little substitute for experience in this area of tax practice. Most practitioners can, however, perform more than adequately, even very effectively in interview situations, with the right preparation – and perhaps a little luck.

9.114 The opening meeting is frequently the key stage of an enquiry. This is so for both the client and the HMRC officer. The latter's training includes help and guidance on interviews. The rapid realisation that the ability to conduct a well-structured and successful meeting is a major factor in conducting successful enquiries should be appreciated by advisers. The accountant or tax practitioner who performs well during interviews is likely to achieve the best settlement for the client.

KEY POINTS

9.115

1 Understand why the meeting is taking place and have a clear view of what the goals of all parties attending are in that meeting.

9.115 *Meetings with HMRC*

2   Prepare for the meeting. Do not go into any meeting without a mastery of the facts.

3   Know who from HMRC you are meeting and what they will want from the meeting. Try to think ahead.

4   Control the meeting and do not allow any 'railroading' by HMRC. Firm but polite is the order of the day.

5   A meeting is seldom the end of the process so ensure there is a clear understanding of what the meeting has achieved and what the next steps are.

Chapter 10

Conduct of a full enquiry

Ian Roberts BA
Partner, The TACS Partnership

Acknowledgement: This chapter includes commentary originally produced by Andrew Burgess

> **SIGNPOSTS**
>
> - **Control is the key to a successful outcome** – Control has to be exercised over the people, the process and the paper (see **10.1–10.6**).
>
> - **Control will allow presentation of the facts but will not change them** – Control can mean damage limitation if the facts are difficult for the taxpayer (see **10.8–10.19**).
>
> - **If you don't control the process HMRC will** – An understanding of the investigation process can allow the adviser to drive and shape the investigation to the benefit of the taxpayer. Failure to do this will leave HMRC in the driving seat. (See **10.31–10.68**.)
>
> - **Meetings are a stage, and a stage needs a director** – An HMRC meeting is a chance for the taxpayer to clarify issues and present the best possible case. An adviser should control the meeting to allow this to happen. (See **10.69–10.93**.)
>
> - **Paper will drown you if not controlled** – The formal and informal paperwork required in an investigation will swamp the unwary. Control from the start is crucial. (See **10.94–10.120**.)
>
> - **Always remember the end game** – The technical debate along the way must always be seen in the context of the final bill the taxpayer will pay. Control is always aimed at driving to an answer to the question 'How much to settle?'. (See **10.130–10.159**.)
>
> - **Key points** – For a list of key points from this chapter, see **10.160**.

10.1 *Conduct of a full enquiry*

WHY IS CONTROL IMPORTANT?

10.1 An HMRC investigation is always a time of great pressure for both the taxpayer and his professional advisers, with the more serious the investigation, the greater the pressure. The taxpayer may find that until the investigation is completed he is distracted from the running of his business and that could be costly in both time and money.

10.2 In addition, the relationship between the taxpayer and his adviser may come under some pressure if the taxpayer sees the adviser as failing in his task of providing protection against the perils of an HMRC enquiry.

10.3 Investigations can run for many months, and almost always lead to significant professional costs. It is only right, therefore, to try to get the matter completed and resolved as quickly as possible.

10.4 Unless the investigation has started with a completely voluntary disclosure by the taxpayer, it is inevitable that HMRC will start off in control of the investigation. It will set the pace and tone of the investigation that it has initiated. It is important, therefore, that the taxpayer's adviser should aim to wrest control of the investigation as soon as possible and retain that control through to the point of settlement.

THE PURPOSE OF THIS CHAPTER

10.5 This chapter is intended to be a guide for the adviser in how to seize and maintain control through all the stages of the investigation from opening exchanges to the final settlement. It is intended to be a practical guide on how to act in a variety of situations. There will inevitably be some overlap with other chapters which look in some detail at some of those aspects and go into more of the legal background. But this chapter hopes to give an insight into the 'on the ground fighting' that can ensure that the taxpayers interests are protected, not just through the use of the legal framework, but also the reality of dealing with HMRC once it is on the attack.

WHO AND WHAT ARE TO BE CONTROLLED?

10.6 There are three important areas that the adviser has to take control over, at the earliest possible time in the investigation. They are:

- control of the client;
- control of HMRC;
- control of the paper.

CASE STUDIES

10.7 To bring out the key points in this chapter two main case studies will be used. The main facts of these cases are set out below. The cases are based on real life but some of the facts have been changed to bring out various points and of course the cases have been tweaked to 'anonymise' the people involved.

> **Case study 10.1 – A serious admission**
>
> Adrian was a successful businessman in the West Country. He had built up a small group of companies primarily involved in importing goods from a Dutch supplier. As far as his local accountant was concerned he was a really good client for whom the firm had done the audit for many years. In addition, they had been able to do some corporate finance and pension scheme work which had provided good fees.
>
> HMRC picked up the main company for a routine enquiry, the first step of which was to have a look at the records. This was done by a visit to the company premises by two officers who spent nearly a day looking at key records. At the end of the day they said they had a few queries and would like to have a short meeting to discuss them. Adrian and the audit partner of the adviser, Barry, who had attended for the day.
>
> At the start of the meeting Adrian seemed a little agitated and said to the officers that, before they went into their questions, there was something he would like to say to them.
>
> At this point it might have been sensible for Barry to have just suggested that before they went any further he would like to speak to his client privately about what he was going to say but Barry didn't take that opportunity.
>
> Instead Adrian went ahead with his statement, the essence of which was that for the previous 15 or so years he had been diverting company income into private bank accounts maintained by himself and his wife in Jersey. The somewhat stunned officers managed to ask the extent of the diversions and were advised that the sum was probably in excess of £500,000.
>
> Adrian had apparently been diverting commission payments which arose where the Dutch company shipped goods direct to significant clients in the UK rather than the usual practice of the goods being imported by Adrian's company and sold on.
>
> Not surprisingly the HMRC officers realised that the case having fallen into their laps would be quickly removed from them to be taken over by the HMRC unit dealing with serious fraud. Barry also realised that he did not have the experience to cope with such an investigation and sought expert assistance.

10.8 *Conduct of a full enquiry*

> **Case study 10.2 – Business economics exercise**
>
> Chris and David were father and son who were respectively a local butcher and farmer in the north of England. Together they ran a partnership whose business was doing hog roasts for parties, fetes, etc. This business was basically seasonal, running from April through to October depending somewhat on the vagaries of the English summer. The profits generated by the partnership in the 2013/14 basis period amounted to a £5,000.
>
> A young officer in the local district, Ms Eager, opened an enquiry which was initially dealt with by Eric, the partnership's accountant.
>
> The initial enquires established that the records of the business were not a full double entry set of books. There was a simplex book, purchase invoices, bank statements and chequebook stubs. Ms Eager had been supplied with the records and had noted in the course of a meeting that these were 'the worst set of records she had ever seen'.
>
> She had then proceeded to do a business economics exercise based on the number of pigs the partnership had roasted in the season under review. This was based on a complex analysis of the records of pigs purchased plus various assumptions about size and development of the animals, etc culminating in a calculation as to how many slices of meat would be obtained. Her conclusions were that 300 pigs had been roasted and the likely profit made by the partnership was in the region of £100,000.
>
> As her conclusions had been reached after almost two years of questions and allegations since the enquiry started, Eric had reached the end of his tether and sought expert help with the case.

> **Focus**
>
> Control means that the taxpayer can put forward the best case possible. Failure to control the investigation can prevent the best case being heard.

CONTROLLING THE CLIENT

10.8 The adviser should have in mind from the beginning that in reality the taxpayer will need to rely on the adviser to assist and guide the taxpayer through a potentially traumatic investigation. It should be made clear from the outset that the adviser will help establish and present the facts of the case, and act at all times to mitigate the potential downside of the investigation, but the adviser will not collude with the taxpayer to mislead HMRC. This level of honesty can build an open trust with the client.

10.9 This can be a hard conversation to have with a taxpayer, particularly if the taxpayer is a long-standing client or if the events under review suggest that the taxpayer has kept things from the adviser in the past. This is one reason why the adviser might introduce an outside expert at an early stage. If the taxpayer cannot accept these ground rules, however, then the adviser must, of course, walk away.

10.10 On a practical note, if an HMRC investigation is being launched it would be helpful if the adviser was able to contact the taxpayer before the taxpayer contacts him. That, of course, will depend on whether or not HMRC has told the adviser of the investigation as well as contacting the taxpayer. In any event, the adviser should set up an early meeting with the taxpayer to establish what has gone on, and to set down the ground rules.

The client must have confidence

10.11 The taxpayer must have complete confidence that the adviser knows what he is doing and is clearly the best person to be handling the case. This can be established by the tone of the initial meeting.

10.12 The taxpayer may start the meeting feeling very aggrieved that he has become the target for an investigation, and will protest innocence. He may also be very critical of the adviser's handling of his affairs. It is advisable to allow him to let off steam whilst remaining professionally calm whilst any allegations are flying about. The following points should be made clear at that initial meeting:

- explain that HMRC has the right to enquire into a return, and that there are clearly issues which have caused an enquiry in this case;
- point out that HMRC is not going to go away without being satisfied that all is well, and that the taxpayer must therefore provide the detailed explanations required;
- the position is a serious one, and if HMRC is successful in its enquiries, the taxpayer will be required to pay the tax involved, interest on that tax and probably also a penalty. The level of that penalty will be determined in part by how the taxpayer deals with the enquiry.
- point out that disclosure is a key element in reducing penalties, and ask the client if there is any substance to the allegations being made and if there are any other matters which need to be disclosed to HMRC.

10.13 *Conduct of a full enquiry*

Take a realistic look at the client

10.13 There is a need, particularly in the initial stages of the investigation, for the professional adviser to take a more critical view of his client's situation. It would be foolhardy and counterproductive to criticise the HMRC officer for starting an investigation and suggest the action was impugning the taxpayer's integrity without having a clear view of the strength of the taxpayer's position.

10.14 The adviser may, of course, already have had some lingering concerns about the taxpayer's position, without having had anything concrete to raise with the taxpayer before the investigation. As a starting point it may be helpful to try to look at the case from the point of view of the HMRC officer. What specific issues are likely to have triggered interest? Particular areas to consider are set out in the checklist below.

Checklist 1   Taking a fresh look at the taxpayer's business

10.15

Do you understand the client's business?	How does the taxpayer actually make his profit?
	What goods/services/facilities is he supplying?
	Where are the customers?
	Where are the suppliers?
	Where does the business operate from?
	How many people are employed?
	Who are the main competitors?
What are the records like?	Were they adequate? Were they the same each year?
	If not, what were the differences and how did they arise?
	Are the sales records complete?
	What scope is there for sales to slip through the books?
	Are there numbers missing from the sequence of invoices?
	Are sales reconciled to other records, eg till roll or order book?
	Are all purchases real?

Conduct of a full enquiry 10.15

What are the key trends in the business?	Are there any significant changes or trends shown by summarising results of accounts over several years in key areas such as: • gross profit ratios; • volume of sales/purchases/stocks; • total P and L expenditure; • various key expense headings; • other significant ratios, eg fuel, takings. What have been the trends in the client's financial benefits from the business: • drawings; • directors remuneration; • dividends; • loan account? Are there reasons for any significant changes? How do the results compare with your general knowledge of the trade?
Look again at the business cash book and bank accounts for the year under review and earlier years if necessary, and consider the following:	Was there any difference on the cash account? If so, how big was it and how has it been treated in compiling the accounts? Do bank lodgements follow a consistent pattern? Are there seasonal fluctuations evident? Were there any notations on bank accounts suggesting the existence of other accounts? Have these been followed up? Do you have full explanations of capital introduced/loan account movements and are they consistent with known facts? Does the actual cash flow reflect what the books show?
The nature and size of the business may require you to consider other specific matters such as the following:	Check year end cut-offs such as debtors and creditors. Is there any stock in the business? If so, what does it consist of? Who valued it and on what basis? Where there is work in progress, what was the basis of valuation? Have disbursements been taken into account? Have personal expenses been properly identified and segregated? Has PAYE/NIC been properly accounted for?

10.16 *Conduct of a full enquiry*

The adviser should be fair but firm with the taxpayer

10.16 However much the taxpayer may complain that there is no reason for the enquiry, the adviser must try to explain that protestations of innocence alone will not convince HMRC to go away. Only facing up to the enquiry and providing rational and documented answers will achieve that objective, and to do this the adviser will need the full cooperation of the taxpayer. This will involve the taxpayer in making sure that all requests for information are dealt with quickly and comprehensively.

10.17 The adviser should make clear why information is being requested, and how it is relevant to the investigation. The adviser should stress that such requests should not be ignored. It should be made clear that without the full co-operation of the taxpayer the adviser simply cannot do his job.

Honesty is paramount

10.18 The adviser must make it clear to the taxpayer at the outset and throughout the investigation that he requires complete honesty from the taxpayer. If, at any stage, it becomes clear that the taxpayer has been less than frank then the adviser must consider his own position. The adviser will need to keep in mind his own reputation with HMRC.

10.19 The taxpayer needs to be reminded continually about the issue of disclosure. Not only is this a vital issue in determining the level of penalties, it could have very serious implications if after the conclusion of the enquiry further facts come to light which will cast doubt on the completeness of any settlement.

Case study 10.1 (continued) – Private bank account deposits

At the first meeting with Adrian, the adviser made it quite clear that he expected total honesty from Adrian throughout. The adviser's role was to prepare a disclosure report for HMRC and if there was any indication that the disclosure was incomplete the consequences would be severe. Adrian indicated his willingness to comply but on several occasions as the investigations proceeded it was clear that he was not being as forthcoming as he could have been.

A review of Adrian's main private bank account showed a couple of significant deposits which could not be reconciled to normal remuneration or dividends or transfers from any other account. The adviser asked Adrian about the first of these, a deposit of £15,000. His reply was that he had sold

Conduct of a full enquiry **10.24**

> a car. The explanation came that this had been his company car and that he had purchased it from the company to sell it on. The adviser was directed to the bank account where he would see the details of the purchase. This turned out to be a cheque for £3,000.
>
> It took a little while for Adrian to grasp that there was a benefit in kind of £12,000 which had not been declared. This was followed by a further disclosure that a second car had been dealt with in a similar way in the following year.

Get disclosure in early

10.20 The fact that an investigation has started will limit some of the benefits of disclosure because the opportunity to make a completely voluntary, unprompted disclosure has been lost. However there may be other issues of which HMRC is blissfully unaware and the disclosure of these at an early stage can influence the level of penalties.

10.21 It may be the case that the initial discussion with the taxpayer does throw up issues which will need to be disclosed to HMRC. In the first instance the adviser needs to probe those issues in detail with the taxpayer to establish the full extent of the disclosures being made and to ensure that they are as complete as possible.

10.22 The next stage will be to consider how and when to make those disclosures to HMRC. It is probably advisable to do that in a meeting and to do it at the start of any meeting to attempt to gain the maximum benefit of the disclosure in negotiation.

10.23 Bear in mind that if the disclosures are significant in amount this may result in the case being passed to the specialist units of HMRC dealing with fraud, with all that entails. Despite the shock of having the word 'fraud' used, this is not always a bad option because the quality of the investigator and the approach he takes may be better from the taxpayer's perspective. At its most basic, if the fraud is serious the disclosure process can protect the taxpayer from HMRC seeking to take action under the criminal code rather than the civil code. At all times the adviser needs to consider whether or not he has the experience to cope with that type of enquiry.

Keep client to a timetable

10.24 Time does become of the essence in investigation cases, although the adviser should try to avoid being 'railroaded' along by the HMRC officer.

10.25 *Conduct of a full enquiry*

It is particularly important to stress to the taxpayer from the outset that time is critical in supplying information. The adviser must build into any timetable scope to review information before submitting it to HMRC. The adviser should keep the pressure on the taxpayer to supply all the information timeously.

10.25 It may be useful for the adviser to remind the taxpayer that time and quality of response will be a factor that the HMRC officer will take into account in considering the penalty loading and anything that the taxpayer can do to assist in bringing that down will ultimately affect the financial cost of the investigation.

Sort out fees

10.26 Investigation work is time consuming and is best conducted by experienced specialist advisers. This combination can lead to significant professional cost implications for the taxpayer. Fee protection insurance may have been taken out which might help ease the pain of these costs but it is important to check that work needed is going to be covered and the extent of the cover.

10.27 The adviser should ensure that the taxpayer understands that the professional costs will be greater (potentially far greater) than the normal costs of dealing with accounts or tax returns. If it seems likely that the investigation will take some time then it would be good practice to establish a pattern of monthly billing to keep matters under control.

10.28 It may be advisable to consider a separate letter of engagement to cover the investigation. This will obviously be necessary if the adviser is only acting in that particular matter for the client.

The adviser needs to eat and only the rich or the foolish adviser would wait for his fees until after HMRC has been paid what it may be owed.

Explain what is happening

10.29 It is important that the taxpayer is always 'kept in the loop'. The adviser needs to explain why information is required. If the adviser has had important discussions with HMRC then the detail of those discussions needs to be conveyed to the taxpayer so that at all times he is aware of what is going on.

Conclusions of the initial discussions with the taxpayer

10.30 The aim of the initial discussions with the client is to end with two main issues resolved:

- A list of the information the adviser requires should be drawn up and third parties from whom information is needed should be identified. This will probably include banks and building societies, and the adviser may have prepared a series of written authorities for the client to sign.

- A decision needs to be taken on the next step as far as dealing with HMRC is concerned. There are three possibilities:

    – submit the information that the officer has requested and hope that this will satisfy the points which triggered the enquiry;

    – arrange a meeting with HMRC once all relevant information has been gathered; or

    – prepare a detailed report to go to HMRC ahead of any meeting.

> **Focus**
>
> Control of the taxpayer means ensuring that realistic expectations are at the heart of the approach to the investigation, Facts will not change, but control will determine how they are presented.

DEALING WITH HMRC

10.31 Once the adviser has ensured that the taxpayer is fully 'on side' with the investigation, the next step will be to attempt to take control of the investigation from HMRC.

10.32 An interesting insight into the view HMRC has of many advisers appeared in an old version of what was then the Inland Revenue Investigation manual. In a significant paragraph the manual noted that:

- agents are reluctant to put much effort into an investigation;

- agents may fear that they will lose the client and don't always let the taxpayer know the full extent of the enquiry;

- agents are reluctant to attend meetings which are expensive.

10.33 The paragraph no longer appears in the latest version of HMRC manuals but clearly, at the time the paragraph was written, HMRC had seen many advisers in action and its view was not entirely favourable. Whilst those

10.34 *Conduct of a full enquiry*

views are no longer the published 'official' view, they may still be held in some quarters of HMRC. They amount to a fairly damning view of the professional adviser, and suggest that there is an instinctive 'stereotype' view that needs to be overcome. The adviser who can demonstrate energy, 'management' of the taxpayer and a willingness to attend meetings may be able to gain some significant ground in his dealings with HMRC, not least because the officer may be taken off guard by such an approach.

HOW DOES AN ADVISER GET CONTROL OF HMRC?

10.34 An investigation is, by its nature, a confrontational affair and in any confrontation it is important to be the party controlling the action.

10.35 It is important to bear in mind that if penalties are likely to arise in the case, a key part of the adviser's work for the taxpayer will be to keep the level of those penalties as low as possible. HMRC will take into account both disclosure and co-operation in calculating penalties. Both of these can be heavily influenced by the actions the adviser and the taxpayer take from the outset: planning to mitigate penalties should be a key part of the investigation strategy and should be in place from the first indication that an investigation is underway.

10.36 In any enquiry case, HMRC starts with a strong advantage and will have the early control. This is particularly true in the more serious cases of tax fraud. It is important that the adviser should try to redress the balance as much as possible without becoming difficult or, even worse, belligerent.

10.37 An interesting section of the Enquiry manual begins at EM1810 and is headed 'Keeping control'. In that section the HMRC investigator is told 'It is essential to retain control of any enquiry's progress'.

10.38 The Enquiry manual then goes on to list ten ways in which the officer should seek to retain control. These 'ten commandments' can be easily restated and can in fact be turned to suggest a mantra for the adviser.

TEN COMMANDMENTS TO ENSURE CONTROL

1 Plan

10.39 HMRC guidance states:

> 'Have an intervention plan and work programme that you can update as the enquiry progresses'

It would be sensible for the adviser to do the same. There should be a key plan from the outset which outlines the ideal way that the enquiry will proceed. After making initial contact with HMRC to acknowledge the existence of the enquiry, the adviser should not be rushed into an early meeting if time is needed to finalise elements of disclosure. If HMRC wants a meeting then the adviser should offer a date which will allow time to complete the initial work.

10.40 It is important to identify the individuals who are going to work on the case. Obviously, this may be limited by the size of the adviser's practice but there is a need to have some consistency. There will be a significant amount of analytical work that can be done by less specialist staff but there are advantages in ensuring that the same person is doing it rather than simply using any staff who are not needed elsewhere. Information builds up in people's minds and the significance of a figure or a piece of information that crops up later in the case may not be seen as relevant by someone who has not previously been involved in the case.

Some cases can develop a number of strands and it is helpful to have a control sheet so that the progress on those different strands can be monitored.

> **Case study 10.1 (continued) – Control of the issues**
>
> It became very clear that there were other issues apart from the large corporate problem and it was necessary to look at benefits in kind (the sale of cars was one of a number of other issues that emerged), some rental income and a general look at private capital and means.
>
> Control of all of these was important from the start to ensure that nothing was missed.

10.41 Some kind of control file is helpful so that anyone involved in the case can see what progress is being made. This can be particularly important if there has to be any change in the personnel involved in the case.

10.42 It is also helpful to have regular meetings of those involved, especially if a major disclosure report is being prepared. This helps keep everyone on their toes and avoids duplication of effort and areas being missed.

2 Control paper

10.43 HMRC guidance states (at EM1811):

'Have a well ordered file.'

10.44 *Conduct of a full enquiry*

Control of paper is discussed in detail at **10.94** *et seq* but it is worth noting the significance that HMRC places on this particular discipline.

3 Don't cause delay

10.44 HMRC guidance (at EM1811) instructs HMRC officers about 'not causing any material delay in the case. If the ball remains in your court for long periods of time it is difficult to complain about delay by others and you may have problems with imposing any penalty'.

10.45 Time can easily run away during an investigation and it is important to always keep an eye on how things are progressing. One particular area for the adviser to watch is the length of time that HMRC takes to reply to correspondence. Nothing is more frustrating than for the practitioner to make every effort to respond to HMRC requests for information within time limits set in correspondence, only to find that weeks, if not months, pass before the officer deigns to reply. This is not acceptable and needs to be dealt with.

10.46 There are anecdotal accounts of cases where the HMRC officer had not replied to correspondence for over six months. When the adviser chased for a reply he was told that the officer had lots of enquiries going on and he would have to take his turn. That is not an acceptable response and the adviser needs to take advantage of that.

10.47 One route might be to put down an early marker. When replying to HMRC within the allotted time limit the adviser might note in the final paragraph of the letter:

> 'You will note that we have replied to your request for a significant amount of information within the time limit you requested. We would now appreciate the courtesy of a response from you within a similar period.'

10.48 If the adviser is feeling particularly bullish he might add:

> 'If we do not receive such a response we will consider taking the matter to the First-tier Tribunal to seek a closure of the enquiry.'

If the stated period elapses without a reply then the adviser should be prepared to take such action and advise HMRC that this is what is being done.

4 Know what you have to do

10.49 HMRC guidance at EM1811 also states:

> 'Make sure that the taxpayer and accountant always know what is expected of them.'

Under the investigation regime in the pre-self-assessment (SA) era an investigation could only be opened if the inspector was not satisfied with the return. There was some onus on the inspector to give an indication of his reasons for not being satisfied.

10.50 The rules for SA do not have the same requirement with the officer having a general right to enquire. If there is clearly an investigation rather than simply a query about a couple of items on a return then it is not unreasonable for the adviser to ask the officer to specify any particular areas of concern.

10.51 There is a reluctance to do this because HMRC feels that if it is too specific in spelling out the grounds for investigation the adviser will concentrate on those and will not consider the possibility of any wider problems which may be around. Whilst that is probably understandable, it should not prevent the HMRC officer giving some clear steer as to key areas of concern whilst making it clear that these are not the exclusive.

10.52 As the enquiry continues and HMRC keeps coming back with further issues, it becomes even more important for it to state why it wishes the enquiry to continue. It is also important for the adviser to be aware of the provisions of *TMA 1970, s 28A*, which allow an application to be made to the First-tier Tribunal for a closure of the enquiry. This is the only legal power that the adviser has at his disposal and it is one that is probably under used.

10.53 Under the provisions of *s 28A*, the onus is placed on HMRC to show why the enquiry should continue and the tribunal is obliged to order a closure if that onus is not properly discharged. In some cases it may be that the threat of such proceedings will be sufficient to elicit the required response from HMRC.

5 Be realistic

10.54 HMRC guidance at EM1811 also states:

'Agree realistic timetables and check progress.'

The adviser should always be realistic in setting and agreeing timetables for action. It does not help to say that information will be supplied by a near date which the adviser knows is unrealistic. Work out carefully what is realistic and add on a couple of weeks for contingencies, then when information is delivered ahead of the deadline the initiative can be retained.

10.55 This should not be a problem area if careful plans have been put in place as discussed in point 1 (**10.39** *et seq*) above. If the adviser is in control of his end of the case, he should be able to control this aspect. If the adviser operates only by responding to deadlines imposed he will be under continual

10.56 *Conduct of a full enquiry*

pressure to deliver and that is when mistakes can occur and opportunities may be lost.

10.56 It is important to keep in mind that if timetables are not adhered to then HMRC may well resort to the use of formal information powers. This will put increased pressure on the adviser and taxpayer and will also result in problems when negotiating penalties. HMRC will argue that some of the conditions relating to disclosure have not been complied with and so important reductions in the penalty loading will not be obtained.

6 Is formal action being taken?

10.57 HMRC guidance at EM1811 also states:

'Raise discovery assessments and make enquiry amendments.'

There are a significant number of powers that HMRC can use to protect its position. It can consider discovery assessments to pick up liability for earlier years; it could consider jeopardy amendments and it could proceed to a formal closure notice. These may well be used in some cases.

10.58 The adviser may consider whether any reluctance on the part of the HMRC officer to use them indicates that he is not sure of his ground or the direction in which the investigation is proceeding. If this is the case then can this uncertainty be exploited to the advantage of the taxpayer by taking the initiative of a closure application to force the officer's hand?

7 Know where you are going

10.59 HMRC guidance at EM1811 also states:

'Bear in mind where you expect the case to go and what you need to know and do to get there.'

The same should hold true for the adviser. Always keep an eye on the objective, which is to ensure that the taxpayer pays the least amount and the enquiry is completed as quickly as possible.

8 Use reminders and powers

10.60 HMRC guidance states (at EM1815):

'You should not issue reminders to taxpayers or agents – either in a letter or on the telephone – without at the same time taking some more positive action. Reminders along the lines of "I do not appear to have heard from you ...." are unlikely to lead to a substantive response and will only drag out the time it takes to bring the enquiry to a conclusion.'

10.61 The adviser who wants to be in control should not act only when action is taken. He should be on top of the case throughout. Having said that, it is important that where progress does appear slow the adviser keeps HMRC in the loop. This can be particularly important in cases of serious fraud where a report is being prepared and a great deal of information is needed. This will take time to collate and there may be delays caused by other parties such as banks being dilatory in responding to information requests.

10.62 It is suggested that in all cases a diary note should be made to contact the HMRC officer every four weeks or so to update on progress. This should keep him aware that progress is being made and will reduce the possibility that he will resort to more formal powers to push the case along.

9 Pay the tax

10.63 HMRC guidance (at EM1811) states:

'Request payments on account.'

There will be cases where it is clear from a very early stage that some additional tax will be payable. The adviser can demonstrate control by advising the taxpayer to make payments before the HMRC officer asks for them.

10.64 In the case of Adrian it was clear that a significant liability was due from the company and so this was quickly calculated based on initial figures and tax was paid.

Doing this puts a stop on the interest accumulating on tax due, and will also be helpful when it comes to looking at penalties.

10 Behave yourself

10.65 HMRC guidance at EM1811 also states:

'[Act] reasonably and courteously so that there are no grounds for the taxpayer to make a complaint.'

It is to be hoped that every HMRC officer will take heed of that point. Some can appear overbearing at times and that needs to be challenged. The adviser and taxpayer will also do well to keep the point in mind.

10.66 *Conduct of a full enquiry*

10.66 Remember that the HMRC officer has a legal right and duty to carry out an investigation and, provided that he continues to act reasonably within the law, that has to be accepted. Being rude to the officer or getting angry with him will serve no useful purpose at all. Indeed it is likely to be counterproductive because it will indicate to the officer, rightly or wrongly, that his enquiries are getting home and that the taxpayer and/or adviser are rattled.

The eleventh commandment

10.67 The cynic would say that the unwritten eleventh commandment is 'Thou shalt not be caught out'. In the investigation context it is perhaps better to say, 'The officer should never be able to tell an adviser anything about the taxpayer that the adviser didn't already know'.

This means that from the outset the adviser must obtain maximum co-operation from the taxpayer, which must include a willingness on the part of the client to be entirely open with him.

The twelfth commandment

10.68 The adviser should not waste any chance to significantly influence the outcome of the enquiry. Sometimes there may be a pivotal moment in an enquiry, where a certain course of action will have a major influence on the overall outcome, whether in time or amount or both. Make sure that you don't miss that chance. An example from the case of Chris and David will illustrate the point.

> **Case study 10.2 (continued) – An important development**
>
> As explained earlier the young officer, Ms Eager, had undertaken a business economics review in the case and had centred her attention on the number of pigs that were roasted. The result of this exercise was that in her view there were 300+ pigs roasted in that season. The accountant, Eric, did his own calculations and came up with a figure of around 120. The discrepancy between the two figures was therefore significant and that was where deadlock had been reached and a specialist adviser was brought in.
>
> Having spent a day looking at the file the adviser decided that it would be sensible to talk to Chris and David face to face. At the start of the meeting the adviser explained the deadlock that had been reached over the number of pigs roasted. Chris said in a quite matter-of-fact way that he couldn't understand why that should be a problem because they had a record of every pig they had roasted. He explained that the environmental health rules

Conduct of a full enquiry **10.70**

required them to record a temperature of the meat each time they roasted a pig and they had to retain that record so that the lady from the local council could look at it any time she wanted. (The lady from the council was perceived as a greater threat than Ms Eager.)

Chris confirmed that they still had the book for the year under review. The adviser, who was about to depart on a short holiday, requested that the book was sent to Eric so it could be examined by the adviser when he got back from holiday. On returning from his break the adviser found a letter from Eric enclosing a letter from Ms Eager. The roasting record had in fact been received and immediately sent on to Ms Eager, who had rejected it out of hand as an unreliable record. She gave two reasons for this. First, there was a date where income had been received but no pig roasted (they had served cold meat on that occasion) and second there was one record which was on a loose sheet of paper which had been stuck in the book (this related to a trip to Ireland where they had recorded the roasting information on paper but had left the book behind in case the lady from the council came around whilst they were away!).

The adviser concluded that the main reason for Ms Eager's reaction was that this was simply unwelcome evidence that went against her view. The book clearly showed that in the year they had roasted around 120 pigs and that Eric's original figures were supported by this additional information. Unfortunately it then took two lengthy meetings to persuade Ms Eager that the book was genuine and the figures tallied with other evidence.

Focus

If the adviser does not control the investigation HMRC will. If HMRC drives the investigation the ability to present the best case may be diminished.

THINK ABOUT MEETINGS

10.69 Meetings are covered in more detail in **CHAPTER 9** of this book but what follows might indicate how careful planning and detail in respect of meetings can make a difference to the control of the case.

Is it cost effective?

10.70 There is no doubt that a meeting can be perceived as a costly exercise as far as the taxpayer is concerned, not least because of the cost of the adviser's time and the time spent by the taxpayer which could otherwise have been utilised in running his business.

10.71 *Conduct of a full enquiry*

10.71 However, in many cases a meeting will actually save costs by cutting down on research time, writing correspondence and avoiding misunderstandings which can creep into correspondence and then develop a life of their own which simply prolong the investigation. In cases where facts are of vital importance and those facts are complex, a meeting will generally be the most economic way of proceeding.

Can the client cope?

10.72 There can be few taxpayers, even those who are completely innocent, who would face the prospect of a meeting with an HMRC officer with any degree of equanimity. The blow can be lessened by arranging for the meeting to take place at the taxpayer's premises or, perhaps a better answer, at the adviser's office as neutral territory, but in some cases that will still not be sufficient.

10.73 The strongest people, both physically and mentally, can break down in front of HMRC officers. The emotional drain that is put on a taxpayer in these meetings should not be underestimated and the adviser must be not just a technical expert, but become a practical expert in human psychology. When a tall, large framed rugby player starts to weep in the middle of a meeting (and that has happened) it perhaps illustrates that no one is immune from the pressure a meeting can produce.

10.74 Where it seems likely that the taxpayer will genuinely be unable to cope with a meeting either because he will be totally overawed by the occasion or where he is likely to go to the other extreme and become belligerent with the HMRC officer, it would be wise to keep the number of meetings he has with HMRC to an absolute minimum.

10.75 In those cases, the adviser should not dismiss the idea of meetings, but should attend them himself so that progress can be maintained. Where the adviser does this he should always make a point of contacting the taxpayer as soon as possible after the meeting and provide him with a full briefing of what has transpired. It may also be helpful to send him a copy of the file note of the meeting. That should prevent any subsequent misunderstanding as to what has been said, etc.

Organising the venue

10.76 The adviser should always try to arrange, where possible, for the meeting to be held at either the taxpayer's premises or at his office, not at the HMRC office. This is less intimidating for the client and less familiar for HMRC. There should be no reason for HMRC to object particularly if it is asking for the meeting and with the closure of many HMRC offices it may welcome the offer as the most practical solution. Indeed, as HMRC offices around the country have been closed, there is often little choice but to meet at the advisor or taxpayers office.

10.77 HMRC's Enquiry manual (at EM1830) indicates that there may be advantages in having the meeting at the business premises or indeed at the taxpayer's home where information about lifestyle can be more easily ascertained. This alone might suggest that it would be preferable to meet at the adviser's office but on some occasions meeting at the taxpayer's premises could help dispel some 'myths' that the HMRC officer may have about the nature of the business or the taxpayer's lifestyle.

Preparation is vital

10.78 The first meeting in an enquiry will be the most important that the taxpayer will attend with HMRC. It will probably be the first meeting he has had with a tax officer and he needs to be carefully prepared. This is not the same as being 'rehearsed'. Where the meeting is likely to be lengthy and significant it can be useful to give the taxpayer the experience of a dry run (assuming the adviser has experience to draw on).

The adviser must also prepare carefully by reviewing all the information collated to date and try to anticipate the likely areas on which the HMRC officer will raise questions.

10.79 The need for a dry run is particularly important where the case involves allegation of serious fraud, because that meeting will have more formal elements and is likely to be lengthy. It can sometimes pay dividends to get someone to play the role of the HMRC officer and ask deliberately awkward questions to see how the taxpayer will react. There are examples where this approach has resulted in taxpayers disclosing items such as a significant bank account previously kept hidden and which were then able to be disclosed at the official meeting.

10.80 On the day of the meeting, the adviser should arrange to meet the taxpayer at the premises where the meeting is being held (assuming it is not in the HMRC office) well before the scheduled start time of the meeting with the officer.

10.81 The likely opening that the HMRC officer will use and the expected questions should be run through carefully. The adviser must tell the taxpayer that he should only answer the questions that he knows he can answer absolutely correctly. He should not make estimates or guesses. It is better to answer 'don't know' and agree to provide a correct answer after the meeting. If it has been decided that the client is going to make disclosures, the adviser

10.82 *Conduct of a full enquiry*

must know what is going to be said. If necessary he should write it down so that the taxpayer can read a statement.

Control the meeting

10.82 If the adviser is hosting the meeting, he should make sure that he is properly organised. Relevant papers should be to hand and he should know where to find key information. Impressions of control soon disappear when the adviser is seen rummaging through papers trying to find key documents which ought to be readily to hand.

10.83 When the HMRC officers arrive they should not be kept waiting unnecessarily. Before arranging for them to be brought in, the adviser should check that everything is in place and take a deep breath! The adviser will be professionally anxious (and so will the officer, especially on a first meeting). If an adviser does not have the adrenaline pumping he is more likely to make mistakes.

The greeting to the HMRC officers should be polite, with introductions made and refreshments offered

10.84 The atmosphere can initially be confrontational because allegations are inevitably being made. The adviser should try to minimise the impact of this as much as possible by keeping the opening as informal as possible. HMRC officers are told to be polite and courteous and not to react when provoked. It follows that the adviser and taxpayer should also be polite and courteous.

10.85 The HMRC officer has a job to do. Sometimes the officer can come across as being overbearing, if not aggressive, particularly when the questioning moves to sensitive areas such as potential allegations or questions about living expenses. If the officer reacts in this way, it is important not to respond in kind and the adviser should point out to the officer that his approach is unnecessary and if he persists the meeting will be terminated.

Get your disclosure in first

10.86 If, as a result of previous discussions with the taxpayer, it is clear that there are errors which need to be disclosed, the adviser should start the meeting by giving details of those matters to HMRC. That will help the subsequent penalty position when disclosure and co-operation are being considered.

10.87 If the issues to disclose are significant then the adviser may consider preparing a statement for the taxpayer to read. There is no requirement that everything in the meeting has to be extempore – the officer will almost certainly have written out his key questions and probably his opening remarks.

Watch your body language

10.88 Facts and information may come out in the course of a meeting which are new to the adviser. It may be information from HMRC or it may be from the taxpayer. It will be helpful if the adviser can avoid registering complete surprise at anything that emerges. HMRC officers are told to look for situations in which the adviser is clearly surprised by what is said. A glare at the taxpayer can easily be picked up and misinterpreted by HMRC. It is perhaps best for the adviser to contain his reaction until after the meeting and then have a 'full and frank exchange of views' with the taxpayer.

Keep control of the client

10.89 It is important for the adviser to keep control over the meeting. This may involve bringing the meeting to a halt – either temporarily or permanently – if things start to get out of hand. This can happen, particularly if the HMRC officer causes the taxpayer to become agitated or angry. It is better to suggest a short adjournment, take the taxpayer out of the meeting and allow time for tempers to cool.

10.90 It can also be important to bring a halt if the taxpayer makes statements about his affairs and brings up issues of which the adviser is unaware. The adviser will need time to talk to the client to find out what is going on.

If it becomes clear that the meeting really cannot continue then the adviser will need to discuss new arrangements with the HMRC officer.

> **Case study 10.1 (continued) – Keeping control at meetings**
>
> You will recall that Adrian took his accountant by surprise at the initial meeting with HMRC and he provided a further example of the problems that can arise at the closing HMRC meeting.
>
> By that stage the basic deal had been thrashed out with HMRC beforehand but the officer, rightly, invited Adrian to make any comments he wished. At this point Adrian started to launch into a tirade about the inequity of the process and other issues. The adviser had seated him too far away for a judicious kick on the ankles, so he stopped the meeting.
>
> He took Adrian out of the meeting and told him in no uncertain terms that if he continued in the way he had started, the deal that they had put to HMRC would not hold and that the consequences would be very serious indeed. He had a choice: to continue in the way he had started, in which case he could negotiate his own deal, or he could go back into the meeting, apologise for his outburst and stay quiet whilst the matter was settled. Thankfully Adrian adopted the latter approach and the case was settled within a matter of a few minutes.

10.91 *Conduct of a full enquiry*

Taking notes

10.91 It is important to have a record of the meeting and so notes need to be taken. It is not possible for the adviser to keep control of the meeting, listen to the client, find papers and fully record what happens, so it is good practice to have someone in the meeting whose sole job is to take the notes. This can prove to be a boon when comparing the adviser's record of the meeting with that of HMRC.

Action points

10.92 At the end of the meeting a list of action points should be drawn up with the HMRC officer to decide what follow up is needed and when it will be done. Realistic time limits should be set. The adviser has nothing to gain by promising a very rapid response which cannot be delivered. It is better to set a longer time but get the action completed earlier. The adviser should not discuss the meeting with the taxpayer until they are both out of the HMRC building or until the officer has left.

After the meeting

10.93 The taxpayer will be physically tired and mentally drained by the meeting and little will be achieved by a detailed post mortem. The adviser should allow the taxpayer a few days to recover and then arrange to meet to follow up the meeting or write to set out the information required.

Focus

Control of any meeting will enable a platform for the taxpayer's case to be heard. Failure to control the meeting will risk that platform being removed.

CONTROL OF PAPER

10.94 It has already been noted that control of paper figures prominently in the HMRC list of ways to keep control and possibly this is where in practice HMRC officers can have an advantage. The author has experience of seeing investigation files in practitioners' offices simply containing all papers piled on top of each other without any attempt to segregate or organise them. This is bad practice in any professional environment and can be detrimental to conducting an investigation case in an efficient and effective manner.

10.95 Investigation work will usually create a considerable amount of paper and information and it is vital that sensible file discipline is instituted from the

Conduct of a full enquiry **10.101**

start. Once it is clear that an investigation covering more than just the latest set of accounts is underway, a separate investigation file should be opened, and the fact that this has been done should be noted on the cover of the adviser's main taxpayer files.

Setting up an investigation file

10.96 At the very least there should *always* be two files established:

1 a correspondence file; and
2 a working file.

10.97 There will also be computer folders which can be used to store spreadsheets, correspondence and the draft of any report being prepared. As a general point on computer documents, the adviser should keep copies of all schedules as the enquiry progresses so that he can see how information has developed. It is good practice to use the date and time footer on the spreadsheet to identify each time a schedule is updated.

Correspondence file

10.98 Correspondence accumulates rapidly in any investigation case and it is extremely important that it should be kept tidily and logically so that important items can easily be found. In a lengthy case it will be very helpful to maintain an index of important correspondence.

10.99 This can be used to record details of notes of meetings with both the taxpayer and HMRC as well as copies of key letters to and from the taxpayer and to and from HMRC. This will help the process of review when the case is nearing settlement. The notes section can be used to indicate action needed or to supplement basic information. HMRC officers are advised in their manual to number all correspondence and advisers may find this a helpful practice to follow.

10.100 A record of open points should be kept on top of the correspondence (or the latest version of an 'action list') so that it is possible to see at a glance what stage the investigation has reached. This can be particularly useful if the taxpayer or HMRC officer phones unexpectedly.

10.101 There used to be an interesting paragraph in a previous version of the HMRC Enquiry manual which was headed 'Communications: Off the Record Conversations'. It stated:

'You should record all contact with the taxpayer and their representatives. This includes all telephone and face to face conversations, however informal.

10.102 *Conduct of a full enquiry*

If the case has to be settled at a Commissioner's hearing, the Commissioners are entitled to consider the evidence of such informal conversations and without a note on file of what was said it will be difficult to rebut any unfavourable hearsay evidence from the taxpayer or agent.

Such notes of conversations are also necessary to give a complete history of a case to anyone reading the case for the first time following:

- a change in personnel; or
- a complaint on the case.

The Revenue Adjudicator has specifically criticised HMRC on a number of cases for failing to keep such records. Any requests that you talk "off the record" should be politely but firmly refused. You can say that you are prepared to discuss matters on a without prejudice basis but you should not at any time say or imply that anything you say is not to be a matter of record.'

The advice to record everything is good practice for the advisor, for exactly the same reasons.

Working files

10.102 This is the heart of the investigation file. It will probably become necessary to hold papers in a lever arch file or indeed several files. It is vital that the indexes for such files are used so that no time is wasted tracking down key schedules. Certain parts of the working file should be regarded as standard as follows:

Record of formal documents

10.103 This should contain copies of all formal documents received such as notices of assessment and appeals made. It should also hold information about payments on account. The summary sheets should be at the top of this section.

Calculations

10.104 These should be updated as the investigation proceeds. A spreadsheet is ideal for this and a printout should be taken of each calculation and filed in the same section of the working file.

Working schedules

10.105 The precise nature of these will vary from case to case. They will include items such as capital statements, analyses of sales, analyses of bank accounts, etc. The adviser should keep all working schedules and print out copies if these are being held on computer. They will provide a useful guide to the progress of the enquiry and show how conclusions have formed over the period of the investigation.

Documents

10.106 Inevitably the adviser will accumulate a huge volume of documents (eg bank statements, property details, etc). It is important that these are carefully indexed and filed so that they can be accessed with ease.

Report preparation file

10.107 For any case in which a report is going to be prepared, it is important to set up a file which will build up the report as it goes along. It is also useful to have a control sheet for the report so that the adviser can keep track of the various issues and monitor progress.

Dealing with information requests

10.108 Detailed commentary about the formal powers of HMRC to require information is set out elsewhere in this book but brief advice on how to handle the situation if formal notices are issued may be useful here.

10.109 It might be said that the fact that an HMRC officer has issued a formal information notice is an indication that the adviser has lost control of the case. If he had stayed in control of the taxpayer then the information that HMRC wants could have been supplied without the need for the notice. The issue of a notice will almost certainly be seen by HMRC as a black mark when it comes to the question of penalties.

10.110 There will be some HMRC officers who may resort to the use of information notices as a matter of course because it is their way of showing they are in control and to 'tick boxes' when their casework is being reviewed by their superiors. In one sense there is not a lot of point in trying to compete at that level.

10.111 It follows that any issue of an information notice should be treated with great seriousness and every attempt should be made to comply, provided that the request is a reasonable one. The test of reasonableness lies at the heart of both the information and inspection powers. In both cases the power can only be used if the obtaining of the information is reasonable to check the tax position of the taxpayer.

10.112 *Conduct of a full enquiry*

10.112 That should be the starting point for the adviser, especially in situations where the information being requested seems a little remote from the issues under investigation. If the adviser feels that the HMRC officer is on some kind of fishing expedition, then he should challenge the officer immediately to say why the latter considers the information request reasonable. This can be particularly important in situations where a request is made for private bank accounts, most obviously where the request is made right at the start of an enquiry.

10.113 There can be situations in which HMRC is justified in asking for private account information, but it is hard to see how this can be justified before the enquiry is fully underway and the officer is aware, for example, of the deficiency in the business records. The adviser could certainly challenge the early request for such information on the grounds of the reasonableness test.

10.114 Compliance with the request should be done on the terms easiest for the taxpayer. The legislation states that compliance must be within the time stated in the notice and documents must be produced at a place agreed by the officer and the taxpayer. HMRC guidance at CH23280 states that the officer should accept any place chosen by the taxpayer provided that it is not an unreasonable location or an unreasonable time.

10.115 The guidance also states that the officer should accept delivery at any HMRC office. It is suggested that this should be the approach adopted, particularly if the investigation is being conducted (as it may well be) from an HMRC office hundreds of miles away from the taxpayer.

10.116 If original documents are being taken by the HMRC officer then a receipt for those documents should be obtained. The adviser should also make clear if any documents are required in the business and early return of these should be requested. HMRC has the power to make copies and if it needs time to look at the documents then it should make the copies needed and return the originals as quickly as possible. The adviser should make this clear in a covering letter and keep chasing if the originals are not returned.

Third party notices

10.117 The broadening of the information powers to third parties does present some issues for the practitioner. *FA 2008, Sch 36* extended the powers to call for documents and information and HMRC is now more likely to want to use third party powers.

10.118 HMRC can obtain a third party notice by simply going to the First-tier Tribunal and it may well choose to do this without the taxpayer being aware of it, until a copy of the notice is actually received by the taxpayer as required under *FA 2008, Sch 36, para 4*.

10.119 The alternative route is to ask permission of the taxpayer for an approach to be made to a third party and this is where the adviser will need to have a policy. If an approach is made along this route there may be an advantage in going along with it not least because, now that the taxpayer is aware of the possibility of the third party involvement, he may be able to explain some issues to the third party before HMRC contacts them. This could be important if the third party is an important customer or supplier to the business (or, indeed, the bank manager).

10.120 Ultimately the adviser has to bear in mind that if the client does not agree then the HMRC officer can go to the tribunal for the notice and will then be able to control that process. In addition the failure to grant approval will almost certainly be seen as an issue to count against the taxpayer in the penalty process.

> **Focus**
>
> The quantity of paper which will be generated in an investigation should not be underestimated. If you do not control it, it will control you.

Dealing with HMRC inspections

10.121 Again the details of the powers now available to HMRC to carry out inspections are dealt with elsewhere and the following comments are limited to the practicalities of dealing with the use of such powers as they relate to controlling an enquiry.

Agreed inspections

10.122 If the HMRC officer wants to visit the client's business premises to have a look around, is that such a bad thing? There may be much to be gained from such a visit, especially if the officer is living with some misconceptions as to the nature and style of the business. HMRC officers do find it helpful to see business premises and often are pleased when the adviser sees the benefits of that. Agreeing to the visit means that the adviser does have some measure of control. The officer is there at the taxpayer's behest and should behave in a different way to a situation in which he is turning up unannounced.

10.123 Better still, the adviser might take the initiative and invite the officer to the premises to see the business for himself. That enables the adviser to have control over how the visit proceeds. If the officer declines the chance it will make it much more difficult for him to request a visit later in the investigation.

10.124 *Conduct of a full enquiry*

Unannounced inspections

10.124 It is much more problematical if the officer turns up unannounced at the client's premises with an order to carry out an inspection. Such a visit may not be a surprise if repeated previous appointments have been missed or requests have been turned down. The officer is now in a very strong position and any measures now are purely defensive on the part of the adviser and client.

10.125 If the visit comes totally out of the blue then it has to be accepted that prima facie things are looking very serious for the client. HMRC clearly will have significant information and grounds for the need for surprise and the adviser needs to start asking some very serious questions of the taxpayer.

10.126 If such a visit takes place the taxpayer should be clearly told to:

- ask the HMRC officer to provide his formal identification, which should be in the form of a warrant card. If there is any doubt as to the identity of the officer, the client should contact the tax office concerned to confirm that a visit has been authorised;

- ask the officer hand to over a copy of the visit notice. This is important because it is necessary to establish whether the unannounced visit has been approved by the First-tier Tribunal. If it has, then a potential penalty position for not allowing the visit will come into play.

10.127 Even if the taxpayer is minded to allow the visit to take place, he needs to buy some time. The HMRC officer will be ready for what he wants to do and will have an obvious advantage. At the very least he might be asked to visit the local café for half an hour or so whilst the client readies himself and importantly contacts his adviser. But it is arguable that in the case of a First-tier Tribunal approved visit even such an action could amount to obstruction and the more cynical HMRC officer might suspect that whilst he is drinking coffee the shredding machine might be in full swing.

10.128 It should be noted that HMRC guidance states that the officer should advise the taxpayer that he can ring his agent if he wishes but the officer will not delay the start of the inspection until the adviser arrives. However, HMRC has no automatic right of entry and so the taxpayer is quite at liberty to ask the officer to wait until the adviser has arrived. This should not be construed as a refusal to allow entry.

10.129 The taxpayer will need to contact the adviser, which may itself cause a problem if the person responsible is not available. This brings another piece of preparedness into play: What steps has the adviser taken to ensure that he is able to respond properly if and when a taxpayer calls to say that an HMRC officer is demanding entry? A proper measured reaction can enable control to be regained in a situation where initially HMRC holds the upper hand.

Bringing matters to a conclusion

10.130 The processes of the investigation will take their course depending on the precise nature of the investigation. Things may move quickly in many cases. In other cases, especially where serious fraud is involved, the process will inevitably be longer because a detailed disclosure report is being prepared. In all cases there will come a time to start to tie up the loose ends and reach agreement if possible on the tax liability before moving on to sorting out the penalty position. A number of 'control' points can be made.

Perfection impossible

10.131 If there are irregularities in the taxpayer's affairs, these obviously need to be quantified. Omissions of income such as bank interest, etc should be capable of accurate quantification but omissions of profits will not be. It is a matter of doing a deal with HMRC based on the reviews that have been undertaken.

10.132 Both sides must remember that achieving a perfect answer is impossible. You are dealing with balance of probabilities and any settlement is going to be subject to negotiation. There is a fine judgement to be made as to whether the adviser takes the lead in these negotiations or whether HMRC makes the first offer. In many respects this is more like poker than professional advice, and each case will be different. It is often easier for the adviser to suggest a realistic but low figure and be argued up from there, rather than allowing HMRC to go first and then having to knock down its figures. But the author remembers well a major case when the HMRC officer made a first offer which was well below what had been anticipated ... and the poker face that had to be maintained whilst the final figures were argued down from that modest starting point!

Keep an eye on the big picture

10.133 The adviser should not let the officer get carried away on minor issues. If there is a way of reaching agreement then go for it.

It is easy to get side-tracked down gross profit alleys, tying down living expenses to the last penny or arguing over technical details of stock valuations. The adviser should always keep in mind what the overall impact is likely to be

10.134 *Conduct of a full enquiry*

on the final tax bill. The adviser should ensure that significant time is not spent on trivial items and not fall into the trap of treating losses as immaterial. The adviser should always try to find pragmatic routes to settle particular issues that, whilst not precise, will save the taxpayer money in both tax and costs.

Watch the number of years

10.134 There are two particular issues here to watch out for. The first is how many years are involved? HMRC will have to be able to justify making assessments for closed years on the grounds of discovery. This may not be difficult if it can show careless or deliberate action by the taxpayer leading to the under-assessment of tax in earlier years. That may not always be the case and the adviser should be prepared to challenge situations in which discovery is simply being assumed by the HMRC officer.

10.135 The second problem that can then emerge is the amount of assessments for earlier years. HMRC like to work on extrapolations from a base year. That may be fine in some situations and can save a lot of time and effort in doing detailed reviews. However, extrapolation can only be valid if all the conditions that existed in the base year are also present in the years covered by the extrapolation. This is where the adviser can make a real impact, challenging the assumptions and if necessary reworking those years.

10.136 As an example, in a PAYE investigation involving a student union bar and casual labour, HMRC tried to take the current year as a basis for the previous six years until it was pointed out that the make-up of the casual labour force in the base year did contain a number of individuals for whom working in the bar was a second job and therefore taxable, whereas in earlier years the staff had comprised students who had no other source of income and for whom there was no tax liability.

What if you cannot reach agreement?

10.137 If a common sense solution cannot be reached there are two approaches to consider.

If the adviser believes that all information has been supplied but HMRC is still demanding more, which the adviser does not consider relevant, then the possibility of seeking a closure at tribunal should be seriously considered. This is the taxpayer's right and should be threatened and followed through if necessary.

10.138 If there is simply a gulf between the two sides and HMRC shows no signs of backing down from a position that is viewed as unreasonable then the outcome may be to get HMRC to issue closure notices and proceed to a contentious appeal at the First-tier Tribunal.

10.139 There are a number of factors to consider:

- There is no guarantee of success.

- There will be costs involved in taking the case. Will those costs outweigh any benefit that may be achieved?

- The adviser is likely to have to put the client on the witness stand. How reliable is he and how will he respond to cross examination?

10.140 Under the new appeal procedures, once an appeal is lodged there is a right to ask for a review of the case by HMRC. In some cases this may be offered by HMRC and it is a route well worth considering.

10.141 The review will be carried out by an HMRC officer independent of the line management of the officer who has been carrying out the enquiry. This may provide an opportunity to get a more balanced view of the case.

Coping with difficult officers

10.142 There are, unfortunately, some HMRC officers who seem so pedantic that they want to deal with every last penny. There are others who get a fixed and unfavourable view of the taxpayer from the outset and this colours every approach that is subsequently made.

10.143 There is no simple solution to such problems. Complaints to their superiors, whether in the office or in the area, usually come back with some vacuous support of the party line: he's only doing his job, client records are useless, lack of meaningful co-operation, etc. At the end of the day the answer is often to be polite and reasonable and count to ten before responding ...

Make payments on account

10.144 If it is clear that there is liability for the year of enquiry or earlier years then the taxpayer should be encouraged to make relevant payments on account. These have the effect of stopping the interest clock running and will also be positive signs of co-operation which will help the overall penalty position.

Planning for penalties

10.145 The final stage in the enquiry and one in which the adviser can do much to help the taxpayer is in the negotiation of penalties. The skill does not

10.146 *Conduct of a full enquiry*

come down to the final negotiation, however. The key is to have the planning of penalties in mind from the outset of the enquiry. If the adviser develops his strategy on penalties the night before the closing meeting with HMRC then that is too late. The correct time to plan strategy on penalties is the night before the *opening* meeting with HMRC.

10.146 The closing meeting is far too late to make any real impact, particularly because HMRC has moved away from a 'horse trade' argument on penalties and far more towards a structured look at the various elements of behaviour that can influence the level of penalty that is appropriate.

The penalty rules are considered elsewhere and the comments here are simply related to the control issue.

Argue behaviour

10.147 The starting point for penalties is to establish the behaviour of the taxpayer in leading to the irregularities. That must be judged in the light of the facts. For example, in the case of Adrian, above, the issue was quite clearly one of deliberate action which was then concealed. It is an issue that ideally the adviser will want to get settled well before the final meeting. The adviser should take every opportunity in correspondence and discussion with HMRC to make the case for the least culpable level and let HMRC respond to that.

10.148 It is also important to recognise that each separate issue should be considered separately. There may be some issues that are clearly the result of at least carelessness on the part of the taxpayer, but that does not mean that every omission is also the result of such behaviour. In some cases the client may demonstrably have taken reasonable care and so penalties should be lower in respect of items related to those items.

Prompted and unprompted

10.149 The issue of prompted or unprompted disclosure can clearly be influenced by identifying disclosure issues and bringing them out as early as possible, as discussed at **10.86** above. Again the issue as to which level of disclosure is appropriate in each situation ought to be established well before the final meeting takes place.

Quality of disclosure

10.150 This will be the area where there is likely to be discussion at the closing meeting but again the planning for this should be taking place throughout the enquiry process.

Conduct of a full enquiry **10.155**

10.151 HMRC takes into account what it terms the 'telling, helping and access' approach, and provides a reduction of the difference between the maximum and minimum penalty positions to reflect this. The impact of this reduction can be significant. For example, at the lowest level the maximum penalty for carelessness is 30% but the minimum penalty for a prompted disclosure is only 15% so getting the quality of the disclosure right can make up to 15% difference on the penalty. In more serious cases the difference can be even more marked.

10.152 The HMRC Compliance Handbook manual gives some guidance to HMRC officers on how to assess the impact of the telling/helping/access approach and it would be sensible for the adviser to be aware of this guidance so that they can react accordingly.

Telling

10.153 HMRC guidance in CH82442 *et seq* should be referred to, so as to see HMRC's view of what it means by telling and the timing of disclosures.

In essence, to gain the maximum reduction for the telling aspect the taxpayer must make a full, frank and prompt disclosure of everything he knows. He must do so freely and not have the information dragged out of him in questioning.

Helping

10.154 This requires the taxpayer (through his adviser) to:

- give reasonable help in quantifying the inaccuracy or under-assessment;
- give positive assistance in the enquiry as opposed to passive acceptance or obstruction;
- actively engage in the work to accurately quantify the inaccuracies; and
- volunteer any information relevant to the disclosure.

These are all areas that the adviser should be alive to throughout the progress of the enquiry. Consider the HMRC guidance at CH82450 on the subject of helping.

Access

10.155 HMRC guidance states that 'giving access' includes a person responding positively to requests for information and documents and allowing access to:

- his business and other records;
- other relevant documents.

10.156   *Conduct of a full enquiry*

This is why reaction to information requests, looking at sensible timetables, etc are all so important. HMRC guidance on giving access is set out in CH82460.

Plan ahead

10.156   The message on penalties is therefore simple: plan ahead. Everything that is done from the outset of the enquiry to the settlement meeting will in some way influence the final penalty loading. Do everything to control that level.

> **Focus**
>
> The eye must always be kept on the endgame. Control of the process should focus on the vital 'How much to settle?' question.

CONCLUSION

10.157   So we reach the end of the enquiry. The taxpayer will not look back on the process with any degree of pleasure. He will be glad that it is all over and he can hopefully resume his business and private life without the shadow of HMRC hanging over him. He will probably vow that he will never go through the same experience again.

10.158   The adviser who has taken the initiative and tried to take and keep control of the case should be able to look back with some satisfaction on a job well done. It should be possible to point to some tangible savings for the taxpayer both in the calculation of tax and the level of penalties.

10.159   There will always be some things that could have been done better, but important experience will have been gained which can be utilised on the next occasion when another taxpayer finds himself in a similar situation.

KEY POINTS

10.160

1   The case must be under the control of the advisor if possible. This control should be aimed for on all aspects of the case.

2   The taxpayer must be supported but his expectations must be managed. At all times he must be aware that honesty and accuracy will allow the adviser to do his job.

3   HMRC must be controlled as far as possible both in terms of its statutory limitations and the general conduct of the case.

4   Plan, pay attention to the detail, think ahead and follow up on all issues. Bring order out of the inevitable chaos that can occur in a complex case.

5   Keep an eye on the 'end-game' and ensure that the conduct of the enquiry is always focussed on allowing the taxpayer to emerge with the least realistic damage.

Chapter 11

Settlement negotiations

Phil Berwick CTA ATT
Director, Berwick Tax Ltd

> **SIGNPOSTS**
>
> - **Scope** – There are a number of potential obstacles to a negotiation involving HMRC. A negotiated settlement is a way of reaching agreement with HMRC without recourse to the legal process. There is statutory authority, supported by case law, which allows the officer to negotiate. (See **11.1–11.4**.)
>
> - **Preparation** – The practitioner should think about settlement negotiations at the beginning of an investigation to gain the best possible outcome for the client. In particular, it is important to consider the relevant penalty rules, and ensure that maximum reduction is obtained for the periods covered by the respective regimes. (See **11.5–11.6**.)
>
> - **The elements of a settlement** – When additional tax is due, interest will be applied and, except in the smallest of cases, HMRC can be expected to seek a penalty. The practitioner needs to be familiar with the current and previous penalty regimes, to ensure that the correct rules are applied (see **11.7–11.14**). HMRC will always seek a payment on account where additional liabilities have been established. The practitioner needs to recognise the advantage to the client of making such a payment (See **11.15–11.18**).
>
> - **VAT** – Practitioners need to consider the possibility of VAT irregularities where there have been omissions, and ensure that the appropriate action is taken (See **11.19–11.20**).
>
> - **Professional costs** – HMRC has stated its view regarding the deductibility of professional fees in relation to enquiries (see **11.21–11.23**). Practitioners should ensure the client is aware of the position on reclaiming VAT on professional costs, and whether a benefit-in-kind needs to be reported to HMRC (See **11.24**).

Settlement negotiations 11.1

- **The advantages of negotiating** – There are numerous advantages to negotiating with HMRC. There should be financial advantages for the client, but the non-financial benefits of negotiating should also be borne in mind (see **11.25–11.28**). Practitioners need to consider their position in the investigation, and the potential impact on their other clients: it is prudent to consider engaging the services of an investigation specialist (see **11.29**). A key consideration for practitioners is establishing what is negotiable, and how the tax, interest and penalty can be reduced (See **11.30–11.32**).

- **Grey areas** – In most investigation cases, there will be issues that need clarifying. Practitioners need to consider whether an item is taxable before agreeing the position with HMRC. There are numerous grey areas, and it is important that practitioners consider all available options, even where the client's case is not absolute. (See **11.33–11.36**.)

- **The Litigation and Settlement Strategy** – The principles HMRC will follow in determining whether to litigate to resolve a tax dispute are provided in the Litigation and Settlement Strategy. HMRC consider that most of their interactions with taxpayers will not constitute a tax dispute for this purpose, but practitioners need to be aware of when they should refer to the guidance. (See **11.37**.)

- **Negotiation elements** – Practitioners should accept that negotiation is an acceptable path to take. Those not comfortable with the concept should seek specialist advice (see **11.38–11.39**). When discussing the position with HMRC, it is important for the practitioner to pitch the client's position at the appropriate level (see **11.40–11.41**). The practitioner must make an objective assessment of the client's position – weaknesses as well as the strengths (see **11.42**). When negotiating, it is important to consider the likely outcome (see **11.43–11.44**). An important part of negotiation is to consider the other party's position, and that is the same when dealing with HMRC (see **11.45**). It is important to get agreement, even if it is, initially, only a relatively minor issue (see **11.46–11.47**). Practitioners should remember that each case is different – there isn't a 'one size fits all' approach that can be taken (see **11.48**). After assessing the client's position, the practitioner should avoid making concessions prematurely (see **11.49–11.50**). The settlement discussions should be planned based on previous experience (See **11.51**).

- **Claims for earlier years** – Where HMRC is able to re-open earlier years, taxpayers are able to make claims that would otherwise be out of time (See **11.52–11.53**).

- **Non-domiciled individuals** – Although the rules regarding non-domiciled individuals have changed significantly in the last ten years, this taxpayer group remains of interest to HMRC (See **11.54**).

11.1 *Settlement negotiations*

- **Culpability and reasonable excuse** – If the practitioner can establish, and convince HMRC that the client took 'reasonable care', a penalty will not be charged. HMRC has tended to take a restricted view when it comes to determining whether a taxpayer has a reasonable excuse. Given the potentially high level of penalties, practitioners should ensure they establish the facts to see whether 'reasonable care' can be demonstrated, or that a 'reasonable excuse' existed. (See **11.55–11.59**.)

- **Consider HMRC** – Practitioners should consider the position from the HMRC officer's point of view (see **11.60**), and the advantages to him of reaching a negotiated settlement. These include time savings (see **11.61–11.63**), and also the impact of his workload (See **11.64**).

- **Alternative solutions** – There may be instances where it is not possible to reach a negotiated agreement with HMRC. Practitioners should be aware of the options, and consider their use where appropriate (See **11.65–11.67**).

- **Look at the package** – The amount of tax to be paid is only one element of the settlement package. Practitioners should consider each component of the settlement, and factor that into their discussions with HMRC and the client. (See **11.68–11.69**.)

- **Paying HMRC** – Practitioners should determine how the client is going to fund the settlement with HMRC. Clients should be made aware of HMRC's more aggressive stance in relation to potential bankruptcy action where they don't have sufficient funds (see **11.70–11.72**). The practitioner should also determine the client's potential timescale for paying HMRC. The officer will expect payment immediately (to the extent that payments on account aren't sufficient to cover the amount due), and time to pay should be discussed as part of the settlement negotiations (See **11.73–11.78**).

- **The letter of offer** – A negotiated settlement is concluded by a written contract between HMRC and the taxpayer. The first part is the submission of a 'letter of offer' by the taxpayer. The letter sets out the terms of the offer, and it is essential that the practitioner ensures the agreed terms are correctly set-out, including with regards to repayment terms. HMRC's formal acceptance letter creates the contract with the taxpayer. (See **11.79–11.82**.)

- **Sub-standard offer** – When the terms of a settlement have been agreed, any temptation to submit a sub-standard offer should be resisted. If the client does not have sufficient funds to make a 'full' offer, this should be factored into the discussions with HMRC. (See **11.83–11.84**.)

- **Settlement meetings** – Formal settlement meetings are unlikely to be requested in smaller cases. Where a meeting is requested, practitioners should note that the client is not under an obligation to attend. If it is considered appropriate to attend such a meeting, the client should be fully briefed beforehand. (See **11.85–11.88**.)

- **Relationships** – Practitioners should consider the various relationships that must be managed during the course of an investigation. It is important to develop a professional relationship with the inspector, and to establish a rapport with him (see **11.89–11.90**). The relationship with the client can be a fractious one, and the practitioner may consider it best to engage the services of an investigation specialist to help (see **11.91**). It is sometimes difficult for the practitioner to view the matter objectively, with potentially disastrous consequences for the client (see *Focus*, **11.91**). The nature of the relationship with the client is likely to change over the course of the investigation. Practitioners should ensure they manage the relationship with the client, and keep the client informed of progress (see **11.92–11.94**). The practitioner's case management should extend to billing arrangements, to ensure maximum recovery of fees (see **11.95**). Practitioners should be aware of the impact of an HMRC investigation on a client (and his family), as the stress can be immense. Successful handling of a client during an investigation can be demanding, and should not be underestimated (See **11.96–11.98**).

- **Key points** – Ten suggestions for the practitioner are included at **11.99**.

INTRODUCTION

11.1 Dictionary definitions of 'negotiate' include 'to reach an agreement or compromise by discussion' and 'to get over an obstacle'. In the context of HMRC investigations, both meanings are equally valid: there are a multitude of potential obstacles to be overcome. These include an intransigent HMRC officer, the client, and the practitioner himself. This chapter will explore ways of navigating the various obstacles that the practitioner may face.

11.2 The practitioner will often be instructed by his client to get the best settlement possible. What is the officer's authority to negotiate? This can be found in *TMA 1970* and common law. *TMA 1970, s 1(1)*, as amended by the *Commissioners for Revenue and Customs Act 2005*, states that the Commissioners for HMRC shall be responsible for the 'collection and management' of income tax, corporation tax and capital gains tax. This authority is an important part of HMRC's powers.

11.3 *Settlement negotiations*

11.3 In the context of an investigation settlement, the authority enables an officer to reach an informal agreement with a taxpayer where complex matters of statutory interpretation are concerned, where precedents derived from case law appear to be in conflict with the particular matter in hand, or even where the facts themselves are open to dispute and different interpretations.

11.4 The 'collection and management' power permits negotiations so that an agreement can be reached which is acceptable to both parties, ie HMRC and the client. The authority permits agreement to be reached without recourse to the legal process, which would be time-consuming, expensive and may result in a decision that was unacceptable to both parties. The Court of Appeal held, in *IRC v Nuttall* [1990] STC 194, that the power to enter into settlement negotiations and make agreements was not overridden by the specific provisions of *TMA 1970, s 54*.

START THE NEGOTIATING GROUNDWORK EARLY

11.5 For the purpose of this chapter, it is assumed that there have been omitted profits, income or capital gains from the client's tax return. Where, in practice, this is established, the practitioner should direct his attention to minimising the level of the additions sought by the officer. The practitioner should also check the basics – that there is a valid enquiry notice. In the *Mabbutt* case (*Michael Mabbutt v HMRC* [2016] UKFTT TC05075), the First-tier Tribunal declared HMRC's enquiry notice invalid because it referred to a non-existent tax year. The taxpayer in the case was a participant in a tax avoidance scheme, but the principle applies to a case involving omitted profits, etc. If the enquiry notice is not valid, the practitioner should challenge the officer. HMRC may, however, have assessing rights under the discovery provisions and that should be established. Assuming that there is a valid enquiry notice, the practitioner should proceed as outlined in this chapter.

Focus

It is important for the practitioner to appreciate that the groundwork for settlement negotiations should start at the beginning of an investigation. Co-operation of the adviser, as well as the client, will be taken into account by the officer when considering the level of penalty at the end of an investigation where the settlement includes penalties under the 'old' regime (see *Focus*, **11.9**). The practitioner should ensure that, from the time of the officer's opening letter, he is not responsible for any unnecessary delays in providing information reasonably requested by the officer, or in respect of the general progress of the enquiry. The practitioner should encourage the client to do the same.

11.6 Where there are going to be delays in, for example, the provision of information, the officer should be kept informed. The practitioner should instil a sense of urgency into his client so that he appreciates the seriousness of the situation, and will qualify for the maximum penalty reduction (abatement for co-operation when penalties under the 'old' regime are in point).

ARE INTEREST AND PENALTIES DUE?

11.7 Historically, HMRC did not pursue a penalty unless omitted profits exceeded £2,000. Following the introduction of the current penalty regime (see **11.9**), HMRC's published instructions do not give details of a *de minimis* limit that will apply in relation to the imposition of a penalty. Unless the practitioner can demonstrate that his client has taken reasonable care, the officer can be expected to seek the imposition of a penalty. As penalties tend to be significantly higher than under the previous regime, which still applies for relevant years (see *Focus*, **11.9**), practitioners must appreciate the importance of establishing whether the client has anything to disclose at the onset of any enquiry, and take appropriate action. This should be done before responding to HMRC's opening enquiry letter.

CALCULATION OF INTEREST

11.8 When the additional liabilities have been agreed, the resulting tax will be calculated together with any interest. This is automatic and there may not be scope for reducing the interest charged. There isn't a specific authority for HMRC to mitigate interest, and only limited circumstances in which they will consider a reduction (principally where there has been excessive HMRC delay). Interest is charged under the provisions of *TMA 1970, s 86*.

PENALTY NEGOTIATION

11.9 Where HMRC has suffered a loss, or potential loss, of tax, the officer will seek, in addition to the tax due, interest and a penalty, except in the smallest of cases. The current penalty regime for inaccuracies in returns or other documents was introduced by *FA 2007, Sch 24, para 1*. The *FA 2007* provisions apply to an inaccuracy contained in a return or other document which was due to be filed on or after 1 April 2009 and the return or other document relates to a tax period beginning on or after 1 April 2008. The regime consists of a series of 'stepped' penalties based on taxpayer behaviour. The penalty is calculated by reference to the 'potential lost revenue' rather than tax lost.

11.10 *Settlement negotiations*

> **Focus**
>
> The previous regime, where the penalty was mitigated by reference to disclosure, co-operation and seriousness (which incorporates size and gravity), will continue to apply in relation to inaccuracies in returns for earlier tax periods. Practitioners will need to ensure that they are applying the appropriate penalty regime when negotiating with the officer. Where an investigation straddles 6 April 2008, both regimes will need to be considered.

11.10 The maximum penalty is, currently, 100% of the 'potential lost revenue', although where the undeclared income or gains arises offshore, a higher level of penalty (up to 200%) will be due (the relevant legislation was introduced in *FA 2010, Sch 10*, and applies to offences committed after 5 April 2011). Under the old regime, the maximum penalty is 100% of the tax lost. The likelihood is that HMRC will recover a higher level of penalty than it would have done for the same offence under the old regime. This increases the importance of negotiation when considering penalties: for example, in determining the appropriate taxpayer behaviour and the corresponding band of penalty that applies. Practitioners should note that the Failure to Correct penalties, which will apply from 1 October 2018, will impose a minimum penalty of 100% of the tax liability which should have been disclosed to HMRC under the Requirement to Correct provisions but was not. Further details of the penalty regime, including the bands of taxpayer behaviour, are considered in **CHAPTER 19**.

11.11 The officer will consider whether there has been a disclosure, and, if so, whether it was prompted or not. He will also take into account what he thinks is the appropriate behaviour and level of mitigation, and, consequently, penalty. It should be noted that the officer's figure is not cast in stone. It is important to remember that it is the client who is making the offer to HMRC: the officer should only be giving an indication of the level of penalty that is likely to be accepted by the Board.

11.12 The penalty process tends to be more formulaic and procedural than the old regime. Practitioners should bear in mind that some officers do not give detailed consideration to each of the relevant steps when calculating the penalty considered due. Practitioners are advised to contact the officer to discuss penalty reduction. When they do so, they should request a breakdown of the penalty loading, as set out in **CHAPTER 19**. If the officer has not fully thought out the penalty reduction in this way, he may have no choice but to agree to a lower figure.

11.13 The penalty reduction does not depend solely on the actions of the client. An inaccuracy by the agent, or delay by him, will count against the client as if it was him who was directly responsible for the inaccuracy or delay. However, where the taxpayer can establish that the inaccuracy relates to information supplied (or not supplied) by another person, and the taxpayer has taken reasonable care to check the information supplied (or not supplied) by the other person the taxpayer will not be liable to a penalty. Practitioners should note that the other person may be charged a penalty where they give the taxpayer false information, or withhold information from the taxpayer, with the intention of the taxpayer submitting a false document. Where the taxpayer suffers an adverse penalty loading because of an inaccuracy or delay by his adviser he may decide to seek compensation from the agent.

11.14 When considering the relevant penalty mitigation, the officer will consider any delays, etc from the time that the investigation started. That is why it is important for practitioners to prepare for their settlement negotiations at the start of an enquiry, by ensuring that the officer's reasonable requests are complied with without unnecessary delay. That does not mean that you agree to unreasonable demands, either in timescale or nature of information requested, by the investigator. Your client should not be penalised because you challenge an overzealous officer.

Focus

The practitioner needs to be particularly careful where he has taken over a case from another adviser. This situation can be fraught with difficulties for the new adviser, who should ensure that the client is fully aware of the seriousness of the position. He should also establish the extent of any disclosure made, and whether that represents the extent of the problem.

PAYMENTS ON ACCOUNT

11.15 Officers are instructed to ask for a payment on account in investigation cases. Making such a payment has, potentially, two advantages for the client. It shows the officer that the client is treating the investigation seriously, and should assist when negotiating the penalty mitigation at the end of the enquiry (for periods covered by the previous penalty regime). Secondly, it helps to mitigate the interest, accruing on a daily basis, where there has been an underpayment of tax. When a practitioner is aware that there are additional liabilities, he should recommend to his client that a payment on account is made.

11.16 During the course of an investigation further liabilities may become apparent, and the practitioner should recommend the making of such additional payments on account as are deemed necessary. If the client is not able to make a lump-sum payment, he should be advised to make monthly payments of such amount as he can afford. It should be noted that the client will not always

11.17 *Settlement negotiations*

make payments on account when recommended to do so by the practitioner. Some may prefer to wait until the settlement figure is known, and then arrange finance to meet the liability in full. It is imperative that the practitioner makes the recommendations regarding payments on account, and, preferably, puts them in writing, even where the client has stated that he will settle in full, so that he is protected against any claims from his client regarding the imposition of interest, or an adverse penalty loading under the 'old' regime.

11.17 The officer's interest computation should be checked carefully. This is particularly important where payments on account have been made, or there are tax repayments due to the client, to ensure that the correct interest credit has been included.

11.18 For a sole trader or partnership, it is important to remember that an increase in the tax payable for years under enquiry will automatically increase the payments on account which should have been made for the following year(s) under *TMA 1970, s 59A*. Surcharges on late-paid tax for self-assessment years under *TMA 1970, s 59C* may also be included within contract settlements, but not where a tax-geared penalty has been charged on the same tax (*TMA 1970, s 59C(4)*).

VAT DISCLOSURE

11.19 Where there has been a disclosure of omitted profits made to the officer, it is extremely likely that there are VAT implications. The practitioner should consider the possibility of VAT irregularities, and make sure that appropriate action is taken. Although the Inland Revenue and HM Customs and Excise merged in April 2005, there are relatively few HMRC officers who are trained in both disciplines.

11.20 It is advisable to put the VAT office on notice at an early stage in the investigation that there is a disclosure to be made. This should assist in minimising the penalty position in relation to the VAT offences. Final details of the irregularities can be provided when the settlement has been agreed with the officer. The VAT officer will usually accept adjustments based on the settlement figures with the officer. It should be borne in mind, that, where there are VAT implications, the figures agreed with the officer take this into account.

PROFESSIONAL COSTS

11.21 HMRC has set out its position regarding accountancy expenses arising out of self-assessment enquiries (EM3981). Where the enquiry does not result in an addition to profits, or there is an adjustment to the profits for the year of enquiry only and that alteration does not arise as a result of a failure to take reasonable care or a deliberate understatement (negligent or fraudulent conduct in relation to periods covered by the old penalty regime) the additional accountancy expenses will be allowable.

11.22 In all other cases, ie where there has been a failure to take reasonable care or a deliberate understatement (fraudulent or negligent conduct in relation to periods covered by the old penalty regime), or there are adjustments for more than one year, the professional costs of dealing with an HMRC investigation are not allowable deductions for income tax or corporation tax purposes. Where the fees include work done in connection with ongoing compliance obligations, eg the preparation of accounts, that element will be allowable in the normal way.

11.23 Where such costs may be allowable, they should be agreed with the officer during the settlement negotiations, rather than waiting until the next tax computation is submitted, when the practitioner's position is weaker.

11.24 When the client is VAT-registered, the VAT element can be reclaimed to the extent that it relates to the business. If the client is not billed separately for the work done on the business affairs and the personal tax affairs of its proprietor or directors, the VAT reclaimed must be restricted. Also, the appropriate entry must be made in the owner's drawings account. When dealing with a company, the relevant amount should be debited to the director's current account, or a benefit returned on form P11D, as appropriate.

WHY NEGOTIATE?

> **Focus**
> Some practitioners may query why they should negotiate with the officer. They should remember that the officer's role is to establish the amount of tax, etc to be paid by the client. The officer has various statutory powers to enable him to do his job. The practitioner's role is to obtain the most favourable settlement for his client. This can usually be best achieved by negotiating the level of additional liabilities, etc with the officer, rather than proceeding down a formal route. There are several practical reasons why it is advantageous for the adviser to reach a negotiated settlement, and these are considered below.

Reduce the length of the investigation period

11.25 If additional profits can be agreed between the officer and the practitioner, this should be quicker than the officer going down the

11.26 *Settlement negotiations*

formal route. Under this process, the officer issues a closure notice for self-assessment years (where there is an open enquiry), discovery assessments for other self-assessment years, and estimated assessments for pre-self-assessment years. The closure notice and, if issued, discovery and estimated assessments must be appealed against, with a subsequent hearing of the appeals before the First-tier Tribunal (or resolution via a statutory review or the alternative dispute resolution process). This process takes time, and will add several months, if not longer, to the investigation period.

Finality for the client

11.26 A negotiated settlement gives the client finality, without the uncertainty of taking the case before the tribunal.

Financial (professional fees)

11.27 Although there may be correspondence, meetings or telephone conversations with the officer to reach a negotiated settlement, the time costs for the client should be cheaper than becoming embroiled in the time-consuming, and costly, process of assessments, appeals and tribunal hearings.

Financial (tax, etc savings for the client)

11.28 The outcome of a negotiated settlement should be that both sides benefit. When reaching an agreement with the officer, without recourse to the formal route, the additions should be lower. This has the consequential effect that the tax, interest and penalty will be reduced, resulting in a lower overall settlement. The negotiated settlement will also be reflected in the penalty loading. In relation to years covered by the previous penalty regime the client will enjoy higher penalty mitigation because the officer has not had to use his formal powers to bring the investigation to a conclusion, and, under the current regime, he will have been deemed to have given a better quality disclosure.

Finality for the practitioner

11.29 It should be remembered that handling an HMRC investigation is time-consuming for the accountant. This is particularly an issue for smaller firms of advisers. The practitioner has a duty to all his clients, not just those under enquiry, and the strain of dealing with only a handful of HMRC investigations, or one large one, can severely stretch the practitioner's resources. A case that may seem complex to a practitioner may be routine for a specialist, dealing with such cases on a regular basis. A practitioner in such a position should consider engaging the services of an investigation specialist.

What is negotiable?

11.30 As in any negotiating situation, when settling an investigation case, anything is potentially negotiable. The officer may say that he cannot give ground on a particular area because of, for example, case law, but the practitioner may be able to obtain a concession in another area.

> **Focus**
>
> The interest and penalty figures follow from the amount of tax due. It makes sense to start by considering how the level of tax can be mitigated. Where the additional tax arises from income, the practitioner should concentrate on minimising the figure for the year under enquiry, as this will determine whether the officer also seeks additions for earlier years, and, if so, for how many.

11.31 It may be possible to restrict the number of earlier years that the officer seeks additions for. Was there, for example, a change in the nature of the business that gave rise to the omissions starting? By reducing the level of additional income, etc the practitioner keeps the tax down, which will lead to lower interest and penalty. Where the enquiry has been ongoing for a number of years, the officer may also seek additions for later years. The comments above also apply to restricting any such additions sought by the officer.

11.32 The practitioner should explore all options when negotiating, including alternative treatments of particular items. Conceding that an item should be taxed under a different provision may result in more tax payable in relation to that aspect, but should not be dismissed if it leads to a lower settlement because of, for example, favourable penalty reduction or mitigation.

CONSIDERATION OF GREY AREAS

11.33 In most investigation cases, there will be three broad areas into which potentially taxable items fall: there will be those items that are agreed by both parties as being taxable; there will be certain items that are accepted as being non-taxable; and there will be those items that fall in between the first two categories.

11.34 *Settlement negotiations*

> **Focus**
>
> Before accepting that an item is taxable, the practitioner should consider all available options. Although the client's case may not be absolute, the officer may be prepared to offer concessions. The practitioner should also be prepared to do the same, although he will be seeking to ensure that he gains more than he concedes!

11.34 There are various examples of grey areas: the distinction between income (liable to income tax) and capital (liable to CGT, or possibly not taxable at all) is a common area of difficulty. Protracted negotiations may be required to agree on the treatment of such items. The practitioner should be aware that different allowances, exemptions and reliefs may apply which reduce or eliminate the tax bill, or transfer liability from the client to another person. A compromise solution can often be the best conclusion for both parties.

11.35 Tax avoidance schemes can be another area of complexity. The client may have implemented a strategy that is at the very edge of current tax understanding. Where HMRC has a contrary view it will challenge any such arrangements. HMRC take an aggressive view of avoidance, and has established specialist units to deal with the more serious or complex cases.

11.36 It is often in the interest of both parties to reach a compromise settlement where there are complex technical issues. This avoids the need for lengthy, and costly, recourse to the legal process to obtain a definitive answer. Once the courts have given their decision, it is too late to negotiate a better settlement if that decision did not go in the client's favour.

LITIGATION AND SETTLEMENT STRATEGY

11.37 HMRC introduced its Litigation and Settlement Strategy (LSS) on 11 June 2007, and refreshed the process in July 2011. The latest guidance (published in October 2017) sets out HMRC's principles for bringing tax disputes to a conclusion. A central theme of the LSS is seeking non-confrontational solutions 'where possible'. The LSS sets out the principles determining whether HMRC will litigate to resolve a case. HMRC anticipates that most of its discussions with taxpayers will not fall within the term 'dispute'. Where there is a substantial and material difference of opinion about tax liabilities in a case, particularly where that difference will not be easily resolved, a practitioner should refer to the detail of the LSS (available on the GOV.UK website) for consideration as to how HMRC may proceed.

THE ART OF NEGOTIATION

> **Focus**
>
> An investigation settlement is no different in many respects to negotiating in other areas of life. Each side wants to win more than it loses. There are numerous publications available which detail negotiating skills, and here it is intended to give a few pointers relevant to tax investigations.

Negotiate

11.38 The first point to remember is that it is perfectly acceptable to negotiate. Tax investigations are contentious and adversarial arenas into which the practitioner is entering on behalf of his client. Some practitioners are wary of negotiating, especially where the officer's case seems cut and dried. It is the practitioner's duty to do whatever he legitimately can, within the law and the ethics of his profession, to seek to minimise the amount of tax, etc that his client has to pay.

11.39 If the practitioner is not comfortable with negotiating, he should seek specialist help for this part of the enquiry process, even if only for a second opinion as to the reasonableness of the officer's proposals, and the merit of the client's position.

Pitch at the right level

11.40 When starting discussions, the practitioner must ensure that his figures are not too high (from the client's point of view). It is inevitable that the opening figures will not be the final ones, so the practitioner should allow room for movement, and be prepared to make concessions from his starting position. The officer can be expected to challenge any figures presented. He will seek an increase on those figures, where appropriate, as he will be looking to maximise the position for HMRC. The practitioner must not pitch too low, as that may have an adverse impact on the penalty position, and should ensure that any figures submitted are tenable.

11.41 With this in mind, the practitioner should work backwards from what he thinks will be the finishing position. It is important not to concede too much before negotiations begin as this will inevitably result in an unsatisfactory settlement figure. As well as dealing with the demands of the client, and managing his expectations, the practitioner must also take into account the officer's position in the negotiations.

11.42 *Settlement negotiations*

How strong is the client's case?

> **Focus**
>
> When deciding where to pitch an offer, the practitioner must take into account the relative strengths and weaknesses of the client's case. Serious irregularities cannot be brushed aside, and must be taken into account in the negotiations. Where the issues concern highly technical matters, ambiguity over the taxability of transactions, etc, this should be brought to the officer's attention.

11.42 It should be remembered that the officer does not have the final say on the level of a settlement. The client can appear before the First-tier Tribunal to present his case, although the risks in taking the dispute there should be stressed. As the practitioner reviews the case, he should consider what view the tribunal might make of the evidence available. This can help the practitioner to plan his dealings with the officer.

Consider the outcome

11.43 When negotiating with the officer, it is important that the practitioner has a clear idea of the best possible outcome, what he thinks will be the result, and the worst position that will be acceptable to the client. These positions may change during the course of the negotiations, if the situation cannot be finalised in one session.

11.44 Discussions with the officer to finalise the additional liabilities may take place over the telephone or at a meeting. It is preferable for the client not to be present, so that you can concentrate on the issues. Thorough preparation is important, so that you know the strengths and weaknesses of your client's case.

The officer is not the enemy

11.45 You should regard the officer as a partner, rather than as an enemy to be defeated. You may have to deal with the same officer in the future, and you do not want him to be seeking revenge for a previous 'defeat'. For the same reason, it makes sense not to say or do anything rash.

> **Focus**
>
> There are some practitioners who take great delight in 'bashing' HMRC. Others relish lengthy delays in dealing with correspondence from the officer and attach little priority to progressing enquiries. These types of attitude are not conducive to effective negotiation.

Agree on minor issues

11.46 If agreement cannot be reached on the level of additional profits, try to see if there are any areas that can be agreed, eg treatment of a particular receipt, or even the level of a private usage adjustment, and then return to the main area.

11.47 The best result is one when both sides are satisfied that the outcome is in their best interests and the best they could have achieved.

No two cases are the same

11.48 The practitioner should approach each settlement for what it is – a unique situation. You cannot treat each case the same because the facts will be different and you are dealing with an individual, the officer. There is no tried and tested formula that can be used in every case. Officers will react differently, depending on the approach taken.

Avoid premature concessions

11.49 After thorough preparation, and having assessed the relative strength of the client's case, the practitioner should not give concessions too soon, or give too many. He should be prepared to stick by his arguments. Investigations are adversarial by nature, and the practitioner must be prepared to argue his side with the officer.

11.50 The practitioner should not be rushed into making concessions by the officer. The investigator is also under pressure to settle for the reasons mentioned earlier. If the practitioner gives in too easily, the officer may regard him as an 'easy touch' and may seek more concessions than he would otherwise do. The practitioner should ensure that concessions are not given away; they should, if possible, be given in exchange for a concession by the officer.

Previous experience

11.51 Your settlement discussions should be planned, taking into account what you have learnt about the officer in your previous meetings and conversations with him. If you have been brought in at a late stage, and are meeting the officer for the first time, you will need to assess the officer at the meeting, and from whatever discussions you have had with him.

11.52 *Settlement negotiations*

CLAIMS, ALLOWANCES AND RELIEFS

11.52 The re-opening of accounts and tax returns for earlier years provides an opportunity to make any claims that have been overlooked, or make claims to relief earlier than has been the case. Before starting negotiations with the officer, the practitioner should conduct a thorough review of the case to establish whether there are any potential claims, allowances or reliefs that should be made. This includes the ability to make claims that would otherwise be out of time.

11.53 The officer can be expected to challenge claims for expenses that are not supported by vouchers. Often, the officer can be persuaded to concede an allowance for some additional expenditure, depending on the circumstances of the case. The officer cannot resist a claim for additional expenditure where he is seeking additional profits that required, for example, additional materials, labour or fuel.

REMITTANCES BY NON-DOMICILED INDIVIDUALS

11.54 Wealthy non-domiciled individuals have long been a favourite target for HMRC. Often, there is considerable difficulty in identifying the source of funds remitted by non-domiciled individuals resident in the UK. The amounts involved can be substantial, and officers are aware of this. The practitioner is advised to undertake a thorough review of funds remitted, and the bank accounts from which the amounts were made, if appropriate, and establish the arguments that can be made. The officer will expect to see an audit trail, demonstrating the origin of the funds. Time spent by the practitioner will usually be worthwhile, because of the substantial sums often involved. The tax treatment of non-domiciled individuals has changed considerably in recent years, including the introduction of the remittance basis charge, which has reduced the risk represented by this group of taxpayers, although they still remain of interest to HMRC.

REASONABLE CARE AND REASONABLE EXCUSE

11.55 Penalties will be due under *FA 2007, Sch 24, para 1* where HMRC can establish that there is an inaccuracy in a tax return and the taxpayer failed to take reasonable care when completing that return or there was a deliberate inaccuracy in the return. (The position was broadly the same under the old penalty regime, although the requirement was whether HMRC could establish fraudulent or negligent conduct: *TMA 1970, s 95*.) Failure to take reasonable care can be likened to the long-standing concept in general law of negligence – the failure to do what a reasonable person should recognise as his duty. A deliberate inaccuracy occurs when a person knowingly and intentionally gives HMRC an inaccurate document. HMRC will usually resist claims that the taxpayer has taken care (which means that HMRC cannot impose a penalty) (innocent error in the previous regime) or that there was a reasonable excuse; although it does recognise that there are situations when penalty reduction is appropriate. Case law is evolving as the tribunals determine what constitutes a deliberate inaccuracy, etc under the *FA 2007* legislation. Reference should be made to **CHAPTER 19** on penalties.

11.56 Where a person has a serious illness this would qualify as a reasonable excuse, and the officer will often be sympathetic. What the taxpayer would have to ensure is that he gets his tax affairs in order following recuperation. Few illnesses are so serious that a person is unable to instruct someone else to deal with matters on his behalf, or advise HMRC of the reason for the delay. The wording of *TMA 1970, s 118(2)* indicates that a 'reasonable excuse' defence will not protect a taxpayer who fails to take the necessary action once the 'excuse' has ceased to apply.

11.57 Ignorance of the law is not a defence, and would not qualify as a reasonable excuse. HMRC will not automatically accept that a person did not know that a receipt or transaction gave rise to a tax charge. The credibility of the excuse will depend on the complexity of the transaction, and the client's background and technical knowledge.

11.58 Where the amounts involved are anything other than minimal, it will be difficult to claim that the client exercised reasonable care. If, however, the client was not aware of, for example, accumulated income from a trust where he was unaware that he was a beneficiary, he cannot be expected to include the details on his tax return. Practitioners should establish the facts to see whether it can be demonstrated that the client took reasonable care. He should seek to determine whether there is documentation to support the contention, including copies of any advice obtained.

11.59 Where the officer cannot establish that an inaccuracy by a person in a document was neither careless nor deliberate at the time the document was sent to HMRC, it will be treated as careless if the person discovers the inaccuracy at some later time and does not take reasonable steps to inform HMRC. There was a similar provision at *TMA 1970, s 97* in relation to the old penalty regime.

ADVANTAGES FOR THE OFFICER

11.60 As with any negotiation situation, it is worthwhile considering the position from the other side: what's in it for the officer?

11.61 *Settlement negotiations*

Time

11.61 The officer does not have the cost issues that the practitioner and his client need to consider. He can spend weeks, or even months, pursuing minor issues. What the investigator does have to consider is his portfolio of investigation cases. Most officers would prefer to bring an investigation to a conclusion rather than let it continue indefinitely. The process of issuing assessments or closure notices is a relatively straightforward task for the officer, with instructions usually passed to a clerical officer, although this can be onerous, particularly where numerous years are involved.

11.62 The investigating officer on a case is not the one who will present the case at a tribunal, as HMRC now use specialist officers. The officer's input will still be needed, particularly if he is going to be called as a witness. The process tends to be labour-intensive and time-consuming process for the officer. Most officers will prefer to reach agreement by negotiation.

11.63 Remember that any 'without prejudice' offers will be withdrawn once formal proceedings have been commenced. Often, though, HMRC will be prepared to reach a negotiated settlement up to, and on, the date of the tribunal hearing.

Workload

11.64 Although the practitioner may handle only a few investigations at any one time, the officer will often have a large portfolio of such cases. He is under pressure to settle cases, and register new ones. When your client's case is finished, he can move on to another taxpayer. A negotiated settlement gives him that opportunity far sooner than finalisation via the formal route.

WHEN AGREEMENT CANNOT BE REACHED

11.65 It is recognised that not every case can be settled by negotiation. There may be particular issues on which agreement cannot be reached, or there may be an intransigent officer who will not move from his unreasonable opening proposals. In these cases, there may be no alternative other than to go to the tribunal, particularly if the officer's manager, or other senior officer, does not encourage him to adopt a conciliatory position. As an alternative to a hearing at the tribunal, the adviser may want to consider a statutory review, or, in appropriate circumstances, HMRC's Alternative Dispute Resolution, a non-statutory process (see **CHAPTER 12**).

11.66 The practitioner faced with this situation should still seek to agree as much as possible with the officer, so that it is only the contentious issues that have to be considered by the mediation hearing or tribunal. Details on presenting a case at the tribunal are contained in **CHAPTER 20**.

11.67 Where there is an assessment under appeal, it should be noted that the officer can issue a further assessment even though the main assessment could be increased under the provisions of *TMA 1970, s 50(7)*. The officer is likely to take this course of action where there is a substantially inadequate assessment under appeal and the client has not made a suitable payment on account. Case law has confirmed that the officer can raise a further assessment under *TMA 1970, s 29(3)* in these circumstances (see *Duchy Maternity Ltd v Hodgson* [1985] STC 764).

THE SETTLEMENT PACKAGE

> **Focus**
>
> When considering what the best possible settlement for the client is, the answer will not usually rest only on the amount of tax to pay. The practitioner needs to consider the overall position and aim to get the most advantageous result for the client in the circumstances of the case. This will include a review of the following:
>
> - the level of tax, interest and penalty;
> - what amounts are included in the settlement (eg the officer may be persuaded to include non-investigation liabilities, effectively giving your client more time to pay);
> - the funding of the settlement;
> - the period of time to repay the liabilities;
> - the level of forward interest charged by the officer in an instalment arrangement; and
> - agreement from the officer on the future treatment of a contentious issue.

11.68 Often, the client is looking at the overall settlement package – what is it going to cost, and over what period does he have to repay HMRC – rather than a detailed consideration of the individual component parts (tax, interest, penalty, etc). Before embarking on negotiations with the officer, it is important that the practitioner discusses the situation with the client. The practitioner can ensure that he is aware of his client's expectations, and that they are reasonable.

11.69 *Settlement negotiations*

11.69 The client must be made aware of the possible outcomes to the negotiations. It will usually be helpful to give the client the 'best-case' and 'worst-case' scenarios. This can help to stabilise the client's level of expectation about the settlement. The client should have been kept informed throughout the investigation process, and this practice should continue until the formalities have been finalised. The client needs to be able to make an informed decision about the level of offer to be made to HMRC.

Focus

During the negotiating process, there will, usually, be various proposals and counter-proposals. The practitioner should recognise when he has gained as many concessions as possible from the officer, taking into account materiality. There is no point continuing to negotiate where the saving to the client may only be a few hundred pounds in tax, etc when it costs him more than that in the adviser's time.

FUNDING THE SETTLEMENT AND TIME TO PAY

11.70 The adviser should discuss the client's means, and how he intends to repay HMRC. A person who has deliberately understated income for tax purposes does not usually make provision for the eventual settlement with HMRC. Banks and building societies are not always agreeable to lending funds to meet an investigation settlement. HMRC generally prefers to reach agreement about the level of settlement, rather than make a person bankrupt. Taking that course of action would result in it only obtaining a proportion of the money due, and it will, usually, reluctantly provide time to pay.

11.71 Practitioners should be aware that HMRC is taking a more robust stance with regard to settlement of liabilities. Bankruptcy is being pursued by HMRC more vigorously than in the past. This course of action is a possible outcome if the client is unable to pay the agreed liabilities. The officer may be prepared to accept a lower figure than might normally be expected, although it will depend on the financial circumstances, and attitude, of the client. Where the client does not co-operate with the officer, or he does not take the necessary steps to sell available assets to meet the liability, he can expect HMRC to be more robust in their dealings with him. The practitioner should notify the client of the risk of bankruptcy if he is not going to be able to obtain the necessary funding.

11.72 If the client is not in a position to make a standard offer, the officer will seek a certified written statement of means. This will include details of all assets and liabilities (including those of his spouse and children or anyone to whom he has transferred assets), full details of current income and outgoings, and details of any likely changes in the following three to five years, for example, the maturing of an endowment policy, or impending retirement.

11.73 The officer will always want any additional liabilities settled as soon as possible, usually within 30 days of the acceptance letter (see below). During the course of an enquiry, the investigator will regularly request further payments on account, and ask the practitioner to ensure that any payments made reflect the additional liabilities established. At the end of the investigation, the officer will want HMRC to be repaid in full in the shortest possible time.

11.74 If the client is unable to make immediate payment, details of his current and future income will need to be established. The client's assets, and liabilities, will already have been identified, from the statement that the officer will have requested as part of the settlement process. The officer will not agree to a lengthy instalment arrangement if the client has substantial funds in a bank account, or, for example, several properties unencumbered by loans.

11.75 In cases where the client does not have sufficient funds to make immediate repayment of the settlement in full, an instalment arrangement must be considered. Repayments can be made over several months, or even years.

11.76 Officers are reluctant to accept instalment offers, particularly those extending beyond two years. An offer where there is a repayment period not exceeding three years can, usually, be agreed locally. A longer instalment period requires approval from HMRC's compliance division. Where an instalment arrangement is accepted, the officer will seek to apply forward interest, in accordance with HMRC policy, for the duration of the repayment period. This should be included in the negotiations with the officer. He may agree not to charge forward interest for a (brief) period.

11.77 The 'time to pay' aspect should not be overlooked when negotiating with the officer. The officer may agree to a period longer than 30 days for repayment to be made, and for this to be interest-free. That will depend on the amounts involved, and the negotiating skills of the practitioner. Readers should be aware that officers are, generally, taking a tougher stance in all matters relating to settlement, and that includes their position on any interest-free period.

11.78 HMRC's Enquiry Manual does not comment on the length of interest-free period that is acceptable. Practitioners should seek as long a period as possible, although the extent of any interest-free period granted will depend on the circumstances. A period of 60 days would not be unreasonable, or longer where the amount involved is substantial. The officer will need to be satisfied that the client needs further time to obtain funding for the settlement, and

11.79 *Settlement negotiations*

the client will be making a cash offer, rather than paying by instalments. The officer can be expected to consider the co-operation of the client, and the action that has been taken to raise the necessary funding. Where a client is selling an investment property to meet the settlement, the officer will expect him to serve notice on the tenant when the extent of the liability is established rather than waiting until the end of the process.

THE LETTER OF OFFER

11.79 Where settlement of an HMRC investigation is by negotiation, the agreement is set out in a written contract, called a 'letter of offer', submitted by the client, detailing the amount to be paid. Where the offer is agreed, HMRC sends the Board's formal acceptance letter, which creates a legally-binding contract with the client. In practice it would be unusual for an offer not to be accepted where agreement had been reached with the officer about the level of offer to be made. An acceptance letter may not be sent when the client has made a sub-standard offer (see below).

11.80 The payment terms are contained in the offer letter. The usual terms are that payment will be made within 30 days from the date of the acceptance letter. Where payment is to be made over a period of time, the offer letter sets out the date of the first and subsequent instalments. As mentioned above, the time granted will depend on several factors, including the practitioner's negotiating skills.

11.81 As with any contract, action can be taken if the terms are broken. The client must be made aware of the implications of, for example, failing to make an instalment payment, before he signs the offer letter. The officer will be reluctant to renegotiate the terms of a contract at a later date if, for example, future income does not meet the projected figure and the client is unable to meet both his obligations under the contract and his ongoing self-assessment liabilities. The practitioner should ensure that the settlement terms are reasonable, and that the client will be able to adhere to them.

11.82 Contract settlements have been the normal way in which investigations are concluded where both parties have been able to reach agreement on the level of additional profits. The process does not sit comfortably with the provisions of *TMA 1970, s 28A(5)* which require the issue of a formal notice at the completion of an enquiry into a self-assessment return. The officer will not normally issue a completion notice where there is a contract settlement. The contract settlement provides finality in the investigation proceedings. The practitioner can seek a completion notice, if desired, although this may not give the client any additional protection.

MAKING SUB-STANDARD OFFERS

11.83 There may be a temptation to submit a sub-standard offer. This should be resisted. Once the level of a settlement has been agreed with the officer it would be unwise to submit an offer in a lower figure. If there are genuine reasons why the client cannot make a 'full' offer, this should be taken into account when negotiating with the officer, before submitting a formal offer. If a sub-standard offer is submitted it may be accepted, providing it is reasonably close to the expected offer, but the officer is likely to exercise extreme caution when negotiating with the practitioner on subsequent cases.

11.84 There may be exceptional circumstances where the submission of a sub-standard offer may be justified, for example, where the officer is intransigent, but it is not recommended that this be done as a matter of course.

SETTLEMENT MEETINGS

11.85 Most officers requested settlement meetings in the past. The purpose of the meeting was for the client to sign the letter of offer, and, usually, for the officer to deliver a moral lecture on tax compliance. Now, most settlements, particularly in smaller cases, are dealt with by correspondence. The officer accepts an assurance that the significance of the various documents signed by the client (typically an offer letter, statement of assets, certificate of bank accounts operated and certificate of full disclosure) has been explained by the practitioner. It is important that the adviser does this in unequivocal terms to the client, in writing, to ensure that he fully appreciates the seriousness of the situation.

11.86 The dangers of signing an incomplete statement of assets or certificate of full disclosure, ie the possibility of a criminal investigation by HMRC, should be stressed to the client. Often, at this late stage in the investigation, the client may disclose additional assets. Although the officer will not be impressed by late disclosure of further assets or sources of income, and this is likely to impact on the penalty reduction, it is preferable to the client signing an incomplete statement or certificate and being prosecuted.

11.87 Although a settlement interview may be requested, particularly in larger cases, there is no statutory obligation on your client to attend such a meeting. If a formal meeting is held, it is important that the client is fully briefed beforehand. The client should be advised merely to listen to the officer, and sign the documentation when requested.

11.88 The practitioner should be aware that the meeting is not for the benefit of the client, but provides the officer with an opportunity to give the client a rap on the knuckles and warn him about his future conduct. The practitioner

11.89 *Settlement negotiations*

should ensure that any debate about, for example, the level of penalty, is agreed before the settlement meeting. At the meeting the client only has to listen, and sign the relevant documentation (which should have been checked in advance by the practitioner).

RELATIONSHIP WITH THE OFFICER

11.89 It is important for the practitioner to establish a good rapport with the officer conducting the investigation. A frosty relationship with the officer will not be helpful when it comes to negotiating a settlement. It is equally important that the relationship does not become 'cosy'. What is desired is a healthy professional respect between the officer and the practitioner.

11.90 If the adviser does not know the officer from previous dealings with HMRC, he should endeavour to establish a rapport at an early stage of the investigation. The following steps can help to achieve this:

- agree the work to be done by the practitioner at the beginning of the investigation;
- carry out the work agreed, within an approved realistic timescale, or keep the officer informed of any unforeseen delays;
- use the telephone, email (where the officer has the facility) or meetings to make progress, rather than lengthy letters, particularly those of a legalistic nature, which tend to prompt replies of similar length and style;
- comply with reasonable requests for information or documentation by the officer, or be prepared to say why certain items are not considered reasonable or relevant to the investigation; and
- adopt an appropriate tone in correspondence; some practitioners adopt an unnecessarily aggressive stance, which is not conducive to establishing a good rapport with the officer.

RELATIONSHIP WITH THE CLIENT

11.91 The relationship with the client can be fraught with difficulty during an HMRC investigation. If the practitioner has acted for the client for many years, there can be a sense of betrayal when it emerges that the client has been guilty of irregularities. The adviser can also feel disappointed that he did not identify the misdemeanours when preparing the accounts. These thoughts must be banished from the practitioner's mind if he is to best represent his client at this difficult time. Often, particularly in large or complex cases, investigation specialists are engaged to deal with HMRC; the client is then handed back to the practitioner 'clean'.

> **Focus**
>
> Many practitioners have reported to me that they are too close to the client, and do not have the required objectiveness for dealing with an HMRC investigation, particularly when dealing with a long-standing client. I have seen numerous cases where clients have come very close to being subject to a criminal investigation, or have suffered higher penalties, because the practitioner has not been able to ask clients the difficult questions that must be addressed when dealing with an investigation.

11.92 Clients will want different outcomes from their advisers at various stages of the investigation. They will all want, initially, to be spared from criminal proceedings. Their priority then shifts to a desire for the settlement cost to be as low as possible. Some clients will let the practitioner get on with his job without much contact other than to supply information or records. Others want to know all the detail of the discussions with the officer. Whatever level of information the client wants, it is imperative that the practitioner makes the client aware of the seriousness of the situation, and the implications where irregularities have been discovered.

11.93 Some clients may try to bury their head in the sand and ignore the consequences of their actions. The practitioner should ensure that his client is not in the dark about the final outcome. The adviser is not doing the client, or himself, any favours in withholding details of the case until presenting the officer's settlement proposal, particularly where the amounts sought are substantial. This can only create difficulties for the practitioner, both in settling the case with the officer and tarnishing the relationship with the client.

11.94 The client should be kept fully informed during the progress of the investigation, and made aware of his options, if any, at a particular stage of the case. Some clients will want to fight all the way, and may seek their 'day in court'; others will take a commercial view and want the investigation concluded as soon as possible, almost regardless of cost. The practitioner needs to deal with both extremes, and every position in between, but must act in accordance with his client's instructions.

11.95 Much of the advice on handling clients is common sense, and good case management. Dealing with the client should extend to billing arrangements. Although the client may normally receive one bill a year, following preparation of the accounts, it is recommended that practitioners bill monthly during an investigation. Time spent in dealing with the officer's enquiries can be substantial. There is a better prospect of recovery where monthly bills are issued, rather than one large bill issued at the end of a lengthy investigation.

11.96 *Settlement negotiations*

11.96 The effect of an investigation on a client should not be underestimated. Even with the practitioner acting as a buffer between the client and the officer, the strain can be immense. There will be a tremendous pressure on the client's business and personal affairs. The practitioner should watch for signs that the stress is taking its toll on the client.

11.97 The penalty reduction and mitigation processes should be explained to the client at the start of the enquiry. The practitioner should highlight the arguments that can be used to reduce the penalty. He should also mention any areas of weakness that the officer will use to argue for a higher penalty. The client may come up with further arguments, and should be encouraged to do so.

11.98 Handling the client during an investigation can be as demanding as the negotiations with the officer. With thorough preparation, a good understanding of the relative strengths and weaknesses of the client's case, and an appreciation of the officer's position, the practitioner will be best placed to negotiate the obstacles in his way during the investigation and achieve a successful conclusion.

KEY POINTS

11.99 The following key points are intended as a guide for the practitioner entering negotiations with HMRC:

1. Start the groundwork early and consider whether you are the best person to negotiate (or even to be conducting the investigation), or whether you should bring in a specialist.
2. Objectively assess the strengths and weaknesses of the client's position (and also HMRC's).
3. Consider the likely end position.
4. Everything is, potentially, negotiable.
5. Minimise the additions in the year under enquiry.
6. Can the number of years for which additions are sought be restricted?
7. How can the penalty be reduced, or mitigated (for periods covered by the 'old' rules)?
   - Consider the client's behaviour.
   - Is there a reasonable excuse, etc?
8. Keep the client informed.
9. Consider the overall settlement package (including the repayment period). Can it be improved?
10. What concessions will be given to the officer, if necessary?

Chapter 12

Alternative Dispute Resolution

Talia Greenbaum
LLB (Hons) FCA CEDR Accredited Mediator; Senior Manager BDO LLP

SIGNPOSTS

- **Alternative Dispute Resolution** – This is well recognised in the commercial field and is increasingly recognised as an effective procedure for resolving disputes. The other option is usually litigation. See **12.1–12.5** for background on why ADR is necessary and increasingly important.

- **Mediation** – The chosen form of ADR. Mediation is often misunderstood as meaning a simple compromise or 'horse trade'. See **12.6–12.9** for a definition and myth buster, also **12.10–12.13** for some ADR highlights and statistics to date.

- **Litigation and Settlement Strategy** – Sets out the principles within which HMRC handles all tax disputes which are not being litigated and are therefore under civil law procedures. The LSS covers most of HMRC's compliance activity, see **12.14–12.22** to understand how and when ADR should be used in the context of LSS. For the types of cases which are suitable for ADR see **12.23–12.24**.

- **Application process** – How to apply for ADR and for tips of the application form see **12.25–12.27**.

- **Guiding principles for a Mediation Day** – There are certain principles which apply to all tax mediations, regardless of the type of dispute or the taxpayer. These include the 'without prejudice' rule, full disclosure, confidentiality, flexibility, decision makers and costs. (see **12.28–12.34**)

- **Structure of the Mediation Day** – The day is split into four distinct phases which are explained in **12.35–12.40**.

12.1 *Alternative Dispute Resolution*

> - **Mediation techniques** – These include relationship building and managing the process, and can be useful in general HMRC meetings as well as formal mediation processes (see **12.41–12.44**).
> - **Conclusion** – see **12.45–12.47** for recent ADR success rates and an idea of the future of ADR in tax disputes.

INTRODUCTION

12.1 This chapter explains how HMRC is developing mediation as a way of settling a tax dispute. It covers what advisers and their clients can expect when they apply to mediate a case with HMRC and also gives some important practical guidance on suitable cases for mediation and how to maximise the benefit of a mediation day.

ADR has been part of normal business at HMRC for about five years and the number of ADR cases is increasing at an accelerated rate. Any practitioner would be wise to consider this method if they have long-running enquiries or investigations, typically those running over twelve months.

HMRC'S ADR PROCEDURE

12.2 Alternative Dispute Resolution (ADR) is available to facilitate a mediated settlement with HMRC and is open to all taxpayers, including individuals, small businesses, trusts, estates and large corporates. It covers all direct and indirect taxes.

Background

12.3 The background is quite straightforward in that an alternative to taking cases to Tribunal is desperately needed. This is largely due to the backlog of cases listed for the First-tier Tribunal, which HMRC's Annual Report and Accounts state is nearly 27,000 as at 2016/17, which is almost triple the cases awaiting tribunal five years ago. HMRC estimates that it takes an average of 18 months just to get to a hearing date. With pressure from the Treasury to collect tax, unresolved disputes are locking up billions of pounds in uncollected tax. ADR is seen as part of the answer to both raise tax revenues and reduce the backlog of listed cases for Tribunal, but it can also benefit taxpayers and their advisers.

It may sound advantageous to have a tax bill that is not yet paid, but HMRC certainly does not think so and this led to the development of accelerated payment notices (see **CHAPTER 8**). However, concerned taxpayers will often keep funds in reserve for tax in dispute so there is no real cash flow advantage. The late payment interest will also mount up during a dispute and many people want certainty about their debts and available capital. The ADR process can speed up a tax resolution and is therefore welcomed by many taxpayers, as well as the tax authority.

12.4 ADR can help to manage the psychological cost of being in dispute with HMRC, and this should never be underestimated. Most taxpayers find a tax enquiry is stressful and distracting. As in divorce cases, an aggressive or uncooperative attitude will often make the dispute harder to resolve as time passes. Once the dispute reaches a time period of over one year there are often entrenched positions and a gradual slide towards litigation. Mistrust of the other side builds and communication will become increasingly difficult the longer the case continues. Mounting professional costs will also add to the pressure of a long-running dispute with HMRC. It is for this reason that most professional fee insurers welcome ADR as an alternative to expensive litigation.

12.5 The ADR route is voluntary and non-statutory so any party can withdraw at any point with no negative implications, making ADR a potentially risk-free strategy if well managed. The nature of the mediation process itself is less confrontational than conventional tax dispute resolution, such as bringing a case to the Tribunal. HMRC's objective for ADR is generally to reach a cost-effective settlement, although as we will see below, this must be within the boundaries of the litigation and settlement strategy.

For many private clients, trustees and executors, the real attraction of ADR is that the process is completely confidential, and all discussions will be on a 'without prejudice' basis (these principles are explored below in more detail). In contrast, for all cases that go to Tax Tribunal the decisions are published in the public domain, which can often lead to unwanted publicity or breaches of privacy.

WHAT IS ADR?

12.6 ADR, in the context of tax disputes, is currently only mediation. HMRC worked closely with the Centre for Effective Dispute Resolution (see www.cedr.com) to develop mediation for tax disputes. It is therefore helpful to refer to the CEDR definition of what the process means:

> 'Mediation is a flexible process conducted confidentially in which a neutral person actively assists parties in working toward a negotiated agreement of a dispute or difference with the parties in ultimate control of the decision to settle and the terms of resolution.'

12.7 Alternative Dispute Resolution

The objective of mediation is to reach a settlement which is owned by the parties, and which is practical and sustainable. Any agreement which is reached in principle is then recorded in a settlement agreement; with HMRC this is usually a contract settlement to close an open enquiry. For settlements were the tax at stake is over £5 million and the decision could have a far-reaching impact on HMRC policy, any settlement proposal may be required to go through the Governance panel before it can be formally accepted by HMRC.

12.7 HMRC will offer to provide a facilitator for the ADR process without charge. This provides taxpayers with the option of having someone who has not been involved in the dispute to work with the two parties. The independence of the facilitator or mediator is a point that HMRC is keen to emphasise; although many practitioners may be skeptical of the independence of the HMRC mediator, this will be borne out by experience.

The person leading the mediation will act as a neutral third party mediator. They do not take responsibility for the outcome of the dispute: the decision making remains with the two parties. However, the mediator or facilitator will work with both sides to explore ways of resolving the dispute through meetings and telephone conversations. They will help the parties to focus on the areas that need to be resolved and, if required, will help re-establish dialogue. In some cases, HMRC and the taxpayer may both agree to jointly pay for a professional independent mediator, for example, from CEDR or another professional firm.

12.8 Unlike the appeals process, a taxpayer can request ADR at any point during the enquiry process provided that the dispute is sufficiently mature ie, the taxpayer has provided the relevant facts and the areas of dispute are identified. ADR can therefore take place before a formal assessment has been issued and a decision is made by HMRC.

It is important for a taxpayer to understand that if a formal assessment has been issued and final decision made by HMRC, they must continue with an appeal or ask for an internal review as well as asking for ADR, because the ADR process is outside of statute and a taxpayer should preserve his legal rights.

Even if a case is not closed via mediation, most parties will find the work and time involved is beneficial as preparation for a Tribunal hearing.

12.9 Mediation is often misunderstood, so it is important to remember and explain to taxpayers *what it is not*. Mediation is not:

- adversarial;
- arbitration;
- a bar to litigation (a listing for the Tribunal can run in parallel);

- a sign of weakness;
- compromising.

Learning from the ADR feedback to date

12.10 HMRC ran a two-year pilot of ADR before it became a permanent offering in 2013. Since then ADR has been 'business as usual' at HMRC. The view of tax practitioners who have used ADR is that, 'carried out properly, ADR has a valuable role to play in dispute resolution involving tax matters'.

The latest HMRC statistics demonstrate that ADR uptake continues to grow with the number of applications in 2017/18 about 2.5 times the level of 2015/16. HMRC consider that the increase in applications is a consequence of them offering ADR to a wider group of taxpayers. In 2017/18 they began trialling ADR in disputes where there were binary, multiple and complex issues. In these cases, taxpayers were offered the opportunity to explore and explain facts to a greater extent than was previously available.

The statistics also show is that the vast majority of applications are accepted into ADR. In the last couple of years there has been a cultural shift within HMRC whereby the default position is now that cases should be accepted into ADR unless there is a specific reason why ADR is not appropriate. Many of the cases rejected for ADR in 2015/16 were rejected either because there was no 'live' dispute (ie no appeal had been made), or the case was stayed behind a lead case or the dispute related to a policy 'red line' matter.

The speed in which HMRC deals with applications is also encouraging with 92% of applications turned around within the 30-day target. The most interesting statistic for taxpayers with long-running disputes is that 85% of cases are closed within 120 days. For cases that have been open in excess of 550 days this is a significant benefit. Feedback supports the statistics and indicate that ADR invariably adds value to cases that have been ongoing for at least 18 months. Whilst ADR doesn't guarantee resolution, it can certainly turbo charge the process.

HMRC statistics for SMEi ADRs show that new evidence or education of the taxpayer or the HMRC decision maker was the key to mediating a settlement in 80% of cases. However, 20% of cases were resolved simply because both sides started communicating again. It is also noted that trust and estate disputes with HMRC can be mediated using the SME and individual route.

12.11 Whilst feedback from both HMRC and taxpayers alike has been very positive, it is important to remember that ADR in tax is still in its relative

12.12 *Alternative Dispute Resolution*

infancy. In order to build on this strong base and continue to grow in relevance and application, HMRC are seeking to learn from the common themes emerging post completion of ADR days.

The following are a summary of the key issues arising:

- Lack of communication in respect of policy 'red lines' in advance of the day. Unwillingness or inability to consider alternative interpretations in these instances.
- Correct identification of the real 'decision maker' in advance of the ADR day. Ensuring that they attend in person on the day or as a minimum on the phone.
- Lack of preparation on the part of the HMRC case worker or indeed the taxpayer or their advisor.
- HMRC's governance position not made clear to the taxpayer or their advisors in advance so that it becomes apparent only on the day itself that there is an additional step that needs to be taken on HMRC's side before settlement can be concluded.

An awareness of the common ADR pit-falls can help taxpayers and their advisors avoid encountering similar hurdles in the future.

12.12 The latest statistics indicate that ADR is used far less frequently in large and complex disputes. The lessons learnt in respect of these type of cases is that they lend themselves more to facilitated discussions rather than one day mediations.

Looking beyond the statistics the more general feedback suggests that, in some tax disputes, simply requesting ADR appears to have motivated the parties to resolve the dispute themselves, without intervention from a mediator.

12.13 Feedback from taxpayers taking part in ADR showed that doubts expressed about the neutrality of facilitators recruited from within HMRC proved unfounded. The general experience was that facilitators are experienced and senior HMRC personnel who tend to have a refreshingly pragmatic approach.

Despite the findings above, both HMRC mediators and taxpayers have indicated that dual mediation can be more effective in more complex mediations. The concept of 'two heads are better than one' is particularly relevant in the context of the mediator role on an ADR day which requires both skill and stamina.

The ADR process itself is a free service provided by HMRC, so paying for a second mediator may be an option that taxpayers are prepared to consider, especially where the tax at stake is, say, in excess of £50,000–£100,000.

Preparing for a mediation day in practice should still be cheaper than preparing for a court case.

HOW DOES ADR FIT INTO THE LITIGATION AND SETTLEMENT STRATEGY?

12.14 In order to understand what is possible via mediation, it is important to appreciate the framework within which HMRC must operate during the ADR process. An understanding of HMRC's litigation and settlement strategy (LSS) is crucial. The Compliance Handbook now includes a chapter on the LSS effectively integrating the existing LSS commentary into the HMRC guidance (see www.hmrc.gov.uk/manuals/chmanual/CH40000.htm).

The principles used in the ADR process and in reaching any dispute resolution are enshrined in LSS. A full reading and understanding of LSS and the latest refresh published in 2017 would be a useful grounding before starting an ADR process; see the full LSS and commentary at www.hmrc.gov.uk/practitioners/lss-guidance-final.pdf.

The LSS sets out the basis on which HMRC will reach agreement in a tax dispute and emphasises the benefits of a collaborative approach to reaching a resolution.

12.15 Set out below are the key paragraphs of the LSS, which form the basis of mediation as developed and operated by HMRC.

ADR should help to articulate the points in dispute in a productive manner as set out in para 9:

'HMRC will seek, wherever possible, to handle disputes non-confrontationally and by working collaboratively with the customer wherever possible. In the majority of cases, this is likely to be the most effective and efficient approach.

- A collaborative approach requires all parties to be open, transparent, and focused on resolving the dispute.
- Working non-confrontationally can offer benefits in terms of effective and efficient dispute resolution in all civil cases.
- HMRC will foster a non-confrontational approach with the customer, but will not be deterred from efficient and effective dispute resolution by other means if collaboration is not forthcoming.
- HMRC will seek to articulate clearly points in dispute and timescales for reaching key decisions will be agreed and adhered to wherever possible.'

12.16 *Alternative Dispute Resolution*

12.16 ADR is a way of getting both parties in a dispute to discuss key facts which may have been lost, misunderstood or not explained in correspondence; this is set out in para 11:

> 'In any dispute, HMRC will seek to establish and understand the relevant facts as quickly and efficiently as possible.
>
> - A non-confrontational approach is likely to help identify and establish relevant facts. For example, HMRC will aim early on to articulate the basis of its enquiries in terms of tax risks. Wherever possible, HMRC will also seek to clarify and confirm its understanding of the relevant facts with the customer.
>
> - Where necessary HMRC will make use of its statutory information powers in order to obtain the relevant facts and documents quickly and efficiently.'

12.17 Specialist advice may have been sought by both parties in a complex and technical tax dispute, although it may be unclear who advised and what the advice was. For example, when corresponding with an inspector during an enquiry, it is not always clear if the HMRC policy leader is giving specialist advice 'behind the scenes'. Likewise, if a taxpayer sought tax counsel's opinion then both technical specialists could meet and share their views through ADR. This is set out in para 12 of the LSS:

> 'In complex cases, once sufficient facts have been established, taking early specialist advice, and ensuring that advice remains current, can bring important efficiency savings. However no single piece of advice is necessarily decisive in determining HMRC's position.'

12.18 The flexible nature of a mediation day allows time for the sharing and testing of views and arguments. After many months or years of correspondence, views are often entrenched and therefore an open discussion can help to see the merits, or otherwise, of each point. This is set out in para 13 of the LSS:

> 'HMRC will seek to work with the customer to understand fully the relevant facts and law, sharing and testing HMRC's own arguments, and fully understanding and testing the customer's arguments, before reaching a considered view on the strength of its case. HMRC will ensure that respective arguments are fully shared. Only exceptionally would HMRC consider the exchange of copies of counsel's or other legal opinions, as opposed to the substance of the arguments supported by such opinions. HMRC would not normally expect legal professional privilege to be waived.'

12.19 It is often the case that one side is uncertain on whether the other side is simply being difficult and 'sticking to their guns' or it actually is a policy issue and must be decided by a judge in Tribunal or the further courts. An ADR application is one way of testing if an issue is 'all or nothing' as referenced in para 14 of the LSS:

'HMRC will always consider whether something that initially appears to be an "all or nothing" issue is in reality "all or nothing" or is a case where there is a range of possible figures for tax due.'

12.20 Paragraph 17 of the LSS encourages settlement by resolution where there is a range of possible tax figures, and this clearly leans towards the use of mediation. It is also helpful if the case is not going to set a precedent for other taxpayers but is an isolated issue, the legislation has since changed or there is a unique set of facts.

'Tax disputes may be resolved either by agreement or through litigation. Where there is a range of possible figures for tax due, the terms on which HMRC will settle by agreement will also take into account which outcome secures the right tax most efficiently. This means:

- in considering how to secure the right tax most efficiently, HMRC's objective of securing the best practicable return for the Exchequer will have regard to future as well as immediate revenue flows, costs and the deterrent effect on customer non-compliance.

- in considering settlement terms for one dispute, HMRC will take account of the potential read across to other open or prospective disputes as well as the impact which settling the dispute could have in releasing HMRC resources to work on other disputes.

- in order to ensure that overall current and future revenue flows and HMRC costs are not prejudiced, the terms on which disputes are resolved will take into account their likely impact on customer behaviour both generally and in relation to the customer concerned, including any question of avoidance, evasion, or a failure to take reasonable care.

- in most cases, resolution by agreement is likely to offer the most effective and efficient outcome. However, HMRC will not compromise on its view of the law to secure agreement, and in that context there will be cases where litigation offers the most effective and efficient means of resolving disputes. In such circumstances, HMRC will seek to reach resolution of the dispute by litigation in an efficient manner.

- where there is a range of possible figures for tax due, HMRC will not settle by agreement for an amount which is less than it would reasonably expect to obtain from litigation.'

12.21 *Alternative Dispute Resolution*

12.21 The LSS expressly mentions ADR and the fact that it is not about 'doing a deal with HMRC'. Collaborative litigation and ADR are both set out in paras 16 and 19 of LSS. Paragraph 16 says:

'Tax disputes must, in all cases, be resolved in accordance with the law. This means:

- HMRC will not usually persist with a tax dispute unless it potentially secures the best practicable return for the Exchequer and HMRC has a case, which it believes would be successful in litigation.

- HMRC must be satisfied that both the substance of any decision leading to resolution of the dispute and the way that resolution is put into effect are fully in accordance with the law.

- where there is more than one dispute between a customer and HMRC, each dispute must be considered and resolved on its own merits, not as part of any overall "package". As a matter of process, however, it may be that a number of disputes will be resolved at the same time (each on their own merits), for example as part of a process of bringing a customer's tax affairs up to date.

- in certain cases Alternative Dispute Resolution can help the resolution of disputes either by facilitating agreement between the parties or by helping the parties to prepare for litigation.'

Paragraph 19 reads:

'A decision to litigate (whether it relates to an "all or nothing" dispute) does not mean that HMRC will stop taking steps to ensure an efficient and effective resolution to the dispute.

- A decision to litigate should be implemented expeditiously. Where possible, litigation should conducted collaboratively as it may reduce the costs or uncertainty of litigation for both parties.

- HMRC will continue to be open to considering the impact of any new information and technical analysis which may be put forward by the customer.'

12.22 Therefore, the LSS puts a responsibility on HMRC to resolve all issues in a non-confrontational and collaborative way *where possible*. The LSS requires that 'all disputes should be dealt with on their own merits and 'package' deals can never be an appropriate basis of settlement'. It also states: 'It is always appropriate to have regard for materiality.' The point here is that every disputed issue will need to be resolved (unless it is agreed to be not material) so there are no areas that can be 'glossed over'. Although package deals cannot be done, conceding on certain points in the spirit of cooperation can help progress towards an overall settlement.

Alternative Dispute Resolution **12.24**

The Code of Governance also applies to ADR if certain thresholds are met. HMRC's Tax Assurance Commissioner is responsible for seeing that tax disputes are resolved efficiently and on a basis that determines the correct tax in accordance with the LSS. The Tax Assurance Commissioner has no role in the tax affairs of specific taxpayers and no line management responsibility for caseworkers. For further guidance on when ADR cases will be impacted by governance procedures please refer to https://www.gov.uk/government/publications/resolving-tax-disputes

SUITABLE CASES

12.23 One of the most important tasks for a practitioner is identifying when a case is suitable for the ADR process. From the pilot and experience to date, a case is ripe for ADR where:

- there is some uncertainty over the facts or you suspect that HMRC has not fully considered or understood the information (eg disputes over valuations);
- there is scope to explore potential alternative technical interpretations;
- there is a lack of understanding and/or articulation of the parties' respective technical interpretation of tax law;
- the dispute has a range of possible outcomes as there is limited factual information (eg because very old records are not available) and therefore the outcome may turn on oral evidence from a credible witness (this may be the taxpayer voluntarily talking to HMRC on a mediation day);
- positions are entrenched and relationships are strained, so applying for ADR may be a way to start to work collaboratively;
- you need to know why HMRC has not agreed evidence that you have provided and why it wants to use other evidence.

12.24 ADR is unlikely to be successful in cases where:

- the case is listed for a Tribunal and the hearing is soon (eg where HMRC has already spent time and money on the preparatory work and the documents are submitted to court);
- HMRC wants to establish a legal precedent on the issue in accordance with LSS, eg a marketed avoidance scheme or a previously untested point of tax law;
- the situation concerns a point of HMRC policy and HMRC would need to change its usual view or practice during mediation;
- HMRC thinks the taxpayer is dishonest or lacks credibility and wants the evidence cross-examined in Tribunal by a judge.

12.25 *Alternative Dispute Resolution*

HMRC has stated that ADR is not appropriate for disputes about the following:

- tax payments, ie debt collection disputes;
- fixed penalties on the grounds of reasonable excuse;
- tax credits;
- PAYE coding notices;
- HMRC delays in using information;
- cases being dealt with by HMRC's criminal investigators;
- default surcharges.

HOW TO ASK FOR ADR

12.25 Larger businesses have either a customer relationship manager (CRM) or customer coordinator (CC) at HMRC. This improves communication but disputes can still become entrenched. CRMs and CCs are trained to help 'resolve issues in real time' with other HMRC officers. They may use dispute resolution techniques and processes outside a formal ADR, but they are not an independent mediator. They are encouraged to promote the use of ADR and may well suggest it as a way of speeding up resolution of a dispute. Likewise, for a wealthy individual who is dealt with by the High Net Worth Individual or Affluent Unit, their CRM may suggest the ADR process is used.

Where a CC or CRM is in place then they should be contacted to discuss why ADR is appropriate to resolve their dispute. If a taxpayer is dealt with by the Large Business Service then it is this unit within HMRC that will handle the ADR application.

12.26 For SMEs or personal taxpayers who do not have a CRM then there is an online form to apply for ADR to HMRC (see https://www.gov.uk/guidance/tax-disputes-alternative-dispute-resolution-adr#how-to-ask-for-adr). A tax agent can do this on behalf of the taxpayer.

HMRC aims to let taxpayers know within 30 days of applying if ADR is suitable for resolving their dispute. There is no right of appeal against a decision by HMRC not to allow the case to use ADR. This, of course, is separate from the statutory right to appeal against a decision such as closure notice, assessment or determination.

Also there is no restriction on applying for ADR again if the reason for the rejection is because the case was not at the right stage. However, clearly if the case is refused ADR because it is a 'red line' policy issue at HMRC that needs to be decided by the Tribunal then there is no point in applying again.

12.27 Tips for applying for ADR include the following:

- list all the disputed issues that you would like a mediation settlement to include;
- be concise, with bullet points;
- do not use it to moan about the history of the enquiry or dispute;
- focus on why mediation may help bring a resolution;
- think about the dispute within the context of LSS;
- highlight any individuals who should be present on the mediation day;
- ensure all relevant information has already been provided.

If the dispute proceeds into ADR then practitioners should ensure their client engagement letter covers the work of mediation.

GUIDING PRINCIPLES AND MEDIATION AGREEMENT

12.28 Before being involved in a mediation day, it is important to appreciate the guiding principles which will apply on the day as set out below. This is also documented between the two parties using a Mediation Agreement (see template at **12.49**).

The 'without prejudice' rule

12.29 The without prejudice rule is frequently used in informal dispute resolution, so meetings or correspondence with HMRC can take place where agents would like to explore possible solutions without being bound by the comments made. The principle applies to all communications passing between the parties on a mediation day. Therefore, these communications cannot be relied on or referred to in a subsequent court hearing if the mediation is unsuccessful. The without prejudice rule is usually stated in the mediation agreement and expressly discussed by the mediator at the start of the mediation day. The Tribunal will uphold this principle and prevent a party from referring to any part of the discussions that took place during the mediation.

The without prejudice rule will cover any oral or written communications made specifically for the purposes of the tax settlement, such as position statements,

12.30 *Alternative Dispute Resolution*

correspondence about the mediation, offers or concessions whether made before, during or after the mediation. It will also cover all the discussions to explore potential settlements and communications for the purposes of agreeing the final tax due and penalty charges.

Full disclosure

12.30 The parties do not have to disclose anything if they do not wish to do so in an ADR process. However, there may be serious consequences of not disclosing documents or facts that are relevant to the tax position.

The mindset for a mediation day should be a 'cards on the table' approach. If the document would have to be disclosed in a Tribunal hearing then it is best to disclose it in the mediation, although it is expected that most documents will already have been shared between both parties in a long-running enquiry. Failure to disclose crucial documents that have a major effect on the case can give rise to a risk of any settlement being overturned in the future.

Most full enquiries or serious investigations will require the taxpayer to sign a certificate of full disclosure at the end of the process, and this will still be the case if mediation is used. Therefore, both parties should have full disclosure as their guiding principle in their mediation discussions.

Flexibility

12.31 Unlike almost every other process that engages a taxpayer and HMRC, a mediation day is flexible and has a notable absence of procedures, guidelines and rules. This is deliberate and enables the mediator to run the day to suit both parties and the nature of their dispute.

For example, some mediation days will be conducted by each party sitting in separate rooms for the majority of the time because it is adversarial. On other mediation days, the parties may spend most of their time together in one room in open discussion about the issues and possible solutions.

Confidentiality

12.32 This is another principle which the mediator will expressly discuss at the opening meeting on a mediation day. HMRC is required to maintain customer confidentiality throughout the entire enquiry process. However, once a matter proceeds to a hearing before the tax Tribunal, the dispute is no longer confidential as the hearing will normally be open to the public and the decision will be published in the public domain. With ADR, the application,

Alternative Dispute Resolution **12.34**

the mediation process itself and the terms of any agreement reached between the parties is entirely confidential.

Clearly, confidentiality is important to create the right atmosphere for open discussions on a mediation day, and this may also tie in with matters concerning legal professional privilege.

Standard confidentiality clauses will be included in the HMRC memorandum of understanding or mediation agreement signed by both parties at the start of the process. However, where a dispute is not fully resolved through mediation, it is possible that certain information provided via mediation could be beneficial at a subsequent Tribunal hearing (eg, where parties narrow down points in dispute). In such circumstances, parties should agree that particular information could be disclosed and used in court proceedings. Where the ADR process is being conducted through an HMRC facilitator, they will need to adhere to confidentiality between the two sides unless express permission is granted to share information with the other party.

The exception to the confidentiality rule is in instances where the taxpayer tells the mediator of tax fraud but refuses to disclosure this to HMRC. In these cases, the HMRC mediator has an obligation as a civil servant to insist that the appropriate disclosure is made by the taxpayer. The obligation to report would also apply in the unlikely event that the mediator had a suspicion of money laundering offences.

Key decision makers

12.33 The presence of the key decision makers on a mediation day is essential for success. As such the taxpayer should be encouraged to be there in person or, for example, the Chief Executive or Finance Director in a company dispute. Likewise, from HMRC, it is expected that the Team Leader and policy adviser will also be physically present for the mediation day, or at least available by telephone. If part of the dispute is, say, a valuations issue then the valuations experts from both sides should attend the mediation day.

Otherwise, the risk is that the dispute cannot be agreed because the decision makers are not available and that could waste time, or worse, jeopardise a mediation day.

Costs

12.34 For HMRC and the taxpayer, there are additional costs associated with every type of dispute resolution in which HMRC may engage. The parties will normally bear their own costs of a mediation day however HMRC

12.35 *Alternative Dispute Resolution*

do offer a neutral HMRC mediator at no additional cost to the taxpayer. It is also worth noting that the financial cost of mediation (such as professional representation on the day) will not be recoverable from HMRC should the taxpayer ultimately succeed before the Tax Tribunal.

THE MEDIATION DAY

12.35 It is the mediator's role to facilitate discussion and negotiations between the taxpayer and HMRC to help them arrive at their own solution. The mediator will try to be encouraging, flexible and forward thinking.

The mediation day can be split into four distinct phases.

Opening phase

12.36 This will be at the start of the day with formal introductions and everyone sitting in one room. The mediator will introduce his or her self, explain the mediator role and outline the mediation process. They will also emphasise the guiding principles such as 'without prejudice' and confidentiality, as described above.

Each party is likely to be asked to make a brief opening statement. The taxpayer can ask their agent to do this for them if they prefer not to speak at this early stage. The statement should explain what they consider the disputed issues to be and what they see as the objectives for the day. It is also an opportunity for either party to ask questions of the mediator or clarify any practical matters.

Exploration phase

12.37 The purpose of the exploration phase is for the mediator to understand the parties' needs and to help air the history of the dispute. The mediator will then try to build a focus on the future and aiming for a settlement. The initial private meetings will clearly be to build rapport and iron out any uncertainties or scepticism about the mediation process. There will also be time to understand what lies beneath the disputed issues and explore each party's perception of the case. Everything that is said in a private room is confidential and the mediator will reiterate this point to each party in their rooms. Therefore, it is likely to include open discussions about the strengths and weaknesses of different positions.

Parties should start to explore options for settlement but possibly not discuss actual tax figures during this phase.

Bargaining phase

12.38 This phase is likely to start after lunch, so early afternoon, on a typical mediation day. Each party will start to identify likely settlement factors and begin work on specific terms of the settlement. The mediator may use a technique called 'reality testing', where appropriate, to push a party to consider the implications of not settling and what the alternatives (such as Tribunal) may mean for them.

Bargaining may happen through the mediator moving between the private rooms or it may be a more open negotiation with both sides in one room.

Concluding phase

12.39 It will often be appropriate to bring the parties together to conclude the mediation. This phase will include refining and finalising the settlement terms and ensuring all matters in the dispute are covered.

For a tax settlement, it will be important to agree the tax figures first, but then not forget the implications of late payment interest. There may also be time to negotiate penalties and time to pay towards the end of the day, if means or cash flow is a problem for the taxpayer.

From a practical point of view, it is helpful to have someone on both sides with a computer to type up a draft settlement agreement on the mediation day. Clearly, it is also important to agree what happens next and the time frame. The final settlement agreement should follow in a few weeks if all the disputed issues are agreed.

12.40 Always remember to think through the 'little things' on a mediation day such as the logistics and practicalities. Together these factors can make a difference to both parties and affect the success of the day. These may include:

- rooms with natural daylight;
- introducing each person and their role;
- the room layout and where each person will sit;
- the timings of the day to allow for travel and arrivals;
- regular 'comfort breaks';
- adequate food and drink to keep everyone refreshed on a long mediation day;
- soundproof rooms to ensure conversations are confidential;

12.40 *Alternative Dispute Resolution*

- provision is made to ensure the taxpayer fully understands what is happening, eg if there is a language barrier or lack of understanding of tax technical points.

Case Study: a private client mediation day

A district enquiry was opened into the tax affairs of an unrepresented taxpayer on the disposal of a residential property in London that the taxpayer did not include on her return (she considered that it was her main residence and, therefore, that no capital gains tax was due).

Following initial submission, HMRC challenged a number of the factual positions included in the capital gains computation. This led to protracted correspondence and eventual stalemate. The factors in dispute included:

- how much principal private residence and lettings relief was available;
- the total base cost of the property (and valuation of property transfers);
- the amount of enhancement expenditure (no invoices were retained).

Two and half years later, HMRC was seeking tax of £560,000 and a 30% penalty, as opposed to the £260,000 (with no penalty) that her advisors argued was due. Her advisors applied to resolve matters through the ADR pilot programme. HMRC agreed and the mediation took place one month after the application.

On the day, the morning progressed relatively slowly, with both parties repeating well-worn arguments. But, as time went on, it became apparent that the previously entrenched positions of both parties were open to significant movement. The first breakthrough was on the property valuation: a relatively quick solution was accepted, with both parties agreeing to meet at about halfway following discussions with the District Valuer who attended the mediation. On the other disputed points, it was again obvious that, in the absence of any further information, reasonable assumptions would have to be accepted. Once HMRC overcame this psychological hurdle, work centred on giving credence to assumptions through the use of general data available on the internet such as tracking house price movements and average cost data.

The penalty was negotiated on the mediation day and it was agreed that the individual should get full mitigation and a zero penalty. With all the issues resolved, the draft settlement agreement that both parties signed showed a final figure of £240,000 tax due. The individual felt this was an excellent resolution to a costly and time-consuming enquiry for HMRC. Likewise, HMRC was paid long overdue tax, plus late payment interest which had been outstanding for nearly four years.

MEDIATION TECHNIQUES

12.41 So what is it about adding a mediator or facilitator to a long-running dispute that can make a difference? An obvious answer is the skills and techniques that are employed by the mediator, and these will include the following.

Relationship building

12.42 The mediator will spend a lot of time with the individuals on both sides to build rapport and read body language. They will try to convey energy and enthusiasm during the day, especially if the mediation becomes a long day. Clear, confident and non-judgmental communication will also be a priority for the mediator.

Techniques will be used to encourage both parties to talk, such as open questions, reframes, paraphrasing and reflecting back on what is discussed. Parties will be allowed to express emotions and the mediator should take care to balance the input of each party.

Managing the mediation process

12.43 For taxpayers and officers of HMRC who have never been involved in a mediation before, it will be the mediator who sets the tone and pace of the mediation day. It will be important for the mediator to summarise positions and move parties forward through each phase of the mediation, and at the appropriate time. The mediator must encourage the use of private and joint meetings as best for the particular dispute on hand. Sometimes it will mean that the mediator sets tasks for a party or puts certain people together to work on one issue. Keeping notes and managing time will be important, as will the use of visual aids such as a flipchart.

The mediator will work hard to maintain control of the day and ensure the guiding principles outlined above are adhered to; they will also be mindful of any ethical dilemmas that may arise.

Facilitating a workable solution

12.44 In order to reach a settlement in one day, the mediator will help both parties to identify and probe all issues that arise. It will be necessary to explore positions and understand beliefs, needs and priorities. Hypothetical questions are used to expand the possibilities of settlement. The mediator is likely to

12.45 *Alternative Dispute Resolution*

use a range of questions, including understanding, probing and challenging. At times it may be helpful for the mediator to help a party to 'save face' in order to reach a solution.

In the later stages of the day, the mediator will encourage movement when the trust of both parties is established; they may also question each party about the risks and benefits of the proposed settlement. The mediation should achieve a solution that is workable and the mediator may want to check details or review the overall settlement to ensure this is the case. Premature commitment to a solution must be avoided and all practical considerations should be discussed. This is often why a mediation day with several disputed issues is expected to last at least 8 hours, often running to 12 hours.

CONCLUSION

Still a role for the Tax Tribunal?

12.45 Despite the success of ADR, there will continue to be many cases where a point of law or public policy merits a full examination at the Tribunal. However the clear intention is to avoid the Tribunal being swamped by cases where one side or the other is clutching at technical straws to support a weak argument. ADR should result in less dubious case law created simply because the Tribunal is faced with an uncooperative taxpayer or an HMRC officer with a poor arguments. Of course, cases where ADR fails or is abandoned will probably still end up in court.

Practitioners cannot use ADR to break any new boundaries of tax law. But, if you use ADR to get a fresh start with entrenched but relatively straightforward tax disputes, it can be a highly cost-effective tool.

Success and the future

12.46 HMRC employees can now be proactive in considering the use of ADR in cases that appear to be stalling. The ADR team within HMRC are actively working on raising awareness of ADR within HMRC and working systematically to educate all staff. This education program along with increasing ADR experience means that knowledge of the process and mediation techniques is steadily growing within HMRC.

A review of all cases that remain unresolved after twelve months is being undertaken, with case workers being encouraged to consider whether ADR would be relevant and suggest its use to the customer. Therefore, practitioners are wise to do the same and make sure they have a clear understanding of when and how ADR can be used to settle tax disputes with HMRC.

12.47 HMRC are keen to promote ADR as a viable and effective alternative to dispute resolution. In order to help with this objective they have set the following Key Performance Indicators:

- Turn around 90% of applications within 30 days of receipt.
- Settle 75% of cases within 120 days of acceptance.
- Partially or fully resolve 80% of cases.

HMRC have comfortably met all three KPI in 2017/18 with 92% of applications turned around in 30 days, 85% of cases settled with 120 days of acceptance and 82% of cases resolved or partially resolved because of ADR.

12.48 Perhaps the most encouraging message to date is that in a survey of taxpayers and practitioners who have been through ADR, the feedback is overwhelmingly positive with 98% saying they would recommend the process.

In an ideal world, ADR would become obsolete because both sides are handling disputes collaboratively with a view to resolving them rather than winning the argument. Unfortunately, a survey following the ADR day found that approximately 82% of participants said that the dispute would not have settled without ADR. It is therefore clear that in the real world there is a long way to go before ADR is no longer required to help resolve disputes. ADR is still somewhat of a method of 'last resort' but compared to the Tribunal it will often be preferred.

On some occasions, a case is already listed for the Tribunal before ADR is called upon. By then it may be necessary to stay the Tribunal proceedings to allow time for the mediation to take place. Most judges will be accommodating if the reasons for mediation are explained. The Tribunal option will always be there but the use of ADR can save time and costs for both sides. The principles of flexibility, confidentiality and 'without prejudice' also ensure it is a relatively stress-free and amicable process for dispute resolution.

12.49 It is evident that awareness of ADR and an appreciation of the benefits is becoming far more commonplace with both agents/taxpayers and HMRC staff alike. With such positive feedback from those participating in the process and on-going education, it is expected that the rate of ADR applications will continue to increase on a year-by-year basis. Looking to the future it is hoped that the ADR process itself will continue to be refined and expanded as HMRC learn from lessons of the past.

12.50 *Alternative Dispute Resolution*

APPENDIX

Template mediation agreement

12.50 Memorandum of Understanding

HMRC facilitator contact details
Name:
Office address:
Phone number:
Email:
Case reference:

Your contact details	Your adviser's details, if you have one
Name in capital letters	**Name in capital letters**
Address	**Address**
Postcode	Postcode
Daytime phone number	**Daytime phone number**
Email	**Email**
Main contact for Alternative Dispute Resolution	

Alternative Dispute Resolution **12.50**

Declaration and Alternative Dispute Resolution (ADR) agreement

Please read and sign the declaration to confirm that you understand this agreement.

I'm entering into dispute resolution because I want to try to settle this dispute. If I don't engage with the process or work within the terms below, my dispute may be removed from the ADR process.

I understand that the HMRC caseworker will also engage with the process on the same terms as this Memorandum of Understanding. If I feel that they're not engaging with the process I'll raise this with the facilitator.

I'll provide any agreed relevant information to the facilitator within 15 working days of their request unless they say otherwise. If I'm unable to meet this deadline I'll explain this to the facilitator and agree if the deadline may be extended.

If I miss a deadline on more than one occasion I accept that this may lead to my case being removed from the process.

During the ADR process I may need to provide more information, attend a meeting or teleconference. I will ensure that, I, and any representative of mine, will be available within the next 90 days for a meeting or a teleconference. I accept that if I'm unavailable in this time, my case may be removed from the process.

I understand that ADR may not result in an agreement on a particular issue or issues and that my dispute may not be resolved. I also understand that if an agreement is not reached the process should help both myself and HMRC better understand the elements that resulted in this dispute and help us work towards a mutual solution.

I understand that ADR is a confidential process carried out on a 'without prejudice' basis. I also accept that any material tax facts (facts which have the potential to result in significant changes to the tax or penalty position) that are shared with the facilitator or HMRC during the mediation can be referred to in any later formal proceedings if agreement cannot be reached.

I accept that the confidentiality of the ADR process does not extend to evidence of criminality. I also accept that if I make a formal complaint about something happening within the ADR process then the facilitator will be expected to comment on the matter when asked to do so by a complaints reviewing officer.

I understand that the facilitator has responsibility for the ADR process. Responsibility for decisions affecting the tax outcomes lies with the parties to the dispute.

12.50 *Alternative Dispute Resolution*

> If I have new information prior to any meeting or teleconference I will make sure that I tell the caseworker, facilitator or both. If additional information is produced at a meeting that the caseworker is unaware of, the facilitator may suspend the meeting to allow the caseworker to analyse it.
>
> If I feel that these terms need to be altered, I'll discuss and agree this in writing with the facilitator at the beginning of the ADR process.
>
> **Your name in capital letters**
>
> **Name of your adviser in capital letters**
>
> **Signature**
>
> **Signature**
>
> **Date DD MM YYYY**
>
> **Date DD MM YYYY**

Chapter 13

Discovery

Helen Adams BSc (Hons) FCA CTA TEP CEDR Accredited Mediator
Tax Principal, BDO LLP

> **SIGNPOSTS**
>
> - **When is discovery irrelevant?** – Sometimes discovery is simply irrelevant so you don't even need to consider it (see **13.6–13.9**).
>
> - **Discovery enquiries?** – Contrary to common belief, there is no such thing enshrined in legislation. HMRC may use a combination of information powers and discovery assessments to somewhat achieve similar results (see **13.10–13.13**).
>
> - **Discovery overview** – HMRC needs to satisfy several criteria in order to successfully make a discovery and issue an assessment. Here is an overview (see **13.14–13.20**).
>
> - **When does a discovery occur?** – The bar is set low as no new information is required, just a change of view or correction of an oversight, although there are some general principles to bear in mind too (see **13.21–13.27**).
>
> - **Assessment time limits** – The legislation provides strict time limits within which HMRC may issue discovery assessments (see **13.28–13.34**). Different time limits apply in relation to deceased persons' tax affairs (see **13.35–13.37**) and following the proposed extension to time limits for offshore matters and offshore transfers (see **13.38–13.42**).
>
> - **When is a discovery assessment made?** – The date of a discovery assessment is critical when considering whether assessment time limits are met (see **13.43–13.45**).

13.1 *Discovery*

- **Discoveries can become stale** – A delay between the HMRC officer making a discovery and the assessment being issued may invalidate the discovery (see **13.46–13.54**).

- **Discovery in the absence of a tax return** – Discovery assessments are an important power enabling HMRC to charge tax despite a return not being submitted (see **13.55–13.58**).

- **Discovery where a tax return was submitted** – If a person submitted a tax return then HMRC may be prevented from successfully issuing a discovery assessment depending on whether the taxpayer provided sufficient information to preclude discovery, can use the generally prevailing practice test or whether HMRC can demonstrate culpability by the taxpayer or someone acting on their behalf (see **13.59–13.65**).

- **Generally prevailing practice** – If the return was prepared in accordance with generally prevailing practice and the insufficiency is attributable to a mistake in the basis of the tax calculation then HMRC cannot successfully issue a discovery assessment. The difficulty is evidencing that the practice was generally prevailing (see **13.66–13.70**).

- **The careless or deliberate behaviour requirement** – If the under-assessment or excessive claim was caused by careless or deliberate behaviour then HMRC can issue a discovery assessment (see **13.71–13.72**). The insufficiency must be caused by the careless or deliberate behaviour (see **13.73–13.76**) so it is important to understand whether someone was acting on behalf of the taxpayer within the meaning of the legislative test (see **13.77–13.83**). Case law setting out the nature of deliberate (see **13.84–13.92**) and careless (see **13.93–13.100**) behaviour helps advisers assess which category their client's case may fall within. If the taxpayer relied on professional advice which was not obviously wrong then the behaviour requirement may not be met (see **13.101–13.104**).

- **Discovery in the absence of culpable behaviour** – HMRC can issue discovery assessments if insufficient information was available to alert them to the insufficiency, even if HMRC did not open an enquiry (see **13.105–13.108**). This test requires consideration of the skills and abilities of the hypothetical officer (see **13.109–13.113**), the time at which the officer's knowledge is tested (see **13.114–13.115**), the information deemed to be available to the officer (see **13.116–13.120**) and the level of awareness needed (see **13.121–13.128**). Two statements of practice are available too (see **13.129–13.130**).

Discovery **13.1**

- **Presumption of continuity** – HMRC may suggest that errors affect other tax years and assert the presumption of continuity to justify discovery assessments for those years (see **13.131–13.136**).

- **Estimating liabilities in the absence of information** – Where factual information is missing, HMRC will extrapolate the amount to be taxed to make good the insufficiency (see **13.137–13.140**).

- **What format should a discovery assessment take?** – There is no standard format for a discovery assessment and various statutory provisions automatically rectify some errors in any assessment (see **13.141–13.146**).

- **Challenging discovery assessments** – Appeals may be made in writing against discovery assessments within 30 days of the assessment being issued. HMRC cannot unilaterally amend a discovery assessment but more than one assessment can be issued for the same matter. On appeal the Tribunal may uphold, increase or decrease the assessment (see **13.147–13.157**).

- **Burden of proof** – The Tribunal will consider whether the burden of proving points is satisfied on the balance of probabilities. HMRC bears the burden of proving that it made a discovery, that culpable behaviour caused the under-assessment and there was objective non-awareness. The taxpayer must discharge their burden of proof to demonstrate that the prevailing practice defence applies and the presumption of continuity does not apply etc. The taxpayer must show not only that the assessment is excessive but also what amount should be assessed (see **13.158–13.165**).

- **When is tax payable following a discovery assessment?** – Tax is generally payable 30 days after the date of the assessment but it may be postponed if an appeal is made against the assessment (**13.166–13.168**).

- **Consequential claims** – Once a discovery assessment is issued, the taxpayer may make additional consequential claims (see **13.169–13.179**).

- **Key points** – For a list of points in conclusion see **13.180**.

INTRODUCTION

13.1 HMRC uses 'discovery' to enable it to assess tax for periods that are not subject to enquiries under *TMA 1970, ss 9A, 12ZM and 12AC* and

13.2 *Discovery*

FA 1998, Sch 18, para 24. This is possible even where no tax return was submitted and/or where a voluntary disclosure is made. HMRC also uses it to bring other tax years into charge whilst an enquiry is ongoing into one year's tax return. It is one of the most important powers in HMRC's arsenal.

13.2 In essence HMRC can make a discovery where an officer changes his mind or another officer takes a fresh look at the case and decides that there is an under-assessment (*Charlton v Revenue and Customs Comrs* [2012] UKUT 770). It is then up to the taxpayer to decide whether to appeal within the standard time limit.

13.3 This power effectively over-rides the sense of finality generated by the limited time within which HMRC is able to enquire into tax returns. It is therefore subject to various restrictions:

- Assessment time limits.
- The Generally Prevailing Practice restriction.
- Behavioural restriction.
- Available information restriction.

The quantity and quality of disclosure on a tax return may be key but may not be determinative as a result.

13.4 This chapter considers when a discovery is made and the conditions that must be met in order for such assessments to be valid. The chapter refers to some case law available at the time of writing as this is an area of tax law for which Tribunal/Court decisions are plentiful.

13.5 The key for an adviser is to understand when HMRC may issue discovery assessments in order to:

- warn a client when they may occur and the possible effect given the overall conduct of the enquiry;
- consider whether there are grounds to challenge the assessment; or
- consider whether any consequential claims might be possible as a result.

WHEN IS DISCOVERY IRRELEVANT?

13.6 It may seem rather strange to start a chapter on discovery by considering when it is irrelevant but time can be saved by not going on to consider whether the conditions for discovery are met if it is not applicable.

Discovery **13.13**

13.7 Discovery is utterly irrelevant where there is a valid open enquiry into the same tax year for the tax in question. Until the enquiry is closed HMRC has an unlimited amount of time within which to issue a partial or full closure notice to assess any additional tax, unless the Tribunal directs HMRC to issue such a notice within a limited period of time.

13.8 The key question is therefore whether the enquiry is valid. Was it issued within the statutory time limits? Is it the right type of enquiry? Cases such as *Revenue and Customs Commissioners v Cotter* [2013] UKSC 69, [2013] 1 WLR 3514 and/or *R (on the application of) De Silva & Another v Revenue and Customs Commissioners* [2017] UKSC 74 may need to be considered. If the enquiry is invalid then HMRC will need to consider using discovery to assess any tax due.

13.9 Also, the concept of discovery does not apply to all taxes. For example, the legislation on inheritance tax (*IHTA 1984, s 240*) does not include this concept in relation to underpayments of IHT.

DISCOVERY ENQUIRIES

13.10 The power to make a discovery, when considered on its own, is a power to issue an assessment not the power to begin an enquiry or investigation.

13.11 As we will see below, once HMRC believes that the triggers for a discovery are satisfied then the officer will consider issuing a discovery assessment. On receipt of the assessment the taxpayer has two choices: accept the assessment and pay the tax or appeal against the assessment.

13.12 However, taxpayers and advisers may consider that when this power is used in practice in conjunction with HMRC's information powers, inspection powers and/or Codes of Practice for investigations (such as COP8 and COP9), discovery can feel like an enquiry.

13.13 HMRC will consider using its information powers in *FA 2008, Sch 36* (as detailed in **CHAPTER 16**) to obtain information and documentation so it can quantify any additional tax due for years for which there are no open self-assessment enquiries. *FA 2008, Sch 36, para 21* permits this in some circumstances after a return is submitted even if a previous enquiry has been closed or where no enquiry was opened within the statutory time limit. However, HMRC should not use their information powers to seek documents

13.14 *Discovery*

and explanations to establish whether there is an issue – only if they already have reason to suspect there is an under-assessment (*Kevin Betts v Revenue & Customs Comrs* [2013] UKFTT 430 (TC)).

DISCOVERY OVERVIEW

13.14 The legislation in *TMA 1970, s 29(1)* or *FA 1998, Sch 18, paras 41–46* says that an HMRC officer or its board need to discover that one of the three conditions below is met before they can consider making a discovery assessment. The conditions are:

(a) that any tax which ought to have been assessed has not been assessed; or

(b) 'that an assessment to tax is or has become insufficient'; or

(c) 'that any relief which has been given is or has become excessive'.

13.15 Once the above conditions are met, if the taxpayer submitted a tax return, then the legislation only permits HMRC to issue a discovery assessment under *TMA 1970, s 29* or *FA 1998, Sch 18, paras 41–46* where:

- the loss of tax is attributable to deliberate or careless behaviour by or on behalf of the taxpayer; or

- HMRC could not have been expected, on the basis of the information available to it at the relevant time, to be aware of the potential loss of tax;

- unless the return was prepared in accordance with the generally accepted prevailing practice at the time.

For discovery in the absence of a tax return see **13.55–13.58**.

13.16 In all cases the discovery assessment must be issued within the applicable statutory time limits (see **13.28–13.42**).

13.17 The assessment is to be 'in the amount, or further amount, which ought in his or their opinion to be charged in order to make good to the Crown the loss of tax'.

13.18 HMRC's power to issue discovery assessment can be summarised as follows:

Discovery **13.18**

Diagram summarising the steps within TMA 1970, s29

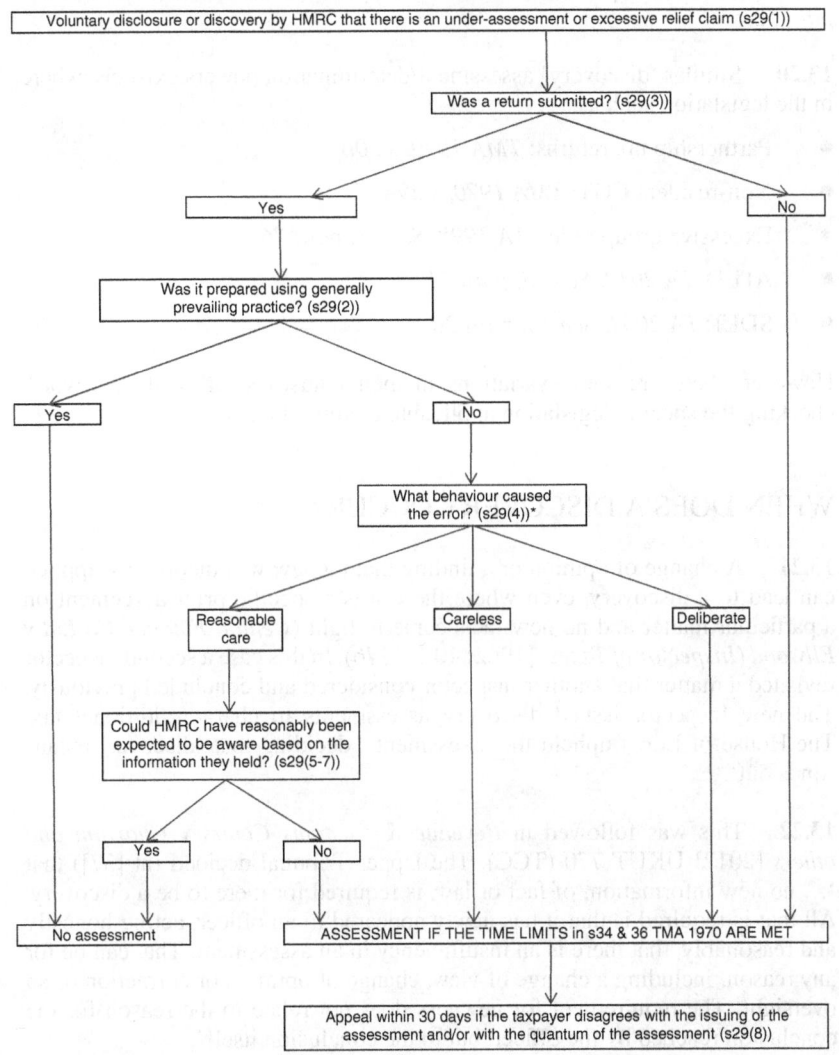

* This refers to behaviour by "the taxpayer or someone acting on his behalf": s29(4)

13.19 *Discovery*

13.19 TMA 1970, s 30 empowers HMRC to recover overpaid tax using *TMA 1970, s 29*. Similar provisions exist for corporation tax at *FA 1998, Sch 18, para 52*.

13.20 Similar 'discovery' assessment/determination powers exist elsewhere in the legislation such as:

- Partnership tax returns: *TMA 1970, s 30B*
- Non-resident CGT: *TMA 1970, s 29A*
- Excessive group relief: *FA 1998, Sch 18, para 76*
- ATED: *FA 2013, Sch 33, para 21*
- SDLT: *FA 2003, Sch 10, para 28*

However, there are some variations in their clauses so it is always worth checking the specific legislation applicable to your client's case.

WHEN DOES A DISCOVERY OCCUR?

13.21 A change of opinion or a finding that the law was incorrectly applied can lead to a discovery, even where there was a specific prior agreement on a particular matter and no new facts came to light (*Cenlon Finance Co Ltd v Ellwood (Inspector of Taxes)* [1962] 40 TC 176). In this case a second inspector revisited a matter that another inspector considered and concluded previously. The new Inspector issued discovery assessments to charge additional tax. The House of Lords upheld the assessments, deciding that 'discover' means 'finds out'.

13.22 This was followed in *Revenue & Customs Comrs v Charlton and others* [2012] UKUT 770 (TCC). The Upper Tribunal decided (at [37]) that '... no new information, of fact or law, is required for there to be a discovery. All that is required is that it has newly appeared to an officer, acting honestly and reasonably, that there is an insufficiency in an assessment. That can be for any reason, including a change of view, change of opinion, or correction of an oversight. The requirement for newness does not relate to the reason for the conclusion reached by the officer, but to the conclusion itself'.

The reference to an 'insufficiency' in the above quote is a reference to one of the three conditions in *TMA 1970, ss 29(1)(a)–(c)* summarised at **13.15** above.

13.23 This sets a relatively low bar for HMRC to surmount as it requires no new information to be identified by the officer – HMRC may therefore hold the information or key document for some considerable amount of time and then make a discovery when the officer currently dealing with the case experiences a 'light bulb' moment.

The light bulb may be set alight by a realisation triggered by the law (or a new interpretation of it) or facts *Cenlon Finance Co Ltd v Ellwood (Inspector of Taxes)* [1962] 40 TC 176.

13.24 However, there can only be one 'light bulb' moment. The Upper Tribunal in *Revenue & Customs Comrs v Raymond Tooth* [2018] UKUT 38 (TCC) confirmed that:

- The same officer can only make the discovery once. Similarly, if two officers independently come to the same conclusion then only the first one makes a discovery.

- However, where two different officers are independently involved and the basis on which they decide to make the discovery is different, they are making different discoveries and both could issue an assessment.

13.25 It is worth bearing mind some additional general principles:

- 'The concept of a "discovery" by an officer involves the application of a subjective test, as to the officer's state of mind, and an objective test as to whether it is open to an officer to have that state of mind' (*Jerome Anderson v Revenue & Customs Comrs* [2018] UKUT 159 (TCC)). Both tests must be satisfied for there to be a discovery within the meaning of *TMA 1970, s 29(1)*.

- 'The exercise of the section 29(1) power is made by a real officer who is required to come to a conclusion about a possible insufficiency based on all the available information at the time when the discovery assessment is made' (*Sanderson v Revenue & Customs Comrs* [2016] EWCA Civ 19).

- In the first instance HMRC needs to consider whether a discovery assessment may be issued i.e. whether there is an insufficiency. At this stage they need not investigate any of the tests referred to in *ss 29(2)* or *(3)* exhaustively (*Hankinson v Revenue & Customs Commissioners* [2011] EWCA Civ 1566)

- The HMRC officer does not need to be certain beyond doubt that there is an insufficiency. 'The statutory condition turns on the situation of which the officer could reasonably have been expected to be aware. Awareness is a matter of perception and of understanding, not of conclusion.' (Moses LJ at [70] in *Revenue & Customs Comrs v Lansdowne Partners Ltd Partnership* [2011] EWCA Civ 1578).

- HMRC is required to exercise best judgement when deciding on the amount of tax to assess. However, it is not obliged to carry out exhaustive investigations (*Van Boeckel v Customs & Excise Comrs* [1981] STC 290).

13.26 *Discovery*

Nevertheless, 'protective' assessments issued by HMRC whilst its investigation is ongoing must also be made to the best of the officer's judgement. The officer must form the opinion and that opinion has to satisfy some objective criteria (*Sanderson v Revenue & Customs Comrs* [2016] EWCA Civ 19). In *William Ritchie & Another v Revenue & Customs Comrs* [2017] UKFTT 449 (TC) the FTT cancelled two of the assessments as they were issued for too little tax and the amounts were wrong based on the information held by HMRC at the time they were issued.

- There is no bar to more than one discovery assessment being made (*Cansick (Murphy's Executor) v Hochstrasser (H M Inspector of Taxes)* 40 TC 151). This was confirmed in *William Ritchie & Another v Revenue & Customs Comrs* [2017] UKFTT 449 (TC) when the FTT decided that HMRC can issue two discovery assessments by reference to the same transaction in the same year as long as the second/subsequent assessments are in addition to the first.

- One discovery assessment can cover multiple sources of income (*TMA 1970, s 30A(2)*). Each source of income or gains being assessed by a discovery assessment must be considered separately when deciding whether the criteria for a discovery assessment is met. One small error cannot be the 'peg' for an assessment on an unrelated, larger tax liability (*Elizabeth Marsh v Revenue & Customs Comrs* [2017] UKFTT 320 (TC)).

- If the assessment is broadly related to the matter that triggered the discovery and the other statutory conditions are met, then the discovery assessment will be upheld (*G Clark v Revenue & Customs Comrs* [2017] UKFTT 392 (TC)).

- It is not necessary for there to be an enquiry into a period (or another period) before a discovery assessment is issued (*Kennerley v Revenue & Customs Comrs* [2007] STC 188).

13.26 Examples of situations in which HMRC may make a discovery may include:

- A taxpayer with lots of high value assets and a luxurious lifestyle who declared only small amounts of income on his tax returns for the last 10 years. It is unclear how he affords the assets or the lifestyle so perhaps he failed to disclose all his taxable income and gains.

- A self assessment enquiry into a company's tax return shows that the company miscategorised capital assets as revenue expenses and failed to disallow charitable donations. The taxpayer admits the situation occurred in previous years too.

- The taxpayer voluntarily discloses that he diverted takings for his UK self employment into an offshore bank account and falsified invoices to

Discovery **13.29**

overstate the business expenses too. Consequently the profits declared on his returns were significantly under-stated.

13.27 As can be seen from the above, the Courts interpreted the word 'discovery' very widely.

ASSESSMENT TIME LIMITS

13.28 The standard time limits within which a discovery assessment must be issued for income tax and capital gains tax depend upon whether they are attributable to:

Deadline	*Behaviour*	*Statutory reference*
4 years from the end of the tax year	innocent error or failure to notify with a reasonable excuse	*TMA 1970, s 34*
6 years from the end of the tax year	careless error*	*TMA 1970, s 36(1)*
20 years from the end of the tax year	– deliberate error – failure to notify liability without a reasonable excuse – failure to comply with an obligation to provide HMRC with information in relation to a tax avoidance arrangement under *FA 2004, ss 309, 310 or 313* – arrangements which were expected to give rise to a tax advantage in respect of which the person was under an obligation but failed to notify of a promoter reference number to HMRC under *FA 2014, s 253*	*TMA 1970, s 36(1A)*

*SI 2009/403 Art 3, however, confirms that the 20 year time limit for failing to notify cannot apply where the tax year is 2008/09 or prior years AND the loss of tax is not attributable to negligence by the taxpayer or someone acting on their behalf. Such cases are likely to be relatively rare.

13.29 The above time limits also apply to corporation tax as set out above except that the deadline is set in relation to the end of the accounting period in question according to *FA 1998, Sch 18, para 46*.

13.30 *Discovery*

13.30 The four year assessment time limit expressly applies to non-resident CGT disposal determinations under *TMA 1970, s 29A (TMA 1970, s 34(1A))*. HMRC will use its discovery assessment power in *TMA 1970, s 29* to assess CGT that is undeclared due to careless or deliberate behaviour.

13.31 The above time limits are extended where the Requirement to Correct applies (*F(No 2)A 2017, Sch 18, Para 26*) (see **CHAPTER 18**). Legislation is expected in the Finance Bill in late 2018 to extend the assessment time limits for non-deliberate behaviour relating to offshore matters and offshore transfers for income tax, CGT and IHT (see **13.38–13.42** below).

13.32 It is important to note that the loss of tax that the discovery assessment seeks to correct can be caused by the behaviour of the taxpayer or someone acting on their behalf. Similarly the above assessment time limits are linked to the behaviour of the taxpayer or someone acting on their behalf (*TMA 1970, s 36(1B) and FA 1998, Sch 18, para 46(2B)(a)*). The behaviour of a person who was a partner of the company is similarly relevant (*FA 1998, Sch 18, para 46(2B)(b)*) This aspect is explored further at **13.77–13.83** below.

13.33 Similar time limits apply for other taxes, although the legislation should be checked for commencement dates etc.

- SDLT – *FA 2003, Sch 10, para 31*.
- ATED – *FA 2013, Sch 33, para 25*.

13.34 Occasionally, income is received in a year of assessment after that in which it was assessable. If this happens then an assessment to income tax in respect of this employment, pension or social security income may be made at any time not more than four years after the end of the year of assessment in which it was received (*TMA 1970, s 35*).

Assessment time limits – deceased taxpayers

13.35 Tax liabilities do not cease to exist when a person dies. Income tax and capital gains tax that is yet to be assessed when a person dies may be charged to the executors or administrators of a deceased person's estate.

13.36 The time limits set out in *TMA 1970, ss 34–36* may not extend more than 4 years after the end of the year of assessment in which the deceased died (*TMA 1970, s 40(1)*).

Where the deceased (or someone acting on his behalf) before to his death brought about a loss of tax carelessly or deliberately, HMRC may assess his personal representatives for the income tax or capital gains tax due for any year of assessment ending not earlier than six years before his death. However, the assessment itself must be made not more than four years after the end of the year of assessment in which he dies (*TMA 1970, s 40(2)*).

13.37

> **Example 13.1**
>
> Gary dies in June 2016 (i.e. in 2016/17) having deliberately not declared the tax due on income and gains arising from the rental and disposal of six UK properties that he sold prior to his death. HMRC has until 5 April 2021 to issue assessments to his personal representatives for income tax and CGT arising in the tax year ending on 5 April 2011 and subsequent tax years until his death.

Assessment time limits – offshore non-compliance

13.38 Draft legislation was published in July 2018 for inclusion in Finance Bill 2018/19. If enacted as drafted this will extend the assessment time limits (summarised at **13.28** above) where there are 'offshore matters' or 'offshore transfers'. The rationale for this extension is that HMRC is starting to receive large quantities of offshore data as a consequence of the Common Reporting Standard and is concerned that existing time limits may expire before it analyses the data and gets sufficiently far with investigations that it can issue discovery assessments.

13.39 The changes to the time limits set out below apply to income tax and capital gains tax in connection with offshore matters and offshore transfers. They also apply to inheritance tax but that is outside the scope of this chapter as explained at **13.9**. The 20 year time limits remain unchanged as do the assessment time limits for UK situs issues.

In brief, the new legislation will extend the 4 and 6 year time limits in the table at **13.28** so that they expire 12 years after the end of the tax year in question.

13.40 However, the proposed 12 year time limits will not apply where:

(a) information is received by HMRC from an overseas jurisdiction as a result of automatic information exchange;

(b) On the basis of this information HMRC could reasonably have been expected to be aware of the loss of tax; and

(c) It was reasonable to expect the assessment to be issued before the current assessment time limits expired.

13.41 *Discovery*

Furthermore, the changes are not intended to apply to the time limits for assessments on personal representatives or for income received after the year for which it is assessable, specified by *TMA 1970, ss 35, 40* respectively.

13.41 The consultation document on these proposals mooted the extension of corporation tax assessment time limits. However, the draft legislation suggests the new time limits will not apply to Corporation Tax or to transfer pricing adjustments.

13.42 The new time limits will apply to periods that remain in date for assessment at 6 April 2019, according to the government's consultation responses.

This will affect income tax and CGT within scope of these changes for:

– 2013/14 and subsequent years where careless errors occur; or
– 2015/16 in all other cases.

In future, advisers may therefore need to take care to ensure that assessments are only issued for the appropriate tax years depending upon the facts of the case, the above time limits and the extension of the time limits under the Requirement to Correct (see **13.31** above).

WHEN IS A DISCOVERY ASSESSMENT MADE?

13.43 Prior to the days of computerised processing, a Revenue inspector would make a note of the discovery in a ledger. The actual assessment was issued as a separate, subsequent stage of the process. The assessment must be made by a HMRC officer (*TMA 1970, s 30A*).

13.44 Now computerisation dominates HMRC's processes. Nonetheless, a discovery assessment is made when the HMRC officer authorises its entry into the computer (*Corbally-Stourton v Revenue and Customs Comrs* [2008] UKSPC 692). The officer who made the discovery may delegate to another officer the assessment's finalisation and the sending of it to the taxpayer (*TMA 1970, s 113(1B)*).

13.45 The date that the assessment is entered onto HMRC's computer system is therefore the critical date when considering the above assessment time limits, rather than the date on which the taxpayer receives the assessment for which there is no deadline (*Honig v Sarsfield* [1986] STC 246 (Court of Appeal) and *Nijjar Dairies Limited v Revenue and Customs Comrs* [2013] UKFTT 434).

DISCOVERIES CAN BECOME STALE

13.46 In *Corbally-Stourton v Revenue and Customs Comrs* [2008] UKSPC 692 and various subsequent cases the courts considered whether a delay between the HMRC officer making a discovery and the issuing of the discovery assessment was a problem.

13.47 The Special Commissioners in *Corbally-Stourton v Revenue and Customs Comrs* [2008] UKSPC 692 said at [44] that '"a discovery" is something newly arising, not something stale and old. The conclusion that it is probable that there is an insufficiency must be one which newly arises (from fresh facts or a new view of the law or otherwise).' The inference from this decision is that a discovery assessment may be invalid if the discovery is stale before the assessment is issued. This is a different point from whether the assessment is issued before the assessment time limits expire and does not usurp it.

13.48 Whilst the FTT in *Miesegaes v Revenue & Customs Comrs* [2016] UKFTT 375 considered that discoveries cannot become stale, this is not the view of cases that set a precedent.

13.49 Indeed the *Corbally-Stourton* approach to staleness was bolstered by the Upper Tribunal in *Revenue & Customs Comrs v Charlton (and others)* [2012] UKUT 770 (TCC). The Tribunal decided that if, after an officer decides that a discovery assessment should be made, 'for some reason the assessment is not made within a reasonable time period after the conclusion is reached, it might, depending on the circumstances, be the case that the conclusion would lose its essential newness by the time of the actual assessment'. In this case it was appropriate for HMRC to wait a few months pending a Supreme Court decision whether to grant an appeal in another case before issuing the discovery assessment so the discovery was not stale.

13.50 The Upper Tribunal in *Pattullo v Revenue & Customs Comrs* [2016] UKUT 270 (TCC) further developed the concept of 'staleness'. The Tribunal confirmed that a discovery assessment can be defeated if the discovery is stale by the time the assessment is made. Lord Glennie decided at [52] that:

> 'So far as ... whether any discovery under s 29(1) has to be acted upon while it remains fresh (or before it becomes stale) ... the requirement for the discovery to be acted upon while it remains fresh appears to me to arise on the natural meaning of s 29(1) itself. ... The context makes it clear that an assessment may be made if and when it is discovered that the assessment to tax is insufficient. It would, to my mind, be absurd to contemplate that, having made a discovery of the sort specified in s 29(1), HMRC could in effect just sit on it and do nothing for a number of years before making an assessment just before the end of the limitation period specified in s 34(1).'

13.51 *Discovery*

13.51 Whilst the HMRC officer is not required to make an assessment instantaneously a discovery is made, *Pattullo v Revenue & Customs Comrs* [2016] UKUT 270 (TCC) indicates that a pause of 18 months or more, depending on the specific case's facts, could cause the discovery to be stale such that an assessment would be invalid. However, Lord Glennie added at [53] '... it would only be in the most exceptional of cases that inaction on behalf of HMRC would result in the discovery losing its required newness by the time that an assessment was made.' Ultimately, the Tribunal decided that the discovery in this case was not stale as it was made between July and November 2009 before the assessment was issued in January 2010. Similarly, a delay of approximately 9 months between the discovery being made and the assessment being issued was not 'exceptional' so the discovery was not stale (*John Hicks v Revenue & Customs Comrs* [2018] UKFTT 22 (TC)).

13.52 The FTT in *Clive Beagles v Revenue & Customs Comrs* [2017] UKFTT 462 (TC) followed *Pattullo* agreeing that 'it is therefore possible for an assessment to loss its "newness" or become "stale"'. Whilst the evidence indicated that HMRC realised its failure to open an enquiry soon after the enquiry window closed, it was not until the Special Commissioner's decision in another case on the technical point in question some years later that they concluded there was an under-assessment. At this point the discovery was made and as the discovery assessment was issued shortly thereafter the discovery itself was not stale.

13.53 In *Revenue & Customs Comrs v Raymond Tooth* [2018] UKUT 38 (TCC), the Upper Tribunal agreed that the assessment must be issued expeditiously after a discovery is made, whilst it is still 'new'. It considered that a five year delay between discovery and assessment would make the assessment invalid as the discovery was stale by this point. However, it should be noted that this comment is not binding or indicative of how long a gap would be needed to make a discovery stale, not least because the case was decided on another point and the Tribunal considered that there was insufficiently clarity in the facts summarised by the FTT to be able to conclude on this point.

13.54 In *Gordon and others v Revenue & Customs Comrs* [2018] UKFTT 307, the FTT decided that two years was too long a delay between the discovery and the assessments being issued. The discovery was stale and the FTT cancelled the assessments.

DISCOVERY IN THE ABSENCE OF A TAX RETURN

13.55 If a person fails to submit a tax return despite HMRC issuing a notice to file under *TMA 1970, ss 8 or 8A*, then HMRC may determine their tax liability (*TMA 1970, ss 28C and 28G*). A similar power exists for corporation tax (*FA 1998, Sch 18, para 36*). This is separate from the power to issue discovery assessments.

13.56 There is nothing in *TMA 1970, s 29(1)* which restricts HMRC to only making a discovery assessment after a tax return is submitted. This is logical as HMRC needs to be able to assess tax where a taxpayer fails to submit any tax returns (e.g. because they are determined to stay under the radar in the hidden economy) as well as after a taxpayer makes a voluntary (unprompted) disclosure.

13.57 A discovery assessment can be made where the taxpayer has not submitted a tax return (*Osborne v Dickinson* [2004] STC 104.) In the absence of a tax return, *TMA 1970, s 29(1)* permits an assessment to be made without the need to consider *TMA 1970, ss 29(2) or (3)* (*Henke & Anor v Revenue & Customs Comrs* [2006] UKSPC 550).

13.58 Once the officer discovers that more tax should be assessed then they just need to issue the assessment in the amount that ought in his opinion to be charged in order to make good the loss of tax, within the appropriate statutory time limits.

Focus: discovery related points to consider when making a voluntary disclosure

When helping a client to make a voluntary disclosure (see **CHAPTER 14**), there are a number of areas linked in some way to discovery that are worth considering after your client explains what it is that needs to be disclosed:

- Consider the application of the discovery legislation and case law combined with assessment time limits to the factual situation.

- Your client should make a full disclosure of all relevant facts for all relevant years. If the error or omission occurred for more years than you think HMRC is able to assess, then HMRC will expect to be made aware. You can explain why it is you believe HMRC cannot assess the tax for some years. By making the full disclosure then the full matter is 'on the table' so, at the end of the process, your client has certainty that HMRC is aware of everything and the settlement reached concludes all years with no 'loose ends'.

- Another reason to ensure that a full disclosure is made for all years is to protect the client in the situation where the disclosure is submitted on the basis that the mistake was not deliberate but HMRC subsequently asserts it was caused by deliberate behaviour. If, ultimately, HMRC's

13.59 *Discovery*

> view prevails and the tax is assessed on this basis then HMRC will consider using its power to publish the taxpayer's details (*FA 2009, s 94*). HMRC's Compliance Handbook manual (CH190692) indicates that if HMRC needs to ask for more information after a voluntary disclosure is made then HMRC considers that this increases the likelihood of HMRC being able to publish the person's details. An example of a situation in which HMRC would ask for more information is to obtain the information to assess tax for earlier years where it believes the under-assessment was caused by more serious behaviour and the information was not submitted with the original disclosure. (See further **3.19**)
>
> - Similarly, providing a full disclosure up front should help maximise the reductions to penalties under *FA 2007, Sch 24, para 9* and *FA 2008, Sch 41, para 12* (see **CHAPTER 5**).

DISCOVERY WHERE A TAX RETURN WAS SUBMITTED?

13.59 Given the very wide interpretation of the word 'discovery' by the Courts, the chances of persuading a court that a discovery did not occur may be relatively slim. The protections offered elsewhere in the discovery legislation are therefore important and may 'save the day' for taxpayers.

This was illustrated clearly by *Revenue & Customs Comrs v Charlton and others* [2012] UKUT 770 (TCC). The HMRC officer was aware of what was on the taxpayer's tax return and wrote a letter opening an enquiry before the statutory deadline. The letter was never posted so the enquiry was not actually opened. The officer was nevertheless found to have made a discovery after the enquiry window closed so HMRC met the criteria in *TMA 1970, s 29(1)*. It was the protection in *TMA 1970, s 29(5)* which meant the discovery assessment was invalid.

13.60 Where a tax return was submitted and there is no open self-assessment enquiry, *TMA 1970, s 29(2)* precludes HMRC from issuing a discovery assessment where the return was made in accordance with the practice generally prevailing at the time it was made (see **13.66–13.70**).

13.61 However, *TMA 1970, s 29(3)* says that where a taxpayer made and submitted a return under *TMA 1970, ss 8* or *8A* in respect of a particular tax year then HMRC cannot issue a discovery assessment to him for that year 'in the same capacity as that in which he' submitted the return unless one of two conditions is fulfilled:

- The insufficiency was brought about carelessly or deliberately by the taxpayer or a person acting on his behalf (*TMA 1970, s 29(4)*); or

Discovery **13.66**

- At the time when an officer either ceased to be able to open an enquiry or informed the taxpayer that his enquiries were completed, 'the officer could not have been reasonably expected, on the basis of the information made available to him before that time, to be aware of the insufficiency.' (*TMA 1970, s 29(5)*).

13.62 These restrictions on HMRC's powers where a tax return was issued are strictly applied. The Special Commissioner confirmed that the prevailing practice exemption was not available to protect against a capital gains assessment despite the taxpayer filing a repayment claim form (R40) and a form SA108 disclosing the disposal of shares (*Osborne v Dickinson* [2004] SSCD 104).

13.63 These three conditions – i.e. prevailing practice, careless/deliberate behaviour and available information - are considered further below.

13.64 The tests in *TMA 1970, ss 29(4)* and *29(5)* are independent of each other. 'The two conditions were clearly intended as alternatives. That is how *s 29(3)* is expressed. It would be wrong to assume that because HMRC could reasonably have been aware of the insufficiency, that the insufficiency was not careless' (*Atherton v Revenue & Customs Comrs* [2016] UKFTT 831 (TC)).

13.65 It should also be noted that *TMA 1970, s 29(7A)* also says that for 2010/11 and subsequent years 'The requirement to fulfil one of the two conditions mentioned above (i.e. in *ss 29(4)* or *29(5)*) does not apply so far as regards any income or chargeable gains of the taxpayer in relation to which the taxpayer has been given, after any enquiries have been completed into the taxpayer's return, a notice under *TIOPA 2010, s 81(2)* (notice to counteract scheme or arrangement designed to increase double taxation relief)'. This applies for corporation tax accounting periods ending on or after 1 April 2010.

GENERALLY PREVAILING PRACTICE EXEMPTION

13.66 It is impossible for HMRC to sustain a discovery assessment to rectify an under-assessment or excessive claim where:

- the return causing this issue was prepared in accordance with generally prevailing practice at that time; and

- the under-assessment, excessive claim etc is 'attributable to an error or mistake in the return as to the basis on which' the liability should be calculated.

(*TMA 1970, s 29(2); FA 1998, Sch 18, para 45*).

13.67 *Discovery*

13.67 The Special Commissioners' explained the scope of this provision in *Rafferty v Revenue & Customs Comrs* [2005] STC (SCD) 484 at [114] as:

> 'We construe s 29(2) as a protection to the taxpayer from an assessment where the Revenue have changed their mind on a doubtful point in a sense adverse to the taxpayer. It would in our judgement go too far to construe it ... as a bar on the Revenue from raising a discovery assessment in particular circumstance where they had not publicly adopted a practice. We agree that a practice generally prevailing has to be a practice, or agreement, or acceptance over a long period whereby the Revenue agreed or accepted a certain treatment of sums in particular circumstances.'

13.68 The 'practice generally prevailing' is one which is 'relatively long established, readily ascertainable by interested parties, and accepted by HMRC and taxpayers alike' at the time in question according to Henderson J in *Revenue & Customs Comrs v Household Estate Agents Ltd* [2007] EWHC 1684 (Ch) at [58]. Consequently, the habit of one taxpayer, regardless of how frequently the taxpayer took that action, cannot be a generally prevailing practice (*Colin Moore v Revenue & Customs Comrs* [2011] UKUT 239).

The principles underlying the tax return's preparation are the more important aspect of this test, rather than the precise methodology of its preparation (*Jacobs Construction Holdings Ltd v Revenue & Customs Comrs* [2016] UKFTT 555 (TC)).

13.69 The prevailing practice defence is more likely to be of relevance to a defence against an allegation of careless behaviour under *TMA 1970, s 29(4)* than one of insufficient disclosure under *TMA 1970, s 29(5)* according to *Daniel v Revenue & Customs Comrs* [2014] UKFTT 173 (TC).

13.70 An example of *TMA 1970, s 29(2)* may be researching a technical point such as whether a receipt is properly categorised as income or capital. If the research indicated that there was no specific case law precedent on the point given the type of the receipt in question and that there was a body of general professional opinion in publications, journals etc that it should be (say) capital then this may be generally accepted practice. However, a taxpayer would be in a better position to assert this point in order to challenge a discovery assessment, if their agent also had on their files and used in evidence a contemporaneous printout of a section of HMRC's manuals or another part of gov.uk confirming that HMRC also understood such a receipt to be capital.

See **13.152–13.159** below regarding the burden of proof in this area.

THE CARELESS OR DELIBERATE BEHAVIOUR REQUIREMENT

13.71 If HMRC makes a discovery within *TMA 1970, s 29(1)* and the generally prevailing practice test in *TMA 1970, s 29(2)* does not help, then HMRC may issue a discovery assessment using extended assessment time limits if the test in *s 29(4)* is met. This states:

> 'The first condition is that the situation mentioned in subsection (1) above was brought about carelessly or deliberately by the taxpayer or a person acting on his behalf.'

For corporation tax, the equivalent legislation is at *FA 1998, Sch 18, para 43*.

13.72 There are a number of facets to this one sentence legislative requirement. They are considered separately below as follows:

- The situation must be 'brought about' (see **13.73–13.76**)
- Who is 'a person acting on his behalf'? (see **13.77–13.83**)
- What does 'deliberately' mean? (see **13.84–13.92**)
- What does 'carelessly' mean? (see **13.93–13.100**)
- What is the impact of the taxpayer relying on professional advice? (see **13.101–13.104**)
- The burden of proof is considered further at **13.158–13.165** below.

The situation must be 'brought about'

13.73 This legislative test refers to 'the situation mentioned in subsection (1)'. This means the under-assessment, insufficient tax assessed or the excessive relief.

13.74 Consequently, in order for the requirements in *TMA 1970, s 29(4)* to be met, the under-assessment, insufficiency or excess relief must be caused by careless or deliberate behaviour by the taxpayer or someone acting on his behalf.

13.75 If there is no causal link or the behaviour is neither careless nor deliberate then this legislative test is failed and a discovery assessment cannot be issued/sustained on these grounds.

13.76 In *Bubb v Revenue & Customs Comrs* [2016] UKFTT 216 (TC) HMRC's assessment was specifically made to correct two errors. It did not

13.77 *Discovery*

correct a third error which was the only one caused by careless behaviour. Consequently, the FTT cancelled the discovery assessment as it did not correct any error attributable to the taxpayer's careless conduct.

Who is 'a person acting on his behalf'?

13.77 Taxpayers engage professional advisers to provide assistance in various situations. These can be grouped into two categories:

1. Assistance with preparing and submitting tax returns and other forms.
2. Advice on a current or future issue such as advice on the consequences of moving to the UK or advice on the tax consequences of a proposed transaction such as selling an asset or a business.

13.78 Case law draws a distinction between these two categories for the purposes of the 'acting on his behalf' test for discovery assessments. It is therefore important to analyse the role that an adviser takes in order to ascertain whether their actions are directly relevant to whether HMRC is able to issue a discovery assessment.

13.79 In *The Trustees of Bessie Taube Discretionary Settlement Trust v Revenue & Customs Comrs* [2010] UKFTT 473 (TC) the First-tier Tax Tribunal (FTT) decided, at para 93, that:

> 'In our view, the expression "person acting on ... behalf" is not apt to describe a mere adviser who only provides advice to the taxpayer or to someone who is acting on the taxpayer's behalf. In our judgement the expression connotes a person who takes steps that the taxpayer himself could take, or would otherwise be responsible for taking. Such steps will commonly include steps involving third parties, but will not necessarily do so. Examples would in our view include completing a return, filing a return, entering into correspondence with HMRC, providing documents and information to HMRC and seeking external advice as to the legal and tax position of the taxpayer. The person must represent, and not merely provide advice to, the taxpayer.'

13.80 The FTT endorsed this approach in *John Hicks v Revenue & Customs Comrs* [2018] UKFTT 22 (TC). The Tribunal specifically considered the meaning of the phrase 'acting on behalf of' in the context of discovery assessments and decided that:

- With regard to *TMA 1970, s 29* 'subsection (4) is not expressed in terms of whether a third party is the taxpayer's agent or adviser. The only question is whether a third party was "acting on behalf" of the taxpayer in (broadly) bringing about an insufficiency in his assessment.' [133]

- 'Construing the statute purposively in this way leads me to a similar conclusion to that reached in *Bessie Taube*. A third party acts on behalf of the taxpayer in this context if he acts as the taxpayer's proxy or representative—a role described in *Mariner v HMRC* [2013] UKFTT 657, at [25] as "a mere agent, administrator or functionary".' [135]
- The behaviour of Mr Hicks and the agent who prepared his tax returns was therefore relevant when considering *TMA 1970, s 29(4)*. The behaviour of the promoter of the tax avoidance arrangement was not directly relevant (i.e. they were only an adviser) even though advised Mr Hicks' agent on his obligations as his representative in preparing and submitting his returns. See also **13.101–13.104** below.

13.81 It should be remembered that it is not a requirement for a person acting on behalf of the taxpayer to be professionally qualified as an accountant or tax adviser for example. Consequently, someone who has a power of attorney or who is helping as a friend could also meet the criteria of this test.

13.82 Finally, the case law above is that of the FTT. Until a higher court sets a formal precedent in this area HMRC may therefore say that it disagrees with this approach and has an alternative interpretation of this part of the discovery legislation. Whilst it is true that the FTT's decisions do not set a binding precedent para 9 of the FTT's decision in *Providence Health Consultants Limited v Revenue & Customs Comrs* [2013] UKFTT 601 (TC) says that 'HMRC should take [it] seriously' when a taxpayer points to a decision of the FTT 'and not merely dismiss it as not setting a precedent. Decisions of the FTT may not set a precedent but they give informed guidance from experienced tax practitioners which may help to determine what the outcome of a set of facts should be. They should not be dismissed lightly as appears to have happened in HMRC's review in this case.' It should also be noted that at para 193 of the judgement in *Richard Atherton v Revenue & Customs Comrs* [2016] UKFTT 831 (TC), the Taube decision was referred to and the judge noted 'HMRC did not suggest it was wrongly decided'.

13.83 In summary,
- a person or firm is acting on behalf of a taxpayer if they complete the return, submit the return and/or correspond with HMRC whilst representing the taxpayer. The taxpayer cannot escape discovery by getting someone else to take these actions i.e. their actions are taken into account and may trigger a discovery assessment.
- The behaviour of someone solely providing advice is perhaps not the subject of direct scrutiny by this legislation (see **13.101–13.104**).

13.84 *Discovery*

What does 'deliberate' mean?

13.84 The Taxes Acts do not clearly define 'deliberate'. However, *TMA 1970, s 118(7)* offers some clarification as it says:

> 'In this Act references to a loss of tax or a situation brought about deliberately by a person include a loss of tax or a situation that arises as a result of a deliberate inaccuracy in a document given to Her Majesty's Revenue and Customs by or on behalf of that person.'

It is important to remember that *TMA 1970, s 118(7)* does not override *TMA 1970, s 29(4)* or *FA 1998, Sch 18, para 43* i.e. the inaccuracy must give rise to the 'situation' (e.g. the insufficiency in the tax assessed so far). The Upper Tribunal in *Revenue & Customs Comrs v Raymond Tooth* [2018] UKUT 38 (TCC) summarised, at para 47, the test as 'In order for s 29(4) to be met there must be an inaccuracy in a document given to HMRC, that inaccuracy must be deliberate and the deliberate inaccuracy must have brought about an insufficiency in an assessment to tax'.

Before we consider the meaning of 'deliberate' we need to consider the use of the words 'document' and 'inaccuracy' in this section.

13.85 In *Tooth* the document was 'the whole return plus the accompanying computations submitted to HMRC' which the Upper Tribunal considered must be looked at as a whole when deciding whether there is an inaccuracy in the document and whether the inaccuracy was deliberate. In other cases the document may differ e.g. it may be a deliberately erroneous claim submitted on a form or in a letter.

13.86 The Upper Tribunal in *Tooth* also considered what is meant by 'an inaccuracy'.

> 'An inaccuracy is something that is not accurate. Something is accurate if it conforms with the truth or with a given standard. In our judgement, where a taxpayer adopts a position in his return which, albeit controversial cannot (at the time of the return) be said to be wrong and takes the trouble to identify the position he has taken (and the fact that it is controversial) in that return cannot be guilty of an inaccuracy when, subsequently, it is established that the position taken by the taxpayer is wrong.' [52]

13.87 The taxpayer's return included entries relating to a tax avoidance arrangement. At the time it was submitted he did not know that the arrangement would later be defeated (shown not to achieve its intended aims) but he did know that HMRC was likely to challenge it i.e. his interpretation was arguable.

The Tribunal decided that the return became inaccurate but was not inaccurate at the time of its submission and *TMA 1970, s 118(7)* does not cover the case where a document 'is rendered inaccurate by subsequent events'. Consequently, there was no inaccuracy so there could be no discovery as *TMA 1970, s 29(4)* was not met.

13.88 Case law in this area includes cases relating to tax-geared penalties and discovery as both consider the taxpayer's behaviour using similar terminology.

13.89 The Upper Tribunal considered what constitutes deliberate behaviour in *Revenue & Customs Comrs v Raymond Tooth* [2018] UKUT 38 (TCC). It decided that:

- 'An allegation of deliberately bringing about a tax loss is a serious one, tantamount to an allegation of fraud.' [63]

- Completing and submitting a tax return cannot of itself amount to 'deliberate behaviour' in the sense required by the legislation. The error must be deliberate.

- Putting an inaccurate figure on a document '... may be a deliberate act, but it is not, necessarily, a deliberate inaccuracy'. [65]

- Mr Tooth had not acted deliberately and that there was 'no evidence of any intent on the part of Mr Tooth to bring about an insufficient assessment of tax or give to HMRC a deliberately inaccurate document'.

13.90 In para 63 of its decision in *Auxilium Project Management Limited v Revenue & Customs Comrs* [2016] UKFTT 249 (TC) the FTT said '... a deliberate inaccuracy occurs when a taxpayer knowingly provides HMRC with a document that contains an error with the intention that HMRC should rely upon it as an accurate document. This is a subjective test'. The FTT also confirmed that there is no need to contrast the taxpayer's actions with those of a hypothetical 'reasonable taxpayer' in order to assess whether the error was deliberate; only the taxpayer's knowledge and intention is relevant.

13.91 In *Changtel Solutions Limited & another v Revenue & Customs Comrs* [2016] UKFTT 399 (TC) the FTT considered that 'deliberate' 'In terms of inaccuracy, we consider it to mean "done with a set purpose". That purpose must be to produce an inaccuracy, within the meaning of Schedule 24. There is an element of intent in "deliberate" which is not present in "careless". It represents a higher degree of fault'. [98]

Furthermore, in *McCloskey v Revenue & Customs Comrs* [2018] UKFTT 352 (TC), the FTT considered that in order to prove deliberate behaviour by the taxpayer it was also necessary to show that the taxpayer consciously knew that the omission of some employees from the PAYE returns would lead to a loss of tax. The judge considered that this 'is supported by the text of s 36(1A) TMA, which speaks of "a case involving a loss of income tax ... brought about

13.92 *Discovery*

deliberately by the person". This suggests that a deliberate failure to file correct returns is not enough, and that the Appellant must know that the inaccuracies in the return will in fact in practice result in a loss of tax'.

13.92 *Anthony Clynes v Revenue & Customs Comrs* [2016] UKFTT 369 (TC) extended the concept of 'deliberate' errors to omissions:

'Our view is that, depending on the precise circumstances, an inaccuracy may also be held to be deliberate where it is found that the person consciously or intentionally chose not to find out the correct position, in particular, where the circumstances are such that the person knew that he should do so. A person cannot simply escape liability by claiming complete ignorance where the person clearly knew that he should have taken steps to ascertain the position. We view the case where a person makes such a conscious choice not to take such steps with the result that an inaccuracy occurs, as no less of a "deliberate inaccuracy" on that person's part than making the inaccuracy with full knowledge of the inaccuracy.' [86]

What does carelessness mean?

13.93 A loss of tax or a situation is brought about carelessly by a person if the person fails to take reasonable care to avoid bringing about that loss or situation (*TMA 1970, s 118(5)*).

A loss of tax or a situation brought about by an inaccuracy is deemed careless by *TMA 1970, s 118(6)* where information is provided to HMRC and:

- the person who provided the information (or the person on whose behalf the information was provided) discovers sometime later that the information was inaccurate, and
- the person fails to take reasonable steps to inform HMRC.

13.94 Case law in this area includes cases relating to tax-geared penalties and discovery as both consider the taxpayer's behaviour using similar terminology.

13.95 The Upper Tribunal in *Colin Moore v Revenue & Customs Comrs* [2011] UKUT 239 (TCC) considered what constitutes reasonable care. It approved and cited Judge Berner's comments at para 22 of the decision in *Anderson (deceased) v Revenue & Customs Comrs* [2009] UKFTT 258 (TC):

'The test to be applied, in my view, is to consider what a reasonable taxpayer, exercising reasonable diligence in the completion and submission of the return, would have done.'

Discovery **13.98**

The taxpayer in *Moore* was careless as he relied on informal advice provided over dinner by an accountant who regularly stayed in the same hotel as him for long periods on business, without checking the Tax Return Guidance notes and working sheets.

Furthermore, workings on sheets attached to the return are not taken into account when deciding if the taxpayer was careless, unlike entries on the actual tax return form.

13.96 After considering the taxpayer's knowledge, experience and abilities, the Upper Tribunal in *Timothy Harding v Revenue and Customs Comrs* [2013] UKUT 575 (TCC) confirmed that an error was 'careless' '... since it was due to the failure by the Appellant to take reasonable care. He failed to take reasonable care because he knew, or should reasonably have known, that there was at least a possibility that the ... payment was liable to tax'. [37]

13.97 By way of an example, in *Auxilium Project Management Limited v Revenue & Customs Comrs* [2016] UKFTT 249 (TC), the taxpayer had no intention to submit an incorrect return. The company's director thought that she knew what she was doing and believed that she was providing accurate information. Unfortunately, she made a mistake. The FTT concluded that it was careless, not deliberate, as she did not intend to submit an incorrect return.

13.98 Unlike the test at *TMA 1970, s 29(5) / FA 1998, Sch 18, para 44*, *TMA 1970, s 29(4) / FA 1998, Sch 18, para 43* does not turn on the quality of any disclosure in the additional information box on a tax return. The under-assessment needs to be brought about by the careless behaviour in order for the *TMA 1970, s 29(4)* test to be met and the taxpayer's abilities need to be taken into account when considering if they were careless.

Nevertheless, the FTT in *Rusling v Revenue & Customs Comrs* [2014] UKFTT 692 (TC) decided the taxpayer was careless such that the *TMA 1970, s 29(4)* test was met as he failed to put a note in the additional information box to tell HMRC that tax may be payable if their interpretation differed. A similar result arose in *Atherton v Revenue & Customs Comrs* [2016] UKFTT 831 (TC).

In contrast, accountants in general practice were not careless when they relied on commercially available software to complete tax returns to calculate relief for foreign tax credits (*Cooke v Revenue & Customs Comrs* [2017] UKFTT 844 (TC)). Also, it was not careless for a taxpayer to use her month 12 payslip to prepare her tax return, rather than her P60. She was entitled to assumer her payslip would be correct so HMRC could not justify the discovery assessment under *TMA 1970, s 29(4)* (*Blum v Revenue & Customs Comrs* [2018] UKFTT 152 (TC)). Clearly, every case turns on its facts.

13.99 *Discovery*

13.99 Taxpayers can mitigate against careless errors by engaging advisers to assist them (see **13.71–13.77**). If that person is a qualified accountant then the test for *TMA 1970, s 29(4)* and *FA 1998, Sch 18, para 43* is what the ordinary competent adviser would do, rather than what an ordinary lay person would do (*Smith v Revenue & Customs Comrs* [2011] UKUT 270 (TCC)). Ignoring the requirements of accounting standards when preparing accounts was considered negligent in that case.

13.100 Where the adviser provided advice rather than acting on behalf of the taxpayer, it is necessary to consider whether the taxpayer was correct to rely on that advice (see **13.101–13.104**).

Reliance on advice

13.101 Tax is complicated. Taxpayers often need help to understand it. A taxpayer is considered to take reasonable care (i.e. is not careless) if they take '… proper and appropriate professional advice with a view to ensuring that [their] tax return is correct, and acts in accordance with that advice (if it is not obviously wrong), would not have engaged in negligent conduct' (*AB (a firm) v Revenue & Customs Comrs* [2006] SpC 572).

13.102 Whether the taxpayer should be expected to identify that the advice was 'obviously wrong' depends on the facts of the case and objective standards of reasonable conduct by reference to the taxpayer's own specific circumstances. The FTT in *Hanson v Revenue & Customs Comrs* [2012] UKFTT 314 (TC) expected the taxpayer to apply their experience so a higher standard will be expected of a person who is experienced or a specialist and taxpayers cannot simply abdicate responsibility to their adviser. The extent to which a taxpayer needs to check the advice provided depends on the circumstances of the case but if the 'matters … would not be straightforward to a reasonable taxpayer and where advice from an agent has been sought which is ostensibly within the agent's area of competence, the taxpayer is entitled to rely upon that advice'.

13.103 In *Sanderson v Revenue & Customs Comrs* [2013] UKUT 623 (TCC), the taxpayer was not considered negligent (careless) as he reasonably relied on his adviser. The adviser relied on advice from the promoter of the tax avoidance arrangement. The Upper Tribunal considered the adviser was entitled to regard them as having particular expertise relating to the arrangements and so was entitled to rely on them.

In *Anderson v Revenue & Customs Comrs* [2016] UKFTT 335 (TC), the taxpayer acted reasonably and diligently when obtaining a valuation for CGT purposes. He relied on advice from the corporate finance team of a leading accountancy firm and fully considered whether it made sense. He was not careless.

13.104 The FTT also considered that it was reasonable for the taxpayer in *Hicks Revenue & Customs Comrs* [2018] UKFTT 22 (TC) to rely on the advice of his accountant as it was not obviously wrong. His accountant was acting on his behalf. He prepared his tax return including details of the tax avoidance arrangement, following the instructions provided by the promoter. The promoter was not acting on behalf of Mr Hicks as they only provided advice. His accountant was not careless either:

> 'In principle, a firm of accountants completing Mr Hicks' return could have done more than Mr Bevis. They could have conducted a thorough review of Montpelier's advice, if necessary obtaining a second opinion. Mr Bevis was, however, effectively a one man band with none of the resources or expertise of a large firm of accountants. He had no prior knowledge of the area of tax law on which the Scheme and Montpelier's advice relied. He had been advised by the partner at his former firm to whom he then reported that the Scheme was effective on numerous occasions and in no uncertain terms. He had become confident after the February 2009 meeting with Montpelier and sight of the two technical documents that the Scheme stood "the best possible chance" of success.'

Focus

Don't forget to consider whether the adviser was given all the relevant information and documentation before the advice was provided.

If they were not and the taxpayer knew they did not know all the facts then HMRC is unlikely to agree that it was reasonable for the taxpayer to rely on advice. HMRC is likely to ask for evidence on this point so be prepared to provide it (see **13.158–13.165** for burden of proof), and consider related matters such as privilege and penalties (see **CHAPTER 18**).

DISCOVERY WITHOUT CULPABLE BEHAVIOUR

13.105 In the absence of careless or deliberate (i.e. culpable) behaviour extending assessment time limits, HMRC's only other avenue to use its discovery assessment powers following submission of a tax return is *TMA 1970, s 29(5), FA 1998, Sch 18, para 44* or the equivalent provisions in the other legislation listed at **13.20** above.

In essence this enables HMRC to make a discovery where insufficient disclosure was included on a tax return even though HMRC did not open a self assessment enquiry (or completed one).

13.106 Before we look in detail at this part of the legislation, it is important to revisit the reason why this provision exists. On the one hand, Parliament

13.107 *Discovery*

wants taxpayers to have certainty as to their tax position within a relatively short period following submission of their return – in the absence of careless or deliberate behaviour. On the other hand, it wants HMRC to have a chance to assess additional tax when an officer realises that it is due. The balance between these two competing interests is set out in this legislative provision.

Conditions

13.107 *TMA 1970, s 29(5)* and *FA 1998, Sch 18, para 44* empower HMRC to issue a discovery assessment if 'the officer could not have been reasonably expected, on the basis of the information made available to him ... to be aware' of the under-assessment or excessive claim for relief. The test is strictly time limited (see **13.114–13.115**).

This test is applied by considering the available information as defined by *TMA 1970, s 29(6)* and *FA 1998, Sch 18, para 44(2)* at the point when HMRC ceased to be able to open a self-assessment enquiry or closed their enquiry (see **13.116–13.120**).

13.108 Overall, there are four parts to the test in *TMA 1970, s 29(5)*:

- identify the officer in question – see **13.109–13.113**;
- the time at which the officer's knowledge is tested – see **13.114–13.115**;
- the information deemed to be available to the officer – see **13.116–13.120**; and
- the level of awareness needed – see **13.121–13.128**.

The 'hypothetical' officer

13.109 *TMA 1970, s 29(5)* and *FA 1998, Sch 18, para 44(1)* considers the officer's awareness of an insufficiency (i.e. the under-assessment). But who is the officer?

13.110 The 'officer' is not the real HMRC officer handling the case and concluding that a discovery assessment should be issued. As this test in the legislation is objective, it refers to a hypothetical officer. The level of skill and experience that this hypothetical officer is deemed to possess is a difficult issue.

This focus on a hypothetical officer contrasts with the test in *TMA 1970, s 29(1) / FA 1998, Sch 18, para 41* which focuses on the actual officer when considering whether there was a discovery and who should make it.

13.111 The hypothetical officer is deemed to have knowledge of basic arithmetic, some knowledge of tax law and some general knowledge, all of which he will use when considering information sources in *TMA 1970, s 29(6) (Langham v Veltema* [2004] EWCA Civ 193). The Court of Appeal endorsed this approach in *D S Sanderson v Revenue and Customs Comrs* [2016] EWCA Civ 19 confirming that the test focuses on a hypothetical officer of general competence, knowledge or skill.

The hypothetical officer is assumed to have reasonable knowledge and understanding. He is not required to resolve points of law or forecast a taxpayer's response (*Revenue & Customs Comrs v Lansdowne Partners LP* [2011] EWCA Civ 1578).

13.112 The Upper Tribunal in *Revenue & Customs Comrs v Charlton & Others* [2012] UKUT 770 (TCC) built on this somewhat by listing the qualities of the hypothetical or notional inspector in the context of an avoidance arrangement. In generic terms these may be summarised as:

1. He would be sufficiently aware of the specific area of tax law to appreciate the unusual nature of the entries in the return.

2. He would be aware of the relevant Court judgements in this area.

3. He does not only require the characteristics of an officer or general competence, knowledge or skill. The notional officer must be assumed to have the level of knowledge and understanding that would reasonably be expected in an officer considering the particular information provided by the taxpayer i.e. the skills and knowledge of the hypothetical officer are dependent on the information deemed to be before him.

4. It is not necessary that the notional officer should be able to comprehend all the workings of the scheme or the legal and factual arguments that might arise or be able to form a reasoned view of those matters.

13.113 This is not a totally settled matter as the Upper Tribunal in *Pattullo v Revenue and Customs Comrs* [2016] UKUT 270 (TCC) acknowledged that their view differed from *Charlton*. The Upper Tribunal thought that the officer 'will be expected to have a reasonable knowledge and understanding of tax law and of HMRC practice, policy and procedure. But he could not be expected to have specialist knowledge of these matters. On that basis, he would reasonably be expected to pick up inconsistencies in the tax return, excessive deductions and the like; but he would not be expected to identify, understand and unravel tax avoidance schemes ...'

Hopefully a future decision by a higher Court may eventually settle this matter once and for all but in the meantime the approach taken by the Court of Appeal in the cases listed at **13.111** provide the precedents.

13.114 *Discovery*

When does the officer cease to be entitled?

13.114 This provision (*TMA 1970, s 29(5)* and *FA 1998, Sch 18, para 44*) is strictly time delimited. It applies if the conditions are met when:

- HMRC ceases to be entitled to open a self-assessment enquiry; or
- HMRC closes the enquiry or the relevant part of the enquiry using a full or partial closure notice.

The awareness of the hypothetical officer is tested at this time.

13.115 It is important to remember that the discovery must be made before the 4 year time limit (see **13.28–13.37**) expires and that this is a wholly separate point to whether the timing aspect of the test in *TMA 1970, s 29(5) / FA 1998, Sch 18, para 44* is met.

Available information

13.116 The only information which can be taken into account when this test is considered is limited by the legislation (*TMA 1970, s 29(6)* and *FA 1998, Sch 18, para 44(2)*) to information:

(a) In the taxpayer's tax return or claim for the year in question or either of the two preceding years.

(b) In any accounts, statements or documents accompanying the return or claim.

(c) In documents, accounts or other information produced or submitted by the taxpayer to the officer for the purposes of any enquiries into the return or claim.

(d) The existence and the relevance of which:

    (i) an officer could reasonably be expected to be infer based on the information falling within (a)–(c) above; OR

    (ii) was notified in writing by the taxpayer to an HMRC officer.

References to the taxpayer's tax return also include references to any partnership returns where the taxpayer is carrying on a trade, profession or business in partnership.

13.117 Paragraph 24 of the FTT's decision in *Blum v Revenue & Customs Comrs* [2018] UKFTT 152 (TC) confirms that information provided by third parties can be referred to as a result of the test in *TMA 1970, s 29(6)(d)(i)*:

'... Information that can reasonably be inferred from information falling within s 29(6)(a) – (c) falls within s 29(6)(d)(i) and thus is "made available" to the hypothetical officer. I do not consider that it is implicit that s 29(6)(d)(i) is referring only to documents provided by the taxpayer. The evident purpose of s 29(6)(d)(i) is to fix the hypothetical officer with knowledge of information that the taxpayer has not actually provided, but which can reasonably be inferred from other information that the taxpayer has provided. In those circumstances, Parliament cannot have intended that s 29(6)(d) could apply only to information provided by the taxpayer ...'

13.118 On first glance, *TMA 1970, s 29(6)(d)(i)* (and its equivalent for corporation tax *FA 1998, Sch 18, para 44(2)(d)(i)*) appear to be helpful to taxpayers. However, unless the case is clear cut, the Courts are reluctant to accept that inferences can be made from the return or claim.

The inclusion of a DOTAS number on a tax return meant that the officer could reasonably be expected to infer that form AAG1 existed containing details of the avoidance arrangement and how it operated under *TMA 1970, s 29(6)(d)(i)*. This meant that the Upper Tribunal in *Revenue & Customs Comrs v Charlton & others* [2012] UKUT 770 (TCC) decided that the hypothetical officer could infer that using the arrangement gave rise to a loss of tax so the assessment was invalid as HMRC did not meet the criteria in *TMA 1970, s 29(5)*.

Nevertheless, in its judgement the Upper Tribunal observed that:

'The correct construction of s 29(6)(d)(i) is that it is not necessary that the hypothetical officer should be able to infer the information; an inference of the existence and relevance of the information is all that is necessary. However, the apparent breadth of the provision is cut down by the need, firstly, for any inference to be reasonably drawn; secondly that the inference of relevance has to be related to the insufficiency of tax, and cannot be a general inference of something that might, or might not, shed light upon the taxpayer's affairs; and thirdly, the inference can be drawn only from the return etc provided by the taxpayer.' [78]

'As we have described, the balance provided by s 29 depends on protection being provided only to those taxpayers who make honest, complete and timely disclosure. That balance would be upset by construing s 29(6)(d)(i) too widely. Inference is not a substitute for disclosure, and courts and tribunals will have regard to that fundamental purpose of s 29 when applying the test of reasonableness.' [79]

13.119 Case law in this area is rather variable, for example:
- Information on the corporation tax file of the company whose shares the appellant (one of two owner managers) held & sold is not 'information available' to the Inspector dealing with the individual's tax affairs (*Brown and another v Revenue & Customs Comrs* [2012] UKFTT 425 (TC)).

13.120 *Discovery*

- Information on a form such as a P35 submitted by an employer may be available. The case law is conflicting – compare *Norman v Revenue & Customs Comrs* [2015] UKFTT 303 (TC) against *Blum v Revenue & Customs Comrs* [2018] UKFTT 152 (TC).

- The officer investigating the beneficiary's tax position could not reasonably infer the existence and relevance of a disclosure in a trust tax return (*Miesegaes v Revenue & Customs Comrs* [2016] UKFTT 375 (TC)).

13.120 Information provided verbally to HMRC does not fall within the above provisions and so does not protect the taxpayer against a discovery.

However, if HMRC made a note of the discussion which the taxpayer then adopted in written correspondence then it does fall within *TMA 1970, s 29(6)(d)(ii)* (*Revenue & Customs Comrs v Lansdowne Partners LP* [2011] EWCA Civ 1578). HMRC accepted that information in notes of a meeting between the taxpayer and HMRC was information made available even though it was unclear whether the meeting notes were adopted by the taxpayer (*While v Revenue & Customs Comrs* [2012] UKFTT 58 (TC)).

The level of awareness

13.121 HMRC may issue a discovery assessment if the officer could not have been 'reasonably expected' to be aware of the insufficiency at the relevant time (*TMA 1970, s 29(5)* and *FA 1998, Sch 18, para 44*). The meaning of this phrase is the subject of a considerable amount of case law.

13.122 This is an objective test of awareness. The Upper Tribunal in *Pattullo v Revenue and Customs Comrs* [2016] UKUT 270 (TCC) considered that 'reasonably' in this context is an objective test by reference to the standards of knowledge and expertise reasonably to be expected of an HMRC officer dealing with tax returns raising 'this kind of question' and giving 'this amount of information'. In this case the Inspector's lack of awareness was not unreasonable and the discovery assessment was valid.

13.123 The Court of Appeal in *Langham v Veltema* [2004] EWCA Civ 193 explained the rationale for this part of the legislative criteria for valid discovery assessments:

'... the key to the scheme is that the Inspector is to be shut out from making a discovery assessment under [TMA 1970, s 29] only when the taxpayer or his representatives, in making an honest and accurate return or in responding to a section 9A enquiry, have clearly alerted him to the insufficiency of the assessment, not where the Inspector may have some other information, not normally part of his checks, that may put the sufficiency of the assessment in question.'

The Court of Appeal decided that:

- 'awareness' means the officer's awareness of an actual insufficiency in the self assessment in question, not an awareness that he needs to do something to determine whether there is an insufficiency; and

- the available information in question must clearly alert the officer to the insufficiency of the assessment if it is to prevent a discovery assessment being valid.

13.124 This approach was followed in *D S Sanderson v Revenue and Customs Comrs* [2016] EWCA Civ 19 in which the Court of Appeal decided that HMRC could make a discovery assessment even where details of the pre-DOTAS tax avoidance arrangement were disclosed on the relevant return. The absence of a DOTAS number on Mr Sanderson's return meant it was 'entirely speculative' for the hypothetical officer to conclude that another part of HMRC may have information on the arrangement. Overall, it was insufficient to enable the officer to decide to raise an assessment so it did not prevent HMRC making a discovery.

This approach is in stark contrast to the decision in *Revenue & Customs Comrs v Charlton & Others* [2012] UKUT 770 (TCC) where a DOTAS number was on the taxpayer's return (see **13.118**).

13.125 Arguably, the first bullet point in **13.123** above, may result in the Tribunal deciding that some 'protective' discovery assessments, issued by HMRC before time limits expire whilst an investigation is ongoing, are invalid if the Tribunal deems the officer to be unaware of an 'actual insufficiency'.

13.126 Whilst the available information must alert the officer to the actual insufficiency, there are limits to this. The Upper Tribunal in *Revenue & Customs Comrs v Charlton & Others* [2012] UKUT 770 (TCC) considered it unnecessary for the information to explain how the tax avoidance arrangement worked or to specify that the taxpayer adopted a different view from that taken by HMRC.

13.127 HMRC is not precluded from making a discovery assessment merely because it would have been reasonable for an officer, had he thought about it, to initiate an enquiry into a return which could have been expected to reveal the true facts (*Revenue & Customs Comrs v Household Estate Agents Ltd* [2007] EWHC 1684).

13.128 The hypothetical officer is not expected to quantify the under-assessment as that is done by the actual officer who decides to raise the

13.129 *Discovery*

assessment based on all the available information, not just that specified in *TMA 1970, s 29(6)* (*D S Sanderson v Revenue and Customs Comrs* [2016] EWCA Civ 19 at [25]).

HMRC'S STATEMENTS OF PRACTICE

13.129 HMRC's two statements of practice in this area are:

- SP8/91 – HMRC considers its right to make a discovery assessment where a prior agreement was reached between the taxpayer HMRC on a particular matter.

- SP1/06 – HMRC considers when it can make a discovery assessment where information was previously provided to HMRC but where there was not necessarily any prior agreement with the officer.

13.130 Both statements of practice are rather out of date. However, they are worth reading if you face these situations although they may be of limited practical assistance.

PRESUMPTION OF CONTINUITY

13.131 If HMRC identifies an error in a tax return which may affect other years' tax returns then it may assert the presumption of continuity thus suggesting that all those other returns are similarly incorrect, before issuing discovery assessments for those years too if it is within time to do so.

13.132 The presumption of continuity is illustrated by Walton J's comments in *Jonas v Bamford* [1973] EWHC 51 TC 1 (Ch):

> 'once the inspector comes to the conclusion that, on the facts which he has discovered, [the taxpayer] has additional income beyond that which he has so far declared to the inspector, then the usual presumption of continuity will apply. The situation will be presumed to go on until there is some change in the situation, the onus of proof of which is clearly on the taxpayer.'

13.133 However, the First-tier Tribunal at para 38 of its decision in *Dr I Syed v Revenue & Customs Comrs* [2011] UKFTT 315 (TC) did not wholly agree with the above statement, considering that this presumption may not always be appropriate:

> 'In our view, this quotation expresses no legal principle. It seems to us that it would be quite wrong as a matter of law to say that because X happened in Year A it must be assumed that it happened in the prior year. An officer

is not bound by law and in the absence of some change to make or to be treated as making a discovery in relation to last year merely because he makes one for this year. This Tribunal is not bound to conclude that what happened this year will happen next year. It seems to us that Walton J is instead expressing a common sense view of what the evidence will show. In practice, it will generally be reasonable and sensible to conclude that if there was a pattern of behaviour this year then the same behaviour will have been followed last year. Sometimes, however, that will not be a proper inference: there will be occasions when the behaviour related to a one-off situation, perhaps a particular disposal, or particular expenses; in those circumstances continuity is unlikely to be present.'

13.134 It is important to remember that the presumption of continuity may be rebutted depending upon factual evidence (*Ignazio Cardazzone t/a Mediterranean Ices v Revenue & Customs Commissioners* [2014] UKFTT 357 (TC)). Explicable one-off errors in one tax return cannot be relied upon by HMRC under the presumption of continuity to constitute a discovery in relation to another year.

13.135 If HMRC asserts that a mistake in one year affects other years then the next step is to establish whether the facts support this assertion. For example:

- If the issue relates to accounting entries such as the calculation of closing stock, work in progress or provisions, was the same methodology used in prior and/or subsequent years? If so, was it inappropriate for those years? Which years are affected?

- If interest from an offshore bank account was omitted, when was the account opened? Did another account exist before this one? Was interest receivable in all the years?

- If a company did not pay salary or interest on a loan from the main director shareholder within 12 months of the end of the year and omitted to disallow the P&L expense in calculating its profits chargeable to corporation tax, how many years has this situation been going on?

- If tax claims or reliefs are affected, then in which years were the claims made? Did the same error occur in them?

13.136 The important thing is never to assume. Instead:

- establish the facts so that it is clear which years are affected;

- explain to HMRC what the facts are and therefore which years are/are not potentially in need of rectification; and

- consider which of those years are either the subject of open valid enquiries or within time for HMRC to issue discovery assessments given the level (if any) of culpability and the statutory assessment time limits.

13.137 *Discovery*

ESTIMATING LIABILITIES IN THE ABSENCE OF EVIDENCE

13.137 Depending on how many years are affected, factual information may be unavailable for some of those years. It may then be necessary to extrapolate the amount of income, gains and profits which are undeclared but still within time to be assessed.

13.138 The extrapolation needs to take into account the circumstances existing e.g. if undeclared interest arising on an offshore bank account needs to be extrapolated in the absence of statements then a reasonable estimate should be possible by taking into account:

- bank base rates;
- the amount by which the bank offered savings rates below or above bank base rate in the years for which statements are available;
- the level of funds in the account at the earliest date for which statements are available; and
- any circumstantial evidence or other evidence from the taxpayer as to what happened to the balance before that.

13.139 Similarly, when attempting to estimate understated turnover in the absence of books and records the First-tier Tribunal in *Barkham v Revenue & Customs Commissioners* [2012] UKFTT 519 (TC) commented that it '… would like the parties to consider the market and economic conditions at the time, trading fluctuations, competition, sales and discounts and non-taxable sources of income among other factors.' It also noted, on the balance of probabilities, that using a fixed percentage to increase turnover during the period in question appeared inaccurate and unfair as the taxpayer had significant debts and the car industry was in recession.

13.140 It is important that any extrapolated taxable income, gains or profits are calculated on a basis which is realistic, fair and reasonable given the circumstances.

WHAT FORMAT SHOULD A DISCOVERY ASSESSMENT TAKE?

13.141 There is no standard format in which discovery assessments must be issued. Taxpayers and advisers should therefore not expect to receive a sheet of paper clearly headed 'discovery assessment' with a computation setting out the income, gains or profits now being assessed and the tax arising thereon. HMRC does issue such documents, but not always.

Discovery **13.146**

13.142 *TMA 1970, s 30A(3)* and *FA 1998, Sch 18, para 47* require a notice of an assessment to be issued to a taxpayer 'stating the date on which it is issued and the time by which an appeal against [it] may be made'.

13.143 *TMA 1970, s 30AA* specifies that income tax charged on income arising may be assessed:

- in the name of any one or more of the assessable trustees of a settlement in the year in which the income arose; or

- in the name of any one or more of the personal representatives of a deceased person in the year in which the income arose.

13.144 There is nothing in legislation requiring an assessment to state the exact statutory provision under which it was issued so the assessment is still valid even if it does not refer to *TMA 1970, s 29*, for example (*Peter G Gunn v Revenue & Customs Comrs* [2011] UKUT 59 (TCC)).

13.145 *TMA 1970, s 114(1)* enables HMRC to issue assessments in any form, so they can be made within a letter. They are unaffected by 'reason of a mistake, defect or omission therein'. However, this is only as long as in substance and effect it conforms with the intent or meaning of the Taxes Acts. Also, the person or property charged should be specified in the assessment in a way which is understandable.

In addition, *TMA 1970, s 114(2)* says that the assessment remains valid despite of a mistake therein about the:

- name or surname of the taxpayer;

- description of any profits or property;

- amount of the tax charged; or

- difference between the notice and the assessment.

13.146 However, there are limits. The FTT cancelled a tax assessment issued by National Crime Agency on the trustee in bankruptcy, rather than the bankrupt person, as serving a notice on the wrong person was such a serious error that it could not be fixed by *TMA 1970, s 114* (*Matthew Chadwick (trustee in bankruptcy of Gloria Oduneye-Braniffe v Revenue & Customs Comrs* [2017] UKFTT 656 (TC)).

Given the requirements of *TMA 1970, s 30A(3)* and *FA 1998, Sch 18, para 47* that a notice of assessment must be issued to the taxpayer, in *Nijjar Dairies Limited v Revenue and Customs Comrs* [2013] UKFTT 434) the FTT decided that a file copy of a letter sent to the company's third party accountant (which was not received by the company) was insufficient and could not be rectified

13.147 *Discovery*

by *TMA 1970, s 114*. The discovery assessment was therefore invalid as it did not:

- refer to *FA 1998, Sch 18, para 41* or to discovery;
- set out the deadline for making an appeal; and
- have the appearance of an official record of a decision to make an assessment.

CHALLENGING DISCOVERY ASSESSMENTS

13.147 HMRC frequently issues discovery assessments in order to protect HMRC's position where a compliance check (not a self assessment enquiry) for the period is ongoing and assessment time limits (see **13.28–13.42**) are soon to expire. Even where progress is being made on the compliance check, it is essential that a written appeal is submitted to HMRC in order to keep the position open.

HMRC often at this stage say that further information can be submitted and discussions will proceed with a view to reaching a mutually acceptable solution. If this proves impossible then HMRC will issue a final decision setting out their view of the matter in question, against which the taxpayer may request a review or notify the Tribunal of their appeal.

13.148 Taxpayers can challenge discovery assessments on the grounds that HMRC did not meet one or more of the tests for their issue and/or the substantive grounds for the assessment or its amount.

Discovery assessments can only be challenged by the taxpayer appealing against them (*TMA 1970, ss 29(8)* and *31(1)(d)*). Appeals must be made in writing within 30 days of the date of the assessment (*TMA 1970, s 31A(1)*). The taxpayer can decide whether to request internal review or a Tribunal hearing (see **CHAPTER 20**). Postponement of collection of the tax assessed may be requested where the statutory conditions are met (*TMA 1970, s 55(3)*).

13.149 Unlike a self-assessment, HMRC has no power to unilaterally amend a discovery assessment (*TMA 1970, s 30A(4)*). Discovery assessments can be revised by mutual agreement under *TMA 1970, s 54*. The outcome of an internal review is treated as an agreement under *TMA 1970, s 54* (*TMA 1970, s 49F(2)*) and may uphold, vary or cancel the assessment. On appeal the Tribunal may increase or decrease the tax charged but otherwise the assessment will remain unchanged (*TMA 1970, s 50*).

13.150 In practice, the limits on HMRC's ability to alter discovery assessments pose practical problems. In *Lyth v Revenue & Customs*

Comrs [2017] UKFTT 549 (TC) the taxpayer appealed against a discovery assessment late, due to mental health issues. HMRC admitted it had over-assessed her but could not unilaterally reduce the discovery assessment. In the interests of justice, the FTT allowed the late appeal and reduced the tax assessed by the discovery assessments.

In *Marsh v Revenue & Customs Comrs* [2017] UKFTT 320 (TC) during a compliance check HMRC issued discovery assessments for two years just within the 6-year assessment time limit for carelessness. Over a year later, following more correspondence and after the statutory assessment time limit, HMRC issued 'amended assessments' both years for reduced amounts of tax against which the taxpayer appealed. The FTT confirmed that HMRC has no power to amend a discovery assessment so the second batch of assessments were invalid. The Tribunal inferred that HMRC effectively accepted late appeals against the initial two assessments by reading into the correspondence. After considering the substantive issues, the Tribunal cancelled the assessments.

13.151 As stated in **13.35–13.37** above, there are different deadlines within which discovery assessments must be issued following a taxpayer's death. But what happens when a taxpayer dies before their appeal against a discovery assessment is heard?

The taxpayer's executor or personal representative is then in the, potentially difficult, position of needing to continue the appeal. In *Wood v Revenue & Customs Comrs* [2015] UKFTT 282 (TC), the taxpayer appealed against a discovery assessment justified on the basis of his deliberate conduct before his death. The FTT determined that the assessments should not be set aside because of the taxpayer's death. Requiring the personal representative to contest the assessments was not at odds with the overall tribunal objective of dealing with cases 'fairly and justly' (Tribunal Procedure Rule 2). The exact basis of the assessments was unclear so it was impossible at this stage for the FTT to conclude whether Mr Wood's personal representative was unduly adversely prejudiced by being required to continue the proceedings. Consequently, the Tribunal required his personal representative to submit the disclosure report within 60 days and HMRC to issue its statement of case within further 60 days.

13.152 On appeal the Courts will consider whether a discovery was made, the time limits met and the other statutory conditions satisfied. Who needs to provide evidence on each point is determined by rules on the burden of proof (see **13.158–13.165**).

13.153 On appeal, *TMA 1970, ss 50(6)* and *(7)* mean that the assessment will remain unchanged unless:

13.154 *Discovery*

- The Tribunal decides the taxpayer was overcharged, in which case it will reduce the assessment.
- It decides that the taxpayer was undercharged, in which case it will increase the assessment.

13.154 It is important to remember that:

'On the appeal, by virtue of s 50(6) and (7), the tribunal is not confined to the reasons for the opinion of the officer when coming to the opinion that there had been a loss of tax, nor is it confined to examination only of the facts on which that opinion was based, or the legal analysis applied at the time ... the tribunal, acting fairly, may apply the law to the facts as it finds them, and is not constrained by the arguments put forward by the parties whether before or at any stage in the proceedings.' (Clark v Revenue & Customs Comrs [2017] UKFTT 392 (TC))

13.155 In other words the Tribunal will want to look at all the relevant facts relating to the issue which triggered the discovery assessment.

In *Clark* HMRC investigated two related pension transfers and issued a discovery assessment on the second of them. The taxpayer, tax liability and tax year was the same regardless of which transfer was taxable. The taxpayer argued that it was the first transfer that led to the liability so the assessment was incorrect. The Tribunal disagreed saying that *TMA 1970, s 29(1)* was framed in terms of opinion not conclusion and the law did not require it to be definitive. The whole set of facts (i.e. relating to both transfers) was therefore relevant and the assessment stood unchanged.

13.156 Taxpayers occasionally try to argue that there should be an initial Tribunal hearing to consider whether HMRC met the criteria for issuing the discovery assessment. Their suggestion is that if HMRC fails on this point then there is no need to consider the substantive points whereas if HMRC winds then a separate hearing could decide the substantive points.

However, *Hargreaves v Revenue & Customs Comrs* [2016] EWCA Civ 174 confirms that the taxpayer has no right to a preliminary hearing on the discovery point. The FTT's exercise of its case management powers protects the taxpayer instead. Mr Hargreaves then asked the FTT to issue case management directions to effectively adjourn the case after HMRC stated its case at the hearing. The FTT rejected this as an attempt to obtain a preliminary hearing via 'the back door'.

In *Addo v Revenue & Customs Comrs* [2018] UKFTT 93 (TC) the FTT directed HMRC to open the case and present its evidence on the points on which it bears the burden of proof. On conclusion of HMRC's case on the discovery issue, the FTT confirmed that Ms Addo may submit that HMRC failed to discharge the burden of proof. The Tribunal can then decide what to do. However, importantly and notwithstanding that this may be varied by the Tribunal during the hearing, both parties should prepare for the hearing on the assumption that, following HMRC's case, Ms Addo must present her case and lead her evidence on the issues on which she bears the burden. Once she presents her case then HMRC may lead their evidence on those issues before both parties make closing submissions in the normal way.

13.157

Tips for challenging discovery assessments

- Ensure that a written appeal is submitted within the statutory time limit. See **20.106** *et seq* if the deadline is missed.

- When reviewing discovery assessments issued by HMRC, the basics should be checked to ensure the assessment is valid (see **13.141–13.146**). If discrepancies are found then they should be added to any grounds of appeal.

- List all the appeal grounds clearly – i.e. adopt a 'kitchen sink' approach

- Don't forget to ask for collection of all or part of the liability to be postponed setting out the amount for which postponement is needed and explaining why the criteria in *TMA 1970, s 55(3)* are met.

- If you think that the case is heading towards Tribunal, consider seeking a second opinion from Tax Counsel on the case's merits and whether there are any additional grounds for appeal before finalising the appeal form that is submitted to the Tribunal Service.

BURDEN OF PROOF

13.158 In basic terms, 'burden of proof' means who needs to demonstrate, using evidence, that a point is correct. Burden of proof is an important element of appeals to the First-tier Tribunal and beyond.

Sometimes HMRC fails to discharge the burden of proof. In such a situation, the discovery assessments are reduced to zero even if under-declarations are established (*Burgess & Brimheath Developments Ltd v Revenue & Customs Comrs* [2015] UKUT 578 (TCC)).

13.159 The Court of Appeal, in *Hankinson v Revenue and Customs Comrs* [2011] EWCA Civ 1566, said that HMRC has no obligation to investigate whether the taxpayer is guilty of negligence or fraud (now careless or deliberate

13.160 *Discovery*

errors), or of failing to supply information sufficient to enable HMRC to be aware of the potential loss of tax, before issuing an assessment. Consequently, if an HMRC officer considers that there is an under-assessment, the officer will issue a discovery assessment in order to bring the under-assessed tax into charge. Effectively the burden of proof therefore does not bite at this early stage.

13.160 According to *Burgess & Brimheath Developments Ltd v Revenue & Customs Comrs* [2015] UKUT 578 (TCC) the burden of proof falls on HMRC to demonstrate to the Tribunal that the relevant conditions for discovery are met – i.e. that the requisite discovery was made. This case and *Revenue & Customs Comrs v Household Estate Agents Ltd* [2007] EWHC 1684 (Ch) also confirm that HMRC bears the burden of proof of demonstrating that there was careless or deliberate behaviour (*TMA 1970, s 29(4)* or *FA 1998, Sch 18, para 43*) or objective non-awareness (*TMA 1970, s 29(5)* or *FA 1998, Sch 18, para 44*). If HMRC fails to discharge the burden of proof on this and demonstrate that the assessment time limits were met, then the assessments are invalid.

13.161 This approach was endorsed by Arden LJ at para 42 of the Court of Appeal's decision in *Hargreaves v Revenue & Customs Comrs* [2016] EWCA Civ 174 who observed that 'Even though the appeal raises other issues, Mr Hargreaves could at the end of HMRC's case, if HMRC open, submit that there was no case to answer on the conduct/officer condition. If he won on that, there would be no valid [discovery assessment]. If he lost on that, he could then call his evidence on the substantive issues in his appeal, including s 29(2).' An example of a case in which this approach was used is *Gordon and others v Revenue & Customs Comrs* [2018] UKFTT 307 (TC). Despite it being clear that HMRC identified the issue several years prior to issuing discovery assessments, HMRC presented little evidence to the FTT on staleness. The FTT forced HMRC to disclose relevant documents. These demonstrated that HMRC made the discovery at least two years before issuing the assessments.

13.162 The burden of proof sometimes causes issues for HMRC following detailed investigations. HMRC may undertake exercises to extrapolate taxable income from details of changes in the taxpayer's assets over the period or from other sources. Such exercises may cause HMRC to assert that the person failed to disclose sufficient income in prior years. If HMRC is unable to identify the source of the unidentified income, beyond general suggestions, then it is insufficient just to label it 'other income'. The FTT decided that HMRC must identify a loss of tax for the years for which discovery assessments are issued and offer an identified or alleged source of the allegedly undeclared money in order to discharge their burden of proof such that the assessments were valid (*Ashraf v Revenue & Customs Comrs* [2018] UKFTT 97 (TC)).

13.163 In contrast, the burden of proof is on the taxpayer to demonstrate that there was an operative mistake in the return, which itself was prepared in accordance with the generally prevailing practice i.e. that *TMA 1970, s 29(2)* or *FA 1998, Sch 18, para 45* applies – *Revenue & Customs Comrs v Household Estate Agents Ltd* [2007] EWHC 1684 (Ch).

In that case, the Court noted that the company failed to discharge the burden of proving that a 'generally prevailing practice' existed. Whilst it stated what it believed the profession's view was of the relevant piece of tax legislation, it did not provide evidence to the Court to support that assertion or that HMRC took the same view. Consequently, there was nothing 'which could support a conclusion that a settled practice existed, let alone a settled practice which could properly be described'.

13.164 In practice, assuming that HMRC *prima facie* demonstrates that the discovery was valid *then Barkham v Revenue & Customs Comrs* [2012] UKFTT 499 (TC) demonstrates that, when preparing for the Tribunal, the taxpayer must be ready to place evidence in front of the Tribunal to support their defence because:

- the burden of proof is on the taxpayer to show, on the balance of probabilities, that the assessment is excessive, including that the presumption of continuity does not exist for all years for which HMRC raised assessments;

- it is possible for taxpayers to disprove the presumption of continuity by providing evidence to show that the amounts assessed should be reduced;

- the taxpayer's explanations of what happened and their understanding may alter the Tribunal's mind as to whether they were careless or deliberate mistakes compared to the evidence which HMRC advances; and

- the taxpayer must show that HMRC's figures are wrong and also what the correct figures should be.

This last point is crucial. The case law is littered with failed appeals by taxpayers who did not give the Tribunal credible evidence demonstrating what their liabilities should be (e.g. *Aziz v Revenue & Customs Comrs* [2018] UKFTT 153 (TC)). This is despite Tribunals trying to give the benefit of the doubt to the taxpayer as the standard of proof for discovery, a civil matter, is on the balance of probabilities (*While v Revenue and Customs Comrs* [2012] UKFTT 58).

13.165 *Discovery*

13.165

Tips for burden of proof & evidence

If an appeal against a discovery assessment is to be appealed by way of internal review or an appeal to the FTT, consider at an early stage:

- What evidence is HMRC likely to advance to support its case on the points on which it bears the burden of proof?

- What evidence can you help your client put before the review officer or FTT to demonstrate that HMRC is incorrect in this respect?

- On points where the taxpayer bears the burden of proof (e.g. what the replacement taxable income figures should be) what evidence can you and your client collate to demonstrate no tax is due or to support alternative figures? What does this show?

- How might HMRC seek to challenge your client's replacement figures? What might the response be to their challenge?

Obtaining advice from Counsel so that high quality evidence is submitted in advance of the hearing and HMRC's points anticipated is an important step to maximising the chances of any appeal succeeding.

WHEN IS TAX PAYABLE FOLLOWING A DISCOVERY ASSESSMENT?

13.166 The tax assessed is payable 30 days following the day on which the assessment was 'given' (*TMA 1970, s 59B(6)*). It is given by posting it to the taxpayer and, unless proved otherwise, it is deemed 'given' when the letter would be delivered 'in the ordinary course of post' (*Interpretation Act 1978, s7*).

13.167 Payments on account of income tax for the next tax year need to be adjusted following a discovery assessment (*TMA 1970, s 59A(4B)*). So if a discovery assessment is issued for 2014/15 then the income tax payments on account will need to be adjusted for 2015/16.

13.168 The above is delayed if HMRC agrees to postpone collection of the tax following an appeal under *TMA 1970, s 55*.

CONSEQUENTIAL CLAIMS

13.169 Once a discovery assessment is issued a taxpayer (or their adviser) may revisit their overall position for the tax in question.

Discovery **13.174**

> **Example 13.2**
>
> Mr B originally submitted his 2013/14 tax return on the basis that he had no taxable income as his income was entirely covered by trading losses arising. He therefore did not claim to offset negligible value claims against income during the same tax year. After an investigation into some tax planning, HMRC decided that he was not entitled to relief for these losses. HMRC therefore issued a discovery assessment to make good the loss of tax that it considered arose as a result of the excessive claim. Mr B asks his adviser to reconsider claims for the capital losses against income.

13.170 The usual rule is set out in *TMA 1970, s 43(2)*. That says that 'a claim (including a supplementary claim) which could not have been allowed but for the making of an assessment to income tax or capital gains tax after the year of assessment to which the claim relates may be made at any time before the end of the year of assessment following that in which the assessment was made'.

13.171 Where the discovery assessment was not issued to make good a loss of tax arising because of deliberate or careless behaviour by the taxpayer or someone acting on their behalf, the above section must be read in conjunction with *TMA 1970, ss 43A* and *43B*.

- *TMA 1970, s 43A* permits relevant claims, elections, applications or notices previously made or given to be revoked or varied unless they were irrevocable.

- *TMA 1970, s 43B* limits taxpayers' ability to exercise the power in *TMA 1970, s 43A* where it alters the liability of another person.

13.172 In the above example, if the assessment was made on 28 February 2018 then the taxpayer has until 5 April 2019 to submit a claim.

13.173 *FA 1998, Sch 18, paras 61–63* contain equivalent provisions for corporation tax. The deadline for submitting a consequential claim for corporation tax is one year from the end of the accounting period in which the discovery assessment was issued (*FA 1998, Sch 18, para 62(1)(a)*).

13.174 The inclusion of the word 'relevant' in *TMA 1970, s 43A* and *FA 1998, Sch 18, para 62(2)* is important. *TMA 1970, s 43A(3)* and *FA 1998, Sch 18, paras 62(2) and (3)* say that a claim, election etc is relevant in relation to a discovery assessment for the year/accounting period if:

(a) it relates to that year or is made or given by reference to an event occurring in that year; and

13.175 *Discovery*

(b) it has or could have the effect of reducing a liability mentioned in *TMA 1970, s 43A(4) / FA 1998, Sch 18, para 62(3)* i.e:

- the increased tax liability resulting from the discovery assessment, or
- the taxpayer's other tax liabilities for the same year of assessment or any subsequent year of assessment ending no later than one year after the end of the year of assessment in which the discovery assessment was made.

> **Example 13.3**
>
> If HMRC issues a discovery assessment to Fred for 2014/15 in June 2018 then he can make consequential claims for 2014/15, 2015/16, 2016/17, 2017/18, 2018/19 and 2019/20 if the claim is made or given by reference to an event occurring in 2014/15. The deadline for making the consequential claims is 5 April 2020.

13.175 However, there are limits on consequential claims.

- *TMA 1970, s 43(2)* permits consequential claims 'which could not have been allowed but for the making of' a discovery assessment. In other words, if a person chose not to make a claim (e.g. a capital allowances claim) previously (perhaps because their personal allowance was covering their taxable income anyway) then they may not be able to make that claim now.

- *TMA 1970, s 43B(3)* and *FA 1998, Sch 18, para 64* limit the effect of consequential claims as it prevents them giving rise to a refund i.e. the consequential claims may eliminate the liability that would arise from the discovery assessment but they cannot generate a refund of tax previously disclosed e.g. via the tax return. This provision does not apply to consequential claims following discovery assessments issued as a result of careless or deliberate behaviour.

13.176 HMRC can use extended time limits when issuing discovery assessments as a consequence of deliberate or careless behaviour (see **13.28–13.42**). In this situation, *TMA 1970, s 36(3)* applies in conjunction with *TMA 1970, s 43(2)* for income tax and CGT. The equivalent provision for corporation tax is *FA 1998, Sch 18, para 65*.

TMA 1970, s 36(3) says 'if the person on whom the assessment is made so requires, in determining the amount of the tax to be charged for any chargeable period in any assessment made ... effect shall be given to any relief or allowance to which he would have been entitled for that chargeable period on a claim or application made within the time allowed by the Taxes Acts'.

Discovery **13.179**

13.177 The Court of Appeal's decision in *Revenue & Customs Comrs v Raftopoulou* [2018] EWCA Civ 818 considered whether the deadlines for making claims (in that case, an overpayment relief claim) can be extended by virtue of the taxpayer having a reasonable excuse for missing the statutory deadline under *TMA 1970, s 118(2)*. The Court concluded that this provision only applies to mandatory acts, rather than voluntary ones such as a decision whether to make a claim. Consequently, this provision cannot be used for extending the deadlines within which consequential claims may be made.

13.178 Consequential claims cannot be made for SDLT and ATED as there are no equivalent legislative provisions to those for income tax, CGT and corporation tax.

13.179 In practice:

- HMRC may work with tax advisers so that, on conclusion of a compliance check or investigation, the assessments issued or contract settlements agreed under *TMA 1970, s 54* take into account consequential claims.

- There must be tax arising in a year in order for a consequential claim relating to the same tax in the same year to be made.

- Capital losses are not allowable losses for CGT purposes unless a notice is given to HMRC quantifying the amount of the loss. *TMA 1970, ss 42 and 43* apply as if the notice was a claim for relief (*TCGA 1992, s 16(2A)*). The standard time limit for these claims is 4 years from the end of the tax year (*TMA 1970, s 42(1)*) and consequential claims may be made for capital losses subject to the limitations in *TMA 1970*.

- These limits may cause practical problems. For example, if Sharon is disclosing an offshore investment portfolio and discovery assessments are being as a result of deliberate behaviour then HMRC can look at 20 years' tax due to the extended assessment time limits (see **13.28–13.42**). In some years she made capital losses. In the years where those losses exceeded any additional capital gains being disclosed now, she cannot claim those losses as a consequential claim is not possible, unless the years fall within the standard time limit in *TMA 1970, s 42(1)*.

- Care should be taken regarding amending group relief. The company to which the discovery assessment is issued may make a new claim using the consequential claim rules. However, it does not necessarily follow that other entities in the same group can revise their group relief claims. Whether they can depends on whether they have open corporation tax enquiries (*FA 1998, Sch 18, para 24*) for the same period or whether they also face discovery assessments. However, HMRC has some discretion in this regard as *FA 1998, Sch 18, para 74(2)* permits a claim to be 'made or withdrawn at a later time' if HMRC permits it.

13.180 *Discovery*

- The deadline for consequential claims is set by reference to when the discovery assessment is issued. If the discovery assessment is appealed, then consequential claims may need to be made whilst the taxpayer waits for their appeal to be heard and concluded.

KEY POINTS

13.180 When faced with a discovery assessment or the possibility of one being issued:

1. Check whether the client submitted a tax return for the period in question and whether there is an open self-assessment enquiry. The answer to these points will determine whether discovery is in point and, if so, which parts of the discovery rules need to be considered.

2. Discuss the matter carefully with the client to check your understanding of the facts including why the error or omission occurred. Check the facts to documentary evidence where it is available.

3. Consider whether, given the wide interpretation by the Courts' of the meaning of 'discover', HMRC has or is likely to make a discovery. Also, is HMRC's discovery stale?

4. Consider why the error or omission occurred and whether it is a failure to notify or an error in a tax return. This will help you decide what years HMRC is in time to assess using its discovery powers. This is worth doing even though the burden of proof is on HMRC – be prepared to submit evidence to persuade them/the Tribunal that actually the behaviour was of a different nature.

5. If a tax return was submitted, consider whether the 'generally prevailing practice' defence may apply and, if so, what contemporaneous evidence can be submitted to HMRC or the Tribunal. Also consider whether sufficient information was available to alert the 'hypothetical officer' to the under-assessment so as to preclude a discovery (e.g. under *TMA 1970, s 29(5)*).

6. Decide whether HMRC may seek to use the presumption of continuity and, if so, how that presumption might be curtailed so as to limit the number of years affected based on the case's facts.

7. In the face of a lack of records, what evidence can be collated to substantiate estimates and what assumptions are needed? The Tribunal needs to be persuaded on the balance of probabilities that the taxpayer's figures are correct if they are to overturn HMRC's assessment.

8. Don't forget that there is no such thing as a discovery enquiry. HMRC can use its information powers to obtain information and explanations

Discovery **13.180**

relating to prior years. Consider with your clients the merits of co-operating as, in a worst case scenario, HMRC may issue assessments to the best of its judgement leaving the client to defend their position. Not co-operating can detrimentally affect penalty mitigation too.

9. If you disagree with a discovery assessment, even if HMRC's calls it 'protective', formally appeal against it within the statutory deadline. This protects the taxpayer's position and the matter can proceed to Tribunal in due course if the matter is not resolved following discussions, mediation (alternative dispute resolution) or internal review.

10. Consider whether consequential claims can be made before time limits expire. In practical terms, this can be done as part of a voluntary disclosure or contract settlement. Alternatively, they can be submitted after a discovery assessment is issued.

Chapter 14

Voluntary disclosures

Phil Berwick CTA ATT
Director, Berwick Tax Ltd

> ### SIGNPOSTS
>
> - **Introduction** – There are a wide range of circumstances in which a voluntary disclosure may need to be made to HMRC, covering a range of culpabilities. Consequently, each case will require a custom solution. Specialist advice may be needed, as the consequences for getting it wrong can be significant. Voluntary disclosures are now categorised as either 'prompted' or 'unprompted', for which there are statutory definitions. (See **14.1–14.2**.)
>
> - **Early considerations** – Practitioners need to establish the extent of irregularities at an early stage in their discussions with the client. There can be a reluctance by clients to make a full confession. As part of the process, practitioners need to determine the period to be covered by the disclosure, requiring consideration of the client's behaviour. Different periods may be appropriate where there is more than one source being disclosed. HMRC may take a different view from the client, and practitioner, as to whether a disclosure is unprompted. Practitioners need to be sufficiently objective when dealing with a voluntary disclosure. Caution is required, to ensure that neither the client nor the adviser are compromised. The practitioner may feel let down by the client, and referral to a specialist adviser can be beneficial to both parties. (See **14.3–14.6**.)
>
> - **Triggers for making a voluntary disclosure** – Each client volunteering a disclosure will have his own motivation for doing so. Practitioners need to establish the reason, as this will impact on the categorisation of the disclosure. Typical examples include sleepless nights, contact from HMRC, recognition that the opportunities for hiding assets are diminishing, the risk of getting caught, and the 'snowball effect', where extractions have started small and then increased significantly over a period of time. (See **14.7–14.12**.).

Voluntary disclosures **14.1**

- **Advantages of making a voluntary disclosure** – Clients may need to be reminded of the benefits of making a voluntary disclosure. The advantages can include professional fees lower than those for dealing with a protracted HMRC investigation, civil resolution of the matter, as opposed to criminal proceedings, which are likely to lead to a confiscation order being issued to the client. Other advantages include a reduction in the penalty sought by HMRC, although practitioners need to be aware of a change in HMRC's policy, even though there hasn't been a change in the relevant legislation. (See **14.13–14.18**.)

- **The old penalty regime** – Practitioners need to be mindful of the old penalty regime where the disclosure pre-dates the current regime. Practitioners should be aware of a change in HMRC's policy regarding the old penalty regime, and the higher penalties that will apply. (See **14.19–14.23**.)

- **HMRC's view** – The Compliance Handbook contains HMRC's view on when a disclosure is prompted or unprompted. The guidance covers the situation where an enquiry has started into a taxpayer's affairs, and where the taxpayer claims that prior notification of the disclosure has been given. HMRC's guidance on penalty reduction is included in the manual. It is not uncommon for there to be differences between a practitioner and HMRC as to what category the voluntary disclosure falls into, and practitioners should challenge the HMRC officer when appropriate. HMRC's guidance includes examples of the penalty reduction, and some of these are included in the chapter. HMRC undertook research into the motivators and incentives for voluntary disclosure, albeit based on a very small sample. (See **14.24–14.35**.)

- **Options for making the disclosure** – In relation to any voluntary disclosure, there is likely to be more than one route for notifying HMRC. The practitioner must determine the best option for the client's circumstances. An obvious route may be to contact the client's usual tax office, or the investigating officer, where the client is under enquiry. This may not be the optimum route for the client, and the practitioner should also consider HMRC's voluntary disclosure opportunities, and the Contractual Disclosure Facility in appropriate circumstances. (See **14.36–14.47**.)

- **Making the disclosure** – Planning is essential when preparing a disclosure. There are various steps that need to be taken prior to submission of the disclosure letter/report (depending on the nature and extent of the irregularities being disclosed). Practitioners need to consider the methodologies to be used, and the narrative required. The client should confirm to the adviser that the disclosure report is complete, and that it may be submitted to HMRC. The practitioner should recommend the making of payments on account to HMRC,

14.1 *Voluntary disclosures*

> and explain to the client the benefits of doing so. The client's financial position should be considered, to establish that he has the means to fund the eventual settlement with HMRC. When appropriate, practitioners should negotiate with HMRC regarding a time-to-pay arrangement. Practitioners need to be aware of what can go wrong when submitting a voluntary disclosure. (See **14.48–14.55**.)
>
> - **HMRC's response to the disclosure** – Practitioners should pre-empt HMRC's likely response to the disclosure. Those with a lack of experience in this area should seek advice from a specialist practitioner to assist with their review. Various aspects should be considered, so that the practitioner can ensure that any risk areas are addressed prior to submission of the report. Examples of typical situations are considered. Practitioners will not be able to pre-empt all of HMRC's queries, but dealing with the obvious ones will help to smooth the processing of the disclosure. After dealing with any queries from HMRC, the case should progress to agreement as to the liabilities. As part of the settlement process, which will usually be by a contract agreement, the client will be expected to sign various documents. (See **14.56–14.58**.)
>
> - **Key points** – Ten key issues for the practitioner are included at **14.59**.

INTRODUCTION

14.1 There are a wide range of circumstances in which it may be necessary to make a voluntary disclosure to HMRC, from the realisation that a simple, and single, innocent error in a tax return has been made, to a deliberate understatement of significant liabilities over a long period of time. When it comes to disclosing these matters to HMRC there is no 'one-size-fits-all' approach that can be taken. Each case must be considered on the facts, and practitioners should contact HMRC in the most appropriate way for those circumstances.

> **Focus**
>
> In some circumstances, specialist advice may be needed. Taking the wrong approach when dealing with a voluntary disclosure can, at best, mean the client faces a bigger bill from HMRC. In more serious cases, it could mean the difference between the client being dealt with under HMRC's civil regime and a criminal investigation. Practitioners should be mindful of advising clients in this area if they do not have sufficient experience or expertise, and the potential for claims under their professional indemnity insurance.

14.2 Following the introduction of the provisions at *FA 2007, Sch 24*, voluntary disclosures are categorised as either 'prompted' or 'unprompted'.

The statutory position is that a disclosure is 'unprompted' 'if made at a time when the person making it has no reason to believe that HMRC have discovered or are about to discover the inaccuracy, the supply of false information or withholding of information, or the under assessment' (*FA 2007, Sch 24, para 9(2)(a)*). Otherwise, the disclosure is 'prompted' (*FA 2007, Sch 24, para 9(2)(b)*). In this chapter, the term 'voluntary disclosure' is used to refer to prompted and unprompted disclosures unless indicated otherwise.

EARLY CONSIDERATIONS

Focus

Where a client volunteers a disclosure, it is important to establish the extent of irregularities at an early stage. Frequently, where the client is in denial, or he has been under-declaring profits for, maybe, 20 years, there can be a reluctance to make a full confession the first time the matter is discussed. In view of the significant impact on penalties, it is imperative that all material facts are established at the earliest opportunity. The client should be made aware of the penalty position, to encourage his early and complete recall of the extent of the problem.

14.3 When assessing the extent of the disclosure, practitioners must consider the relevant period. Where the client has failed to notify liability, a 20-year period must be considered (*TMA 1970, s 36(1A)(b)*). When income or gains have been under-declared to HMRC, and it can be demonstrated that the client has taken 'reasonable care', the disclosure only needs to cover the last four years. Evidence will need to be obtained to support the client's position in this regard. Where it cannot be established that the client has taken reasonable care, the practitioner must determine whether the client's behaviour has been careless or deliberate, in which case 6 and 20-year periods respectively must be considered. In a straightforward disclosure, the position may be clear. Where a client is disclosing multiple sources, different rules may apply to each element, and the disclosure should reflect this.

14.4 HMRC's view is that a disclosure will not be treated as unprompted where an enquiry has started. This should not be accepted by the practitioner without considering the facts. There may be circumstances where the contra position can be demonstrated.

14.5 *Voluntary disclosures*

> **Example 14.1**
>
> HMRC starts an aspect enquiry into the client's pension contributions shown on his tax return. If the client makes a disclosure of undeclared business takings, it could be argued that HMRC would not have established the under-declaration from its enquiry.
>
> **Example 14.2**
>
> HMRC starts a business records enquiry into a taxpayer's return. If, following receipt of the opening enquiry letter, the client wishes to make a disclosure of undeclared business takings, HMRC is unlikely to accept that the disclosure was 'unprompted'.
>
> If, however, the client makes a disclosure of undeclared rental income, an argument could be made that the disclosure was 'unprompted', as HMRC's enquiry is not addressing rental income. HMRC is likely to argue that a 'full' enquiry would cover all of a taxpayer's affairs, and the disclosure of rental income is, therefore, 'prompted'. The practitioner should consider the scope of HMRC's enquiry and whether it is likely that it would encompass the matter being disclosed, before accepting that a disclosure is 'prompted'.

14.5 It is better that the client makes a prompted disclosure rather than HMRC uncovering the irregularities. Whenever a practitioner receives an enquiry notice or 'nudge letter' (typically a bulk-issue letter issued to taxpayers in a particular business sector suggesting they may want to review their tax affairs) in relation to a client, he should establish whether there are any matters which need to be disclosed to HMRC. The consequences of failing to make a disclosure, where one is needed, should be explained to the client. This can be done in a non-accusatory way by the practitioner, and he should explain that it is in the client's interest to make a disclosure where one is due.

Focus

Part of the problem for the practitioner when handling these situations is being sufficiently objective in his dealings with the client. This is particularly the case where the adviser has been acting for a long time. Even where a client indicates that there is a disclosure to make, practitioners can fail to ask the probing questions that are often required to determine the full extent of the irregularities. I have come across this situation numerous times when working with advisers. A variety of explanations are offered, including, frequently, that he was the last client the practitioner would expect to be hiding anything from him. Whatever the explanation, the end result is the same: the client's position is compromised, and he is likely to

> face a more serious sanction from HMRC than would otherwise be the case. A consequence for the practitioner is that he could face a claim of negligence if he has failed to advise the client correctly.

14.6 Often, the practitioner feels let down by the client, and this can distort the way the matter is handled. I have been asked to assist on many such occasions – the adviser is disillusioned by the client, but recognises that it is not the time to disengage him. In such circumstances, it can be prudent to bring in a specialist to handle the disclosure, giving the practitioner an opportunity to reflect on the position and to repair the relationship with the client. In such circumstances, the client is often embarrassed that he has deceived his adviser, and the introduction of a specialist third party can be beneficial to client and practitioner.

TRIGGERS FOR MAKING A VOLUNTARY DISCLOSURE

14.7 There are many reasons why taxpayers choose not to comply with their obligations, and fail either to notify HMRC of their chargeability or to disclose the extent of their income and capital gains. Each client volunteering that he has undeclared tax liabilities will have his own motivation for doing so, and for doing so at that time. Practitioners should establish the reason why a client has decided to confess to HMRC, particularly whether there has been any contact from HMRC, to categorise the disclosure as 'prompted' or 'unprompted'. The following are a few typical examples.

Sleepless nights

14.8 The client may have been aware that he had a problem for some time, but was not sure what to do. Over time, the pressure in such circumstances increases, as the client wrestles with his conscience. The strain that this situation places on the client, his business and his family life can lead the client to confess to HMRC.

HMRC contact

14.9 At other times, the decision to make the voluntary disclosure may follow contact from HMRC. This could take the form of a formal enquiry notice, one of HMRC's 'nudge' letters, some other intervention, or perhaps HMRC advertising. It is important to determine the particular circumstances of each case, as they enable the practitioner to form a view as to whether HMRC will deem the disclosure to be 'prompted' or 'unprompted'.

14.10 *Voluntary disclosures*

The world is changing

14.10 From a tax perspective, the world is a very different place from five years ago, never mind ten or 20 years ago. More than 100 jurisdictions have signed up to the automatic exchange of information, which will result in even more data being passed to HMRC about UK taxpayers' global affairs. The outcome is that there are fewer places in the world where taxpayers can hide their assets from HMRC. For those who wish to continue to hide their assets, they will, in the main, be left with riskier jurisdictions in which to deposit their wealth, and from which there may not be certainty that they can withdraw their funds on demand.

'Had a good run'/Risk of getting caught

14.11 This situation arises where the client has been deliberately suppressing profits, capital gains, or a source of income. The client knows it is likely that HMRC will catch up with him eventually, and he wants to 'come clean' before that happens. Often in these circumstances, the client has used the unpaid tax to build a property portfolio, or otherwise improve his financial position. The decision to 'come clean' is often accompanied by the knowledge that the client is now in a position to settle the undeclared liabilities.

'Snowball' effect

14.12 Where a client has extracted money from his business, it may not have started as a dishonest act. An opportunity may have presented itself, and the client took it, perhaps with the intention of repaying the funds. As the business grows, more opportunities may arise, or the opportunities involve larger sums. What started as a relatively small problem can quickly grow. As more funds are extracted from the business, the client may have resorted to concealment by, perhaps, creating, or altering, documentation, in an attempt to cover his tracks. This situation can frequently lead to sleepless nights, and the escalation created by the 'snowball' effect can make it harder for the client to take advice.

ADVANTAGES OF MAKING A VOLUNTARY DISCLOSURE

Professional fees

> **Focus**
>
> Practitioners should remind clients of the benefits of making a voluntary disclosure, where one is needed. Some clients may take more convincing

> than others of the need to make such a disclosure. The client should not be left in any doubt as to the dire consequences that may follow where he decides not to make a disclosure where there are irregularities in his tax affairs.

14.13 The professional fees for dealing with a voluntary disclosure should be a cost-effective option for the client, when compared to the alternatives. The costs for preparing a disclosure report, in whatever form is considered appropriate, and the negotiations with HMRC, should be compared to the likely costs of dealing with an HMRC investigation, and the potential outcome of those investigations (whether conducted along civil or criminal lines).

Civil resolution

14.14 If clients are reticent to make a voluntary disclosure, they should be reminded that HMRC may use its criminal investigation powers to pursue a taxpayer who has under-declared his income or gains, or who has failed to notify his liability. A conviction in the criminal courts can result in a custodial sentence, and also have significant financial consequences for the client.

14.15 When a criminal conviction has been obtained, HMRC will consider using the *Proceeds of Crime Act 2002* (POCA 2002) to obtain a confiscation order. An example of such a case is *R v Steed (Gareth Edward)* [2011] EWCA Crim 75, which was a complex one. The defendant was convicted of cheating the public revenue after failing to notify HMRC of a liability to tax (for the year ending 5 April 2003). The judge accepted that the client had been undertaking 'moonlighting activities' (meaning legitimate trading activities on which tax had not been paid). There were also suggestions of illegal activities by the defendant. The outcome was that there was a confiscation order for £707,200, even though the tax due on undeclared earnings was only £3,558 for the year, with a further £3,558 due as a payment on account for the following year (the significance of these amounts is that the prosecution must demonstrate, among other requirements, that the defendant has obtained a benefit from criminal conduct (*POCA 2002, s 76(4)*).

Penalty reduction

14.16 Making a voluntary disclosure, particularly when HMRC accept it as being unprompted, will result in a significant reduction in the level of penalty suffered by the client. Details of the relevant statutory minimum penalties that apply are at **14.30**. Even when the disclosure is prompted, the client should benefit from a penalty lower when making a full disclosure than that which would be charged if HMRC established the nature and extent of the irregularities

14.17 *Voluntary disclosures*

without assistance from the client. Practitioners should note HMRC's revised penalty policy (see CH403204), which applies to disclosures made after 5 September 2016. HMRC will seek to restrict the maximum reduction by 10% where the taxpayer has taken a 'significant period' to correct their non-compliance. HMRC consider a 'significant period' to be over three years, but it may be less where the overall disclosure covers a longer period. Practitioners should note that there has not been any change in the relevant legislation.

For disclosures that straddle the old penalty rules (see **14.19** *et seq*), a reduced penalty should also apply in relation to the years that precede the current penalty regime.

The 'naming and shaming' provisions

14.17 HMRC publishes details of certain deliberate tax defaulters under its Publishing Details of Deliberate Defaulters ('PDDD') process. Although pictures of offenders are not published, their names and addresses are listed on HMRC's website for a period not exceeding one year. Even if national newspapers do not reproduce the information, there is the likelihood that publications in the offender's town, or professional or trade publications, may. Although some taxpayers may view their 'naming and shaming' as a 'badge of honour', many taxpayers would not welcome that type of publicity. It is important for practitioners to understand the circumstances in which HMRC may publish details of their clients.

14.18 The relevant provisions are at *FA 2009, s 94* and give HMRC the ability to publish details of taxpayers who have received penalties for deliberate errors in their tax returns, or who have deliberately failed to comply with their tax obligations. The taxpayer's details may be published if, after an HMRC investigation, the person has been charged one or more penalties for deliberate defaults and those penalties involve tax of more than £25,000. Publication can be avoided if the person receives the maximum reduction of the penalties (by fully disclosing details of the defaults). When handling a voluntary disclosure, the practitioner should manage the client, and the disclosure process, such that 'naming and shaming' is not a realistic prospect. Practitioners should note that HMRC's new penalty policy (see **14.16**, above) makes it impossible to avoid the client being referred for inclusion in the PDDD process where the relevant threshold has been met, and the client has significantly delayed making their disclosure.

THE OLD PENALTY REGIME

14.19 Practitioners should remember that in a case involving a voluntary disclosure spanning the old and current penalty regimes each must be viewed

Voluntary disclosures **14.24**

separately. The appropriate rules must be applied to each year contained in the disclosure.

14.20 Briefly, practitioners are reminded that the current penalty rules relate to inaccuracies in returns or other documents with a filing date on or after 1 April 2009 where the return or document relates to a tax return beginning on or after 1 April 2008. For inaccuracies relating to earlier returns, the old rules apply. In such cases, the language of 'prompted' and 'unprompted' disclosures does not apply. The starting point for the penalty calculation under the old rules is 100% of the tax lost. Abatement is made for disclosure (usually a maximum of 20%), co-operation (maximum 40%) and seriousness (maximum 40%), to arrive at the appropriate penalty loading.

14.21 HMRC's guidance on contract settlements and the calculation of the penalty at EM6070 (which relates only to direct tax) has been amended in a similar way as that regarding the current penalty regime (see **14.16** above).

14.22 The amended HMRC guidance (EM6070) states that where a taxpayer has taken a 'significant period' to correct their non-compliance (whether in relation to an onshore or offshore matter, or they could have previously made a disclosure through one of HMRC's offshore disclosure facilities) they will no longer get the full abatement for disclosure. HMRC regard a 'significant period' to be over three years but may be less where the overall disclosure covers a longer period. Where there has been a delay of this type, HMRC will seek to reduce the abatement for disclosure by 10 percentage points. In practical terms, this means that for any client where the old rules are in point, HMRC will seek to restrict the penalty reduction in this way.

14.23 HMRC used to grant an additional 10% reduction in the penalty where there was a voluntary and spontaneous disclosure. The amended guidance on this abatement (EM6071) applies the same restrictions as are included at EM6070 (see **14.22**, above), meaning that the extra reduction will not be given. The practical effect is that, in certain circumstances, clients are being penalised twice for the delay in making a disclosure. As a consequence, some clients will be paying a significantly higher penalty under the old regime than would have been the case. This is part of HMRC's tougher stance on penalties.

HMRC'S VIEW

14.24 HMRC sets out its views on what constitutes prompted and unprompted disclosures at CH403202. The guidance states that:

'A disclosure is unprompted if it is made at a time when the person making it has no reason to believe that HMRC have discovered or are about to

14.25 *Voluntary disclosures*

discover the inaccuracy, under-assessment, failure to notify, deliberate withholding of information or wrongdoing. Otherwise it is prompted.'

14.25 The guidance comments on disclosures made once an enquiry has started into a taxpayer's affairs:

'Disclosures made during a compliance check will usually, but not always, be prompted. A disclosure could be considered unprompted if the inaccuracy, under-assessment, failure or wrongdoing disclosed was outside the scope of the compliance check and would not have been found in the normal course of the check.

A disclosure made at the start of a compliance check by a person because they think that HMRC will discover it later, cannot be unprompted. Such early and complete disclosure is to be encouraged but any credit due must be given by an improved reduction for the quality of the disclosure (telling, helping, and giving access) ... and not treating it as unprompted.'

14.26 Officers are instructed not to pre-judge whether a disclosure is unprompted or prompted:

'Judgement should be left until the end of the compliance check, even if you are pressed to do so by the person or their agent. Further investigation may reveal that what initially appeared to be an unprompted disclosure was in fact prompted.'

14.27 The guidance at CH403202 concludes by advising officers what to do where the taxpayer claims his disclosure was unprompted because he made earlier contact with HMRC. Evidence of the prior contact with HMRC will be requested. Where a claim is made that a call was made with a Contact Centre, details of the date and time of the call will be requested so that the officer can check the recording of the call. In practice, clients may not have kept details of such telephone calls, particularly where the call was made several months previously. Itemised telephone statements should be reviewed, or obtained if no longer held by the client, to help determine the time and date of the contact with HMRC. I have, on numerous occasions when assisting clients, been able to provide details of calls made to HMRC so that the officer can verify what was said to, and by, the client.

14.28 The HMRC guidance regarding penalty reductions where there has been a voluntary disclosure differs in its interpretation of whether a disclosure can be unprompted if a compliance check is in progress, compared to that at CH403202, as stated at **14.24** above.

14.29 The relevant guidance, at CH82421, states that 'It will be exceptional for a disclosure to be unprompted if a compliance check is in progress'. This appears to take a harder line than that suggested at CH403202. The guidance at CH82421 also states that 'Whether a disclosure is unprompted or prompted is an objective test. The particular facts and circumstances which led to the disclosure are the basis of the test, not the belief that it was either unprompted or prompted'.

14.30 Practitioners should not be afraid to challenge HMRC in its consideration of whether a disclosure is prompted or unprompted. The difference in penalty between the two types of voluntary disclosure can be significant (the statutory minimum penalty for a prompted disclosure (where the behaviour is careless) is 15%, whereas for an unprompted disclosure it is 0%; where the behaviour is deliberate with concealment the minimums are 50% and 30% respectively (these apply to UK-source disclosures)). There can be a tendency for practitioners to accept what HMRC says, including with regard to the level of penalty. Practitioners should establish the facts, and reach an objective view on the appropriate level of penalty, taking specialist advice if necessary, before agreeing a penalty proposal from HMRC.

HMRC's manuals give examples of unprompted and prompted disclosures in the context of penalty reductions for the quality of disclosure, and some of these are reproduced below.

14.31 The following relate to penalties for inaccuracies (CH82422):

Example 14.3

Jemima returned a capital gain which is the subject of a compliance check. There is no intention to expand the scope of the compliance check during the review. She discloses that she has not declared her car benefit. This is an unprompted disclosure.

Example 14.4

During a VAT assurance visit considering the credibility of Alphonse's sales records, he discloses that his sales have also been understated for income tax. This would be related to the subject under review and so is a prompted disclosure.

Example 14.5

During an Employer Compliance review the employer makes a disclosure that the basis of the transfer pricing calculation for corporation tax is wrong. This is unrelated to the subject under review and so there is an unprompted disclosure.

14.32 *Voluntary disclosures*

14.32 The following relate to penalties for failure to notify (CH73160):

> **Example 14.6**
>
> Simon inherits a property from his grandmother. He decides to rent the property rather than sell. Simon receives the rental income from June 2009 but he does not notify HMRC. In January 2011, following a national campaign by HMRC to remind people to send in their SA returns, Simon decides to contact HMRC and declare his rental income. As Simon had no reason to believe HMRC was looking at his tax affairs this is an unprompted disclosure.
>
> **Example 14.7**
>
> Simon inherits a property from his grandmother. He decides to rent the property rather than sell. Simon receives the rental income from June 2009 but he does not notify HMRC. In January 2011 he receives a letter from HMRC asking if he is receiving rental income. Simon realises that HMRC has some information with regards to this so he decides to tell it about the rent. This is a prompted disclosure because HMRC made contact with him.

Failure to file on time

14.33 When considering the penalty reduction for disclosure where there has been failure to file on time, HMRC state its position to be that 'we want to encourage unprompted disclosures' (CH63140). Officers are advised that 'You need to consider all the facts before deciding whether a disclosure is unprompted or prompted. You should apply a common sense approach in deciding whether or not a disclosure is unprompted and avoid making hasty judgements'.

VAT wrongdoing

14.34 Similar comments are made in relation to the penalty reduction for VAT wrongdoing as to whether the disclosure is prompted or unprompted, and that being an objective test (CH94700). The guidance states that 'It is not what the person believed but what the particular facts and circumstances gave him reason to believe'. When considering a case of voluntary disclosure, practitioners must remember that the HMRC manuals are only 'guidance' and reference should be made to the statutory position, as outlined at **14.2** above.

14.35 HMRC undertook research on the motivators and incentives for voluntary disclosure. The research, published in September 2015, was based on a very small sample of taxpayers, but interested practitioners can view the document at www.gov.uk/government/publications/motivators-and-incentives-for-voluntary-disclosure.

OPTIONS FOR MAKING THE DISCLOSURE

14.36 When a client notifies his adviser that he has a voluntary disclosure to make, the practitioner must consider the optimum route for notifying the position to HMRC. There will, usually, be several options available to the practitioner, and he must assess which gives the best outcome for the client:

(a) notify the client's usual tax office, or the investigating officer where the client is already under enquiry;

(b) HMRC voluntary disclosure opportunities (including offshore facilities); and

(c) the Contractual Disclosure Facility (Code of Practice 9).

The investigating officer (or usual HMRC office)

14.37 The obvious choice may be to notify the client's usual tax office or the investigating officer, where the client is already under enquiry. This may not be the best option for the client. That is particularly so where the amounts involved are significant, or the client's circumstances fall within HMRC's criminal investigation policy. In such circumstances, the officer will refer the case internally, and HMRC will, in the first instance, consider whether the case is suitable for criminal investigation. If a criminal route is not pursued, HMRC may pursue the case using the Contractual Disclosure Facility (for more details on which, see **CHAPTER 2**). In such circumstances, the officer may be expected to request full details of the irregularities.

Voluntary disclosure opportunities

14.38 HMRC has offered various voluntary disclosure opportunities for taxpayers to regularise their tax affairs. In recent years, these have comprised HMRC campaigns and offshore disclosure facilities. At the time of publication of this book, HMRC provides the Digital Disclosure Service for persons with a disclosure to make in relation to income tax, capital gains tax, National Insurance contributions and corporation tax.

14.39 HMRC's campaigns are dedicated to particular business sectors or groups of taxpayers. The voluntary disclosure opportunities available at the time the client notifies the adviser of the irregularities must be considered. The terms of the disclosure facilities vary from time to time and those available should be assessed to see whether they are suitable for the client.

14.40 *Voluntary disclosures*

14.40 There is, at the time of publication of this book, only one offshore disclosure facility. The Worldwide Disclosure Facility (WDF), announced by HMRC on 5 September 2016, runs from that date until 30 September 2018. The facility is open to those with an undeclared UK tax liability wholly or partly connected to an offshore issue. HMRC have stated that this will be the final 'last chance' for those with offshore irregularities to come forward. The WDF is an online process but does not offer any special terms for those coming forward (HMRC do not feel the need to offer any such terms, given previous disclosure facilities and the Failure to Correct penalty regime, with its minimum penalty of 100% of the tax involved, that will apply after the WDF ends).

14.41 Unfortunately, the WDF does not offer any of the practical, non-financial, benefits that the Liechtenstein Disclosure Facility offered to clients, advisers and HMRC (that process closed to new registrations on 31 December 2015). Aside from the lack of immunity from prosecution, the WDF has numerous disadvantages (including only 90 days to submit the disclosure after registration, no guarantee of technical support, and restrictions where there are outstanding tax returns) and potential pitfalls for the unwary (particularly in that the onus for categorising the taxpayer's behaviour – and the consequential assessing and penalty ramifications – rests with the taxpayer/adviser). There are too many restrictions for the WDF to be a practical option unless the disclosure is simple and straightforward, and the client already has all relevant documentation to enable the adviser to quantify the disclosure. Advisers should carefully consider whether the WDF is the best option for the client, and seek specialist advice.

The Contractual Disclosure Facility

14.42 When an application is made for the Contractual Disclosure Facility, the practitioner is not required to reveal details of the irregularities. The process should only be used where tax fraud has been committed, or the taxpayer's behaviour is such that HMRC would regard his conduct as fraudulent, and the amounts involved are material. Further details on the Contractual Disclosure Facility are contained in **CHAPTER 2**. The details below are those relevant in the context of a client making a voluntary disclosure. Practitioners who are not familiar with the process should obtain specialist advice before using this facility to make a voluntary disclosure (see Example 14.8 below).

14.43 HMRC provides a form online, CDF1, so that you can ask HMRC to consider the client for a contract under the Contractual Disclosure Facility. The form must be printed, signed by the client, and sent to HMRC's Fraud Investigation Service for consideration. The client's contact details, together with his date of birth, tax reference number, VAT number, where appropriate, National Insurance number, and confirmation that the client is UK-resident

Voluntary disclosures **14.47**

must be provided. When the client is already under enquiry, those details must also be included on the form.

14.44 HMRC don't have to offer the client a contract under the process, and won't do so if the client is already involved in a criminal investigation by HMRC or another law enforcement agent (such as the police).

14.45 When a client voluntarily requests the protection afforded by the Contractual Disclosure Facility, it is very unlikely that HMRC would seek to pursue a criminal investigation. Generally, HMRC will not deny the client an opportunity to use the Contractual Disclosure Facility, except as indicated above. To do otherwise would deter taxpayers from making voluntary disclosures through that process.

14.46 Practitioners should consider the implications of registering a client for the Contractual Disclosure Facility, particularly where the client may have a reporting obligation to a professional body, and advise the client accordingly.

14.47 Where the client has used the Contractual Disclosure Facility, or a previous incarnation of HMRC's Code of Practice 9 process, extra care should be taken before approaching HMRC. The adviser should establish whether the previous disclosure submitted to HMRC was incorrect, or whether a false statement was provided during that process. Legal advice should be obtained before proceeding, as HMRC may not be willing to give the client a second opportunity to use the Code of Practice 9 route to regularise his tax affairs.

Example 14.8

I was asked to assist in a case where HMRC had written to the client under the Contractual Disclosure Facility. The accountant advised me that the client's undeclared income was around £20,000 (much less than the usual level at which HMRC will use the Contractual Disclosure Facility), and they had not been able to establish any additional risk areas from the client that would justify the use of the process. I subsequently met with the client, and established that he had asked the accountant to make a voluntary disclosure on his behalf – the undeclared income was in the region of £20,000. The accountant had voluntarily registered the client for the Contractual Disclosure Facility. Although the client's behaviour had been deliberate, the amounts involved did not merit using that process, and registering the client for that process was over-kill. After I had obtained various assurances from the client, HMRC agreed to withdraw the Contractual Disclosure Facility invitation. The disclosure was submitted to HMRC, and a conclusion reached within a few weeks. Thanks to my involvement, the client saved

14.48 *Voluntary disclosures*

a considerable amount of time, and also the professional costs that would otherwise have been incurred in dealing with the Contractual Disclosure Facility.

MAKING THE DISCLOSURE

Focus

Planning and preparation are essential before the disclosure is made to HMRC. Although time constraints may mean that the full extent of the quantum of the additional liability will not be known, a broad understanding of the offences that have been committed, and an approximation of the amounts involved, should be established at an early stage. The practitioner can then determine the route by which notification will be made to HMRC.

14.48 The typical steps in making the disclosure to HMRC are outlined below:

1　Establish the nature and quantum of the disclosure (to determine the best route for disclosing to HMRC).

2　Put HMRC on notice that a disclosure will be made (or register for a disclosure facility).

3　Analyse and quantify additional income and gains.

4　Prepare the disclosure narrative (this may be a letter for a simple disclosure, or a substantive report where matters are more complex).

5　Make tax and interest calculations.

6　Consider and, potentially, quantify the appropriate penalty (when a disclosure opportunity is used, quantification of the penalty is usually required).

7　Gain approval of the disclosure by the client.

8　Submit the disclosure to HMRC.

14.49 Practitioners should refer to **CHAPTER 17** for consideration of the content of the disclosure letter/report, and the methodologies to use. The disclosure report should set out the background to the under-declaration, and include any mitigating circumstances, such as bereavement or serious illness. The practitioner should ensure that all relevant liabilities are included, and should also consider the non-domicile rules, if they are applicable to the client, as failure to apply them correctly can lead to additional liabilities, and they are an area of particular interest for HMRC.

Voluntary disclosures **14.55**

14.50 It is important to note that, although the practitioner should get the client to confirm his agreement to the disclosure report, the document should not be sent to HMRC with a certified statement of adoption. The client should also be asked to confirm in writing that the report can be sent to HMRC.

14.51 When notification has been made to HMRC that a voluntary disclosure will be made, it is prudent for practitioners to recommend that the client makes a payment on account towards the eventual tax liability. A payment can be made at the time of the notification to HMRC. As quantification of the liability is refined, further payments on account should be recommended. The making of payments on account will help to reduce the overall liability, as interest will be accruing on a daily basis. When a disclosure covers the old penalty regime, the making of payments on account may also impact on the level of penalty sought by HMRC.

14.52 Practitioners should establish whether the client has the means to fund the likely settlement. If the client will need time to pay, that should be established at the earliest opportunity, and discussed with HMRC. That will maximise the likelihood of HMRC agreeing an instalment arrangement. Practitioners should ensure that any instalment arrangements are reasonable, and that the client will be able to meet the payments as they fall due. Failure to meet the terms of the arrangement can mean that HMRC will take recovery action against the client, including bankruptcy or liquidation. The client's financial status will need to be demonstrated to HMRC, and the officer may require evidence that the client has, for example, exhausted sources of finance.

14.53 An example of what can go wrong when making a voluntary disclosure is illustrated by the First-tier Tribunal decision in the case of *D'Souza v Revenue and Customs Comrs* [2012] UKFTT 210 (TC). Mr D'Souza voluntarily disclosed to HMRC that he had failed to declare the interest arising on an offshore bank account. HMRC requested sight of bank account statements to verify that the disclosure was complete, even though the reported tax at stake was only £44.61. The taxpayer resisted HMRC's informal request for the statements.

14.54 HMRC subsequently issued a formal notice, under *FA 2008, Sch 36*, requesting 'bank statements in relation to accounts you may have held outside the UK between 6 April 2006 and 5 April 2009'. Mr D'Souza did not provide the statements and appealed against the notice. The First-tier Tribunal dismissed the appeal, deciding that the information notice was lawful.

14.55 Practitioners should be aware that the above represents a typical response from HMRC, and pre-empt the outcome when dealing with a voluntary disclosure. HMRC will want to verify the information provided, and is likely to ask for supporting documentation. Where there is a bank account

14.56 *Voluntary disclosures*

involved, HMRC will also want to establish the source of any funds deposited therein.

HMRC'S RESPONSE TO THE DISCLOSURE

> **Focus**
>
> Before submitting the substantive disclosure report or letter to HMRC, practitioners should consider the likely response. They should objectively review the available documentation and information, and consider whether it makes sense. Practitioners without sufficient experience in this area should seek assistance from an investigation specialist.

14.56 Practitioners should consider whether:

- the report adequately covers the risk areas;
- HMRC will view the disclosure as complete, or whether there are any obvious holes in the information or documentation that are not adequately addressed;
- the facts stand up to close scrutiny:
- they have included the appropriate period in the disclosure (this requires a consideration of the nature of the disclosure and the client's behaviour to determine whether there should be a four/six/20-year disclosure period).

14.57 Although the client is making a voluntary disclosure, whether prompted or unprompted, HMRC will want to verify that the disclosure is complete. As noted in the example at **14.53**, HMRC can be expected to request supporting documentation to satisfy itself that the disclosure has been accurately quantified, and that all relevant matters have been disclosed.

> **Example 14.9**
>
> Where a client makes a disclosure of undeclared rental income, HMRC will want to establish that the funding of the property and, potentially, the mortgage, can be demonstrated. Practitioners should verify the position with the client, and comment on this matter in the disclosure report. If the client has used undeclared business takings to fund, or part-fund, the acquisition of the property or any expenditure thereon, the practitioner should ensure that is included in the disclosure computations.

> **Focus**
>
> Pre-empting HMRC's likely questions can reduce the overall time that a case takes to be resolved, and help to minimise the penalty sought by HMRC. Although the adviser may not be able to pre-empt all of HMRC's likely queries, he should address the most obvious ones. This will help to smooth the processing of the disclosure, and to manage the client's expectations.

> **Example 14.10**
>
> Where the client's disclosure concerns undeclared business takings, practitioners should ensure that they have reviewed the client's private financial affairs. This ensures that the client's private spending, and acquisition of assets, can be reconciled to the undeclared takings. A reconciliation of this type will help to reassure HMRC that the disclosure is complete.

14.58 Subject to any queries that the officer may have, agreement should be reached as to the additional liabilities. The case will usually be formally settled by a contract agreement between the client and HMRC. Practitioners should note that any VAT liabilities will not be included in the contract settlement, but will be subject to assessments by HMRC. The client will be expected to sign various forms, and these should be explained to the client. For more information, please refer to **CHAPTER 17**.

KEY POINTS

14.59 The following are ten key points for the practitioner to consider:

1 Establish all relevant facts from the client.

2 Determine the reason for the disclosure, to establish whether it is 'prompted' or 'unprompted'.

3 Impress on the client the need for a complete disclosure to be made.

4 Determine the period to be included in the disclosure (be aware of the old and new penalty regimes).

5 Consider the best route for making the disclosure to HMRC.

6 Do not use the Contractual Disclosure Facility without taking specialist advice (unless you have significant experience of that process).

7 Pre-empt HMRC's response, and likely queries, following receipt of the disclosure.

14.59 *Voluntary disclosures*

8   Consider engaging a specialist if you are not able to be sufficiently objective, or lack sufficient expertise.

9   Advise making payments on account to HMRC.

10 Agree an instalment arrangement if the client does not have the means to pay.

Chapter 15

Private records: are they 'private'?

Ian Roberts BA
Partner, The TACS Partnership

Acknowledgement: This chapter includes commentary originally produced by Chris Chadburn BSc

---

SIGNPOSTS

- **HMRC's right to ask for information is constrained by statute** – The rules set out what can and cannot be demanded (see **15.1–15.27**).

- **HMRC must also follow its own guidance** – The adviser must be aware of the stated approach of HMRC and hold it to this (see **15.28–15.32**).

- **The tax tribunal and courts have given guidance on the interpretation of the rules** – The adviser should be aware of decisions and how they inform what HMRC can request (see **15.33–15.35**).

- **Information can be provided voluntarily outside these rules if it supports the taxpayer's position** – The question is whether additional information gives a more positive picture of the position.

- **Key points** – For a list of key points from this chapter, see **15.36**.

INTRODUCTION

15.1 A request by HMRC for records will relate to a compliance check of some description. At one extreme it may be a dozen dividend vouchers are sought to validate an entry in a tax return or, at the other, non-business bank statements for several years will be requested to move forward a tax fraud investigation into a substantial business. HMRC's powers to obtain such information are very wide but they are finite.

15.2 HMRC officers have significant powers to obtain information through *FA 2008*, and in particular *Sch 36*. For a detailed consideration of these see **CHAPTER 16**.

15.3 *Private records: are they 'private'?*

See also HMRC Compliance Check factsheet 2 issued when an information notice is given (www.gov.uk/government/collections/hm-revenue-and-customs-leaflets-factsheets-and-booklets#compliance-checks-factsheets-general-information).

THE POWER TO OBTAIN INFORMATION AND DOCUMENTS

15.3 At the outset of any check the HMRC officer will typically make an informal request for information and usually suggest a date by which this information should be supplied. This will normally be 30 days from the date of the letter requesting the information: see HMRC's Enquiry manual (EM) at EM1580. If the deadline is not met then the next step is often the immediate issue of a taxpayer notice requesting the information.

15.4 HMRC's Compliance Handbook (CH) at CH223100 gives examples of when a formal notice might be appropriate. As well as cases where informal requests have been refused they also cover cases where;

- there is a history of non-compliance and HMRC have reason to believe that information will not be provided if requested informally;
- an informal request is likely to cause an unacceptable delay;
- pre-approval of a taxpayer notice is appropriate, for example when large sums are at stake, there is a fear documents might be destroyed etc. (see CH223400); or
- an investigation into a tax avoidance scheme would benefit from the early use of formal powers.

15.5 The information or document covered by a *FA 2008, Sch 36, para 1* notice must be reasonably required by the officer for the purpose of checking the taxpayer's tax position. 'Tax position' is an extremely wide term and relates to most foreign taxes as well as any UK tax. It includes past, present and future liabilities and is only subject to the application of the time limits for HMRC assessing the tax.

15.6 There are general restrictions on what a person has to produce to HMRC and these are covered in **CHAPTER 16**.

There is also a right of appeal (and HMRC internal review) against the taxpayer notice, unless the notice:

- reflects information or documentation forming part of the taxpayer's statutory records (these are what the taxpayer is required to keep for tax purposes under the Taxes and VAT Acts); or
- has been approved by the First-tier Tribunal.

Private records: are they 'private'? **15.11**

15.7 HMRC's Compliance Handbook at CH212100 gives details of what ranks as a statutory record (which must be delivered to HMRC upon request) and a supplementary record which can be requested only if they are reasonably required by HMRC. A notice requiring the delivery of a supplementary record can be appealed against.

15.8 CH212100 *et seq* also sets out the general requirements relating to record keeping, as required by specific statute (for example as it relates to VAT) and the general requirement that records must be kept to enable any person to make and deliver a correct and complete return.

15.9 Similar powers are used to issue notices to third parties but only after either the taxpayer agrees or approval is obtained from the First-tier Tribunal. CH23620 advises the HMRC officer to try to obtain details from the person whose tax position is being checked before approaching any third party.

Focus

HMRC must be reminded of the rules of the game, which some HMRC officers are prone to forget.

HMRC'S CONDUCT OF ENQUIRIES

15.10 HMRC's stated view is that it operates a system of 'openness and early dialogue' across many areas of compliance checking.

HMRC's approach to enquiry work can be seen in a series of compliance factsheets which can be found at www.gov.uk/government/collections/hm-revenue-and-customs-leaflets-factsheets-and-booklets#compliance-checks-factsheets-general-information.

Non-business information and documents

15.11 Access to private bank account statements and the like can be a major source of friction between taxpayers and HMRC. Clarity on what does and what does not comprise a private record can be crucial. EM1561 sets out the documents and information that HMRC considers may be needed to check the accuracy of the returns of a business taxpayer. In broad terms these are:

- documents on which the return is based;
- business accounts (including detailed analyses, eg drawings or director's loans accounts) and computations;

15.12 *Private records: are they 'private'?*

- items needed to prepare the accounts or returns;
- reconciliations between PAYE and subcontractor records and the accounts;
- details on particular technical points being queried; and
- other documents.

15.12 As far as these 'other documents' relating to business taxpayers are concerned, HMRC state that they adopt the following approach:

- in principle private details can be reasonably required using *FA 2008, Sch 36* powers, but the HMRC officer needs to consider whether it is appropriate to use these powers at the stage reached in each particular case;
- private bank, building society or credit card details should not be requested as a matter of course;
- if the records on which the return was based include private records, these may be requested;
- if means are identified as a risk or accounts are not based on a complete and effective record system, HMRC can request private records;
- the basis of any request should be explained and this should be specific.

15.13 Advice on information requests for non-business taxpayers is at EM1570. Where HMRC wishes to examine private documents it should first consider if it can verify information using third party information already held (eg from banks or building societies). In addition HMRC tells its inspectors:

> 'you should only ask to see private bank statements if you can demonstrate their relevance to the return and that you reasonably require them for the purpose of checking its accuracy.'

15.14 CH207310 refers to proportionality as well as reasonableness in that an HMRC inspector 'must ensure that the administrative burden [he] place[s] on the person is proportionate to the risk'. This is not only an issue of time and cost but also of intrusion into the taxpayer's private life. To avoid any issues under the *Human Rights Act 1998, Sch 1, Article 8*, the HMRC officer is advised that to assess the issue proportionally the following must be considered:

- the nature and degree of the interference;
- whether the interference is reasonable in the circumstances; and
- whether the information can be obtained in a less intrusive manner.

15.15 The greater the interference the more justification is needed. HMRC suggest that discussing the reasons before asking for information will help the taxpayer understand the need for particular information or documents. See CH21360 and CH21380.

15.16 A former version of the HMRC Enquiry Manual included a number of useful examples of situations where such requests would appear to be reasonable. These included situations where HMRC considered:

- undeclared income or gains had been credited to the private account;
- there were doubts or questions about means or capital growth;
- the tax return was based to a degree on the private account;
- where taxable receipts or expenditure were not vouched or were estimated; and
- where payments to the business from an account are treated as non-taxable (say capital introduced) and were not verified.

15.17 There should generally be little argument if the HMRC officer is requesting statutory records or other records used in drawing up the accounts and/or return. More contentious will be cases where there is a dispute around whether the particular information is reasonably required to check the return.

Business models

15.18 There may be other non-financial records relating to the business where it is less obvious that the information being requested is relevant to a check of the return. When investigating business returns, particularly in 'cash trades', officers may request information they believe will help them validate the declared turnover, at least in broad terms. So the hairdresser may be asked for an appointment diary or the pub for its menu and price lists for the relevant periods. The HMRC officer will be looking to use such information to help create a business model to estimate turnover. See EM3502 *et seq* for details of the approach.

15.19 Such models can be simplistic and over-reliant on broad estimates. Considerable time, money and effort can be spent on these exercises with minimal useful output. Objecting to requests for information relating to such models should focus on establishing with the officer what he wants to check and why. The stronger the books and records the easier it will be to get evidence to conclude whether the request is reasonable, and whether HMRC's perception of risk is valid. The taxpayer will invariably be on the back foot if the books and records are demonstrably weak.

15.20 *Private records: are they 'private'?*

> **Focus**
> The adviser should be wary of challenging requests for information which clearly relates or is linked to the business of the taxpayer.

Private finances

15.20 Another common method of testing risks and recalculating profits is a review of private finances. See EM3550 for details of the various approaches adopted by HMRC. The degree of detail requested may vary, but an analysis of private bank statements will be at the heart of any significant review. It is worth repeating the EM1561 advice to HMRC officers at this point:

'the basis of your request should be explained and this should be specific'

15.21 If the officer has followed this guideline then all well and good. Usually the information provided by HMRC will be fairly general but it will hopefully allow the taxpayer or his adviser to decide whether the request is reasonable. It may be helpful to discuss whether there is a better way forward to deal with any HMRC request. For example:

- at least in the first instance, would a review of a sample period (rather than a full tax year) minimise costs?
- can any specific issues raised be addressed? For example, if there is a question of how a new house and other assets were financed, can it be demonstrated that there were loans, gifts etc?

15.22 If the HMRC officer has not provided any substantive reasons for the request then a discussion needs to take place. You can only sensibly decide on the reasonableness of the request if you understand on what basis the request has been made.

15.23 In conducting a detailed private side review, the HMRC officer may well ask for additional personal records in addition to bank statements, for example:

- credit, debit and store card statements;
- paying in slips, cheque counterfoils, specific paid cheques;
- evidence of the purchase of major assets, eg completion statements or vehicle invoices;
- evidence of how the assets were financed, eg mortgage or loan agreements.

Private records: are they 'private'? 15.28

15.24 HMRC's statutory power to obtain information and documents, etc (in *FA 2008, Sch 36*) is subject to certain restrictions (*Sch 36, Pt 4*). For example, *Sch 36, para 19(2)* provides that an information notice does not require a person to provide or produce personal records.

15.25 'Personal records' are defined in the *Police and Criminal Evidence Act 1984, s 12* as:

'documentary and other records concerning an individual ... who can be identified from them relating:

(a) to his physical or mental health;

(b) to spiritual counselling or assistance given or to be given to him; or

(c) to counselling or assistance to be given to him for the purposes of his personal welfare by any voluntary organisation'

15.26 However, an HMRC information notice may require a person to provide documents or copies that are personal records, omitting any 'personal information' (ie information whose inclusion makes the original document a personal record), and to provide any information contained in the records that is not personal information (*Sch 36, para 19(3)*).

15.27 In practice, the above restriction in HMRC's information powers is therefore limited. For example, in *Smith v Revenue and Customs Comrs* [2015] UKFTT 200 (TC), the First-tier Tribunal held that, on the basis that the taxpayer's private bank and credit card statements included business and personal transactions, HMRC's notice requesting such information should be varied in accordance with *Sch 36, para 19(3)*, such that the taxpayer was required to provide the bank and credit card statements, but omitting any personal information.

Focus

The information HMRC is allowed to request is subject to restrictions, which the adviser should be fully aware of.

15.28 The purpose of the detailed reviews is set out at EM3560 and EM3593 in relation to:

- identifying spending patterns;
- checking incoming and outgoing transfers;
- reconciling credits with drawings, director's loan account, etc;

15.29 *Private records: are they 'private'?*

- indications of other accounts and use of cash;
- checking claimed non-business sources of funds;
- seeing how regular payments and large payments were met; and
- taking a view on the taxpayer's lifestyle.

15.29 The HMRC officer may seek information from the taxpayer's spouse or partner to complete the review of private finances. CH207325 advises that in smaller cases the officer can ask the taxpayer to obtain from the spouse a statement of gifts, loans or whatever. If the private side is a 'material consideration' then the officer may need to consider the spouse's:

- income and gifts;
- assets; and
- spending habits.

Such requests should be made direct to the spouse and in the absence of the required information a third party information notice may be issued.

Progressing the enquiry

15.30 At the early stages of an enquiry HMRC will have identified a number of risks but may well have little if any damning information. The worse the state of the records the more likely it will be for HMRC to push hard for details that might help in establishing a view of those risks. As the investigation unfolds, HMRC will develop a clearer picture of potential problems and this will influence requests for further and better particulars in relation to the business and/or the private side. In simple terms, HMRC will be looking to put itself in a better position to argue its case before the tax tribunal if matters were to progress through such action.

15.31 A common request is for certain working papers of the accountant to be provided. These are 'link papers', ie those explaining an entry in the records and the corresponding entry in the return. HMRC's view is that where necessary these can be obtained formally through the taxpayer or the accountant (EM10023 and EM10150). Provision of the trial balance may save time and trouble in answering basic questions.

15.32 HMRC's position on information requests for directors of close companies is set out in EM8211. If the enquiry is into the company and the private finances of the director are a 'particular concern':

- the company should be asked (voluntarily) to provide private bank statements of the director;

- if these are not produced and there are clear risks present on the director's return, an enquiry into that return may be opened and an information notice issued to the director;
- if this is not appropriate or not possible because of expired time limits, a third party information notice may be issued to the director.

TAX CASES

First-tier Tribunal

15.33 Cases under *Sch 36* have involved matters where it is clear that there are issues arising in the returns and HMRC's approach has been upheld as reasonable as a question of fact.

'It is not for the Tribunal to determine how HMRC conduct their review ... provided what is done is within the rules as laid down by the legislation and case law.'

(*Paul Whight v Revenue and Customs Comrs* [2011] UKFTT 60 (TC))

'The Tribunal finds as a fact that the information sought by HMRC was to verify the Appellant's returns and accounts and to ensure that all sources of income and liabilities had been declared and paid.'

(*D Midgley & Sons Ltd and Stuart Midgley v Revenue and Customs Comrs* [2011] UKFTT 187 (TC))

'The information relating to the account held ... with the bank of East Asia Ltd in Hong Kong was reasonably required ... because the Inspector of Taxes ... was not in a position to satisfy himself as to the lodgements in the Hong Kong account.'

(*Wong Yau Lam v Revenue and Customs Comrs* [2012] UKFTT 118 (TC))

'Mr Beckwith's First Direct Account is a business record and so forms part of his statutory records .... As a result he has no right of appeal ... to the extent that it asks for the bank statements relating to the First Direct account.'

The account was used to pay 90 business expenses in relation to purchases, rent and rates, materials and phone purchases (*Beckwith v Revenue and Customs Comrs* [2012] UKFTT 181 (TC) (see **6.53**)).

'information and documents are statutory records if and for as long as Mrs Lee is required by the Taxes Acts to preserve them and Mrs Lee has no right of appeal against an Information Notice in respect of them.'

(*Priti Lee v Revenue and Customs Comrs* [2012] UKFTT 312 (TC))

15.34 *Private records: are they 'private'?*

In *Alvi* [2016] UKFTT 0201 (TC) (a case involving a tax avoidance scheme), the Tribunal held that the information requests were entirely proper, reasonable and directly concerned with the taxpayer's tax position, and that whilst the taxpayer may not have had the relevant documentation or have been given an oral summary of the scheme, HMRC should insist on the taxpayer obtaining documents from the other material parties to the scheme.

15.34 See also:

- *Singh v Revenue and Customs Comrs* [2014] UKFTT 299 (TC) – dealing with bank statements delivered in response to an information notice which had certain names redacted.

- *Spring Capital Ltd v Revenue and Customs Comrs* [2015] UKFTT 8 (TC) – where the tribunal held that HMRC was entitled to check a company's tax return without having 'grounds for suspicion'. There was nothing in *Sch 36, para 1* that required HMRC to suspect that the return was incorrect before issuing an information notice.

- *Betts v Revenue and Customs Comrs* [2013] UKFTT 430 (TC) – where HMRC failed to convince the tribunal that it had a real and genuine belief (and to provide evidence) of the fact that the amount that ought to have been assessed may not have been assessed.

Special Commissioners and the courts

15.35 Earlier cases include:

- Re *TMA 1970, s 19*

    - *Mother v HM Inspector of Taxes* Sp C [1999] SSCD 279

    - *Siwek v CIR* Sp C [2002] SSCD 247

    - *Sokoya v HMRC* [2008] EWHC 2132 (Ch)

    - *Murat v HM Inspector of Taxes* [2000] SSCD 522

    - *Guyer v Walton* Sp C [2001] SSCD 75

    - *Taylor v Bratherton* Sp C 2004 [2005] SSCD 230

        This is a rare occasion where the taxman did not satisfy the Commissioner that the request for private records from the taxpayer (a taxi driver) was reasonable. The notices were valid in 'so far as the documents and information specified in the notices relate to the taxpayer's income and allowable deductions.' As far as details of his personal expenditure was concerned 'the request

Private records: are they 'private'? **15.35**

was intrusive and should not be required ... if that could be avoided'.

- *Murphy v Gowers* [2005] Sp C 434
- *Guest House Proprietor v Kendall* [2005] SSCD 280

  Concerned comprehensive list of documents required with many points settled by agreement.

- *Alan Humphreys v Revenue and Customs Comrs* [2010] UKFTT 204 (TC)

• Re *TMA 1970, s 20*, whether notices unreasonable

- *Monarch Assurance Co Ltd v Special Commissioners* (1986) 59 TC 594

  Upheld, company engaged in share option scheme.

- *Kempton v Special Commissioners of Income Tax* (1992) 66 TC 249

  Upheld, although the extent and cost of the material required was extensive.

- *R v O'Kane & Clarke, ex p Northern Bank Ltd* (1996) 69 TC 187

  Not upheld as considered too general.

- *R v IRC, ex p Ulster Bank Ltd* (1997) 69 TC 211

  Upheld, Northern Bank principles overturned by Court of Appeal.

- *R v IRC and Connolly, ex p Mohammed and Electrowide Ltd* (1998) 73 TC 128

  Upheld notices to bank although prejudicial to the taxpayer.

- *R v IRC, ex p Banque International a Luxembourg SA* (2000) 72 TC 597

  Upheld as significant and dubious avoidance scheme.

- *R (on the application of Werner) v IRC* [2002] STC 1213

  Upheld although taxpayer in prison for tax fraud.

- *R v IRC, ex p David Frankel and Mead* (2000) 73 TC 185

  Upheld, significant burden to the taxpayer's solicitors but not disproportionate.

15.36 *Private records: are they 'private'?*

KEY POINTS

15.36 When faced with a request for information the following questions need to be considered:

1   Are the records or documents requested 'statutory'?
2   If not, is HMRC acting within its own guidelines?
3   Do they relate to out of time periods?
4   Is the basis for the request understood?
5   If so, is it reasonable to require these to check the return?
6   Essentially, is the request irrelevant to the check, onerous, intrusive or disproportionate?
7   In any event is it in the interests of the client to provide the details requested and/or any other information not requested?

Chapter 16

HMRC's information powers

Hartley Foster
Partner, Fieldfisher LLP

SIGNPOSTS

- **Scope** – HMRC's information powers are to be found in primary and secondary legislation. HMRC's civil information powers that enable HMRC officers to obtain information and documents for the purpose of checking a taxpayer's tax position are to be found in *FA 2008, Sch 36* (see **16.24–16.89**). HMRC's powers in relation to criminal tax matters are to be found in the *Police and Criminal Evidence Act 1984, ss 60–70*, the *Serious Organised Crime and Police Act 2005, Sch 1, Pt 2* and *TMA 1970, s 20BA* (see **16.193–16.233**). HMRC's interpretation of its powers is to be found in its Compliance Handbook.

- **Preliminary issues** – Clients should be educated regarding record keeping and practitioners should ensure that, wherever possible, clients keep and maintain adequate records from the outset. Ideally, documents held by clients should be segregated, according to whether or not they constitute 'business records' and whether they may be protected from disclosure, particularly by reason of legal professional privilege. (See **16.108–16.110**.)

- **The people involved** – HMRC officers are trained in enquiries and in relation to information powers. Practitioners must be prepared fully. Consideration should be given to whether it would be in the client's best interest for the matter to be handled in-house, or whether an external specialist should be engaged instead.

- **Practicalities** – With regard to HMRC's civil information powers, practitioners should have the requisite knowledge and understanding of the tax legislation as it applies to HMRC's information powers, and an awareness of HMRC practice from guidance such as the

16.1 *HMRC's information powers*

> Compliance Handbook. Advising in relation to a criminal investigation requires specialist expertise, from the day of a raid onwards.
>
> - **Controversial points** – Areas of potential difficulty include HMRC requests for a taxpayer's private records (namely, whether such requests are justified), and unannounced visits by HMRC officers to taxpayers' business premises (see **16.42** and **16.115–16.116** respectively). Regarding the latter, it is important to ensure that the officers comply with their obligations, including, for example, providing a copy of the requisite notice of inspection.
>
> - **Other issues** – HMRC requests for documents that pertain to both business and non-business matters, such as diaries, should be addressed with care, particularly where such documents contain sensitive personal information. Practitioners should be prepared to seek expert professional help in appropriate cases.
>
> - **Key points** – For a list of key points from this chapter, see **16.235**.

INTRODUCTION

> **Focus**
>
> This chapter aims to provide practical guidance to assist practitioners in relation to the powers of information that are possessed by HMRC. It comprises an analysis of HMRC's civil investigatory powers and an analysis of the powers that are available to HMRC in relation to criminal investigations.

16.1 Before the bodies were merged (in 2005), HM Customs and Excise and the Inland Revenue had powers that were set out in legislation that applied only to each department; and there were significant differences between the powers available to each department.

16.2 It was an aim of the Government that, post-merger, the powers available to HMRC officers should be rationalised in accordance with a fundamental underlying principle, namely that the nature of the activity, rather than the tax, should determine the ambit of the statutory power. HM Revenue and Customs' system of information powers (which reflects that aim) has been introduced in stages. The new system was introduced by *FA 2007* and *FA 2008*. In general terms and on each occasion, the powers that the new legislation replaced were repealed at the same time and consequentially. There are, however, transitional provisions that keep in force the pre-1 April 2009 rules relating to appeals and penalties for information notices that were issued before 1 April 2009.

HMRC's information powers **16.3**

1   *FA 2007* included enabling legislation under which the criminal investigatory powers of HMRC in England, Wales and Northern Ireland became based on the powers contained in the *Police and Criminal Evidence Act 1984 (PACE 1984)*.

2   *FA 2008* introduced a new regime of civil information powers that enable HMRC officers to obtain information and documents for the purpose of 'checking a taxpayer's tax position'.

16.3   The Government has amended the scope of HMRC's information powers in virtually every Finance Act that has been introduced since *FA 2008*. Key amendments include:

1   *FA 2009* amended and extended the regime that had been introduced by *FA 2008*.

2   *FA 2010* extended the regime to include bank payroll tax.

3   *F(No 3)A 2010* aligned the record-keeping rules and time limits for excise duties in accordance with the changes that had been made to other taxes and duties.

4   *FA 2011* introduced a consolidated set of powers that enable HMRC to require data-holders who hold information on third parties to provide HMRC with 'relevant' data.

5   *FA 2012* introduced a new power for HMRC to obtain information about a taxpayer whose identity is not known where HMRC is unable to demonstrate a likelihood of serious prejudice to the assessment or collection of tax (which is required under the 'identity unknown' power in *FA 2008, Sch 36*).

6   *FA 2013*:

   (a)   aligned HMRC's powers under the *Proceeds of Crime Act 2002*, so that its powers pertaining to income tax and corporation tax issues are the same as its powers in relation to indirect taxes; and

   (b)   introduced a power that allows HMRC to issue information notices to merchant acquirers, who process credit and debit card transactions, requiring them to provide bulk data to HMRC about businesses accepting card payments.

7   *FA 2014* inserted new provisions into *FA 2004* that empower HMRC to require persons who have made DOTAS disclosures to provide additional information and documents (in such form and manner as HMRC specifies); and ensure that 'high-risk promoters' of tax avoidance structures are made subject to stricter monitoring, and information disclosure rules.

16.4 *HMRC's information powers*

8   FA 2015 introduced a requirement for promoters of DOTAS structures to provide updated information to HMRC (and extended the information that promoters must give clients).

9   FA 2016 extended HMRC's data-gathering powers to electronic payment service providers and online business intermediaries.

10   F(No 2)A 2017 extended HMRC's data-gathering powers to money service businesses.

16.4 After this introductory section, this chapter comprises two sections. The first section contains an analysis of HMRC's civil investigatory powers (under *FA 2008, Sch 36*); and the second contains an analysis of the powers that are available to HMRC in relation to criminal investigations (under *PACE 1984*, the *Serious Organised Crime and Police Act 2005* (*SOCPA 2005*) and *TMA 1970, s 20BA*).

The rationale for change

16.5 The Commissioners for Revenue and *Customs Act 2005* (*CRCA 2005*) received Royal Assent on 7 April 2005. It provided the legal basis for the integrated department of HM Customs and Excise and the Inland Revenue (HMRC) and for the independent prosecutions office – the Revenue and Customs Prosecutions Office (RCPO).

16.6 Under *CRCA 2005*, HMRC became responsible for all the functions that were previously the responsibility of the Commissioners of Inland Revenue and the Commissioners of Customs and Excise, absent prosecutions (for which, as a result of *CRCA 2005, s 35*, RCPO had responsibility). On 1 January 2010, RCPO was merged with, and formed a new Revenue and Customs division within, the Crown Prosecution Service.

16.7 Prior to the merger, HM Customs and Excise and the Inland Revenue had powers that were set out in legislation that applied only to each department. Although the two bodies had different functions, responsibilities and powers, the powers of each body were transferred unchanged to HMRC. The powers were 'ring fenced' so that they could be used only for their original purpose. Thus, the basis on which it was determined which powers were available to HMRC was by reference to the specific tax that was being investigated. The powers of the former Inland Revenue were applicable to direct taxes; and the powers of the former HM Customs and Excise were applicable to indirect taxes, and to customs and excise duties.

16.8 However, the Government had recognised, prior to the merger of the departments, that it was important to consider whether the heterogeneous powers of HMRC could be rationalised. This would make it easier for taxpayers to understand and comply with their tax obligations, and potentially could reduce the administrative burden of the tax system that fell on them.

16.9 A major review of HMRC's powers, deterrents and safeguards was undertaken. During the second reading of *CRCA 2005*, the Paymaster General announced that a consultation process entitled 'Modernising Powers, Deterrents and Safeguards: A Consultation on the Developing Programme of Work' would be commenced in 2006. This consultation process included a review of the information powers available to HMRC in relation to civil tax matters, as well as where criminal activity was suspected. HMRC indicated that, in its view, *PACE 1984* should become the statutory framework for the investigation of all tax-related criminal activity.

16.10 Following the review of HMRC's powers and a subsequent consultation, including consultation on draft clauses, the Government, in *FA 2007*, introduced enabling legislation under which HMRC's investigatory powers in England, Wales and Northern Ireland became based on the powers contained in *PACE 1984*. (A statutory code was introduced for Scotland, where PACE does not apply.) By Treasury Order that was introduced with effect from 1 December 2007 (see further below), these powers apply across all taxes and mean that HMRC criminal investigations are subject to the statutory codes of practice and safeguards that attach to criminal investigations generally. A notable change therefore was that, from 1 December 2007, HMRC officers have had the *PACE 1984* powers of search, seizure and arrest in connection with ex-Inland Revenue matters.

Finance Act 2007

16.11 The amendments in *FA 2007* increased the powers available to ex-Inland Revenue investigators; and mean that HMRC no longer needs to follow different procedures in the same investigation where both direct and indirect tax fraud are suspected.

16.12 *FA 2007* repealed *TMA 1970, s 20C*, and *para 10(3), Sch 11* of the *Value Added Tax Act 1994* (*VATA 1994*) and *ss 82(2)* and *83(2)* of that Act enabled the Treasury to make an order applying the provisions of *PACE 1984* to investigations conducted by Officers of HMRC. The Police and Criminal Evidence Act 1984 (Application to Revenue and Customs) Order 2007, SI 2007/3175 was laid before Parliament on 9 November 2007; it applies the relevant provisions of *PACE 1984* to all functions of HMRC (except where the department acts as an agent for other government departments) with effect from 1 December 2007.

16.13 Thus, since 1 December 2007, HMRC officers have had access to the appropriate powers in *PACE 1984* to investigate all tax matters where criminal

16.14 *HMRC's information powers*

activity is suspected. In particular, since that date, search warrants have been obtained under *PACE 1984, s 8 and Sch 1*, rather than *TMA 1970, s 20C* (for offences concerning direct tax) or *VATA 1994, Sch 11, para 10(3)* (for offences concerning indirect tax).

16.14 The changes introduced by *FA 2007* resolved a number of the problems that arose when HMRC officers sought to investigate combined instances of direct and indirect tax fraud. For example, prior to the introduction of these changes, if a taxpayer was suspected of both VAT and corporation tax fraud, separate warrants for each of these offences were required to search and seize evidence from the same premises and, technically, the taxpayer had to be arrested twice (once by the police for the suspected direct tax offence and once by HMRC officers for the suspected indirect tax offence).

It is to be noted, however, that there remain a number of police powers (such as the power to charge and bail suspects and the power to take fingerprints) that HMRC is unable to exercise.

16.15 FA 2007 also introduced a new regime for penalties for incorrect declarations and returns. The Finance Act 2007, Sch 24 (Commencement and Transitional Provisions) Order 2008, SI 2008/568, brought into force the provisions of *FA 2007, Sch 24* in relation to return periods beginning from 1 April 2008, but provides that *Sch 24* shall not apply to any tax period for which a return is required to be made before 1 April 2009.

16.16 Under *FA 2007, Sch 24*, a single penalty regime applies to returns (and similar documents) for income tax (including PAYE), capital gains tax, the construction industry scheme, corporation tax, National Insurance contributions and VAT. *FA 2010* included legislation to align the remaining VAT (and other indirect tax) penalties and introduced new penalty rules for unauthorised issue of VAT invoices and for breach of the obligation to notify chargeability to tax. Under the current penalty regime, an error in a 'taxpayer's document' (which is broadly a tax return or the accounts that accompany the return) gives rise to a penalty if that inaccuracy amounts to or leads to an understatement of the taxpayer's liability to tax and that inaccuracy was 'careless or deliberate'.

16.17 This approach relates the determination of penalties to the underlying behaviour that gave rise to the inaccurate return or assessment. If it was caused by a mistake or misinterpretation of fact or law and reasonable care was taken, then there is no penalty. Otherwise, to reflect the increasing seriousness of the behaviour, penalties at three different levels may be imposed:

1   failure to take reasonable care;

2   deliberate understatement; and

3   deliberate understatement with concealment.

HMRC's information powers **16.22**

16.18 There are reductions for disclosure. In general terms, early and truthful explanation of why the arrears arose and their true extent, supplying information promptly, including full written disclosure, will result in mitigation of the penalty.

Finance Acts 2008 and 2009

16.19 *FA 2008* homogenised HMRC's powers in relation to civil tax matters. It introduced a new regime of information powers that enable HMRC officers to obtain information and documents for the purpose of 'checking a taxpayer's tax position' (*Sch 36*).

16.20 As introduced, with effect from 1 April 2009 (under the Finance Act 2008, Sch 36 (Appointed Day and Savings) Order 2009, SI 2009/404), *Sch 36* applied to enquiries into income tax, corporation tax, capital gains tax, VAT, PAYE, NICs and construction industry scheme (CIS) liabilities.

16.21 *FA 2009, ss 95* and *96* and *Schs 47* and *48* contained amendments to the information and inspection powers contained in *Sch 36*, and extended the *Sch 36* regime to:

(a) insurance premium tax;

(b) inheritance tax;

(c) stamp duty land tax;

(d) stamp duty reserve tax;

(e) petroleum revenue tax;

(f) aggregates levy;

(g) climate change levy;

(h) landfill tax; and

(i) relevant foreign taxes.

16.22 These provisions also provided for the repeal (by statutory instrument in due course) of other information and inspection powers that are no longer required. The Finance Act 2008, Schedule 36 (Appointed Day and Savings) Order 2009 repealed, with effect from 1 April 2009, a number of the old HMRC information powers (including *TMA 1970, s 20*) and self-assessment information powers (including *TMA 1970, s 19A*), subject to transitional provisions. The transitional provisions keep in force the pre-1 April 2009 rules relating to appeals and penalties for information notices issued before 1 April 2009. Documents in respect of which a penalty is exigible under *TMA 1970, s 98* are expressly excluded from the *FA 2007, Sch 24* penalty regime. Thus, the

16.23 *HMRC's information powers*

'old' regime remains in force in relation to penalties for failure to comply with a *s 20* notice.

16.23 *FA 2009, Sch 48* also introduced the concept of an 'involved third party', namely a person who is 'closely involved' in a potentially taxable event or transaction and who has obligations to provide information in relation to certain taxes that are similar to the obligations of a taxpayer. Involved third parties were specifically defined; they included, for example, a manager of an individual investment plan, a body approved for the purposes of payroll giving to charity and an account provider in relation to a child trust fund.

FINANCE ACT 2008, SCH 36

Summary

16.24 *FA 2008, Sch 36* introduced a common compliance checking structure. It is intended to provide a more flexible approach than was possible with the heterogeneous information powers that HMRC possessed previously. Under *Sch 36*, it is different taxpayer behaviours, rather than different taxes, that determine the approach to be taken by HMRC. *Sch 36* provides a framework for:

- the records to be kept and the requirement to make them available to HMRC;
- the powers to obtain information from taxpayers and third parties;
- inspection powers; and
- time limits for assessment.

Scope of HMRC's information and inspection powers

16.25 *Sch 36* introduced two classes of information powers:

- the power to obtain information and documents; and
- the power to inspect premises.

16.26 These powers apply in relation to:

- income tax;
- capital gains tax;
- corporation tax;
- value added tax (for taxpayer and third party notices, this includes both UK VAT and VAT charged by other member states);

HMRC's information powers **16.30**

- insurance premium tax;
- inheritance tax;
- stamp duty land tax;
- stamp duty reserve tax;
- petroleum revenue tax;
- aggregates levy;
- landfill tax;
- relevant foreign tax; and
- bank payroll tax.

16.27 'Relevant foreign tax' is either tax due to an EU member state which is covered by the EU Council Directive 2011/16EU on administrative co-operation in the field of taxation or tax imposed by a country with which the UK has either a double tax treaty containing an exchange of information article or a tax information exchange agreement.

The power to obtain information and documents

16.28 Under *Sch 36*, an HMRC officer may, by notice in writing ('an information notice'), require the taxpayer or a third party to provide information or documents if the 'information or document is reasonably required for the purpose of checking the taxpayer's tax position'.

Tax position

16.29 'Tax position' is defined in *Sch 36, para 64* as a person's position as regards any tax, including:

(a) past, present and future liabilities to pay tax;

(b) penalties and other amounts payable in connection with any tax; and

(c) claims, elections, applications and notices in relation to that person's liability to pay tax.

16.30 HMRC take the view that an officer does not have to have evidence that a document will definitely affect the tax position, only that it is 'reasonably required' to carry out a check. In *Long v Revenue and Customs Comrs* [2014] UKFTT 199 (TC), the First-tier Tribunal rejected HMRC's contention that a doctor's appointment diary was reasonably required. The tribunal accepted the doctor's evidence that the diary contained no financial information, observing

16.31 *HMRC's information powers*

that the diary was 'not necessarily an accurate record of patients seen and services provided or charged for' and that there was 'no way of correlating the numbers of patients with the turnover generated'.

16.31 A person served with an information notice must provide the information or documents within such period as is 'reasonably specified or described' in the notice (*para 7*). There is no minimum limit that can be set for compliance. Whether the time limit for compliance is 'reasonable' will depend on the circumstances of the notice and the information sought under it.

The legislation also gives HMRC the right to 'reasonably specify' the place where the information should be produced for inspection (*para 7(2)*).

16.32 A person who receives an information notice is only required to produce a document if it is in that person's possession or power (under *Sch 36, para 18*). However, 'information' can require the creation of new documents on service of an information notice. The information requested in an information notice may be specified or 'described' by HMRC (*para 6(2)*). This means that HMRC is not restricted to asking for documents that it can identify specifically. In the Explanatory Notes to the Finance Bill 2008, it was indicated that 'information' includes both explanations and the creation of schedules or documents that do not already exist.

16.33 In *R D Utilities Ltd v Revenue and Customs Comrs* [2014] UKFTT 303 (TC), the First-tier Tribunal allowed a company's appeal against a notice that required 'subjective' information. The tribunal held that 'information notices should be expressed in clear terms' and it said that

'it should be a straightforward matter for both parties to know whether an information notice has been complied with. That is why HMRC guidance states that the information notice should request facts and not opinion. In this case, the built-in assumptions on which the requests for information were based made it impossible for the parties to know whether the notice had been complied with because the accuracy of the assumptions was disputed.'

Similarly, in *Gold Nuts Limited and others v HMRC* [2017] UKFTT 354 (TC), the First-tier Tribunal held that a taxpayer could not be required, under an information notice, to provide an opinion on a point of law. In this case, HMRC had asked the taxpayer to explain why it considered that a loan was not within the loans to participators rules. The tribunal noted that it was open to the HMRC officer to ask the taxpayer why it had adopted a particular tax position. But, that was part of the enquiry process; it was not the purpose of an information notice.

16.34 Provision is also made that the information should be supplied in such form (if any) as is specified by HMRC. It is considered that this means that HMRC may request information and/or documents in electronic form. *FA 2008, s 114* gives HMRC, at any reasonable time, access to computers used in connection with relevant documents and a power to insist (with threat of a penalty for obstruction) on 'reasonable assistance' in relation to the same. HMRC regularly requires that business records be supplied in electronic form and demands that computer records be produced.

16.35 *Sch 36, para 7(2)* allows HMRC to specify physical production at a place other than a dwelling. In *TELNG Ltd v Revenue and Customs Comrs* [2015] UKFTT 327 (TC), the First-tier Tribunal observed, in passing, that a notice that failed to provide an option for physical production at a place might be found invalid, on the basis that the concomitant requirement to post or email the documents involved was not, in all the circumstances, a reasonable one.

Information not reasonably required

16.36 An information notice only requires the recipient to produce information or documents 'reasonably required' for checking the relevant person's tax *position (Sch 36, para 1)*. However, HMRC's conduct is not relevant to the question of whether information is reasonably required (see *Whitefields Golf Club Ltd v Revenue and Customs Comrs* [2014] UKFTT 458 (TC).

Burden of proof

16.37 *R (on the application of Derrin Brother Properties Ltd) v Revenue and Customs Comrs* [2014] EWHC 1152 (Admin) established that the burden of proof in relation to the 'reasonably required' test lies on the taxpayer. However, in *Mathew v Revenue and Customs Comrs* [2015] UKFTT 139 (TC), the First-tier Tribunal, having noted *Derrin Brothers* decided to proceed 'on the working assumption that HMRC had the burden of showing that it was reasonable to require the information or documents' and said that 'had we found that HMRC had not met that burden, we would have adjourned the case for further submissions in relation to the burden of proof'.

16.38 In practice, in a dispute about whether the information or document should be produced, HMRC will be obliged to provide the reasons why it considers the information to be reasonably required. In *Behague v Revenue and Customs Comrs* [2013] UKFTT 647 (TC), the First-tier Tribunal held that HMRC was justified in requesting a large amount of information and documents in relation to an unusually large tax deduction claimed on the appellant's tax return. However, the First-tier Tribunal also held that, once an engagement letter between lawyer and client had been redacted to remove the

16.39 *HMRC's information powers*

paragraphs that were covered by legal professional privilege, the remainder of the letter was irrelevant to the enquiry and so did not need to be disclosed.

'Non-business' records

16.39 A frequent area of disagreement is where HMRC requests information contained in 'non-business' records, such as private bank accounts. Requests for details of personal expenditure may be intrusive and the Special Commissioners held that they should not be sought if that can be avoided (*Taylor v Bratherton (Inspector of Taxes)* [2005] STC (SCD) 230). However, requests for documents and information concerning the taxpayer's income are reasonable for the purposes of an enquiry into the taxpayer's affairs (*Commane v Revenue and Customs Comrs* [2006] STC (SCD) 81). It is sensible to keep personal and business transactions and bank accounts separate. In *Beckwith v Revenue and Customs Comrs* [2012] UKFTT 181 (TC), a large number of business transactions had been undertaken through the taxpayer's personal bank account. The First-tier Tribunal held that the taxpayer's personal bank account statements were business records and therefore statutory records for the purposes of *Sch 36* and that they were reasonably required for checking the tax position of the taxpayer's business.

16.40 There are three main information notices that HMRC may issue under *Sch 36*:

- a taxpayer notice;
- a third party notice; and
- an identity unknown notice.

These notices are addressed in turn below.

16.41 *FA 2009, Sch 48* introduced a power that enabled HMRC to issue 'involved third party notices'. That power was replaced, with effect from 1 April 2012, by a power that applies to a range of 'data holders', under *FA 2011, Sch 23*. An additional 'identity unknown' power was introduced with effect from 1 April 2010 by *FA 2012*. These additional powers are addressed subsequently.

Taxpayer notice (Sch 36, para 1): key points

16.42 Paragraph 1 bestows on HMRC a free-standing power to obtain information and documents. The issue of a notice requiring production of information is no longer related, as it was in respect of the self-assessment information powers, to the issue of a notice of enquiry Nor is it issued for the purpose of 'determining whether a return is incomplete'. Instead, it is issued

HMRC's information powers **16.45**

for the purpose of checking the taxpayer's 'tax position' (which includes future liabilities to pay tax).

Thus, the power allows HMRC to inspect records before a return is filed.

16.43 A restriction on the use of notices under *Sch 36, para 1* is, however, provided by *para 21*, which provides that if the taxpayer has already filed a corporation tax or personal self-assessment return, then an HMRC officer cannot issue a taxpayer notice in relation to the period covered by the return in order to check that person's corporation tax position or income or chargeable gains tax position unless one of the following conditions is satisfied:

1 there is an open enquiry in relation to that period; or

2 the officer has reason to suspect one of the following:

    (a) an amount that ought to have been assessed to tax for the chargeable period may not have been assessed;

    (b) an assessment to tax for the chargeable period may be or have become insufficient; or

    (c) relief from tax given for the chargeable period may be or have become excessive;

3 the notice is given for the purpose of obtaining any information or document that is required for the purpose of checking that person's position as regards any tax other than income tax, capital gains tax or corporation tax;

4 the notice is given for the purpose of obtaining any information or document that is required for the purpose of checking the person's position as regards any deductions or repayments of tax or withholding income (eg under PAYE or CIS).

16.44 HMRC is not restricted to the seeking of existing identifiable documents. The information that can be requested by a taxpayer notice may be specified or 'described' by HMRC.

As is indicated in the Explanatory Notes to the Finance Bill 2008, 'information' includes both explanations in respect of existing documents and the creation of schedules or documents that do not already exist.

16.45 There is no statutory pre-condition that HMRC asks the taxpayer to provide the information or documents voluntarily before service of a taxpayer notice. HMRC's Compliance Manual provides that HMRC will consider using an information notice only when:

(a) the taxpayer has not responded to an informal request for information or documents; or

16.46 *HMRC's information powers*

(b) HMRC does not consider it appropriate to ask the taxpayer to supply the information voluntarily, for example where:

 (i) the taxpayer has a history of non-compliance and HMRC has reason to believe that information will not be provided if requested informally;

 (ii) an informal request is likely to cause an unacceptable delay;

 (iii) pre-approval of a taxpayer notice by the tribunal is appropriate (see below); or

 (iv) an investigation into a tax avoidance scheme would benefit from the early use of formal powers.

16.46 There is no obligation on HMRC to obtain prior judicial approval of the taxpayer notice Under *FA 2008, Sch 36*, the HMRC officer can choose whether or not to seek approval from the First-tier Tribunal in advance. HMRC may make an application to the First-tier Tribunal for approval without notice to the taxpayer (*Sch 36, para 3(2A)*).

Whether or not the officer has sought approval has consequences for the ability of the taxpayer to appeal the notice to the tribunal (see further below).

16.47 FA 2009 ensures that the taxpayer has no right to appeal against a decision of the First-tier Tribunal to approve the issue of a notice (*FA 2008, Sch 36, para 6(4)*, inserted by *FA 2009, Sch 47, para 4*).

16.48 A taxpayer notice can require the taxpayer to produce documents more than six years old, provided that the request has been made by an 'authorised officer' of HMRC (defined in *para 58* as an HMRC officer who has been authorised by HMRC for the purposes of *Sch 36*).

16.49 A taxpayer who is required to provide information or documents must do so within the period, at the time, and by the means and form reasonably specified in the notice (*FA 2008, Sch 36, para 7*).

Third party notice (Sch 36, para 2)

16.50 An HMRC officer may by written notice to any person require that person to provide information or to produce a document if either is reasonably required for checking the tax position of a known person (a 'third party notice').

Third party notice: key points

16.51 As with taxpayer notices, third parties can be required to provide 'information' (as well as existing documents), potentially by creating new documents. The power is frequently used by HMRC to obtain documents from banks that concern the tax affairs of their customers.

16.52 HMRC may also, for example, seek explanations for transactions from bank employees in the context of seeking evidence for or understanding the 'motive' of taxpayers when entering into transactions.

A copy of the third party notice must be given to the taxpayer to which it relates, unless the First-tier Tribunal disapplies this requirement.

16.53 The tribunal may not disapply the requirement unless the application for consent has been made by (or with the agreement of) an authorised officer of HMRC and it is satisfied that the officer has reasonable grounds for believing that giving a copy of the notice to the taxpayer might prejudice the assessment or collection of tax.

16.54 The issue of a third party notice requires judicial approval, unless the taxpayer consents to the issue of the notice. Under *FA 2008, Sch 36, para 3(3)(b)*, the First-tier Tribunal must be satisfied that, in the circumstances, the HMRC officer is justified in issuing a third party notice. As with a taxpayer notice, HMRC can make an application to the First-tier Tribunal for approval without notice.

Judicial approval of taxpayer and third party notices

16.55 As indicated above, HMRC may request approval from the First-tier Tribunal for the giving of a taxpayer notice, but it is not obliged to do so. However, it may not issue a notice to a third party without the approval of the First-tier Tribunal, unless the taxpayer has agreed.

16.56 The First-tier Tribunal will not approve the giving of a taxpayer or third party notice unless the conditions in *FA 2008, Sch 36, para 3(3)* are satisfied:

1   The application is made by an authorised HMRC officer.

2   The First-tier Tribunal is satisfied that, in the circumstances, the HMRC officer is justified in issuing an information notice.

3   The person to whom the notice is addressed is given a summary of the reasons why HMRC requires the information or documents and has had an opportunity to make representations to HMRC concerning the information request.

4   A summary of the representations made by the person to whom it is addressed (ie either the taxpayer or the third party) has been given to the First-tier Tribunal.

16.57 *HMRC's information powers*

>The legislation does not specify whether the summarising is to be undertaken by HMRC or the person to whom the notice is to be addressed. It is recommended that taxpayers or third parties that wish to make representations should send these directly to the First-tier Tribunal, with a copy to the relevant HMRC Inspector.

5   In the case of a third party notice, the taxpayer has received a summary of the reasons why the officer requires the information and/or documents from the third party.

16.57   The First-tier Tribunal may disapply requirements 3–5 above if it is satisfied that taking the specified action might prejudice the assessment or collection of tax. Accordingly, HMRC can obtain a third party notice without notice to either the third party or the taxpayer.

There is no right of appeal against a tribunal's decision to disapply any of these conditions (*Sch 36, para 6(4)* (inserted by *FA 2009, Sch 47, para 4*)).

An information notice that is given with the approval of the First-tier Tribunal must state this (*para 6(3)*).

16.58   If the First-tier Tribunal has approved the issue of an information notice, then there is no route of appeal available to the taxpayer or to the third party (see *paras 29(3)* and *30(3)* respectively, and *Sch 36, para 6(4)* (inserted by *FA 2009, Sch 47, para 4*)) The only routes that are available to the taxpayer or the third party are judicial review of the First-tier Tribunal's decision to approve the notice or challenging the imposition of a penalty on the basis that the notice was not lawfully issued. In *Whitefields Golf Club v Revenue and Customs Comrs* [2014] UKFTT 495 (TC), the First-tier Tribunal suspended the effect of a notice whilst the taxpayer sought judicial review of the tribunal's decision to approve the notice

16.59   If HMRC serves the taxpayer with an information notice that has not been approved by the First-tier Tribunal, then the taxpayer has a right of appeal to the First-tier Tribunal against the notice itself, or any requirement in it. However, this right of appeal does not apply to a requirement in a notice to produce any document that forms part of the taxpayer's statutory records.

There is no right of appeal from the First-tier Tribunal to the Upper Tribunal. *FA 2008, Sch 36, para 32(5)* provides:

>'Notwithstanding the provisions of sections 11 and 13 of the Tribunals, Courts and Enforcement Act 2007 a decision of the tribunal on an appeal under this Part of this Schedule is final.'

This restriction on the rights of appeal was considered in *Jordan v Revenue and Customs Commissioners* [2015] STC 2314. The taxpayer appealed

HMRC's information powers **16.63**

against a *Sch 36* notice. The FTT concluded that the notice was valid in principle, but allowed the appeal in part by removing certain items from the list of required documents and information that had been attached to the notice. Notwithstanding *Sch 36, para 32* the First-tier Tribunal gave permission to appeal. HMRC applied to the Upper Tribunal to strike out the appeal on the ground that the tribunal had no jurisdiction to hear it The Upper Tribunal held that the First-tier Tribunal should not have given permission to appeal, and that HMRC's application to strike out the appeal would, accordingly, be allowed. The Upper Tribunal added:

> 'That conclusion is, moreover, consistent with what I perceive to be the legislative purpose: to exclude any appeal against a requirement to produce those records a taxpayer is obliged to keep and, ..., to restrict judicial scrutiny to one stage. It is perhaps worth pointing out that para 32(5) applies to HMRC as well as to a taxpayer.'

16.60 If approval from the First-tier Tribunal was not obtained in relation to the service of a third party notice (which would only be in the case where the taxpayer agreed to the issuing of notice on the third party), then the third party may appeal to the First-tier Tribunal against the notice; the only basis on which the third party may appeal against the notice is on the ground that it would be 'unduly onerous' to comply with *(Sch 36, para 30(1))*.

16.61 'Statutory records' are defined by *Sch 36, para 62(1)* as 'information or a document which a person is required to keep and preserve ... under the Taxes Acts or any other enactment relating to a tax'.

In relation to VAT, for example, the cross-referencing is to the *Value Added Tax Act 1994* and to SI 1995/2518. This was considered in *Shimlas Ltd v HMRC* [2016] UKFTT 0670 (TC). The First-tier Tribunal concluded that the company's bank statements were business records and that they fell within the meaning of statutory records 'by virtue of the bank account being a necessary operative part of the appellant's business through which income and expenditure related to the business passed.'

16.62 To the extent that any information or document that is required to be kept and preserved does not relate to the carrying on of a business and is not also required to be kept or preserved under any other enactment relating to tax, it only forms part of a person's statutory records to the extent that the chargeable period or periods to which it relates has or have ended *(Sch 36, para 62(2))*.

16.63 In *Beckwith v Revenue and Customs Comrs* [2012] UKFTT 181 (TC), the First-tier Tribunal held that a self-employed VAT-registered taxpayer's personal bank account statements were statutory records for the purpose of *FA 2008, Sch 36*. It also determined that they were 'reasonably required by

16.64 *HMRC's information powers*

HMRC to check the taxpayer's tax position' at the time HMRC issued a notice requesting them. The tribunal noted that there is no link between the underlying tax under enquiry and the source of the obligation to keep tax records for the purposes of *Sch 36*. As the taxpayer was VAT registered, his bank statements were business records for VAT purposes (see *VATA 1994, Sch 11, para 6*, VAT Regulations 1995, SI 1995/2518, reg 31 and VAT Notice 700/21). Further, that over 90 business transactions had been undertaken through the taxpayer's personal bank account demonstrated that the account was not one from which the taxpayer simply made occasional capital injections into his business (as he had asserted) but was an operational part of the business.

16.64 Information and documents cease to form part of a person's statutory records when the period for which they are required to be preserved by the enactments referred to above has expired (*Sch 36, para 62(3)*).

HMRC has said that, although there is provision for it to specify further the records to be kept, it has no plans to do this.

The position of a trustee in bankruptcy

16.65 In *HMRC v Ariel* [2016] EWHC 1674 (Ch), the position of a trustee in bankruptcy who receives a third party notice was considered by the High Court.

Mr Ariel, a potential recipient of a third party notice, had submitted to the First-tier Tribunal that his position as a trustee in bankruptcy raised special issues. In particular, he was, under the *Insolvency Act 1986*, an officer of the court subject to the statutory regime imposed by that Act and certain of the documents in which HMRC had expressed an interest were ones that he had acquired either under compulsion, exercising his powers under the Act, or subject to undertakings as to their use. The First-tier Tribunal deferred approving a *Sch 36* notice pending his seeking advice from the Bankruptcy Court as to his obligations under the *Insolvency Act*. The Bankruptcy Court opined in terms that severely restricted Mr Ariel's obligations under *Sch 36*.

The High Court held that it was the First-tier Tribunal that had exclusive jurisdiction to determine whether or not to approve the issuance of the notice. It went on to say that, to some extent, the position of a trustee in bankruptcy raised special issues, potentially as regards confidentiality and costs:

> 'The fact that documents held by the recipient of a third party notice have emanated from another person, and particularly where they were obtained under compulsion, and even more particularly where undertakings have been given to a foreign court or other body, is something to which those deciding on further disclosure must be sensitive. It does not follow that the

information should not be further disclosed, but the point needs addressing with proper consideration given to the interests of those who disclosed the information to the trustees in the first place.'

It disagreed with HMRC's assertion that the fact that the costs of complying with a notice could exceed the assets available in the bankruptcy (with the consequence that the costs would have to be borne by the trustee) was irrelevant.

The High Court said also that, although *Sch 36* did not give the third party the right to be heard, there was nothing to prevent the First-tier Tribunal from allowing a trustee in bankruptcy to make direct representations; and, indeed, it considered that 'in the more complex (though not necessarily in all) cases the [First-tier Tribunal] would be much assisted'. It is considered that there is a reasonable argument that that applies, by implication, to any third party.

Identity unknown notice (Sch 36, para 5)

16.66 The power under *Sch 36, para 5* enables HMRC to obtain, from a third party, information about a taxpayer whose identity is not known (an 'identity unknown notice').

Under *para 5*, an HMRC officer may by written notice to any person require that person to provide information or to produce a document if that is reasonably required for checking the tax position of either of the following:

- a person whose identity is not known to the HMRC officer; or
- a class of persons whose individual identities are not known to the officer.

16.67 HMRC may not issue an identity unknown notice to a third party without the approval of the First-tier Tribunal. The First-tier Tribunal must be satisfied that:

- the information or documents are reasonably required by the officer;
- there are reasonable grounds for believing that the person or any of the class of persons to whom the notice relates may have failed or may fail to comply with any provision of the Taxes Acts or *VATA 1994*;
- any such failure is likely to have led or lead to serious prejudice to the assessment or collection of UK tax; and
- the information or documents are not readily available from any other source.

The like preconditions applied to notices under *TMA 1970, s 20(8A)* (absent the references to 'information' and to VAT).

16.68 *HMRC's information powers*

The approach of the tribunal as regards identity unknown notices

16.68 The approach taken by the First-tier Tribunal and the Special Commissioners in a series of cases relating to applications by HMRC to obtain, from banks, information in relation to individuals with a UK address and a non-UK bank account or a credit card that was associated with a non-UK bank account suggests that the 'right' of HMRC to obtain information and documents outweighs the rights of third parties.

16.69 By *TMA 1970, s 20(7)*, a Special Commissioner was to give his consent to, inter alia, a *s 20(8A)* notice 'only on being satisfied that in all the circumstances the Inspector was *justified* in proceeding under that section'. There was thus a balancing act between the reasonable requirements of HMRC to obtain information, in order to carry out the effective investigation of tax affairs, and the protection of the personal property rights of taxpayers against invasion to be carried out by the Special Commissioner.

16.70 The obligation on the Special Commissioner to carry out this balancing act was most stringent in the case of *s 20(8A)* notices. Here, not only did the burden fall on a third party (as was the case with all *s 20(3)* notices), but also there was the likelihood that the burden would be a significant one. That this is so was recognised by the courts. It was also recognised by Parliament. (In the Standing Committee debates on Finance (No 2) Bill 1988 with regard to the clause that was to introduce what became *ss 20(8A)* and *(8B)*, an amendment was tabled that a person complying with a *s 20(8A)* notice be entitled to claim from the Revenue his reasonable expenses for so complying (ie as per the recommendation in the Keith Report). Mr Howarth MP, for example, referred, in particular, to the 'enormous obligation' that would be imposed, on, for example, banks who might be required to provide details of a class of taxpayers who might have drawn cheques over a number of years.)

16.71 Further, contrary to the express recommendation of the Keith Report, there was no possibility of reimbursement from HMRC of any reasonable costs incurred by a third party in complying with the significant burden.

16.72 However, the approach taken by the Special Commissioner in relation to 16 applications by HMRC where the power under *s 20(8A)* was sought to be used to obtain, from banks, information in relation to individuals with a UK address and a non-UK bank account or a credit card that was associated with a non-UK bank account suggests that, even in relation to *s 20(8A)* notices, the scales were strongly weighted in HMRC's favour.

16.73 The first six cases are: *Re an Application by Revenue and Customs Comrs to serve section 20 notice* [2006] STC (SCD) 71; *Re an Application by Revenue and Customs Comrs to serve section 20 notice (No 2)* [2006] STC (SCD) 360; *Re an Application by Revenue and Customs Comrs to serve* *section 20 notice* [2007] STC (SCD) 202; *Re an Application by Revenue and Customs Comrs to serve section 20 notice* [2007] STC (SCD) 208; *Re an Application by Revenue and Customs Comrs to serve section 20 notice* [2007] STC (SCD) 216; and *Re an Application by Revenue and Customs Comrs to serve section 20 notice* [2007] STC (SCD) 222.

16.74 In these cases, the Special Commissioner considered that the statistical evidence presented by HMRC in relation to the additional tax yield that would be generated consequent on the disclosure of the information sought was sufficient to enable him to conclude that the 'class' of taxpayers was in default and that this non-compliance by the class had led to serious prejudice to the proper assessment or collection of tax.

16.75 In the first two cases to be decided (which concerned the same bank), HMRC's estimate was that 20% of the cases investigated following disclosure would result in additional tax yield. The total additional tax yield from customers of that bank who fell within the 'class' was estimated at £1,855 million. The figure given in relation to the following four banks was £40 million, £55 million, £36 million, and £150 million respectively. Given that the estimated anticipated total additional tax yield in the four subsequent cases was based on a similar percentage of cases leading to additional tax yield, but the average anticipated total additional tax yield consequent on the notices served on each bank was only approximately 4% of the tax yield that was estimated would be generated from customers of the first bank (and all five banks were (broadly) comparable in size), it would have been incumbent on the inspector to provide a reasonable explanation for that extremely significant difference. For the judicial control introduced by *s 20(8A)* to have been effective, the Special Commissioner should have evaluated that explanation and accepted it as legitimate before giving his consent. There is nothing in the decisions to suggest that any explanation at all was either given or requested by the Special Commissioner.

16.76 In *Re an Application by Revenue and Customs Comrs to serve section 20 notice; Note* [2009] UKFTT 69 (TC), which concerned a similar application by HMRC for a *s 20(8A)* notice, the Special Commissioner noted that the estimate of £1.5 billion additional tax yield given in [2006] STC (SCD) 360 was an overestimate by HMRC, stated that 'this error had been made known to me earlier' and concluded that this had no effect on his conclusion that the condition that there must be serious prejudice to the proper collection of tax is satisfied. This was notwithstanding that the estimate of serious tax prejudice was approximately six times its true quantum.

A similar approach to the legislation was adopted by the Special Commissioner in relation to all 16 *s 20(8A)* applications that were made against banks between 2006 and 2009.

16.77   HMRC's information powers

16.77   There is no 'balancing act' to be carried out by the First-tier Tribunal in relation to *para 5* notices. This and the decision of the First-tier Tribunal in *Application by the Commissioners for Her Majesty's Revenue and Customs to serve 308 notices under paragraph 5 of Schedule 36 to the Finance Act 2008 on Financial Institutions in respect of customers with UK addresses holding non-UK accounts* [2009] UKFTT 224 (TC) gives rise to a concern as to whether tribunal approval, under *para 4*, provides any form of check against HMRC's use of the power under *para 5*.

16.78   In *Application to serve 308 notices*, the First-tier Tribunal approved the issue of 308 *para 5* notices (seeking details of non-UK bank accounts held by persons with a UK addresses) to be served by HMRC on financial institutions.

16.79   In determining whether failure to have complied with the tax legislation 'is likely to have led or to lead to serious prejudice to the assessment or collection of tax', the tribunal considered that generic evidence (rather than evidence specific to each financial institution) was sufficient. The approach that the tribunal seems to have adopted was to hold that, as the disclosures made under the offshore disclosure facility (ODF) proved that the tests had been satisfied in relation to the previous 16 applications made by HMRC for *s 20(8A)* notices, the tests also must be satisfied in relation to these (similar) applications. Yet, *para 5* bestows on HMRC a power to require 'a' person to provide information and documents if the relevant conditions are met.

16.80   Thus, even though the First-tier Tribunal was right in its decision that 'there is nothing in the statute preventing the issue of many notices in the same form', the relevant conditions should have been met in relation to each recipient individually. That clearly did not occur; and, in any event, many of the recipient banks were operating in a way that meant that their accounts were dissimilar to accounts (held with other banks) in respect of which ODF disclosures were made. Moreover, it seems that HMRC was not put to proof as to whether the information could have been obtained 'from another source'; particularly given that it seems that the purpose of obtaining the information and documents was to enable HMRC to carry out a 'cross-check' against disclosures made under the New Disclosure Opportunity or under the Liechtenstein Disclosure Facility, it is at best moot as to whether this test would have been satisfied had it received any detailed judicial consideration.

The approach taken by the First-tier Tribunal, which is combined with the lack of an appeal route, means that there is little effective judicial control of HMRC's use of its *Sch 36* powers.

16.81 If HMRC chooses to undertake *Micawberish* 'fishing expeditions', based on a generalised suspicion, by serving generic notices that impose a massive compliance burden on third parties, it is unlikely that it will be precluded from doing so by the tribunal.

Key points regarding identity unknown notices

16.82

- There is no statutory pre-condition that HMRC asks a person to produce the information or documents voluntarily before service of an identity unknown notice.

- As with third party notices, information (as well as documents) can be sought under identity unknown notices.

- An identity unknown notice can be appealed, but the basis of appeal is that it would be 'unduly onerous' to comply with the notice (*Sch 36, para 30*). The test under *TMA 1970, s 20(8B)* was that the *s 20(8A)* notice would be 'onerous' to comply with. In the cases referred to above concerning financial institutions with offshore bank accounts, the Special Commissioner gave (at most) limited consideration of the estimated cost of compliance with the notices, on the basis that the financial institutions had a separate right of appeal against the notice on the basis that compliance with the notice would be onerous. In *Rincham Ltd v Revenue and Customs Comrs* [2010] UKFTT 502 (TC), the First-tier Tribunal rejected the company's arguments that it would be onerous for it to provide details of some 40 capital redemption policies, particularly as it had no direct employees. The tribunal stated that it considered that it should be a relatively inexpensive matter for them to employ, if necessary, a temporary or part-time person to obtain the details and provide them to HMRC.

Relevant information identity unknown notices (Sch 36, para 5A)

16.83 *FA 2012, s 224* introduced a new *FA 2008, Sch 36, para 5A* (with effect from 1 April 2012). HMRC indicated that a peer review by the Global Forum on Transparency and Exchange of information for Tax Purposes had identified a deficiency in its information powers. Where an overseas authority requested information about a taxpayer who was identified not by name, but by some other identifying information, HMRC would have to have recourse to an identity unknown notice, but the precondition that any such failure is likely to have led or lead to serious prejudice to the assessment or collection

16.84 *HMRC's information powers*

of UK tax would not be satisfied, and so an identity unknown notice could not be obtained.

16.84 *Sch 36, para 5A* enables HMRC to obtain, in respect of a taxpayer, 'relevant information' (name, address and, if an individual, date of birth) from a third party, where HMRC holds identifying information about the taxpayer, but does not know his identity. Having established the taxpayer's identity, HMRC can then use its other *Sch 36* powers to obtain whatever further information may be required.

16.85 There are four conditions that must be met before a relevant information identity unknown notice can be issued:

(i) HMRC must reasonably require the information to check the tax position of the taxpayer (*para 5A(2)*);

(ii) the taxpayer's identity is not known to HMRC, but HMRC holds information from which the taxpayer's identity can be ascertained (*para 5A(3)*);

(ii) HMRC must believe that the third party will be able to identify the taxpayer from the identifying information that HMRC holds and that the third party obtained relevant information regarding the taxpayer in the course of a business (*para 5A(4)*); and

(iv) the taxpayer's identity cannot readily be ascertained by other means from the information held by HMRC.

In contrast to *para 5* notices, there is no requirement on HMRC to obtain approval from the tribunal in advance.

16.86 The only right of appeal against a *para 5A* notice is the same as with a *para 5* notice: that it would be unduly onerous to comply with the notice. Accordingly, if the four conditions described above are not satisfied, the third party can challenge the notice only by waiting for a penalty notice for non-compliance to be imposed and appealing the penalty on the basis that the notice was not lawfully issued. Similarly, if, for example, the third party no longer has the relevant information (say, having destroyed it once the required record-keeping period has ended), but HMRC does not accept this, then the only option is to challenge the penalty notice issued by HMRC for non-compliance with the notice.

Involved third party notices (Sch 36, para 34A)

16.87 *FA 2009* introduced a hybrid regime between taxpayer notices and third party notices, namely 'involved third party' notices. Involved third parties

HMRC's information powers **16.91**

are, in essence, third parties who are involved in transactions that may have given rise to a taxable transaction. In broad terms, involved third parties are intermediaries of taxpayers. *FA 2008, Sch 36, para 61A* specifies 12 categories of 'involved third parties', and what constitutes a 'relevant tax' and 'relevant information or relevant documents' for each category. *Paragraph 61A* provides a list of the relevant information and relevant documents which can be requested in relation to that involved third party, in relation to a specified tax.

16.88 Between 1 April 2010 and 1 April 2012 an information notice could be issued to an 'involved third party', by which HMRC could require a person acting as an intermediary for a taxpayer in specified circumstances to provided certain information. If an 'involved third party' was given a third party notice for the purposes of checking the position of a person in relation to the 'relevant tax' and referring only to 'relevant information or relevant documents', then the involved third party was treated as if he had received a taxpayer notice, rather than a third party notice (*FA 2008, Sch 36, para 34A*).

16.89 With effect from 1 April 2012, HMRC use their data-gathering powers under *FA 2011, Sch 23* (which powers are analysed below). *Schedule 23* provides a power that applies to a range of 'data holders'. It can be used to collect data in connection with any of the taxes administered by HMRC (including diverted profits tax), as well as certain foreign taxes.

The power to inspect the business premise of an involved third party, under *Sch 36, para 10A* remains in force. It is addressed at **16.120** below.

HMRC'S POWERS IN RELATION TO DATA-HOLDERS (FA 2011, SCH 23)

16.90 *FA 2011, Sch 23* came into force on 1 April 2012. It provides HMRC with a consolidated set of powers under which data-holders that hold information on third parties can be required to provide relevant data (as defined in the Data-gathering Powers (Relevant Data) Regulations 2012, SI 2012/847, which also came into force on 1 April 2012).

16.91 Schedule 23 applies to all UK taxes and to relevant foreign tax (defined as tax of a EU member state (other than the UK) which is covered by the exchange of information provisions under Directive 77/799/EEC, and any other tax imposed under the territory's law and covered by the international tax enforcement arrangements under *FA 2006, s.173*).

16.92 *HMRC's information powers*

Categories of data and data-holders

16.92 Sixteen broad categories of data, data-holders, and the information and documents that can be obtained by HMRC as regards each of the categories were introduced by *FA 2011*:

Data	Data-holders	Information
Salaries, fees, commission, etc	An employer, a person making payments to another's employees, an approved agent for payroll giving, and a person in a business connected with making relevant payments (being payments for services provided by non-employees and for certain IP rights).	Employment-related payments made by the employer, information on payments made by non-employers, apportioned expenses relating to employment-related payments and donations under payroll giving.
Interest, etc	A person by or through whom interest is paid or credited.	Account details where relevant interest is payable (being money received or retained in the UK with or without interest deductions).
Income, assets, etc belonging to others	A person who is in receipt of money or value of or belonging to another person.	Information on money or value received and the name and address of the beneficial owner.
Payments derived from securities	A registered holder of securities, a recipient under a company share buy-back under *Corporation Tax Act 2010, s 1033*, a recipient of a chargeable payment in a demerger, and a person who makes a payment derived from securities received from or paid on behalf of another.	Details of the beneficial owner(s) of securities, the person for whom the securities are held or to whom the payment is made, and details of amounts paid that are received from or paid on behalf of another person.
Grants and subsidies out of public funds	A person who makes a payment out of public funds by way of grant or subsidy.	Details of the recipient of the payment or on whose behalf it has been received, the amount of the payment, and the address of any property in respect of which the payment has been made.

HMRC's information powers **16.92**

Data	Data-holders	Information
Licences, approvals, etc	A person who issues licences or approvals or who maintains a register.	The name and address of any licence holder, particulars of the licence or approval, and information relating to any licence application or approval.
Rent and other payments arising from land	A lessee or successor in title of a lessee, an occupier of land, a person having the use of land, and a person who, as agent, manages land or is in receipt of rent or other payments arising from land.	The terms of the lease, occupation or use of land, the consideration given for the grant or assignment of a tenancy, information relating to any person on whose behalf the land is managed, and the payments received.
Dealing, etc in securities	A person who is a party to securities transactions as agent or principal, a registrar or administrator for securities transactions, a person who makes a securities-derived payment, a person who makes a payment derived from bearer securities, and an accountable person in respect of stamp duty reserve tax regulations.	Information relating to the issue, allotment or placing of public issues or placings.
Dealing in other property	Persons responsible for managing a clearing house, an auctioneer, a dealer in tangible movable property, an agent or intermediary in dealings of tangible movable property.	Particulars of any transaction effected through a clearing house, and where tangible moveable property is disposed for more than £6,000.
Lloyds	A registered managing agent at Lloyds for a syndicate of underwriting members.	Information and documents relating to the activities of any syndicate of underwriting members of Lloyds.

16.92 *HMRC's information powers*

Data	Data-holders	Information
Investment plans	An investment plan manager under *ITTOIA 2005, s 696*, or an account provider for a child trust fund.	Details of investments held under the plan and information on any child trust fund including investments held under the fund.
Petroleum activities	A licence holder under *Petroleum Act 1998, Part 1* or a responsible person in relation to an oil field under *Oil Taxation Act 1975*.	Particulars of transaction authorised by a petroleum licence resulting in a person being taxable under *TCGA 1992, s 276, CTA 2009, ss 276, 1313* or *ITTOIA 2005, s 874*, and of earnings which is employment income, or other payments relating to duties or services performed under a petroleum licence.
Insurance activities	Any person involved in an insurance business or in making arrangements for persons to enter into insurance contracts.	Information relating to contracts of insurance entered into in the course of an insurance business.
Environmental activities	A person involved in UK aggregate exploitation, making or receiving supplies of taxable commodities, or landfill disposal (including connected activities).	Information relating to aggregates levy matters, climate change levy matters, and landfill disposal.
Settlements	A person who makes a settlement, trustees, beneficiaries and any person to whom income is payable under a settlement.	Information relating to the settlement in question including income or gains arising to the settlement.
Charities	A charity as defined in *FA 2010, Sch 6*.	Information relating to donations to the charity eligible for tax relief under the various provisions of the Taxes Acts.

HMRC's information powers **16.95**

16.93 FA 2013 extended the definition of data-holder to include any person who has a contractual obligation to make payments to retailers in settlement of payment card transactions, including credit, debit and charge cards (by inserting *FA 2011, Sch 23, para 13A*) (such persons are colloquially known as 'merchant acquirers').

16.94 For this type of data-holder only, relevant data is:

- In relation to a retailer, information relating to payment card transactions recorded against a merchant account, including the currency these payment card transactions were made in.

- The reference number of the account into which payments are made by the relevant data-holder to the retailer and, where necessary for identifying the account, the branch where the account is held.

- Any unique identifier which has been allocated to a retailer, for the purposes of identifying the retailer, as part of the business arrangement between the relevant data-holder and the retailer.

- Any identifier which has been allocated to a retailer, for the purposes of classifying the trade of the retailer, as part of the business arrangement between the relevant data-holder and the retailer. Any unique identifier which has been allocated to a retailer's merchant account, for the purposes of identifying this merchant account, as part of the business arrangement between the relevant data-holder and the retailer.

- The name, address, telephone number, email address, website address and VAT number (relevant details) of a retailer and, if different, the relevant details associated with a merchant account.

16.95 A merchant account is an account held by a retailer with the relevant data-holder, by reference to which the amount due to be paid by the relevant data-holder to the retailer in settlement of payment card transactions is calculated. The Merchant acquirer data-gathering regulations came into force on 1 September 2013 (the Data-gathering Powers (Relevant Data) (Amendment) Regulations 2013, SI 2013/1811).

The Data-gathering Powers (Relevant Data) (Amendment) Regulations 2016 (SI 2016/979) came into force on 1 November 2016. These Regulations specify the information that electronic stored-value payment service providers and business intermediaries must provide to HMRC (on receipt of a data-holder notice). The relevant data that HMRC may seek is, broadly:

- For electronic stored-value payment service providers, information identifying the payment recipient (such as name, address, company

16.96 *HMRC's information powers*

registration number, VAT registration number, NICs reference number), information about the transactions (including the currency the transactions were made in) and information identifying the accounts or systems into which payments were made or credited.

- For business intermediaries, information identifying suppliers, information about the transactions that the data-holder enabled or facilitated, information about the quantity or value of transactions and information identifying the accounts or systems into which payments were made or credited to or on behalf of suppliers.

The regulations also made changes to the information that can be sought from merchant acquirers to align the merchant acquirers provisions with these provisions.

16.96 HMRC accepts that the data-gathering powers in *Sch 23* do not empower UK financial institutions to collect the national insurance and other tax identification numbers of holders of interest bearing accounts. HMRC had intended to collect that data for all interest bearing accounts opened on or after 6 April 2013, but has now accepted that further legislation would be required to empower the collection of such data. It has been indicated that any future legislation will be discussed with the industry before its introduction.

Money service businesses

16.97 *F(No 2)A 2017, s 69* extended the definition of relevant data-holder (by adding a new *para 13D* to *FA 2011, Sch 23*) to encompass money service businesses ('MSBs'). MSBs are persons to whom the Money Laundering, Terrorist Financing and Transfer of Funds (Information on the Payer) Regulations 2017 (SI 2017/692) apply and who operate a currency exchange office, transmit money by any means or cash cheques that are payable to customers. MSBs do not include excluded credit institutions (for example, banks or building societies). Relevant data as regards MSBs is defined to include:

(i)   records required to be kept by the data-holder under the Money Laundering, Terrorist Financing and Transfer of Funds (Information on the Payer) Regulations 2017 (2017/692) reg 40;

(ii) the quantity and value of transactions carried out by the data-holder for a customer during any period;

(iii) identifying information relating to a customer; and

(iv) where, in a transaction carried out by the data-holder for a customer, there is a beneficial owner (as defined in the Money Laundering, Terrorist Financing and Transfer of Funds (Information on the Payer)

Regulations 2017 (2017/692) regs 5 and 6) who is not the customer, identifying information relating to the beneficial owner.

Data-holder notices

16.98 The data-holder notice must specify the matter and form in which the relevant data should be provided to HMRC and when it is to be provided.

HMRC may copy documents and may retain documents for a reasonable period.

As with taxpayer notices, HMRC may (but is not obliged to) obtain the approval of the First-tier Tribunal before issuing a data-holder notice.

16.99 There are three permitted grounds of appeal:

1   The notice is unduly onerous to comply with (this cannot apply in respect of data forming part of the data-holder's statutory records).

2   The notice is addressed incorrectly.

3   The data is not relevant data.

There is no right of appeal against the decision of the First-tier Tribunal.

Penalties for failure to comply with a data-holder notice

16.100 Failure to comply with a data-holder notice attracts an initial penalty of £300 and, if the failure continues, a daily default penalty of £60. An increased daily default penalty can be imposed by the First-tier Tribunal or the Upper Tribunal on an application by HMRC if a daily default penalty has been imposed, the failure to comply with the data-holder notice has continued for more than 30 days and the data-holder has been told that an application for increased daily penalties may be made.

16.101 Neither the initial penalty nor the daily default penalties will be sought if the data-holder notice is complied with outside the original time limit provided that it is complied with within 'such further time (if any) as an officer of Revenue and Customs may have allowed'.

16.102 There is also a penalty for providing inaccurate information or a document containing an inaccuracy where:

- the inaccuracy is careless or deliberate;
- the data-holder knows of the inaccuracy at the time that the data is provided but fails to tell HMRC at that time; or

16.103 *HMRC's information powers*

- the data-holder discovers the inaccuracy some time later and fails to take reasonable steps to inform HMRC.

The maximum penalty is £3,000 for each inaccuracy.

These penalties mirror the penalties in *FA 2008, Sch 36*. All penalties must be assessed within a prescribed time. The data-holder may appeal against the penalty or the amount of the penalty.

The power to inspect premises

16.103 HMRC's power of inspection is provided by *FA 2008, Sch 36, Pt 2*.

'Inspect' means to examine; this power does not give HMRC the right to force entry, or to search. The power to inspect is restricted to the business premises of the person whose tax liability is being checked, other than in relation to VAT or the premises of involved third parties in certain circumstances. Absent involved third parties, the ambit of the power does not extend to third parties.

POWER TO INSPECT TAXPAYER'S BUSINESS PREMISES (SCH 36, PARA 10)

16.104 An HMRC officer may enter a person's business premises and inspect the premises and business assets and business documents on the premises, if the inspection is reasonably required for the purpose of checking that person's tax position.

HMRC has indicated that this power is not to be used routinely, and that it will carry out an inspection only where it considers it to be the best and most effective way to tackle tax risk.

What can be inspected?

16.105 The premises that HMRC can inspect are those used by the person whose liability is being checked. The inspection may extend to the premises and to business assets and business documents on the premises, if their inspection is reasonably required for the purposes of checking the person's tax liability.

The power does not extend to inspection of any part of the premises used solely as a dwelling.

16.106 'Business premises' are any premises (or a part thereof) that an HMRC officer has reason to believe are used in connection with the carrying on of a business by or on behalf of the taxpayer. They include land, buildings, and 'means of transport'.

16.107 *Sch 36, para 10* does not give HMRC a power of entry to premises that are used wholly as a dwelling. HMRC considers that there are circumstances where it may be reasonable to conduct an inspection at a person's home. These include the following:

> 'In the case of an outworker – the stock or assets kept at their home may be inspected. The person should be given an opportunity to make the items available for inspection elsewhere if this is practical.
>
> At a farm – the office, fields, barns and areas involved in business activity can be visited. The private areas of the farm house and private garden cannot be visited without invitation.
>
> In a pub – the cellar, bar, commercial kitchen, store rooms and any vacant rooms which are let can be visited. The private living accommodation cannot be visited without invitation.'

16.108 'Business assets' are assets that an HMRC officer has reason to believe are owned, leased or used in connection with the carrying on of a business by any person.

The definition of business assets excludes documents other than documents which are trading stock or plant *(Sch 36, para 10(4)* (inserted by *FA 2009, Sch 47, para 5)).* 'Business documents' means documents that relate to the carrying on of a business by any person and that form part of any person's 'statutory records' (statutory records are defined in *Sch 36, para 62* as information or documents required to be kept and preserved under the Taxes Acts and enactments relating to VAT).

16.109 Thus, any person's business records can be reviewed if they are found on the inspected premises, but only if that inspection is reasonably required for checking the tax position of the person in connection with whose business the premises are used.

16.110 HMRC cannot review documents that could not have been required to be produced had the occupier been given an information notice at the time of inspection *(Sch 36, para 28).*

In particular, this means that HMRC cannot view documents that are protected by legal professional privilege.

16.111 *HMRC's information powers*

16.111 As with information notices, HMRC is not required to obtain judicial approval before conducting an inspection; under *Sch 36, para 13(1)*, an officer may ask the First-tier Tribunal to approve an inspection.

There is no appeal to the First-tier Tribunal against an inspection.

16.112 A person who deliberately obstructs an HMRC officer in the course of an inspection that has been approved by the First-tier Tribunal is liable to a penalty of £300 and a daily default penalty of £60. There is no penalty if there is a reasonable excuse for the obstruction (Sch 36, paras 39 and 45).

In the event that the First-tier Tribunal has not approved the notice, then the penalty regime in *Sch 36, para 39* (and in *para 40*), does not apply.

Timing of inspections

16.113 Inspections should normally take place at a time agreed with the occupier of the premises.

Absent agreement, HMRC may carry out an inspection 'at any reasonable time' in two circumstances:

- where the occupier has been given at least seven days' notice; or
- where an authorised HMRC officer has agreed that the inspection can be carried out *(Sch 36, para 12)*.

16.114 HMRC has indicated that, in practice, the notice period is likely to be longer than seven days and the time and date of the inspection will be both by negotiation and at the taxpayer's convenience.

16.115 Inspections can be made without advance warning *(Sch 36, para 12(2)(b))*. In 'A New Approach to Compliance Checks: Responses to Consultation and Proposals' (issued on 10 January 2008), HMRC indicated that unannounced visits would be 'the exception, and need higher levels of safeguards to reassure the majority of the population'.

16.116 As indicated above, no external judicial authorisation is required for unannounced visits; such visits need only the agreement of an 'authorised' HMRC officer. An 'authorised officer' is defined in the legislation simply as an HMRC officer authorised by HMRC for the purposes of *Sch 36*. It is understood that HMRC does not consider that officer grade is the appropriate criterion, but rather someone with the appropriate training. Information on the training that is required for an officer to become authorised is awaited.

There is also no right of appeal to the tribunal.

Inspection of premises used in connection with taxable supplies (Sch 36, para 11)

16.117 As originally enacted, *para 11* provided for the inspection of premises used in connection with VAT taxable supplies where an HMRC officer had reason to believe any of the following:

- the premises were being used in connection with the taxable supply of goods and such goods were on those premises;
- the premises were being used in connection with the taxable acquisition of goods from other member states and such goods were on those premises;
- the premises were being used as a fiscal warehouse.

16.118 This reproduced the power in *VATA 1994, Sch 11, para 10(2)*. The power was widened slightly by *FA 2009* (with effect from 21 July 2009). Since then, HMRC officers have been able to inspect premises if they have reason to believe that documents relating to a taxable supply or taxable acquisition of goods are on the premises or if the premises are used in connection with a fiscal warehouse (*FA 2009, Sch 47, para 6*).

16.119 Under *para 11*, the HMRC officer may inspect the premises, any goods that are on the premises and any documents on the premises that appear to relate to the goods. This power to inspect is not restricted to the premises of the person whose tax liability is under enquiry (unlike the general inspection power: see above), but it only applies to VAT.

Power to inspect premises of involved third parties (Sch 36, para 10A)

16.120 *FA 2009* introduced a power for an HMRC officer to inspect:

- an 'involved third party's' business premises; and
- business assets and 'relevant documents' on those premises,

for the purpose of checking the position of any person in relation to any 'relevant tax' (*FA 2008, Sch 36, para 10A* inserted by *FA 2009, Sch 48, para 3*). The power came into force on 1 April 2010.

16.121 *FA 2008, Sch 36, para 61A* (inserted by *FA 2009, Sch 48, para 14*) includes a table which comprises a list of 'involved third parties' and the 'relevant tax' and 'relevant documents' to which the inspection of that third party's premises must relate. Involved third parties are closely related to a potentially taxable event or transaction.

16.122 *HMRC's information powers*

16.122 The ambit of this power is fairly narrow; it is restricted to those involved in payroll giving, individual investment plans and child trust funds for income tax purposes, managing agents of Lloyd's syndicates, those involved in insurance business or contracts of insurance for the purposes of insurance premium tax, accountable persons for the purposes of stamp duty reserve tax and certain persons in relation to petroleum revenue tax and environmental taxes.

Power to inspect premises for valuation (Sch 36, para 12A)

16.123 *FA 2009* introduced a power for HMRC to inspect any premises (business or private) for the purpose of valuing, measuring or determining the character of the premises, provided that the valuation is reasonably required for the purpose of checking any person's position as regards income tax, corporation tax, capital gains tax, inheritance tax, stamp duty land tax or stamp duty reserve tax (*FA 2008, Sch 36, para 12A* introduced by *FA 2009, Sch 48, para 5*). The power came into force on 1 April 2010.

The HMRC officer can be accompanied by any person whom the officer considers is needed to assist with the valuation, such as a surveyor.

16.124 An inspection can be carried out only if one of the following two conditions is met:

- the occupier (or person who controls the premises, if the occupier cannot be identified or the premises are vacant) has agreed the time of the inspection and has been given a written notice; or
- the inspection has been approved by the First-tier Tribunal and the occupier (or person who controls the premises) has been given at least seven days' notice in writing of the inspection.

16.125 The First-tier Tribunal may not approve the inspection unless the person whose tax position is being checked and the occupier have been given a reasonable opportunity to make representations to HMRC about the inspection and the tribunal has been given a summary of those representations (*FA 2008, Sch 36, paras 12B* and *13* as amended by *FA 2009, Sch 48, para 6*).

RESTRICTIONS ON THE USE OF THE POWERS BY HMRC

16.126 A number (but, by no means all) of the restrictions that applied in relation to the old HMRC information powers (including under *TMA, s 20*) and self-assessment information powers (including under *TMA, s 19A*) have been carried over to *FA 2008, Sch 36*.

16.127 These include:

- an information notice only requires a person to produce a document if it is in that person's 'possession or power';
- privileged communications are excluded from disclosure; and
- auditors and tax advisers' documents are protected from disclosure.

These concepts are analysed further below.

Possession or power

16.128 *Sch 36, para 18* provides that an information notice only requires a person to produce a document if it is in that person's 'possession or power'. This restriction does not apply:

(a) to the provision of 'information' on service of an information notice; or

(b) in respect of HMRC's power to enter business premises and inspect.

The terms 'power' and 'possession' are not defined in any of the taxing statutes; and there is little case law on the meaning of the phrase 'power or possession' in the context of requests for information from HMRC.

Possession

16.129 The term 'possession' applies in a variety of contexts and has a number of meanings (Palmer, *Bailment* (2nd edn, 1991) notes, at p 103 that 'Possession is a ductile and intuitive concept'; and Stroud's *Legal Dictionary* (5th edn, 1986) lists 49 different meanings).

16.130 The meanings of the term 'possession' include:

(a) de facto control or 'custody', that is, actual physical possession;

(b) the right to possession where actual physical possession is not present;

(c) ownership; and

(d) 'legal' possession in the sense of physical possession combined with a right to possession.

16.131 The most relevant to the meaning of the term in the context of *s 20* is the phrase that formerly appeared in the Rules of the Supreme Court in relation to the inspection and discovery of documents for the purposes of civil litigation in the High Court. (The duty of disclosure under the Civil Procedure Rules is limited to documents which are or have been in a party's control; and so does

16.132 *HMRC's information powers*

not assist interpretatively here.) Under these Rules a party was required to list, for the purposes of disclosure, the documents that were in his 'possession, custody or power' (with the term 'custody' being added in 1964).

16.132 The meaning of the threefold test was considered in a matrimonial case, *B v B* [1978] Fam 181, where Dunn J said that:

> 'for this purpose "possession" means the right to the possession of a document. "Custody" means the actual, physical or corporeal holding of a document regardless of the right to its possession, for example, a holding of a document by a party as servant or agent of the true owner. "Power" means an enforceable right to inspect the document or to obtain possession or control of the document from the person who ordinarily has it in fact. The requirements of the rules are disjunctive in their operation, so far as possession, custody and power are concerned.'

16.133 Thus, it is clear that Dunn J was of the view that 'possession' is limited to lawful possession. *De facto* control, or physical possession without a right to possession is not sufficient. If a document has been entrusted to an individual who is acting as the owner's agent or bailee, and is physically held by that individual subject to an obligation of confidentiality to the owner, then that document is not in the legal possession of the agent or bailee, because although he has custody (or physical possession) of the document, he does not have an unfettered right to possession of the document.

16.134 Although this definition was in the context of a threefold test of 'possession, custody or power', there seems to be no reason why that definition should not apply equally in *s 20*, which refers to 'possession or power'.

16.135 Documents that are in the custody or physical possession of an officer or employee of a company, if held as servant or agent of the company, or by such individual in his capacity as an officer or an employee of the company, will be treated as being in the possession of the company (see *Skoye v Bailey* [1971] 1 WWR 144 and *Williams v Ingram* (1900) 16 TLR 451).

Power

16.136 Although 'power' has a number of meanings, its meaning in the context of access to information is clear in the view of the author, despite the decision of the First-tier Tribunal in *Parissis* (see **16.146**).

16.137 The term 'power' was defined by the House of Lords in *Lonhro Ltd v Shell Petroleum* [1980] 1 WLR 627. In *Lonhro*, the claimants sought disclosure of documents held by foreign subsidiaries of Shell. The claimants argued that, even though the subsidiary companies had refused to supply the documents further to a request from Shell, the documents were in the 'power' of Shell and were thus disclosable under RSC Ord 24, r 2 (which provided that 'all documents must be disclosed which the party giving discovery has or has had in his possession, custody or power'). Shell owned 100% of the shares of the subsidiary companies; and so it could remove the directors or change the articles so as to require disclosure of the documents.

16.138 This argument was rejected by the Court of Appeal ([1980] QB 358). Shaw LJ noted that, in a general philosophical sense, there was a latent power that could be used to achieve possession of the relevant documents. However, no note of futurity could be read into Ord 24. As it specified documents that 'were or had been' within a party's power, that constituted the limits on what could be obtained. It could only be in the situation where company A was so subservient to the wishes of company B that compliance was guaranteed that it could be said that company B had the documents in its power.

16.139 The House of Lords upheld the decision of the Court of Appeal, Lord Diplock saying (at p 635) that the term 'power' means 'a presently enforceable legal right to obtain from whoever actually holds the document inspection of it without the need to obtain the consent of anyone else'.

16.140 The following observation (at p 634) was made:

'The articles of association of all the subsidiaries vest the management of the company in its board of directors. It is the board that has control of the company's documents on its behalf; the shareholders as such have no right to inspect or to take copies of them. If requested to allow inspection of the company's documents, whether by a shareholder or by a third party, it is the duty of the board to consider whether to accede to this request would be in the best interests of the company.'

16.141 The rule was caveated, however: 'I say nothing about one-man companies in which a natural person and/or his nominees are the sole shareholders and directors. It may be that, depending upon their own particular facts, different considerations apply to these' (at pp 636–637).

16.142 In the context of the *s 20(8A)* and *para 5* notices served against financial institutions (described above), HMRC indicated that it considered that *Lonhro* was incorrectly decided by the House of Lords and/or does not apply in a tax context.

16.143 The decision of the House of Lords in *Lonhro* has been considered in the context of the information powers of HMRC in two cases: *Meditor Capital Management v Feighan (Inspector of Taxes)* [2004] STC (SCD) 273 and *Revenue and Customs Comrs v Parissis* [2011] UKFTT 218 (TC).

16.144 *HMRC's information powers*

16.144 *Meditor* concerned, inter alia, documents that were held by Meditor Capital Management (Bermuda) Limited ('MCM(B)') in Bermuda and sought by HMRC by service of a notice under *FA 1998, Sch 18, para 27* on Meditor Capital Management Ltd ('Meditor'), a UK resident 100% subsidiary of MCM(B). Meditor adduced evidence of correspondence between itself and MCM(B), which showed that it had asked MCM(B) twice to supply to it the documents requested by the Revenue and that MCM(B) had twice refused to do so. The Special Commissioner held that these letters were not sufficient proof that the particular documents were not in the power or possession of Meditor. He hinted that the *Lonhro* test may not be the correct test to apply for these purposes, and that simply a *de facto* ability to obtain the documents or particulars might suffice.

16.145 However, this decision was in the context of Meditor having previously agreed to provide the particular documents (under the terms of agreed directions) and having provided other information that had been, both legally and factually, held on an identical basis to the particular information that it claimed was not in its power or possession.

16.146 In *Parissis*, the taxpayers were variously settlors and beneficiaries of three Guernsey trusts that were administered by a commercial trustee company. HMRC issued a *s 20* notice requiring production of various documents that related to the establishment and operation of the trusts and a British Virgin Islands company held by the trusts. The taxpayers did not comply, arguing, *inter alia*, that these documents were not in their power.

16.147 The tribunal considered that, following *Meditor*, 'power' should be construed more widely for *s 20* purposes than it had been by the House of Lords in *Lonhro*. It held that, in the context of the *TMA 1970, s 20*, 'power' should be considered in terms of both legal power and 'practical' power.

16.148 The tribunal indicated that the test as to whether documents are in a person's power for the purposes of *s 20* is whether the person '*can obtain them, by influence or otherwise, and without great expense, from another person even where that person has the legal right to refuse to produce them.*' The tribunal provided no guidance as to what it meant by 'great expense' or 'influence or otherwise'. Whether 'great expense' is a subjective or objective test is not known, nor is it known as to what methods 'otherwise' extends. The decision of the tribunal that introduces a nebulous and ill-defined concept of 'power' is wholly unsatisfactory. The taxpayers' appeal to the Upper Tribunal was withdrawn. The decision in *Parissis* has not been referred to in any case subsequently.

Notwithstanding *Parissis*, it is considered that the current state of the law in respect of documents held offshore by non-UK resident companies in a group of companies with a UK-resident parent company is that, provided the relevant

HMRC's information powers **16.151**

company is a separate legal entity and it cannot be said that it is so subservient to the wishes of the parent company that, with regard to requests from that company, compliance will always be guaranteed, it cannot be said that all documents in the possession of a subsidiary company are in the power of the parent company.

16.149 If the parent company is unable to recover the documents without taking further steps, such as amending the articles to allow the shareholders to have a right of inspection of the documents, then the parent company does not have power over the documents. This is on the assumption that the autonomy which the overseas subsidiaries enjoy is conferred on them *bona fide*, and that the local directors 'run their own show' with comparatively little interference from the parent company.

This issue is addressed further below with regard to the territorial limits of Sch 36.

16.150 The First-tier Tribunal took a robust line against the settlors and protectors of a trust who argued in *H A Patel & K Patel (a partnership) v Revenue and Customs Comrs* [2014] UKFTT 167 (TC) that the relevant documents were not in their power or possession because they were held by the trustees and the trustees had refused to deliver them up. The tribunal found that the taxpayers had made no serious attempt to obtain the information and documents from the trustee, and had demonstrated a passive acceptance of the trustee's refusal to provide the items in the taxpayer notice. Therefore, the tribunal was not satisfied that the items in the taxpayer notice were not in the taxpayers' possession or power and dismissed their appeal.

Territorial limits of Schedule 36

16.151 There is no express statutory limitation on the territorial scope of *Sch 36*. And, HMRC has expressed the view that, for example, the reporting obligations imposed on professionals under *Inheritance Tax Act 1984, s 218* have extra-territorial effect.The issue as to whether *Sch 36* provides HMRC with the power to issue notices outside the UK will be heard by the Court of Appeal in December 2018, in *Jimenez*. In *R (on the application of) T M Jimenez v the FTT and HMRC* [2017] EWHC 2585, the High Court held (contrary to the First-tier Tribunal) that *Sch 36* does not provide HMRC with the power to issue notices outside the UK. It said that the question of whether a taxpayer notice can be given to a British national who is resident abroad must be assessed by considering *Sch 36* as a whole and not by isolating taxpayer notices. Although the overall purpose of *Sch 36* was to provide a 'credible and effective system of checking and investigation', that did not lead to the conclusion that Parliament had intended *Sch 36* to have effect outside the UK. Rather, the UK should rely on mutual assistance agreements to seek information about the liability

16.152 HMRC's information powers

to UK tax of individuals resident outside the UK (in accordance with the principle established in *Clark v Oceanic Contractors* [1983] 2 AC 130 that: 'English legislation ... is applicable only to English subjects or to foreigners who by coming to this country ... have made themselves ... subject to English jurisdiction'). The court noted that the existence of such mutual assistance agreements undermined HMRC's arguments based on public interest. The idea that a taxpayer would move abroad to avoid a fiscal investigation was 'imaginary'. A sufficient 'footprint' would be left in the UK, and HMRC would retain the ability to rely on mutual assistance agreements, as well as the ability to serve third party notices. The court noted also that the 'teeth' given to *Sch 36*, in the form of enforceable provisions for penalties and criminal sanctions, meant that it could only apply in the UK, as a practical matter.

Legal professional privilege

16.152 *Sch 36, para 23* provides that an information notice does not require a person to provide information or produce any part of a document which is protected by legal professional privilege.

Similarly, the business premises inspection power does not permit HMRC to inspect a business document that is protected by legal professional privilege (*Sch 36, para 28*).

16.153 Legal professional privilege is a fundamental aspect of the legal system in this country. It allows a person to consult a lawyer without fear that the information that he reveals will be disclosed in court contrary to his wishes. It thus enables the client to have confidence in the confidentiality of his legal adviser and so encourages him to 'make a clean breast of it to the gentleman whom he consults' (per Sir George Jessell MR, *Anderson v Bank of British Columbia* (1876) 2 ChD 644 at 649).

16.154 Further, legal professional privilege has been recognised as an aspect of the right to privacy under Article 8 of the European Convention on Human Rights by the European Court of Human Rights and by the European Court of Justice to be part of European Union law.

16.155 That privilege is a fundamental human right has been recognised in the UK by the House of Lords in a series of cases. (See *R (on the application of Morgan Grenfell & Co Ltd) v Special Comr of Income Tax* [2002] UKHL 21, per Lord Hobhouse of Woodborough at 798f and Lord Hoffmann at 796g–j and 790d, where he said that: '[privilege] has been held by the European Court of Human Rights to be part of the right of privacy guaranteed by art 8 of the Convention for the Protection of Human Rights and Fundamental Freedoms'.) There are two heads of privilege: legal advice privilege and litigation privilege.

Legal advice privilege

16.156 There is no requirement that such documents be produced for the 'dominant purpose' of legal advice. Provided that there is a 'relevant legal context', a lawyer/client communication will be privileged. This will cover most lawyer/client communications.

16.157 Internal communications between employees of a company, even if for the purpose of seeking legal advice or preparing 'raw material' in respect of which advice may be given are not privileged, unless those employees are the 'client'.

Only those employees in an organisation who are given the role of obtaining or receiving legal advice can be classified as 'the client' for the purposes of privilege.

Communications between third parties and lawyers or clients are not privileged under this head, even if they are made in connection with the seeking or giving of legal advice.

16.158 The only exception to this rule is if that third party is an agent of either the lawyer or the client and is simply a medium of communication. This is strictly construed (see *Price Waterhouse v BCCI Holdings* [1992] BCLC 583 where Millett J (as he then was) held that reports produced by accountants and sent to lawyers were not privileged, as the accountants acted as more than mere agents of communication).

16.159 Communications with other professionals, such as accountants or chartered tax advisers, will not attract legal professional privilege under this head, even if such individuals are giving advice on strictly legal matters, such as tax law. This was confirmed by the Supreme Court in *R (on the application of Prudential plc) v Special Commr of Income Tax* [2013] UKSC 1.

16.160 In *Prudential*, the specific issue was whether Prudential (Gibraltar) Ltd and Prudential plc were entitled to withhold from HMRC advice given to them by their accountants (PricewaterhouseCoopers LLP), on the basis that that advice was protected by reason of legal professional privilege. The more general question raised by that issue was whether legal advice privilege extends, or should be extended so as to apply, to legal advice that is given by someone other than a member of the legal profession. The focus of the Supreme Court, understandably, was on the general question only; its answer (by a 5:2 majority) was 'no'.

16.161 *HMRC's information powers*

16.161 Lord Neuberger (with whom Lords Hope, Walker, Mance, and Reed agreed) delivered the lead judgment. A summary of his analysis is as follows:

It is universally accepted that legal advice privilege applies only to communications in connection with advice given by members of the legal profession. All sources, which include the following, are wholly consistent on this point:

(a) over 130 years' jurisprudence, commencing with the decision of Sir George Jessel MR in *Slade v Tucker* (1880) 14 Ch D 824;

(b) the courts' refusal, for example, to extend legal advice privilege to legal advice given by a trade mark agent, a patent agent, or a personnel consultant (see, respectively, *Dormeuil Trade Mark* [1983] RPC 131, *Wilden Pump Engineering Co v Fusfeld* [1985] FSR 159, and *New Victoria Hospital v Ryan* [1993] ICR 201);

(c) the official reports, such as, for example, the 16th Report of the Law Reform Committee (Privilege in Civil Proceedings) (1967) (Cmnd 3472) and the Keith Report (the 1983 Report of the Committee on Enforcement Powers of the Revenue Departments (Cmnd 8822));

(d) the government's rejection (in 2003) of a proposal, which had been made by the Director General of Fair Trading that legal advice given by accountants should be subject to the same privilege as that given by members of the legal profession;

(e) the discussion by the House of Commons Public Bill Committee as to whether legal advice privilege should be extended to tax advice given by accountants (in the context of the replacement of the information and document gathering provisions of *TMA 1970* by what became *FA 2008, Sch 36* (Hansard (HC Debates) 10 June 2008, cols 606–608)).

16.162 Accordingly, contrary to Prudential's submissions at the Supreme Court, were the Supreme Court to allow the appeal, it would be extending legal advice privilege beyond its current limits, and, indeed, what had been understood universally, for well over 100 years, to be its limits. Moreover, as it would follow ineluctably from the acceptance of Prudential's argument that legal advice given by at least some other professional people would be covered also, the court would be extending the ambit of the principle considerably.

16.163 Legal advice privilege is based on the need to ensure that a person can seek and obtain legal advice with candour and full disclosure, secure in the knowledge that the communications involved can never be used against that person. It is conferred for the benefit of the client, and may be waived only by the client. Accordingly, as a great deal of legal advice now is tendered by professional advisers other than members of the legal profession, in principle, the argument for allowing the appeal is a strong one.

16.164 However, legal advice privilege should not be extended, for three reasons:

1. The consequences of allowing the appeal are hard to assess and would be likely to lead to what is currently a clear and well understood principle becoming unclear and uncertain.

   As well as the profession of chartered accountant, occupations such as actuaries, auditors, architects, surveyors, town planners, engineers and pension advisers require training and qualifications. All have associations, with rules and disciplinary procedures; and such professionals often have considerable specialist legal expertise, on which their clients draw and expect to be able to draw. However, when members of such professions give legal advice, often it will not represent the totality of the advice, and, indeed, it may be only a subsidiary part. In contrast, lawyers normally only give legal advice.

   With legal advice privilege limited to advice from members of the legal profession, the strong, and justified, presumption has been that legal advice privilege applies to all communications in that context. If the privilege were to be extended, the presumption could not apply. It is likely that there would be difficult questions to resolve, as to whether, and, if so, in respect of which documents, legal advice privilege could be claimed.

2. The question raises questions of policy which should be left to Parliament.

   The implications of extending the generally understood limits of legal advice privilege could clearly be significant and the extension could have consequences that would need to be considered through the legislative process, with its wide powers of enquiry and consultation and its democratic accountability. For example, if legal advice privilege is to be extended, it may not be appropriate to extend it other than on a conditional or limited basis. When, in 1983, the Keith Committee recommended that communications in connection with tax advice given by chartered accountants should be protected, that new privilege was to be subject to various controls and an override in certain circumstances. It is not realistically open to the courts to impose such restrictions or conditions; but, it would be open to Parliament.

3. Parliament has enacted legislation relating to legal advice privilege, which, at the very least, suggests that it would be inappropriate for the court to extend the law in the way proposed by Prudential.

   In particular, Parliament has legislated in the very field with which this appeal is concerned (*TMA 1970, s 20B*, and *FA 2008, Sch 36, paras 23–26*) on the basis that legal advice privilege applies only to advice given by lawyers.

16.165 *HMRC's information powers*

Litigation privilege

16.165 Litigation privilege covers communications that came into existence for the dominant purpose of being used in connection with or in contemplation of litigation.

There is an overlap between advice and litigation privilege in that, once litigation is in prospect, then lawyer/client documents produced for that litigation will be protected under both heads.

16.166 There are two important limits on litigation privilege. First, it does not arise in respect of non-adversarial proceedings. In *Re L* [1997] AC 16, the House of Lords held (by a majority) that litigation privilege could not apply to proceedings under the *Children Act 1989, Pt IV* in respect of child care orders, because the proceedings were not adversarial in nature; privilege was excluded by necessary implication from the terms and overall purpose of the Act.

16.167 Second, the documents must be produced for the 'dominant purpose' of litigation. In *Waugh v British Railways Board* [1980] AC 521, the House of Lords adopted and applied the 'dominant purpose' test that had been put forward by Barwick CJ in his minority judgment in the High Court of Australia in *Grant v Downs* [1976] 135 CLR 674, at 677 to determine whether a report that had been prepared both for safety purposes and for the purpose of obtaining legal advice in anticipation of litigation was privileged (Lord Edmund-Davies described the 'dominant purpose' test as the 'touchstone' of the privilege).

16.168 The dominant purpose test (which must be applied at the time of creation) acts as a filter mechanism and prevents privilege attaching to documents brought into existence for purposes other than that of legal advice. If a document has been produced partly for the purpose of litigation and partly for another purpose, that document will not be privileged if the relevant litigation purpose is a secondary or even an equal purpose. Thus, for example, communications by a tax authority with third parties in order to ascertain the value of goods for the purpose of tax legislation, even though such communications would also enable the authority to meet an inevitable challenge by taxpayers, were not protected by litigation privilege (*Alfred Crompton Amusement Machines Ltd v Customs and Excise Comrs (No 2)* [1974] AC 405).

16.169 There is a further important difference between the two privileges in that communications between the client or lawyer with third parties can be protected by litigation (but not advice) privilege. Although no lawyer need, in fact, have been engaged at the time of the communication, as the dominant purpose for which the communication is made must be either:

(a) obtaining legal advice from the client's lawyer; or

(b) use by the lawyer in aid of litigation that has commenced or is contemplated, whether litigation privilege applies to third party/client communications when no lawyer is contemplated is doubtful.

16.170 This is particularly the case in the light of the recent judicial trend to seek to limit the ambit of litigation privilege. Lord Scott, for example, in *Three Rivers District Council v Governor and Company of the Bank of England* [2004] UKHL 48 suggested that there should be a limit on third-party communications being protected under the head of litigation privilege. In Lord Scott's view, even if such documents were produced for the dominant purpose of litigation, they should not be privileged unless they constitute or disclose the seeking or giving of legal advice. (See also Scott V-C in *Secretary of State v Baker (Re Barings)* [1998] Ch 356.)

16.171 The consequence of this is that if an accountant or tax adviser is instructed in relation to a tax dispute and instructing a legal adviser is not anticipated, then it is likely that communications between the adviser and the client will not be protected by litigation privilege.

Such documents may, however, be protected by the statutorily created quasi-privileges under *Sch 36, paras 19, 24* and *25.*

Resolving privilege disputes

16.172 Regulations have been issued covering disputes about privileged information for the purposes of *FA 2008, Sch 36.*

The Information Notice: Resolution of Disputes as to Privileged Communications Regulations 2009, SI 2009/1916, which came into force on 7 August 2009, provide a procedure for the First-tier Tribunal to resolve disputes about whether a document or information is protected from disclosure by reason of legal professional privilege.

16.173 Where a dispute arises in correspondence, the recipient of an information notice must serve on HMRC a list of the documents that the recipient believes are privileged. The list must describe the nature and contents of each piece of material, unless that description would itself give rise to a dispute about privilege.

16.174 The recipient must serve the list within the time for complying with the information notice. HMRC then has 20 working days in which to tell the recipient which material on the list it requires and which it considers is not privileged. Assuming that the matter is not resolved between the parties, the recipient must then make an application (which notice must be accompanied

16.175 *HMRC's information powers*

by the disputed material) to the First-tier Tribunal for it to resolve the dispute, The application must be made within a reasonable time, to be agreed between HMRC and the recipient, but no later than 20 working days after HMRC has indicated which material it requires and which it considers is not privileged.

16.175 Where the dispute arises during an inspection of premises, the recipient of the information notice must tell the HMRC officer carrying out the inspection which material it considers is privileged and any disputed material must be placed in a sealed opaque container. The HMRC officer must then deliver the container to the First-tier Tribunal within 42 working days, with an application that it resolve the dispute about privilege.

16.176 The process under the Regulations is potentially of particular use in relation to premises inspections, first, because there is no appeal against an inspection and, second because a reasonably held belief that a document is or may be privileged amounts, in the author's view, to a reasonable excuse for obstructing the HMRC officer by not providing that particular document. (A person who deliberately obstructs an HMRC officer in the course of an inspection that has been approved by the First-tier Tribunal is liable to a penalty, unless there is a reasonable excuse for that obstruction (*FA 2008, Sch 36, paras 39* and *45*).)

HMRC and the recipient of the information notice can also resolve a dispute about privilege by agreement at any time.

16.177 A recipient who complies with these regulations is treated as having complied with the information notice in relation to the disputed material until the tribunal decides whether privilege applies or the dispute is settled by agreement.

16.178 *Behague v Revenue and Customs Comrs* [2013] UKFTT 596 (TC) concerned the issue as to whether a solicitor's engagement letter was protected from disclosure by legal professional privilege. The First-tier Tribunal noted that engagement letters are not *per se* privileged (*Dickinson v Rushmer* [2002] 1 Costs LR 128), and held that the parts of the letter that went beyond setting out the terms on which the firm would act and which detailed the particular matters involved (including the fact that advice was sought on a particular matter) were privileged.

16.179 The tribunal held subsequently (*Behague v Revenue and Customs Comrs* [2013] UKFTT 647 (TC)) that the information in the redacted engagement letter was not reasonably required by HMRC.

Schedule 36, para 19(1)(a)

16.180 *FA 2008, Sch 36, para 19(1)(a)* protects documents 'relating to the conduct of any pending appeal relating to tax' from disclosure under service of an information notice. It is not coterminous with litigation privilege.

16.181 The reference to 'conduct' of appeals indicates that only documents that are brought into existence for the purposes of the preparation and presentation of the appeal are protected (see *Monarch Assurance Co Ltd v Special Comrs* [1986] STC 311). It applies only in respect of 'pending' appeals; thus, until an appeal has been made by the taxpayer, para 19(1)(a) does not apply to protect documents, even if they came into existence for the purpose of contemplated litigation.

Auditors and tax advisers' documents (FA 2008, Sch 36, para 24)

16.182 *FA 2008, Sch 36, para 24* provides that, subject to certain qualifications, which are described below, an auditor cannot be required either to provide information held in connection with the performance of carrying out a statutory audit or to produce documents that are his property and that were created in the course of carrying out a statutory audit.

16.183 In practice, HMRC continue to allow equivalent protection where an accountant has been appointed to carry out a non-statutory independent audit to standards similar to those required for a Companies Act audit, provided that the work on the audit was kept separate from any work on the preparation of the accounts.

16.184 *Para 25* provides that, subject likewise to the qualifications described below, anyone appointed to give advice about the tax affairs of another person cannot be required to produce documents that are his property and which consist of 'relevant communications' with his taxpayer client or another tax adviser of the client for the purpose of giving or obtaining advice on that client's tax affairs.

HMRC considers that the term 'relevant communications' can include notes of meetings and telephone calls, and internal memoranda, as well as client correspondence.

16.185 The protection for documents of tax advisers and auditors is subject to two qualifications:

- Under *para 26(1)*, no protection is provided in relation to information or documents that contains workings or analytical information showing how a particular entry on the return, accounts, etc was arrived at.

16.186 *HMRC's information powers*

- Under *para 26(2)*, where the notice requiring production of documents or information relates to an unidentified taxpayer (ie it is a notice under para 5), no protection is provided for such part of a document which contains information as to the identity or address of a taxpayer to whom the notice relates or in respect of any person who has acted on behalf of such a taxpayer.

16.186 *Paras 26(1)* and *(2)* are subject to *para 26(3)*, which provides that the protection for a document or information in the possession of an auditor or tax adviser is not lost, as a result of these qualifications, if the explanatory information or the information identifying the taxpayer or adviser respectively is also contained in another document that has already been produced to HMRC.

16.187 In relation to *TMA 1970, s 20* notices, HMRC stated that the formal power to require access to an accountant's working papers was to be used only where the information needed could not be obtained on a voluntary basis and HMRC had no other means of satisfying itself that a taxpayer's accounts or returns are accurate.

A like assurance has yet to be given expressly in relation to the current regime.

Who can exercise the Sch 36 powers?

16.188 *Sch 36* provides that certain aspects of HMRC's information and inspection powers can only be exercised by or with the agreement of an 'authorised officer' of HMRC. *Para 59* defines an 'authorised officer' as an HMRC officer who has been authorised by HMRC for the purposes of *Sch 36*. HMRC's Compliance Handbook indicates the grade of officers who are authorised (see CH262000: How to do a compliance check: Authorisation levels: Classes of authorised officer: Contents). The handbook contains guidance on the approvals and authorisations needed to use the powers contained in *Sch 36*.

The grades of officer authorised to carry out the various *Sch 36* functions are set out below.

Action requiring agreement	Authorised officer
Applications to the First-tier Tribunal for issue of an information notice and permission not to send a copy to the taxpayer	Officers at Grade 7 and above
Request for documents more than six years old	Officers at Grade 7 and above

Action requiring agreement	Authorised officer
Short-notice or unannounced inspections and applications for tribunal approval for an inspection	Officers at Grade 7 and above, except in missing trader intra-community (MTIC), Large Payers Unit (LPU) and excise where Senior Officer (SO) managers are also authorised
Identity unknown notice	Officers at Grade 6 and above (director's agreement also required where tribunal approval is to be sought)
Authorised actions in sensitive cases	Sensitive Case Manager
Penalty functions to enforce powers	Officers at Grade 7 and above
Application to the Upper Tribunal for tax-related penalty on information powers	Officers at Grade 7 and above
Inspection of premises which could be wholly private	Officers at Grade 7 and above, except in MTIC, LPU and excise where SO managers are also authorised

Penalties

16.189 Transitional provisions keep in force the pre-1 April 2009 rules relating to appeals and penalties for information notices issued before 1 April 2009. Documents in respect of which a penalty is exigible under *s 98* are expressly excluded from the *FA 2007, Sch 24* penalty regime. Thus, the 'old' regime remains in force in relation to penalties for failure to comply with a *TMA 1970, s 20* notice.

16.190 Failure to comply with an information notice issued under *Sch 36* renders the taxpayer liable to a penalty of £300 and an additional £60 for each day on which the failure continues after the day on which such penalty was imposed (*Sch 36, paras 39 and 40*). Failure to comply within the time limit will not necessarily attract a penalty, provided that there is compliance within such further time as HMRC may allow (*Sch 36, para 44*). A further tax-geared penalty may be imposed for continued failure to comply (*Sch 36, para 50*).

16.191 A penalty does not arise if the person satisfies HMRC (or the First-tier Tribunal on appeal) that he has a reasonable excuse and, if relevant, the failure is remedied without unreasonable delay after the excuse ceases (*Sch 36, para 45*).

16.191 *HMRC's information powers*

The taxpayer may appeal against HMRC's decision that a penalty is payable (under *paras 39* or *40*) or against the amount of such penalty (*para 47*). Recent examples of successful appeals by taxpayers include:

Chohan v HMRC [2017] UKFTT 779 (TC)

The First-tier Tribunal held that it was reasonable for the taxpayers, who had relied on their accountant to conduct their tax affairs for more than 30 years, to rely on him to comply with the notices. Accordingly, they had a reasonable excuse as regards the initial penalty; that did not, however, extend to the daily penalties charged thereafter. The tribunal also reduced the penalty by 10% to reflect that, of the ten documents requested in the information notice, one had been requested unlawfully (as it originated more than six years before the date of the information notice).

Anstock v HMRC [2017] UKFTT 307 (TC)

The First-tier Tribunal held that the information notice issued was so poorly thought through and so inadequately drafted that it failed the fundamental requirement of certainty and precision. It quashed the penalty that had been imposed, holding that a taxpayer could not be in breach of a notice unless it was a valid notice, meaning one which met the requirements of certainty and precision.

However, arguably, the tribunal has no jurisdiction to consider an appeal against the discretionary decision of HMRC to impose a penalty (see *R&J Birkett t/a The Orchards Residential Home v HMRC* [2017] UKUT 89 (TCC)). In *Birkett*, the Upper Tribunal noted that the tribunal's power under *para 47(b)* enables it to consider whether the amount is within the permissible range in *para 40(2)* and where in that range the penalty should be levied. But, as an appeal under *para 47(b)* is concerned with quantum, not liability, it held that the appellant's argument for a penalty of £0 a day was effectively an argument that the penalty should not have been imposed at all and so could not be determined by the tribunal.

The decision of the Upper Tribunal in *Birkett* was approved by the Administrative Court in *PML Accounting Ltd v HMRC* [2017] EWHC 733 (Admin), which held that the validity of a notice could not be challenged in an appeal against penalties for non-compliance with the notice. However, in *Goldsmith v Revenue and Customs Commissioners* [2018] UKFTT 5 (TC), the First-tier Tribunal declined to follow *PML Accounting*, and held that the interpretation in that case was not binding on it (as the appeal before it concerned a different statutory provision and issue (namely, penalties imposed on a taxpayer for his failure to deliver income tax returns by their due dates)).

As at the date of writing, the decision in *PML* is the subject of an appeal to the Court of Appeal. It is considered that the analysis in *Goldsmith* is to be preferred, and particularly the conclusion by the First-tier Tribunal that there was no reason to think that Parliament, when it provided for '*an appeal against a decision of HMRC that a penalty is payable*' should be taken to have intended that phrase to be construed so narrowly as to exclude consideration of whether the relevant notice that led to the imposition of the penalty had been issued lawfully.

As indicated above, a tax-geared penalty can be imposed for continued failure to comply. In *HMRC v Tager* [2015] UKUT 0040 (TCC), the Upper Tribunal held that the *para 50* penalty is designed to be punitive (in contrast to *paras 39* and *40*, the purpose of which is to encourage compliance). The taxpayer had failed to comply with three information notices. HMRC had imposed penalties under *paras 39* and *40*, but the information remained outstanding. The tribunal imposed penalties of 100% of the estimated tax (with a modest reduction for mitigation). The taxpayer's appeal was heard by the Court of Appeal in April 2018; its decision is awaited at the time of writing.

16.192 There is also a penalty regime for providing inaccurate information or a document containing an inaccuracy in complying with an information notice where both of the following conditions are satisfied that:

- the inaccuracy is careless or deliberate; and
- the person who provided the inaccurate information or document discovers the inaccuracy some time later and fails to take reasonable steps to inform HMRC.

The maximum penalty in relation to inaccurate information is £3,000 (*FA 2008, Sch 36, para 40A* introduced by *FA 2009, Sch 47, para 15* from 21 July 2009).

THE CRIMINAL INVESTIGATORY POWERS OF HMRC

PACE powers

16.193 Not all the powers that are available to the police under *PACE 1984* are available to HMRC officers. In particular, the power to take fingerprints, and the power to charge and bail suspects have not been made available to HMRC officers. Article 4 of the Police and Criminal Evidence Act 1984 (Application to Revenue and Customs) Order 2007, SI 2007/3175, ensured that HMRC officers do not have powers to charge a person, release a person on bail or to detain a person after charge. Police and Criminal Evidence Act 1984 (Application to Revenue and Customs) Order 2015/1783 repealed that Order with effect from 4 November 2015; its Article 4 replicates these exceptions.

16.194 *HMRC's information powers*

16.194 *PACE 1984* has been amended so as to apply four categories of PACE powers to all taxes. These categories are:

- search warrants;
- production orders;
- arrest powers; and
- search and entry powers in order to arrest.

16.195 In 'Criminal Investigation Powers: Publication of Draft Clauses and Explanatory Notes' (which was published on 17 January 2007), it was proposed that the use of the PACE powers would be restricted to suitably trained officers authorised by the Commissioners of HMRC; and at para 7.7 of 'The Explanatory Memorandum to The Police and Criminal Evidence Act 1984 (Application to Revenue and Customs) Order 2007 SI No 2007 3175', it was indicated that, before 1 December 2007, HMRC would publish material on its Internet site in respect of 'how criminal investigation work is organised in HMRC, which officers are entitled to use the powers and how use of the powers is authorised'.

16.196 This proposal has, to an extent, been superseded by the introduction of the enabling Treasury Order. Nonetheless, on 6 December 2007, HMRC issued a release in which it was stated, inter alia:

'**Authorisation to use powers**

The criminal investigation powers can be used only by officers who are authorised to use them. An authorised officer is an officer of HM Revenue and Customs, appropriately trained and engaged on operational duties in Criminal Investigation, Detection, Risk and Intelligence and Internal Governance Directorates. PACE provides that some powers can be exercised only by police constables of a particular rank. When those powers are applied to HMRC the police ranks are converted to HMRC grades of an equivalent authority –

- Sergeant   Officer
- Inspector   Higher Officer
- Chief Inspector   Higher Officer
- Superintendent   Senior Officer'

16.197 HMRC has set internal authorisation levels requiring an authorised officer to obtain the approval of a higher graded officer before using certain powers. The authority levels for HMRC are set no lower than the authority levels in the police, the primary user of PACE powers.

16.198 However, in most cases, HMRC has set the main authority level required at a minimum of senior officer grade (including, for example, applications to a magistrate or court for a production order or search warrant). The majority of authorities in the police service are held at inspector level, which is equivalent to HMRC's higher officer grade.

The PACE power to search

16.199 On an application by an HMRC officer, a magistrate may issue a warrant for the HMRC officer to enter and search premises if he has reasonable grounds for believing that an indictable tax offence has been committed and that there is material on the specified premises that is likely to be of substantial value (whether by itself or together with other material) to the investigation of the offence and is likely to be admissible at the trial for the offence.

16.200 The powers of seizure under PACE have been considerably extended under the *Criminal Justice and Police Act 2001 (CJPA 2001)*.

Its provisions aim to overcome the problems that arose either where it could not be conveniently determined in situ whether a particular item (such as a computer) was subject to seizure or where there were issues relating to whether or not material was protected by reason of legal professional privileges.

16.201 Under *CJPA 2001, Sch 1, Pt 1*, the *s 50* powers of seizure under that Act are extended to *PACE 1984, s 8*. This power applies where it is not reasonably practicable to determine on the premises whether the material is, or contains, something HMRC is entitled to seize. It entitles HMRC officers to remove material (eg computer hard drives) if they have reasonable grounds to believe that the material may contain items they are authorised to seize.

16.202 In *R (on the application of H) v IRC* [2002] EWHC 2164 (Admin), which concerned a *TMA 1970, s 20C* warrant, the High Court held that a hard disk could not be regarded as simply a container of the files visible to the computer's operating system. It was a single object: a single thing. There was no basis, therefore, for a computer not being considered a 'thing' within the meaning of *s 20C(3)(b)*. The fact that there was also on the hard disk irrelevant material did not make the computer any less of a thing that might be required as evidence for the purposes of criminal proceedings. Accordingly, if an HMRC officer who entered into premises under the authority of a warrant under *s 20C* found a computer, and he had reasonable cause to believe that the data on the computer's hard disk might be required as evidence for the purpose of relevant proceedings, then he was entitled to seize and remove that computer, even though it contained irrelevant material also.

It is considered that the ratio of this case applies equally to PACE warrants.

16.203 *HMRC's information powers*

16.203 Once the material is removed from the premises, HMRC is empowered to sift the material to determine whether it contains any relevant items that it wishes to seize.

When powers of seizure under *s 50* are exercised by an HMRC officer, the taxpayer or third party must be provided with a written notice of this in accordance with *CJPA 2001, s 52*. The warrant must be endorsed to provide a record of those documents or items that have been removed.

16.204 Access to all the documents or items may be permitted, on request and under supervision. Copies may be taken at the time of access, or requested. If requested, the copies must be provided within a reasonable time. There is no right to allow a copy to be taken at the time of search.

16.205 An HMRC officer exercising powers under *PACE 1984, s 8* is bound by the PACE Codes of Practice.

Code B provides, inter alia, that a person from whom any items are seized must, on request, be provided with a list or description of the property within a reasonable time. If an original document has been removed and is of such a nature that a copy would be sufficient:

(a) for use as evidence at a trial for an offence; or

(b) for forensic examination or for investigation in connection with an offence;

it may not be retained longer than is necessary to establish that fact and to obtain the copy.

16.206 Items held with the intention of furthering a criminal purpose are not subject to legal privilege.

In *R v IRC and Middlesex Guildhall Crown Court, ex p Tamosius and Partners* [1999] STC 1077, the High Court held that *TMA 1970, s 20C(4)* prevented only the removal of documents with respect to which a claim to professional privilege could be 'maintained': the seizure did not become unlawful merely because the firm of American lawyers that had been raided claimed that the documents were privileged.

16.207 HMRC will often adopt the practice of nominating counsel and then using that counsel to review material to determine whether or not legal privilege applies. However, this process is undertaken only to protect HMRC; it does not preclude a taxpayer or third party challenging a decision by counsel that material is not privileged.

16.208 If there is a dispute as to whether legal privilege applies, attempts should be made, at the time of the search, to persuade HMRC to put the material in opaque, sealed envelopes and the issue of privilege resolved subsequently.

Key points in respect of the PACE search powers

16.209
- There must be reasonable grounds for 'believing' that an offence has been committed (suspicion is not sufficient). The judge is only able to issue an order where he is satisfied that there are reasonable grounds for believing that an offence 'has been' committed (that it is 'being, or is about to be' committed will not suffice).
- An application for a warrant under *PACE 1984, s 8* is made to a magistrate. If special procedure material is involved, a search warrant cannot be issued under *s 8*, and a warrant can be issued only by a circuit judge (see further below).
- Applications for search warrants under *PACE 1984* do not require the approval of the Board of HMRC (although, as a matter of practice, they do need internal authorisation at a senior level).

Production orders

16.210 'Special procedure material', items subject to legal professional privilege, and 'excluded material' are excluded from the scope of a *s 8* warrant. Special procedure material consists broadly of business records that are held by a person under an obligation of confidence to a third party (see *PACE 1984, s 14*).

16.211 If it is suspected that special procedure material needs to be obtained, HMRC can apply to a circuit judge (ex parte) for a warrant under *PACE 1984, Sch 1, para 12*. If granted, this enables an Officer to enter premises and search for excluded material or other special procedure material (there are a number of conditions as to access and other criteria that must be satisfied (see Code B of the PACE Codes of Practice)).

16.212 An alternative to an order authorising such material to be seized under a search and seizure exercise is a production order (under *PACE 1984, Sch 1, paras 7–11*).

If a circuit judge is satisfied that there are reasonable grounds for believing that an indictable tax offence has been committed, he may consent to the issue

16.213 *HMRC's information powers*

of a PACE production order. The hearing before the judge is *inter partes* (in contrast to applications under *TMA 1970, s 20BA*).

Currently, the production order powers under *TMA 1970, s 20BA* (direct tax) and *VATA 1994, Sch 11, para 11* (VAT) are preserved.

16.213 However, if the documents sought are believed to include special procedure material, then those documents may not be obtained under the *s 20BA* or *para 11* production order process: a production order under *PACE 1984, Sch 1* must be used instead. Prior to its repeal, Article 7 of the Police and Criminal Evidence Act 1984 (Application to Revenue and Customs) Order 2007, SI 2007/3175 provides that PACE is to be interpreted as if *s 14B* was inserted after s 14A, with *s 14B* providing that an HMRC officer may only make an application under *TMA 1970, s 20BA* or *VATA 1994, Sch 11, para 11* if the officer considers that an application under *PACE 1984, Sch 1* would not succeed because the material required does not consist of or include special procedure material. Article 6, Police and Criminal Evidence Act 1984 (Application to Revenue and Customs) Order 2015/1783 provides the like provision.

Safeguards

16.214 The PACE Codes of Practice apply when PACE powers are exercised by HMRC officers and when HMRC officers are investigating tax offences (see *PACE 1984, s 67*). They contain detailed regulations on the exercise of PACE powers and notes for guidance. They are admissible in evidence and any relevant provision must be taken into account by a court (under *PACE 1984, s 67(11)*).

PACE Code B deals with the powers to search premises and to seize and retain property found on premises and persons.

The SOCPA powers

16.215 *SOCPA 2005, ss 60–70, Sch 1, Part 2*, introduced, inter alia, new investigatory powers in relation to tax crimes.

The offences to which the powers relate include common law cheat of the public revenue and false accounting (*Theft Act 1968, s 17*), provided that, in the opinion of the investigating officer, the potential loss to the public revenue is of an amount not less than £5,000. The powers came into effect on 1 April 2006.

HMRC's information powers **16.222**

16.216 An HMRC prosecutor can give, or can authorise an officer of HMRC to give, a disclosure notice to any person who has information which relates to a matter relevant to the investigation of the offence, provided that there are reasonable grounds for belief that the information in question, whether or not by itself, is likely to be of 'substantial value' to the investigation.

16.217 A recipient of the notice not only has to produce documents relevant to the investigation, but also has to 'answer questions with respect to any matter relevant to the investigation' and to 'provide information with respect to any such matter as is specified in the notice' (under *SOCPA 2005, s 62(3)*).

16.218 There is a similar protection for privileged information or documents as was contained in *TMA 1970, 20C(4)*; a person may not be required to answer any privileged question, or provide any privileged information, or produce any privileged document (except that a lawyer may be required to provide the name and address of his client).

16.219 Two offences have been created with regard to *SOCPA 2005* disclosure notices.

The first is failure to comply with the requirements set out in a disclosure notice (punishable by a maximum sentence of 51 weeks' imprisonment, with a 'reasonable excuse' for failure to comply being a defence); and, second is making a false or misleading statement in response to the requirements imposed by a disclosure notice (punishable by a maximum of two years' imprisonment).

16.220 If the recipient of a disclosure notice fails to comply with its terms, then the HMRC prosecutor can obtain a search and seize warrant from a justice of the peace. Such a warrant will enable an HMRC prosecutor to enter and search premises, using force where necessary, and to take possession of any documents that appear to be of a description specified in the disclosure notice, or to take any other steps that appear to be necessary for preserving, or preventing interference with, any such documents.

16.221 A warrant can also be issued if it is not practicable to issue a disclosure notice, or where the service of a disclosure notice might seriously prejudice the investigation (under *SOCPA 2005, s 66(2)*).

16.222 It was intended that these powers would be used primarily against third parties, including professional advisers. (See the comments of the Parliamentary Under-Secretary of State for the Home Department at the Committee stage of the Serious Organised Crime and Police Bill.) However, to date, HMRC only rarely makes use of these powers.

16.223 *HMRC's information powers*

Section 20BA – the production power

16.223 HMRC's ability to obtain possession of documents in the case of suspected serious fraud was enhanced by the introduction of *TMA 1970, s 20BA* (and *Sch 1AA*), which was inserted by *FA 2000, s 149(1)*.

16.224 *Section 20BA* does not require HMRC to apply for a search and seizure warrant to obtain documents from a third party, who may have evidence relating to suspected fraud; a judge may issue an order requiring the person to deliver the documents to HMRC. The appropriate judicial authority (a circuit judge in England and Wales (see *s 20D(1)*) may, if satisfied on information on oath given by an authorised officer of the Board of the grounds set out below, make an order under *s 20BA* requiring a person who appears to have in his possession or power the documents specified in the order to deliver them to a specified HMRC officer within ten working days (working days exclude Saturdays, Sundays and public holidays), or such other period as may be specified.

16.225 *Section 20BA* was intended to limit the occasions on which it is necessary for HMRC to enter the premises of persons not themselves suspected of fraud; a warrant could be issued under *s 20C* if the production order procedure under *s 20BA* is more appropriate. *Section 20C(1AA)* provided that the Board of HMRC shall not approve an application for an *s 20C* warrant unless 'they have reasonable grounds for believing that use of the procedure under s 20BA ... might seriously prejudice the investigation'. There is no such equivalent requirement to consider *s 20BA* before applying for a warrant under *PACE 1984, s 8*.

16.226 *Section 20BA* has been amended in one regard following the changes introduced by *FA 2007*: the procedure under *s 20BA* cannot be used to obtain 'special procedure material' (see Article 6, Police and Criminal Evidence Act 1984 (Application to Revenue and Customs) Order 2015/1783, and further below); instead an application under *PACE 1984, Sch 1* must be made.

16.227 The grounds for issuing the order are that:

- there is reasonable ground for suspecting that an offence involving serious fraud in connection with, or in relation to, tax is being, has been or is about to be committed; and

- documents which may be required as evidence for the purposes of any proceedings in respect of such an offence are or may be in the power or possession of any person (under *s 20BA(2)*).

16.228 A person is entitled to notice of the intention to apply for an order against him under *s 20BA* and to appear and be heard at the hearing of the

HMRC's information powers **16.231**

application, unless the appropriate judicial authority is satisfied that this would seriously prejudice the investigation of the offence (under *Sch 1AA, para 3*).

16.229 A recipient of the notice of intention to apply for an order must not do any of the following:

- conceal, destroy, alter or dispose of any document to which the application relates; or

- disclose to any other person information or any other matter likely to prejudice the investigation of the offence to which the application relates (under *Sch 1AA, para 4*) unless permission is obtained from the appropriate court, or in writing from an HMRC officer, or after the application has been dismissed or abandoned, or after any order has been complied with.

16.230 This is an exception to the anti-tipping off provision in the case of professional legal advisers. A professional legal adviser may disclose information to his client in connection with the giving by the adviser of legal advice, or to any other person in contemplation of, or in connection with, legal proceedings and for the purposes of those proceedings.

However, this exception does not apply in circumstances where disclosures are made with a view to furthering a criminal purpose.

Sch 1AA, para 5 provides the same protection to privileged materials with regard to the exercise of a power under *s 20BA* as *s 20C(4)* did in the context of *s 20C* notices.

16.231 In addition, Orders for the Delivery of Documents (Procedure) Regulations 2000, SI 2000/2875, reg 7 sets out a procedure for the resolution of disputes as to legal privilege. If there is a dispute as to whether any document or parts of documents are protected by legal privilege, the person concerned may apply to the appropriate judicial authority (in England and Wales, a circuit judge) to resolve the dispute. If the application is made within the time allowed for the delivery of the documents, then they are deemed to have been delivered in accordance with the notice until the dispute is resolved. In the meantime, all the documents concerned are to be lodged with and held by the court. The Board of HMRC is entitled to at least five working days' notice of the hearing of the application, and to attend and be heard at the hearing. If the authority upholds the claim for legal privilege in whole or in part, the costs of the application are to be met by the Board of HMRC.

Before the hearing of the dispute, it may be resolved by agreement between the Board and the applicant.

16.232 *HMRC's information powers*

16.232 HMRC does not have a statutory duty to provide copies or an inventory, although there are rights to access/request copies: if an original document has been delivered and is of such a nature that a copy would be sufficient:

(a)   for use as evidence at a trial for an offence; or

(b)   for forensic examination or for investigation in connection with an offence;

the original shall not be retained longer than is necessary to establish that fact and to obtain the copy (*s 20CC* and *Sch 1AA, para 8*).

SECTION 20BA OFFENCES

16.233 Failure to comply with an order made under *s 20BA* is punishable as a contempt of court. Failure to comply with the obligations under *Sch 1AA, para 4* is also punishable as a contempt of court.

TAX ACCOUNTANTS AND AGENTS

16.234 Prior to 1 April 2013, HMRC could only demand documents from a tax accountant who had been convicted by a UK court of any tax offence or had had a penalty imposed on him for assisting in the preparation of a tax return or accounts which he knew to be incorrect or in the preparation or delivery of any information or document to be used for tax purposes which he knew to be incorrect. And, these powers applied only to direct taxes.

In February 2010, draft legislation that sought to provide HMRC with powers to address deliberate wrongdoing by tax agents was published. A further consultation document and revised draft legislation were published in July 2011. Slightly revised draft legislation was published on 6 December 2011, and was enacted in *FA 2012, s 223* and *Sch 38*. *FA 2012, Sch 38* introduced (with effect from 1 April 2013) new powers, which apply across all taxes, to take action against tax agents who HMRC determine as having engaged in dishonest conduct. These powers enable HMRC to impose a civil penalty on dishonest tax agents and to access their working papers (to determine the extent of their dishonesty).

There are three main elements:

(*a*)   the power to issue a dishonest conduct notice;

(*b*)   the power to require access to all the working papers of an agent to whom such a notice has been issued; and

(*c*)   a civil penalty of up to £50,000.

The term 'tax agent' is widely defined, for the purpose of *Sch 38*, as an individual who, in the course of business, assists others with their tax affairs. An individual may be a tax agent even if appointed indirectly or at the request of someone other than the client. Assistance with a client's tax affairs includes providing advice to, or acting for, a client in relation to tax, as well as assistance with regard to any document that is likely to be relied upon by HMRC to determine the client's tax position. If assistance is provided in the knowledge that it is likely to be used in connection with the client's tax affairs, then, even if it is provided for a 'non-tax' purpose, that may amount to assistance for these purposes.

If HMRC conclude that a tax agent is, or has been, engaging in dishonest conduct, they may make a formal determination to that effect by sending a conduct notice to him. The notice can be only issued by, or with the approval, of an authorised officer of HMRC. It must set out the grounds on which the determination is made.

If a conduct notice has been issued (and not overturned on appeal), HMRC have power (under *Sch 38, para 8*) to issue a 'file access note'. A file access notice allows an HMRC officer to require 'relevant documents' to be provided from either the tax agent or any other person that the officer believes may hold them. Relevant documents are defined as the agent's working papers, and any other documents used by him in assisting clients with their tax affairs. Clients includes past clients; and the power is not limited to obtaining documents relevant to those clients for whom the tax agent has been engaging in dishonest behaviour. *Para 9(2)* provides that: 'it does not matter who owns the papers.'

The notice:

(a) may require provision of either specified relevant documents or all relevant documents in the power or possession of the document holder;

(b) does not need to identify the tax agent's particular clients;

(c) must name the tax agent where it is addressed to a third party; and

(d) may specify the time limit, form and location for the provision of the documents.

A file access notice can not require documents that

(*a*) are not in the document holder's power or possession;

(*b*) contain material that relate to a pending tax appeal or which is journalistic or personal material (within the meaning of *PACE, s 12*);

(*c*) are privileged; or

(*d*) are more than 20 years old (unless they are relevant to later tax periods);

to be provided.

16.235 *HMRC's information powers*

HMRC may copy or take extracts from any document provided. They may retain a document for a 'reasonable period'. If they do so, must provide a copy to the document holder if requested. Once a file access notice has been given, or the individual has been informed by HMRC that such a notice will be, or is likely to be given, then the individual is guilty of a criminal offence if he conceals, destroys or otherwise disposes of a material document.

KEY POINTS

16.235 The following six key points are intended as a guide for the practitioner whose client has received a request for information or documents from HMRC:

1. HMRC possesses very extensive powers to obtain information and documents from taxpayers and third parties.

2. The legislation provides various 'checks and balances' on HMRC's exercise of its powers. Since the new system of information powers was introduced by *FA 2007* and *FA 2008*, the Government has amended the legislation at least annually; hence ensuring cognisance with the changes is critical.

3. Certain categories of documents, particularly documents that are subject to legal professional privilege, are protected from disclosure to HMRC.

4. Objectively assess the strengths and weaknesses of the client's position, and of HMRC's position.

5. Consider whether you should bring in a specialist to assist, particularly if HMRC is alleging criminal conduct.

6. Keep the client informed.

Chapter 17

Preparing reports for HMRC

Phil Berwick CTA ATT
Director, Berwick Tax Limited

SIGNPOSTS

- **Scope** – There are many different occasions on which the adviser may consider submitting a report to HMRC. Typically, these are disclosure reports, whether requested by HMRC, or initiated by the adviser or client (see **17.1**). There are numerous other situations in which a report may be required (see **17.3**), and the adviser must consider why the preparation of a report may be beneficial.

- **The advantages of a report** – The preparation of a report is, usually, an expensive process. A report can, however, be a cost-effective route for dealing with a client's tax affairs (see **17.5–17.7**). Professional fees will be one of the major components of the costs associated with preparing a report. Care must be taken to ensure that an objective view is taken (see **17.6–17.7**). The adviser needs to consider the impact on likely additional liabilities, including interest and penalty charges (see **17.8**). In a typical investigation, the process is controlled by the inspector. Preparing a report can help to regain some of the initiative. The adviser can take a pro-active approach, instead of answering a seemingly endless stream of questions or information requests from the inspector, but preparation of a report must be risk-based (see **17.9–17.11**). Preparation of a report enables the facts to be presented in a favourable light, rather than the issues being detected by HMRC, following a detailed records examination (see **17.12–17.13**). A considered report can pre-empt HMRC queries, and have a positive impact on penalty reduction (see **17.14**). The preparation of a report can have a tactical advantage, particularly where the client may be in denial about his position (see **17.15–17.16**).

- **Establishing the ground rules** – After the decision has been made to prepare a report, the next step is to establish, and agree, the parameters and content. The responsibility for the preparation, and

17.1 *Preparing reports for HMRC*

> cost, of the report rests with the client, but the inspector will want to provide input. Failure to take the inspector's position into account may result in a subsequent investigation by HMRC (see **17.17–17.18**). The planning stage should include a consideration of any gaps in the client's records so that approaches can be made to third parties if necessary, to avoid delay (see **17.19**). The adviser needs to have a frank discussion with the client to establish the nature and extent of irregularities. The adviser can then agree the parameters of the report with the inspector before detailed work is undertaken. The content should, ideally, be agreed with the inspector, but it is the client's report, and the adviser may need to make a judgement call about what is included (see **17.20–17.23**). The agreed content, and timescales, should be given in writing to the client and inspector (see **17.24**).
>
> - **Preparing the report** – After the content has been agreed, work should start in earnest. There are two basic elements to the report that must be considered. Also, the adviser should consider the style required – plain language wins over fancy prose. The report will be read by HMRC and the client, and the document should be prepared with that in mind, also taking into account the agreed content and parameters. (See **17.25–17.29**.)
>
> - **Typical methodologies** – Appropriate methodologies must be used, to identify and quantify the disclosure, and also to demonstrate that there aren't any other irregularities. Each case is different, but at least some of the common methodologies will be used (see **17.30–17.31**). Analyses of bank accounts is always a primary task. A key aspect is to agree an acceptable de minimis limit with HMRC, to reduce the amount of work necessary. Success of the analysis will depend on the records available (see **17.32–17.33**). Lodgements to the accounts will need to be verified, subject to the de minimis limit or on a sample basis. The adviser needs to consider HMRC's policy regarding unidentified lodgements, and to approach the bank for further information where necessary (see **17.34–17.36**). Withdrawals from bank accounts need to be treated in the same way as lodgements, ensuring that material items are identified. The review will need to consider the client's known lifestyle, to ensure that expected expenditure is identified The acquisition of significant assets during the review should be identified through the analysis (see **17.37–17.39**). The analysis of the bank accounts should be compared to the information provided on tax returns submitted to HMRC, to identify any differences (see **17.40–17.41**). When dealing with a close company, the directors' loan accounts should be reviewed in the same way as a bank account. The account should be adjusted for any understated profits. The adviser

Preparing reports for HMRC **17.1**

should pay attention to the timing of dividends or remuneration in the company's records, to ensure they are consistent with the facts. The review of the loan accounts will help to build an overall picture of the client's financial position (see **17.42–17.43**). A cash flow test may be needed, particularly where the business has cash takings. It can be difficult to accurately determine the levels of cash income and expenditure, particularly given the changing sources of cash, but this is an area that must be considered by practitioners (see **17.44–17.48**). When considering a client's credit card expenditure, there are two key areas to address. Where a full set of credit card statements have not been retained, it may be sufficient to obtain duplicates for a sample period. The review of the credit card statements should include identification of any cash withdrawals (see **17.37–17.39**). Benefits in kind that have not been included on annual P11D returns need to be identified. Information obtained from other reviews should be compared with data previously supplied to HMRC (see **17.52–17.53**). A schedule of personal assets and liabilities will need to be included, usually certified. In some cases, annual schedules may need to be prepared, although the use of capital statements is less common than it was (see **17.54–17.55**).

- **Working papers** – Any working papers created during the investigation process should be retained, and made available to HMRC, if required. Copies of correspondence with third parties should also be retained, and, potentially, made available to the inspector, helping to reduce the likelihood of HMRC making enquiries to those persons. (See **17.56–17.57**.)

- **COP9 reports** – Cases conducted under the Contractual Disclosure Facility require careful handling because of the threat of criminal investigation. Failure to submit a formal disclosure report, where one is required, can have a significant effect on the level of penalty sought by HMRC, assuming a criminal investigation is not undertaken (See **17.58–17.61**.)

- **Voluntary disclosures** – The same general rules apply when making a report in the context of a voluntary disclosure. Advisers should consider the most appropriate way of contacting HMRC to make the submission. (See **17.62–17.65**.)

- **Disclosure facility submissions** – Practitioners should consider the options available, whether the client is making an unprompted disclosure or where there is an existing enquiry. The guidance on the submission of reports is equally applicable to disclosures being made

17.1 *Preparing reports for HMRC*

> under one of HMRC's dedicated disclosure processes, subject to the particular requirements of that process. (See **17.66–17.67**.)
>
> - **Formal certificates** – There are several formal, but not statutory, certificates that the inspector will ask the taxpayer to sign when a disclosure report has been prepared. The significance of the forms must be explained to the client (see **17.68–17.69**). In a COP9 case, HMRC will also want the formal disclosure report to be formally adopted by the client (see **17.70**).
>
> - **Client sign-off** – Advisers should consider getting their clients sign-off on any report, whether or not formally adopted, and obtaining authorisation for its submission to HMRC (see **17.71**).
>
> - **Key points** – Ten key issues for the practitioner are included at **17.72**.

INTRODUCTION

17.1 There are many different circumstances in which it may become appropriate to submit a report to HMRC. The most common circumstance, and the one that this chapter will mainly focus on, is a disclosure report. A report of this nature may be prepared at the specific prompting of HMRC or, alternatively, on the initiative of the taxpayer and/or his adviser. The adviser must consider the most appropriate manner of submitting the disclosure to HMRC.

17.2 For many years, disclosure reports have been an integral part of investigations carried out under HMRC's Code of Practice 9 (COP9), the civil investigation of fraud procedure. The latest incarnation of that process, the Contractual Disclosure Facility (introduced on 31 January 2012, with a subsequent update on 30 June 2014), is no different. The relevance of COP9 to disclosure reports will be considered in more detail later in the chapter. For more information on the COP9 process, please refer to **CHAPTER 2**.

17.3 Outside of COP9 cases, reports may be prepared in a variety of situations. These may include the following examples, the list of which, however, is far from exhaustive:

- other investigations conducted by HMRC's specialist investigations units (including Code of Practice 8 – see **CHAPTER 2**);

- a submission under a HMRC disclosure facility, or similar process;

- a specific review of a tax or accounting issue, eg capital allowances;

- a review of employment tax and NIC compliance;

- an unprompted disclosure of tax irregularities; or
- a review of a taxpayer's affairs in response to an HMRC enquiry or challenge.

17.4 Whatever the particular set of circumstances that prompt the preparation of a report, there are some well-established ground rules to bear in mind. Before we look at them, it is important to consider the reasons why the preparation of a report might be strategically advantageous.

THE CASE FOR PREPARING A REPORT

Focus

Reports can be expensive to prepare. The adviser should explain to his client that, if done well, and HMRC's subsequent direct involvement is managed properly, the cost of preparing a report will often pay for itself by reducing the overall fees that would have arisen if the HMRC enquiry or challenge had been handled directly.

17.5 There is only ever a case for preparing a report if the adviser and his client believe that such an approach will be cost-effective.

Professional fees

17.6 The cost in point will include the amount of professional fees that might arise under different scenarios. This is always a difficult estimation to make at the outset of an enquiry. All manner of unexpected and unforeseeable factors may arise that could have a significant impact on the length and extent of the enquiry. Some of these may be avoided if there is a very open and frank relationship between the adviser and his client from the start of the enquiry. Costs may also be avoided where the adviser has a detailed knowledge of the client's business and private affairs. This is especially true where that knowledge extends to the books and records kept by the client. A potential downside is that an adviser who is too close to the client may not be objective enough to carry out the work necessary. That can have adverse implications for the client and adviser.

17.7 There are therefore many potential pitfalls in trying to assess the cost-efficiency of preparing a report. Of itself this potential positive factor for preparing a report will rarely be enough to persuade an adviser or client to go ahead with the report.

17.8 *Preparing reports for HMRC*

Additional liabilities

17.8 Another important ingredient of the overall cost is the amount of additional tax and the accompanying interest and penalty charges. If the adviser and his client feel that the preparation of a report will impact favourably on these potential additional financial liabilities, then that must be a persuasive reason for going ahead. In short, will the preparation of a report be a positive force for damage limitation?

Control

17.9 Another, strategically important, reason for preparing a report is to retain or recover control over the investigation process. Typically investigations are managed and controlled by the inspector. He decides:

- whether to enquire into a taxpayer's return;
- what aspects of that taxpayer's affairs to focus on;
- when to develop or extend the issues under enquiry;
- when to ask to see and examine the prime records; and
- when to seek a meeting with the taxpayer and/or adviser.

17.10 The adviser and client often simply keep responding to successive questions, and requests for records and meetings as they arise. The initiative remains with the inspector, and he remains in control of events throughout the investigation.

17.11 If the client remains convinced of his innocence and there is no reason to fear the inspector's enquiries, then there will rarely be any need to consider preparing a report. The adviser should explore all relevant risk areas with the client before adopting this approach.

17.12 Where, however, at the beginning or early stages of an HMRC enquiry, it becomes obvious that there are problems or apparent irregularities, it may be appropriate to suggest to the inspector that a report be prepared. This allows the adviser and client an opportunity to both:

- evaluate the extent and quantum of the irregularities; and
- present them in the best possible light to HMRC.

17.13 This will almost certainly be a better way forward than simply leaving the inspector to carry out a detailed and potentially damaging examination of the relevant records, etc and presenting him with a gift-wrapped opportunity to tear apart the returns, accounts and underlying records. Their obvious unreliability will be used much more forcibly by the inspector if uncovered as a result of his efforts rather than by a properly-packaged disclosure from the taxpayer.

> **Focus**
>
> A disclosure presented in a report that is thorough and complete will go a long way towards pre-empting HMRC questions and actions, and demonstrating the client's desire to regularise his tax affairs. Early and appropriate payments on account should also be considered, as this helps to convey that the client is keen to co-operate and to make amends.

17.14 This leads to the issue of penalty reduction. The level of penalty for an incorrect return is influenced by the way in which any disclosure is made and the assistance given to HMRC. A well-prepared report with a full and complete disclosure will help reduce the level of penalty, under both the old and new regimes. Additional reduction will be given where the report is in respect of an unprompted disclosure. Advisers should bring this matter to the attention of the client at an early stage, so that the best possible penalty reduction is achieved, and the client is aware of the consequences if he does not co-operate with the preparation of the report. Advisers should be aware that HMRC have, without any change in the relevant legislation, changed their policy in relation to the penalty reduction given (under the old and current penalty regimes) where a taxpayer has taken a significant period to correct their non-compliance, or would previously have been able to make a disclosure through one of HMRC's offshore disclosure facilities.

Tactics

17.15 Another good reason for opting to prepare a report may be to save the client from himself. Some clients cannot bring themselves to admit to either their adviser or HMRC that their returns are incorrect. They will often only eventually do so when faced with incontrovertible evidence. By that time, the whole enquiry process has gone on for far too long, at considerable cost in fees and with the penalty reduction severely dented. The enquiry can sometimes unnecessarily become a war of attrition.

17.16 Advisers need to assess the position, spell out the advantages of making a disclosure (where appropriate) and persuade the client to accept the benefits of addressing the problem(s) and making a prompt and complete disclosure.

17.17 *Preparing reports for HMRC*

The ground rules: planning the report and agreeing the parameters with HMRC

> **Focus**
>
> Once a decision has been taken to proceed by way of the preparation of a report, it is vital that the parameters are agreed with the investigating inspector before work commences. Failure to do so may mean additional, and preventable, enquiries are raised by the inspector after submission of the report.

17.17 In cases other than COP9, the HMRC officer will normally make it clear that the report is being prepared at the instigation of the taxpayer. The inspector will want to distance himself from any responsibility as to the cost or quality of the report. Inspectors will be prepared however to provide input into the issues and time periods to be covered.

17.18 It is very important that the report focuses on the aspects of the taxpayer's affairs about which the inspector has concerns. The report must review or investigate those aspects in a way that will satisfy the inspector. Unless this is agreed, there is always the danger that the inspector will prefer to conduct a separate and detailed review, adding to the length of the enquiry and potentially to the final amount of additional tax payable.

17.19 The author of the report needs to have a detailed knowledge and understanding of the taxpayer's business and private affairs. An early assessment should be made of the available underlying records. If there are gaps or missing records (eg bank statements), arrangements should be put in place at the earliest opportunity to apply to third parties for the records or information that is required. Although some clients will be able to make the necessary arrangements, the adviser should consider obtaining letters of authority so that he can approach the third party directly. Practitioners should retain copies of correspondence with third parties, in case it is requested by HMRC, or it is considered beneficial to share with the officer.

These types of enquiries can take an unexpectedly long time to produce the missing paperwork so failure to identify and apply for missing material can significantly increase the time needed to complete the report.

17.20 Where there is an admission of irregularities, the adviser should have a full and frank discussion with his client. It is important to get an early idea of how the irregularities arose and over what period. If it is a case of defalcations, care should be taken to understand how they were effected, how they were hidden or omitted from the prime records, their regularity or pattern, the approximate

Preparing reports for HMRC **17.23**

amounts and what was done with the money taken. This information does not have to be necessarily disclosed to the inspector at this stage. Without such knowledge, however, the initial planning for the preparation of the report's approach to describing and quantifying the irregularities will be incomplete.

17.21 With this knowledge the adviser is equipped to discuss and agree the report's parameters with the inspector. The objective must be to finish up with a report that not only provides HMRC with a full and complete disclosure, but also leaves the inspector with little or no reason to investigate further.

17.22 The areas to agree with the inspector before starting detailed work on the report may include the following:

- the period or years of assessment to be covered;
- the specific aspects of the client's affairs to be reviewed and/or analysed;
- the extent and nature of any analytical work to be carried out;
- identification of sample years/periods to be examined, if appropriate;
- mutually acceptable *de minimis* limits to be applied;
- the third party enquiries that need to be made and/or the information needed to ensure that the report is complete;
- in the case of defalcations, the methods used to quantify the underdeclared profits, eg business economics (ie gross profit or mark-up rates), cash flow analyses, capital statements (single or double entry), means tests, etc;
- what, if any, reconciliation there should be between the results of any business exercise and the private affairs and known lifestyle of the taxpayer;
- any particular technical issues that need to be addressed;
- which records need to be examined, and for what periods;
- the extent and basis of any extrapolation into past, or subsequent, years of the results of work carried; and
- the timetable for the submission of the report, including the dates for any progress meetings with the inspector.

17.23 Although it is good practice to agree the content of the report with the inspector, it is for the adviser to determine. The client will be paying for the report, and the content should be sufficient to cover his circumstances. There is not a standard template that can be used for each situation. Many inspectors, if given the opportunity, will request far more information than is reasonable. I acted for a client where the inspector had sought a report from his adviser covering a 20-year period, including full analysis of the business, and a

17.24 *Preparing reports for HMRC*

comprehensive review of his property transactions for that period. After I was appointed, I re-negotiated the content of the report with the inspector to reflect the circumstances of the client. This resulted in the report being completed quicker than would otherwise have been the case.

17.24 It is good practice to encapsulate the agreed parameters into a transmittal letter to the client, and in a confirmatory letter to the inspector. There should be no doubt or confusion amongst any of the parties about what needs to be done, for what years, by whom and to what timescale.

PREPARING AND COMPLETING THE REPORT

17.25 Once the parameters and timetable for the report are agreed between the parties, work can commence in earnest. By this time, any obvious third party enquiries will have been sent out and all relevant records and documents assembled and listed.

17.26 There are usually two basic elements to a report. One is the results of analytical and computational work, typically forming appendices to the report. The other is the narrative that will describe the work carried out and generally take the reader through the:

- background history;
- issues;
- descriptions of work carried out; and
- arguments and conclusions.

17.27 Style is a very subjective matter, but experience suggests that simplicity of wording and concise references to appendices are the best way forward. A report will always make a good initial impression with an inspector when, after the first read, he can see what the disclosure is and the basis on which it has been arrived at and quantified. As in many things in life, first impressions count. Inspectors are human and will often sub-consciously decide after the first read just how much they are prepared to accept and/or challenge in the report.

17.28 The other important subscriber to the report is the client. He must also be able to understand the way in which the disclosure has been qualified and quantified. The client will be required to adopt the report as a full and complete disclosure. It is essential that the client is satisfied that all relevant issues have been disclosed, and adequately dealt with.

17.29 The report must be prepared in accordance with the parameters agreed with HMRC and the client. The adviser will have significant input into the content and approach. That is what he is engaged for. In the end, however, it is the responsibility of the client to ensure that it is complete and correct.

COMMON METHODOLOGIES USED IN PREPARING THE REPORT

17.30 In many ways, a disclosure report is like a jigsaw. Pieces interlock and support each other to create an overall picture. So many of the most common methodologies used support and create further pictures of an individual's affairs. There are two main purposes behind the use of these methodologies. One is to identify and quantify the disclosure. The other is to provide first-hand evidence that there are no further irregularities. They are used to prove a negative.

17.31 What are the most typical methodologies? They will certainly include some, or all, of the following, depending on the purpose of the report:

- analyses of banking accounts;
- reviews of lodgements into those accounts;
- analyses of withdrawals from banking accounts;
- where appropriate, scheduling income from various sources and comparing the result with submitted tax returns;
- where appropriate, tracking all movements and transactions on a director's loan or current account with the company;
- cash flow tests;
- analyses of credit card expenditure;
- review of P11Ds and potential benefits in kind; and
- tracking the acquisition and disposals of assets, and drawing up statements of assets and liabilities as at given dates.

This list is far from exhaustive as every case may have its own idiosyncrasies. Having said that, it would be unusual in a typical disclosure report not to have most of these methodologies used in its preparation.

Analyses of banking accounts

17.32 This is always a primary task. It will paint a good picture of the individual's lifestyle and throw up any obvious discrepancies or odd-looking patterns. It is important to agree an acceptable *de minimis* limit with HMRC in advance of starting this work. The higher the limit agreed, the less specific

17.33 *Preparing reports for HMRC*

queries will arise. All transactions below the limit can be pooled together and no time and effort expended to tie down their source or destination, or any such review work can be conducted on a sample basis, if necessary.

17.33 The completeness of such analyses will depend on the records available. On the one hand, there are individuals who keep meticulous records, and all their bank statements, paying-in slips and chequebook stubs (where used) will have been retained. On the other hand, there are individuals who do not keep any records regarding deposits made into accounts, nor do they keep cheque stubs or, if they do, they do not complete them. With the increasing move to online statements, it is important to obtain the documents early in the enquiry process, when they are more likely to be available, particularly where statements for earlier years are required

Review of lodgements

17.34 Inevitably, there will still be a list of lodgements for which further explanation is required. This will to some extent depend upon the records the client has kept. It is amazing just how many sundry amounts are deposited in bank accounts for which the individual keeps no record and has no memory of at a later date. It is important to try to eliminate as many as possible.

17.35 In cases where there are irregularities, especially of an extractive nature, HMRC's well-oiled policy is to treat any unidentified lodgements as further amounts of undisclosed taxable income. The client can end up having to pay tax (plus interest and a penalty) on amounts when nobody knows whether they are genuinely taxable or not. This, incidentally, is why inspectors ask about loans, gifts, windfalls, gambling wins and inheritances at interviews with taxpayers. They are trying to close off these obvious avenues of explanation for unidentified lodgements should they subsequently be put forward by the taxpayer.

17.36 The analysis of lodgements will also dovetail with the schedules of annual income for comparison with submitted tax returns and with disposals of assets. It will also tie-down all transfers into the accounts, enabling the reviewer to spot any funds coming in from an account of which there is no previous knowledge. Where this happens, the adviser has the opportunity to follow this up by writing to the bank or building society from where the funds were transferred and get full details of the account held with them.

Analyses of withdrawals from banking accounts

17.37 In much the same way as with lodgements, this provides the adviser with an opportunity to pick up any transfers from known accounts, to ensure

Preparing reports for HMRC **17.42**

that there are not any previously unidentified banking accounts. If there are, then, again, the adviser must follow this up and complete a full picture of all the accounts he comes across.

17.38 If possible, the withdrawals need to be posted to different expense headings. This analysis will only be as good as the available records. Where there are completed cheque stubs, or other records available, then the analysis can be quite detailed. The adviser will draw up an annual picture of the private expenditure so as to ensure that all normal types of expense are included (ie utility bills, food, taxes) and that the amounts expended are commensurate with the individual's known lifestyle. In particular, special events (weddings, holidays, etc) or times of the year (Christmas, birthdays, etc) should throw up additional expense. Often, regular payments are the subject of direct debits or standing orders that can be easily picked out and scheduled.

17.39 The acquisition of assets such as properties, shares and motor vehicles will all be tracked in accordance with the analyses of these withdrawals. Any loans or gifts made should also be identified.

Cash drawn will normally be the subject of a separate analysis (see below).

Scheduling income for comparison with submitted tax returns

17.40 The analysis of lodgements should enable a detailed schedule of income to be completed. This is a fundamental task that should prove the accuracy or otherwise of the tax returns previously submitted to HMRC. In particular, details of interest received and dividends should reconcile with the amounts returned each year.

The same applies to remuneration or drawings, whichever applies.

17.41 Together with the quantum of private expenditure and movements on assets, the report should be able to paint a full picture of the individual's personal financial affairs. It will either show that all is correct and satisfactory, or that there are clear indications that potentially taxable income is missing.

Directors' loan or current accounts

17.42 In cases where there is a close company, it is always necessary to review the director's loan or current account. It is just like another banking account. There is, however, a significant difference with a banking account. That is because if there are understated profits extracted by the director, then the bookkeeping is straightforward. Sales are credited, and the director's account

17.43 *Preparing reports for HMRC*

is debited. If the result of such revision is that the account becomes overdrawn, or has an increased overdrawn balance, an additional tax liability arises, under *Corporation Tax Act 2010, s 455*. There may also be a beneficial loan for *ITEPA 2003, s 175* purposes. HMRC guidance (at EM8510) acknowledges that the benefit will not arise until there is an intention that the loan be repaid.

17.43 The reviewer should have a careful eye for the timing of movements on this account. It is not uncommon to find remuneration or dividends credited at a date that does not correspond with the historical facts. The same may apply to debits to the account.

The analysis will add further ingredients to the overall picture of the individual's income, expenditure and assets.

Cash flow tests

17.44 The availability, quantum and pattern of cash income and spending is always of interest to inspectors. Traditionally, it is their experience that many extractive frauds involve cash as it is easiest to take and hide. It does not necessarily appear on bank account statements, and is hard to trace or track. This applies to any case being investigated by HMRC, but is especially the case where the business has cash takings.

17.45 A cash flow test is designed to check:

- whether there is sufficient cash to meet the typical types of expenditure met in that way; and
- whether there is a satisfactory pattern of available cash.

17.46 In the first place, it is necessary to try to establish just what dependency a client has on cash to meet private expenditure. Habits vary considerably on this. Some individuals use cash quite sparingly, and rely extensively on debit or credit cards to fund private expenditure. The increased use of contactless payment methods will reduce the cash requirement for low-value purchases. It is important to establish the client's habits before gauging the quantity of cash that would be required to meet whatever level of expenditure applies. Care must be taken to ensure that between cash, debit and credit cards, and contactless payment methods, all obvious types of expenditure have been accounted for. The analysis should be reviewed to verify that, for instance, food has been purchased. It would be no good preparing these schedules only to find that there is no sign of food being bought by any of these methods.

17.47 The cash available, and the timing of that availability, should be identified from either the bank account statements or the business records, depending on how the individual draws cash. Often, it is not possible to be

100% accurate when determining either the level of cash available, or cash expenditure. This exercise has become more problematic, particularly given the availability of cashback withdrawals at supermarkets and other retail outlets, which do not show the component parts of the transaction on the bank statement. Other sources of cash, for example, credit card withdrawals, should also be established and verified.

17.48 Any unusual trends in the pattern of cash drawings and spending will need to be addressed before the report is submitted. Inspectors are liable to draw unhelpful conclusions from unsatisfactory patterns of cash drawings and spending if there is no reasonable explanation for such unusual trends.

Analyses of credit card expenditure

17.49 There are two main aspects to the analysis of credit card expenditure. The first concerns determining how the credit card bill has been paid; the second relates to the nature of expenditure incurred on the credit card. Both are largely dependent on the availability of records. Some individuals keep the monthly statements; others dispose of them as soon as they have made their monthly payment. With the increasing move to online statements, it is important to obtain the documents early in the enquiry process, when they are more likely to be available, particularly where statements for earlier years are required.

17.50 Determining the source of payment for the credit card bill is the first aspect to address when considering the client's credit cards. Payments to the credit card company will be identifiable from the bank account statements, if made by regular direct debit. If paid by cheque, payments will be picked up from cheque stubs, if they have been retained. If statements have not been retained, and many people destroy them for fear of identity theft, the normal remedy is to obtain copies. There will usually be a charge for this, so it makes sense to consider what statements, if any, are available. If there are only a few missing, it may not be necessary to put the client to the expense of obtaining duplicate statements. Where there is a significant gap in the records available, or statements have not been retained, it may be prudent to obtain duplicate statements only for a sample period in the first instance. Following a review of those statements, the adviser can consider whether it is necessary to obtain duplicate statements for other periods.

17.51 When considering the type of expenditure incurred on the client's credit card, the adviser should determine whether there have been any cash withdrawals. Any cash withdrawn in this way will need to be included in the client's cash flow analysis. Whatever results can be gleaned from a review of credit card expenditure have to be included in the statements of annual income and expenditure, and also in the schedules of personal assets and liabilities, as appropriate.

17.52 *Preparing reports for HMRC*

Review of P11Ds and potential benefits in kind

17.52 This applies only where the individual concerned is a director or employee of a company. In companies owned by families or individuals, HMRC is always concerned to find out whether benefits have been enjoyed that are not included in annual P11D returns.

17.53 To address the inspector's concerns, it is good practice to review P11Ds submitted to HMRC, and to compare them with information coming out of all the other reviews and critical analyses carried out in preparing the report. If it is not done in the preparation of the report it is very likely an area that the inspector will explore. Should he find discrepancies and establish that incorrect P11Ds have been submitted, it is likely to undermine the credibility of the rest of the report.

Schedules of assets and liabilities and/or capital statements

17.54 All of the methodologies discussed above will paint a picture of the individual's private financial affairs. The report may need to include a schedule of assets and liabilities at each relevant year end, with a figure of annual movement. This together with known spending has to be compared with known available income. This comparison is the result of compiling capital statements. It begs the question, has the individual saved and spent more than the known available income? Any discrepancy will be additional taxable income unless there is another acceptable explanation.

17.55 A well-prepared and thorough report should be able to summarise all income and expenditure and all movements on assets and liabilities, and provide this overall picture. Although the use of capital statements is less common than was the case, there will be a need to include at least a schedule of assets and liabilities or a formal, certified, statement. The statement will provide a snapshot of the client's wealth at a specified date. Where a report covers the period, say, 6 April 2012 to 5 April 2018, the statement of assets will be prepared as 5 April 2018. A statement of assets at other dates may be requested by the officer, and such requests should be considered for their reasonableness in the client's circumstances.

WORKING PAPERS

17.56 The working papers created during the preparation of the report should be retained, as the inspector may wish to examine extracts to satisfy himself on any areas of the report. There is always a mountain of detail when a disclosure report is prepared, and easy reference and access to any specific areas may help speed up the inspector's review of the report and also hopefully negate duplication of effort. If the inspector can see papers that demonstrate an orderly and well-organised approach this creates a very good impression, and may influence the inspector on just how much review and investigative work he needs to do.

17.57 It is also good practice to keep copies of all correspondence with third parties, and make these available to the inspector, if requested. The inspector may consider asking the client to sign general or specific mandates so third parties can be approached. This can be a sensitive subject, and also an avoidable issue of contention, if the potential avenues for third party enquiries have been closed-off by the adviser. A review of copies of the relevant correspondence between the adviser and third parties may lead the inspector to conclude that further independent enquiries are unnecessary.

DISCLOSURE REPORTS IN COP9 CASES

17.58 HMRC uses the COP9 process where it suspects that a taxpayer has committed tax fraud, but does not commence a criminal investigation. Under the COP9 process, the Contractual Disclosure Facility (CDF), introduced on 31 January 2012 (and updated on 30 June 2014), there is an ongoing risk of criminal investigation, unless the client complies with the process, and meets their various obligations. That applies even where they admit, in an Outline Disclosure, that there has been an underpayment of tax due to their deliberate behaviour, and the Outline Disclosure has been accepted as valid by HMRC. Immunity from criminal investigation exists only for those offences admitted in the Outline Disclosure, subject to the provisos mentioned above.

17.59 In most COP9 investigations, after the outline disclosure has been accepted by HMRC, there will be a need to submit a formal disclosure report. There should be no difference in the use of the various methodologies just because it is a disclosure under COP9. Great care should be taken, and the adviser and his client should never lose sight of the fact that an incomplete disclosure could lead to a criminal investigation by HMRC.

17.60 HMRC's Investigation of Fraud statement, contained in COP9, states that where the taxpayer 'fails to make a full disclosure of the tax frauds they have committed, the Commissioners reserve the right to commence a criminal investigation with a view to prosecution'. The warning is stern and there is a serious onus on the taxpayer to ensure a full disclosure is made. Failure to submit a comprehensive formal disclosure report where one is required will have significant consequences for the client, even if HMRC does not pursue

17.61 *Preparing reports for HMRC*

a criminal investigation. The inspector's internal guidance on this matter (see HMRC's Fraud Civil Investigation Manual (FCIM) 209030) states that in those circumstances 'the disclosure reduction must be significantly less', where the CDF offer was made from 30 June 2014 onwards, with a similar comment at FCIM109030 in relation to cases where the CDF offer was made before 29 June 2014.

17.61 Preparation of a disclosure report in a COP9 investigation can be an onerous and time-consuming process. Advisers without experience of COP9 investigations should consider obtaining support or assistance from a specialist in this area. Handling a COP9 investigation without the requisite experience can have serious implications for an adviser's client, and, by inference, for the adviser. A client is likely to consider legal action against his adviser where he has acted negligently.

VOLUNTARY DISCLOSURES

17.62 When submitting a report in the context of a voluntary disclosure, the adviser should follow the general rules set out above regarding the areas to be covered. The content of the report will vary greatly, depending on the client's circumstances. Given the significant impact of penalties, it is essential that the report is as comprehensive as possible, without including unnecessary detail.

17.63 Where there is a straightforward disclosure to make (for example, undeclared rental income without any issues regarding the source of funding for the rental property), the report may be no more than a three- or four-page letter, with accompanying schedules. If there are multiple properties, and the funding of those properties has come from diverted business takings, for example, a more comprehensive report will be needed.

17.64 With HMRC's increasing move to online digital services, including in relation to disclosure facilities, the need to prepare a comprehensive report, particularly in straightforward cases, may be diminished. Where there is a significant disclosure to be made, the preparation of a report, as outlined in this chapter, should continue to be beneficial to the client.

17.65 Advisers must consider the best route for making the disclosure to HMRC. Particular care must be taken not to prejudice the client's position and leave him vulnerable to criminal investigation. For more guidance on voluntary disclosures, refer to **CHAPTER 14**.

DISCLOSURE FACILITY SUBMISSIONS

Focus

HMRC's dedicated disclosure facilities can provide a favourable route for making either an unprompted disclosure, or, potentially, transferring an existing HMRC enquiry or investigation. The historical facilities have been specific to a particular trade or business sector, or connected to an overseas jurisdiction. The practitioner must ensure he has identified all options available to a client, and that the optimum route is taken.

17.66 The guidance in this chapter is equally applicable to disclosures being made under a dedicated disclosure facility. Although HMRC's disclosure facilities have moved online, the disclosure report still has a part to play in bringing the client's affairs up to date. The practitioner should ensure that the client meets the relevant qualifying criteria for the facility. One factor that must be borne in mind when using a dedicated facility is that there is a short timescale within which the disclosure must be submitted. A consequence of this is that the analyses and review work must be tailored accordingly. The timetable is a good discipline and should ensure that only the most necessary work is undertaken.

17.67 The disclosure report, where one is required, should be significantly shorter than would otherwise be the case. A good discipline to adopt is to restrict the disclosure submission to a maximum of four pages, unless the circumstances are particularly complex. The key issues are to address the disclosure, and major risk areas.

FORMAL CERTIFICATES

Focus

There are certain formal certificates that HMRC may request a taxpayer to complete and sign when a disclosure report has been prepared. The certificates require serious consideration by the client before signature, as HMRC may instigate a criminal investigation if it establishes that a false statement has been given. This should be brought to the client's attention, in writing, before he is asked to sign any of the certificates mentioned below. Practitioners should note that the certificates mentioned below are not statutory documents. Where there is an HMRC enquiry or investigation, the investigating officer is unlikely to finalise the process without the forms listed. Each case should, however, be considered on its merits.

17.68 *Preparing reports for HMRC*

17.68 The certificates referred to above include a certificate of bank accounts, etc operated in the period under review or enquiry. The inspector will provide a standard form for completion, but the adviser should check the wording. The period to be covered by the certificate will need to be agreed with the inspector. The certificate should include details of private and business accounts. It will also include any accounts operated jointly with another person(s), or in any other name but over which the taxpayer has control. A similar document is the certificate of debit and credit cards operated, which requires the treatment outlined in relation to the certificate of bank accounts.

17.69 Another important certificate is a Statement of Personal Assets and Liabilities and Business Interests. HMRC uses a standard form, MS142, for this. If the report includes a schedule of assets and liabilities at each year end the inspector may decide to dispense with the need for a separate certificate. At the very least, the adviser should expect to have to complete a statement at the end of the review period. Where the client has a means problem, and will be seeking an instalment arrangement with HMRC, the inspector will also request a statement of assets at a current date.

A Certificate of Full Disclosure will be requested by the inspector at some stage in the process, but should not be completed and signed until the quantum of additional income, profits or gains has been agreed.

17.70 In COP9 cases, HMRC will expect the report to be adopted by the taxpayer as his full disclosure, with the client signing a formal certificate to that effect. Completion of an adoption certificate reinforces to the client that the onus for making a full disclosure rests with him and not the professional adviser who has prepared the report. In other cases, the adviser should resist a request for formal adoption of the report. Completion of a Certificate of Full Disclosure (see above) at the end of the investigation process should give HMRC the necessary comfort regarding the completeness of the disclosure.

17.71 Advisers should consider obtaining their client's sign-off on any report prepared, confirming that they have made a full disclosure, and that they have made all documents available. Any such sign-off by the client should include his authority to submit the document to HMRC.

KEY POINTS

17.72 The following are ten key points for the practitioner to consider:

1   Determine whether a (disclosure) report is appropriate or necessary.

2   Remember the advantages of preparing a disclosure report, including tactical benefits, and explain these to the client.

Preparing reports for HMRC **17.72**

3   Preparation of the report must be cost-effective.

4   Agree the parameters of the report (and the timetable for submission) with HMRC.

5   The adviser must consider the methodologies that will be most appropriate, given the client's circumstances.

6   Extra care is needed with COP9 reports.

7   When preparing a voluntary disclosure, consider the options for reporting to HMRC.

8   Health warnings must be given to the client before he is asked to sign the various formal certificates that will be required.

9   Seek specialist support if you do not have sufficient experience in this area.

10 Obtain the client's written authority before submitting the report to HMRC.

Chapter 18

Penalties for error and failure to notify

Russell Cockburn BSc (Hons) FFTA
Taxation consultant, lecturer and author; former Inspector of Taxes

---

Focus

This chapter aims to provide an introduction to the concept of tax penalties under the current UK regime but it is important to recognise that in practice this is a still a developing area of tax law and practice and constant reference to the growing body of court and tribunal case law decisions will be essential so as to have an up-to-date understanding of why and how penalties are commonly imposed. This chapter also provides an introduction to, and an outline of, a number of additional penalty situations which can arise where taxpayers fail to comply with certain extra tax obligations. It is therefore important that taxpayers and their advisers are fully aware of all their various obligations under statute. Whilst some of these penalties are not particularly onerous, the implications of such failures occurring as regards HMRC's view of a taxpayer's overall compliance with his obligations and the likely impact this may have on HMRC's approach to dealing with a taxpayer generally cannot be understated.

The following chapter, **CHAPTER 19**, looks at the methods available to taxpayers and advisers seeking to negotiate with HMRC as regards the mitigation of tax penalties, and suggests techniques and strategies to follow, together with a consideration of reasonable excuse and special reduction issues.

INTRODUCTION

History

18.1 Early in the twenty-first century HMRC undertook a review of the regime of financial penalties for tax offences. Various consultation documents were issued as part of this review. The end result was the introduction of a new penalties regime, with the bulk of the relevant legislation contained in *Finance Acts 2007* to *2009*. Much of the new system took effect from 1 April 2009.

18.2 Broadly the objective of the new regime was to seek to achieve a harmonisation of the approach of all penalties legislation so that the same principles and procedures would apply across all taxes wherever possible.

HMRC's stated aim for the new penalties regime from the outset was 'to influence positive customer behaviours and encourage voluntary compliance'.

Objectives of this chapter

18.3 This chapter will provide readers with a summary of the current UK tax penalties regime as it applies to cases involving penalties for 'error'. It should be noted that in some cases the legislation has been applicable for tax return periods starting on or after 1 April 2008 although most changes took effect from later dates.

18.4 The objective is to provide an overview and give information about how these penalties arise and why they are imposed, as well as some guidance on their computation and factors which can be used to mitigate their effects.

HMRC guidance

18.5 There is a mass of published information available on this subject. Of particular relevance will be the HMRC's own internal Compliance Handbook at CH80000 *et seq* which gives a detailed exposé of the department's own opinions and views on the penalties legislation. The HMRC manual can of course be regarded as an authoritative and comprehensive handbook and is an invaluable resource in its own right.

18.6 However, it should always be remembered that HMRC's manuals do of course offer the reader the department's own interpretation of the application of the law to any particular situation. There is no substitute for reference to the original statute itself for confirmation of any particular issue.

THE RELEVANT PENALTIES LEGISLATION

Finance Act 2007, Sch 24

18.7 *FA 2007, Sch 24* provided a revised statute for the imposition of penalties for 'inaccuracies in returns or other documents'; it is headed 'Penalties for Errors'. The areas of tax legislation affected by these provisions are:

- VAT;
- construction industry scheme (CIS);

18.8 *Penalties for error and failure to notify*

- income tax;
- corporation tax (CT);
- capital gains tax (CGT);
- PAYE (Pay As You Earn) and National Insurance contributions (NICs).

Finance Act 2008

18.8 *FA 2008* extended the *FA 2007* regime for penalties for incorrect returns to all excise duties, environmental taxes, inheritance tax, insurance premium tax, stamp duties and petroleum revenue tax.

18.9 *FA 2008* also introduced legislation in respect of HMRC's own information and inspection powers, computer records, record keeping, disclosure of tax-avoidance schemes, time limits for assessments, claims, etc, correcting and amending tax returns and penalties for failure to notify liability to tax.

Finance Act 2009

18.10 *FA 2009* made some further amendments to the regime and subsequent legislation has also included some further 'tidying up' changes and revisions.

Hence the main thrust of the legislation in *FA 2007, Sch 24* is to provide penalties where there is an error or a mistake in a return or some other document on which HMRC relies for the purposes of taxation. There are of course other penalty provisions dealing with failures to submit returns on time, pay tax on time and other matters and these are discussed in the next chapter.

The statute

18.11 *FA 2007, Sch 24* states:

'1(1) A penalty is payable by a person (P) where –

(a) P gives HMRC a document of a kind listed in the Table below, and

(b) Conditions 1 and 2 are satisfied.

(2) Condition 1 is that the document contains an inaccuracy which amounts to, or leads to –

(a) an understatement of [a] liability to tax,

(b) a false or inflated statement of a loss ..., or

Penalties for error and failure to notify **18.15**

(c) a false or inflated claim to repayment of tax.

(3) Condition 2 is that the inaccuracy was [careless (within the meaning of paragraph 3) or deliberate on P's part].

(4) Where a document contains more than one inaccuracy, a penalty is payable for each inaccuracy.'

The types of 'inaccuracy'

18.12 Thus it is important to note that it is HMRC's view and also the statutory position that there has to be an 'inaccuracy in a document' for a penalty to arise and that the inaccuracy has to have been either 'careless' or 'deliberate'. This identifies the first line of defence which may be possible for the taxpayer, ie the concept of *innocent error*. If the taxpayer has made a simple mistake without carelessness, ie having taken reasonable care in the preparation of the document then there is no penalty.

On the other hand, it is important to note that it is technically possible for a document which has multiple errors to lead to multiple penalties!

18.13 It is also important to note that if HMRC takes the view that an inaccuracy was neither careless nor deliberate at the time it was sent to HMRC, it will however, be treated as careless by HMRC if the person:

- discovered the inaccuracy at some later time, *and*
- did not take reasonable steps to inform HMRC.

DOCUMENTS SUBJECT TO THE PENALTY REGIME

18.14 The documents within the inaccuracies penalties regime are listed in *FA 2007, Sch 24, para 1*. Broadly the penalties can apply to documents which contain an inaccuracy which amounts to or leads to:

- an understatement of an individual's liability to tax;
- a false or inflated statement of a loss by an individual; or
- a false or inflated claim to repayment of tax.

18.15 There is no statutory definition of the scope of the word 'document' here but HMRC has indicated that it is its opinion that penalties can apply to 'any document likely to be relied upon by HMRC to determine a person's liability to tax or repayment due'.

18.16 *Penalties for error and failure to notify*

18.16 The department has also indicated that 'documents' can in its opinion include information given to HMRC in an email or letter, by fax or even during a telephone call! It remains to be seen whether or not HMRC will ever seek to impose a penalty for incorrect information given over the telephone, but it is perhaps worth remembering that calls to HMRC are routinely recorded.

Documents relevant for income tax

18.17 Documents relating to income tax and capital gains tax subject to the penalty regime within *FA 2007* are:

- personal tax returns under *TMA 1970, s 8*;
- trustee returns under *TMA 1970, s 8A*;
- a return, statement or declaration in connection with a claim for an allowance, deduction or relief;
- partnership returns under *TMA 1970, s 12AA*;
- statements or declarations in connection with a partnership return under *TMA 1970, s 12AB*;
- accounts in connection with a partnership return;
- a return for the purposes of PAYE regulations;
- returns under the CIS Scheme.

Documents relevant for corporation tax

18.18 Corporation tax documents within these penalty provisions are:

- company returns under *FA 1998, Sch 18, para 3*;
- a return, statement or declaration in connection with a claim for an allowance, deduction or relief;
- accounts in connection with ascertaining liability to tax.

Documents relevant for VAT

18.19 For VAT, documents described in the legislation are:
- VAT returns;
- returns, statements or declarations in connection with a claim.

Documents relevant for all taxes

18.20 Also included within the penalty regime is any document which is likely to be relied upon by HMRC to determine without further enquiry a question about the taxpayer's liability to tax, eg:

- payments made by the taxpayer by way of or in connection with tax;
- any other payment by the taxpayer including penalties;
- repayments or any other kind of payment or credit to the taxpayer.

ASSESSMENTS

18.21 Penalties can also be imposed if HMRC finds it necessary to issue a determination or an assessment to recover tax underpaid because there has been an 'understatement' of someone's income (eg business profits). Alternatively, this scenario may arise where HMRC sends someone a return to fill in and he fails to send it back. As the legal onus is on the taxpayer to tell HMRC when he has a liability his failure to submit a return in these circumstances can lead to a penalty.

18.22 Where an assessment is issued the taxpayer must also inform HMRC if he has reason to believe that assessment could be insufficient. If he does not do this then this also may lead to a penalty being imposed. Thus, a taxpayer can be charged penalties where the HMRC assessment issued understates the taxpayer's liability to income tax, capital gains tax, corporation tax or VAT, and HMRC has reason to believe that the taxpayer has failed to take reasonable steps within 30 days of the date of the determination or assessment to tell HMRC that it represents an under assessment of his true tax position.

PENALTY PERIODS

18.23 A penalty has to be imposed by reference to a tax period having legal status. Statute specifies quite simply therefore that penalties can be charged with reference to inaccuracies for a tax year, an accounting period or any other period for which tax is charged or due, or a repayment of tax is claimed.

THE 'RELEVANT PERSON'

18.24 A taxpayer for the purposes of the penalty legislation is any individual, company, partner, trustee, personal representative, executor, or an

18.25 *Penalties for error and failure to notify*

administrator. In the case of a VAT group, the nominated member of the group is also a person.

THE PREVIOUS PENALTIES REGIME

18.25 The current penalties regime introduced by *FA 2007* applied initially to errors in returns for periods commencing after 31 March 2008 where the return is filed after 31 March 2009. It was then subsequently extended in *FA 2008* to return periods commencing on or after 1 April 2009 where the return is due on or after 1 April 2010.

18.26 For earlier return periods the old penalties regime is applicable and can produce penalty charges where there are incorrect tax returns for periods commencing before 1 April 2008 submitted to HMRC prior to 1 April 2009. The previous regime was substantively different from its replacement. Broadly under the old regime penalties could be imposed where it was shown that a person had 'fraudulently or negligently' delivered:

(i) an incorrect return;

(ii) an incorrect statement or declaration in connection with a claim for any allowance, deduction or relief; or

(iii) incorrect accounts to HMRC.

Thus, the new regime differs quite significantly from the old one and is potentially applicable in a much wider range of circumstances.

18.27 There was no statutory definition of fraudulent or negligent conduct under the old regime so HMRC and advisers alike had to rely on the judicial interpretation of these terms as developed by case law over the years. Thus 'fraudulent' would generally be held to mean something done deliberately with an intention to deceive whilst 'negligence' would mean carelessness or a simple failure to do something. As can be seen the new regime relies much less on interpretation of legal terminology and much more on a fact-based review of the documents or tax returns under review.

18.28 Under the old regime therefore the onus was on HMRC to show that there had been fraudulent or negligent conduct whereas effectively under the new regime all it has to show is that there is an inaccuracy in the return and then determine the type of 'behaviour' that led to this inaccuracy arising. This is a conceptually very different route to the imposition of penalties from that which subsisted under the old regime.

18.29 Mitigation of penalties under the old regime was also very different from that which subsists now. Broadly an HMRC officer could mitigate penalties by reviewing three factors for which set percentage mitigation amounts were available. These were 'disclosure', 'co-operation' and 'size and gravity'.

18.30 The old penalty charges and provisions will therefore still apply to return periods before the commencement of the new regime where these are the subject of compliance checks that are continuing over the transition to the new regime or where those earlier periods become the subject of enquiry now under HMRC's powers to review earlier years under its 'extended time limits' powers, which broadly can mean, in effect, that in serious cases it can investigate return periods up to 20 years old. If a return period prior to the commencement of the new regime is the subject of enquiry and errors, omissions or other offences are found in those earlier periods then it is the old penalty rules which apply to tax lost for those earlier periods, not the new regime.

PENALTIES FOR INCORRECT RETURNS/INACCURACIES

Introduction

18.31 The provisions of *FA 2007* impose financial penalties on taxpayers where 'inaccuracies in documents and returns' are identified. The relevant statute is *FA 2007* (*s 97* and *Sch 24*). Technically the statute deals with 'defaults and errors in documents' whilst the HMRC guidance talks about *inaccuracies in documents*.

The legislation provides a mechanism for the imposition of graduated financial penalties based on what HMRC terms 'taxpayer behaviour and corresponding errors which result in any inaccuracy'.

The scale of penalties

18.32 The potential penalties range from:

- 0% for a simple mistake, to
- 30% for a mistake made for failure to take reasonable care, to
- 70% for a 'deliberate inaccuracy', and possibly
- 100% cent for 'deliberate and concealed inaccuracies'.

HMRC's guidance on these penalties can be found in its Compliance Handbook at CH81001–CH84950.

18.33 *Penalties for error and failure to notify*

18.33 The *FA 2007* legislation took effect for income tax periods which commenced after 31 March 2008, where the return is filed after 31 March 2009. Correspondingly the legislation commenced for corporation tax periods for the year ended 31 March 2009 and later where the company has a 12-month accounting period.

The percentages refer to the tax underpaid or over-repaid as a result of the inaccuracy. This is referred to as potential lost revenue (PLR).

18.34 The potential penalties are to be calculated as a percentage of the extra tax payable, or not repayable, as a result of HMRC identifying action which is necessary to correct any inaccuracy. This percentage is generally determined by the 'behaviour that gave rise to the inaccuracy'.

Assessing the taxpayer's 'culpability'

18.35 The penalty provisions recognise differing degrees of 'culpability' which are used to decide the level of penalty to be imposed in any particular case. As already stated these range from 0% for a simple mistake through to 100% for deliberately concealed inaccuracies.

18.36 At this stage it is also perhaps worth mentioning that in cases involving offshore tax evasion the maximum civil penalty which can nowadays be imposed has been increased to 200%. The use of 'tax havens' or offshore tax jurisdictions has long been a means for some individuals seeking to hide their income and or gains from the UK tax authorities. There are a number of places around the world which have traditionally been viewed as suitable for this sort of practice. Indeed, it might be said that some such places have even been host to businesses which at times have actively encouraged such practices! In recent years HMRC working together with other tax authorities around the world has adopted a practice of seeking to persuade overseas territories and other countries to enter into tax exchange agreements with the UK in order to obtain information about UK taxpayers holding funds in such jurisdictions and many have now done so.

18.37 Of course there can also be criminal sanctions for cases of tax evasion so the 200% maximum civil penalty may not always be the maximum that HMRC seeks to impose but where cases are settled by a civil action on behalf of HMRC then this 200% represents a very significant increase in the financial imposts which are now available to HMRC.

18.38 There is nothing illegal about holding funds or other assets offshore and many UK-based individuals do so for perfectly legitimate reasons. Similarly, the use of offshore companies or trusts is not illegal in the UK even where it is adopted for tax planning reasons, provided of course that it is done properly and with the correct disclosures being made to the UK tax authorities. On the other hand, simply hiding income or gains somewhere overseas when they have not been properly disclosed for tax purposes in the UK is essentially fraudulent activity and will nowadays be pursued rigorously by HMRC where it is discovered and can be the cause of criminal prosecutions.

Where are there no penalties?

18.39 The concept of 'innocent error' can still be found within the penalties regime today and is of considerable importance when dealing with cases where HMRC is pursuing a penalty. Indeed, being able to recognise the differences between the different types of penalties and how HMRC applies them is an increasingly important part of the tax practitioner's role in dealing with compliance checks on behalf of their clients. The difference in the amounts due arising from the application of different types of penalty can be very substantial indeed.

18.40 An individual may be able to argue that no penalty is due when he can show that although there was an error or inaccuracy in his return he had taken 'all reasonable care' in its preparation and submission to HMRC and can thus argue that there is no element of culpability on his part.

18.41 Hence the penalty regime does still recognise the possibility that a taxpayer may be guilty of nothing more than an 'innocent error'. This is in fact something of an improvement over the penalty regime which existed for about ten years after the introduction of the self-assessment regime in the UK in the mid-1990s for both individuals and corporates.

18.42 Although some commentators would argue that the regime has not really changed here, in practice under the old regime it was in fact technically quite difficult to have an innocent error. This was because the old penalty regime in practice did not explicitly recognise this category of mistake. If there was a mistake on a return then technically there was a penalty position and the practitioner was left to argue that the level of culpability was purely nominal in order to seek to reduce the penalty to a very low level, or possibly zero.

18.43 Under the *FA 2007* regime the 'innocent error' category is given official recognition. The lowest level of penalty is therefore 0% for a taxpayer who makes a simple mistake having 'taken all reasonable care'. It is important however to stress that an innocent error can still carry a tax penalty if the taxpayer fails to inform the HMRC of the error within a reasonable time of discovering it, generally 30 days.

18.44 *Penalties for error and failure to notify*

18.44 HMRC has given some indications that it might regard the following as innocent errors:

- an error after taking reasonable care;
- taking a reasonable view of the law that proves to be wrong or is not pursued;
- an act or omission that does not form part of a pattern of behaviour and is untypical of the taxpayer concerned;
- the adoption of a treatment for tax purposes that is clearly disclosed to HMRC in a return or accounts, even if it is subsequently changed by agreement or tribunal decision.

18.45 Some specific examples given by HMRC include:

- an arithmetical error but not so big so as to produce an error which should have been noticed by the taxpayer;
- misclassifying an unusual item which is not big enough to prompt the need for professional advice;
- a mistake made by an assistant or employee;
- omitting a small (relative to overall liability) item from a return;
- a reasonable judgement is made (eg on a valuation);
- a reasonable view of the law is adopted even if this differs from HMRC guidance.

Other actions that would be regarded as taking reasonable care are set out in CH81130, with some examples in CH81131.

18.46 In CH81141, HMRC states:

'People do make mistakes. We do not expect perfection. We are simply seeking to establish whether the person has taken the care and attention that could be expected from a reasonable person in similar circumstances.'

18.47 CH431010 sets out factors that may demonstrate that the taxpayer was not taking reasonable care with his affairs, and CH431020–CH431040 give illustrations of such behaviour. CH84540 then illustrates the issues that HMRC will consider when deciding whether the taxpayer has taken reasonable care.

18.48 Some examples given by HMRC of cases where the taxpayer would be regarded as having taken 'reasonable care' are as follows:

- the taxpayer takes a reasonably arguable view of situations but this view is not subsequently upheld;

- the taxpayer makes a simple arithmetical or transposition error which is not so large either in absolute terms or relative to the taxpayer's overall liability so as to produce an obviously odd result or be picked up by some internal quality control procedure or similar checks;
- the taxpayer follows advice from HMRC that later proves to be wrong, so long as all the details and circumstances were fully provided to HMRC when the advice was being asked for;
- the error was made by the taxpayer after seeking and acting on advice from a 'competent adviser' but that advice subsequently proves to be wrong even though the adviser was provided with all the relevant and material facts;
- the taxpayer used and accepted information from a third party and placed reliance on that information in circumstances where it was not possible to verify the accuracy or completeness of that information.

18.49 The HMRC manual on this aspect indicates that an official can treat a person as taking reasonable care if:

- arrangements or systems (such as comprehensive internal accounting systems and controls with specific reference to tax sensitive areas) exist that, if followed, could reasonably be expected to produce an accurate basis for the calculation of tax due by the internal tax department, or external agent;
- despite the above, inaccuracies arise in processing or coding items through the person's accounting system which result in a mis-statement of tax liability; and
- the effect of the inaccuracies is not significant in relation to the person's overall tax liability for the relevant tax period.

Some practical examples of an inaccuracy despite taking reasonable care are to be found at CH81131.

18.50 The current UK compliance penalties regime can perhaps be described as an *automatic* system. Penalties for even simple compliance failures are often imposed automatically by HMRC's ubiquitous computer system recognising that a document or payment has not been made at the correct time and then automatically sending out a penalty notice.

18.51 A prime example of this could be said to be the issue of the first penalties under the Real Time Information (RTI) PAYE tax system early in 2014 for late submissions by employers of their payroll information under RTI. HMRC had already said in 2013 that it intended not to penalise these early failures as the new system 'bedded in' but contrary to this the computer seems to have issued a significant number of such penalty notices and this has

18.52 *Penalties for error and failure to notify*

resulted in a number of complaints to HMRC apparently and the department having to urgently review the situation.

18.52 In order to mitigate or avoid a penalty the taxpayer can initially either seek an internal review from HMRC or appeal against it. In either case this will require the taxpayer to demonstrate that he had a 'reasonable excuse' for failing to meet his compliance obligations.

18.53 The concept of reasonable excuse is a difficult one, requiring as it does reference to the facts of any particular case and a detailed exposition to the authorities of sound evidence and reasons pertaining to the failure which has occurred.

18.54 Examples which have been accepted by tax tribunals have included serious illness of a taxpayer or a key employee leading to record-keeping failures, misunderstandings between an accountant and a taxpayer leading to confusion over who was responsible for the submission of returns, and extreme business difficulties as the result of cash-flow problems following the recession. However, it has to be stressed that each case will turn on its own facts and there will be no substitute for a detailed presentation to HMRC or a tax tribunal of all the available evidence.

18.55 'Reasonable excuse' is taken to mean something that happened which was *exceptional and unforeseeable* to such an extent that it can be said to have been beyond the control of the taxpayer. Each case will have to be reviewed on its on facts and a detailed exposition of those facts and all the detailed circumstances may have to be presented to HMRC in support of an appeal.

18.56 In a recent case, *Hanson v Revenue and Customs Comrs* [2012] UKFTT 314 (TC), a claim for roll-over relief against redemptions of loan notes was made on a tax return by agents acting for a client. HMRC disputed the validity of the claim and this was eventually accepted by the accountants acting.

18.57 The tribunal judge, Jonathan Cannan, decided that the taxpayer in this case had taken reasonable care because he was entitled to rely on the expertise of his advisers who had acted for him for many years without himself consulting the legislation or the technical guidance made available on such matters by HMRC. In this case therefore the appeal was allowed, and the penalty was cancelled.

18.58 See also *Auxilium Project Management Ltd v Revenue and Customs Comrs* [2016] UKFTT 249 (TC5024) in which an appeal against a penalty imposed for the submission of an incorrect VAT return was allowed by the Tribunal. It was held that the taxpayer had made an innocent error having

Penalties for error and failure to notify **18.63**

failed accidentally to account for output tax on a transaction in one return in what appears to have been a misunderstanding about the way the cash basis operates for VAT. The judge decided that the taxpayer had not 'knowingly and intentionally' provided an inaccurate document and so allowed the appeal after giving due allowance for the good co-operation provided to HMRC throughout the process once the matter had come to light.

18.59 In a somewhat similar case, *Shakoor v Revenue and Customs Comrs* [2012] UKFTT 532 (TC), capital gains on two flat sales were omitted from tax returns and the taxpayer claimed that this was the fault of incorrect advice about a claim for 'main residence relief' received from his accountants.

18.60 However, in this case the tribunal decided that the accountant's advice had obviously been wrong, and that the taxpayer should have realised this or at least sought some further explanation or justification from the accountant before proceeding on the basis of his advice. The decision was taken that the penalty was correct although in recognition of the client's reliance on his accountant's advice the tribunal did decide to reduce the penalty significantly from 70% to 30%.

18.61 As can be seen there are a variety of circumstances in which a taxpayer may be able to argue that an error in his return arises through some external or internal factor over which he arguably has had no control or on which he was inevitably forced to rely, which was either unforeseeable or so exceptional as to be beyond his control.

18.62 For example, in *Connaught Contracts v Revenue and Customs Comrs* [2010] UKFTT 545 (TC) a carpet and flooring contractor had its gross payment status under the construction industry subcontractors' scheme withdrawn by HMRC because tax had not been paid on time and so the department contended that the 'compliance test' had been breached. The taxpayer claimed reasonable excuse on the basis that the business was in a very serious financial position caused directly by the economic downturn and also that whilst partnership funds were inadequate to meet its tax liability and its current wages bill all the outstanding tax had actually been paid as soon as possible and its previous tax compliance history had been good. The company also stressed that losing its gross payment status would severely damage its business because many of its customers would not deal with it in future and so this might result in the closure of the business and redundancy for the employees. In this case the tribunal decided that there was indeed a reasonable excuse, the business's cash-flow difficulties having coincided with one of the worst financial crises in the UK's history.

18.63 An error in a return which is blamed on an adviser or accountant rarely receives acknowledgement by HMRC as having a reasonable excuse but there have been cases where in extreme circumstances, ie where the state of mind

18.64 *Penalties for error and failure to notify*

of the business proprietor can clearly be demonstrated as such that complete reliance had been placed on a third party and the business had no reason to believe that tax returns were not being filed timeously, might in some cases be accepted by a tribunal as a reasonable excuse.

18.64 In *Rich v Revenue and Customs Comrs* [2011] UKFTT 533 (TC) the tribunal allowed an appeal in August 2011 where the appellant's defence was simply that he had relied on his accountant to deal with a self-assessment tax return and the judge accepted that it was reasonable in the circumstances of the case for the taxpayer to rely on the accountant to deal with the matter and that there was no reason why the appellant should think that the accountant would fail in dealing with the matter. It was the reliance upon the accountant that had led to the failure and this was the 'causal factor' of the subsequent chain of events.

18.65 Subsequently in *Lithgow v Revenue and Customs Comrs* [2012] UKFTT 620 (TC), a case where reliance on an accountant was not accepted as a reasonable excuse, the judge indicated that reliance on a third party would not be acceptable and would not be considered a reasonable excuse if the accountant acts as 'an administrator or functionary' as the taxpayer's agent so that a default (whether negligent or not) will not normally provide a taxpayer with opportunity to claim reasonable excuse. However, the judge went on to say that where the adviser acts in a truly professional advisory capacity reliance placed upon properly provided professional advice, where there is no obvious reason to believe that said advice might be wrong or unreliable or constrained, substantial 'caveats' can indeed be acceptable as an excuse that the taxpayer has not been negligent where he has taken and acted upon that advice.

18.66 Similarly, in *Mariner v Revenue and Customs Comrs* [2013] UKFTT 657 (TC) a tribunal allowed a taxpayer's appeal when she claimed that she had not been negligent, having relied on her adviser to complete her tax return on the basis that the negligent advice or service of a professional, 'is not to be imputed to the taxpayer'.

18.67 The main point to come out of this sort of case then is that a taxpayer cannot be argued to have been negligent where he perceives that there is a need to take professional advice and having done so he then relies upon that properly provided advice, even if it turns out to be wrong.

18.68 See also *J & W Brown* (TC51010) in which penalties for late VAT returns were reduced on appeal to the Tax Tribunal from 30% to only 10% after the tribunal decided that the taxpayer had done sufficient in communicating the nature of a change of business entity to HMRC to entitle him to significantly more mitigation than HMRC were prepared to offer. Whilst there had been delays in providing the returns and providing the relevant information

HMRC had shown a 'surprising failure to engage in correspondence with the taxpayer' which had to be taken into account in reducing the penalty impact. Clearly wherever there is the situation that a late penalty arises the courts will take every effort that the taxpayer takes to set their affairs in order in to account these days.

18.69 There is also a clear and obvious difference between the current penalties regime for errors or inaccuracies in returns or other tax documents and that which exists for failures to meet the various assessment time limits or due dates for delivery of documents. Whilst it is becoming more common to see tribunals' acceptance of the concept of reasonable excuse for errors or inaccuracies in documents, it is less so for cases where there has been a failure to deliver a document or return on time. The penalties for failures in these areas are imposed much more 'automatically' and currently are proving much harder to defend on the grounds of reasonable excuse. The train of thought here in the tribunals seems to be that tax deadlines and time limits are generally so well known now and are widely publicised by HMRC that the occasions on which a taxpayer may rely on the reasonable excuse escape route will be much less common.

Two more recent cases on the concept of reasonable excuse are *Schotten and Hansen (UK) Ltd v HMRC* and *Steiner v HMRC*. In the first case the firm had appointed reputable accountants and had relied on their advice in connection with a CIS matter. The Tribunal concluded that it was not unreasonable for an appellant to assume that their advisers would have advised them about any compliance issues which might arise from the information that their clients had provided to them and so allowed their appeal. In the second case a newly appointed firm of accountants identified errors in a tax return and amended it to correct those errors which increased the tax liability. The Tribunal decided that because insufficient details had been given of precisely what the errors were or how they had arisen this could not be held to be a reasonable excuse.

It has become clear in recent penalty cases that whilst HMRC does accept now that reliance on an agent may well be used as a reasonable excuse, in some cases it expects a taxpayer to tell it in some detail what actions they took themselves personally to ensure that their tax affairs have been dealt with properly and timeously.

Penalties for careless errors

18.70 Carelessness is defined as a failure to take reasonable care resulting in an inaccuracy in a document. A failure to take reasonable care is not easy to define in statute and it is therefore left largely to the courts to decide when a taxpayer appeals against a penalty on the grounds of 'reasonable excuse'.

18.71 *Penalties for error and failure to notify*

18.71 The penalty for 'carelessness' is 30% of the PLR. This is subject to mitigation down to nil where there is an 'unprompted disclosure' and to 15% where there is a 'prompted disclosure'.

This penalty can also be imposed in respect of a document submitted to HMRC on the taxpayer's behalf (eg by an accountant or tax adviser).

The carelessness penalty applies equally when HMRC itself discovers an inaccuracy in a document at some later time and the taxpayer has taken no reasonable steps to inform the department.

18.72 Mitigation of this penalty is only granted for differing levels of 'disclosure'. This can however include consideration of the degrees of co-operation by the taxpayer and also the seriousness of the case when assessing the level of this 'disclosure'. HMRC has given some examples of behaviour that would be construed as not taking reasonable care as follows:

- a breach of duty existing at a time when the duty should have been performed;
- not doing something that the person knew or should have known ought to have been done and which the person concerned had the power to do;
- the absence of such skill, care and diligence as was the duty and capacity of the person to bring to the work;
- omitting to do something that a reasonable person would do and the person concerned could do, or doing something that a reasonable person would not do;
- negligence, implying some neglect of duty in relation to facts or the interpretation of the law, provided the capacity to perform the duty is present.

18.73 Specific examples of carelessness in HMRC's view are as follows:

- making large arithmetical mistakes;
- mis-classifying items of income and expenditure without giving the matter adequate consideration or after taking professional advice;
- keeping incomplete books and records;
- omitting occasional items of income and gains;
- having insufficient quality control over the work of others;
- applying PAYE wrongly, occasionally or to an unusual item without checking on the correct treatment.

CH81145 gives some other specific examples of careless inaccuracies.

Penalties for 'deliberate errors'

18.74 Some might argue that there can be no such thing as a 'deliberate inaccuracy', that this is a contradiction in terms. Be that as it may the statute provides for a penalty for this civil offence and proscribes that a significantly higher level of charge is to be imposed.

18.75 Where a taxpayer deliberately understates his tax liability, but such understatement is not 'concealed', the maximum penalty is 70%. This is mitigable by 50% in the case of an 'unprompted disclosure' and 35% in the case of a 'prompted disclosure'.

Note therefore that the current regime presupposes that there are no circumstances in which this penalty may be mitigated to zero, a significant change to the pre-existing penalties mitigation regime.

18.76 Deliberate understatement of tax without concealment is defined as:

- deliberately not doing something which ought to be done; or
- deliberately getting something wrong.

18.77 Examples of this behaviour include:

- not recording all sales, especially where a pattern of under-recording appears to rule out a genuine misunderstanding;
- including personal expenditure in business expenditure in circumstances that rule out a genuine misunderstanding;
- making inadequate private use adjustments where the amounts are significant;
- omitting significant amounts of income;
- adopting inappropriate accounting treatment;
- describing transactions in a misleading way;
- deliberately misinterpreting the law with a view to understatement.

CH81150 gives other examples of deliberate inaccuracies, with illustrations at CH81151, and CH432030 gives examples of indirect evidence of such behaviour.

18.78 Other situations in which it can probably be envisaged that HMRC will seek to invoke the 70% penalty level would be the use by a taxpayer of an artificially structured tax avoidance scheme which in the event turns out to be defective. In these circumstances HMRC could clearly contend that

18.79 *Penalties for error and failure to notify*

the taxpayer has deliberately taken some action to reduce his tax liability and his actions have turned out to be inaccurate or mistaken and result in an inaccurate tax return. This could clearly come within the ambit of the deliberate mistake category.

Penalties for deliberate errors with 'concealment'

18.79 Again, some commentators might suggest that this description rather understates the nature of the inaccuracy. It might even perhaps be suggested that a deliberate *and* concealed inaccuracy in a tax return could actually represent fraudulent behaviour worthy of categorisation as tax evasion deserving of criminal prosecution.

18.80 There will always be circumstances in which HMRC will reserve the right to prosecute offenders, but where it seeks a civil settlement this category will represent the highest potential level of penalty except in circumstances where offshore evasion is detected.

Where the taxpayer understates his tax liability deliberately, and this understatement is also concealed, the maximum penalty is 100% of the PLR. Once again this can be mitigated.

This level of penalty also applies to an inaccuracy due to the deliberate behaviour of another person.

18.81 Mitigation of up to 70% can be gained in the case of an 'unprompted disclosure', making the penalty 30%. In the case of a 'prompted disclosure' mitigation of up to 50% is available, which would produce a penalty of 50%. The 'quality of the disclosure' is clearly all important.

18.82 There is no statutory definition of concealment. However, an example is the making of a deliberate error for tax purposes, covering it up, perhaps by producing a false document, and then destroying incriminating documentary evidence. Basically, it is submitting false evidence in support of figures known to be incorrect. This type of default is clearly very close if not identical with circumstances in which HMRC could and indeed probably would, initially consider a criminal prosecution.

18.83 Examples given of deliberate understatement with concealment are:

- creating false invoices or altering invoices;
- backdating or post-dating contracts or invoices;
- creating false minutes of meetings or minutes of fictitious meetings;

Penalties for error and failure to notify **18.86**

- destroying books and records;
- deliberately misleading accountants or HMRC;
- systematic diversion of income into undisclosed bank accounts and covering up the traces of this action;
- invoice routing, for example the purported sale or purchase of goods through a tax haven company (with no activity undertaken by that company even though contracts exist showing the contrary) leaving profits untaxed in that company;
- creating sales records that deliberately understate the value of the goods sold, the balance of the full price being paid separately to the person;
- describing expenditure in the business records in such a way as to make it appear to be business related when it is in fact private (possibly with the supplier agreeing to change the description on the relevant invoices);
- alteration of genuine purchase invoices to inflate their value.

18.84 CH81160 also includes compiling false business accounts to support the availability of a claim to agricultural or business relief for IHT and mis-declaring the strength of alcoholic products for excise duty purposes. Specific examples are given at CH81161.

18.85 It is important to recognise that in any case where these types of behaviour are identified the possibility that HMRC might seek initially to prosecute an offence of tax evasion should always be considered. It will therefore be important to ascertain at an early stage in the disclosure process what actions, civil or criminal, HMRC will be considering.

See also *Pendergate Ltd* (TC4956) where a taxpayer's appeal against penalties imposed by HMRC for errors in operating PAYE procedures incorrectly was accepted by the Tribunal. Confusion had arisen over whether or not HMRC had actually notified the employer about PAYE coding changes via the normal Coding Notice procedure and as a result of which an underpayment of PAYE taxes had arisen. HMRC claimed that paper notices had indeed been sent but it was not at all clear whether in fact the employer had ever received them. The Tribunal allowed an appeal on the grounds of reasonable excuse after taking into account the taxpayer employer's previously general 'high level of compliance' on such tax matters.

18.86 Any situation which involves the creation of false documents or the alternation of documents is a case where there is the potential for prosecution and specialist advice will probably be needed by both the tax adviser and certainly by his client. An immediate disclosure to HRMC

18.87 *Penalties for error and failure to notify*

will normally be essential but that disclosure should be made with the appropriate legal advice.

FAILURE TO NOTIFY PENALTIES

18.87 The legislation providing for the imposition of penalties for failure to notify liability to tax is to be found in *FA 2008, s 123* and *Sch 41*. It applies to obligations entered into on or after 1 April 2009 and took effect from 1 April 2010.

18.88 Penalties will be imposed under this legislation for acts that are 'deliberate and concealed' or 'deliberate but not concealed'. The maximum rate of penalty is:

- 100% for acts that are deliberate and concealed;
- 70% where the default was deliberate but not concealed;
- 30% in other cases.

18.89 Once again, the penalty is applied to potential lost revenue (PLR), and for income tax and capital gains tax relates to tax unpaid on 31 January after the end of the tax year. For corporation tax purposes the date is 12 months after the end of the accounting period.

Schedule 41, para 2 imposes a penalty on the unauthorised issue of a VAT invoice.

18.90 *FA 2008, Sch 41*, para 1 provides a detailed table listing all the penalties applicable to the various taxes for which a failure to notify penalty can be imposed. These cover income tax, corporation tax, VAT, and a miscellany of other taxes and levies such as the new diverted profits tax introduced in *FA 2015*.

18.91 Penalties are due under these provisions where any 'person' fails to comply with one of the tax obligations specified under the relevant legislation listed in the table.

- For income tax the notification obligation arises generally under *TMA 1970, s 7* and provides that the period for notification of chargeability to the tax is generally six months after the end of the relevant UK tax year, ie generally 5 October, although this can be revised in certain specified circumstances.

- For corporation tax the notification obligation arises under *FA 1998, Sch 18, para 2* and provides that the notification must be given within 12 months of the end of the relevant company corporation tax accounting period.

OTHER PENALTIES

Failure to notify an under-assessment

18.92 The current penalty regime includes a penalty for a failure to notify HMRC of an under-assessment of income tax, corporation tax, capital gains tax or VAT.

This penalty can be imposed when a taxpayer fails to take 'reasonable steps' to notify the under-assessment of tax to HMRC within 30 days of it becoming apparent.

As for other penalties this one is mitigable up to a total 30% of the PLR, but again can be reduced to 0% for an unprompted disclosure or 15% in the case of a prompted disclosure.

18.93 In assessing whether this penalty should be imposed, HMRC will take account of the 'competence of the taxpayer to recognise that tax has been under-assessed', and will then consider what steps ought reasonably to have been taken by him if the under-assessment was recognised. This initial review is quite apart from the consideration of mitigation for disclosure. Some examples of penalties for under-assessment based on PLR are illustrated in CH82162.

Errors by third parties

18.94 *FA 2008, Sch 40, para 3* provides that where an error in a taxpayer's document is attributable to another person, penalties of up to 100% of PLR may be imposed, but subject to reductions and possibly the special reduction based on taxpayer behaviour

Computer records

18.95 *FA 2008, s 114* provides that a penalty of £300 may be imposed for obstruction in or failure to provide computer records required by HMRC.

HMRC information powers

18.96 *FA 2008, Sch 36, para 39(2)* imposes a penalty of £3,000 for obstruction and failure to comply with HMRC requirements under notices issued pursuant to its information and inspection powers. This includes concealment, destruction or disposal of documents and is subject to the reasonable excuse provisions.

18.97 *Penalties for error and failure to notify*

18.97 *FA 2009* extended this legislation to provide for the penalty to apply where a person carelessly or deliberately provides inaccurate information and produces inaccurate documents in response to an HMRC information notice.

18.98 A daily penalty of up to £60 may be imposed where the offence continues. Both the initial and daily penalty must be imposed within 12 months of the 'relevant date'. An appeal procedure is available. Where the offence continues HMRC may apply to the tax tribunal for a tax-related penalty, which is additional to the initial and daily penalties. All penalties under these provisions must be paid within 30 days.

18.99 Concealment, destruction and disposal of relevant documents are treated very seriously. The penalty can be a fine, or imprisonment for up to two years in addition to the fine.

These provisions apply to obligations entered into after 31 March 2009.

Senior accounting officers

18.100 *FA 2009, s 93, Sch 46* provides for penalties to be imposed on company senior accounting officers and potentially also the company itself may suffer a tax penalty, in certain circumstances.

18.101 This penalty can be imposed where a company and its senior accounting officer fail to take reasonable steps to:

- establish and maintain appropriate tax accounting arrangements;
- monitor the accounting arrangements; and
- identify any respects in which the arrangements are not 'appropriate' for the accurate calculation of taxes and duties.

18.102 Additionally, a company must certify annually on or before the statutory accounts filing deadline that appropriate arrangements were in place throughout the year; or provide an explanation of why arrangements were not appropriate.

18.103 Failures under these rules can lead to penalties of up to £5,000 which may be imposed on the company for failing to notify the identity of the senior accounting officer during the financial year, and/or up to £5,000 on each count on the senior accounting officer personally for failure to meet the conditions specified above.

18.104 Currently the senior accounting officer legislation limits these penalty provisions to a company or group which has at the end of its financial year:

- turnover of more than £200 million; and/or
- a balance sheet total of more than £2 billion.

Notices for details of debtors

18.105 *FA 2009, s 97 and Sch 49* provides that HMRC may issue notices requiring third parties to provide contact details for those in debt to HMRC.

A person who fails to comply with such a notice is liable to a penalty of £300. The procedures for penalties are similar to those for information powers under *FA 2008, Sch 36*.

FAILURES TO MAKE RETURNS

18.106 *FA 2009, s 106* and *Sch 55* provide penalties for late filing of tax returns for income tax, corporation tax, PAYE, National Insurance contributions, the construction industry scheme (CIS), stamp duty land tax, stamp duty reserve tax, inheritance tax, pension schemes and petroleum revenue tax.

Taxpayers have a right of appeal against all penalties and no penalty can be charged if the taxpayer has a reasonable excuse for his failure.

Amount of these penalties

18.107 The initial penalty here is fixed at £100, provided that the taxpayer's failure continues after the end of the period of three months beginning with the penalty date.

A daily penalty of £10 is imposed for each day that the failure continues during the period of 90 days beginning with the date specified in the penalty notice.

18.108 A penalty of the greater of £300 or 5% of the liability to tax shown in the return is imposed where the return is still outstanding six months after the filing date and there would have been a liability to tax shown in the return.

18.109 Where the failure continues after the end of a period of 12 months, and the taxpayer withholds information that would enable HMRC to assess the liability to tax:

- if the withholding of the information is deliberate and concealed the penalty is the greater of:
    - 100% of the liability to tax; and
    - £300.

18.110 *Penalties for error and failure to notify*

- if the withholding of the information is deliberate but not concealed the penalty is the greater of:
  - 70% of the liability to tax; and
  - £300.
- in any other case the penalty is the greater of:
  - 5% of the liability to tax; and
  - £300.

Note that there are other specific penalty regimes for failures to make PAYE and CIS returns

FAILURE TO PAY TAXES

18.110 *FA 2009, s 107* and *Sch 56* provide a penalty regime for late payment of income tax, corporation tax, PAYE, National Insurance contributions, tax due under the CIS, stamp duty land tax, stamp duty reserve tax, inheritance tax, pension schemes and petroleum revenue tax.

18.111 The Schedule defines the taxes to which this penalty applies by reference to a detailed table. The penalty is 5% of the unpaid tax. The penalty is incurred if the taxpayer fails to pay the tax in full by the date provided for in column 4 of the table. This date is normally 30 days after the due date for the tax.

No penalty arises under these provisions where the taxpayer satisfies HMRC or the tax tribunal that there is reasonable excuse for the failure.

BREACH OF MINIMUM WAGE RULES

18.112 From 6 April 2009, the Minimum Wage Rules impose penalties where employers fail to pay the minimum wage. Such failures can bring automatic penalty of between £100 and £5,000 based on the amount they owe to their workers. This penalty will apply even if the underpayment was a mistake. In the most serious cases employers could also face an unlimited fine.

THE COMMON CAUSES OF PENALTIES

18.113 Where a taxpayer is the subject of a 'compliance check' (perhaps more commonly termed an enquiry or investigation) by HMRC there is always the potential for penalties to be imposed if inaccuracies or errors come to light and HMRC takes the view that tax offences have been committed.

Late returns

18.114 Sometimes compliance checks may actually be started because a taxpayer has been consistently late in submitting his tax returns or has not actually sent in a tax return for a particular year.

18.115 The submission of a late tax return is probably the most common reason for the imposition of penalties by HMRC. Generally late return penalties will be relatively minor in amount; the initial late return penalty is £100 but this can rise very sharply to £1,600 when a return is a year late and eventually the daily penalties and tax-geared penalties for returns later than this, as mentioned earlier in this chapter, will mount up to seriously large sums indeed!

Inaccuracies in documents

18.116 During the course of a compliance check or enquiry the penalty most likely to be encountered will be that which HMRC will seek to impose for inaccuracies in a return or other documents. This is a tax-geared penalty and is based on 'potential lost revenue'. In most cases this will be the difference between the tax which is eventually payable as the result of the enquiries raised by HMRC and the tax that would have been paid had the return been accepted as originally submitted with the error or inaccuracy.

18.117 It should however be noted that the words 'potential lost revenue' have a somewhat wider meaning that might be imagined. Thus, if an inspection visit takes place at a business's premises, for example to carry out a review of payroll records, and HMRC discovers an error in the business's record keeping, then in theory at least it is possible for HMRC to seek to impose a penalty based on the difference between the tax that would have been paid, based on those errors, and the tax that will now be paid. Note that this means that in theory at least HMRC can seek to impose a penalty for an inaccurate return that has yet to be submitted. The potential for this to happen first came to light during the HMRC's business records checks pilot in 2011 and practitioners and advisers alike have become concerned about this possibility. In practice it seems that this is not in fact happening now but where such penalties are indeed pursued by HMRC specialist advice should probably sought as to the technicalities involved.

18.118 Incorrect return penalties can arise for a variety of reasons. These may range from the submission of an incorrect claim for a simple tax deduction,

18.119 *Penalties for error and failure to notify*

to an incorrect decision about the eligibility of an item of plant for capital allowances, to the setting of an incorrect transfer price between related companies in a group at an excessive or inadequate level. There is a multitude of possibilities.

18.119 The most common cause of an incorrect return penalty is probably a 'control systems failure' by a business. This can arise for example where the internal record keeping or data capture systems put in place by a business are found to be inadequate and have led to tax leakage. This could perhaps arise by overpaying mileage allowances to employees or incorrect posting of capital expenditures to repairs in the profit and loss accounts for a company. The permutations are endless. Businesses with sound record-keeping systems that have built in control checks and review procedures will generally be much less vulnerable to such penalties but even they can sometimes find that their systems have weaknesses which come to light during an HMRC compliance check.

18.120 In most such cases HMRC will pursue the 'carelessness' or simple negligence penalty starting at the 30% level with mitigation available for the 'quality of disclosure' as outlined earlier. It will however be rare nowadays for this penalty to be reduced below 15% once it has been accepted by the business that there has indeed been an 'inaccuracy'.

Failure to notify chargeability

18.121 Sometimes an adviser will be asked to represent a taxpayer who has not in fact even told the HMRC about a source of income or capital gains; the taxpayer may actually have been in business for some time without notifying HMRC at all. This is known as a 'failure to notify chargeability'.

18.122 Where the failure has only persisted for a short time and notification is made thereafter without undue further delay it is likely that HMRC will accept the position, seek a fairly small level of penalty and then be content to register the source of income or business and get the taxpayer into the system and paying his taxes, etc on time for the future.

18.123 Where however the failure has persisted over a number of years HMRC will normally take a less lenient view. If the failure has persisted over many years HMRC may take the view that this was deliberate tax evasion and in large cases will even consider prosecution to be in the public interest.

18.124 The maximum tax penalty for a failure to notify case is 100% of the tax eventually found to be due. It is rarely this large and often much lower. Cases as low as 15% have been encountered recently. Where however the failure has occurred over many years and HMRC does not seek to prosecute then the penalty can be very large indeed!

18.125 It should also be noted that where a failure to notify case does extend over a number of years it is likely once the disclosure has been made to HMRC that it will wish to enquire into the taxpayer's affairs in detail to satisfy itself that the disclosure now being made is indeed comprehensive.

Compliance with information notices

18.126 HMRC has very significant information gathering powers nowadays, indeed some commentators feel that the balance has shifted very definitely in favour of HMRC. Since the inception of the new compliance regime on 5 April 2009 the ability of an officer of HMRC to demand information from a taxpayer has increased to the point where the enforcement powers now available to HMRC are probably stronger than they have ever been.

18.127 The phrase 'documents and information in the taxpayer's possession or power' has effectively been extended to cover almost all records kept by a business, whether financial or non-financial. This probably extends to records that are kept for the purposes of business management but which may not be used in the preparation of accounts or tax returns. Certainly, HMRC's interpretation of the phrase 'supplementary information' which is now included in the scope of its information powers is very broad indeed. Its own compliance manuals on the subject suggest that 'diaries, minutes of meetings and similar records' are within the scope of an information notice for the purposes of carrying out a compliance check where the taxpayer is unwilling to disclose such information.

18.128 Virtually the only protection now available to a taxpayer (apart from personal journalistic, spiritual and medical information) is that provided by legal professional privilege. This provides some protection to the taxpayer for papers containing tax advice provided by a lawyer but not by an accountant. There have been various attempts in court to get this protection extended to cover tax advice provided by an accountant or qualified tax adviser but as yet all these have failed.

18.129 It is thus not uncommon to see information notices for the production of information or documents being issued during the course of a compliance check. Failure to comply with such notices can lead to the imposition of penalties.

18.130 What is important here is not so much the potential for penalties to arise but that the client and his advisers understand the procedures that apply and which may lead to the issue of a notice for information. Tax officials

18.131 *Penalties for error and failure to notify*

conducting compliance checks have to operate within defined protocols and internal compliance procedures. The compliance checks for which they are responsible are subjected to regular internal reviews and control checks. If at the start of a compliance check they ask for information from the taxpayer and/or the acting tax agent and this is not forthcoming within a reasonable deadline (they usually allow 30 days but will grant longer on request) without an adequate explanation then they are as a matter of practicality left with little room for manoeuvre.

18.131 If no explanation for a delay or lack of response for not providing information which has been requested is forthcoming from the taxpayer or adviser then internal procedures will rapidly result in the issue of an information notice. The taxpayer then has two choices: whether to comply with the notice and provide the information or appeal against the notice. Failure to comply with the notice without submitting an appeal will result in the imposition of penalties, automatically. There is no escape and the HMRC official has little or no discretion here.

18.132 The watchwords therefore have to be 'timely compliance'. This can either be sending in the information demanded by the notice or the timely submission of an appeal against the notice. This is a matter entirely within the discretion of the taxpayer, presumably after seeking advice from his tax agent or accountant.

18.133 Sending the information within the time allowed or submitting an appeal will therefore obviously avoid the initial imposition of penalties. If the taxpayer or his agents believe that they have a genuine reason for non-compliance then it should be put to the HMRC official immediately, without delay. It is not that the penalties are inevitable, rather that the internal control systems operated by the department make it very difficult, as a matter of practicality, for the official to delay issuing an information notice once he has asked for something and either it has not been provided or a reasonable excuse for not providing it has not been sent in reply.

ARE COMPANY OFFICERS LIABLE FOR PENALTIES?

18.134 *Schedule 41, para 22* provides that where a penalty is chargeable on a company for a 'deliberate action' offence, but the action is attributable to an officer of that company, HMRC may pursue all or part of the penalty from that officer.

18.135 The position of 'officer of the company' means:

- a director;
- a manager;

- a secretary; and
- any other person managing or purporting to manage any of the company's affairs.

In these circumstances, the company officer is liable to pay such proportion of the penalty (which may be up to 100%) as is specified by HMRC within 30 days of the issue of the relevant notice.

18.136 Note that if the company pays this penalty on behalf of the officer this will then be a taxable benefit in kind and arguably, as the employer will be meeting a personal pecuniary liability of an employee, ought to be dealt with via the PAYE system in the month of payment.

PENALTIES AND TAX AVOIDANCE SCHEMES

18.137 As was explained earlier in this chapter, the amount of a penalty imposed for an inaccuracy in a tax return or other tax document will depend on the type of tax offence committed (ie the penalty category ranging from careless to deliberate and concealed, the quality of the disclosure made and then any mitigation available for telling, helping and giving access).

18.138 The fundamental principle is that a penalty liability will potentially arise where there is an inaccuracy in a return or other tax document unless the error was a simple mistake with no element of carelessness. The more serious the behaviour leading to the error, the more serious the penalty which can be imposed.

18.139 One significant issue which can arise will be determining what level of penalty might be applicable when a taxpayer has used a 'tax avoidance' scheme or where HMRC takes the view that a taxpayer has deliberately avoided tax by his actions either in entering into a bespoke tax avoidance scheme or himself taking certain actions, or even perhaps omitting to take certain actions, which HMRC then views as deliberate tax avoidance.

18.140 Volumes have been written about the difference between tax evasion and avoidance and such a narrative would be beyond the scope of this chapter. What is important in this context is a recognition that HMRC currently seeks higher penalties in situations it regards as tax avoidance entered into deliberately. Clearly the two higher penalty categories lend themselves to this sort of 'offence' and were presumably drafted with this in mind as well!

18.141 Additionally, recent Finance Acts have seen the introduction of a range of sanctions aimed specifically at those individuals and businesses that

18.142 *Penalties for error and failure to notify*

seek to avail themselves of perceived tax avoidance opportunities or who purchase bespoke tax avoidance 'schemes' which are found not to be effective either legally or commercially. Again there is a considerable body of case law on this subject beyond the scope of this chapter but the recent introduction of sanctions against users of avoidance schemes, such as 'accelerated payment' and 'follower notices' for the users of such 'failed schemes' and the development of sanctions against the promotors of tax avoidance schemes from July 2014 stand as clear testimony to recent governments' declared intent to clamp down on such activities and to deter both individuals and corporates from indulging in such tactics. Furthermore, the current climate of negative press and media attention to the users of such schemes and what might perhaps be categorised as the current 'fairness' agenda amongst politicians who clearly see the use of such avoidance strategies as unacceptable, has led to an increasing emphasis on the introduction of new statute and regulations to counter these sorts of activities.

18.142 For users of tax avoidance strategies, this current climate and the development of the growing body of case law represents a real dilemma. Is the use of such strategies even now acceptable at all? Many companies in particular seem to be adopting a much more cautious approach to their tax affairs than perhaps was the case in the past; indeed many large companies are regularly commenting that they have moved away from the use of such strategies in what might be characterised as a clear publicity move to garner populist support or at least to avoid potential boycotts when the use of such schemes attracts press attention as it seems to do with increasing regularity these days.

18.143 The problem for the users of such tax avoidance schemes is knowing if or when HMRC will seek to impose a penalty should the scheme prove to be ineffective or is eventually defeated in the courts by HMRC. Will a penalty be sought when a taxpayer has legitimately sought to reduce his liabilities only to find additional tax becoming due because the scheme he has purchased proves to be ineffective? Or can reliance be placed upon the fact that the scheme came with fully developed and written tax advice which provided reassurance that all was perfectly legal and above board.

18.144 In the first instance there can be little doubt that HMRC will seek a penalty in the 'deliberate' category for the users of such schemes in most cases. There *have* been examples where the department has offered 'early settlement' opportunities for the users of historic avoidance schemes with the offer of considerably reduced penalties for early settlement, such as the settlement opportunity recently offered for users of employee benefit trusts but this seems likely to become a thing of the past.

18.145 What then should the position of the taxpayer and his advisers be in such situations when the scheme was apparently believed to be perfectly legal from the outset? Cases have appeared in which HMRC has sought to impose significant penalties and has argued that the very use of such schemes merits a severe penalty when they fail simply because the strategies followed were clearly deliberate. Its argument seems to turn on a belief that the users of such schemes, being generally well-informed individuals and having a clear understanding of what they were embarking upon from the outset, ought to have understood that should the scheme fail this would merit a higher penalty categorisation. This is a controversial view on HMRC's part and it is going to take some time before it is really clear how the courts will view this sort of case going forward.

18.146 Examples such as *Litman v Revenue and Customs Comrs* [2014] UKFTT 089 (TC) illustrate HMRC's willingness to seek tax-geared penalties even in cases where the taxpayer had made clear disclosure on his tax returns of his use of a tax avoidance scheme. HMRC will argue that the returns have been submitted negligently at the very least, on the grounds that the taxpayer should have understood that what he was doing might well ultimately fail and that more tax would then be due. In cases which rely to some extent on what the department will seek to categorise as 'artificial and highly structured' tax avoidance planning, their contention is commonly that any reasonable person with commercial and financial experience should have understood that what he was doing could be defeated by HMRC and that commonly the signing of a multiplicity of deliberately tax-structured documents should be seen as a clear indication that the tax structure being set up could be seen as artificial and therefore not in truth reflective of real commercial transactions.

18.147 On the other hand, the taxpayer in such situations will frequently have purchased a tax scheme genuinely believing that it was effective and will have taken comprehensive advice, presumably from experts in their field who can surely be relied upon to know their job and to be selling schemes which 'work' and are legal. If a taxpayer purchases a bespoke tax scheme and follows the necessary transactional steps through correctly, many would argue that it ought to be impossible for HMRC to argue that he has negligently submitted his tax return let alone that he has perpetrated a 'deliberate' inaccuracy therein. This remains a very controversial area and HMRC continues to pursue such cases vigorously.

18.148 Ever since the introduction of the self-assessment tax regime in the UK in the mid-1990s it has been a fundamental tenet of the system that a taxpayer who has made a complete and accurate disclosure of his affairs (ie has notified HMRC on his return that he has used a particular tax avoidance scheme), for example, should have protection from the imposition of penalties, but this does not seem to be HMRC's view and users of such schemes in future will have to take cognisance of this approach. The higher levels of 'deliberate' penalties are being sought in such cases in what some commentators view as an

18.149 *Penalties for error and failure to notify*

unacceptably aggressive manner by HMRC and it remains to be seen whether the courts will generally support this view.

RECENT DEVELOPMENTS

2015 Consultation on Penalties

18.149 Early in 2015 HMRC issued a consultative document looking at the future shape the UK's tax penalties regime should take and proposing various reforms and options. The consultation finished and a summary of responses was issued in September 2015. The main proposals were that any new penalties regime should not punish simple errors and that the penalties should be understandable and more easily explained to taxpayers than the existing regime. Also, HMRC acknowledge that even in the post *FA 2008* era there remains a confusing plethora of differing penalty offences and that these should be simplified and harmonised further to make the regime much more easily applicable and relevant to the future modern digital age of tax administration.

18.150 HMRC's stated overall objectives which came out of the consultation process are now stated as recognising the distinction between the majority of taxpayers who are compliant and those who are not, a small minority, and providing a penalty system that works to encourage the non-compliance back into full compliance in the future. The ultimate goal is therefore to charge fewer penalties and to introduce a system of prompts in future to encourage improved taxpayer compliance.

18.151 HMRC fully expects penalties for inaccuracies to continue to be linked to the size of the error and the seriousness of the mistake but also intends to explore the imposition of increased reporting and other compliance obligations as an encouragement to improved compliance after an error has been identified. Penalties will also be set at varying levels according to a taxpayer's previous compliance history as well as considering whether de-minimis levels should apply and whether these should be varied for different types of taxpayers and possibly businesses as well as imposing increasing penalty levels according to a taxpayer's individual compliance history, the degree or inaccuracy identified and the extent of the taxpayer's cooperation in sorting things out to HMRC's satisfaction.

All this clearly indicates that the future shape of the UK's tax penalty regime may differ very considerably from that detailed in this chapter and in **CHAPTER 19**. These reforms will take time but much has already been announced in the recent consultation documents issued under the 'Making Tax Digital' heading and makes interesting reading, (see below).

Making Tax Digital – penalty proposals

18.152 In 2015 the Chancellor announced that HMRC intends to move towards a fully digital tax administration system in the UK by 2020. As part of this change, which represents probably the most significant alteration of the personal and business tax administration regime in the UK for thirty years, since the introduction of the current self-assessment regime, it proposes to significantly alter the current penalties regime for late submission of tax filing obligations and late payment of taxes.

Late filing penalties

18.153 In August 2016 HMRC outlined its preferred options and/or alternatives for the shape of the new penalties regime. What follows is a summary of those proposals which at the time of writing are still the subject of consultation but which seem certain to be introduced as part of the making tax digital reforms over the next three to four years.

18.154 It is proposed that after a period of time to allow 'customers' to become familiar with their new obligations under the digital tax regime a new 'points-based' system of late filing penalties will be introduced. The current proposal is that this will be a 12-month familiarisation period, effectively a period of grace, before any new style penalties are to be imposed.

18.155 Thereafter the new penalties will be imposed according to a weighing system of points awarded for consecutive and cumulative failure to meet the various new style filing obligations that are to arise within the new digital regime.

18.156 The main proposal is that the new style points-based system would ensure customers will not be charged any penalty at all for their first failure to file their electronic submissions on time but would instead draw this to their attention and thus give them the opportunity to put their errors right for the future and thereafter take account of their recent compliance history in determining what penalty points should be awarded and then what sanction might be appropriate.

18.157 There are two main proposals contained in the consultation documents:

> **Option 1** – this proposes that the taxpayer would incur one or more penalty points each time they fail to send in the required information on time and that a penalty would only then be imposed when a total of four penalty points had been accrued. Thereafter their compliance record

18.158 *Penalties for error and failure to notify*

would be reset once a period of full compliance had elapsed, currently proposed at two years.

Option 2 – this proposes that another alternative model could be to impose further penalty weighting points increasing over time when a submission remains outstanding. The intention would be to focus taxpayers' attention on remedying mistakes already made as well as encouraging good compliance in future. This proposal would allow the accrual of five penalty points for failed submission building up over time the longer submissions are outstanding.

The proposal under either of the above two 'models' is for fixed penalties rather than tax geared penalties so that the system is clear and easy to understand for all taxpayers. Higher penalties are under consideration for continued and repeated failures but little details have as yet been put forward for these.

18.158 Whatever the final shape of the late filing penalties regime there is little doubt that the advent of the new making tax digital regime will inevitably include continued emphasis on penalties as a deterrent for incorrect behaviour but with the emphasis on encouraging good taxpayer compliance and giving incentives to improve compliance before penalties are actually imposed. Overall this looks to be something of an improvement on the current regime but time will tell how the new regime develops and what its final shape will look like.

Penalties for late payment

18.159 The making tax digital consultation documents also put forward some new proposals for late payment sanctions. HMRC argues that a points basis cumulating regime, such as that proposed for late filing, would not be appropriate for late payment as it might not encourage taxpayers to pay on time. Therefore, late payment penalties are to be separate and distinct from those for late filing.

Two alternative proposals are under consideration: penalty interest for failures to pay within 14 days of a due date:

1. Revisions of the existing penalties payment regime to align the legislation for all taxes. Penalty interest is apparently seen as widely acceptable to taxpayers and their advisers and as easily understood.

2. Revisions of the existing regime towards alignment is also seen as attractive but probably would entail some carry over of existing provisions and might not result in as clear a regime as HMRC would prefer to introduce.

Again, these are all just proposals at the moment and only time will tell what the final shape of the new sanctions will actually be.

Finance Act 2016 changes

18.160 *Finance Act 2016* includes new tax-geared penalties for HMRC challenges to cases under the UK's General Anti-Abuse Rules (GAAR). The new penalty will be set at a level of 60% of the value of the 'tax advantage that HMRC has challenged and taken counteraction against'. The penalty is to be imposed once a counteraction notice has been successfully imposed by HMRC.

18.161 It is noteworthy that in such cases there is an existing 'inaccuracy' penalty which is tax geared and that the new penalty can be imposed alongside it but that the total penalties will never rise above 100% of the tax avoided or challenged by HMRC although this can be subject to enhanced maximum 200% penalty charges for offshore matters.

The new regime applies to tax arrangements entered into on or after the date of Royal Assent for *FA 2016*.

18.162 'Enablers of Offshore tax Evasion' also face an added potential penalty under *FA 2016*. This will apply to individuals and businesses who have deliberately assisted taxpayers to disguise or hide taxable assets or income sources overseas in order to evade UK tax obligations.

This new penalty only applies where it can be shown that the action of the enabler was deliberate and the evader has been subjected to an offshore tax evasion penalty. The enabler thereafter faces a penalty of up to 100% of the tax evaded. These new provisions also include a facility for the HMRC to 'name and shame' the enabler although this apparently is to be reserved for the 'most serious' of cases.

18.163 *Finance Act 2016* also includes as a new offence strict liability for criminal offences by individuals who fail to notify HMRC of their liability to income and gains arising offshore where they are liable to UK taxes in respect of those income and gains, or where they fail to submit a correct return of such sources to the UK Revenue. This offence will only be invoked where the tax involved exceeds £25,000 for a single tax year.

18.164 Following new rules contained in *FA 2016*, HMRC will henceforward be able to issue a formal notice to the user of a notified tax avoidance scheme when the scheme has been defeated, presumably via court action. Such notice will then put the taxpayer on notice for a period of five years during which time the taxpayer will have to notify HMRC that they have not used

18.165 *Penalties for error and failure to notify*

any further such schemes or if they have to provide HMRC with full details and the tax saving they expect to benefit from. A rising scale of penalties is to apply where such further schemes *are* used by the taxpayer during this period if they are subject to defeat by HMRC. This measure takes effect as from 6 April 2017.

OTHER CHANGES INTRODUCED IN 2017

Partial Closure Notices

18.165 *Section 63* of *Finance Bill (No 2) 2017* introduces (via *Sch 15*) provisions for the introduction of 'Partial Closure Notices' to be available to HMRC in connection with the carrying out of tax compliance checks on taxpayers' returns under the relevant provisions of the *Taxes Management Act 1970* and *Finance Act 1998*.

The new provisions are detailed and complex but in essence mean that in future during the course of a compliance check an officer of HMRC may decide to issue a closure notice on any particular aspect or matter of the areas under review during the compliance check at any stage during the process. In particular this will give HMRC powers to effectively 'force' the progress of a compliance check where there are matters in dispute which cannot be agreed between the parties. Rights of appeal will remain against the issue of a closure notice.

An alternative way of viewing the new provisions is to point out that they also give the parties a way to formally agree, as the compliance check progresses, which aspects have been agreed between the parties rather than leave everything to the end of what can sometimes be protracted discussions, negotiations and review procedures.

Presumption of 'carelessness'

18.166 *Section 64* of *Finance Bill (No 2) 2017* introduces a new feature of the penalty regime where 'errors' are identified in taxpayers' documents filed with HMRC which can be deemed to have arisen as the result of the use of 'avoidance arrangements'.

In future where specific tax documents, returns etc, are provided to HMRC and those documents contain an inaccuracy which has arisen because specific and identified tax avoidance arrangements have been used within the meaning of the statute and which have in the event turned out to be ineffective (ie they have not achieved the tax savings that the taxpayer set out to achieve by using the particular avoidance 'scheme'), the statute will now include a specific presumption, for the purposes of the penalties legislation, that the inaccuracy was a matter of 'carelessness' for the purposes of the penalties legislation, unless it can be identified as deserving of one the more serious 'deliberate' levels of penalties provided by the statute. In effect this new provision denies the taxpayer reliance on the 'innocent error' defence in circumstances where HMRC forms the view that the taxpayer used the scheme for tax avoidance purposes. The only defence will be where the taxpayer can demonstrate to HMRC, or on appeal to the Tribunal) that the taxpayer took *reasonable care* to avoid inaccuracy.

A particular feature of this new provision is that the taxpayer will not be able to rely on the 'adviser defence' (ie reliance on the advice of a person (defined as an 'interested person') who was involved in some way in the promotion, marketing or sale of the tax avoidance arrangements or who has themselves participated in the scheme or who facilitated the use of the scheme by the taxpayer in return for payment).

Once again, the statute contains detailed explanatory and extending provisions which anyone using or advising on the use of tax avoidance arrangements in future will need to become very familiar with.

Penalties for enablers of tax avoidance

18.167 *Section 65* and *Sch 16* of *Finance Bill (No 2) 2017* introduce the new regime for the imposition of penalties on those who are identified as 'enabling' tax avoidance arrangements which are defeated by the courts in the UK.

These provisions are lengthy and complex and represent another part of the gradual shift in power to HMRC in the continuing battle between it and those who actively promote and facilitate the use of artificial and complex strategic tax avoidance arrangements and schemes. They will become required reading for the firms, businesses and individuals involved in this field and can result in the imposition of serious financial penalties and will probably also have a significantly deleterious impact on the future of any business on which such penalties are imposed.

The provisions come in from 2017 and the new penalties apply to those whom the statute identifies specifically as 'enablers' of failed tax avoidance arrangements. The new rules also introduce a change in the way penalties are applied to those taxpayers who are identified as having used 'failed' tax avoidance schemes.

These new penalties will apply to what are to be termed 'abusive schemes' which have been defeated by HMRC and the potential is for the imposition

18.168 *Penalties for error and failure to notify*

of a 100% penalty, based on the fees charged to the clients involved. This will be imposed on anyone and everyone who HMRC or the Tribunals identify as having any involvement in the so-called 'supply chain' for the provision of the tax advice concerned in the particular defeated scheme. The new penalties under these provisions are to apply to advice provided or actions taken after Royal Assent to the Finance Bill.

More VAT penalties for breaches of VAT record-keeping rules

18.168 *Section 68* of *Finance Bill (No 2) 2017* contains additional penalty provisions targeting VAT fraud involving more than one person.

The existing penalty provisions for VAT are revised to stipulate that a person will in future be liable to a penalty where they have entered into a transaction involving the making of a supply for the purposes of VAT and three conditions are satisfied:

1   the transaction is connected with the fraudulent evasion of VAT by another person;

2   the person knew or should have known this to be the case;

3   that HMRC has issued a decision which prevents the first person exercising or relying on a right to recover VAT input tax.

PENALTIES FOR OFFSHORE MATTERS

Offshore disclosure facility cases

18.169 Special penalty arrangements have been offered in recent years for taxpayers who make disclosures of offshore income and/or gains under either the general offshore disclosure facility or the special Liechtenstein Disclosure Facility. Penalties here can be limited to only 10% of the tax at stake in most cases.

General approach to offshore evasion penalties

18.170 Penalties for offshore tax evasion can otherwise be as much as 200% of the tax lost to HMRC (ie twice the normal maximum penalty for a 'civil' offence). These higher levels of penalties are designed to be a significant deterrent to the use of offshore jurisdictions (traditionally known as tax havens) by determined tax evaders seeking to hide money or other financial assets overseas.

18.171 The provisions first applied from 6 April 2011 for income and capital gains tax. The additional penalties will not however normally apply to an individual taxpayer who makes a full disclosure to HMRC of his overseas assets and pays his income tax. Furthermore, in recent years HMRC has made available specific 'disclosure opportunities' for individuals with offshore bank accounts, etc in a number of locations as well as offering initially a general offshore disclosure facility for those with overseas bank accounts under which a low penalty, commonly 10%, would be applied if the taxpayer made a full and complete disclosure within certain time limits and agreed to pay his tax liabilities in full.

18.172 The amount of any applicable penalty for offshore tax evasion is initially applied on a scale according to three levels or categories which are determined according to the ease with which the UK tax authorities can obtain tax information from the overseas jurisdiction or, alternatively, how readily the overseas jurisdiction shares information with the UK tax authorities. These categories are as follows:

1   Territories in category 1 – the penalty rate is the same as for existing penalties, up to 100% of the tax due.

2   Territories in category 2 – the penalty is 1.5 times the existing penalties, up to 150% of tax due.

3   Territories in category 3 – the penalty is double the existing penalties, up to 200% of tax due.

18.173 HMRC publishes a list of the countries which are in categories 1 and 3 and any other territories are in category 2. The list can be found at www.gov.uk/government/publications/territory-categorisation-for-offshore-penalties/territory-categorisation-for-offshore-penalties-from-24-july-2013.

18.174 Similar reductions to the size of any offshore evasion penalty can be obtained for a 'prompted or unprompted' disclosure and then for 'telling', 'helping' and 'giving access' as described earlier in this chapter for inaccuracy penalties.

18.175 HMRC acknowledges that the penalty can be disapplied altogether in cases where the taxpayer can demonstrate that he had a 'reasonable excuse' for his failure in connection with his overseas accounts which he characterises as some unusual event that is either unforeseeable or beyond the taxpayer's control and which applied throughout the period when the individual failed to comply with his tax obligations.

Similarly HMRC will not charge an inaccuracy penalty if the individual can demonstrate that he took 'reasonable care' to file his tax return correctly but still made a mistake.

18.176 *Penalties for error and failure to notify*

18.176 FA 2015 included new legislation to extend the offshore penalty regime. These provisions:

- extended the offshore penalty regime to include inheritance tax from 1 April 2016;

- extended the offshore penalty regime so that it will in future apply where the proceeds of a deliberate error or failure in the UK have been moved to an overseas jurisdiction on or after 1 April 2016;

- increased the applicable penalty by a further 50% if money or assets have been moved to an overseas tax jurisdiction to avoid engagement with the OECD's common reporting standard (CRS);

- introduced a fourth category of penalties for countries which sign up to the CRS which will be less than the penalties that can be due for assets or income derived in other jurisdictions. This will come into effect from 1 April 2016.

OTHER CONSEQUENCES OF 'DELIBERATE' PENALTIES

Managing serious defaulters

18.177 HMRC operates a specific programme to monitor closely the tax compliance of taxpayers whom it categorises as 'serious defaulters'. They describe these as people who deliberately get their tax affairs wrong. This is a deliberate programme of monitoring aimed at deterring repetition of serious tax defaults and ensuring future compliance by these individuals. Details are contained in summary form in the HMRC factsheet at: www.gov.uk/government/uploads/system/uploads/attachment_data/file/372579/CC-FS14_11_14.pdf.

18.178 Deliberate defaulters are categorised as people who have been:

- charged a penalty because of their deliberate behaviour;

- identified, during a civil investigation of fraud, as presenting a continuing high risk to HMRC;

- successfully prosecuted by the Director of Revenue and Customs Prosecutions, or another prosecuting authority, for a tax matter;

- charged a civil evasion penalty for dishonesty;

- required to give, and have given, security to HMRC as a guarantee against potential future default;

- successfully pursued, by an insolvency practitioner, for a claim on behalf of HMRC for recovery of money or assets.

18.179 HMRC's stated reasoning behind this programme is based on its perception of the risk posed by these taxpayers to the Exchequer as regards their potential to continue to seek to deliberately evade their tax obligations or to fail to pay the taxes that they owe.

18.180 Where HMRC identifies someone who can be categorised as a serious defaulter it will thereafter monitor the tax compliance of these people much more closely than the generality of other taxpayers. Their tax returns will be scrutinised more closely than normal and for a period of time they may be asked to provide extra detail with their tax returns than they would otherwise be obliged to (eg they might be asked to submit detailed accounts for their business each year whilst they are in the programme whereas this is not a strict requirement for most unincorporated businesses).

18.181 HMRC notifies taxpayers in writing when it decides to enter them in the serious defaulters programme and explains what conditions they will have to comply with and for how long. The programme can last for between two to five years and HMRC formally notifies taxpayers when they have been removed from the programme.

18.182 Clearly inclusion in this programme represents an additional compliance burden on any taxpayer so that additional advice will normally be needed in order to satisfy the extra requirements. It will mean that the taxpayer will need to ensure that he is keeping adequate and comprehensive records from the outset of the programme in order to be able to fully comply with the conditions that HMRC imposes. Anyone who has been found to have committed a tax offence in one of the two deliberate categories is potentially vulnerable to inclusion in this programme and will therefore need to take specific advice when settlement with the HMRC is imminent about what he will need to do to meet the compliance conditions and for how long.

18.183 This therefore adds an additional aspect to any case where an adviser is dealing with the settlement of a compliance check on behalf of a client. Whilst the negotiations towards settlement with HMRC are continuing the practitioner will need to bear in mind that an extra consequence of the acceptance that the penalty will be categorised as 'deliberate' could well lead to the inclusion of the client in the serious defaulters programme after the settlement of the case and hence the imposition of additional and possibly onerous extra compliance burdens on the client.

Naming and shaming

18.184 *FA 2009, s 94* contains provisions under which HMRC is permitted to publish information (including names) of persons who have been

18.185 *Penalties for error and failure to notify*

penalised for deliberate defaults (eg inaccuracies, failing to notify, and certain VAT and excise duty wrongdoings, in each case where the tax lost exceeds £25,000).

18.185 No details will be published if the person has made a full disclosure, either prompted or unprompted, within a time considered appropriate by HMRC. Any details must be published within 12 months from the relevant penalties becoming final and may not continue to be published beyond 12 months from when first published.

Details of the HMRC's approach to this issue can be found in summary form via its helpsheet at www.gov.uk/government/uploads/system/uploads/attachment_data/file/367393/cc-fs13_1_.pdf.

18.186 This programme of publishing the details of deliberate defaulters, commonly known as the 'naming and shaming' programme, has proved controversial from the outset as many commentators felt initially that it represents a major step away from the fundamentals of the relationship between taxpayers and the tax authorities. However it is now in place and advisers and clients alike need to be aware of the implications that inclusion in this programme might have on their lives and the public perception of them as individuals.

18.187 Before including a taxpayer in the naming and shaming programme and thereafter deciding to publish his details via its website, HMRC considers five separate aspects of the case:

1 Is the penalty being imposed in the 'deliberate' category?

2 Does the penalty apply in relation to an inaccurate return or other tax document for a period starting on or after 1 April 2010?

3 Was the penalty imposed as the result of an HMRC investigation?

4 Is the penalty subject to less than the maximum available mitigation?

5 Does the PLR exceed £25,000?

18.188 If the answer to all five of these questions is 'yes' then HMRC can enter the taxpayer in the naming and shaming publishing programme. It may not always do so but it will be able to consider doing so if the above five questions can be answered in the affirmative.

18.189 Once an investigation has been completed and the HMRC officer determines that the five questions can be answered positively, the case is referred internally to a specialist team for a decision on whether publication of the taxpayer's details is to proceed.

18.190 The HMRC's guidance on this issue states that where the answer to each of the five questions is 'yes' then publication will be effected in all but exceptional circumstances, in other words publication in such cases is to become a matter of routine.

18.191 The details that can be published are the taxpayer's name, address, the amount of the penalties charged, additional tax that those penalties were based on, the nature of the taxpayer's business where relevant, the period over which tax was evaded, and any other details necessary to clearly identify the taxpayer.

HMRC publishes taxpayers' details online at www.hmrc.gov.uk/defaulters/defaulters-list.pdf and normally the details stay there for up to 12 months from the date they are first published.

18.192 It is important also to recognise that a taxpayer has very limited influence over HMRC's decision on whether or not to publish his details once it has been determined that the answers to the five questions are all yes. HMRC will normally ask the taxpayer whether he thinks there are any reasons why it should not publish his details.

18.193 Normally the taxpayer then has only 30 days to reply and make any representations on the matter, after which a 'Senior Civil Servant' is given the task of considering those representations in detail and making the final decision on whether or not to publish. This is clearly a very important issue and advantage should always be taken of the opportunity to make such representations as are permitted as experience suggests that HMRC can be persuaded in some cases not to proceed with publication.

ADMINISTRATIVE MATTERS – DEADLINES FOR IMPOSING PENALTIES

Assessments

18.194 In assessing any particular level of penalty HMRC indicates in its guidance notes that it will proceed by:

- fixing a penalty for the nature of the action;
- basing the penalty on the PLR;
- taking into account whether any disclosure was prompted or unprompted;
- considering the 'quality' of the disclosure.

CH82510–CH82512 describe the penalty calculation process.

18.195 *Penalties for error and failure to notify*

Time limits

18.195 The time limit for making a penalty determination is up to three years after the final determination of the PLR. This is reduced to 12 months from either:

- the end of the appeal period for the decision correcting the inaccuracy;
- if there is no assessment, the date on which the inaccuracy is corrected; or
- where the taxpayer has failed to tell HMRC of an under-assessment, the end of the appeal period in respect of the assessment relating to the tax understated.

Appeals

18.196 Taxpayers can appeal to the First-tier Tax Tribunal against the imposition or amount of any penalty or a decision not to suspend a penalty. Where the appeal relates to whether a penalty should be suspended or whether HMRC should reduce the penalty due to special circumstances, the appeal body may consider whether HMRC's decision is reasonable. *FA 2009, Sch 57, para 6* makes it clear that the taxpayer is not required to pay a penalty until the appeal against the penalty has been determined.

Multiple penalties

18.197 More than one penalty may be charged in respect of the same failure. Each penalty can be applied and pursued in isolation and a person has a right of appeal against each of them. This is subject to the proviso that tax-geared penalties may not exceed 100% of the relevant liability to tax.

Transition

18.198 Finally it is important to note that the current penalties legislation is not retrospective. This means that the old and new penalty regimes will run side by side for the 20 years or so following its introduction as explained earlier in this chapter. The current regime applies to defaults occurring after 31 March 2008 for defaults in connection with the main taxes and to defaults occurring after 31 March 2009 for other taxes, failure to notify chargeability and obstruction of HMRC information powers.

18.199 The previous legislation under what were *TMA 1970, ss 7, 93* and *95, FA 1998, Sch 18, paras 17–18* and other existing legislation will continue to apply to tax defaults occurring before either 1 April 2008 or 1 April 2009.

SOME MISCELLANEOUS PENALTY MATTERS

Group relief

18.200 Penalties are normally calculated by reference to PLR, as explained earlier in this chapter. It is important however to note that in cases where there are claims or provisional claims for group relief involved in a tax computations, PLR is normally to be calculated before any group relief claim or surrender.

18.201 If however the subject of a compliance check is a group relief claim itself which proves to contain an inaccuracy then clearly PLR can be computed by reference to the difference between the tax payable before and after the group relief claim that contained the inaccuracy.

18.202 The above rule stipulating that group relief is not taken into account when calculating PLR could in some circumstances be said to potentially penalise groups if there was no additional tax becoming due as the result of an error. This could arise as the result of the availability of losses within a group. To cover this situation the current penalties statute permits a group to make group relief claims which can then be taken into account where the error has the effect of creating or increasing an aggregate loss.

It is understood that HMRC will treat aggregate losses as including understatements of a profit which reduce net losses available to a group.

18.203 The exact way in which the calculation is to be made in a group loss situation is also not defined. It seems that in HMRC's view, the basic PLR includes additional amounts of tax payable by other group companies as a result of the withdrawal of group relief, even though the claimant companies may not themselves have been careless. Consequently, only the part of the overall group loss which would have been carried forward to a future year attracts the special 10% tariff.

Losses

18.204 Again in contrast to the position which subsisted under the previous penalties regime *FA 2007* introduced a new concept of overstated loss relief to the penalty regime in the UK. Under this regime now the overstatement

18.205 *Penalties for error and failure to notify*

of a loss relief claim can be penalised even though no loss relief claim which reduces the amount of tax actually payable has been made.

18.205 There is however a restriction which applies here such that the PLR is deemed to be no more than a maximum of 10% of any such part of the loss. HMRC has stated that this rule will apply where the error in the loss calculations creates or increases a loss. Where the loss is potentially the subject of a group relief claim or there is a group situation which may affect the loss relief claim the calculations as above are to be applied after any claims for group relief.

18.206 HMRC has also confirmed that a 'nil' penalty can apply in circumstances where there is no reasonable prospect of a loss being used to reduce a tax liability. Additionally if a loss claim related error arises as the result of some timing issue rather than giving rise to an absolute loss of tax and payment of tax has been delayed HMRC will treat only 5% of any deferred tax arising from these sort of circumstances as lost revenue liable to the penalty.

Multiple penalties

18.207 There are a number of circumstances where a taxpayer can become potentially liable to more than one penalty simultaneously. HMRC instructs its officials to 'exercise discretion' when deciding how many penalties to impose, taking into account the circumstances of the case and the perceived compliance effect of the imposition of more than one penalty at the same time. Clearly it recognises that this might be perceived as unfair and oppressive but it should not be ignored that this is strictly possible under current legislation. Advisers will therefore need to point this out to their clients and to be prepared to negotiate on this matter with HMRC in specific cases.

It is also clear from HMRC's own instructions to its officers that where there are multiple penalties capable of imposition this is not a reason for mitigating any of the penalties.

18.208 HMRC recognises three broad categories of situations which can lead to potential multiple penalty liabilities:

Category A A taxpayer in breach of only one regulation or condition but who has breached the same regulation numerous times because of the nature of his business.

Category B A single act of misconduct by a taxpayer results in breaching a number of regulations.

Category C A taxpayer who fails to submit a return is liable to a fixed penalty which is issued automatically and then another for failure to pay it.

Some examples of the types of situations that might give rise to the above multiple penalty situations are given by HMRC at www.hmrc.gov.uk/manuals/ecpmanual/ecp5810.htm.

The double jeopardy rule

18.209 In addition to the regime of civil penalties described in this chapter and the next, the UK does of course have a parallel system of judicial and criminal sanctions which can be imposed for tax evasion. HMRC operates a 'selective' regime of criminal prosecutions which will normally be used for one of the three following types of offence:

- cheating the public revenue;
- the fraudulent evasion of income tax;
- offences under the *Fraud Act 2006*.

Where HMRC pursues a prosecution against any taxpayer for one or more of the above offences there can be no civil imposition of penalties for the same offences.

KEY POINTS

18.210 Penalties can result in a very significant increase in the eventual amounts payable on the settlement of any tax compliance check carried out by HMRC. It is therefore very important that the taxpayer and adviser are aware of the risk of penalties being imposed from the outset and take steps to achieve maximum mitigation wherever possible.

1   Identify any errors as early as possible.

2   Make an early disclosure to HMRC.

3   Make comprehensive disclosures to HMRC.

4   Do not make piecemeal disclosures or partial disclosures.

5   Encourage active co-operation on the part of the client/taxpayer.

6   Consider at an early stage whether suspension of 'negligence penalties' may be a possibility.

18.210 *Penalties for error and failure to notify*

7   Ensure comprehensive assistance and access to records is given to HMRC to ensure that maximum mitigation is available for 'co-operation' as part of the 'good quality disclosure' process.

8   Detailed legislation on penalties is to be found in *FA 2008* and *FA 2009*.

9   Penalties are now driven by an 'automatic' regime for simple compliance failures.

10 Penalties for inaccuracies are likely to be much more common in future.

11 HMRC operates penalties for inaccuracies according to a 'fixed scale'.

12 Mitigation of penalties can be achieved but only according to the HMRC's criteria for a 'prompted' or 'unprompted' disclosure.

13 HMRC provides guidance on penalties to which close attention should be paid when dealing with cases of failure or potential failures.

14 The amount of penalties is directly related to 'potential lost revenue' in cases of inaccurate returns accounts or documents.

15 It is important to establish the facts on any specific case in order to establish whether there are grounds for 'reasonable excuse'.

16 Reasonable excuse means something 'unforeseen' or 'exceptional' beyond the taxpayer's control.

17 It will be rare to be able to use the actions of a third party, especially an adviser, as a reasonable excuse although this can be accepted in some cases.

18 There are statutory mechanisms for appealing against penalties imposed by HMRC. It will be important to establish clearly all the pertinent facts in making such an appeal.

19 Many penalties can be avoided by paying close attention to tax compliance deadlines and time limits.

20 The most common penalties for inaccuracies arise from simple system and control failures, particularly in business records and data capture systems.

21 The lowest level of penalties imposed for 'carelessness' failures can be the subject to 'suspension' period by HMRC on request by the taxpayer.

Chapter 19

Penalty Mitigation

Russell Cockburn BSc (Hons) FFTA
Taxation consultant, lecturer and author; former Inspector of Taxes

---

Focus

This chapter looks at the methods available to taxpayers and advisers seeking to negotiate with HMRC as regards the mitigation of tax penalties, and suggests techniques and strategies to follow, together with a consideration of reasonable excuse and special reduction issues.

REDUCTIONS FOR DISCLOSURE

19.1 The main avenue available to taxpayers seeking to mitigate penalties is provided by statute, which offers a consideration to the taxpayer for the 'quality of their disclosure' and details various factors to be taken into account when deciding if the disclosure has been of a level and quality sufficient to entitle the taxpayer to complete or partial mitigation for the disclosure they have made to HMRC once a penalty has been established to be eligible for a particular tax offence.

19.2 The penalty regime in *FA 2007 et seq* deals with reductions for disclosure by the taxpayer. The actions that will trigger this are:

- letting HMRC know about the default;
- giving HMRC reasonable help in quantifying the tax unpaid by reason of the default;
- allowing HMRC access to the business or other records for the purpose of checking how much tax.

19.3 In a similar manner to the penalties that can be imposed for inaccuracies, mitigation of this penalty is related solely to the quality of a

19.4 *Penalty Mitigation*

'disclosure' In the context of a failure to notify a penalty is now quantified by HMRC on the basis of the following:

- whether the disclosure of the act of failure by the taxpayer was unprompted and the taxpayer has no reason to think that HMRC has discovered or is about to discover the relevant act or failure;

- whether the act of disclosure of the failure was prompted.

19.4 HMRC considers the quality and completeness of the disclosure and its timing (ie how promptly it was made). The nature of the disclosure is also considered, in the sense of the level of evidence provided and the degree and extent of access provided to test the disclosure.

19.5 The potential reductions in penalties are:

- the unprompted disclosure penalty of 100% can be reduced to not less than 30%;

- the prompted disclosure penalty of 100% can be reduced to not less than 50%;

- the unprompted disclosure penalty of 70% can be reduced to not less than 20%;

- the prompted disclosure penalty of 70% can be reduced to not less than 35%;

- in the case of an unprompted disclosure where the 30% penalty could be imposed, HMRC may reduce the penalty to nil or 10% where it becomes aware less than 12 months after tax becomes unpaid by reason of failure to notify the relevant items. This reduction will depend on the quality of the disclosure;

- in the case of a prompted disclosure where a 30% penalty could be imposed, this may be reduced to not less than 10%, or in any other case 20%, depending on the quality of the disclosure, where HMRC becomes aware of the failure within 12 months.

MITIGATION OF PENALTIES FOR FAILURE TO MAKE RETURNS

19.6 As is the case for other penalties these penalties may be mitigated according to the quality of the disclosure that the taxpayer makes where there has been a failure to make a return.

19.7 Reductions of penalties these will be made as follows:

- Where the person who is otherwise liable to a 100% penalty makes an unprompted disclosure, HMRC must reduce the 100% penalty to not less than 30%.

- Where an individual liable to a 100% penalty makes a prompted disclosure, HMRC must reduce the 100% penalty to a percentage of not less than 50%.

- Where a person who is liable to a 70% penalty makes an unprompted disclosure, HMRC must reduce the penalty to not less than 20%.

- Where a person who would otherwise be liable to a 70% penalty makes a prompted disclosure, HMRC must reduce the penalty to not less than 35%.

19.8 Note however that HMRC may not reduce the penalty for occasional returns and annual returns below £300, and the CIS penalty to less than £3,000 where the failure to submit information was deliberate and concealed or £1,500 where the failure was deliberate but not concealed

MITIGATING PENALTIES BY MAKING GOOD QUALITY 'DISCLOSURE'

19.9 The penalty regime in *FA 2007 et seq* offers taxpayers and their advisers the opportunity to obtain penalty mitigation in a very different way from the old regime. Whereas previously mitigation was arrived at by taking into account the three long-established and fairly well-known factors, disclosure, co-operation and size and gravity, the new system places the emphasis for the mitigation and negotiation process solely on the concept of 'disclosure'. Whilst it is true that the old factors do form part of this disclosure process to some extent, the emphasis is now very different indeed. Disclosure represents the sole factor that will determine the level of penalty to be imposed and will be the major factor considered by HMRC in such negotiations.

19.10 The concept of disclosure does not initially sound too difficult. Clearly it represents the degree of openness that a taxpayer exhibits in providing HMRC with the necessary information to enable it to assess and collect any unpaid taxes arising as the result of taxpayer errors or inaccuracies in returns and other documents. What is important however is the *type* of disclosure that a taxpayer makes and thereafter the speed and accuracy with which the taxpayer facilitates the disclosure process. HMRC places great emphasis on whether or not the taxpayer made his disclosure voluntarily or had to be encouraged to make it by the department. Thus, a disclosure will be categorised as either 'prompted' or 'unprompted'.

19.11 There is nothing new in HMRC offering greater mitigation for a taxpayer who voluntarily discloses past defaults. There has always been some

19.12   Penalty Mitigation

mitigation of penalties for this. However, the whole process now deals with mitigation in terms of the *quality* of the disclosure made by the taxpayer.

19.12   HMRC has stated that an *unprompted* disclosure occurs when the person making it 'has no reason to believe HMRC has discovered or is about to discover the inaccuracy or under-assessment'. On the other hand, an unprompted disclosure (ie all other types of disclosure), will occur when HMRC has already taken some action towards identifying inaccuracies in returns or other documents which prompts the taxpayer into providing details of those matters. Prompted disclosures will carry significantly lower levels of mitigation although it is still possible to obtain a high level of reduction of the penalty weighting in any case by adopting a constructive and co-operative approach to the disclosure process after the 'prompt'.

What is very different from the old regime is that it is now virtually impossible to obtain a very low level of penalty when the case falls into the 'prompted' category. Indeed, in the years since the new regime was introduced it has become apparent that there is in practice a 'floor' of 15% below which prompted penalties cannot fall.

HRMC has adopted three criteria which will be examined when deciding the level of mitigation to be allowed for the various types of penalty. These are 'telling', 'helping' and 'giving access'.

19.13   The statute in *FA 2007, Sch 24, para 9(1)* defines disclosure in the following terms:

- informing HMRC about the return inaccuracy or under-assessment of tax;
- providing reasonable help to HMRC in quantifying the potential tax loss; and
- allowing HMRC access to books, records and information for the purpose of ensuring that the inaccuracy or understatement has been completely corrected.

19.14   The criteria HMRC has said it will use in mitigating penalties draw on and expand the statute so that 'telling' includes admitting a document (or documents) was inaccurate or that there was an under-assessment, disclosing the inaccuracy in full, and explaining how and why it arose. 'Helping' includes giving HMRC officials reasonable help in quantifying the inaccuracy or under-assessment. 'Giving access' is defined by HMRC as where a person 'responds positively to requests for information and documents, and allows access to their business and other records, or other relevant documents'.

Penalty Mitigation **19.20**

19.15 The levels of penalty which HMRC will impose for the different types taking into account differing categories of disclosure are as follows:

Maximum and minimum penalties for each type of inaccuracy

Type of disclosure	Penalty	Careless	Deliberate	Deliberate and concealed
Unprompted	Maximum penalty	30%	70%	100%
	Minimum penalty	0%	20%	30%
Prompted	Maximum penalty	30%	70%	100%
	Minimum penalty	15%	35%	50%

19.16 HMRC guidance indicates that the penalty charged for each inaccuracy can be the maximum, the minimum *or any amount in between*, but it is clear that the only 0% penalty on offer is for an unprompted disclosure of a 'carelessness' penalty. The most common type of penalty encountered in practice, the carelessness penalty imposed during a compliance check where inaccuracies are identified as the result of HMRC review or other action, can never be mitigated below 15%, or so it would appear.

19.17 CH82410 outlines the HMRC's views on the penalty reductions for disclosure, and CH82430 and CH82432 its views on the weighting that may be given to the elements of disclosure. CH82440–CH82460 explain the penalty reductions for 'telling', 'helping' and 'giving access'.

19.18 Whilst to some extent the table above is the only explicit indication of percentages for mitigation that are available, the HMRC Compliance Handbook at CH82430 does provide some further detail by indicating that the 'telling', 'helping' and 'giving access' elements may be weighted as follows:

- telling – 30%;
- helping – 40%;
- giving access – 30%.

19.19 HMRC has given little further indication of its approach to penalty mitigation than those comments in the Compliance Handbook referred to above. Practitioners and taxpayers will need to take considerable care therefore during any compliance check or investigation process to pay attention from the outset to the factors that will secure greatest mitigation of penalties likely to be imposed at the end of any enquiry process.

19.20 Whilst this has always been the case the emphasis on the 'disclosure' aspects of a case will mean that taxpayers need to understand from the start of any compliance check that it is in their interest to make as complete and

19.21 Penalty Mitigation

detailed a disclosure as is possible and to thereafter facilitate the rest of the disclosure process in as timely and co-operative a fashion as is practical. Even then the most commonly imposed penalty, the 'carelessness' penalty for a system failure (eg errors in business records), will not fall below 15% of the PLR.

19.21 Thus, if the taxpayer himself, or his adviser, identifies any error or inaccuracy in his tax returns, the possibility exists that the taxpayer can get the tax paid, plus interest of course, with no penalty at all where it can be demonstrated that the error was one of simple carelessness and so long as HMRC has been provided with the necessary information in as speedy and helpful a manner as possible. Thus, a disclosure is only 'unprompted' if it is made at a time when the taxpayer has no reason to expect that HMRC has discovered the problem or is about to discover it. In any other circumstances the disclosure will therefore be regarded by HMRC as 'prompted'. Mitigation for 'prompted' penalties will never offer any reduction greater than 50% of the total possible penalty.

19.22 What exactly constitutes 'prompting' can clearly be a matter of some debate and conjecture. If an error becomes apparent during the compliance check process there can be little debate that this is a 'prompted' disclosure, once it has been agreed with HMRC. However, whether or not a general discussion of something over the telephone or during a meeting which leads to the client and his adviser identifying some other separate issue which should be disclosed to HMRC constitutes prompting might perhaps be open to question.

19.23 If, for example, some general discussion about the taxpayer's tax affairs takes place which triggers a train of thought on the part of the taxpayer leading to a disclosure, could this be regarded as 'prompting' when the new issue was totally unconnected with the matters discussed?

See also *M Baines-Stiller* (TC 5233) in which a taxpayer who had filed his return late appealed on grounds of reasonable excuse claiming that injuries suffered in a car accident had rendered him unable to attend to his tax affairs which excuse the Tribunal readily accepted.

In *G MacDonald* (TC5246) a taxpayer's appeal against a penalty for the late submission of a tax return was refused. The appellant argued that she had relied on her accountant to deal with her tax affairs and that he should have notified her appointment as a director to HMRC timeously and that this was a reasonable excuse. However, the tribunal took the view that this excuse was only available in more exceptional cases where the appellant could show that there was clear miscommunication between agent and client and that the taxpayer could not abrogate their ultimate responsibility for their own tax affairs in such a case and ought to have enquired about the tax return progress more carefully and kept track of her affairs more satisfactorily.

MITIGATION BY 'SPECIAL REDUCTION' OR 'SPECIAL RELIEF'

19.24 Across the range of penalties now provided by the current statutory regime HMRC also allows the possibility that mitigation outside the normal 'disclosure' concept can sometimes be given in circumstances described as 'special relief' or 'special reduction'.

This is another new concept not available under the previous penalty regime.

19.25 HMRC is at some pains in its guidance and published statements to make the point that this relief is reserved for unusual cases and only where a strong case can be made that special circumstances can be shown to be relevant. It has not really gone into any greater detail and it remains to a large extent unclear what this really means and how much mitigation can be obtained via this route for any particular penalty.

19.26 HMRC has indicated that factors such as inability to pay the tax or the penalty will not be accepted. Neither will the proposition that tax underpaid has been covered by an overpayment by another taxpayer. CH82490 outlines HMRC thinking on the subject in a little more detail.

19.27 Recent examples of settled tribunal cases include:

- *White v Revenue and Customs Comrs* [2012] UKFTT 364 (TC) in which a judge decided that a taxpayer had clearly received confusing information from her employers and HMRC about a redundancy payment, and that she had made a genuine effort to sort out the matter. The judge therefore decided that this amounted to special circumstances and ruled that a 60% reduction in the penalty was justified.

- *Roche v Revenue and Customs Comrs* [2012] UKFTT 333 (TC) in which some bank interest and a substantial redundancy payment had been omitted from the taxpayer's return. The 'special circumstances' in this case are not reported in detail but the tribunal did decide that whilst the taxpayer had indeed been careless, there had been circumstances which HMRC ought to have taken into account when requested to suspend the penalty and that these could be accepted. The tribunal decided to reduce the penalty on the omitted redundancy payment by 50% to take account of these special circumstances.

- *Fane v Revenue and Customs Comrs* [2011] UKFTT 210 (TC), in which the tribunal judge accepted that HMRC guidance indicating that a 'one-off' error will not normally be suitable for the suspension of a penalty could be regarded as an 'understandable and justified' approach.

19.28 *Penalty Mitigation*

- See also *E Porter v Revenue and Customs Comrs* [2016] UKFTT 0401 (TC5156) in which appeals against penalties for late submission of returns were partially allowed by the Tribunal. The taxpayer argued that she had been prevented from accessing necessary business and partnership records as these were held by her ex-husband after a divorce and that it was reasonable for her to have assumed that the partnership's accountants would be handling the partners' tax returns properly and promptly.

- See also *Group One (A Mehmood) v Revenue and Customs Comrs* [2016] UKFTT 198 (TC) (TC4986) in which an appeal against penalties for errors relating to input VAT on returns was dismissed. HMRC had disallowed some claims for input tax on the relevant returns which showed no entries for output tax at all. The tribunal found 'material inconsistencies' in some of the taxpayer's explanations about the existence of a business and business activities being carried on and concluded that there was evidence that the taxpayer had acted 'deliberately' in filing inaccurate returns. The penalty was, however, reduced significantly to reflect the degree of co-operation given by the taxpayer in resolving the issues involved in the case.

CALCULATING PENALTIES AND POTENTIAL LOST REVENUE

19.28 Tax penalties are applied to PLR. The penalties regime is intended to focus on taxpayer behaviour. Therefore, penalties are 'graduated so that they will increase depending on the seriousness of the taxpayer's failure, although the old concepts of 'size and gravity' are not mentioned in the legislation or associated literature. Accordingly, the amount charged moves up from a 'nil' penalty for an innocent mistake to much higher penalties for deliberate understatements of tax, particularly when compounded by concealment.

19.29 Guidance as to how HMRC will interpret taxpayer behaviour has been published. Some notes on this interpretation are included below.

Schedule 24, para 5(1) describes as PLR the additional amount due or payable in tax and National Insurance as a result of correcting the inaccuracy or assessment.

19.30 This includes over-repayments made by HMRC. Calculations of group relief and close company relief for loans taxable under the provisions in *CTA 2010, s 455 et seq* are ignored for the purposes of assessing PLR, but this does not prevent a penalty being imposed for an inaccurate claim for relief (see CH82282–CH82284).

The HMRC Compliance Handbook at CH82301–CH82370 makes it clear that losses over-claimed will contribute to PLR.

Examples of the calculation of the penalty based on PLR are given at CH82161 and at CH82260 and CH82272 for overstatements.

19.31 It is important to note that the interpretation of PLR is very wide indeed. In practice the application of this definition can be very different from the traditional view of *culpable taxes* in an enquiry situation. Historically penalties were charged on the difference between tax due on a return and the tax which was eventually payable. Thus, in an investigation situation, the extra taxes and any other duties etc becoming due after the completion of the investigation would have been those to which the penalty percentages were applied.

19.32 Whilst this will still be so in many cases, perhaps the majority, it is also important to realise that the definition of PLR can bring other considerations into the penalty equation. An example would be the difference between a repayment claim originally made and a lower repayment amount eventually agreed with HMRC (eg a corporation tax loss carry back claim resulting in a repayment of corporation tax from an earlier accounting period). Even if the original amount claimed by the company was never repaid to the taxpayer but was held over pending the result of an enquiry into the claim, there can be a penalty. The PLR would be the difference between the amount originally claimed as a repayment and the amount eventually repaid to the taxpayer. Although HMRC would have never over-repaid any tax, there will still be a penalty by reference to the amount that would have been over-repaid if the original return had not been challenged.

19.33 Thus, the amount to which a penalty charge is to be applied and by which the level of penalty will be calculated is either the actual tax lost to the Exchequer as the result of the taxpayer's default or failure (ie the amount that has not been paid), or it can be the amount that *would not have been paid* as the result of the taxpayer's default or failure.

19.34 So, the circumstances can range from a situation in which a return accepted and processed by HMRC turns out to have been incorrect and tax is underpaid as a direct result of that inaccuracy, to a situation in which a company submits a return which on being checked turns out to contain an inaccuracy and which on the inaccuracy being corrected the company pays the corrected amount of tax on time. In the latter case, whilst there has been no actual loss of tax to HMRC there could still be a penalty based on the difference between what was actually paid and what would have been paid had the original return been accepted as a correct self-assessment.

19.35 *Penalty Mitigation*

19.35 As has been seen earlier the amount of the penalty to be imposed in any particular case will vary according to the type of offence committed and the type of disclosure made by the taxpayer.

19.36 Thus, as can be seen, the adviser's ability to negotiate on the level of penalty to be imposed is to a very significant extent constrained by these limits from the outset. The first and a very significant consideration will be determining the specific level of penalty to be applied and, in most cases, this will be between the careless and the deliberate category.

19.37 Recent experience suggests that officers are increasingly seeking to argue that the deliberate criteria are to be applied on a wider variety of cases than would probably have been the case under the previous penalty regime. In particular, cases are being encountered where failures to identify errors over a number of years are being categorised as deliberate by HMRC on the grounds that a persistent failure which recurs should be regarded as more serious than one which only happens once, even if the error which led to the failure was a simple failure of some internal control or reporting/recording system (eg in the area of employee benefits to be reported on forms P11D). Officers increasingly focus on examining closely the 'behaviour' which has led to a failure and seek to contend that where a pattern emerges of a failure to identify a particular benefit which persists over a number of years or where an internal business control system fails to properly quantify a taxable benefit or non-deductible expense over a similar period, this must be categorised as a deliberate inaccuracy simply because of the length of time period involved.

19.38 The adviser will need to be able to demonstrate that any failure leading to a penalty situation arose not because the client persistently or with intent included an error or inaccuracy in his return or other tax document on which HMRC relies for tax purposes, but that the failure was a simple mistake. The concept of intent is at the heart of the 'deliberate' category of penalty although as yet this seems to be an area where professionals and tax advisers differ significantly from HMRC's interpretation of the legislation. An adviser will need to obtain from his client a detailed exposition of the circumstances which led to the particular failure, how it happened and why, what misunderstandings or errors in communication have led to the erroneous behaviour or record keeping and to be willing to explain this in detail to HMRC based on the client's detailed statement of the facts which are relevant. Even then current experience is such that HMRC officials are being tenacious in arguing that penalties across a wider range of circumstances than hitherto included must be regarded as in the deliberate category.

19.39 There is a second and equally important reason for the adviser to argue strenuously that his client's failure should be within the carelessness category and this is concerned with the opportunity to have the penalty suspended (see **19.40** *et seq* below). Only penalties in the carelessness category are eligible for suspension so that once HMRC accepts that an offence can be categorised as such then there is the very real possibility that after a suspension period has been served the penalty might well be cancelled altogether (ie reduced to zero on successful performance of the conditions imposed for suspension to be granted). The adviser therefore has a very significant incentive to negotiate hard for carelessness.

The other aspect of negotiation on penalties is the categorisation of a disclosure as either 'prompted' or 'unprompted' as has been discussed earlier in this chapter.

SUSPENDED PENALTIES

19.40 The opportunity for the agreed suspension of a penalty is a new concept which was introduced by *FA 2007, Sch 24*. HMRC said in its initial guidance and training notes issued to officers that suspended penalties are 'intended to encourage the taxpayer to prevent further occurrence of errors, by improving their systems and processes so that they can make correct returns in future'.

19.41 It is important to recognise that suspension is not available for all penalties. Only the lowest level penalties (ie those imposed for a 'careless inaccuracy'), are eligible to be considered as potentially suitable for suspension. HMRC has been at some pains to make it clear that it will only consider suspension of a penalty where it takes the view that the nature of the identified failure is such that it will be able to impose specific conditions which will 'help the person avoid penalties for careless inaccuracies in the future'.

19.42 The principle behind suspension is to encourage taxpayers to improve their behaviour in such a manner so as to render the likelihood of a repeat failure in the future very small if not impossible. Thus, the aim is to provide guidance and educational support to taxpayers (mainly in practice, it has to be said, in smaller businesses), so that sufficient time can be allowed for corrective actions to be taken and revised systems and procedures put in place.

19.43 The aim is to provide the taxpayer with an opportunity for 'remedial action to be taken'. Once HMRC has subsequently agreed that the corrective actions have properly been taken and the original behaviour which led to the failure has been properly and adequately addressed then no penalty will eventually payable. This will be on the basis that any conditions imposed by HMRC have been fully complied with at that stage. The time allowed for suspension can be up to two years but in practice it is likely to be much shorter and generally between six and nine months.

19.44 The objective of suspension is to provide the taxpayer with a period of respite in which to correct his failure, or more specifically the behaviour which

19.45 *Penalty Mitigation*

caused it. For this reason, it is essential that the agreed period of suspension should be long enough to provide a reasonable period of time in which to comply with all the conditions agreed with HMRC. It is important therefore that the negotiation process should be approached carefully when this is under consideration as part of a compliance check. The adviser and the taxpayer will need to consider very carefully how long it will take to put corrective measures in place and, of equal importance, how the effect of these corrective measures can be demonstrated to HMRC's satisfaction.

19.45 HMRC will agree a review date and carry out a repeat inspection at that stage to ensure compliance. It is therefore of considerable importance that all those involved in this process are agreed on precisely what those corrective measures actually are. Indeed, it is recommended that the corrective measures should be agreed with HMRC in writing. It is important to recognise that by entering into the 'suspension' facility the taxpayer is effectively sacrificing his right of appeal against the penalties. For this reason, suspension should not be entered into lightly.

19.46 The conditions to be fulfilled to satisfy HMRC must be identified and listed in advance so that when the subsequent review is carried out it should be a relatively straightforward matter to demonstrate that the conditions have indeed been met. Failure to adequately agree the conditions from the outset could produce the worst possible result: the eventual imposition of the penalty with no means of disputing it further.

19.47 That said, the facility to have a penalty suspended is a very useful and indeed welcome innovation as it provides taxpayers with a fairly straightforward means of mitigating potential penalties to zero. Indeed, in many cases this will be the only means of getting the penalty cancelled altogether. If at the end of the agreed suspension period the person has met all the conditions the penalty is cancelled.

19.48 In HMRC's opinion only certain categories of failure are likely to be relevant when the ability to use suspended penalties is being considered. For example, it has indicated that suspension might be appropriate for systemic or record-keeping weaknesses leading to inaccuracies. Thus, a suspended penalty would give the taxpayer the facility to correct these weaknesses in a short space of time. Obviously the more complex the failure then the more time is likely to be required to correct the problem.

Case decisions on suspension

19.49 In *Boughey v Revenue and Customs Comrs* [2012] UKFTT 398 (TC) the taxpayer made an error on his tax return claiming a relief against a redundancy payment which had already been dealt with via the PAYE system, thus resulting in a double claim. The tribunal decided that HMRC's decision not to suspend the penalty here was flawed, taking the view, contrary to HMRC's position, that there is no restriction in the legislation in respect of a 'one-off event' that was unlikely to be repeated.

19.50 In *Cobb v Revenue and Customs Comrs* [2012] UKFTT 40 (TC), a tribunal decided that HMRC is indeed able to suspend all or part of the penalty which it was seeking to impose for a careless error by an individual who had been made redundant, especially where the circumstances of the case showed quite clearly that this had been a relatively 'complex redundancy settlement' and as such difficult for the lay person to fully understand. Furthermore, the tribunal ruled that in this case HMRC could not use the 'one-off event' justification for refusal used in the *Fane* case mentioned at **19.27** above because 'being made redundant may not be a "one-off" event'.

19.51 See in this context also *I Hall v Revenue and Customs Comrs* [2016] UKFTT 0412 (TC5166); an appeal to have a penalty suspended following refusal of the request by HMRC was accepted. The HMRC officer seems to have given no real reasons for rejecting the suspension request and the Tribunal indicated that simply stating that 'it was not likely' that the taxpayer would repeat the error in future returns was not a sufficient reason for refusing suspension which could be granted so long as there was the possibility of a recurrence in future returns.

19.52 See also *P Steady* (TC5225) in which the Tribunal allowed an appeal against HMRC's refusal to suspend a penalty which had been imposed on a taxpayer who had reported bank interest on a tax return for the wrong year. The error came about as the result of the bank in question supplying a certificate for the wrong year and the Tribunal clearly had some difficulty in accepting HMRC's stance in such a case indicating that the decision not to suspend was 'flawed' and 'unreasonable'.

In *E Eastman v Revenue and Customs Comrs* [2016] UKFTT 0527 (TC5276) a taxpayer's appeal against a refusal by HMRC to suspend a penalty was accepted by the Tribunal because HMRC had misunderstood the limitations on its discretion in such cases. HMRC argued that an omission of a capital gain relating to the disposal of business premises from the appellant's tax return had been careless but the penalty could not be suspended because there was no likelihood that the error would recur, this being a one-off capital gain. The Tribunal took the view that suspension should be offered in such a case if such an action would assist the taxpayer in avoiding such an error in future. Whilst a one-off error would indeed not normally be suitable for suspension there had already been earlier tribunal judgements which had indicated that such a condition did not have to be specific and that in this case there could indeed be scope for future errors by the same taxpayer to be minimised.

19.53 *Penalty Mitigation*

Suspension of a penalty is a formal procedure which can only be commenced by agreement with the HMRC officials dealing with a case and only once a formal penalty notice has been issued. This penalty must then be the subject of a formal suspension notice in writing issued by HMRC and that suspension notice must include details of the following:

- which part of the penalty is to be suspended;
- the period of suspension (not more than two years);
- the conditions of suspension; and
- how compliance with the conditions is to be evidenced.

19.53 CH83130–CH83160 explain in more detail in which circumstances a penalty might be suspended. CH83190 details the remedial action taken by the taxpayer that will affect penalty suspension, and CH450660 and CH450670 outline the issues that HMRC will consider before granting a suspension. CH450680–CH450730 deal with conditions for granting a suspension and CH450740 with the period of suspension. HMRC has used the acronym SMART in the Compliance Handbook at CH83250 to illustrate the conditions that must be fulfilled, as follows:

- specific – directly related to the business or individual being penalised;
- measurable – in order to have a penalty cancelled the person needs to be able to demonstrate that conditions have been met;
- achievable – the person must be able to meet the conditions;
- realistic – unrealistic conditions cannot be imposed (for instance a condition that a business employ a full-time resource may be unreasonable for a small business with few business transactions);
- time bound – the conditions must be met by a certain date.

19.54 Practitioners, clients and advisers alike should note that, contrary to the impression given by some HMRC officials, there is a procedural obligation on HMRC to consider suspension of penalties. CH83131 states: 'You can only consider suspending a penalty for a careless inaccuracy. You must consider suspension for every penalty for a careless inaccuracy'!

Examples

19.55 The following are situations in which HMRC has agreed to suspend penalties. In these cases, the period of suspension varied from three to six months.

1   An unrepresented taxpayer prepared his own tax return and included a claim for 'use of home as office' based on information gleaned from

reading various tax publications. On enquiry HMRC decided that the claim was excessive and reduced it considerably but agreed to suspend the penalty on the basis that the taxpayer was inexperienced in running a business and had taken at least some reasonable care in researching the matter before preparing his incorrect claims.

2　A business operating in the construction industry paid its employees a mileage allowance for travel between the main depot and various building sites. The system in use for checking employees' claims proved to be inadequate and open to abuse resulting in the overpayment of mileage allowances on numerous occasions spread over a two-year period. HMRC agreed to suspend the penalty for a six-month period having agreed with the business's directors the new record-keeping procedures that would be put in place and the methods that they would use to check the actual mileages being travelled.

3　A business operating in the hotel sector had agreed a specific 'sampling' method with its tax inspector some years ago for the submission of capital allowances claims using the 'short life asset' regime. On carrying out a compliance review HMRC identified that as the business had grown rapidly in more recent years the agreed sampling method had become inadequate and inappropriate for the revised scope of the current business. This had probably led to inaccuracies in the most recent two years' capital allowances claims although it was difficult to quantify the likely amount. Revised data capture and record-keeping systems were agreed upon and HMRC agreed to suspend the penalties for a nine-month period after which the operation of the new systems would be reviewed and, if accepted by HMRC, the penalties cancelled.

19.56　Once a penalty has been suspended it is important to recognise that the onus is going to be very much on the taxpayer and his advisers to ensure that the conditions imposed by HMRC (usually after a process of discussion and agreement with the taxpayer) must be met in full within the agreed timescale. It is therefore of crucial importance to the process that at the stage when agreement of suspension is being discussed the taxpayer, be it an individual or a business, gains a very comprehensive understanding from HMRC of exactly what is to be required in order to meet the conditions of the suspension. This should ideally be set out in writing in the formal suspension notice to be issued by the officer of HMRC and time should be taken to get this set out in as much detail as possible. This is very important. It will be much easier after the suspension period has elapsed to obtain agreement from HMRC that the conditions have been fulfilled and revised systems and procedures put in place to meet those conditions if everyone is clear from the outset exactly what is to be done.

19.57 *Penalty Mitigation*

MITIGATION FOR 'REASONABLE EXCUSE'

19.57 As is the case for the 'inaccuracy' penalties described in **CHAPTER 18** the concept of reasonable excuse can be used to obtain mitigation of the penalties described in this chapter. Indeed, experience in recent years of tax tribunal decisions has been that they are perhaps willing to accept a wider range of 'excuses' than might normally be expected and certainly to countenance a wider range of excuses than perhaps HMRC is generally willing to accept.

19.58 This is not to suggest that spurious or frivolous excuses stand any chance at all before the tribunals; they do not and are generally seen through very rapidly indeed. However, there is little doubt that increasingly advisers are finding that a well-explained and presented case providing detailed facts concerned with why a particular company or individual has found itself in its particular circumstances or predicament may well in fact stand a reasonable chance of success in front of the tribunal.

19.59 In *Needs v Revenue and Customs Comrs* [2011] UKFTT 424 (TC) appeals were dismissed against penalties for late submission of a self-assessment return and late payment of income tax. Mr Needs claimed that because he had moved from being self-employed to PAYE employment and so was paying his taxes as he worked, he should be excused the penalty but the tribunal did not accept this and moreover pointed to the fact that there was no evidence that he had informed HMRC that his self-employment had ceased.

19.60 In *Westbeach Apparel UK Ltd v Revenue and Customs Comrs* [2011] UKFTT 561 (TC) the company's appeals against penalties for the late filing of its employer's annual P35 return for the year 2009/10 were refused.

19.61 Apparently in this case the failure had occurred because the company's tax agent had unwittingly submitted the form electronically via its software system in 'test mode' but had received a notice indicating 'confirmation of submission'. However, this was not a genuine confirmation but a 'test' notice and so the actual return was not finally submitted until October 2010 well after the May deadline and after the penalty notice had been issued by HMRC.

19.62 The tribunal held in this case that the company's reliance on a third party could not amount to a reasonable excuse. It would seem that the tribunal took the view that because the company had used a specialist payroll bureaux such an agent ought to have a higher level of expertise in such matters and should have known the difference between test and real mode.

19.63 This can be seen in contrast to others where accountants have succeeded in multiple appeals against non-submission penalties on behalf of their clients for failure to get tax returns in on time via their electronic software where test mode has been used in error.

19.64 In *Davies v Revenue and Customs Comrs* [2011] UKFTT 303 (TC), a business operating within the CIS submitted its return for the period to 5 June 2010 and paid the tax due on 19 June. However, whilst the cheque was received on time the return was not received until 22 June after the deadline although Mr Davies had posted the cheque and the return to separate addresses on the same day at the same post office. In this case the tribunal accepted that it was very unlikely that Mr Davies would have made two separate trips to post the return and the cheque and whilst there was no proof of posting, the cheque had arrived in good time and so it was accepted that the delay was on the part of the post office and hence there was a reasonable excuse.

19.65 In *Khan Properties Ltd V HMRC* [2018] TC06225 the tribunal judge ruled that penalty notices issued to a company for failure to submit CT returns were invalid as they were not signed by an officer of HMRC. In a perhaps rather surprising judgement the decision given was that a 'flesh and blood' officer had to at least be mentioned as the issuing officer for such penalty notices for them to be valid in law. Now, whilst the judge was quite specific that this ruling only applied to corporation tax penalties and not the wider panoply of self-assessment taxes, the case has potentially very significant implications for HMRC as regards its current internal procedures for issuing automatic penalties for late returns. Some commentators have suggested that the ruling may indeed be capable of wider application across the full range of UK tax penalties for failure offences; that remains to be seen, but the case does seem to offer a possible route for mitigation of penalties where unsigned or apparently unauthorised penalty notices have been issued. It seems almost inevitable that HMRC will now have to specifically revise its procedures and documentation to deal with this ruling.

19.66 In *R Morris V HMRC* (TC6160) the taxpayer was under the impression that he had correctly filed his 2013/14 and 2014/15 returns with HMRC electronically, having received an e-mail confirmation for them both. He received late filing penalties in late 2016 and so filed the returns again, this time successfully. The penalty notices went to the wrong address, as Mr Morris had moved house; he had informed HMRC of this move. The Tribunal decided that the taxpayer had a reasonable excuse and quashed the penalties for both returns.

19.67 In *P Saunders v HMRC* [2017] UKFTT 765, under new legislation in force from April 2015, a non-resident owner of UK residential property faced a UK capital gains tax liability and was thus obliged to report the gain within 30 days of making the sale.

19.68 *Penalty Mitigation*

Ms Saunders, who was living in Saudi Arabia, had failed to meet this notification deadline and HMRC imposed a penalty. The gain was eventually notified in August 2016. Ms. Saunders was apparently completely unaware of the change in the legislation and notified HMRC as soon as she realised her mistake.

HMRC argued that there had been 'ample publicity' about this change in the law but the tribunal accepted that Ms Saunders had a reasonable excuse because it would only have been reasonable to expect her to be aware of the changes if she had been specifically notified of them, or alerted to them directly by HMRC. The tribunal effectively said that it is unreasonable to expect non-residents to keep up to date with changes in UK tax law

19.68 In *Thomas Richter v HMRC* (TC05816) a taxpayer was allowed his appeal against a late filing penalty for being six and 12 months late; ie. these were 'tax geared' penalties based on HMRC's assessment of the taxpayer's income and resultant liabilities arising. The Tribunal had to consider whether or not the taxpayer being in prison could be a mitigating factor in deciding on mitigation of penalties. The tribunal allowed the appeals on the grounds that it could not be said that HMRC had properly assessed the tax due to its 'best of knowledge and belief', as it could not communicate with the taxpayer to realistically assess his outstanding tax liability due to his detention at Her Majesty's pleasure!

19.69 HMRC's manuals give some indication of its attitude to the concept of 'reasonable excuse' across a variety of areas. For example in the context of the submission of late appeals it has commented as follows:

'The following examples are a guide to, but not an exhaustive list of circumstances, which might amount to a reasonable excuse.

- The customer is a sole trader, or only director of a company, and has suffered a sudden and serious illness during the dates when they could have sent an appeal to HMRC or accepted a review offer, or have been affected by a prolonged and serious illness throughout this same period

- Unavoidable and unexpected absence close to the dates when they could have sent an appeal or accepted a review offer because of business commitments or domestic emergencies

- Accidental destruction of the records through fire or flood

- Exceptional postal delays because of a strike by postal workers or other civil disturbance

- Although we have not received the appropriate appeal or review acceptance from the customer, they claim nevertheless to have posted it to us in good time. Unless there is evidence to the contrary this explanation should be accepted on the first occasion

- Sudden disruption to a business or its records by a break-in installation of a new computer system which has hit unexpected teething problems

It will not be a reasonable excuse for the customer to claim that

- the failure is due to their agent not taking action in time
- information relevant to the appeal or review acceptance was not available by the due date
- their affairs are too complicated for them to have sent us an appeal or accepted the review on time
- they were too busy running their business
- they are not liable to pay any tax for the period for which the appealable decision was made, or have overpaid tax.'

KEY POINTS

19.70

1   Disclosure and the quality of the disclosure are the essential elements required to obtain any mitigation of penalties for UK taxes.

2   The ability to negotiate on the basis of factual evidence plays an important part in convincing HMRC that any mitigation of penalties is to be made available.

3   Cooperation throughout the process of negotiating penalties is essential to the whole process of settling the level of any tax penalty in the UK.

CHECKLIST

19.71   The following are a few essential points and tips on mitigation of penalties

- Always start by checking the statutory position: has there actually been an 'offence' under the taxes acts? An HMRC officer has to establish 'culpability' in order for a penalty to be exigible.
- Is there a 'reasonable excuse'? Did something unforeseeable, exceptional or beyond the taxpayer's control occur?
- Penalties are best avoided; ensure timely compliance with all statutory deadlines and time limits wherever possible.
- Ensure record-keeping systems and control procedures are adequate for ensuring accurate tax reporting wherever possible.

19.72 *Penalty Mitigation*

- Have regular 'compliance health checks' in a business to review all systems and procedures.

- Diarise compliance time limits and deadlines well in advance and keep under review.

- If penalties are likely, ensure timely compliance with HMRC request for information.

- Watch for information notices and ensure timely compliance or make sure that appeals are submitted on time.

- Establish the facts clearly and concisely when negotiations are to take place on penalties.

- Ensure speedy and accurate reporting on penalty mitigation, ie tell HMRC immediately an offence is identified, help it by providing access to the information and allow access to the relevant information in order to quantify the errors or inaccuracies as quickly as possible.

- When an error or inaccuracy is identified without a compliance check taking place always make an immediate disclosure to HMRC so as to ensure access to the 'unprompted' disclosure mitigation category of penalties.

- Consider what alternative avenues are available to the taxpayer when facing penalties, ie 'internal independent review' with another HMRC officer, appeal to the tax tribunals, alternative dispute resolution or possibly even complaints to a senior officer, an MP or the official Parliamentary Ombudsman in extreme cases.

APPENDIX

LIST OF STATUTES

19.72 The full list of provisions on tax penalties now contained in statute is as follows:

- *FA 2007, s 87, Sch 24* – penalties for errors.

- *FA 2008, s 113, Sch 36* – information and inspection powers.

- *FA 2008, s 114* – computer records.

- *FA 2008, s 115, Sch 37* – record keeping.

- *FA 2008, Sch 38* – disclosure of tax avoidance schemes.

- *FA 2008, s 118, Sch 39* – time limits for assessments, claims, etc.

- *FA 2008, s 119* – correction and amendment of tax returns.

Penalty Mitigation **19.72**

- *FA 2008, s 122, Sch 40* – penalties for errors.
- *FA 2008, s 123, Sch 41* – penalties for failure to notify, etc.
- *FA 2009, s 93, Sch 46* – responsibilities of senior accounting officers of large companies.
- *FA 2009, s 94* – naming and shaming tax defaulters.
- *FA 2009, s 95, Sch 47* – amendment of some existing information powers.
- *FA 2009, s 96, Sch 48* – amendment of information powers included in *FA 2008, Sch 36*.
- *FA 2009, s 97, Sch 49* – provision that HMRC may issue notices requiring third parties to provide contact details for those in debt to HMRC.
- *FA 2009, s 98, Sch 50* – extension of record-keeping rules to other taxes.
- *FA 2009, s 99, Sch 51* – amendment of time-limits applying to certain taxes.
- *FA 2009, s 100, Sch 52* – explanation of changed rules regarding overpaid income tax, corporation tax and capital gains tax.
- *FA 2009, ss 101–105, Schs 53–54* – provisions regarding interest on tax paid to and by HMRC.
- *FA 2009, s 106, Sch 55* – creation of new penalty regime for late filing of tax returns.
- *FA 2009, s 107, Sch 56* – creation of new penalty regime for late payment of taxes.
- *FA 2009, s 108* – cancellation of penalties where taxpayers have entered into an agreement with HMRC to defer payment of taxes.
- *FA 2009, ss 106–109, Sch 57* – amendments to *FA 2007, Sch 24* (penalties for errors) and *FA 2008, Sch 41* (penalties for failure to notify and certain other wrongdoing).
- *FA 2010, Sch 10* – new penalties for offence in relation to failures to disclose offshore income and gains.
- *F(No 2)A 2010, Schs 10 and 11* – amendments to the rules on penalties for failures to make returns and failures to pay tax on time.
- *FA 2013, Sch 50* – minor changes to penalties for late filing, late payment and errors. With specific reference to the RTI system from April 2013.

Chapter 20

Tax appeals

Hartley Foster
Partner, Fieldfisher LLP

> **SIGNPOSTS**
>
> - **Scope** – Primary and secondary legislation provides the rules that govern the operation of the tax tribunals. The *Tribunals, Courts and Enforcement Act 2007* (*TCEA*) is an enabling Act, under which, along with the secondary legislation issued thereunder (Transfer of Tribunal Functions and Revenue and Customs Appeals Order 2009, SI 2009/56, arts 3 and 4), the General Commissioners, Special Commissioners, s 706 Tribunal, and VAT and Duties tribunals were abolished and their functions and jurisdiction transferred, with effect from 1 April 2009, to a unified tribunal that comprises a first tier and an upper tier. The procedural rules for the First-tier Tribunal, Tax Chamber and the Upper Tribunal are set out in the Tribunal Procedure (First-tier Tribunal) (Tax Chamber) Rules 2009, SI 2009/273 and the Tribunal Procedure (Upper Tribunal) Rules 2008, SI 2008/2698 respectively. (See **20.26–20.33**.)
>
> - **Preliminary issues** – Many tax practitioners have little or no experience of taking an appeal to the tax tribunals. Indeed, there is a school of thought that regards the reaching of some form of compromise settlement with HMRC as a panacea. Although, as a general rule, reaching a negotiated settlement is preferable to resolution via litigation, that is only a general rule. The approach that should be adopted in any particular case can be arrived at only after considering fully what is best for the taxpayer, and should not be influenced by any pre-disposition against litigation.
>
> - **The people involved** – Practitioners must be prepared fully. Although approximately 66% of taxpayers are not represented on appeals to the First-tier Tribunal, that statistic disguises the fact that a very significant percentage of appeals are simple matters

Tax appeals **20.1**

(such as late filing penalties) that are allocated to the 'paper track' and are dealt with by means of written submissions only. For matters that are more complex (whether as a matter of law or fact or both), consideration should be given to whether it would be in the clients' best interest for the matter to be handled in-house, or whether an external specialist should be engaged instead. (See **20.129–20.147**.)

- **Practicalities** – Being mindful of the adage 'if you want peace, prepare for war' and thus dealing with enquiries from the perspective that, ultimately, the underlying issues may be heard by a tribunal or court, can achieve considerable improvements, both in terms of the cost of compliance and the ultimate outcome of the case. Valuable protection is provided to the taxpayer by *TMA 1970, ss 28A(4)* and *28B(5)* and *FA 1998, Sch 18, para 33* (in relation to personal, partnership and company returns respectively), which enable the taxpayer to apply to the First-tier Tribunal, during the enquiry, for a direction that the enquiry should be closed. The burden of proof is then on HMRC to show that there are 'reasonable grounds' for not closing the enquiry. (See **20.51–20.77**.)

- **Controversial issues** – Currently, fees are not charged by the First-tier Tribunal or the Upper Tribunal. In 2016, the Ministry of Justice consulted on the introduction of a split fee structure, under which a charge would be levied on both the issue of an appeal and on hearings. The rationale for this was to enable 25% of operating costs in the tax tribunals to be recouped by the Government (it is understood that the annual running costs of the tax tribunals is approximately £8.7 million). The Government noted that there was strong opposition to the proposals, but concluded that it would introduce them, regardless.

- However, in June 2017, the Supreme Court held in *R (Unison) v Lord Chancellor* [2017] UKSC 51 that the introduction of fees in respect of the Employment Tribunal (by the Employment Tribunals and the Employment Appeal Tribunal Fees Order 2013, SI 2013/1893 made under the general power in *TCEA, s 42(1)*) was unlawful, both under common law and as a matter of EU law. The theoretical assumptions and justifications that lay behind the Government's desire to introduce fees to tribunals ignored completely the public function of individual tribunal claims in delivering rights at the systemic level.

- It is to be hoped that the consequence of *Unison* is to persuade the Government to abandon, rather than just delay, the introduction of fees to the tax tribunals. The majority of appeals to the First-tier

20.1 *Tax appeals*

> Tribunal involve small amounts of money, comparatively simple matters of fact and law, and unrepresented taxpayers. But, the First-tier Tribunal also hears cases where the money at stake is in the hundreds of millions, the issues arising are complex (both factually and legally) and both parties are represented by teams of advisers. The introduction of tribunal fees would dissuade the former, but not often the latter, from pursuing appeals.
>
> • **Key points** – For a list of key points from this chapter, see **20.280**.

INTRODUCTION

The tax appeals system

> **Focus**
>
> This chapter aims to provide practical guidance to practitioners regarding tax related litigation. It encompasses:
>
> (i) the procedures that apply in tax matters before cases are notified to the First-tier Tribunal;
>
> (ii) the jurisdiction and powers of the First-tier Tribunal and Upper Tribunal; and
>
> (iii) the various tax-related matters that may be heard by other judicial bodies.

20.1 The tax appeals system in the UK changed fundamentally on 1 April 2009. Before that date, rather than having one specialist tax tribunal that could hear all tax-related appeals, different taxes carried with them different methods and routes of litigation.

20.2 Litigation that concerned income tax, corporation tax, capital gains tax and the stamp taxes fell within the purview of the General Commissioners and the Special Commissioners (the Commissioners) (with the division of jurisdiction being complicated; some were reserved to the General Commissioners, some to the Special Commissioners, and some could be heard by either body); the jurisdiction of the *s 706* tribunal was limited to determining whether a person being in a position to obtain, or having obtained, a 'tax advantage' in consequence of a transaction in securities or of the combined effect of two or more transactions in securities could suffer the nullification of that tax advantage; and the jurisdiction of the VAT and duties tribunals encompassed VAT, customs duties, excise duties, insurance premium tax, landfill tax, aggregates levy, climate change levy, and airport passenger duty.

20.3 The rules governing the reform and operation of the tax tribunals are set out in the *Tribunals, Courts and Enforcement Act 2007* (*TCEA 2007*). *TCEA 2007* received Royal Assent on 19 July 2007. It is an enabling Act, under which, and the secondary legislation issued thereunder (Transfer of Tribunal Functions and Revenue and Customs Appeals Order 2009, SI 2009/56, arts 3 and 4), the General Commissioners, Special Commissioners, s 706 tribunal, and VAT and duties tribunals were abolished and their functions and jurisdiction transferred, with effect from 1 April 2009, to a unified tribunal that comprises a first tier and an upper tier (the First-tier Tribunal (FTT) and Upper Tribunal (UT), respectively).

20.4 The procedural rules for the FTT and the UT are set out in the Tribunal Procedure (First-tier Tribunal) (Tax Chamber) Rules 2009, SI 2009/273 (the First-tier Rules) and the Tribunal Procedure (Upper Tribunal) Rules 2008, SI 2008/2698 (the Upper Tribunal Rules) respectively.

20.5 References to HM Revenue and Customs (HMRC) include references to its statutory predecessors. Reference to the term 'tax tribunal' means either the UT or FTT. If the expression 'tax tribunals' is used, it means both bodies.

20.6 This chapter is divided into five sections, after this introductory section.

The first section, by way of summary and introduction, describes briefly the new tribunal system, and contains a short history of why the system was introduced. Section two explains the procedures that apply in tax matters before cases are notified to the FTT. The third section sets out in detail the jurisdiction and powers of the FTT. The fourth section comprises an analysis of the UT, and an outline of the procedure on appeals from the FTT to the UT. The fifth section comprises an analysis of the various matters that may be heard by judicial bodies that adjudicate on tax-related matters outside the new tribunal system.

Use of litigation as a tactic

20.7 Many tax practitioners have little or no experience of taking an appeal to the tax tribunals. Indeed, there is a school of thought that regards the reaching of some form of compromise settlement with HMRC as a panacea. Although, as a general rule, reaching a negotiated settlement is preferable to resolution via litigation, that is only a general rule and the approach that should be adopted

20.8 *Tax appeals*

in any particular case can be arrived at only after considering fully what is best for the taxpayer, and should not be influenced by any pre-disposition against litigation.

20.8 Being mindful of the adage '*if you want peace, prepare for war*' and thus dealing with enquiries from the perspective that, ultimately, the underlying issues may be heard by a tribunal or court, can achieve considerable improvements, both in terms of the cost of compliance and the ultimate outcome of the case.

Litigation and Settlement Strategy

20.9 The approach referred to at **20.7** is particularly relevant since, under its Litigation and Settlement Strategy (LSS), HMRC adopt a litigation-focused approach to disagreements with taxpayers. LSS was published in June 2007. It has been revised 3 times since then (in 2011, 2013 and 2017). LSS is the strategy that inspectors are required to adopt to all contentious matters.

The original LSS

20.10 In an article in the *Tax Journal* (11 June 2007), Dave Hartnett (who was, at the time, HMRC Director General, Business) set out the aims of HMRC's LSS strategy:

> 'The LSS sets consistent standards for the way we settle disputes with our customers, whether by agreement or litigation. It ensures that where we are confident about the strength of our case and the disputed point is a significant one, we will insist on 100% of the tax or other liabilities that HMRC believes to be due. Where we accept that we do not have strong grounds for our position or the issue is less important to us, we will aim to avoid disputes altogether.'

20.11 LSS is part of HMRC's wider aim of promoting positive customer behaviours and deterring non-compliance with the tax laws. LSS covers all types of dispute about liability to pay taxes or duties, or entitlement to tax credits, absent litigation to recover debts or concerning employment matters. The term 'dispute' means any situation where HMRC is in disagreement with a taxpayer and 'the disagreement is not readily resolved'. Once this stage has been reached, LSS must be applied by the inspector to the matter and a litigation-focused approach adopted.

20.12 The two fundamental aspects of LSS (as introduced) are as follows:

1 Each dispute is to be settled on its own merits. There are no 'package deals' that settle a range of issues for a single undifferentiated sum of money.

2   Disputes that have an 'all-or-nothing' character involving a single point of law that would be decided one way or the other by the courts must be settled on an 'all-or-nothing' basis. Thus, for example, no discount will be provided for an agreement not to litigate.

These fundamental aspects remain key, although there has been an element of nuance added subsequently.

Mr. Hartnett (then as the Permanent Secretary for Tax) announced a change to LSS in an interview that he gave to the *Financial Times* on 19 August 2010. He indicated that 'increasingly, inspectors will be encouraged to reach agreement' in relation to disputes with businesses, and that inspectors may conclude a settlement, provided that the amount of tax payable is based on a 'plausible' technical conclusion on the point at stake.

20.13 Subsequently, in July 2011, HMRC 'refreshed' LSS, following the criticism that there was not a consistency of understanding by HMRC officers as to the flexibility permitted in settling disputes. The re-launch of LSS was intended to make the message clearer. It does not, according to HMRC, involve any significant revisions to the stated strategy.

In November 2012, HMRC published its Tax Disputes Governance Code, which is designed to improve transparency regarding how HMRC approaches tax disputes. It is emphasised in the code that the way in which HMRC handles all tax disputes is as set out in LSS. In the code it is indicated that the Tax Disputes Resolution board, which is made up of directors from business areas across HMRC, makes recommendations in all cases where the tax at stake is more than £100 million and in a sample of cases where the tax at stake is between £10 million and £100 million. Tax settlements for more than £100 million reached with large companies are overseen by the Tax Assurance Commissioner (currently Jim Harra).

Further updates were made to LSS in 2013. And, in 2017, a new version of LSS was published.

The 2017 version

20.14 In this version, collaborative working, or seeking to resolve disputes by agreement is described as HMRC's 'default approach', departure from which is described as a 'rare exception'. It is stated that:

'A key part of HMRC's overall customer strategy is to help reduce the likelihood of situations arising which may give rise to a dispute.'

2017 LSS refers to HMRC's use of random enquiries 'to validate the risk-based approach to compliance work', with the overall aim being to 'secur[e] the best practicable return for the Exchequer' (rather than the aim of 'maximis[ing]

20.15 *Tax appeals*

revenue flows' that appeared in previous versions). HMRC's random enquiry programme involves the selection of a sample of returns for enquiry before there is any consideration of risk.

2017 LSS contains a modified definition of 'risk'. This is the term that HMRC use to describe the disputed tax treatment of a specific transaction or entry on a return with a particular taxpayer. Where the same risk applies to several taxpayers, HMRC refer to that as an 'issue'.

HMRC's 'behavioural approach' is summarised. In particular, it is indicated that:

(i) in certain circumstances, HMRC will suspend inaccuracy penalties; it is indicated that the rationale is 'only penalising those who do not agree to changes, or fail to implement them properly'; and

(ii) where the outcomes are finely balanced, HMRC will consider not only the absolute amounts at stake, but also:

　　(a) the taxpayer's past and potential future behaviour; and

　　(b) the precedent value of the issue.

It is stated that decisions on judicial review will be referred to the Tax Disputes Resolution Board (for to determine whether or not to contest the matter) only in the circumstance where HMRC is considering not defending the judicial review. The default position, accordingly, is that HMRC will contest applications for judicial review.

20.15 The dominant factor in determining whether or not to litigate is the chance of success. If HMRC considers that it is unlikely to succeed in litigation, then it will not pursue the case unless it can be justified by the particular circumstances, such as a very large amount of tax in question (in the case itself or from immediate precedent value), or a fundamental point of principle at stake. In all cases, the legal advice from HMRC Solicitor's Office will be a critical factor in decision making.

An analogous approach by the taxpayer from the enquiry stage onwards not only brings greater rigour and enables greater focus when responding to HMRC, but also allows litigious tactics to be used.

INTRODUCTION OF THE TRIBUNAL SYSTEM

The origin for change

20.16 The pre-April 2009 tax appeals system was a complex one. As indicated above, rather than (as is the case in many other European countries) having one specialist tax tribunal that could hear all tax-related appeals, in the UK different taxes carried with them different methods and routes of litigation.

Moreover, not all tax-related matters could be litigated before the specialist tax tribunals (eg only the High Court could hear applications for judicial review pertaining to the actions of HMRC).

20.17 Reform of this labyrinthine system had been mooted for many years. In 2001, a consultation document was issued by the Lord Chancellor's Department (LCD). It was released as part of the consultation exercise that was undertaken to ensure that all government departments operated in a way that was compatible with individuals' rights under the European Convention of Human Rights.

20.18 In essence, the LCD proposed refinements to the existing system. The LCD paper proposed a move to a unified tax tribunal that would hear all tax appeals. The other significant issue that was addressed in the LCD paper was that of costs, and, in particular, the divergence of regimes between the Special Commissioners, the General Commissioners and the VAT and duties tribunals.

The Leggatt Inquiry

20.19 In contrast to the reforms suggested in the LCD paper, which were, in essence, refinements, rather than changes, to the existing system, in his report, Sir Andrew Leggatt proposed a revolutionary change: a single homogeneous system for all tribunals. Sir Andrew Leggatt was concerned that the tribunals, as they had developed in piecemeal fashion, were not cost-effective, and often appeared to lack independence:

> 'Because they are many and disparate, there is considerable waste of resources in managing them, and they achieve no economies of scale. Most importantly, they are not independent of the departments that sponsor them.'

20.20 It was stated in relation to the General Commissioners that:

> 'although now sponsored by the Lord Chancellor's Department, [they] are still wholly dependent on the Inland Revenue for case listing and for the flow of information to enable them to take decisions.'

20.21 It was proposed by Sir Andrew Leggatt that the existing 'system' of tribunals, where each tribunal had evolved its own rules and procedure as a solution to the particular requirements in its particular area of law, should be replaced by a single consistent procedure and structure for all tribunals. Thus, regardless of the area of law within which the particular tribunal operated, the same procedure would apply. The tax tribunals were expressly included within the proposed new system.

20.22 *Tax appeals*

20.22 As it pertained to tax, the proposed outline structure was as follows:

- a general tax tribunal (the general tax tribunal), with jurisdiction to hear the cases heard by the General Commissioners and straightforward VAT cases, such as those dealing with 'reasonable excuse';
- the second-tier tribunal (that would largely be a successor to the Special Commissioners and the VAT and duties tribunal) would hear appeals from the general tax tribunal and would be able to set precedent binding on the general tax tribunal;
- the second-tier tribunal would also hear, at first instance, the most complex appeals arising from decisions made by HMRC;
- appeals from the second-tier tribunals would go direct to the Court of Appeal;
- permission would be needed for an appeal from the general tax tribunal to the second-tier tribunal; and
- permission would be needed for an appeal from the second-tier tribunal to the Court of Appeal.

20.23 In July 2004, the government published its response to the Leggatt Report in a White Paper entitled 'Transforming Public Service: Complaints, Redress and Tribunals'. The key proposal that was set out in the White Paper was a unified tribunal service organisation. Most of the proposals of Sir Andrew Leggatt were accepted.

20.24 A further impetus to reform the system was the merger in April 2005 of the Inland Revenue and HM Customs and Excise and the creation of HMRC. Although each of HM Customs and Excise and the Inland Revenue had different functions, responsibilities and powers, these were transferred unchanged to the new body, and 'ring-fenced', so that they could be used only for their original purpose.

The consequence was that different rules and procedures applied across different taxes that were now administered by a single department.

The Tribunals, Courts and Enforcement Act 2007

20.25 *TCEA 2007* reflects the approach set out in the Leggatt Report. *TCEA 2007* is divided into eight parts. The principal reforms relating to tax appeals are contained in two parts:

- Part 1: Tribunals and Inquiries (*ss 1–49*).

    This created a new statutory framework for the tribunals, and brought the tribunal judiciary together under a senior president.

- Part 2: Judicial Appointments (*ss 50–61*).

  This revised the minimum eligibility requirements for appointment to judicial office, and enabled eligibility to be extended by order.

Summary of the tax tribunal system

20.26 A single UK-wide first-instance tribunal with the competence to hear every form of tax appeal and every tax-related application by either the taxpayer or HMRC with one set of procedural rules (including a notice of appeal that is common to all tax appeals) was introduced in April 2009. The Special Commissioners and chairmen of the VAT and duties tribunals transferred into the new tribunal system, with the majority transferring to the First-tier (where they are known as 'judges of the First-tier Tribunal').

The membership of both the FTT and the UT consists of legally qualified judges (tribunal judges) and of members with specialist expertise in tax matters (tribunal members) (see *TCEA 2007, Schs 2* and *3*).

20.27 The FTT is the first instance tribunal for most jurisdictions; the majority of appeals commence in this tier. The FTT is organised into specialist divisions or 'chambers'. Each chamber is headed by a chamber president and the tribunals' judiciary is headed by the Senior President of Tribunals, currently Sir Ernest Ryder (who is also a Court of Appeal judge). The chambers are intended to be flexible groupings, able to maintain and expand expertise and to incorporate new jurisdictions where most suitable.

20.28 There are five chambers in the FTT:

1 social entitlement;

2 general regulatory;

3 health, education and social care;

4 taxation; and

5 land, property and housing.

20.29 The UT is divided into three chambers:

(1) administrative appeals;

(2) tax and chancery; and

(3) land.

A system of 'ticketing' has been introduced within each chamber. The president can issue tickets to judges and members that identify their suitability to sit in a particular jurisdiction.

20.30 *Tax appeals*

20.30 Thus, for example, many Special Commissioners, who were also VAT and Duties Tribunal chairmen, were issued with indirect and direct tax tickets that enable them to hear both such appeals.

A procedure known as 'assignment' has also been introduced; this enables cross-chamber transfer (with the consent of the relevant president). Judges of the UT may sit in the FTT where the weight of the case justifies it.

20.31 In essence, the FTT replaced the General and Special Commissioners, the VAT and Duties tribunal, and the *s 706* tribunal, and the UT replaced the High Court as an appellate jurisdiction. Appeals from the FTT to the UT are possible only on points of law and with permission.

20.32 Whilst the role of the UT is primarily to hear appeals from the decisions of the FTT, it also hears some first-instance appeals in more complex tax cases and it may take over the judicial review function of the High Court in certain cases. For a case to be heard by the UT at first instance, the parties must consent to the transfer. The FTT refers the matter to the President of the Tax Chamber with a request that the case be considered by the UT. The agreement of the President of the Tax and Finance Chamber of the UT is also required.

HMRC does not perform any listing or case management procedures. That function is performed by the tax tribunals' administration.

20.33 There are two concepts that are likely to seem novel to many tax practitioners, but which are likely to be familiar to those who have experience of litigation before the civil courts, that were introduced to the tax tribunal system. These are the 'overriding objective' and alternative dispute resolution.

The overriding objective

20.34 Lord Woolf introduced the overriding objective that courts deal with cases 'justly' as a fundamental part of his reforms to civil court procedure. Rule 1 of the Civil Procedure Rules 1998 (CPR) provides that 'these Rules are a new procedural code with the overriding objective of enabling the court to deal with cases justly'.

20.35 Dealing with a case justly includes, so far as is practicable:

1 ensuring that the parties are on an equal footing;

2 saving expense;

3   dealing with the case in ways which are proportionate –

   (a)   to the amount of money involved,

   (b)   to the importance of the case,

   (c)   to the complexity of the issues, and

   (d)   to the financial position of each party;

4   ensuring that it is dealt with expeditiously and fairly; and

5   allotting to it an appropriate share of the court's resources, while taking into account the need to allot resources to other cases.

20.36 The First-tier Rules, r 2 and the Upper Tribunal Rules, r 2 introduce a similar concept to the tax tribunal system; they provide that the overriding objective of the Rules is to enable the tribunal to 'deal with cases fairly and justly'. Rule 2(2) states that:

'Dealing with a case fairly and justly includes –

(a)   dealing with the case in ways which are proportionate to the importance of the case, the complexity of the issues, the anticipated costs and the resources of the parties;

(b)   avoiding unnecessary formality and seeking flexibility in the proceedings;

(c)   ensuring, so far as practicable, that the parties are able to participate fully in the proceedings;

(d)   using any special expertise of the Tribunal effectively; and

(e)   avoiding delay, so far as compatible with proper consideration of the issues.'

20.37 There are some important differences between the CPR's overriding obligation and the tax tribunal's version. For example, the obligation in the CPR that the courts seek to ensure that the parties are 'on an equal footing' is not included in the tax tribunal's version of the overriding objective. This obligation has been interpreted in the civil courts as referring to equal financial footing and has been used by the courts to allow parties that are in a weaker financial position than their opponents to be given, for example, additional time to comply with deadlines.

20.38 Given that, in tax matters, the taxpayer's 'opponent' will invariably be the State, and so the parties to a tax case will never be on an equal footing, this obligation would have been difficult to impose in a reasonable or meaningful sense.

20.39 *Tax appeals*

Also, there is no equivalent provision to that found in CPR r 3.9 in the tax tribunals' rules. Rule 3.9, CPR provides:

'(1) On an application for relief from any sanction imposed for a failure to comply with any rule, practice direction or court order, the court will consider all the circumstances of the case, so as to enable it to deal justly with the application, including the need—(a) for litigation to be conducted efficiently and at proportionate cost; and (b) to enforce compliance with rules, practice directions and orders. ...'

This is relevant to applications made under r 8 of the First-tier Rules (the provision that provides for the striking out of a party's case of the barring of HMRC from taking further part in the proceedings); and is addressed at **20.168** below.

Rule 2(4) imposes on the parties an obligation to help the tribunal to further the overriding objective and an obligation to co-operate with the tribunal generally.

Alternative Dispute Resolution

20.39 The First-tier Rules, r 3 and the Upper Tribunal Rules, r 3 impose an obligation on the respective tribunals to bring the availability of any appropriate alternative procedure for the resolution of the dispute to the attention of the parties.

20.40 In 2011, HMRC began examining whether the involvement of a mediator might be used in some tax disputes to facilitate agreement. Two separate ADR pilot studies aimed at clarifying the criteria for when mediation might be most appropriate for resolving tax disputes were commenced. The first was a small-scale pilot study involving large businesses or taxpayers with complex tax affairs. Third-party accredited mediators were used. In phase one of the pilot study (which concluded on 31 March 2012), about 65% of the applications were rejected. The acceptance criteria were changed for phase two, and applications from HMRC were also accepted. The overall rejection rate dropped to 32%.

One of the findings from the pilot study was that a dispute is less likely to be resolved through ADR if the tribunal hearing is imminent.

20.41 The second pilot study involved around 150 mainly small and medium-sized enterprises. A number of 'disputes' were resolved in this way. However, the approach differed from standard mediation, as the facilitator was an HMRC officer. Also, the approach was applied only in respect of disputes that were at the stage before the enquiry had been closed (ie before the matter falls within the jurisdiction of the tribunal). On 4 February 2013, HMRC announced that, following the pilot study, ADR for SMEs and individuals would become part of its 'business as usual' approach.

In addition, HMRC recently has also indicated a willingness to consider 'collaborative dispute resolution' or 'facilitated dispute resolution' in relation to the large corporate sector.

20.42 Given that HMRC has, in recent times, adopted a far more aggressive stance towards tax disputes, and, in particular, has a compliance goal of changing what it considers is unacceptable behaviour in relation to taxation, it is considered that the extent to which ADR can be used to resolve tax disputes is limited.

20.43 ADR is likely to be of most use in cases where, as described in LSS, there is 'a range of plausible figures for tax due', ie where there is a dispute over facts or valuation. In HMRC's published *Guidance on Mediation*, the interaction between mediation and the LSS is described as follows:

> 'Any decision by HMRC to settle a case during a mediation process will still be governed by the terms of the LSS, and any settlement/agreement reached as a result of mediation will be subject to exactly the same governance and decision making process as any other case.
>
> One of the fundamental principles of the LSS is that settlement of the full tax due is to be sought wherever possible. Another is that disputes should be resolved in the most efficient and cost-effective method possible. In this way, mediation, where it is used, is supportive of LSS principles as a cost effective way of trying to reach agreement and to provide a process which allows for a better shared understanding of each other's arguments/contentions regarding what is the "right tax" to enable HMRC and the customer to make a more informed decision.'

20.44 Paragraph 18 of the LSS provides that, in relation to disputes that are, according to HMRC 'genuinely of an all or nothing nature':

> 'Where HMRC believes that it is likely to succeed in litigation and that litigation would be both effective and efficient, it will not reach an out of court settlement for less than 100% of the tax, interest and penalties (where appropriate) at stake. It therefore follows that, if the customer is unwilling to concede in such cases, HMRC will seek to resolve the dispute by litigation as quickly and efficiently as possible.'

20.45 This paragraph reinforces the concept that disputes that turn on points of law (which is a significant proportion of tax disputes) are unlikely to be suitable for resolution via mediation. The obligation on HMRC to consider the impact of an issue on other taxpayers and the constraints of LSS mean that

20.46 *Tax appeals*

HMRC will not often be in a sufficiently flexible position to resolve a dispute via ADR. For more detailed commentary on ADR, see **CHAPTER 12**.

PRE-APPEAL PROCEDURES

Introduction

20.46 Whilst the tribunal procedure, after an appeal has been notified to the FTT, is now, broadly, the same across all the taxes, the procedures before appeals are made against HMRC decisions remain the same as they were before 1 April 2009 and there are different 'pre-appeal' procedures for direct and indirect tax matters.

The fundamentally different ways in which direct and indirect tax disputes were dealt with before 1 April 2009 have, in this way, been perpetuated post April 2009.

Starting an appeal: direct taxes

20.47 Following the introduction of self-assessment for both individuals and corporations, most assessments are made either by the taxpayer or by an HMRC officer on his behalf, based on the information in the taxpayer's tax return. There is no right of appeal against such assessments.

20.48 Instead, under *TMA 1970, s 31(1)*, there is a right of appeal against:

- an amendment to a self-assessment by an HMRC officer during an enquiry in order to prevent loss;
- any conclusion stated or amendment made by a closure notice under *ss 28A* or *28B* following completion of a formal enquiry;
- any amendment of a partnership return under *s 30B(1)*; or
- any assessment to tax which is not a self-assessment.

20.49 Similar provisions exist in relation to other direct tax matters (*FA 1998, Sch 18, para 48* for appeals relating to company tax matters and *FA 2003, Sch 10, para 35* for appeals relating to stamp duty land tax assessments). Appeals must be made within 30 days of the relevant date under the statute (broadly the date that the decision, be it an assessment or closure notice, was issued).

20.50 The appeal must be made in writing to HMRC. Notwithstanding the fundamental changes to the procedures for appeals with effect from

Tax appeals **20.56**

1 April 2009, which changes emphasise that notification of an appeal to the FTT is the taxpayer's role, not HMRC's, this requirement remains. However, after appealing to HMRC, the taxpayer may then immediately notify that appeal to the FTT (under *TMA 1970, s 49D(2)*).

Self-assessment closure procedure

20.51 Under *TMA 1970, s 28A* (personal self-assessment) and *FA 1998, Sch 18, para 32* (corporate self-assessment), an enquiry is completed when, by closure notice, the HMRC officer informs the taxpayer that he has completed his enquiries and states his conclusions.

20.52 The closure notice must either state that no amendment of the return is required, or make the amendments of the return that the officer considers are necessary to give effect to his conclusions. The taxpayer may then appeal against any conclusion stated or any amendments of the return.

Closure notice applications

20.53 HMRC not only has very wide powers during the enquiry stage, but also considerable scope for prolonging this stage. This is significant for taxpayers, as, in general, they can appeal only after the enquiry has been completed.

20.54 However, valuable protection is provided to the taxpayer against HMRC by *TMA 1970, ss 28A(4)* and *28B(5)* and *FA 1998, Sch 18, para 33* (in relation to personal, partnership and company returns respectively), which enable the taxpayer to apply to the FTT, during the enquiry, for a direction that the enquiry should be closed. The burden of proof is then on HMRC to show that there are 'reasonable grounds' for not closing the enquiry.

20.55 As the Special Commissioner noted in *Jade Palace v Revenue and Customs Comrs* [2006] STC (SCD) 419:

> 'the issue on [a closure notice] application is not simply whether a closure notice should be directed, but whether it should be directed within a specified period. The reasonable grounds must cover the setting of a period.'

This procedural rule is intended to protect taxpayers against protracted and unfocused enquiries and to enable taxpayers to take control of a dispute with HMRC.

20.56 In *Eclipse Film Partners No 35 LLP v Revenue and Customs Comrs* [2009] STC (SCD) 293, the Special Commissioner noted that

20.57 *Tax appeals*

s 28B (and the corresponding provisions relating to companies discussed in *Revenue and Customs Comrs v Vodafone 2* [2005] EWHC 3040 (Ch)) are:

> "'constructed so as to produce a reasonable balance" between the taxpayer's "legitimate concern that the enquiry is concluded as soon as it is reasonable so to expect, so that he has the certainty of knowing either that his return is accepted unamended, or that he may appeal so as to determine any matter of dispute identified in the closure notice" and HMRC's caution as to "when their enquiries may be regarded as sufficiently complete to enable them to issue a closure notice"'.

The Special Commissioner concluded that:

> 'it is implicit in the powers given to the General or Special Commissioners to give a direction requiring the issue of a closure notice, and is part of that "reasonable balance", that a closure notice can be required notwithstanding that the officer has not pursued to the end every line of enquiry or investigation – what is required is that he should have conducted his enquiry to a point where it is reasonable for him to make an informed judgment as to the matter in question, so that, exercising such judgment, he can state his conclusions and make any related amendments to the taxpayer's return. The exercise of that judgment may require the officer to express his conclusions in broad terms, or even express alternative conclusions (see the observations made in the case of *D'Arcy v HMRC* [2006] UKSPC 549 at [12]) – which should at the practical level allow an officer of the Commissioners to avoid the pitfalls identified in the *Tower MCashback* case of a closure notice too restrictively drafted in its conclusions.'

The purpose of a closure notice

20.57 *Section 31(1)(b)* provides that an appeal may be brought against 'any conclusion stated or amendment made by a closure notice'. The legislation thus distinguishes between 'a conclusion stated' and 'an amendment required to give effect to the conclusion'. The ambit of any appeal is delimited by reference to the conclusion stated and/or amendment made to the return.

20.58 In the closure notice, the inspector's conclusions can be stated in the alternative (see *D'Arcy v Revenue and Customs Comrs* [2006] STC (SCD) 543 at [12]) and there is no obligation on the inspector to give reasons for them (see *Tower MCashback v Revenue and Customs Comrs* [2011] UKSC 19). What matters for the purpose of *TMA 1970* is the conclusions, not the process of reasoning by which the conclusions are reached.

Tower MCashback v HM Revenue and Customs Commrs

20.59 The role of the closure notice in the context of a subsequent appeal was considered by the Special Commissioner, High Court, Court of Appeal and Supreme Court in *Tower MCashback v Revenue and Customs Comrs* [2011] UKSC 19.

20.60 As both the High Court and Court of Appeal undertook a detailed analysis of the self-assessment provisions, but reached a different view, and, in contrast, the Supreme Court adopted a 'broad-brush' approach (by way of contrast, the Court of Appeal's decision comprises 103 paragraphs, 68 of which pertain to the closure notice issue; only 17 paragraphs of the Supreme Court's 94 paragraph decision concern the issue), the approach taken at each stage is summarised below.

Background facts

20.61 The Tower MCashback LLPs (the LLPs) claimed first-year allowances (FYAs) in respect of certain software licences under *CAA 2001, s 45*. HMRC opened enquiries and formed the view that the structure failed in its object of generating 100% FYAs under *s 45(4)*, which disqualified expenditure from being first-year qualifying expenditure if the person potentially entitled to FYAs incurred the expenditure 'with a view to granting another person a right to use or otherwise deal with' any of the software in question.

20.62 After various exchanges of correspondence between the LLPs and HMRC, the LLPs indicated that they intended to apply for a direction from the Special Commissioners that the enquiries be closed. The officer issued closure notices in which he stated that, 'as previously indicated', his conclusion was that the claim under s 45 was excessive and that the return had been amended as follows: 'Capital Allowances £nil; Allowable loss £nil.' In his covering letter, the officer stated: 'I am satisfied that [the structure] fails on the [CAA 2001 s 45(4)] point alone.' The officer also said that he had not been able to review all of the papers that had been provided to him, but 'in the circumstances, I have to accept that any additional points that may arise will make no difference to the bottom line that no loss relief is due because of s 45(4)'.

20.63 A few weeks before the Special Commissioner's hearing, HMRC raised two new points (the 'expenditure issue' (the LLPs had not 'incurred' the full expenditure, but only an equivalent amount to the capital contribution) and the 'trading issue' (whether LLP1 had begun to trade on or before 5 April 2004). During the hearing itself, HMRC abandoned its initial contention (*s 45(4)*), leaving only the new points (and a further point that was raised by the Special Commissioner during the hearing) as the subject

20.64 *Tax appeals*

matter of the appeal. The LLPs argued that the *s 45(4)* argument was the only issue that could be raised in the appeal: the Special Commissioner had no jurisdiction to hear legal arguments on the wider question as to whether the other requirements of *s 45* had been satisfied, because then the appeal would no longer be an appeal against the conclusion stated in the closure notice.

Decision of the Special Commissioner

20.64 The Special Commissioner rejected the LLPs' argument. He said that each closure notice denied the allowances under the section under which they were claimed; it was only the covering letter that had referred to a particular sub-section.

20.65 However, even if the closure notice had referred just to *s 45(4)*, he still would have held that HMRC could have raised arguments on appeal other than those in the closure notice. The factual compass of the matter and the subject of the closure notice was the purchase of the software and all related transactions, not just whether a third party had obtained licence rights. HMRC could raise any arguments in support of its conclusions and adjustments related to those transactions.

High Court

20.66 Henderson J reversed the decision of the Special Commissioner. He undertook a detailed review of the relevant statutory provisions (*TMA 1970, ss 28B, 31(1)(b)* and *50*) and reached the following three conclusions:

(i) the duty of the tribunal is not to evaluate HMRC's reasons for its conclusion, but to consider whether the amounts contained in the return are excessive or insufficient and to reduce or increase the amounts accordingly; and

(ii) thus, the tribunal is free to entertain legal arguments that played no part in reaching the conclusions set out in the closure notice; but

(iii) the scope and subject matter of the appeal are defined by the conclusions that are set out in the closure notice.

20.67 Henderson J treated the covering letter from the officer as a 'conscious decision to pin his colours to the mast of s 45(4)'. Once he had done so, it was too late for HMRC to go back on that decision and seek to widen the ambit of the appeals (issue of a closure notice being an irrevocable step).

20.68 The significance of HMRC relying on *s 45(4)* was that this approach carried with it an implicit acceptance that the LLPs qualified for relief, but

Tax appeals **20.72**

were then disqualified for relief because of a perceived licence to a third party. Accordingly, HMRC's approach only put a particular element of the structure (perceived third-party licensing arrangements) at issue, rather than the entire structure.

The Court of Appeal

20.69 The Court of Appeal (Arden LJ dissenting on this issue) held that the Special Commissioners had jurisdiction to hear any legal argument relevant to the subject matter of the conclusions stated in a closure notice. To a large extent, there is little difference between the majority of the Court of Appeal and Henderson J as to the principles to be applied. The difference, and the reason for allowing HMRC's appeal was by the application of those principles. The Court of Appeal (Moses and Scott Baker LJJ) held that the question as to the subject matter of the appeal was one of fact for the Special Commissioner, and he had correctly identified the conclusions; and that the conclusion stated in the closure notices was, in plain terms, a refusal of relief under *s 45*.

20.70 They went on to say that *s 45(4)* was the reason for the officer issuing the closure notice, but it was not the conclusion stated in the notice (which was that the *s 45* claim was excessive). The Court of Appeal also emphasised that the tribunal may entertain any evidence or legal argument relevant to the subject matter of the enquiry, subject to its obligation to ensure a fair hearing.

The Supreme Court

20.71 The Supreme Court dismissed the LLPs' appeal on the procedural issue.

It held that it preferred the approach of Moses LJ to that of Henderson J as regards the application of the principles (on which principles there was broad agreement). Lord Hope added the comment that, although the scope and subject matter of the appeal was defined by the conclusions in the closure notice, *TMA 1970, s 50* meant that the tribunal was not tied to the precise wording of the closure notice when hearing the appeal.

Application of *Tower MCashback*

20.72 Part of the reason as to why answering what may seem to be a straightforward question (what is the ambit of a tax appeal?) was so difficult and why it has also arisen in a number of other cases (such as

20.73 *Tax appeals*

D'Arcy v Revenue and Customs Comrs [2006] STC (SCD) 543 and *Bayfine v Revenue and Customs Comrs* [2009] STC (SCD) 43) is the issue identified by Special Commissioner Avery-Jones in *D'Arcy*: there is a tension between the rules that set out the powers of the tribunal on the hearing of an appeal (particularly *TMA 1970, s 50*) and the procedure for assessing taxpayers' liability to tax under self-assessment. This tension has not been resolved by the introduction of the new tribunal system.

20.73 Under self-assessment, the taxpayer is under a statutory duty to set out his correct tax liability in his return. This new burden has been balanced by new protections. The self-assessment return constitutes the final determination of liability unless HMRC amends the return in accordance with a closure notice under *TMA 1970, s 28A* or makes a discovery assessment (under a far more restricted power than existed previously).

20.74 The closure notice comes at the end of the enquiry process, during which time HMRC may use its considerable information gathering powers. In broad terms, these powers cease on completion of the enquiry (*FA 2008, Sch 36, para 21*), and the intended finality of the closure notice is reinforced by the release of the taxpayer from his record-keeping obligations (under *TMA 1970, s 12B*). The taxpayer's right of appeal is confined to an appeal against the conclusions reached or amendments made in the closure notice (under *TMA 1970, s 31(1)(b)*). This limits the ambit of the appeal to the subject matter of the conclusions stated in the closure notice.

20.75 Under the tribunal system, the taxpayer's notice of appeal must include the grounds for making the appeal; and the statutory provision that enabled the taxpayer to put forward grounds not specified in the notice of appeal has been repealed. Yet, *s 50* remains in force in similar wording to the wording that applied under the old assessment regime. Moreover, it is in broadly similar terms to the equivalent wording that was in place when the tribunal also had an assessing function (this function was ended in 1965). Accordingly, it is not the case that the closure notice fixes the maximum amount of tax payable. It is inherent in *s 50* that the tribunal may take the initiative and apply the law to the facts in a manner that appears to it to be correct, regardless of the arguments advanced by the parties.

20.76 The decision of the Supreme Court is to be welcomed in one particular regard. After the decision of the High Court had been released, HMRC adopted a defensive position in relation to the closing of enquiries. First, it would resist issuing closure notices, even when it seemed clear what its conclusion was, on the basis that investigations must be undertaken to ensure that every question, however tangential to the issues, was answered before closure. Secondly, when forced to close enquiries, often this would be undertaken either by simply amending returns without providing any reasons or by expressing the closure notices in such broad terms that the questions in issue were left completely open-ended.

20.77 The Supreme Court emphasised that this second element of HMRC's approach should not be adopted. The issuing of the closure notice in bald and uninformative terms was criticised. In issuing closure notices, HMRC officers' aim should be that of being helpful, both to the taxpayer and to the tribunal and they should, wherever possible, set out the conclusions that they have reached on each point that was the subject of enquiry that has resulted in their making an amendment to the return. As regards the first element, because the Supreme Court has confirmed that the tribunals are not limited by the precise wording of a closure notice when hearing an appeal, it will be harder for HMRC to contend that there are reasonable grounds for keeping the enquiry open, because the officer has not pursued to the end every line of enquiry or investigation. Accordingly, it should now be easier to obtain closure notices than the period when the decision of the High Court in *Tower MCashback* applied.

Examples of where the *Tower MCashback* analysis has been considered and applied include:

- *B & K Lavery Property Trading Partnership* [2015] UKFTT 470. Here, it led to the First-tier Tribunal concluding that there was no basis for striking out HMRC's case under Rule 8(2)(a) of the Tribunal Procedure (First-tier Tribunal) (Tax Chamber) Rules 2009 and holding, instead, that HMRC should be allowed to amend their statement of case.

- *Fidex v HMRC* [2016] EWCA Civ 385. The Court of Appeal held that the scope of the appeal was defined by the conclusions stated in the closure notice but that HMRC was not restricted to the process of reasoning by which it had reached those conclusions; it was free to deploy new arguments in support of them.

- *BNP Paribas SA (London Branch) v Revenue and Customs Commissioners* [2017] UKFTT 487 (TC). The FTT held that the appeal's scope was to be determined essentially by the subject matter of the conclusions and amendments set out in the closure notice, and allowed HMRC to raise an argument based on the context of the issuance of the closure notice.

- *Towers Watson Limited v HMRC* [2017] UKFTT 846. The conclusion stated in the closure notice was that charging a full year's amortisation in the year of acquisition did not comply with generally accepted accounting principles ('GAAP'). HMRC sought to extend the appeal to encompass the question of whether the valuation of the goodwill, upon which the amortisation was carried out, was in accordance with GAAP. The FTT refused, holding that a reasonable recipient

20.78 *Tax appeals*

of the closure notice would not have understood it to encompass a challenge to the valuation of the goodwill.

Referral of questions during enquiry

20.78 *FA 2001* inserted a new Part IIIA ('Referral of questions during enquiry') into *TMA 1970*. Sections *28ZA–28ZE* set out a procedure for personal self-assessment that enables questions relating to the subject matter of an enquiry to be referred to the Tax Tribunal whilst the enquiry is still in progress. A similar procedure of referral was also introduced with regard to corporation tax self-assessment (see *FA 1998, Sch 18, paras 31A–31D*).

20.79 Referral can be made only jointly by the taxpayer and HMRC. Whilst proceedings on a referral are in progress in relation to an enquiry and until the matter referred is finally determined, no closure notice will be issued, nor can an application for a direction to give such a notice be made. A question is not finally determined whilst there remains a possibility of a determination by the tribunal being set aside (eg by appeal on a point of law).

20.80 The determination is binding on both parties, subject to any further appeal rights, in the same way as a decision on a preliminary issue in an appeal. HMRC must take the determination into account in reaching its conclusions on the enquiry and in formulating amendments to the return. The referred point cannot be reopened on an appeal against HMRC's conclusions at the end of the enquiry.

The circumstances when a referral of questions may be sought have been reduced by the introduction of the partial closure notice procedure by *FA 2017*.

Partial Closure Notices

20.81 *Finance Act 2017* amended *TMA, ss 28A and 28B* (including by introducing ss 28A and 28B(1A)), and *FA 1998, Sch 18, paras 32 and 33*, with effect from 16 November 2017.

This procedure enables HMRC and taxpayers to resolve a specific matter (or matters) during an enquiry into an income tax or corporation tax self-assessment return where more than one issue is open.

HMRC have said that they will issue partial closure notices only in enquiries where:

(a)   a taxpayer's tax affairs are complex;

(b) there is avoidance; or

(c) large amounts of tax are at risk.

The taxpayer may, at any time during the course of an enquiry ask the tribunal to direct HMRC to issue a partial closure notice within a specified period (under *TMA, s 28B(5)*). It is considered that the approach that the tribunal will take to such applications will be analogous to its approach to final closure notices.

Where HMRC issue a partial closure notice and amend a person's tax return, the taxpayer has a right to appeal and can ask for payment of the tax to be postponed.

STARTING AN APPEAL: INDIRECT TAXES

20.82 HMRC conducts various checks to ensure that the correct amount of tax has been reported and paid. If HMRC considers that insufficient tax has been paid, then it has the power to issue a decision on a number of aspects of a taxpayer's affairs, including, for example:

(i) whether a taxpayer should be registered for VAT purposes; or

(ii) the amount of input tax credited to a person.

20.83 A taxpayer can appeal against decisions made by HMRC to the extent that the decision comes within the statutory jurisdiction of the tax tribunals.

For example, in relation to VAT, an appeal will lie to the tax tribunal for any matters listed in *Value Added Tax Act 1994* (*VATA 1994*), *s 83* and for matters relating to landfill tax, *FA 1996, s 54* lists those that are appealable.

20.84 There is no equivalent to a closure notice application in indirect tax. If HMRC does not issue an appealable decision, then the taxpayer's remedy is to issue an application for judicial review. This is a route that was followed in a number of cases concerning HMRC's application of its policy of 'extended verification' in MTIC fraud cases (the exercise of tracing the taxpayer's purchases of goods back through the chain of supply to establish whether, and if so in what circumstances, the chain included a fraudulent loss of VAT).

20.85 For example, in *Livewire Telecom Ltd* (VTD 20533), the company, after seven months of extended verification by HMRC, brought judicial review proceedings. These were concluded by HMRC issuing a decision to deny recovery of input tax two days prior to the hearing of the application for judicial review.

20.86 *Tax appeals*

20.86 There are no provisions in the VAT legislation that specify who may appeal to the tribunal (*VATA, s 83* states simply that an appeal 'shall be to the tribunal'). *Williams & Glyn's Bank v Customs and Excise Comrs* [1974] VATTR 262 established that a taxable person who was the recipient of a supply has a right to appeal if he has sufficient legal interest in the outcome of the appeal. As at the date of writing, *Jolyon Maugham QC v HMRC* was to be heard by the FTT. The matter concerns the tax treatment of a supply of Uber minicab services made to the taxpayer; he has asserted that the FTT has jurisdiction (under *VATA, s 83*) to hear the appeal.

THE REVIEW PROCEDURE

Introduction

20.87 The review procedure applies before any notification of an appeal to the FTT. A review is carried out by an HMRC case officer who has no connection to the decision under review. The outcome of a review will be that the decision is upheld, varied or cancelled. Use of the review process is voluntary. The aim of the review process is to provide an inexpensive means of resolving disputes without the need for a hearing. The statistics released by the government with regard to the first five years of the review system (2009/10 to 2013/14) demonstrate the following:

- The average number of review requests made each year was 41,610.

- The vast majority of reviews pertained to penalties (for example, in 2012/13 there were 39,156 reviews, of which only 5,932 were non penalty cases).

- Approximately one-third of reviews in non-penalty cases resulted in the original decision being cancelled or varied.

- Approximately 60% of reviews in VAT penalty cases resulted in the original decision being cancelled or varied (this stems from HMRC accepting, on review, in a significant percentage of cases explanations that have been provided for late returns or payments).

- Approximately 40% of reviews in other penalty cases resulted in the original decision being cancelled or varied.

- The majority of taxpayers (approximately 85%) were not represented at the review stage.

20.88 There are certain differences between the review procedure for direct and indirect tax matters. In particular, in indirect tax matters only, the review process is not part of an appeal, but precedes it. Any indirect tax decision that is subject to a review remains enforceable. Its effect is put in abeyance whilst the review is being conducted. The indirect tax procedures are addressed first.

Indirect taxes

20.89 Prior to 1 April 2009, there was a semi-formal procedure under which HMRC encouraged taxpayers, who disagreed with decisions of HMRC, to seek a reconsideration by their local VAT office, before commencing an appeal. This local reconsideration procedure did not form part of the appeals procedure.

20.90 Whilst there was, initially, some doubt as to whether or not this procedure had been replaced by the new statutory review process, in Revenue and Customs Brief 10/09 it was stated: 'This new legal right to a review will replace reconsiderations ... in indirect taxes'. Taxpayers may still, however, make informal representations to HMRC.

20.91 At the time of notifying an appealable decision to a taxpayer, HMRC must also offer the taxpayer a review of that decision. The taxpayer has 30 days within which to accept the offer; and, if the offer is accepted, HMRC must conduct a review unless there has already been an appeal made to the tax tribunal against the decision (*VATA 1994, s 83C*). A request for a review can be made out of time (under *VATA 1994, s 83E*), but HMRC is required to conduct a review only if it is satisfied that the person requesting the review had a reasonable excuse for not accepting the offer and that the request was made without unreasonable delay after the reasonable excuse had ceased to apply.

20.92 Any person other than the recipient of the decision who has a right to appeal against the decision (see above) can also request a review, provided that this is done within 30 days of the date when that person became aware of the decision.

20.93 The taxpayer can choose not to accept the offer of a review and to appeal the decision by HMRC to the tax tribunal (by lodging a notice of appeal). If the taxpayer chooses not to accept the offer of a review the notice of appeal must be lodged within 30 days of the date of the document notifying the decision to which the appeal relates.

Direct taxes

20.94 After a taxpayer has notified HMRC of his decision to appeal, he has three options:

- to request that HMRC review its decision;

20.95 *Tax appeals*

- to respond to any offer from HMRC to review its decision; or
- to bypass the review procedure by notifying the tax tribunal of the appeal.

20.95 There is no time limit on HMRC to offer a review. HMRC's internal guidance provides:

> 'If the appeal can not be settled by agreement, and at a time the decision maker considers is appropriate, the decision maker will write to the customer to give and explain HMRC's view of the matter and offer a review.'

(Tribunals Reform Review Officer Guided Learning Unit (GLU), para 2.1.3).

20.96 The offer of a review by HMRC must be accompanied by a 'notification of HMRC's view of the matter in question' (*TMA 1970, s 49C(2)*). If the taxpayer requires a review, this notification must be sent to the taxpayer within 30 days of the request (*s 49B(2)*). Accordingly, if a review is requested or offered, the decision first must be considered by the officer who made it. The officer's 'view of the matter in question' may remain the same as when the appeal was made (and, as a general rule, it tends to). The matter is then referred to a specialist review team.

20.97 If HMRC offers a review, the taxpayer has 30 days to accept the offer, unless HMRC extends the time period. HMRC must review a decision out of time where it is satisfied that the taxpayer had a reasonable excuse for not accepting the offer for a review in time and the request was made thereafter without unreasonable delay. A taxpayer need not accept the offer of a review, and may not accept the offer if an appeal against the decision has already been lodged at the tax tribunal.

20.98 If the taxpayer neither accepts the offer of a review nor notifies the appeal to the tax tribunal within 30 days after having been offered a review then the decision is deemed to be upheld and is treated as a settled appeal (*TMA 1970, s 49C(4)*).

As stated above, the taxpayer has the option of notifying the tax tribunal of the appeal, rather than having a review undertaken. This starts the appeal process before the tribunal.

20.99 If the taxpayer proceeds to a review, then it is not be possible to notify the tax tribunal of the appeal until after the review has been concluded. If the taxpayer disagrees with HMRC's post-review decision, then it is the taxpayer's responsibility to notify the tax tribunal of the appeal within 30 days. Failure to do so means that HMRC's original decision stands.

Tax appeals **20.103**

20.100 *TMA 1970, ss 49A–49I* specify the rules as to when the taxpayer may notify the tax tribunal of its appeal, namely:

- at any time after an appeal has been notified to HMRC, provided that –

    – a review has neither been requested nor an offer of a review accepted, or

    – the appeal is one to which the review process does not apply (*s 49A*);

- within 30 days of the conclusion of a review (*s 49G(5)(a)*);

- within 30 days of the end of the period when HMRC should have given notice of its review conclusion but has failed to do so (*s 49G(5)(b)*); or

- if HMRC offers to conduct a review, but the taxpayer has not accepted, within 30 days from the date that HMRC notified the taxpayer of the offer to review the matter (*s 49H*).

The review process for all taxes

20.101 HMRC determines the nature and extent of the review as appears appropriate, having regard to the steps taken by HMRC to reach the decision and it should take account of representations made by the taxpayer. The review is carried out by specially trained staff, who are not only independent of the officer responsible for the case, but also outside his management chain. HMRC has confirmed that the review is a genuine 'second look' at the case. However, it is stated in HMRC Manual ARTG4080 that it is not the purpose of the review 'to assess new facts or evidence.'

20.102 HMRC is required to 'take account of any representations made by the appellant at a stage which gives HMRC a reasonable opportunity to consider them' (*TMA 1970, s 49E; VATA 1994, s 83F(4)*). If the review process is followed, it is generally advisable to make representations, and to agree a suitable timetable with the review officer.

20.103 The role of the reviewing officer is to 'review the basis of the decision made by the decision maker', rather than 'carry out the case work as such' (GLU, paras 3.1.3 and 3.17). In this regard, the internal guidance to review officers provides also that if the decision 'was subject to extensive internal checking, perhaps including two or more layers of informal review separate from the decision maker, and/or requiring input from specialist technical advisers or counsel, the review officer is not expected to challenge the technical advice unless there is reason to do so' (GLU, para 3.1.4).

20.104 *Tax appeals*

20.104 HMRC must notify the taxpayer of the conclusions of the review within 45 days of the 'relevant day'. This is either:

Direct taxes

(i) where the taxpayer requested the review, the date that the initial officer notified the taxpayer of his view of the matter; or

(ii) where HMRC offered the review, when HMRC received notification from the taxpayer that the offer of a review was accepted.

Indirect taxes

(i) the date when HMRC received the taxpayer's acceptance of the offer of a review;

(ii) the date when HMRC received a third party's notification requiring a review; or

(iii) the date when HMRC decided to conduct a review out of time.

20.105 Where HMRC is required to undertake a review, but it does not give notice of its conclusion within the relevant period, then the review is to be treated as having concluded that the decision is upheld. Although HMRC is required to notify the taxpayer of this conclusion that the review is treated as having reached, there is no applicable time limit for provision of this notification of the deemed conclusion.

Appealing to the tax tribunal after the review process

Direct taxes

20.106 The taxpayer's immediate right to notify his appeal to the tax tribunal is suspended during the review process. Once the review has been concluded, or has been deemed to have been concluded, the taxpayer may notify the appeal to the tax tribunal (if he does not accept the result or deemed result). An appeal must be notified within 30 days of the date of the document notifying the conclusions of the review. HMRC has no power to extend this time limit; the taxpayer who wishes to notify an appeal to the tax tribunal outside this period must obtain permission from the tax tribunal (under *TMA 1970, s 49G(3)*).

20.107 If HMRC has not given notice of its conclusion within the relevant period, the view of the original officer is deemed to have been upheld, and so the taxpayer may notify the appeal to the tax tribunal at any time after the date that the review should have been completed. The 30-day time limit for notifying the tax tribunal only commences by reference to the date of the document notifying the conclusions of the review. Accordingly, if HMRC does not give notice of the conclusions of the review, then there is no applicable time limit by which the taxpayer must notify the appeal to the tax tribunal.

Indirect taxes

20.108 The taxpayer appeals the decision by HMRC by lodging a notice of appeal at the tribunal. If a review has been requested and the taxpayer has received notice of the review conclusion, the time limit for appealing is within 30 days of receiving the conclusion of the review.

20.109 If a review has been requested, but HMRC has not notified the taxpayer of its conclusions within the 45-day time limit, then the decision is deemed (under *VATA 1994, s 83F(8)*) to be upheld. Accordingly, the taxpayer may appeal to the tribunal at any time after the date that the review should have been completed. HMRC is required to notify the taxpayer of the deemed review conclusion (under *VATA 1994, s 83F(9)*). The 30-day time period within which to appeal commences from the date of this notification.

Application for postponement of tax

20.110 The default position in relation to both direct and indirect taxes is that the disputed tax must be paid, irrespective of the appeal. Accordingly, either HMRC or the tax tribunal must agree that the tax need not be paid to ensure that it is postponed pending the outcome of the appeal.

The criteria, and procedures, for obtaining postponement are different in respect of direct and indirect tax appeals.

Indirect tax appeals

20.111 *VATA 1994, s 84(3)* requires all the disputed tax to be paid or deposited. It does not matter whether the assessment is in relation to input or output tax (see *Safegold Fashions Ltd v Customs & Excise Commissioners* [1992] VATTR 105.

VATA 1994, 84(3B) provides that the appeal can proceed without payment of the tax if that would cause the appellant to suffer hardship. There is a two-stage process in making a hardship application. First, an application must be made to HMRC. If HMRC refuses the application, then to obtain postponement it is necessary to apply to the tax tribunal.

The factors, other than just the financial consequences for the appellant, that the tribunal will consider in determining whether there is financial hardship

20.111 *Tax appeals*

were considered by the VAT & Duties Tribunal in *Peter and Linda Kemp v Customs and Excise Comrs* (VTD 19479) to be:

(i) the public interest, particularly as regards ensuring that there was no unfairness as regards appellants who paid VAT and those who did not; and

(ii) whether or not HMRC would receive the VAT then payable if it succeeded with the appeal.

In *Elbrook Cash & Carry Ltd v The Commissioners for Her Majesty's Revenue & Customs* [2016] UKFTT 0191, the FTT considered *Kemp* and 5 other cases:

1   *R (on the application of ToTel Ltd) v First-tier Tribunal (Tax Chamber)* [2011] EWHC 652 (Admin) (*'ToTel 1'*).

2   *ToTel Ltd v HMRC* [2014] UKUT 485 (TCC) (*'ToTel 2'*).

3   *Buyco Ltd & Sellco Ltd v HMRC* [2006] VTD 19752.

4   *Seymour Limousines Ltd v HMRC* [2009] VATD 20966.

5   *Tricell (UK) Ltd v CCE* [2003] VATTR 18127.

It noted that, whilst there was a substantial measure of agreement on the principles to be derived from the cases, there were differences of nuance. Having considered the cases, it set out eight principles that it considered should be applied in relation to hardship:

1   Decisions on hardship should not stifle meritorious appeals (*ToTel 1*, 82(i)).

2   The test is one of capacity to pay without financial hardship, not just capacity to pay (*ToTel 1*, 82(ii), *ToTel 2*, 55, approving *Seymour*, 57).

3   The time at which the question is to be asked is the time of the hearing (*ToTel 1*, 77, approving *Buyco*, 6, and *ToTel 2*, 37).

   Save that this may be qualified if the appellant has put themselves in a current position of hardship deliberately (eg by extraction of funds otherwise readily available from a company by way of dividend), or if there is significant delay on the part of the appellant (*ToTel 1*, 78, *ToTel 2*, 44–47, *Buyco*, 6).

4   The question should be capable of decision promptly from readily available material. (*ToTel 1*, 82(iii)).

5   The enquiry should be directed to the ability of an appellant to pay from resources which are immediately or readily available (*ToTel 1*, 82(iii), *Buyco*, 8).

   A corollary of this is that a business is not expected to look outside its normal sources for funding, nor is it required to sell assets, especially if to do so would take time (*Buyco*, 6 and *Tricell*, 55, 56) (The First-tier Tribunal disagreed with that which had been suggested to the contrary by the VAT & Duties Tribunal in *Kemp*).

6   The test is all or nothing: ability to pay part of the VAT without hardship does not matter (*Buyco*, 6).

7   If the tribunal has fixed a cut off point for the admission of material, it is not an error of law for the tribunal to ignore any later furnished evidence (*ToTel 1*, 86).

8   The absence of contemporaneous accounting information is a justification for the tribunal to conclude that it can place little if any weight on the appellant's assertion that it is unable to afford to pay (*ToTel 2*, 79).

The FTT's decision was upheld on appeal by the UT ([2017] UKUT 0181 (TCC)) (although it expressed the view that the FTT's decision 'might in places have been more felicitously worded'). The UT emphasised in its decision that 'the test for financial hardship is an "all or nothing" one. The only question is whether payment or deposit of the whole of the disputed tax would cause financial hardship. It is of no relevance that payment of some lesser amount might be capable of being achieved without hardship.'

Direct tax appeals

20.112 Where the taxpayer has lodged an appeal and he considers that the tax charged is excessive, he can apply to HMRC, under *TMA 1970, s 55*, for postponement of payment of part or all of the tax charged, pending the determination of the appeal. This application must be made within 30 days of the date of the closure notice. An application after that period can be made only where there has been a 'change in circumstances of the case', as a result of which the taxpayer has grounds for believing that he has been overcharged to tax (*TMA 1970, s 55(3A)*).

20.113 HMRC may agree with the taxpayer the amount of tax in respect of which payment may be postponed; and most cases are determined in this way. However, if agreement cannot be reached, then the taxpayer may refer the application for postponement to the FTT. The application must be made within 30 days from the date of the document informing the taxpayer of HMRC's decision on postponement. The taxpayer is not required to prove all the facts or succeed in the legal arguments that will have to be proved or established at the substantive appeal; instead, the taxpayer just must show 'reasonable grounds' for believing that he has been overcharged to tax. 'Reasonable' means that the grounds must be based on reason and must not be irrational, absurd or ridiculous (see *Sparrow Ltd v Inspector of Taxes* [2001] STC (SCD) 206).

20.114 Only the amount of tax that depends on the outcome of the appeal is postponed until the appeal is heard. In the meantime, HMRC is entitled

20.115 *Tax appeals*

to seek payment of the balance (which is payable within 30 days of the agreement or the tax tribunal's decision under *TMA 1970, s 55(5)*: see *Parikh v Back* [1985] STC 232). In the event that the taxpayer does not apply for postponement, then the whole of the tax charged is payable as if there had been no appeal (but without prejudice to the appeal).

Follower Notices and Accelerated Payment Notices

Introduction

20.115 *FA 2014, Pt 4* introduced the concept of 'follower notices', which notice HMRC may give to a taxpayer where it considers that a judicial ruling is 'relevant to' a tax 'arrangement' entered into by the taxpayer. Since its introduction, HMRC has issued follower notices in respect of 130 arrangements. If a follower notice is issued (which is at HMRC's discretion) then the taxpayer must either withdraw his appeal against HMRC's decision that tax is payable or face (significant) additional penalties for not doing so if the appeal is eventually unsuccessful.

The same part of *FA 2014* also introduced the power for HMRC to issue 'accelerated payment notices' (APNs). These require the disputed tax to be paid in advance of resolution of an appeal. HMRC may (and is likely to) issue an accelerated payment notice when a follower notice has been given. It is understood that over 60,000 APNs have been issued to date.

Accelerated payment notices

20.116 HMRC may issue an APN where:

(i) the arrangement is a notifiable scheme under the DOTAS rules;

(ii) a follower notice has been given in relation to the scheme; or

(iii) a GAAR counteraction notice has been given.

As the intent of *FA 2014, Pt 4* is to enable HMRC to require that the tax in dispute is paid prior to resolution of the dispute, the taxpayers' ability to seek postponement is excluded. If payment of tax under appeal has already been postponed, the APN has the effect of cancelling that postponement.

20.117 There is no right of appeal against the issue of an APN (see *FA 2014, s 219*). The only remedy is to send written representations to HMRC (under *FA 2014, s 222*); and, if these are not successful, to seek judicial review. There have been a number of judicial review challenges by which the taxpayers have argued that the APN system is unlawful *in toto*. All have failed comprehensively.

The main cases are:

(i) *R (on the application of Rowe) v Revenue and Customs Commissioners* [2015] EWHC 2293 (Admin);

(ii) *R (on the application of Dr Walapu v Revenue and Customs Commissioners* [2016] STC 1682;

(iii) *R (on the application of Graham and others) v Revenue and Customs Commissioners* [2016] EWHC 1197 (Admin); and

(iv) *R (on the application of Vital Nut Co Ltd and another) v Revenue and Customs Commissioners* [2016] EWHC 1797 (Admin).

The first of these cases to be heard was *Rowe*. In this case, around 150 investors in various film partnerships challenged HMRC's issue of partner payment notices (which are analogous to APNs) on numerous grounds. Ultimately, the High Court considered five of the grounds:

(i) breach of natural justice;

(ii) an *ultra vires* act by HMRC;

(iii) legitimate expectation;

(iv) irrationality; and

(v) incompatibility with the individuals' human rights.

20.118 Each of the grounds was dismissed in turn.

In each of the further three cases, the challengers sought (unsuccessfully) to point to a distinguishing feature that set that case apart from the similar grounds deployed in the previous cases.

The approach of the Administrative Court in these cases was to accept that APNs achieve a simple rebalancing in direct tax appeals pertaining to avoidance structures, namely that, in such cases, it will be HMRC, rather than the taxpayer, who holds the tax in dispute pending resolution of the dispute.

The decisions of the High Court in *Rowe* and *Vital Nut* were upheld by the Court of Appeal ([2018] STC 462). The Court of Appeal held that it was the clear intention of Parliament to deter the use of tax avoidance schemes through the use of the APN regime. It confirmed that the APN regime can be applied to arrangements entered into before the legislation came into force.

With regard to the argument that there was a breach of Article 1 of the First Protocol to the Convention on Human Rights, the court asked:

1. Is the article engaged at all by interfering with the 'peaceful enjoyment of ... possessions'?

20.118 *Tax appeals*

2. If so, is the interference 'provided for by law'?

3. Is the interference 'proportionate'?

It held that the claimants' rights were not infringed. The High Court had held that *Kopecký v Slovakia (2005)* 41 EHRR 43 applied; in *Kopecký*, the applicant was claiming a 'right in money' and, accordingly, his claim was not a 'possession' for Article 1 purposes. The Court of Appeal disagreed; McCombe LJ said (at §§ 168 and 169):

> 'Under the APN/PPN procedures, it [the state] simply has a money claim conferred on it by legislation, in anticipation of a possible future tax liability which may or may not be established. It makes no claim whatsoever to the money as tax. The appellants' money remains their money. It is to turn the matter around 180 degrees to say that it is the appellants who only have a claim to keep their money because of the demand made by the state to deprive them of it ... It is difficult to see how the state's statutory claim prevents the cash being a "possession" of the appellants.'

But, the Court of Appeal concluded that, even if Article 1 was engaged, the interference was provided for by law. It noted that the interference was not wholly retrospective: the taxpayers knew that they may have to pay amounts back to HMRC at some future date, should the arrangements that they had entered into be found to be ineffective. The court also concluded that if the APN regime constituted interference, it was proportionate in the circumstances, which included the legislative objective of eliminating tax avoidance.

As regards the challenge under Article 6 (right to a fair trial), the Court of Appeal held that the availability of the procedure for making representations against the issuance of notices, together with the availability of judicial review, provided sufficient safeguards.

Although the Court of Appeal dismissed the challenges on all grounds, it agreed with the claimants in relation to the role of the 'designated officer', who considers representations made against APNs. HMRC asserted it is not the duty of the designated officer to determine the effectiveness of the underlying scheme. The court disagreed with the claimants. Arden LJ said (at 61):

> 'The courts are entitled to approach these unusual powers on the basis that (unless the legislation clearly provides the contrary) Parliament would not confer power to serve an APN/PPN unless there were reasonable grounds for concluding that the tax would ultimately be found to be payable. That would result in APNs/PPNs only being capable of being used in a proportionate manner when the interests of the state and of the taxpayers involved are fairly balanced. The contrary proposition would involve

allowing the state arbitrarily to deprive individuals of their property, even only in anticipation of an obligation that has not yet become complete in law.'

and went on to say, at 67:

'As I see it, Parliament has taken the view that the new powers to exact accelerated payments should only be available if the designated officer forms the view that the tax scheme does not work having diligently weighed up to the appropriate extent all the information available and not before, and the designated officer has no reason to doubt that information

…

I appreciate that this interpretation makes the legislation less easy for HMRC to operate but that is not a reason for departing from the statute's meaning as I understand it to be. It can, moreover, equally be said that it is difficult to see why Parliament would have legislated for the interpolation of a designated officer, a senior officer of HMRC, if it was not intended that HMRC should have to take a view on effectiveness.'

Arden LJ was also critical of HMRC's hardship policy. The claimants said that HMRC had not considered whether issuing the notices would cause financial hardship to the recipients. Nor had they taken into account the fact that the delay in determining the tax appeals was largely the fault of HMRC, rather than the taxpayers. HMRC's response was that it has a hardship policy that enables taxpayers who have received an APN to contact HMRC with a view to agreeing a 'time to pay' arrangement, if they cannot pay without incurring financial hardship. Arden LJ said that HMRC's application of its hardship policy may not be sufficient as a means of safeguarding taxpayers' rights; she said at 91:

'HMRC may be dealing with individual taxpayers on whom an APN/PPN may have a draconian effect. Some may be wealthy taxpayers but others may have to sell their homes or make decisions about involvement in that business and about that financial expenditure which may turn out to have been unnecessary if the scheme in question is effective … In deciding whether to issue or confirm an APN/PPN, HMRC may, in performance of their duty to act fairly, have to take into consideration that there is a significant failure rate (20%), and that taxpayers should not be required to comply with APNs/PPNs where the result would be arbitrary or oppressive, as where a taxpayer is forced to sell his home and is not given enough time to do so in a way that will produce a good price or leave him with an acceptable alternative.'

The claimants have sought permission to appeal to the Supreme Court. As at the date of writing, that application remains pending.

20.119 Tax appeals

One of the grounds for challenging an APN is that the particular arrangement was not a notifiable scheme under the DOTAS rules. DOTAS arrangements are defined, for the purpose of APNs, as 'notifiable arrangements to which HMRC has allocated a [DOTAS] reference number'. HMRC have accepted that the allocation of a DOTAS reference number is not sufficient by itself; the structure must also have been 'notifiable'. A number of APNs has been withdrawn on this basis.

Follower Notices

20.119 Where a follower notice ('FN') has been issued, the taxpayer is required to take corrective action (which includes amending the tax return or withdrawing his appeal) and pay the disputed tax within a specified time. If the taxpayer fails to do so, he risks the imposition of a 50% penalty.

An FN may be issued if 4 conditions are met:

(A) there is an open enquiry into a person's return or an open appeal in relation to a relevant tax.

(B) the return subject to the enquiry, or the appeal, is made on the basis that the taxpayer obtains a tax advantage from the use of particular tax arrangements;

(C) HMRC are of the opinion that there has been a judicial ruling relevant to that return/claim or appeal; and

(D) no previous FN has been given to the person in respect of the same tax arrangements and tax advantage and has not been withdrawn.

A relevant judicial ruling is a final ruling made by a court or tribunal that relates to tax arrangements and where the 'principles laid down, or reasoning given, in the ruling would, if applied to the chosen arrangements, deny the asserted advantage or a part of that advantage.' (*FA 2014, ss 205(3), (4)*) A 'final ruling' is a decision made by any court or tribunal that has not been appealed. This includes decisions of the FTT, even though they are not binding precedent. To date, there are 28 decisions that HMRC consider are relevant judicial rulings.

An FN may not be given after 12 months after release of the relevant judicial ruling. The FN must identify the judicial ruling on which it is based and must explain why HMRC consider that that is relevant to the recipient's tax arrangements. It is to be noted that Condition C is not that the judicial ruling is relevant, but that HMRC is of the opinion that the judicial ruling is relevant.

HMRC has published guidance regarding the operation of follower notices. This includes: 'Guidance; Follower notices and accelerated payments'

Tax appeals **20.119**

(updated 23 July 2015) and 'CC/FS25a Tax avoidance schemes—follower notices' (dated 19 June 2017). In the 2017 Guidance, it is stated, inter alia:

> '*Followers*
>
> When we have a large number of very similar avoidance cases, we often investigate 'representative cases'; taking them to litigation if necessary. If the court or tribunal finds that the scheme doesn't achieve the tax or NICs advantage in those cases, the disputes in those cases are settled. We can then recover the tax and/or NICs due.
>
> '*Followers*' are people who have used:
>
>> the same scheme that was used in a representative case
>>
>> a different scheme but where a principle in that scheme is sufficiently similar to the scheme used in a representative case.'

This suggests that the intent of the follower notice legislation is limited; it is to ensure that identical or 'very similar' cases to a case that has been determined judicially are resolved without the need for hearing. The 2015 Guidance has a similar purport:

> '1.2.1 Overview
>
> A follower notice can be given to a person (P) who has used an avoidance scheme that has been shown in another person's litigation to be ineffective
>
> ...
>
> 1.7.1 Intention of legislation
>
> The intention of the legislation is to tackle behaviour by those who use avoidance schemes; primarily schemes marketed to a large number of people. Those schemes can have small variations – for example, the avoidance may be based around a different type of asset in different variants, or may be set up slightly differently depending on whether an individual, company or partnership is involved.
>
> This does not mean that follower notices will automatically be given to users of variants: each case will be considered by a senior HMRC panel (see section 1.19 of this guidance for more details about the governance process).'

The approach taken by HMRC to FNs has been, on occasions, to adopt a significantly more expansive interpretation of the intent of the legislation than that which is indicated in their own published guidance.

In *R (on the application of Haworth) v Revenue and Customs Commissioners* [2018] EWHC 1271 (Admin), the issue as to 'relevance' of a judicial ruling was considered by the Administrative Court. The taxpayer asserted that

20.119 *Tax appeals*

'principles' or 'reasoning' (in *FA 2014, s 205(3)(b)*) necessarily must be legal principles and reasoning, since it is not possible to apply the factual findings of one case to another. The Administrative Court disagreed. It held that test is not the same as for legal precedent (i.e. does the *ratio decidendi* of case 1 determine the outcome of case 2?). Important facts could be taken into account when applying the principles and reasoning of the judicial ruling: 'to the documents, evidence and representations in the claimant's case to determine whether there was a scheme ... which would deny the asserted advantage.'

There is no right of appeal against the issue of an FN or against a notice that closes an enquiry where that notice gives effect to any amendment made by the taxpayer in response to the FN. The only remedy available to the recipient of a FN is to send written representations to HMRC (under *FA 2014, s 207*) objecting to the FN, and judicial review of the review officer's decision (to uphold the FN). In *R (on the application of Haworth) v HM Revenue & Customs Commissioners* [2018] EWHC 1271 (Admin), Cranston J. rejected an argument that, following the Court of Appeal's decision in *Rowe*, the review officer must consider whether the arrangement is effective when considering representations in relation to an FN: 'With a follower notice the context is that conclusion has been reached as to the effectiveness of the scheme, albeit elsewhere in HRMC.'

The penalty for not taking corrective action in respect of an FN is 50% of the value of the denied advantage. That can be reduced if the recipient has co-operated with HMRC, but not to below 10%. The recipient of an FN may appeal the penalty to the FTT. *FA 2014, s 214* sets out the grounds on which an appeal may be made. These include:

(*a*) that the judicial ruling was not 'relevant' to the arrangements.

(*b*) that Condition A, B or D in *FA 2014, s 204* was not met (see above); and

(*c*) that it was reasonable in all the circumstances for the taxpayer not to have taken the corrective action.

In *Onillon v HMRC* [2018] SFTD 728, the FTT allowed the taxpayer's appeal against a penalty imposed for failing to take corrective action following the issue of an FN on the basis that it was reasonable in all the circumstances for the taxpayer not to take such action. The FTT said that 'reasonable' must be construed objectively, not subjectively; and that this means that the taxpayer must have done what a prudent and reasonable hypothetical person would have done in his situation in light of all the facts and the legislative context. The taxpayer had been issued with an APN and an FN simultaneously. The APN was unlawful. It required him to pay over £260,000. There were no grounds for HMRC to issue an APN requiring payment of this sum; even after the tax advantage that he had sought had been denied, he was entitled to a refund of tax. There was no payment due by the taxpayer, as he had never received the repayment which he sought. The FTT held that the taxpayer's 'failure to follow instructions in a FN sent at the same time as the APN, in circumstances where the FN, while correctly issued, contained potentially contradictory instructions to its covering letter' was reasonable.

It is clear from the interaction of the statutory provisions that, with regard to appeals, corrective action in the form of withdrawing the appeal can be taken by the recipient of a FN only if he has made an appeal on the basis of a 'particular tax advantage' (the asserted advantage) to which the judicial ruling pertains. That may be straightforward in a case where the taxpayer is seeking to run exactly the same argument as in a case which has already been decided adversely to taxpayers. However, as Nugee J. recognised in R, on the application of *Broomfield v Revenue and Customs Commissioners* [2017] EWHC 2926 (Admin), the provisions are not at all straightforward where the taxpayer is running 2 arguments, only 1 of which is such an argument. Nugee J. addressed the first circumstance at paras 23–25:

> '23. In a case where the taxpayer is running the same argument as in a case which has already been decided adversely to the taxpayers, these provisions work without great difficulty. Suppose, for example, Ms Broomfield's appeal to the FTT in this case had been solely based on the Huitson argument, the same argument as was rejected by the FTT in Huitson. Then there would be no doubt that Condition B in s.204(3) would be satisfied. The appeal would be made on the basis that a particular tax advantage resulted from the Montpelier arrangements, the particular tax advantage being that asserted in her return, namely that she was entitled to exemption under the UK-Isle of Man DTA and hence the income was not subject to UK income tax.
>
> 24. ... under s.208(3) the denied advantage would be the exemption under the DTA which was denied by the reasoning in Huitson, and under s.208(4), (5) and (6) the necessary corrective action is not difficult to identify.
>
> 25. By s.208(5)(b) in the case of an FN given by virtue of s.204(2)(b), which is where the taxpayer has made a tax appeal, the taxpayer has as a first step to take all necessary action to enter into an agreement with HMRC in writing for the purpose of relinquishing the denied advantage. That would mean in effect giving up the appeal.'

He went on to say, however, that interpreting whether the 'particular tax advantage' in *FA 2014, s 204(3)* refers to either: (a) the particular relief or exemption relied upon by the taxpayer or (b) the end result asserted by the taxpayer is not straightforward. Either interpretation leads to contradictions in

20.120 *Tax appeals*

the cases where the taxpayer is relying on more than one argument (where only one is the subject of the FN). Permission to bring judicial review proceedings was granted to the taxpayer. A full hearing is awaited.

Agreements settling appeals

Direct taxes

20.120 Litigation which has been commenced by notice of appeal can be validly settled by agreement only if the agreement complies with the relevant statutory provision, namely *TMA 1970, s 54*. In short, a *s 54* agreement has the same consequences as a determination to the same effect by the tax tribunal; and the agreement binds the parties to it in the same way as a determination binds the parties to an appeal (see *Tod v South Essex Motors (Basildon) Ltd* [1988] STC 392). It cannot be determinative of tax liabilities for years after that to which the assessment in question relates (see *MacNiven v Westmoreland Investments Ltd* [2001] UKHL 6 in which, although the inspector's reasoning in the agreement referred to the amount of excess management expenses that were intended to be carried forward, the House of Lords held that this did not bind HMRC to take those into account in future years). Save as otherwise provided in the Taxes Acts, the determination of the tax tribunal is final and conclusive (under *s 46(2)*).

Thus, a *s 54* agreement is similarly final and conclusive and the issues that are resolved by it cannot be re-litigated by the parties. In *Easinghall Limited v HMRC* [2016] UKUT 105 (TCC), the Upper Tribunal confirmed that where an agreement has been reached with HMRC under *Taxes Management Act 1970, s 54*, HMRC can not commence an enquiry or issue a discovery assessment unless either concerns an issue which was not the subject of the agreement.

20.121 An agreement between HMRC and a taxpayer made outside *s 54* will be binding only in limited circumstances. Whilst HMRC, under its care and management powers, may enter into 'back duty' agreements (whereby it agrees to settle for less than the tax that may be due), HMRC does not have power to enter into 'forward tax agreements' (where it is agreed, in advance, that specified amounts will be paid annually in lieu of tax that otherwise would be due, because HMRC does not have power to agree not to perform its duty to collect tax in accordance with the statutory procedure (see *Al Fayed v Advocate General for Scotland* [2004] STC 1703). If a taxpayer enters into such an agreement, it will be enforceable only by way of judicial review proceedings, and HMRC will be bound only if its failure or refusal to abide by the agreement amounts to an abuse of power.

Indirect taxes

20.122 The provisions for settlement by agreement of appeals in indirect taxes are very similar to those in direct taxes. The applicable statutory provision is *VATA 1994, s 85*. It is paramount that there is an agreement for *s 85* to apply ('in the absence of an offer and an acceptance, there was no meeting of minds and no agreement, either within the meaning of s 85 or at common law', *R (on the application of DFS Furniture Company plc) v Customs and Excise Comrs* [2002] EWCA Civ 1708, per Mummery LJ at para 42).

WITHDRAWAL OF AN APPEAL

20.123 Rule 17 of the First-tier Rules enables either party to withdraw all or part of his appeal at any time before the FTT makes its decision either in writing to the FTT before the hearing starts, or orally during the hearing. A taxpayer who has given notice of appeal may notify an HMRC officer, orally or in writing, that he does not wish to proceed with the appeal. Within 30 days of such notification, the officer may refuse to accept withdrawal, in which case the proceedings will continue. If the officer does not refuse to accept withdrawal, the appeal is treated as settled as if the parties had come to an agreement that the assessment should be upheld without variation.

20.124 Where the appeal is withdrawn orally, HMRC normally will ask for that to be confirmed in writing. If written confirmation is not forthcoming, the officer may confirm acceptance of the withdrawal in writing, in which case the issue will be treated as having been confirmed by the FTT.

20.125 Either the taxpayer or HMRC may withdraw all or part of their appeal at any time before the FTT makes its decision either in writing to the tribunal before the hearing starts, or orally during the hearing. The taxpayer has the right to withdraw his appeal without the permission of either HMRC or the FTT. An appeal may also be withdrawn where the case has been adjourned part heard. The FTT will notify the other parties of any withdrawal.

20.126 A party who has withdrawn his case may apply subsequently to the FTT for the case to be reinstated. In *St Anne's Distributors Ltd v Revenue and Customs Comrs* [2011] STC 708, the company sent an email to the Tribunal Centre purporting to withdraw its appeals; and then, a few weeks later, sent a message in which it stated that it wished to proceed with the appeals. The FTT treated the second communication as an application to reinstate the appeals, which it refused. The UT allowed the company's appeal. It held that the email did not comply with r 17(1); and so the company's subsequent

20.127 *Tax appeals*

message should not have been treated as an application for reinstatement. Also, it was observed that:

> 'the scheme of rule 17(1) and (2) is to give an appellant the unilateral right to withdraw the appeal without permission of the Tribunal and without the intervention of HMRC. The formalities for withdrawal are required to enable the Tribunal and anyone with an interest in the outcome of the proceedings to satisfy themselves that a notice describing itself as a 'notice of withdrawal' means what it says. Rule 17(3) and (4) are there to protect the appellant who for some reason has, deliberately and in good faith, withdrawn his appeal but, for an acceptable reason (e.g., because he has insufficient funds to continue the fight or has come to see the implications of withdrawal), has applied to reinstate the appeal within the 28-day cooling-off period. Rule 17 is not a weapon to enable the Tribunal to cull unmeritorious appeals of non-cooperative traders.'

THE FIRST-TIER TRIBUNAL

Introduction

20.127 The FTT is the court of first instance for nearly all tax appeals. The judges, for every appeal, are selected on a case-by-case basis from a pool that comprises both legally qualified and non-legally qualified members. The composition of the panel of judges that hears the case depends on the nature of the case. All members of the UT are able to sit as members of the FTT. A substantial number of Special Commissioners transferred to the FTT.

The FTT sits in local centres, with larger centres in London, Manchester and Edinburgh having been established to deal with matters of greater complexity.

20.128 A central processing centre (based in Birmingham) has been established to handle the administration of all appeals. It receives and registers cases, creates case files and categorises cases according to the First-tier Rules. To commence an appeal, the taxpayer submits a notice of appeal to the FTT. Appeals can be submitted electronically (by being sent to taxappeals@tribunals.gsi.gov.uk) or can be made by post (to First-tier Tribunal – Tax, HM Courts and Tribunals Service, 3rd Floor, Temple Court, 35 Bull Street, Birmingham, B4 6EQ). The relevant forms are available on the HM Courts and Tribunals Service website. The unit in Birmingham processes all new work, undertakes the basic checks, registers the appeals on the system and allocates them an FTT reference number. After administrative checks have been undertaken, the Birmingham team undertakes the initial categorisation of the appeal. It allocates each case to one of four categories: (1) default paper; (2) basic; (3) standard; or (4) complex.

After a case has been allocated to a category, either party may apply (or the FTT may decide on its own initiative) for the case to be reallocated to a different category.

The categories

Default paper cases

20.129 The simplest appeals (such as late filing penalties) are dealt with under this track. They are dealt with by means of written submissions only, unless either party requests a hearing.

An appeal against, for example:

(i) penalties for late income tax and corporation tax self-assessment returns (including penalties under *TMA 1970, ss 93(2)* and *93(4)*, and *FA 1998, Sch 18, para 17(2)* and *(3)*), and

(ii) fixed percentage surcharges for late payment of income tax under *TMA 1970, s 59C*,

must be allocated to the paper track, unless the FTT considers that there is a reason why it is appropriate to allocate the case to a different category.

20.130 Once a case has been categorised as a default paper case, a copy of the notice of appeal is sent to HMRC by the FTT. HMRC then has 42 days within which to file its statement of case (which must set out the legislative provision under which the decision under appeal was made and their position in relation to the appeal) with the FTT and serve it on the appellant. HMRC may ask for the appeal to be dealt with at a hearing (First-tier Rules, r 25(3)). HMRC is unlikely to do this, unless it considers that there is an important issue that arises.

20.131 The appellant may (but is not obliged to) respond to HMRC's statement of case by sending a reply to the tribunal. If the appellant wishes to reply, then he must do so within 30 days of receiving HMRC's statement of case.

20.132 In the reply, the appellant may address the arguments raised by HMRC in its statement of case and may also bring any information that he considers is relevant to the appeal to the attention of the FTT. The appellant may request an oral hearing (First-tier Rules, r 26(3)(c)).

20.133 If neither party has made a written request for a hearing, then the FTT will determine the case on the papers. However, if either party has requested a hearing, the FTT must hold a hearing before determining the

20.134 *Tax appeals*

case; such a hearing will be heard by a single tribunal judge or tribunal member (see *Tribunal Composition Practice Statement*, 10 March 2009, para 3).

20.134 Only a small number of default paper track cases proceed to a hearing. An example is *Royal Institute of Navigation v Revenue and Customs Comrs* [2012] UKFTT 472 (TC), which concerned a penalty for late filing of a P35 (the FTT reduced the penalty from £400 to £200).

Basic cases

20.135 Appeals where it is considered that little or no case management is required (and which do not fall within the default paper category) will be categorised as basic appeals. All standard tax penalties and surcharges that are not suitable for the default paper category will be allocated to the basic track, as will appeals against information notices.

20.136 In addition, applications for:

- permission to make a late appeal,
- postponement of the payment of tax pending an appeal (under *TMA 1970, s 55*), and
- a direction that HMRC close an enquiry,

will generally be classed as basic.

20.137 Basic cases, generally, proceed directly to a hearing without the need for further documents to be exchanged.

The procedural rules in relation to the preparation and service of a statement of case do not apply to basic cases.

20.138 However, if HMRC wishes to raise at the hearing any grounds for contesting the proceedings that it has not raised previously, then it must inform the appellant of these before the hearing (under First-tier Rules, r 24(3)) and as soon as reasonably practicable (under First-tier Rules, r 24(4)). No particular time is specified in relation to this; the length of the time allowed varies according to the nature of the appeal and the issues raised.

20.139 Basic cases are heard by a panel of one, two or, where the Chamber President considers it appropriate, three, consisting of judges or members as determined by the Chamber President (see *Tribunal Composition Practice Statement*, 10 March 2009, para 4).

Standard cases

20.140 Any case that does not fall within the basic or default paper categories will, as a rule, be allocated as a standard case. The cases that will be allocated as standard (or complex) cases are those that require substantial case management, exchanges of documentary evidence and witness statements.

20.141 The rules governing the composition of the panel are similar for both standard and complex cases. If preliminary issues are to be determined or the panel is disposing of the case, the panel must consist of at least one tribunal judge, who may sit with two others, who may be either tribunal judges or tribunal members, as determined by the Chamber President. Any other decision, including giving directions (whether or not at a hearing) must be presided over by a single tribunal judge.

Complex cases

20.142 For a case to be allocated to the complex track, the FTT must consider that one or more of the following criteria are satisfied:

(*a*) the case will require lengthy or complex evidence or a lengthy hearing;

(*b*) it involves a complex or important principle or issue; or

(*c*) it involves a large financial sum (First-tier Rules, r 23(4)).

20.143 The circumstances when it is appropriate to categorise a case as complex were considered by the FTT and the UT in *Capital Air Services Ltd v HMRC* ([2010] UKFTT 160 (TC) and [2010] UKUT 373 (TCC) respectively). The FTT declined to categorise the case as complex, holding that, in order to be complex, it must be the type of case that ought to be treated exceptionally and start in the UT. The UT disagreed. It allocated the case as a complex case.

20.144 The UT also made a number of observations regarding the general approach that should be taken to allocation:

1   A case has to satisfy one or more of the three criteria. Accordingly, a case which is, overall, complex within the ordinary meaning of the word but does not quite meet any of the criteria separately cannot be allocated as a complex case.

2   Alternatively, a case that is not complex as a matter of ordinary meaning, but which nonetheless satisfies one or more of the criteria could be allocated as complex. However, if for example, a case would involve no lengthy or complex evidence and no complex or important principle or issue, then it may be appropriate not to allocate the matter

20.145 *Tax appeals*

as complex simply because it involves a large amount of tax. This could be either because a case must be complex, as that term is ordinarily understood, in order to be allocated to the complex category or because the FTT has a discretion not to allocate such a case to the complex category. (It is considered by the author that the latter is the better justification.)

3   There is an element of objectivity to be applied. Thus, for example, a hearing of half a day can never be 'lengthy', whereas a three-month hearing always would be. Likewise, a case involving tax of £1,000 could never be said to involve a large financial sum and a case involving tax of £100 million always would. Absent broad indicative limits such as these, there is not a single 'right' answer that could be ascertained objectively as a matter of law.

20.145 The analysis at 2 above was applied by the tribunal in *Dreams plc v Revenue and Customs Comrs* [2012] UKFTT 614 (TC), where the taxpayer was unsuccessful in persuading the FTT that its case should be reallocated as a complex case. The tribunal emphasised that an appeal 'must have some feature out of the ordinary' to be categorised as complex. Whilst the amount in issue (more than £5 million) was self-evidently a large financial sum and accordingly the r 23(4)(c) test was satisfied, neither of the other complex tests was met. The FTT noted that the only distinguishing feature of the case was a sufficiently large sum in issue for it to pass through the rule 23(4)(c) gateway, and exercised its discretion not to allocate the case to the complex category: 'the amount of tax in issue does not 'trump' the fact that, by reason of its failure to pass through the other gateways, the appeal is more suitable for allocation to the Standard category.'

20.146 In *JSM Construction Ltd v Revenue and Customs Comrs* [2015] UKFTT 474 (TC), the FTT noted that the parties did not disagree about the nature or volume of the evidence in the case or the likely length of the hearing, but the taxpayer urged it to regard both as lengthy and HMRC sought to persuade it that the evidence was straightforward and the hearing nothing out of the ordinary. The FTT concluded that, having regard to *Capital Air Services* and *Dreams*, it should form its own view. It held that five witness statements and a six-day hearing were not lengthy or complex and that the appeal could not be categorised as complex.

20.147 Once an appeal has been allocated as a complex case, the FTT may, with the agreement of the parties, refer the case to the Chamber President with a request that the case be transferred directly to the UT. The agreement of the President of the Tax and Finance Chamber of the UT is also required (First-tier Rules, r 28). The first appeal to be heard in the UT, *John Wilkins (Motor Engineers) Ltd v Revenue and Customs Comrs* [2009] UKUT 175 (TCC) was so transferred. Only small numbers of cases are transferred to the UT.

Where a complex case is transferred to the UT, the rules relating to the composition of the panel are the same as those governing complex cases in the FTT.

Statement of case/exchange of documents

20.148 For all categories, except the basic category, HMRC must file a statement of case that sets out HMRC's position in relation to the case. The statement of case must also include the legislative provision under which the decision under appeal was made.

20.149 In standard and complex cases, HMRC has 60 days from the date that the FTT sent the notice of appeal to provide its statement of case (First-tier Rules, r 25(1)(b)); and in default paper cases it has 42 days. Requests by HMRC for an extension of time to serve its statement of case are made routinely.

In standard and complex cases, unless any other directions are given, each party must send to the FTT and to each other, within 42 days after the date that the statement of case is sent by HMRC, a list of the documents that it has in its possession or power and which it intends to rely on in the proceedings (First-tier Rules, r 27).

Case management powers

20.150 Rule 5 of the First-tier Rules provides that, subject to *TCEA 2007*, the FTT may regulate its own procedure.

The FTT has wide-ranging powers to manage the proceedings before it, such as the ability to require expert evidence, to compel the production of documentary evidence or the attendance of witnesses, and to select preliminary issues, consolidate cases and appoint lead cases.

20.151 The aim of directions is to prepare the appeal for hearing. The practice in all courts is now to require that all evidence and argument be committed to writing in advance of the hearing. This means that all witnesses (including the appellant) are required to prepare written statements of the evidence that they will give and both parties are required to set out their legal arguments in outline.

These documents, together with any other document which is to be produced in the appeal, must be lodged with the FTT, and served on the other side, in advance of the hearing.

20.152 *Tax appeals*

20.152 There are many advantages to this approach. It shortens the length of the hearing, because all the evidence and argument can be read by both sides and the FTT1 before the hearing begins. It means that each witness can prepare his evidence in advance and it means that each party is fully aware of the other's case. It is no longer regarded as reasonable, or in the interests of justice, for late evidence (oral or written) or argument to be sprung on the opposing party at or during the hearing of the appeal.

20.153 In *Mobile Export 365 Ltd, Shelford IT Ltd v Revenue and Customs Comrs* [2007] EWHC 1737 (Ch), the Administrative Court criticised the approach that counsel had adopted before the VAT Tribunal. In relation to counsel having produced 'from his papers (as a conjurer produces a rabbit out of his hat) a skeleton argument and a bundle of authorities', Lightman J said:

> 'I should conclude by saying a word about springing surprises on opponents, as were sprung on the Commissioners and the Tribunal in this case. Such tactics are not acceptable conduct today in any civil proceedings. They are clearly repugnant to the Overriding Objective laid down in CPR 1.1 (where applicable) and the duty of the parties and their legal representatives to help the court to further that objective. The objection to them is not limited to proceedings to which the CPR are applicable.'

20.154 Under the First-tier Rules, r 15(2), the FTT has the power to admit evidence and the power to exclude evidence that is admissible but would otherwise be unfair to admit. In considering what is 'unfair to admit', the FTT will start from the presumption that all relevant evidence should be admitted, unless there is some other compelling reason not to admit it. In identifying whether there is a compelling reason not to admit evidence, the FTT will weigh up the fairness to the parties in admitting it or not admitting it.

20.155 So, for example, the FTT may conclude that a party would be unfairly prejudiced if the other party were able to adduce evidence shortly before or at the hearing, such that there is a compelling reason that the evidence should not be admitted.

20.156 The FTT may issue a specific direction itself on its own initiative or, alternatively, the parties may apply for directions. If a direction is requested, it must be made in writing (unless it is requested at a hearing) and reasons must be given for the request.

Once promulgated by the FTT, the directions must be sent to the parties and to any person affected by the direction (unless the FTT considers that there is good reason not to do so).

20.157 The only procedural directions that are prescribed by the First-tier Rules are in respect of service of a statement of case by HMRC and exchange of lists of documents by the parties. In nearly all complex cases (and in many standard cases), further directions will be required.

20.158 In general, the parties will agree directions for the management of the case between themselves, but if they are unable to do so, the FTT will list the matter for a preliminary hearing at which a tribunal judge will issue relevant case management directions.

20.159 Case management directions will typically include some or all of the following steps:

1 exchange of witness evidence of fact;

2 exchange of expert evidence;

3 agreement of a statement of agreed facts;

4 agreement of a statement of issues;

5 exchange of skeleton arguments;

6 preparation of a paginated bundle of documents.

20.160 The time estimate of the length of the hearing is left to the parties. If there is any doubt as to the length of hearing, time should be over-estimated rather than under-estimated. If a hearing has to be adjourned part-heard and further dates fixed, the gap between hearings can be weeks or even months, depending on how much further time is required and the availability of the particular FTT judge or judges who heard the first part of the appeal. For example, in *Degorce v Revenue and Customs Comrs* [2013] UKFTT 178 (TC), the hearing dates were 1, 2, 3, 4, 8, 9 May and 15 June 2012 (and the decision was released on 4 March 2013).

Strike out

20.161 The case management powers under the First-tier Rules are backed up by sanctions. If a taxpayer fails to comply with a direction that states that failure to comply would lead to the striking out of the proceedings or part of them, then the proceedings, or an appropriate part of them, will be struck out automatically.

20.162 The FTT may strike out the whole or part of the proceedings if:

- the taxpayer has failed to comply with a direction that states that failure to comply could lead to the striking out of the proceedings;
- the taxpayer failed to co-operate with the FTT to such an extent that the FTT cannot deal with the proceedings fairly and justly; or

20.163 *Tax appeals*

- the FTT considers that there is no reasonable prospect of the taxpayer's case (or part of it) succeeding.

20.163 The FTT may not strike out under the second or third heads above without first giving the taxpayer an opportunity to make representations in relation to the proposed striking out. The power to strike out hopeless cases without need for a full hearing is rarely exercised by the FTT. However, the FTT has struck out a number of cases on the ground that it does not have jurisdiction to hear the matter. Examples include *Prince v Revenue and Customs Comrs* [2012] UKFTT 157 (TC), where the FTT held that there was no right to challenge the terms of an extra statutory concession, and *Taylor v Revenue and Customs Comrs* [2013] UKFTT 483 (TC), where the FTT concluded that it had no jurisdiction to hear an appeal against a calculation raised by HMRC.

20.164 If the proceedings have been struck out by reason of the taxpayer's failure to comply with a direction, then the taxpayer may apply in writing within 28 days after the notice of the striking out was sent to have the proceedings reinstated. The cogency of the reasons given by the taxpayer for failure to comply with a direction is often determinative of whether or not the appeal will be struck out. A failure to give any reasons (or any proper reasons) for the breach is likely to result in the case being struck out (see *Customs and Excise Comrs v Young* [1993] STC 394).

20.165 The FTT does not have an inherent jurisdiction to review an assessment outside a taxpayer's appeal. Thus, if the appeal is struck out (for whatever reason), the assessment of tax payable by the taxpayer stands and the tax thereunder is due, even if it is incorrect or unlawfully demanded.

The above rules apply to HMRC, save that, under r 8(7), the references to 'striking out' must be read as references to 'the barring of HMRC from taking any further part in the proceedings'.

20.166 This limitation of the strike out rule in respect of HMRC was criticised by, inter alia, the Tax Appeals Modernisation Stakeholder Group, because it would have had the consequence that the taxpayer would have had to discharge the burden of proof (in the normal manner), but without being able to cross-examine HMRC's witnesses. A last minute amendment was introduced to r 8 by the inclusion of a new r 8(9):

> 'If a respondent has been barred from taking further part in proceedings under this rule and that bar has not been lifted, the Tribunal need not consider any response or other submissions made by the respondent, and may summarily determine any or all issues against the respondent.'

20.167 Accordingly, if HMRC is barred from taking part in the proceedings, the FTT is not obliged to consider any submissions made by it. The FTT *may* summarily determine any or all the issues against HMRC, but it is not obliged to do so. It is considered that this discretionary power may be used by the FTT to prevent taxpayers from receiving 'windfalls' in cases where it considers that the tax has been correctly demanded, but HMRC is barred from taking part in the proceedings due to, for example, contumelious conduct. Whether the bias in the rules in this way in favour of HMRC is appropriate is moot.

BPP Holdings

20.168 *BPP Holdings Ltd v Revenue and Customs Commissioners* [2017] STC 1655 concerned an application by the taxpayer for a debarring order.

HMRC served their statement of case 14 days late, which document failed to set out clearly the facts on which they would rely to support their contention that VAT was owed by BPP. BPP requested further information and an order was made by the FTT that directed HMRC to reply by a particular date. The order was accompanied by a warning that failure to comply could result in an order barring HMRC from taking further part in the proceedings. HMRC responded in time, but wholly inadequately. BPP applied for a debarring order against HMRC.

The FTT granted the order. The UT allowed HMRC's appeal. The Court of Appeal restored the debarring order; and the Supreme Court upheld that decision. The Supreme Court considered the interplay between the High Court's focus on enforcing compliance with rules, practice directions and orders necessitated by the Civil Procedure Rules, and the First-tier Rules and UT rules that include a requirement of ensuring that parties are able to participate fully in the proceedings and that are based on a recognition that a significant proportion of those who appeal to the tribunals will be unrepresented. With regard to the former, a strict line had been taken by the Court of Appeal in *Mitchell v News Group Newspapers Ltd* [2014] 1 WLR 795; and one of the issues that was considered was the extent to which the *Mitchell* line of authority should be applied in the tax tribunals.

The FTT's decision

20.169 The FTT issued directions that barred HMRC. In reaching its decision, it noted the *Mitchell* line of authority (but did not apply it), and said, *inter alia*:

> 'There is very clear prejudice to the appellant in not knowing HMRC's case. Litigation is not to be conducted by ambush. The appellant has the right to be put in the position so that it can properly prepare its case ...

20.170 *Tax appeals*

'... the real prejudice to the appellant is in the delay. Only now can the parties proceed to exchange list[s] of documents and witness statements. ... it is in my view fair to say that HMRC's continued failure to make a proper statement of their case has delayed the progress of this appeal by about 8 months.'

The FTT barred HMRC from further involvement in the appeal. It held that both the Statement of Case served by HMRC and the reply failed, despite repeated requests, to provide any facts on which HMRC intended to rely in its argument. BPP had not been given any indication of the facts to be relied on until shortly before the hearing, when HMRC produced a skeleton argument setting out the basis of its case.

At the time of the FTT's decision, differently constituted Upper Tribunals had reached different conclusions on the question as to whether *Mitchell* applied in the tax tribunals. In *McCarthy & Stone (Developments) Ltd v HMRC* [2014] UKUT 196 (TCC), Judge Sinfield held that it was appropriate for the tax tribunals to follow the *Mitchell* approach. In *Leeds City Council v HMRC* [2014] UKUT 350 (TCC), Judge Bishopp held that the differences in the wording of the overriding objectives in the CPR and UT rules meant that, until such time as there was an equivalent amendment to the UT rules to reflect the CPR, the tribunal should adopt a more relaxed approach to compliance with rules, directions and orders than the courts.

The UT's decision

20.170 The decision of the FTT was overturned on appeal by the UT (Judge Bishopp). The UT held that *Mitchell* does not apply in the FTT. It concluded:

'As I have made clear, there is much in its conduct of this appeal for which HMRC deserve criticism. But in my judgment their failings are not so grave as to warrant a barring order, once one puts aside the notion, engendered by Mitchell before it was explained in Denton, that the enforcement of rules and directions is a factor of particular importance, to be afforded substantial weight. The most compelling factor, in my assessment of this case, is that there is no risk to the hearing, nor of compromise to the FTT's ability to apply the overriding objective.'

The Court of Appeal's decision

20.171 The Court of Appeal re-imposed the barring order that had been granted by the FTT. It held that, whilst, technically, the CPR did not apply to proceedings before the FTT (and it noted that there is no equivalent provision to that found in CPR r 3.9 in the tax tribunals' rules), the need for litigation to be conducted efficiently and at proportionate cost and the need to enforce compliance with rules, directions and orders was equally important in such proceedings. Accordingly, there was no reason to depart from the *Mitchell* line of authority or to apply a more lenient test. To do so would run the risk that non-compliance with all orders, including final orders, would have to be tolerated. The Court of Appeal said:

> 'Flexibility of process does not mean a shoddy attitude to delay or compliance.'

The Court of Appeal approved the FTT's comments cited above.

The Court of Appeal was also scathing in its criticism of HMRC's argument that, as an impecunious agent of the State, it should be accorded 'special treatment':

> 'I found the approach of HMRC to compliance to be disturbing. At times it came close to arguing that HMRC, as a state agency, should be treated like a litigant in person and that the constraints of austerity on an agency like the HMRC should in some way excuse unacceptable behaviour. I remind HMRC that even in the tribunals where the flexibility of process is a hallmark of the delivery of specialist justice, a litigant in person is expected to comply with rules and orders and a state party should neither expect to nor work on the basis that it has some preferred status—it does not.'

The decision of the Supreme Court

20.172 In a single judgment delivered by Lord Neuberger, the Supreme Court dismissed HMRC's appeal against the Court of Appeal's decision. It held that that the FTT's original decision was not unreasonable and was not one with which an appellate court should interfere.

Lord Neuberger said that, when examining issues of procedure, tribunals may rely on standards that have been developed by the courts. Tribunals 'should generally follow a similar approach' to the court system where sanctions are concerned. But, there are two important matters that tribunals should take into account when seeking guidance on procedure from the court system.

First, as the jurisdiction of some tribunals extends to the whole of the UK, tribunal judges, when seeking guidance from civil procedure standards, should be wary of focusing solely on the procedural jurisprudence developed in the English and Welsh courts. The approaches in Northern Ireland and Scotland should also be taken into account.

20.173 *Tax appeals*

Secondly, there are differences between the civil courts and the tax tribunals. These must be taken into account, rather than simply importing wholesale the standards and rules of the CPR to the tribunal system.

HMRC's argument that it should be accorded special treatment in relation to its compliance with rules and orders was, again, given short shrift. HMRC contended that the FTT should have taken into account the fact that the barring order would prevent HMRC from carrying out its public duty to ensure that the correct amount of tax was collected. Lord Neuberger said that this argument, if accepted, could set a 'dangerous precedent'. He emphasised that public bodies should, at the least, live up to the same standards expected of private individuals in the conduct of litigation: 'There is at least as strong an argument for saying that the courts should expect higher standards from public bodies than from private bodies or individuals.'

Jurisdiction of the First-tier Tribunal in respect of public law matters

20.173 There is a long line of authority that includes the decision of Jacob J in *Customs and Excise Comrs v National Westminster Bank plc* [2003] EWHC 1822 (Ch) to the effect that 'the proper remedy for unfair treatment is judicial review, not an appeal to the tribunal'. Although there was a subsequent detour from those principles occasioned by comments by Sales J in *Oxfam v Revenue and Customs Comrs* [2009] EWHC 3078 (Ch), it is considered that that statement of principle by Jacob J is correct and applies as regards the FTT.

20.174 In *Oxfam*, Sales J commented that, on the basis that *VATA 1994*, s *83(1)(c)* brought within the FTT's jurisdiction the amount of input tax which may be credited to a person, the FTT jurisdiction extended to the public law issue which arose between Oxfam and HMRC (being legitimate expectation) as far as that issue related to the amount of input tax to be credited.

20.175 This caused the FTT on some occasions to conclude that it had been bestowed with a judicial review jurisdiction; see, for example, *Hanover Company Services Ltd v Revenue and Customs Comrs* [2010] UKFTT 256 (TC) and *Revenue and Customs Comrs v Noor* [2011] UKFTT 349 (TC). This was notwithstanding that in *Thorpe v Revenue and Customs Comrs* [2010] EWCA Civ 339 Lloyd LJ described the jurisdictional question in *Oxfam* as *obiter*.

20.176 In other instances, the FTT held that it did not have jurisdiction: see, for example, *Space 2 Build Ltd v Revenue and Customs Comrs* [2010] UKFTT 66 (TC) and *Health Response UK Ltd v Revenue and Customs Comrs* [2010] UKFTT 123 (TC).

20.177 The issue was determined by the UT in *Revenue and Customs Comrs v Noor* [2013] UKUT 71 (TCC), where it distinguished *Oxfam*. The UT held that the jurisdiction of the FTT derives wholly from statute; and noted that it was clear from *TCEA 2007* that Parliament had not intended, and had not, conferred a judicial review jurisdiction on the FTT. As the FTT had no general supervisory jurisdiction over decisions of HMRC, it could not adjudicate a claim to a credit for VAT based on legitimate expectations.

Hearings

20.178 Hearings in basic cases are informal; in many cases, the taxpayer represents himself. Hearings in standard and complex cases are more formal, and representation is more common. Either party can appoint someone to represent him at the hearing (First-tier Rules, r 11), but that person need not be a legal representative (regardless of which category the case has been allocated to).

20.179 If a party does not attend the hearing, then the FTT has a discretionary power to continue to hear the appeal if it is satisfied that:

(*a*)   the party has either been informed of the hearing or reasonable steps have been taken to notify him of it; and

(*b*)   it considers that it is in the interests of justice to continue (First-tier Rules, r 33).

20.180 All hearings are held in public, unless the tribunal directs that all or part of the proceedings are to be held in private (First-tier Rules, r 32). The tribunal will give a direction to this effect only if it considers that restricting access to the proceedings can be justified:

- in the interests of public order or national security;
- to protect a person's right to privacy;
- to maintain the confidentiality of sensitive information;
- to avoid serious harm to the public interest; or
- because it is in the interests of justice.

20.181 The number of cases that are held in private is very small. To date, there has been only one reported decision of the FTT: *A v Revenue and Customs Comrs* [2012] UKFTT 541 (TC), which is analysed below at **20.189–20.190**.

20.182 Whether a similar approach to that taken by the tribunal in *A* (dismissing Mr A's request for a hearing in private) will be applied in cases

20.183 *Tax appeals*

where the subject matter of the appeal is not a marketed tax avoidance structure remains to be seen; the author considers that the tribunal may have been more sympathetic to the taxpayer's request, had the subject matter of the appeal been different. The approach that was taken by the Special Commissioners and the VAT and Duties tribunals to the issue of publicity provides some guidance; and this is summarised first.

THE POSITION BEFORE THE PREDECESSOR TRIBUNALS

20.183 Prior to September 1994, proceedings before the Commissioners were held in private. After 1994, the general rule was that proceedings of the Special Commissioners were held in public; and, in December 2002, legislation was introduced to make General Commissioners' hearings open to the public.

In contrast, proceedings before the VAT and Duties Tribunals were held in public.

20.184 Until 31 December 2002, an appellant before the Commissioners had the right to have his appeal heard in private. However, since that date there was no longer an unqualified right. A hearing before the Commissioners could be held in private only if the particular tribunal was satisfied that this was necessary in the interests of morals, public order, national security, juveniles or for the protection of the private life of the parties, or if they considered that publicity would prejudice the interests of justice (see the Special Regulations, reg 15 and the General Regulations, reg 13). Agreement by the parties that the appeal should be heard in private was not sufficient.

20.185 The Practice Statement that accompanied the Standard Directions in respect of proceedings before the Special Commissioners stated that: 'The Special Commissioners will rule on applications for hearings in private even where these are agreed.' If such a Direction was applied for, it was considered by the Special Commissioners on its merits having regard to the facts of the case.

However, if the only argument that was put forward is that the appellant did not want his tax affairs discussed in public, then that was unlikely to satisfy the conditions for a Direction.

20.186 In *Red Discretionary Trustees v Inspector of Taxes* [2004] STC (SCD) 132, a company related to the appeal owned a high-profile asset that had attracted a considerable amount of press attention; the settlor's family wealth had made the family a target for theft and violence. They had suffered a serious personal attack in which members of the family were handcuffed by robbers at the home and a substantial amount of property was stolen. Press reports of the event were provided. HMRC indicated that it had no objection to the hearing in private.

20.187 The Special Commissioners allowed the application for the hearing to be heard in private. They said:

> 'As we believe this is only the second such application under the amended rule we are setting out the chairman's reasons for granting the application in this decision for the benefit of those reading this decision when it is published in an anonymised form. The rules clearly state that consent of both parties is in itself not enough; the tribunal must be satisfied about the matters set out in (i) or (ii) of reg 15(2). There is a public interest in open hearings and a presumption that sittings will be in public unless sufficient reasons are shown that one of those matters is satisfied. In this case given the circumstances of the robbery and its press publicity the chairman considered that sitting in private is necessary for the protection of the private life of the appellant to a greater extent than would ordinarily be the case. Protecting the taxpayer's private life could not be achieved if part of the hearing were in private. Accordingly the chairman agreed that the hearing would be in private. If it had not been for the press publicity about the robbery the tribunal would probably have decided to sit in public and for figures to be omitted where these were not necessary to an understanding of the decision.'

(The decision of the Special Commissioners was appealed directly to the Court of Appeal, where it was heard in public: *Howell v Trippier (Inspector of Taxes)* [2004] EWCA Civ 885. The anonymity protection afforded by the tribunal did not automatically extend to the higher courts.)

20.188 A party in proceedings before the VAT and Duties tribunals could apply for the hearing or any part of the hearing to take place in private (under the VAT Tribunals Rules, r 24). A direction that a hearing be held in private would only be made in exceptional circumstances.

An example of where such circumstances were found to arise was where the disclosure of information could have caused harm to an appellant's business (see *Consortium International Ltd* (VTD 824)).

APPROACH OF THE HIGH COURT

20.189 In *Revenue and Customs Comrs v Banerjee (No 2)* [2009] EWHC 1229 (Ch), the High Court refused an application from a taxpayer that its judgment be anonymised in order to protect her private life. The application was

20.190 *Tax appeals*

made after the proceedings had taken place in open court; and Dr Banerjee's previous appeal to the General Commissioners had been heard in public. The application was opposed by HMRC. Henderson J said:

> 'It is relevant to bear in mind, I think, that taxation always has been, and probably always will be, a subject of particular sensitivity both for the citizen and for the executive arm of government. It is an area where public and private interests intersect, if not collide; and for that reason there is nearly always a wider public interest potentially involved in even the most mundane seeming tax dispute. ... in tax cases the public interest generally requires the precise facts relevant to the decision to be a matter of public record, and not to be more or less heavily veiled by a process of redaction or anonymisation. The inevitable degree of intrusion into the taxpayer's privacy which this involves is, in all normal circumstances, the price which has to be paid for the resolution of tax disputes through a system of open justice rather than by administrative fiat.'

20.190 Henderson J also went on to note that there was nothing 'inherently sensitive or embarrassing about the information disclosed'. The judge concluded that 'it will only be in truly exceptional circumstances that a taxpayer's rights to privacy and confidentiality could properly prevail in the balancing exercise that the court has to perform'.

APPROACH OF THE FIRST-TIER TRIBUNAL

20.191 To date, there have been only a few reported cases of the FTT.

In *A v Revenue and Customs Comrs* [2012] UKFTT 541 (TC). A was a well-known broadcaster who participated in a marketed tax avoidance structure. He asked that his appeal be heard in private and that the decision be anonymised. This was on the basis that, if it were to become publicly known that he had used a tax avoidance structure, it was likely that he would receive adverse media comment that could damage his career and his future earning capacity. This was particularly relevant, in his view, because of recent public anger about the tax avoidance structures used by other media celebrities. He indicated that his concerns were such that he may withdraw his appeal rather than forfeit his anonymity.

20.192 The FTT followed *Bannerjee* and dismissed his application:

> 'There is an obvious public interest in its being clear that the tax system is being operated even-handedly, an interest which would be compromised if hearings before this tribunal were in private save in the most compelling of circumstances. The fact that a taxpayer is rich, or that he is in the public

eye, do not seem to me to dictate a different approach; on the contrary, it may be that hearing the appeal of such a person in private would give rise to the suspicion, if no more, that riches or fame can buy anonymity, and protection from the scrutiny which others cannot avoid. That plainly cannot be right.'

In *Clunes v Revenue and Customs Commissioners* [2017] UKFTT 204 (TC), the taxpayer (a well-known actor) sought a direction that his appeal against HMRC's decision that he was not entitled to set the cost of cosmetic treatment against his earnings in the calculation of his income tax liability should be heard in private and that any resulting published decision should be anonymised. The application was refused. The FTT held that the public interest in the outcome of tax litigation outweighed the desire of the taxpayer for anonymity. The inevitable resultant intrusion into matters which might otherwise remain confidential was the price that had to be paid for open justice, however unpalatable the individual taxpayer might find it to be.

It is to be noted that non-parties may be able to obtain copies of documents that have been filed at the tax tribunals. *Aria Technology Ltd v Revenue and Customs Commissioners* [2018] UKUT 111 (TCC) concerned an application by the company for an order that certain documents pertaining to a dispute between it and HMRC should not be disclosed to a (third party) publisher. The UT said that, although the CPR did not apply to the UT, it could provide helpful guidance where the UT Rules were silent or uncertain in scope and that, generally, the UT should follow a similar approach in exercising its powers (following *BPP Holdings*). There was no equivalent to CPR, r 5.4C in the UT Rules but there was also nothing that prohibited the UT from allowing a non-party to have access to documents that had been filed and were in the records. There was a strong presumption, founded on the open justice principle, that, where access was sought for a proper journalistic purpose, non-parties should be allowed access to documents relating to proceedings held in the UT. The company had not demonstrated that allowing access to its notice of appeal and HMRC's response would lead to any unfairness or was likely to cause it or any other person real harm. Its application was, accordingly, refused.

Decisions

20.193 The First-tier Rules, r 35 provides that the FTT may give an oral (extempore) decision at the hearing. The decision also must be communicated in writing to the parties within 28 days after making a decision by a decision notice that states the FTT's decision and informs the party of its appeal rights.

20.194 *Tax appeals*

20.194 Unless both parties agree that it is unnecessary, the decision notice must either include a summary of the findings of fact and the reasons for the decision or be accompanied by full written findings of fact and reasons for the decision. If the decision notice includes summary findings and reasons only or does not include any reasons or findings then either party may apply in writing (to be received within 28 days of the date that the decision notice was sent) for full written findings and reasons to be provided. On receiving such an application, the FTT is obliged to send the full statement of findings and reasons within 28 days 'or as soon as practicable thereafter' (First-tier Rules, r 35(6)).

A party who wishes to apply for permission to appeal the FTT's decision must apply for full written findings and reasons before making such an application.

The general practice is that, in basic appeals, decisions are given orally at the hearing, but, in standard and complex appeals, judgment will be reserved and full written decisions will be provided subsequently.

20.195 Decisions where full reasons have been provided are published on the tribunal's website and are reported in *Simon's First-tier Tax Decisions* (LexisNexis). The First-tier Rules do not contain any specific provisions regarding anonymisation of decisions. In *Reddleman Properties Ltd v Revenue and Customs Comrs* [2011] UKFTT 395 (TC), the FTT held that it was appropriate for the tribunal to apply the same criteria as are applicable to having a hearing heard in private. It said: 'It follows that there must be some compelling reason why any part of the proceedings must be in private. It is not enough that a taxpayer wishes to conceal his private affairs from others' and dismissed the application for anonymity.

In *Mr and Mrs Chan v Revenue and Customs Comrs (aka Mr and Mrs B v Revenue and Customs Comrs)* [2014] UKFTT 256 (TC), the FTT rejected the taxpayer's application for the decision to be anonymised, but agreed to anonymise the decision until the appeal process had been exhausted. The taxpayer did not appeal to the UT, and the decision was subsequently republished without anonymisation. The case concerned a solicitor's challenge to a penalty that had been imposed on him for a deliberate inaccuracy in a stamp duty land tax return. In refusing his application for anonymity, the FTT said:

> 'My conclusion is that this case, similarly to that in Mr A, concerns a taxpayer in an exceptional position, but that exceptional position, so far from justifying anonymity, positively favours full publication. Mr B wishes to hide alleged misdemeanours from the SRA, his clients and his potential clients. The Tribunal is here to administer justice: it is inimical to justice for the Tribunal to help Mr B keep from his professional body and his clients matters which even he thinks the SRA would consider relevant to his practice as a solicitor.'

Review of decisions

20.196 The FTT has power to correct administrative or clerical errors (such as spelling mistakes) in decisions, either of its own motion or consequent on an application by either party.

If a decision or direction is amended, a copy will be sent to all parties and the FTT will amend the published version (First-tier Rules, r 37).

20.197 A decision may be set aside if there has been a procedural irregularity and the FTT considers that it is in the interests of justice to do so (First-tier Rules, r 38). In *Jumbogate Ltd v Revenue and Customs Comrs* [2015] UKFTT 0064 (TC), the company had appealed against PAYE and NIC determinations. HMRC applied for the appeals to be struck out, on the basis that the substantive issue had been determined by the Court of Appeal's decision in *PA Holdings Ltd v Revenue and Customs Comrs* [2011] EWCA Civ 1414. The company did not attend the hearing of HMRC's application, and the FTT struck out the appeal, saying that:

> 'it is not open to an appellant simply to take no part in the proceedings, and to expect the tribunal to undertake its own analysis. That, in effect, is expecting the tribunal to stand in the shoes of the appellant and to make out a case for the appellant before making a determination as between that case and the case put forward by the respondents'.

20.198 The company subsequently applied for that decision to be set aside and for its appeal to be reinstated. Its application was successful, with it being observed that the amounts of tax and NICs at stake were substantial, and that the company's 'declared intention not to take part in the appeal were not due to deliberate disregard of its responsibilities but to the difficult financial situation in which it found itself'.

Procedural irregularities include documents either not being sent or being sent late or one party's representative not being present at the hearing.

An application to set aside a decision must be made to the FTT in writing within 28 days of the decision having been sent by the FTT (First-tier Rules, r 38(3)).

20.199 A party wishing to challenge a decision of the FTT must apply in writing to the FTT within 56 days of the latest date of receipt of:

(i) the fully reasoned decision;
(ii) notification of amended reasons for, or correction of, the decision following a review; or

20.200 *Tax appeals*

(iii) notification that an application for the decision to be set aside has been unsuccessful (First-tier Rules, r 39(2)).

20.200 The FTT has the power to extend time under First-tier Rules, r 5(3)(a). An application for permission to appeal outside this period must include a request for an extension of time and state the reason why the application is being made late.

20.201 On receiving an application for permission to appeal, the FTT must first consider, in accordance with the overriding objective, whether to review the decision (First-tier Rules, r 40). The FTT may only undertake a review if it is satisfied that there was an error of law in the decision (First-tier Rules, r 41(1)(b)) and it may not take any action without first having given all parties the opportunity to make representations. If the FTT decides not to review the decision or, having reviewed it, decides to take no action then it must consider whether to give permission to appeal. There is no prescribed test; and, as a general rule, the FTT judges tend to allow permission unless there is no reasonable prospect of success.

20.202 If the FTT refuses permission to appeal, then it must send to the parties a statement of its reasons for such refusal and notification that the party wishing to appeal may make an application direct to the UT for permission to appeal.

Costs

20.203 There are four circumstances when the FTT may award costs. These are:

(i) wasted costs;

(ii) unreasonable conduct;

(iii) complex cases; and

(iv) pre-April 2009 costs.

The quantum of costs may be ascertained by the tribunal by summary assessment, by agreement between the parties or by assessment upon application to the High Court or county court (First-tier Rules, r 10).

In *Bastionspark LLP (and others) v HMRC* [2016] UKUT 0425 (TCC), the UT considered an appeal against the decision of the FTT that the LLPs pay two-thirds of HMRC's costs. The UT noted that, in summary, the FTT had allowed the appeal of all five LLPs to a limited extent, but rejected the most significant of the claims that had been made by them. Given that, as a matter of common sense, neither party was wholly successful, but both parties were successful in some respects, it was necessary to apportion costs. In purely arithmetical terms, HMRC had succeeded to the extent of about 85% to 86%; and, as the case was entirely about how much (if any) of the sums disallowed by HMRC should have been allowed, the UT held that that did not seem to be an unreasonable way of measuring the relative success of the parties. The LLPs' appeal was accordingly dismissed.

Wasted costs

20.204 *TCEA 2007, s 29(4)* enables the FTT to make a wasted costs order. Wasted costs are costs that have been incurred by a party either:

(i) as a result of improper, unreasonable or negligent conduct by any legal or other representative; or

(ii) which the FTT considers that it would be unreasonable to expect that party to pay.

The costs of a hearing to deal with a failure to comply with directions, for example, could give rise to a wasted costs order being made against a party's representative.

20.205 In *Morris v Roberts (Inspector of Taxes)* [2005] EWHC 1040 (Ch), a wasted costs order was made against solicitors who had appealed against penalty determinations to the High Court and then withdrawn the appeal shortly before the proposed hearing. Lightman J considered that the appeal lacked merit. He noted the taxpayer's failure to pay previous adverse costs orders and penalty determinations and concluded that the appeal had been brought for delaying purposes only.

Unreasonable conduct

20.206 Under First-tier Rules, r 10(1)(b), the FTT may award costs if it considers that a party (or their representative) has acted unreasonably in bringing, defending or conducting the proceedings. The adverb 'wholly' that was in the Special Commissioners Regulations, reg 21 is not included and there is no requirement that the unreasonable conduct be 'in connection with the hearing', as had been the case before the Special Commissioners. Although this test is less stringent than the reg 21 test, costs are rarely awarded against a party under this head unless that party has acted in a capricious or vexatious fashion. It is considered that it is *prima facie* reasonable for a taxpayer to assert that a taxing statute does not apply to his particular factual circumstances, if there is a tenable argument to support that. It is to be noted that in *Homeowners Friendly Society Ltd v Barrett (Inspector of Taxes)* [1995]

20.207 *Tax appeals*

STC (SCD) 90, the Special Commissioner indicated that he did not consider that HMRC was acting wholly unreasonably in pursuing a point even though it had little confidence in the arguments.

20.207 As indicated above, the FTT makes costs orders under r 10(1)(b) relatively sparingly. An example of costs being awarded against HMRC under r 10(1)(b) is *Thomas Mawdsley & Son v Revenue and Customs Comrs* (TC/2010/05147), where HMRC withdrew the assessment one week before the hearing of the appeal was due to take place. HMRC submitted that it was not until it was served with the appellant's witness statement that it appreciated what the appellant's case was. The tribunal rejected this submission by HMRC. It said that *'the case for the appellant had been set out clearly both prior to and throughout proceedings'*, and held that, because HMRC had failed to consider properly the documents provided by the appellant or the appellant's case as a whole, its conduct had been unreasonable. Other similar examples include *Atkins' Executors v Revenue and Customs Comrs* [2011] UKFTT 468 (TC) (where HMRC withdrew an assessment shortly before the hearing) and *Bogle v Revenue and Customs Comrs* [2014] UKFTT 201 (TC) (where HMRC withdrew a penalty shortly before the hearing).

Complex cases

20.208 If the proceedings have been allocated as a complex case under First-tier Rules, r 23 then the FTT has a costs jurisdiction. The default costs approach is as in the High Court: the losing party pays the costs of the successful party.

20.209 However, a taxpayer can elect to opt out of the default approach and submit to a 'no costs' environment, as for default paper, basic and standard cases, by making a written request to the tribunal within 28 days of receiving notice that the case has been allocated as a complex case. Such a decision is irrevocable. Once made, the FTT has no power to make an order in respect of costs (save in respect of wasted costs or because it considers that a party has acted unreasonably): see *Revenue and Customs Comrs v Atlantic Electronics* [2012] UKUT 45 (TCC).

This means also that the FTT may not make an order that the costs of preparing hearing bundles for a substantive appeal should be shared between the taxpayer and HMRC: see *Eclipse Film Partners No 35 LLP v Revenue and Customs Comrs* [2016] 1 WLR 1939.

In *Eclipse*, the appeal had been allocated to the complex track, and Eclipse then opted out of the costs regime. At a case management hearing before the FTT, the tribunal judge, having ordered that Eclipse should prepare the hearing bundles, made an oral direction that the costs of doing so should be shared. Eclipse prepared the hearing bundle and, after it had lost the substantive case, sent HMRC a bill for half the cost of preparing the bundle. HMRC refused to pay and applied to the FTT to set aside the direction, on the ground that the tribunal's jurisdiction to make a costs order was limited to the circumstances set out in rule 10(1), namely appeals allocated as complex cases where the taxpayer had not exercised the right to disapply the power, and cases where the tribunal decided to make a wasted costs order or considered that a party or the party's representative had acted unreasonably in bringing, defending or conducting the proceedings. The UT, the Court of Appeal, and the Supreme Court agreed with HMRC.

Eclipse raised two arguments. First, that an order to share costs was not the same thing as an order to pay costs and that what was prohibited was the latter. And, secondly, that the FTT's power to make various case management orders must include, by implication, the power, incidentally, to make awards of costs. It was argued that it was clearly implied that, even where the taxpayer had opted for the no-costs regime, the Tribunal could allow amendment or adjournment conditional on the payment of expenses to compensate the other party.

The Supreme Court rejected both arguments. The case management powers, set out in the First-tier Rules r 5(3), did not confer jurisdiction on the FTT to make costs orders, as to do so would have a significant adverse effect on the regime under r 10(1) which limited the tribunal's power to order costs to situations where either wasted costs or unreasonable behaviour could be invoked.

If the taxpayer wishes to opt out of the costs regime, but is desirous of receiving a contribution from HMRC to the costs of preparing hearing bundles for the appeal, it is recommended that this be addressed before opting out of the costs regime. Failing that, a direction should be sought that the parties prepare the bundles jointly. Both the Court of Appeal and the Supreme Court said that the FTT could have ordered both parties to prepare the bundles, in which case there would have been a powerful argument for saying that Eclipse could have recovered half the costs, on the basis of a contribution between two jointly liable parties.

20.210 A written ministerial statement that sets out HMRC's policy in relation to costs was made by the Financial Secretary to the Treasury (Mr Stephen Timms) and the Financial Services Secretary to the Treasury (Lord Myners) on 30 March 2009 (Hansard HC Vol 490, col 29WS and Hansard HL Vol 709, col WS60). This replaces the statement that was made on 12 March 1980 by Mr Peter Rees, then Minister of State at the Treasury.

20.211 *Tax appeals*

20.211 In the 2009 ministerial statement, it is indicated that HMRC may waive its right to seek costs in certain circumstances:

'The general rule in the appeal courts is that the losing party risks having to pay the other side's costs, and I do not think it would be right to treat tax cases differently as a matter of course.

However, HM Revenue and Customs (HMRC) exercise their discretion and are willing in appropriate circumstances, and in particular where it is they who are appealing against an adverse decision, to consider waiving any claim to costs in cases before the Upper Tribunal or the appeal courts, or to consider making other arrangements – this may also extend to cases before the First-tier Tribunal.

In the minority of cases categorised as complex, where costs can be awarded in the Tax Chamber of the First-tier Tribunal other than for unreasonable behaviour, the appellant can ensure that there is no risk of them bearing HMRC's costs by opting for the costs rules not to apply.

In considering the exercise of HMRC's discretion, influential factors include the risk of financial hardship to the other party, the involvement of a point of law the clarification of which would be of significant benefit to taxpayers as a whole and the efficient collection and management of revenue for which HMRC have responsibility.

If HMRC are to come to an arrangement of this nature, they would expect to do so in advance of the hearing and following an approach by the taxpayer involved.'

20.212 It is considered that, if the outcome of a particular appeal may affect a significant number of taxpayers (and particularly where the tax in issue for the appellant taxpayer is not significant), then the taxpayer should, at an early stage, approach HMRC to discuss whether an agreement under which he has no liability to HMRC's costs can be reached in advance of an appeal.

Pre-1 April 2009 appeals

20.213 Where a taxpayer has appealed against a decision before 1 April 2009, but the hearing has not taken place before that date, the FTT may make directions to apply the old procedural rules (Transfer of Tribunal Functions and Revenue and Customs Appeals Order 2009, Sch 3, para 7(3)) in order to deal with cases fairly and justly. Under the transitional rules, an order for costs may be made only if, and to the extent that, an order for costs could have been made before 1 April 2009, regardless of when the costs have been incurred (Transfer of Tribunal Functions and Revenue and Customs Appeals Order 2009, Sch 3, para 7(7)).

20.214 In *Surestone Ltd v Revenue and Customs Comrs* [2009] UKFTT 352 (TC), the FTT held that r 23 (allocation of costs to categories) applies only to appeals made after 1 April 2009. Accordingly, appeals that commenced before April 2009 cannot be allocated as complex cases, even if they satisfy one or more of the complex case tests. In order for a pre-April 2009 appeal to be within a costs regime, a taxpayer must rely on the transitional provisions. A similar approach was taken by the FTT in *Hawkeye Communications v Revenue and Customs Comrs* [2010] UKFTT 636 (TC). However, in *Babergh District Council* [2011] UKFTT 341 (TC) and *Everest Ltd* [2010] UKFTT 621 (TC), the FTT took the opposite view and said that allocation is possible.

20.215 Although the transitional rules were considered by the UT in *Atlantic Electronics v Revenue and Customs Comrs* [2012] UKUT 45 (TCC), the issue as to whether or not allocation for pre-April 2009 appeals is possible was not decided. Warren J held that the default position is that the post-April 2009 provisions apply. He identified two policy considerations: 'One policy is to give the taxpayer in a Complex case a choice as to the applicable costs regime, a choice which a taxpayer must make at an early stage of the proceedings' and the second policy 'is to provide certainty about the applicable costs regime at an early stage of the proceedings. ... If a taxpayer was able to exercise his right of election at a late stage, or even until the result of the appeal was known, he would be able to elect for the regime which he knew was the more favourable to him; this would amount, effectively, to one-way costs shifting which was obviously never intended'.

20.216 He held that the transitional rules permit the FTT to direct that costs incurred at different stages in the proceedings be dealt with differently and that the FTT should take the following factors into account when deciding which rules apply:

(*a*) the extent to which work relating to the case was done before or from 1 April 2009;

(*b*) how soon after 1 April 2009 the costs application was made; and

(*c*) any representations made by the parties to one another in relation to costs.

20.217 In *National Exhibition Centre Ltd v Revenue and Customs Comrs* [2014] SFTD 107, the FTT said:

'We note that the Upper Tribunal in *Atlantic Electronics Ltd* [2012] STC 931 expressed the view obiter (at [14]) that the decision in *Surestone* 'might have come as a surprise to some people' but declined to rule whether it was right or wrong. On balance we feel that, for the reasons set out by Judge Clark in *Babergh District Council*, allocation is possible.'

20.218 *Tax appeals*

20.218 It directed that the (pre-2009) appeal be allocated to the complex category. The issue was not considered by the UT on appeal ([2015] UKUT 23 (TCC)). Accordingly, there remains jurisprudential uncertainty regarding the issue. It will be addressed, *de facto*, when all appeals that have been lodged before 1 April 2009 have been heard by the FTT (or otherwise concluded). But, even though it is fast approaching the 10 year anniversary of the new system, particularly due to the number of appeals that have been made and then stayed, that has yet to occur.

THE UPPER TRIBUNAL

The function of the Upper Tribunal

20.219 The UT's main role is to act as a court of appeal from the FTT. It has replaced the High Court as an appellate tax court in this regard. The UT also has jurisdiction to hear references against decisions of the Financial Services Authority (FSA) and the Pensions Regulator. In some cases, such as tax and FSA cases, the UT's jurisdiction is UK-wide; in other cases the geographical jurisdiction is slightly more limited.

20.220 In *National Exhibition Centre Ltd v Revenue and Customs Comrs* [2015] UKUT 23 (TCC), the UT considered whether, when it sat in England, it was bound by a decision of the Scottish Court of Session. It concluded that English and Scottish courts (and tribunals) are not bound to follow the judicial decisions of the other jurisdiction; a decision in a Scottish court does not create a precedent in an English court (and vice versa). However, it added that, for a UK tax to be applied uniformly across England and Scotland it needs to be interpreted uniformly and that, consequently, cross-border decisions should be followed as far as possible.

The UT also has jurisdiction in relation to judicial review cases in certain instances. This is analysed in more detail at **20.234** *et seq*.

20.221 In addition to tax appeals from the FTT, some cases go directly to the UT:

- direct referrals;
- appeals in which there are conflicting FTT decisions;
- some tax-related judicial review cases; and
- applications by HMRC for the imposition of additional penalties where they consider that significant tax is at risk (under *FA 2008, Sch 36, para 50*).

Direct referrals to the Upper Tribunal

20.222 Complex cases may, with the consent of the parties, be referred directly to the UT by the FTT. In order to transfer a complex case directly to the UT, the FTT may, with the consent of the parties, refer a case to the President of the Tax Chamber, who may, with the agreement of the President of the Tax and Finance Chamber of the UT, direct that the case be transferred to the UT (First-tier Rules, r 28).

Once a complex case has been transferred to the UT, the rules relating to the composition of the panel are the same as those that govern complex cases in the FTT.

20.223 For a case to qualify for such a referral, it has to:

(*a*)   raise a point of law of wide importance or particular complexity; and

(*b*)   not involve a complex factual dispute.

20.224 The policy intention is that the number of cases that will be heard by the UT acting as a first instance tribunal will be very small. Since the establishment of the UT in 2009, only a handful of cases have been so heard. The first case to be heard by the UT in such capacity was that of *John Wilkins (Motor Engineers) Ltd v Revenue and Customs Comrs* [2009] UKUT 175 (TCC). This was an unusual case procedurally; it was the tribunal limb of claims by taxpayers for compound interest on overpaid VAT, where the same substantive legal issue had already been heard by the High Court (*FJ Chalke and AC Barnes v Revenue and Customs Comrs* [2009] EWHC 952 (Ch)).

Appeals from the First-tier Tribunal

20.225 There is no automatic right of appeal from a decision of FTT to the UT. This is in contrast to the pre-1 April 2009 position, where taxpayers could appeal to the High Court as of right in most cases.

20.226 The following decisions are not appealable:

- a decision by the FTT not to review its own decision;
- a decision by the FTT to take no action following a review;
- a decision to set aside an earlier FTT decision;
- a decision that has already been set aside; and
- any other decisions of the character specified in the Appeals (Excluded Decisions) Order 2009, SI 2009/275.

20.227   Tax appeals

20.227   Appeals from the FTT are on points of law only (*TCEA 2007, s 11(1)*) (as was the case with appeals from the Special or General Commissioners or the VAT and Duties Tribunals to the High Court). Although *TCEA 2007, s 12* which prescribes the powers of the UT to make determinations on an appeal involving an error on a point of law, expressly bestows on the UT a power to make 'findings of fact', an appeal to the UT does not give the appellant the opportunity to re-litigate factual issues in respect of which the FTT has made findings (see para 7.19 of the 2004 White Paper *Transforming Public Services: Complaints, Redress and the Tribunals*), and the hearing will not be a rehearing.

20.228   The ability of the UT to make findings of fact is limited and is analogous to the ability that the High Court possessed under *TMA 1970, s 56A*, applying *Edwards v Bairstow* [1956] AC 14. In essence, findings of facts may be challenged only if they are outside the ambit of 'reasonable judgment'. This can be a difficult test to meet; see, for example, *MJP Media Services Ltd v Revenue and Customs Comrs* [2012] EWCA Civ 1558.

20.229   As set out above, an application for permission to appeal a decision of the FTT must first be made to the FTT. The legal test applicable to applications for permission to appeal to the Upper Tribunal is whether 'it is arguable that there is an error of law and that the case is an appropriate one for the Upper Tribunal' (*ATEC Associates Ltd v Commissioners for HM Revenue and Customs*, unreported, 4 December 2009).

If the FTT refuses permission to appeal, an application may be made to the UT (*TCEA 2007, s 11(4)(b)*). Applications for permission to appeal must be made in writing. The application for permission to appeal is considered in the first instance by the UT on the papers filed.

20.230   The application for permission must be received by the UT within one month of the date on which the FTT previously refused the application (Upper Tribunal Rules, r 21(3)(b)). If the application is filed outside the one-month period, it must include a request for an extension of time giving the reasons why it is late. In *Revenue and Customs Comrs v McCarthy & Stone Developments Ltd* [2014] UKUT 196 (TCC), the UT rejected an application by HMRC to lodge a late appeal. It noted that HMRC had not advanced any reason for its failure to comply with the rules other than administrative error. The UT said that 'it would not be consistent with the need to ensure that appeals in the Upper Tribunal are conducted efficiently to allow HMRC to serve a notice of appeal almost two months after the time limit has expired'.

20.231   If permission is refused on the papers, the party seeking to appeal the decision may apply in writing (to be received within 14 days of the UT sending notice of its refusal to give permission to appeal) for an oral hearing before the

UT of the application (Upper Tribunal Rules, r 22(3)–(5), as substituted by the Tribunal Procedure (Amendment) Rules 2009, SI 2009/274, r 14).

20.232 If permission is granted, the appellant must provide a notice of appeal to the UT within one month after permission to appeal has been sent to the appellant. If it is the UT (rather than the FTT) that has given permission to appeal, generally the application for permission will be treated as the notice of appeal and a copy of it will be sent to the respondents by the UT (Upper Tribunal Rules, r 22(2)(b)). The UT may, with the agreement of all parties, determine the appeal without the need for any further papers (although, in practice, this power is exercised rarely).

20.233 In cases where the FTT gave permission to appeal, the UT, having received notice of the appeal sends a copy of the notice of appeal to the respondents to the appeal. The respondents then have one month within which they may file a written response. The response must state whether the respondent opposes the appeal and give the grounds on which they intend to rely. It must also state whether or not the respondent wants the case to be dealt with at a hearing (Upper Tribunal Rules, r 24). The appellant then has one month within which they may reply to the response (Upper Tribunal Rules, r 25). Having received the papers, the UT will either decide the appeal without a hearing, if the parties have agreed, or will arrange for the case to be listed and heard.

20.234 The UT must decide if the FTT made an error of law. If it does so decide, then it may set aside the original decision (although it is not obliged to do so). If the decision is set aside, the UT must either remit the matter back to the FTT for it to reconsider or give a new decision itself.

20.235 If the UT does not remit the case to the FTT, it may make any decision on the case that the FTT could have made (under *TCEA 2007, s 12(4)(a)*). In the event that the UT remits the case to the FTT, it may give directions as to how the case should be managed by the FTT. This can include directing that the case be heard by a differently constituted panel (under *TCEA 2007, s 14(3)(a)*).

Judicial review

20.236 TCEA 2007 created a statutory regime that enables the UT to exercise judicial review powers in appropriate cases. Where it has jurisdiction, the UT has power to grant the following kinds of relief:

(i)   a mandatory order;

(ii) a prohibiting order;

20.237 *Tax appeals*

(iii) a quashing order;

(iv) a declaration; or

(v) an injunction ('the judicial review reliefs').

20.237 These powers may be used either where:

- a direction has been made by the Lord Chief Justice, with the agreement of the Lord Chancellor, specifying a class of case that is to be heard in the UT, rather than the High Court (under *TCEA 2007, s 18*); or
- the High Court has ordered the transfer of an individual case, because it considers that it is just and convenient to do so (under *TCEA 2007, s 19(3)*).

20.238 Whilst the legislation allows for an application for permission to judicially review a matter to be made in the first instance to the UT, the UT must transfer such an application to the High Court unless it meets the four conditions set out within *TCEA 2007, s 18*, so that the UT has the function of deciding the application.

20.239 The first condition is that the application does not seek anything other than the judicial review reliefs. The second condition is that the application does not call into question anything done by the Crown Court. Condition three is that the application falls within a class specified for the purposes of s 18 in a direction given in accordance with the *Constitutional Reform Act 2005, Sch 2, Pt 1*. A Practice Direction was made for this purpose by the Lord Chief Justice on 28 October 2009. It specifies the class of cases that fall within condition three as decisions of the FTT where there is no right of appeal to the UT only. The fourth condition is that the judge who will hear the application is either a judge of the High Court or the Court of Appeal or 'such other persons as may be agreed from time to time between the Lord Chief Justice ... and the Senior President of Tribunals'. Conditions 1, 2 and 4 are likely to be met in the majority of tax judicial review cases; however, condition 3 will be met (at present) in very few cases. Consequently, the present situation (ie unless and until a further Practice Direction is released in this regard) is that almost all judicial review cases need to be commenced in the High Court.

20.240 Where a claim for judicial review has commenced in the High Court, a different condition 4 applies. It is highly unlikely to be relevant to a tax case, and, accordingly, condition 4 is likely to be satisfied in the vast majority of tax cases. If all four conditions are met, then the High Court must transfer the application to the UT. Where only conditions 1, 2 and 4 are met, the High Court may transfer the application if it appears to be just and convenient to do so.

20.241 Accordingly, although the majority of tax judicial review cases must be started in the High Court, the majority of these applications will be suitable to be considered for transfer from the High Court to the UT. After transfer, the case will then be decided by a High Court judge sitting in the UT, applying the rules of the UT.

In many instances, there will be both a tax appeal and judicial review proceedings pertaining to connected issues. The appropriate procedure to be adopted has to be decided on a case-by-case basis.

20.242 In *Reed Employment plc v Revenue and Customs Comrs* [2010] UKFTT 596 (TC), the tax appeal and the legitimate expectation issues were highly interconnected, both factually and in law. Warren J and Judge Avery Jones (sitting as judges of both the UT and the FTT) considered the appropriate procedure to be adopted. Warren J exercised his casting vote and directed that the tax appeal be heard in the FTT (by Judge Avery Jones) and the judicial review proceedings be stayed until after release of the tax appeal decision.

However, it was indicated by the judges that they did want this case to be seen as a pointer towards any practice.

20.243 In *Revenue and Customs Comrs v Dhanak* [2014] UKUT 68 (TCC), there was what was described by the judge as a 'procedural thicket.' The taxpayer had appealed against amendments made to his tax returns by HMRC that denied relief under *ITEPA 2003, s 386*, and also had issued protective judicial review proceedings. HMRC made an application to strike out the taxpayer's appeal, on the basis that the FTT had no jurisdiction to consider the refusal of relief. That application was dismissed by the FTT; HMRC was given permission to appeal to the UT. The judicial review proceedings were transferred to the UT. It was directed that all three matters be heard together, with the statutory appeal being heard by the FTT and the two other matters being heard by the UT. The judge allocated to hear the matters was not authorised to sit in the FTT. In order to cut through the thicket, he transferred the statutory appeal to the UT during the hearing, and heard all matters together.

Case management powers

20.244 The UT may regulate its own procedures and it has the same case management powers as the FTT. In addition, under Upper Tribunal Rules, r 5 it may also, *inter alia*:

- suspend the effect of a decision where a party has made an application for permission to appeal or whilst an appeal is ongoing; and

20.245 *Tax appeals*

- ask the FTT to provide information or documents in relation to any decision and the reasons for that decision.

20.245 Under Upper Tribunal Rules, r 7, the UT may take any action that it considers 'just' to deal with a failure to comply with directions. There is no definition as to what would be considered just in the legislation; each case is likely to be considered by the UT by reference to the circumstances of the failure, and in accordance with the overriding objective. The actions that can be taken include:

- waiving the requirement;
- requiring the failure to be remedied;
- striking the case out; or
- restricting a party's participation in the proceedings.

Also, as a superior court of record, the UT has the power to treat failure to comply with an order of the UT as contempt; a custodial sentence can be imposed.

Hearings

20.246 Whilst the UT may make any decision without an oral hearing, it must have regard to the views of the parties when deciding whether to hold a hearing (Upper Tribunal Rules, r 34). This is in contrast to the FTT, which can decide cases without a hearing only if both parties consent. Absent this difference, the rules applying to hearings before the two tribunals are broadly the same. Legal representation before the UT is not mandatory; and a party's representative need not be legally qualified (see Upper Tribunal Rules, r 11).

Generally, most cases are heard by one UT judge. The Chamber President may require a hearing before up to three UT judges.

20.247 As in the FTT, a hearing will be held in public unless the UT directs that all or part of it should be heard in private. The Upper Tribunal Rules do not specify when it is appropriate for the UT to so direct. It is considered extremely unlikely that the UT would direct that a hearing be heard in private unless it was for the one of the reasons that the FTT is obliged to consider (ie the interests of public order or national security, protection of a person's right to a private or family life, confidentiality of information, the avoidance of serious harm to the public interest). In *Revenue and Customs Comrs v Sir AF Morrison* [2013] UKUT 497 (TCC), the UT rejected an application for a hearing to take place in private saying that *'the court will not depart from the principle of open justice simply to save one or other party from embarrassment'*.

Decisions

20.248 The UT may give a decision orally at the hearing (Upper Tribunal Rules, r 40). A written decision, with reasons, together with information on appeal rights, must be sent to all parties as soon as is 'reasonably practicable' after making the decision (the term 'reasonably practicable' is not defined) under Upper Tribunal Rules, r 40(2).

The UT is a superior court of record and its decisions are published.

Costs in the Upper Tribunal

20.249 The UT has a full costs jurisdiction. However, the UT may not make an order for costs against a person without first (i) giving that person an opportunity to make representations; and (ii) if the person is an individual and either the proceedings were a judicial review or if the UT considers the person (or his representatives) has acted unreasonably, considering the person's financial means.

Appeals from the Upper Tribunal

20.250 As in the FTT, the UT has power to correct clerical errors (such as spelling mistakes) in decisions by sending notification of the amended decision to all parties and making any necessary amendments to any information published in relation to the decision (under Upper Tribunal Rules, r 42).

20.251 Also as at the FTT, the UT may set aside a decision if there has been a procedural irregularity and the UT considers that it is in the interests of justice to do so (Upper Tribunal Rules, r 43). A written application to set aside a decision must be made to the UT so that it is received within one month of the decision being sent by the UT.

20.252 An appeal from the UT lies to the Court of Appeal. In the first instance, permission to appeal must be sought from the UT (Upper Tribunal Rules, r 44(1)). Following the UT's decision, the unsuccessful party has one month in which to seek permission to appeal.

20.253 In *Grogan v Revenue and Customs Comrs* (unreported, 20 November 2010), the UT indicated that it viewed this power with circumspection. It considered that permission should not be granted by the UT unless the appeal has a real prospect of success and that, in cases of doubt, it should leave the matter to the Court of Appeal. If the UT refuses to give permission, it must inform the parties in writing of the reasons for refusal. If permission is refused, the party then may apply to the Court of Appeal.

20.254 *Tax appeals*

20.254 The available grounds for appeal are the same as those for an appeal from the High Court to the Court of Appeal (as set out in *Access to Justice Act 1999*): first it must be an appeal on a point of law; and, secondly, the proposed appeal must raise an important point of principle or practice or there must be some other compelling reason for the Court of Appeal to hear the appeal (Appeals from the Upper Tribunal to the Court of Appeal Order 2008, para 2).

20.255 Under the Access to Justice Act 1999, s 55(1) 'second appeals' are to be granted only in exceptional circumstances. The above test applied for appeals from the High Court even if the taxpayer succeeded at first instance, but lost on appeal. Although the change was introduced to ensure that 'second appeals would ... become a rarity' (per Brooke LJ in *Tanfern Ltd v Cameron-MacDonald* [2000] 1 WLR 1311 at 1320C), it was often not too difficult to demonstrate an 'important point of principle' in tax matters when applying for permission for a second appeal to the Court of Appeal.

20.256 The Court of Appeal grants permission for appeals from specialist tribunals more sparingly. The fact that the Upper Tribunal (Tax and Chancery Chamber) is a specialist tribunal (whereas the High Court was not, even when it heard tax cases) does not seem to have a significant impact on the number of tax appeals that are granted permission to be heard by the Court of Appeal.

20.257 *Access to Justice Act 1999, s 54(4)* provides that there is no appeal from a decision of the Court of Appeal refusing permission to appeal to that court.

Consequently, if the Court of Appeal refuses to grant permission, the appeal process ends.

THE TAX COURTS

The High Court

20.258 As set out above, prior to 1 April 2009, the High Court sat as an appellate court from the Commissioners, the *s 706* tribunal, and the VAT and duties tribunals. The UT has effectively assumed the jurisdiction of the High Court as regards this appellate function.

20.259 In very general terms, before 1 April 2009, the High Court also existed as a potential jurisdiction of first instance where, in a tax-related matter, there was no statutory route of appeal to the tax tribunals.

The High Court's jurisdiction has not been expressly transferred to the UT and so the extent to which this jurisdiction has been assumed also by the UT is, to a degree, unclear.

20.260 The principle of 'exclusive jurisdiction' applies to delimit the jurisdiction of the High Court. In very broad terms, the principle of 'exclusive jurisdiction' has the consequence that the jurisdiction of the High Court is ousted at first instance if there is a statutory scheme containing its own system of remedies in place to deal with claims and Parliament has assigned resolution of such disputes to that scheme.

20.261 Whether the correct analysis of the principle is that, where the proceedings come within the area that has been assigned to a statutory tribunal and thus concern matters over which the specialist tribunal should have exclusive jurisdiction, but jurisdiction has not been explicitly confined by statute to that tribunal (as, for example, *Taxes Management Act 1964, s 5(6)* and (as originally enacted) *s 29(6)* confined the right to challenge assessments to the tax tribunals), then the jurisdiction of the High Court is excluded (cf the House of Lords' decision in *Barraclough v Brown* [1897] AC 615) or, alternatively, retained, but subject to the rule that the High Court should exercise its discretion to refuse jurisdiction (cf the House of Lords' decision in *Re Vandervell's Trusts* [1971] AC 912) remains an open question.

20.262 It is the author's view that it is only where a taxpayer's High Court claim is an indirect way of seeking to achieve exactly the same result as it would be open to the taxpayer to achieve directly by appealing to the tax tribunals, that the High Court's jurisdiction is excluded absolutely (as this is, or is tantamount to, abuse of process). However, if there are elements of the claim that differ, including, for example, the seeking of a remedy that the tribunal has no power to grant, the High Court jurisdiction is not ousted and it is an issue of discretion.

20.263 Matters that could be taken to the High Court before 1 April 2009 included:

- claims to recover overpayments of tax (although, if *TMA 1970, s 33* applied, this potentially provided an exclusive procedure. See *Woolwich Equitable Building Society v IRC* [1992] STC 657, and *Deutsche Morgan Grenfell Group plc v IRC* [2006] UKHL 49);
- claims for declaratory relief (see, for example, *Buxton v Public Trustee* (1962) 41 TC 235, where a declaration was sought that trusts were charitable);
- claims for damages in tort (such as proceedings for negligence or misfeasance in a public office against HMRC); and
- judicial review of decisions of HMRC or the tax tribunals.

20.264 *Tax appeals*

20.264 It is considered that the matters listed above may still be taken to the High Court, save that the position regarding: (i) judicial review; and (ii) claims to recover overpayments of tax with effect in relation to claims made on after 1 April 2010 is now more complicated. The issue of judicial review is addressed further above at **20.234** *et seq*.

20.265 *TMA 1970, Sch 1AB* (which was inserted by *FA 2009*) is intended to provide a complete code with regard to claims to recover overpayments of tax; consideration as to whether it achieves that purpose is outside the scope of this chapter.

20.266 Under *IHTA 1984, s 222(3)*, the High Court is also an alternative first-instance venue for certain inheritance tax appeals. An appeal against a determination by HMRC may be notified to the High Court where either the appellant and the Board agree that the matters for decision on appeal 'are likely to be substantially confined to questions of law' or, in the absence of such agreement, if the appellant applies for and obtains leave from the High Court, having satisfied the court that the subject matter falls within that category.

20.267 In *Bennett v IRC* [1995] STC 54, where Lightman J gave leave for an inheritance tax appeal to be heard at first instance at the High Court, he held that, whilst it was a precondition for leave that the appeal be substantially confined to questions of law, it was also necessary to determine whether the issue, by reason of its novelty, importance or otherwise, was one which could and should proceed by way of appeal directly to the High Court. Leave was granted on the basis that a short but important issue of law was raised and it was likely that any decision of the Special Commissioners would be appealed.

Court of Justice of the European Union

20.268 The jurisdiction of the Court of Justice of the European Union (CJEU) is defined in the EU treaties. It has jurisdiction over the following matters:

- failure by a Member State to fulfil an obligation under the Treaty on the Functioning of the European Union (previously known as the EC Treaty);
- legality of acts of the institutions of the European Union; and
- interpreting EU law at the request of national courts and tribunals (preliminary rulings).

20.269 The CJEU comprises one judge from each of the member states. The court may sit as a full court, but rarely does so. It usually sits in chambers of

Tax appeals **20.275**

three or five judges, depending on the importance or complexity of the issues, and occasionally as a Grand Chamber of 13 judges.

20.270 Cases are dealt with via a two-stage procedure. The first stage requires the parties and any interested member states (and the European Commission) to submit written statements to the CJEU (known as 'written observations'). An appointed judge then summarises the statements into a report. The second stage of a case is the oral hearing, at which the parties and the interested member states (and the European Commission) have the opportunity to give short, oral submissions to the court.

20.271 The court is assisted by Advocates General. At the end of a hearing, the Advocate General appointed to the case may prepare a detailed written opinion which is publicly released. Since 2003, Advocates General are only required to give an opinion where the court decides that the case deals with a new point of law. If the Advocate General does provide an opinion, it is authoritative, but not binding on the CJEU. However, the CJEU does often (albeit not always) follow the Advocate General's opinion.

20.272 The general rule is that, where a question concerning EU law arises before a national court or tribunal, the matter may be referred to the CJEU if a decision on the question is necessary to enable the national court to give judgment. However, under Article 267 of the Treaty on the Functioning of the European Union (previously Article 234 of the EC Treaty), the matter must be referred to the CJEU if there is no right of appeal from a decision of the court or tribunal.

20.273 Thus, courts of last resort (typically the Supreme Court in the UK) do not have a discretion as to whether to make a reference on an EU law issue which it is necessary to resolve before judgment can be given (although the court in question retains its discretion to decide whether a decision on a question of EU Law is necessary to enable it to give judgment (see *Henn and Darby v DPP* [1981] AC 850). If the answer to the EU law point is '*acte clair*' (in essence so obvious that there is no scope for any reasonable doubt), then there is no obligation to refer the question to the CJEU.

20.274 The decision to make a reference is a matter for the national court or tribunal, not for the parties to the case. The court is not even bound to accept a joint submission by the parties that an issue of EU law that is not *acte clair* arises (see *Rheinmuhlen-Dusseldorf v Einfuhr-und Vorratsstelle fur Getreide und Futtermittel (Case 166/73)* [1974] ECR 33). Similarly, a reference may be made by a court against the wishes of all the parties (see, for example, *Direct Cosmetics v Customs and Excise Commissioners* [1984] 1 CMLR 99).

20.275 Thus, if one of the parties disagrees with the decision regarding the making of a reference to the CJEU, he must appeal under national law

20.276 *Tax appeals*

to challenge that decision: there is no direct right of access to the CJEU (see for example, *Marks and Spencer v Halsey* [2003] STC (SCD) 70: the Special Commissioners declined to refer questions to the CJEU; that decision was appealed to the High Court, where Park J referred questions to the CJEU).

20.276 In *R v International Stock Exchange, ex p Else Ltd* [1993] QB 534, Sir Thomas Bingham set out guidelines that courts should be mindful of when deciding whether or not to refer issues of EU law to the CJEU. If the issues are almost certain to be conclusive of the outcome of these appeals, and it cannot be said that the court can resolve the issue itself 'with complete confidence', the issues should be referred.

20.277 If the delay and costs of an appeal can be avoided by the making of a reference at an early stage, then that is a relevant consideration for a court to consider (see Bingham J in *Customs and Excise Commissioners v ApS Samex (Hanil Synthetic Fiber Industrial Co Ltd)* [1983] 3 CMLR 194).

20.278 It is the responsibility of the UK court, rather than the parties, to settle the terms of the reference, although, in practice, the parties are normally involved in the drafting process. *Practice Direction (ECJ References: Procedure)* [1999] 1 WLR 260 states that the reference should 'identify as clearly, succinctly and simply as the nature of the case permits the question to which the British court seeks an answer. It is very desirable that language should be used which lends itself readily to translation.'

If a reference is made, the CJEU will not concern itself with the question of whether or not a reference was necessary; it will simply give a decision.

20.279 When questions are referred to the CJEU by national courts or tribunals, the CJEU's sole function is to decide what the EU law is and to assist the referring court on the point of law in abstract. It does not have jurisdiction to interpret national law; and it is for the referring court or tribunal to apply the relevant rule of EU law, after it has been interpreted by the ECJ, in the specific case pending before it (see, for example, *Marks and Spencer plc v Halsey (Case C-446/03)* [2006] STC 237, where the decision of the CJEU was applied by the referring High Court ([2006] STC 1235), and further by the Court of Appeal ([2008] STC 526)).

On 23 June 2016, an 'In/Out' referendum was held in the UK. The decision (by a small margin) was to leave the European Union. Following the enactment of the *European Union Notification of Withdrawal Act 2017*, the Prime Minister sent a notification of the UK's withdrawal from the EU to the European Council President on 29 March 2017. The UK remains subject to EU law unless and until an Article 50 withdrawal agreement comes into force; the CJEU has confirmed that it will consider all references that have been made to it by UK courts prior to March 2019. Accordingly, the above explanation as regards references to the CJEU remains accurate (see *BAT Industries PLC v R & C Comrs* [2017] UKFTT 558 (TC)). As the UK will remain subject to EU law during the proposed transitional period, it seems likely that, if the Withdrawal Agreement that is currently the subject of debate between the EU and the UK is agreed, that will remain the position until 31 December 2020.

KEY POINTS

20.280 The following six key points are intended as a guide for the practitioner considering the merits of litigation:

1 Whilst, as a general rule, reaching a negotiated settlement with HMRC is preferable to resolution via litigation, that is a general rule only.

2 The approach that should be adopted in any particular case can be arrived at only after considering fully what is best for the taxpayer.

3 Start the consideration of litigation (and use of litigious tactics) as early as possible. Dealing with enquiries from the perspective that, ultimately, the underlying issues may be heard by a tribunal or court can achieve considerable improvements, both in terms of the cost of compliance and the ultimate outcome of the case.

4 Objectively assess the strengths and weaknesses of the client's position, and of HMRC's position.

5 Consider whether you should bring in a specialist to assist.

6 Keep the client informed.

Chapter 21

Tackling 'tax avoidance'

Dawn Register
BSc (Hons) CTA TEP CEDR Accredited Mediator; Partner, BDO LLP

SIGNPOSTS

- **Introduction** – HMRC can remove the cash flow advantage from tax scheme users by issuing an Accelerated Payment Notice (APN), or link a tax appeal success by issuing a Follower Notice (FN) to users of similar arrangements (see **21.1–21.2**).

- **Primary targets** – Focusing enforcement and collection action on specific areas of tax and disclosed tax schemes allows HMRC to use APNs and FNs rapidly on a systematic basis (see **21.2**).

- **Accelerated Payment Notice** – HMRC must meet certain conditions to issue an APN and there is a set process and timeline to be followed once a notice is issued (see **21.6–21.11**).

- **Follower Notice** – A notice to help clear the backlog of tax cases on schemes and with different criteria for HMRC to meet and their own processes and timeline (see **21.12–21.19**).

- **Promoters of tax avoidance schemes** – The POTAS rules operate in tandem with FNs and impose substantial controls on firms seeking to promote aggressive tax schemes (see **21.20–21.22**).

- **Enablers & Offshore Enablers** – new penalties for enablers of defeated abusive tax arrangements, including those involved at any step (see **21.23–21.24**).

- **PCRT & Spotlights** – The Professional Conduct in Relation to Taxation and the published list of HMRC spotlights are two important areas of awareness for tax agents (see **21.25**).

- **The General Anti-Abuse Rule (GAAR)** – deterring taxpayers from entering into abusive arrangements, and would-be promoters from promoting such arrangements (see **21.26**).

- **Contesting an APN or FN** – There is no formal right of appeal against an APN or FN but it is possible to make representations to HMRC (see **21.27–21.28**).

- **Differences for partnerships** – There are several important differences to the APN and FN processes for partnerships to cater for the legal specifics of partnership structures (see **21.29–21.31**).

- **Serial Tax Avoidance Regime** – designed to tackle what HMRC perceive to be continuing use of tax avoidance arrangements, and seeks to impose new regulatory sanctions on users of schemes to deter them from further use (see **21.32**).

- **Disguised Remuneration** – HMRC action to tackle the provision of loans to employees through third parties, by imposing a new charge on loans outstanding at 5 April 2019 (see **21.33**).

- **Penalties on tax avoidance arrangements** – changes in Finance (No 2) Act 2017 which make it much easier for HMRC to charge penalties for errors on the tax arising when an avoidance arrangement fails (see **21.34**).

- **The taxpayer's options** – The options available to a taxpayer affected or potentially affected by an APN or a FN will vary depending on where in the process you begin advising the client (see **21.39–21.42**).

- **Summary** – For a list of key learning points from this chapter (see **21.43**).

INTRODUCTION

21.1 Tax avoidance is not illegal and many people still muddle the term 'avoidance' with evasion (which is against the law). The safest definition is probably HMRC's published view from 2016 which defines avoidance:

'Tax avoidance involves bending the rules of the tax system to gain a tax advantage that Parliament never intended. It often involves contrived, artificial transactions that serve little or no purpose other than to produce this advantage. It involves operating within the letter, but not the spirit, of the law.' (https://www.gov.uk/guidance/tax-avoidance-an-introduction.) It is also helpful to set out from the start some of the standard hallmarks which HMRC would expect see in an 'avoidance scheme':

- A promise to lower your tax bill for little or no real cost.
- Similarly, the benefits are disproportionate to the cost.

21.1 Tackling 'tax avoidance'

- An arrangement means you are paid in the form of a loan.
- The money goes round in a circle.
- Involves artificial steps with no commercial justification;
- HMRC has given it a Scheme Reference Number (SRN).

HMRC allocates significant resources to tackling tax avoidance and created a whole new Directorate in 2014 called the 'Counter Avoidance Directorate' ('CAD'). CAD is devoted to tackling tax avoidance arrangements and users. Tackling tax avoidance takes many forms; investigating whether tax avoidance arrangements achieve their intended aims, deterring users of tax avoidance arrangements, and removing the attractiveness of using arrangements going forwards.

The term tax avoidance 'arrangement' is used interchangeably with tax avoidance 'scheme', and each such scheme has a designated HMRC inspector within CAD who is responsible for the enquiries and subsequent court action against the scheme. This is done to streamline the process and ensure that all scheme participants are dealt with in the same way to comply with HMRC's Litigation and Settlement Strategy.

Most schemes are dealt with under normal enquiry provisions, though complex arrangements (and 'multiple scheme users') are typically dealt with under HMRC's Code of Practice 8. Some scheme enquiries are escalated to Code of Practice 9 (suspected serious fraud) which are handled through HMRC's Fraud Investigation Service.

The Government's strategy to tackle avoidance continues to spark much debate about the associated moral and political impact and factors; all of which we will leave aside to examine the actual rules and practical application.

The original problem identified in 2012 was that those taking part in a tax avoidance scheme could claim (via Self-Assessment) that the arrangement was effective when completing their tax returns and pay their tax accordingly (or not!). Where a scheme is disclosable under the disclosure of tax avoidance scheme (DOTAS) rules and is given a scheme number, this must be recorded on the self-assessment return. Further white space disclosures may also be prudent. However, the taxpayer can assume that the scheme is effective for tax purposes and it is up to HMRC to challenge the return. If a tax refund arises as a result of the scheme or less tax is paid then so be it. However, now many more schemes are identified earlier than ever before and refunds are withheld as a result of enquiries soon after returns are submitted.

There remains a backlog of tax avoidance cases being litigated through the Tribunal Service. These cases commonly take several years to be resolved with fighting funds created by the promoters to finance appeals – sometimes all the way to the Supreme Court.

For the Treasury, this previously meant a large amount of tax not being collected for many years and the taxpayers and scheme promoters had a cash flow incentive to drag out each legal dispute. This is largely eliminated with the introduction of Accelerated Payment Notices.

HMRC are eager to publicise cases won through the tax tribunal and frequent press releases state that it 'wins at least 80% of avoidance cases that go to court'.

21.2 The regime of accelerated payment notices (APNs) and follower notices (FNs) introduced in *FA 2014* is designed to remove the cash flow advantage of using a disclosable avoidance scheme. While taxpayers can still complete their tax returns and calculate and pay tax on the basis that a scheme they have taken part in is effective, when HMRC challenges the return, it can demand payment of the disputed tax. Where similar tax schemes are concerned, once HMRC has won a lead case it can use an FN to effectively shut down the disputes on 'follower' cases. Although both APNs and FNs can be contested, there is no formal right of appeal.

PRIMARY TARGETS FOR APNs

21.3 HMRC's primary targets so far for the use of APNs are tax schemes that involve:

- Sideways loss relief;
- Stamp duty land tax (SDLT);
- Film tax relief;
- Capital gains tax losses;
- Contractor loan schemes;
- Enterprise Zone Trusts; and
- Remuneration/bonus arrangements, including Employee Benefit Trusts (EBTs).

Target list

21.4 HMRC publishes a list of 'tax avoidance schemes on which users may be charged an upfront tax payment' at www.gov.uk/government/publications/tax-avoidance-schemes-on-which-accelerated-payments-may-be-charged-by-hmrc. This list is updated regularly so do always check the latest version.

21.5 *Tackling 'tax avoidance'*

> **Example 21.1 – How HMRC uses APN's and FN's in practice**
>
> Schemes that involve sale and leaseback arrangements for film distribution were early targets for APNs. Similarly, having won its case against a scheme that claimed to create trading losses, such as the Working Wheels 1 arrangement (which focused the financing of dealing in second hand cars), HMRC was able to issue FNs against later iterations of the scheme and a variant for high value watches.

Any scheme promoted by a firm that falls within the promoters of tax avoidance schemes (POTAS) rules or that has high profile individuals participating in it, is also likely to be near the top of HMRC's list for issuing notices.

However all taxpayers who have previously taken part in any of the listed schemes can expect to receive a request for payment of the disputed tax in due course.

TAXES COVERED

21.5 APNs and FNs can be used to pursue payments of and closure of disputes involving:

- Income tax;
- National insurance contributions;
- Capital gains tax;
- Inheritance tax;
- Corporation tax (now including group relief);
- Stamp duty land tax; and
- the annual tax on enveloped dwellings (ATED).

Group loss relief claims were not originally covered in *FA 2014* but *FA 2015, Sch 18* covers that omission.

Note that there is no time limit in terms of how far back the disputed tax goes, provided that a notice can be validly issued.

There is no set order in which APNs and FNs must be issued: commonly an APN will be issued first or both can be issued at the same time. An FN may be issued on its own.

ACCELERATED PAYMENT NOTICES

Qualifying conditions

21.6 The primary legislation for APNs is set out in *FA 2014, ss 219–229*, with special rules for partnerships set out in *FA 2014, Sch 33* and amendments in the *National Insurance Contributions Act 2015 (NICA 2015)* to ensure that the rules also apply to NIC.

HMRC can only issue an APN to a taxpayer if **all three** of the following are met.

(a) HMRC is enquiring into the taxpayer's tax return or claim or there is an ongoing appeal (against an assessment, closure notice or determination) regarding entries on a return or a claim or, in the case of NIC, a 'relevant contributions dispute' is in progress or there is an open appeal against an HMRC decision. As there is no formal enquiry procedure for NIC, *NICA 2015, Sch 6, para 4* now defines a relevant contributions dispute as occurring where HMRC has written to the taxpayer to notify him or her that HMRC considers NIC to be due and the taxpayer writes back to dispute the NIC liability.

Enquiries covered include	Appeals covered include
• Self-assessment returns for income tax and capital gains tax under *TMA 1970, ss 9A* or *12AC*.	• Income tax appeals against amendments of self-assessment under *TMA 1970, s 31* or amendments made by closure notices under *TMA 1970, ss 28A* or *28B*.
	• Income tax: appeals against amendments made by closure notices under *TMA 1970, Sch 1A, para 9* or by virtue of regulations in *ITEPA 2003, Pt 11*.
	• Against income tax counteraction notices under *ITA 2007, s 705*.
• Company tax return for corporation tax under *FA 1998, Sch 18, para 24* or under or *TMA 1970, s 12AC(6)*.	• Corporation tax appeals against amendment of a company's return by closure notice, assessments other than self-assessments, under *FA 1998, Sch 18, paras 34(3)* or *48*.
	• Corporation tax: appeals against counteraction notices under *CTA 2010, s 750*.

21.6 *Tackling 'tax avoidance'*

Enquiries covered include	**Appeals covered include**
• IHT account (or statement amending one) delivered under *IHTA 1984, ss 216* or *217*.	• IHT appeals against determinations under *IHTA 1984, s 222*.
• Inheritance tax information provided under *IHTA 1984, s 256*.	
• SDLT returns under *FA 2003, Sch 10, para 12*.	• SDLT appeals against amendment of self-assessment, discovery assessments under *FA 2003, Sch 10, para 35*.
• Annual tax for enveloped dwellings returns under *FA 2013, Sch 33, para 8*.	• Annual tax on enveloped dwellings: appeals against amendment of self-assessment, discovery assessments – under *FA 2013, Sch 33, para 35*.
• Claims made outside a return – under *TMA 1970, Sch 1A, para 5*.	

(b) The tax return or claim was submitted on the basis that the taxpayer could reduce their tax liability (or claim a repayment) as a result of a tax avoidance arrangement.

(c) The tax avoidance arrangements are caught by this legislation.

The arrangements or scheme used by the taxpayer falls within the legislation under (c) if **any one** of the following applies:

1. The arrangement was notifiable to HMRC under DOTAS.
2. HMRC has (or is) issuing a follower notice to the taxpayer in relation to the tax avoidance arrangement.
3. The General Anti-Abuse Rule (GAAR) Advisory Panel has given a counteraction notice for all or part of the tax avoidance arrangement.

In the APN, HMRC must set out which one or more of the sub-conditions of (c) are relevant. This is required because the circumstances surrounding this sub-condition may change. For example, from time to time, HMRC removes notification requirement for some tax schemes that were originally given a DOTAS number. If the DOTAS listing is the only reason that condition (c) is met HMRC must withdraw the APNs. It is also possible for a late appeal to be allowed against a case which has led to the issue of an FN.

It is important to note that the amount of the payment required by the APN may relate to different sub-conditions of (c) so that, if one no longer applies,

Tackling 'tax avoidance' **21.7**

a lower payment may be appropriate. In such circumstances HMRC must issue a revised APN to the taxpayer.

Not all arrangements notifiable under DOTAS where conditions (a) and (b) are also met will trigger the issue of an APN to the user. HMRC advises that only users of the notifiable schemes that it has listed are likely to receive an APN.

Just because a listed DOTAS number is declared on a taxpayer's return, that does not mean that an APN can be issued if there is no open appeal or assessment.

Given the strong link between DOTAS and APN, there is fresh impetus in the need to test the process for forcing disclosure of arrangements. Since 2007, HMRC has had the power to force disclosure of schemes, but very little case law followed. In *Mercury Tax Group* [2009] STC 307, the taxpayer won, and then in *HMRC v Root2tax Ltd and Root3tax Ltd* [2017] UKFTT 696 (TC) HMRC was successful in forcing disclosure of an arrangement.

Process and timeline

21.7 First it is important to note that, provided the case remains open (see conditions below) there is no time limit within which HMRC must issue an APN. This has enabled HMRC to carry out a huge catch-up exercise on historic scheme enquiries since the introduction of *FA 2014*.

Secondly, it must be remembered that the issue of an APN is not an end in itself, it is simply a payment on account of the disputed tax. It is not the end of the formal tax enquiry process. In practice, HMRC usually write to the affected taxpayer and their agent two weeks before the APN is issued to give the taxpayer a copy of its factsheet CC/FS24 – see www.gov.uk/government/publications/compliance-checks-tax-avoidance-schemes-accelerated-payments-ccfs24. The ostensive purpose of this advance warning is to give taxpayers more time to locate the funds required to make the payment required. However, the arterial motive is often seen as HMRC putting pressure on the taxpayer to withdraw from the scheme altogether before an APN is issued and, in our experience, it can prompt such action.

Note that there are no deadlines for issuing NIC decisions. Therefore, where a scheme involves NIC, it is possible for HMRC to issue separate APNs for the income tax and NIC elements of the same scheme as the NIC decision may not have been issued so there is not yet a relevant contribution dispute under which an APN can be issued (see the conditions above).

21.8 *Tackling 'tax avoidance'*

The notice

21.8 The APN and a calculation of the accelerated payment required is sent to the taxpayer (with a copy to his or her agent) with a covering letter briefly setting out 'What you need to do now' – see appendix at the end of this chapter for an example of an APN. In the covering letter, HMRC again encourages the taxpayer to formally withdraw from the scheme that was used.

The information shown on the APN will vary slightly depending on whether there is an on-going enquiry or an appeal is pending – see table.

An APN must show:

Enquiry in progress	Appeal pending
The amount of the accelerated payment.	Set out the amount of the disputed tax (ie the amount under appeal related to that scheme – may not be all the tax under appeal).

The date by which the payment must be made.

Set out the late payment penalty terms, rates and structure.

Make clear that there is no right of appeal but that representations may be made to HMRC before the payment date.	Explain that the tax cannot be postponed as there is no right of appeal but set out how representations may be made to HMRC before the payment date.

What HMRC must do if representations are made (see **21.23**).

How the conditions A–C have been met (including each of the sub-condition of (c) that are met).

That the accelerated payment is to be treated as a payment on account of the tax in dispute.

Warn the taxpayer that even if they win in court, HMRC may appeal and apply to not repay the tax pending that appeal.

Calculating the tax due

21.9 HMRC calculates the tax payable under an APN on the basis that all or part of the tax advantage of the scheme is removed. For example, the loss relief claimed for particular years is no longer taken into account.

Where an FN is issued, this is relatively straightforward as HMRC will have established how the tax return should be amended. Similarly, where a GAAR counteraction notice is issued, the payment due should be straightforward

Tackling 'tax avoidance' **21.10**

to establish. However, complexities will naturally arise where an individual or entity has used multiple schemes or where corporation tax loss relief is involved.

The original legislation did not cater for cases where the withdrawal group loss relief but *Finance Act 2015* amended *FA 2014, s 220* so that where a loss arose as a result of a scheme and the loss was then surrendered to another company, the APN will reduce the loss arising in the year in which the scheme applied. Changes to *FA 2014, s 221* enable the restriction of losses available for surrender to be set out in the APN and representations made against such restrictions.

In effect, the legislation removes the excessive group relief thus increasing the tax payable by the recipient company. The mechanism for this is not straight forward – it is achieved by preventing a company from consenting to a surrender of group relief an amount which is subject to an APN. It also provides a mechanism for overriding existing time limits for amending corporation tax returns – specifically overriding *FA 1998, Sch 18, para 31(3)*.

If an APN is eventually overturned because the tax arrangements are ruled to be tax-effective (or withdrawn after representations are made – see Contesting an APN or FN) then the group relief will again be available. However, the original group relief claim is not reinstated and the companies affected only then have 30 days after the date of the withdrawal/revision of the APN to lodge new group relief claims to utilise those losses.

HMRC's ability to demand taxpayer's money before a dispute is resolved is considered in detail in the Court of Appeal's decision in *R (on the application of Rowe and Others) v HMRC* [2017] EWCA Civ 2105.

Payment

21.10 The payment must be made within 90 days of the date of the APN or 30 days after HMRC issues a determination against any representations made following the notice's issue (see below).

Generally, HMRC sends the taxpayer a payment reminder 45 days after the issue of the APN if payment has not been made. Taxpayers will be expected to raise external finance or sell assets to pay the tax, as with any tax bill. For taxpayers that have participated in multiple schemes, funding multiple accelerated payments could pose a major cash flow problem (see **CHAPTER 22**).

If the payment requested by an APN is not made within the 90 days HMRC will charge interest from the due date that the tax should have been paid until it

21.11 *Tackling 'tax avoidance'*

is paid. HMRC can also charge tax geared penalties if notices are not complied with before the deadline:

- A 5% penalty will be charged for the initial failure to comply;
- Further penalties of 5% of the unpaid amount will be charged five and 11 months after the original payment date.

However, these penalties will not be charged if the taxpayer has a time to pay (TTP) arrangement in place before the payment deadline or has a 'reasonable excuse' for non-payment and pays when that excuse ends.

A TTP arrangement may be agreed with HMRC's Debt Management and Banking (DMB) department before the payment deadline. TTP arrangements are generally limited to those who can demonstrate that they have tried to raise monies by all other means.

If the taxpayer instead decides to withdraw from participating in the scheme (see below) and chooses to settle the outstanding liabilities in full, it is possible to do this by way of a contract settlement following discussions with the HMRC officer. In suitable cases, HMRC may be prepared to include in the contract settlement instalment payments which may be made over a period in excess of 12 months.

It is important to highlight that finalising their tax position with a contract settlement means the taxpayer will not benefit if the scheme is ultimately found to achieve its original aims through litigation.

Resolving the underlying tax dispute

21.11 As outlined above, the primary purpose of an APN is to collect tax payments from individuals. In theory, accelerated payments have no legal impact on the conduct of the tax dispute between HMRC and the taxpayer – both can still have their day in court.

However, once HMRC has got the money, it is unlikely to press for a case to be taken forward quickly – cash flow disadvantage now sits with the taxpayer. In our experience, it is not uncommon for a taxpayer to decide to withdraw from a scheme as soon as it becomes clear that an APN will be issued. Indeed, if a settlement is reached quickly and full payment made including interest and any penalties, HMRC will withdraw the APN when payment is made.

Where the taxpayer does not want to exit the scheme and the case eventually goes to Tribunal, when the tax case is finally resolved, any payment made under an APN will be treated as a payment on account of the overall final liability or refunded if the taxpayer wins. Note that if HMRC wins its case, it will seek late payment interest and potential penalties from the tax year in dispute onwards and this could significantly increase the taxpayer's overall liability beyond the tax paid on account under an APN. HMRC will provide computations of the additional tax due plus late payment interest.

FOLLOWER NOTICES

Purpose of an FN

21.12 HMRC wants to reduce the number of outstanding appeals on tax schemes without having to take each taxpayer and each scheme to court. While some scheme promoters have been content to stand their legal argument with HMRC behind a lead case addressing the technical issues, others have sought to differentiate the schemes they have promoted so that a separate court hearing is required.

FNs are designed to address this issue by giving HMRC:

1. A mechanism to quickly apply lead case rulings to all the cases and taxpayers stood behind them;
2. A mechanism to apply some or all of a technical ruling to other cases that are not formally stood behind that particular lead case.

Note that for the second mechanism, the case for which the ruling is given need not be identical or 'on all fours' with the scheme for which the FN is issued, the ruling must simply address a point of law which HMRC interprets as determinative for a particular scheme or schemes.

There are no time limits on HMRC issuing an FN and it can be issued after, at the same time as or before the issue of an APN.

Where an FN is issued, under the POTAS rules, HMRC can then issue a stop notice to known promoters of the scheme involved or similar schemes. The idea is to ensure that no further taxpayers enter schemes that, in HMRC's view, are proven not to be effective for tax purposes.

Qualifying conditions

21.13 HMRC can only issue a follower notice (FN) to a taxpayer **if all three** of the following are met:

(a) HMRC is enquiring into the taxpayer's tax return or claim, or there is an ongoing appeal regarding entries on a return or a claim;

(b) The tax returns or claims or appeals were submitted on the basis that the taxpayers could reduce their tax liability (or claim a repayment) as a result of a tax avoidance arrangement;

21.14 *Tackling 'tax avoidance'*

(c) HMRC believes that avoidance arrangement does not succeed because there is a final (see below) judicial ruling on the key issues relevant to the arrangement.

For a judicial ruling to be relevant to another arrangement, the circumstances of the original decided case need not be identical to the new taxpayer's arrangements. HMRC can rely on a ruling to issue an FN where the ruling:

- addresses tax arrangements;
- HMRC believes that the principles set out in the decision mean that the new taxpayer's arrangements are not tax-effective (in whole or in part); or
- the ruling is final.

A ruling is treated as final if it is from the Supreme Court or, if from a lower court or tribunal, the time for appeal has expired or permission to appeal is refused. Note that a ruling from the First-Tier Tribunal can be the basis for HMRC to issue an FN even though it does not set a legal precedent.

Clearly, the scope for technical interpretation here is considerable (see **21.23**) and HMRC accepts that there will be some cases where a subsequent judicial ruling may conflict with the one on which it relied to issue a FN. In such a situation, HMRC accepts that it may have to withdraw or adapt FNs that are already in issue.

Process and timeline

21.14 HMRC has 12 months to issue a valid FN with the clock starting from the later of the date:

- Of the final ruling on the original case;
- The new taxpayer's return of claim was received;
- The appeal was made.

As with APNs, FNs for NICs may be issued later for the NIC element of a scheme if the relevant contribution dispute condition, under which an FN can be issued, has not yet been met.

The notice

21.15 The notice will inform the taxpayer that, in HMRC's opinion, a judicial decision is relevant to their case and determines their dispute and that

Tackling 'tax avoidance' **21.18**

as a consequence, the taxpayer should amend their return or enter a written agreement to resolve an outstanding appeal within 90 days of the date of the notice.

This deadline may be extended where the taxpayer makes representations against the FN, see **21.27**.

Amended returns

21.16 Unless there is an outstanding appeal (see below), the taxpayers who receive an FN must amend their returns for the relevant years to reflect the effect of the technical ruling relevant to their circumstances. The amended return must then be submitted to HMRC with a revised tax calculation and any balancing tax payment required.

Outstanding appeals

21.17 Here a contract settlement will be required. With the FN, HMRC will send the taxpayers a template contract under which the taxpayers will formally:

- accept that the judicial ruling cited in the FN is relevant to their own arrangements;
- agree that the their own arrangement is not effective for tax and or NIC purposes;
- agree to withdraw their appeal within 14 days;
- confirm that any extra tax and or NIC due will be paid by the required date (or has already been paid).

Signing such a contract settlement will, of course, commit the taxpayer to meet its terms and can lead to further substantial penalties if they are not met.

Penalties for failure to comply with a follower notice

21.18 Where taxpayers fail to amend their return or reach a contact settlement with HMRC within the 90 day time limit, HMRC can impose a penalty. This penalty is in addition to any penalties charged by HMRC for the error in the return, failing to file the return on time or failing to notify HMRC that the taxpayer was liable to tax.

The penalty notice must be issued within 90 days of the issue finally being resolved (ie enquiry completed or amended return sent/contract

21.19 *Tackling 'tax avoidance'*

settlement made). The penalty will be 50% of the additional tax due because of the FN but can be mitigated down to 10% depending on how cooperative the taxpayer has been.

The taxpayer has 30 days after a penalty is charged to appeal against the imposition or amount of the penalty. The tribunal may affirm, amend or cancel the penalty.

Payment and resolving the dispute

21.19 Payment of tax and NIC connected to a FN will be triggered either by:

- Amending the relevant tax returns;
- Entering into a contract settlement;
- The issue of an APN on the same tax arrangements.

As with APNs (above), it may be possible to agree a time to pay arrangement with HMRC but, without one, later payment will trigger a penalty as well as interest.

For further guidance issued by HMRC on the APN and FN processes introduced in the *Finance Act 2014 (Pt 4)*, the *National Insurance Contributions Act 2015 (s 4 and Sch 2)*, and the *Finance Act 2015 (s 118 and Sch 18)* see www.gov.uk/government/publications/follower-notices-and-accelerated-payments.

PROMOTERS OF TAX AVOIDANCE SCHEMES

21.20 In tandem with APNs and FNs, *FA 2014, Pt 5* introduced powers for HMRC to tackle a 'limited number' of firms promoting high risk tax avoidance schemes. These are intended to curb the activities of such promoters and have little direct impact on the way APNs and FNs are used. However, they have significant practical impact where individuals use a scheme promoted by a firm that falls within the POTAS rules.

The POTAS rules allow HMRC to issue conduct notices to promoters and approach the First-Tier Tribunal (FTT) to request that a monitoring notice is issued.

The detailed guidance for the POTAS rules is https://www.gov.uk/government/publications/promoters-of-tax-avoidance-schemes-guidance

HMRC has made significant efforts to deter people from working with a 'promoter', including the publishing of a list about the 10 things a POTAS will not always tell you. https://www.gov.uk/government/publications/ten-things-a-promoter-of-tax-avoidance-schemes-wont-always-tell-you/ten-things-a-promoter-of-tax-avoidance-schemes-wont-always-tell-you

Conduct notices

21.21 Where a promoter fails to live up to certain standards of professional behaviour (eg ignoring a stop notice, not fulfilling its reporting obligations under the disclosure of tax avoidance schemes rules, not complying with an information notices from HMRC, being sanctioned by its professional body), HMRC can issue the firm with a conduct notice. There is no right of appeal and the notice lasts for two years.

Having issued a conduct notice, HMRC can then issue various directions to the promoter to regulate its conduct, including directing the promoted to:

- comply with any stop notice it issues;
- supply adequate information to its clients and any intermediaries about schemes that it is promoting;
- meet its obligations under DOTAS and any notice to provide information and documents to HMRC under *FA 2008, Pt 1, Sch 36* (and not discourage others from doing so);
- not enter into restrictive contractual terms that prevent the client from making a disclosure to HMRC;
- not promote schemes that rely on one or more contrived or abnormal steps to produce a tax advantage.

Where a promoter fails to comply with the terms of the conduct notice, HMRC can approach the FTT to request that a monitoring notice is issued.

Monitoring notices

21.22 The FTT will only issue a monitoring notice for certain types of breach of a conduct notice but, if it does, the impact on the promoter would be far reaching and probably terminal: none have been issued at the time of writing.

Once a monitoring notice is in place, HMRC can publicly name the promoter as a monitored promoter and will give it a promoter reference number (PRN) which the promoter must:

- provide its PRN to clients and intermediaries (who may also have to pass the PRN on to other parties, eg other group companies or employees, it knows have used the scheme);

21.23 *Tackling 'tax avoidance'*

- publish the PRN on its website; and
- refer to it in its publications and correspondence.

In addition, once the promoter has become a monitored promoter, there will be a direct impact on its clients and intermediaries. HMRC can request information and documents from clients where the promoter is non-resident (which must be provided to within just 10 days).

The promoters' clients will be required to report the PRN on their tax returns and other communications. They will also be subject to extended time limits (20 years) where failure to disclose the PRN leads to any loss of income tax, capital gains tax and inheritance tax.

Needless to say, there are numerous information powers available to HMRC where conduct notices and monitoring notices are issued and substantial penalties for failing promoters who fail to comply with them (*FA 2014, Sch 35*).

ENABLERS OF TAX AVOIDANCE

21.23 *F(No 2)A 2017, Sch 16* introduced new penalties for enablers of defeated abusive tax arrangements that are entered into on or after 16 November 2017. These new penalties extend beyond those who promote tax avoidance schemes to those involved at any step in their development, design, management or implementation. Enablers who are penalised may also have their details published by HMRC.

The new legislation incorporates an exemption for facilitating the taxpayer's withdrawal from arrangements, but only as long as it's reasonable to assume that the obtaining of a tax advantage is not one of the taxpayer's purposes in withdrawing from the arrangement.

HMRC's guidance follows the order of the legislation in explaining to whom and how the penalties will apply. It also sets out how the GAAR 'double reasonableness' test will apply and how the legislation interacts with the guidelines on Professional Conduct in Relation to Taxation (PCRT), see **21.25**.

Offshore enablers

21.24 On 1 January 2017 HMRC was given the power to penalise and publish the details of firms which 'enable' offshore 'non-compliance' (*FA 2016, Sch 20* & SI 2016/1249). Non-compliance includes failure to take reasonable care or lacking a reasonable excuse.

Tackling 'tax avoidance' **21.24**

HMRC can charge the enabler with a penalty of up to 150% of the tax, as well as publishing their details e.g. name, business address, amount of the penalty.

HMRC can penalise anyone who encouraged, assisted or otherwise facilitated a taxpayer to carry out 'offshore tax evasion or non-compliance' if:

- the enabler knew when their actions were carried out that they enabled or were likely to enable the taxpayer to carry out 'offshore tax evasion or non-compliance'; and
- one of the following applies:
  - the taxpayer is liable for a penalty for an error in their return, failure to notify a liability or failure to file returns within 12 months re: an offshore activity, even if that penalty is not charged by agreement; or
  - the taxpayer has been convicted of an offence re: an offshore activity e.g. fraudulent evasion of income tax, cheating the public revenue or a strict liability criminal offence.

In this context an 'offshore activity' includes:

- income arising outside the UK;
- assets held outside the UK;
- activities wholly or mainly located outside the UK;
- funds received in a jurisdiction outside the UK or transferred to a territory outside the UK (such that *FA 2007, Sch 24, para 4AA* is met); or
- anything triggering an 'offshore asset moves penalty'.

Again, an enabler is any person who is responsible, to any extent, for the design, marketing or otherwise facilitating another person to enter into abusive tax arrangements. When such arrangements are defeated in court or at the tribunal, or are otherwise counteracted, each person who enabled those arrangements may be liable to a penalty.

The penalty for each enabler is equal to the amount of consideration either received or receivable by them for enabling those arrangements. The General Anti-Abuse Rule (GAAR) Advisory Panel provides an important safeguard for the purpose of applying the legislation. No penalty can be charged unless HMRC has obtained an opinion of the GAAR Advisory Panel in relation to the tax arrangements or equivalent arrangements.

Any penalty HMRC charges, having considered the relevant GAAR Advisory Panel opinion, is appealable.

21.25 *Tackling 'tax avoidance'*

Throughout the HMRC guidance, such arrangements are referred to as 'abusive tax arrangements'. Those who provide clients with services in respect of genuine commercial arrangements will not be impacted.

The Penalties, appeals, and publishing details of enablers guidance explains how the information powers at *FA 2008, Sch 36* are modified for the purposes of checking whether a person is liable to a penalty under the enablers legislation. HMRC will make use of these powers to help check or obtain information that will help determine whether a penalty under the enablers legislation is appropriate for a particular person.

This article on the CIOT's website addresses what the penalties for enablers rules mean in practice for members by considering some *Frequently Asked Questions* (FAQs).

https://www.tax.org.uk/professional-standards/general-guidance/faqs-penalties-enablers

See also the HMRC guidance at https://www.gov.uk/guidance/tax-avoidance-enablers-of-defeated-tax-avoidance-legislation

PCRT & HMRC Spotlights

21.25 'The Professional Conduct in Relation to Taxation' (PCRT) came into force on 1 March 2017. This was jointly signed by the seven UK professional bodies involved in providing tax services. It was a Treasury initiative with the stated aim of 'doing more to tackle the creation and promotion of tax avoidance schemes'.

Within the PCRT is the 'The New Standards for Tax Planning' and this sets out five 'Standards' that all tax practitioners must adhere to. Please see your institute website for the latest information on PCRT in relation to tax avoidance, for example the ICAEW:

https://www.icaew.com/-/media/corporate/files/technical/tax/tax-faculty/29-10-16-professional-conduct-in-relation-to-tax.ashx

The HMRC website contains a list which is regularly updated of schemes that HMRC deems to be tax avoidance, there are currently over 40 arrangements. This should be seen as a warning for those who implement arrangements after they are published on Spotlights that more severe sanctions or penalties are likely to apply in any subsequent investigation. Arrangements in the Spotlights list are already identified as having the features of tax avoidance, and are already being investigated by HMRC. View the latest list at https://www.gov.uk/government/collections/tax-avoidance-schemes-currently-in-the-spotlight

THE GENERAL ANTI-ABUSE RULE (GAAR)

21.26 The primary policy objective of the GAAR is to deter taxpayers from entering into abusive arrangements, and to deter would-be promoters from promoting such arrangements. There may be tax avoidance arrangements that are challenged by HMRC using other parts of the tax code, but if they are not abusive they should not within the scope of the GAAR.

Underlying the GAAR legislation is the recognition that, under the UK's tax code, in many circumstances there are different courses of action that a taxpayer can quite properly choose between. The GAAR therefore includes a number of safeguards that ensure that any reasonable choice of a course of action is kept outside the target area of the GAAR.

For example, it is stated in HMRC's guidance that a tax payer deciding to carry on a trade can do so either as a sole trader or through a limited company and such a choice is completely outside the target area of the GAAR. Similarly, choosing to invest in an ISA rather than a savings account the interest on which would suffer income tax is also merely using a statutory relief in a straightforward way. It is only where taxpayers set out to exploit the rules by entering into contrived arrangements where the arrangements bring themselves into the target area of the GAAR.

The GAAR operates alongside and independently of other anti-avoidance rules. This means that HMRC may use either one or both of these mechanisms in order to tackle arrangements that it considers produce tax advantages that fall outside the range of acceptable tax planning.

In broad terms, the GAAR applies to 'tax arrangements' which are 'abusive'. A tax arrangement is any arrangement which, viewed objectively, has the obtaining of a tax advantage as its main or one of its main purposes. The term 'tax advantage' is given a wide definition and so the main focus of any analysis of a tax arrangement will be to determine whether it is abusive. A tax advantage includes:

- relief or increased relief from tax;
- repayment or increased repayment of tax;
- avoidance or a reduction of a charge to tax or an assessment to tax;
- avoidance of a possible assessment to tax;
- a deferral of a payment of tax or an advancement of a repayment of tax; and
- avoidance of an obligation to deduct or account for tax.

21.26 Tackling 'tax avoidance'

The legislation defines an abusive arrangement as one which, it is not reasonable to conclude, is a reasonable course of action, taking all of the circumstances into account. In applying the GAAR, the burden of proof is on HMRC to demonstrate that an arrangement is abusive. Furthermore, as a result of the 'double reasonableness test', if a reasonable conclusion can be reached that an arrangement is a reasonable course of action then that arrangement will not be abusive, even if it is also reasonable to conclude that it is not a reasonable course of action.

Determining whether an arrangement is a reasonable course of action can be very tricky and so the legislation gives some examples of the 'circumstances' in the light of which the arrangement can be assessed which form the basis of the checklist below.

HMRC has used these circumstances to analyse a list of examples at section E of its guidance notes to determine whether it believes that examples are or are not abusive. These include examples in which HMRC would expect the GAAR to apply:

- 'double dipping' tax deductions;
- schemes to obtain a credit or repayment for overseas tax which has not been paid;
- using prescriptive legislation in an artificial way to generate a deemed tax deduction where the economic loss is either much smaller or does not exist; or
- exploitation of double tax treaties to engineer double non-taxation;

and examples in which HMRC would not expect the GAAR to apply:

- intra-group arrangements to ensure losses are not stranded in a group company where there are unrelieved profits in other group companies;
- using a conditional contract to delay a tax event to take advantage of future tax rate reductions;
- use of the main residence election for 'flipping' property transactions; and
- transfers between spouses and civil partners in order to reduce CGT liabilities.

There have now been a number of GAAR advisory panel opinions. To date these cases are aimed at the highly artificial end of the tax planning spectrum. To read more on GAAR and for the latest opinions from the GAAR Advisory Panel, and the HMRC guidance see https://www.gov.uk/government/collections/tax-avoidance-general-anti-abuse-rule-gaar.

CONTESTING AN APN OR FN

21.27 There is no formal right of appeal against either notice – this would defeat the purpose of the notices by leading to further postponement of tax payment. In addition, the NIC rules have been amended so that there is no longer a need for HMRC to issue a formal NIC decision (and resolve any related appeal) before payment can be collected.

However, the legislation allows for 'representations' to be made in writing to HMRC within 90 days of the date of the APN or FN being issued.

The grounds for making such representations set out in the table:

APN	FN
That any one of the three conditions for issuing an APN was not met.	That any one of the three conditions for issuing an FN was not met.
The amount of tax and or NIC specified in the notice is incorrect.	The judicial ruling cited by HMRC is not relevant to the individual's tax arrangements.
	The notice was not issued within the time limit.

It is particularly important to consider what tax years are formally under enquiry and if HMRC has the power to open other tax years.

HMRC must consider the representations and either confirm, amend or withdraw the notice (whether it is an APN or an FN) but there is no deadline by which this must be done. The representations will be considered by an HMRC officer who is not involved in the team issuing the notices.

Our experience of making representations to HMRC to date is unsurprisingly that HMRC reject the points made and generally continue to pursue the full payment of the APN or FN. However, do always check the calculation of the notice amounts carefully as we have seen instances of incorrect calculations being used as a basis for the notice.

21.28 The next step is for HMRC to issue a 'determination' on the representations to the taxpayer although there is no deadline by which a determination must be issued. At this point HMRC may either, confirm, withdraw or amend the notice.

If the notice is confirmed or amended more than 60 days after it was originally issued, the taxpayer then has a further 30 days to make the payment or amend the tax return/enter a contract settlement. If the representations are made and the determination issued quickly, the original 90 day deadline for compliance may remain in place.

21.29 *Tackling 'tax avoidance'*

DIFFERENCES FOR PARTNERSHIPS

21.29 *FA 2014, Schs 31* and *32* set out special rules for partnership follower notices (PFNs) and partnership payment notices (PPNs). Although the key principles behind the notice system for partnerships are broadly the same as the rules for other taxpayers there are several important differences to cater for the legal peculiarities of partnership structures. The following tables highlight the key differences.

	PFNs	**PPNs**
Issue to	Representative partner (or successor) ie the person responsible for submitting the partnership tax return rather that individual partners.	Each individual partner. A PFN will fulfil condition C for each of the partners allowing a PPN to be issued. Individuals can also receive an APN in their personal capacity.
Representations	Made by representative partner.	Individual partner.
Amended return/contract settlement	Representative partner must arrange amended return/ agree settlement as instructed by majority of partners.	Individual partners decide whether or not to withdraw from scheme.
Denied advantage/ calculation	Is a part of the profit or loss on the partnership return.	Tax advantage for individual partner based on his or her own returns.
Penalty for failure to comply	20% with mitigation down to 4% possible. All partners have joint liability for payment.	Individual partner.
Payment	PPNs issued to each individual partner.	Individual partner responsible.

21.30 In addition to these differences, the way that partnerships are taxed for SDLT and ATED means that further rules are required in *FA 2014, ss 230* and *231*. The key differences are summarised in the following table:

	SDLT	**ATED**
Responsible partners	All who are members on the day of the transaction.	All who are members on the first day of property ownership in the chargeable period.

	SDLT	**ATED**
Issue notices to	Each partner.*	Each partner.*
Representations	Can be made individually or jointly.	Can be made individually or jointly.
Amended return/ contract settlement	All partners have joint and several liability.	All partners have joint and several liability.
Penalty for failure to comply	All partners have joint and several liability (apart from those who joined after the failure).	All partners have joint and several liability (apart from those who joined after the failure).
Payment	Each individual partner (apart from those who joined after the transaction).	Individual partner responsible.

*'partner' includes two or more individuals acting jointly (so that they have joint and several liability)

Practical issues for partnerships

21.31 The fact that the deadlines for dealing with PFNs and PPN are also set at 90 days can be problematic as it will almost inevitably take longer to arrive at decisions for partnership – giving far less time to make effective representations or agree amended returns and payments.

It will also be essential to check that individual partners do not receive duplicate APNs/PPNs where the partnership has engaged in several tax schemes so that appropriate representations can be made.

The Court in *Cotter* [2013] UKSC 69 dismissed the argument that HMRC had failed to open the correct form of enquiry into carry back claims within the relevant statutory time limits. Then the decision in *De Silva* [2017] UKSC 74 concluded that an enquiry into the partnership by HMRC was sufficient to enquire into any claim made by a partner to utilise losses with the result that HMRC could, in theory, collect any additional tax.

SERIAL TAX AVOIDANCE REGIME

21.32 The Serial Tax Avoidance Regime (STAR) was introduced by *FA 2016, s 159, Sch 18* and affects all taxpayers who participate in tax avoidance arrangements (TAAs) regardless of whether they are individuals, partnerships or companies.

21.32 Tackling 'tax avoidance'

This regime is designed to tackle what HMRC perceive to be continuing use of TAAs, and seeks to impose regulatory sanctions on users of schemes to deter them from further use.

Despite its name, this regime applies if a taxpayer participates in **one** or more TAAs which are 'defeated' after 5 April 2017.

HMRC's guidance on this regime is as issued in November 2016: www.gov.uk/guidance/serial-tax-avoidance.

HMRC will issue a warning notice to the taxpayer within 90 days of a 'relevant defeat', which broadly occurs when:

- a GAAR counteraction notice becomes final;
- a follower notice is complied with or becomes final; or
- DOTAS (or the VAT equivalent) arrangements are counteracted eg via an assessment or contract settlement (such as one reached via a settlement opportunity).

A five year 'warning period' starts from the day after the warning notice is issued, although it is extended if the taxpayer suffers another relevant defeat.

The taxpayer must submit information notices to HMRC annually during the warning period. These annual information notices (AIN) give HMRC details of TAAs the taxpayer used during the year. Late submission of an AIN and submission of an incorrect AIN will both result in the warning period being extended to finish five years after this failure. Special rules will apply for corporate groups, associated persons and partnerships.

The STAR legislation imposes penalties of 20–60% of the tax if a taxpayer uses a TAA in a warning period which HMRC subsequently defeats. In addition, the STAR legislation imposes consequences if a taxpayer uses three TAAs during a warning period which HMRC subsequently defeats:

- restriction of tax reliefs; and
- publishing of taxpayers' details.

FA 2016, Sch 18, para 55 broadly defines 'use' as occurring on submission of a tax return or claim containing entries relating to the TAA.

The legislation confirms that taxpayers who participated in TAAs prior to 15 September 2016 and from which they are yet to withdraw (ie where HMRC's enquiry into the arrangement is ongoing or there is an open appeal) will escape the regime if, before 6 April 2017, they:

- reached an agreement with HMRC to exit the TAA; or

- fully disclosed to HMRC the matters to which the 'relevant counteraction' relates; or

- agreed to fully disclose to HMRC the matters to which the 'relevant counteraction' relates by a future date specified by HMRC.

Taxpayers who did not take one of these steps before 6 April 2017 will be issued with a warning notice if the TAA is defeated after 5 April 2017 and will then need to file AINs for five years.

Taxpayers who participate in TAAs, even if they were put on their returns many years ago, will need to carefully consider what to do in relation to STAR.

DISGUISED REMUNERATION

21.33 HMRC continues to tackle Disguised Remuneration ('DR') arrangements which it sees as tax avoidance. This will normally involve a loan or other form of a payment from a third-party which (in reality) may never be repaid. These arrangements can be implemented by employers or individuals, and usually minimise or avoid Income Tax on employment, PAYE, and National Insurance Contributions. They are also commonly used by contractors, and are known as 'contractor loan schemes'.

DR arrangements includes Employee Benefit Trusts, and EFRBS or Employer-Financed Retirement Benefits Schemes. HMRC is keen to publicise their win in the Supreme Court for Scotland regarding the EBT used by Rangers Football Club. In para 39 of the Court's decision, the principle is set out that employment income paid from an employer to a third party is still taxable as employment income. RFC 2012 Plc (in liquidation) (formerly The Rangers Football Club Plc) v Advocate General for Scotland [2017] STC 1556. https://www.supremecourt.uk/cases/docs/uksc-2016-0073-judgment.pdf

Following this decision, Follower Notices were issued by HMRC to other users of EBT type arrangements.

Many participants in disguised remuneration arrangements are reviewing their options in light of the new loan charge announced at Budget 2016 which will apply to all disguised remuneration loans outstanding on 5 April 2019. The 'loan charge rules' are contained in *F(No2)A 2017, Sch 11* and *FA 2018, Sch 1*, which build on the 2011 DR rules which are now in ITEPA 2003, Pt 7A. In summary, the rules require a repayment of funds borrowed from a DR arrangement (for example a contractor loan) in full by 5 April 2019. A failure to do this will give rise to an income tax and NIC liability in the 2019–20 tax year, with a deadline to report information to HMRC before 1 October 2019.

21.34 *Tackling 'tax avoidance'*

In view of this HMRC is writing to those with outstanding loans and has introduced standard settlement terms for those who wish to rectify their tax position for past tax years rather than suffer the loan tax charge from 5 April 2019. HMRC state that they expect to collect £2.5billion from the loan charge by 2021. [HMRC's Annual Report 2017–18]

HMRC currently list nine disguised remuneration arrangements under Spotlights which it considers are tax avoidance and in HMRC's view do not work. These include arrangements such as contractor loans, EBTs, annuities to avoid PAYE and those that seek to avoid the April 2019 loan charge or re-describing loans.

For tax agents wishing to settle taxpayers' affairs with HMRC, the detailed guidance can be found at https://www.gov.uk/government/publications/disguised-remuneration-detailed-settlement-terms

Particular care is needed where the employer no longer exists or it is an employee only settlement. Please check any implications under the 'Requirement To Correct' and 'Failure To Correct' legislation in *F(No 2)A 2017, Sch 18*. PAYE and NIC are not within the scope of this legislation, however income tax and IHT are within scope and therefore some DR arrangements and settlements could be impacted where there is an offshore element, for example an EBT located outside the UK.

Some settlements of historical tax years with HMRC are agreed on the basis of voluntary restitution, and here no late payment interest and no penalties will apply.

PENALTIES ON TAX AVOIDANCE ARRANGEMENTS

21.34 It is no longer safe to assume (if in fact it ever was) that where tax advice was given on the structure and implementation of an avoidance arrangement, that 'no penalties' will apply on the settlement or conclusion of an enquiry with HMRC. Changes in *F(No 2)A 2017* make it much easier for HMRC to charge penalties for errors on the tax arising when an avoidance arrangement fails.

Tax geared penalties for errors in tax returns

21.35 If a TAA fails to achieve its aims e.g. because HMRC wins the litigation and the Courts decide that it does not work or because it was not implemented properly then HMRC will consider whether to charge penalties. This will either be under the legislation in *FA 2007, Sch 24* or its predecessor, *TMA 1970, s 95*. Penalties may be imposed if the taxpayer is found to be careless or deliberate in their submission of incorrect returns. The penalties are up to 100% of the tax that becomes payable as a result of the TAA's failure, although they may be higher if the TAA was offshore such that the offshore uplift also applies.

Almost all taxpayers who use TAAs will be advised by professional advisers. The adviser may also assist the taxpayer with the implementation of the TAA and/or advise of the entries and wording to be put on the taxpayer's tax return. Following all this advice may not be sufficient to avoid penalties for TAAs entered into before 6 April 2017, particularly if there was an implementation failure (e.g. a step in the arrangement did not occur & was such that the taxpayer was able to check before submitting their tax return relying on the TAA's expected tax saving).

F(No 2)A 2017, s 64 changed *FA 2007, Sch 24* for periods starting on or after 6 April 2017 where the document (e.g. tax return) was submitted on or after Royal Assent (16 November 2017). It is now the case that advice given to the taxpayer by advisers and/or a tax barrister may be deemed 'disqualified' and ignored when the decision on penalties is made by HMRC or the Tribunal. The rules are complicated and a careful analysis of what happened on a case by case basis will be necessary.

Other ways in which HMRC can penalise taxpayers who participate in tax avoidance arrangements are detailed below.

Failures to deal with APNs or FNs on time

21.36 As detailed above, if a taxpayer fails to amend their return to remove the entries relating to the TAA, within 90 days of the FN's issue, then a penalty of 50% of the tax advantage can be charged.

Failing to pay the tax demanded by an APN leads to further penalties unless a time to pay arrangement is requested before the payment date and agreed with HMRC. The penalties are up to 15% of the tax due.

GAAR Penalty

21.37 If a TAA is deemed to fall foul of the GAAR, then Finance Act 2016 enables HMRC to charge penalties of 60% of the tax advantage set out on a taxpayer's tax return as a result of them using such an arrangement. Penalties may also be levied under the penalties for error rules, as above, but the cumulative penalties should not exceed 100% of the tax advantage. HMRC has discretion to mitigate penalties. If the taxpayer amends their return to remove the TAA before the matter is referred to the GAAR Panel then no penalties will be charged.

21.38 *Tackling 'tax avoidance'*

Serial Tax Avoiders Regime (STAR)

21.38 As above, using a TAA within a warning period which is subsequently defeated then HMRC may impose additional penalties of 20%–60% of the tax saving that the arrangements set out to make.

The person is not liable to a penalty under this section if they satisfy HMRC that they have a reasonable excuse for the failure to which the defeat relates. However, lack of funds or reliance on a third party (unless the taxpayer took reasonable care to avoid the failure) are not reasonable excuses. Reliance on advice does not constitute a reasonable excuse if the advice was addressed to or was given to another person or if it takes no account of the taxpayer's circumstances. The taxpayer must remedy the failure without unreasonable delay after the excuse ceases. Again, HMRC has some discretion to mitigate penalties.

THE TAXPAYER'S OPTIONS

21.39 APNs are a mechanical tool and, provided HMRC follows the legal requirements for issuing an APN, the taxpayer may have little choice but to comply with the payment request. With a follower notice, there may be more scope to argue that the judicial ruling cited is not relevant to an individual taxpayer's own circumstances.

Where are we now?

21.40 In practice, the options open to the taxpayer will, of course, depend on the point in time when you are considering them.

As noted above, when faced with an APN, many taxpayers choose to exit the tax scheme that they have used and pay all the disputed back tax and interest – effectively backing out of the legal dispute before the case is tested in court. Reputational reasons often play a key role here as the public mood against scheme users has hardened considerably in past years. Taking this route will inevitably lead to the individual paying over more to HMRC than is requested in the APN (due to late payment interest and potential tax geared penalties) but many taxpayers are willing to do this for finality.

Individual scheme participants taking this route need to carefully review engagement letters with scheme providers to understand the implications of continuing to defend or withdrawing their appeals. If they are uncertain then legal advice may be needed.

Tackling 'tax avoidance' **21.42**

Some schemes are effectively 'dead in the water' anyway because they, or identical schemes, have been through the courts and found to not work – so that an FN is issued or expected.

> **Example**
>
> Many film schemes were replicated on an annual basis with the basic template of the arrangement unchanged. If HMRC wins an appeal on a template arrangement for year one, it will issue FNs for schemes based on this template for all subsequent years. Individuals who entered the later year's schemes will have few options once the lead case has been won by HMRC and may well be best to see a contract settlement before an FN and APNs are issued.

Other schemes may need to be reviewed in light of recent court hearings to understand the merits of continuing to defend the scheme.

Of course, where the case has yet to go to court, some taxpayers are content to pay the tax demanded by an APN and continue the tax dispute with HMRC in the belief that their case is strong and that the courts will eventually uphold their argument so that the tax paid over now will eventually be returned to them (with interest).

In such cases, it is important to remember that it is not only the technical merits of the scheme that are important: usually a successful appeal depends on how the scheme was implemented and the quality of the paperwork retained.

It is also vital to estimate the potential costs of each course of action. For example, it is important to take into account that HMRC takes the view that penalties may be payable on tax avoidance enquiries: if it believes that elements of the scheme amount to fraud, such penalties can be up to 200% or more of the tax due where offshore arrangements are involved.

Judicial review

21.41 Various action groups have grown, alongside some individuals, to challenge the use and fairness of the avoidance legislation (see **CHAPTER 20**).

Early stage options

21.42 Clearly, Individuals whose scheme (or a similar scheme) has yet to come to court have the most options. The benefits and downsides of various

21.42 *Tackling 'tax avoidance'*

potential courses of action **before** notices are issued are summarised in the following table. It is important to consider these early in the process because, once notices are issued, the taxpayer is likely to perceive time to be short and will be keen to make quick decisions.

Possible course of action	Possible benefits	Potential downsides	Other points to check/consider
Exit the scheme now	• Peace of mind and finality. • No need to contribute further to the promoter's fighting fund. • No further information requests from HMRC or correspondence with them after the matter is concluded. • Can be done by way of a contract settlement under *TMA 1970, s 54* taking into account any consequential claims needed.	• Individual does not benefit if the scheme ultimately succeeds. • Will need to pay the tax and late payment interest now. • May need to pay penalties or surcharges (eg for late payment of tax, errors in the return).	• Does the promoter's engagement letter entitle it to receive or retain fees if the client withdraws from the scheme before the courts decide whether it works? • Does the taxpayer need to obtain external finance (HMRC prefers this to be tried) or an instalment plan to pay HMRC?
Wait for APN	• Pay APN and stay in the scheme and benefit if it ultimately succeeds.	• Potential reputational damage if the press publicise the taxpayer's participation in the scheme.	• Check tax return and all relevant scheme papers so quick decision can be made on whether representations can be made on APN.

900

Possible course of action	Possible benefits	Potential downsides	Other points to check/consider
	• Payment will be repaid together with repayment supplement if the scheme succeeds. • If the taxpayer participated on more than one scheme and wants to continue participating, then may be able to obtain a global time to pay agreement.	• Will need to pay the tax and late payment interest. • May need to pay penalties or surcharges (eg for late payment of tax, errors in the return) if the scheme fails. • May need to continue contributing to the promoter's fighting fund. • May get further information requests from HMRC or correspondence with them until the matter is concluded.	• Establish whether you need to work with the scheme promoter centrally if representations are to be made to HMRC. • How will the taxpayer fund the tax payment within 90 days? • Is external finance (eg loan, mortgage) needed? HMRC prefers this to be explored before any request for time to pay. • Will the taxpayer need a time to pay agreement? If so, information such as a statement of assets and liabilities and/or details of their income and expenditure will be needed.

21.42 *Tackling 'tax avoidance'*

Possible course of action	Possible benefits	Potential downsides	Other points to check/consider
Wait for the FN?	• Continue to participate in the scheme and benefit if it ultimately succeeds. • APN payment will be repaid together with repayment supplement if the scheme succeeds. • If the taxpayer participated on more than one scheme and wants to continue participating, then may be able to obtain a global time to pay agreement.	• Potential reputational damage if the press publicise the taxpayer's participation in the scheme. • Will need to pay the tax when the APN is issued plus late payment interest when the scheme fails. • May need to pay penalties or surcharges (eg for late payment of tax, errors in the return) if the scheme fails. • May need to continue contributing to the promoter's fighting fund. • May get further information requests from HMRC or correspondence with them until the matter is concluded.	• Obtain the tax return that included the scheme plus any other relevant papers so that the FN can be checked quickly and a decision on making representations (or not) can be made quickly. • Establish whether you need to work with the scheme promoter centrally if representations are to be made to HMRC. • HMRC may issue an enquiry closure notice instead of a follower notice. • Consider whether any consequential claims need to be made/given effect to.

KEY POINTS

21.43

1   HMRC's powers to issue APNs and FNS are designed to help them bring in tax that has been tied up in long running disputes.

2   The fact that there is no formal right of appeal against APNs and FNs swings the practical balance in HMRC's favour.

3   The reputational risk attached to use of tax avoidance schemes is likely to have increased exponentially since the client entered their particular scheme. Especially in view of the Serial Tax Avoidance Regime from 6 April 2017.

4   A simple warning letter from HMRC that an APN is to be issued may be sufficient to persuade a taxpayer to fully withdraw from a scheme.

5   A full withdrawal from a scheme means using a contract settlement or settlement deed to close all open tax enquiries – a process that is not to be taken lightly. Legal advice may also be necessary on the implications of withdrawing from a scheme.

6   Paying the tax demanded by an APN is far from the end of the matter, clients can still have their day in court and may get the money back.

7   Great care is required with FNs: some may be based on rulings in identical circumstances to your client's whereas others may stretch technical interpretation too far and be ripe for challenge.

8   Always remember that just because your client has entered tax avoidance schemes in the past does not guarantee that he or she can afford to pay the tax now. You will need to handle financing discussions with tact and empathy as a time to pay agreement with HMRC may be necessary.

9   If a client has used a disclosable scheme but has not received an APN, don't assume that the issue has gone away. HMRC is continuing to issue notices in a phased and sometimes haphazard way.

10 Following court success and Disguised Remuneration Settlement Opportunities, HMRC is focussed on tackling remuneration arrangements designed to avoid PAYE and NIC.

21.43 *Tackling 'tax avoidance'*

APPENDIX

AN EXAMPLE OF AN ACCELERATED PAYMENT NOTICE

HM Revenue & Customs
Counter Avoidance AP Teams S0987
PO Box 30002
GLASGOW
G70 6AG

Phone   03000 574 367
Mon-Fri 8.30am to 5pm

Web   www.gov.uk

Date   26 September 2014
Our ref
Your ref

Dear Sir or Madam

Your client:

We enclose a copy of the letter that we have sent to your client today.

We have also sent your client a copy of factsheet CC/FS24, 'Tax avoidance schemes - accelerated payments'.

If you want to read factsheet CC/FS24, you can get a copy online. Go to www.hmrc.gov.uk/compliance/factsheets.htm If you prefer, you can phone us on the number shown at the top of this letter and we will send you a copy.

If you have any questions, please phone us.

Yours faithfully

Accelerated Payments
Team 2

Information is available in large print, audio and Braille formats.
Text Relay service prefix number – 18001

CADAcc18   HMRC 08 14   Director: David Richardson

904

Tackling 'tax avoidance' **21.43**

HM Revenue & Customs
Counter Avoidance AP Teams S0987
PO Box 30002
GLASGOW
G70 6AG

Phone   03000 574367
Monday to Friday 8:30am - 5:00pm

Web   www.gov.uk

Date   26 September 2014
Our ref

Dear

About the tax avoidance scheme that the partnership used

Name of partnership:

We wrote to you on 12 September 2014, to tell you that we were going to send you a partner payment notice. I now enclose that notice, which shows the amount due.

What you need to do now

Please read the notice carefully as it requires you to take action and it contains important information, including about surcharges for not paying on time. The notice requires you to pay the amount due by the date shown, but if you object to the notice and make representations, this date may change. The notice explains this.

You should also read factsheet CC/FS24, as it also contains important information. We sent you a copy with our letter dated 12 September 2014.

If the partnership now wants to settle the current appeal

If the partnership now wants to settle the current appeal, the nominated partner should phone us straightaway on the number shown at the top of this letter. We will then tell them what they need to do next.

It is entirely up to the partners whether the partnership settles. If the partnership does not want to settle, the appeal will remain open.

Problems paying

If you think you will have problems paying the amount due, please phone us straightaway on the number shown at the top of this letter.

Getting advice

We have sent a copy of this letter to y   . You may want to discuss this matter with them.

Information is available in large print, audio and Braille formats.
Text Relay service prefix number – 18001

CADAcc16b   HMRC 09 14   Director: David Richardson

21.43 *Tackling 'tax avoidance'*

More information

If you need another copy of factsheet CC/FS24, you can get one online. Go to www.hmrc.gov.uk/compliance/factsheets.htm or you can phone us and we will send you a copy.

Contacting us

If you have any questions about the enclosed notice, please phone us.

Yours sincerely

Accelerated Payments
Team 2

To find out what you can expect from us and what we expect from you go to www.gov.uk/hmrc/your-charter and have a look at 'Your Charter'.

Tackling 'tax avoidance' **21.43**

 **Partner payment notice – issued under Part 4, Chapter 3 and Schedule 32 of the Finance Act 2014**

HM Revenue & Customs
Counter Avoidance AP Teams S0987
PO Box 30002
GLASGOW
G70 6AG

Phone	03000 574 367
Mon-Fri 8.30am to 5pm	
Our ref	
Payment ref	
Date	26 September 2014

Notice for the year ended 5 April

Amount due in respect of this notice:

Payment due on or before:
2 January 2015
(Payment may be due on a later date if representations are made under paragraph 5 of Schedule 32 of the Finance Act 2014.)

This partner payment notice relates to:
Scheme name
Scheme reference

Name of partnership:

About this notice
We are giving you this partner payment notice under section 228 and paragraph 3(5)(b) of the Finance Act 2014.

The legislation allows us to give you this notice because certain conditions have been met. Those conditions are that:
- the partnership named above has made a tax appeal in relation to Income Tax and that appeal has not yet been determined by the tribunal or court to which it is addressed, or been abandoned or otherwise disposed of - Schedule 32, paragraph 3(2)(b) of the Finance Act 2014
- the appeal is made on the basis that a tax advantage ("the asserted advantage") results from particular arrangements ("the chosen arrangements"), namely the scheme referred to above - Schedule 32, paragraph 3(3) of the Finance Act 2014
- the arrangements are DOTAS arrangements - Schedule 32, paragraph 3(5)(b) of the Finance Act 2014

About the accelerated partner payment
The amount that you have to pay ("the accelerated partner payment") is shown above. You must pay this amount by 2 January 2015. However, if you make representations to us about this notice, and they do not result in this notice being completely withdrawn, then you must pay this or any amended amount by the later of 2 January 2015 or 30 days after we have notified you of our decision in respect of your representations. There is more information about this in the section below headed 'what to do if you disagree with this notice'.

The amount of the accelerated partner payment is determined by virtue of Schedule 32, paragraph 3(5)(b) of the Finance Act 2014.

The accelerated partner payment is to be treated as a payment on account of "the understated partner tax" as defined by schedule 32, paragraph 4(3) of the Finance Act 2014. The understated partner tax is the amount of the charge to tax in accordance with our view of the effect of the DOTAS arrangements.

CADAcc13   1   HMRC 08/14

21.43 Tackling 'tax avoidance'

Postponing payment

You have no right to apply to us or to a tribunal to postpone the payment of any understated partner tax to which this notice relates

If a court or tribunal later decides that our view of the effect of the DOTAS arrangements is incorrect, then we would normally be required to repay the amount (or part of the amount) that you paid us under this notice. However, if we appeal against the decision to a higher court or tribunal, in certain cases we may also ask for their permission not to repay you. We would do this if we believed that there was a risk that, if we were successful with our appeal, you would not then pay the amount due. If the relevant court or tribunal considered it necessary for the protection of the revenue, then it could give us permission to withhold all or part of any repayment, or require you to provide security before we repaid you.

Surcharges for not paying on time

If you do not pay in full and on time, you may be liable to surcharges. Any such surcharges would be payable in addition to the amount due. If your payment is not made in full:

- within 28 days of the date it is due, you will be liable to a surcharge of an amount equal to 5% of the amount you still owe
- on or before 6 months of the date it is due, you will be liable to a further surcharge of an amount equal to 5% of the amount that you still owe – this is as well as the 5% explained in the previous bullet

If we charge you a surcharge, we will send you a notice telling you how much the surcharge is and the period to which it relates. You will then have 30 days to pay the surcharge. If you disagree with the surcharge you will be able to appeal. You can find out more about this in factsheet HMRC1 'HM Revenue & Customs decisions – what to do if you disagree. You can get a copy online. Go to **www.hmrc.gov.uk/factsheets/hmrc1.pdf**

How to pay

We recommend that you pay electronically using Bacs Direct Credit, CHAPS or Faster Payments by online/telephone banking. For details of other electronic payment methods go to, **www.hmrc.gov.uk/payinghmrc/misc.htm**

Whichever method you use, you will need to use the bank and payment details shown below:

Name of bank:	CITI Bank
Account name:	HMRC Shipley
Amount due:	▬▬▬▬
Payment reference number:	▬▬▬▬▬▬
If paying from a UK bank account, use:	• account sort code 08-32-10 • account reference number 12001020
If paying from a non-UK bank account, use:	• ▬▬▬▬▬▬▬▬▬ • ▬▬▬▬▬▬▬▬▬▬▬▬▬

If you cannot pay electronically, please send a cheque to:
HM Revenue & Customs
BRADFORD
BD98 1YY

Your cheque should be made payable to 'HM Revenue and Customs', followed by the reference XW005043264180.

What if you have problems paying

If you think you will have problems paying the amount due, please phone us straightaway on the number shown at the top of this notice.

What to do if you disagree with this notice

You cannot appeal to us against this notice, or to a tribunal or court. However, under paragraph 5 Schedule 32 of the Finance Act 2014, you can make representations to us objecting to the notice and/or the amount of the accelerated partner payment if you believe that one or both of the following applies:

- one or more of the conditions shown earlier in this notice for issuing this notice have not been met

CADAcc13

- the amount shown on the notice is not correct - if this is the case you will need to tell us what you think the correct amount is and why

If you want to make representations, you need to write to us to let us know what they are. You need to make sure that we receive your letter no later than 2 January 2015.

We will then consider your representations and let you know our decision. If you make representations in relation to the conditions for issuing the notice we will either confirm this notice (with or without amendment) or withdraw it. If you make representations about the amount specified in this notice we will decide whether a different amount should have been specified and then either confirm the amount specified in this notice or amend the notice to specify a different amount.

If you make representations **before** the date the payment is due, and we do not withdraw the notice, payment will be due on or before the later of:

- the original date the payment is due (shown above)
- 30 days after the date on which we notify you of our decision in respect of your representations

21.43 *Tackling 'tax avoidance'*

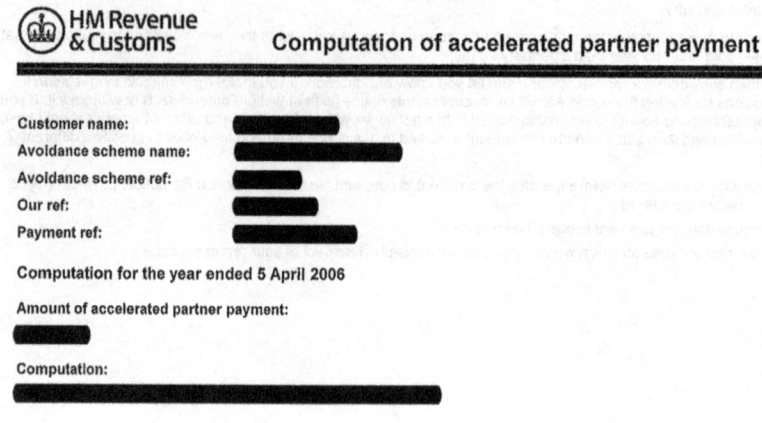

Tackling 'tax avoidance' **21.43**

HM Revenue & Customs

Tax Calculation for 2002-03

Tax Reference:
Date: 23 September 2014

Summary
Tax and Class 4 National Insurance contributions due (Declared) £39,594.77
Tax and Class 4 National Insurance contributions due (Revised) £75,631.21
Difference £36,036.44

Tax Calculation for 2002-03 (year ended 5 April 2003) (based on declared figures)

Income		
Partnerships	227,039	
Foreign Income	47	
UK Interest (before tax)	3,013	
UK Dividends & tax credits	328	
Total Income		230,427

minus Deductions and Allowances		
Losses	90,092	
Retirement Annuity Relief etc.	1,901	
Loan Interest payments	18,502	
Annuities	6,256	
Personal Allowance	4,615	
Total Deductions and Allowances		121,366

Taxable Income 109,061

How I have calculated your Income Tax
Your basic rate limit has been increased by £4240 to £34140 for pension payments etc.
This reduces the amount of income charged to higher rates of tax.

Non-savings income etc.
1,920 @ 10% = 192.00
32,220 @ 22% = 7,088.40
70,234 @ 40% = 28,093.60

Savings (other than Dividend income) etc.
0 @ 10% = –
0 @ 20% = –
3,622 @ 40% = 1,448.80

Dividend income etc.
0 @ 10% = –
1,066 @ 32.5% = 346.12

Taxable Income 109,061

Income Tax 37,168.92
minus Foreign Tax Credit Relief 7.18
Income Tax due after Allowances and Reliefs 37,161.74
Tax due on annuity payments 6,256 at 22% = 1,376.32
minus non-payable tax credits on Dividends 101.80
plus Class 4 National Insurance contributions 1,806.00
Income Tax and Class 4 National Insurance contributions 40,242.26

minus tax deducted at source from
Partnerships 45.21
UK Interest 602.64
Total deducted at source 647.85

Tax and Class 4 National Insurance contributions due 39,594.41

Adjustment to agree the Self Assessment –0.36

Tax and Class 4 National Insurance contributions due 39,594.77

Tax Calculation for 2002-03 (year ended 5 April 2003) (based on revised figures)

Income		
Partnerships	227,039	
Foreign Income	47	
UK Interest (before tax)	3,013	
UK Dividends & tax credits	328	
Total Income		230,427

minus Deductions and Allowances		
Retirement Annuity Relief etc.	1,901	
Loan Interest payments	18,502	
Annuities	6,256	
Personal Allowance	4,615	
Total Deductions and Allowances		31,274

Taxable Income 199,153

How I have calculated your Income Tax
Your basic rate limit has been increased by £4240 to £34140 for pension payments etc.
This reduces the amount of income charged to higher rates of tax.

Non-savings income etc.
1,920 @ 10% = 192.00
32,220 @ 22% = 7,088.40
160,326 @ 40% = 64,130.40

Savings (other than Dividend income) etc.
0 @ 10% = –
0 @ 20% = –
3,622 @ 40% = 1,448.80

Dividend income etc.
0 @ 10% = –
1,066 @ 32.5% = 346.12

Taxable Income 199,153

Income Tax 73,205.72
minus Foreign Tax Credit Relief 7.18
Income Tax due after Allowances and Reliefs 73,198.54
Tax due on annuity payments 6,256 at 22% = 1,376.32
minus non-payable tax credits on Dividends 101.80
plus Class 4 National Insurance contributions 1,806.00
Income Tax and Class 4 National Insurance contributions 76,279.06

minus tax deducted at source from
Partnerships 45.21
UK Interest 602.64
Total deducted at source 647.85

Tax and Class 4 National Insurance contributions due 75,631.21

911

Chapter 22

Tax debt collection

Jennifer Jones CTA
Senior Tax Manager, BDO LLP

This is my first year as author of this chapter and credit for much of the content must go to the previous author, Helen Adams. My approach has been to continue Helen's good work and simply update the material she originally contributed.

SIGNPOSTS

- **Managed payment plans** – Before a tax liability becomes a debt, taxpayers can apply to HMRC to put a payment plan in place to cover certain liabilities to spread the cost by making payments both before and after the due date with no interest or late payment penalties (see **22.3–22.6**)

- **The early collection stages** – HMRC's systems automatically recognise tax debts but where debtors cannot be traced, in some circumstances, responsibility for some taxes can be transferred to others. Tax codes are used to collect certain debts but for others HMRC issues a series of reminders for other debts. Debts arising from tax in dispute because of a tax avoidance Scheme are collected using accelerated payment notices (see **22.7–22.23**).

- **Time to pay agreements** – Any tax or duty can be part of a time to pay (TTP) arrangement. HMRC is most likely to agree a TTP arrangement if it is requested in advance of the payment deadline, only spread over up to 12 months and you can show the taxpayer has started economising to help meet the payments (see **22.24–22.31**).

- **Direct recovery of debts from taxpayer's bank accounts** – Where strict conditions are met, HMRC is able to recover cash directly from taxpayers' bank and building society accounts and cash ISAs but must leave a balance of at least £5,000 available to the taxpayer in most circumstances. HMRC can also issue an information notice and a hold notice (to freeze a specified amount in the account – see **22.36–22.37**) before issuing the final deduction notice. Affected parties have 30 days to object to a hold notice but HMRC can penalise financial institutions that do not cooperate (see **22.32–22.53**).

- **Court action** – HMRC may use civil debt collection proceedings through the magistrates' or higher courts to collect tax debts as well as interest and penalties (see **22.54–22.55**).

- **Notice of enforcement (taking control of goods)** – These can be issued to taxpayers who are 'habitual defaulters' and take a charge over their assets for tax debts. The assets cannot be sold by the taxpayer and, if the debt is not settled within 14 days, HMRC will send the bailiffs in to take control of them and sell them to settle the debt (see **22.56–22.62**).

- **Liquidation and bankruptcy** – Like any creditor, HMRC can petition the court to put a company into liquidation or bankrupt an individual to settle tax debts even where an assessment is under appeal and awaiting a tax tribunal hearing (see **22.63–22.70**).

- **Requirement to give security for tax** – Where it is concerned that a business may fail, to limit its exposure to bad debts for certain taxes HMRC can require that a business provides financial security which may also result in the business entering the Managing Serious Defaulters programme (see **22.71–22.80**).

- **HMRC enforcement of non-UK tax debts** – Under the European Union Mutual Assistance for Recovery of Debts HMRC collects tax debts in the UK for other EU member states and can also collect debts under other international agreements including for the signatories to the OECD's Convention on Mutual Administrative Assistance in Tax Matters (see **22.81–22.96**).

- **Summary** – for a list of key points from this chapter see **22.97**.

INTRODUCTION

22.1 HMRC is responsible for the collection and management of taxes, duties and National Insurance contributions as a consequence of the Commissioners' responsibilities set out in the *Commissioners for Revenue and Customs Act 2005*. HMRC has an impressive and growing range of powers to collect the cash owed to it by taxpayers, which was added to by the Enforcement by Deduction from Accounts legislation included in the *Finance (No 2) Act 2015*.

22.2 *Tax debt collection*

22.2 This is a crucial aspect of the government's efforts to reduce the deficit and taxpayers who do not pay what is owed on time are likely to experience one or more of the collection methods available to HMRC. Where possible taxpayers should consider obtaining a time to pay arrangement proactively before a payment date is missed. HMRC, in a similarly proactive vein, may require a taxpayer to provide security in advance of a tax debt.

MANAGED PAYMENT PLANS – PRE-EMPTING CASHFLOW ISSUES

22.3 Before a tax liability becomes a debt, *TMA 1970, s 59G* enables taxpayers to apply to HMRC for a managed payment plan (MPP) to cover amounts due which are:

(a) payments on account of income tax due on 31 January and 31 July under *TMA 1970, s 59A(2)*;

(b) income tax and capital gains tax payable on 31 January after the end of a tax year by virtue of *TMA 1970, s 59B*; and

(c) corporation tax payable nine months after the end of an accounting period under *TMA 1970, s 59D*.

MPPs are not available to companies who settle their corporation tax liabilities via quarterly instalment payments.

22.4 As set out in *TMA 1970, s 59G(2)(b)*, the payments due under an MPP are made by instalments before and after the usual due date of the payment which is being settled via the MPP. Payments made before the due date must equal those paid after the due date in terms of amount and intervals as a result of *TMA 1970, s 59H*.

22.5 If all payments are made in accordance with the pre-agreed instalments then the liability is treated as having been paid at the due date (*TMA 1970, s 59G(4)*) so no late payment interest or penalties/surcharges are charged. Failure to pay instalments on time may result in interest, penalties and/or surcharges.

22.6 Overall, this provision should help taxpayers budget for their tax liabilities although taxpayers must ensure that they do have sufficient funds to meet all MPP payments to which they commit as HMRC expects payments to be made via direct debit. This, however, does reduce the risk of taxpayers inadvertently missing payments.

Similarly, time to pay arrangements may be obtained prior to a debt's due date – see **22.24** below.

THE EARLY COLLECTION STAGES

Identifying the debt and debtor

22.7 HMRC's systems allow it to automatically recognise when tax payments have not been made on time. This triggers many automated processes but the key point is that the debt is flagged up to HMRC's Debt Management and Banking (DMB) department. Where the debtor's contact details are unclear or not known, HMRC can issue a notice to a third party under *FA 2009, Sch 49* to obtain the debtor's contact information.

Transfer of debt to other parties

22.8 Where debtors cannot be traced, in some circumstances, responsibility for PAYE and NIC debts may be transferred to other parties, eg where there is a deliberate failure to pay in cases involving a managed service company (MSC), employment intermediary or even an employee. For cases involving MSCs, *ITEPA 2003, s 688A(2)*, allows the debt to be transferred to:

- a director, other office holder or associate of the MSC;
- the MSC provider (director, office holder or associate of the MSC);
- any other person who was directly or indirectly involved in the Scheme (or its director, or other office holder or associate).

22.9 The debt must be incurred after 6 January 2008 for the transfer provisions to apply. Further information on these regulations and the exclusions from it can be obtained from HMRC's Employment Status manual (ESM) at ESM3625.

The intermediaries' legislation also includes specific provision to transfer a debt to an individual by way of the issue of a 'personal liability notice' to company directors after 5 April 2014.

22.10 Effectively, *ITEPA 2003, ss 44(4)–(6)* and *46A* may be used to deem another party to be the employer of the workers for both tax and NIC purposes. The other party may be a company (or LLP) and if it then fails to pay HMRC the PAYE on time then HMRC may issue a personal liability notice to the company's directors to make them responsible for paying the PAYE plus late payment interest personally. The notice specifies the amount payable within 30 days of the notice's date. Personal liabilities notices may be issued to more than one director of a company for the same debt thus making the individuals jointly and severally liable to pay HMRC. The individuals may appeal against the notice which may be withdrawn if the tribunal cancels it.

22.11 Tax debt collection

22.11 The legislation enabling HMRC to collect the sums due to it as a consequence of a personal liability notice was introduced by *FA 2014, s 17*. This amended the Income Tax (Pay As You Earn) Regulations 2003, SI 2003/2682, to include regs 97ZA–97ZF inclusive. Regulation 97ZF also enables HMRC to repay any surplus amounts collected with interest. Further information is available via ESM2046.

22.12 *O'Rorke v Revenue and Customs Comrs* [2011] UKFTT 839 (TC) considered personal liability notices transferring a company's liabilities to NICs to a director after the company failed to pay HMRC. This was a decision on a preliminary issue and, after much consideration, the tribunal decided that such notices are effectively criminal matters and therefore 'neglect' is a subjective test, ie the court should not consider a hypothetical man but instead consider whether the director must have intended the negligent act. Consequently, medical evidence about director that was excluded at an earlier directions hearing needed to be readmitted for the tribunal's consideration.

22.13 Generally an employer is liable to pay both primary and secondary Class 1 NICs to HMRC (*Social Security Contributions and Benefits Act 1992, Sch 1, para 3(1)*). However, Social Security (Contributions) Regulations 2001, SI 2001/1004, reg 86(1)(a) provides that the employee, not the employer, becomes responsible for paying the primary Class 1 NICs when:

- the employer fails to pay primary Class 1 NICs on behalf of the employee; and
- the failure is caused by the employee's act or omission rather than that of the employer; or
- the employee knows that the employer wilfully failed to pay HMRC and has not recovered amount due from the employee.

22.14 *R v IRC, ex p Chisolm* [1981] STC 253 established that 'wilful' means 'intentional' or 'deliberate' and *R v IRC, ex p Sims* [1987] STC 211 and *R v IRC, ex p Keys* (1987) 60 TC 405 both decided that a director receiving a payment without deduction of PAYE must have known about that failure. *R v IRC, ex p McVeigh* [1986] STC 91 also examined the issue in relation to bonuses paid to directors.

22.15 HMRC may also refer to a non-tax case, *HL Bolton (Engineering) Co Ltd v TJ Graham & Sons Ltd* [1956] 3 All ER 624, in which Lord Denning considered that a company was like a body and the directors and managers its brain such that the state of mind of these individuals is that of the company and the law would treat it as such.

Further information on HMRC's approach to these regulations can be accessed via HMRC's National Insurance manual (NIM) at NIM01022 and NIM12116.

Tax collection via coding notices

22.16 HMRC will alter taxpayers' coding notices to collect self-assessment tax, Class 2 National Insurance debts, contract settlement debts and tax credit overpayments by deduction at source from their salary or pension.

22.17 The amount that can be collected in this way varies depending on a person's earnings. If a person earns less than £30,000 per annum then HMRC can collect up to £3,000 via his tax code. If a person earns more than this, then HMRC can collect more – up to £17,000 if the person earns £90,000 or more – although the limit for collecting self-assessment balancing payments and PAYE debts remains £3,000.

If the amount owed exceeds these limits, HMRC will not collect the debt via the individual's coding notice but will use other methods instead.

Reminders

22.18 The lump sum collection process starts with the issue of a demand, or payment reminder, to the taxpayer by post (*TMA 1970, s 60(1)*). Following a series of reminders (the number depends broadly on the size of the debt), a DMB officer will telephone the taxpayer to demand payment.

22.19 At this stage the next steps may include:

– payment of the debt (for which a receipt may be requested under *TMA 1970, s 60(2)*);
– applying for a time to pay agreement;
– direct recovery of debts;
– court action to enforce payment;
– the issue of a notice of enforcement.

22.20 Occasionally, the debt slips through the reminder process and the taxpayer hears nothing from HMRC for some time. It is important to remember that, after the assessment or demand is issued, there is no time limit within which HMRC must pursue a debt for tax or interest according to the *Limitation Act 1980, s 37* (although *ss 9* and *24* do apply six-year time limits for NIC and related penalties). HMRC's DMB teams work through lists of old debts (sometimes referred to as Arrears Control lists) issuing letters to taxpayers with a statement setting out all liabilities which HMRC believes are overdue for payment. These may arrive unexpectedly at a taxpayer's home or business premises and will need to be either paid, contested (to demonstrate payment was made some time ago) or a time to pay arrangement obtained otherwise HMRC will follow its standard collection procedures.

22.21 *Tax debt collection*

Accelerated payment notices for Scheme users

22.21 Where the 'debt' arises from tax in dispute because of a tax avoidance Scheme, under *FA 2014, ss 219–229* HMRC may issue an accelerated payment notice (APN) to a taxpayer – see **CHAPTER 21**.

22.22 The notice effectively prevents postponement of tax while an enquiry or appeal is ongoing. The payment must be made within 90 days of the APN or 30 days after HMRC issues a determination in response to any representations made following the notice's issue. However, a TTP arrangements can be agreed with HMRC's DMB team and provided that the taxpayer meets the conditions of the TTP arrangements, the APN penalty should not be payable (see **22.26**).

22.23 If the taxpayer instead decides to withdraw from participating in the Scheme and settle the outstanding tax then it may be possible to do this by way of a contract settlement following discussions with the HMRC officer. In suitable cases, HMRC may be prepared to include in the contract settlement instalment payments which may be over a period in excess of 12 months. A better result may be achieved in terms of time to pay than via a TTP agreement negotiated with DMB but, having finalised his tax position, the taxpayer will not benefit if the Scheme is ultimately found to achieve its original aims.

Time to pay agreements

22.24 Since 2008, HMRC has allowed companies and individuals to defer paying taxes and duties through time to pay (TTP) arrangements facilitated by its limited discretion under its care and management responsibilities. Detailed guidance on TTP is available via HMRC's Debt Management and Banking (DMB) manual at DMBM 800000 *et seq* and via the Government website at www.gov.uk/difficulties-paying-hmrc.

22.25 Any tax or duty can potentially be part of a TTP arrangement. The overarching point is that HMRC is concerned with collecting the money it is owed. For the same reason, while a bank may not be prepared to lend more money, taxpayers may find that their bank may be inclined to support a TTP application as it will enable a business to continue operating so that the bank does not lose a client, for example.

22.26 Whilst interest is still charged on late payments, the benefits to taxpayers of agreeing TTP are:

- greater certainty over their cash flow;
- avoiding default surcharges and late payment penalties on the debt (provided the payments are made as agreed and the TTP arrangement

was in place before the date on which the default surcharge or late payment penalty is levied) see **CHAPTER 21** (for APN penalties see the case decision below); and

- HMRC should suspend further steps to enforce the debt.

The decision in *BW Hills Southbank Limited v Revenue and Customs Comrs* [2016] UKFTT 423 (TC) confirms that it is sufficient for the taxpayer to have requested a TTP arrangement in respect of the APN before the deadline in order to avoid the APN penalty being charged. It is not necessary for the taxpayer to have agreed the TTP arrangements with HMRC before the payment deadline.

22.27 It is best to request a TTP arrangement before the payment deadline (as soon as default looks likely) and it is helpful to show that the taxpayer has taken steps or put plans in place to cut costs. In addition, all taxes on which there are arrears should be covered by a TTP arrangement. HMRC should be the last option, not the first; the taxpayer should approach other sources of finance (eg banks for loan finance) before approaching HMRC. HMRC may expect this to be demonstrated in addition to requiring businesses to provide other information in support of a TTP request, such as cash-flow projections. Where an individual owes HMRC funds, HMRC may request an up-to-date statement of assets and liabilities to determine the individual's net assets in addition to a statement detailing the individual's monthly income and outgoings.

22.28 The reason for this is that HMRC will only agree to TTP if the taxpayer has sufficient means to meet the proposed instalments in addition to paying his other liabilities and other tax liabilities that will become due during the proposed period of the TTP arrangement. Realistic terms for a TTP are crucial because enforcement action or liquidation/bankruptcy applications may follow a failure to meet TTP instalment payments.

22.29 HMRC is unlikely to agree to instalments over more than 12 months. Regular monthly payments, even if small to start with, are preferable. However, HMRC is less likely to agree heavily back loaded payment schedules. Similarly, HMRC is unlikely to agree to payment holidays unless the taxpayer has no funds available until an asset (eg a property) is sold and active steps are being taken to sell it. Where HMRC does allow the taxpayer time to release funds through the sale of an asset, it will likely still require the taxpayer to pay some instalments in the interim to demonstrate the taxpayer's commitment to settling the debt. HMRC is often reluctant to agree a TTP arrangement where a taxpayer has had one previously.

22.30 According to DMBM800520, the Business Payment Support Service Helpline (0300 200 3835) should be contacted when the taxpayer is yet to

22.31 *Tax debt collection*

receive a demand from HMRC's DMB team. Once a demand is received, the first step is to contact the number shown on the demand.

22.31 Once TTP is agreed HMRC will, from 3 August 2015, expect payments to be made by direct debit. One reason for this is that direct debits reduce the chance of payments being missed. Where a taxpayer does not have a bank account that permits direct debits, HMRC may consider reaching a TTP agreement based on other payment methods. HMRC is bound by any TTP agreements it makes but can withdraw from them in some circumstances, eg if the taxpayer defaults from the payments, if HMRC subsequently realises that it was misled or if new facts come to light.

Direct recovery of debts from taxpayer's bank accounts

22.32 Legislation is included in *F(No 2)A 2015, s 51* and *Sch 8* to enable HMRC to collect tax and duties due to them directly from taxpayers' bank and building society accounts in England, Wales and Northern Ireland. In this legislation, this new power is called 'enforcement by deduction from accounts' and is also known as direct recovery of debts (DRD). This legislation has been introduced to enable HMRC to collect debts from those taxpayers who have the means to pay but have not settled their debts. In Scotland, HMRC can already apply for a warrant to enforce debts with Sherriff Officers enforcing it – where necessary through arrestment on bank accounts.

22.33 The legislation permits HMRC to amend the regulations at any time via Statutory Instruments (*Sch 8, paras 19–21*). The Enforcement by Deduction from Accounts (Imposition of Charges by Deposit-takers) Regulations 2016, SI 2016/44 came into force on 10 February 2016. These Regulations prevent the bank or building society (deposit-taker) from charging a fee in respect of administrative costs for the DRD process other than in the circumstance where:

- it has agreed with the account holder that a fee can be charged;
- the direct recovery of debts process has concluded; and
- no previous fee for the administrative costs has been charged by the deposit-taker.

Regulation 4 limits the charge that can be imposed by the deposit-taker to the lesser of:

- the amount of those administrative costs reasonably incurred by the deposit-taker; or
- £55.

22.34 Based on HMRC's 'Issue Briefing: Direct Recovery of Debts' of 5 August 2015, HMRC intends that every debtor will receive a face-to-face visit from HMRC agents before his debts are considered for recovery under DRD. Whilst this safeguard is not included in the legislation, in summary the new legislation will mean that:

- HMRC will be able to recover cash directly from taxpayers' bank and building society accounts and cash ISAs (not stocks and shares ISAs);

- taxpayers (including individuals, partnerships and companies) that owe money to HMRC by virtue of an assessment, determination, APN, enquiry closure notice or contract settlement will be affected by these provisions;

- when determining the amount of funds available to settle the taxpayer's debt, an amount of at least £5,000 must be left in the debtors account(s) with the bank/building society in most cases; and

- the debt due from the taxpayer must also meet all of the following conditions (set out in *F(No 2)A 2015, Sch 8, para 2*) for it to be subject to direct recovery:

    (a) the debt must be at least £1,000;

    (b) the debt must be an 'established debt' meaning it results from a decision or assessment by HMRC against which no appeal (or further appeal) can be made *or* it is a debt demanded in an accelerated payment notice (APN); and

    (c) HMRC is satisfied that the person is aware of the sum that is due and payable.

22.35 Reports suggest that HMRC is taking a measured approach to the introduction of the DRD powers. DRD was introduced gradually, with the results being analysed to help improve the process in the future.

Information and hold notices

22.36 Where HMRC considers a person has failed to pay a debt, *para 3* enables HMRC to issue an 'information notice' to the bank/building society to obtain certain information about the accounts held by the debtor, including joint accounts. HMRC will use this information to determine whether a 'hold notice' should be issued to the bank/building society ('the deposit taker') in respect of those accounts as the next step towards the direct recovery of the debt. The deposit taker will only have ten working days to reply to the information notice. *F(No 2)A 2015, Sch 8, para 3(3)* confirms that HMRC may only use this information power to determine whether to give a hold notice.

22.37 *Tax debt collection*

22.37 Effectively, if issued, the hold notice requires the bank or building society to ensure that the account's balance does not fall below the 'held amount'. The alternative is that the deposit taker may transfer the held amount into a suspense account. The hold notice must specify:

- the taxpayer's name and address;
- the 'specified amount', ie the debt to be collected from the account;
- the 'safeguarded amount' which is a minimum of £5,000 in most circumstances (*F(No 2)A 2015, Sch 8, para 4(6)*). This is the amount that will continue to be available to the debtor whilst the hold exits. According to the notes published with the Finance (No 2) Bill 2015 prior to its consideration by Parliament, HMRC will have discretion to set this amount higher where it is reasonable to do so (eg to safeguard funds to pay employees' salaries);
- the order or priority of accounts subject to the notice.

The deposit taker must give effect to the notice 'as soon as reasonably practicable' (*Sch 8, para 6(2)*) and within five working days after the notice is issued.

22.38 A copy of the hold notice will be sent to the account holder. If the account is a joint account then the notice will be sent to all those individuals/entities with a beneficial interest in the account. The amount held will relate to the proportion of the account balance that the relevant individual holds. If the debtor has more than one account and HMRC issues hold notices to more than one bank/building society, the total amount which may be held under all the notices cannot exceed the total debt due to HMRC (*F(No 2)A 2015, Sch 8, para 4(4)*).

22.39 *F(No 2)A 2015, Sch 8, para 7* specifies that the 'held amount' is:

- nil, where the account has less funds than the safeguarded amount; or
- an amount up to the specified amount, where the account has more funds than the safeguarded amount.

22.40 A multi-part calculation is set out at *F(No 2)A 2015, Sch 8, para 7(2)* for situations where there is more than one account in existence. In effect, the deposit taker must check whether the total account balances exceed the safeguarded amount. If it does, then there is an order of priority set out at *Sch 8, para 7(5)* which determines the affected accounts. The safeguarded amount is offset against current accounts in preference to savings accounts and to the debtor's own accounts in priority to joint accounts.

22.41 According to *F(No 2)A 2015, Sch 8, para 8*, the deposit taker must notify HMRC that it applied a hold notice to one or more accounts. HMRC is then obliged to notify the affected parties. *Sch 8, para 8(10)* enables the deposit taker, if he wishes, to similarly notify the affected parties after the hold notice is imposed. The affected parties in this context will be the debtor, the other account holder if the account is a joint account and anyone 'who is an interested third party in relation to the account' (para 8(10)(c)). An interested third party is defined in *Sch 8, para 8(11)* as:

'a person other than [the taxpayer] who has a beneficial interest in –

(a) an amount standing to the credit of the account, or

(b) an amount which has been transferred from that account to a suspense account.'

22.42 HMRC can cancel or reduce the specified amount in the hold notice at any time by issuing a notice of cancellation or variation under *F(No 2)A 2015, Sch 8, para 9*. A copy of the notice must be given to the taxpayer and any other affected parties.

22.43 *F(No 2)A 2015, Sch 8, para 5(1)* states that before using their powers to issue an information or a hold notice 'HMRC must consider whether or not, to the best of HMRC's knowledge, there are any matters as a result of which the person is, or may be, at a particular disadvantage in dealing with the person's Revenue and Customs affairs'. If so, *para 5(2)* says that HMRC must take these matters into account. HMRC published a policy paper on 10 February 2016 titled 'Direct Recovery of Debts – vulnerable customers'. This guidance describes the following four categories to help identify disadvantaged and vulnerable individuals:

- **A disability or long-term health condition** – This could be a long term or temporary disability, mental health condition or learning difficulty. The condition affects the taxpayer's ability to manage their affairs and they are unable to understand or appreciate their indebtedness.

- **A temporary illness, physical or mental health condition** – The taxpayer is diagnosed with a serious illness or condition. The condition affects the taxpayer's ability to understand or appreciate their indebtedness.

- **Personal issues** – Issues affecting the taxpayer, or someone close to them, to such an extent that the taxpayer cannot understand or cope by themselves.

- **Lower levels of literacy, numeracy and/or education** – The taxpayer is unable to fully understand their indebtedness without advice or support.

22.44 *Tax debt collection*

The guidance is not intended to provide an exhaustive list and factors not covered by the above categories should also be considered. Taxpayers who are identified as vulnerable will not be subject to DRD, instead they will be given alternative support to settle their debt.

Objecting to and appealing against hold notices

22.44 The affected parties (as defined above) have 30 days to object to a hold notice under *F(No 2)A 2015, Sch 8, para 10*. The debtor can object on the grounds that the debt has been paid in part or in full. All affected parties can object on other grounds set out in *Sch 8, para 10(3)* which include that the notice is or will cause exceptional hardship to the person objecting or another person. The objection must be made in the form of a 'notice of objection' and must state the objector's grounds. HMRC may accept a late notice of objection if the objector had a reasonable excuse for not submitting the notice within the usual time limit and submits it without unreasonable delay after the excuse ceases (*Sch 8, paras 10(6)–(8)*).

22.45 HMRC has 30 days to consider the notice of objection before it must, according to *F(No 2)A 2015, Sch 8, para 11*, either:

- cancel the hold notice;
- cancel the effect of the hold notice in relation to the held amount or part thereof relating to a specific account(s); or
- reject the objection.

22.46 Where the hold notice is not cancelled in full following an objection, *F(No 2)A 2015, Sch 8, para 12* permits one or more of the affected parties to make a formal appeal against the hold notice, within 30 days, stating the grounds of appeal. The appeal must be made to a county court. The court may cancel the notice, cancel the effect of part or all of the notice or dismiss the appeal. If the appeal is allowed in full or in part, the court will serve an order on the deposit taker which it must action within five working days. The legislation contains a provision at *Sch 8, para 12(9)* to enable a person to apply to the court to suspend the effect of a hold notice pending its appeal decision.

Deduction notices

22.47 If the debtor fails to pay the relevant debt after the issue of a hold notice, a 'deduction notice' can be issued by HMRC under *Sch 8, para 13* after the appeal period expires for the hold notice (or when an appeal against the hold notice is resolved). This deduction notice requires the bank/building society to make the specified payment to HMRC by a set deadline to complete the direct recovery process *(Sch 8, para 13(2)(c))*. Once all payments are made, the deduction notice automatically expires *(Sch 8, para 13(11))*.

22.48 The notice must specify the name of the debtor, one or more affected accounts and the amount that the deposit taker must deduct and pay to HMRC from each account. HMRC must give a copy of the notice to the debtor and other affected people, eg joint account holders. Should HMRC amend or cancel the deduction notice then a copy of any revised notice must also be given to the debtor and other affected people *(Sch 8, para 13(10))*.

A deposit-taker is not liable for damages as a consequence of complying in good faith with a hold notice or a deduction notice *(Sch 8, para 18)*.

Penalties

22.49 Under *F(No 2)A 2015, Sch 8, para 14* HMRC may charge penalties to the bank/building society for failure to comply with:

- an information, hold or deduction notice;
- obligations to notify HMRC of the effects of a hold notice or that there are no affected accounts; and/or
- obligations to cancel or modify the effect of a hold notice or to cancel or adjust arrangements to give effect to HMRC's decision following objections.

22.50 The penalty is £300. However if the failure continues after the penalty is charged then daily penalties of up to £60 day may be charged *(F(No 2)A 2015, Sch 8, para 14(4))*. No penalties are charged if the deposit taker rectifies the situation within 'such further time, if any, as HMRC may have allowed' *(Sch 8, para 14(5))* or if the deposit taker has a reasonable excuse for the failure *(Sch 8, para 14(6))*.

22.51 In addition, HMRC may charge a £300 penalty if the deposit taker 'tips off' the debtor or another person which 'is likely to prejudice HMRC's ability to recover a debt using this legislation' following an information or a hold notice *(F(No 2)A 2015, Sch 8, para 14(1)(g))*.

22.52 HMRC has 12 months to impose the penalty by written notice starting from the day on which the deposit taker becomes liable to the penalty for failure to comply with an information notice. In all other cases HMRC has until 12 months of the later of the following dates set out in *F(No 2)A 2015, Sch 8, para 15(3)*:

- the day on which the deposit taker becomes liable to the penalty;

22.53 *Tax debt collection*

- the end of the period in which a notice of an appeal against the hold notice could have been made; and

- the date on which an appeal against the hold notice is determined or withdrawn.

22.53 The deposit taker may appeal against the penalty under *F(No 2)A 2015, Sch 8, para 16* by giving HMRC a notice within 30 days of being notified of the penalty's imposition. The appeal must include the grounds of the appeal. The penalty is payable within 30 days of the date on which it is imposed or the date on which the appeal is determined or withdrawn, whichever is the later.

COURT ACTION

22.54 HMRC may apply to the magistrates' court for a debt of up to £2,000 to be recoverable summarily under civil debt proceedings where the amount owed is income tax, capital gains tax or corporation tax (*TMA 1970, s 65* and DMBM660040).

22.55 Larger amounts may be sued for and recovered via other courts such as the county courts or High Court (*TMA 1970, ss 66 and 68*). Similar regulations exist for Scottish and Northern Ireland courts. Detailed information on HMRC's procedures can be found in HMRC's Debt Management and Banking manual from the indexes at DMBM665000, DMBM670000, DMBM675000 and DMBM680000.

Interest and penalties can be collected through similar action as if they were tax (*TMA 1970, s 69*).

NOTICE OF ENFORCEMENT – TAKING CONTROL OF GOODS

22.56 Information about the steps that HMRC may take to collect tax debts can be found at www.gov.uk/if-you-dont-pay-your-tax-bill.

DMB teams are able to issue a notice of enforcement to taxpayers who are 'habitual defaulters' (eg those who fail to pay PAYE and NIC for three months). The notice gives up to just 14 days to pay, although it is still possible to agree a TTP arrangement after the notice has been issued (albeit on much less favourable terms). Issuing the notice effectively blocks taxpayers from removing or selling their goods until the tax is paid. New rules under the

Tribunals, Courts and Enforcement Act 2007, Pt 3 now allow a charge for this 'service' – HMRC currently charges £75 to issue a notice of enforcement.

22.57 Failure to pay within the 7 days will lead to HMRC commencing a taking control of goods enforcement action (also known as 'distraint') under the Taking Control of Goods Regulations 2013, SI 2013/1894 and *TMA 1970, s 61*. Such visits from HMRC's Field Force (bailiffs) will result in an additional charge to the taxpayer of £235 (plus 7.5% of the amount of the debt over £1,500) – even if the taxpayer pays immediately.

22.58 If the taxpayer cannot pay immediately, the bailiffs take a note of the assets that they wish to confiscate and ask the taxpayer to sign this 'Controlled Goods Agreement' (termed 'Walking Possession' in Northern Ireland). If the tax is not paid within a further five days, the bailiffs will return, confiscate the assets and auction them to settle the debt (and charge a fee of £110 plus 7.5% of the amount of the debt over £1,500). Please note that different fees are charged in Northern Ireland.

22.59 If the result of the auction is that more funds are raised, net of fees such as auctioneers and advertising costs, then the excess balance is returned to the taxpayer. However, if the funds (net of costs) are less than the debt due to HMRC (including fees for the enforcement action) then HMRC will pursue collection of the remaining debt.

Further information on HMRC's procedures for enforcement can be found in its Debt Management and Banking manual's sub-menus at DMBM575000 and DMBM650000.

22.60 HMRC and the Border Force also have the power to seize goods and vehicles under the *Customs and Excise Management Act 1979, s 139*, when the correct duty or Import VAT has not been paid. In May 2016 HMRC reissued 'Notice 12A: what you can do if things are seized by HM Revenue and Customs' containing guidance on what can be done by those who have items seized under these rules, there are three options:

- **Challenge** – The legality of the seizure can be challenged by sending a Notice of Claim to HMRC or the Border Force.
- **Restoration** – Ask HMRC or the Border Force for the seized item to be returned even if there is an acceptance that it was seized legally.
- **Challenge & Restoration** – Do both of the above.

Challenge and Restoration are separate processes and will be dealt with differently. The legality of the seizure is likely to be considered by the magistrates' court, whilst Restoration is decided by HMRC or Border Force.

22.61 *Tax debt collection*

Notice 12A contains more details on how to make the claims, including example claim letters and a helpline number.

Who is the bailiff?

22.61 Historically HMRC used external debt collection agencies to pursue tax debts and tax credit debts. In 2015 the government announced that it was working with Integrated Debt Services Ltd, a company jointly owned by the government and TDX Group (an Equifax company) to provide a single point of access to a wide range of debt management and collection services. Consequently it may be the case that the bailiff is not an HMRC employee.

22.62 The presence of bailiffs at business premises can be disruptive even if they are not seizing goods. Their visit may cause reputational damage even if it is a mistake or the debt is then paid. Consequently, it may well be advisable to encourage clients to authorise you (their agent) to:

- engage with HMRC's DMB team in an attempt to avoid such action; and/or

- pro-actively consider placing the company into administration or entering into an individual voluntary arrangement in order to manage cash flow issues without confiscation of property.

LIQUIDATION AND BANKRUPTCY

22.63 HMRC can petition the court as a creditor to put a company into liquidation or to make an individual bankrupt if they have failed to settle tax debts. This is permitted even where an assessment is under appeal and awaiting a tax tribunal hearing, where collection of tax is not postponed.

22.64 In *Biffin and others v HMRC* [2016] EWHC 2926, the High Court granted an injunction prohibiting HMRC from commencing enforcement action in respect of tax liabilities that were the subject of appeal and postponement applications before the FTT. The Court did not view the claimants' claims as 'totally without merit' and considered damages would not be an adequate remedy in the event that HMRC took steps to enforce the unpaid tax because of the adverse impact of such a judgment on the company's business. The Court noted that if HMRC were successful in its claims as to the tax assessed, it would be compensated for the delayed receipt of the tax by way of interest and penalties, whilst the consequences of enforcement for the claimants were far more significant.

In *Parkwell v Wilson* [2014] EWHC 3381 (Ch), HMRC was successful in seeking the liquidation of the company to recover tax debts despite the tax being subject to an ongoing appeal to the First-tier Tax Tribunal (FTT). The court referred to the Court of Appeal's decision in *Revenue and Customs Commissioners v Rochdale Drinks Distributors Ltd* [2011] EWCA Civ 1116 during its deliberations. Whilst ordinarily a disputed debt precludes a winding up order, the appeal to the other court on substantive grounds needs to have merit. If the tribunal hearing was imminent the winding up petition may have been stayed.

22.65 Consequently, in *Parkwell* the High Court ruled that it was obliged to consider the likelihood of the success of the appeal. The company could not prove its appeal had merit as it failed to produce evidence to substantiate the entries on its VAT returns. As a result and because the company had insufficient assets to pay the VAT debt, the High Court approved the company's liquidation. A similar conclusion was also reached by the Court of Appeal in *Changtel Solutions UK Ltd (formerly Enta Technologies Ltd) v Revenue and Customs Comrs* [2015] EWCA Civ 29.

22.66 In committal proceedings after the *Parkwell* case, *Revenue and Customs Comrs v Munir* [2015] EWHC 1366 (Ch), it was decided that the directors actions in making payments from the company and impeding the provisional liquidator amounted to contempt of court.

22.67 Clearly, when making an appeal, a request should be made to postpone collection of the tax due under *TMA 1970, s 55*. However, it should be noted that if the case is lost by the taxpayer, then the tax may be payable despite an appeal to a higher court under *TMA 1970, s 56*.

22.68 Company directors should be aware that, in addition to the liquidation of the company, they themselves may face disqualification where the company fails to pay its tax debts. An October 2016 press release by the Insolvency Service describes the case of a director who was disqualified for 15 year following an investigation that started with the winding up of the company for unpaid VAT debts.

HMRC procedure for dealing with tax debts for companies in insolvency

22.69 In 2014, HMRC published Revenue and Customs Brief 42/2014 'Integration of HMRC Claims in Insolvencies'. Historically HMRC had separate teams dealing with direct and indirect taxes on insolvency. From 1 December 2014, integrated claims will be issued to insolvency practitioners covering direct and indirect tax debts.

22.70 The full text of the brief contains instructions on where forms will need to be sent and how to de-register for VAT and is available via

22.71 *Tax debt collection*

www.gov.uk/government/publications/revenue-and-customs-brief-42-2014-integration-of-claims-in-insolvencies.

REQUIREMENT TO GIVE SECURITY FOR TAX

22.71 Security can be demanded for debts of PAYE, NIC, VAT, insurance premium tax, aggregates levy, climate change levy and landfill tax. HMRC uses this power to limit its exposure to potential bad debts when it is concerned that a business may fail to pay its debts in future.

22.72 HMRC will issue a notice of requirement to give security to companies and their directors or LLPs and their partners if:

- they failed to comply with their tax obligations in their previous or current business; or
- HMRC identifies that the directors were connected or associated with multiple business failures.

22.73 An example of this is directors of companies who go into liquidation with significant debts due to HMRC before those same directors form a new company from which to trade. HMRC will therefore seek to understand:

- why the original company went into liquidation; and
- what the involvement of the directors and shareholders was prior to the liquidation (and how much money they lost as a result).

22.74 The notice requires that security is given within 30 days: the company and its directors are jointly and severally liable to give the full amount of security. The security can only be provided by:

- cheque or bank transfer;
- opening a joint bank account with HMRC;
- providing a guarantee in the form of a performance bond from an approved financial institution.

In addition, the taxpayer may be entered into the Managing Serious Defaulters regime (see **CHAPTER 8**).

22.75 The security is normally held for 24 months but, if the company or LLP meets its normal tax obligations (including payments), the holding period may be reduced. When it is no longer required, the security is either repaid or set against outstanding tax debts.

22.76 If the taxpayer disagrees with anything in the notice then they must appeal to HMRC within 30 days of the date of the notice setting out what they disagree with and why. HMRC will then contact them to discuss it. If no agreement is reached then the matter may be referred for internal review or a hearing before the FTT.

22.77 Such an appeal was considered by the FTT in *Mistral Promotions & Marketing (UK) Ltd* [2015] UKFTT 112 (TC) which considered a notice of requirement to give security for VAT. The tribunal noted the VAT debt and non-compliance of a company carrying out a similar business whose director was also director of the appellant. However, the FTT considered HMRC's decision to issue the notice was flawed as it did not state the reasons for the notice's issue and because HMRC failed to consider whether an appeal against an assessment issued to the previous company had been withdrawn. However, the FTT decided that HMRC's decision to issue the notice was not otherwise unreasonable and considered that if the flaws in HMRC's decision had not happened it was inevitable that security would still be required. Consequently, the taxpayer's appeal was dismissed.

School Estates Consultancy Ltd [2018] TC 06283 also highlights the use of these provisions where it is necessary 'for the protection of the revenue'. The FTT concluded HMRC's decision to require security was reasonable, specifically referring to the shareholders involvement in previous businesses that had gone into liquidation which operated the same types of trade from the same premises.

22.78 *D-Media Communications v HMRC* [2016] UKFTT 430 (TC) clarifies the FTT's role in the appeal process against a notice of requirement to give security. The tribunal confirmed that for PAYE and NIC it has appellate jurisdiction over the issue of a notice of requirement to give security. It therefore has the power to, confirm, vary or set aside the notice under the Income Tax (Pay As You Earn) Regulations 2003, reg 97V(5). These powers are not present in the VAT legislation so the tribunal's role in VAT cases is supervisory in nature. It can only consider if the requirement to give security is reasonable and then allow or dismiss the taxpayer's appeal. In this case the tribunal found that, although it was not unreasonable for HMRC to require security from D-Media Communications, the amount of security requested was too high and the company could not pay the amount demanded. The tribunal reduced the amount of security to the previous four months PAYE and NIC liabilities and stated that HMRC must consider a taxpayer's ability to pay when determining the amount of the security required.

22.79 Failure to give security is a criminal offence and HMRC may prosecute the company and directors or the LLP and partners: convicted parties will be fined up to £5,000. If the company cannot fund the security then it can seek a TTP agreement before the deadline for paying the security. If it is refused then it has a further 30 days after HMRC notifies its decision to pay the security to HMRC.

22.80 *Tax debt collection*

22.80 Further information about the requirement to give security can be found in HMRC's Security Guidance manual and in its series of factsheets: SS/FS1, SS/FS2a, SS/FS2b and SS/FS3 to 6 inclusive. The legislation may be found in various places as follows:

Tax/Duty	Legislation
PAYE	Income Tax (Pay as you earn) Regulations 2003, SI 2003/2682, Pt 4A
NIC	Social Security (Contributions) Regulations 2001, SI 2001/1004, Pt 3B, Sch 4
VAT	VATA 1994, Sch 11, para 4(2)(a)
Insurance premium tax	FA 1994, Sch 7, para 24
Landfill Tax	FA 1996, Sch 5, para 31
Aggregates levy	FA 2001, s 26(1)
Climate change levy	FA 2000, Sch 6, para 139(1)

HMRC ENFORCEMENT OF NON-UK TAX DEBTS

22.81 It is sometimes overlooked that HMRC does enforce collection of other jurisdictions' tax debts in some circumstances. HMRC's activities in this area are detailed in its HMRC's Debt Management and Banking manual at DMBM560000 *et seq.*

European Union Mutual Assistance for Recovery of Debts (MARD)

22.82 The EU's rules on mutual assistance for the recovery of debts are set out in European Union Council Directive 2010/24/EU which was implemented by Commission Implementing Regulation (EU) No 1189/2011.

22.83 This is incorporated into UK law at *FA 2011, s 87* and *Sch 25* and implemented as a consequence of the MARD Regulations 2011, SI 2011/2931. The Treasury can amend these regulations at any time, for example if the EU Directive is altered.

22.84 The regulations enable states to obtain information that would help them recover tax etc. However, the main effect of MARD is to oblige the UK to enforce the recovery of other EU countries' tax debts as if they were amounts owed to HMRC if the taxpayer is living/established in or has his assets in the UK. Other EU states are similarly required to enforce liabilities due to HMRC. Liabilities include tax, interest and penalties. The full list of countries and debts covered can be found at DMBM560015.

22.85 It should be remembered that in most cases, the UK cannot enforce an overseas tax authorities' debt if it is being contested by the taxpayer. If the taxpayer overturns the overseas' tax liability then the UK has to stop enforcement action.

22.86 According to DMBM560100, a member state may make a recovery request to HMRC if either:

- '• it is obvious that there are no assets for recovery in the applicant member state and information indicates that the debtor has assets in the requested member state

- • to exhaust all domestic means of recovery would give raise to disproportionate difficulty.'

A member state can only refuse to provide assistance on limited grounds, eg where the total debt is less than €1,500 including interest and costs.

22.87 In addition, an EU country can request assistance in the collection of Social Security Debts as a consequence of:

- EU Council Regulation (EC) No 883/2004 (as amended);
- EU Council Regulation (EC) No 987/2009;
- the Recovery of Social Security Contributions Due in Other Member States Regulations 2010, SI 2010/926.

Further information on this is available via DMBM560500 and DMBM 560520.

Mutual Assistance to non-EU countries for tax debts

22.88 HMRC has obligations to assist countries outside the EU to collect tax debts. These obligations derive from the Council of Europe/Organisation for Economic Co-operation and Development (OECD) Convention; and bilateral arrangements, typically articles within a double taxation agreement.

22.89 Article 11 of the OECD's Convention on Mutual Administrative Assistance in Tax Matters contains similar provisions to enable one jurisdiction to collect tax owed to another jurisdiction on request, as if the liability was a liability owed to it. This applies to non-contested debts. It also covers claims concerning a deceased person or his estate but the claim is limited to the value of the estate or the property acquired by each beneficiary, depending on whether the claim is to be recovered from the estate or beneficiaries thereof. The Convention was given effect in UK law by the International Mutual Administrative Assistance in Tax Matters Order 2007, SI 2007/2126 and came into force in the UK on 1 May 2008.

22.90   *Tax debt collection*

22.90   The other UK legislation that applies when HMRC assists non-EU countries to collect tax debts is:

- *FA 2006, ss 173, 175*;
- the Recovery of Foreign Taxes Regulations 2007, SI 2007/3507;
- the Recovery of Foreign Tax (Amendment) Regulations 2010, SI 2010/794.

HMRC's manuals for non-EU mutual assistance can be found at DMBM560200 and the countries affected are detailed at DMBM560205.

22.91   Generally mutual assistance will be given for the collection of debts that are less than five years old unless exceptional circumstances (eg fraud) warrant older debts being pursued. The age of the debt is usually calculated from the date the debt was established or confirmed following a dispute. However, local laws in the country in which the debt is situated may limit the time within which a debt may be pursued.

22.92   The types of assistance that may be offered include:

- checking addresses, employment information and assets;
- arranging for legal documents to be served;
- using normal debt collection procedures to pursue payment from the debtor, third party holding assets or another person liable to settle a claim; and
- protecting a claim by seizing assets or freezing bank accounts.

22.93   In addition, DMBM560900 provides information regarding 'Debt and Return Pursuit: Foreign Cases: Manual Assessments and Penalty Determinations on Tenants and Letting Agents of Non-resident Landlords'.

HMRC mutual assistance teams

22.94   According to DMBM560020 and DMBM560220 in practical terms, the parts of HMRC that are involved in such cases are:

Team	Role
Enforcement Technical Team	Policy lead in HMRC
The MARD Team	Operational matters – receives and processes inbound and outbound requests for assistance

Team	Role
National Non-resident Unit	Deal with UK direct taxpayers who live abroad and/or liaise with the countries in which the taxpayer resides to collect the tax (see DMBM560850)
Debt Management and Banking	Collection of liabilities

22.95 Strict confidentiality provisions apply to all information received from foreign countries. Information and documents sent to HMRC a part of a request for assistance from a foreign country can only be provided to:

- the person mentioned in the request for assistance;
- those persons and authorities responsible for the recovery of the claims and solely for that purpose; or
- the judicial authorities dealing with issues concerning the recovery of claims.

22.96 However, according to DMBM560070, some information can be provided despite it not being requested by the other jurisdiction. An example of this is the UK telling another state about a tax refund it intends to pay to a taxpayer resident in the other state, although the information sharing should not delay the refund to the taxpayer.

KEY POINTS

22.97

1   Managed payment plans may be sought in some circumstances before a debt becomes due, in order to spread the payments over a period before and after the due date.

2   HMRC has numerous ways to collect tax debts (including APNs) which usually start with letters or calls to the debtor.

3   Where possible, taxpayers may be best advised to contact HMRC at the earliest time to discuss their options and seek a mutually acceptable TTP agreement when it becomes clear that they have insufficient funds to pay a liability or foresee cashflow issues.

4   HMRC will use more disruptive methods to collect the debts if they remain unpaid.

5   HMRC should issue guidance before it starts using the new legislation enabling it to enforce payment by deduction from bank accounts.

22.97 *Tax debt collection*

6   HMRC may also collect debts by using bailiffs or petitioning to put a company into liquidation or an individual into bankruptcy, even where a matter is outstanding before the tax tribunals.

7   HMRC is able to enforce collection of non-UK tax debts and may call on assistance from some overseas tax authorities to enforce collection of UK debts in those jurisdictions.

8   Where HMRC is concerned that a business may fail, it can require security to be provided.

Chapter 23

Complaints about HMRC

Simon Oakes
Consultant, former Head of the Adjudicator's Office

SIGNPOSTS

- **Scope** – If, when conducting an investigation, HMRC fails to act or make decisions in accordance with its guidance – or otherwise mishandles the case – it can be held to account through HMRC's complaints process (see **23.1–23.9**).

- **Timing** – This can be done either at the conclusion of the investigation or, in appropriate cases, while the investigation is still ongoing (see **23.50–23.56**).

- **Ongoing investigations** – In the case of ongoing investigations, even when HMRC admits to serious mishandling this will not necessarily result in the investigation being closed down. It can, however, effect an appropriate change in how HMRC conducts the case. (See **23.52–23.54**.)

- **Viability of a complaint** – Except in the most straightforward of cases, it very much depends on the facts of the case whether there is a viable complaint. There are also judgements to be made concerning both the client's expectations and the extent to which he feels aggrieved. (See **23.42–23.49**.)

- **Financial redress available** – If the complaint is upheld, HMRC will (on an ex-gratia basis) pay financial redress in respect of all the costs incurred as a *direct* consequence of the *relevant HMRC mishandling* (including the costs of making the complaint). In appropriate cases tax and/or interest may also be written off. (See **23.82–23.83**.)

- **Interaction with any litigation** – Where the investigation is being litigated, and there are associated HMRC mishandling issues, a complaint should be considered as, following a recent UT decision,

23.1 *Complaints about HMRC*

> it is unlikely that these issues will be ruled upon at any tribunal hearing. (See **23.59–23.61**.)
>
> - **Accessibility** – HMRC has an accessible complaints process that is there to be used in the right circumstances. This includes large clients with a designated HMRC Customer Relations Manager. Its use will *not* prejudice either the client or the agent's relationship with HMRC. (See **23.57–23.58**.)
>
> - **Interaction with judicial review** – If an application for judicial review is being considered, it needs to be borne in mind that the courts regard this as a remedy of last resort and, where an adequate alternative remedy such as HMRC's complaints process is available (as was the case here), the court will usually refuse permission to apply for judicial review unless there are exceptional circumstances justifying the claim proceeding. (See **23.62–23.63**)

INTRODUCTION

23.1 A feature common to all of the topics covered in this book is that, alongside the relevant statutory framework, HMRC's actions and decisions are also governed by a body of published guidance.

23.2 This comprises both the guidance bespoke to the particular type of HMRC investigation or intervention (eg any specific accompanying guidance, HMRC compliance check factsheets, Codes of Practice, relevant extracts from HMRC's internal guidance, and so on) together with more generic guidance on how HMRC will treat its customers. The latter includes HMRC's Charter, its published leaflets, Extra-Statutory Concessions and Statements of Practice, and its Litigation and Settlement Strategy (which covers all HMRC civil disputes).

23.3 This guidance sets out:

(a) the principles by reference to which HMRC will make its decisions;

(b) how HMRC will act; and

(c) the circumstances when, and the extent to which, HMRC can exercise discretion.

There is little point in HMRC promising to act and make decisions in accordance with such guidance, however, if there are no accessible mechanisms in place to hold them to account in respect of that undertaking.

23.4 So, how can HMRC be held to account in investigation cases where:

(a) HMRC is failing, or has failed, to follow this guidance;

(b) the relevant guidance (or the legislation) allows HMRC to exercise discretion, but it does so unreasonably, unfairly or disproportionately; or

(c) HMRC otherwise acts mistakenly, gives misleading advice, acts with unreasonable delay, or in some other way behaves unacceptably?

There are legal remedies available (discussed further at **23.59–23.63** below), but in most practical instances this is done by way of using HMRC's complaints process.

23.5 HMRC has a complaints process that aims to be accessible and customer focused. To quote from its Complaints Handling Guidance (CHG805):

'It is important that we adopt a positive attitude to receiving and dealing with complaints. We must never pre-judge the issue and should always investigate any complaint thoroughly and fairly. Adopting a defensive attitude is rarely helpful and can lead to unnecessary escalation of a complaint. It is important to remember that the complaint is almost certainly not directed at you personally and you are dealing with it on behalf of the Department.'

23.6 HMRC is also ultimately accountable to the Parliamentary Ombudsman on how it operates this process, who herself investigates complaints by reference to a set of published standards (discussed further at **23.77** below).

23.7 While non-statutorily based, therefore, HMRC has to deal with complaints by way of a process that follows principles common to all government departments. This promotes trust and transparency in HMRC's complaints process, as it means it cannot make up the rules on a case-by-case basis.

23.8 Reinforcing this is the fact (flagged up at **23.32** below) that where HMRC has not handled a complaint as well as it could have, its complaints process can, and does, provide for the giving of redress in such cases.

It also means HMRC is required to make its complaints process accessible to all and easy to use.

HMRC's complaints process is there to be used; and in the right circumstances can be an effective means of holding HMRC to account in respect of both ongoing and settled investigations.

23.9 Complaints about HMRC

23.9 There is an HMRC Complaints Factsheet giving further details of its complaints process, together with two internal staff manuals that govern how that process should be administered, ie the Complaints Handling Guidance (CHG) and the Complaints Remedy Guidance (CRG).

23.10 The above is discussed in more detail below under the following headings:

(a) What does HMRC's complaints process cover? (**23.11** *et seq*);

(b) What HMRC's complaints process does *not* cover (**23.33** *et seq*);

(c) Other factors that need to be taken in to account when deciding to complain (**23.42** *et seq*);

(d) Interaction with legal routes to securing redress (**23.59** *et seq*);

(e) HMRC's complaints process (**23.64** *et seq*);

(f) Redress available if the complaint is upheld (**23.81** *et seq*).

WHAT DOES HMRC'S COMPLAINTS PROCESS COVER?

23.11 There is useful material covering this in both the introduction to HMRC's Complaints Handling Guidance (CHG115) and the Adjudicator's webpage (www.adjudicatorsoffice.gov.uk). To summarise this, the following can come within the scope of HMRC's complaints process:

(a) mistakes;

(b) unreasonable delays;

(c) unreasonable/misinformed decisions;

(d) disproportionate/unfair/inconsistent decisions;

(e) HMRC not following its published guidance;

(f) misleading advice;

(g) unacceptable HMRC staff behaviour;

(h) any mishandling by HMRC of the complaint.

Taking each of these in turn:

Mistakes

23.12 This takes its simple, natural meaning, eg use of an incorrect address, misspelling of names, and so on. As well as straightforward mistakes, for the purposes of HMRC's complaint process, 'mistake' is also often used to embrace breaches of confidentiality and failures by HMRC to follow its own guidance (discussed further at **23.24–23.26** below).

Unreasonable delays

23.13 This is not defined mechanistically, neither does any breach by HMRC of one of its published customer service standards relating to turnaround times automatically render that delay unreasonable.

23.14 Rather, judging whether any delay by HMRC in actioning correspondence or otherwise progressing the investigation was unreasonable or not is a highly context sensitive decision. In other words, was it reasonable for HMRC to take the time it did to respond or act given the particular facts of the case?

23.15 The circumstances can be such that a relatively short delay by HMRC can be unreasonable (eg if the delay impacts on other, time critical deadlines relevant to the investigation and of which HMRC was aware).

23.16 In other circumstances, it can be reasonable for HMRC to delay progressing the investigation for relatively long periods of time (eg if an issue requires extensive research or relevant issues are being litigated elsewhere). In such cases HMRC should explain the reasons for such a delay.

In the absence of such exceptional circumstances and explanations, however, if any HMRC delays exceed a few months then prima facia there is a case for arguing there has been unreasonable delay.

Unreasonable/misinformed decisions

23.17 The role of the Parliamentary Ombudsman in HMRC's complaints process is discussed in more detail below. Briefly, when investigating complaints against government departments she is guided by the Parliamentary Ombudsman's Principles of Good Administration, Principles of Good Complaints Handling and Principles for Remedy. Details of these can be found on the Parliamentary Ombudsman's website (www.ombudsman.org.uk/improving-public-service/ombudsmansprinciples).

In respect of these Principles, HMRC's CHG 115 states: 'Our policy on complaints and remedy recognises the Ombudsman's Principles so you should be aware of and familiar with them.'

23.18 Complaints about HMRC

23.18 The Ombudsman's Principle 'Getting it right' has this to say on government decision making:

> 'In their decision making, public bodies should have regard to the relevant legislation. Decision making should take account of all relevant considerations, ignore irrelevant ones and balance the evidence appropriately.'

23.19 In other words, HMRC's decisions have to be both reasonable and appropriately informed. Given what CHG says, *all* of HMRC's decision-making both when initiating, and then conducting, investigations should meet this criteria. If any such decisions fail to do this, then there is a case for making a complaint.

23.20 In this regard, it needs to be borne in mind that, when exercising the discretion available to it in an investigation, the circumstances might be such that more than one reasonable option was available for HMRC to take. In such cases, HMRC's complaints process *cannot* be used to substitute one reasonable decision for another.

For a complaint to be viable, the relevant HMRC decision has to be *unreasonable* (and/or misinformed).

Disproportionate/unfair/inconsistent decisions

23.21 Linked to the above is the requirement for HMRC's actions and decisions, when both initiating and conducting investigations, to be proportionate, fair and consistent. In this regard, the Ombudsman's Principle 'Acting fairly' has this to say:

> 'People should be treated fairly and consistently, so that those in similar circumstances are dealt with in a similar way. Any difference in treatment should be justified by the individual circumstances of the case.
>
> When taking decisions, and particularly when imposing penalties, public bodies should behave reasonably and ensure that the measures taken are proportionate to the objectives pursued, appropriate in the circumstances and fair to the individuals concerned.'

23.22 One of the intentions of the HMRC-published guidance relevant to investigations is to place HMRC's duty to collect the right amount of tax within a framework of obligations to those subject to such investigations that ensure the above-stated aims are met.

23.23 If HMRC fails to act by reference to these aims, therefore, it is likely that it is also acting in breach of its guidance. Nonetheless, the Ombudsman's

Principle 'Acting fairly' can be invoked on a standalone basis in complaints concerning heavy handed, unfair or inconsistent actions by HMRC.

HMRC not following its published guidance

23.24 CRG3025 of HMRC's Complaints and Remedy Guidance states that a mistake (and thus within the scope of HMRC's complaints process) includes HMRC not following its published technical and operational guidance:

> 'According to the Ombudsman's Principles of Good Complaints Handling:
>
> > "All public bodies must comply with the law and have regard for the rights of those concerned. They should act according to their statutory powers and duties, and any other rules governing the service they provide. They should follow their own policy and procedural guidance on complaints handling, whether published or internal."
>
> If we fall short of this in any regard, it is likely that we have made a mistake.
>
> By "any other rules" we would include our own technical and operational guidance.'

23.25 As mentioned earlier, the relevant technical and operational guidance here covers both published guidance bespoke to the particular type of HMRC investigation or intervention, together with more generic guidance on how HMRC will treat its customers. The latter includes the obligations to its customers set out in HMRC's Charter (explicitly flagged up by CRG3025), its published leaflets, Extra-Statutory Concessions (ESCs) and Statements of Practice, and its Litigation and Settlement Strategy (LSS – which covers all HMRC civil disputes).

23.26 This renders the potential scope of HMRC's complaints process to be very wide ranging. In particular:

(a) HMRC's complaints process is thus the means by which HMRC can be held to account in respect of its published guidance (eg its ESCs, Statements of Practice, guidance on legitimate expectation following the giving by HMRC of misleading advice) where significant sums of tax may be at stake.

(b) HMRC's LSS, setting out as it does clear protocols (including those for establishing the facts and identifying the risks) as to how HMRC will conduct civil disputes within the law in ways that minimise both its costs and those of its customers, can be a means of holding it to account in respect of all disproportionate or over-long investigations (eg where HMRC keeps making unreasonable requests for further information, keeps raising new points, or otherwise prolongs the investigation in an unreasonable way).

23.27 *Complaints about HMRC*

Misleading advice

23.27 Cases of misleading advice that require HMRC to refrain from collecting tax that might otherwise be legally due are covered by its published guidance entitled 'When You Can Rely on Information or Advice Provided by HM Revenue & Customs (HMRC)'. Where HMRC is in breach of this guidance, it can be held to account under HMRC's complaints process for the reasons given above.

23.28 CRG3200 of HMRC's Complaints and Remedy Guidance makes clear, however, that the scope of its complaints process extends to other cases of misleading or incorrect advice. In such cases, where there is lack of conclusive evidence HMRC may well be reluctant to give the complainant the benefit of the doubt.

23.29 In this regard, CRG3200 says the following:

'When it is clear that we have given a customer misleading or incorrect advice, whether in person, by phone or in writing (including in a leaflet or published guidance), that usually means we have made a mistake. Regardless of whether or not we are bound by what we have said or written, you will still need to consider if financial redress is appropriate in respect of the mistake. The nature and amount of any financial redress will depend, as with any other sort of mistake, on the circumstances and on the impact the misleading advice had on the customer. The same principles apply if we have given misleading advice in a public notice or leaflet, but in such circumstances you will need to liaise closely with the author division of the notice or leaflet in order to agree a co-ordinated approach.

In many cases there will be insufficient documentary evidence to establish exactly what happened, making it hard to determine beyond doubt that we made a mistake. That is particularly the case where the customer's complaint is based on a face to face meeting or unrecorded telephone conversation that took place some time before. Memories inevitably fade over time and interpretations of what was said may vary. This means that the customer's recollection of what happened may be different from that of the staff member concerned. In these cases, carefully consider the customer's version of what happened, especially if they made a note at the time. Consider also any note of the conversation made by the member of staff concerned. In deciding what weight to give to this evidence you will need to make a judgement about the extent to which the customer's recollection fits in with what you know of the circumstances at the time; for example, whether the point at issue was frequently the cause of misunderstanding and the subject of other complaints. In such cases you should normally give the customer the benefit of the doubt and pay what financial redress, if any, you consider appropriate.

However, in many cases, there won't be any evidence apart from what the customer and the staff member recall, and their recollections will frequently be different. In these cases, you may have to accept that it is simply not possible to make a decision about what happened, and will need to explain to the customer that you are unable to uphold the complaint. You may need to explain that this is not because you think they are not telling the truth about their recollection of what happened but because, without further evidence, you are unable to favour one version of events over the other.'

23.30 The lesson to be drawn regarding HMRC's conduct of investigations is that any verbal advice or undertakings given by HMRC, either at a meeting or during any phone calls, should *always* be contemporaneously recorded and then communicated to HMRC (see **9.64–9.70**).

If HMRC subsequently wishes to resile from such advice or undertakings, the client should then be in a strong position to remedy this by way of the making of a complaint.

Unacceptable HMRC staff behaviour

23.31 If a member of HMRC's staff acts or behaves unprofessionally or otherwise inappropriately, this can come within the scope of HMRC's complaints process.

If the staff misbehaviour is serious and/or potentially criminal, see **23.41** below.

Any mishandling by HMRC of the complaint

23.32 The above extends to HMRC's handling of a complaint. HMRC can be held to account for any mishandling of a complaint through its complaints process.

WHAT HMRC'S COMPLAINTS PROCESS DOES NOT COVER

23.33 HMRC's complaints process is essentially concerned with HMRC handling issues. The following lie outside its scope:

(a) issues of statutory construction per se;

(b) court decisions.

23.34 It is pointless, therefore, invoking the complaints process if HMRC's actions and decisions unambiguously follow what is required of it under the

23.35 Complaints about HMRC

law – no matter how draconian or unfair the consequences, accelerated payment notices (APNs – see **Chapter 21**) being perhaps a good example here.

Handling issues associated with how HMRC interprets tax legislation and court decisions

23.35 An important qualification, however, needs to be made in this regard. Associated with all of the legislation for which HMRC is responsible (and some court decisions) will be published guidance or explanations concerning how this legislation will be applied and administered. There might also be a relevant Extra-Statutory Concession or other guidance that precludes HMRC from applying that legislation in some circumstances.

This guidance *does* come within the scope of HMRC's complaints process for the reasons explained above at **23.24–23.26**.

23.36 So to return to the APN example quoted earlier, what some might see as the inherent unfairness of this regime lies outside the scope of HMRC's complaints process. HMRC *can*, however, be held to account under that process in respect of how it administers the accompanying guidance and other published statements.

Interest charges arising from unreasonable delays by HMRC

23.37 In this regard, while coming within the scope of HMRC's complaints process, in some cases it will consider writing off interest charges arising from unreasonable delays. Such cases are considered by its Interest Review Unit (IRU). Complaints on this issue cannot be sent directly to the IRU, however, but should be made to the relevant local office.

23.38 This extract from DMBM405020 gives further details, including how this process interacts with complaints:

> 'The Interest Review Unit (IRU) is a specialist team handling objections to paying interest charged under the relevant sections of law dealing with individuals; partnerships; companies; employers and National Insurance contributors.
>
> Central Policy-Tax Administration Policy (CP-TAP) gives the law and policy overview for the guidance and the way in which we apply our responsibility for care and management under Section 5 Commissioners for Revenue and Customs Act (CRCA) 2005.
>
> The terms under which interest is charged are well defined.
>
> There is no scope for cancelling correctly charged interest.

There is no automatic right to have the amount of interest due reduced or given up. Where the charge is legally correct, HMRC is entitled to recover payment in full, regardless of the circumstances.

Unlike most commercial debt, the sums HMRC seeks to collect are due under law and not as a result of a contract between two parties. All taxpayers are expected to make full payment by the due date. Charging interest is simply our way of recognising that tax has been paid later than when it was due. As a result the scope for setting aside interest on late payment is not as wide as it may be in a commercial setting.

However the IRU will look at the facts of every interest objection passed to them in a fair and impartial manner. They will only look at cases where a customer or their representative has made an objection to the interest charge in writing or over the phone. A case will not normally be considered before the underlying tax has been paid and the interest charged.

Objections sent direct to the unit are not accepted. Customers or their representatives should make their objection to the appropriate local office that handles their affairs.

In most cases, the nature of the objection and the associated evidence will be clear at an early stage and will be covered in this guidance.

Some cases will need special attention, and care will be taken to give every case the proper consideration. The key principle is that giving up interest is based on the fact that HMRC error or unreasonable delay financially disadvantaged the customer by making an interest charge that would not otherwise have had to be paid or increasing the amount of an interest charge that already existed or was building up.

Where necessary all relevant papers and reports will be reviewed by the IRU to enable a reasoned judgement based on the facts of the case.

A decision will not be influenced by a customer's persistence or willingness to complain. It will be based on the facts alone.

Interest that arose because a customer failed to meet their statutory duty will not normally be given up. Customers are responsible for making sure their tax affairs are in order if an interest charge is to be avoided.

Claims that HMRC error or unreasonable delay has caused, or added to the build up of interest will be carefully examined. Where the facts prove the claim we will consider giving up part or full.

Any continued claim for the interest charged will be in line with the law. The overall aim of looking at the case is to make sure that the individual customer is being treated fairly, while taking account of the wider body of customers, the Treasury and the law. The objector will normally be advised directly of the decision. The aim is to avoid drawn out and needless contact.

23.39 *Complaints about HMRC*

So when upholding interest, a full and reasoned explanation for the decision will be given.

Where a decision has been made to uphold interest, we will consider further representation where new facts not previously looked at are presented. If there are no new facts the case will be closed and the customer advised that the interest remains due.

The decision is not open to being negotiated in order to get a settlement figure. Any relief given is non-statutory and based on the facts. It is calculated to remove only the part of interest that was caused by HMRC error or unreasonable delay and nothing more, and is given only at the IRU's discretion.

An interest charge arises because of precise conditions. The IRU's role is to make a judgement on the interest based on the facts presented. A customer will normally be advised to make a complaint to the appropriate Complaints Handlers for appropriate business stream if they continue to be unhappy with HMRC handling of the case.

That team is best placed to look at all the issues involved and respond fully to a complaint. But they have no capacity to overturn or vary the IRU's decision. They can only answer the various points of the complaint and deal with any other non-interest areas.'

Unnecessary or vexatious complaints

23.39 For the client, HMRC investigations can be stressful, intrusive and potentially very costly. Even when the investigation establishes no culpable wrongdoing, however, that does not necessarily bring HMRC's decisions and actions within the scope of its complaints process. Whether it does is a question to be decided by reference to the principles discussed above.

23.40 Likewise, any complaint made during an investigation will be considered by HMRC on its merits. However, HMRC's complaints process *cannot* be used per se to delay or deflect an HMRC investigation.

Complaints concerning serious and/or potentially criminal misbehaviour by HMRC staff

23.41 These lie outside HMRC's normal complaints process, and should instead be sent by post to:

PO Box 64353
London
EC30 3AW

OTHER FACTORS THAT NEED TO BE TAKEN IN TO ACCOUNT WHEN DECIDING TO COMPLAIN

Impact on the client

23.42 When advising the client on whether to complain, as well as scoping out the viability of the potential complaint by reference to the above discussed principles, the impact on the client also has to be considered.

23.43 There is little point in making a complaint if the impact on the client of the relevant HMRC mishandling is minimal or immaterial. In such cases, even if the complaint is upheld the redress on offer – or any wider impact on HMRC's handing of the investigation (if it is still ongoing) – will be insignificant.

23.44 As the discussion at **23.81** below on the financial redress offered in respect of upheld complaints makes clear, while such payments can be very large, it is not possible to make any kind of meaningful 'profit' from making a complaint. There are no payments analogous to tort or punitive damages available.

23.45 There are also some important subjective factors to consider, ie how aggrieved does the client feel. Where the impact on the client of HMRC's mishandling of a concluded investigation is more serious, with perhaps a considerable amount of potential financial redress at stake, the client might still prefer to move on rather than invest time and money in taking forward a complaint (even though that money can be recovered if the complaint is upheld – see **23.81** *et seq*).

23.46 Even if the case against HMRC is clear cut, this may still be the right option for such clients. This is especially so if the issues are likely to be considered contentious by HMRC and/or potentially large sums of financial redress are at stake. Such complaints may well encounter strong resistance from HMRC; and if that happens, the client will need to have the level of determination and commitment necessary to see the process through.

Management of expectations

23.47 If the client does feel aggrieved sufficiently to want to hold HMRC to account for its decisions and actions, it is important that expectations are properly managed. Determining whether there has been any HMRC mishandling depends on the individual facts of the case, and cannot be decided mechanistically except in the most straightforward of cases (eg where it is an obvious HMRC mistake).

23.48 *Complaints about HMRC*

23.48 It all depends on the facts, and it is important that the strength of the complainant's case is scoped out as far as possible before a complaint is made. Likewise, the position needs to be kept under review as the complaint progresses in the light of HMRC's explanations and any new facts that emerge.

23.49 It is also important that expectations as to the redress available if the complaint succeeds are managed for the reasons mentioned at **23.40** and **23.44** above. Complaints in respect of what – in the eyes of the client – might be regarded as serious HMRC mistakes (eg inappropriate staff behaviour or a breach of confidentiality) may well result in just an apology from HMRC and a small, token worry and distress payment.

Likewise, other instances of HMRC mishandling with serious consequences for the client (eg on his health) might at most be expected to generate a similar outcome.

When to complain: ongoing investigations and the seeking of other outcomes

23.50 HMRC can, and does, investigate and uphold complaints in respect of ongoing investigations. If, during the investigation, there is a clear case to be made that it is being mishandled by HMRC, then the making of a complaint should be considered.

23.51 One caveat: The Adjudicator's website (see **23.73**) makes clear it will only investigate complaints in respect of concluded HMRC investigations. Given its place in the process (see **23.64** *et seq*), however, this does not seriously curtail the benefits of complaining in respect of HMRC of an ongoing investigation in the right circumstances.

When should a complaint in respect of a mishandled ongoing HMRC investigation be made? The answer depends on the outcomes being sought.

23.52 The first point to make is that, even if such a complaint is fully upheld, this will not necessarily result in the investigation being terminated. It is important the client's expectations in this regard are properly managed.

A realistically possible outcome, however, from such a complaint is that the mishandling will cease and, going forward, HMRC will conduct the investigation properly.

23.53 For example, if in a dispute HMRC is inappropriately litigating an issue (by reference to the principles set out in its LSS) then the complaint might result in HMRC dropping the litigation and, instead, seeking to resolve the issue in a more reasonable and proportionate manner.

23.54 Getting the investigation properly 'back on track' in this way can be an important outcome for both the client and HMRC. The client benefits from being treated in accordance with the appropriate guidance while HMRC, having been put on early notice of its mishandling of the investigation, is given the opportunity to mitigate the impact of this by capping its exposure to any resultant financial redress that might be payable as a consequence.

23.55 Key to securing this outcome is the copying of the letter of complaint to an appropriate, senior HMRC official of director level or above. From HMRC's perspective, a mishandled investigation is often both inefficient and the consequence of poor management. HMRC's senior management, therefore, also has an interest in having such cases drawn to its attention and helping get the mishandled investigation 'back on track'.

Also helpful in promoting this outcome is copying the complaint letter to the client's MP.

23.56 Finally, as discussed in the next section, the scope of tribunals to rule on the sort of HMRC mishandling discussed here has now been severely curtailed. If it is likely the investigation will be the subject of a tribunal hearing, therefore, it is likely any associated HMRC handling issues will *not* be considered at the hearing.

In such cases, consideration should be given, therefore, to getting into a complaint process alongside the hearing.

Other implications of complaining

23.57 Are there any consequences of complaining, either for practitioners or their clients, for their future relationship with HMRC?

In short, no. Providing and funding a customer-focused and accessible complaints process forms an integral part of how HMRC operates. Unless the complaint specifically concerns staff behaviour, complaining should not be seen as a personal questioning of individuals within HMRC. Rather, it is a means by which the department itself can be held to account.

23.58 Of course, resolving any issues informally and by agreement where possible is much to be preferred. But if that isn't possible, HMRC's complaints process is there to be used.

This applies even when the client has a designated HMRC Customer Relations Manager.

23.59 *Complaints about HMRC*

INTERACTION WITH LEGAL ROUTES TO SECURING REDRESS

Interaction with tribunal hearings

23.59 There is a degree of overlap between the scope of HMRC's complaints process and that of the tribunal. For example:

(a) how HMRC exercises any discretion afforded it by the legislation; and

(b) the reclaiming of costs.

23.60 The recent decision, however, in *Revenue and Customs Comrs v Abdul Noor* [2013] UKUT 71 (TCC), where the Upper Tribunal decided that the First-tier Tribunal does not have jurisdiction to consider a claim based on legitimate expectation, looks to have curtailed significantly their scope to consider HMRC handling issues.

23.61 Thus if, in any investigation likely to be resolved by way of a tribunal hearing, there are associated HMRC handling issues, it cannot assume these will be resolved at any tribunal hearing. As mentioned above, consideration in such cases should be given to whether resolution should be sought through HMRC's complaints process alongside any tribunal proceedings.

Interaction with Judicial Review

23.62 There is a high degree of overlap between the scope of HMRC's complaints process and that of Judicial Review. HMRC's complaints process, however, offers much greater flexibility and cheapness compared with the court-based routes. This greater flexibility ensures that HMRC has to account for all the issues raised by the complainant.

23.63 Furthermore, the comments of Mrs Justice Swift in the case of *The Queen (on the Application of NCM 2000 Ltd) and The Commissioners for HM Revenue & Customs* [2015] EWHC 1342 (Admin) make it clear that judicial review is a remedy of last resort and, where an adequate alternative remedy such as HMRC's complaints process is available (as was the case here), the Court will usually refuse permission to apply for judicial review unless there are exceptional circumstances justifying the claim proceeding. Here is a link to that case: www.bailii.org/ew/cases/EWHC/Admin/2015/1342.html.

If a client feels strongly enough about an HMRC handling issue to contemplate funding Judicial Review proceedings, therefore, then as a matter of course the complaints route should also be considered.

HMRC'S COMPLAINTS PROCESS

23.64 HMRC has a three tier complaints process, the first two tiers of which are handled within the relevant HMRC Business Unit conducting the investigation.

Complaints can be made by agents on behalf of their clients, and should, in view of the above, be sent in to the investigating officer.

This might seem odd. That officer, however, will forward the complaint straight away to that unit's relevant specialist complaints team.

23.65 There is no set format for making a complaint. HMRC's guidance defines a complaint as 'Any expression of dissatisfaction that is not resolved at initial contact and requires a response'. For the avoidance of doubt, however, it is good practice at the start of a complaint letter to make it clear this is an issue that requires dealing with by HMRC's complaints process.

23.66 The complaint letter should explain the relevant issues and set out:

(a) why HMRC has mishandled the investigation by reference to the principles discussed above;

(b) details of the redress and/or other outcomes sought.

In accordance with its guidance HMRC is required to provide at least a holding reply within 15 working days.

Time limits for complaining

23.67 CHG510 states the following on this:

'In practice, the vast majority of customers make their complaint soon after the event and, where they remain unhappy with our first response, escalate matters quickly.

Although our complaints factsheet asks customers who are unhappy with our service to let us know "as soon as possible", we do not impose a strict deadline. While we would expect most customers to contact us shortly after the issue giving rise to the complaint occurred, there may be reasons why a particular customer was either unable to or chose not to. Rejecting a complaint because it is made too long after the event will be the exception rather than the rule, and in any case where you are contemplating taking such a line, you should first consult CCAST. Remember, if we refuse to take on a complaint and it is subsequently taken on by the Adjudicator or the Ombudsman, we will have missed the opportunity to put right any mistakes beforehand.'

23.68 *Complaints about HMRC*

23.68 Please note that, when considering whether *their* time limits have been met, the Parliamentary Ombudsman is now taking a critical look at the length of time between the event giving rise to the complaint and the making of the complaint itself. As far as possible, therefore, this gap should be kept to a minimum as, if there is a significant delay then, in the absence of a good reason, it may prove difficult escalating the complaint as far as the Parliamentary Ombudsman. Please see **23.78** below.

What if there is more than one area of HMRC involved?

23.69 Where there is more than one Business Unit dealing with the investigation, or the complaint covers a number of issues that span more than one part of HMRC, but it is clear one of the Business Units is in the lead, the complaint should be sent to that Unit.

23.70 If it is not obvious which area of HMRC is in the lead then you can send the complaint to any of the relevant Business Units – it is the responsibility of HMRC to 'join the dots' and decide where the complaint should be dealt with, not the complainant.

Tier 1

23.71 This is HMRC's first attempt to resolve the complaint. It is its stated policy to attempt to resolve as many complaints as it can at this level.

Tier 2

23.72 If the complainant remains dissatisfied, however, he can ask HMRC to look at the complaint again. A different HMRC officer in the same Business Unit will handle this tier 2 review to provide, in HMRC's own words, a 'fresh pair of eyes'.

If the tier 2 review fails to resolve the complaint, then the complainant has the option – within six months of the tier 2 decision – to escalate his complaint to the Adjudicator.

Tier 3: the Adjudicator

23.73 The Adjudicator offers an independent review of the complaint. She is not an officer of HMRC. Instead, she operates under a service level agreement (SLA) with HMRC under which she is provided with an HMRC office (the Adjudicator's Office) to support her in her role.

Further details are given at www.adjudicatorsoffice.gov.org.

23.74 The SLA requires the Adjudicator to look at complaints about:

- mistakes;
- unreasonable delays;
- poor or misleading advice;
- staff behaviours; and
- unreasonable use of discretion by HMRC.

23.75 Outside her scope are complaints about government or departmental policy, any matters arising from a commercial or employment contract between a complainant and HMRC, or any matters where there is a specific right of determination by any court, tribunal or other body with specific jurisdiction over the matter.

23.76 If an agent is acting on the client's behalf, a fresh, bespoke authorisation is required. The relevant form can be downloaded from the Adjudicator's website.

The Parliamentary Ombudsman

23.77 If the complainant remains dissatisfied after the Adjudicator's review, he can take his complaint (via his MP) to the Parliamentary Ombudsman. This MP channel has been adapted to ensure non-resident complainants are not excluded. Further details of how to do this are provided on the Parliamentary and Health Ombudsman Office's website at www.ombudsman.org.uk/make-a-complaint/how-to-complain.

23.78 Please note that the legislation says that complaints have to be made to the Parliamentary Ombudsman with a year of the event giving rise to the compliant having taken place. They will, in practice, take into account the time taken to take the complaint first through HMRC's complaints process when applying this rule. If there are significant, unexplained delays between either the event and the initial complaint to HMRC, or between the date of the Adjudicator's decision and the complaints submission to the Parliamentary Ombudsman, however, the complaint may well be timed out. In order to maintain the option of escalation to the Parliamentary Ombudsman, therefore, delays between the event giving rise to the complaint and its initial making to HMRC, and that complaint's subsequent escalation through HMRC's complaints process, should be kept to a minimum.

23.79 The Parliamentary Ombudsman operates under a legal framework that requires her to investigate complaints about maladministration. Whether there

23.80 *Complaints about HMRC*

has been maladministration by HMRC, and if so how it should be remedied, is decided by reference to the Parliamentary Ombudsman's Principles of Good Administration, Principles of Good Complaints Handling and Principles for Remedy.

23.80 HMRC's own complaints guidance (CHG115) states that its policy on complaints and remedy recognises the Ombudsman's Principles, so they play an important underpinning role in HMRC's own complaints process, as well as assisting the Ombudsman in deciding whether HMRC's decisions and actions in a particular case have been maladministrative.

REDRESS AVAILABLE IF THE COMPLAINT IS UPHELD

23.81 If a complaint is upheld, HMRC's redress policy provides for:

- an apology and explanation by HMRC;
- a payment by HMRC of a sum in recognition of any worry and distress caused to the taxpayer by its mishandling (these amounts are not large, and rarely amount to more than a few hundred pounds);
- an ex-gratia financial redress payment by HMRC to compensate for any financial loss directly arising from its mishandling (this includes the costs incurred by the complainant in making his complaint).

Compensation for financial losses

23.82 HMRC's redress policy for making these payments follows the Treasury's guidelines on complaints handling and remedies for all government departments ('Annex 4.14 Complaints and Remedy, Managing Public Money') and are intended (as far as is possible) to put the complainant back into the position he would have been in if the relevant HMRC mishandling had not occurred.

Unnecessarily incurred professional fees (including those incurred in making the complaint) are a common example but they can embrace other costs.

23.83 Such amounts must have been *already paid* by the client and can only be claimed in respect of financial losses *directly* resulting from this mishandling. As stated earlier, they are not intended as a form of punitive damage and the process does not allow for a complainant to make a monetary 'profit' out of using HMRC's complaints process.

The writing off of tax, interest or a tax credit repayment

23.84 HMRC's complaints process is also a means of holding HMRC to account in respect of how it applies its Extra-Statutory Concessions, Statements of Practice, or other guidance concerning the amount of tax or interest payable in specific circumstances. If such complaints are upheld, therefore, the complainant may also be entitled to the writing off by HMRC of tax, interest or a tax credit repayment.

See **23.37** *et seq* above for further details regarding the writing off of interest.

Chapter 24

VAT aspects

Kendra Hann
Partner, Deloitte LLP

SIGNPOSTS

- **Scope** – Businesses will be subject to VAT assurance visits at various times, based on their risk profile. Larger businesses can expect more interaction with HMRC than small and mid-sized businesses.

- **Preliminary issues** – Risk profiling is based on maximising compliance yield, not necessarily on where the risk of VAT losses is greatest (see **24.1–24.6**).

- **Practicalities** – HMRC may carry out joint visits checking a number of taxes. HMRC officers will have access to details of VAT returns submitted and other information about the business, including sales of goods and services to other EU member states. A first HMRC visit will involve assembling or checking basic information about the business, including a review of at least one VAT return. A review of Intrastat returns may be undertaken separately, especially for large businesses. (See **24.7–24.18**.)

- **Routine checks** – HMRC's computer system will also conduct routine checks on VAT returns. This will sometimes result in an HMRC officer contacting a business to look into a particular issue, for example if a refund is claimed. HMRC will also carry out checks of business records. (See **24.19–24.34**.)

- **Preparation for an HMRC visit** – An assurance visit should not be treated as a routine meeting. Preparation should be undertaken and procedures put in place before the visit. On a more ongoing basis, period-end routines should be put in place for VAT returns, with appropriate review and sign-off procedures. (See **24.48–24.58**.)

- **Search and entry powers** – HMRC has wide powers to visit businesses and request information in respect of the business' tax and VAT affairs, and, where dishonesty or fraud is suspected may undertake surveillance operations (see **24.59–24.68**).

VAT aspects **24.4**

- **Assessments and disputes** – Businesses are entitled to request an internal independent HMRC review, within 30 days (or longer if an extension is agreed with HMRC) of an assessment or other appealable tax decision. HMRC has 45 days to review the decision (or a longer period if agreed with the taxpayer). Where a taxpayer does not want an internal review, or disagrees with the outcome of a review, the taxpayer can appeal to the tax tribunal within 30 days. Alternative Dispute Resolution (ADR) is becoming a more common way to resolve disputes, instead of proceeding though the court system. (See **24.72–24.85**.)
- **Key points** – Suggestions for businesses facing an assurance visit are included at **24.86–24.87**.

OVERALL CONCEPT

24.1 HM Revenue and Customs (HMRC) is responsible for the control and management of all taxes. In respect of VAT, all VAT registered businesses are reviewed by HMRC based on their risk profile. Businesses will be selected for an assurance visit at certain points of trading. The risk profile for VAT purposes is often determined in conjunction with the direct tax teams within HMRC, and is always determined this way for businesses that are deemed to be 'large and complex'.

24.2 The risk profile of the VAT-registered business drives HMRC's assurance plan and is determined by factors such as the size of the business, its global or national footprint, compliance history and nature of its business activities. Profiling businesses in this way ensures HMRC can allocate its resources to businesses which it believes are most likely to pose a risk and where the financial return for HMRC is likely to be greatest. These businesses receive a greater number of, and longer and more frequent, targeted VAT assurance visits.

24.3 Businesses can register for VAT using HMRC's online services or by sending in paper forms. When the registration is approved, the business is allocated a VAT number. The VAT numbers are always in the same format: they consist of seven digits and two check numbers, eg 123 4567 89. The validity of any VAT number (including those issued by other EU member states) can be checked at http://ec.europa.eu/taxation_customs/vies/vieshome.do?selectedLanguage=EN. If required, a certificate showing that the number has been checked can also be obtained.

24.4 For online applications, HMRC will send a message within three working days advising of the VAT registration number or that there will be a

24.5 *VAT aspects*

delay because further information is required. For paper applications, HMRC aim to send a VAT registration number certificate within 15 working days of receiving the application form.

> **Example 24.1**
>
> There are sometimes considerable delays in processing applications to register for VAT, especially for overseas businesses. HMRC will generally try to work to resolve these by deploying additional resources, but this can be a source of frustration and it is recommended that businesses plan well ahead when applying for VAT registration.

24.5 The Large Business (LB) Directorate of HMRC deals with, generally, the 2,000 largest businesses, which are allocated Customer Compliance Managers (CCM). HMRC also has support for mid-sized businesses; HMRC defines 'mid-sized' as having a UK turnover of £10 million or more and/or a minimum of 20 employees. HMRC's approach is based on managing tax risks and compliance resources. A dedicated specialist may be able to help a mid-sized business with tax for a specific period of time.

For businesses without an HMRC contact, there is VAT helpline: 0300 200 3700.

For online queries, see https://www.gov.uk/government/organisations/hm-revenue-customs/contact/vat-online-services-helpdesk.

HMRC recommends that VAT queries are submitted by email, but the postal address for written queries is:

HM Revenue and Customs – VAT Written Enquiries Service
Alexander House
21 Victoria Avenue
Southend-on-Sea
SS99 1BD

24.6 Under Making Tax Digital for VAT (MTDfV), from April 2019, businesses with a turnover above the VAT threshold (currently £85,000) will have to maintain records digitally for VAT purposes, and provide VAT return information to HMRC via MTD functional compatible software using an Application Programming Interface (API). HMRC is also requesting that VAT data should pass through an organisation's systems via digital links.

This initiative is consistent with a global trend of tax authorities digitising tax systems and processes.

ASSURANCE VISITS

24.7 When VAT was introduced in 1973, the first visit to a business was a registration or educational visit. This was to ensure that a new business was aware of its obligations, the accounts maintained by the business were adequate for VAT purposes and the liability treatment of the supplies made by the business was correct. In the past, a newly registered business could expect to receive its first assurance visit from the local VAT office (LVO) within about 18 months of being registered. These visits formed the basis of control of the tax.

24.8 More recently, the majority of assurance visits are assigned by a computer-based model based on a series of factors that assess the risk of errors, and the potential for negligent or fraudulent returns. Now, as set out in the *Report by the Comptroller and Auditor General* published alongside the 2012/13 HMRC accounts, 'HMRC's current risk profiling of VAT returns identifies cases where compliance yield can be maximised, rather than where the risk of VAT evasion may be greatest' (para 28).

Smaller businesses may not receive such a visit for many years, whereas larger businesses may have regular visits and/ or telephone discussions.

24.9 HMRC may choose to carry out joint visits using officers checking more than one tax. For large businesses that are allocated a CCM, joint visits by usually two or more officers (looking at different taxes) are often undertaken. In normal circumstances however, HMRC will make it clear before the visit which taxes it will be inspecting and, usually, how many officers can be expected on the visit.

24.10 When a business is selected for an assurance visit, the officer will have access to the business's electronic folder which contains details of VAT returns submitted together with other relevant information about the business.

24.11 Additionally, if the business sells goods or supplies services to other EU states, the officer will be able to obtain information relating to the aggregate value of dispatches and sales by that business for each quarterly period. Each VAT authority in every member state submits the data from the individual EC Sales Lists (ESLs) into the VAT Information Exchange System (VIES). The data contained on ESLs enables VIES to identify, by VAT number, the value of sales from each supplier/member state. The officer can use this information to gain knowledge of where a business sells its goods and the level of such sales prior to his visit.

24.12 The officer will also check acquisitions of goods made from other EU member states. Clearly, if the value ascribed to a particular UK business by VIES is different from the acquisition value shown on the VAT returns, some questions can be expected.

24.13 *VAT aspects*

24.13 Businesses are also required to complete ESLs for the majority of services supplied to businesses in other EU member states. The officer will then also verify these to ensure sales of services have been declared appropriately and, in addition, will be able to check (using data received from other EU states) that the taxpayer has declared reverse charge VAT on services received from businesses established in other member states.

24.14 Usually, for businesses other than those in LB, the visit will be arranged by a centralised visit booking team, which usually telephones to make an appointment. This will generally be followed up in writing to confirm the arrangements. HMRC will normally give at least seven days' notice of a visit.

24.15 When the VAT officer arrives for the visit he will have an identity card bearing his photograph. This should always be inspected before allowing the officer into the working area since bogus VAT visits have been known and are an effective way of finding out a lot about a business.

24.16 An assurance visit typically splits into three parts. First, general questions about the structure of the business, the way it operates and the build up to the VAT account; secondly a check of the VAT account and a detailed review of at least one VAT period; and, lastly, an overview of the business accounts including a number of credibility checks that will assist the officer in assessing the credibility of the figures on the returns.

General questions

24.17 For the first visit, the officer will be required to assemble/check basic information concerning that particular business such as:

- name, status and contact details for the person responsible for VAT at the business;
- name, address and contact details for the auditors;
- financial year end;
- address of the principal place of business and registered office if different, and of any branches from which the business operates;
- confirmation that the details on the VAT4 (VAT registration certificate) are still correct;
- a description of the main and, if applicable, subsidiary business activities;
- whether the business has contact with other parts of HMRC, eg whether the business has a bonded warehouse or operates under any HMRC customs duty regime;
- whether the business imports or exports goods;

- whether the business imports or exports services;
- principal sales (outputs) and purchases (inputs);
- which retail schemes are operated (if applicable);
- a list of the main, subsidiary and other non-accounting records maintained by the business;
- structure of the business;
- details of bank and building society accounts;
- tax point information (eg whether the business uses the 14-day rule for invoices);
- rulings given to the business;
- risk areas and special or unusual features; and
- any errors made by the business that the officer may need to be aware of prior to inspecting the records.

On subsequent visits to the business this information will be reviewed and amended as necessary to reflect changes in the business.

24.18 The above information is generally obtained whilst conducting a general discussion about the business. The information obtained allows the officer to establish an understanding of the business and how it is organised. Depending on the nature of the business, it is often followed by a request to see/inspect the premises. This general walk around adds to the officer's general understanding and allows him to see whether there are any trading activities which were not mentioned in the general discussion and may have an impact on the VAT due or recoverable by the business, eg the officer will note specific items of stock or machinery so that he can check these out later when inspecting the accounting system.

Review of VAT returns submitted

24.19 As mentioned earlier, the officer will usually check at least one VAT return in detail. This involves checking from source documents, eg orders, purchase and sales invoices, etc, through the various accounting records to the VAT account and the completed VAT return.

24.20 The officer will also make other checks in order to verify the credibility of the VAT returns. For example, he will check that the sales figures indicated on VAT returns for a 12-month period correspond with the turnover figure disclosed in the annual accounts for the same period. Similarly, officers will check the annual accounts for any disposal of assets to ensure that output

24.21 *VAT aspects*

tax has been charged and declared and that the level of expenses declared in the accounts agrees with the input figures declared on the VAT returns. The credibility checks used will vary according to the specific activities of the business and the records available to the officer. Other credibility checks used include cash reconciliations (more commonly used in smaller cash businesses such as restaurants and pubs), bank reconciliations and mark-up exercises.

Focus

An assurance visit will include a review of at least one VAT return in detail, including checks to verify the credibility of the VAT returns.

24.21 Officers will often cross-refer invoices inspected at one business with the information disclosed at another business. For example, sales of confectionery items sold by a wholesaler will be checked against purchases declared by the wholesaler's customers. Although on the surface, the absence of purchases in the retailer's records might seem to suggest that eligible input VAT has not been claimed by the business, it is often a good indication, particularly in a cash business, that the business is not recovering input VAT in order to suppress sales and the corresponding output VAT. To continue to claim all input VAT whilst suppressing sales will eventually show that the business is being run on uneconomical margins. This will either mean that the business is in financial trouble or raise suspicions with HMRC that the business is failing to account for VAT on all of its sales.

24.22 Following the visit HMRC may write to the business summarising the visit, including any agreements or recommendations, any corrections that are required to be made to the VAT account, any over- or underpayment of VAT, and/or any penalty, and asking for further information details if required.

Focus

Following an assurance visit, HMRC may write to the business confirming various details and steps to be taken.

24.23 Depending on the size and complexity of the business and its accounting system, more than one officer may attend. It is unusual, however, for three or more officers to attend on the same day as this is regarded by HMRC as over-burdensome on the business.

24.24 If the business uses a sophisticated computerised accounting system, it is possible that the visit will be made by an officer with specialist computer training who may, for example, ask for interrogation software to be run against the business accounts, or for electronic data for interrogation off site. If interrogation software is loaded on the business's computers it is imperative that HMRC is denied running the checks against online data, since this could corrupt current data. It is always advisable to run interrogation checks offline.

24.25 Again, depending on the sophistication of the system, the officer may document the procedures and processes conducted by the computer. This will highlight, from a VAT perspective, the key controls and any weaknesses in the system. Any areas where there are perceived weaknesses in controls or processes will then be subject to further review by HMRC. Subsequent assurance visits will check to see whether the key controls are still in place. The removal of a key control could mean that the VAT accounting of that system is flawed or weakened in some manner.

There are also specialist accountants with HMRC who may become involved in visits to businesses with particularly complex accounting issues.

24.26 Sometimes, officers carrying out routine visits may be accompanied by specialist anti-avoidance officers interested in any planning measures adopted by the business. Occasionally, independent visits may be undertaken by such officers outside the routine verification process. If a business becomes aware that it is being visited by HMRC's anti-avoidance teams, it would be well advised to obtain professional advice on how to deal with the situation.

24.27 If an assurance visit becomes uncomfortable or an investigation team arrives at the business, the business's advisers should be contacted immediately. Trying to handle situations where interviews are being conducted under caution can be fraught and create a high degree of distress. The following are points to remember:

- phone the professional adviser immediately to seek specific advice;
- be polite and helpful at all times, as it is an offence to obstruct an officer in the course of his duties;
- politely but firmly refuse to give interviews under caution, whether taped or written, until you have taken professional advice;
- say something to the effect that 'we are happy to answer your questions, however, could you please outline your areas of concern so that due consideration can be given to providing the correct answer'; and

24.28 VAT aspects

- always remember that when an investigation is instigated, it is an indication that the officer believes that offences may have been committed. If a comment is made under caution, it cannot be retracted. Trying to persuade HMRC that something said in a statement was wrong or inaccurate can be very difficult and expensive.

> **Focus**
>
> If a business is visited by HMRC's anti-avoidance team or investigators, or if an assurance visit becomes uncomfortable, professional advice should be sought.

CREDIBILITY QUERIES

24.28 A business may not just see the VAT officer on assurance visits. HMRC's computer system conducts routine checks on each VAT return submitted. The credibility routine, for example, not only checks that the figure shown in box 1 (VAT due in this period on sales and other outputs) is not significantly less than the VAT calculated on the box 6 figure (total value of sales and other outputs excluding any VAT), but it also conducts a series of comparison exercises.

24.29 When a business completes a VAT1 (Application for registration), it is required to describe its main business activity. This allows HMRC to assign a trade classification to the business. For example, all petrol filling stations will be allocated to the same trade classification. Thus, when each filling station puts in its VAT return, HMRC can compare any single VAT return for a petrol filling station with all other filling stations submitting VAT returns for that period. Trends can, therefore, be detected. If all other petrol filling stations are showing an upturn in trade in any particular period and one filling station is claiming a repayment then this may generate a query.

24.30 Often this type of verification will simply prompt a phone call to the business asking why an unusual VAT return was submitted. It may, for example, simply be that the business is stocking up or has incurred significant refurbishment costs on a building, etc. However, if the amount is large, the officer may decide to visit. The officer should agree the visit in advance, but it is usual to arrange the visit soon after the initial telephone call, particularly when it is a repayment return. This will usually simply be to verify the single queried VAT return and the checks will just be to satisfy the officer that the return is credible in the circumstances before the VAT repayment is made. It is worth noting that whilst the return is being queried, the clock for a repayment supplement is stopped. Thus, it is in the interests of the business

VAT aspects **24.34**

to ensure that such credibility queries are dealt with and agreed with HMRC as soon as possible.

> **Focus**
>
> Sometimes HMRC's systems and checks may identify a particular issue that an HMRC officer will need to verify. These issues may be resolved by a simple phone call. A business should deal with these credibility checks as promptly as possible, especially if the business is in a repayment position.

BUSINESS RECORDS CHECKS

24.31 HMRC carries out checks on how businesses keep their records, essentially to determine whether adequate records are being maintained and that those records are sufficient to enable accurate returns to be filed.

HMRC may write to a business and then contact the business by phone to ask about business records. During the phone call, which typically will last about 10 to 15 minutes, HMRC will ask questions to enable it to determine whether the necessary records are maintained.

24.32 From the replies given, HMRC will determine whether the business:

- is able to submit an accurate return from the records, in which event, HMRC will advise the business of this, and confirm it in writing;
- requires additional assistance, in which event, HMRC will tell the business so, and provide a link for help and support; or
- is at risk of keeping inadequate records, which will normally lead to a face-to-face visit, and HMRC will contact the business to agree details.

24.33 If business records are found to be inadequate, there may be a record-keeping penalty, but HMRC will generally allow time to bring the records up to an adequate standard, and will follow up with a visit within three months to check that the improvements have been made. If the record-keeping has improved, and the records are adequate, HMRC may reduce the penalty to nil. If not, a penalty of £500 will apply for a first offence; for new businesses (in their first year of trading) the penalty will be £250. There is a penalty of £3,000 if records have been deliberately destroyed; which may be reduced to £1,500 if only some records have been destroyed.

24.34 Where records are inadequate, HMRC will refer the business for another business records check in two years. If the business records check identifies that the tax returns may be inaccurate, the records will be passed to other teams, who may contact the business to carry out a check on the return.

24.35 *VAT aspects*

> **Focus**
>
> HMRC may impose penalties for inadequate records, but will normally work with a business to improve record-keeping.

INTRASTAT VISITS

24.35 Businesses involved in the sale and movement of goods and the supply of services to other EU member states are required to prepare and submit EC Sales Lists (ESL) and supplementary statistical declarations (Intrastat declarations), subject to the value of these sales or movements being over a certain value. The ESL is used by all EU VAT administrations as a control document to monitor and check on the movement of goods and services across EU borders. The information contained on the Intrastat declaration is used by HMRC to build up the statistical data on what goods have been 'dispatched' from the UK and the 'arrivals' of goods in the UK from other member states. The Intrastat information, as it is called, is compiled from two sources: first, boxes 8 and 9 of the VAT return, and second the Intrastat declaration.

24.36 Businesses are required to complete an ESL for goods supplied to other EU member states and for services supplied to businesses in other EU member states where the business in the destination country is required to account for 'reverse charge' VAT. Businesses report the supplies of goods using form VAT101 on a monthly basis, and services using the same form on a calendar quarterly basis (businesses already reporting monthly have the option to report cross-border services monthly as well).

24.37 ESLs must be submitted:

- for online submissions, within 21 days from the end of the reporting period; and

- for paper ESLs, within 14 days from the end of the reporting period.

24.38 Intrastat declarations must be submitted each calendar month when the level of dispatches and arrivals exceed a prescribed minimum threshold. Currently the annual threshold for arrivals is £1,500,000 and for dispatches is £250,000. These forms must be submitted and amended online, via the HMRC website, or through the Electronic Data Interchange (EDI)/EDIFACT. Intrastat declarations must be submitted by the twenty-first day of the month following the end of the month to which they relate.

24.39 Depending on the level of activity, businesses may be required to submit returns only for dispatches or for arrivals or both. The information required to be gathered and declared on the supplementary declaration by

VAT aspects **24.43**

each member state can be different. However, the core information is always required. Failure to submit declarations or submitting persistently late, missing or inaccurate declarations could result in penalties.

24.40 Besides the header information (VAT registration number, number of items, period covered, etc) the statistical information required on a supplementary declaration in the UK is:

- commodity code;
- goods value;
- delivery terms (unless the value of dispatches or arrivals is less than £24,000,000);
- nature of transaction;
- net mass;
- supplementary units;
- member state to which/from which consigned;
- trader's reference (optional).

24.41 The above information is not always contained on the main accounting system and it can then be time consuming to collate the required data from a number of sources. As a basic check, it is always worth comparing the values declared on the monthly Intrastat declarations against the monthly/quarterly VAT returns for the same period. If the figures do not agree, a problem may have arisen in capturing the data and HMRC may also question the difference.

24.42 HMRC officers may inspect and check Intrastat declarations as part of an ordinary assurance visit, although there are dedicated Intrastat officers who will arrange a visit specifically to verify the declarations. For large businesses a few days each year may be set aside by HMRC to verify the data supplied on the declarations. This will usually be undertaken by a specialist Intrastat officer. HMRC will also question when declarations have not been completed when it is aware intra-EU supplies are made and/or received in order to ascertain why the returns have not been submitted.

MUTUAL ASSISTANCE THROUGH EXCHANGE OF INFORMATION

24.43 MTIC fraud, a fraud which exploits the intra-community trade system by inserting in supply chains a trader that defaults on its VAT liabilities and then disappears, represents one of the most high-profile and serious attacks on the tax system. As such, it has prompted HMRC and the tax authorities in other

24.44 *VAT aspects*

member states to work closely together to combat this and other international tax frauds. HMRC can conduct MTIC investigations under its civil or criminal powers and teams within Special Investigations and Criminal Investigations deals with these enquiries.

24.44 Member states are obliged to exchange information that might enable them to effect a correct assessment of taxes on income and capital under a Mutual Assistance Recovery Directive, which includes VAT. The extent of this co-operation seems set to increase with the European Commission's recent proposals to combat VAT fraud with increased cooperation and information sharing.

24.45 A number of multilateral VAT assurance visits have been carried out as member states focus on the joint control of multi-national companies. In addition, visits by HMRC are sometimes prompted by information requests from the tax authorities in other member states, acting under the 'mutual assistance' regime. Typically, such information requests relate to cross-border trade and are directed towards establishing that the correct treatment has been applied in both the member states concerned.

24.46 However, the national legislation of some member states has prohibited this type of exercise, even though EU legislation permits it. The EU Commission believes that these EU-wide controls should become a common part of each member state's national control strategies. As such, it seems likely that these types of visits will increase in number and scope as EU member states update their legislation in line with EU law.

24.47 From 16 November 2017, a new penalty has come into force for businesses and directors that fail to take adequate steps to avoid becoming unwittingly involved in fraudulent supply chains. The penalty is set at 30% of the revenue at risk.

PREPARING FOR VISITS

24.48 An assurance visit from HMRC must not be treated as a routine meeting. A degree of planning and preparation is required. Generally, prior to a VAT visit a letter should be issued from HMRC which should set out who is coming, which part of HMRC the officer is from and the information and records he will require on the day. This provides an opportunity to review the material that the visiting officer will see and, perhaps, identify any issues that may exist in advance.

24.49 Preparation for assurance visits must start well before the visit. Any business registering for VAT must accept that it will be visited by VAT officers.

VAT aspects **24.51**

Generally, the larger and more complex the business is, the longer and more frequent the visits will be. When establishing accounting systems, the following points should, therefore, be borne in mind:

- establish documented procedures for all accounts staff;
- understand what system controls are in place and if staff can override these;
- prepare guidance manuals for staff dealing with VAT;
- define default procedures should system failures occur; and
- ensure that staff dealing with VAT are trained.

24.50 Before the visit, try to arrange an office or meeting room for the VAT officer to use away from the normal office routine. This prevents the officer from overhearing conversations which may be misinterpreted. The office should be comfortable and tidy and any confidential documents should be locked away securely. The following points should also be considered:

- upon arrival, check the officer's identity;
- give clear instructions to all staff that HMRC officers are on the premises and how to react if they are approached/asked questions by any of the visiting officers;
- make notes of the meeting with the HMRC officer, noting documents inspected and if possible checks performed;
- write to confirm rulings given verbally by HMRC during the visit;
- use HMRC's own controls, flowcharts/interrogation software;
- be polite but firm in dealings with HMRC; and
- do not allow the officer free run of the premises.

Focus

Assurance visits from HMRC should not be treated as a routine meeting, and procedures should be put in place to manage the visit.

24.51 Preparation for any visit from HMRC should also be part of the ongoing routine for any business. If any business ignores good accounting practice, a period of, say, two weeks' notice of a visit would not be enough to get accounts into good order. As indicated above, good accounting routines should always be established. It is also important that, wherever possible, the

24.52 *VAT aspects*

accounting procedures should be familiar to more than one person. There have been many appeals to the VAT tribunals against a default surcharge in which the business has argued that VAT returns were submitted late due to the absence of a director or holiday of a key accounts staff member. Some of these cases were successful, but only where it was established that the missing person was away unexpectedly. Good accounting practices and procedures allow a business to be prepared for the unexpected.

24.52 It is worth taking time to establish a period end routine when completing VAT returns; a best practice approach to VAT. Among the rights under HMRC's Charter is that HMRC will 'treat you as honest' and also that HMRC will 'Tackle those who bend or break the rules'. The more that a business can demonstrate that it is managing its tax affairs correctly, the less time HMRC is likely to spend inspecting that business – and that can only be good news.

24.53 Businesses also seek to efficiently manage VAT costs and cash flow. Effective planning for VAT can assist in achieving this. Period-end routines can assist in recognising differences from the norm and serve to identify under- or over-declarations of VAT. Whilst HMRC officers are obliged to adjust for errors they discover that are in the taxpayer's favour, the checks undertaken during visits are generally aimed at identifying under-declarations. HMRC officers are unlikely to undertake detailed checks designed to ascertain whether a business has failed to take credit for input VAT or if it has been taken late. It is important, therefore, that each business has its own checks and procedures in place to ensure that it is not over-declaring its VAT liability, as well as checks to identify any under-declarations. When VAT is under-declared, HMRC can impose interest and penalties.

24.54 HMRC will impose a penalty if a business cannot show that it has taken 'reasonable care' to get things right. The penalty will depend on the type of inaccuracy involved, whether the error was careless, deliberate or deliberate and concealed, and whether any notification of the error to HMRC was prompted or unprompted. The penalty can range from 0% to 100% of the potential lost revenue (PLR) (see **CHAPTER 18**). Taking reasonable steps to help avoid a penalty includes keeping accurate records, checking the position when a VAT liability is unclear, and telling HMRC promptly about any error discovered on a VAT return that has already been submitted.

24.55 The concept of the credibility visit which, from HMRC's perspective, often identifies the one-off error made by a business has already been explained. Simply having a second person to check the figures for a VAT return and making sure that the figures shown are credible is a good plan. Businesses can utilise software or spreadsheets to compile and check the VAT return data.

Various checks can be built into these processes. It is also best practice to have a different person signing the VAT return from the person who prepares it and for the signatory to perform some independent credibility checks on the return to ensure that it does not contain obvious errors, is consistent with the activities of the business, etc.

24.56 A common criticism from HMRC is that the signatory to the VAT return is often at too low a level within a large business. A routine period-end procedure is an ideal way to get VAT taken more seriously within a business, especially if the finance director is required to check and sign the VAT return.

VAT return processes should be well documented and kept up to date. They should be available and readily accessible to all relevant staff.

> **Focus**
>
> Period-end routines should be in place for completing VAT returns, so that VAT is not under-declared, but also so that VAT liability is not over-declared. A second person should check the VAT return, and the return should be signed off at an appropriate level of seniority.

24.57 One reaction to concerns about how seriously VAT (and other taxes) is taken in some organisations is the legislation that makes senior accounting officers (SAOs) of large UK companies (who are liable to taxes and duties in the UK) responsible for ensuring and certifying that appropriate tax accounting arrangements have been established and maintained. The legislation only applies to a UK-registered company with a turnover of more than £200 million or with gross assets of more than £2 billion, but it may be a hint of things to come for smaller businesses if it achieves the objective of persuading those large businesses to take tax (including VAT) compliance more seriously at a high level within the organisation.

24.58 The 'main duty' of the SAO is to take reasonable steps to monitor the accounting arrangements of the company and to identify any respects in which those arrangements are not appropriate tax arrangements. The SAO is a director or officer who in the company's opinion has overall responsibility for the company's financial accounting arrangements. The SAO must provide HMRC with a certificate for each financial year of the company stating whether the company had appropriate arrangements in place throughout the year. Breaches of the SAO regime may result in penalties for both the SAO, personally, and the company.

24.59 *VAT aspects*

SEARCH AND ENTRY

24.59 HMRC has one set of powers covering VAT, PAYE, income tax, capital gains tax, corporation tax and the construction industry scheme to:

- visit businesses to inspect premises, assets and records;
- ask taxpayers and third parties for more information and documents; and
- set record-keeping requirements.

The powers are principally contained in *FA 2008, Sch 36*.

24.60 For Intrastat purposes, HMRC's powers are contained in the Statistics of Trade (Customs and Excise) Regulations 1992, SI 1992/2790. All that will be dealt with here are the powers generally exercised during a routine VAT inspection.

24.61 *VATA 1994, Sch 11* (amended in accordance with *FA 2008*) deals with the administration, collection and enforcement of the tax. *Paragraph 6* requires a business to keep records. Under *para 11*, a justice of the peace (or justice in Scotland) may make an order giving an officer the right to access and remove information where there are reasonable grounds for believing a VAT offence has been or is about to be committed and the information may be required as evidence.

24.62 Following consultation with the ICAEW and the Chartered Institute of Taxation, HM Customs and Excise (HMCE as it was then known) issued VAT Leaflet 700/47 (February 1993) 'Confidentiality in VAT Matters (Tax Advisers) – Statement of Practice'. This leaflet acknowledged the confidential nature of such tax advice and recognised that tax advisers have a duty of confidentiality to their clients. The former HMCE policy in this area, therefore, is not normally to request the business to produce confidential opinion letters. This will typically include auditors' working papers and management letters, except to the extent that they contain information relating to a supply of goods or services. Where advice letters contain mixed information, ie general advice and guidance and advice relating to a supply of goods or services, HMRC will normally accept an extract from the document supported by a written statement from the tax adviser or business that in his opinion HMRC do not have the power to see the other part(s) of the document. This Notice was withdrawn in February 2012, because the information in it has been incorporated into HMRC's Compliance manual.

24.63 If any business is in doubt as to whether to give any documents to HMRC it should consult its advisers. If documents of a confidential nature are shown to HMRC – which should be resisted – ensure, as far as possible, that no copies are taken. It is worth remembering that, in dispute cases involving appeals, HMRC may seek, and the tax tribunal may order, disclosure of documents viewed as 'confidential'.

SURVEILLANCE OPERATIONS

24.64 In general terms, surveillance operations cover two types of activity: first, test purchases and secondly observation of premises and/or people. If VAT officers have reason to believe that a business is suppressing the value of its sales, for example, one device that can be used to good effect is to conduct a test purchase operation. This is a low-key investigation technique typically employed against retailers, particularly restaurants and hairdressers. A small team of VAT officers is sent to the target premises to, for example, purchase a meal and to observe the waiters and other staff to see what happens to the money, ie what procedures are operated.

24.65 The officers will complete a report (sometimes a witness statement) which typically details:

- what they purchased (a receipt is an essential feature);
- what the cash-taking routine is for the business, ie what does the waiter do with the cash or credit card slips, etc;
- the number of diners in the restaurant between certain times; and
- the general atmosphere in the restaurant.

24.66 This type of activity may go on for several days, or if the business and suspected misdeclarations are large enough, over a period of weeks. The output from this type of activity gives a rough idea of the level of takings for the restaurant for a given period. By extrapolation, an idea of the actual level of takings for a VAT period or year can be ascertained.

24.67 The 'test meal' will be followed fairly quickly by an assurance visit. The VAT officer, armed with the intelligence gained from the test meal operation, can compare known takings against the takings declared in the record of daily gross takings that must be maintained by every retailer. Clearly, if the test meal operation identifies a significant difference between declared and actual takings, the assurance visit is likely to turn very swiftly into an investigation.

24.68 If HMRC wants to obtain information about premises and/or people it will, on occasion, mount an exercise to observe those premises or people (known colloquially as 'obs'). This procedure demands considerable skills which would not normally be expected of a VAT officer. Because of the level of expertise required and the manpower needed to conduct this type of operation, these techniques are usually employed only by trained investigators within HMRC.

24.69 *VAT aspects*

ROLE OF THE PROFESSIONAL ADVISER

Business review

24.69 A professional adviser can, of course, take many roles and provide a variety of services. In an ideal world every accounting system should have rigorous procedures all of which are documented and involve staff having split responsibilities. However, in practice this utopian ideal may not always translate to the real world. It should also be remembered that professional advice is not cheap. A business invariably strikes a balance between the perceived risks and the cost of implementing a rock-solid accounting system.

24.70 Although the vast majority of businesses are subject to an annual audit, VAT errors or mistakes are rarely material to the accounts and VAT does not, therefore, form a large part of a typical audit. The role of the professional VAT adviser is something beyond the scope of an audit.

24.71 A typical role for a professional adviser can be to conduct an overview of the system operated by a business to determine key weaknesses and controls and to ensure that the systems suit that particular business. This type of VAT review is often likened to an HMRC assurance visit; the question then posed by the business is 'why do we pay an adviser to do that, when HMRC do it for free?' There are two fundamental reasons why a separate review should be considered by a business. First, HMRC's role is to maximise revenue. This means that HMRC will be looking mainly for errors where VAT has been under-declared or over-recovered. If such errors are found by HMRC, as stated earlier, this will result in an interest charge and, in some circumstances, a monetary penalty. Secondly, HMRC is not in the business of giving bespoke tax advice. Generally speaking, opportunities will not be pointed out by a visiting VAT officer.

ASSESSMENTS AND DISPUTES

Assessments

24.72 If a business has received an assessment following a VAT visit, it should be confirmed that it is correct and has been validly issued, eg is it out of time? Does the assessment reflect the law, rather than just HMRC's view or its interpretation of the law?

24.73 It must be remembered that most public notices and leaflets are simply HMRC's interpretation of the law, albeit some elements of the published guidance do have the force of law. The number of successful appeals against HMRC's view is a testament to the fact that HMRC's interpretation can be and, where appropriate, should be challenged. It should also be appreciated that UK VAT legislation must reflect the provisions of EU VAT legislation. A business has the right, on appeal, to challenge HMRC's interpretation on both UK and EU law. HMRC can only defend the UK legislation, it cannot rely on EU law that has not been implemented properly into the domestic legislation. A professional adviser should be aware of the vast amount of UK and EU legislation and legal precedent and often has greater resources available than a normal business to ascertain the correct position.

Appeals

24.74 This can be a daunting thought for many businesses. The tribunal procedures can be obscure for the uninitiated as can the idea of building the legal arguments and giving evidence at the tribunal. A professional adviser can put the case together and remove a lot of the concerns usually experienced by a business going to a tribunal for the first time. Although businesses can take a case on their own, with the complexity of today's legislation, particularly if a case involves a VAT liability issue, they are well advised to seek professional guidance.

24.75 There is a two-tier tribunal system hearing all tax appeals. The First-tier Tribunal hears the majority of appeals, with larger and more complex cases being considered by the Upper Tribunal, which also hears appeals from decisions of the First-tier Tribunal. Costs will not generally be payable to the successful party in an appeal to the First-tier Tribunal. In the more complex cases, however, the usual costs regime can apply and either party could find itself meeting its own and the opponent's costs. Experience has shown that even when a successful appellant is awarded costs, these will rarely cover the full economic cost of the appeal so it would be wrong to regard even a successful appeal as a 'no cost option'.

24.76 Businesses are entitled (but not obliged) to request an internal review of appealable tax decisions. Reviews are optional and will be undertaken by a trained review officer, who has not previously been involved with that decision and who will be able to offer a balanced and objective view. If the taxpayer does not agree with the result of the review, he can appeal to the tribunal or seek to resolve the dispute through Alternative Dispute Resolution (ADR).

Appeal time limits

24.77 In circumstances where HMRC issues an appealable decision (including a VAT assessment), the taxpayer has 30 days (this can be extended with HMRC's agreement) to notify HMRC that he wants the decision

24.78 *VAT aspects*

reviewed, and should back up his request with relevant information that supports the case for review.

24.78 Once a taxpayer has notified HMRC of his desire for a review, HMRC has 45 days to review the decision (a longer period can be agreed with the taxpayer if necessary). The taxpayer cannot appeal to the tribunal until the review is carried out.

24.79 Where a taxpayer does not want a review of a decision or disagrees with the outcome of the review, he can appeal to the tribunal. This should be done within 30 days of HMRC's decision letter, or within 30 days of receipt of HMRC's review decision.

Focus

Businesses can request from HMRC an internal, independent review of an appealable tax decision, within 30 days of the decision. If the business does not want an internal review or disagrees with the outcome of a review, it can appeal to the tribunal within 30 days of the decision letter or HMRC's review decision.

Alternative dispute resolution

24.80 In the more complex disputes involving liability issues, disputes about the relevant facts or the way the law applies, HMRC is now willing to consider ADR as a means of resolving tax disputes.

24.81 ADR refers to any form of dispute resolution that is not litigation. The tool that has been used most by HMRC so far is 'facilitative mediation'. This is a process whereby a trained mediator or mediators (who can be independent, from HMRC and/or the business's advisers, or a combination of these) will try to bring the parties together to try to reach an agreement, or at least narrow the issues for litigation if a resolution cannot be reached. A mediator's role is not to suggest a solution or to impose a view one way or the other. The mediator's role is to use a variety of techniques which assist the parties in reaching a settlement.

24.82 ADR is becoming more popular as a cost-effective and efficient way to resolve disputes, especially where the discussions between the parties have stalled or reached an impasse. Allowing a third-party presence can change the dynamics of the dispute and bring a fresh perspective. It can also resolve the issues between the parties in a day as opposed to years.

> **Focus**
>
> The author is aware of a number of disputes where both HMRC and the taxpayer were at an impasse, and that were successfully resolved via the ADR process, much more efficiently and quickly than if the disputes had ended up going through the court process.
>
> The option of ADR is one that businesses should certainly consider if they feel they are no longer making progress through HMRC's appeal processes.

The Revenue and Customs adjudicator

24.83 If a business has a grievance about the way it has been dealt with by HMRC, and the complaint has not been resolved through HMRC's complaint procedures, the business may be able to complain to the Adjudicator for HMRC. Appropriate complaints concern the way in which HMRC has conducted itself in relation to a business's affairs and may include, for example:

- Mistakes.
- Unreasonable delays.
- Poor or misleading advice.
- Inappropriate staff behaviour.
- The use of discretion.

24.84 The Adjudicator must resolve the complaint in accordance with HMRC's own procedures and practices. This may include asking HMRC for an apology, to meet additional costs incurred, and/or to make a small compensatory payment. The Adjudicator does not examine cases which are appealable to a VAT tribunal.

Judicial review

24.85 In some cases where it is not possible to settle a dispute or to appeal it under the 'normal' appeal process to the tax tribunal, it may be possible to seek judicial review, either in the Administrative Court or the Upper Tribunal (which has power to consider certain judicial review cases that are transferred to it from the Administrative Court). Judicial review cases tend to be complex and involve tight time limits. Early professional advice would be essential in any situation where this process might be adopted.

24.86 *VAT aspects*

KEY POINTS

24.86 Where a business is subject to an assurance visit it should:

1   ensure that the person responsible for the business's VAT affairs is present;

2   collate the information detailed in **24.17** if this is the business's first assurance visit; and

3   have all VAT return source documents ready for inspection on the basis that HMRC will generally inspect at least one VAT return in detail.

24.87 A business should consider the following:

1   upon arrival, check the officer's identity;

2   give clear instructions to all staff that HMRC officers are on the premises and how to react if they are approached/asked questions by any of the visiting officers;

3   make notes of the meeting with the HMRC officer, noting documents inspected and if possible checks performed;

4   write to confirm rulings given verbally by HMRC;

5   use HMRC's own controls, flowcharts/interrogation software;

6   be polite but firm in dealings with HMRC; and

7   do not allow the officer free run of the premises.

By undertaking the above, and familiarising itself with the rules and process in relation to an HMRC visit, a business should be in a good position to deal with a visit from an HMRC officer.

Chapter 25

National Insurance aspects

Alastair Kendrick
(based on the original text drafted by David Heaton FCA CTA and Peter Arrowsmith FCA)

> **SIGNPOSTS**
>
> - **Background** – NICs used to be under the separate control of the Department of Social Security and its Contributions Agency, with compliance provisions rules set out in social security legislation. The Agency and responsibility for NICs policing were transferred to the Inland Revenue in 1999, and NICs came to be policed by what is now HMRC. The Department now monitors and enforces compliance for £124 billion per year of NI Fund income, which pays for the state pension and part-funds the NHS (**25.02–25.12**);
>
> - **Inspectorate powers** – The powers in the social security acts have now been largely superseded by parallel powers in *TMA 1970* and those introduced as common powers for tax and NICs by the HMRC Powers Review between 2007 and 2010, with the aim of ensuring that all due contributions are collected so as to replenish the NI Fund (**25.13–25.22**);
>
> - **Triggers for investigation** – HMRC has come to rely increasingly on technology and data mining to trigger its compliance interventions, but there are some regular and fairly obvious areas of difficulty for employers that automatically attract HMRC's attentions. These triggers have taken on a slightly different character since the advent of universal RTI reporting, but many remain the same as they always have been (**25.23–25.73**);
>
> - **Practical aspects of the investigation** – HMRC rarely makes unannounced visits, and the reasons for a visit, its timing and how the process works will be explained by the issue of a number of factsheets (**25.74–25.102**);
>
> - **Inspection report and future visits** – The outcome of the visit will generally be summarised in writing, with an explanation of the arrears estimated to be due. The employer's risk rating will be added

25.1 *National Insurance aspects*

> to the HMRC file so that the need for future visits may be noted (**25.103–25.107**);
>
> - **Offences, penalties and interest** – When inaccuracies are found, they will be assessed against a series of criteria to determine whether a penalty will be charged, and whether further sanctions might be necessary. Interest will almost always be assessed on the statutory basis. The system of follower notices and accelerated payment notices in avoidance cases has been extended to the NICs regime (**25.108–25.165**);
>
> - **Appeals** – Where alleged arrears are not settled by agreement, HMRC may exercise powers to issue formal notices of decision, charging NICs on the employer and/or individual contributors. These may, as with income tax assessments, become the subject of an appeal to the First-tier Tribunal (**25.166–25.217**);
>
> - **Conclusions** (**25.218–25.224**);
>
> - **Key points** (**25.225**).

INTRODUCTION

25.1 Over a number of years employer compliance officers have adopted a much higher profile and there is clear evidence that considerably more thought is going into deciding which employers will be selected for a visit or investigation. In very simple terms HM Revenue and Customs (HMRC) is making the best use of the resources it has for visiting duties and it is clearly seeking value for money. To help it achieve this aim it has sought help from accountancy firms and management consultants and, from the way in which it now conducts investigations, that was clearly money well spent. In addition, computer-based risk assessment is increasingly being undertaken by teams in the Knowledge, Analysis and Intelligence (KAI) units in the Customer Compliance Directorate, so that ever more scarce human resources can be directed to the most fruitful targets. Around 50% of HMRC staff are now classed officially as dealing with enforcement and compliance, but there are no current public statistics about how many deal with employer compliance, and HMRC has stopped publishing data about how many employer investigations, enquiries or interventions it undertakes. Many of the staff in 'enforcement and compliance' are those who collect the pay as you earn (PAYE) and National Insurance contributions (NIC), those who process tax codes and those who man the call centres, so it is not clear how many are involved in what was once called 'PAYE Audit' or 'NIC Field Operations'.

25.2 Following the merger between the Inland Revenue and Contributions Agency on 1 April 1999 inspections are now, almost without exception, made into both tax and NIC – including statutory sick pay (SSP), statutory maternity pay (SMP), statutory paternity pay (SPP), statutory adoption pay (SAP) and now statutory shared parental pay (SShPP) – at the same time in a single visit. HMRC also undertakes audits of employers' national minimum wage (NMW) compliance, on behalf of the Department of Business, Energy and Industrial Strategy (BEIS), but the teams do not combine NIC compliance with their NMW work. It seems likely that the payroll compliance teams will, in future, also monitor compliance by large employers with the new apprenticeship levy regime, once it is in place, which is also a policy that falls under BEIS.

25.3 Another significant factor is the modern attitude of government where the lawful use of mismatched or ill-considered legislation to avoid or reduce National Insurance contributions is regarded as akin to evasion if it may be described as 'avoidance' or even 'aggressive tax planning'. With such a prevailing attitude, many employers are likely to suffer an investigation which is not really justified. Such activity is also affected by the application of the disclosure of tax avoidance schemes (DOTAS) regime to any National Insurance contributions avoidance schemes that are not already reportable due to a tax saving too – the extension to National Insurance took effect from 1 May 2007 – as well as the subsequent 'disguised remuneration' provisions (which took effect for NIC purposes from 6 December 2011). It is notable that no NIC planning schemes were notified under the DOTAS provisions in 2014/15, and only seven in total in 2013/14, suggesting that employers now are not being sold NIC avoidance schemes because HMRC's compliance response makes it uneconomic to devise and market new schemes. The extension of the accelerated payment notice and follower notice regime to NICs by the *National Insurance Contributions Act 2015* will have reduced the allure of NIC avoidance schemes even further, as will the 2016 proposals to make the scheme vendors liable to a penalty.

25.4 According to HMRC's annual report for 2015/16, total HMRC receipts were £537 billion, of which £112 billion (21%) related to National Insurance (and most of that to Class 1 contributions) – the HMRC accounts clearly use a slightly different accounting basis than the Government Actuary, whose report in January 2016 estimated 2015/16 NIC collections at £113 billion. Consequently, there is no disputing that a certain amount of check visiting is necessary to ensure that employers and the self-employed pay what is due and otherwise comply with the many NIC legislative requirements. The amount of public money involved effectively makes this mandatory, although the number of employers visited by HMRC employer compliance officers (out of a total of around 2.6 million enterprises, with over 1.9 million PAYE schemes between them) was only around 18,000 in a recent year.

25.5 However, with substantial staff reductions ordered by successive governments now largely implemented and yet more ordered under a series of spending reviews, the likelihood of visits must inevitably reduce, with ever

25.6 *National Insurance aspects*

more effort focused on automated processes and 'big data' to identify errors. It might be expected, however, that penalties will be applied with ever more frequency and ever less flexibility, and the review of HMRC's powers that took place during 2006 and 2007 also provided from April 2009 a more rigid regime to discourage non-compliance without the need for too much human intervention. At the same time, HMRC has adopted a 'nudge' strategy to encourage compliance, setting up a behavioural insights team in 2010 with a target of using psychology to subtly alter taxpayer behaviour.

25.6 The first fruits of this approach have not been encouraging. HMRC in 2015 published a proposal to reform the penalty regime once more. It might at first be surprising to find that the proposals involve relaxing some requirements rather than tightening them, but in retrospect this must have been inevitable. HMRC has said repeatedly that it wants taxpayers to comply with the rules rather than pay penalties, but it has created automated systems that sometimes simply baffle employers and their agents (and HMRC's own staff), or behave in unexpected ways, which makes PAYE, NIC, construction industry scheme (CIS) and student loan compliance more difficult, with the inevitable consequence that more penalties are charged. An experiment with automated CIS penalties was abandoned very quickly, and payroll penalties are currently back on a manual process.

25.7 For example, the Real Time Information (RTI) regime was meant to include automated penalties for late filing and late payment, but they had to be deferred because the volume of apparent errors was overwhelming HMRC's limited resources. The moratorium on automated RTI penalties was supposed to end, along with the relaxation of deadlines for small employers, in April 2016, but there were simply too many errors built into the systems to allow the penalty process to recommence.

25.8 The first late filing of a Full Payment Submission (FPS) in a year was meant to be penalty-free, with escalating penalties thereafter as the number of errors mounted. HMRC created a 'generic notification system' (GNS) to send employers a warning via a secure online mailbox that they had filed late or omitted to file, but when the system produced hundreds of thousands of non-specific warnings every month (it is normally impossible to identify the exact error from the contents of the notice, especially in large payrolls), many of them for errors that existed only on HMRC's computer, or could only be identified with lengthy telephone calls to HMRC's call centres, a re-think was required.

25.9 One of the first responses was not to correct the processes that produced the incorrect penalties, but instead to introduce a new automated 'Penalty Appeals Service', so that employers who had received an incorrect penalty notice could appeal online, without human intervention. In a sure sign that the general penalty system was not working as intended, these online appeals could even be accepted automatically by HMRC's computers, without human intervention. The introduction of automated penalties therefore had to be deferred, with HMRC reverting to a 'risk-based' approach instead, meaning that compliance staff would issue penalties by manual intervention when they found errors worthy of a penalty.

25.10 As a temporary 'sticking plaster', HMRC also announced that any late filing of an FPS until April 2016 would be disregarded if the submission was no more than three days late. This apparently removed around 90% of the volume of penalty notices, but it has never been explained why so many employers seem to be missing the RTI filing deadlines. Part of the problem is undoubtedly the requirement placed on employers to file an FPS on or before the date of payment, which is feasible for civil service employees with stable and predictable earnings and earnings periods but impossible in a significant minority of commercial contexts. Part is also the confusion about the meaning of 'payment', which has different meanings in PAYE, NIC and universal credit contexts but is treated as the same by HMRC's RTI system. Another big part is that HMRC requires employers to operate HMRC's computer systems, knowing exactly how every aspect of the software works, without having been trained. Employers frequently need help, but HMRC's call centres have until very recently been under-resourced and unable to provide prompt support.

25.11 The review of the penalty regime is therefore very welcome, but a review of the whole RTI system is also required, since there are parts of it where employers simply cannot comply, and parts where HMRC's processes produce unpredictable outputs that waste time for all concerned. It appears that the tight deadlines are imposed by the Department for Work and Pensions' (DWP) requirements, which dictate that universal credit entitlements are recalculated each week or month as claimants' earnings fluctuate, a policy that rests on real-time information from HMRC's PAYE systems about those earnings. The structure for providing prompt information from HMRC's RTI systems to DWP's universal credit systems is in place – data received by HMRC for any record flagged as of interest to the DWP are passed to the DWP computer four times per day – but any queries about discrepancies have to be passed back to HMRC for clerical intervention.

25.12 The Government have asked the Office of Tax Simplification to consider the possible merger of income tax and National Insurance but despite initially there being positive re-actions to the proposed changes we have seen no further steps to introduce change.

INSPECTORATE POWERS

25.13 From 6 April 2005, the tax and National Insurance powers of HMRC officers to inspect records and obtain information were aligned and *TMA 1970*,

25.14 *National Insurance aspects*

ss 20B and *20BB* – with appropriate modifications – applied to NIC (s 20 also applied prior to 1 April 2009). From that date, the *Social Security Contributions and Benefits Act 1992 (SSCBA 1992)*, *s 110ZA* was rewritten. The rewritten *s 110ZA* does not deal with Class 3 contributions as they are entirely voluntary, and Class 4 contributions were already within the TMA regime in any event.

25.14 A revised compliance checking regime across most taxes was introduced from 1 April 2009 with reformed information powers contained in *FA 2008, Sch 36*. This applies equally to National Insurance contributions, *SSAA 1992, s 110ZA* having been further amended by *FA 2008, Sch 36, para 84*.

25.15 All employer compliance officers carry a warrant card setting out their powers in addition to a standard identification card. Employers should ask to see such warrants if they are unsure of the rights to enter business premises, review documents and ask questions that the employer compliance officers have.

Before looking at what can trigger a National Insurance investigation, it is worthwhile looking at the overall National Insurance funding position.

NATIONAL INSURANCE FUNDING

25.16 NICs are no longer cheap – the abolition of the employer's upper earnings limit in October 1985, the extension of employee liability from April 2003 and the increase in the main rate of employee contributions to 12% from 2011/12 have seen to that.

25.17 In the 2015/16 tax year, according to the Government Actuary, HMRC collected around £113 billion in NIC, of which around £22 billion were directed to the NHS while the rest was spent on paying benefits that depend on contributions, the principal one being the state pension. The total cost of paying pensions was £90 billion, so the NI Fund overspent, mainly because the 'triple lock' policy led to a 2.9% increase in pension rates when earnings (and the resultant NIC income) were static. The total NIC amount vies with VAT as the second largest source of government revenue after income tax. Of the money collected, nearly 98% comes in the shape of Class 1 contributions, ie from employees and employers. Estimated social security expenditure on contributory benefits for 2015/16 was around £92 billion, according to the Government Actuary. There are in addition other benefits, means tested rather than paid as of right based on contributions history, such as income support, tax credits (very gradually being replaced by the new universal credit on a phased basis from October 2013) and child benefit which are funded from general taxation, taking the total 'welfare' bill to £244 billion in 2015/16. Allowing for the fact that NICs also make a contribution to the running of the National Health Service (which is not within the 'welfare' budget), the

National Insurance aspects **25.20**

National Insurance Fund is expected to show a small surplus in 2016/17 of around £1.65 billion. The impact of increasing the state pension age to save money was not expected to bring the NI Fund back into balance until 2019/20, according to the Government Actuary's report on the National Insurance Fund in January 2015, but the abolition of the contracting out rebate from April 2016 has contributed to a forecast of a big surplus for the next few years, with the NI Fund balance (ie, the accumulated excess of contributions collected over benefits paid out) now scheduled to rise from £25 billion in April 2016 to £58 billion by April 2021.

25.18 The Government Actuary recommends a working balance of one-sixth of annual benefit expenditure, and for several years from 2008/09 to 2012/13 there was an excess surplus in the medium term of well over £15 billion. It seemed that National Insurance rates were higher than they needed to be. However, the cumulative effect of the pensions triple lock in a period of very low inflation turned the surplus into a series of deficits, and the National Insurance Fund balance was forecast at one point to fall to no more than one and a half weeks of benefit expenditure in the next few years. The need for HMRC's enforcement and compliance teams to bring in more NI 'yield' became urgent, although the January 2016 estimates from the Government Actuary suggested that the various recent policy changes on contributions and state pension reform might have removed that urgency.

25.19 The UK social security system is based on a pay-as-you-go principle – the contributions now being paid are used to fund the current payment of social security benefits. The money collected should be enough to cover HMRC's and DWP's administrative costs (around £859 million in 2016/17) and to pay all contributory benefits in the year.

25.20 For a few years from 1985 the Government Actuary consistently underestimated the NIC yield mainly because earnings grew at a faster rate than expected. The result was a large surplus in the National Insurance Fund and one government minister actually described the Fund as being awash with money. In hindsight, it seems clear that the surplus had been created with future benefit increases in mind: in April 2010, the qualifying period for a full basic state pension was reduced from 44 years for men and 39 years for women to 30 years for both, before any increase in state pension age could have any effect, so expenditure grew quickly without a matching rise in contributions. The Labour government had also committed to raising the basic state pension even if there was no price or earnings inflation, after Gordon Brown had been embarrassed by a programmed rise of only 25p per week based on the longstanding indexation regime and a year of almost no inflation. It was therefore no surprise when an extra 1% was added to both employee and employer rates of Class 1 and the self-employed rate of Class 4 in April 2011. After the introduction of the employment allowance in April 2014, giving employers relief worth £1.25 billion in the first year (initially forecast to rise to £1.7 billion by 2017/18,

25.21 *National Insurance aspects*

even before the 2015 announcement that the employment allowance would rise to £3,000 in April 2016), the problem of underfunding was exacerbated, so it was again no surprise when the Government Actuary announced that the National Insurance Fund would need a subsidy from general taxation (a 'Treasury grant') of £6.6 billion in 2015/16. In the event, the NI Fund actually needed £9.6 billion, but only as a temporary measure.

25.21 To some extent, the National Insurance Fund numbers are just accounting entries in the government's ledgers, but governments have tended to adhere to the long-established principle that NICs should raise enough to fund contributory benefits and the use of a Treasury grant is to be avoided. But NICs are as susceptible to political tinkering as any tax: National Insurance rates for employers were reduced for a time (thus reducing the income into the National Insurance Fund) to counterbalance the imposition of the climate change levy and aggregates tax – yet the proceeds from these duties go to the Treasury, not the National Insurance Fund. Because of the instability of the policymaking, projections by the Government Actuary sometimes seem to be out of date before they have been published, as the impact of new measures changes assumptions about future revenues, expenditure and behaviour. There is also a necessary amount of guesswork in the estimates made: the Government Actuary's annual report on the draft annual benefits uprating order is issued in January, in advance of the actual uprating. The economic data on which it is based are necessarily those for the period before the previous September, when the uprating is actually set (usually, the figures from the Office for National Statistics on employment levels that form the basis of the estimates are extrapolations from the period May to July of the previous year). The report does not use 'live' data from HMRC either, so it can only ever provide a very broad-brush picture, although it does function as part of the evidence base for any proposed new measures.

25.22 The most far-reaching measure, however, has been a change in the attitude of HMRC. Employer compliance officers rarely visit back-street garages or corner shops to confirm that the basic NIC rules are being complied with, but will visit large employers and investigate all aspects of social security going back as far as six years (as well as tax, of course). They will pay particular attention to those employers who have used structured NIC mitigation schemes and to those with an international exposure because that is where significant contributions are thought, often correctly, to have been underpaid.

TRIGGERS FOR INVESTIGATIONS

Triggers for visit

25.23 There are many reasons why an employer compliance officer would want to visit an employer. Although much less common now due

National Insurance aspects **25.26**

to resource constraints, it could be because he is a new employer and the employer compliance officer wants to introduce himself and check that the employer is familiar with the basic rules for NIC, SSP, SMP, SPP, SAP and SShPP (the latter five collectively known as 'statutory payments') and those for PAYE and the collection of student loans. New businesses in the construction industry will also face checks on their CIS compliance. Given the shortage of manpower at HMRC, employers are very likely to receive a series of educational emails with pointers to guidance and basic webinars, with face-to-face checks restricted to those employers who exhibit a poor RTI compliance record in their first year.

25.24 In the past, there might have been a small discrepancy in the year-end reporting forms, causing the employer compliance officer to need a quick look at the employer's records. Now that RTI is classed as 'business as usual' by HMRC and year-end P14s and P35s are a thing of the past, discrepancies on FPS or Employer Payment Summaries (EPS) are likely to appear only in the employer's 'dashboard', possibly accompanied by 'specified charges' generated by the HMRC computer in respect of (allegedly) missing FPSs. It will then be the employer who initiates the contact with HMRC and most queries will be dealt with by telephone. It was always, and remains, a possibility that a special check is being made of businesses in a specific industry type or an employer has been selected for a more in-depth examination based on information prepared by the KAI team, possibly prompted by a large number of queries to HMRC's helpline by employees of that business (see, eg, the decision of the First-Tier Tribunal in *Reed Employment plc v Revenue and Customs Comrs* [2010] UKFTT 596 (TC), which notes that HMRC faced a large volume of questions from workers about the company's salary sacrifice scheme and the way its earnings were being calculated and taxed).

Which employers are chosen for investigation?

25.25 Although some random visits continue to be made, employer compliance officers are likely to have been prompted by a KAI report identifying employers worthy of a visit. They are under some pressure to collect additional NICs (and tax too) and so they will not want to waste time visiting employers who are unlikely to have underpaid or made other serious errors.

25.26 Employer risk-profiling is used to identify suitable targets and factors taken into account include size, geographical location, industry type and make-up of workforce etc. Computer programs are regularly used to identify such targets. HMRC uses software called 'Connect' to carry out data mining, matching information from numerous public sources, commercial databases (eg Experian credit references) and tax return submissions of all kinds (from individuals, companies – RTI, VAT, CIS and P46(Car) returns – banks, conveyancers, trustees and pension administrators) to look for information that

25.27 *National Insurance aspects*

suggests non-compliance. Typically, attention will be drawn to an employer by an error in a return, or a return that has gone astray and been flagged as missing, a query from an employee, or a complaint (malicious or not) from an ex-employee or competitor. Occasionally, the employer may draw attention to a problem by asking HMRC for agreement to a particular tax treatment that suggests to HMRC that there is an attempt at avoidance (although in the *Reed* case, it appears to have taken HMRC some years to take a detailed interest in the company's remuneration arrangements, despite being asked for dispensations based on round-sum allowances each year).

25.27 With virtually the whole social security system to police, employer compliance officers could realistically pop up anywhere and look at anything. In reality, however, there are a few specific instances where they are likely to show most interest.

25.28 As regards National Insurance contributions and related matters, they include:

- errors or omissions in an employer's RTI submissions (and pre RTI, employer end of year return);
- errors or omissions in P11D returns (giving exposure to Class 1A arrears);
- persistent late reporting or late payment of PAYE and NICs;
- a large employer (where a small error across a large workforce can lead to significant under-declarations);
- an employer with an international exposure (because cross-border NIC and tax rules are different and complex, leading to frequent error);
- an employer with an employee benefit trust or other suspected 'disguised remuneration';
- an employer with multiple tax-advantaged share schemes;
- a national drive against a specific industry;
- an employer failing to reply to correspondence;
- a routine audit visit;
- a complaint from an employee;
- a local HMRC initiative, though becoming less common since regionalisation.

RTI submissions

25.29 Under RTI, employers are required to provide pay and deductions information (including details of National Insurance deducted) to HMRC each

National Insurance aspects **25.32**

time that a payment is made to an employee. At or before sending their first RTI submission to HMRC, large employers had to undergo a payroll alignment process to ensure that the data that they held on their employees, including National Insurance numbers, matched that held by HMRC.

25.30 HMRC systems automatically check an employee's National Insurance number (NINO) on the FPS and, when it was used during the first phase of RTI's introduction, it was checked from the employer alignment submission (EAS). If an employer does not have an employee's NINO, or the employee does not have one (eg inbound expatriates who are insured under the rules of another state by virtue of the EU regulations or a reciprocal social security agreement, or who need a UK NINO but are waiting for one to be issued) this field should be left blank on the submission. Employers can check NINOs under RTI by submitting a National Insurance number verification request (NVR), and a blank NINO field in an FPS is taken as an NVR. Years ago, when employer returns were rejected by HMRC if submitted without a NINO, it was common to create a temporary NINO using 'TN' followed by the employee's date of birth and gender, in the format 'TN dd mm yy M' (or 'F' for a female), which helped the DSS or HMRC match the employee contributions to a record by manual intervention after the year-end. The advent of RTI required such TNs to be removed from records, to avoid creating duplicate records. Date of birth and gender are discrete fields in the FPS record, so matching is automated. Employers should by now have purged their records of any TNs. Any that remain will simply result in the duplication of employee records, followed by demands from HMRC for phantom underpayments and the issue of multiple tax codes for non-existent second jobs. This will automatically raise a flag over the employer's payroll compliance record inviting an educational visit from an employer compliance officer.

25.31 HMRC undertakes a series of compliance checks on data submitted under RTI and, in particular, analyses trends and inconsistencies, and will follow up errors and inconsistencies that come to light. Most difficulty is caused to employers where HMRC's system processes data that it, rather than the employer's payroll software, has generated.

25.32 For example, if the system's algorithms estimate that one or more FPSs should have been submitted when none have in fact been submitted, the HMRC system will automatically create a 'specified charge', an estimate of the PAYE and NIC under-declared, which it then adds to the employer's account. Employers who do not track their online account regularly have been known to find out about the specified charges only when debt collectors arrive at the employer's premises seeking to collect the alleged underpayment. This can even happen where an employer is registered as having an annual scheme, where only one FPS is expected each tax year: specified charges have nevertheless been added for several months because the system has not been programmed with the correct pay frequency (despite the number

25.33 National Insurance aspects

being included in each FPS). The specified charge is an automated version of the determination that the 'collector of taxes' used to be able to make if no payment had been received from an employer in a particular month, but the old paper-based routine was more reliable, because all charges were authorised by a human and employers were notified by letter.

25.33 Employers sometimes also face being chased by HMRC Debt Management and Banking staff for unpaid PAYE or NICs as a result of HMRC allocating payments to a different reference, either in error or for reasons known only to HMRC, as far as the employer can see. A recent real life example may serve to illustrate the point.

> **Example 25.1**
>
> X Ltd paid a number of large bonuses using a remuneration scheme, expecting no NIC liability. The scheme was duly disclosed, the scheme challenged, and a settlement figure was agreed. HMRC issued a payslip for the agreed sum, incorporating a payment reference. The total sum due exceeded the employer's BACS limit, so the employer split the payment into four payments, and made all four e-payments using the same HMRC-generated and correct payment reference. HMRC subsequently contacted the company to query why the full amount had not been paid, and it emerged on investigation that only one of the four payments had been posted against the payment reference, two had been posted to a suspense account and one to the company's normal PAYE and NIC account. None of the confusion was caused by the employer, who had paid on time and in the correct amount.

End-of-year returns (pre-RTI)

25.34 Prior to the introduction of RTI (and for employers who, due to one of the very limited exceptions, do not operate online reporting), information on pay and deductions was provided to HMRC at the end of the tax year by means of an employer annual return. The P35 and P14 no longer exist, even for paper filers: they now use a paper RT2 full quarterly payment submission and RT5 employer payment summaries to report the set-off of statutory payments.

25.35 Before the introduction of RTI, every employee who earned an amount equal to the National Insurance lower earnings limit in any week in a tax year required the submission at the end of the year of a P14 on his behalf. This was so even though no actual contributions might have been payable – if earnings were below the earnings thresholds – because earnings at or above the lower earnings limit give rise to benefit entitlement. Prior to RTI, the P14 was the only real contact the National Insurance Contributions and Employer Office

(NIC&EO) of HMRC had with most employees and it is not surprising that the form was subjected to a number of checks, both immediately upon electronic submission and then at Newcastle, using various computer routines which had been developed over the years.

25.36 The very first check at Newcastle was to ensure that there was enough information to match the contributions paid against an individual's record on the NPS (the National Insurance and PAYE System) computer system (previously called NIRS2). Did the National Insurance number match with the identity details held for that number? These checks are now automatic, every time an FPS is submitted.

25.37 Where there was no match or a number was missing HMRC would attempt to trace the individual from the other information supplied. However, if it was a common name and no meaningful date of birth or address was supplied on the P14, then there was little chance of HMRC making a successful trace and it would have had no option but to come back and ask further questions of the employer who had submitted the P14. If there were too many enquiries for a single employer, then that was frequently enough to trigger some form of investigation on the grounds that if an employer could not be bothered getting numbers correct, he was probably making other errors. Obtaining the correct National Insurance number is no longer an onerous task under RTI.

25.38 The former Contributions Agency identified that they were spending an inordinate amount of time sorting out missing numbers and so they introduced procedures to help employers. This included the introduction of a separate enquiry form which could be sent to NIC&EO, and the ability to contact NIC&EO by telephone. Under RTI, National Insurance numbers can be checked by submitting an NVR. These various measures reduce the number of enquiries coming from Newcastle and employers should supply the additional information where it is easy to do so, and avoid unnecessary queries by checking carefully employee standing data before including it in the payroll records.

25.39 Once sufficient identity details have been established, then HMRC has two separate types of checks. The first concerns matching the contributions paid against those expected. For instance, if contracted-out contributions have been paid and HMRC has no record of an individual joining a company pension scheme then questions will be asked. The seeds of this problem disappeared along with contracting out in April 2016, although there will inevitably be some legacy cases that take a year or two to investigate. HMRC insisted from April 2014 that every FPS for any employee paying contracted-out NICs include a scheme contracting out number (SCON) so that scheme members could be easily identified. Any FPS submitted showing Table D or Table E contributions (COSR scheme members) without a corresponding SCON was

25.40 *National Insurance aspects*

being rejected, although numbers were reportedly dwindling as the end of contracting out approached. Now that contracting out has been abolished, it should be practically impossible for employers to make an FPS submission showing contracted out rates, as all payroll software should have removed the option to use such rates.

25.40 The same sense-check used to happen in reverse where they were expecting contracted-out contributions, but they received full-rate contributions. When did the individual leave the pension plan and how had his pension rights been secured were obvious questions that needed to be answered.

25.41 It is this type of checking, called compatibility checking, which raises queries regarding individuals who have paid a lower rate of contribution and there is no evidence to support that level of contribution. Examples will now include married women paying the reduced rate of contribution where no valid certificate is held, individuals paying the pensioners' rate when they have not yet reached state pension age and so on. For any employee where full rate standard contributions are not paid the employer should have valid evidence. This will be, for example, a married woman's reduced rate election, an age exemption certificate or copy of birth certificate or an A1 or equivalent for EEA and reciprocal agreement country secondments. A new issue in 2015/16 is likely to have been the payment of secondary NICs in respect of the earnings of workers who are under the age of 21, since they ceased to be due on earnings up to the UEL in any earnings period. As most employers now use computerised payrolls and employee records must include dates of birth, the problem seems likely to be limited, possibly to those cases where young earners receive a bonus that takes their earnings for a particular week above the upper earnings limit (UEL) for that week, when employer NICs are indeed payable on the excess. The issue may nevertheless still arise under the new rules in 2016 setting a nil secondary NI rate for employers of apprentices under the age of 25. The RTI record will now show the date of birth and flag the contribution as falling under the appropriate table (G or H), but it cannot link to any official record of the worker having a valid apprenticeship agreement, so employer compliance checks of this aspect of payroll may still be expected.

25.42 Millions of enquiries are raised each year by basic compatibility checks and thousands of man hours are wasted by the authorities. They are showing less and less patience with employers who make regular errors and to bring these employers into line a check visit of some sort is likely to be made.

25.43 The second type of checking is called ratio checking and this is a consideration of the financial aspects of the payments.

For example, has the employer paid roughly 11–12% of the taxable pay (if for 2010/11 or an earlier year) or 12–13% for later years by way of employer NIC? Does the employer portion come out as disproportionately more than the employee share? Do the total contributions exceed the employee contribution liability? If not there is likely to be something wrong. Has SSP been paid beyond a certain acceptable level? A similar sort of check is carried out for SMP, although here it is much more difficult because there is no maximum rate payable for the first six weeks. Where the SMP paid looks excessive, however, or exceeds a certain amount, NIC&EO may very well ask an employer compliance officer to check the validity of the figures. Among other issues he will want to satisfy himself that any bonus payment used to calculate the entitlement has been treated properly. The advent of ShPP in April 2015, which allows the mother's maternity leave and SMP or SAP to be shared with the father, who will generally be employed by a different employer, has given the HMRC compliance staff yet another confusing item to check.

25.44 Other checks carried out at Newcastle used to include a simple arithmetical check on the amounts on the individual P14 forms to ensure that the total agreed with that shown on the summary form P35. The checks will also confirm that the correct year's rates and limits have been used along with confirmation that the appropriate additional rate contributions have been paid on earnings that exceed the employee upper limit. A number of checks would be automatically included where electronic filing was undertaken, and this is now a constant feature of compliance checking under RTI. Where the data are not satisfactory the return(s) will be rejected. If correct and valid data are not resubmitted in time and/or electronically, then standard penalties may be imposed.

25.45 The introduction of RTI has improved the National Insurance data available to HMRC in that details of National Insurance contributions deducted must be notified to HMRC on the FPS every time that a payment is made to an employee, with set-offs of statutory payments reflected in a monthly EPS. The introduction of RTI removed the need to submit year end forms P35 and P14 and instead HMRC carry out automated checks on data submitted under RTI, which are much more voluminous than on the P14, since each FPS includes over 100 data fields, most of which are susceptible to rapid analysis by the RTI system.

Category X notations

25.46 One important area where employer compliance officers show an interest is in the area of Category X, the contribution category letter which signifies that no contributions are payable. This creates some difficulty for HMRC simply because they have no earnings or contributions on which to base their validation checks. The Newcastle computer is simply programmed to accept the validity of such entries, but it would be a bit of a nonsense for NIC&EO to accept these returns without question. It would only be a matter of time before unscrupulous employers made fraudulent use of the X notation.

25.47 *National Insurance aspects*

25.47 In the past checking has been restricted to a sample of returns every few years, but the additional contribution yield from those checks has encouraged the authorities to instigate an annual check and so employers can now expect to see a considerable amount of activity on this front. Confusingly for employers of expatriates who are not covered by the UK NIC scheme, the RTI instructions require the NI fields of the FPS to be left completely blank: no earnings for NIC purposes, no NINO, no table letter should be reported. The use of Table X is likely to result in a letter or, occasionally, an educational visit.

25.48 Because of this increased activity, employers should be aware of when it is in order to use Category X. The following uses will be accepted by employer compliance officers although they may well investigate the matter before giving approval:

- The employee is under age 16 at the time the payment of earnings is made. Employers should ensure that they have a record of when the employee reaches 16 so that liability begins with the correct payment (the FPS requires a date of birth to be reported in every case).

- The earnings are below the relevant earnings limit. Care needs to be taken to ensure that the earnings fall below the lower earnings limit in each earnings period. Unless a company director (or other employee in respect of whom an annual earnings period has been imposed by a direction) is involved it is wrong to look at the total earnings at the end of the year and compare the amount paid with the annual limits. Another common mistake is the assumption that if an employee is given a weekly or monthly payment which is equal to the appropriate lower earnings limit then no NIC entries are required. This is incorrect because benefit entitlement starts at the lower earnings limit itself rather than at a penny over it. This mistake is common where a spouse helps out in the family business and the wage/salary payments are made to make use of tax allowances.

- The only payment being made is a pension. Employer compliance officers are wary of payments made in the form of pensions and are likely to want to satisfy themselves that the pension is genuine and not some other payment wrongly described: in family businesses, it is easy for controlling directors to cause the company to pay a pension instead of a salary once they reach retirement age, which has the advantage of attracting no NICs of any kind. Special attention will also be paid where there are contributions into or benefits from unapproved pension arrangements, in light of the Supreme Court decision in *Forde & McHugh Ltd v Revenue and Customs Comrs* [2014] UKSC 14 and the introduction in 2011 of the disguised remuneration rules.

25.49 As noted above, expatriates bring complexity to payroll, and they used to be a source of many Table X entries on payroll, but that has changed under RTI, because those employees outside the UK NIC regime should have blank NIC fields on their FPSs:

- The employee is working temporarily in the UK and is paying contributions to another country's social security scheme. All will be well if the employee has come from a treaty or EC/EEA country and holds the appropriate certificate of coverage. Employers should check every so often to ensure that certificates have not expired and that the employment details quoted on the certificate have not changed in any material way. Table X was used pre-RTI but now should no longer be used.

- The employee has been sent from a non-treaty country by his overseas employer to work temporarily in the UK. In such instances there is no contribution liability for the first 52 complete calendar weeks in the UK. To avoid difficulties employers should ensure that they have a workable system whereby they identify when the contribution liability begins.

- The employee has been sent to a treaty country in continuation of a UK employment and the appropriate certificate of coverage issued by the UK authorities has expired. If any earnings were still paid in the UK no contribution liability would arise (because in most cases the posted worker would fall under the host country's social security laws to the exclusion of UK law).

- The employee is working abroad for a UK employer in a non-treaty country and has been out of the UK for more than 52 weeks (note that the issue and application of an NT PAYE code – possibly even on departure in a split year – and the cessation of UK NIC liability – possibly a year later – will be at different dates).

25.50 Whilst the above circumstances are perfectly acceptable to HMRC, many employers continue to use Category X in other situations and so are of interest to an employer compliance officer when the matter finally comes up for investigation. The following are the more common examples of where employers incorrectly use Category X:

- no entries are made where earnings are below the earnings threshold, even though they exceed the lower earnings limit;

- a non-working director, etc has some earnings in the form of fees or bonuses which reach or exceed the relevant limit;

- an employee from a non-treaty country has been in the UK for more than the exempt first 52 weeks;

- an employee from a treaty country holds a certificate of coverage which is either invalid or out of date;

25.51 *National Insurance aspects*

- the earnings are thought to be exempt from NIC liability, eg paid via some avoidance scheme which is flawed. This is an area almost certain to provoke an investigation because officials believe that few avoidance schemes now work on account of the many changes to the exemptions in the Contributions Regulations and HMRC's claimed successes in defeating 80% of schemes before the courts and tribunals.

25.51 Employers should not be surprised to hear that when an employer compliance officer investigates matters and finds something amiss he will not restrict his actions to recovery of outstanding contributions to the year in question. In fact, employer compliance officers are likely to try to collect arrears for as far back as the particular circumstances have existed.

25.52 Since the merger in 1999, requests for more than six years' arrears are now almost unheard of, but should still be resisted where they occur. The time limit for NIC under the *Limitation Act 1980* remains at six years (except in Scotland, where a different law applies – see the *Prescription and Limitation (Scotland) Act 1984*) and is not affected by the April 2010 changes to various tax time limits (including PAYE).

25.53 Although HMRC cannot be expected to issue any guidance on this matter, it would be reasonable for it to restrict the cases it selects for investigation. There will always be times when the Category X notation is quite correct and allowance will have to be made for this. Employer compliance officers will not want to waste time investigating matters which are unlikely to result in additional contributions yield.

25.54 For instance, it is unlikely that employer compliance officers would want to look at cases where an employee is out of the UK or has been out of the country for part of the year. They are also unlikely to be very keen spending time looking at cases where the employee is dead or where it is likely that the payment could be some sort of occupational pension and the introduction of an internal age limit is probable, with employer compliance officers not looking at cases where the employee is, say, 55 or over. A P14 with Category X contributions shown along with some other category of contributions would also have been less likely to be examined on the reasoning that if an employer has shown at least one category letter in addition to Category X then he would seem to know that there are different table letters and might be expected to understand why they were different.

Investigation of Category X cases now features strongly in an employer compliance officer's regular routine work and any irregularities found in this area may well provoke a more detailed investigation.

Complaints from employees

25.55 From time to time complaints are received from employees alleging that:

- contributions are being deducted but not sent on to HMRC;
- too much is being deducted as employee contributions;
- the employee has to pay the employer's share;
- the individual is being made to work on a self-employed basis;
- the individual is not being paid the national minimum wage (NMW).

25.56 Whilst a single complaint will not be ignored it may not generate any activity other than a phone call or a letter to the employer, but it is reasonable to assume that a series of complaints will result in some sort of investigation. Such matters should never be taken lightly and steps should be taken to allay employee fears. Indeed, HMRC now actively solicits calls from people who have information relating to businesses or individuals that are not paying tax and/or National Insurance on the Tax Evasion Hotline 0800 788 887 or online at www.gov.uk/report-an-unregistered-trader-or-business.

Separate staff in HMRC deal with all NMW matters. However, these employees are now allowed freely to exchange information with colleagues in other sections of the organisation.

Regional initiatives

25.57 It is entirely up to regional HMRC managers to decide whether they want to set up any local investigations, though with a scarcity of resources and various national initiatives these are now rare.

Nonetheless, as an example, a specific industry may be based in a particular area and bad habits creep in, particularly where one employer obtains a commercial advantage and others follow. It is not uncommon for employer compliance officers to be sent in to tidy up matters. It is also quite common for personal prejudices to creep in and perhaps public houses, market traders and mini-cab drivers are singled out for investigation. More often than not the purpose behind a local initiative is to check that employees at a specific location are not working and claiming benefits at the same time. If employees at a particular location are prone to defraud the DWP, then some thought will be given to whether the employer has been in collusion with the employee. Now that Universal Credit (UC) is beginning to replace certain other benefits, and earnings data from FPSs are being passed daily to the DWP for UC purposes, there are already reports of employers being called with questions about

25.58 *National Insurance aspects*

disputed FPS figures that have come to light as a result of a UC claim, and of employees rapidly withdrawing UC claims once they realise that the DWP already knows exactly what they have earned in the relevant period. Often a regional initiative will be the result of a national decision to create a task force to test compliance in a particular sector, such as restaurants.

National programme

25.58 It has long been recognised that employers with operations at many locations create problems for employer compliance officers. At one time, employer compliance officers usually had to remain in their specific geographical area and so the larger employers often slipped through the net. Nowadays teams of employer compliance officers from the Customer Compliance Directorate will assume responsibility for visiting all the branches irrespective of where they are located.

25.59 Specific industries or employment groups will sometimes be targeted for some form of investigation and, when that happens, control will be exercised from some central point to ensure continuity of action and equity of treatment.

Routine visits

25.60 Employer compliance officers used to have a purely theoretical and underlying objective to visit every employer via a five-year rolling programme but, given the more sophisticated targeting arrangements now in place along with the quest for additional contributions combined with significant staff reductions, this aspiration has inevitably fallen by the wayside, as work is focused on problems and employers already identified by statistics from the KAI team.

25.61 Employer compliance teams, however, will still be responsible for policing their own geographical area and can decide to make a visit whenever they deem it to be necessary. A surprise visit (usually with the approval of a tribunal, unless an urgent anti-fraud step is required) especially where the findings are publicised, will often have the result of making many others fall into line and so the value of such visits should never be underestimated and equally, small employers should never assume that they are exempt from investigation. If they are found to have evaded over £25,000 by deliberate suppression or misreporting of information, they may now be 'named and shamed' on HMRC's website.

Failing to reply to correspondence

25.62 Most of the sections that make up HMRC will have to write to employers from time to time. The most common reason for them getting in touch is that their records are not complete enough to allow a benefit claim to be decided (HMRC at NIC&EO operates the NPS computer – formerly known as NIRS2 – on behalf of both itself and DWP).

25.63 Because a benefit claim is involved there is a fair degree of urgency, and if there is a delay in replying, the papers are likely to be referred to an employer compliance officer to visit and collect what is needed. Such visits might then not be restricted to collecting purely what is needed, and a full check of the other National Insurance and perhaps tax issues may well be carried out. To avoid such an investigation is simple: reply quickly, but if that is not possible then tell the writer accordingly and indicate when a reply will be sent.

Large employers

25.64 As already mentioned above, some larger employers were historically left alone simply because of the effort needed to carry out an investigation coupled with the fact that a number of different locations might be involved. Sometimes businesses were completely missed because local offices dealt only with small employers while national teams dealt with those having at least 1,000 employees, and those between the two target populations were nobody's responsibility. The former Contributions Agency worked out that the bigger the employer the bigger the potential yield and so matters changed. Special teams of inspectors began to work together to investigate these larger employers.

25.65 This approach continued after the 1999 merger, these special teams being subsumed at first into what was the Large Business Office and, after the 2005 merger with the former HM Customs and Excise, the Large Business Service (later renamed simply 'HMRC Large Business') dealing with all indirect taxes as well. The name of the game is additional contributions and as long as they are likely to be collected an investigation will continue. A large employer is generally one who has at least 1,000 employees either at a single location or spread all over the country. The employer compliance officers looking after the larger employers also have some responsibility for investigating the many structured National Insurance contribution avoidance schemes, irrespective of the size of the employer, although the response will be coordinated centrally in the Counter-Avoidance Directorate. Large employers within the scope of Large Business will have a dedicated customer relationship manager (CRM) who should be the first point of contact for employers who have queries about their NIC arrangements and any enquiries, although the CRM in question may not be NIC-trained and may therefore have to act merely

25.66 *National Insurance aspects*

as a coordinator and facilitator of the relationship between the employer and HMRC.

Employers with an international exposure

25.66 HMRC believes that employers who send employees abroad are significantly underpaying their NICs and so in-depth investigations are likely to be carried out again by employer compliance officers from Large Business.

25.67 It is usually a simple task to identify the relevant employers because (in the case of many countries) the employer needs to hold a certificate confirming the contribution position and they are only issued by a central point at NIC&EO in Newcastle. Income tax issues for expatriates are centred in Chapel Wharf in Manchester.

25.68 Employer compliance officers will want to satisfy themselves that where UK certificates are held contributions have been paid on the full remuneration package, with particular emphasis placed on the various allowances linked to employment abroad, payments made at the foreign location and the local income tax position.

25.69 In summer 2003, a revised approach to handling enquiries in relation to inbound expatriates was outlined. HMRC recognises that enquiries are often easier if it has established a working relationship with the relevant in-house tax department or professional advisers. Given the complex issues that are usually involved, there will be situations where the apparent Exchequer risk means that HMRC may need to pursue enquiries that will have substantial compliance costs for the employer.

25.70 HMRC recognises, however, that:

- such enquiries often relate to individuals not familiar with the UK tax and NIC system;
- directors and employees on tax-equalised packages can sometimes fail to understand the need for the UK tax authorities to make detailed enquiries into their financial affairs;
- there can be considerable compliance costs in retrieving documentation, especially from overseas.

25.71 HMRC has stated that it is aware of these factors when handling enquiries, and that it is increasingly undertaken by specialist units, for example suspected cases of serious fraud and evasion are handled by the Fraud Investigations teams (until recently known as 'Specialist Investigations' and before that as the Special Compliance Office. Certain aspects relating to expatriates may be referred to specialist offices such as the Non-Residents teams, which deal with residence and domicile issues, principally out of offices in Longbenton (NIC), Salford or Bootle (tax) and Cardiff (seafarers/mariners).

25.72 With the Brexit proposals we may see the current position over A1 certificates within EEA countries change. The position is unclear, as is whether any change will be in place at the time Brexit occurs. This could create an added complexity for employers which would give the opportunity for error.

Unlucky

25.73 Some employers may not have been selected for a visit but, nevertheless, an employer compliance officer writes to notify the employer that a compliance visit is planned. While most visits are initiated on the basis of computer analysis that has identified potential problems, a small percentage of cases is selected at random, so that no employer can ever feel totally safe from scrutiny.

HMRC VISITS

Purpose of visit

25.74 Protecting the National Insurance Fund is the primary purpose of the NIC element of any visit but another very important purpose is ensuring that employees' state benefit rights are fully maintained by confirming that the correct amount of NIC has been paid. Other reasons for a visit are to identify instances where too little or too much NIC has been paid and to correct any errors, and to check that the statutory payments are being correctly and timeously paid out to employees when due.

25.75 For several years, starting in 2011, HMRC also ran a programme of 'business record checks', including payroll records, as it suspected that some employers were under-declaring income and payments and hiding the fraud behind poor record-keeping. As many as 60% of small businesses were thought to have inadequate records, but a review of the programme found that the number was only 12%, so the process was changed to a telephone interview rather than a visit. By October 2014, 29,000 businesses had been reviewed and not a single penalty had been imposed, and HMRC announced after a review in 2015 that the business record check programme was to be closed down. Instead, it was announced in late 2015, businesses would be forced within a few years to make quarterly returns online, which would require them to keep computerised records on a timely basis. This became part of the proposals for Making Tax Digital which are still out for further consultation at the time of writing.

25.76 *National Insurance aspects*

Timing of visit

25.76 Employer compliance officers will not want to visit too often, although where serious errors have been found or significant NICs collected, check visits will be made more often because the risk of error has been flagged. Following the 1999 merger of the former Inland Revenue and the former Contributions Agency all inspection visits dealt with both tax and NIC (including the related statutory payments issues) at the same time.

25.77 This continued to be the case following the subsequent 2005 merger between HM Customs and Excise and the Inland Revenue. For larger employers, there will be a combined corporation tax, VAT and PAYE/NIC review, with the CRM acting as 'ringmaster' for the various HMRC compliance teams involved.

Notification of visit

25.78 It is extremely rare these days for employer compliance officers to make unannounced visits, as these are generally reserved for cases of suspected fraud where advance notice of a visit might lead to evidence being destroyed. HMRC also generally needs permission from a tribunal (without the business's involvement or knowledge) before carrying out an unannounced visit. Employers are instead very likely to receive a telephone call or letter at least two weeks in advance.

25.79 Employers should not hesitate to seek to delay or defer a visit if there are work pressures caused by, for example, being at or near the end of the financial or trading year or because of staff shortages. However, the authorities are aware that sometimes requests for later dates are attempts to avoid a visit at all costs. Deliberately attempting to avoid being audited is unlikely to lead to the inspection being cancelled.

Following wider tax changes effective from 1 April 2009, visits with less than seven days' notice and unannounced visits will have been approved beforehand by a specially trained HMRC officer. CH25500 makes it clear that nearly all visits under the powers in *FA 2008, Sch 36* will be pre-arranged.

25.80 In larger employers, employer compliance officers may want to make a preliminary visit to explain how they see the inspection progressing whilst at the same time obtaining some background information such as who will be able to deal with the queries, the form in which the various records are kept and for how long the records are held and whether there is suitable accommodation for them to use.

25.81 At that preliminary meeting the employer is likely to find out how many employer compliance officers and support staff will be involved in the inspection, how long it is likely to take and any specific areas in which the employer compliance officers are interested.

25.82 The visiting officer will generally have used an internal risk assessment report from the KAI team to identify the areas of interest. KAI will have reviewed all data held about the employer and will have a picture of its compliance record as an employer.

Length of visit

25.83 It is virtually impossible to estimate in advance just how long an inspection will take and they will range from an hour to several weeks. It is safe to say that where there are, say, at least 1,000 employees the inspection will last for at least two weeks.

25.84 It may well be that employer compliance officers are not on the premises for a continuous period but will simply check an aspect at a time, go away and put together their findings and then return and check something else. This is especially the case where there are status or IR35 aspects to the case, as the officers will need to interview other parties outside the organisation.

Place of visit

25.85 Employer compliance officers will generally want to carry out their inspection at the employer's place of business and if the records are not readily available there they are likely to ask for the records to be brought to the place of business. Sometimes employer compliance officers can be persuaded to visit another location such as a payroll bureau or an accountant but that is the exception rather than the rule. The Contributions Regulations 2001, Sch 4, para 26 used to provide NIC-specific inspection powers and required the records to be made available at the employer's principal office unless otherwise arranged, but that was superseded by the powers and record-keeping rules in *FA 2008, Schs 36* and *37*.

Employer compliance officers will, however, want to visit other work locations to check paperwork held locally and maybe even to count the number of heads to make sure that they are all on the payroll.

Preparation for the visit

25.86 There is a lot an employer can do beforehand to make sure that the inspection runs smoothly. He should, for example, make sure that all the records requested by the employer compliance officer are readily available and that

25.87 *National Insurance aspects*

someone with knowledge of the employer's system and procedures is available to deal with any queries. That person should be senior enough to be able to answer queries without needing to refer matters elsewhere. HMRC staff are not permitted to operate an employer's computer system, even if the employer gives permission, because of the risk of corruption to the employer's data. The employer is expected to make someone available to extract information from the computer on request.

25.87 An employer should also ensure that accommodation is made available for the employer compliance officers and it would be courteous to ensure that the room is lockable, that there is access to a telephone and that there are tea, coffee and toilet facilities.

Commencement of the visit

25.88 At the beginning of the visit the employer compliance officer(s) should make the necessary introductions and explain the process of conducting the examination of the records. This is the time for both the employer compliance officer and the employer to ask any questions and also to ensure that all the required records (listed below) are available. The employer compliance officer should also establish who should be contacted in the event of queries and questions.

25.89 During the course of the inspection the records of all employees and directors may be checked to ensure that contributions (including Class 1A, Class 1B and, in the case of unincorporated businesses, Class 2) are being correctly assessed and paid and also that SSP, SMP, SPP, SAP and SShPP are being paid to employees who qualify and that only the correct recoveries are being made from the employer's monthly (or quarterly) remittances. While they will start with the current year they will usually check back into the preceding year and earlier years if they feel it is necessary.

Records to be made available

25.90 Employer compliance officers need to be able to examine any of the employer's records that could involve a liability for National Insurance contributions. It should be noted that HMRC officers have the power to inspect, but no power to search for information: they must ask the employer for any information they reasonably need and can then examine it. The list of documents that may be required for examination for NIC purposes is extensive and, while not exhaustive, includes:

- *Accident book*: Where there is a legal requirement to keep such a book, employer compliance officers may want to ensure that it is held and that

National Insurance aspects **25.90**

it is being correctly completed (there is unlikely to be any NIC yield, so such requests are now rare).

- *Bank statements*: Employer compliance officers will want to identify payments which do not go through the payroll and which could attract an NIC liability.
- *Cash book*: Employer compliance officers will want to confirm that payments subject to NIC have been transferred to the payroll and have been correctly treated.
- *Certificates of deferment*: The visiting officers will want to ensure that these certificates are actually held.
- *Certificates of age exception*: Employer compliance officers will want to ensure that these certificates are valid and have been correctly used, although they are in fact not required if the employer has some other proof of the employee's date of birth.
- *Certificates of election for married women paying reduced rate National Insurance*: Again employer compliance officers will want to ensure that these certificates continue to be valid.
- *Cheque stubs*: Employer compliance officers will want to identify payments that should have gone through the payroll for NIC purposes.
- *Company accounts*: Employer compliance officers will want to examine these as there are various clues to the NIC position. For example, does the employer NIC bill broadly equal 13.8% of the total employee remuneration shown in the accounts, after allowing for each employee's secondary threshold and the employment allowance, and has all the remuneration paid to directors been considered for NIC purposes?
- *Contracting-out certificate*: Is this valid and has the employer correctly identified those employees covered by the contracting-out arrangements?
- *Deduction working sheets (P11s)*: Very few employers will use the standard P11s but they will have equivalent documentation (normally as part of a payroll software package, following the introduction of RTI) and employer compliance officers will check a number of calculations to ensure that the correct NIC figures have been reached, often downloading electronic records onto their own computerised audit program for further analysis work off the premises.
- *Sickness absence records*: Employer compliance officers used to look to see if employers had correctly dealt with sickness absences and in the main this would be to ensure that employees had received the equivalent of SSP, but since SSP is now irrecoverable this check may be skipped.

25.91 *National Insurance aspects*

- *Maternity absence records*: Employer compliance officers will want to check a few SMP calculations and confirm that employers are holding the correct evidence of pregnancy.

- *Paternity pay, shared parental pay and adoption pay records*: Employer compliance officers will look to see if employers have correctly dealt with such absences and in the main this will be to ensure that employees have received the correct payments and the employer holds the appropriate certification from the employee(s) in question.

- *Minute book*: This is where employer compliance officers will identify additional payments to company directors and senior executives (this may include the awarding of shares, share options and other similar securities).

- *P30BC paying-in book/P32 (or equivalent electronic records)*: Employer compliance officers used to want to ensure that monies had been paid over to HMRC when due, but this is now a matter that the RTI system should identify. It is now much more likely that officers will check that the date of payment of earnings reported on an FPS tallies with the date of payment in the employer's bank records.

- *Petty cash book*: Again, officers will be looking to identify payments that should have gone through payroll for NIC purposes.

- *Petty cash vouchers*: This is another area where the officers will be looking for payments liable for NIC which have not gone through the payroll arrangements.

- *Wage book/payroll*: This is where employer compliance officers will pay close attention and they will take a sample of entries to ensure that NIC liabilities have been fully met and that the correct reporting mechanisms are in place.

- *Dispensation*: When looking at periods before 6 April 2016, officers will want to ensure that where NIC liabilities have not been met that this is because the terms of a dispensation granted by HMRC have been fully complied with. In appropriate cases HMRC can, and will, withdraw dispensations retrospectively if the terms on which they were issued have ceased to apply or if the circumstances were misrepresented in the original application. It should be noted that, despite the abolition of dispensations in April 2016, HMRC retains the power to withdraw old dispensations retrospectively.

25.91 When checking the above documentation employer compliance officers will pay close attention to the following aspects:

- *Basic pay*: They will want to ensure that NICs have been paid on the full amount and that the correct contribution category letter and earnings period have been used.

- *Bonuses*: Employer compliance officers will want to ensure that these have been added to the basic pay in the correct earnings period and that NICs have been assessed on the total. Employer compliance officers will pay very close attention to any bonus arrangements that have avoided NIC liabilities (eg where employers pay large bonuses at quarterly intervals in order to take some of the earnings above the UEL for the employees concerned).

- *Company cars, fuel expenses and other benefits in kind*: Officers are likely to carry out an in-depth examination of Class 1A contribution liabilities. They will also look to identify fuel used for private motoring and to ensure that all NIC liabilities are met. They will also look at mileage rates and allowances paid by employers to ensure that there is no profit element (ie an excess over the authorised mileage rate, or payments for private mileage), as well as considering all other benefits in depth.

- *Other payments in kind*: The officers will want to satisfy themselves that payments in kind are genuine and that if they have not been subjected to NIC liabilities such payments fall within the general Class 1 NIC exclusion provisions and, where appropriate, Class 1A is accounted for nonetheless.

- *Casual and part-time workers*: They will want to ensure that they go through the payroll, even when earnings do not reach the NIC lower earnings limit so that no NICs are due, and that National Insurance numbers (NINOs) are held.

- *Directors*: Employer compliance officers will want to identify all individuals who fall within the definition of a company director for NIC purposes and verify that an annual earnings period (or pro-rata in the year of appointment) has been used. They will also look closely at any arrangements that are an attempt to avoid NIC liabilities.

- *Employees with pension scheme contracted-out number (including directors)*: Employer compliance officers will want to confirm for periods up to 5 April 2016 that the correct category letter has been used and that the scheme numbers go on the full payment submission or, prior to the introduction of RTI, end-of-year returns (P35 only for a salary-related scheme and, prior to 6 April 2012, both the P35 and all affected P14s in the case of a money purchase occupational scheme).

- *Expenses payments*: This is an area where employer compliance officers will pay very close attention and they will be seeking to identify profit elements within payments as well as entirely non-business payments so that NIC liabilities can be assessed. They will look closely at what expenses employees are allowed to claim and the steps that employers have put in place for authorising such expenses.

25.92 National Insurance aspects

- *Fees/commissions*: Employer compliance officers will want to make sure that such payments are added to the basic salary in the correct earnings period and that full NIC liabilities are met.
- *Overtime*: Employer compliance officers will again check that this has been added to basic pay.
- *Self-employed workers*: This is always an area which excites employer compliance officers simply because of the likely additional NIC yield if the individuals are in fact employees. They will look closely at the employment arrangements and in particular at any supervision, control or direction that is evident.
- *Workers to whom the Categorisation of Earners Regulations apply*: This may apply, inter alia, where self-employed workers are engaged through an agency. or prior to 6 April 2012 as teachers, lecturers or instructors, or prior to 6 April 2014 as entertainers.
- *Workers exempt from payment of National Insurance/paying reduced rate National Insurance/not liable to pay National Insurance*: Employer compliance officers will be looking for documentation to support the NIC position. This may involve employers in having to provide certificates of reduced rate authority, deferment certificates, age exception certificates and certificates of coverage issued by foreign social security authorities.
- *Shares and other securities, including options*: Employer compliance officers will examine all arrangements carefully including those in relation to tax-advantaged (formerly known as 'approved') schemes where transactions outside normal rules may give rise to liability.

25.92 More generally, the officers will also want to ensure that none of the business activities are such that either the personal service companies ('IR35') or managed service companies provisions are applicable. In the case of employment agencies and 'umbrella' employers, particular care will be devoted to checking the employment contracts and travel expense payments, which frequently give rise to disputes, especially where some kind of salary sacrifice arrangement for expenses has been implemented. Following the introduction of the block on claiming tax and NIC relief for commuting expenses for intermediary workers from 6 April 2016, and the block from the same date on the exemption of ordinary travel expenses if paid under a salary sacrifice arrangement, this is an area that is likely to receive close scrutiny for the next few years.

RECORD KEEPING

25.93 The legislation requires employers to keep records for the current tax year and the three previous years. It is likely that employer compliance officers will restrict their initial action to the current year and the last closed tax year. If errors are found they will go back further. If employers have records going back more than three years employer compliance officers are likely to look at the last four years, and if any careless errors are identified, the last six years. It is arguable, however, that if an employer only holds records for the three years the wording of the social security legislation precludes an employer compliance officer from going back any further simply because he would be unable to identify a named employee who received a payment of earnings on a specific date. However, in practice, employer compliance officers, after finding a careless error, will normally seek six years' arrears in all cases. It should be noted that whilst tax arrears are, at first instance, restricted to the collection of only four years' arrears with effect from April 2010, the pre-existing six-year limit under the relevant *Limitation Act 1980* is still applicable for NIC (except in Scotland).

25.94 It is understood that the government was considering a review of the Limitation Acts generally and no changes to National Insurance legislation have been made pending this. It remains unclear whether the current government will proceed with the review that was planned or in what timescale, given that many justice matters are now devolved.

25.95 It is the employer's responsibility to make sure that the relevant records are made available to employer compliance officers. If the records are going to take a time to put together or to collect from different locations then employer compliance officers are usually agreeable to delay the inspection for a short time.

25.96 Employers who do not make the relevant records available to the officers within a reasonable time may find that the employer compliance officer will issue formal information notices and, if the information is not forthcoming, take proceedings.

25.97 It is always open to an employer compliance officer to take records away from the business premises but he will generally return them as quickly as possible. If an employer needs the records for his business purposes then the employer compliance officer will arrange for copies to be supplied to him.

ERRORS AND OMISSIONS

25.98 One of the main purposes of an inspection is to ensure that employers are not making errors. Yet with such a complicated scheme to operate it is inevitable that employers will make mistakes. The opportunities to get it wrong are wide and varied – some of the common areas include:
- accepting a person as being self-employed when the facts do not support the decision;

25.99 *National Insurance aspects*

- treating casual workers paid in cash as being irrelevant to the payroll (while such a worker may earn below the LEL, it is likely in many cases that there is a PAYE deduction due at basic rate);
- omitting to account for Class 1 contributions where self-employed workers are engaged to whom the Categorisation of Earners Regulations apply;
- using the wrong year's NI tables, whether hard-copy tables or through not having updated, or incorrectly updated, software either at all or on time;
- having incomplete identity details, usually the lack of NI numbers;
- deducting reduced rate contributions without holding the appropriate certificate;
- continuing to deduct reduced rate contributions when a woman has been divorced;
- for periods before 6 April 2016, continuing to pay contracted-out rates (employer and employee) after the contracting-out certificate had been withdrawn and/or (prior to 6 April 2012) paying employers contracted-out contributions as if the pension scheme was salary related when it was in fact money purchase;
- directors' annual earnings periods;
- errors with statutory payments;
- failing to account for employees' contributions without the required proof of age exception or failing to account for any National Insurance contributions without the appropriate international coverage certification;
- treating a contractual payment in lieu of notice as compensation rather than earnings;
- applying the 0% rate of employer NICs to workers who have passed their twenty-first birthday or apprentices who have passed their twenty-fifth birthday;
- deducting employment allowance when it is not due or has already been claimed by an associated employer; or
- simply failing to treat as 'earnings' an item that is earnings in the opinion of HMRC.

25.99 Using the wrong year's NI tables or having incomplete identity details – at least – caused PAYE schemes filed electronically for 2005/06 onwards to be immediately rejected upon submission. Paper, etc returns – where used in the past – containing such errors were also returned in due course for correction by the employer. In either situation, the P35 was not then treated as having been submitted until the errors were successfully corrected.

25.100 The introduction of RTI (applying to almost all employers from 2013/14 onwards) has removed the need to file employer annual returns. Under RTI, identity details were checked as part of the payroll alignment process when the payroll was switched to RTI reporting, and discrepancies between details held by the employer and by HMRC should have been investigated. An FPS for a new employee is now checked on submission against the existence of an employee record on the NPS database. Indeed, this automatic alignment check resulted in severe problems in the first few years of RTI operation, as minor differences between the standing data on the FPS and the equivalent data already on HMRC's system led to the automated creation of numerous duplicate records, as the computer had been programmed to assume that the FPS was for a different employee. Even something as simple as adding a '0' to the beginning of an employee payroll ID could cause the problem. The problems with duplicate tax codes (usually showing different values, because at least one would be issued for an assumed second employment) and alleged non-submission of FPSs for the phantom employees led HMRC to defer the introduction of automatic RTI penalties to 2016 at the earliest, and then until 2017 at the earliest. HMRC does not publicise the numbers of duplicate records its systems hold, but it is known to have taken steps to re-programme its systems during 2015/16 in an attempt to avoid the creation of further duplicates and save a lot of effort in resolving unnecessary discrepancies.

25.101 Very few employers make mistakes deliberately. During visits, employer compliance officers try to ensure that employers both understand and can operate the system. Where errors are found then the employer compliance officer will draw it to the employer's attention with guidance as to how the position should be rectified and how it should be avoided in future. Where the error results in an overpayment or underpayment of NIC then the employer compliance officer will again give guidance as to how this should be rectified. Employers will often now be directed towards educational material on HMRC's website and even on YouTube.

25.102 In simple terms, if the error is in the current tax year then an adjustment can be made, but if it is in a closed tax year then either a refund application can be made, or the employer compliance officer will issue a demand for arrears.

INSPECTION REPORT

25.103 At the end of the inspection, the employer compliance officer will explain, in some detail, what has been discovered, answer questions, try to

25.104 *National Insurance aspects*

ensure that the employer (and staff) will be able to deal with problems in the future and know who to contact when faced with difficulties. Afterwards the employer will usually receive a written report of some kind, and will definitely do so, along with calculations, if arrears of NIC (and/or tax) are being demanded. It could merely be a letter or it could be a much more formal document, such as a notice under *SSCTFA 1999, s 8* (usually alongside a determination made under PAYE Regulations 2003, Reg 80). Where the officer has discovered the use of a NIC avoidance scheme, the issue of the s 8 notice and the subsequent appeal made by the employer may also lead to the issue of an accelerated payment notice, provide the conditions are fulfilled (although the APN will be handled by a different team in Counter-Avoidance, so there will inevitably be a delay between the conclusion of the inspection, the issue of assessments, the appeals and the issue of the APNs).

25.104 Whatever is issued will highlight the officer's findings and contain his recommendations to improve the record keeping. What employers will really be interested in is the usual demand for NIC arrears. Such demands will almost certainly accompany the inspection report with a request for payment. It is likely that some interest charge will also be levied, and in most cases penalties too (the NIC regulations adopted the *FA 2007, Sch 24* penalty regime for inaccuracies). It is up to employers to pay over what is due or, if they consider that there is no liability, to set out in writing why they believe that is the case. This is often when advisers become involved and they will take the matter forward on behalf of the employer. Generally speaking, the bigger the employer the more likely it is that employer compliance officers will want to have a formal meeting at the end of the inspection to discuss all the findings.

25.105 It should not be overlooked that there remain a number of differences between the National Insurance and tax regimes. Compliance officers tend to know about those instances where National Insurance arises, but not tax, but in other cases have been known to proclaim, incorrectly in some cases, that the tax and National Insurance treatment is identical. Differences may be as to actual existence of liability, timing, or manner of reporting. Further, it should be appreciated that deep technical expertise within HMRC on National Insurance matters is concentrated in a group of technical advisers, so differences of opinion on how the law works will usually have to be referred to one of this team.

25.106 When assessing any arrears, the employer compliance officers will also advise the employer of the implications of interest charges on contributions (and tax) that have not been paid. Interest on Class 1 used to run only from 19 April (22 April where the payment was made electronically) in the tax year following that in which the NICs were due, but interest began to be charged monthly from April 2014, ie from the normal remittance date for a month's deductions.

National Insurance aspects **25.109**

Interest on Class 1A NICs runs from 19 July after the end of the year in which the benefit was provided (again, from 22 July for e-payers), and on Class 1B it runs from 19 (or 22) October. Penalties may also be assessed where payments were late in-year, on a sliding scale according to how many late payments were made. Penalties for inaccuracies are assessed in the same way as those applied to inaccuracies in tax returns, their level dependent on whether the error was disclosed voluntarily or found by HMRC ('prompted' or 'unprompted'), and whether the error was a simple mistake, a careless inaccuracy, a deliberate inaccuracy or a deliberate inaccuracy that was concealed. Discounts will be applied, as for income tax, for 'telling, helping and showing' HMRC where the errors are and how much is owed, and penalties for careless errors may, as for income tax, be suspended subject to conditions. See further below.

FUTURE VISITS

25.107 When the employer compliance officer decides to make a further visit will depend greatly on what he finds at the inspection. If there is little of concern then it is likely to be five years or more before he returns. If, however, there are a large number of errors or significant NIC due then he may very well make a check visit within 12 months or so.

OFFENCES AND PENALTIES

Background

25.108 New penalties came into effect in respect of underpayments associated with incorrect returns in the case of return periods commencing on and after 1 April 2008 where the return was lodged on and after 1 April 2009: see **25.136–25.139** and **25.149–25.150**. Further penalties for payroll errors under RTI have also been legislated, but they are currently not automatic because HMRC's data are not yet reliable enough as a basis. Instead, HMRC will apply them on a 'risk-assessed basis', ie, when employers have made persistent errors or persistent late returns, and when they have been caught out and the case has been handled by an HMRC officer rather than just the HMRC computer.

False information, delays and obstruction

25.109 The criminal penalties which once applied have been dealt with as civil offences since 1 April 1999, following the transfer of responsibility from the former Contributions Agency to what was then the Inland Revenue and which merged with HM Customs and Excise in April 2005 to become HMRC. Outright fraud may still be dealt with under the common law offence of

25.110 *National Insurance aspects*

cheat. Such cases are very rare, but HMRC has committed itself to increasing significantly the number of prosecutions for tax fraud that it instigates, and where wages are suppressed or overstated there will usually be an NIC angle to the case. HMRC's annual report for 2015/16 noted 880 prosecutions for tax-related offences, although no breakdown was provided and it is likely that a large majority were for customs and excise offences, although a small number will have involved fraudulent claims for tax and NIC relief (eg, in respect of home-to-work travel expenses paid for non-qualifying journeys on an organised and persistent basis).

Contravention of regulations

25.110 The previous criminal offences under *SSAA 1992, s 113* were replaced with effect from 6 April 1999 by new *s 113*, inserted by the *Social Security Act 1998, s 60*. This provides for regulations to be made setting out a scheme of civil penalties. It should be noted that, in the case of Class 1 NICs, it is the employer who is guilty of an offence, even if he delegated his duties of compliance to another (*Godman v Crofton* [1913] 110 LT 387).

25.111 There is an extensive scheme of penalties applying to employers' failures in relation to SSP, SMP, SPP, SShPP and SAP (*SSAA 1992, ss 113A, 113B; Employment Act 2002, ss 11, 12, Sch 1*). These include:

- failure to produce documents or records or to provide information: up to £300, and for continuing failure a possible penalty of up to £60 per day;
- failing to maintain records: up to £3,000;
- repeated failure to make payments to employees: up to £3,000;
- incorrect payments due to fraud or neglect: up to £3,000;
- excessive advance funding by reason of fraud or neglect: up to £3,000.

These latter penalties will also be reformed in due course, but did not change in April 2009 (see **25.108**) and, as yet, have not changed subsequently.

Offences relating to contributions

25.112 If an employer deducts or tries to deduct all or part of the employer's Class 1 secondary liability from the employee's pay he is guilty of an offence unless the transfer of liability is expressly permitted, such as in the case of elections to transfer in respect of employment-related securities (*SSCBA 1992, Sch 1, paras 3A, 3B* and SI 2001/1004, Sch 4, para 6(2), (3)). Refusing to employ a worker directly but offering him a contract via his own personal service company has the same effect – the employee funds the employer contributions due – but is not (yet?) an offence.

25.113 The *Social Security Act 1998* introduced a new *criminal* offence of fraudulent evasion and being knowingly involved in fraudulent evasion of contributions. The offence is brought to trial summarily or on indictment. When tried summarily the maximum fine is expressed as being at level 5 on the standard scale as stated in the *Criminal Justice Act 1982, s 37(2)*. For offences committed from 12 March 2015, as a result of a change to the top of the standard scale brought about under the *Legal Aid, Sentencing and Punishment of Offenders Act 2012, s 85*, the maximum fine is now technically unlimited, whereas it used to be capped at £5,000). When tried on indictment the maximum penalty is seven years' imprisonment and/or an unlimited fine (*SSAA 1992, s 114* inserted by the *Social Security Act 1998, s 61*).

It should be noted that this offence relates to 'any person' and so may extend to an accountant, tax adviser or junior payroll clerk.

Offences by bodies corporate

25.114 Where a company commits an offence by failing to pay a contribution, and it is proved that the offence was committed with the consent or connivance of, or to be attributable to any neglect on the part of a director, manager, secretary or other similar officer of the company, proceedings may also be taken against that individual (*SSAA 1992, s 115 (1)*). This applies equally to a company which is managed by its members (*SSAA 1992, s 115 (2)*).

25.115 The former Contributions Agency (CA) successfully prosecuted a director of two 'phoenix' companies under *s 115* in 1995. Directors of such companies typically incur large debts through the non-payment of creditors and then liquidate the company, relying on its limited liability status to protect themselves. NICs are often deducted correctly from employees' wages, but are not passed on to what is now HMRC. This was the first criminal case of its kind (CA Press Release of 27 September 1995).

Employer failing to pay Class 1 and Class 1A contributions

Notice of amount due

25.116 Under the pre-RTI rules, if, within 17 days of the end of any income tax period, an employer had either failed to pay, or paid insufficient, Class 1 or Class 1A contributions and HMRC's Debt Management and Banking service believed that contributions were due, HMRC could issue a notice to the employer instructing him to make a return within 14 days, showing the amount of contributions which he was liable to pay in respect of the period in

25.117 *National Insurance aspects*

question (SI 2001/1004, Sch 4, para 14(1), (3)). This rule continues in force for the small number of non-RTI employers.

25.117 The Debt Management and Banking service may alternatively, upon consideration of the employer's record of past payments, to the best of its judgment, specify the amount of contributions which it considers the employer is liable to pay and give notice of the amount (SI 2001/1004, Sch 4, para 15(1)). This process has now been automated to a great extent for RTI employers, with 'specified charges' added by the system to employers' accounts based on computer algorithms intended to identify non-payment and underpayment by them based on the suspected non-submission of FPSs for the month in question.

25.118 Such specified charges, even if they are a made-up number based on false assumptions by the HMRC system, qualify as contributions (or PAYE, CIS or student loan deductions) due and are enforceable until displaced. Employers can only displace such a specified charge by submitting the missing FPS or EPS. If the specified charge for a period is discovered only after 19 April following the end of the tax year, an earlier year update (EYU) is required.

25.119 If the computer has guessed incorrectly and raised a charge where none was due, the employer must send a nil EPS for the month in question. HMRC's guidance states:

> 'If you do not send an EPS, HMRC will assume that you have failed to file a Full Payment Submission (FPS) and pay what you owe. Based on your previous submissions they will contact you for payment. As soon as you send in an EPS HMRC will update your records and stop pursuing the debt.'

25.120 Some commercial payroll software has no facility for submitting a nil EPS, but the employer can use the HMRC Basic PAYE Tools (BPT) package to do so, even if the employer has more than nine employees, which is the normal limit for the BPT. There is no legal requirement to file a nil return and employers cannot be penalised for not doing so, but HMRC's systems have somewhat perversely been written so that only a nil return can displace the specified charge.

Evidence of non-payment of contributions

25.121 If the employer has not paid either the estimated liability or the actual amount due within the seven days allowed in the notice, Debt Management and Banking's certificate of the amount due is, until the contrary is proved, sufficient evidence in any proceedings before the courts that the sum mentioned in the certificate is unpaid and due (SI 2001/1004, Sch 4, para 15(4)). A document purporting to be such a certificate is deemed to be such a certificate until the contrary is proved (SI 2001/1004, Sch 4, para 15(4)).

25.122 The *Social Security Act 1998* provides for distraint action to be taken in England and Wales where a person served with a certificate confirming their debt fails to make payment within seven days (*SSAA 1992, s 121A*). A magistrate's warrant is required for forced entry to premises and, where necessary, the assistance of a constable may also be secured. Any goods distrained will be held for a five-day period and then sold by auction.

25.123 In Scotland, poinding proceedings under the *Debtors (Scotland) Act 1987, Sch 5* can be instituted where a person has been served with a certificate confirming the debt but fails to make payment within the longer period of 14 days. A sheriff's summary warrant is required for recovery and sale by way of poinding. Applications must be accompanied by the certificate of debt and a certificate stating that the certificate of debt was served on the person in question and the debt remains unpaid (*SSAA 1992, s 121B* inserted by the *Social Security Act 1998, s 63*).

Recovery of Class 1 contributions

25.124 The provisions of *ITEPA 2003* and PAYE Regulations relating to the recovery of tax apply also to Class 1 contributions which an employer is liable to pay to HMRC, as if they had been tax charged by way of an assessment on the employer as 'general earnings' (*ITEPA 2003, s 684* and SI 2001/1004, reg 67(1)).

Proceedings may be brought for recovery of Class 1 and Class 1A contributions in the same way as they are for income tax charged on 'general earnings' (*TMA 1970, s 65(3)*).

Where an employer has used a remuneration arrangement that is notifiable under DOTAS and there has been a *s 8* notice and appeal, the accelerated payment notice and follower notice provisions of *FA 2014* imported into NIC law by *NICA 2015, Sch 2* may mean that the employer has to pay the disputed contribution liability pending settlement of the dispute. Any such payment is deemed to be a payment of contributions, rather than simply a payment on account of such contributions. This is logical: the contributions payable in any one tax year may entitle the employee concerned to a short-term social security benefit in the calendar year following the end of that tax year, or may affect the employee's state pension. There is no statutory provision for repayment of any such advance contributions that are later found not to have been due, or for the retrospective adjustment of benefits in such a case, but HMRC has stated that

25.125 *National Insurance aspects*

any contributions that were ultimately found not to have been due will always be repaid.

Class 1, Class 1A and PAYE penalties

25.125 Under RTI, penalties for late RTI submissions were introduced from October 2014, although not quite in the form originally intended, which had been that all employers would be liable for failures as soon as the new regime was commenced (see **25.130** below). Penalties were charged for 2012/13 and 2013/14 for late final submissions where the submission was received after 19 May. The penalties mirrored those previously applying for late year end returns.

25.126 *FA 1989* introduced significant changes to the penalty regime for PAYE failures, including the penalty in respect of late and incorrect year end returns (forms P14 and P35) (*TMA 1970, s 98A*). With effect from 22 October 1990, these penalties also applied in relation to returns required under NI regulations of Class 1 and Class 1A contributions. For NIC purposes, *SSCBA 1992, Sch 1, para 7* still mirrors the PAYE penalty provisions in *TMA 1970, s 98A* subject to the following modifications, although the RTI penalty rules are now different, which is no surprise in view of the abolition of annual PAYE and NIC reporting:

- where a person has failed to render a tax return for a particular tax year within the time prescribed and is thus liable for (has been required to pay) a penalty for a default in the first 12 months, he is not liable for a similar penalty in respect of the associated contributions return (*SSCBA 1992, Sch 1, para 7(3)*);

- where a person has failed to render a tax return and an associated contributions return for a particular tax year and the failure has continued beyond 12 months, a single penalty may apply of up to the sum of any tax and contributions remaining unpaid at the end of 19 April following the end of the tax year to which the return relates. An authorised officer must determine that a penalty is to be imposed in respect of both returns (*SSCBA 1992, Sch 1, para 7(4), (5)*);

- where a person has fraudulently or negligently made an incorrect tax return and an associated contributions return for a particular tax year, a single penalty may apply of up to the sum of any tax and contributions remaining unpaid at the end of 19 April following the end of the tax year to which the return relates. Again, an authorised officer must determine that a penalty is to be imposed in respect of both returns (*SSCBA 1992, Sch 1, para 7(4), (5)*).

25.127 The provisions in *FA 2009, Sch 55* (Penalty for failure to make returns, etc), which came into effect on 6 April 2011 as regards income tax self-assessment (and therefore the Class 4 NIC element included therein) were not extended to Classes 1, 1A and 1B, or PAYE, for which they would not work. Instead, specific RTI-focused penalty rules were created, but the old rules remained in place to deal with defaults in pre-RTI years. The transfer by NICA 2015 of Class 2 NIC collection onto almost the same basis as Class 4 through the self-assessment regime has brought Class 2 into scope for *Sch 55* penalties, although the amounts are tiny.

For the RTI pilot year, 2012/13, the Contributions Regulations 2001 (SI 2001/1004), reg 21A(8) continued to apply *FA 2007, Sch 24* to inaccuracies and reg 21F(12) extended it to SSP, SMP, etc.

25.128 *TMA 1970, s 98A* continued to apply to late filing of returns. At the end of the pilot year, ie from 6 April 2013, a new reg 21EA was inserted into the Contributions Regulations 2001 (SI 2001/1004), Sch 4. When an employer does not make an FPS return as required by reg 21A or 21D, the missing information must be supplied with the next return, or by 20 May after the end of the tax year at the very latest. The *s 98A* penalty continued to apply only from 20 May after the tax year end.

25.129 The result was that a penalty of £100 per 50 employees per month of delay applied only to final payments for 2013/14 not reported before 20 May 2014. The original intention was to introduce in-year late filing penalties from April 2014, but this was deferred until 6 October 2014 because the RTI system was generating too many false reports of errors and was unreliable as a basis for automated penalties.

25.130 After assessing the volume of apparent mistakes reported by the RTI system, from 6 October 2014, HMRC decided to apply late filing or non-filing penalties only to large employers, with the remainder to be brought in from April 2015, but after the issue of the first batch of quarterly penalties, and the number of errors experienced, HMRC put the new system back on hold, which is where it still remains pending a review of how penalties are used to encourage compliance.

25.131 The size of the theoretical late filing penalty is set by reference to the number of employees within the PAYE scheme for the relevant month:

No of employees	Amount of monthly penalty
	£
1–9	100
10–49	200
50–249	300
250+	400

25.132 *National Insurance aspects*

Penalty notices should be issued quarterly in mid-July, October, January, and April for the quarter just ended. If returns remain outstanding for more than three months, an additional 5% penalty may be charged. Such penalties are now being charged only where an HMRC officer has identified serious non-compliance.

25.132 All penalties are open to a reasonable excuse defence and can be appealed automatically through the online Penalty Appeals Service or by contacting the Customer Operations Employer Office, BP4102, Chillingham House, Benton Park View, Newcastle-upon-Tyne, NE98 1ZZ and quoting the penalty notice's unique ID number.

Any penalties collected by HMRC in respect of NICs are, after the deduction of the collection costs, paid to the National Insurance Fund (*SSCBA 1992, Sch 1, para 7(6), (8)*). HMRC's accounts do not make clear how much of the £1 billion collected in fines and penalties in 2015/16 related to NICs.

Personal liability notices

25.133 With effect from 6 April 1999, officers of bodies corporate may be issued with a personal liability notice where the business has failed to pay the correct contributions at the correct time and the failure *appears* to be attributable to fraud or neglect on the part of one or more individuals (*SSAA 1992, s 121C* inserted by the *Social Security Act 1998, s 64*).

25.134 The personal liability notice will transfer the whole or a specified part of the company's NIC debt to the director or company secretary as a personal debt of the individual, including the associated interest accrued to date. Further interest will accrue until payment is made. Appeals may be made against such notices.

25.135 It is worth noting that when this provision was introduced it was stated to be targeted at, and would only be used in the case of, 'phoenix companies'. In fact, the first two cases (in which HMRC was successful) did not involve phoenix companies: see *Inzani v Revenue and Customs Comrs* [2006] STC (SCD) 279 and *Livingstone* (TC 369).

25.136 Subsequent cases have involved phoenix companies: see *Roberts and Martin* (TC 1130), *Christine Roberts* (TC 1994) and *Smith* (TC 2110). Christine Roberts was successful in getting the 100% of NIC liability attributed to her reduced to one-third by being shared out with two other directors. In the preliminary case of *O'Rorke* (TC 1675) the FTT agreed with the appellant that 'neglect' is to be interpreted subjectively (ie a question of the accused person's state of mind) and not objectively (a question of his actual conduct), but the decision was appealed by HMRC to the Upper Tribunal which decided

([2013] UKUT 499 (TCC)) that it bore its ordinary, objective meaning and the case was remitted to the First-Tier Tribunal.

The concept of transferring liability for arrears to directors has also been adopted in connection with the managed service company rules introduced in 2007, the intermediary worker rules introduced in 2014 and the intermediary travel expenses rules introduced in 2016, although the transfer regime is found in *ITEPA 2003, ss 688A–688B* and the PAYE Regulations 2003 rather than the NIC legislation and, technically, only applies to PAYE debts.

Penalties for late returns (pre- and post-RTI)

25.137 As mentioned above, prior to the introduction of RTI (which applies to most employers from 2013/14 onwards), for 1994/95 and subsequent years, an employer who had not filed his end of year return of tax and NICs by the due date (19 May following the year of assessment) was liable to an automatic penalty of £100 for each month or part month it is delayed, in respect of every 50 employees (or part thereof) who should be on the return.

25.138 For example, a return for 51 employees which was late by one day would attract an automatic penalty of £200 (*TMA 1970, s 98A*). Where the delay continued beyond 12 months, an additional penalty was due, equal to the amount of tax and NICs unpaid at 19 April following the end of the year to which the return related.

25.139 The penalty provisions in *FA 2009, Sch 55*, which came into effect on 6 April 2011 as regards income tax self-assessment (and therefore the Class 4 NIC element included therein), were extended to real time information returns from 6 April 2014 (by virtue of *FA 2013, s 230* and *Sch 50, paras 3, 4*). Penalties for late RTI submissions applied from October 2014, rather than April 2014 as originally intended, and only to large employers initially. Smaller employers were due to fall into the regime from April 2015, but the introduction led to so many penalties that HMRC had to retrospectively change the rules by concession to disregard any return that was no more than three days late. The concession was stated to be available only until April 2016, but it was extended in modified form without fanfare in an article on page 2 of the June 2016 Employer Bulletin as follows:

> '… employers will not necessarily incur penalties for delays of up to three days in filing PAYE information during the current tax year and late filing penalties will continue to be reviewed on a risk assessed basis rather than be issued automatically.
>
> We won't charge a late filing penalty for occasional delays of up to three days after the statutory filing date. However, employers who persistently

25.140 National Insurance aspects

file after the statutory filing date but within three days may be contacted or considered for a penalty.

The three day easement is not an extension to the statutory filing date which remains unchanged and employers are required to file on or before each payment date unless the circumstances set out in the "sending an FPS after payday guidance" are met.

We will continue to review our approach to PAYE late filing penalties beyond 5 April 2017 in line with the wider review of penalties. We will focus on penalising those who deliberately and persistently fail to meet statutory deadlines, rather than those who make occasional and genuine errors for which other responses might be more appropriate.'

So it seems HMRC will still permit occasional late filing under the three-day concession, but will take compliance action against employers who persist in filing after the deadline but within three days to ensure that they have a genuine reasonable excuse for the delay.

Penalties for late final submission under RTI

25.140 The introduction of RTI removed the need to file year-end returns as pay and deductions information is submitted to HMRC progressively by means of the FPS each time that a payment is made to an employee.

Under RTI, instead of submitting year end returns, the employer must make a final submission, either by means of the FPS, or where no payments are made in the final pay period, by means of the EPS. The final submission requires the employer to confirm that it is the last submission of the tax year and to complete the declaration. The year-end questions that used to appear on the P35 and the early RTI final submissions have now been dropped from the year-end routine, although HMRC has re-introduced one of them, an online form to notify HMRC that no P11D(b) is required, separately.

The *TMA 1970* penalty is still available, but the advent of quarterly penalty charges based on FPSs filed late in the previous three months should mean that it is no longer applicable to RTI employers.

Penalties for incorrect returns

25.141 In the case of return periods commencing on and after 1 April 2008 where the return is lodged on and after 1 April 2009, the penalty regime under *FA 2007, Sch 24* applies. This regime applies to NIC because *FA 2007, Sch 24* applies the provisions of that schedule to *SSCBA 1992, Sch 1, para 7*.

National Insurance aspects **25.145**

25.142 The penalties are determined by reference to the amount of tax/NIC understated, the nature of the behaviour that gives rise to the understatement and the extent of disclosure made by the 'taxpayer'. No penalty is charged where 'reasonable care' has been taken. The penalty is 0–30% where there has been failure to take reasonable care (with a minimum of 15% where disclosure was prompted by HMRC), 20–70% where there has been deliberate understatement (with a minimum of 35% where disclosure was prompted by HMRC) and 30–100% where there has been deliberate understatement with concealment (with a minimum of 50% where disclosure was prompted by HMRC). In some circumstances, penalties may be suspended for up to two years, eg if the error is due to systems or record-keeping failure and objective criteria for measuring future behaviour can be set.

25.143 In the case of older returns, the penalty for an incorrect return, fraudulently or negligently made, is an amount up to the difference between the amount paid for the year of assessment to which the return related and the amount which would have been payable if it had been correct (*TMA 1970, s 98A(4)* and SSCBA *1992, Sch 1, para 7(2)*).

Penalties for incorrect manner of payment

25.144 Prior to 6 April 2010, a surcharge applied to large employers who failed to make payments of PAYE and NIC to HMRC electronically. In respect of Class 1 NIC and PAYE liabilities (for 2004/05 and years following), large PAYE schemes (those with 250 or more employees) had to make their monthly remittances by electronic means. Where the full amount due was not paid electronically then the employer was in default. The only ground for an appeal against a default notice was that there was no default. A surcharge was imposed for defaults on an increasing scale. This remained the case even where all payments were on time and complete but paid by cheque.

There were three extra days to pay if doing so electronically, though cleared funds had to be received within those extra three days (SI 2001/1004, regs 90F–90H).

The surcharge was replaced by the penalty for late payment of PAYE, which applies from 6 April 2010.

Penalties for late payment

25.145 From April 2010, penalties are applied to employers who are late in making in-year (ie monthly/quarterly) PAYE/NIC remittances (SI 2001/1004, reg 67A) on more than one occasion in the tax year. The penalty applies irrespective of the number of employees that the employer has.

25.146 *National Insurance aspects*

25.146 The amount of the penalty depends on the number of defaults in any 12-month period. The first occasion on which payment is made late is not counted as a default, except for those small companies that pay their director only annually – it would make no sense to allow the sole annual payment to be made late without a penalty. The next occasion is the first default and so on. The penalty (as a percentage of the tax paid late) depends on the number of defaults, starting at 1% and rising to 4% of the deductions paid late.

25.147 There are further cumulative penalties of 5% of any amounts still unpaid at six months after the due date and again at 12 months after the due date. These penalties are not charged during an agreed time to pay arrangement (unless the taxpayer defaults or 'misuses' the arrangement).

25.148 Such penalties apply equally under RTI. They are currently imposed after the end of the tax year. It had been intended to move to charging the penalties in-year on a quarterly basis from 2014/15. However, the introduction of in-year late payment penalties was delayed by at least two years, due to the volume of incorrect data on HMRC's systems, and still did not commence in April 2016. Late payment penalties for 2015/16 will be charged after the end of the tax year on a 'risk-assessed basis', which means that HMRC will issue a penalty notice only when it actually finds late payments being made after due investigation of the case, and this continues to be the case.

Class 1A contributions

25.149 In the case of Class 1A, there is a penalty of up to the amount of contributions underpaid where there is fraud or neglect (SI 2001/1004, reg 81(1)), otherwise £100 per 50 earners (the number of employees being rounded up to the nearest 50) per calendar month (or part) for the first 12 months, or the amount of contributions underpaid if the failure extends beyond 12 months (SI 2001/1004, reg 81(2), (3) and (4)).

25.150 The *FA 2007, Sch 24* regime mentioned in **25.141–25.142** also applies to Class 1A contributions but in a different way. In respect of the 2010/11 liability onwards, there are penalties of 5% on Class 1A contributions unpaid 30 days after the due date and a further 5% (each time) as at six months and 12 months after the due date (SI 2001/1004, reg 67B).

Class 1B contributions

25.151 The *FA 2007, Sch 24* regime mentioned in **25.141–25.142** also applies to Class 1B contributions, but in a different way. In respect of the 2010/11 liability onwards there are penalties of 5% on Class 1B contributions unpaid

National Insurance aspects **25.157**

30 days after the due date and a further 5% (each time) as at six months and 12 months after the due date (SI 2001/1004, reg 67B).

Class 4 contributions

25.152 In the case of return periods commencing on and after 1 April 2008 where the return is lodged on and after 1 April 2009 the new scheme of penalties under *FA 2007, Sch 24* applies.

The penalties are determined by reference to the amount of tax/NIC understated, the nature of the behaviour that gives rise to the understatement and the extent of disclosure made by the 'taxpayer'.

25.153 The penalty is zero for mistakes made despite 'reasonable care' having been taken, 0–30% where there has been failure to take reasonable care (with a minimum of 15% where disclosure was prompted by HMRC), 20–70% where there has been deliberate understatement (with a minimum of 35% where disclosure was prompted by HMRC) and 30–100% where there has been deliberate understatement with concealment (with a minimum of 50% where disclosure was prompted by HMRC).

25.154 In some cases penalties may be suspended for up to two years, eg if the error is due to systems or record-keeping failure and checks can be instituted to ensure that there is no recurrence of the error for the period of suspension.

25.155 Where an inaccuracy does not result in tax/NIC being lost altogether but being declared in a later period than it should have been, the penalty is 5% for each year of delay.

There is a right of appeal against the imposition and amount of a penalty. The onus of proof is on HMRC.

25.156 In the case of older return periods, the penalty provisions of *TMA 1970, Pt X* applied to Class 4 contributions that were payable by way of assessment made in accordance with income tax legislation (*SSCBA 1992, s 16*).

INTEREST

Overdue contributions

25.157 Interest has been applied automatically since 1992/93 to payments of PAYE and subcontractors' deductions outstanding at 19 April after the end of the tax year.

25.158 *National Insurance aspects*

Before this, and only from April 1988, interest arose in cases where tax, which the employer had failed to deduct under PAYE, was formally determined under what was then the Income Tax (Employments) Regulations 1993, SI 1993/ 744, reg 49. A similar charge did not apply for NIC purposes prior to 1992/93.

25.158 For years up to 5 April 2014, interest is automatically charged on Class 1 contributions paid more than 14 days after the end of the year in respect of which the contributions were due, eg 19 April 2013 for 2012/13 Class 1 contributions, or paid more than 17 days after the end of the year if payment was made electronically for 2004/05 onwards (SI 2001/1004, Sch 4, para 17).

25.159 From 2014/15, interest is charged in-year on late paid PAYE and NIC once the overdue amount has been paid and the dates of payment are known. When RTI was conceived, HMRC expected nearly all employers to pay their staff via BACS, which would mean that every payment could be traced by HMRC's system, but this was a misunderstanding, and only payments that are clearly late (ie received after the 19th or 22nd of the month) are likely to attract automatic interest additions in the employer's tax account. Where underpayments are established as a result of a compliance visit, interest will be calculated manually from the relevant original payment date.

25.160 Interest on late-paid Class 1A contributions is also charged automatically. Since 2000/01, interest on overdue Class 1A has run from the due date (normally 19 July) (SI 2001/1004, reg 76). The due date was extended by three days for 2004/05 onwards for payment made electronically (SI 2001/1004, reg 71).

25.161 Interest on late-paid Class 1B contributions is automatically charged and runs from the due date (normally 19 October) (SI 2001/1004, Sch 4, para 17(1)(a)).

The due date is extended by three days if payment (in respect of 2004/05 onwards) is made electronically (SI 2001/1004, Sch 4, para 17(3)).

In all cases, the rate of interest charged is the same as for late-paid income tax as set by *FA 1989, s 178* (*SSCBA 1992 Sch 1, para 6(3)*).

Repaid contributions

25.162 Class 1, 1A and 1B contributions which are repaid after the 'relevant date' carry interest. The relevant date is:
- for Class 1 contributions, 14 days after the end of the tax year in respect of which the contribution is payable; for Class 1A contributions, 14 days after the end of the tax year in which the contribution is payable; for

Class 1B contributions, 19 October after the end of the tax year to which the contribution relates; or

- if later, the date of payment.

(SI 2001/1004, reg 77, Sch 4, para 18).

Repayment and remission of interest

25.163 Where an employer has paid interest on late-paid Class 1, Class 1A or Class 1B contributions which is subsequently found not to have been due, the interest will be repaid (SI 2001/1004, reg 78, Sch 4, para 19).

Interest will be remitted if the contribution in respect of which it was charged was paid late as a result of an official error on the part of HMRC or its predecessor bodies where the employer or his agent did not cause or materially contribute to the mistake or omission (SI 2001/1004, reg 79, Sch 4, para 20).

Interest on Class 4 and Class 2 contributions

25.164 Class 4 contributions collected by assessment may attract an interest charge under *TMA 1970, s 86* (*SSCBA 1992, Sch 2, para 6*).

Class 4 arrears may technically be enforced up to six years after they fell due, but they depend on there being an assessment under *ITTOIA 2005, Pt 2, Ch 2*, so in practice HMRC will only look back four years unless a careless error means that tax may be assessed for six years.

25.165 Until the reform of Class 2 by NICA 2015, interest was not chargeable in respect of Class 2 contributions that were paid late, although a 'penalty rate' applied instead. This ensured that where payment was made later than one tax year after the end of the year to which the contributions related they would be charged at the highest rate in force from the time payment was due to the time it was made (inclusive). Since 6 April 2015, when Class 2 became chargeable together with Class 4 via the annual self-assessment tax return, on the basis of the same calculation of earnings, and payable with the balancing income tax payment for the tax year on 31 January, interest applies to late paid Class 2 contributions from 1 February until the date of payment.

APPEALS

25.166 Historically, until April 1999 there was, in the Social Security Acts, no provision for appeals in connection with contribution matters and the appellate

25.167 *National Insurance aspects*

bodies which operate in connection with state benefits had no jurisdiction so far as the contribution side of the state scheme was concerned. However, there was *effectively* an appeal procedure in connection with contributions, but it was not widely known or understood and entailed asking a formal 'question' of the Secretary of State for Social Security, who then determined the matter in a quasi-judicial capacity.

25.167 A decision of the Secretary of State in favour of a contributor or employer could not be further appealed by the authorities, but an employer or contributor could appeal against a decision unsatisfactory to them, although only to the High Court (Queen's Bench Division, and no further) and only on a point of law.

25.168 However, with the transfer of the former Contributions Agency to the then Inland Revenue with effect from 1 April 1999 and the transfer of contributions policy functions from DSS to the Treasury from the same date, the opportunity was taken to modernise the appeals system, such as it was. It is now brought almost entirely into line with those procedures encountered in dealing with most other imposts for which HMRC is now responsible.

25.169 This means that for exactly ten years National Insurance appeals were heard by the General and Special Commissioners but are now (since 1 April 2009) heard by the tax tribunals. Although SMP, SAP, SPP and SShPP are in effect state benefits, they are nevertheless a matter for the tax tribunals, although somewhat bizarrely tax credits are handled by the Social Security and Child Support Tribunal.

25.170 The fact that there remain some small differences, and the previous absence of a formal appeal system in relation to contributions, is explained by the fact that the Social Security Acts (unlike the Taxes Acts) make no provision for formal assessments of their levies, other than Class 4 contributions. The liability is either self-assessed at a fixed rate or employer-assessed by reference to earnings paid (eg Class 1 contributions) or to company cars, fuel and other taxable benefits made available to employees (ie Class 1A contributions) or in respect of minor payments made to employees (ie Class 1B contributions).

25.171 Save for the Commissioners having been replaced by the tax tribunal, the current system has operated from 1 April 1999 and remains, after the 2009 change, still largely regulated by the *Social Security Contributions (Transfer of Functions, etc) Act 1999* (*SSCTFA 1999*) and the Social Security Contributions (Decisions and Appeals) Regulations 1999 (SI 1999/1027).

Decisions of officers of HMRC

25.172 Where a contributor or his employer is faced with a demand for payment that is considered to be wrong or excessive, the matter will first be considered informally.

If the dispute cannot be resolved in this way, it will then be for an officer of HMRC to issue a formal 'decision' under *SSCTFA 1999, s 8*.

The formal decision is then appealable in much the same way as an old-style tax assessment or an amendment to a self-assessment. HMRC and the contributor may also opt to try the Alternative Dispute Resolution (ADR) process if that provides a possible route to settlement before formal appeal proceedings are instituted before a tribunal.

The subject matter of a decision

25.173 An officer may decide:
- whether a person is or was an earner and, if he is or was, in which category of earners he should be included;
- whether a person is or was employed in employed earner's employment for industrial injuries purposes (*SSCBA 1992, Pt V*);
- whether a person is or was liable to pay any contributions of any class and the amount of the liability (a notice of decision charging Class 1 NICs on earnings will often be issued together with the equivalent determination under the PAYE Regulations, reg 80);
- whether a person is or was entitled to pay contributions, notwithstanding that there is no liability to pay, eg payment of voluntary contributions;
- whether contributions of a particular class have been paid for any period;
- on any issue in connection with SSP, SMP, SPP, SAP or SShPP;
- on matters concerning the issue or content of any notice under *SSCBA 1992, s 121C* (notices of company officer's personal liability for unpaid contributions);
- any issue arising under the *Jobseekers Act 1995, s 27* (back to work schemes for long-term unemployed);
- whether to give or withdraw approval for the transfer to the employee of the employer's Class 1 liability in respect of certain unapproved share options;
- whether a person is liable to a penalty and the amount;

25.174 *National Insurance aspects*

- other issues as may be prescribed by regulations made by the Commissioners of HMRC.

(SSCTFA 1999, s 8(1))

25.174 Decisions relating to the regional NIC Holiday that ran for new businesses set up from 22 June 2010 to 5 September 2013 inclusive were included within the above *(National Insurance Contributions Act 2011, s 8(6))*.

25.175 The third and fifth items above do not include decisions relating to Class 4 contributions which have, because they are invariably collected along with income tax, always been dealt with under tax appeal procedures *(SSCTFA 1999, s 8(2))*.

25.176 The sixth item above does not extend to any decision as to the making of subordinate legislation since policy for SSP and SMP remains with the Secretary of State for Work and Pensions (formerly the Secretary of State for Social Security), even though it is now administered by HMRC. Nor does it extend to any decision as to whether the liability to pay SSP, SMP, SPP, SAP or SShPP is that of HMRC or the employer.

25.177 Likewise, policy responsibility for SPP, SAP and SShPP lies with the Secretary of State for Business, Energy and Industrial Strategy (BEIS) (formerly BIS or BERR) *(SSCTFA 1999, s 8(3))*.

25.178 With regard to the final item in the list in **25.173**, further matters have been prescribed as follows:

- whether a notice should be given under SI 2001/1004, reg 3(2B) (directions as to a change of earnings period to counter avoidance) and if so the terms of such notice;
- whether a notice given under SI 2001/1004, reg 3(2B) should cease to have effect;
- whether a direction should be given under SI 2001/1004, reg 31 (counteracting abnormal practices designed to avoid or reduce liability) and if so the terms of the direction;
- whether the condition in SI 2001/1004, reg 50(2) (Class 3 paid late through ignorance or error) is satisfied;
- whether late applications under SI 2001/1004, reg 52(8), reg 54(3) or reg 55(3) for the refund of (respectively) contributions generally, Class 1 contributions paid at the wrong rate, or Class 1A contributions should be admitted;

National Insurance aspects **25.179**

- whether, where a secondary contributor has failed to pay primary contributions that failure was with the consent or connivance of the primary contributor, as is mentioned in SI 2001/1004, reg 60;
- whether the condition in SI 2001/1004, reg 61(2) (Class 2 paid late through ignorance or error) is satisfied;
- whether in the case of Class 2 contributions remaining unpaid at the due date, the reason for non-payment is the contributor's ignorance or error, and if so whether that is due to failure to exercise due care and diligence (SI 2001/1004, reg 65(2));
- whether the reason for non-payment of Class 3 within the prescribed period is the contributor's ignorance or error, and if so whether that is due to failure to exercise due care and diligence (SI 2001/1004, reg 65(3));
- whether the reason for non-payment of Class 3 within two years of the end of the year to which the contributions relate is the contributor's ignorance or error, and if so whether that is due to failure to exercise due care and diligence (SI 2001/1004, reg 65(4));
- whether a late application under SI 2001/1004, reg 110(3) for the return of a special Class 4 contribution should be admitted;
- whether a contribution (other than a Class 4 contribution) has been paid in error (SI 2001/1004, reg 52(1)(a));
- whether there has been a payment of contributions in excess of the amount specified in SI 2001/1004, reg 21 (SI 2001/1004, reg 52(1)(b));
- whether certain delays mentioned in the now superseded National Insurance (Contributions) Regulations 1969 were reasonable, etc;
- whether the delay in making payment of primary Class 1 contributions was neither with the consent nor connivance of the primary contributor (Social Security (Crediting and Treatment of Contributions, and National Insurance Numbers) Regulations 2001, SI 2001/769, reg 5);
- whether in the case of a contribution paid after the due date, the failure was due to ignorance or error and not failure to exercise due care and diligence (SI 2001/769, reg 6);
- from 6 August 2007, whether the circumstances are such that the managed service company provisions apply.

25.179 The Board may make regulations with regard to the making of decisions and an officer may direct that he shall have the assistance of an 'expert' where it appears that a question of fact requires special expertise (*SSCTFA 1999, s 9(1), (2)*).

25.180 *National Insurance aspects*

'Expert' means a person appearing to the officer of the Board to have knowledge or experience which would be relevant in determining the question of fact (*SSCTFA 1999, s 9(3)*).

The Board may make regulations enabling decisions under s 8 to be varied or superseded (*SSCTFA 1999, s 10*) and have done so.

25.180 A decision must be made to the best of the officer's information and belief and must state the following (SI 1999/1027, reg 3(1)):

- the name of every person in respect of whom it is made; and
- the date from which it has effect; or
- the period for which it has effect.

25.181 An officer may entrust responsibility for completing procedures to some other officer, whether by means involving the use of a computer or not, including the responsibility for serving the notice on any person named in it (SI 1999/1027, reg 3(2)).

Giving notice of the decision

25.182 Notice of a decision must, under the regulations, be given to every person named in it or, in the case of a decision relating to entitlement to SSP, SMP, SPP, SAP or SShPP to the employee and employer concerned (SI 1999/1027, reg 4(1)).

25.183 In the case of Class 1 contributions, the notice will name the employer and each affected employee. Where the number of employees exceeds six, HMRC will normally seek to agree a representative sample of employees with the employer or the agent and will name only those selected employees (as well as the employer) in the notice. This is an extra-statutory arrangement, there being no legal basis for the selection of six employees as the number beyond which not to look at each case individually.

25.184 In *Westek Ltd v Revenue and Customs Comrs* [2008] STC (SCD) 169, a notice of decision sent to the employer had merely referred to 'earnings of employees' without naming the employees in question. W, inter alia, challenged the validity of the notices.

25.185 The Special Commissioner upheld the view of HMRC that the decisions had been made under *SSCTFA 1999, s 8(1)(c)* and it was only the employer that in the first instance was liable to pay both the primary and the secondary contributions. Accordingly, the notice needed only to name, as it did, the employer and it was therefore only the employer who had to be sent a copy of the decision notice (SI 1999/1027, reg 4).

National Insurance aspects **25.193**

25.186 In 1999 the then Inland Revenue had stated that the affected employees would always be named in notices of decision. Following Sp C 629 it must therefore be assumed that this policy is no longer followed consistently.

25.187 Where the dispute relates to Class 1A contributions only the employer is affected as no employee's contribution arises. However, whilst there is therefore no obligation on the part of HMRC to name employees in the notice, they will usually do so where the decision concerns the provision of particular benefits. Similar procedures apply, as far as possible, in the case of disputed Class 1B liability.

25.188 In the case of Class 2, Class 3 or Class 4 decisions (the latter relating only to cases where Class 4 is not collected through the self-assessment tax return, eg deferment cases), there will invariably be only one person named in the notice.

25.189 The notice must state the date on which it is issued and may be served by post addressed to any person at his usual or last known place of residence or his place of business or employment. Notice to a company may be addressed to its registered office or its principal place of business (SI 1999/1027, reg 4(2), (3)).

25.190 A decision may be varied by an officer if he has reason to believe that it was incorrect at the time it was made. Notice of such variation must be given to the same persons and in the same manner as the original decision (SI 1999/1027, reg 5(1), (2)).

If a decision is under appeal, it may be varied at any time before the tax tribunal determines the appeal (SI 1999/1027, reg 5(4)).

25.191 A decision may be made superseding an earlier decision, including a varied decision, which has become inappropriate *for any reason*. A superseding decision will have effect from the date of the change in circumstances which rendered the previous decision (or varied decision) inappropriate.

The previous decision ceases to have effect immediately the superseding decision comes into effect (SI 1999/1027, reg 6(1), (2)).

25.192 Decisions are issued on Form DAA1(A), effectively a standard letter, which tells the recipient to let their professional adviser or agent, if they have one, see it. Copies will be issued direct to agents, if known to be acting. Where copies are sent to more than one person, the notes on the face of the notice will be varied on each copy to reflect the differing effects of the decision on different categories of people affected, eg where copies are sent to employers and one or more employees.

25.193 The notice of decision also includes a payslip for making payment of the National Insurance contributions in question and will be sent with a letter

25.194 *National Insurance aspects*

of explanation which will, in practice, usually be a summary of what has been established in previous correspondence. A guide will also normally be sent to every recipient, although the standard text may simply be included in the letter serving the notice. Notices cannot be served by fax or email, only by post or by hand.

Appeals against officer's decisions

25.194 Any person named in a notice of decision has the right of appeal to the tax tribunal. The same right also extends to personal liability notices issued to company officers in respect of company contribution debts (*SSCTA 1999, s 11(1), (2), (4); SSAA 1992, s 121D*, as inserted by the *Social Security Act 1998, s 64*). Contributors also have the right to ask for a decision to be reviewed internally by an independent HMRC office before any appeal is made to a tribunal, in just the same way as a tax determination.

Manner of making an appeal

25.195 Once a notice of decision has been issued any person named in it can appeal to HMRC with or without immediately also notifying the tax tribunal of the appeal. HMRC should offer a formal internal review, but the appellant may request a review even if not offered. If the review does not change the decision, then the appeal can still be notified to the tribunal at that stage.

25.196 An appeal must be made in writing to HMRC within 30 days after the date on which the notice of decision was issued or the review decision notified. The letter sent with every notice of decision contains a tear-off appeal form (DAA3) which may be used, but an appeal made in any format – provided it is in writing and made within the specified 30 days – is legally valid (*SSCTFA 1999, s 12(1), (2)*).

25.197 Whilst National Insurance law specifies no particular form, the tax tribunal does provide one (T240) for notifications of appeals to it at www.justice.gov.uk/forms/hmcts/tax which it says 'can' be used to make an appeal. It may be that the appeal will proceed more smoothly if the form provided is in fact used. The form can also be obtained by phone on 0300 123 1024. Once completed it should be sent to HM Courts and Tribunals Service, First-tier Tribunal (Tax), PO Box 16972, Birmingham B16 6TZ or by email to taxappeals@hmcts.gsi.gov.uk.

25.198 The notice of appeal must specify the grounds of appeal, but on hearing by the tribunal it may allow additional grounds, not stated in the notice of appeal, to be put forward if satisfied that the omission was neither wilful nor unreasonable (*SSCTFA 1999, s 12(3)*).

25.199 The Board have the power to make regulations, with the concurrence of the Lord Chancellor and (in Scotland) the Lord Advocate, in respect of contributions, SSP, SMP, SPP, SAP and SShPP appeals, and may also make regulations regarding matters arising, pending a decision of an officer under s 8, pending the determination by the tax tribunal, out of the variation of a decision or out of the superseding of a decision (*SSCTFA 1999, ss 13, 14*).

Place of hearing of appeal

25.200 The Tribunals Service has a network of 130 hearing centres across the country and the facility for additional private hearings, although the main centres are in Birmingham, London and Manchester for English appeals, Belfast for Northern Ireland cases and Edinburgh for Scottish cases. The Tribunals Service maintains permanent hearing centres in Newport, Cardiff, Swansea, Colwyn Bay and Wrexham (all of which offer Welsh language hearings).

Late appeals

25.201 Late appeals may be admitted if the officer of the Board is satisfied that there was a reasonable excuse for not bringing the appeal within the normal time limit, provided that application is made without undue delay thereafter (SI 1999/1027, reg 9, applying the provisions of *TMA 1970, s 49*).

25.202 If HMRC declines a late appeal (which it may do if there is no 'reasonable excuse'), the potential appellant may apply to the tribunal to make a late appeal and the tribunal may consider factors beyond those that HMRC is required to consider.

Determination by tax tribunal

25.203 The tribunal may decide at the hearing that the decision shall be varied in any manner or that it shall stand good. The tribunal may examine the appellant on oath or affirmation or take other evidence (SI 1999/1027, reg 10).

Settling appeals by agreement

25.204 Appellants may, before an appeal is heard by the tax tribunal, come to an agreement with an officer that the decision under appeal should be treated as:

- upheld without variation, or

25.205 *National Insurance aspects*

- varied in a particular manner, or
- superseded by a further decision,

and the same consequences will then ensue as would have ensued if the officer had made a decision in the same terms as that under appeal, had varied the decision or made a superseding decision, as the case may be. In any of these circumstances, all appeals against the original decision shall lapse and notice of the agreement must be given by the officer to all persons named in the decision who did not appeal against it (SI 1999/1027, reg 11(1), (2), (3)).

25.205 If such an agreement is not made in writing it is necessary for the officer to confirm by written notice to every appellant the fact that an agreement was come to and details of its terms (SI 1999/1027, reg 11(4)).

An appellant may, before an appeal is heard by the tax tribunal, notify the officer and every other person named in the decision, either orally or in writing, that he does not wish to proceed with the appeal.

25.206 Unless, within 30 days, any person to whom that notice is given indicates that he is unwilling that the appeal should be treated as withdrawn then the appellant, the officer and every person named in the decision are treated as having reached an agreement that the decision should be upheld without variation (SI 1999/1027, reg 11(5)).

25.207 Where an appeal is to be settled by agreement in any manner mentioned above, the agreement may be made with any person acting on behalf of an appellant or any other person named in the decision and notices may be validly given to such persons (SI 1999/1027, reg 11(6)).

Dissatisfaction with tribunal's determination

25.208 If HMRC, the appellant or another party to the proceedings think that the tribunal's decision is wrong on a point of law, then an appeal may be made to the Upper Tribunal.

At this stage, the contributions in dispute must, if that is not already the case, be paid. If the appellant is successful, the amount will be repaid. If the hearing is with regard to SSP, SMP, SPP, SAP or SShPP, employers do not have to pay amounts alleged to be due until the courts have finally settled the appeal.

25.209 The First-tier Tribunal may initially review its own decision on receipt of an application of appeal to the Upper Tribunal (TPC, r 41; Tribunals, *Courts and Enforcement Act 2007, s 9*). A refusal of appeal by the First-tier Tribunal must be accompanied by an explanation and an option to have the rejection reviewed by the Upper Tribunal. Appeals against the Upper Tribunal decisions will be heard by the Court of Appeal in England and Wales or by the Inner House of the Court of Session in Scotland.

Upper Tribunal hearings will generally be held in London, Manchester, Birmingham, Belfast or Edinburgh.

Decisions under the Pension Schemes Act 1993 and in respect of the award of credits, etc

25.210 An officer is to make decisions in relation to questions concerning contracting out matters referred to in the *Pension Schemes Act 1993, s 170(1)* (*SSCTFA 1999, s 16(1)*).

A dissatisfied party will not, however, appeal to the tax tribunal but has the right of appeal to the Social Entitlement Chamber of the Tribunals Service (which deals with State benefit disputes) (*Social Security Act 1998, s 12*, as amended by *SSCTFA 1999, s 16(6)*).

25.211 The same procedure applies in the case of appeals against decisions of officers concerning the award of National Insurance credits, Carers' credits or (until replaced in 2010 by Carers' credits) Home Responsibilities Protection.

Class 4 appeals

25.212 Because Class 4 contributions are payable in accordance with assessments made under the Taxes Acts, the provisions of *TMA 1970, Pt V* have always applied with necessary modifications in relation to such contributions as they apply in relation to income tax and this continued to be the case after 31 March 1999 (*SSCBA 1992, s 15(1), (2), (5), Sch 8*).

25.213 The effect of this is that an appeal against any Class 4 assessment must be made in writing within 30 days of the issue of the notice of assessment or an unfavourable HMRC internal review decision and must state the grounds on which it is based. An appeal may be brought out of time if there is a reasonable excuse for the delay. An appeal against the decision of the tax tribunal may be made in the same manner as described in **25.208**.

25.214 Under 'self-assessment' few tax assessments are issued. However, in the case of a dispute, whether for income tax, Class 4 contributions or both, it will be necessary for HMRC, exceptionally, to issue a closure notice (ie, in effect an assessment) in order to enable an appeal to be made by the taxpayer/contributor.

25.215 *National Insurance aspects*

25.215 The only questions concerning Class 4 contributions which are excluded from this jurisdiction are:

- whether by regulations made under *SSCBA 1992, s 17(1)* a person is excepted from Class 4 liability or his liability is deferred; and/or

- whether he is liable for Class 4 contributions that may be collected directly by the NIC&EO (eg because deferment proves to have led to an underpayment) under *SSCBA 1992, ss 17(3)–(6), 18*.

25.216 These two matters previously fell within the Secretary of State's remit. However, from 1 April 1999, they became matters for a decision of an officer of the Board under *SSCTFA 1999, s 8* and then, only by those means, will the matter fall to be put before the tax tribunal.

Publication of decisions

25.217 The Social Security (Adjudication) Regulations 1986, SI 1986/2218, reg 16(1) gave the Secretary of State the authority to publish decisions 'in such manner as he thinks fit'. A decision is specific to an individual's contribution position and, while it was binding on the former CA, Benefits Agency, Social Security Commissioners, social security appeals tribunals and the courts, in respect of the person (or persons) named in the decision, it had no wider application. Between 1950 and 1958 'Selected Decisions of the Minister on Questions of Classification and Insurability' were published but are now out of print. Subsequently, the Secretary of State, for reasons of cost and confidentiality, chose not to publish them.

As with other types of cases, National Insurance appeals heard by the Special Commissioners were published – anonymised where appropriate – and this continues to be the case under the new tax tribunal.

CONCLUSIONS

25.218 Despite the potential for up to 70,000 visits that used to be expected per year, in a recent year only 18,000 visits were conducted. Whether this number might yet revert to former levels remains to be seen but either way the arithmetic shows that there is a less than 1 in 80 chance of any employer suffering an investigation involving a visit and considerably less than that if staff resources remain constrained or are further constrained by budget cuts.

These numbers, however, are not the real story and given that the smaller employers will generally be ignored the odds move quickly against larger employers.

National Insurance aspects **25.224**

25.219 Little can be done to avoid an investigation if an employer is deemed to be large, although it will usually be possible to delay the event, provided there are genuine grounds for doing so. What employers should aim to do is keep a low profile by ensuring that their RTI and end-of-year returns are as complete and accurate as possible, that payments due are made promptly and accurately, and that any enquiries from the authorities are dealt with as quickly as possible.

25.220 With employer compliance officers' growing ability to target firms for inspection with greater effectiveness using risk-management tools, the potential for discovering financial irregularities is greater and the accent is now firmly on yield discovered rather than the number of visits carried out.

25.221 Targeting, by its very nature, involves the selection of businesses where experience indicates that there is more likelihood of employers making mistakes. Coming into this area are companies with a high turnover of staff, companies who employ large numbers of casual staff, those with staff coming into or leaving the UK on secondment, etc, those with numerous widespread sites with consequential long lines of communication, companies engaging large numbers of temporary workers through intermediaries, and companies who make large numbers of mistakes in their returns.

25.222 However, while being able progressively to identify such businesses employer compliance officers also have a duty to protect the NIC records of all types of employers because of the potential consequences in state benefit terms for their workers. There must therefore be a balance between concentrating purely upon yield with the need to demonstrate that it is protecting employees in all types and sizes of employers.

25.223 From the above comments, it will be appreciated that there is not a lot that employers can do to avoid inspection visits. They will be selected as a target for any number of reasons and the employer compliance officer will follow that through. What employers can do, however, is check their procedures and ensure that they are following the legislative requirements. They could, in fact, mirror the type of checks that employer compliance officers carry out on a regular basis and ensure that all is in order.

25.224 To this end, the HMRC Expenses and Benefits from Employment 'Toolkit' and/or the National Insurance Contributions and Statutory Payments Toolkit might be used (available at www.gov.uk/government/collections/tax-agents-toolkits). However, users should appreciate that these documents are not comprehensive checklists but merely developed from the main errors that HMRC encounter in the respective fields covered.

25.225 *National Insurance aspects*

KEY POINTS

25.225

1 Whilst some visits are still entirely random and include small employers, most are specifically targeted at large employers because small errors are more likely to give a greater yield due to employee numbers.

2 Compliance officers are likely to be especially interested in internationally mobile workers, self-employed workers, employee benefit trusts and anything with a sniff of 'disguised remuneration'.

3 The time limit for collection of National Insurance arrears remains six years from the time payment was due notwithstanding the relatively recent reduction in the basic limit for tax to four years.

4 There remain a number of differences between the tax treatment and National Insurance treatment of various items.

5 The special provisions for fraudulent evasion of contributions (later matched with a similar tax provision) and personal liability notices should not be overlooked.

6 The appeals process uses the First-tier Tax Tribunal in the majority of instances. In very rare cases a different Chamber of the Tribunals Service is utilised.

Chapter 26

Employment tax issues

Alastair Kendrick
Employment Tax Specialist

> ### SIGNPOSTS
> - In this chapter we aim to give you an understanding of the technical aspects of employment tax/National Insurance so you can work your way through any HMRC enquiry.
> - The chapter also covers the topical areas you need to be aware of when working in this area (see **26.7, 26.20, 26.47, 26.54, 26.73–26.75, 26.93** and **26.171**).
> - Dealing with an employer compliance review can involve coming to grips with a lot of technical issues and understanding HMRC working practice. Given the wide number of areas which could be covered you need to be mindful of this.
> - We are seeing recently a significant updating of some of the historical rules in relation to employment tax and those involved in fronting an HMRC review will need to be aware of these and be careful of understanding when the changes occurred (see **26.20, 26.92** and **26.171**). In addition, we are seeing change to the tax rules to salary sacrifice, termination payments and the harmonisation of tax/NIC.
> - Whilst an employer may decide it does not need to engage a professional adviser to assist with any HMRC review, it may be sensible that it at least gets some pointers on how to proceed at the outset.
> - It is important to understand the scope of any HMRC review. This could be to look at a specific area of compliance or to do a total review of the business. It is also important to understand who is involved at HMRC – is this a general employer compliance team or is a more important team involved? (See **26.5, 26.16** and **26.17**.)

26.1 *Employment tax issues*

> - We are seeing HMRC take more of an aggressive approach and this results in it being less willing to negotiate a settlement and more willing to take disputes to tribunal.
>
> - It is the case that many employers do not appreciate the cost of getting this area wrong. It is important that therefore you are careful to understand the extent of the position before you concede to HMRC's position.

26.1 The review of employees and directors historically was carried out by a number of different Revenue agencies. This changed with the setting up of Employer Compliance Units, who cover both the tax and the NIC implications of both salary and benefits paid to employees and directors. We are now seeing the emphasis on compliance reviews conducted with HMRC also prepared to take more disputes through to tribunal. HMRC have a number of particular compliance activities in this area with particular trade reviews and also reviews relating to particular aspects of tax compliance. There is also specific targeted activity by units set up to review tax avoidance schemes.

26.2 The purpose of this chapter is to look specifically at the points which an audit or investigation team may raise in respect of employee/director tax issues. It aims to identify those points which are most vulnerable to challenge and, where possible, it suggests how such challenges can be best dealt with. It cannot cover all areas and in particular does not attempt to deal with the tax rules applicable only to certain occupations, such as those of footballers, divers and farm-workers. In general, directors are swept up in the category of 'higher paid employees' although when a particular point is relevant to directors only, this is identified.

26.3 Another chapter of this work covers the penalties and interest which HMRC may charge following a review of employee tax issues. The way negotiations should in general be conducted is also separately dealt with, and this chapter will thus only identify those negotiation points which are specific to employees and directors. Self-assessment is also dealt with elsewhere although where this has a significant impact on PAYE / Schedule E tax compliance, it is referred to briefly in this chapter. The review requirements relating to certain National Insurance contributions (NICs) are covered elsewhere in this book, but the NIC treatment of payments and benefits is also mentioned here, where appropriate.

INTRODUCTION

26.4 As is well known, an employee is taxable on all 'emoluments' from his employment (*ITEPA 2003, s 6 and 7*). Emoluments are defined to include

Employment tax issues **26.8**

'all salaries, fees, wages, perquisites and profits whatsoever' (*ITEPA 2003, ss 10(2), 62(2)*). Emoluments may include payments from third parties.

NICs are payable on 'earnings'. This is similar to the HMRC definition of emoluments, and now includes most benefits in kind.

26.5 In order to review compliance with the tax legislation, HMRC has broad authority to examine records held by the employer. These include:

- copies of P9Ds and P11Ds;
- HMRC's started checklist (which replaced the form P46);
- petty cash records;
- expense claims;
- cash book/purchase ledger/cheque requisition records;
- timesheets and clock cards;
- tachographs or other similar technology;
- chequebook stubs; and
- bank statements.

26.6 We now have real time information (RTI) in place in respect of payroll which requires employers to file payroll details to HMRC online. This means that HMRC can review the payroll operation during the course of the tax year and from this ensure that the scheme is being correctly applied and that the right amount of income tax and National Insurance is being paid to HMRC during the year. This process is supported by new penalties which can apply if the scheme is not being fully complied with. In view of RTI the need for HMRC to visit the office of the employer to check payroll is reducing and if a request is received for such a visit it is likely that this is prompted by some error detected in the online process.

26.7 In addition, such powers extend to enable HMRC to ensure the following aspects have been correctly dealt with:

- national living wage;
- student loan repayment; and
- tax credits.

26.8 With the introduction of Real Time Reporting, HMRC can keep a remote eye on the employer's compliance in this area by looking at the monthly reports it provides. One of the specific areas being monitored is whether it was possible any of the workers had been paid below the national living wage.

26.9 Employment tax issues

26.9 HMRC will occasionally request, in addition, wish to carry out what is called a 'payroll cleanse' which is to ensure that the employer is using the correct National Insurance number for the employee. Whilst this review is voluntary it is sensible to permit it to be undertaken, given there is the threat that the rules may at some point be changed which would enable penalties to be imposed for the use of an incorrect National Insurance number.

26.10 It is the inspection of these records which allows HMRC to check both compliance with the PAYE regulations and the more general rules for the taxation of benefits. The appropriate application of National Insurance is likely also to be reviewed. The way HMRC carries out compliance checks changed in April 2009. This change is said by HMRC to make the arrangement simpler and more consistent. Also with the introduction of real time information HMRC can undertake a significant amount of checking of information provided online without the need to request a site visit.

At the time of writing HMRC are piloting a further change in the process. This requires employers to initially complete a detailed questionnaire which is followed with a conference call to consider potential issues. This may then lead to a review of records.

26.11 This chapter analyses the review/investigation approach in four main areas:

- compliance with the PAYE regulations;
- directors;
- Schedule E benefits; and
- liability for tax arising.

PAYE COMPLIANCE ISSUES

26.12 The overall reason for reviewing PAYE records is to ensure that the correct amount of PAYE and NICs has been deducted from the earnings of the employees and directors of the business. This requires that the company has:

- deducted PAYE and NICs from all relevant payments;
- calculated the correct amount of PAYE and NICs; and
- included all employees and directors on the payroll.

26.13 It is in the employer's interest that these areas are regularly reviewed, either by in-house specialists or an external adviser, so as to ensure that an HMRC visit will not produce unwelcome and expensive surprises. It is

Employment tax issues **26.16**

recommended that the employer apply for appropriate dispensations and make himself aware of any working rule agreements applicable to his industry.

26.14 If the company is conducting any pre-review or check, it is worth noting that HMRC standard procedures require it to question those responsible for completing wages and similar records. Similar discussions should be conducted by the internal review team. It is common to find, in the course of such a review, that the procedures actually being carried out in practice are not exactly as management imagine.

26.15 The employer should also not forget that HMRC officials carrying out a PAYE or Schedule E review are under instructions to keep their eyes open for any indications that the employer has been deliberately evading tax. This includes VAT, for example; the HMRC team will then introduce colleagues responsible for those areas. It is now a common practice for details of any employer compliance visit to be shared with the corporate tax and VAT colleagues of the review.

26.16 The following are some review points relevant to employee/director issues:

- Does the workforce on the books look like the workforce on the premises?
- Are there indications of shift work (and possibly an additional workforce paid through a second set of books)?
- Does the business look prosperous?
- Have there been any recent improvements or alterations to the premises?
- Is the apparent lifestyle of directors in keeping with the level of remuneration?
- Are any directors paid less than employees?
- Is the wages clerk related to the directors?
- Are cash wages paid?
- Are significant round sum payments made? (Even if it seems reasonable that these represent genuine business expenditure, large amounts paid without supporting documentation point to a lack of control.)
- Is there a large casual wages charge (ie large relative to the size of the business)?
- Are wages paid to domestic staff or gardeners?
- Do spouses or other relatives receive excessive wages?
- Is there the opportunity to earn extra income?

26.17 Employment tax issues

- If the main income is by cheque, is there a subsidiary business generating cash?
- Are the directors personally in control of cash/petty cash/chequebooks?
- Is there a poor system of cash control?
- Are there cash takings where you would not expect them?
- If there is a high level of cash takings, is it all banked?
- Is cash in hand kept at a steady level or does it fluctuate?
- What was the cash in hand figure at the beginning and end of the year?
- Are the records inaccurate, not up to date, written up after a period from memory and not from vouchers and receipts?
- How often is the cash book balanced?
- Is personal expenditure paid by the business?
- Is the expenditure not supported by receipts or vouchers?
- Is there evidence of altered or false invoices, that is where Special Civil Investigation Office (previously Special Compliance Office (SCO)) have not taken up the case?
- Are unusual benefits provided (for example yachts, caravans, holiday homes, trips abroad, fines paid, school fees, upkeep of animals, prizes awarded by third parties)?
- Are round sum entertaining expenses paid?
- Are any company vehicles rarely used for business (including those used by relatives)?

26.17 If the employer is using a computerised payroll system (or if this is outsourced to a third-party payroll provider) the HMRC team will be interested to know the particular system and what security is in place over the overrides to the system. One area looked at would be payroll parameter reports which show that payments made through the system are dealt with for income tax and National Insurance. It will also be interested to ascertain who is authorised to override electronic systems and what exception reports are then generated. Is the system kited? This means has HMRC carried out the appropriate checks of the payroll software and satisfied itself that the calculations it performs are correct? In the world of RTI HMRC will be aware of the gross pay for each earnings period and the resulting income tax and National Insurance withheld. It will however, be seeking comfort that there are not overrides to take certain amounts of the income out of the payroll system.

26.18 As well as a review of employment taxes being the trigger for an investigation of other areas, the reverse can also be true. When HMRC reviews

Employment tax issues **26.20**

business accounts it is instructed to consider whether costs in the profit and loss account may point to PAYE irregularities. Such costs may include:

- payments to casuals;
- commissions, fees, or consultancy payments;
- wages payments where there is no evidence of a PAYE scheme; and
- suspiciously large items which may conceal additional payments to employees or uncertified subcontractors.

With the significant interest at present over the engagement of workers off payroll, HMRC are likely to take a keen interest over whether those paid off payroll should be considered for tax purposes 'employed workers'.

In particular, whenever a close company is investigated for whatever reason, the official is required to review the company's compliance with its PAYE obligations.

Subjecting earnings to PAYE/NICs

26.19 As has been stated above, not all emoluments are within the scope of PAYE and/or NICs. Even a cursory overview shows up significant differences in tax and NIC treatment, despite recent attempts at greater alignment of the two systems. Some particular points to note are set out below.

Focus

HMRC will carry out checks to see that the gross to net pay looks reasonable and that the tax paid during the course of the tax year appears in line with what HMRC would be expecting.

It is sensible therefore periodically to check that the payments are in line and that there are no payroll errors. In the world of real time information this should be identified by HMRC from the information they receive via the payroll software.

Round sum allowances

26.20 The tax rules changed significantly at April 2016. These are allowances paid to an employee whether or not he spends them in a particular way. As such they are taxable and subject to NICs (*Fergusson v Noble* (1919) 7 TC 176). However, where an allowance is set at a level which is simply intended to reimburse the employee's actual expenditure for 'a specific and distinct business expense', prior to April 2016 it will not be regarded as a 'round

26.21 *Employment tax issues*

sum allowance'. Ideally such flat rate payments, eg for travel or subsistence, should be discussed with the local inspector in advance and a dispensation agreed. HMRC published set rates which it considers to be reasonable. Whilst it is not necessary to comply with these rates if the payment exceeds the amount set, HMRC would want to be satisfied that the amounts paid do not give rise to a profit in the hands of the employee.

26.21 Where there is no dispensation, and an audit review identifies the payments, the employer should see how far he can establish that his allowances were a reasonable estimate of actual necessary expenditure incurred by employees in performing their duties and seek to exclude this from the settlement. It will be the practice of HMRC to ensure that the specific arrangements in place for payment of round sums, which had been disclosed when the dispensation was agreed, is being followed.

26.22 From April 2016 such payments will fail to be taxable unless the amount paid are at the HMRC benchmark rates or the employer has agreed a specific bespoke allowance for overnight rates etc. From April 2016 there will be a major overall of the expenses and benefit reporting system. One of these changes is the ending of dispensations and the placing of the onus is now with the employer over whether a particular expense or benefit needs to be reported. In this situation the 'risk' is with the employer and in case of doubt the particular expense or benefit should be reported and the employee claim relief in his self-assessment return.

Focus

It is important that a 'round sum' allowance is agreed with HMRC before it is paid free of income tax/National Insurance.

Sick pay

26.23 Sick pay paid to employees is generally within the scope of PAYE. Exceptions do occur, eg where sick pay is provided by a third party after an employment has ceased, or when an employee has contributed to a sickness insurance scheme. In the latter case only the part of the sick pay attributable to the employer's contribution, if any, attracts PAYE and NICs.

Tips and service charges

26.24 This is an area in which we have seen significant interest over recent years and the approach of HMRC change. The position is now set out in booklet E24 which clarifies that there is little change from the historical position save that where the employer is using tips to form part of the minimum wage of the employee then National Insurance arises on these irrespective of how the tips are paid.

26.25 Tips paid in cash to the employee or into a communal pool are taxable as earnings from the employment, and may be subject to PAYE and NICs, depending on the role of the employer. The table below summarises the position.

Employer decides basis of distribution	Employer distributes tips	Employer to deduct/ account for:
Yes	Yes	PAYE/NICs
Yes	No	NICs
No	Yes	PAYE

26.26 Service charges are more complex. Where employees receive a share of the service charge made by the employer to customers, the employer must *always* account for NICs.

26.27 However, PAYE has to be deducted by the person responsible for distributing the service charge to employees. This may not be the employer, but may, for example, be the bar steward or head waiter. Such an arrangement is generally known as a tronc. Where the troncmaster has been found not to operate PAYE satisfactorily, the principal employer can be made responsible, but only for future amounts. The troncmaster is still responsible for amounts underpaid in the past. However, it is true to say that in such cases an auditor will look very carefully at the arrangements to see if the troncmaster was genuinely independent of the employer. It is in my experience rare for anyone to be willing to take on the responsibility of running the tronc and when they fully understand the implications of this role they resign.

HMRC has made the point that it is essential that the employee is earning in excess of the minimum wage without account taken of any tips.

26.28 We are seeing a considerable level of HMRC interest in the tipping arrangements in particular hotels and restaurants to ensure that there is full compliance by the employer. Where tips are paid to the employee personally there is also interest to ensure these are being reported by the employee concerned. There have been a number of HMRC challenges to individual workers who, because of the incorrect reporting of cash tips, have claimed excessive tax credits.

> **Focus**
>
> Is the employer involved in the collection of the monies to be paid out? If the tip is collected by the employee personally from the customer then there is no problem. In other cases you need to think of the position for the employer.

26.29 *Employment tax issues*

Remuneration in non-cash form

26.29 Over recent years a number of schemes have sought to avoid NICs and PAYE by paying remuneration other than in cash, eg by using gold bullion, coffee beans or fine wines. However, successive anti-avoidance legislation has sought to prevent the use of such devices. HMRC has also had some success when challenging schemes before the courts: see *DTE Financial Services Ltd v Wilson* [1999] STC 1061 and *NMB Holdings v Secretary of State* (2000) 73 TC 85. Whether a particular method or asset is caught may thus depend on the years for which it was in force and the case law position. It is surprising though that there are still promoters who are trying to sell such arrangements to employers.

26.30 There have been a number of methods used to provide bonuses to employees without the requirement to apply PAYE or National Insurance at the time of the award. These have largely been the subject of HMRC scrutiny and in many cases it is not possible for the payer of the bonus to receive any tax relief for the payments made until the PAYE and National Insurance is settled. The most popular route adopted in this area was the payment of the bonus via an employee benefit trust (EBT). It is generally the case that HMRC in discovering such an arrangement in place will refer the matter to a specialised team to consider. It is essential that payments passed in to an EBT were not contractually entitled to be paid to the employee and that he sacrificed his rights to the remuneration to be paid into the EBT. This is an aspect which HMRC will wish to consider.

26.31 We have seen of late a considerable amount of HMRC attention in regard to EBT arrangements, looking for those who have these in place to make voluntary settlement. This arrangement is set out in the HMRC 'Spotlight' document. Employers who have used EBT arrangements or similar had been encouraged to make their intention to settle known to HMRC by 1 June 2018. Those making that approach will be expected to settle their historical tax liabilities by 5 April 2019 when there are changes to the tax rules.

26.32 Much of the above types of arrangements have been closed with the introduction of 'disguised remuneration' rules which came into effect on 6 April 2011. However, it is important to bear in mind that in the period between 9 December 2010 and 5 April 2011 anti-forestalling rules were introduced which largely mirrored the 'disguised remuneration' legislation. Care should be taken when considering adopting any remuneration planning to ensure this is not caught by these rules. The legislation is widely drafted and catches a variety of arrangements.

26.33 HMRC has announced windows for the voluntary disclosure of these schemes by employers which if adopted provide preferential settlement terms. If an employer does not use that particular window with HMRC then it means more significant amounts will be sought in settlement and HMRC has suggested it will take the matter to tribunal. With the advent in April 2015 of the accelerated payment notice many of those employers who had participated in these arrangements will have received demands for the resulting tax liabilities on the monies paid into the EBT. There is now the intention to levy additional sums from employers who ignore the opportunity to settle the liabilities prior to April 2019 with the introduction of a tax charge on the funds held in the trust fund using the beneficial loan tax rules.

> **Focus**
>
> Are you still in time to make an offer? Have there been accelerated payments and if so, can these be offset against any potential settlement?

Terminations

26.34 A pre-audit review should also check that any termination payments have been correctly included for PAYE purposes. While it is widely known that there is an exemption for the first £30,000 of a termination payment (*ITEPA 2003, s 403*) this does not apply to every payment made on cessation of an employment, and a single lump sum may be composed of a number of different amounts. Points to note are set out below. It should be noted that there is a significant change in the tax rules relating to termination payments at April 2018 and a further change in regard to National Insurance at April 2019.

Contractual payments

26.35 HMRC will seek to tax any termination payment, which is contractual. It has sought to tax termination payments both where the contract provided explicitly for such a payment, and where there was an expectation that such a payment would be made. In the latter situation HMRC argues that the payment is an implied contract term. This situation was the subject of the case of *SCA Packaging Ltd v HMRC* [2007] EWHC 270 (Ch). We are still seeing HMRC paying significant interest in the arrangements of the employer and whether there is clear evidence of a pattern over how such payments are dealt with. If it is, for instance, customary for the employer to not permit employees in to work following their termination to serve out any notice period then it is possible HMRC will argue that the case of *SCA Packaging Ltd v HMRC* is in point and their pay for this period is taxable. It is therefore very important for an employer to ensure that payments in lieu of notice (PILONs) (see below) cannot be considered contractual on grounds of custom.

26.36 *Employment tax issues*

26.36 NICs are also sought on contractual amounts, and the same comments apply. However, with NICs there is an extra point: the employer should also resist any attempt to charge NICs on any redundancy payment, as such payments are specifically excluded from NIC liability.

Payments in lieu of notice

26.37 The HMRC view of contractual payments extends to PILONs. If a PILON is contractual, HMRC will seek to exclude it from *ITEPA 2003, s 403*. HMRC's view was supported in *EMI Group Electronics Ltd v Coldicott* [1999] STC 803. However, in this case, the Revenue accepted that payments in lieu of notice to junior employees were not taxable emoluments, since the employees had no contractual right to them.

There is a substantial change in the rules from April 2018 in that, irrespective of the contractual terms, the tax position is to identify the element of the payment which relates to the PILON and to tax this on the basis that this represents earnings and not compensation. There is a further change at April 2019 which will revise the National Insurance position so that this will arise under Class 1A.

Restrictive covenants

26.38 HMRC has also sometimes sought to argue that part or all of the termination payment is in respect of a restrictive covenant and therefore taxable (*ITEPA 2003, s 225*). However, HMRC significantly reduced the scope and believe these to only be of relevance if the payment being made is a restriction on the employee, which is not specified in his employment contract. Where a restrictive covenant would apply, the employer should seek to apportion the payment being made to apportion the covenant and the balance.

Dismissals

26.39 There have also been attempts to argue that *s 403* is only applicable to redundancies, and not, for example, where someone is dismissed. There are no grounds for this restrictive interpretation within the very broad wording of the section:

> 'This section applies to any payment (not otherwise chargeable to tax) which is made, whether in pursuance of any legal obligation or not, either directly or indirectly in consideration or in consequence of, or otherwise in connection with, the termination of the holding of the office or employment or any change in its functions or emoluments.'

Employment tax issues **26.44**

Retirement

26.40 A further line of HMRC attack has been on payments made to individuals nearing retirement. It has sought to argue that the termination payment is in effect a non-approved retirement benefits scheme, which would make it taxable (*ITEPA 2003, s 394*). This should be resisted as it is difficult to believe that a court would agree with HMRC, and it is doubtful whether HMRC would be prepared to take such a case to court.

26.41 If this point is raised by HMRC it should be noted that in particular the termination of employment because of redundancy or inefficiency is frequently referred to as 'early retirement' even though the employee has been deprived of his employment prematurely, often against his wishes. In both these situations, any ex-gratia lump sum paid by the employer should not be regarded as chargeable. This is so even if the employee also becomes entitled, at the time of termination, to immediate pension benefits from the employer's approved superannuation scheme.

Continuing benefits

26.42 On termination some employees are provided with continuing benefits, such as the use of a company car or a beneficial loan. New rules were introduced by *FA 1998, s 58* which rewrote *TA 1988, s 148* (*ITEPA 2003, s 403*). These rules apply to payments received after 5 April 1998, unless the sums were already taxed in earlier years. It is necessary to monitor the benefits provided to former employees and to report these at the end of the tax year. Since the changes to the pension rules there is a significant change in approach to benefits provided to retired employees.

Employment termination settlements

26.43 The HMRC view of continuing benefits pre-*FA 1998* is explained in the HMRC Press Release of 17 March 1997: 'Taxation of Benefits Received after the Year of Termination'. This Press Release also describes special arrangements available for employment termination agreements entered into from 6 April 1996. These special arrangements offer taxpayers a simpler approach to taxing such continuing benefits.

26.44 Employers who are attacked under the continuing benefits rules for these years are advised to read the Press Release and *Tax Bulletin*. However, despite the detailed arguments set out therein by HMRC, it is arguable that continuing benefits which cannot be transferred have no market value and thus were not assessable. The only reported case on the point is

26.45 *Employment tax issues*

George v Ward [1995] STC (SCD) 230 (SpC30), when the taxpayer lost the argument that there was no tax to pay on a continuing benefit. It was, however, held that tax should be charged by reference to the period for which the benefit was actually made available rather than for the longer period set out in the termination agreement. If *George v Ward* is raised by HMRC in support of its taxation of continuing benefits, it should be reminded that it is merely a Special Commissioner's case, and thus does not create a binding precedent. It is also the view of many tax advisers that it was wrongly decided.

26.45 *ITEPA 2003, s 403* only applies where an item is 'not otherwise chargeable to tax', but the HMRC official may argue that certain continuing benefits cannot form part of the £30,000. Targets include gifts of assets, taxable under *ITEPA 2003, s 203*, and loan write offs, taxable under *ITEPA 2003, s 188*. Such problems could be avoided if the employee was given the cash which was then used to buy the asset at its market value, or to repay the loan. If this route was not taken, and the official seeks to argue that the amounts are taxable, reference should be made to the HMRC Press Release of 17 March 1997 which clearly suggests that both cars and loans can fall within the £30,000.

Where the 'continuing benefit' is a small regular gift, such as a Christmas box to pensioners, the employer could argue that, if it is taxable at all, it should be exempted.

Other issues

26.46 Terminations are complex and are occurring with increasing frequency. Their cumulative cost and the value of the tax-free amounts are significant, and thus can be expected to draw an inspector's attention. In addition to the points raised above, other relevant issues arise where:

- The employee has been made redundant and then subsequently re-employed. The inspector will review such cases to ensure that the redundancy was genuine at the time it was made.

- The employee has 'retired', received a lump sum from his pension tax free, and then been re-employed. In these cases the Pension Schemes Office may challenge the tax-free status of the lump sum and may even threaten the qualifying status of the pension scheme itself. For a discussion of this issue, see Adrian Waddingham's article in *Taxation*, 18 May 2000. Therefore, it is important to demonstrate that there has been a genuine cessation of employment, with a re-employment on wholly different terms. It may be worth consulting an employment lawyer.

- The employee is given 'garden leave', ie continues to receive his salary but is not required to report to the office. This is taxable under Schedule E in the normal way.

- The employee has spent some time abroad. In this case a higher amount can be paid tax free; if he is retiring through ill-health, there is no £30,000 limit (*ITEPA 2003, s 413*) but this concession ceases to apply in regard to terminations from 6 April 2018.

26.47

> **Focus**
>
> Is there a compromise agreement in place? Does this show the breakdown of the proposed payment to the former employee? What elements of this payment can be paid free of tax/National Insurance? It is important to bear in mind that the £30,000 limit is for income tax not National Insurance at present. For National Insurance the entire payment (if non-contractual) can be paid gross.

> **Example 26.1**
>
> An employee is made redundant and his compromise agreement suggests that the employer is offering to make a payment to its respective employee of £50,000 which is said to be in full and final settlement.
>
> On review of the employee's contract you see that he is entitled to 30 days' notice period but the contract says the employer reserves the right to not require the worker to work his notice period but to receive the payment in lieu. Given this option £5,000 of the £50,000 is clearly relating to the notice period and is taxable and caught to National Insurance given the option.
>
> Of the balance of £45,000 it appears that the employee is being paid for annual leave not used which totals £2,000. This is a contractual payment and is therefore caught to National Insurance.
>
> You are comfortable that the balance of £43,000 is compensation and therefore £30,000 of this sum can be paid free of income tax with the balance paid under deduction of income tax at the employee's marginal tax rate. However, for National Insurance the total sum of £43,000 can be paid without deduction.

Salary sacrifice arrangements

26.48 A salary sacrifice is an arrangement under which the employee agrees to take a cut in future remuneration in exchange for some other benefit, such as an increased employer contribution to the employee's pension fund. It is

26.49 *Employment tax issues*

becoming very common to use salary sacrifice to avoid the employer National Insurance and to pass on some savings in employee National Insurance to the employee. It is the case that HMRC are keen to ensure that the rules around salary sacrifice are observed and difficulties with compliance can prove expensive.

26.49 An HMRC official may check a sample of such salary sacrifices to ensure that they:

- are in writing, signed and dated;
- stating clearly that the employee is varying his right to remuneration;
- are not retrospective; and
- they are also likely will want comfort that the salary sacrifice is dealt with in the payroll records.

26.50 Failure in any respect will mean that HMRC will view the sacrifice as ineffective, so that the employee remains entitled under his contract to the originally sacrificed amount and should thus have been taxed on it. The NIC implications will follow, plus a possible over-funding of the pension scheme if the re-categorised amount takes the employee above his contribution limit.

26.51 There are special rules relating to life changing circumstances. HMRC has given guidance of what significant lifestyle changes warrant an early exit from a salary sacrifice arrangement. HMRC at the time of any review will want to be satisfied that those who have exited early from a salary sacrifice were in circumstances which it would consider to fall within its guidance.

26.52 HMRC has issued significant guidance on what it considers is essential to meet the qualifying conditions for a salary sacrifice arrangement. The HMRC guidance makes clear that the arrangement, which must be available to 'all employees', must not discriminate against employees who for instance cannot obtain credit, ie employees below 18. In addition, in respect of the 'bike to work' scheme, the price at which the bike is transferred to the employee at the end of the hire period must represent market value. HMRC has issued guidance over what it considers that value to be. From April 2011 the provision of canteen meals using salary sacrifice is stopped.

26.53 We have recently seen HMRC succeed in the Court of Appeal with its dispute with Reed Employment over its employee salary sacrifice scheme (TC1727). The court found the scheme documentation was unclear and did not accept that a salary sacrifice had occurred. This reinforces the need to ensure that there are clear changes made to the contract for the employee and any guidance issued is clear.

26.54 With the ever increasing number of items available to be covered within a salary sacrifice arrangement employers need to be comfortable exposed. They need to ensure that the tax rules are being followed and that employees are not left with earnings which are below the national living wage. There are now significantly increased penalties which can be levied for national living wage failures and there is also the risk of the employer being 'named and shamed'.

The tax rules have significantly changed from April 2017 although certain arrangements are left unchanged eg childcare vouchers and pensions. There are other arrangements which have been permitted to continue until April 2021 but this is dependent on there being no change to the employer's contractual terms in this period. It should also be noted that in the case of an arrangement which provides a cash or benefit arrangement then, from April 2017, the employee is taxed on the greater of the cash sacrificed or the taxable benefit under the optional remuneration rules (OPRA).

This is an area which is complex, and it is easy for employers to misunderstand the rules that apply. It is important for those who are continuing to offer schemes to their employees to get the appropriate tax advice.

Focus

- Is there a genuine change in the employee's contract of employment to take account of the salary sacrifice?
- Does this arrangement still work given the changing tax rules from April 2017?
- Is that change of contractual term not able to be terminated for a period of at least 12 months except in a case of 'lifestyle change'?
- Have you considered whether the particular benefit in kind needs to be reported on form P11D?
- Are you sure this will not take the respective employees below the national living wage?

Example 26.2

An employee who works 20 hours a week earning £7,280 wishes to take a salary sacrifice scheme offered by the employer for an iPad. The salary sacrifice means a reduction in salary of £600 in the year which will leave the employee below the NMW assuming a rate of £6.50 per hour. In view of this the salary sacrifice cannot be approved.

Example 26.3

An employee asks to join a company car salary sacrifice arrangement and takes a Ford Fiesta. Having joined the scheme the employee concerned decides within 30 days he does not like the vehicle and agrees with the lease provider that the car can be returned and the agreement cancelled. Given that the reason for the cancellation is unlikely to qualify for a 'lifestyle event', HMRC is likely to consider that the particular salary sacrifice arrangement was not robust and the payments sacrificed would be taxable.

The Government stopped the tax relief available under salary sacrifice. The change is proposed at April 2017 and will catch all but:

1   Pension salary sacrifice arrangements.
2   Child care.
3   Bike to work schemes.

However, there are transitional rules for certain benefits until April 2021.

Calculation of the correct amounts of PAYE/NICs

26.55 In these days of computerised PAYE, it is often thought that calculation errors are unlikely to occur. This is not the case, although some of the errors occur not because of the system itself but through faulty inputs – the 'garbage in, garbage out' principle. Particularly vulnerable are PAYE systems which are supplied with information from more than one source, such as two or more departments or subsidiaries. As part of any *pre-audit* review some mechanical checks on the operation of the system are therefore useful. HMRC's review will make similar checks. Some areas where the wrong amounts may be erroneously brought into the calculation are set out below.

Timing of taxing the earnings

26.56 Specific rules exist to establish when earnings are taxable, and these are different for employees and directors. Employees are taxable on the earlier of receipt and entitlement (*ITEPA 2003, s 10*). Particular care needs to be taken with bonus payments and commission.

26.57 The special rules for the taxing of directors' remuneration are likely to be checked by HMRC. The remuneration is taxable on the earliest of:

- receipt of the emoluments;
- entitlement to the emoluments;

- determination of the emoluments; or
- crediting the emoluments to an account with the company.

26.58 It is the fourth of these which most commonly gives problems, because companies do not always realise that the account in question does not have to be the director's own account. A credit in the company's salaries account is enough, or a written note in a minute book. Neither does a restriction (a 'fetter') on drawing out the money prevent the credit from being regarded as remuneration (*TA 1988, s 203A(1)(c)*), although in such cases there are no NICs until payment is made. Companies should also be aware that 'director' includes a shadow director (*TA 1988, s 202B(6)*). However, the company should note that to be taxable:

- the entry must identify the director, and
- it must be for an emolument. In particular, an accounts provision which has not been agreed, or remuneration which is contingent on the happening of some future event, is not an emolument.

(SE 5351)

26.59 Inspectors will review this area by:

- asking if any directors' remuneration has been deferred; and
- paying particular attention, when examining records, to any annual fees, bonuses, etc and establishing the date on which they should have been subject to PAYE.

26.60 There are also special NIC rules for directors, under which the earnings period is a year rather than a month or a week (their regular earnings period). This has the effect of accelerating the payment of NICs. Directors may now pay primary contributions for 11 months as if they were employees, with a recalculation and 'catch-up' payment in month 12 if necessary. Failures in earlier periods are often treated leniently by auditors as long as the correct amount of NICs has been paid in the tax year. However, problems can arise with directors who leave in the year.

26.61 This is an area often overlooked by payroll departments especially when using electronic payrolls. This special rule does, however, only apply to statutory directors and not those who simply carry the title of 'director'.

26.62 With effect from April 2010 it is proposed that interest and penalties can be sought from an employer if income tax or National Insurance is not paid on time. HMRC has confirmed that its approach to penalties continues following the introduction of RTI.

26.63 *Employment tax issues*

New employees

26.63 Sometimes the first month's salary is paid by cheque whilst the administrative arrangements to include the employee on the payroll are in process. Ensure that any such payments are included in PAYE pay.

NICs, SSP and SMP issues

26.64 The cost of errors in these areas, and particularly in employer's NICs, can be substantial. HMRC will check that these amounts have been correctly calculated for a sample of employees. The accuracy of the following may be reviewed:

- any non-standard calculations, such as reduced rate NICs and small employer's relief for SSP;
- contracted-out amounts;
- NICs;
- SMP amounts paid and the amounts offset against NICs due – the SMP rules are complex and in general less well supported by either computer systems or trained staff than PAYE. For employers with relatively low numbers of women on maternity leave, the cost of errors in this area may be small, but for organisations with large female workforces it may be worth checking that the rules are understood and being operated correctly; and
- correct application of the NIC aggregation rules.

26.65 One important point for employers is the limited scope they have to collect under-deductions of NICs from employees. Such sums can only be recovered if they occur in the current tax year; if later, the cost is purely one for the employer.

Payroll giving schemes

26.66 If the company is operating a payroll giving scheme, the inspector will ask to see:

- the employer's contract with the approved agency;
- form CHY 140(1) if for a period prior to 2000;
- the employer's written authority to make deductions from the employees' pay.

Employment tax issues **26.72**

26.67 He will also check that:

- PAYE is being operated on a 'net pay' basis but that NICs are calculated on the true gross pay;
- for years before 2000/01, that the deductions are within the maximum annual limit; and
- the company has paid the donations to the agency within 14 days of the end of the income tax month in which they were deducted.

Third parties

26.68 Where a cash payment, such as a round sum allowance, is paid as a reward in connection with an individual's employment, the paying company has to deduct PAYE. This is because of *ITEPA 2003, s 684*.

26.69 An 'employer' is defined as 'any person paying emoluments'. This means that PAYE obligations may stretch more widely than is sometimes presumed. It should, however, be noted that the client is not liable for the NICs on these payments. For the position of benefits paid to third parties see **26.175–26.176** below.

Including all employees and directors on the payroll

26.70 Ensuring that all employees are correctly included on the payroll is a key audit task. HMRC will look particularly closely at any individuals paid by the company who have not been included in PAYE, such as casuals, agency workers, students, those regarded as self-employed, and one-man companies. Recently it has paid particular attention to subcontractors.

26.71 There will also be particular attention paid to directors. HMRC review instructions say that all directors should be identified at the time of interview, and that the records should be checked to see if there is any director whose remuneration has been concealed.

Self-employment v employment: basic principles

26.72 There is no definition of either 'employment' or 'self-employment' in the legislation, and the HMRC/CA will thus rely on the principles established in a series of tax cases. These have sought to distinguish between the individual who works under a contract of service (and is thus employed) and one who

26.73 Employment tax issues

works under a contract for services. The distinction was summarised in the case of *Market Investigations Ltd v Minister of Social Security* [1969] 2 QB 173:

> 'Is the person who has engaged himself to perform these services performing them as a person in business on his own account? If the answer to that question is "yes" then the contract is a contract for services. If the answer is "no" then the contract is a contract of service.'

26.73 This is a developing area and regard should always be had to recent case law in establishing the latest position. There is increasing interest in this area caused by the introduction of the personal services legislation.

26.74 It is understood by HMRC that this is the number one focus on mainstream employment taxes. We have seen a number of significant challenges in recent months in this area. There are a growing number of Employment Tribunal cases which test the status of the worker and give grounds for HMRC to attack this issue.

26.75 The Office of Tax Simplification has recently undertaken a review of status and made various recommendations for HM Treasury to consider. These proposals are now being considered by Department for Business, Innovations and Skills (BIS) but if introduced then unless a worker meets the particular criteria they will be considered 'employed' for tax purposes.

26.76 Currently the basic principles which a court would adopt in deciding whether an individual is an employee or not are:

- Is the person in business on his own account? This was discussed in the case of *Hall v Lorimer* [1994] STC 23, in which the judge said:

> 'In order to decide whether a person carries on business on his own account it is necessary to consider many different aspects of that person's work activity. This is not a mechanical exercise of running through items on a check list to see whether they are present in, or absent from, a given situation. The object of the exercise is to paint a picture from the accumulation of detail. The overall effect can only be appreciated by standing back from the detailed picture which has been painted, by viewing it from a distance and by making an informed, considered, qualitative appreciation of the whole.'

Some of the details that will be considered (*Market Investigations Ltd v Minister of Social Security* [1969] 2 QB 173) include:

(a) How much control is exercised over the individual? Control includes control over *where* the individual does his work, *when* he does it, *what* he does and *how* he does it. The relative importance of each will vary, eg a surgeon is not told how to perform an operation (*Morren v Swinton and Pendlebury Borough Council* [1965] 1 WLR 576).

(b) Does he provide his own equipment? There is a presumption that employers will generally provide major items of equipment which are necessary for employees to do their job. Similarly many self-employed people own their own equipment. However, there are many exceptions to this. 'Little significance can be attached to the provision of small tools (or even major items) where it is customary for them to be provided' (SE 604). Cases on this point include *Ready Mixed Concrete (South East) Ltd v Minister of Pensions and National Insurance* [1968] 2 QB 497.

(c) Can he hire his own helpers? If he can, he is more likely to be self-employed.

(d) Does he take financial risk, so that he can make a loss as well as a profit? If he can, he is likely to be self-employed. If there is no financial risk, it is still possible, albeit unusual, that the individual will be self-employed (*Addison v London Philharmonic Orchestra Society Ltd* [1981] ICR 261).

(e) Can he 'profit from sound management'? A self-employed person is often in this position: the efficiency with which he carries out his job will affect his income. The same may, however, apply to some employees, such as those paid on piecework.

- Can the individual send a substitute to do the job? If he can, this is almost conclusive evidence in favour of self-employment, as the requirement for personal service is a normal ingredient of most service contracts.

- What were the intentions of the parties? Although not conclusive, what the parties intended should be taken into account.

- How is the individual paid? Again, this is not conclusive, but generally only employees have paid holidays, sick pay, maternity pay and pensions.

- Is the individual effectively selling his skills to a succession of different companies? This is a very difficult test to apply, and the tax case of *Hall v Lorimer* is the best illustration of its application. Mr Lorimer was a vision mixer who customarily worked for 20 or more production companies. Most of his engagements lasted for only a single day. HMRC has said that it believes that *Lorimer* will have particular relevance to engagements where:

    (a) the worker provides similar services to many engagers; and

    (b) there is a mutual intention not to create employment; and

    (c) the worker has a business-like approach to obtaining and organising his engagements and incurs expenditure in this area of a type not normally associated with employment.

26.77 *Employment tax issues*

In addition the following pointers may be present although their absence would not inevitably mean employment:

(d) the worker has many short-term engagements;

(e) the worker is providing professional services or services requiring the exercise of rare skill and judgment;

(f) the worker is engaged for a specific task;

(g) as a result of the number of different engagers the worker incurs expenditure travelling to various workplaces similar in nature to 'home to work' travel but considerable in amount when compared to the level of expenditure that is likely to be incurred by an employee who resides close to his workplace;

(h) the worker bears a greater financial risk than an employee because payment is made after the payer has been invoiced, exposing the worker to the risk of delayed payment and bad debt; and

(i) the extent to which the worker is able to influence the rate of pay is greater than is normally the case in employment situations, for example evidence of tendering.

- It is, however, possible for a person to be neither an employee, nor in business on his own account: see the comments of Nolan J in *Wickens v Champion Employment* [1984] ICR 365.

Self-employment v employment: the audit approach

26.77 We are seeing a lot of HMRC activity on the status of workers which includes resourcing teams to specifically identify and review those workers who are engaged off payroll. It is understood from HMRC sources that this is their main target area in employer compliance. We are seeing a lot of HMRC activity looking jointly at the National Living Wage and status.

As stated above, in seeking to establish whether individuals are employees, HMRC will apply the above case law principles to the facts of each case. To establish these it will:

- interview some or all of the individuals. This may well occur without the engager being aware;

- ask to see any documentation concerning the terms under which the individual was engaged. This may include the original job advertisement, any oral instructions given when he started work, the written contract (if any) and written company procedures;

- seek to confirm actual practice which may be other than described in the written agreements. (Remember that this works both ways: the written documentation may not be helpful, but if the company can establish that the actual procedures are otherwise, this should also be taken into account.);

- seek to discover whether there are other workers doing similar duties and if so, whether they are employed or self-employed;

- ask whether the worker was previously an employee of the 'employer' – if so it will ask when the change occurred and what differences exist in the terms of engagement.

26.78 HMRC has developed an employment status tool indicator on its website into which the detailed terms of a contract can be populated and from which it will give an indication of whether that person engaged should be treated on a self-employed or employed basis. Clearly in any HMRC review in this area it will want to see if the status tool was used and also whether the information fed in to this was correct and therefore its conclusion can be relied upon. This may result in a formal ruling that the individuals the company has been treating as self-employed are in fact employees. If the company disagrees with the ruling it may be necessary to take a test case to the courts. Whether the ruling is to be applied for past years or only for the future is a matter for negotiation, often as part of an overall audit settlement.

26.79 Where an individual is retrospectively re-categorised as an employee, there will be a recalculation of the outstanding tax and NICs. In such cases the Schedule D tax and Class 4 NICs should be allocated against the Schedule E tax, and the Class 2 against the Class 1 NICs (Hansard (1984), vol 55 No 108 cols 62–63). The shortfall (plus possibly interest and penalties) is to be paid by the employer, with the limited recovery rights. The position is now changed following the principles outlined in the case of *Demibourne Ltd v Revenue and Customs Comrs* [2005] STC (SCD) 667. HMRC will now only accept an offset which is equivalent to the Schedule D tax paid by the contractor. This could leave an employer facing a significant liability in respect of the past and any penalties arising will be calculated prior to the '*Demibourne* offset' which can prove expensive for the engager.

26.80 Even before their merger, HMRC and the CA used the same case law in arriving at their status decisions, and agreed that they would accept each other's rulings. However, the CA, and now HMRC, had the power to *determine* that particular groups of workers should be treated as Class I (employed) or Class II (self-employed). They made use of these powers for the following groups of workers:

- electoral workers (generally exempt from NICs);
- examiners, moderators, etc of certain examining bodies (generally treated as self-employed);

26.81 *Employment tax issues*

- domestic employment by close relatives (generally exempt from NICs);
- ministers of religion (generally treated as employees);
- office and telephone cleaners (generally treated as employees);
- engaging of a person by his spouse (generally treated as an employee).

26.81 The practice of HMRC in this area is currently changing, following the case of *Demibourne Ltd*. This case outlined the position of how income tax paid under Schedule D by the worker could be used against the tax liability of the engager. Whilst the future approach is still not final HMRC is now only prepared to offset tax paid by the worker if that person consents and this will be given in the form of a credit against the engager which is still likely to leave a balance of liability payable.

At the time of writing, this is an area of Government consultation following a review under the Taylor report, and there are proposals for the possible introduction of a statutory test of self employment.

Focus

Getting the status of a worker wrong can prove expensive. It is not just a case of looking at the written contract but how it works in practice (substance over form).

Even if the worker had paid Schedule D tax it is likely there will be PAYE arising on expenses claimed under Schedule D which would not be permitted under PAYE. Also penalties will be sought on the gross tax before the *Demibourne* offset.

Example 26.4

An engager takes on an independent consultant to work for the company three days a week and it pays him £50,000 on an annual basis for the work undertaken. When HMRC undertakes an employer compliance review of the company it decides this worker is an employee and whilst the worker is registered with HMRC under Schedule D he had claimed expenses against his profits of £5,000 which would not be allowable under PAYE. HMRC is satisfied therefore that of the balance of £45,000 tax is paid and can be offset under the *Demibourne* rules but seeks from the employer PAYE/National Insurance on the balance of £5,000 covering the current and proceeding four tax years. HMRC, however, decides to seek penalties against the engager for not applying PAYE/National Insurance and in so doing this is calculated on the income tax/National Insurance on the full earnings (£50,000) and not just the £5,000.

Employment tax issues **26.87**

Casual workers

26.82 A 'casual' in common parlance is someone who is not permanently employed by an organisation. There is no special legislation covering such people, and the normal rules for employment status, described in the preceding section, therefore apply.

26.83 However, it is in the case of casuals that the concept of mutuality of obligation comes into its own. For an individual to be an employee there must be an ongoing obligation on the part of the person who employs him to supply him with work and an ongoing obligation on the part of the worker to take work which is offered. There is a long line of cases on this point, of which *O'Kelly v Trusthouse Forte plc* [1984] QB 90 is perhaps the most significant.

26.84 From the employer's point of view, casuals represent a review vulnerability. The company may genuinely believe the casual worker to be self-employed, eg because the worker has no sick pay or holiday pay and is known to undertake a succession of similar contracts. However, the individual may nevertheless be an employee: see the comments of Lord Griffiths in *Lee Ting Sang v Chung Chi-Keung* [1990] 2 AC 374:

> 'the picture emerges of a skilled artisan earning his living by working for more than one employer as an employee and not as a small businessman venturing into business on his own account as an independent contractor with all its attendant risks. The applicant ran no risk whatever save that of being unable to find employment which is, of course, a risk faced by casual employees who move from one job to another'

26.85 Organisations with a large number of branches are particularly vulnerable if the branch manager has authority to cover short-term staff shortages. The amounts paid to each casual may be small, but if multiplied across a branch network and carried back for six years, the total cost can be substantial.

26.86 Another risk area is casual payments made to existing employees for extra duties such as unscheduled overtime. This may also not have been correctly dealt with under the NIC aggregation rules. A classic case is the teacher who does occasional evening classes for the same local authority which employs him during the day.

26.87 In dealing with an audit attack on casuals, the company should:
- check whether there is any scope for arguing that some of the individuals are genuinely self-employed, applying the principles set out above, and in particular *O'Kelly v Trusthouse Forte* and the *Hall v Lorimer* case;
- review whether any of the workers were supplied by bona fide employment agencies, in which case the agency rules may apply;

26.88 *Employment tax issues*

- perform a detailed sample check to establish whether and how many workers are below the threshold for taxation and NICs – this may be possible where the casuals are known to other workers in the organisation, eg family members or friends;

- consider writing to the individuals asking them to complete forms P46 on a retrospective basis;

- if the payment should have been taxable, seek to have it reduced by the personal allowance which would have been available, on the basis that such individuals are unlikely to have used it elsewhere. Likewise full use should be made of the lower rate band in assessing tax underpaid (this argument may be resisted by HMRC but may be useful when negotiating an overall settlement).

Agency workers

26.88 People supplied by a third-party agency who are not employed either by the agency or the company can be *deemed* employees (*ITEPA 2003, s 44*). In this case PAYE is operated by whoever pays them. The deeming provision operates where: 'an individual ('the worker') renders or is under an obligation to render personal services to another person ('the client') and is subject to, or to the right of, supervision, direction or control as to the manner in which he renders those services' (*ITEPA 2003, s 44*). Exceptions to this deeming provision include musicians, entertainers, models and (until 6 April 1998) subcontractors (*ITEPA 2003, s 44*).

Where an organisation engages a worker through a foreign agency without a branch or agent in the UK, the UK organisation is deemed to be the employer for PAYE and NIC purposes.

26.89 The inspector will seek to establish whether the deeming provisions should be applied, and in so doing will:

- review the contractual relationships. If the agency has only introduced the worker to the company then the deeming provisions will not apply (*Brady v Hart (t/a Jaclyn Model Agency)* (1985) 58 TC 518). However where this is the case the auditor will then review whether the worker is an employee of the organisation for which he is working;

- check whether any travelling expenses or associated subsistence have been paid to cover the workers' travel costs in getting to the job. Such expenses are regarded as home to work travel and as such are taxable. PAYE is deductible by the person making the payments, which may be the company for whom the individual is working. Before settling on this point with the auditors, the company should check whether in fact some of the expenses cover detached duty away from the normal place of

Employment tax issues **26.91**

work, in which case they will be allowable. There is also a concessional relief available for travel between clients.

26.90 There have been considerable changes in this regard since April 2014. There are three specific categories:

- If the worker is supplied by an overseas agency/intermediary then from April 2014 the end client is responsible to operate PAYE and National Insurance on payments made to the third party agency.

- If the worker is supplied by a UK agency/intermediary then the responsibility for PAYE and National Insurance sits with them. Since April 2014 the circumstances in which payments can be paid gross to a worker is limited and will only be relevant when there is no control or management of the worker by either the end client or intermediary. The intermediary is required from April 2015 to provide HMRC with a list of persons who have been paid gross. This is a quarterly requirement and penalties can arise if this is not complied with.

- If the worker is involved in the gas or oil industry then special rules apply which require the worker to be registered with HMRC.

26.91 This is new legislation and it creates a significant change in practice. It is important that those who supply workers to a third party either on a formal agency basis or on a less formal basis are familiar with their requirements and comply with these. Also those who are supplied with workers via a third party will need to be comfortable that they are complying with the obligations for those who are supplied by a non-UK intermediary. It is clear that going forward we are likely to see a considerable amount of HMRC activity in this area, particularly at the time of an HMRC review.

Focus

Do you have workers provided by a third party? Are these workers being engaged by the third party outside of PAYE/National Insurance? Where is the intermediary based?

Example 26.5

An employer engages a worker via an agency but does not check where it is based and pays the intermediary gross for the services provided. HMRC undertakes a review of the employer and discovers that the agency is located in the Isle of Man (so not UK resident). It therefore claimed the PAYE/National Insurance arising on the payments made to the agency for the services of the worker together with interest and penalties.

26.92 *Employment tax issues*

> **Example 26.6**
>
> A worker is provided by an agency to undertake duties for a client. The individual is clearly controlled by the engager in the work he undertakes. HMRC discovers that the intermediary is not accounting for PAYE/National Insurance on payments made or providing the quarterly return to HMRC. Given that the intermediary is based in the UK then there is no failure by the end client, with the responsibility sitting with the intermediary.

One-man companies

26.92 The tax rules are changing in this area and HMRC are concerned to ensure those caught to IR35 are preparing their tax computation on this basis. HMRC are also considering whether the contract is really with the personal service company and not the individual worker. This is a matter of fact. Also are there managed service company implications because of the involvement of the adviser undertaking the management of the company.

One-man companies are common in some industries, such as computer consultancy. There should be no problem with using the services of such companies: an attempt to make the client liable for the PAYE and NICs on payments to such personal service companies was defeated (IR Press Release, 23 September 1999). The company is registered and will receive its own tax return; the salary paid to the director will be subject to PAYE by the one-man company. There will only be a liability on the payer if the amount represents non-business costs, such as a round sum allowance (see Frequently Asked Question on IR35, no 17). The personal service company's client may also have a reporting obligation if benefits are provided and should also:

- ensure that the individual *has* such a company and not be misled by business names on headed paper, such as 'Jim Brown Computing' which may simply be a trading name with no corporate identity;
- be sure that a formal contract has been entered into with the company to make it clear that the individual is not being employed directly.

HMRC is likely to ask to see copies of the contracts between the service companies and the organisation using the company's services.

26.93 If however, the one-man limited company is not UK resident for tax purposes it is likely that HMRC will expect the engager of the services to withhold tax on payments it makes. It is sensible though that the engager should take the precaution of deducting tax on the payments made. There are proposed changes from April 2017 to limit the use of personal service

Employment tax issues **26.94**

companies within the public sector. These changes were announced in the 2016 Autumn Statement and follow consultation. These proposals will require in many instances the engager to operate tax/NIC on payments made to the one-man limited company. It is worth bearing in mind that the issues in IR35 are very topical and HMRC is presently consulting over introducing restrictions on when personal service companies can be used. The proposal is to prevent their use to any persons who are integral to the running of an organisation.

26.94 In May 2012 HMRC launched the Business Entity Tests, which are as follows:

Test 1	Business Premises test	Does your business own/rent separate business premises which are separate from your home and client's premises?	Yes = 10
Test 2	PII test	Do you need professional indemnity insurance?	Yes = 2
Test 3	Efficiency test	Has your business had the opportunity in the last 24 months to increase your business income by working more efficiently, eg by finishing the work/project earlier than projected but still receiving the full agreed payment?	Yes = 10
		For example you originally agreed with the client/engager that the work would take 3 months and cost 10,000 but you finished in 2 months and still received the full 10,000 at the end of the 2 month period.	
Test 4	Assistance test	Does your business engage one or more workers who generate at least 25% of your business turnover annually?	Yes = 35
Test 5	Previous PAYE test	Have you been engaged on PAYE employment terms by your current client/end user within the last financial year with no significant changes to your working arrangements?	Yes = (minus) -15
		If you are doing the same work you should answer yes to this question. Current engager also includes working at a different location owned by your engager or working at a different company but which is connected, eg part of the same group.	

26.95 *Employment tax issues*

Test 6	Advertising test	Has your business invested over £1,200 on advertising, excluding entertainment in the last 12 months?	Yes = 2
Test 7	Business Plan test	Does your business have a business plan with cash flow forecast, that is regularly updated, and a business bank account which is separate from your personal account and identified as a business bank account by the bank?	Yes = 1
Test 8	Repair at Own Expense test	Would your business have to bear the cost of having to rectify any mistakes?	Yes = 4
Test 9	Client Risk test	Has your business been unable to recover payment for work done during the last 24 months in excess of 10% of annual turnover?	Yes = 10
Test 10	Billing test	Do you invoice for work carried out prior to being paid and negotiate payment terms?	Yes = 2
Test 11	Personal Service test	Does your business have the right to send a substitute?	Yes = 2
Test 12	Substitution test	Has your business hired anyone in the last 24 months to do the contracted work you have taken on? This could be demonstrated by sending a substitute in your place or by sub-contracting, but in both cases your business remains responsible for the work and for paying the substitute or sub-contractor. You can still pass this test if you had to notify the end client of the name of the individual you sent as a substitute.	

26.95 HMRC has also published details of how it will interpret the scoring. This is as follows:

The total score/risk bands are as follows:

- less than 10: high risk;
- 10 to 20: medium risk;
- more than 20: low risk.

> **Focus**
>
> We are seeing a significant amount of compliance resource applied by HMRC in checking that those who are engaged via a personal service company are accounting correctly for their tax and National Insurance. The particular concern centres on whether the requirement to account under IR35 is applied. We are seeing a number of personal service companies who because of the nature of their contract now face a liability under IR35 together with interest and penalties.

26.96 The position over the engagement of non-executive directors via a personal service company changed in April 2014. If the director concerned is still paid off the payroll, it is now a requirement that IR35 is applied to the calculations of the fees received in his personal service company. If a company engaging a non-executive director does not operate PAYE/NIC on the payment, whilst no loss of tax will result because of the use of IR35, HMRC may still seek payroll to be applied going forward.

The rules changed in April 2017 for those personal services who provide their services within the public sector. These changes are significant and require the public sector body to satisfy itself that the terms of the engagement will fall outside of IR35. HMRC have provided a tool which can be used for this test. If the terms do not fall outside of IR35 then the public sector body is required to operate PAYE and National Insurance on the payments it makes. It is now proposed that these rules be adopted by all engagers from possibly 2020. This is currently the subject of consultation.

Students

26.97 Students are likely to be outside PAYE, but to establish this they need to have completed a form P38(S). Where this has not been completed HMRC will seek back tax. The employer should try to obtain the forms retrospectively. Other points to watch are that:

- there is no exemption from NICs, so that the normal rules apply – thus NICs should be operated where the student's earnings exceed the lower earnings limit;
- where a student's period of vacation work is at Easter, two tax years may be straddled. In such cases a form P38(S) is required for each year.

Special arrangements may apply to foreign or agricultural students.

Cleaners

26.98 Certain cleaners are deemed to be employees for NIC purposes. These deeming provisions apply to cleaners who work in an office or other non-domestic premises and are accepted as self-employed for tax purposes. However, the deeming rules will not be applied if the cleaners are operating in partnership or have their own employees. The rules also do not apply to window cleaners, but do apply to cleaners of telephone kiosks.

26.99 The employer in the office which they clean must operate Class 1 NICs on what it pays them. An official will seek back payment of Class 1 NICs on payments to a 'self-employed' cleaner if non-deduction is discovered during a review.

DIRECTORS

26.100 In many respects the investigation of directors is the same as that for higher paid employees, but there are a number of special points:

- HMRC takes a special interest in anyone who may be able to override an organisation's normal accounting controls. Apart from deliberate fraud, the HMRC official will also look for expense claim forms from directors where the expenses are not fully vouched, or are self-certificated. It will be for the company to prove that the payments were for genuine business expenses, rather than a benefit to the director.

- For the same reason the interface between the individual's own returns and the company's may also be checked. In the case of a more complex investigation each director may be asked whether his own returns are correct and complete to the best of his knowledge and belief. The personal files of the directors may also be called for.

- Directors of close companies are subject to particularly close examination, eg to ensure that personal expenditure has not been put through as a business expense.

SCHEDULE E BENEFITS AND REIMBURSED EXPENSES

Dispensations

26.101 A dispensation releases an employer from the obligation to include expenses payments and benefits on employees' P11Ds. It also releases the employee from including the items on his tax return. Without a dispensation HMRC may argue that *all* reimbursed expenses and all benefits must be

Employment tax issues **26.106**

reported on the P11D and the individual's tax return, even where the reimbursed expenses were incurred solely for business purposes. From April 2016 the rules change and it is proposed that from then onwards dispensation applications will cease and the onus will sit with the employer (see below).

26.102 However the legal position is that only 'benefits provided for the employee such as give rise to any charge to tax' need to be reported. Thus if the business reason is quite clear, the employer should resist any penalty for not having included an amount on the P11D. It is of course simpler if employers pre-empt such problems by applying for dispensations where appropriate (IR Leaflet IR 69 explains how to do this).

26.103 To obtain a dispensation the employer will need to show that:

- the expenses are necessarily incurred in the performance of the employees' duties;
- claims to expenses are independently checked and authorised;
- where possible expense claims are accompanied by receipts or other evidence;
- the employer has procedures to ensure that advances of expenses are fully accounted for, and any excess advance has been repaid by the employee.

26.104 HMRC will check current dispensations at the beginning of its review. Problems can arise where:

- an examination of the company's records shows that the terms of the dispensation have not been complied with, eg if amounts in excess of agreed subsistence allowances have been paid;
- the dispensation was for a limited period and has not been renewed;
- the dispensation only covered some companies or individuals in the group but has been applied to others.

26.105 If either the second or third point are found to apply, the employer should seek to prove that, had a dispensation been applied for, the company would have satisfied the requirements. We have recently seen HMRC move to bring all dispensation applications to be reviewed in one office so that it can ensure consistency of treatment.

26.106 In the new world the employer is only required 'post April 2016' to report expenses and benefits which would be taxable in the hands of the employee. With this change the 'risk' sits with the employer who will on P11D completion need to be comfortable with which items need to be included. Clearly at the time of HMRC reviews, this will be an area which will be the subject of review. It would be sensible if the employer is in doubt of the tax position that it shows the respective items on the form P11D and lets this be dealt with by the individual employee.

Working rule agreements

26.107 Working rule agreements (WRAs) are collective agreements drawn up between representatives of employers and trade unions to govern rates of pay and conditions of work in a number of industries. HMRC is not a party to these agreements but has agreed that certain WRA allowances paid for daily travel and lodging should not be taxed or liable for NICs.

26.108 This is broadly on the basis that the employees would otherwise be able to claim a deduction for the expenses under *ITEPA 2003, s 336*, although HMRC has indicated that 'it now seems likely that many such expenses payments might not be deductible under the general expenses rule, with the result that the tax treatment of WRAs is, at least in part, concessionary'.

26.109 The WRA allowances generally cover travel, accommodation and subsistence and are normally payable only to specific groups of employees within the construction and allied industries. The modified tax procedures are negotiated nationally and apply only where the employer adopts the terms and conditions of the relevant WRA. However, the employer does not have to be a member of the relevant employers' federation, nor do employees have to belong to the union negotiating the allowances, for these procedures to operate.

26.110 It is possible that some payments made by an employer could fall within a WRA, but the employer is ignorant of its existence. HMRC may point out the WRA and apply its provisions to past payments; if the employer wishes to check for himself, a complete listing of current WRAs and their tax consequences is available and this should be available at every tax office and on the HMRC website.

26.111 If the employer is aware of the WRA but has not been operating it correctly, he will be invited to make a settlement to cover the difference between the WRA amounts and the amounts actually paid. Should such a settlement be resisted, HMRC can make a determination under the legislation, which would of course be on the stricter provisions of *ITEPA 2003, s 336* without the concessional WRA elements.

Focus

Working rule agreements only apply if there is an agreement for their use by HMRC.

Scope of benefits

Benefits assessable on all employees

26.112 Although the benefits legislation is commonly thought of as applying to 'higher paid' employees, some benefits are assessable on *all* employees. These are:

- all vouchers (other than those for meals worth less than 15p per day). Note that:
    - (a) vouchers exchangeable for cash are taxable as earnings (*ITEPA 2003, s 7*), and
    - (b) a travel voucher includes a season ticket;
- gifts of assets. The second-hand value is assessable. It may be possible to argue that the gift was not 'by reason of the employment' but was made to the employee in a personal capacity, see *Reed v Seymour* (1927) 11 TC 625, HL, although HMRC can be expected to challenge this;
- living accommodation, where the rules in *ITEPA 2003, s 7* apply to determine the value;
- payments made by the employer to meet the employee's pecuniary liability, such as telephone bills or school fees (*Hartland v Diggines* (1926) 10 TC 247; *Nicoll v Austin* (1935) 19 TC 531).

26.113 It is proposed that at April 2016 the concessionary treatment for lower paid workers will be removed (those earning less than £8,500 per annum). From this point there will be no difference in tax treatment to the basis of the benefit in kind irrespective of the individual's earnings

It is also proposed that an employer may elect to payroll benefits and thereby avoid the need to complete form P11D. The precise nature of this arrangement is still to be announced.

National Insurance

26.114 From 6 April 2000, Class 1A NICs are due on all benefits unless *either* Class 1 already applies, *or* the benefit is:

- covered by a dispensation;
- included in a PAYE settlement agreement;
- provided to employees (other than directors) earning less than £8,500;

26.115 *Employment tax issues*

- a reimbursed expense which is wholly for business; or
- shares or options. In some cases these will already be subject to a Class 1 NIC charge.

26.115 In years before 2000/01, benefits in kind were not generally subject to NICs. However, Class 1A NICs have been due on cars and fuel since 1991, and NICs were also payable where the company settled the employee's liability rather than providing the asset or benefit directly. Thus if a company provided clothing for its employees, there were no NICs; if it reimbursed the employees for the cost of the clothing, NICs were payable. It was generally possible to replace contracts between the employee and a supplier with a contract between the company and the supplier, and thus avoid the NICs. However, the inspector may resist this where the benefit being provided is clearly an individual's personal liability, such as a child's school fees, although a properly structured contractual agreement may withstand attack.

26.116 The reimbursement of expenses is strictly subject to NICs, ie there is no deduction equivalent to the tax rules. However, reimbursements could be excluded if 'they are specific and distinct payments of, or a contribution towards, expenses actually incurred by the employee in carrying out his work'.

26.117 It is important to bear in mind that Class 1A National Insurance only arises on benefits provided to employees who are themselves liable to Class 1 National Insurance on their earnings. If, therefore, benefits are provided to inpat employees who are continuing to have social security deductions collected in some overseas territory then Class 1A National Insurance will not arise on any benefits they may receive.

Benefits assessable on higher paid employees and all directors

26.118 A 'higher paid' employee is one who is remunerated at the rate of £8,500 per year (*ITEPA 2003, s 66(4)*). There are two potential traps for the unwary:

- benefits and reimbursed expenses must be included in calculating the £8,500, even if these are covered by a dispensation or would be allowable under the normal expenses rules;
- the £8,500 is a *rate* of pay. Thus an employee paid £2,000 a month for three months of the year is 'higher paid' within the definition.

The £8,500 upper earnings limit is being removed at April 2016 and from then irrespective of salary the benefit in kind will be calculated on the same basis.

However, employee pension contributions on a 'net pay' basis and payroll giving amounts are both deductible in this calculation.

26.119 Following a review by the Office of Tax Simplification the Government has decided to abolish the tax breaks for lower paid workers from April 2016.

26.120 A director is within the scope of the benefits legislation irrespective of his earnings level unless he has no material interest in the company and either is a full-time working director or the company is a charity or non-profit-making concern (*TA 1988, ss 167–168*).

26.121 Benefits and reimbursed expenses are taxable if they are made or provided 'by reason of the employment'. Although the HMRC Manual says that 'the legislation deems this to be the case if it is the employer who is making or providing them' (*ITEPA 2003, s 71*), there remain cases where something can be provided by the employer to the employee which is not a benefit, if it is not given in return for 'acting as or being an employee' (*Hochstrasser v Mayes* (1959) 38 TC 673; *Mairs v Haughey* [1993] STC 569). Nevertheless it must be accepted that the deeming provision is wide ranging in scope.

26.122 Points which may be picked up on an HMRC review include the following:

- any amounts paid to the employee's family or household must also be included on the P11D (or P9D, where applicable). Note, however, that 'family or household' does not include an unmarried partner who is not a dependant or a member of the employee's household (*ITEPA 2003, s 721(5)*);

- the amount included on the P11D or P9D must be the full VAT-inclusive cost. The fact that some or all of the VAT may be recovered by the employer from Customs and Excise is irrelevant.

Self-assessment

26.123 Under self-assessment the employer is required to show the cash equivalent value of the items included on P11Ds and P9Ds. Suffice it to say that under self-assessment the need to understand the benefits legislation and the penalties for non-compliance are both greater than before 1996/97 (when self-assessment came in to force).

Value of benefits

26.124 The general rule on valuing a benefit is that the employee is taxable on the money's worth of the benefit, ie its cash equivalent. *ITEPA 2003, s 203(2)* and *ITEPA 2003, s 204* states that the cash equivalent of the benefit is its cost, less any part made good by the employee to those providing the benefit. VAT is included whether or not it is recoverable by the employer.

26.125 *Employment tax issues*

26.125 The case of *Pepper v Hart* (1992) 65 TC 421 established that by 'cost' the statute did not mean full cost but marginal cost. Thus an airline employee who has the use of a spare seat on the airline which would otherwise be unused is only taxed on the extra cost to the airline of carrying one more passenger, not on the total cost of the flight divided by the number of passengers.

26.126 HMRC has agreed that the marginal cost principle should apply to in-house benefits and to the use of assets employed in the business. Thus where a telephone is provided for business use it is accepted that the employee does not have to pay a proportion of the line rental or any other standing charges. However, there are cases other than in-house benefits and assets used in the business where marginal cost can be applied. Where appropriate HMRC can be successfully challenged on this restrictive interpretation of *Pepper v Hart*.

26.127 A further point to note is that where an employee is charged for part of the cost of the benefit, there may be VAT on the amount so charged, depending on the normal VAT rules. The area in practice most affected by this used to be payments for the private use of company cars but this has now changed. However, the same point continues to apply to other supplies, such as the use of holiday accommodation.

Areas likely to be investigated

26.128 In investigating the taxation of benefits, the HMRC official will concentrate on areas where the employer is most likely to have made mistakes. Some of the main ones are covered below. It should, however, be emphasised that this is a review of vulnerabilities and not a complete summary of the benefits legislation. In particular, for years 2000/01 and subsequently, the National Insurance costs should be taken into account.

Accommodation (ITEPA 2003, ss 97–113)

26.129 Where living accommodation is provided by the employer for employees, HMRC may check that:

- any job-related accommodation (*ITEPA 2003, s 99(1)*) is so in fact. Accommodation is job-related and thus exempt from tax if it is either:

    (a) *necessary* for the proper performance of the duties;

    (b) provided for the *better* performance of the duties in an employment where the provision of accommodation is *customary*; or

    (c) required to protect the employee's *security*.

    The difficult area here is (b), which is subject to erosion by HMRC. For example, it is currently challenging the customary right of certain public

Employment tax issues **26.130**

sector workers to be provided with accommodation. This covers people like school caretakers and police officers. In job-related accommodation cases it may be worth considering an appeal to the tribunal if the facts are strong and HMRC continues to challenge the position.

The job-related exemption does not, however, apply to the payment by the employer for household furniture, which is subject to the 20% rule for assets. Nor does it apply to the payment by the employer of household bills or ancillary costs such as cleaning. However, it should be noted that:

(a) P9D employees escape tax if the liability is met directly by the employer, but not if the employer reimburses the employee's costs;

(b) structural alterations, or alterations which would be the landlord's responsibility under the *Landlord and Tenant Act 1985, s 11* are also not taxable;

(c) where the accommodation is provided in an institution, such as a hospital or school, the benefit of such ancillary costs as cleaning can be reduced using *Pepper v Hart* principles;

(d) where there is a liability, it is capped at 10% of the employee's net emoluments, ie his emoluments after deducting pension contributions, capital allowances and allowable expenses and before including the benefit of the household costs (*ITEPA 2003, s 315*);

- the calculation has been carried out correctly. This is based on the rateable value, for new properties with no rateable value an estimate is used;

- 'expensive' accommodation (broadly that which cost more than £75,000 (*ITEPA 2003, s 105*)) has been correctly identified and that the benefit has been accurately calculated. Note here that properties which originally cost less than £75,000 do not fall within the 'expensive' category even if the current market value is more than that, unless improvements subsequent to the purchase and before the year of assessment, together with the purchase price, have taken the cost above £75,000;

- any 'perk' accommodation, such as London flats or holiday homes, have been correctly assessed;

- any accommodation provided to a shadow director has been taxed.

26.130 Many employers who provide expensive accommodation set up lease premium arrangements to minimise the benefit in kind charge. These arrangements work with the employer paying a premium to the landlord which then means that the monthly rent is reduced. On this basis given the rent is reduced then the benefit in kind is reduced. The premium lease arrangements is the subject of HMRC attack and from 22 April 2009 are no longer available to be used for leasing entered into after the 2009 Budget. For employers who

26.131 *Employment tax issues*

have existing arrangements in place it is important these arrangements are not varied following the 2009 Budget otherwise they will cease to benefit from the previous tax position.

26.131 If such arrangements have been organised, HMRC at the time of any review would want to be satisfied that there is a valid arrangement in place and it is worth checking whether the arrangement was cleared with HMRC at the outset. It is the opinion of HMRC that these arrangements are only applicable when the lease premium covers a extensive period. At present HMRC is challenging employers who have set schemes up for a period below what it would consider acceptable. It is likely that HMRC will seek to take cases on this matter to tribunal. For those employers who previously used the lease premium arrangement, we are finding that despite the change of tax rules going forward, HMRC is looking to seek a settlement of the liability in regard to the past.

26.132 Where an asset remains the property of the employer but the employee can use it privately, the taxable benefit is on the 'annual value' of the use of the asset, unless specific provisions exist to tax it separately, such as company cars. The 'annual value' is 20% of the market value of the asset when first used privately. Points to note in an audit context are that:

- the 20% charge is replaced by the actual cost of hiring the asset if this is greater;
- if the original cost is enhanced by further expenditure, this must be added when calculating the annual value;
- if ownership of an asset is transferred to an employee, the normal rule is that there is only a benefit if the asset is transferred at less than market value at the date of transfer. However, these rules are amended where there has been private use: see *ITEPA 2003, s 203(3)*;
- the cost of the asset includes VAT, whether or not this can be recovered by the employer;
- if the asset is provided part way through the fiscal year, there is no pro-rating of the benefit charge;
- if the private use of an asset has been prohibited, the company can argue that there was no benefit (*Gilbert v Hemsley* (1981) 55 TC 419);
- from 2000/1 there is a specific exemption for any assets where the private use is 'not significant'. This covers the use of telephones, photocopiers and fax machines, as well as computers provided for work which do not fall within the *ITEPA 2003, s 320* exemption. Unsurprisingly, this relief does not extend to the private use of aeroplanes, boats or cars, even if private use is not significant.

Cars

26.133 The provision of cars for employees is a fruitful area for a compliance review. Under self-assessment employers are required to calculate the cash equivalent of the benefits. This will increase the employer's exposure to interest and penalties.

26.134 The cost of incorrect handling of company cars is compounded when one looks at Class 1A contributions. If an error is made in calculating the value of the car, or the business miles, this will affect the value of the car and the fuel for both tax and Class 1A purposes. Thus an error in this area can prove extremely expensive.

26.135 Particular points to note are that:

- All cars with private use have been included on the P11Ds. A fleet listing may be used for this purpose. Check especially:
    (a) new cars;
    (b) second cars;
    (c) cars provided other than by the company's fleet department, eg by a branch for use by a salesman;
    (d) hire cars provided before the employee's company car could be made available.

- Since 1994/95 cars have been included on the P11D at original market value, not cost.
    (a) The original market value is broadly the manufacturer's list price, and is defined as the price which was 'published by the car's manufacturer, importer or distributor (as the case may be) as the inclusive price appropriate for a car of that kind if sold in the United Kingdom singly in a retail sale in the open market on the relevant day' (*ITEPA 2003, s 216(3)*). The inclusive price means the price including delivery, VAT, customs duty and car tax.
    (b) Particular care is needed when the car is acquired second-hand, as the original market value must still be used, not the second-hand cost.
    (c) As the definition in *s 216(3)* quoted at (a) above makes clear, cars obtained by the employer at a volume discount must be included at the price that would have been charged if only a single car had been bought by a retail customer.

26.135 *Employment tax issues*

- Any accessories also need to be treated correctly (*ITEPA 2003, s 125*). Standard accessories will be included in the car's list price. If optional accessories are provided with the car, then their price must be added to the list price when calculating the total price of the car. Note that:

    (a) car phones provided by the employer are exempt;

    (b) only those optional accessories attached to the car are added to the price (this includes accessories such as a roof-rack which is attached although it can be removed, but does not include emergency triangles, first aid kits, car rugs, etc – in practice the value of such excluded items can be regarded as *de minimis*, although strictly there is an annual value charge of 20% on their cost;

    (c) optional accessories paid for by the employee such as car stereo equipment are not added to the car price;

    (d) optional accessories necessarily required for the employee's job, such as a towbar, are also not added to the price;

    (e) the removal of an item from the car which would have been provided as standard does not reduce the list price;

    (f) the price to be used for accessories, as for the car, is the open market list price and not the actual cost (*ITEPA 2003, s 126*). Personalised number plates on a company car are not generally assessable;

    (g) complex rules apply to replacement accessories.

- Where the individual 'in the year concerned ... is required, as a condition of the car being available for his private use, to pay any amount of money for that use' the scale charge can be reduced. The strict wording here means that if the payment is not *required*, or the requirement was not *in the year concerned*, the inspector may argue that the payment was ineffective. He may also question whether the payment was for private use, or merely, for example, to obtain a better model than that otherwise available at his grade. The company should have made clear the purpose of the contribution in its documentation (*Tax Bulletin* 1, November 1991).

    From 1 August 1995 there is no need to charge VAT on the private use payment, provided the input tax is also excluded (VAT Information Sheet 12/95, 1 June 1995).

- Capital contributions to the cost of the car by the employee reduce the price of the car for assessment purposes, as long as the contribution does not exceed £5,000 (*ITEPA 2003, s 132*). Note that this only applies to reduce the value of the car when used by that employee and not when it is transferred to another employee.

- Where a car is classified as a pool car, the inspector will check that the strict conditions in *ITEPA 2003, s 167(1)* are being complied with. These are that:
    (a) the car is available to, and actually used by, more than one employee and is not ordinarily used by any one of them to the exclusion of the others;
    (b) any private use of the car by any of the employees is merely incidental to its business use;
    (c) it is not normally kept overnight at or in the vicinity of the residence of any of the employees except while it is being kept on premises occupied by the person providing the car.

    Note that *all* the conditions must be met. Pool cars are a frequent target of inspectors and can cost employers significant sums in settlement where cars do not in practice meet the requirements.

    Particularly difficult is the second requirement and the interpretation of 'merely incidental', which is a qualitative test. If the private use follows from the business use then the incidental test is passed, but not if the private use of the car is independent of its business use (HMRC has a rule of thumb that a car is not regarded as 'normally kept overnight' at employees' homes if the total number of nights on which it is taken home by employees, for whatever reason, is less than 60% of the total number of nights in the period under review (IR Booklet 480)). However it warns that:

    'If a car is taken home often enough to approach the 60 per cent limit – though without breaking it – it is unlikely that all the home to work journeys will satisfy the "merely incidental" test.'

    Note that where a chauffeur employed to drive pool cars is obliged to take the car home overnight this will not disqualify the car from being a pool car.

- The inspector will also check that there has been correct calculation of the total taxable car benefit. In addition to items 1 to 6 above this will include adjustments to the list price for:
    (a) business mileage;
    (b) periods when the car was unavailable – the period of unavailability must be for at least 30 consecutive days and it is not enough that the driver cannot drive for the period, eg because of illness or a driving ban (*TA 1988, Sch 6, paras 6 and 9*).

- Where a company car is sold to an employee at less than the open market value the difference will be assessable as a benefit on the employee. If the price at which the car was transferred is significantly different from

26.136 *Employment tax issues*

that given for a car of that age and type in, say, *Glass's Guide*, then the employer may need to prove that the market value of this particular car was less than would be expected, eg because the car was in poor condition.

- Although car parking is exempt from tax under *ITEPA 2003, s 237(2)* there is an NIC cost if the car parking charge at an employee's permanent place of work is reimbursed to the employee (CWG2 (2000), p 75).

- Where a chauffeur is used by an employee for private journeys, his costs are taxable on the employee. SP 2/96 discusses HMRC's view on the use of a chauffeur to collect senior personnel from home so they can work in the car. While discouraging, the statement of practice does not preclude a claim that such a car is a pool car and that the private use is incidental, but it does increase the difficulty of having such a claim accepted. If it is not, then the inspector will seek the cost of both car and fuel benefit, as well as the chauffeur costs.

  The latter is based on the relevant proportion of his wages, including waiting time, overtime, pension contributions, and NIC costs. The amount of exposure can be reduced if the chauffeur does other jobs.

- Parking fines are taxable on an employee if the penalty notice was actually handed to him at the time of the offence, or if the employee owns the car. But if the notice was fixed to a car owned by the employer, and the employer pays the fine as the registered owner, there is no Schedule E liability on the employee. The Revenue Manual says that:

  'If the employee voluntarily pays a fine in these circumstances, and the employer reimburses it, the employee will be chargeable on the emolument arising. A deduction for the expense may then be allowed to the employer.'

  Where the fine is not taxed on the individual, HMRC will, however, seek to disallow it in the company's tax computations. This is on the basis that it was not 'wholly and exclusively' in the course of the company's trade (*CIR v Alexander von Glehn & Co Ltd* (1920) 12 TC 232).

26.136 A number of employers have offered employee car ownership schemes which use their purchasing power to obtain discounts for employees to permit the employee to purchase a car from a third-party provider. This provider offers an arrangement to manage the vehicle to ensure the vehicle is maintained and with a guaranteed buy back price on the vehicle at the end of the loan period. In addition employers involved in this area will often provide insurance on the vehicle to ensure this is adequately insured for any business travel.

26.137 It is the case that the employer will often support the employee car ownership scheme with some financial support which is either paid directly

Employment tax issues **26.141**

to the employee or to a third party, eg the provider. It is the case at the time of any employer compliance review that HMRC will wish to ensure that any financial support met by the employer is identified and tax/NIC on this correctly dealt with.

26.138 To make employer car ownership schemes financially viable many employers will use the approved mileage allowance payments (AMAP) to cushion the tax impact on any payment made to the employee. This is an area which will be of particular interest to HMRC who will want to be certain the payment fits in to the category of approved mileage allowances and, in regard to National Insurance, falls within the appropriate earnings period. The rules in the Social Security (Contributions) Regulations 2001, SI 2001/1004, reg 22A are complex but need to be followed to ensure that the NIC relief can be obtained. This is a very topical issue for HMRC. There is a growing interest in company cars being provided to employees via a salary sacrifice arrangement. These schemes need to be robust with a clear change in the employees' Contract of Employment to reflect the amount of the sacrifice. The employee is still taxed on the car under the normal benefit in kind rules.

26.139 The rules on vans changed over recent years and the level of the benefit is now significantly increased to £3,000. However, the benefit only arises if the van is made available for private use. The change in the rules however takes account of private use as well as normal commuting journeys. Therefore if the van's use is available to the employee for business travel but is taken home each day then no benefit will arise subject to the employee not being permitted to use the van for additional private use. At the time of any HMRC compliance visit it will want to ensure that the policy and practice of employers do not permit unlimited private use.

Credit cards

26.140 These are taxed under the vouchers legislation (*ITEPA 2003, s 7*). Employers should ensure that any corporate credit cards are properly controlled, so that expenditure is analysed between private and business. There is no tax liability if all private expenditure is reimbursed to the employer, and there is also no tax on credit card interest or annual/joining fees for the card (SE 2011).

Commissions and discounts

26.141 Until the publication of HMRC Statement of Practice SP4/97, the taxation of commissions, rebates and discounts was in disarray. SP4/97 states that where an employee receives commission by reason of his employment, this

26.142 *Employment tax issues*

is taxable. If in cash, the amounts should be subjected to PAYE. If invested, for instance in a financial product, then the value of the uplift should be reported on the employee's P11D. Particular areas of interest or difficulty include:

- If the employee receives a discount rather than a commission, there will be no tax if either the discount is also available to the public or the amount paid by the employee is above cost to the employer (*Pepper v Hart* (1992) 65 TC 421).

- The taxable commission can be reduced by any rebate which passes the 'wholly exclusively and necessarily' test. This is likely to be the case where the product is sold to a third party at arm's length, but employers should beware of rebates passed on to friends and relatives.

Conferences

26.142 The official is likely to ask if the employees attend conferences, and be particularly interested in any which are overseas and/or where a partner is invited. He will ask to see itineraries and programmes for the conference, as well as other relevant documentation, such as invitations. Because of the cost of such meetings, especially those overseas, and the number of attendees, the expense of a settlement in this area can be substantial. The official is likely to ask a number of questions.

26.143 *What is the business content?* The HMRC official may argue that any business purpose was *de minimis*, indeed a mere front for the overseas trip. The Schedule E Manual (SE 4261) instructs him as follows:

> 'Overseas trips variously described as conferences, conventions or seminars are often no more than incentives intended either to reward past performance or to motivate employees for the future. Although a minimal 'business' element such as an address by a company executive may have been included in the programme do not give a deduction if it otherwise consists of social occasions, excursions and leisure activities.'

Where the conference does have some business content, the best the company can achieve is a reasonable apportionment of costs between business and private, but HMRC now discourage this.

26.144 *Was the trip necessarily incurred?* Here HMRC may not accept that a conference was necessary if the employee himself decided to go (*Owen v Burden* (1971) 47 TC 476). Senior employees should therefore ensure that they are 'instructed' to attend, and do not simply authorise their own attendance. Similarly HMRC may argue that a seminar to improve an employee's qualifications to do his job or to keep his knowledge up to date is not allowable (*Humbles v Brooks* (1962) 40 TC 500; *Parikh v Sleeman* (1990) 63 TC 75), unless the education forms an integral part of the performance of the duties of the employment.

26.145 *Did partners attend?* Attendance of partners at a conference is likely to increase HMRC's doubts about the business purpose of the conference. In addition it will check whether the cost of the spouse's attendance has been included on the P11D for the employee. Note that there is no benefit where the person attending is not a member of the employee's family or household (*ITEPA 2003, s 721(5)*). The employee must show that the expense of taking his spouse with him is necessarily incurred in the performance of his duties. In assessing whether the 'necessarily' test is satisfied, HMRC will ask whether his duties would have required someone else to go with him, such as a secretary or interpreter. The company will need to prove that either:

- the spouse has some special skill or qualification associated with the employee's job which is needed on the trip (although not necessarily full-time). An example might be where the spouse is a competent linguist and acts as an interpreter at business meetings; or
- the spouse's presence is essential to act as host at a series of business entertaining occasions which the employee is required to organise as part of his duties. It is insufficient that the employee and his spouse merely attend functions where other guests are accompanied by their spouses; or
- the employee's health is so poor that it would be unreasonable for him to travel alone.

Entertaining clients

26.146 This has long been a favourite of HMRC, which has a dual weapon:

- *CAA 2001, Sch 2 para 51(1)(a)* prohibits a deduction for entertaining costs from *trading profits*;
- *ITEPA 2003, s 356(1)* states that no deduction for such expenses shall be made from emoluments chargeable to tax under Schedule E.

26.147 However, *ITEPA 2003, s 357* prohibits a double disallowance where the employer pays for, or reimburses, the cost of the entertaining, and the cost is disallowed in the trading computation. Where this is the case, the employee still has to satisfy the test in *ITEPA 2003, s 328(1)*.

26.148 HMRC may thus wish to check that there was a genuine business reason for the entertainment, and that the company is not simply being used as a tax-efficient vehicle for private entertaining by senior management or directors.

26.149 *Employment tax issues*

26.149 It is true that genuine entertainment of third-party business contacts, such as customers or suppliers, would qualify. However, in such cases HMRC may check that the amounts have been correctly identified as disallowable in the company's corporation tax return (*TA 1988, s 577(3)*). Indeed, under self-assessment the P11D requires the employer to state whether any entertaining expenses included on the P11D (ie those not covered by a dispensation) have been or will be disallowed.

26.150 The position is different where the employer is a non-trading entity, such as a local council or charity. These organisations, and their employees, are not affected by *s 577* because any entertainment which they may provide is not 'in connection with a trade' and therefore is not 'business entertainment' as defined in *s 577(5)*. The employees of such organisations are therefore entitled to a deduction for any entertainment expenses they may incur which satisfy the conditions of *ITEPA 2003, s 328(1)* provided only that the expense is incurred out of their taxable emoluments.

26.151 The position is different again where the employer is a representative office of an overseas company. In that case the company's profits, whilst chargeable to tax overseas, are not subject to UK tax. As a result there can be no disallowance on the company under *s 577(1)(a)*, and *s 577(3)* thus cannot operate to protect the employee, while *s 577(1)(b)* denies the employee a deduction for business entertainment expenses irrespective of whether the expenses are, or are not, reimbursed by the employer. This often results in the employees being taxed under Schedule E in respect of their reimbursed entertainment expenses with no possibility of an off-setting deduction under *s 198*. However, it may be possible to change HMRC's mind if the overseas company is in a treaty country, on the grounds that the tax exemption derives from the treaty. There is always the possibility of arguing that the position is unfair and not within HMRC's commitment to human rights which requires that all taxpayers should be treated equally.

Entertaining – staff

26.152 For many years, HMRC adopted a tolerant attitude where staff entertaining was concerned. As long as the cost was either included as a benefit on their P11D (the technically correct position) or disallowed in the company's tax computation, it accepted the position. However, a stricter approach was set out in *Tax Bulletin* 42, August 1999, which said that the disallowing of staff entertaining 'is inconsistent with the concept of self-assessment, and should no longer be adopted'. The old approach will continue to apply for accounting periods ending not later than 30 April 2000 (*Tax Bulletin* 45, February 2000); thus for these earlier periods it should be possible to agree a disallowance in the company computations in preference to the more onerous (and usually more expensive) adjustment to an individual's emoluments.

26.153 There remain many areas of difficulty, eg where the employer entertains an employee or two employees have lunch 'on the firm', this is taxable on the employees as a benefit. This includes a meal out as a reward for doing a good job, or having lunch in a restaurant to provide a relaxed ambience for a team meeting. In general HMRC takes the view that 'meetings over a meal with other members of the same organisation are normally social, with work matters being insufficient to make the meeting a necessary business occasion'. You can therefore expect that such costs will be challenged.

26.154 However, HMRC is prepared to accept that there is no benefit where the nature of some meetings would qualify for *ITEPA 2003, s 328(1)* relief, eg:

- meetings for the negotiation of the renewal or alteration of a service contract; or
- a briefing visit where local staff are detained beyond normal hours to fit in with a visit from head office.

26.155 However, the employer is on weaker ground when the person being entertained is from a branch rather than a connected company, as a branch has no separate existence. Here some use may be made of HMRC's agreement that 'where the colleague being entertained would be entitled to tax-free subsistence, [his] costs can be discounted'.

26.156 The company has no grounds for a defence where the individuals are from the same site, unless the costs involved are no more than they would have been had they eaten in the company's subsidised or free restaurant.

26.157 A problem may arise where one employee has paid for the mutual staff entertaining, in that the full bill should have been entered on his P11D. However, HMRC will normally agree that the bill should be shared among all attendees. Where a higher rate taxpayer paid the bill, this apportionment will have the effect of reducing the overall tax charge. In practice, the company may wish to include such items in a PAYE settlement agreement.

Gifts

26.158 Gifts provided by the employer are generally taxable under the deeming provisions of *ITEPA 2003, s 71*. However, HMRC will accept that there is no benefit if the gift is either provided on personal grounds (eg a wedding present) or as a mark of personal esteem. See also long service awards and third party benefits.

26.159 *Employment tax issues*

Loans

26.159 Cheap or interest-free loans supplied by or by arrangement with the employer are taxable if they fall within the detailed rules of *ITEPA 2003, s 7(5)*. Particular points to note are as follows:

- Certain loans are classed as 'qualifying' and are exempt from these provisions (*ITEPA 2003, s 180*). These include loans to buy into a partnership, to buy shares in, or lend money to, a close company, and to buy machinery or plant for use by the partnership or employment. From 6 April 2000, loans to acquire a main residence are no longer qualifying, and from the same date qualifying loans do not have to be included on a P11D (*ITEPA 2003, s 180(5)*). For earlier years the loan should have been reported by the employer, leaving it for the individual to claim *ITEPA 2003, s 328(1)* relief. However, it would be unusual for HMRC to take this point.

- Allowable relocation loans are also not a benefit, but see **26.166** *et seq* for details of the rules which must be satisfied here.

- Loans on the same terms as those provided to members of the public are excluded (*ITEPA 2003, s 180(5)*), if the lending of money is part of the business of the employer. A deregulatory amendment introduced by *FA 2000, Sch 10(5)(1)* improved the position for such loans, and the rules were backdated to cover the previous six years. Previously the 'same terms' requirement was strictly interpreted, so that a relaxation of lending criteria or a waiver of fees for staff loans, as compared to those for the public, caused the loan to fall outside this exemption (IR Interpretation, August 1994).

- There is a *de minimis* exemption for cheap or interest-free loans below £5,000 (from April 2014 £10,000). Where the total amount loaned has exceeded £5,000, the full amount, and not just the excess, will come within the rules. The total value of loans to each individual must therefore be checked. In practice loans can be granted from different sources within the company, eg one department may provide season ticket loans, and another loans for car purchase. Because all season ticket loans are below the *de minimis* amount, they may have been ignored when looking at whether there is a benefit.

- The *de minimis* exemption is only valid if the loan does not exceed the £5,000 limit at *any time* in the tax year.

- The loan interest must not simply be *payable* in a tax year, it must actually be paid (*ITEPA 2003, s 7(5)*). Where the loan is interest bearing but the interest has not been paid, the loan must be reported on the P11D. The employee can recover the tax charged once he has paid the interest (*s 174(1)*). In an audit situation the employer should check whether the

Employment tax issues **26.161**

- employee has now paid the interest, and if so should seek to limit the cost of settlement to sufficient interest to cover the period during which HMRC would have had the tax if the P11D had been correct originally.

- Loan guarantees are also included within the loan benefits legislation.

- In some cases the company may argue that the loan has not been granted 'by reason of' the employment, but because of the private circumstances of the employees. They may find support for this in *Hochstrasser v Mayes* (1959) 38 TC 673.

- Loans written off are taxable, even when the write-off happens after the individual has left (*ITEPA 2003, s 188(2)*).

- For years before 2000/01 a benefit could arise if the loan interest rate fell below the HMRC approved rate for any part of the tax year. This could happen where the company follows a market rate and HMRC's rate falls more slowly. For 2000/01 and subsequent years, the official rate is set at the beginning of the tax year, making it easier to monitor whether a benefit has arisen (IR Press Release, 25 January 2000).

- Under self-assessment the actual benefit of the loan must be calculated. HMRC will check a sample of such calculations to ensure that they have been carried out correctly.

Long service awards

26.160 The tax rules exempt certain long service awards from tax. However, the requirements of the concession have to be met; it is not enough that, for example, the total sum spent is less than that allowed by the Concession but the gifts are made more frequently. A small gift made every five years can cause expensive gifts made after 20 years to be taxed.

Mobile phones

26.161 *FA 1999* changed the rules for mobile phones, to the enormous relief of all those involved in PAYE reviews with the possible exception of the HMRC official (*ITEPA 2003, s 316(1)*). For years from 1999/2000 onwards, the following points are relevant:

- mobile phones provided by the employer are exempted from tax from 6 April 1999 (however, limited to one phone per employee);

- however this does not cover the reimbursement of private calls made on the employee's own phone, which remain taxable; and

- neither does it cover the cost of vouchers used by employees to make calls, unless covered by *ITEPA 2003, s 328(1)*.

26.162 *Employment tax issues*

Incidental expenses (ITEPA 2003, s 240)

26.162 Employees often incur incidental expenses when staying away from home, such as laundry, personal phone calls and newspapers. Until *FA 1995* these items tended to be covered by dispensations, although under strict law they do not meet the requirements of *ITEPA 2003, s 328*.

26.163 From 6 April 1995 a specific relief was introduced. Now, an employee is not taxable on personal incidental expenses up to £5 per night (£10 outside the UK) if he is away on business for at least one night. The new relief was heralded as deregulatory, in practice it is more likely to cause problems for employers when audited.

26.164 Particular note should be taken of the following:

- If the payment is more than £5, the whole amount is taxable and subject to NICs.

- If an employee stays away for several nights consecutively, the total allowance is five times the number of nights away. For example, where an employee stays away for four nights and claimed £5 on the first night, £5 on the second, £6 on the third and £4 on the fourth he would be within the exemption because the total does not exceed £5 × 4. Where the number of nights is not consecutive, no averaging is allowed.

- Where the limit is exceeded the employer should check that the employee was not bearing some costs of other employees. If he was, HMRC will accept an apportionment (HMRC Booklet 480 App 8).

Prizes

26.165 A prize won in a competition only open to employees is within the scope of Schedule E. See also gifts (**26.158**), suggestion schemes (**26.173**), and third-party benefits (**26.175** *et seq*).

Relocations

26.166 The rules for relocations were made infinitely more complex by the introduction in 1993 of *TA 1988, Sch 11A*. This lays down detailed rules as to which relocation costs are allowable, or, as the legislation puts it, eligible. Eligible expenses of up to £8,000 per relocation will not be taxed.

26.167 Note that there is no requirement for overpayments of such eligible expenses to go through PAYE, even where the excess is a cash sum. However, payments of ineligible amounts must be taxed under the normal rules, which include the application of PAYE where appropriate.

26.168 In particular a reviewer will check that:

- The employer has clearly separated eligible and ineligible relocation costs, and that the latter have been either taxed under PAYE or included on the employee's P11D as appropriate. Ineligible costs include:

    (a) abortive relocation costs (ie where the employee doesn't actually relocate after all);

    (b) council tax;

    (c) duplicate costs of any items which are not 'domestic', such as school fees or season ticket costs;

    (d) higher cost housing payments for moving to a more expensive area – these were allowed, within limits, until the new legislation was introduced;

    (e) transport and installation costs of non-domestic items, such as boats or horses; and

    (f) travel allowances paid to employees who choose not to relocate.

- The £8,000 limit on eligible expenses has not been exceeded in the tax year, and if it has, whether the excess has been included on the employee's P11D.

- Where a relocation crosses a tax year, the amount spent in the previous tax year has been carried forward in calculating whether the £8,000 limit has been exceeded.

- The time limits on paying or providing eligible relocation expenses/ benefits have been adhered to. If expenses have been paid after the time limit, has permission been sought from the local inspector to extend the limit? In practice, where permission has not been sought but it is reasonable to believe that an extension would have been granted had a request been made, the inspector will generally accept this.

- The payment of any flat rate allowances as part of the £8,000 limit has been agreed in advance with the local inspector of taxes. If not, the employer can argue that the allowance should be accepted if it is:

    (a) required to be spent on eligible costs; and

    (b) broadly within the limits allowed to the civil service. Unfortunately these are no longer published, as each government department has been given authority to set its own limits. The most recent allowances were set in 1993 as follows:

Married householder	£2,705
Single householder	£1,645
Single non-householder	£635

26.169 *Employment tax issues*

- Reasonable increases on these amounts to allow for inflation should be accepted by HMRC.
- The complex rules for beneficial bridging loans have been complied with. Interest on bridging loans can be included as an eligible cost but only insofar as the £8,000 limit has not been used to cover other eligible relocation expenses. Interest therefore forms the top slice of eligible costs. This unused slice of relocation relief is then used to determine how long the beneficial loan can be outstanding before it becomes taxable. The formula for calculating this is given in *ITEPA 2003, s 288(4)*.
- Any guaranteed price scheme is being correctly operated. Again, this is complex, and failure may mean that significant sums fall into tax. HMRC explained the legal position in *Tax Bulletin* 16, April 1995.

26.169 Note that until 6 April 1998 the Contributions Agency rules on relocation were not affected by the Sch 11A rules and thus some elements of a relocation package were taxable but not subject to NICs (CWG2 (1998) 78). However for relocations after 6 April 1998 the NI rules broadly follow the tax legislation, although a number of important differences remain. In particular, there is no £8,000 cap for NI purposes, so if an expense qualifies as allowable, no NI was charged, irrespective of the amount. A further year of grace was allowed for relocation payments made via a PSA agreement, with no contributions being due until 1999. Employers should thus analyse the position of their relocated employees with care before agreeing to any audit settlement.

Staff social functions

26.170 The inspector will check whether staff social functions fall within *ITEPA 2003, s 264*. It is important to ensure that:

- the allowable limit (currently £150 per attendee) has not been exceeded;
- in calculating the £150 the employer has:
    (a) included VAT, and
    (b) where relevant, travel to the function and accommodation, and
    (c) that the cost is on a per head basis of those who actually attended, not those who could have attended;
- the function was open to employees generally. In practice a number of departmental functions which are of a similar nature will be accepted as falling within this condition;
- if the allowable limit for a single function has been exceeded, the full amount is taxable and not just the excess; and

Employment tax issues **26.174**

- if there have been a number of functions and the total cost is more than £150, HMRC will disregard those functions which total £150 or less but will tax the others in full.

Note that the concession currently in place is more generous than the previous version, and that more restricted rules apply to tax years before 1995/96.

Subsistence

26.171 Along with travel, this is perhaps the most fruitful area of review for an HMRC official. Particular points which will be checked are whether:

- the payments of subsistence allowances or the reimbursement of actual costs are reasonable in amount. HMRC has now published rates that it considers can be paid free of income tax (benchmark allowances). If there are round sums paid for other than meals an agreement will be with HMRC to the sum being paid tax free (bespoke allowances). These limits do not apply if an employer simply met the costs incurred by the employee;

- allowances are paid or amounts reimbursed only when the employee is away from his normal place of work or holding a travelling appointment;

- meals for late working have been taxed. However, the concession can be argued to apply if the meals are available to all who work late; and

- where a working rule agreement applies, the terms have been followed.

26.172 Complex new rules on travel and subsistence were introduced with effect from 6 April 1998 (*ITEPA 2003, s 328*). However, it should be noted that subsistence is treated as part of travel, and thus any food or accommodation provided in conjunction with travel which does not fall within the new rules, will itself be taxed and subject to NIC.

Suggestion schemes

26.173 These are exempt from tax if they fall within *ITEPA 2003, s 321*. Note that the NIC rules are more generous.

Telephones

26.174 The official will check whether the employer has reimbursed any part of home telephone costs. See also mobile phones at **26.161**.

- all home telephone calls paid should have been included on the P11D (other than necessary business calls). Evidence will be required to support the business calls unless they are covered by a dispensation;

26.175 *Employment tax issues*

- line rental is regarded as taxable (*Lucas v Cattell* (1972) 48 TC 353) unless:

    (a) employees can show that it is genuinely part of their duties to deal with emergencies; or

    (b) the employee's home is the place of employment; or

    (c) the contract for the telephone is in the employer's name; or

    (d) the telephone is used exclusively for business.

In (a) and (b) a proportion of the rental charge is allowable. HMRC generally seeks to allow only the same proportion as the business use of the telephone is of the overall use. In (c) there is no charge to either tax or NICs (*Pepper v Hart*; CWG 2: 79 and (d)).

Third-party benefits

26.175 To date this has not been a significant review area but the position is changing with self-assessment. Many gifts are covered by the concession, which exempts from tax gifts received by employees from a third party by reason of their employment and totalling £150 or less from the same source in a single tax year. Until 1995/96 the limit was £100. This concession does not cover gifts provided by, or by arrangement with, the employer. The only review risk here is that if the limit is exceeded the full amount, not just the excess, is taxable.

26.176 The reporting rules for third parties under self-assessment have increased the risks to employers. These cover expenses payments or benefits provided to employees by a third party other than those covered by the concession. They took effect for 1996/97 onwards and require that where a third-party benefit is provided, the third party must provide the employee with details of the cash equivalent of the benefit in writing by 6 July after the end of the tax year. The employer of the employee who has received these third-party benefits is also required to tell HMRC the name and address of the provider (*FA 1995, s 106(9)(c)*; SAT2 and SAT3). Where the benefit has been provided by arrangement with the employer, the latter must provide details of both the amounts and the name and business address of the other person (*FA 1995, s 106(9)(b)*).

These are extensive requirements and, combined with the self-assessment enquiry powers will have a significant effect on companies' audit settlements.

Travel

26.177 Reimbursing employees' travel expenses, or paying an allowance to cover travel costs, is invariably the subject of an HMRC review. Legislation

Employment tax issues **26.179**

on travel and subsistence was finally introduced with effect from 6 April 1998 (*ITEPA 2003, s 337*). This was supplemented by the publication, in January 1998, of the Revenue's 'Employee Travel: A Tax and NIC Guide for Employers'. This booklet is destined to become the reviewers' bible, and any employer who wishes to ensure compliance with the rules would be advised to study its numerous examples.

26.178 Problems are likely to arise when considering the operation of:

- the two-year rule for site-based employees;
- the interpretation of 'substantially ordinary commuting';
- whether an employee has more than one permanent workplace;
- the difference between employees with an 'area' and those with 'travelling appointments'.

It should be remembered that the Guide is only a guide, not dogma. In cases of dispute, reference should be made both to the legislation and to its purpose: see IRPR 24 September 1997 and 9 January 1998.

26.179 For earlier years, HMRC will look in particular for:

- Payment of travel costs other than those necessarily for business. Note that the 'wholly and exclusively' test does not apply to travel, see *ITEPA 2003, s 337*. This will include any reimbursement of home to work travel other than those included in a WRA, eligible relocation costs, emergency call outs (see point 4 in **26.180** below) and amounts payable on a secondment which is expected to last less than a year (see point 5 in **26.180** below). Note that where an employer reimburses home to work costs HMRC may seek to recover the fuel scale charge which applies when petrol costs for private use are paid by the employer.

- Cases where employers reimburse business miles. Here the HMRC applied the 'triangular travel' principle. This only allowed the employer to reimburse on a tax-free basis the lower of the actual miles travelled on business and the miles which would have been travelled to reach that location if the employee had set off from his normal place of work rather than from home. Failure to tax any payments in excess of this can be very expensive for the company. However, it should be noted that this principle is a derivation by HMRC from the law, and has never been established as such in either statute or case law. It is unclear whether HMRC would be prepared to take a contested case to court, and an employer faced with a large retrospective liability may want to obtain a counsel's opinion on the law as it stands.

- Proper controls over mileage reimbursements to ensure that only allowable business miles, according to HMRC's definition, are being

26.180 Employment tax issues

reimbursed. The rates of reimbursement will also be reviewed: are they in line with the fixed profit car scheme rules? Have they been agreed with the local inspector? Excess payments for mileage can be an expensive part of a review settlement, as what appear to be relatively small amounts are spread over a large number of miles and employees. Note that under self-assessment the employer must report details of the mileage paid, including any profit, on P11Ds, unless this has been covered by a dispensation.

- Transport vouchers (including season tickets and travel passes) provided for any employees by reason of their employment, including those in the form P9D category. These are taxable unless the travel is genuine business and does not include home to work. Employees who worked at a succession of different places (site-based employees) were regarded as having a 'normal place of work' at each site, and thus any reimbursement of travel costs or a travel allowance was taxable as was subsistence. Since the employee was likely to have counted this travelling as business rather than private, the reclassification was also likely to affect his car benefit calculation and the employer's NICs. This has in practice resulted in some very large settlements following HMRC reviews. Contrast this with secondments at point 5 in **26.180** below. Both areas are significantly affected by the new rules.

26.180 In addition, the following general points on the review of travel should be noted:

1 Cases where an employer pays for or reimburses the cost of late night travel home. This is taxable unless it falls within the concession, which requires that:

(a) public transport has ceased or could not reasonably be used; and

(b) the employee travels from home to work by public transport; and

(c) normally works fairly regular hours; but

(d) is occasionally required to work late (HMRC in practice accepts that 60 occasions a year or fewer is occasional); and

(e) the pattern of late working must not be regular, eg every Friday.

The same rules apply to NICs.

2 Where an employee holds a travelling appointment, the reimbursements or allowances are more flexible and are likely to include travel from home. It may be necessary for the employer to establish that an employee or a group of employees hold a travelling appointment, for which there is no definition in law. HMRC's view is that 'for an employee to hold a travelling appointment ... travel must be a fundamental part of the job and not just to put the employee in a position to do the job'.

3   Employees who are based at home and travel from there. These are regarded by HMRC as working from home usually as a matter of personal choice. To have the costs of home to office travel allowed, the employer must demonstrate that it is an objective requirement of the employment that the employee must work at home. Often the inspector will ask whether the employee has a desk and other facilities on the employer's premises, and if he does will reject the premise that the employee is home-based. Such a finding is expensive for the employer with a number of employees who work in this fashion. It is advisable to obtain clearance in advance of any review that the employees are 'home-based'. The current HMRC position is described at para 2.13.1 of the Consultative Document on Employee Travel of 13 May 1996. For a defence, see *Horton v Young* (1971) 47 TC 60.

4   Where an employer pays emergency call-out expenses, these will be taxable unless the employee has given instructions before leaving home and had continuing responsibility for the emergency whilst travelling to the normal place of employment (*Pook v Owen* (1969) 45 TC 571). Health service employees have for some time generally been required to certificate any such travel expenses to say that they met these criteria. If this is not done, the inspector is likely to attack any such reimbursement.

5   Under the pre-*FA 1998* rules, home to work travel (and subsistence) was not taxable if the employee had a normal place of work and was temporarily seconded to another. For periods before 6 April 1998 the payment was tax free if:

(a) the absence did not exceed 12 months; and

(b) the employee returned to his normal place of work at the end of the secondment.

If it became obvious at some point in the period that the employee would not return within 12 months, payments were taxable from that date. The same rules applied to NIC.

LIABILITY FOR TAX ARISING

26.181 Where an employer does not tax an item which should have been included in PAYE, the primary liability for any back tax, interest and penalties is with the employer. The employee cannot currently be made to pay the tax unless it was reasonable to assume that he knew the item should have been taxed and that it had not been onwards.

26.182 There is a statutory exception for directors, on the basis that 'in practice the failure to deduct tax from remuneration nearly always occurs in respect of certain directors'. So special legislation was introduced to treat

26.183 *Employment tax issues*

the amount of any tax paid by someone other than the director as a benefit chargeable on the director (*ITEPA 2003, s 223(7)*). Note that this only applies to directors as defined at **26.120**.

26.183 The position is different for benefits. Here the primary liability for paying the tax rests with the employee, and the employer can therefore refuse to settle the unpaid tax on benefits which is uncovered during a review, and require that HMRC assesses the individuals. However, HMRC can penalise the company for filing an incorrect P11D, and this can result in fines of up to £3,000 for each incorrect form.

26.184 The refusal to settle the tax under-deducted on P11Ds can be used judiciously to reduce the costs of a settlement, as HMRC will often be reluctant to go to the trouble and expense of assessing hundreds of employees on what is, individually, often a fairly small amount.

Case study 26.1

An employer applies for a dispensation in regard to P11D reporting which results in HMRC deciding to select him for an employer compliance review. The review identified significant levels of entertaining and travel and subsistence expenditure which should have been reported on employees' forms P11Ds year on year. HMRC calculated that the tax arising on these benefits amounted to a liability in seven figures. HMRC also sought penalties for incorrect forms P11D.

After a great deal of review it was possible to show that the vast majority of expenditure was allowable in the hands of the employee and HMRC decided to seek a token sum in settlement.

Case study 26.2

A public sector employer had engaged a significant number of self-employed workers and on HMRC ascertaining this it (without knowledge of the engager) interviewed the workers to consider whether they had actually been subject to PAYE/Class1 NIC on earnings.

Some of the workers concerned had not registered for Schedule D tax and because of this said they thought they were employed. HMRC approached the engager for a considerable amount of PAYE/ Class 1 NIC. This resulted in my firm being engaged when we considered the status of the workers.

There was no one standard engagement and we ruled which workers should be correctly employed and those self employed. For the employed workers we negotiated an offset under the guidance following *Demibourne* and the net liability.

We also set up systems with the HR team over the engagement of workers to ensure those who should be considered employed workers were identified and dealt with correctly from the outset of the engagement.

Case study 26.3

A client was challenged by HMRC at the time of an employer compliance review over the mileage claims of employees using company cars on business travel. HMRC believed the mileage looked in rounded figures and suggested it seeks a fuel scale charge on each vehicle when the data looked suspect.

We agreed a sample population to review and went back over an agreed period to look at mileage claims. We used autoroute to test the distances claimed. We found a small error rate of below 10% and negotiated a settlement based on the results of our review.

We assisted the client in tightening its expenses policy and undertook a further review three and six months later to check the new policy was working.

Case study 26.4

We had a public sector client who at the time of an employer compliance review was challenged over expenses claimed by a number of employees. These employees had claimed expenses based on them being home-based but HMRC considered them to be office-based.

We met with a few of these workers and looked at their working patterns and the agreements that they had with their employers. We found significant evidence that the staff did work from home. We prepared a report which was passed to HMRC who, after significant discussion, accepted this view.

Case study 26.5

An employee of a client approached HMRC over a termination payment he had received from his employer. This resulted in HMRC contacting the employer and asking for details of termination payments made over the previous six years. HMRC had decided that, because it was custom for employees not to serve their notice period that the PILON element of the payment was taxable.

After significant review we found that we had no case for sales-facing staff but this was not the case for clerical staff who had been made redundant. A settlement was agreed on this basis.

Index

A
Accelerated payment notice (APN)
  appeals 20.115, 20.116–20.118, 21.6, 21.27
  artificial loss deductions 21.8
  calculation of tax due 21.8, 21.9
  capital gains 21.8
  contesting 21.27, 23.34
  delivery 21.8
  determinations 21.24
  DOTAS 21.2, 21.6
    arrangements notifiable under 21.6
  enquiries 20.117, 21.6
  example of 21.32
  follower notice, and 21.5, 21.6
  generally 21.1–21.7, 22.22–22.23
  group loss relief 21.5, 21.9
  introduction 21.6, 21.9
  judicial review 20.118–20.119, 21.41
  key points 21.43
  legislation 21.6
  National Insurance contributions 21.5–21.7
  options open to taxpayer 21.39–21.42
  partnership payment notices (PPNs) 21.29–21.31
  payment reminders 21.10
  payments under 21.10
  penalty regime 21.10, 21.36
  promoters of tax avoidance schemes (POTAS) rules 21.10, 21.20
  qualifying conditions 21.6
  resolving underlying dispute 21.11
  sale and leaseback 21.9
  self-employment 21.8
  sideways loss relief 21.8
  stamp duty land tax 21.3, 21.5
  status 21.7
  summary 21.32

Accelerated payment notice (APN)
  – *contd*
  target list 21.3–21.4
  taxes covered 21.5, 21.6
  time limits 21.5, 21.7, 21.10
  time to pay (TTP) arrangements 21.10
Accelerated payment rules
  DOTAS 4.31
  follower notices 4.30
  general anti-abuse rule (GAAR) 4.31
  generally 4.29
Accessories and Abettors Act 1861
  offences under 3.7
Accommodation
  provided by employer 26.129–26.132
Accountanta
  reliance on advice 18.60, 18.64–18.65
    reasonable excuse 18.63
  tax advice not privileged 19.49
  working papers, access to 1.48
Accounting date
  change of 7.40
Advertising and promotion costs
  selection for enquiry 7.62–7.63
Advisers
  notifying, inspection of premises 1.102
  papers, protection 4.115–4.117
Agency workers
  PAYE compliance 26.70, 26.88–26.91
Aggregates levy
  HMRC information gathering powers 16.26
  security for tax, requirement to give 22.67–22.75
Aiding and abetting
  enabling offshore evasion 31
  tax fraud offences 3.4, 3.7
Alternative dispute resolution (ADR)
  application for 12.18, 12.48
  availability 12.3
  bargaining phase 12.37

1107

Index

Alternative dispute resolution (ADR)
  – *contd*
  confidentiality 12.31
  costs 12.33, 12.35
  direct taxes 12.3
  disclosure 12.29, 12.31
  flexibility 12.47
  generally 6.85–6.87, 12.1–12.12, 19.65, 20.39–20.45
  guiding principles 12.27–12.33
  high net worth individuals 12.24
  indirect taxes 12.3
  key decision makers, presence 12.32
  large businesses 12.24
  Litigation and Settlement Strategy (LSS) 12.13–12.21
  mediation 12.9–12.14
    guiding principles 12.27–12.33
    mediator's role 12.34–12.35
    techniques 12.40–12.43
  Mediation Agreement 12.27, 12.49
  mediation day 12.1, 12.17–12.26
    case study 12.39
    confidentiality 12.31
    costs 12.33
    flexible nature 12.30
    full disclosure 12.29
    opening statements 12.35
    practical considerations 12.43
    presence of key decision makers 12.32
    structure 12.34–12.39
    'without prejudice' rule 12.28
  non-confrontational approach 12.14–12.15
  non-statutory status 12.7
  objective 12.4–12.8, 12.14
  personal taxpayer 12.25
  pilot 12.2, 12.15–12.21
  requesting 12.24–12.24
  resolving an enquiry 4.175–4.176, 8.127–8.128, 8.130
  resolving disputes with 1.121–1.122
  settlement agreement 12.6, 12.38
  SMEs 12.25
  specialist advice 12.26
  suitable cases 12.22–12.23
  tribunal system, and 12.44–12.48, 20.33, 20.39–20.45

Alternative dispute resolution (ADR)
  – *contd*
  value added tax disputes 24.80–24.82
  voluntary nature 12.7
  withdrawal from 12.7
  without prejudice rule 12.28
Annual tax on enveloped dwellings (ATED)
  accelerated payment notices 21.5
  follower notices 21.5
Appeals
  accelerated payment notices 20.115, 20.116–20.118, 21.6, 21.27
  closure notices 1.110–1.111, 20.59–20.77
    applications 20.53–20.56
    purpose 20.57–20.58
    self-assessment 20.51–20.52, 20.60–20.77
    Tower MCashback v HMRC Comrs 20.59–20.77
  Court of Appeal 20.250–20.255
  discovery assessments 1.110–1.111
  follower notices 20.115, 20.119, 21.27
    outstanding appeals 21.16, 21.17
  FSA decisions 20.219
  generally 20.1–20.6
  High Court 20.189–20.190, 20.258–20.267
  hold notices 22.44–22.46
  information notices 1.94
  legislation 20.1–20.6
  litigation
    key points 20.280
    tactical use 20.7–20.8
  Litigation and Settlement Strategy (LSS) 20.9–20.15
  National Insurance contributions
    award of credits 25.211
    Class 4 appeals 25.212–25.216
    contracting out matters 25.210
    determination by tribunal 25.203, 25.208–25.209
    further appeal to Upper Tribunal 25.208–25.209
    generally 25.166–25.171
    HMRC officers' decisions 25.172–25.194
    late appeals 25.201–25.202

1108

Index

Appeals – *contd*
National Insurance contributions
– *contd*
manner of making appeal
25.195–25.199
place of hearing 25.200
publication of decisions 25.217
settlement agreements
25.204–25.207
notice of enquiry 1.37–1.38
offshore tax non-compliance,
RTC offence 5.142
penalties 18.52, 18.55, 18.196
data-holder notices 16.102
pending, documents relating to
16.180–16.181
Pensions Regulator
decisions 20.219
position before predecessor tribunals
20.183–20.188
postponement of tax, application for
direct taxes 20.112–20.114
generally 20.110
indirect taxes 20.111
pre-appeal procedures 20.46
direct taxes 20.47–20.50
indirect taxes 20.82–20.86
referral of questions during enquiry
20.78–20.80
self-assessment closure procedure
20.51–20.52, 20.60–20.77
review procedure
all taxes 20.101–20.105
appeal after 20.106–20.109
direct taxes 20.94–20.100, 20.104
generally 20.87–20.88
indirect taxes 20.89–20.93, 20.104
settlement by agreement
direct taxes 20.120–20.121
indirect taxes 20.122
tribunal system
ADR 12.44–12.48, 20.33,
20.39–20.45
direct taxes 20.106–20.107
First-tier Tribunal, *see* First-tier
Tribunal
indirect taxes 20.108–20.109
introduction 20.16–20.45
Leggatt Inquiry 20.19–20.24
origin for change 20.16–20.18

Appeals – *contd*
tribunal system – *contd*
overriding objective 20.33,
20.34–20.38
summary 20.26–20.33
Tribunals, Courts and Enforcement
Act 2007 20.25
Upper Tribunal, *see* Upper Tribunal
Upper Tribunal, from 20.250–20.257
value added tax disputes
24.74–24.76
ADR 20.39–20.45
time limits 24.77–24.79
withdrawal 20.123–20.126
Appointment diary
HMRC access to 1.48, 6.80–6.81
Appropriate arrangements
annual certification 18.102
Arrest
HMRC powers 3.43–3.44, 3.48, 3.50,
3.52, 3.54, 3.60, 3.123
PACE powers 16.194
Assessments
discovery 1.17, 1.22–1.23, 8.107
cancellation 8.105
challenging 13.147–13.157
estimates 8.106
format 13.141–13.146
issue 8.112
power to make 8.113
time limits 8.109, 13.28–13.34
deceased taxpayers
13.35–13.37
offshore non-compliance
13.38–13.42
when made 13.43–13.45
when tax payable 13.166–13.168
offshore tax non-compliance,
RTC offence 5.139
penalty regime 18.21–18.22
failure to notify under-assessment
18.92–18.93
level of penalty 18.194
time limits 8.110
value added tax 24.72–24.73
Assurance visit, *see* Value added tax
Auditors
HMRC information gathering powers
16.127, 16.182–16.187
Avoidance, *see* Tax avoidance

1109

Index

B
Bad debts
 selection for enquiry 7.65
Bail
 release on 3.44
Balance sheets
 selection for enquiry 7.69–7.82
Bank accounts
 certificate, HMRC requesting 8.114, 8.117
 directors' loan or current accounts 7.80, 17.31, 17.42–17.43
 disclosure reports 17.31–17.43
 estimates and assumptions where source of deposit unknown 8.105
 joint 1.48
 record keeping 1.75
 see also Private records
Bank payroll tax
 HMRC information gathering powers 16.26
Banking information
 HMRC information gathering powers 1.104–1.105, 8.6–8.10
 offshore banks 8.8
 see also Private records
Bankruptcy
 tax debt collection 22.63–22.68
Base Erosion Profit Shifting (BEPS)
 OECD's action points 4.37, 4.39
Benefits and reimbursed expenses
 accommodation 26.129–26.132
 areas likely to be investigated 26.128
 assessable on all employees 26.112–26.117
 benefits in kind 26.4
 cars 26.133–26.139
 commissions and discounts 26.141
 conferences, employees attending 26.142–26.145
 credit cards 26.140
 directors 26.118–26.122
 dispensations 26.101–26.106
 entertaining clients 7.62–7.63, 26.146–26.151
 entertaining staff 7.62–7.63, 26.152–26.157
 gifts 26.158

Benefits and reimbursed expenses
 – contd
 higher paid employees 26.118–26.122
 liability for tax arising 26.10, 26.181–26.184
 loans 26.159
 long service awards 26.160
 mobile phones 26.161
 National Insurance contributions 26.114–26.117
 personal incidental expenses 26.162–26.164
 prizes 26.165
 relocation costs 26.166–26.169
 review for disclosure reports 17.31, 17.52–17.53
 self-assessment 26.123
 staff social functions 26.170
 subsistence allowances 26.171–26.172
 suggestion schemes 26.173
 telephone costs 26.174
 third party benefits 26.175–26.176
 travel and subsistence costs 26.171–26.172, 26.177–26.180
 value of benefits 26.124–26.127
 working rule agreements 26.107–26.111
Body corporate, *see* Corporate entity
Books, *see* Records and documents
Bribery
 offences 3.6
Business inspection
 agreed 10.122–10.123
 inspection of documents 1.100, 9.63
 search warrants, *see* Search warrant
 unannounced 1.99, 1.102, 6.55–6.60, 10.124–10.129
 see also Business record checks/examinations; Inspection of premises
Business premises
 costs, selection for enquiry 7.57
 employer compliance checks 9.77–9.110
 inspection, *see* Business inspection; Inspection of premises
 meaning of premises 3.70
 private home as 1.99

Index

Business record checks/examinations
  business records checks (BRCs),
    failure of 7.27, 9.43
  generally 9.43
  private homes 1.99
  record-keeping, making tax digital
    project (MTD) 7.27
  selection for enquiry 7.27
  senior accounting officer (SAO) rules,
    penalty regime 18.100–18.104
  unannounced inspections 1.99, 1.102,
    6.55–6.60, 10.124–10.129
  value added tax 24.31–24.34
  see also Private records; Records and
    documents

C
Capital account
  selection for enquiry 7.81–7.82
Capital gains
  accelerated payment notices 21.8
  selection for enquiry 7.87–7.88
Capital gains tax
  accelerated payment notices 21.5
  debt recovery 22.56
  failure to notify liability 18.89
  follower notices 21.5
  HMRC information gathering
    powers 16.26
  managed payment plans 22.3–22.6
Cars
  provided by employer 26.133–26.139
Carelessness, *see* Discovery; Penalty
  regime
Cash
  cash flow tests 17.31, 17.44–17.48
  indications of use 15.28
Casual worker
  PAYE compliance 26.70, 26.82–26.87
Certificate of full disclosure
  HMRC requesting 8.114, 8.122
Cheating the public revenue
  aiding and abetting 3.7
  double jeopardy rule 18.209
  offence, generally 3.6–3.7, 3.139
  penalties 3.6
Children
  income of 1.48
  statement of assets and liabilities
    (SOAL) 8.121

Civil Investigations
  false statements or documents 3.36
  Specialist Investigations, *see* Specialist
    Investigations Office (SI)
  see also Code of Practice 8; Code of
    Practice 9
Civil Investigation of Fraud (CIF), *see*
  Code of Practice 9
Civil resolution
  voluntary disclosure leading to
    14.14–14.15
Cleaners
  PAYE compliance 26.98–26.99
Climate change levy
  security for tax, requirement to give
    22.67–22.75
Closure notices
  amendments 1.106, 1.108, 1.110
    appeal against 1.110–1.111
  appeals 1.110–1.111, 8.106,
    20.59–20.77
  application for 1.109–1.111,
    6.95–6.103, 20.53–20.56
  ADR 1.121–1.122
  case law 1.112–1.120
  contents 1.106–1.108
  corporation tax 1.108
  estimates 8.106
  income tax 1.106
  issue 1.106
  partial 1.123–1.125, 18.165, 20.81
  partnerships 1.107
  time of effect 1.106
  Tower MCashback v HMRC Comrs
    20.59–20.77
Code of Practice 8 (COP8)
  CDF, complete and unprompted 2.13,
    2.59–2.60, 3.35, 3.38
  Criminal Investigation Directorate,
    cases passed to 2.82
  fraud
    abuse of position 2.19–2.20
    failure to disclose information
      2.19–2.20
    false representation 2.19–2.20
    generally 2.82–2.83
  generally 2.3, 2.9, 2.82–2.84
  marketed avoidance schemes 2.84
  non-evasion cases 2.9
  offshore investigations 2.82

1111

Index

Code of Practice 8 (COP8) – *contd*
  practice management 2.85–2.92
  professional indemnity insurance 2.85
Code of Practice 9 (COP9)
  case study 2.98
  circumstances leading to investigation 2.12, 2.36
  Civil Investigation of Fraud (CIF)
    criminal investigations 2.32–2.33
    disclosure 2.36
      voluntary 2.13, 2.39, 2.59–2.60, 3.38
    exceptions 2.13–2.14
      see also Code of Practice 8 (COP8)
    generally 1.30, 2.31–2.40
    introduction 2.31
    meetings under 2.35–2.39
      preparation for 2.40–2.43
    previous investigations 2.12, 3.36
    replacement 2.43
  Contractual Disclosure Facility (CDF)
    closing the investigation 2.78
    contract, contents 3.25
    criminal investigations following 2.44, 3.25–3.27
    denial of fraud 2.44, 2.52, 3.25
      with offer of cooperation 2.52, 2.54–2.56
    disclosure 2.49–2.51, 2.57–2.60, 3.25, 3.38, 14.36–14.37
      reports 17.2, 17.58–17.61
    formal questions 2.61
    from June 2014 2.54–2.56
    generally 1.31, 2.3, 2.8, 2.43–2.46, 3.23–3.25, 14.42–14.47
    HMRC approach 2.10–2.14
    HMRC Investigation of Fraud Statement 2.47–2.48
    introduction 2.43
    meetings under 2.62–2.63
      preparation for 2.64–2.77
    non-cooperation 2.44, 2.53, 3.25
    outline disclosure 2.57–2.58
    payment of taxes and penalties due 3.25
    settlement 2.79–2.81
    suitability of cases 2.45–2.46
  cooperation 2.44
    withdrawal 2.44

Code of Practice 9 (COP9) – *contd*
  cost effectiveness 3.12
  direct tax questions 2.38, 2.41
  disclosure
    case study 2.98
    CDF procedures 2.49–2.51, 2.57–2.60, 3.25, 3.38, 14.36–14.37
    certificate of full 17.68–17.71
    failure to make 17.60
    outline 2.57–2.58, 2.98
    reports 2.98, 17.2, 17.58–17.61
    voluntary 2.13, 2.39, 2.59–2.60, 3.35, 17.62–17.65
  failure to notify chargeability 2.42
  fraud
    definition 2.15–2.20
    denial of 2.44, 2.52, 2.54–2.56
    intention to make gain or loss 2.20
    suspected serious 2.2, 2.8, 2.10–2.14
  handling enquiries 1.31
  'Hansard' investigations 2.21
  historical background 2.21–2.30
  HMRC Investigation of Fraud Statement 2.47–2.48
  HMRC policy 2.10–2.14, 3.12
  indirect tax questions 2.42
  key forms HMRC may request 8.114–8.125
  meetings under
    CDF procedures 2.62–2.77
    CIF procedures 2.35–2.46
  notification by HMRC 2.34
  practice management 2.85–2.92
  professional indemnity insurance 2.85
Commissions and discounts
  Pay As You Earn 26.141
Company
  failure to prevent facilitation of foreign tax evasion 5.122–5.124
  insolvency 22.65–22.66, 22.69
  international tax planning
    background 4.37
    BEPS action plan 4.39
    diverted profits tax 4.38
  liquidation 22.63–22.68
  security for tax, requirement to give 22.67–22.75

Company car, *see* Cars
Company officers
 liability for penalties 18.134–18.136
Company residence
 generally 5.17
 international planning, fact finding 4.121–4.125
Complaints procedure
 Adjudicator 23.73–23.76
 client
  considering impact on 23.42–23.46
  managing client's expectations 23.47–23.49
 compensation for financial losses 23.80–23.81
 consequences of complaining 23.57–23.58
 court decisions 23.33–23.34
  HMRC interpretation 23.35–23.36
 delays 23.11, 23.13–23.16, 23.74
 disproportionate decisions 23.11, 23.21–23.23
 enquiries 6.121–6.127
 generally 23.1–23.10, 23.64–23.66
 HMRC guidance 23.1–23.5, 23.9
  HMRC not following 23.11, 23.24–23.26
 HMRC staff behaviour 23.11, 23.31, 23.41, 23.74
 inconsistent decisions 23.11, 23.21–23.23
 Interest Review Unit (IRU) 23.37–23.38
 legal remedies, interaction with
  generally 23.4
  judicial review 23.52–23.63
  tribunal hearings 23.59–23.61
 legislation 23.33–23.34
  HMRC interpretation 23.35–23.36
 legitimate expectation 23.60
 matters covered by 23.11–23.41
 mishandling by HMRC 23.11, 23.32
 misinformed decisions 23.11, 23.17–23.20
 misleading advice 23.11, 23.27–23.30, 23.74
 mistakes 23.11, 23.12
 more than one HMRC area involved 23.69–23.76

Complaints procedure – *contd*
 Ombudsman 23.6, 23.77–23.80
 ongoing investigations 23.50–23.56
 poor advice 23.74
 redress for inadequate handling 23.8
 redress where complaint upheld 23.81–23.84
 three tier process 23.64–23.66, 23.69–23.76
 time limits 23.67–23.68
 unfair decisions 23.11, 23.21–23.23
 unnecessary or vexatious complaints 23.39–23.40
 unreasonable decisions 23.11, 23.17–23.20
 unreasonable discretion 23.74
Complex enquiries
 HMRC's approach to working, *see* Working of complex enquiries
Compliance check
 areas likely to be reviewed 9.108–9.110
 business inspections 1.98
 contractors 9.77
 disclosure made during 14.25–14.26, 14.29
 employment income 26.10–26.11
 generally 7.3–7.7, 9.77–9.103, 26.10
 HMRC powers 7.3, 9.79
 National Insurance contributions 25.14, 25.23, 25.31–25.32
 on-site meetings 7.6–7.7
 pre-planning checklists 9.104–9.108
 purpose 9.77–9.78
 real-time record review 7.6–7.7
 reason to suspect 7.4, 7.5
 tax position, meaning 7.3
 use of term 7.3
 see also Business inspection; Business record checks/examinations
Computer records
 criminal investigations 3.78, 3.90
 evidential material 3.78, 3.90
 obstruction/failure to provide 18.95
Concealment
 deliberate 2.12, 3.36, 18.96–18.99
 deliberate errors, of 18.32, 18.77–18.84
 failure to notify liability 18.88
 proceeds of crime 3.172

1113

Index

Conferences
benefits and reimbursed expenses 26.142–26.145
Confiscation order
court powers 3.151–3.152
Conspiracy to defraud
offence, generally 2.12, 3.6, 3.36, 3.139
penalties 3.6
Construction Industry Scheme (CIS)
compliance checks 25.23
failure to make return 18.106, 18.109
Contractor
employer compliance checks 9.77
Contractual Disclosure Facility (CDF), *see* Code of Practice 9
Control of paper, *see* Controlling the investigation (documents)
Controlled Goods Agreement
debt recovery 22.56
Controlling the investigation
act reasonably and courteously 10.65–10.66
areas to be controlled 10.6
avoid being sidetracked 10.133
avoid delay 10.44–10.48
business inspections
agreed 10.122–10.123
unannounced 10.124–10.129
case studies 10.7, 10.40, 10.68, 10.90
client's cooperation 10.144
concluding the investigation 10.131–10.144
controlling client
client's confidence in practitioner 10.11–10.12
early disclosure 10.20–10.23, 10.86–10.87, 10.149–10.152
fees 10.26–10.28
generally 10.6, 10.8–10.10
honesty paramount 10.18
keeping client informed 10.29
keeping client to timetable 10.24–10.25
meetings with HMRC 10.89–10.90
objective assessment of client 10.13–10.17
disclosure reports 17.9–17.14

Controlling the investigation – *contd*
documents
calculations, record-keeping 10.104
correspondence file 10.98–10.101
formal 10.103
generally 10.6, 10.43, 10.94
indexing and filing 10.106
information requests 10.108–10.116
investigation file, setting up 10.96–10.97
report preparation file 10.107
retention of working papers 17.56–17.57
third party notices 10.117–10.120
working files 10.102–10.103
working schedules 10.105
formal action 10.57–10.58
generally 10.68, 10.76, 10.121, 10.158
HMRC officers
difficult 10.142–10.143
generally 10.6, 10.31–10.38
importance of control 10.1–10.5
knowing what is expected 10.49–10.53
meetings with HMRC
action points 10.92
body language at 10.88
cost effectiveness 10.70–10.71
early disclosure 10.86–10.87
follow-up action 10.93
generally 10.69, 10.72–10.75, 10.82–10.85
keeping control of client 10.89–10.90
preparation for 10.78–10.81
taking notes 10.91
venue 10.76–10.77
number of years, associated problems 10.134–10.136
objectives, importance 10.59
payment of tax 10.63–10.64
payments on account 10.144
penalties, negotiating 10.145–10.156
powers, using 10.60–10.62
preparation and planning 10.39–10.42
realism, importance 10.54–10.56
reminders, using 10.60–10.62
reports to HMRC 17.9–17.14
where agreement cannot be reached 10.137–10.141

1114

Index

Corporate entity
　failure to prevent tax evasion 3.8, 3.10
　NIC offences 25.114–25.115
　personal liability notices
　　25.133–25.136
Corporation tax
　accelerated payment notices 21.5
　debt recovery 22.56
　errors in returns, penalty regime 18.18
　failure to make return 18.106
　failure to notify liability 18.89–18.91
　follower notices 21.5
　HMRC information gathering
　　powers 16.26
　managed payment plans 22.3–22.6
Corruption
　deliberate 2.12, 3.36
Costs
　ADR 12.33
　First-tier Tribunal
　　complex cases 20.203,
　　　20.208–20.212
　　generally 20.203
　　pre-1 April 2009 appeals 20.203,
　　　20.213–20.218
　　unreasonable conduct 20.203,
　　　20.206–20.207
　　wasted costs 20.203, 20.204–20.205
　Upper Tribunal jurisdiction 20.249
　see also Fees; Legal and professional
　　fees
Counter Avoidance Directorate (CAD)
　role 25.65
Court of Appeal
　appeal from Upper Tribunal
　　20.250–20.255
Credit cards
　analyses of expenditure 26.140
　certificate, HMRC requesting
　　8.114, 8.117
　credit card data, selection for
　　enquiry 7.11
　expenditure analysis for disclosure
　　reports 17.31, 17.49–17.51
　HMRC access to private records 15.23
Criminal investigations
　ADR inappropriate where 12.36
　aiding and abetting tax evasion 3.4, 3.7
　arrests 3.43–3.44, 3.48, 3.50, 3.52,
　　3.54, 3.60, 3.123

Criminal investigations – *contd*
　authorised officers 16.196–16.198
　avoidance schemes 2.12
　background 3.1–3.5
　CDF procedures 2.44, 3.25–3.27
　CIF procedures 2.32–2.33
　circumstances leading to 2.12, 2.36
　Criminal Investigation Directorate 2.6
　Crown Prosecution Service (CPS)
　　2.5, 3.44–3.45, 3.139
　dawn raids 3.69, 3.122–3.127, 6.82
　decision to charge 3.44–3.45
　deterrence 3.29
　disclosure, complete and unprompted
　　2.13, 3.25, 3.38
　dishonesty 3.1, 3.147
　evidential material 3.77–3.96
　　electronic form, in 3.78, 3.90
　　enter and search powers 3.85
　　excluded material 3.77–3.96
　　legal professional privilege 3.42,
　　　3.77–3.96, 3.124, 3.128–3.133,
　　　16.127, 16.152–16.155, 19.49
　　records to be kept 3.86
　　removal from premises 3.84
　　special procedure material
　　　3.77–3.96
　factors leading to 3.33–3.38, 3.42
　false statements or documents 2.12,
　　2.36, 3.36
　forged documents 2.12, 3.36
　generally 3.41, 3.42–3.47, 8.28–8.31
　government policy 3.11–3.19
　government subsidies, false claims for
　　3.2–3.3
　HMRC enquiries 3.5, 8.28–8.31
　　enquiry triggers 8.17–8.19
　HMRC prosecution policy
　　2.10–2.14, 3.11–3.19
　HMRC Risk and Intelligence Service
　　3.39, 7.9
　human rights issues 3.31
　increasing use of 3.1, 3.12, 3.16
　individuals holding position of trust or
　　responsibility 2.12, 3.26
　information gathering, *see* Information
　　and data gathering powers
　inspection of premises, *see* Inspection
　　of premises
　international offences 2.12, 3.36

1115

Index

Criminal investigations – *contd*
  interviews 3.42–3.43, 3.45, 3.134–3.138
  LDF, registration with 5.73
  money laundering 2.12
  NIC evasion 3.2
  officer training 3.59–3.61
  organised crime 2.12
  PACE powers 3.88–3.92, 3.112–3.116, 3.131, 16.2, 16.10, 16.12–16.13, 16.193–16.214
    safeguards 16.214
  powers and safeguards 3.48–3.49
    arrests 3.43–3.44, 3.48, 3.50, 3.52, 3.54, 3.60, 3.123
    dawn raids 3.69, 3.122–3.127
    entry and search without warrant 3.85
    external independent approval 3.68
    external oversight 3.67
    interception of communications 3.62–3.65
    officer training 3.59–3.61
    PACE 3.42, 3.88–3.92, 3.112–3.116, 3.131, 16.2, 16.10, 16.12–16.13, 16.193–16.214
    production orders, *see* Production orders
    property interference 3.62–3.65
    removal of material for examination elsewhere 3.84
    safeguards, generally 3.66–3.68
    search of persons 3.71
    search warrants, *see* Search warrant
    searching premises 3.42, 3.69–3.76
    surveillance operations 3.62–3.68, 24.64–24.68
  previous offences 2.12, 3.36
  production orders, *see* Production order
  prosecution policy 3.28–3.32
  release on bail 3.44
  search warrants, *see* Search warrant
  selective prosecution 3.28–3.30, 3.36
  SOCPA powers 3.117–3.121, 16.215–16.222
  state benefits, false claims for 3.2–3.3
  surveillance powers 3.62–3.68, 24.64–24.68

Criminal investigations – *contd*
  suspected serious fraud 2.6, 2.8
    HMRC's published prosecution policy 2.11
  tax evasion, generally 3.1
  trial preparation 3.139–3.158
Criminal Investigation Directorate
  officer training 3.59–3.61
Criminal lifestyle
  defendants with 3.151–3.154
Criminal offences, *see* Offences
Criminal prosecution
  burden of proof 3.140–3.141
  confiscation orders 3.151–3.152
  conviction 3.140, 3.147
    determination of appropriate sentence 3.149
  criminal lifestyle, defendants with 3.151–3.154
  Crown Court 3.6, 3.46–3.47, 3.142
  decision to charge 3.44–3.45
  defence statement 3.144–3.145
  disclosure of documents to defendant 3.142–3.143
  dishonesty must be proven 3.1, 3.147
  guilty plea 3.46
  jury 3.148
  Magistrates' court 3.6, 3.46–3.47
  majority verdicts 3.148
  not guilty plea 3.46
  order of events 3.139–3.158
  procedure 3.46–3.47, 3.139–3.158
  witnesses 3.146
Crown Court
  prosecutions 3.6, 3.46–3.47, 3.142
Crown Dependency disclosure facilities
  generally 5.107–5.112
Crown Prosecution Service (CPS)
  decision to charge 2.5, 3.44–3.45, 3.139
  Specialist Fraud Division 3.11
Customer relationship manager (CRM)
  National Insurance contributions 25.65
  promoting ADR 12.37–12.38
  value added tax 24.5, 24.9
Cyber fraud
  specialist teams 3.34

Index

D

Data gathering, *see* Information and data gathering powers

Data-holder notice
failure to comply, penalties 16.100–16.102
generally 16.98–16.99

Data-holders
categories 16.92–16.96
generally 16.90–16.91
money service businesses 16.97

Dawn raids
engaging solicitor 6.82
generally 3.69, 3.122–3.127
tips for handling 8.97

Debt collection, *see* Tax debt collection

Debtor
debt collection, *see* Tax debt collection
habitual defaulters 22.56
non-UK 22.81–22.93
notices for details of 18.105
untraced 22.8–22.15

Deceased person
time limits
assessment 13.35–13.37
information notices 1.93

Deception
deliberate 2.12, 2.36

Deduction notice
failure to comply 22.49–22.53
generally 22.47–22.48

Default surcharge
ADR inappropriate 12.36

Delay by HMRC
complaints procedure 23.11, 23.13–23.16, 23.74
interest charges resulting from 23.37–23.38

Determination
appeal against 8.106
issue, generally 8.106

Deterrence
HMRC prosecution policy 3.29

Direct taxes
ADR 12.3
appeals, *see* Appeals
SI office 3.23

Directors
benefits 26.118–26.122
close company 15.32

Directors – *contd*
current accounts 7.80
employment income 26.71, 26.100
liability
for penalties 18.132–18.134
for tax arising 26.182
loan or current accounts 15.28
disclosure reports 17.31, 17.42–17.43
notice requesting statements 1.48
PAYE compliance 26.71, 26.100
personal assets and liabilities 1.48
reports to HMRC 17.52–17.53
security for tax, requirement to give 22.67–22.75

Disclosure
ADR 12.45–12.47
certificate of full 17.68–17.71
civil or criminal investigations 2.13, 2.59–2.60, 3.35
Code of Practice 9, *see* Code of Practice 9
complete and unprompted 2.13, 2.59–2.60, 3.35, 3.38, 10.149, 11.11
Contractual Disclosure Facility, *see* Code of Practice 9
discovery, preventing 6.13
DOTAS, *see* Disclosure of Tax Avoidance Schemes (DOTAS)
early 10.20–10.23, 10.86–10.87, 10.149–10.152
HMRC returning disclosed documents 1.19
importance 6.13
key forms HMRC may request 8.114–8.125
LDF, *see* Liechtenstein disclosure facility
non-submission of return 8.26
offshore facility, *see* Offshore disclosure
penalty reduction 10.145–10.153, 11.9, 19.1–19.5
prompted 10.149, 11.11, 19.7, 19.29
quality 10.150–10.152, 19.1
mitigating penalties 18.120, 19.6, 19.9–19.23
relevance to return 1.19–1.22

1117

Index

Disclosure – *contd*
  report, *see* Disclosure report
  risk reduction, generally 1.14–1.23
  selection for enquiry 7.12
  unprompted 2.13, 2.59–2.60, 3.35,
    3.38, 10.149, 11.11, 19.7, 19.29
  value added tax 11.19–11.20
  voluntary, *see* Voluntary disclosures
Disclosure of Tax Avoidance Schemes (DOTAS)
  accelerated payments
    notices 21.2, 21.6
    rules 4.29, 4.31
  arrangements impacted 4.14
  background 4.12–4.13
  changing role, practical
    issues 4.22
  hallmarks 4.16
  information powers 4.19
  introducers 4.17
    information from 4.20
  National Insurance contributions 25.3
  penalties 4.18
  promoter 4.15
  publication of schemes and/or
    promoters 4.21
Disclosure report
  admission of irregularities 17.20
  agreeing parameters with HMRC
    17.17–17.24
  circumstances prompting
    17.1–17.4
  controlling investigation process
    17.9–17.14
  COP9 reports 17.2, 17.58–17.61
    failure to make 17.60
  cost-effectiveness 17.5, 17.7
  costs involved 17.5–17.7
  formal certificates 17.68–17.71
  key points 17.72
  persuading client to disclose
    17.15–17.16
  planning and preparation
    17.17–17.24, 17.30–17.31
  preparation and completion
    17.25–17.56
  responsibility of client 17.29
  see also Report for HMRC
Discounts
  Pay As You Earn 26.141

Discovery
  assessment 1.17, 1.22–1.23, 8.107
    cancellation 8.105
    challenging 13.147–13.157
    estimates 8.106
    format 13.141–13.146
    issue 8.112
    power to make 8.113
    time limits 8.109, 13.28–13.34
      deceased taxpayers 13.35–13.37
      offshore non-compliance
        13.38–13.42
    when made 13.43–13.45
    when tax payable 13.166–13.168
  becoming stale 13.46–13.54
  burden of proof 13.158–13.165
  careless or deliberate behaviour
    requirement 13.71–13.72
    'a person acting on his behalf'
      13.77–13.83
    carelessness, meaning
      13.93–13.100
    'deliberate', meaning 13.84–13.92
    reliance on advice 13.101–13.104
    situation must be 'brought about'
      13.73–13.76
  compulsory production of documents
    or information 1.132
  consequential claims 13.169–13.179
  contract settlement 1.135–1.138,
    8.145–8.156
  enquiries 13.10–13.13
    enquiry window 1.17, 7.2
  estimating liabilities in absence of
    evidence 13.137–13.140
  fraud 1.127, 1.130
  generally 13.1–13.5
  generally prevailing practice
    exemption 13.66–13.70
  HMRC's Statements of Practice
    13.129–13.130
  increased threat of 4.184–4.197
  irrelevance 13.6–13.9
  key points 13.180
  negligence 1.127, 1.130
  occurrences leading to 13.21–13.27
  overview 13.14–13.20
  powers generally 1.126–1.127
  presumption of continuity
    1.133–1.134, 13.131–13.136

Index

Discovery – *contd*
  prevention 6.13
  professional fee protection policy 1.139
  requirements for valid 1.23, 1.128, 1.133
  returns
    absent 13.55–13.58
    submitted 13.59–13.65
  speculative enquiry 6.43
  time limits 1.129–1.131
  volunteering information 1.14–1.23
  without culpable behaviour 13.105–13.106
    available information 13.116–13.120
    conditions 13.107–13.108
    'hypothetical' officer 13.109–13.113
    level of awareness 13.121–13.128
    when officer ceases to be entitled 13.114–13.115
Disguised remuneration
  National Insurance contributions 25.3, 25.48
  tax avoidance 21.33
Dismissal from employment
  payments on 26.39
Dispensation
  benefits and reimbursed expenses 26.101–26.106
Dispute resolution
  accelerated payment notices 21.11
  alternative, *see* Alternative dispute resolution (ADR)
  generally 6.84–6.87
  LSS, *see* Litigation and Settlement Strategy (LSS)
  meaning of dispute 20.14
  Ombudsman 19.65
  tactical use of litigation 20.7–20.8
  Tax Disputes Governance Code 20.13
Distraint
  debt recovery 22.56–22.60
Diverted profits tax (DPT)
  failure to notify liability 18.90
  generally 4.38
Documents, *see* Private records; Records and documents
Domicile
  offshore tax investigations 5.12–5.14

Double jeopardy rule
  generally 18.209
Double taxation treaties
  liaison with overseas authorities 2.94

E

Emoluments, *see* Employment income
Employee benefit trust (EBT)
  National Insurance contributions 25.28
  sub-trust, payment into 4.76–4.77
Employee costs
  selection for enquiry 7.55–7.56
Employer compliance check, *see* Compliance check
Employment income
  benefits and expenses, *see* Benefits and reimbursed expenses
  benefits in kind 26.4
  compliance checks 26.10–26.11
  directors 26.71, 26.100
  earnings 26.4
  emoluments 26.4
  generally 26.1–26.10
  minimum wage 26.7, 26.8
    breach of rules, penalties 18.112
  National Insurance numbers 25.30, 26.9–26.10
  PAYE compliance, *see* Pay As You Earn (PAYE)
  payroll cleanse 26.9
  real time information 26.6, 26.8
  records which may be examined 26.5
  Schedule E benefits and reimbursed expenses, *see* Benefits and reimbursed expenses
  student loan repayment 26.7
  tax credits, HMRC powers 26.7
Enquiries
  accelerated payment notices 21.6, 21.7
  appeals to tribunal 6.88–6.90, 8.129–8.130
  area office network 1.33
  aspect enquiry 1.6, 1.8
  business record checks and examinations, *see* Business record checks/examinations
  categories 1.6
  change of direction 1.13
  Civil Investigations of Fraud 1.30, 1.32
  closure notices, *see* Closure notices

1119

Index

Enquiries – *contd*
Code of Practice 9 (COP9) 1.31, 1.33
common reporting standard,
   effect of 7.9
complaints procedures 6.121–6.127
completion
   deliberate inaccuracy findings 6.58
   see also Closure notices
complex, HMRC's approach to
   working, *see* Working of complex enquiries
contentious 4.1–4.2
Contractual Disclosure Facility
   (CDF) 1.31
controlling, *see* Controlling investigation
costs 6.6–6.9, 6.127
   professional 11.21–11.24, 11.27
criminal investigations 3.5, 8.28–8.31
deadlock, resolving 8.126–8.130
delays in progress 8.95–8.99
   settlement affected by 11.14
disclosure 1.14–1.23
discovery, *see* Discovery
dispute resolution 6.84–6.87
   ADR 4.175–4.176, 6.85–6.87, 8.127–8.128, 8.130
   Litigation and Settlement Strategy (LSS) 4.180–4.183
engagement letter 6.18
enquiry notice 6.41–6.43
   aspect or full enquiry 6.44
   speculative discovery enquiry 6.43
   time limit for 6.41–6.43
escalation 1.8
estimation in absence of full
   information 8.100–8.106
evidencing facts/purpose 4.147
   courts' approach to evidence 4.148–4.149
expanding into other tax years 8.107–8.113
fact finding, HMRC approach, *see*
   Working of complex enquiries
fee protection insurance 6.8, 6.38–6.40, 6.127
for cause 1.11
formalities 6.41–6.51
Fraud Investigation Service (FIS) 1.28–1.29, 1.33

Enquiries – *contd*
full 1.6–1.7
   controlling, *see* Controlling investigation
generally 1.1–1.8, 1.24–1.35, 1.140, 6.1–6.3, 8.123–8.126
HMRC Compliance Handbook 6.2
HMRC Enquiry manual 6.2
HMRC practice
   generally 6.1–6.5
   spreading 6.91–6.94
HMRC's strategy for dealing with tax avoidance, *see* Tax avoidance
information gathering, *see* Information and data gathering powers
information notices 6.45, 6.46–6.51
   formal 15.4–15.6
   generally 15.3–15.9
   informal 15.4
   private records 15.3–15.6
key forms HMRC may request 8.114–8.125
key points 8.176
looking for obvious flaws 6.10–6.13, 6.127
maintaining progress despite delays 8.95–8.99
managing, *see* Managing the enquiry
meetings with HMRC, *see* Meetings with HMRC
multi-tax 8.48–8.61
   departments using 8.55
   meetings 8.60–8.61
   tips for handling 8.62
   taskforces 8.52, 8.55
      cross agency 8.54
      Offshore Property Developers Task Force (OPDTF) 8.53
network enquiries 1.33–1.34
non-compliance, history of 15.4
non-statutory interventions 1.12–1.13
non-statutory rules 1.24
objectives 1.4–1.5
parties involved
   HMRC officer 6.22–6.28
   solicitor 6.82
   specialist consultants 6.83
   taxpayer 6.19–6.21
partnerships 1.2, 1.18

Index

Enquiries – *contd*
  penalty regime, *see* Penalty regime
  practice management 6.14–6.18
    at enquiry's end 6.119–6.120
    key points 6.128
  preparation for
    key points 6.127
    research and training 6.33–6.37
  professional indemnity
    insurance 2.85
  random 1.6, 1.10–1.11, 9.9
  records and documents
    appointment diaries 1.48, 6.80–6.81
    client records 6.17
    enquiry notices 6.41–6.43
    information notices 6.45, 6.46–6.51
    private records 6.52–6.54, 15.3–15.9
    time limit for production 6.45
    see also Business record checks/
      examinations; Records and
      documents
  reducing likelihood 1.14–1.23
  referral of questions during
    20.78–20.80
  risk assessment 1.10, 7.2, 7.8–7.12
  selection for, *see* Selection for enquiry
  self-assessment system
    6.1, 6.4–6.5, 7.1
  settlement 6.104–6.118, 8.145–8.156
  specialist investigations, merger
    1.28–1.29
  Specialist Investigations Office (SI)
    1.29, 2.85–2.92
  spreading 6.91–6.94
  start of, *see* Start of enquiry
  statutory record, definition 15.7
  statutory rules 1.24–1.26
    compliance 6.127
  tax debt collection 8.157–8.158
  tax planning arrangements 4.3–4.6
    international, *see* International tax
      planning
  triggers 8.17–8.19
  unannounced HMRC inspections
    6.55–6.60
  useful publications 1.35
  volunteering information 6.127
  window, *see* Enquiry window
  Worldwide Disclosure Facility
    (WDF) 7.9

Enquiry window
  discovery assessment 1.17
  enquiry notice to be within
    6.41–6.43
  selection for enquiry 7.2
Entertainment expenses
  clients 26.146–26.151
  selection for enquiry 7.62–7.63
  staff 26.152–26.157
Entrepreneurs' relief
  problems arising 6.11
Escalated enquiry
  generally 1.8, 4.174
Estimates
  use of 1.77
European Court of Justice (ECJ)
  jurisdiction 20.268–20.279
European Union Directives
  exchange of information
    5.26–5.30
  money laundering 3.162–3.169
  mutual assistance 24.41–24.45
**European Union Mutual Assistance for
  Recovery of Debts (MARD)**
  generally 22.77–22.87, 22.94
Evasion, *see* Money laundering;
  Tax evasion
Exchange of information
  value added tax 24.43–24.47
Excluded material
  definition 3.81
  evidential material 3.77–3.96
Expatriates
  National Insurance contributions
    25.47, 25.49, 25.71
Expenses
  reimbursed, *see* Benefits and
    reimbursed expenses
Exports
  breach of prohibitions or restrictions
    2.12, 3.36

F
Failure to make return
  penalty regime 18.106–18.109
  mitigation 19.6–19.8
Failure to notify chargeability
  Code of Practice 9 (COP9) 2.42
  generally 3.9, 16.16, 18.198
  penalties 18.121–18.125

1121

Index

Failure to notify liability
capital gains tax 18.89
concealment 18.88
COP9 procedures 2.42
disclosure 14.3
diverted profits tax 18.90
income tax 18.89–18.91
offshore evaders 3.9
penalty regime, *see* Penalty regime
Failure to notify under-assessment
penalty regime 18.92–18.93
Failure to pay tax
penalty regime 18.110–18.111
Failure to prevent facilitation of foreign tax evasion
generally 5.122–5.124
False accounting
cheating the public revenue 3.7
offence, generally 3.6
penalties 3.6
False statements or documents
cheating the public revenue 3.7
criminal investigation following 2.12, 2.36
Fees
discussing with client 6.9
fee protection insurance 6.8, 6.38–6.40, 6.127, 10.26
generally 6.6–6.9, 6.118, 10.26–10.28
see also Legal and professional fees
Finance charges
selection for enquiry 7.66
Financial intermediary
money laundering, *see* Money laundering
tax evasion, *see* Tax evasion
Financial Services Authority (FSA)
appeals against decisions of 20.219
First-tier Tribunal
ADR 20.33, 20.39–20.45
appeals to Upper Tribunal 20.219, 20.225–20.235
approach, generally 20.191–20.192
basic cases 20.128, 20.135–20.139
case management powers 20.150–20.160
chambers 20.27–20.28
complex cases 20.128, 20.142–20.147
costs 20.203, 20.208–20.212
constitution 20.26–20.29, 20.127

First-tier Tribunal – *contd*
costs
complex cases 20.203, 20.208–20.212
generally 20.203
pre-1 April 2009 appeals 20.203, 20.213–20.218
unreasonable conduct 20.203, 20.206–20.207
wasted 20.203, 20.204–20.205
decisions 20.193–20.195
review 20.196–20.202
default paper cases 20.128, 20.129–20.134
exchange of documents 20.148–20.149
function and jurisdiction 20.26–20.33
generally 20.3, 20.26–20.33, 20.127–20.128
hearings 20.178–20.182
HMRC enquiries, appeals relating to 6.88–6.90, 8.129–8.130
overriding objective 20.33, 20.34–20.38
public law matters 20.173–20.177
standard cases 20.128, 20.140–20.141
statement of case 20.148–20.149
strike out 20.161–20.172
Fixed assets
risk analysis 7.36
Follower notices
accelerated payments
notices 21.5, 21.6
rules 4.29, 4.30
amended returns 21.16
appeals 20.115, 20.119, 21.27
outstanding 21.16, 21.17
contesting 21.27
delivery 21.15
determinations 21.28
failure to comply 21.18
group loss relief 21.5
introduction 21.9
key points 21.43
lead case rulings 21.12
National Insurance contributions 21.5, 21.14, 21.19
options open to taxpayer 21.39–21.42

1122

Index

Follower notices – *contd*
  partnership follower notices (PFNs) 21.29–21.31
  payments under 21.19
  penalty regime 21.18, 21.36
  promoters of tax avoidance schemes (POTAS) rules 4.11, 21.12
  purpose 21.12
  qualifying conditions 21.13
  resolving underlying dispute 21.19
  taxes covered 21.5
  technical rulings 21.12
  time limits 21.5, 21.12, 21.14
Foreign tax
  evasion, *see* Offshore tax evasion
  relevant, HMRC information gathering powers 16.26–16.27
Forged documents
  criminal investigation following 2.12, 3.36
  criminal prosecution 3.139
Forms
  forms HMRC may request 8.114–8.125
Fraud
  abuse of position 2.19–2.20
  Code of Practice 8, *see* Code of Practice 8
  Contractual Disclosure Facility (CDF) 2.45
  definition 2.15–2.20
  discovery powers 1.127, 1.130
  dishonesty 3.1, 3.137
  double jeopardy rule 18.209
  failure to disclose information 2.19–2.20
  failure to notify chargeability 2.42, 3.9, 16.16, 18.198
  penalties 18.121–18.125
  false representation 2.19–2.20
  intention to make gain or loss 2.20
  missing trader intra-Community (MTIC) fraud 2.14, 3.37, 24.43
  serious, *see* Code of Practice 9; Criminal investigations
  SI, *see* Special Investigations Office
  suspected, HMRC's approach 4.200
  see also Tax evasion
Fraud Investigation Service (FIS)
  generally 1.27–1.28, 1.31, 1.33, 2.1
  multi-tax enquiries 8.55, 8.59

Full Payment Submissions (FPS)
  National Insurance contributions 25.8, 25.24, 25.30, 25.100
  specified charges 25.32

G
General anti-abuse rule (GAAR)
  accelerated tax payment rules 4.29, 4.31
  final counteraction notice 8.68
  tax avoidance 4.25–4.28, 21.26
  penalty 21.37
  tax geared penalties 18.160
Generally Accepted Accounting Practice (GAAP)
  estimates, use of 1.77
Generic notification system (GNS)
  generally 25.8
Gifts
  Pay As You Earn 26.158
Government policy
  generally 3.11–3.19
Government subsidies
  false claims 3.2–3.3
Gross profit
  selection for enquiry 7.50–7.53

H
Hansard investigation, *see* Code of Practice 9
High Court
  generally 20.189–20.190, 20.258–20.267
  jurisdiction 20.258–20.267
High Net Worth Unit (HNWU)
  ADR process 12.37
HM Revenue & Customs (HMRC)
  Adjudicator
    complaints procedure 23.73–23.76
    value added tax disputes 24.83–24.84
  approach to working complex enquiries, *see* Working of complex enquiries
  campaigns to encourage voluntary disclosures 8.32–8.47
  Charter 23.25
  civil investigations, *see* Civil investigations

1123

Index

HM Revenue & Customs (HMRC)
 – *contd*
  collaborative working 8.63–8.68,
   9.3–9.4
  collection and management power
   11.2–11.4
  complaints procedure, *see* Complaints
   procedure
  Criminal and Enforcement Policy
   (CEP) 3.40–3.41
  criminal investigations, *see* Criminal
   investigations
  Customer Compliance
   Directorate 25.1
  data gathering, *see* Information and
   data gathering powers
  debts, recovery and account
   deduction 1.136
  delays 23.11, 23.13–23.16
   in using information 12.36
  discretion, unreasonable 23.74
  disproportionate decisions 23.11,
   23.21–23.23
  Enforcement and Compliance
   Assurance Team (ECAT)
   3.40–3.41
  enforcement strategy 3.11–3.19
  enquiries, *see* Enquiries
  Extra-Statutory Concessions
   (ESCs) 23.25
  generally 8.1–8.5, 16.5–16.10
  generic notification system
   (GNS) 25.8
  HMRC documents, theft, misuse or
   destruction 2.12, 3.36
  HMRC guidance, not following 23.11,
   23.24–23.26
  inconsistent decisions 23.11,
   23.21–23.23
  information gathering, *see* Information
   and data gathering powers
  Internal Governance 3.39
  key forms, request for 8.114–8.125
  Knowledge, Analysis and Intelligence
   (KAI) units 25.1
  liaison with other government
   agencies 2.94
  liaison with overseas authorities 2.94
  Litigation and Settlement Strategy
   (LSS) 23.25

HM Revenue & Customs (HMRC)
 – *contd*
  Managing Serious Defaulters (MSD)
   regime 8.159–8.166,
   18.177–18.183
  meetings with, *see* Meetings with
   HMRC
  mishandling complaints 23.11, 23.32
  misinformed decisions 23.11,
   23.17–23.20
  misleading advice 23.11,
   23.27–23.30, 23.74
  mistakes 23.11, 23.12
  multi-tax enquiries 8.48–8.61
   departments using 8.55
   meetings 8.60–8.61
    tips for handling 8.62
   taskforces 8.52, 8.55
    cross agency 8.54
    Offshore Property Developers
     Task Force (OPDTF) 8.53
  officers
   assault on or threats to 2.12, 3.36
   identification cards 25.15
   impersonation 2.12
   obstruction 1.95, 1.99, 1.103, 1.114,
    16.112, 16.176, 18.96–18.99,
    25.109
   refusing entry to 6.58–6.59
   tax enquiries, generally 6.22–6.28
   training 3.59–3.61
   unannounced visits by 6.55–6.60
   warrant cards 25.15
  Offshore Coordination Unit (OCU)
   2.95, 5.44, 8.34
  penalty regime, *see* Penalty regime
  prosecution policy 3.28–3.32
   factors leading to 3.33–3.38
   human rights issues 3.30
   selective 3.28–3.30, 3.36
  *Qualitative Research with People
   Convicted of Tax Evasion* report
   3.20–3.22
  restrictions on powers, *see* Restrictions
   on powers
  Risk and Intelligence Service
   3.39, 7.9
  road fuel testing 3.39
  staff behaviour 23.11, 23.31,
   23.41, 23.74

Index

HM Revenue & Customs (HMRC)
– *contd*
Statements of Practice 23.25
discovery 13.129–13.130
unannounced visits by 6.55–6.60
unfair decisions 23.11, 23.21–23.23
unreasonable decisions 23.11,
23.17–23.20
Hold notice
appeals 22.44–22.46
failure to comply 22.49–22.53
objecting to 22.44–22.46
tax debt collection 22.36–22.43
Human rights
HMRC's prosecution policy 3.30

I
Identity unknown notice, *see*
Information notice
Imports
breach of prohibitions or restrictions
2.12, 3.36
Income tax
accelerated payment notices 21.5
debt recovery 22.56
errors in returns, penalty
regime 18.17
failure to notify liability 18.89–18.91
follower notices 21.5
fraudulent evasion 3.6, 3.17–3.18,
3.139
HMRC information gathering
powers 16.26
managed payment plans 22.3–22.6
possible merger with NICs 25.12
see also Employment income
Indirect taxes
indirect taxes 3.23
see also Appeals; Value added tax
Information and data gathering
powers
appointed day statutory instrument
16.20, 16.22
authorised officers 16.188,
16.196–16.198
banking information
1.104–1.105, 8.8
offshore banks 8.8
business inspections, *see* Business
inspection; Inspection of premises

Information and data gathering
powers – *contd*
business records checks, *see* Business
record checks/examinations
challenging information requests
documents not within power or
possession 4.165–4.171
generally 4.160–4.161
information not reasonably required
4.162–4.163
legal professional privilege 4.164
summary 4.172
child's income 1.48
civil powers 16.4, 16.9
close company directors 15.32
concealment 2.12, 3.36, 18.96–18.99
deliberate errors 18.32, 18.77–18.84
failure to notify liability 18.88
'Connect' data analysis system
7.10–7.12, 8.9–8.10, 25.26
controlling the investigation
10.108–10.116
copied and original documents 1.85
credit card data 7.11
criminal investigations 16.4,
16.12–16.18, 16.193–16.214
data, categories 16.92–16.96
data-holder notices
failure to comply, penalties
16.100–16.102
generally 16.98–16.99
data-holders 16.90–16.91
categories 16.92–16.96
money service businesses 16.97
deceased persons 1.93
destruction of documents 18.96–18.99
disclosure 1.14–1.23
disposal of documents 18.96–18.99
documents
concealment 2.12, 3.36,
18.96–18.99
copied and original 1.85
destruction 18.96–18.99
disposal of 18.96–18.99
must be in possession or power
1.86, 16.127–16.150, 19.48
power to obtain 16.25–16.35
DOTAS
information from introducers 4.20
powers 4.19

1125

Index

Information and data gathering powers – *contd*
  enquiry triggers 8.17–8.19
  errors or unexplained items 1.50
  excluded material 3.77, 3.81–3.94, 16.210
  Finance Act 2007 amendments 16.2, 16.10, 16.11–16.18
  Finance Act 2008, Sch 36
    civil powers under 16.2, 16.4, 16.19–16.20, 16.24
    HMRC information and inspection powers 16.25–16.35
    information notices 16.28
    inspection of premises, *see* Inspection of premises
    penalty regime 16.190–16.191
    restrictions, *see* Restrictions on powers
    territorial limits 16.151
    who can exercise powers 16.188
  Finance Act 2009 16.3, 16.21–16.23
  Finance Act 2010 16.3, 16.16
  Finance (No 3) Act 2010 16.3
  Finance Act 2011 16.3, 16.90–16.91
  Finance Act 2012 16.3, 16.234
  Finance Act 2013 16.3
  Finance Act 2014 16.3
  Finance Act 2015 16.3
  Finance Act 2016 16.3
  Finance (No 2) Act 2017 16.3
  generally 1.81–1.83, 1.95, 8.6–8.16, 15.1–15.9, 16.1–16.4, 16.25–16.35
  identity unknown notices 16.40–16.41, 16.66–16.67
    key points 16.82
    relevant information 16.83–16.86
    tribunal's approach to 16.68–16.81
  inaccurate information or document, providing 16.192, 18.7, 18.12, 18.97, 18.116–18.120
  information not reasonably required 16.36
    burden of proof 16.37–16.38
  information notices, *see* Information notice
  inspection of premises, *see* Inspection of premises

Information and data gathering powers – *contd*
  international information exchange agreements 5.23–5.38, 8.8
  Internet sources 7.12, 8.7, 8.10
  involved third party notices 16.87–16.89
  joint bank accounts 1.48
  key points 16.235
  legal professional privilege, *see* Legal professional privilege
  link papers 15.31
  maintaining progress despite delays 8.95–8.99
  mandate from taxpayer 1.104–1.105
  merchant acquirers 16.93–16.95
  National Insurance contributions 25.13–25.15
  non-business records 16.37–16.39
  non-compliance 1.95
  obstruction, *see* Obstruction of officers
  PACE powers 3.42, 3.88–3.92, 3.112–3.116, 3.131, 16.4, 16.10, 16.12–16.13, 16.193–16.214
  penalty regime 1.95, 16.189–16.192, 18.96–18.99, 18.198
  personal records 15.25–15.27
  place documents produced 1.85
  private home, business premises at 1.99
  private records 1.48–1.49, 15.3–15.9
  rationale for change 16.5–16.10
  rental income 8.8
  restrictions on 1.86–1.92, 16.126–16.127
  sharing of information 3.159
  SOCPA powers 3.117–3.121, 16.215–16.222
  special cases 1.95
  special procedure material 3.77–3.96, 16.210–16.213
  spouse/partner's income and expenditure 1.48, 15.29
  start of enquiry, request for information 1.39–1.48
    challenging 1.42–1.43, 1.48
    formal requests 15.4
    private records 15.3
    relevance of information requested 1.46
  unreliable accounts 1.50

1126

Index

Information and data gathering powers – *contd*
supplementary information 19.48
tax position of taxpayer, checking 16.28–16.35
taxes covered 16.26
Taxes Management Act 1970
   s 20A 16.240–16.242
   s 20BA 3.87, 3.96, 3.97–3.102, 3.103–3.111, 16.223–16.232, 16.233
taxpayer notices 1.84, 1.87, 16.40
   judicial approval 16.55–16.64
   key points 16.42–16.49
   time limits 1.93
third party notices 1.85, 1.104–1.105, 8.8, 10.117–10.120, 15.9, 16.28, 16.40–16.41, 16.50
   involved 16.87–16.89
   judicial approval 16.55–16.64
   key points 16.51–16.54
   trustee in bankruptcy 16.65
trust assets where taxpayer trustee 1.48
use of information 3.159
who can exercise Sch 36 powers 16.188

Information notice
appeal against 1.94
controlling the investigation 10.108–10.116
failure to comply 22.49–22.53
generally 16.28, 16.40
identity unknown notices 16.40–16.41, 16.66–16.67
   key points 16.82
   relevant information 16.83–16.86
   tribunal's approach to 16.68–16.81
inaccurate information or document, providing 16.192, 18.7, 18.12, 18.97, 18.116–18.120
information not reasonably required 16.36
burden of proof 16.37–16.38
issue during enquiry 6.45, 6.46–6.51
non-business records 16.37–16.39
penalty regime 16.189–16.192, 18.126–18.133, 22.49–22.53
power to obtain information and documents 16.28

Information notice – *contd*
tax debt collection 22.35
taxpayer notices 1.84, 1.87, 16.40
   judicial approval 16.55–16.64
   key points 16.42–16.49
   time limits 1.93
third party notices 1.85, 1.104–1.105, 8.8, 10.117–10.120, 15.9, 16.28, 16.40–16.41, 16.50
   involved 16.87–16.89
   judicial approval 16.55–16.64
   key points 16.51–16.54
time limits, deceased taxpayers 1.93

Information sharing
generally 3.159

Inheritance tax
accelerated payment notices 21.5
failure to make return 18.106
follower notices 21.5
HMRC information gathering powers 16.26

Insolvency
tax debt collection 22.65–22.66, 22.69

Inspection of premises
agreed inspections 10.122–10.123
business assets 16.105
business documents 16.105
   meaning 16.108
business premises
   HMRC inspection powers 1.98–1.103
   meaning 16.106
criminal investigations, generally 3.42, 3.69–3.76
dawn raids 3.69, 3.122–3.127, 6.82
entry and search without warrant 3.85
generally 1.99–1.102
HMRC internal instructions 1.101
inspect, meaning 16.103
judicial approval 16.111
notice of 1.99
notifying advisers 1.102
obstruction of officers 16.112, 16.176
part of premises used as dwelling 1.99
power to inspect, generally 16.24, 16.103, 16.104–16.105
premises of involved third parties 16.120–16.122

1127

Index

Inspection of premises – *contd*
  premises used in connection with
      taxable supplies 16.117–16.119
  refusal of entry 1.99, 3.69, 6.58–6.59
    penalties for 1.99, 1.103
    reasonable force 1.103
    to allow for advice to be taken 1.103
  restrictions 1.100
  search warrants, *see* Search warrant
  timing 1.99, 16.113–16.116
  unannounced 1.99, 1.102, 6.55–6.60,
      10.124–10.129
  valuation purposes, for 16.123–16.125
  what can be inspected 16.105–16.112
  see also Business inspection; Business
      record checks/examinations
Insurance premium tax
  HMRC information gathering
      powers 16.26
  security for tax, requirement to give
      22.71–22.80
Interception of Communications Commissioner
  role 3.62
Interest
  charges, deduction from
      income 7.66
  delays by HMRC, resulting from
      23.37–23.38
  late payment interest
    calculation 11.8
    generally 12.5
    LDF requirement 5.71
  NI contributions, *see* National
      Insurance contributions (NICs)
  PAYE, liability 26.181–26.184
  writing off following complaint 23.82
Interest Review Unit (IRU)
  complaints to 23.37–23.38
Internal independent review
  generally 19.71
International offences
  criminal investigations 2.12, 3.36
International tax planning
  companies
    background 4.37
    BEPS action plan 4.39
    diverted profits tax 4.38
    liability for penalty for failure to
        correct 4.36

International tax planning – *contd*
  new guidance on comparability
      factors 4.40
  personal tax 4.35
  working of complex enquiries,
      HMRC's approach, *see* Working
      of complex enquiries
Internet
  as information source 7.12, 8.7, 8.10
Interviews
  cautions 3.43, 3.135–3.137
  criminal investigations 3.42–3.43,
      3.45, 3.134–3.138
  right to silence 3.43, 3.137
Investment income
  selection for enquiry 7.85–7.86

J
Judicial review
  HMRC complaints procedure, and
      23.52–23.63
  search warrants, challenging 3.93–3.96
  Upper Tribunal, powers and
      jurisdiction 20.236–20.243
  value added tax disputes 24.85

K
Known tax evader
  close scrutiny 3.19

L
Landfill tax
  HMRC information gathering
      powers 16.26
  security for tax, requirement to give
      22.71–22.80
Large and complex businesses
  NIC investigation triggers 25.28,
      25.64–25.65, 25.219
  record checks, *see* Business record
      checks/examinations
  value added tax 24.1, 24.5
Large Business Services
  customer relationship managers
      (CRMs), adoption 8.51
  multi-tax enquiries 8.55
Legal advice privilege (LAP)
  generally 16.127, 16.156–16.164
  resolving privilege disputes
      16.172–16.179

1128

Index

Legal and professional fees
reports for HMRC 17.6–17.7
selection for enquiry 7.64
settlement negotiation
11.21–11.24, 11.27
Legal professional privilege
criminal investigations 3.42,
3.77–3.96, 3.124, 3.128–3.133
definition 3.129
documents protected by 4.164, 16.127, 19.49
generally 16.152–16.155
production orders 3.130
resolving privilege disputes
16.172–16.179
search warrants 3.77, 3.80
Leggatt Inquiry
generally 20.19–20.24
Legitimate expectation
complaints procedure 23.60
Letter of offer
settlement negotiation 11.79–11.82
Liechtenstein disclosure facility (LDF)
beneficial interest, definition of
5.52–5.55
calculation of UK tax liabilities
5.64–5.70
composite rate option
5.67–5.69, 5.76
eligible persons 5.56
five-year taxpayer assistance
compliance programme
5.49–5.50
generally 3.15, 5.45–5.48, 5.55,
5.74–5.80, 14.40–14.41, 18.147
immunity from criminal
investigation 5.73
interest on late payment 5.71
materiality test 5.78
Memorandum of Understanding
(MOU) 5.45
penalty regime 5.72, 5.76, 18.169
relevant persons 5.51
replacement 5.55, 5.81–5.82
single rate charge 5.70, 5.76
Tax information Exchange Agreement
(TIEA) 5.45
Liquidation
tax debt collection 22.63–22.68

Litigation
key points 20.280
tactical use 20.7–20.8
Litigation privilege
generally 16.127, 16.165–16.171
resolving privilege disputes
16.172–16.179
Litigation and Settlement Strategy (LSS)
2017 version 20.14–20.15
ADR 12.13–12.21
collaborative working 8.63–8.68
fundamental aspects 20.15
generally 4.180–4.183, 20.9, 23.25
original version 20.10–20.13
settlement negotiation 11.37
Lloyds cases
selection for enquiry 7.40
Loan agreement
HMRC access to private
records 15.23
Loans
cheap or interest free, to employee
26.159
Local Compliance
multi-tax enquiries 8.55, 8.58
Long service award
Pay As You Earn 26.160
Losses
artificial loss deductions 21.8
group loss relief 21.5, 21.9
overstated, penalty regime 18.14,
18.204–18.206

M
Magistrates' court
debt recovery 22.56
prosecutions 3.6, 3.46–3.47
Making tax digital (MTD)
penalty proposals 18.152
late filing 18.153–18.158
late payment 18.159
record-keeping 7.27
Making tax digital for VAT (MTDfV)
generally 24.6
Managed payment plan (MPP)
debt collection, generally
22.3–22.6
Manager
liability for penalties 18.132–18.134

Index

Managing Serious Defaulters programme
  generally 8.159–8.166, 18.177–18.183
Managing the enquiry
  engaging with HMRC
    constructive engagement –
      collaborative working 4.152
      challenging failure to engage 4.155
      summary 4.159
      techniques/features of collaborative working
        decision trees 4.153
        documenting facts and legal arguments agreed and those in dispute 4.154
        use of meetings 4.156–4.158
      generally 4.150–4.151
  evidencing facts/purpose 4.147
    courts' approach to evidence 4.148–4.149
  formal challenges to information requests
    documents
      not within power or possession 4.165–4.171
      subject to legal professional privilege 4.164
    generally 4.160–4.161
    information not reasonably required 4.162–4.163
    summary 4.172
  framing contentions 4.145–4.146
  generally 4.143
  importance of maintaining compelling narrative throughout enquiry 4.144
  resolving an impasse
    ADR 4.175–4.177
    escalation 4.174
    generally 4.173
    proceeding formally 4.178–4.179
Mediation, *see* Alternative dispute resolution (ADR)
Meetings with HMRC
  action points 10.92
  ADR, *see* Alternative dispute resolution (ADR)
  agenda 6.69–6.72
    issue in advance 1.60

Meetings with HMRC – *contd*
  agent refusing to countenance 1.52
  agreeing to 1.58
  alternatives to 9.13–9.22
  ascertaining who will attend 6.65
  body language at 10.88
  business premises 1.39
  Civil Investigations of Fraud (CIF) 2.35–2.43
  Code of Practice 9 (COP9) 2.32–2.43, 2.62–2.77
  collaborative working 9.3–9.4
  compliance checking 7.6–7.7
  compliance officer's objectives 9.41–9.46
  concluding 9.71
  conduct 9.64–9.70
  contentious enquiries 4.156–4.158
  Contractual Disclosure Facility (CDF) 1.31, 2.62–2.77
  controlling the investigation 10.69–10.93
  cost effectiveness 10.70–10.71
  during the visit, checklist 9.90
  early, advantages of 1.59
  early disclosure 10.86–10.87
  employer compliance checks, *see* Compliance checks
  follow-up action 10.93
  format 9.49
  generally 6.61–6.65, 9.1–9.6, 9.111–9.115
  HMRC approach 6.62
  HMRC guidance 9.7–9.8
  importance 1.51–1.53, 1.70
  keeping control of client 10.89–10.90
  key points 9.76, 9.115
  length 6.72
  multi-tax enquiries 8.60–8.61
    tips for handling 8.62
  no power to compel attendance 9.13
  notes 1.64–1.69, 6.73–6.79, 9.72–9.75, 10.91
    challenging 1.69
    errors or omissions 1.68
    requesting copy 1.64–1.69
  preparation for
    checklist 9.47–9.48
    Civil Investigations of Fraud 2.40–2.43

1130

Meetings with HMRC – *contd*
preparation for – *contd*
Contractual Disclosure Facility
2.64–2.77
generally 6.69–6.72, 9.23–9.40,
10.78–10.81
identifying problem areas
9.25–9.28
reviewing knowledge of
client 9.24
purpose 9.6, 9.7–9.12
compliance officer's objectives
9.41–9.46, 9.69
resistance to 1.52, 1.54
settlement meetings
11.85–11.88
taking clients to 1.60
taxpayer's presence
6.61, 6.63
those attending 9.50–9.57
timing 9.58–9.63
venue 1.55, 1.60, 6.66–6.68,
9.58–9.63, 10.76–10.77
business premises 1.61–1.62, 9.6,
9.59–9.61
voice recordings 6.73
voluntary nature 1.57–1.58
see also Controlling the
investigation
Minimum wage
breach of rules, penalties 18.112
HMRC powers 26.7, 26.8
**Missing trader intra-community
fraud (MTIC)**
value added tax 2.14, 3.37, 24.43
Mistake by HMRC
complaints procedure
23.11, 23.12
Mitigation of penalties, *see* Penalty
regime
Mobile phones
provided by employer 26.146
Money laundering
breach of prohibitions or
restrictions 2.12
criminal conduct 3.175
criminal investigations 3.36
definition 3.177
engaging solicitor 6.82
EU Directives 3.162–3.169

Money laundering – *contd*
financial intermediaries and
professional advisers
guidance for 3.190–3.206
Auditing Practices Board
3.196–3.197
Chartered Institute of
Taxation 3.195
Consultative Committee of
Accountancy Bodies 3.194
HM Revenue & Customs
3.199–3.201
Institute of Chartered
Accountants in England and
Wales 3.190–3.193
knowledge or suspicion of an
offence 3.202–3.203
Law Society 3.198
procedures for processing reports
3.204–3.206
risk to 3.214–3.234
fiscal authorities, role 3.207–3.208
foreign tax evasion 3.182–3.186
generally 3.160–3.161
HMRC's strategy 3.209–3.213, 3.329
key points 3.235
knowledge or suspicion of
3.187–3.189, 3.202–3.203
offences, generally 3.6
proceeds of crime,
generally 3.166
Proceeds of Crime Act 2002
acquisition, use and
possession 3.174
arrangements 3.173
concealing 3.172
generally 3.171
interpretation (section 340)
3.175–3.181
professional advisers 3.36
Regulations 3.170
Serious Organised Crime Agency
(SOCA) 2.95–2.96
terrorism, financing 3.167
Regulations 3.170
what constitutes 3.176–3.180
Mortgage agreement
HMRC access to private records 15.23
Motor expenses
selection for enquiry 7.59–7.60

Index

Multi-national company
VAT assurance visits 24.45
Multi-tax enquiries
departments using 8.55
generally 8.48–8.61
meetings 8.60–8.61
tips for handling 8.62
taskforces 8.52, 8.55
cross agency 8.54
Offshore Property Developers Task Force (OPDTF) 8.53

N
Naming and shaming
avoiding 14.17–14.18
HMRC powers 3.10, 3.19, 3.36
penalties for deliberate errors 8.159–8.166, 18.184–18.193
tax agents 3.36
National Insurance contributions (NICs)
accelerated payment notices 21.5–21.7
appeals
award of credits 25.211
Class 4 appeals 25.212–25.216
contracting out matters 25.210
determination by tribunal 25.203, 25.208–25.209
further appeal to Upper Tribunal 25.208–25.209
generally 25.166–25.171
HMRC officers' decisions 25.172–25.194
late 25.201–25.202
manner of making 25.195–25.199
place of hearing 25.200
publication of decisions 25.217
settlement agreements 25.204–25.207
apprentices, nil secondary employer rate for 25.41
arrears, time limit 25.52
avoidance, investigations, and 26.3
benefits legislation 26.114–26.117
Brexit proposals and A1 certificates 25.72
calculation 26.55
casual workers 25.98
category X notations 25.46–25.54

National Insurance contributions (NICs) – *contd*
coding notices 22.16–22.17
compatibility checking 25.40–25.42
compliance checking regime 25.14, 25.23, 25.31–25.32
Construction Industry Scheme 25.23
debt collection, *see* Tax debt collection
disguised remuneration 25.3, 25.28
DOTAS regime 25.3
DWP, information sharing with 25.11
employee benefit trusts 25.28
employer compliance checks 9.77–9.103
Employer Payment Summaries (EPS) 25.24
errors and omissions 25.28, 25.98–25.102
penalty regime 25.108
evasion 3.2
expatriates 25.47, 25.49, 25.71
failure to make return 18.106
follower notices 21.5, 21.14, 21.19
Full Payment Submissions (FPS) 25.8, 25.24, 25.30, 25.100
funding 25.16–25.22
generally 25.1–25.12
HMRC Toolkits 25.224
inspectorate powers 25.13–25.15
interest
Class 2 contributions 25.164–25.165
Class 4 contributions 25.164–25.165
overdue contributions 25.157–25.161
repaid contributions 25.162
repayment and remission of 25.163
investigation triggers
category X notations 25.46–25.54
complaints from employees 25.28, 25.55–25.56
employer compliance team visits 25.61
employers with international exposure 25.28, 25.66–25.72
end-of-year returns (pre-RTI) 25.34–25.45

1132

National Insurance contributions (NICs) – *contd*
  investigation triggers – *contd*
    failing to reply to correspondence 25.28, 25.62–25.63
    generally 25.25–25.28, 25.218–25.224
    large employers 25.28, 25.64–25.65
    multiple tax-advantaged share schemes 25.28
    national programme 25.28, 25.58–25.59
    random visits 25.25, 25.73
    regional initiatives 25.57
    risk analysis 25.26, 25.220
    routine visits 25.60–25.61
    RTI submissions 25.28, 25.29–25.33
    triggers for visits 25.23–25.24, 25.107
    unannounced HMRC visits 25.73
  investigations
    both tax and NIC covered 25.2
    employers chosen for 25.25–25.28
    further visits 25.107
  key points 25.225
  NI numbers 25.30, 25.98, 26.9–26.10
    employer questionnaire 26.10
    payroll cleanse 26.9
  offences and penalties
    bodies corporate 25.114–25.115
    Class 1 and 1A penalties 25.125–25.132
    Class 1A contributions 25.125–25.132, 25.149–25.150
    Class 1B contributions 25.151
    Class 4 contributions 25.152–25.156
    contravention of regulations 25.110–25.111
    contributions offences 25.112–25.113
    delays 25.109
    employers' contributions 25.116–25.136
    false information 25.109
    generally 25.108
    incorrect manner of payment 25.144
    incorrect returns 25.141–25.143

National Insurance contributions (NICs) – *contd*
  offences and penalties – *contd*
    late final submission 25.140
    late payment 25.145–25.148
    late reporting 25.28
    late returns 25.28, 25.137–25.139
    Pay As You Earn 25.125–25.132
    personal liability notices 25.133–25.136
    'risk assessed basis' 25.108
  P11D returns 25.28
  payments allocated to different reference 25.33
  possible merger with income tax 25.12
  ratio checking 25.43
  Real Time Information regime 25.7, 25.24, 25.28, 25.29–25.33, 25.90, 25.100
    penalties for late final submission 25.140
  records
    record keeping 25.93–25.97
    to be available for inspection 25.90–25.92
  reduced rate 25.41, 25.90, 25.91, 25.98, 26.64–26.65
  risk analysis 25.26
  routine visits 25.60–25.61
  security for tax, requirement to give 22.71–22.80
  self-employed working for employee 25.98
  Universal Credit claims and 25.57
  visits
    annual numbers 25.218
    commencement 25.88–25.89
    errors and omissions 25.28, 25.98–25.102
    inspection reports 25.103–25.106
    IR35 aspects 25.84
    length 25.83–25.84
    notification 25.78–25.82
    preparation for 25.86–25.87
    purpose 25.74–25.75
    random visits 25.25, 25.73
    records to be made available 25.90–25.92
    timing 25.76–25.77

Index

National Insurance contributions (NICs) – *contd*
  visits – *contd*
    unannounced 25.73
    venue 25.85
  see also Pay As You Earn (PAYE)

Negligence
  discovery powers 1.127, 1.130

Negotiated settlement, *see* Settlement negotiations

Non-cash remuneration
  PAYE and NICs 26.29–26.33

Non-domiciled individuals
  remittances and negotiated settlements 11.54
  see also UK/Swiss tax cooperation agreement

Non-evasion investigations
  generally 2.9
  see also Code of Practice 8

Northern Ireland
  HMRC powers 3.49
  Public Prosecution Service 3.11

Notice of enforcement
  debt recovery 22.56–22.60

Notices
  business inspections 1.99
  closure, *see* Closure notices
  information, *see* Information notice
  start of enquiry 1.36–1.39
    appeal against notice 1.37–1.38
    information requests 1.39–1.48, 15.3–15.6
      challenging 1.42–1.43, 1.48
      relevance of information requested 1.46–1.48
      unreliable accounts 1.50
      volunteering information 1.42–1.45
    opening letter 1.39–1.41
    time limit 1.39–1.40
    validity of notice 1.37–1.38

O

Obstruction of officers 18.96–18.99, 18.198, 25.109
  business inspections 1.99, 1.103
  computer records 18.95
  generally 16.112, 16.176
  reasonable excuse 16.112, 16.176

OECD tax convention
  liaison with overseas authorities 2.94

Offences
  Accessories and Abettors Act 1861 3.7
  aiding and abetting 3.4, 3.7
  bribery 3.6
  charge to tax, failure to give notice of 3.8
  cheating the public revenue 3.6–3.7, 3.139
  commission of 3.8
  conspiracy to defraud 2.12, 3.6, 3.36, 3.139
  corporate failure to prevent tax evasion 3.8, 3.10
  facilitation of foreign tax evasion 5.122–5.124
  criminal facilitation, principles to prevent 3.8
  elements of 3.8
  encouraging 3.7
  false accounting 3.6
  forgery 2.12, 3.139
  income tax, fraudulent evasion 3.6, 3.17–3.18, 3.139
  intent 3.10
  money laundering
    knowledge or suspicion of 3.187–3.189, 3.202–3.203
  National Insurance contributions, *see* National Insurance contributions (NICs)
  new criminal offences 3.8–3.10
  offshore evaders, *see* Offshore tax evasion
  penalties for, *see* Penalty regime
  perjury 3.139
  proceeds of crime 3.166
  requirement to correct (RTC), *see* Offshore tax non-compliance
  return, failure to deliver 3.8
  strict liability 3.9
  tax evasion, *see* Tax evasion
  terrorism, financing 3.165
  Theft Acts 3.139

Offshore bank accounts
  HMRC's information gathering powers 8.8

Index

Offshore Coordination Unit (OCU)
  generally 2.95, 5.44, 8.34
  multi-tax enquiries 8.55
Offshore disclosure
  campaigns 5.39–5.43
  facilities 14.38, 14.40–14.41
    penalty arrangements 18.169
  Worldwide Disclosure Facility (WDF)
    8.35–8.39, 8.42–8.43, 14.40,
    14.41
'Offshore move' penalty
  generally 5.116
Offshore tax avoidance
  generally 5.1
  HMRC compliance strategy 5.1–5.5
  see also Offshore tax investigations
Offshore tax evasion
  civil deterrents 5.126–5.128
  corporate failure to prevent facilitation
    of 5.122–5.124
  criminal offences 3.9–3.10,
    5.117–5.118
  deliberate 3.9–3.10, 5.1
  enabling 3.10
    civil sanctions for enablers 5.119
  foreign offence
    associated person 5.125
    reasonable procedures
      defence of 5.126
      HMRC guidance 5.127
  HMRC compliance strategy
    5.1–5.5
  intent 3.10
  key points 5.144
  money laundering 3.182–3.186
  penalty regime 5.113–5.116, 5.120,
    18.36, 18.170–18.176
    civil sanctions for
      enablers 5.119
    'offshore move' penalty 5.116
  Worldwide Disclosure Facility (WDF)
    5.128–5.134
  see also Offshore tax investigations
Offshore tax investigations
  anti-avoidance legislation
    5.18–5.20
  cases 5.21–5.22, 5.128
  Code of Practice 8 (COP8) 2.82
  Crown Dependency disclosure
    facilities 5.107–5.112

Offshore tax investigations – *contd*
  domicile 5.12–5.14
  generally 5.1–5.4
  HMRC offshore disclosure campaigns
    5.39–5.43
  international exchange of information
    common reporting standards
      5.37–5.38
    EU Savings Directive
      5.26–5.30
    HMRC information gathering
      powers 8.8
    LDF, *see* Liechtenstein disclosure
      facility
    OECD 5.23–5.25
    US FATCA/IGA agreements
      5.31–5.37
  Offshore Coordination Unit (OCU)
    2.95, 5.44, 8.34
  LDF, *see* Liechtenstein disclosure
    facility
  UK/Swiss tax cooperation
    agreement, *see* UK/Swiss tax
    cooperation agreement
  offshore disclosure
    facility 18.147
  penalty regime 5.113–5.116
    offshore move 5.116
  residence 5.5–5.11
    companies 5.17
    statutory residence test
      (SRT) 5.7
    trustees 5.15–5.16
  trustee residence 5.15–5.16
  UK/Swiss tax cooperation agreement,
    see UK/Swiss tax cooperation
    agreement
Offshore tax non-compliance
  assessment time limit
    13.38–13.42
  requirement to correct (RTC)
    offence 5.135
    appeals 5.142
    assessments 5.139
    correcting offence and disclosure
      5.136–5.138
    penalties 5.140
      failure to correct (FTC) 5.140
      reduction 5.141
    reasonable excuse 5.143

1135

Index

Ombudsman
  complaint to 19.65, 23.77–23.80
  HMRC accountability 23.6, 23.17
  Principles guiding, generally 23.17, 23.21, 23.24
One-man company
  PAYE compliance and IR35 26.92–26.96
Online trading
  information source for HMRC 8.7
  risk analysis 7.12, 8.7
Opening an enquiry, *see* Start of enquiry
Organisation for Economic Cooperation and Development (OECD)
  exchange of information 5.23–5.25
Organised crime
  HMRC investigations 2.12, 3.34, 3.36
  Serious Organised Crime Agency (SOCA) 2.95–2.96
  production orders 3.117–3.121
Overseas fiscal authorities
  liaison with 2.94

P
P11D
  review for disclosure reports 17.31, 17.52–17.53
Parliamentary Ombudsman, *see* Ombudsman
Partial closure notices
  generally 1.123–1.125, 18.165, 20.81
Partnership
  bank statements 1.48
  closure notices 1.107
  enquiries 1.2, 1.18
  partnership follower notices (PFNs) 21.29–21.31
  partnership payment notices (PPNs) 21.29–21.31
  security for tax, requirement to give 22.71–22.80
Pay As You Earn (PAYE)
  agency workers 26.70, 26.88–26.91
  back tax 26.181–26.184
  bike to work schemes 26.54
  calculation 26.55
  cash payments 26.68–26.69
  casual workers 26.70, 26.82–26.87

Pay As You Earn (PAYE) – *contd*
  child care 26.54
  cleaners 26.98–26.99
  coding notices 12.36
  directors 26.71, 26.100
  earnings subjected to 26.19–26.55
  failure to make return 18.106, 18.109
  generally 26.10, 26.12–26.18
  interest, liability 26.181–26.184
  liability 26.181–26.184
  new employees 26.63
  non-cash remuneration 26.29–26.33
  offences and penalties 25.125–25.132
    liability 26.181–26.184
  one-man companies 26.92–26.96
  payroll giving schemes 26.66–26.67
  reduced rate NICs 26.64–26.65
  round sum allowances 26.20–26.22
  salary sacrifice arrangements 26.48–26.54
  security for tax, requirement to give 22.71–22.80
  self-employment v employment 26.70, 26.72–26.81
    audit approach 26.77–26.81
    basic principles 26.72–26.76
    employment status issues 26.77
  statutory maternity pay 26.64–26.65
  statutory sick pay 26.23, 26.64–26.65
  students 26.70, 26.97
  subcontractors 26.70
  termination of employment
    continuing benefits 26.42–26.45
    contractual payments 26.35–26.36
    dismissals 26.39
    other issues 26.46–26.47
    payments 26.34
    payments in lieu of notice (PILONs) 26.37
    restrictive covenants 26.38
    retirement 26.40–26.41
    settlements 26.43–26.45
  third parties 26.68–26.69
  timing taxation 26.56–26.62
  tips, tronc and service charges 26.24–26.28
Payments in lieu of notice (PILONs)
  generally 26.37

Index

Payments on account
  advantages of making 10.144, 11.15
  managed payment plans 22.3–22.6
  settlement negotiation 11.15–11.18
  voluntary disclosure 14.51
Payroll giving schemes
  Pay As you Earn 26.66–26.67
Penalty regime
  2015 consultation 18.149–18.151
    making tax digital,
      proposals 18.152
      late filing 18.153–18.158
      late payment 18.159
  accelerated payment notices 21.10
  alternative avenues 19.65
  appeals 18.52, 18.55, 18.196
  appropriate arrangements 18.102
  assessing level of 18.172
  assessments 18.21–18.22, 18.194
  calculation of penalties 11.9
  cheating the public revenue 3.6
  checklist 19.65
  common causes 18.113–18.133
  company officers' liability
      18.134–18.136
  computer records, obstruction/failure
      to provide 18.95
  conspiracy to defraud 3.6
  data-holder notice, non-compliance
      16.100–16.102
  deduction notices 22.49–22.53
  directors, liability 18.132–18.134
  DOTAS rules 4.18
  double jeopardy rule 18.209
  errors in returns, etc
    assessments 18.21–18.22
    carelessness 18.11, 18.12–18.13,
        18.70–18.73, 18.120
      presumption of 18.166
    company officers, liability
        18.134–18.136
    corporation tax 18.18
    culpability, assessing
        18.35–18.38
    deliberate errors 8.159–8.166,
        18.11, 18.12, 18.32,
        18.74–18.78
      concealment 18.32, 18.79–18.86
    documents subject to regime
        18.14–18.20

Penalty regime – *contd*
  errors in returns, etc – *contd*
    generally 8.131–8.144, 18.3–18.4,
        18.7, 18.14
    group relief 18.200–18.203
    inaccuracy discovered later 18.13
    inaccurate documents 18.7,
        18.12–18.13, 18.116–18.120
    income tax 18.17
    innocent error, concept of 18.12,
        18.39–18.69
    losses, overstated 18.14,
        18.204–18.206
    multiple errors 18.11, 18.12
    multiple penalties 18.175,
        18.185–18.186
    negligence 18.120
    offshore tax evasion 18.36, 18.38,
        18.78, 18.170–18.176
    penalty periods 18.23
    potential lost revenue 11.9–11.10,
        18.33, 18.200–18.203
    presumption of 'carelessness' 18.166
    previous regime 18.25–18.30
    reasonable care 18.32, 18.47–18.49,
        18.70, 18.130, 18.153
    reasonable excuse 18.52–18.55,
        18.61–18.63, 18.65, 18.69,
        18.153
    relevant person 18.24
    scale of penalties 18.32–18.34
    tax liability, false claims 18.14
    tax repayment, false claims 18.14
    types of inaccuracy 18.12–18.13
    VAT documents 18.19
  failure to comply with data-holder
      notice 16.100–16.102
  failure to correct offshore tax
      non-compliance 4.36
  failure to make returns 18.21,
      18.106–18.109
    mitigation 19.6–19.8
  failure to notify chargeability 2.42,
      3.9, 18.121–18.125, 18.198
  failure to notify liability
    deliberate and concealed 18.88
    deliberate but not concealed 18.88
    generally 14.3, 18.9, 18.87–18.91
    penalty rates 18.88
    reductions for disclosure 19.1–19.5

Index

Penalty regime – *contd*
  failure to notify under-assessment
    18.92–18.93
  failure to pay tax 18.110–18.111
  false accounting 3.6
  follower notices 21.50–21.51
  fraudulent evasion of income tax 3.6
  generally 3.3, 8.131–8.144, 18.1–18.2
  historical background 18.1–18.2
  HMRC guidance 18.5–18.6
  hold notices 22.49–22.53
  inaccurate information or document,
    providing 16.192, 18.7, 18.12,
    18.97, 18.116–18.120
  increased threat of 4.198–4.199
  information notices 1.95,
    16.189–16.192, 18.126–18.133,
    22.49–22.53
  key points 18.210
  late returns 18.114–18.115
  LDF regime 5.72, 5.76
  legislation 18.7–18.13
    Finance Act 2007 18.7, 18.11
    Finance Act 2008 18.8–18.9
    Finance Act 2009 18.10
    Finance Act 2016 changes
      18.160–18.164
    list 19.72
  managers, liability 18.132–18.134
  Managing Serious Defaulters
    programme 18.177–18.183
  minimum wage rules, breach of 18.112
  mitigation
    access 10.151–10.152, 10.155,
      19.10, 19.12
    checklist 19.71
    client's behaviour 10.147–10.148,
      10.154–10.155, 11.99
    cooperation 11.9
    disclosure 2.13, 2.59–2.60, 3.35,
      3.38, 10.145–10.153, 11.9,
      11.11, 14.2, 14.16,
      14.28–14.32
      quality 10.150–10.153, 18.120,
        19.1, 19.6, 19.9–19.23
      reductions for 19.1–19.5
    failure to make returns 19.6–19.8
    helping 10.151–10.152, 10.154,
      19.10, 19.12
    inaccuracy or delay by agent 11.13

Penalty regime – *contd*
  mitigation – *contd*
    key points 19.70
    reasonable care 11.55–11.59, 18.12,
      18.32, 18.47–18.49, 18.70,
      18.130, 18.153
    reasonable excuse 11.55–11.59,
      11.99, 18.52–18.55,
      18.61–18.63, 18.65, 18.69,
      18.153, 19.57–19.69
    special reduction/special relief
      19.24–19.27
    telling 10.151–10.153, 19.10, 19.12
  multiple penalties 18.197,
    18.207–18.208
  naming and shaming 3.10, 3.19, 3.36,
    8.159–8.166, 18.184–18.193
    avoiding 14.17–14.18
  National Insurance contributions
    bodies corporate 25.114–25.115
    Class 1, 1A and PAYE penalties
      25.125–25.132
    Class 1A contributions
      25.125–25.132, 25.149–25.150
    Class 1B contributions 25.151
    Class 4 contributions
      25.152–25.156
    contravention of regulations
      25.110–25.111
    contributions offences
      25.112–25.113
    employers' contributions
      25.116–25.136
    generally 25.108
    incorrect manner of
      payment 25.144
    incorrect returns 25.141–25.143
    late final submission under RTI
      25.140
    late payment 25.145–25.148
    personal liability notices
      25.133–25.136
  negligence 18.120
  negotiating penalties 10.145–10.156,
    11.7–11.14
  potential lost revenue 11.9–11.10,
    18.33
  non-submission of returns
    8.25–8.26
  notices for details of debtors 18.105

Penalty regime – *contd*
  obstruction of officer 1.95, 1.99, 1.103, 1.114, 16.112, 16.176, 18.96–18.99, 18.198, 25.109
  computer records 18.95
  offshore 5.113–5.116
    civil sanctions for enablers 5.119
    offshore move 5.116
    requirement to correct offence (RTC) 5.140
    reduction of penalties 5.141
  tax evasion 18.36
  old penalty regime, cases spanning 14.19–14.23
  planning 10.145–10.146, 10.156
    access 10.151–10.152, 10.155, 19.10, 19.12
    arguing behaviour 10.147
    disclosure
      prompted and unprompted 10.149, 11.11
      quality 10.150–10.152
      helping 10.151–10.152, 10.154, 19.10, 19.12
    telling 10.151–10.153, 19.10, 19.12
  potential lost revenue (PLR)
    calculating penalties 19.28–19.39
    generally 11.9–11.10, 18.33
    group relief 18.200–18.203
  previous regime, transition 18.198–18.199
  records
    computer, failure to provide 18.95
    failure to keep 1.79–1.80
  senior accounting officer (SAO) 18.100–18.104
  suspended penalties 19.40–19.48
    case decisions 19.49–19.54
    examples 19.55–19.56
  tax avoidance schemes 8.131–8.144, 18.137–18.148, 21.34
    enablers 18.167
    failures to deal with APNs or FNs on time 21.36
    general anti-abuse rule (GAAR) 21.37
    Serial Tax Avoidance Regime (STAR) 21.38
    tax geared penalties for error in returns 21.35

Penalty regime – *contd*
  tax evasion 3.3
  third party errors 18.48, 18.62, 18.63, 18.94
  time limits 18.195
  value added tax 24.53
    breaches of record-keeping rules 18.168
    VAT invoice, unauthorised issue 18.89
Pensions Regulator
  appeals against decisions of 20.219
Perjury
  criminal offence 3.139
Personal incidental expenses
  Pay As You Earn 26.162–26.164
Personal tax
  international tax planning 4.35
Petroleum revenue tax
  failure to make return 18.106
  HMRC information gathering powers 16.26
Police and Criminal Evidence (PACE) Act 1984
  access to appropriate powers 16.13
  application of provisions 16.12
  codes of practice 3.42–3.43, 3.50–3.58, 3.59
  HMRC investigatory powers based on 16.2, 16.10
Post
  interception 3.62–3.65
Postponement of tax
  appeal process 20.110–20.114
Potential lost revenue (PLR)
  calculating penalties 19.28–19.39
  generally 11.9–11.10, 18.33
  group relief 18.200–18.203
Practice management
  'anti-Revenue' approach 7.89–7.90
  record-keeping 6.14–6.18
Premises
  business, *see* Business premises; Inspection of premises
Presumption of 'carelessness'
  penalty regime 18.166
Presumption of continuity
  re-opening other tax years 6.91–6.94
Private home
  business premises at 1.99

1139

Index

Private records
appointment diaries 1.48, 6.80–6.81
bank statements 1.48, 15.20–15.29
business models 15.18–15.19
cheque counterfoils 15.23
child's income 1.48
close company directors 15.32
credit, debit and store cards 15.23
directors' loan or current accounts 1.48
dividends 1.48
evidence of purchase 15.23
generally 6.52–6.54, 15.1–15.9, 15.10
information gathering powers 1.48–1.49
joint bank accounts 1.48
journalistic information 19.49
key points 15.36
link papers 15.31
loan agreements 15.23
medical information 15.25, 19.49
mortgage agreements 15.23
non-business information and documents 15.11–15.17
paying in slips 15.23
personal assets and liabilities 1.48
personal records 15.24–15.27, 19.49
power to obtain 15.3–15.9
private finances 15.20–15.29
progressing the enquiry 15.30–15.32
requests for
  during enquiry 6.52–6.54, 15.3–15.9, 15.10
  questions for considerations 15.26
spending patterns, identifying 15.28–15.29
spiritual information 15.25, 19.49
spouse/partner's income and expenditure 1.48, 15.29
statutory record, definition 15.7
tax advice 19.49
tax cases
  First-tier Tribunal 15.33–15.34
  Special Commissioners and courts 15.35
  unreasonable notices (TMA s 20) 15.35
third parties 15.9
trust assets where taxpayer trustee 1.48
what constitute 15.7

Prizes
employee competitions 26.165
Proceeds of crime
generally 3.166
see also Money laundering
Production orders
excluded material 3.77, 3.81–3.94, 16.210
generally 3.17, 3.48, 3.69–3.76, 3.87–3.88, 16.210–16.213
legal professional privilege 3.128–3.133, 16.210
PACE 3.88–3.92, 3.112–3.116, 3.131, 16.194, 16.210–16.213
safeguards 16.214
service 3.88, 3.91
SOCPA powers 3.117–3.121, 16.215–16.222
special procedure material 3.77–3.96, 16.210–16.213
TMA 1970, s 20BA
  compliance 3.103–3.111, 16.233
  generally 3.87, 3.96, 3.97–3.102, 16.223–16.232
Professional advisers
business reviews 24.69–24.71
failure to advise client correctly 14.5
fees, *see* Fees
inaccuracy or delay by 11.13
money laundering 3.36
  guidance 3.190–3.206
    Auditing Practices Board 3.196–3.197
    Chartered Institute of Taxation 3.195
    Consultative Committee of Accountancy Bodies 3.194
    HM Revenue & Customs 3.199–3.201
    Institute of Chartered Accountants in England and Wales 3.190–3.193
    knowledge or suspicion of an offence 3.202–3.203
    Law Society 3.198
    procedures for processing reports 3.204–3.206
  risk 3.214–3.234
offences 16.234
reliance on 18.65–18.67

Index

Professional Conduct in Relation to Taxation (PCRT)
generally 21.25
Professional expenses insurance
generally 6.8, 6.38–6.40, 6.127, 10.26
Profit ratio
varying or low 6.12
Promoters of tax avoidance schemes (POTAS)
accelerated payment notices 21.10, 21.20
conduct notices 21.21
follower notices 21.12
generally 4.23, 21.10, 21.20
monitoring notices 21.22
non-resident promoters 21.22
promoter 4.15
promoter reference numbers (PRNs) 21.22
stop notices 21.12, 21.20
Property
HMRC information gathering sources 8.7, 8.10
multiple ownership 7.13
Publishing of taxpayer's details, *see* Naming and shaming

Q
Qualitative Research with People Convicted of Tax Evasion
findings 3.20–3.22

R
Ramsay principle, *see* Tax avoidance
Real Time Information (RTI)
employment income 26.6, 26.8
National Insurance contributions 25.7, 25.24, 25.28, 25.29–25.33, 25.90, 25.100
payroll errors 25.108
penalties for late final submission 25.140
Reasonable care
disclosure 14.3
generally 18.32, 18.47–18.49, 18.70, 18.130, 18.153
penalty mitigation 11.55–11.59, 18.12, 18.32, 18.40–18.49, 18.57, 18.68, 18.70, 18.130, 18.153
value added tax 24.53

Reasonable excuse
generally 18.52–18.55, 18.61–18.63, 18.65, 18.69, 18.153
obstruction of officers 1.114, 16.112, 16.176
offshore tax non-compliance, RTC offence 5.143
penalty mitigation 11.55–11.59, 11.99, 18.52, 18.153, 19.57–19.69
Records and documents
business inspections 1.100
business record checks (BRCs) 7.27, 9.43
see also Business record checks/ examinations
calculations, record-keeping 10.104
concealment 2.12, 3.36, 18.96–18.99
control of paper, generally 10.94
copied and original 1.85
correspondence file 10.98–10.101
credit card provider data analysis 7.11
destruction 18.96–18.99
disposal of 18.96–18.99
electronic
criminal investigations 3.78, 3.90
obstruction/failure to provide 18.95
employer compliance checks 9.78
estimates, use of 1.77
formal 10.103
generally 10.6, 10.43
inaccurate, providing 16.192, 18.7, 18.12, 18.97, 18.116–18.120
indexing and filing 10.106
information requests 10.108–10.116, 15.3–15.6
investigation file, setting up 10.96–10.97
missing 17.19
National Insurance contributions 25.90–25.92
power to obtain 16.25–16.35
private, *see* Private records
production orders, *see* Production orders
record-keeping
client's 6.14–6.18
National Insurance contributions 25.93–25.97

1141

Index

Records and documents – *contd*
  record-keeping – *contd*
    practice management 6.14–6.18
    records to be kept 1.74–1.76
    VAT, penalties for breaches of rules 18.168
  report preparation file 10.107
  requirements as to 1.71
    HMRC powers 1.79–1.80
    penalties 1.79–1.80
    period of retention 1.72
    records to be kept 1.74–1.76
    statutory obligation, satisfying 1.73
  selection for enquiry 7.11, 7.27–7.28
  third party notices 10.117–10.120
  working files 10.102–10.107
  working schedules 10.105
  see also Business record checks/ examinations; Private records
Redundancy, *see* Termination of employment
Relocation costs
  Pay As You Earn 26.152–26.155
Remuneration, *see* Employment income
Rental income
  HMRC's information gathering powers 8.8
Repairs
  expenditure on 7.58
Report for HMRC
  admission of irregularities 17.20
  agreeing parameters with HMRC 17.17–17.24, 17.29
  basic elements 17.26
  circumstances prompting 17.1–17.4
  controlling investigation process 17.9–17.14
  costs involved
    additional liabilities 17.8
    cost-effectiveness 17.5, 17.7
    professional fees 17.6–17.7
  formal certificates 17.68–17.71
  generally 14.49–14.50
  key points 17.72
  missing records 17.19
  persuading client to disclose 17.15–17.16

Report for HMRC – *contd*
  planning 17.17–17.24
  preparation and completion 17.25–17.56
  preparation methodologies
    analyses of credit card expenditure 17.49–17.51
    analysis of bank accounts 17.32–17.41
    cash flow tests 17.44–17.48
    comparing income with tax returns 17.40–17.41
    directors' loan or current accounts 17.31, 17.42–17.43
    generally 17.30–17.31
    review of P11Ds and potential benefits in kind 17.52–17.53
    schedules of assets and liabilities 17.54–17.55
    schedules of capital statements 17.54–17.55
  responsibility of client 17.29
  retention of working papers 17.56–17.57
  style 17.27
  voluntary disclosure 17.3, 17.62–17.65
  see also Disclosure report
Requirement to correct (RTC)
  offence 5.135
  appeals 5.142
  assessments 5.139
  correcting offence and disclosure 5.136–5.138
    Worldwide Disclosure Facility (WDF) 5.136
  penalties 5.140
    failure to correct (FTC) 5.140
    reduction 5.141
  reasonable excuse 5.143
  voluntary disclosure 8.44–8.45
    failure to correct (FTC) penalty 8.44
Residence
  companies 4.121–4.125, 5.17
  individuals 4.126–4.128
  offshore tax investigations 5.5–5.11
  overseas workday relief 5.9
  statutory residence test (SRT) 5.7
Restrictions on powers
  auditor or tax adviser's documents 16.127, 16.182–16.187

Restrictions on powers – *contd*
  authorised officers 16.188,
    16.196–16.198
  generally 16.126–16.127
  information requests 1.86–1.92
  legal advice privilege 16.156–16.164
  legal professional privilege 3.42,
    3.77–3.96, 3.124, 3.128–3.133,
    16.127, 16.152–16.155, 19.49
  litigation privilege 16.127,
    16.165–16.171
  pending appeal, documents relating to
    16.180–16.181
  possession or power, documents
    must be in 1.86, 16.127–16.150,
    19.48
  resolving privilege disputes
    16.172–16.179
  territorial limits on Sch 36 16.151
Restrictive covenants
  termination payments 26.38
Retirement
  continuing benefits 26.42
  individual nearing, termination
    settlements 26.40–26.41
Returns
  changes in, selection for enquiry
    7.20–7.21
  comparing income with, for disclosure
    reports 17.31, 17.40–17.41
  Construction Industry Scheme
    18.106, 18.109
  discovery
    absent return 13.55–13.58
    submitted return 13.59–13.65
  employer compliance checks 9.78
  estimation in absence of full
    information 8.100–8.106
  failure to make 18.106–18.109
  failure to notify 8.24
  follower notices 21.16
  inaccuracies or errors
    penalties, *see* Penalty regime
    types 18.12–18.13
  incomplete 9.42
  key forms HMRC may request
    8.114–8.125
  late filing 7.13, 7.40, 18.114–18.115
  NIC investigation, *see* National
    Insurance contributions (NICs)

Returns – *contd*
  non-submission 8.20–8.27
  offshore evaders 3.9
  Pay As You Earn 18.109
  penalties, *see* Penalty regime
  personal returns, selection for enquiry
    7.83–7.88
  provisional figures 7.40
  review 7.41–7.47
  selection for enquiry 7.40
  value added tax 24.51, 24.55
**Revenue and Customs Prosecution
    Office (RCPO)**
  generally 2.5
Risk analysis
  Affluent Unit 7.12–7.16
  avoidance schemes 7.13
  behavioural risk 7.16, 7.22–7.26
  business record checks (BRCs)
    7.27, 9.43
  'Connect' data analysis system
    7.10–7.12, 8.9–8.10, 25.26
  credit card data 7.11
  generally 1.10, 7.2, 7.8–7.12, 7.35, 7.39
  inadequate record keeping 7.27–7.28
  key points 7.98
  late filing 7.13
  multiple property ownership 7.13
  National Insurance contributions
    25.26, 25.220
  net profit 7.68
  online trading 7.12, 8.7
  selection for enquiry 1.10, 7.2,
    7.8–7.12
  Swiss bank accounts 7.13
  see also Selection for enquiry
Risk and Intelligence Service (RIS)
  selection for enquiry, *see* Selection for
    enquiry
Road fuel testing
  HMRC Specialist Investigations 3.39
Round sum allowance
  generally 26.20–26.22
  Pay As You Earn 26.68–26.69

S
Salary sacrifice arrangements
  generally 26.48–26.54
Sale and leaseback
  accelerated payment notices 21.4

Index

Scotland
  Crown Office and Procurator Fiscal Service 3.11
  NIC arrears 25.52
  search warrants 3.57
Search and entry
  HMRC powers 3.85, 24.59–24.63
  PACE powers 16.194
  see also Search warrant
Search warrant
  challenging by judicial review 3.93–3.96
  criminal investigations 1.99, 1.103, 3.42, 3.48, 3.69–3.76
  dawn raids 3.69, 3.122–3.127
  excluded material 3.77
  legal privilege 3.77, 3.80, 3.128–3.133
  meaning of premises 3.70
  PACE powers 16.194, 16.199–16.208
    key points 16.209
  reasonable grounds for believing offence committed 16.209
  records to be kept 3.86
  removal of material for examination elsewhere 3.84
  Scottish and English courts 3.57
  search of persons 3.71
  special procedure material 3.77–3.96, 16.210–16.213
Selection for enquiry
  accounts and return review 7.41–7.47
  advertising, promotion and entertainment costs 7.62–7.63
  Affluent Unit 7.12–7.16
  avoidance schemes 7.13
  bad debts 7.65
  bad practice management 7.89–7.90
  balance sheets 7.69–7.82
  behavioural risk 7.16, 7.22–7.26
  capital accounts 7.81–7.82
  capital gains 7.87–7.88
  cash aspect of business 7.77–7.78
  changes in returns 7.20–7.21
  compliance checking 7.3–7.7
  'Connect' data analysis system 7.10–7.12, 8.9–8.10
  credit card data 7.11
  debtors and sales ratio 7.75–7.76
  deductions from income 7.54–7.67
  directors' current accounts 7.80

Selection for enquiry – *contd*
  disclosure of selection parameters 7.17–7.18
  employee costs 7.55–7.56
  enquiry triggers 8.17–8.19
  estimates and percentage abatements 7.48
  fixed assets 7.71
  for cause 1.11
  generally 1.9, 7.91–7.98, 9.9
  gross profit 7.50–7.53
  inadequate record keeping 7.27–7.28
  interest and other finance charges 7.66
  investment income 7.85–7.86
  key points 7.98
  late filing 7.13
  legal and professional costs 7.64
  Lloyds cases 7.40
  loans 7.79
  local level, at 7.29–7.34
  meetings with HMRC, selection for 9.41–9.46
  motor expenses 7.59–7.60
  net profit 7.68
  non-submission of returns 8.20–8.27
  overdrafts 7.79
  personal tax returns 7.83–7.88
  premises costs 7.57
  problems arising 7.1–7.3
  process, generally 7.35–7.40
  random 1.6, 1.10–1.11, 9.9
  record-keeping 7.11
  repairs, deduction of costs 7.58
  risk analysis, *see* Risk analysis
  stock and work in progress 7.72–7.74
  toolkits, using 7.19
  travel and subsistence costs 7.61
  turnover 7.49
Self-assessment
  appeals 20.47–20.50
  benefits and reimbursed expenses 26.123
  business inspections 1.98
  closure procedure 20.51–20.52, 20.60–20.77
  coding notices 22.16–22.17
  debt collection, *see* Tax debt collection
  enquiries, generally 1.1, 1.4, 6.1, 6.4–6.5, 7.1
  process, generally 6.1

1144

Index

Self-employment
  accelerated payment notices 21.8
Self-employment v employment
  audit approach 26.77–26.81
  basic principles 26.72–26.76
  Pay As You Earn, generally 26.70
Senior accounting officer (SAO)
  penalty regime 18.100–18.104
  value added tax 24.56–24.57
Serial Tax Avoidance Regime (STAR)
  generally 21.32
  penalties 21.38
Serious Organised Crime Agency (SOCA)
  generally 2.95–2.96
Service charges
  PAYE and NICs 26.24–26.28
Settlement
  ADR 12.10
  civil tax investigations 2.79–2.81
  enquiries 6.104–6.118
  finality for client 11.26
  finality for practitioner 11.29
  funding 11.70–11.78
  generally 8.145–8.156
  letter of offer 11.79–11.82
  negotiation, *see* Settlement negotiation
  savings for client 11.28
  time to pay 11.74–11.78
Settlement negotiation
  advantages of negotiating 11.25–11.29
    for investigating officer 11.60–11.64
  agreeing on minor issues 11.46–11.47
  claims, allowances and reliefs 11.52–11.53
  client's expectations 11.68–11.69
  collection and management power 11.3–11.4
  delays in progress of enquiry 11.14
  funding the settlement 11.70–11.78
  generally 11.1–11.4, 11.38–11.39, 11.43–11.44, 11.99
  grey areas 11.33–11.36
  groundwork 11.5–11.6, 11.99
  inaccuracy or delay by agent 11.13
  interest, calculation 11.8
  key points 11.99
  letter of offer 11.79–11.82
  Litigation and Settlement Strategy (LSS) 11.37

Settlement negotiation – *contd*
  making sub-standard offers 11.83–11.84
  negotiation techniques 11.38–11.51
  objective assessment of client's position 11.99
  payments on account 11.15–11.18
  penalty negotiation 11.7–11.14, 11.99
  pitching at right level 11.40–11.41, 11.83–11.84
  premature concessions 11.49–11.50
  preparation 11.14, 11.43–11.44
  professional costs 11.21–11.24, 11.27
  reasonable care/reasonable excuse 11.55–11.59
  reducing investigation period 11.25
  relationship with client 11.91–11.98
  relationship with investigating officer 11.45, 11.51, 11.89–11.90
  remittances by non-domiciles 11.54
  settlement meetings 11.85–11.88
  settlement package 11.68–11.69
  strength of client's case 11.42
  tax avoidance schemes 11.35
  time to pay 11.74–11.78
  VAT disclosure 11.19–11.20
  what is negotiable 11.30–11.36
  when agreement cannot be reached 11.65–11.67
Sick pay
  generally PAYE/NICs 26.23, 26.64–26.65
Sideways loss relief
  accelerated payment notices 21.8
Single Compliance Process (SCP)
  generally 6.1
Special Investigations (Fraud and Avoidance) Office (SI)
  case study 2.98
  civil investigations, generally 3.23
  Code of Practice 8, *see* Code of Practice 8
  Code of Practice 9, *see* Code of Practice 9
  Contractual Disclosure Facility (CDF), *see* Code of Practice 9
  direct taxes 3.23
  Fraud Investigation Service (FIS) 1.28–1.29, 1.33
  indirect taxes 3.23

1145

Index

Special Investigations (Fraud and Avoidance) Office (SI) – *contd*
  office locations 2.7
  Offshore Coordination Unit (OCU) 2.95, 5.44
  overseas authorities, liaison with 2.94
  practice management 2.85–2.92
  professional indemnity insurance 2.85
  role 2.2–2.7
  Serious Organised Crime Agency (SOCA) 2.95–2.96
  specialist areas 2.4, 2.85
  specialists within 2.93–2.98
  suspected serious fraud 2.2–2.3
  tax avoidance cases 2.2–2.3
    large scale 2.3
  UK government agencies, liaison with 2.94
Special procedure material
  definition 3.82, 16.210
  generally 3.77–3.96, 16.210–16.213
Spouse
  income and expenditure, HMRC information-gathering powers 1.48, 15.29
Spreading
  re-opening other tax years 6.91–6.94
Staff social functions
  Pay As You Earn 26.170
Stamp duties
  accelerated payment notices 21.3, 21.5
  follower notices 21.5
Stamp duty taxes
  failure to make return 18.106
  HMRC information gathering powers 16.26
Start of enquiry
  information requests 1.39–1.48, 15.3–15.6
    challenging 1.42–1.43, 1.48
    relevance of information requested 1.46–1.48
    time limit 1.39–1.40
    unreliable accounts 1.50
  notice of 1.36–1.39
    appeal against 1.37–1.38
    opening letter 1.39–1.41
    validity 1.37–1.38
  volunteering information 1.42–1.45

State benefits
  false claims 3.2–3.3
  fraudulent evasion of income tax 3.17–3.18
  organised fraud 2.14, 3.37
Statement of assets and liabilities (SOAL)
  HMRC requesting 8.118–8.121
Statutory maternity pay (SMP)
  Pay As You Earn 26.64–26.65
Statutory sick pay
  Pay As You Earn 26.64–26.65
Student
  PAYE compliance 26.70, 26.97
Student loan repayment
  HMRC powers 26.7
Subcontractor
  Pay As You Earn 26.70
Subsistence allowance
  Pay As You Earn 26.171–26.172
Suggestion scheme
  tax treatment 26.173
Surveillance Commissioners
  role 3.64
Surveillance operations
  criminal investigations 3.62–3.68
  VAT officers 24.64–24.68
Suspected serious fraud
  COP9 *see* Code of Practice 9
  production orders, *see* Production orders
Swiss banks
  Affluent Unit 7.13
  untaxed funds held in 3.15

T

Taking control of goods enforcement action
  debt recovery 22.56–22.60
Tax
  writing off following complaint 23.82
Tax accountants
  offences 16.234
Tax advisers
  HMRC information gathering powers 16.127, 16.182–16.187
  sanctions 8.167–8.175

Index

Tax agents
  corporation failing to prevent offence by 3.8, 3.10
  dishonest conduct, HMRC powers 3.36, 16.234
  naming 3.36

Tax avoidance
  accelerated payments, *see* Accelerated payment notice (APN); Accelerated payment rules
  Affluent Unit 7.13
  anti-avoidance legislation 5.18–5.20
  APN, *see* Accelerated payment notice (APN)
  arrangements impacted 4.14
  artificial loss deductions 21.8
  capital gains 21.8
  case law, evolution and importance
    domestic planning 4.47
      planning based on literal interpretation of statute 4.48
      Ramsay principle
        current status as principle of purposive construction 4.53–4.67
        watershed in judicial thinking 4.49–4.52
      summary 4.68–4.70
    employee benefit trust (EBT) arrangements 4.76–4.77
    evasion distinguished 4.97–4.98
    generally 4.45–4.46
    international planning – central management and control 4.89–4.95
    summary 4.96
    trading and loss generation schemes 4.71–4.75
    unallowable purpose
      AH Field (Holdings) Ltd v R & C Comrs 4.78–4.82
      summary 4.88
      Versteegh Ltd v R & C Comrs 4.83–4.87
  Code of Practice 8 (COP8) 2.3, 2.9, 2.82–2.84

Tax avoidance – *contd*
  countering 8.69–8.94
    Counter Avoidance Directorate (CAD) 8.69, 8.73
    serial tax avoidance (STA) legislation/regime 8.82–8.87
    tax avoidance arrangements (TAAs) 8.69–8.94
  defeated schemes
    enables 4.24
    further sanctions 4.34
    serial avoiders 4.32
  disguised remuneration 21.33
  DOTAS regime, *see* Disclosure of Tax Avoidance Schemes (DOTAS)
  enablers 21.23
    defeated schemes 4.24
    further sanctions 4.34
    offshore 21.24
    penalties 18.167
  false or altered documents 2.12, 3.36
  follower notices, *see* Follower notices
  further sanctions for promoters/enablers/users of schemes 4.34
  general anti-abuse rule (GAAR) 4.25–4.28, 21.26
    accelerated tax payment rules 4.31
    generally 21.1–21.7
    HMRC's approach 4.7
    legislative initiatives 4.11
    moral dimension 4.8, 21.1
    operational initiatives 4.9–4.10
  HMRC Spotlights 21.25
  key points 21.43
  large scale cases 2.3
  marketed avoidance schemes 2.84
  offshore 5.1–5.4
    see also Offshore tax investigations
  penalties 8.131–8.144, 18.137–18.148, 21.34
    enablers 18.167
    failures to deal with APNs or FNs on time 21.36
    general anti-abuse rule (GAAR) 21.37
    Serial Tax Avoidance Regime (STAR) 21.38
    tax geared for error in returns 21.35
  POTAS rules, *see* Promoters of tax avoidance schemes (POTAS)

1147

Index

Tax avoidance – *contd*
　Professional Conduct in Relation to Taxation (PCRT) 21.25
　Serial Tax Avoidance Regime (STAR) 21.32
　　penalties 21.38
　settlement negotiation and avoidance schemes 11.35
　SI, *see* Special Investigations (Fraud and Avoidance) Office
　sideways loss relief 21.8
　specialist Directorates
　　background 4.41
　　Counter Avoidance (CA) 4.42–4.44
　stamp duty land tax 21.3, 21.5
　tax evasion distinguished 3.1, 4.97–4.98
　tax strategy, requirement to publish 4.33

Tax credit
　ADR inappropriate 12.36
　false claims 3.2–3.3
　HMRC powers 26.7
　organised fraud 2.14, 3.37
　writing off following complaint 23.82

Tax debt collection
　APNs, *see* Accelerated payment notice
　bailiffs 22.61–22.62
　coding notices 22.16–22.17
　Controlled Goods Agreement 22.56
　court action 22.54–22.55
　debtor not traced, where 22.8–22.15
　deduction notices 22.47–22.48
　　failure to comply 22.49–22.53
　direct recovery 22.32–22.35
　　hold notices 22.35–22.51
　　information notices 22.35
　established debts 22.34
　European Union Mutual Assistance for Recovery of Debts (MARD) 22.77–22.82, 22.89
　follower notices, *see* Follower notices
　generally 8.157–8.158
　HMRC mutual assistance teams 22.89–22.91
　HMRC responsibility 22.1
　hold notices 22.36–22.43
　　appeals 22.44–22.46
　　failure to comply 22.49–22.53
　　objecting to 22.44–22.46

Tax debt collection – *contd*
　identifying debt 22.7
　identifying debtor 22.7
　information notices 22.36
　　failure to comply 22.49–22.53
　insolvency, company 22.69–22.70
　key points 22.92
　liquidation and bankruptcy 22.63–22.68
　managed payment plans 22.3–22.6
　non-UK debts 22.81–22.93
　notice of enforcement 22.56–22.60
　reminders 22.18–22.20
　security for tax, requirement to give 22.71–22.80
　taking control of goods enforcement action 22.56–22.60
　time to pay (TTP) agreements
　　accelerated payment notices 21.9
　　generally 22.24–22.31
　transfer of debt 22.8–22.15
　Walking Possession 22.56

Tax Disputes Governance Code
　generally 20.13

Tax evasion
　Accessories and Abettors Act 1861 3.7
　aiding and abetting 3.4, 3.7
　avoidance distinguished 4.97–4.98
　cheating the public revenue 3.6–3.7
　criminal investigations 2.12
　dishonesty 3.1, 3.147
　double jeopardy rule 18.209
　enabling offshore evasion 3.10
　encouraging offence 3.7
　money laundering, *see* Money laundering
　National Insurance contributions 3.2
　offences, generally 3.1, 3.6–3.7, 3.245
　offshore
　　corporate failure to prevent facilitation of offences 5.122–5.124
　　penalties 18.36, 18.38, 18.170–18.176
　　see also Offshore tax evasion; Offshore tax investigations
　penalty regime 3.3
　suspected serious fraud 2.10–2.14
　tax avoidance distinguished 3.1

1148

Tax Evasion Hotline
  HMRC information gathering sources 8.7
Tax fraud, *see* Fraud; Tax evasion
Tax gap
  size, generally 3.13–3.14
Tax liability
  false claims 18.14
Tax planning
  generally 4.3–4.6
  international, *see* International tax planning
Tax repayment
  false claims 18.14
Taxpayer notice, *see* Information notice
Telecommunications
  interception 3.62–3.65
Telephone
  telephone costs, PAYE 26.174
Termination of employment
  continuing benefits 26.42–26.45
  contractual payments 26.35–26.36
  dismissals 26.39
  other issues 26.46–26.47
  payments 26.34
  payments in lieu of notice (PILONs) 26.37
  restrictive covenants 26.38
  retirement 26.40–26.41
  settlements 26.43–26.45
Terrorism
  financing 3.167
    Regulations 3.170
Third party
  errors by, penalty regime 18.48, 18.62, 18.63, 18.94
  involved 16.87–16.89
  notices for details of debtors 18.105
  obligation of confidence to 16.210
Third party benefits
  Pay As You Earn 26.175–26.176
Third party notice, *see* Information notice
Time limits
  accelerated payment notice 21.5, 21.7, 21.10
  assessments, *see* Assessments
  complaints 23.67–23.68

Time limits – *contd*
  deceased person
    assessment 13.35–13.37
    information notices 1.93
  follower notices 21.5, 21.12, 21.14
  penalties 18.195
  taxpayer notices 21.5, 21.12, 21.14
  value added tax appeals 24.77–24.79
Time to pay (TTP) agreement
  accelerated payment notices 21.9
  advantages 22.26
  generally 22.24–22.31
  interest 22.26
  requesting 22.27–22.28
Tips
  PAYE and NICs 26.24–26.28
  tronc 26.27
Tower MCashback v HMRC Comrs
  closure notice and subsequent appeal 20.59–20.77
Travel and subsistence costs
  Pay As You Earn 26.171–26.172, 26.177–26.180
  selection for enquiry 7.61
Trial
  preparation for, serious fraud investigations 3.139–3.158
Tribunal
  HMRC complaints procedure, and 23.59–23.61
  see also First-tier Tribunal; Upper Tribunal
Trust
  ADR 12.3
Trustee
  enquiries generally 1.2
  residence 5.15–5.16
Turnover
  selection for enquiry 7.49

U

UK GAAP
  estimates, use of 1.77
UK/Swiss tax cooperation agreement
  clearance 5.95–5.100
  generally 5.83–5.85
  historical issues, regularising 5.90
  inheritance tax changes by protocol 5.106

Index

UK/Swiss tax cooperation agreement *– contd*
  non-domiciliary certification 5.105
  non-UK domiciliaries 5.94
  objectives 5.84
  one-off payment 5.91–5.93
  post-1 January 2013 withholding tax 5.101–5.104
  relevant assets 5.85, 5.87
  relevant person 5.85, 5.88–5.89
  Swiss paying agent 5.86
Unannounced visit
  business inspections 1.99, 1.102, 6.55–6.60, 10.124–10.129
  National Insurance contributions 25.73
United States
  Foreign Account Tax Compliance Act (FATCA) 5.31–5.37
  Intergovernmental Agreement (IGA) 5.31–5.37
Universal Credit (UC)
  National Insurance contributions 25.57
Upper Tribunal
  ADR 20.39–20.45
  appeal from 20.250–20.257
  appeals to 20.219, 20.225–20.235
  case management powers 20.244–20.245
  chambers 20.29
  constitution 20.26, 20.29
  costs 20.249
  decisions 20.248
  direct referrals 20.221, 20.222–20.224
  FSA decisions, appeals 20.219
  function and jurisdiction 20.26–20.33, 20.219–20.221, 20.258
  generally 20.3, 20.26–20.33
  hearings 20.246–20.247
  judicial review 20.236–20.243
  overriding objective 20.33, 20.34–20.38
  Pensions Regulator decisions, appeals 20.219
  'ticketing' system 20.29–20.30

V
Value added tax (VAT)
  appeals 24.74–24.76
  assessments 24.72–24.73

Value added tax (VAT) *– contd*
  assurance visits
    checking more than one tax 24.9
    detecting trends 24.29
    general questions 24.16, 24.17–24.18
    generally 24.1, 24.7–24.16
    multi-national companies 24.45
    preparing for 24.48–24.58
    review of returns submitted 24.16, 24.19–24.27
  bogus registration repayment fraud 2.14, 3.37
  business records checks 24.31–24.35
  business reviews 24.69–24.71
  credibility queries 24.28–24.30, 24.54
    preparing for 24.46–24.56
  customer compliance managers (CCMs) 24.5, 24.9
  disclosure 11.19–11.20, 14.34–14.35, 14.58
  disputes
    Adjudicator 24.83–24.84
    ADR 24.80–24.82
    appeals 24.74–24.79
    judicial review 24.85
  EC Sales Lists (ESLs) 24.11–24.13, 24.35–24.37
  errors in returns, penalty regime 18.19
  EU countries, mutual assistance 24.41–24.45
  generally 24.1–24.6
  HMRC control and management 24.1
  HMRC information gathering powers 16.26
  Intrastat visits 24.35–24.42
    search and entry 24.59
  key points 24.86, 24.87
  large and complex businesses 24.1
  making tax digital for VAT (MTDfV) 24.6
  mid-sized businesses 24.5
  missing trader intra-community (MTIC) fraud 2.14, 3.37, 24.43
  mutual assistance through information exchange 24.43–24.47
  penalty regime 24.53
    breaches of record-keeping rules 18.168
    invoice, unauthorised issue 18.89

1150

Value added tax (VAT) – *contd*
  premises used in connection with
    taxable supplies 16.117–16.119
  professional advisers 24.67–24.69
  reasonable care 24.53
  registration 24.3–24.4
    online 24.4
  returns 24.51
    signatory 24.55
  risk profiling 24.1–24.2, 24.8
  search and entry powers
    24.59–24.63
  security for tax, requirement to give
    22.71–22.80
  SOA duties 24.56–24.57
  surveillance operations
    24.64–24.68
  trade classification 24.29
  unpaid debts 22.68
  VAT Information Exchange System
    (VIES) 24.11–24.12
  VAT numbers 24.3
Voluntary disclosures
  advantages 14.13–14.18
  Civil Investigation of Fraud 2.13, 2.39,
    2.59–2.60, 3.38
  civil resolution, leading to
    14.14–14.15
  client/practitioner relationship
    14.5–14.6
  Code of Practice 9 (COP9) 2.13, 2.39,
    2.59–2.60, 3.35, 8.43,
    17.62–17.65
  comparative costs 14.13
  cost-effective option 14.13
  Digital Disclosure Service (DDS)
    8.42–8.43, 14.38
  disclosure reports 17.3
  early considerations 14.3–14.6
  encouraging 8.32–8.47
    requirement to correct (RTC)/
      failure to correct (FTC)
      8.44–8.45
    Worldwide Disclosure Facility
      (WDF) 8.35–8.39, 8.42–8.43
  failure to file on time 14.33
  failure to notify liability 14.3
  generally 14.1–14.2
  HMRC's response 14.56–14.58
  HMRC's view 14.24–14.35

Voluntary disclosures – *contd*
  key forms HMRC may request
    8.114–8.125
  key points 14.59
  making 14.48–14.55
    notifying investigating officer
      14.36–14.37
    options 14.36–14.47
    triggers 14.7–14.12
    typical steps 14.48
  offshore facilities 14.38, 14.40–14.41
  payment by instalments 14.52
  payments on account 14.51
  penalties
    former penalty regime,
      cases spanning
      14.19–14.23
    reduction 14.16, 14.28–14.32
  planning and preparation 14.47
  practitioner negligence 14.5
  prompted and unprompted
    14.2, 14.4, 14.9
  what constitutes 14.24–14.32
  'reasonable care' 14.3
  specialist third parties, engaging
    14.6, 14.59
  value added tax 14.58
  wrongdoing 14.34–14.35

W
Wages, *see* Employee costs
Walking Possession
  debt recovery 22.56
**Wealthy and Mid-sized Business
  Compliance Teams**
  ADR process 12.37
  risk analysis 7.12–7.16
  selection for enquiry
    7.13–7.16
Working of complex enquiries
  case identification 4.99–4.100
  case profiling 4.101
  case sampling 4.118–4.119
  fact finding
    domestic planning 4.105–4.107
    requests for tax advice 4.108
    legal basis 4.109–4.114
    protection for advisers' papers
      4.115–4.117
    generally 4.102–4.104

1151

Index

Working of complex enquiries – *contd*
  fact finding – *contd*
    international planning
      approach to determining
        residence for individuals
        4.126–4.128
      company residence 4.121–4.125
      generally 4.120
    impact of operational and legislative
      changes 4.129–4.130
  recommended responses,
    overview 4.131
      adopt realistic view of facts and
        ensure proper evidence
        4.133–4.135

Working of complex enquiries – *contd*
  recommended responses,
    overview – *contd*
      prepare for worst 4.132
      rigour in execution and
        documentation processes 4.136
      domestic planning 4.137–4.140
      international planning 4.141–4.142
Working rule agreement (WRA)
  benefits and reimbursed expenses
    26.107–26.111
Worldwide Disclosure Facility (WDF)
  5.128–5.134, 5.136,
  7.9, 8.35–8.39, 8.42–8.43, 8.125,
  14.40, 14.41